Handbook of
Stainless Steels

Other McGraw-Hill Handbooks of Interest

Aljian • Purchasing Handbook

American Institute of Physics • American Institute of Physics Handbook

American Society of Mechanical Engineers • ASME Handbooks

   Engineering Tables   Metals Engineering-Processes

   Metals Engineering-Design   Metals Properties

Azad • Industrial Wastewater Management Handbook

Baumeister and Marks • Standard Handbook for Mechanical Engineers

Brady and Clauser • Materials Handbook

Brater and King • Handbook of Hydraulics

Burington • Handbook of Mathematical Tables and Formulas

Burington and May • Handbook of Probability and Statistics with Tables

Callender • Time Saver Standards for Architectural Design Data

Chow • Handbook of Applied Hydrology

Condon and Odishaw • Handbook of Physics

Conover • Grounds Maintenance Handbook

Crocker and King • Piping Handbook

Croft, Carr, and Watt • American Electricians' Handbook

Davis and Sorensen • Handbook of Applied Hydraulics

DeChiara and Callender • Time-Saver Standards for Building Types

Fink and Carroll • Standard Handbook for Electrical Engineers

Flügge • Handbook of Engineering Mechanics

Hamsher • Communication System Engineering Handbook

Harper • Handbook of Plastics and Elastomers

Harris • Handbook of Noise Control

Harris and Crede • Shock and Vibration Handbook

Havers and Stubbs • Handbook of Heavy Construction

Hicks • Standard Handbook of Engineering Calculations

Ireson • Reliability Handbook

Juran • Quality Control Handbook

Karassik, Krutzsch, Fraser, and Messina • Pump Handbook

Korn and Korn • Mathematical Handbook for Scientists and Engineers

LaLonde and Janes • Concrete Engineering Handbook

LeGrand • The New American Machinist's Handbook

Lewis • Management Handbook for Plant Engineers

Lewis and Marron • Facilities and Plant Engineering Handbook

Machol • System Engineering Handbook

Mantell • Engineering Materials Handbook

Maynard • Handbook of Business Administration

Maynard • Industrial Engineering Handbook

Merritt • Building Construction Handbook

Merritt • Standard Handbook for Civil Engineers

Merritt • Structural Steel Designer's Handbook

Morrow • Maintenance Engineering Handbook

O'Brien • Scheduling Handbook

Parmley • Standard Handbook of Fastening and Joining

Perry • Engineering Manual

Raznjevic • Handbook of Thermodynamic Tables and Charts

Rothbart • Mechanical Design and Systems Handbook

Smeaton • Switchgear and Control Handbook

Society of Manufacturing Engineers • Die Design Handbook

Society of Manufacturing Engineers • Tool and Manufacturing Engineers Handbook

Streeter • Handbook of Fluid Dynamics

Truxal • Control Engineers' Handbook

Tuma • Engineering Mathematics Handbook

Tuma • Handbook of Physical Calculations

Tuma • Technology Mathematics Handbook

Urquhart • Civil Engineering Handbook

Watt and Summers • NFPA Handbook of the National Electrical Code

Woods • Highway Engineering Handbook

Handbook of
Stainless Steels

DONALD PECKNER

Consultant
Santa Monica, California

I. M. BERNSTEIN

Professor of Metallurgy and Materials Science
Carnegie-Mellon University
Pittsburgh, Pennsylvania

DUANE S. REYES,
BOX 293,
BRUNO, SASK.

McGraw-Hill Book Company

New York   St. Louis   San Francisco   Auckland   Bogotá
Düsseldorf   Johannesburg   London   Madrid   Mexico
Montreal   New Delhi   Panama   Paris   São Paulo
Singapore   Sydney   Tokyo   Toronto

Library of Congress Cataloging in Publication Data

Main entry under title:

Handbook of stainless steels.

Includes index.
1. Steel, Stainless—Handbooks, manuals, etc.
I. Peckner, Donald.   II.   Bernstein, Irving Melvin.
TA479.S7H28   669'.142   76-54266
ISBN 0-07-049147-X

The editors for this book were Harold B. Crawford and Betty Gatewood,
the designer was Naomi Auerbach, and the production supervisor was
Teresa F. Leaden. It was set in Caledonia by University Graphics, Inc.

To our families
Doris, Lloyd, Nancy, and Amy Peckner
and
Kathie Bernstein

Contents

Index follows the Appendixes.

Preface

The commercial development of stainless steels has continued to expand because materials in this alloy class exhibit the highly attractive combinations of excellent corrosion resistance, good formability, an aesthetically pleasing appearance, and a wide range of strength levels. New classes of stainless alloys and new applications are continually being introduced. Yet surprisingly, there is no single comprehensive English-language publication dealing with either wrought or cast stainless steel. Moneypenny's excellent work, published in 1951, is now out of print, and anyone dealing with stainless steel must resort to a shelf-full of publications to obtain anything more than the simplest data.

The editors believe that this multipurpose handbook fills the following needs:

1. It is an up-to-date source for metallurgists on constitution, effects of alloying elements, metallurgical reactions, and necessary tradeoffs between structure and properties.

2. It can be used by design engineers to help them specify stainless steels both for properties and fabricability. The depth and readability of the various sections will allow design engineers to make such decisions even if their metallurgical background is limited.

3. It can be used as a single rapid reference source for all types of data on properties, corrosion, heat treatment, compositions, etc. Much of this data has never been available in one convenient source.

The usefulness of this handbook to a broad spectrum of the technical community rests with the diversity of the material. Each individual need should be accommodated, whether it be a broad overview on melting practice or an in-depth analysis of precipitation-hardenable stainless steels.

The first section presents an overview of stainless steel metallurgy designed to introduce the more detailed subject matter in the following sections. The next section deals with the detailed metallurgy of wrought and cast stainless steels. A chapter on a relatively new family of alloys, the microduplex stainless steels, is included to give the reader an understanding of this important class of structural alloys and their potential areas of application. The effects of alloying elements on structure and properties concludes the section on metallurgy.

This is followed by comprehensive chapters dealing with the theoretical and practical aspects of corrosion. This ubiquitous problem is the keystone for stainless steel development. The chapters in this section will not only provide the reader a choice of materials for specific environmental situations, but also will provide the basic knowledge to permit more predictive alloy selection processes for future applications.

Physical and mechanical properties are reviewed over broad temperature and structural ranges. The data are not exhaustive—but they will serve to advise the reader as to the properties he or she may expect to encounter over widely varying conditions.

The authors of the section dealing with fabrication and design practices discuss common fabrication operations. In addition to explaining the problems that may be encountered—and how to solve them—they also discuss the design parameters of each of the processes. The rationale for this entire section is that the design engineer should be able to consider a variety of fabrication techniques before deciding on the one that will produce a component at the lowest unit cost. The emphasis in this section is twofold: how the process works with stainless steels and the design parameters which must be considered before finally determining which production process to use.

Finally, a large number of application areas are discussed. These areas define the technological forefront of stainless steel applications and should provide to the reader not only uses of direct interest, but also an awareness of new applications and how industry meets the challenges of more and more demanding service conditions.

The book ends with two appendixes. The first is designed to familiarize the readers with the major stainless steel specifications of the producing nations. Appendix 2 gives the reader the nominal composition of many commercial stainless steels and alloys as well as the nonstandard stainless steels mentioned in the book.

It is important to note that the editors did not ask the authors of the chapters to define their subjects exhaustively, but rather to present an informative overview to make the reader aware of the basics of the subject and problems to consider. A book of this type, covering such a broad range of topics within a single field, cannot offer an exhaustive discussion of each topic. The reader is encouraged to pursue specific subjects of interest in greater detail through the extensive literature references at the end of most chapters. Also, readers are encouraged to use the extensive subject index, since many topics are covered in detail but with a different perspective in more than one chapter.

It is our hope that the reader will find this collection of practical use. With some exceptions, the units of measurement used in the book are presented both in English and the new SI metric units. The reader should note that during the long period involved in obtaining and editing manuscripts for the chapters, the standard SI unit for pressure was changed from Newton per square meter (N/m^2) to Pascal (Pa). Both units appear in the book and they are exactly equivalent.

We would like to offer our sincere thanks to the chapter authors, most of whom worked on their own time to prepare the chapters that make up this handbook. And our special thanks to Dr. Bernstein's secretary, Mrs. Jean Gibson, for the help she always gave at critical moments which enabled us to meet some semblance of a schedule. We are deeply grateful to our families for their patience during the several thousand hours which were expended to edit this handbook.

DONALD PECKNER
I. M. BERNSTEIN

Handbook of
Stainless Steels

Part 1

Introduction to Stainless Steels

Chapter **1**

The Wrought Stainless Steels

GEORGE J. FISCHER
**Professor of Metallurgical Engineering,
Polytechnic Institute of New York, Brooklyn, New York**

ROBERT J. MACIAG
Executive Assistant to the Provost, Polytechnic Institute of New York, Brooklyn, New York

Stainless steels contribute properties and characteristics which are otherwise unavailable within the alloy systems of the various ferrous alloy groups. In order to understand the utilization of these alloys, consideration must be given to their historic development and to their relationship to other alloy systems.

Figure 1 is a diagram demonstrating the position of stainless steel alloys with respect to all of the ferrous alloy systems. Alloys with compositions and structures suitable for wrought products will be discussed in this chapter. Casting alloys will be considered in Chapter 2.

In perspective, AISI-SAE* carbon and low-alloy steels are far more important on a tonnage basis. However, in view of the corrosion- and oxidation-resisting qualities of stainless steels, the function they perform cannot be duplicated by the other systems for their cost. The stainless steels were developed because other ferrous alloys lacked sufficient corrosion resistance or oxidation resistance as service temperatures increased.

Over 50 years ago, it was discovered that a minimum of 12% chromium would impart corrosion and oxidation resistance to steel. Therefore, the definition: stainless steels are those ferrous alloys which contain a minimum of 12% chromium for corrosion resistance.

*American Iron and Steel Institute—Society of Automotive Engineers.

This development was the beginning of a family of alloys which have enabled the advancement and growth of chemical processing and power-generating systems upon which our technological society is based. Table 1 indicates the approximate equivalency of the AISI designations of stainless steels with those of other producer nations.

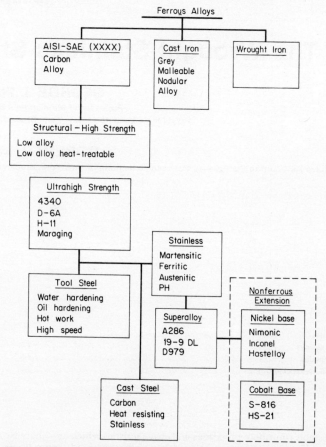

Fig. 1   Relationship of stainless steels to other families of ferrous alloys.

The subsequent development of several important subcategories of stainless steels, namely the ferritic, austenitic, martensitic, and precipitation-hardenable grades, are based on compositional, microstructural, and crystallographic factors which will be discussed in connection with their mechanical and chemical effects (corrosion).

The basis for stainless steels is the binary iron-chromium system. Modifications resulting from the addition of specific elements, which may profoundly influence the resulting alloys with regard to structure and properties, are best first considered by viewing their effects on the iron-chromium binary.

Figure 2 is an iron-chromium phase diagram, which is the foundation of stainless steels.

Ferritic Grades   It will be noticed that the alpha (α) ferrite phase is quite extensive whereas the gamma (γ) phase is restricted and enclosed in a loop. The diagram in Fig. 2 forms the basis of two major subgroups: the ferritic and martensitic grades of stainless steel. The ferritic grades consist of a microstructure of alpha ferrite which has a body-centered cubic (bcc) crystal structure with chromium contents varying from 14.5% chromium to approximately 27% chromium.

Some of the typical AISI grade ferritic steels and their compositions are shown in Table 2.

TABLE 1   Comparison of AISI and SAE Stainless Steel Standards with Approximately Equivalent Standards of Other Stainless Steel Producing Countries

| USA | | West Germany | | Great Britain | | Poland | |
AISI	SAE	Standard no.	DIN designation	BS970:Part 4:1970	En steel replaced	Spec. no. PN	Type
201							
202		1.4371	X8CrMnNi189	284S16		86020	OH17N4G8
301	30301	1.4310	X12CrNi177	301S21			
302	30302	1.4300	X12CrNi188	302S25	58A	86020	1H18N9
302B	30302B	1.4330					
303	30303	1.4305	X12CrNiS188	303S21	58M		
303Se	30303Se	1.4305	X12CrNiS188	303S41	58M		
304	30304	1.4301	X5CrNi189	304S15	58E	86020	OH18N9
304L	30304L	1.4306	X2CrNi189	304S12		86020	OOH18N10
305	30305						
308	30308						
309	30309	1.4828	X15CrNiSi2012	309S24		86022	H20N13S2
309S	30309S						
310	30310	1.4841	X15CrNiSi2520	310S24		86022	H25N20S2
310S	30310S	1.4845	X12CrNi2521			86022	H23N18
314	30314						
316	30316	1.4401	X5CrNiMo1810	316S16	58J		
316L	30316L	1.4404	X2CrNiMo1810	316S12		86020	OOH17N14M2
317	30317	1.4449	X5CrNiMo1713	317S16			
317L		1.4435	X2CrNiMo1812	317S12			
318		1.4583	X10CrNiMoNb1812				
321	30321	1.4541	X10CrNiTi189	321S20			OH18N9T
				321S12	58B&58C	86020	OH18N10T
347	30347	1.4550	X10CrNiNb189	347S17	58F&58G	86020	OH18N12Nb
348	30348						
384							
385							
403	51403	1.4006	X10Cr13	403S17			
405	51405	1.4002	X7CrAl13			86020	OH13J
410	51410	1.4006	X10Cr13	410S21	56A		
414	51414						
416	51416	1.4005	X12CrS13	416S21	56AM		
416Se	51416Se			416S41	56AM		
420	51420	1.4021	X20Cr13	420S37	56C	86020	2H13
420F	51420F						
429							
430	51430	1.4016	X8Cr17	430S15	60	86020	H17
430F	51430F	1.4104	X12CrMoS17				
430FSe	51430FSe	1.4104	X12CrMoS17				
431	51431	1.4057	X22CrNi17	431S29	57	86020	2H17N2
434	51434	1.4113	X6CrMo17	434S19			
436	51436						
440A	51440A	1.4109	X65CrMo14				
440B	51440B	1.4112	X90CrMoV18				
440C	51440C	1.4125	X105CrMo17				
442	51442						
446	51446						
501	51501					86022	H5M
502	51502					86022	H5M

It will be noted from the phase diagram that beyond approximately 12% chromium, alloys do not transform to any other phase up to the melting point and, as a result, these steels cannot be strengthened by heat treatment. They can, however, be cold-worked and annealed. Because of the composition of these alloys, they have good resistance to oxidation and corrosion and are also used for high-temperature applications. They have resistance to some reducing gases. They are subject to grain growth when held for long times at temperatures above 1850°F (1008°C). As a group they are more corrosion resistant than the martensitic grades but generally inferior to the austenitics. The sigma (σ)-phase loop in the phase diagram may be disregarded at this point but will be more important

TABLE 1   Comparison of AISI and SAE Stainless Steel Standards with Approximately Equivalent Standards of Other Stainless Steel Producing Countries *(Continued)*

AISI	Romania Spec. no. STAS	Type	Soviet Union GOST	Sweden SIS-14-	Czechoslovakia CSN	Hungary Spec. no. MSZ	Type	Bulgaria Spec. no. BDS	Type
201	3583	10AzMNC170							
202			12Kh17G9AN4		17460	4360	KO31	6738	14
301									
302	3583	10NC180	12Kh18N9	2330/2331	17241	4360	KO32	6738	16
302B									
303				2346					
303Se				2346					
304	3583	7NC180	08Kh18N10	2332/2333	17240	4360	KO33	6738	15
304L				2352	17249	4360	KO41		
305	6855	T12MSNC180	10Kh18N9L	2333					
308					17251				
309	3583	15SNC200	20Kh20N14S2					6738	21
309S									
310	3583	15SNC250	20Kh25N20S2		17255			6738	22
310S				2361					
314				2361					
316	6855	T12MSMoNC180		2347/2343	17352			5084	21
316L				2353	17350	4360	KO38		
317									
317L			03Ch17N14M2						
318									
321	3583	7TNC180	1Kh18N10T	2337	17248	4360	KO36/KO37	6738	18
347	3583	7NbNC180	08Kh18N12B	2338		4360	KO34		
348									
384									
385									
403	3583	12C130	12Kh13	2302	17021	4360	KO2	6738	4
405									
410	3583	12C130	12Kh13	2302	17021	4360	KO2	6738	4
414									
416									
416Se									
420	3583	20C130	20Kh13	2303	17022	4360	KO11	6738	5
420F									
429									
430	3583	10C170	12Kh17	2320	17041	4359	H16	6738	8
430F									
430FSe									
431			20Kh17N2	2321		4360	KO17		
434						4360	KO6		
436									
440A									
440B									
440C									
442									
446				2322					
501									
502									

*See Appendix 1 for specification numbers.

when specific discussions are centered about the effects of precipitation of this phase later on in the text.

Martensitic Grades   The martensitic grades were developed in order to provide a group of stainless alloys which would be corrosion resistant and hardenable by heat-treating. This is accomplished by adding carbon to the binary iron-chromium system which produces an alloy which responds to a quench temperature cycle. Carbon enlarges the gamma-loop phase field and makes it possible for martensite to transform

East Germany			France	Italy	Japan
Spec. no. TGL	Type	Characteristic number	AFNOR	UNI	Notation*
					SUS 201
7143	X10CrMnNiN17.9.4	9840			SUS 202
7143	X12CrNi17.7	6980	Z12CN17-08	X12CrNi1707	SUS 301
7143	X10CrNi18.9	6940	Z10CN18-09	X10CrNi1809	SUS 302
			Z10CNF18-09	X10CrNiS1809	SUS 303
				X10CrNiS1809	SUS 303Se
7143	X5CrNi18.10	6950	Z6CN18-09	X5CrNi1810	SUS 304
7143	X3CrNi18.10	6970	Z2CN18-10	X2CrNi1811	SUS 304L
			Z8CN18-12	X8CrNi1812	SUS 305
					SUS 308
7061	X15CrNiSi20.13			X16CrNi2314	SUH 309
					SUS 309S
7061	X15CrNiSi25.20	8130		X22CrNi2520	SUH 310
					SUS 310S
7143	X5CrNiMo18.11	8870	Z6CND17-11	X5CrNiMo1712	SUS 316
			Z2CND17-12		SUS 316L
			Z2CND17-13	X2CrNiMo1712	SUS 317
					SUS 317L
				X6CrNiMoNb1713	
7143	X8CrNiTi18.10	8940	Z10CNT18-11		SUS 321
			Z6CNT18-11	X6CrNiTi1811	
			Z6CNNb18-11	X8CrNiNb1811	SUS 347
					SUS 384
					SUS 385
7143	X10Cr13	4640	Z6C13	X12Cr13	SUS 403
			Z6CA13	X6CrA113	SUS 405
7143	X10Cr13	4640	Z6C13	X12Cr13	SUS 410
			Z12C13		
			Z12CF13	X12CrS13	SUS 416
7143	X20Cr13	4650	Z20C13/Z40C14	X20Cr13	SUS 420J1
			Z30C13		
					SUS 420F
7143	X8Cr17	4620	Z8C17	X8Cr17	SUS 430
7143	X12CrMoS17	7090	Z10CF17	X10CrS17	SUS 430F
7143	X12CrMoS17	7090		X10CrS17	
				X16CrNi16	SUS 431
			Z8CD17-01	X8CrMo17	SUS 434
					SUS 440A
7143	X90CrMoV18	9260			SUS 440B
			Z100CD17		SUS 440C
					SUH 446

from austenite in a manner similar to that in carbon steels. The heat treatment normally involves soaking in the austenitic range, quenching to form martensite, and tempering to tempered martensite. Some of the martensitic grades in the stainless steel group are indicated, with their AISI designations, in Table 3.

The martensitic stainless steel alloy group provides a means of making available stainless grades of steel that can be strengthened and hardened by heat treatment. However, these alloys are not as corrosion resistant as the ferritic or austenitic groups.

Strengths of up to 270,000 psi (1862 MN/m²) are achievable with martensitic grades. The choice of whether to select martensitic or ferritic stainless steel is based on the balance of corrosion resistance against the hardness, strength, and wear resistance required.

Austenitic Grades Austenitic stainless steels are formed by the addition of a face-centered element, such as nickel or manganese, to the iron-chromium system shown in Fig. 2. The gamma loop is expanded by virtue of the face-centered cubic (fcc) alloy

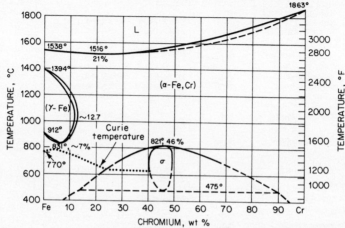

Fig. 2 The iron-chromium phase diagram. *(From "Metals Handbook," vol. 8, p. 291, 8th ed., American Society for Metals, Metals Park, Ohio.)*

addition and this results in the enhancement and enlargement of the gamma phase. This phase is called *austenite* and, when sufficient nickel or manganese is added to the austenite transformation, it suppresses the formation of alpha ferrite.

It is, therefore, possible to alloy iron-chromium steels with a minimum of 8% nickel to obtain an austenitic structure stable at room temperature. The austenitic stainless steels are those iron and chromium alloys which have been sufficiently alloyed with nickel or manganese and nitrogen to have an austenitic structure at room temperature.

The austenite is nonmagnetic as compared with the magnetic ferritic and martensitic

TABLE 2 AISI Ferritic Steels
Body-centered cubic, magnetic, not heat treatable

AISI Type no.	Nominal composition, %			
	C	Mn	Cr	Others
430	0.08 max.	1.0	16.0–18.0	
430F	0.12 max.	1.25	16.0–18.0	0.6Mo max.
430F Se	0.12 max.	1.25	16.0–18.0	0.15Se min.
446	0.20 max.	1.5	23.0–27.0	0.25N max.

TABLE 3 AISI Martensitic Steels
Body-centered cubic, magnetic, heat treatable

AISI Type no.	Nominal composition, %				
	C	Mn	Cr	Ni	Others
403	0.15 max.	1.0	11.5–13		
410	0.15 max.	1.0	11.5–13		
416	0.15 max.	1.2	12–14		0.15S min.
420	0.15 min.	1.0	12–14	……	
431	0.20 max.	1.0	15–17	1.2–2.5	
440A	0.60–0.75	1.0	16–18	……	0.75Mo max.
440B	0.75–0.95	1.0	16–18	……	0.75Mo max.
440C	0.95–1.20	1.0	16–18	……	0.75Mo max.

stainless steels. The most common austenitic alloys are iron-chromium-nickel steels and are widely known as the 300 series. These austenitic stainless steels, because of their high chromium and nickel content, are the most corrosion resistant of the stainless steels group. Typical Type 300 stainless steel compositions are shown in Table 4.

TABLE 4   AISI Austenitic Grades—Type 300
Face-centered cubic, nonmagnetic, not heat treatable

AISI Type no.	Nominal composition, %				
	C	Mn	Cr	Ni	Others
301	0.15 max.	2.0	16–18	6.0–8.0	
302	0.15 max.	2.0	17–19	8.0–10	
304	0.08 max.	2.0	18–20	8.0–12	
304L	0.03 max.	2.0	18–20	8.0–12	
309	0.20 max.	2.0	22–24	12–15	
310	0.25 max.	2.0	24–26	19–22	
316	0.08 max.	2.0	16–18	10–14	2–3Mo
316L	0.03 max.	2.0	16–18	10–14	2–3Mo
321	0.08 max.	2.0	17–19	9–12	(5 × %C) Ti min.
347	0.08 max.	2.0	17–19	9–13	(10 × %C) Cb-Ta min.

Since these alloys do not undergo any transformation during heat treatment, they cannot be hardened by heat treatment but can be hardened significantly by cold-working. The yield strength of a 301 stainless steel can be increased from 33,000 to 200,000 psi (228 to 1379 MN/m²) by cold-working 45%. Type 301 steel does harden and strengthen to this degree because of the transformation to martensite during severe cold-working, which also renders the alloy slightly magnetic.

It will be noted that some 300 grades contain considerable percentages of alloying elements, with chromium contents up to 26% and nickel contents up to 22%. Some grades contain molybdenum, which improves the alloy's resistance to pitting in chloride solutions.

Carbon is held to a minimum or stabilized by addition of titanium or columbium. This avoids intergranular attack and loss of toughness due to grain-boundary carbide precipitation after exposure between 850 and 1050°F (454 to 565°C). Manganese may be substituted for part of the nickel in the austenitic grades. Alloys of this type are categorized as Type 200 grades (Table 5).

TABLE 5   AISI Austenitic Grades—Type 200
Face-centered cubic, nonmagnetic, not heat treatable

AISI Type no.	Nominal composition, %				
	C	Mn	Cr	Ni	Others
201	0.15 max.	7.5	16–18	3.5–5.5	0.25N max.
202	0.15 max.	10.0	17–19	4.0–6.0	0.25N max.

These alloys are not hardenable by heat treatment but, like the 300 series, work harden rapidly. The substitution of manganese, and in some cases, nitrogen, for nickel provides economic advantages with minimal sacrifice in corrosion resistance.

Precipitation-Hardenable Grades   The last group of alloys to be considered is the general category called *precipitation hardenable*. The ordinary stainless steels of the 300 series are not heat treatable and give up strength for corrosion resistance, while the 400 series contain higher carbon contents, and therefore higher strength, but have reduced resistance to the environment. A technique utilized in aluminum-, magnesium-, and nickel-based alloys, among others, was applied to ferrous-based corrosion-resisting alloys, namely precipitation hardening or age-hardening.

The need for strength leads to the reintroduction of carbon and the development of alloys with low-carbon martensite matrices further strengthened by precipitation hardening. Thus as the group of alloys evolved, three families of alloys emerged: austenitic; semiaustenitic, and martensitic. Table 6 shows examples of each.

The martensitic types have compositions such that martensite forms on cooling above room temperature, usually between 250 and 100°F (121 and 38°C). They are based on an

TABLE 6 Nominal Compositions of PH Stainless Steels

Element	Martensitic							Semiaustenitic						Austenitic	
	W	17-4PH	13-8	Custom 455	Pyromet X15	AM 362	AM 363	15-5	17-7	15-7	14-8	AM 350	AM 355	A266	HNM
C(max.)	0.12	0.07	0.05	0.05	0.03	0.03	0.03	0.07	0.09	0.09	0.05	0.12	0.15	0.08	0.30
Mn(max.)	1.00	1.00	0.1	0.5	0.1	0.3	0.2	1.0	1.0	1.0	0.1	0.9	0.95	1.5	3.5
Si(min.)	1.00	1.00	0.1	0.5	0.1	0.2	0.15	1.0	1.0		0.1	0.5	0.5	0.7	0.5
Cr	17	16	12.5	12	15	14.5	11.5	15	17		15	16.5	15.5	15	18.5
Ni	7.0	4.0	8.0	8.5		6.5	4.25	4.5	7.0		8.5	4.5	4.5	26	9.5
Mo			2.5	0.5							2.5	3.0	3.0	1.3	
Cu		4.0		2.0	2.9										
V				0.5											
Ti	1.0 max			1.1		0.8	0.5							35	
Al	1.0 max		1.1						1.0		1.1			20	
Cb & Ta		0.15–0.45		0.3				0.35						0.35	
Co				13.5	20.0										
N	0.2											0.1	0.09		

18Cr-8Ni austenitic composition with the addition of small amounts of carbon and a slight decrease in nickel, chromium, and manganese. Initial cooling from temperatures in the range of 1850 to 1950°F (1008 to 1063°C) produces a soft ($R_c \approx 30$) martensite which is aged at 900 to 1200°F (482 to 648°C) to produce precipitation of compounds of nickel with aluminum, titanium, and columbium. The latter three elements are present either alone or in combination in the precipitation-hardenable grades. Complex carbides may also contribute to the final properties which typically are in the range:

$$\begin{array}{ll} \text{Hardness} & \text{40–45 } R_c \\ \text{Tensile strength} & \text{200 ksi (1379 MN/m}^2) \\ \text{Yield strength (0.2\%)} & \text{180 ksi (1241 MN/m}^2) \\ \text{Elongation} & \text{3–9\%} \end{array}$$

The semiaustenitic grades have M_s temperatures below room temperature. On cooling from a solution annealing the steel maintains its face-centered cubic structure and is relatively soft, ductile, and workable. Strengthening is achieved by first producing martensite by quenching from an elevated temperature and then precipitation of compounds by a subsequent multistep process.

1. If sufficient carbon is present, the precipitation of chromium carbide at a suitable elevated temperature depletes the matrix of alloy addition and produces martensite on cooling. The depletion of alloy content in the matrix moves the M_s from below 0°F (−18°C) to above room temperature. Subsequent age-hardening cycles develop final properties.

2. The alloys may be cooled to below their M_s. Refrigeration for 8 h at 100°F (38°C) is typical for a 15-7PH alloy. Aging again follows.

3. Mechanical deformation may induce the martensitic transformation. This may be accelerated or completed by refrigeration followed by aging.

Strengths some 10 to 15% higher than in the martensitic grades are attainable.

Austenitic alloys are basically 300-series alloys modified with higher nickel, aluminum, and titanium to produce precipitates. The maximum strengths do not match the other grades and yield strengths on the order of 100 to 125 ksi (690 to 862 MN/m²) are typical. Since aging is done at about 1300°F (704°C) compared to a nominal 900°F (482°C) treatment for the martensitic and semiaustenitic grades, the austenitic alloys may be used at higher service temperatures. Tables 7 and 8 show the various grades discussed and examples of properties which they attain with various heat treatments.

TABLE 7   Effect of Processing on Semiaustenitic Grades

Type	Condition	Ultimate tensile strength		Yield strength (0.2%)		Elongation, %, in
		ksi	MN/m²	ksi	MN/m²	2 in. (50.8 mm)
17-7PH	As-annealed	130	896	40	276	35
	Reheat/cond. to martensitic	200	1379	185	1276	9
	Refrigerate/age	230	1586	217	1496	6
	Cold-rolled/age	260	1793	260	1793	2
15-7PH	As-annealed	130	896	55	379	30
	Reheat/cond. to martensitic	210	1448	200	1379	7
	Refrigerate/age	240	1415	225	1551	6
	Cold-rolled/age	265	1827	260	1793	2
14-8PH	As-annealed	125	862	55	379	25
	Reheat/cond. to martensitic	210	1448	200	1379	6
	Refrigerate/age	230	1586	215	1482	6
	Cold-rolled/age					
AM 350	As-annealed	150	1034	63	434	39
	Reheat/cond. to martensitic	195	1345	155	1069	11
	Refrigerate/age	201	1386	172	1186	13
	Cold-rolled/age	225	1551	195	1345	13
AM 355	As-annealed	185	1276	56	386	29
	Reheat/cond. to martensitic	195	1345	155	1069	10
	Refrigerate/age	216	1489	181	1248	11
	Cold-rolled/age	235	1620	200	1379	16
	Refrigerate/cold-roll/age	290	2000	280	1931	2

TABLE 8   Effect of Heat Treatment on Martensitic Grades

Material	Treatment, °F (°C)	Ultimate tensile strength		Yield strength (0.2%)		Elongation, %, in 2 in. (50.8 mm)	Hardness, Rockwell C (R_c)
		ksi	MN/m²	ksi	MN/m²		
Stainless W	1900 (1036) soak 1050 (565) age	200	1379	100	690	7	42
13-8	1700 (926) soak 950 (510) 4h	225	1551	210	1448	12	47
13-8	1700 (926) soak 1050 (565) 4h	190	1310	180	1241	15	43
13-8	1700 (926) soak 1150 (620) 4h	130	896	85	586	22	28

Chapter 2

The Cast Stainless Steels

ERNEST A. SCHOEFER

Consultant, Alloy Casting Institute Division, Steel Founders' Society
of America, Rocky River, Ohio

COMPARISON OF CAST AND WROUGHT STAINLESS STEELS

Stainless steel alloys are available for castings in all the grades used for wrought forms and in many additional grades or modifications for special end uses. Whereas the alloys formed by rolling or forging generally must have reduced strength and considerable ductility at hot-working temperatures, and sufficient ductility for cold-working for some products, the range of usable casting alloys is not restricted by such requirements; hence castings are made successfully of compositions that are difficult or impossible to form by mechanical means. For this reason the family of stainless steels in cast form includes two distinct series of alloys: one, closely corresponding to the wrought grades, used mainly for resisting corrosive media at temperatures below 1200°F (650°C); and the other, of compositions modified to provide considerably higher strength at elevated temperatures, used for structural components operating up to 2200°F (1205°C). Because of the variations in chemical composition and mechanical and physical properties between the wrought and cast grades, the casting alloys are generally known by the designation system adopted by the Alloy Casting Institute (ACI) and, when users specify particular alloys, these ACI symbols should be used in preference to the type numbers assigned to the wrought alloys by the American Iron and Steel Institute (AISI).

The ranges of iron, chromium, and nickel for the compositions most widely used are shown in Fig. 1 and identified with a letter that is an arbitrary part of each grade designation. It will be observed that as the nickel content increases the letters progress from A toward Z. Through the use of initial letters C or H, designations indicate whether the alloy is for corrosion or high-temperature service. Those with the initial C are normally used to resist corrosive attack at temperatures less than 1200°F (650°C), and those with the initial H are generally used under conditions where the metal temperature is in excess of 1200°F. The second letter of the designation represents the nominal chromium-nickel type as shown on the diagram. Numerals following the letters indicate the *maximum* carbon content of the corrosion-resistant alloys; carbon content may also be designated in the heat-resistant grades by following the letters with a numeral to indicate the *midpoint* of a ±0.05% carbon range. If special elements are included in the composition, they are indicated by the addition of a letter to the symbol. Thus, CD-4MCu is an

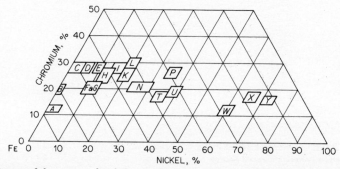

Fig. 1   Ranges of chromium and nickel in standard grades of heat- and corrosion-resistant castings.

alloy for corrosion-resistant service of the 26Cr-5Ni type with a maximum carbon content of 0.04% and containing molybdenum and copper.

Grades Used for Corrosion-Resistant Service   These fall within the following brackets for each major element: 11 to 30% chromium, 0 to 31% nickel, and 50 to 88% iron. All the alloys contain carbon, silicon, manganese, sulfur, and phosphorus in minor amounts introduced either as the result of melting practice or from impurities in the raw materials. Some alloys have small additions of molybdenum, columbium (niobium), copper, or selenium for the purpose of obtaining specific properties such as resistance to particular corrodents, improved strength, or better machinability.

Most of the corrosion-resistant "standard grades" are covered by Specification A 296 (Iron-Chromium and Iron-Chromium-Nickel Casting Alloys for General Corrosion-Resistant Service) of the American Society for Testing and Materials (ASTM), and are related to similar alloys among the AISI wrought types. Table 1 lists the chemical composition of each casting alloy and the most closely corresponding wrought grade, if any. In general, the wrought and cast alloys have equivalent resistance to corrosive media and are frequently used in conjunction with each other.

There are differences in physical and mechanical properties, however, between wrought and cast alloys of the same type because the chemical compositions *are not the same*. The variations in chemistry may appear small but they are not trivial—they provide for optimum forgeability on the one hand and optimum castability on the other. As a result, the balance among the alloy constituents is different in each case and influences the microstructure on which the properties depend. This is the reason why use of cast alloy designations is important when ordering castings. For example, Type 316 is the AISI type number for a wrought alloy containing the following percentages of elements: 0.08C max.-2.00Mn max.-1.00Si max.-0.045P max.-0.030S max.-16 to 18Cr-10 to 14Ni-2 to 3 Mo. The corresponding cast grade is designated CF-8M. Reference to Table 1 will show that the silicon and chromium contents of the cast alloy are higher and the nickel content lower than in the wrought alloy. Chapters 11 to 14 on metallurgy contain detailed

TABLE 1   Alloy Casting Institute Designations and Chemical Composition Ranges for Corrosion-resistant Casting Alloys

Cast alloy designation	Wrought alloy type*	Composition, %								
		C†	Mn†	Si†	P†	S†	Cr	Ni	Fe	Other elements
CA-6NM		0.06	1.00	1.00	0.04	0.04	11.5–14	3.5–4.5	Bal.	0.4–1.0Mo
CA-15	410	0.15	1.00	1.50	0.04	0.04	11.5–14	1.0†	Bal.	
CA-15M		0.15	1.00	0.65	0.040	0.040	11.5–14	1.0†	Bal.	0.15–1.0Mo
CA-40	420	0.40†	1.00	1.50	0.04	0.04	11.5–14	1.0†	Bal.	
CB-30	431 442§	0.30	1.00	1.50	0.04	0.04	18–22	2.0†	Bal.	
CB-7Cu	17-4PH	0.07	1.00	1.00	0.04	0.04	15.5–17	3.6–4.6	Bal.	2.3–3.3Cu
CC-50	446	0.50	1.00	1.50	0.04	0.04	26–30	4.0†	Bal.	
CD-4MCu		0.04	1.00	1.00	0.04	0.04	25–26.5	4.75–6.00	Bal.	1.75–2.25Mo 2.75–3.25Cu
CE-30		0.30	1.50	2.00	0.04	0.04	26–30	8–11	Bal.	
CF-3	304L	0.03	1.50	2.00	0.04	0.04	17–21	8–12	Bal.	
CF-8	304	0.08	1.50	2.00	0.04	0.04	18–21	8–11	Bal.	
CF-20	302	0.20	1.50	2.00	0.04	0.04	18–21	8–11	Bal.	
CF-3M	316L	0.03	1.50	1.50	0.04	0.04	17–21	9–13	Bal.	2.0–3.0Mo
CF-8M	316	0.08	1.50	2.00	0.04	0.04	18–21	9–12	Bal.	2.0–3.0Mo
CF-8C	347	0.08	1.50	2.00	0.04	0.04	18–21	9–12	Bal.	Cb 8xC, 1.0Cb†
CF-16F	303	0.16	1.50	2.00	0.17	0.04	18–21	9–12	Bal.	1.5Mo† 0.20–0.35Se
CG-8M	317	0.08	1.50	1.50	0.04	0.04	18–21	9–13	Bal.	3.0–4.0Mo
CG-12		0.12	1.50	2.00	0.04	0.04	20–23	10–13	Bal.	
CH-20	309	0.20	1.50	2.00	0.04	0.04	22–26	12–15	Bal.	
CK-20	310	0.20	2.00	2.00	0.04	0.04	23–27	19–22	Bal.	
CN-7M		0.07	1.50	1.50	0.04	0.04	19–22	27.5–30.5		2.0–3.0Mo 3.0–4.0Cu
CW-12M		0.12	1.00	1.50	0.040	0.030	15.5–20	Bal.	7.5†	5.25W†, 0.4V† 2.5Co†
CY-40		0.40	1.50	3.00	0.015	0.015	14–17	Bal.	11.0†	
CZ-100		1.00	1.50	2.00	0.015	0.015		95 min.	1.5†	
N-12M		0.12	1.00	1.00	0.040	0.030	1.0	Bal.	6.0†	0.6V†, 2.5Co†
M-35		0.35	1.50	2.00	0.015	0.015		Bal.	3.5†	26–30Cu

*Wrought alloy type numbers shown are for grades most closely corresponding to the casting alloys. It should be noted that the wrought alloy and cast alloy composition ranges *are not the same*.
†Maximum.
‡0.20 minimum.
§See discussion in text of influence of composition balance on properties of CB-30 grade.

discussion of the effects of the individual elements on microstructure. It is sufficient here to point out that the composition balance normal for Type 316 produces an alloy with a structure that is nonmagnetic; whereas the normal CF-8M alloy is perceptibly magnetic because of substantial amounts of the ferrite phase in the structure. This difference is frequently the cause of misunderstandings by users who are unaware that such a distinction exists between wrought and cast alloys of the same type. Consequently, a person familiar with the nonmagnetic character of wrought Type 316 may erroneously believe that magnetic castings of supposedly the same alloy are the wrong composition or have been improperly heat-treated. Experienced high-alloy foundries when accepting an order, therefore, usually state that they will supply the "cast equivalent" of alloys identified by wrought alloy designations.

Grades Used for Heat-Resistant Service   These alloys are listed in Table 2. The ranges for the elements are: 8 to 32% chromium, 0 to 68% nickel, and 13 to 90% iron. Except for type HA, all the grades are covered by ASTM specification A 297 (Heat-Resistant Iron-Chromium and Iron-Chromium-Nickel Alloy Castings for General Application); type HA is included as Grade C12 in ASTM specification A 217 (Alloy Steel Castings for Pressure Containing Parts Suitable for High-Temperature Service). Like the corrosion-resistant alloys, the heat-resistant grades also contain minor amounts of carbon, silicon

TABLE 2 Alloy Casting Institute Designations and Chemical Composition Ranges for Heat-resistant Casting Alloys

Cast alloy desig- nation	Wrought alloy type*	Composition, %								
		C	Mn†	Si†	P†	S†	Cr	Ni	Fe	Other elements
HA		0.20†	0.65†	1.00	0.04	0.04	8–10		Bal.	0.90–1.20Mo
HC	446	0.50†	1.00	2.00	0.04	0.04	26–30	4†	Bal.	0.5Mo†
HD		0.50†	1.50	2.00	0.04	0.04	26–30	4–7	Bal.	0.5Mo†
HE		0.20–0.50	2.00	2.00	0.04	0.04	26–30	8–11	Bal.	0.5Mo†
HF	302B	0.20–0.40	2.00	2.00	0.04	0.04	19–23	9–12	Bal.	0.5Mo†
HH	309	0.20–0.50	2.00	2.00	0.04	0.04	24–28	11–14	Bal.	0.5Mo†, 0.2N†
HI		0.20–0.50	2.00	2.00	0.04	0.04	26–30	14–18	Bal.	0.5Mo†
HK	310	0.20–0.60	2.00	2.00	0.04	0.04	24–28	18–22	Bal.	0.5Mo†
HL		0.20–0.60	2.00	2.00	0.04	0.04	28–32	18–22	Bal.	0.5Mo†
HN		0.20–0.50	2.00	2.00	0.04	0.04	19–23	23–27	Bal.	0.5Mo†
HP		0.35–0.75	2.00	2.00	0.04	0.04	24–28	33–37	Bal.	0.5Mo†
HT		0.35–0.75	2.00	2.50	0.04	0.04	15–19	33–37	Bal.	0.5Mo†
HU		0.35–0.75	2.00	2.50	0.04	0.04	17–21	37–41	Bal.	0.5Mo†
HW		0.35–0.75	2.00	2.50	0.04	0.04	10–14	58–62	Bal.	0.5Mo†
HX		0.35–0.75	2.00	2.50	0.04	0.04	15–19	64–68	Bal.	0.5Mo†

*Wrought alloy type numbers shown are for grades most closely corresponding to the casting alloys. It should be noted that the wrought alloy and cast alloy composition ranges *are not the same.*

†Maximum. (Except for type HA, molybdenum is not intentionally added to these alloys.)

‡0.35 minimum.

manganese, sulfur, and phosphorus, but the carbon content is considerably higher than for the other series. In general, the chromium and nickel contents are also higher: whereas the CF (19Cr-9Ni) types account for the bulk of corrosion-resistant-alloy output, the HH (26Cr-12Ni) and HT (17Cr-35Ni) types constitute the major portion of heat-resistant-alloy casting production. Although molybdenum is a constituent of type HA, it usually is not added to any of the other grades. For improved performance in special service conditions, however, cobalt, columbium (niobium), molybdenum, tungsten, and zirconium are sometimes added individually or in various combinations to the standard types and to proprietary alloys, but by far the greatest tonnage of castings is confined to the standard grades.

In contrast to the situation with the corrosion-resistant alloys, the list of 15 heat-resistant casting alloys shows that only 4 have corresponding standard wrought grades. Even among these the 302B, 309, and 310 types are comparable only in the chromium and nickel levels since they are substantially lower in carbon content than the HF, HH, and HK casting alloys. It is this higher carbon content that contributes greatly to the superior strength of the cast alloys at high temperatures. Even at low working stresses, wrought alloys have relatively short life at minimum creep rates with respect to their total life before rupture. Cast alloys, on the other hand, tend to spend the greater portion of their lives in second-stage (minimum-rate) creep. For this reason, the distortion of the cast alloys is considerably less than that for corresponding wrought alloys over comparable periods. In addition, for a given life span, the cast alloy can sustain a stress two to three times that possible for the wrought grade.

An example of the difference between wrought and cast alloys in their behavior when exposed to elevated temperatures for long periods of time is illustrated in Fig. 2. Here characteristic time-deformation curves are plotted for specimens of the HK-40 cast alloy and the Type 310 wrought alloy stressed at 1700 and 550 psi (11.7 and 3.8 MN/m²), respectively, in creep-rupture tests at 1800°F (982°C). Although the rupture life for both alloys is in the same general order of magnitude and the minimum creep rates are roughly the same, the shapes of the curves are quite different. The cast alloy specimen did not start the accelerated deformation rate of third-stage creep until after 9000 h. Conversely, the wrought alloy (carrying only one-third the load) began the third stage at 250 h and by 9000 h had elongated 40% in contrast to an elongation of only 0.15% for the cast alloy at that time. Thus, the maximum design stress for the high-carbon cast heat-resistant alloys in long-time elevated temperature service generally is limited by the stress that will produce rupture after a desired life span; whereas, for corresponding wrought alloys or relatively low-carbon cast corrosion-resistant alloys, the design stress criterion for the same life span is the stress that will result in an acceptable total deformation over the useful life.

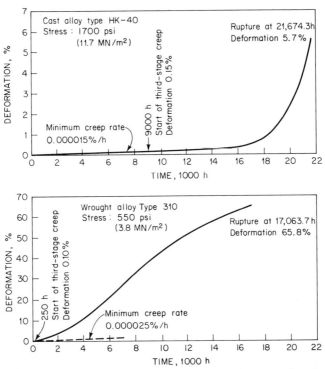

Fig. 2 Time-deformation curves for creep-rupture test specimens of cast HK-40 (0.44% carbon) and wrought type 310 (0.06% carbon) 25Cr-20Ni alloys at 1800°F (982°C). Note that the vertical scale for type 310 is *10 times* the scale for type HK-40. *(Adapted from Van Echo, Roach, and Hall.[1])*

MANUFACTURE OF HIGH-ALLOY CASTINGS AND GENERAL AREAS OF APPLICATION

The exacting requirements of the severe service conditions in which high alloys are employed demand close control of all foundry operations for the production of acceptable castings. Accordingly, intimate knowledge of the intended application is helpful to both the user and the casting manufacturer. For this reason no one foundry customarily produces all of the various alloy types. Because the alloys and the types of castings used for resistance to aqueous corrosive media at relatively moderate temperatures are distinctly different from those used to resist gaseous corrodents at high temperatures, producers of high-alloy castings have tended to concentrate on either heat- or corrosion-resistant alloy categories. Similar considerations have prompted most high-alloy casting producers who also manufacture castings in other metals to confine their high-alloy operations either to an individual section of the main plant or to an entirely separate foundry where special melting, molding, cleaning, and inspection equipment and personnel can be devoted to making only high-alloy castings.

Use of stainless steel castings has been growing steadily over the past 40 years. Current production (1974) is more than 10 times the output of the immediate pre-World War II years—an average annual growth rate of about 7%. Corrosion- and heat-resistant castings are indispensible components of many severe service industrial process systems. As such they contribute in large measure to the efficient operation of modern industrial equipment, especially in those industries where continuity of operation and freedom from contamination are essential. The chemical producers, food processors, oil refiners, pharmaceutical manufacturers, pulp and paper mills, textile dyers, and so on (wherever corrosive materials are encountered) are substantial users of corrosion-resistant castings for liquid handling and control equipment, as are the water supply and nuclear power utility systems. Most heat-resistant castings are used in industrial furnaces of various types as parts of the structures or for containing or conveying material being processed. Heat-treating furnaces, petrochemical stills, power plant boilers, refractory and cement kilns, refuse incinerators, steel mills, and roasting ovens for ore reduction are major consumers.

DESCRIPTION OF INDIVIDUAL ALLOYS

Corrosion-Resistant Types   Iron-chromium alloys are "stainless" in many media, particularly those that are highly oxidizing, their corrosion resistance increasing with their chromium content. Those at the lower chromium levels are hardenable by transformation of austenite to martensite and can be given a wide range of mechanical properties. At higher chromium contents the alloys are ferritic at all temperatures up to the melting point and cannot be hardened by heat treatment. As nickel content is increased, resistance of the alloys to weakly oxidizing acids and neutral chloride solutions is improved. Additions of molybdenum to the alloys increases their resistance to pitting in chloride-containing media. Alloys containing substantial amounts of nickel are either wholly austenitic in microstructure or a combination of austenite and ferrite (as previously noted in the discussion of the cast grade CF-8M in comparison to the wrought Type 316). Like the nonhardenable ferritic alloys, the austenitic grades cannot be hardened by the austenite-martensite transformation process. There are, however, some chromium-nickel compositions that can be hardened by a heat treatment that results in a martensite transformation, a precipitation of another phase, or a combination of both mechanisms. Thus there are five types of corrosion-resistant casting alloys:
1. Martensitic
2. Ferritic
3. Precipitation-hardening
4. Austenitic-ferritic
5. Austenitic

Martensitic Grades. The alloys included are CA-15, CA-40, CA-15M, and CA-6NM. Type CA-15 is an Fe-Cr alloy containing the minimum amount of chromium necessary to make it essentially rustproof. It has good resistance to atmospheric corrosion as well as to many organic media in relatively mild service. Type CA-40 is a higher carbon modification of CA-15 that can be heat-treated to higher strength and hardness levels. Type CA-15M is a molybdenum-containing modification of CA-15 that provides improved elevated temperature strength properties. Type CA-6NM is an Fe-Cr-Ni-Mo alloy of low carbon content. The addition of nickel to the composition offsets the ferritizing effect of low carbon content so that strength and hardness properties are comparable to CA-15 and the impact strength is substantially improved. The molybdenum addition confers increased resistance on the alloy to seawater corrosion.

A wide range of mechanical properties can be obtained in the martensitic alloy group. Tensile strengths from 90 to 220 ksi (621 to 1520 MN/m^2) and hardness as high as 500 BHN are obtainable through choice of heat treatment. Frequently used heat treatments and resulting properties are set forth in Table 3. The alloys have fair to good machining and welding properties if proper techniques are employed, with type CA-40 considered the poorest and CA-6NM the best in this regard. The tough, erosion-resistant microstructure of the martensitic alloys makes them useful as castings for pumps, compressors, valves, hydraulic turbines, propellers and machinery components.

Ferritic Grades. These are designated CB-30 and CC-50. Type CB-30 is a borderline alloy that is practically nonhardenable by heat treatment. As normally made, the balance among the elements in the composition results in a wholly ferritic structure similar to the wrought alloy Type 442. By balancing the composition toward the low end of the chromium and the high ends of the nickel and carbon ranges, however, some martensite can be formed through heat treatment, and the properties of the alloy approach those of

TABLE 3   Representative Room-Temperature Mechanical Properties of Cast Corrosion-resistant Alloys[2] (*Not* specification values)

Alloy type	Heat treatment condition	Tensile strength		Yield strength, 0.2% offset		Elongation in 2 in. (50 mm), %	Reduction of area, %	Brinell hardness number	Charpy impact		
		ksi	MN/m²	ksi	MN/m²				ft-lb	kg-m	J
CA-6NM	a	120	827	100	689	24	60	269	70†	9.7	94.9
CA-15	b	115	793	100	689	22	55	225	20‡	2.8	27.1
CA-40	a	150	1034	125	862	10	30	310	2‡	0.3	2.71
CB-30	c	95	655	60	414	15		195	2‡	0.3	2.71
CB-7Cu	d	190	1310	170	1172	14	54	400	25†	3.5	33.9
CC-50*	e	97	669	65	448	18		210			
CD-4MCu	f	108	745	81	558	25		253	55†	7.6	74.6
CE-30	g	97	669	63	434	18		190	7‡	1.0	9.5
CF-3	h	77	531	36	248	60		140	110†	15.2	149.2
CF-3A	h	87	600	42	290	50		160	100†	13.8	135.6
CF-8	h	77	531	37	255	55		140	74‡,¶	10.2	100.3
CF-8A	h	85	586	45	310	50		156	70‡	9.7	94.9
CF-20	g	77	531	36	248	50		163	60‡	8.3	81.4
CF-3M	h	80	552	38	262	55		150	120†	16.6	162.7
CF-3MA	h	90	621	45	310	45		170	100†	13.8	135.6
CF-8M	g	80	552	42	290	50		170	70‡	9.7	94.9
CF-8C	h	77	531	38	262	39		149	30‡	4.2	40.7
CF-16F	g	77	531	40	276	52		150	75‡	10.4	101.7
CG-8M	h	82	565	44	303	45		176	80†	11.1	108.5
CH-20	g	88	607	50	345	38		190	30‡	4.2	40.7
CK-20	i	76	524	38	262	37		144	50§	6.9	67.8
CN-7M	g	69	476	31	214	48		130	70‡	9.7	94.9

Heat treatment code:

a—Air-cooled from above 1750°F (954°C), tempered at 1100 to 1150°F (593 to 621°C).
b—Air-cooled from above 1800°F (982°C), tempered at 1200°F (649°C).
c—Annealed at 1450°F (788°C), furnace-cooled to 1000°F (538°C), then air-cooled.
d—Oil-quenched from 1900°F (1038°C), aged 925°F (496°C) 1 h, then air-cooled.
e—Air-cooled from 1900°F (1038°C).
f—Solution-annealed at 2050°F (1121°C) minimum, furnace-cooled to 1900°F (1038°C), then water quenched.
g—Water-quenched from above 2000°F (1093°C).
h—Water-quenched from above 1900°F (1038°C).
i—Water-quenched from above 2100°F (1149°C).
*Composition containing over 2.0% nickel and 0.15% nitrogen.
†Charpy V-notch.
‡Charpy keyhole notch.
§Izod V-notch.
¶Charpy keyhole notch value at −423°F (−253°C): 52 ft-lb (7.2 kg-m, 70.5 J).

the hardenable wrought alloy Type 431. Type CB-30 castings have greater resistance to most corrodents than the CA grades and are used for valve bodies and trim in general chemical production and food processing. Because of its low impact strength, however, the alloy has been supplanted in many applications by the higher-nickel-containing austenitic grades of the CF type. The high-chromium CC-50 alloy has good resistance to oxidizing corrodents, mixed nitric and sulfuric acids, and alkaline liquors. It is used for castings in contact with acid mine waters and in nitrocellulose production. For best impact strength, the alloy is made with over 2.0% nickel and 0.15% minimum nitrogen.

Precipitation-Hardening Grades. CB-7Cu and CD-4MCu are the alloys in this group. Type CB-7Cu is a low-carbon, martensitic alloy containing minor amounts of retained austenite. The contained copper precipitates submicroscopically in the martensite when the alloy is heat-treated to be in the hardened condition. Corrosion resistance of CB-7Cu lies between that of the CA types and the nonhardenable CF alloys, so it is used where both high strength and improved corrosion resistance is required. CB-7Cu castings can be machined readily in the annealed condition and then through-hardened by a low-temperature aging treatment (900 to 1100°F) (482 to 593°C). Because of this capability the CB-7Cu grade has found wide application for highly stressed, machined castings in the aircraft and food processing industries.

Type CD-4MCu is a two-phase alloy with an austenite-ferrite structure which, due to its high chromium and low carbon contents, does not develop martensite when heat-treated. Like the CB-7Cu grade, the alloy can be hardened by a low-temperature aging treatment, but it is normally used in the solution-annealed condition in which its strength is double that of the CF grades. This alloy has corrosion resistance equal to, or better than, the CF types and has excellent resistance to stress-corrosion cracking in chloride-containing media such as seawater. It is highly resistant to sulfuric and nitric acids and is used for pumps, valves, and stressed components in the marine, chemical, textile, and paper industries where a combination of superior corrosion resistance and high strength is essential.

Austenitic-Ferritic Grades. The alloys in this group include CE-30, CF-3, CF-3A, CF-8, CF-8A, CF-20, CF-3M, CF-3MA, CF-8M, CF-8C, CF-16F, and CG-8M. The microstructure of these alloys usually contains from 5 to 40% ferrite, depending on the particular grade and the balance among the ferrite-promoting and austenite-promoting elements in the chemical composition. This ferrite content improves the weldability of the alloys, increases their mechanical strength, and raises their resistance to stress-corrosion cracking. The amount of ferrite in a corrosion-resistant casting can be estimated from its composition by use of the Schoefer diagram[3] (see Fig. 12, Chapter 10), or from its response to magnetic measuring instruments. The diagram is related to the Schaeffler constitution diagram developed for determining the structure of weld deposits, and is constructed to read in "ferrite number" to agree with the calibration procedure for magnetic measurement of the ferrite content of austenitic stainless steel weld metal and castings adopted by the High Alloys Committee of the Welding Research Council. In producing controlled-ferrite alloy grades, the Schoefer diagram is useful in adjusting the preliminary analysis of a furnace charge to obtain the composition balance necessary for a specified ferrite-content range.

Type CE-30 is a high-carbon, high-chromium alloy that has good resistance to sulfurous acid and can be used in the as-cast condition. It has been applied extensively in the pulp and paper industry for castings and welded assemblies that cannot be heat-treated effectively. A controlled-ferrite grade, designated CE-30A, is used in the petroleum industry for its high strength and for resistance to stress-corrosion cracking in polythionic acid.

The CF alloy types, as a group, constitute the major segment of corrosion-resistant casting production. When properly heat-treated, the alloys are resistant to a great variety of corrodents and are usually considered the best general-purpose types. They have good castability, machinability, and weldability, and are tough and strong at temperatures down to −423°F (−253°C). Type CF-8, with a nominal composition of 19Cr-9Ni-0.08C max. can be viewed as the base grade and all the others as variants of this basic type. The CF-8 alloy has excellent resistance to nitric acid and all strongly oxidizing conditions. The higher-carbon-content CF-20 grade is used satisfactorily for less corrosive service than that requiring CF-8, and type CF-3 is used where conditions are more severe. Type CF-3 is specifically designed for use where castings are to be welded without subsequent heat treatment as in field-welded construction. The molybdenum-containing grades CF-8M and CF-3M have improved resistance to reducing chemicals and are used to handle dilute sulfuric and acetic acids, paper mill liquors, and a wide variety of industrial corrodents. The CF-8M alloy has become the most frequently used grade for corrosion-resistant pumps and valves because of its versatility in meeting many corrosive service demands. Type CF-3M has a low carbon content permitting use of the alloy without heat treatment after welding. Type CF-8C contains columbium (niobium) which, by suitable heat treatment, combines with carbon and helps the alloy to avoid intergranular corrosion if exposed to chromium carbide formation temperatures. Castings of type CF-8C, therefore, are used to resist the same corrodents as CF-8 but where field welding or service temperatures around 1200°F (649°C) are involved.

Higher mechanical properties are specified for grades CF-3A, CF-8A, and CF-3MA than for the CF-3, CF-8, and CF-3M alloys because the compositions are balanced to provide a controlled amount of ferrite that will ensure the required strength. These grades are being used in nuclear power plant equipment.

The CF-16F grade has an addition of selenium to improve machinability of castings that require extensive drilling, threading and the like. It is used in service similar to CF-20. Type CG-8M has a higher molybdenum content than CF-8M and is preferred to the latter in service where improved resistance to sulfuric and sulfurous acid solutions and to the pitting action of halogen compounds is needed. Unlike CF-8M, however, it is not suitable for use in nitric acid or other strongly oxidizing environments.

Austenitic Grades. Included in this group are CH-20, CK-20, and CN-7M. The CH-20 and CK-20 alloys are high-chromium, high-carbon, wholly austenitic compositions in which the chromium exceeds the nickel content. They have better resistance to dilute sulfuric acid than CF-8 and have improved strength at elevated temperatures. These alloys are used for specialized applications in the chemical and paper industries for handling paper pulp solutions and nitric acid. For handling hot sulfuric acid at various concentrations, the nickel-predominant CN-7M grade containing molybdenum and copper is widely used. This alloy is also usefully resistant to dilute hydrochloric acid and hot chloride solutions. It is used in steel mills for nitric-hydrofluoric pickling solutions and in many industries for severe service applications where the chromium-predominant CF-type alloys are inadequate.

In addition to the alloys previously discussed which are customarily classed as stainless steels, there are a number of nickel-based casting alloys that are produced by high-alloy foundries for corrosion-resistant service. These include the standard grades CW-12M, CY-40, CZ-100, N-12M, and M-35 (shown in Table 1) and several proprietary alloys. The cost of these alloys normally confines their use to specific critical applications where their improved corrosion resistance over that of the stainless steel grades makes them economically justified.

Heat-Resistant Types   There are three classes of heat-resistant casting alloys and they have the following general characteristics:

1. Those containing from 8 to 30% chromium and little or no nickel. They have low strength at elevated temperatures but excellent resistance to oxidation and are used under oxidizing conditions and uniform heating at very low static loads.

2. Those containing in excess of 19% chromium and in excess of 9% nickel, with the chromium content greater than the nickel content. They are used under oxidizing conditions to withstand moderate changes in temperature and considerably greater loads than can be supported by the Class 1 alloys.

3. Those containing in excess of 10% chromium and in excess of 23% nickel, with the nickel content greater than the chromium content. They are used in reducing as well as oxidizing conditions to withstand severe temperature gradients such as in quenching fixtures and in parts that are not heated uniformly.

Surface stability is essential for any part intended for exposure to elevated temperatures for long times. Heat-resistant castings have the ability to withstand corrosive attack from hot gases because they tend to form adherent, protective scales that diminish the rate of corrosion with time. The protectiveness of the scale increases with either increasing chromium or increasing nickel depending on the constituents of the atmosphere to which the alloys are exposed. Structural stability is another property essential to long life of alloys used at high temperatures. Freedom from major phase changes (such as from ferrite to austenite and back) avoids the distortion that would otherwise occur. In addition, the alloy must not dissolve its strengthening constituents (such as carbides) nor precipitate embrittling constituents (such as sigma phase) at the operating temperature of the part or else its serviceability may be destroyed.

Although specifications for heat-resistant casting alloys call for minimum mechanical properties at room temperature, such values are relatively unimportant since they have little relation to the behavior of metals at high temperature. They may be of interest if castings are subjected to high stresses when cold, as in furnace shutdowns for repairs, but for design purposes, elevated temperature property data are essential. Elongation under load (creep) and life before rupture are time- and temperature-dependent properties. Comparative typical values for stresses that will produce minimum creep rates of 0.0001%/h, and rupture in 10,000 h at temperatures of 1400 and 1800°F (760 and 982°C) are given in Table 4 for the various grades. It must be recognized that the values shown are derived from laboratory tests and that the actual conditions of service may cause substantial departures from the indicated life or deformation. Variations in temperature (particularly heating above the designed maximum) can shorten life considerably. Contaminants in the atmosphere (high sulfur or vanadium pentoxide, for example) can result in drastic loss of metal section through corrosive attack.

TABLE 4   Representative Long-Time Elevated Temperature Mechanical Properties of Cast Heat-resistant Alloys[4]

Alloy	Stress at 1400°F (760°C) for								Stress at 1800°F (982°C) for							
	Minimum creep rate of 0.0001%/h		1% total elongation in 100,000 h		Rupture in 1000 h		Rupture in 10,000 h		Minimum creep rate of 0.0001%/h		1% total elongation in 100,000 h		Rupture in 1000 h		Rupture in 10,000 h	
	ksi	MN/m²	ksi	MN/m²	ksi	MN/m²	ksi	MN/m²	ksi	MN/m²	ksi	MN/m²	ksi	MN/m²	ksi	MN/m²
HA	16.0*	110*			27.0*	186*										
HC	1.3	9			2.3	15			0.4	3			0.6	4		
HD	3.5	24			7.0	48			0.9	6			2.5‡	17‡		
HE	4.0	28	4.4	30	11.0‡	76‡	6.1	42	1.4	10			2.5‡	17‡		
HF	6.8	47	2.0	14	9.1	63	4.8	33								
HH†	6.3	43			8.0	55			2.1	14			1.6	11	0.9	6
HI	6.6	46			8.5	59			1.9	13			2.6	18		
HK	10.2	70	6.3	43	12.0	83	8.8	61	2.5	17			2.8	19	1.7	12
HL	7.0	48			15.0‡	103‡			2.2	15	0.9	6	5.2‡	36‡		
HN									2.4	17	1.1	8	3.4	23	2.1	14
HP									2.8	19	2.1	14	3.6	25	2.2	15
HT	8.0	55			12.0	83	8.4	58	2.0	14			2.7	19	1.7	12
HU	8.5	59							2.2	15			2.9	20	1.8	12
HW	6.0	41			7.8	54			1.4	10			2.6	18		
HX	6.4	44							1.6	11			2.2	15		

*Stress at 1000°F (538°C).
†Wholly austenitic type.
‡Stress for rupture in 100 h.
Note: Values are for constant-temperature operation. If alloys are exposed to cyclic temperatures, lower values would apply.

Class 1 Iron-Chromium Grades. HA, HC, and HD are included in this group. Type HA is recommended for use only up to 1200°F (649°C). The molybdenum content of the alloy enhances the strength in the temperature range 1000 to 1200°F (538 to 649°C) and castings of this grade are used extensively in the petroleum industry. The HC and HD alloys can be used for moderate load-bearing applications up to 1200°F (649°C) and, where only light loads are involved, up to 1900°F (1038°C); type HD has a somewhat greater strength than type HC at elevated temperatures because of its higher nickel content. Both HC and HD are especially useful in high-sulfur-containing atmospheres, and in applications where high-nickel-content alloys cannot be used. Accordingly, high-sulfur-atmosphere applications not requiring high strengths (such as ore-roasting furnace rabble arms and blades, grate bars, and fan blades for hot gases) are among the uses for these types. The HC and HD alloys will become embrittled from sigma-phase formation if held for long periods in the temperature range 1300 to 1500°F (704 to 816°C).

Class 2 Iron-Chromium-Nickel Grades. Alloys in this class include HE, HF, HH, HI, HK, and HL. Being partially or completely austenitic, they have greater high-temperature strength than Class 1 alloys. They can be used in either oxidizing or reducing atmospheres containing moderate amounts of sulfur. Type HE is suitable for service up to 2000°F (1093°C). It has excellent corrosion resistance at high temperatures. Its relatively low nickel content makes it useful in very-high-sulfur environments, and it is the strongest grade available for such service. Typical applications, therefore, are in ore-roasting and steel mill furnaces. Type HF is similar in composition to the CF corrosion grades except that the carbon content is higher. Castings of this alloy operate in the 1200 to 1600°F (649 to 871°C) temperature range in oil refineries for tube supports, and in cement mills, ore-roasting and heat-treating furnaces.

Type HH exhibits high strength and resistance to oxidation at temperatures up to 2000°F (1093°C). These properties make it an extremely useful alloy, and it accounts for about one-third of the production of all heat-resistant castings. Depending on composition balance, the alloy can be partially ferritic or wholly austenitic. The austenitic type is preferred for operation below 1600°F (871°C); for service above 1600°F either of the compositions will serve—the ferritic for highest hot ductility and the austenitic for highest hot strength. Typical applications for the HH alloys are tube supports and beams in oil refineries, and for a wide variety of parts in cement mills, steel mills, and heat-treating furnaces. They are not generally recommended for service where severe temperature cycles are encountered, such as in quenching fixtures.

Type HI is more resistant to oxidation than type HH and can be used up to 2150°F (1176°C). Similar to the HH alloy in mechanical properties, the HI grade has been used mainly for cast retorts operating above 2100°F (1149°C) in magnesium production. Type HK is also similar to a fully austenitic HH alloy; it has high resistance to oxidation and is one of the strongest heat-resistant cast alloys at temperatures above 1900°F (1038°C). It can be used in structural applications up to 2100°F (1149°C), but it is not recommended for high-sulfur-bearing atmospheres or where severe thermal shock is a factor. The HK grade is widely used for parts requiring high creep-rupture strength. The HK-40 variety (0.35 to 0.45% carbon) has become a standard for centrifugally cast tubing used in petrochemical and petroleum refinery processes.

Type HL is similar to type HK but has higher chromium content. The composition of this alloy is among the most resistant to corrosion in high-sulfur-containing atmospheres up to 1800°F (982°C). It is used where higher strength is required than that obtainable with the HE grade or the Class 1 alloys. Typical applications are for gas dissociation equipment fixtures, radiant tubes, and stack dampers.

Class 3 Iron-Nickel-Chromium Grades. These include HN, HP, HT, HU, HW, and HX. These alloys have nickel as the predominant alloying element or as the base metal, and have a stable austenitic structure that is not as sensitive to variations in composition as the chromium-predominant Class 2 grades. This high-nickel group normally constitutes about 40% of the total production of heat-resistant castings. The alloys can be used up to 2100°F (1149°C); they have good hot strength, do not carburize readily, and give excellent service life where subject to rapid heating and cooling. Because of their high nickel content, however, they are not recommended for use in high-sulfur-bearing atmospheres.

Type HN has high strength comparable to the HK-40 type at 1800°F (982°C) and has been used successfully up to 2100°F (1149°C). It is used in high-temperature brazing

TABLE 5 Physical Properties of Corrosion and Heat-resistant Casting Alloys[2, 4]

Cast alloy designation	Tensile modulus of elasticity, million		Density		Specific heat		Specific electrical resistance at 70°F (21°C) μΩ/cm³	Melting point approx.		Thermal conductivity		Mean coefficient of linear thermal expansion 21–100°C		Magnetic permeability
	psi	kN/m²	lb/in.³	kg/m³	Btu/(lb)(°F) at 70°F	cal/(g/°C) at 21°C		°F	°C	Btu/(h)(ft²)(ft/°F) at 212°F	Cal/(s)(cm²)(cm/°C) at 100°C	70–212°F μin./(in.)(°F)	21–100°C μm/(m)(°C)	
CA-6NM	29	200	0.278	7695	0.11		78.0	2750	1510	14.5	0.060	6.0	10.8	Ferromagnetic
CA-15	29	200	0.275	7612	0.11		78.0	2750	1510	14.5	0.060	5.5	9.9	Ferromagnetic
CA-40	29	200	0.275	7612	0.11		76.0	2725	1496	14.5	0.060	5.5	9.9	Ferromagnetic
CB-7Cu*	29	200	0.282	7806	0.11		77.0	2750	1510	10.3	0.043	6.0	10.8	Ferromagnetic
CB-30	29	200	0.272	7529	0.11		76.0	2725	1496	12.8	0.053	5.7	10.3	Ferromagnetic
CC-50	29	200	0.272	7529	0.12		77.0	2725	1496	12.6	0.052	5.9	10.6	Ferromagnetic
CD-4MCu	29	200	0.280	7750	0.11		75.0	2700	1482	8.8	0.036	6.3	11.3	Ferromagnetic
CE-30	25	172	0.277	7667	0.14		85.0	2650	1454	8.5	0.035	8.7	15.7	Over 1.7
CF-3	28	193	0.280	7750	0.12		76.2	2650	1454	9.2	0.038	9.0	16.2	1.20–3.00
CF-8	28	193	0.280	7750	0.12		76.2	2600	1427	9.2	0.038	9.0	16.2	1.00–1.30
CF-20	28	193	0.280	7750	0.12		77.9	2575	1413	9.2	0.038	9.6	17.3	1.01
CF-3M	28	193	0.280	7750	0.12		82.0	2600	1427	9.4	0.039	8.9	16.0	1.50–3.00
CF-8M, CG-8M	28	193	0.280	7750	0.12		82.0	2550	1399	9.4	0.039	8.9	16.0	1.50–3.00
CF-8C	28	193	0.280	7750	0.12		71.0	2600	1427	9.3	0.038	9.3	16.7	1.20–1.80
CF-16F	28	193	0.280	7750	0.12		72.0	2550	1399	9.4	0.039	9.0	16.2	1.00–2.00

									At 1000°F	At 538°C	70–1000°F	21–538°C	
CH-20	28	193	0.279	7723	0.12	84.0	2600	1427	8.2	0.034	8.6	15.5	1.71
CK-20	29	200	0.280	7750	0.12	90.0	2600	1427	7.9	0.033	8.3	14.9	1.02
CN-7M	24	165	0.289	8000	0.11	89.6	2650	1454	12.1	0.050	8.6	15.5	1.01–1.10
HA	29	200	0.279	7723	0.11	70.0	2750	1510	15.7	0.065	7.1	12.8	Ferromagnetic
HC	29	200	0.272	7529	0.12	77.0	2725	1496	17.9	0.074	6.3	11.3	Ferromagnetic
HD	27	186	0.274	7584	0.12	81.0	2700	1482	17.9	0.074	7.7	13.9	Ferromagnetic
HE	25	172	0.277	7667	0.14	85.0	2650	1454	12.4	0.051	9.6	17.3	1.30–2.50
HF	28	193	0.280	7750	0.12	80.0	2550	1399	12.3	0.051	9.9	17.8	1.00
HH	27	186	0.279	7723	0.12	75–85	2500	1371	12.0	0.050	9.5	17.1	1.00–1.90
HI	27	186	0.279	7723	0.12	85.0	2550	1399	12.0	0.050	9.9	17.8	1.00–1.70
HK	27	186	0.280	7750	0.12	90.0	2550	1399	11.8	0.049	9.4	16.9	1.02
HL	29	200	0.279	7723	0.12	94.0	2600	1427	12.2	0.050	9.2	16.6	1.01
HN	27	186	0.283	7833	0.11	99.1	2500	1371	11.0	0.045	9.3	16.7	1.10
HP	27	186	0.284	7861	0.11	102.0	2450	1343	11.0	0.045	9.2	16.6	1.02–1.25
HT	27	186	0.286	7916	0.11	100.0	2450	1343	10.8	0.045	8.9	16.0	1.10–2.00
HU	27	186	0.290	8027	0.11	105.0	2450	1343	10.8	0.045	8.8	15.8	1.10–2.00
HW	25	172	0.294	8138	0.11	112.0	2350	1288	11.1	0.046	8.0	14.4	16.00
HX	25	172	0.294	8138	0.11	116.0	2350	1288	11.1	0.046	7.8	14.0	2.00

*In hardened condition.

fixtures, radiant tubes, heat-treating furnace parts and petrochemical furnace tubes and tube supports. Its properties are similar to the HT grade but it has better ductility. Type HP has higher nickel and higher chromium contents than type HN which give the alloy improved resistance to hot gas corrosion in both oxidizing and reducing atmospheres in the higher temperature range. Creep-rupture strength of type HP castings in the 1800 to 2000°F (982 to 1093°C) range is comparable to, or better than, the HN and HK-40 types.

Type HT can be used satisfactorily at temperatures up to 2100°F (1149°C) in oxidizing atmospheres, and 2000°F (1093°C) in reducing atmospheres. This alloy is very resistant to carburizing environments and is used widely for heat-treating furnace parts such as rails, disks, chains, belt links, boxes, pots, and fixtures subject to cyclic heating. It is also used for glass rolls, and radiant heater tubes. Type HU is a higher-nickel, higher-chromium modification of type HT. Although used for the same general applications as HT, it is often recommended for severe service conditions because the increased alloy content improves both hot strength and resistance to corrosive attack.

Type HW is not as strong at elevated temperature as the HT and HU alloys, but has better life in service involving drastic thermal shock and temperature cycling. It performs satisfactorily up to about 2050°F (1121°C) in strongly oxidizing atmospheres and up to 1900°F (1038°C) in oxidizing or reducing products of combustion provided that sulfur is not present in the gas. Sulfur will react with the protective scale on this alloy to form a low-melting-point compound which, by fluxing action, causes a rapid removal of scale and accelerates the corrosion. In sulfur-free atmospheres, however, the generally adherent nature of the oxide scale on type HW castings makes this grade suitable for enameling furnace service where even small flakes of dislodged scale could ruin the work in process. The type HX alloy is related to the HW grade in the same way that type HU is related to type HT. It is higher in both nickel and chromium and the increased alloy content confers substantially improved resistance to hot gas corrosion on HX, even in the presence of some sulfur. In other properties it is essentially the same as type HW and is suitable for the same applications in situations where corrosion must be minimized. Both grades are highly resistant to carburization when in contact with tempering and cyaniding salts; they are not recommended for use with neutral salts, however, nor salts used in hardening high-speed steels. The high electrical resistance of these alloys makes them attractive for use as cast electric heating elements. Their tolerance of steep thermal gradients and thermal shock under high stress has made them frequently used for intricate heat-treating fixtures that are quenched with the load.

INFLUENCE OF PHYSICAL PROPERTIES

The physical properties listed in Table 5 must be given consideration for their influence on application, design, and fabrication of the various alloy grades. For example, in comparison with carbon steel these alloys have about five times the electrical resistance, 50% greater thermal expansion, and 50% less heat conductivity. Although all the grades are machinable and weldable, as described elsewhere in this handbook, these thermal and electrical characteristics of the alloys have an important effect on such operations and proper techniques must be employed for satisfactory results. The low thermal conductivity can cause development of steep thermal gradients which, in conjunction with the large thermal expansion coefficients, can create damaging high stresses in high-temperature applications unless carefully avoided through appropriate component design.

PURCHASING CONSIDERATIONS

In ordering heat-resistant or corrosion-resistant castings, the purchaser must bear in mind that these products are custom-made in closely controlled alloy compositions and are to be used for exacting service conditions. For this reason, timely delivery of satisfactory castings often depends on the extent to which the buyer has supplied the foundry with complete information at the outset. Understanding the properties of the casting alloys and consultation with the producing foundry before "freezing" a casting design will help to prevent misunderstandings between producers and purchasers that can cause delays in production. The following guides should be observed for best results:

1. Specify the desired alloy composition by *casting type designation.* Use of ASTM specifications that have been developed as a consensus of consumers, producers, and disinterested experts is often the most effective way to ensure understanding of the requirements.

2. Provide as much service information as possible to the foundry. Conditions of temperature, corrosive environment, and loading are important in assessing the suitability of a casting design. In addition, the foundry should be informed of fabrication, i.e., machining or welding, and specification or construction code requirements that might be applied later to the casting as a component of the purchaser's product.

3. Give complete dimensions and detailed drawings. Designs based on forgings or welded assemblies frequently can be improved as castings with respect to strength-weight distribution or streamlining of contours; in addition, design changes may be required to enhance the soundness of wall sections. Early consultation between the engineering department of the purchaser and the foundry is helpful to both.

4. Use good pattern equipment. Proper patterns are just as important as proper part design in the production of successful castings. Patterns used in making high-quality, high-alloy castings must be designed and rigged specifically for this purpose. It must be recognized that the physical properties of high alloys differ among themselves and markedly from those of gray iron or steel. Patterns suitable for those metals cannot be counted on for production of sound, dimensionally accurate castings of heat- or corrosion-resistant Fe-Cr-Ni alloys. (See Table 6 for comparative patternmakers' shrinkage allowances for the various grades.)

TABLE 6   Comparative Patternmakers' Shrinkage Allowance[*2, 4]

| | Shrinkage allowance | |
Material	in./ft	mm/m
Gray iron, bronze	1/8	10.4
Aluminum, magnesium	5/32	13.0
Steel, brass	3/16	15.6
HC, HD, CC-50	7/32	18.2
HA, CA-6NM, CA-15, CA-40, CB-30, CD-4MCu	1/4	20.8
HE, HF, HW, HX	9/32	23.4
HH, HI, HK, HL, HN, HP, HT, HU, CE-30, CF-3, CF-8,		
CF-3M, CF-8M, CF-16F, CG-8M, CH-20, CK-20, CN-7M	5/16	26.0
CF-20, CF-8C	11/32	28.6

*These values are for unhindered contraction; considerable variation may occur, depending on the shape of the casting.

5. Be realistic in delivery requirements. Unusual or unnecessary special inspection and testing specifications delay deliveries. The best assurance of obtaining promised deliveries of castings meeting the desired quality is procurement from a foundry *experienced* in producing castings of the types and alloys involved.

SPECIFICATIONS

Organizations in the United States issuing specifications covering corrosion-resistant and heat-resistant high-alloy castings are: American Society for Testing and Materials (ASTM), American National Standards Institute (ANSI), American Society of Mechanical Engineers (ASME), Department of Defense (MIL), and Society of Automotive Engineers, Aeronautical Materials Specifications (AMS). ASTM specifications are adopted by ANSI and ASME codes.

Corrosion-resistant and heat-resistant casting alloys are listed by ACI type designations in Tables 7 and 8 with the applicable ASTM, MIL, and AMS specifications. Also listed are the nearest equivalent alloys covered by specifications or designations in Germany, Great Britain, India, Italy, Japan, France, Russia, and Sweden.

TABLE 7 American and Foreign Nearest Equivalent Casting Specifications or Alloy Designations for Corrosion-resistant Castings[6]

ACI type	USA ASTM A296	USA ASTM A351	USA MIL-S867 (Ships)	USA AMS	USA MIL-S16993A	Germany DIN 17445 reference (DIN 17006)	GB BS1504	GB BS1630	GB BS1631	GB BS1632	GB BS1965	India IS:3444	Italy UNI 3161	Japan JIS G5121	French AFNOR	Russian GOST	Swedish SIS
CA-6NM	*																
CA-15	*	*		5351B	(I)	G-X25Cr14	713	A				(1)	X20C12	SCS1			
CA-40	*							B				(3)		SCS2			
CB-30	*											(4)					
CB-7Cu				5398A													
CC-50	*	*										(5)	X25C26				
CD-4MCu		*				G-X40CrNi274											
CE-30	*	*															
CF-3	*	*							C		C801L		X3CN1911	SCS19	Z3CN18-10	Kh18N8	
CF-3A	*	*															
CF-8	*	*	(I)	5371		G-X6CrNi189	801		A		C801		X10CN188	SCS13	Z6CN18-10	0 Kh18N9	2332
CF-8A	*	*															
CF-20	*	*				G-X15CrNi188			D			(6)	X17CN188	SCS12	Z12CN18-10	1Kh18N9	2330
CF-3M	*	*								F	C845L			SCS16	Z3CND18-12		
CF-3MA	*	*															
CF-8M	*	*	(III)	5361B		G-X5CrNiMo1810			D	D	C845B	(9)	X10CND188	SCS14	Z6CND18-12	Kh18N9M	2342
CF-12M		*															
CF-8C	*	*	(II)	5363B		G-X10CrNiNb189	821		B		C821Nb	(7)		SCS21	Z10CNNb18-10	0 Kh18N9B	2333
CF-16F		*	(I)						D								
CG-12		*															
CG-8M	*	*									C846	(10)		SCS17			
CH-20	*	*								A				SCS18	Z15CNS25-13	Kh23N15	
CK-20	*	*		5365A							C805	(15)		SCS23	Z15CNS25-20	Kh25N20	
CN-7M	*	*															

*ACI type designations are used to identify grades in these specifications.

TABLE 8 American and Foreign Nearest Equivalent Casting Specifications or Alloy Designations for Heat-resistant Castings[6]

ACI type	USA ASTM A217	USA ASTM A297	USA ASTM A351	Germany Stahl-Eisen-Werkstoffblatt 471-60 Ref.: DIN 17006	Great Britain BS1504	Great Britain BS1648	Great Britain BS4238	India IS:3038	Italy UNI3159	Japan JIS G5122	Alloy designation French AFNOR	Alloy designation Russian GOST
HA	C12				629†							
HC		*		G-X40CrSi29		B1		(7)	X45CN28	SCH2		
HD		*		G-X40CrNi274		B2				SCH11		
HE		*				D				SCH17		
HF		*		G-X40CrNiSi229						SCH12		0Kh18N9S2
HH(1)‡		*		G-X35CrNiSi2512		E	EC2		X25CN2412	SCH13		
HH(2)§		*		G-X40CrNiSi2614			EC1					
HI		*				F				SCH18		
HK			*	G-X40CrNiSi2520			FC		X25CN2420	SCH21		
HK30			*				FC					
HK40		*				G				SCH22		
HL		*				H2						
HN		*				H1				SCH19		
HP		*					H1C					
HT		*	*	G-X40NiCrSi3616					X25CN1533	SCH15	Z20NCS36-18	Kh15N35
HT30						H2	H2C					
HU		*				K				SCH16		
HW		*				K				SCH20		
HX		*										

*ACI type designations are used to identify grades in these specifications.
†Also BS1463.
‡Partially ferritic.
§Wholly austenitic.

REFERENCES

1. Van Echo, J. A., D. B. Roach, and A. M. Hall: Short-Time Tensile and Long-Time Creep-Rupture Properties of the HK-40 Alloy and Type 310 Stainless Steel at Temperatures to 2000°F, *Trans. Am. Soc. Mech. Eng.,* 1967.
2. Schoefer, E. A.: High Alloy Data Sheets, Corrosion Series, Alloy Casting Institute Div., Steel Founders' Society of America, Rocky River, Ohio, 1973.
3. Schoefer, E. A.: Appendix to paper, Mössbauer-Effect Examination of Ferrite in Stainless Steel Welds and Castings, *Weld. J.,* Vol. 39, p. 10-s, January 1974.
4. Schoefer, E. A., and T. A. Shields: High Alloy Data Sheets, Heat Series, Alloy Casting Institute Div., Steel Founders' Society of America, Rocky River, Ohio, 1973.
5. Schoefer, E. A.: How to Buy High Alloy Castings, *Purchasing,* Jan. 18, 1960.
6. "British and Foreign Specifications for Steel Castings," 3d ed., Steel Castings Research and Trade Association, Sheffield, England, December 1968.

Chapter 3

Melting of Stainless Steels

DONALD C. HILTY
Metallurgical Consultant

THOMAS F. KAVENY
Manager, Electric Furnace Market Development, Metals Division,

Union Carbide Corporation, Niagara Falls, New York

OPERATIONS

As this handbook is being prepared, stainless steel melting is undergoing a substantial transition. After years during which melting and refining were done exclusively in the arc furnace (with a small amount of production reserved for the induction furnace), the electric furnace is becoming solely a melting unit, with refining moved to another vessel. Also, a small-to-moderate tonnage is being produced in basic oxygen furnaces (BOF), sometimes using other vessels or facilities for refining.

To lay the groundwork for exploring the technology of the stainless steelmaking process, we should review the basic mechanics of the more important processes.

Air-Melt—Electric-Arc Furnace   Figure 1 is a drawing of a basic-lined electric-arc furnace. There is no difference between a furnace intended for stainless melting and one intended for carbon steel production. Commonly, one furnace is used for both.

The stainless steel melting process can be visualized as a number of steps frequently overlapping. These are: charging, melting, decarburizing, reducing, and finishing. A log of a well-made heat is given in Table 1.

Charging. After tapping the previous heat and fettling the furnace hearth with magnesite or dolomite, the furnace is charged. The mix consists of stainless and carbon steel scrap, charge chrome*, and possibly a nickel or molybdenum source. Lime is commonly added to neutralize silica formed during meltdown. The exact makeup varies with such things as analysis to be produced, availability of materials, and shop or process limitations. There is no "perfect" charge and even what is best for a given shop is influenced by subjective judgments. The matter of process restrictions will be discussed later.

Charge placement is no different from carbon-steel operations. It is desirable to have heavy material on the bottom both to protect the hearth and to avoid the possibility of its falling against and breaking an electrode should the charge shift during melting. Light scrap should be charged last, so as to be at the top of the furnace where it will absorb heat radiated from the arcs and hence help protect roof and sidewalls.

In many instances, the volume of the furnace is insufficient to contain the entire charge before at least a portion of it is melted; one or more recharges may therefore be necessary. Melting the first charge completely before adding the second charge is unnecessary and even undesirable. Doing so takes time and power, increases refractory wear, and increases the possibility of splash when the second charge is added. As a rule of thumb, the first charge should be about 75% melted when the second charge is added.

Alloy, such as charge chrome, is frequently added between charges.

Roughly speaking, the densities of various types of scrap are as follows:

$$
\begin{array}{ll}
\text{Light scrap} & 300\text{--}800 \text{ kg/m}^3 \\
\text{Medium scrap} & 1600\text{--}2500 \text{ kg/m}^3 \\
\text{Heavy scrap} & 4300\text{--}4800 \text{ kg/m}^3
\end{array}
$$

Meltdown. After a brief period of reduced power while the electrodes bore into the charge and the gap between arc and roof widens, the meltdown should be as rapid as possible. There are two schools of thought regarding the extent of melting prior to continuing to the next (decarburizing) operation: one school prefers complete liquefaction; the other prefers less complete liquefaction, leaving up to 30% of the bath solid as the process continues. The former method tends to lead to lower oxidation of chromium on subsequent processing, although meltdown time is extended. Again, neither option is right or wrong, but the choice should reflect what is best for the shop and involves factors such as furnace and transformer size, oxygen injection rate, etc. There is also a good deal of subjective judgment involved in the decision.

Decarburization. Decarburization is at the heart of the stainless melting process. It involves the injection of gaseous oxygen into the bath to oxidize and remove carbon. The necessity of removing carbon to low levels in the presence of chromium creates the special character of stainless steel melting.

Two techniques of oxygen injection are widely employed. The older method is the use of a straight-pipe consumable lance which is fed into the bath as it is burned. The tip of this lance is usually positioned at the slag-metal interface and feeding is normally by hand. A bare or a coated lance may be used; the former lasts about 5 to 10 min (for a 20-ft [6.1-m] pipe), while the latter will have a life of up to 30 min.

In large furnaces—and increasingly in smaller ones—an oxygen "gun," frequently water-cooled, is used. The "gun" blows oxygen at very high velocity onto the slag which is parted by the force of the jet to give the oxygen access to the metal.

---

*A type of high-carbon ferrochromium alloy.

No precise comparison of the efficiency of oxygen utilization by hand-held lances and guns has been made, but it is assumed commonly that the differences are not great.

The rate at which oxygen is injected into steel is influenced by furnace size. Total volume per unit of time is greater on the large furnaces, but smaller furnaces require a greater volume per unit of time per ton of capacity. There are lower limits below which

Fig. 1   Direct arc furnace. *(Carbon Products Division, Union Carbide Corporation, New York)*

oxygen injection is ineffective, about which much will be said in the technology section. No practical maximum has been established although for a given furnace one must exist.

Reduction. Oxygen injection for carbon removal, unfortunately, leads to substantial oxidation of chromium. In the interest of economy this chromium is recovered by addition to the slag of a reducing agent (normally a silicon alloy) as soon as oxygen injection is terminated. The reducing agent is generally accompanied by lime which, along with lime that may have been added in the charge, creates a basic slag from which chromium is best reduced.

The reducing period is also used to make other additions, notably scrap and low-carbon ferrochromium (FeCr). At the completion of oxygen injection, because of heat generated by the oxidation of C, Si, Cr, Fe, and Mn, the bath is quite hot, e.g., 1875°C (3400°F). It is much hotter, in fact, than the refractories are expected to withstand. These temperatures are helpful in reducing oxidation of chromium, but once decarburization is completed the bath must be cooled as quickly as possible to preclude excessive refractory wear. Hence, scrap is added as soon as the oxygen lance is withdrawn. The scrap should be heavy, clean, and well-identified, for very little refining (except for sulfur removal) is accomplished after decarburization. At the time scrap is added, an amount of low-carbon FeCr known to be needed is also added. This further cools the bath, minimizes later additions which must be melted-in with power, and brings the analysis of the bath close to the final specification for chromium.

As a rule, power is applied during slag reduction. While there is enough excess heat in

TABLE 1 Grade 304 Heat Log*

	C	Mn	P	S	Si	Cr	Ni	Mo	Cu
Spec.:	0.055/0.075	1.50/1.80	0.025 max.	0.015 max.	0.40/0.70	18.00/18.25	8.00/8.50	0.50 max.	0.50 max.
Aim:	0.07	1.65	0.021	0.006	0.55	18.15	8.30		
Final:	0.069	1.69			0.58	18.18	8.49	0.18	0.37

PRELIMINARY CHEMISTRY

Sent	Received	C	Mn	P	S	Si	Cr	Ni	Mo	Cu
8:47	9:02	0.52	0.84	0.021	0.032	0.13	14.94	8.57	0.21	0.44
9:42	9:50	0.066	1.45	0.023	0.013	0.70	18.19	8.35	0.17	0.37
10:37	11:04	0.070					18.23	8.45		
								8.49		

Material	Amount, lb (kg)	
18-8 scrap	40,820	(18,516)
18-8 H. M.	11,600	(5262)
Graphite	300	(136)
Charge Cr	2200	(998)
NiO sinter	2100	(953)
Low P scrap	12,040	(5461)
Lime	2300	(1043)

Time	Operation
5:36–5:40	Tap previous heat
5:45–6:16	Repair furnace
6:25–7:05	Charge furnace
	→ Overage from previous heat
7:05	Power on
7:50	Add second charge
8:45	Complete meltdown T-2920°F (1605°C)

Time	Addition	ft³	(m³)	Remarks
8:47				Take meltdown chemistry; returned at 9:02
9:09				Temperature check 2970°F (1632°C)
9:10–9:39	O_2	21,500 ft³	(609 m³)	Blow with O_2
9:42				Take C test; returned at 9:50
9:43–9:46				Add reduction mix
	FeCrSi	5300	(2404)	
	FeMnSi	700	(318)	
	Low-carbon FeCr	2100	(953)	
	18-8 scrap	3400	(1542)	
	NiO sinter	200	(91)	
	Lime	3800	(1724)	
9:46–10:15				Fuse and refine reducing slag
10:20–10:25				Tap metal
10:25–10:30				Decant slag
10:30–10:35	Low P scrap	1000	(454)	Refurnace
	Lime	650	(295)	
	Fluorspar	200	(91)	
10:35	75% FeSi	125	(57)	Add refining slag
10:37				Temperature check 3065°F (1685°C)
10:37				Take chemistry check; returned at 11:04
11:05	Elec. Mn	175	(79)	Make final additions
	Low P scrap	200	(91)	
11:25				Blow 2 min with argon
11:27				Temperature check 3060°F (1682°C)
11:27				Blow 2 min with argon
11:35				Temperature check 3060°F (1682°C)
11:35				Tap—38.7 tons (35.1 metric tons)
Time, tap to tap				5:59
O_2 used				555 ft³/ton (17.3 m³/metric ton)
Power used				439 kWh/ton (484 kWh/metric ton)

*Courtesy, S. E. Wolosin, Melt. Supt., Washington Steel Corporation.

the system to fuse the slag and melt the additions, mixing of slag and metal is not good and excess heat is not always where it is needed; hence, a nominal use of power to liquify slag.

The most commonly used reducing agent is ferrochromium silicon (FeCrSi). FeCrSi is selected on the basis of its cost, which is usually less than equivalent additions of ferrosilicon (FeSi) and low-carbon FeCr. Ferromanganese silicon (FeMnSi) is also widely used, when its use is less costly than equivalent but separate manganese plus silicon additions. The amount of addition is determined by the amount of chromium to be reduced from the slag, which in turn depends on the conditions which existed during decarburization.

On completion of reduction, which would normally take about 20 min, the reducing slag is removed and replaced with a finishing slag. This slag is made up of lime, fluorspar, and generally, a reducing agent such as relatively fine ferrosilicon.

Reduction and slag removal are combined in many shops in a refurnacing operation. In this instance, after the various additions are made at reduction and the slag fused, metal and slag are poured together into a ladle. The slag is decanted and the metal returned to the furnace for finishing. Refurnacing accomplishes a number of desirable aims:

1. It accomplishes the intimate mixing of metal and slag and improves the efficiency of slag reduction.

2. It cools the metal.

3. It enables operators to patch the furnace and it very effectively aids cooling the refractory.

4. It simplifies slag removal. (Slag is decanted from the ladle.)

5. It mixes the metal thoroughly, so that a representative chemical sample can be obtained.

6. In some cases, it allows the metal to be weighed before return to the furnace so that more precise final additions can be calculated.

Finishing. This period starts with the addition of the so-called finishing slag and incorporates tasks such as sampling, alloying, desulfurizing, and adjusting temperature for tap. Slags are generally dressed with FeSi or calcium silicon (CaSi). Carbon dressing is, of course, out of the question because of probable carbon pickup. Aluminum-dressed slags are seldom used, although they are employed in special cases where very low sulfur levels are needed or where highly oxidizable elements, e.g., titanium, are to be added through the slag.

In many foundries and under some conditions in an ingot shop, the reducing slag may not be removed. In this case, the separation of the reducing and the finishing period becomes indistinct.

Deoxidation. With its high levels of Si, Mn, and Cr, stainless steel is self-deoxidizing. On the other hand, in pursuit of cleanliness and inclusion control, aluminum may be used in some grades—primarily in the ferritic and martensitic steels. Occasionally, such aluminum additions are immersed in the bath below the slag, and often an aluminum addition is made to the ladle.

On austenitic grades, aluminum is seldom used; most American producers consider it detrimental to the surface appearance of polished strip. There is a similar aversion to using aluminum in martensitic steels destined for highly polished cutlery use.

CaSi or calcium-barium silicon (CaBaSi) are used in some plants for inclusion modification with improvement in internal cleanliness and surface quality.

Ladle additions in stainless steel are not the rule. If needed, aluminum and calcium alloys are so added, but aside from those, only titanium and columbium (as an exothermic alloy) are sometimes put in the ladle.

For a similar carbon content, stainless steel is tapped at a lower temperature than are carbon grades, although it is difficult to set a level in view of differences in casting techniques in each shop (e.g., small versus large ingots, pressure casting versus ingot casting, etc.). Also, stainless steels tend to pour more sluggishly than carbon steels and melters generally use a larger nozzle size.

Air-Melt—Basic Oxygen Practice A number of techniques have been suggested for producing stainless steel in a basic oxygen vessel since the process first became successful. For a number of reasons few of these were adopted into commercial practice.

There is no technical reason why most stainless grades could not be made in a basic oxygen vessel, but the absence of a heat source other than chemical makes a precise heat balance most critical. Also, if a broad range of grades is to be made and if the scrap cycle is to be closed, a source of chromium- and nickel-bearing hot metal of low phosphorus content is critical. A hot-blast cupola has been used as a source of such hot metal. Also, considerable research was done to determine the suitability of using a small blast furnace to smelt chromium, iron, and nickel ores to supply feed metal for the basic oxygen vessel, but the process was never put into commercial practice.

In the United States, there is only one producer of stainless steel using a basic oxygen vessel for such materials. Basically, the practice described by its users[1] parallels electric furnace practice but has obvious mechanical differences.

The charge consists of stainless steel scrap, charge chrome, and low-phosphorus hot metal from a water-cooled, hot-blast cupola. In this shop, the cupola is used primarily to supply metal for silicon steel production so no alloying elements are used in its operation. Were the metal to be alloyed, the process would gain in flexibility relative to scrap use and grades produced.

The heat is blown with gaseous oxygen to the required carbon level. During the blow, lime and fluorspar are added to the bath.

As in electric furnace practice, chromium, manganese, and iron are oxidized during the blow and must be recovered in the interest of economy. Also, the bath must be cooled after blowing to minimize attrition of refractories. The reduction period begins with the addition of cooling scrap and continues as reducing agents and fluxes are added. Solution of these materials in the bath and slag is aided by rocking the furnace and continued when metal and slag are tapped together into a "dummy ladle" (a ladle without provision for teeming) in which mixing is continued by argon bubbled through a porous plug set in the bottom of the ladle.

When reduction is judged to be completed, the reduced slag is decanted, the bath is sampled, and the required additions prepared. Solution of added alloys is aided and metal mixed using porous plug gas bubbling.

Minor adjustments in temperature are achieved by either bubbling argon (to cool) or injecting oxygen to burn silicon (to heat). When ready, the metal is tapped into a teeming ladle.

The basic oxygen vessel has been used commercially in combination with vacuum decarburization in Europe[2] and in Japan. A charge of chromium-bearing (and sometimes nickel-bearing) hot metal prepared in a cupola is blown with the slag of a previous heat. Presumably, the mixing of the high-carbon charge reduces chromium put into the slag in the previous heat. After a short blow, the first slag is decanted and discarded. At this point, alloy additions may be added as required, and lime and fluorspar are added. The injection of oxygen is begun again and continued until a carbon level of about 0.40% is attained. The heat is then tapped into a ladle and transferred to a vacuum tank for further decarburization.

In the practice, chromium oxidation is minimized by discontinuing the blow at a relatively high carbon level. No attempt is made at this time to recover the chromium that is oxidized. Instead, the slag is retained in the vessel where it is acted upon by the charge of the succeeding heat.

The vacuum decarburization step which follows this preparatory practice is discussed later in this chapter.

Argon-Oxygen Decarburization (AOD) The argon-oxygen decarburization practice is part of a duplex process. Molten metal is prepared in a supplying furnace and is transferred to the argon-oxygen unit for decarburization and further refining.

As will be discussed in some detail later, in the air-melt practices described above, reduction of carbon by oxidation to a low level is impossible, practically, if the chromium content of the bath is in the range normal to finished stainless steel. Carbon oxidation, however, is greatly aided if the partial pressure of CO formed by carbon oxidation is reduced. In the AO process, this is accomplished by diluting CO with an inert gas.

Figure 2 is a drawing of an argon-oxygen refining vessel. It is quite similar to a basic oxygen vessel except for the presence of one or more tuyeres located at the bottom of the furnace within an arc of 45° around the back of the vessel just above the bottom of the lining. The tuyeres are immersed in the metal when the vessel is in the upright position, but when it is tilted for charging or sampling, they are exposed. In most installations, the vessel can be removed from the trunnion ring and replaced with another vessel while the first is relined.

The ratio of oxygen to argon ranges from about 3:1 to pure argon. During the blow, the ratio is changed as conditions in the bath change: The high O_2/A ratio is used at the start when carbon is high and is reduced in steps to $1O_2/3A$, or even pure argon as carbon drops. No maximum injection rates have been established per ton of steel, although the norm seems at present to be 31 m^3 of O_2 per metric ton and 31 m^3 of total gaseous mixture per metric ton.

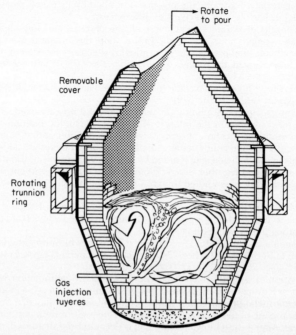

Fig. 2 Argon-oxygen decarburizing vessel. *(Linde Division, Union Carbide Corporation, New York)*

A log of a typical heat produced in an AOD vessel is given in Table 2.

The charge is prepared in a feed vessel (most generally an electric-arc furnace, although it could be partially refined metal from a BOF). Chemistry of the heat should be close to final specification for chromium, nickel, and molybdenum. Carbon and silicon are allowed to float to some extent, although it is desirable to have silicon at 0.25% maximum. This reduces lining wear, and reduces time and excessive temperature increase to some extent. Carbon, too, is desirably low for much the same reason (although it is not quite so detrimental as silicon); but generally, the substantial use of charge chrome leads to a higher carbon level in the metal transferred to the vessel than would be preferred.

The temperature of the metal in the vessel before beginning oxygen flow is desirably about 1525°C (2777°F).

Oxygen injection is begun at a ratio of $3O_2/1A$. In one practice, this blow is continued until carbon is reduced to 0.25% or temperature is 1700°C (3092°F) (whichever comes first). The ratio of gases is changed to $1O_2/1A$ and continued at this level to a carbon of 0.12% or a temperature of 1730°C (3146°F). The blow is continued to the end point at a ratio of $1O_2/3A$.

An alternate method of operation has been evolved to permit the melting of stainless steel scrap or other materials in the vessel. In this instance, the bath is blown at each oxygen/argon ratio to a specific carbon content rather than to a given temperature. The temperature is allowed to vary as determined by the equilibrium of the system. At the end of each blowing period, stainless steel scrap is added to reduce the temperature to a predetermined maximum before oxygen and argon injection is resumed. Further development has allowed continuous additions during decarburization. Since the melting of cold metal requires the

TABLE 2   Vessel Log: Argon-Oxygen Decarburization*

Time, min	Operation	Temp., °C	Gas flow, Nm³/h O₂	A
0	Charge liquid metal (slag free)	1510		
	Weight 13.15 metric tons			
	0.70C-0.39Mn-0.14Si-0.072S-17.42Cr-			
	8.60Ni			
3	Begin stage 1 blow		538	170
	Adjust alloy			
	125 kg std. FeMn; 320 kg charge Cr			
30	Complete stage 1 blow	1670		
31	Begin stage 2 blow		453	227
36	Complete stage 2 blow	1720		
	C = 0.117%			
38	Begin stage 3 blow		227	453
46	Complete stage 3 blow	1720		
51	Add reduction mix and stir		0	396
	725 kg CaO; 125 kg Fluorspar;			
	342 kg 75% FeSi			
	Sample:			
	0.04C-1.07Mn-0.48Si-			
	0.012S-18.33Cr-9.20Ni			
63	Slag off	1630		
83	Make final additions			
	16 kg FeMn; 43 kg 75% FeSi			
	14 kg nickel; 72 kg lime			
87	Tap	1570		
	Ladle temperature	1550		

*The heat described was melted in an electric furnace and transfered, slag-free, to the decarburizing vessel.

generation of heat in the system, this alternate practice results in somewhat higher oxidation of chromium than does that represented in Table 2. Nevertheless, in some operations where capacity limitations and production requirements outweigh the need for conservation of alloys, it may have merit.

As can be seen in the chemistry of Table 2, some chromium is oxidized even under reduced p_{co}. As a rule, this is about 2%. To recover this chromium as well as to fluidize the slag, which after decarburization is quite dry and lumpy (actually nodular), it is necessary to use a slag reduction step.

As in the electric furnace, silicon-bearing agents are used together with lime and fluorspar to adjust basicity and speed fluidization. If necessary to reduce bath temperature, well-identified, clean, stainless steel scrap is also added. During reduction, the metal is stirred quite vigorously with argon. No external heat is added and no chemical heat generated except that created by the reducing reactions themselves, that is, $Cr_3O_4 + 2Si = 3Cr + 2SiO_2$. Because of the near-perfect mixing of slag and metal, slag reduction is close to optimum. Recovery of chromium from the charge is about 98% and that of manganese in the charge close to 80 to 85%.

When reduction is completed, the heat can be tapped—if the melter has confidence in the precision of the operation—or it can be sampled and alloying adjustments made.

If required, sulfur removal can be accomplished in the AO vessel. By removing the reduced slag, replacing it with a basic slag of lime, fluorspar, and a deoxidizer, e.g., CaSi, and churning metal and slag with argon, sulfur is easily dropped to less than 0.010%. Of course, desulfurizing, involving as it does the fusion of a new slag, reduces bath temperature. Consequently, it is proper for the melter to plan the additions prior to desulfurizing (especially cooling scrap) in anticipation of the heat losses involved in the sulfur-removing steps to be taken.

An AOD heat can easily be cooled by extending the argon bubbling time or even by adding scrap. If it is too cold, silicon can be added and then blown out with oxygen. It is not considered desirable to do the latter, but there may be no practical alternative.

To a substantial extent, nitrogen can replace argon as the inert gas in the AOD process. The resultant higher nitrogen level in the steel is not necessarily a detraction. If it is used in the first two stages of blowing only, the nitrogen pickup is only about equal to a level normally found in arc-furnace-produced alloy. In some austenitic steels, this slight pickup is a positive benefit. If nitrogen is required as an alloying element, its use as a gas in the

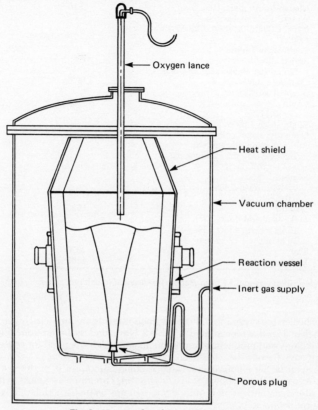

Oxygen lance

Heat shield

Vacuum chamber

Reaction vessel

Inert gas supply

Porous plug

Fig. 3   Vacuum decarburizing vessel.[25]

late stages of blowing and in mixing can introduce a residual as high as its inherent solubility in the steel.

Decarburization in Vacuum   In many ways vacuum decarburization is similar to the argon-oxygen process. It provides a reduced partial pressure of CO, although in a different way, to minimize chromium oxidation. Also, it is the last part of a duplex (or even triplex) process and relies on a liquid charge.

A schematic illustration of a vacuum decarburization apparatus is shown in Fig. 3. The unit is essentially a modified ladle degassing system, except for the addition of a lance for injecting oxygen into or onto the bath. A system for mixing the metal and breaking the slag cover is imperative in the process. Induction stirring has been used, but the agitation imparted by argon stirring and its action to break slag cover seems to be more effective. The gas volume introduced through the plug is small [about 10 ft³/min (0.005 m³/s)]. It is considerably less than used in the AOD process and its action is considered mechanical rather than as a diluent for CO. The required low p_{co} is attained by reducing pressure through pumping action and reduction of total pressure.

An example of the vacuum decarburizing technique is the AVR (Allegheny Vacuum Refining) process.[3] This process utilizes a modified Asea degassing unit. The heating unit of the installation is not necessarily utilized in the process so description of the process parallels other similar operations. The AVR unit is the only vacuum decarburizing installation operating on a broad spectrum of grades in the United States.

As in AOD, the charge as disclosed by operators is adjusted close to its ultimate specification prior to transfer to the vacuum station. The silicon is kept low (0.25% maximum) and to some extent, carbon is allowed to float. Preferably, carbon is held to 0.60% but in instances where a large amount of charge chrome is used, the carbon may climb. Above 1% C, the heat may be preblown in the furnace as a much higher carbon could result in too violent a boil in the vacuum.

The temperature of the metal in the ladle as vacuum pumping is begun is preferably 1600 to 1625°C (2912 to 2957°F).

Oxygen is injected into the bath through a five-hole spiral lance immersed 6 in. (15 cm) deep. This lance is consumable and fed throughout the heat. The pressure above the metal at which injection is begun depends on carbon content—higher for high carbon charges. It is gradually reduced to the system minimum.

When the calculated oxygen volume is fed into the vessel, injection is discontinued, the system backfilled with N_2, and the vacuum broken. The temperature at this point is 1700 to 1730°C (3092 to 3146°F); if higher, stainless steel cooling scrap is added.

The reduction mix consists of FeCrSi, FeMnSi, lime, and spar. When added, the ladle is returned to vacuum and the metal-slag system stirred using argon through a porous plug.

When reduction is completed, the vacuum is again broken, the metal sampled and alloy additions made. If necessary, in the AVR system, arc power can be applied to melt additions, although, as a rule, additions found to be necessary are small.

Other vacuum systems work in similar ways, although techniques of lancing, the pressure cycle, and method of judging end-point carbon are different.

TECHNOLOGY

Chemistry of Decarburization   The economics of materials costs and the need to recycle chromium steel scrap dictate that stainless steel must be produced (except in a few special cases) by processes involving removal of carbon from liquid iron in the presence of chromium. Such decarburization is best accomplished by oxidation. Thus, the various processes make use of some form of oxygen injection.

The principles of physical chemistry require that in the Fe-Cr-C-O system, liquid metal must coexist with a liquid or solid oxide phase and a gas phase which is essentially carbon monoxide. Thus, even though the source of oxygen may be injected gas, the chemical equilibria controlling oxidation of carbon from molten Fe-Cr alloys are described by equations of the following type:†

$$Cr_xO_y(s) + Y\underline{C} = YCO(g) + X\underline{Cr} \tag{1}$$

in which the equilibrium constant K is defined by

$$K = \frac{a_{Cr}^x \, p_{co}^y}{a_{Cr_xO_y} a_c^y} \tag{2}$$

and

$$\log K = \frac{-\Delta F°}{4.575\, T} \tag{3}$$

where a = the thermodynamic activity of the substance
   $F°$ = the standard free energy of the reaction
   p = pressure in atmosphere
   T = absolute temperature in degrees Kelvin

In investigations of the solubility of oxygen in molten Fe-Cr alloys, three oxide phases have been identified: chromite (nominally $FeCr_2O_4$), a modified form of chromite designated as "distorted spinel" (nominally $Fe_{0.67}Cr_{2.33}O_4$), and chromium oxide (Cr_3O_4). The limits of occurrence of these phases is shown in Figs. 4 and 5.[4]

By combining earlier data for the chromium-carbon-temperature relationship in molten iron under oxidizing conditions[5] with information on the effect of chromium on the

---

†In this chapter, the following conventions are used: underlining a chemical symbol indicates that element is in solution in liquid iron; (l), (g), and (s) mean liquid, gas, and solid, respectively.

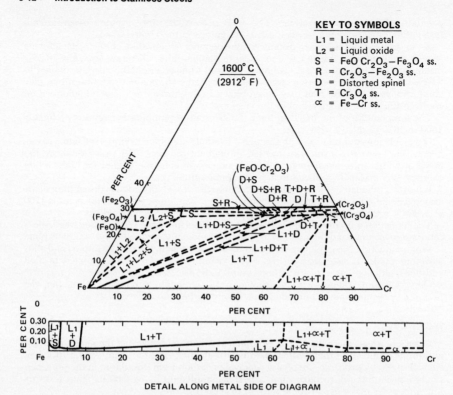

KEY TO SYMBOLS

L1 = Liquid metal
L2 = Liquid oxide
S = FeO Cr$_2$O$_3$−Fe$_3$O$_4$ ss.
R = Cr$_2$O$_3$−Fe$_2$O$_3$ ss.
D = Distorted spinel
T = Cr$_3$O$_4$ ss.
∝ = Fe−Cr ss.

DETAIL ALONG METAL SIDE OF DIAGRAM

Fig. 4 Isothermal section of the Fe-Cr-O system at 1600°C.[4]

thermodynamic activity of carbon,[6] the equilibrium constants for the reactions in the above oxide phase regions have been evaluated empirically as follows:[7]

Chromite range (0 to 3% Cr):

$$FeCr_2O_4(s) + 4\underline{C} = Fe(l) + 2\underline{Cr} + 4CO(g) \tag{4}$$

$$4 \log \% \, C + \frac{1432}{T} \, \% C = 2 \log \% \, Cr + \left(\frac{7326}{T} - 3.762 \right) \% \, Cr$$
$$+ \log \frac{\% \, Fe}{100} + 4 \log p_{co} + \frac{44{,}250}{T} - 28.32 \tag{5}$$

Distorted spinel range (3 to 9% Cr):

$$\tag{6}$$

$$Fe_{0.67}Cr_{2.33}O_4(s) + 4\underline{C} = 0.67 \, Fe(l) + 2.33 \, \underline{Cr} + 4CO(g)$$

$$4 \log \% \, C + \frac{1432}{T} \, \% C = 2.33 \log \% \, Cr + \left(\frac{160}{T} + 0.057 \right) \% \, Cr + 0.67 \log \frac{\% \, Fe}{100}$$
$$+ 4 \log p_{co} + \frac{60{,}760}{T} - 37.32 \tag{7}$$

Chromium oxide range (>9% Cr):

$$Cr_3O_4(s) + 4\underline{C} = 3\underline{Cr} + 4CO(g) \tag{8}$$

$$4 \log \% \, C + \frac{1432}{T} \, \% C = 3 \log \% Cr + \left(\frac{160}{T} - 0.0476 \right) \% \, Cr$$

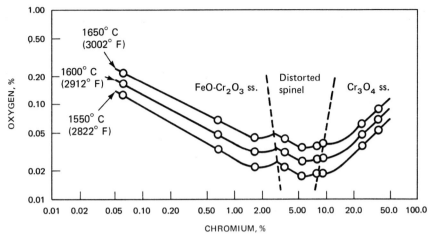

Fig. 5 Effect of temperature and chromium level on solubility of oxygen in Fe-Cr alloys.[4]

$$+ 4 \log p_{co} + \frac{57,100}{T} - 35.16 \quad (9)$$

Equations (5), (7), and (9) are rather cumbersome and must be solved mainly by iterative methods. Between 3 and 30% Cr, however, the relationship between log Cr and log C approaches linearity, so that for practical purposes it can be approximated for air-melting conditions at atmospheric pressure by Eq. (10):

$$\log \frac{\% \text{ Cr}}{\% \text{ C}} = -\frac{13,800}{T} + 8.76 \quad (10)$$

By interpolation from Eqs. (7) and (9), Eq. (10) can be modified to include the effect of CO pressure, Eq. (10a):

$$\log \frac{\% \text{ Cr}}{\% \text{ C}} = \frac{-13,800}{T} + 8.76 - 0.925 \log p_{co} \quad (10a)$$

Accurate data to validate Eq. (10a) are unavailable. In fact, work done in vacuum-melting equipment suggests that actual measured (gauge) pressures and what might be termed "effective" CO pressures can differ substantially from one another, particularly at low pressures. This difference is presumably associated with the ferrostatic head of the metal and the internal pressure necessary to generate CO bubbles. Similar differences are commonly observed in vacuum degassing plain-carbon steels. Nevertheless, Eq. (10a) can be a useful guide for estimating pressure effects on the chromium-carbon-temperature relationship in stainless steels refined by reduced pressure processes.

Since nickel dissolved in molten iron has a small but significant influence on the thermodynamic activities of carbon and oxygen, Eq. (10) was modified to reflect this effect at one atmosphere to produce Eq. (11)[8]

$$\log \frac{\% \text{ Cr}}{\% \text{ C}} = -\frac{13,800}{[T + 4.21(\% \text{ Ni})]} + 8.76 \quad (11)$$

Generalized to show the effect of pressure, Eq. (11) becomes

$$\log \frac{\% \text{ Cr}}{\% \text{ C}} = -\frac{13,800}{[T + 4.21(\% \text{ Ni})]} + 8.76 - 0.925 \log p_{co} \quad (12)$$

The relationship among chromium, carbon, and temperature in oxygen-saturated baths at atmospheric pressure is shown graphically in Fig. 6. Figure 7 illustrates the relation as it is affected by reduced partial pressure of carbon monoxide.

For practical application of these fundamental data to prediction and control of actual stainless steel melting operations, the term % Cr in the various equations really means % (Cr + Mn). Estimates of the free energy of formation of the oxides of chromium from chromium dissolved in molten iron place them very close to that of manganous oxide (MnO) per atom of oxygen.[9] Consequently, adding the manganese normally present in stainless steel heats during the carbon-oxidation period to the chromium content should improve the utility of the established equilibrium data without introducing serious error. It has also been found that the chromium/manganese ratio in an oxygen-blown bath (Cr_2/ Mn_2) is determined by the chromium/manganese ratio in the bath prior to oxygen injection (Cr_1/Mn_1). The relationship is given in Fig. 8.[10]

From the standpoint of maximizing the chromium retained in solution while carbon is being oxidized to the low levels usually required in stainless steel, it is desirable to reach a relatively high temperature at the end of the decarburization period. Although this temperature is lower if the partial pressure of CO in the system is reduced, its attainment requires thermal energy which may be electrical (e.g., electric arcs) or chemical (oxidation of C, Si, Cr, and other metallics). Practical considerations of time, refractories, etc., dictate that the energy input be mainly chemical in nature. On the other hand, generation of any chemical energy by oxidation of chromium and other metallics must be minimized in the interest of economy and conservation of materials. The stainless steel melting process is thus controlled by a materials and energy balance. Greatest economy in stainless steel production is achieved by optimizing the materials and energy balance within the restrictions imposed by the chemistry of the decarburization process. Understanding of the way in which this balance operates is therefore fundamental to prediction and control of stainless steel refining in any of the current commercial processes.

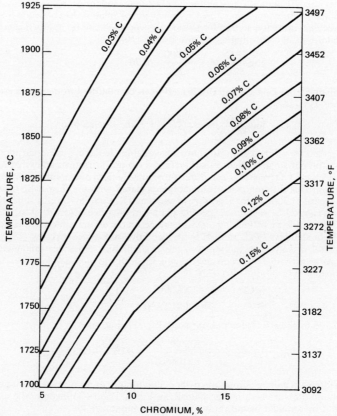

Fig. 6 Relation among chromium, carbon, and temperature in oxygen-saturated bath.

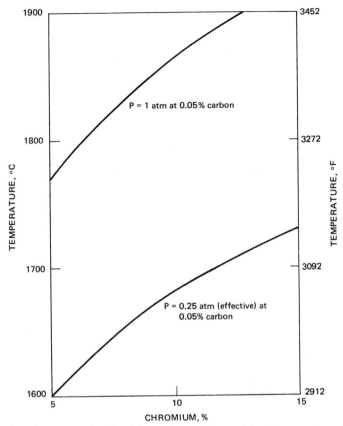

Fig. 7 Effect of pressure on the relation between temperature and chromium retention at 0.05% C in an oxygen-saturated bath.

Energy Balance The generalized statement of the energy balance for the decarburization period of a stainless steel heat is as follows:

$$\Delta H_C + \Delta H_{Si} + \Delta H_M + E = C_p \Delta T + q_0 t \tag{13}$$

where ΔH_C = heat of oxidation of carbon
$\quad\quad \Delta H_{Si}$ = heat of oxidation of silicon
$\quad\quad \Delta H_M$ = heat of oxidation of chromium, manganese, and iron
$\quad\quad E$ = electrical energy
$\quad\quad C_p'$ = apparent heat capacity of the metal-refractory system
$\quad\quad \Delta T$ = temperature change during the decarburizing period
$\quad\quad q_0$ = steady-state external heat-loss rate
$\quad\quad t$ = total elapsed time from start of oxygen injection until the beginning of the reduction period

In other words,
Chemical energy + electrical energy = heat absorbed by the metal and its container + heat losses

Oxidation of Carbon. The oxidation of carbon from molten stainless steel proceeds according to the reaction:

$$\underline{C} + \tfrac{1}{2}O_2(g)_{298} = CO(g) \tag{14}$$
$$\Delta H_{2000} = -26{,}276 \text{ cal}$$
$$= -21{,}900 \text{ kcal/(1\% C)(metric ton)}$$

If the CO generated by reaction (14) comes in contact with air while still at high temperature, it is converted to CO_2 by the following reaction:

$$CO(g) + (\tfrac{1}{2}O_2 + 1.88N_2)(g)_{298} = CO_2(g) + 1.88N_2(g)^1 \qquad (14a)$$
$$\Delta H_{2000} = -34,391 \text{ cal}$$
$$= -28,658 \text{ kcal}/(1\% \text{ C})(\text{metric ton})$$

When such combustion of CO occurs above the steel bath within the furnace, the heat of reaction (14a) can supplement that of reaction (14).

The original evaluations of the energy balance during decarburization of stainless steel were carried out on the older, conventional arc furnace practice.[11] The investigators

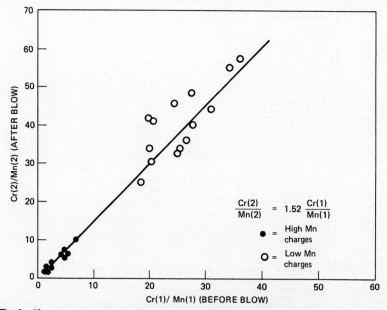

Fig. 8 Chromium-manganese relationship in stainless steel heats during oxygen injection.[10]

assumed that carbon in the steel was oxidized to CO by injected oxygen according to Eq. (14) and that reaction (14a) then operated to convert the CO to CO_2 by reaction with air inside the furnace. The assumption fit their observations quite well. Later experience has indicated that the assumption is probably valid for conventional arc furnace practice until the carbon content of the bath exceeds about 1% at the start of decarburization. The removal of 1% carbon under these conditions requires 10 m³ of injected oxygen per metric ton of steel plus an equal amount of oxygen as air. Thus, a total of 60 m³ of gas per ton of steel is involved in the decarburization.

Observations of stainless steel heats during oxygen injection give visual evidence of CO burning to CO_2 outside the furnace when the carbon content exceeds 1%, simply because of the large volume of gas involved. Moreover, if modern, direct-withdrawal fume control is in operation on the furnace to meet antipollution regulations, much oxidation of CO to CO_2 may take place in the ductwork rather than in the furnace. Thus, if carbon content of the steel exceeds 1%, or if fume collection devices are connected to the furnace, not all of the heat generated by reaction (14a) will be effective in the energy balance.

Measurements show that during decarburization of stainless steel in a basic oxygen vessel only about 10% of the CO formed is converted to CO_2. An even lower conversion can be assumed for argon-oxygen or vacuum-decarburizing operations. Consequently, in stainless processes other than the arc furnace, only reaction (14) need be considered as the contribution of carbon oxidation in the energy balance.

For practical application of Eq. (13) to conventional arc furnace stainless steel practice, therefore, the value of ΔH_C ranges from 21,900 to 50,558 kcal/(1% C oxidized)(metric ton of steel). If carbon content of the bath is under 1% at the start of decarburization and if the furnace is operating without direct fume withdrawal, the latter figure should be used. If carbon exceeds 1% or direct fume evacuation is employed, ΔH_c will be within the stated range; independent estimation for the specific conditions should be made. In the case of the other commercial processes, ΔH_c is approximately 21,900 kcal/(% C oxidized)(ton of steel).

Oxidation of Silicon. Silicon is oxidized by injected oxygen. The reaction is

$$\underline{Si} + O_2(g)_{298} = SiO_2(l) \tag{15}$$
$$\Delta H_{2000\,K} = -180,752 \text{ cal}$$
$$= -64,374 \text{ kcal}/(1\% \text{ Si})(\text{metric ton})$$

In stainless steel processes such as the conventional arc furnace or the basic oxygen furnace, silicon is removed completely during the decarburizing period. In practices such as argon-oxygen or vacuum decarburization, silicon removal may be incomplete. In the latter instances, some operators report as much as 0.05% Si remaining in the steel after decarburization.

Oxidation of 1% Si from a metric ton of steel requires 8.6 m³ of oxygen.

Oxidation of Chromium, Manganese, and Iron. Evaluation of the contribution of the oxidation of chromium, manganese, and iron (which is often referred to for convenience as "metallic oxidation") is more complicated than in the case of carbon and silicon because of variability in the composition of the oxide with composition of the steel.

As illustrated by Figs. 4 and 5, the oxide phases of interest are FeO, $FeCr_2O_4$, distorted spinel, and Cr_3O_4, none of which are of constant composition. The heats of formation of FeO, $FeCr_2O_4$, and Cr_3O_4 have been estimated.[11,12] That of distorted spinel has not. Since the heats of formation of the companion oxides of chromium are not greatly different, however, the presence of distorted spinel can be ignored for practical purposes. The oxide slag that forms when chromium and iron are burned during oxygen injection can be treated for calculation purposes as if it were a mixture of FeO and $FeCr_2O_4$, or $FeCr_2O_4$ and Cr_3O_4, the division between the two occurring at about 6% Cr in the oxidized bath. The reactions assumed for estimation of ΔH_M in the energy balance are

$$Fe(l) + \tfrac{1}{2}O_2(g)_{298} = FeO(l) \tag{16}$$
$$\Delta H_{2000} = -49,826 \text{ cal/gfw} \ddagger$$
$$Fe(l) + 2\underline{Cr} + 2O_2(g)_{298} = FeCr_2O_4(s) \tag{17}$$
$$\Delta H_{2000} = -315,304 \text{ cal/gfw}$$
$$3\underline{Cr} + 2O_2(g)_{298} = Cr_3O_4(s) \tag{18}$$
$$\Delta H_{2000} = -328,504 \text{ cal/gfw}$$

As explained previously, the relatively small amount of manganese usually present in stainless steel is considered equivalent to chromium in the thermochemistry of the process. It is, however, a significant component of the materials balance and its presence must be recognized and included for quantification of Eq. (13).

The proportion of chromium plus manganese oxidized to iron oxidized is almost wholly dependent on the chromium plus manganese content of the steel after decarburization. [13] The empirical relationship, applicable to both plain chromium and nickel-bearing steels is shown in Fig. 9. The equation of the line in Fig. 9 is

$$\log\left(\frac{\% \text{ Cr} + \% \text{ Mn}}{\% \text{ Fe}}\right)_{slag} = \log\left(\% \text{ Cr} + \% \text{ Mn}\right)_{metal} - 0.438 \tag{19}$$

With the help of Eq. (19), the proportions of the oxide phases produced by reactions (16) to (18) can be calculated and thus ΔH_M determined in relation to composition of the steel after oxygen injection. The results of this computation are given by Fig. 10 and Eq. (20)

$$\Delta H_M = 44,900 - 3.60 \times 10^3 \times Cr_2 + 2.87 \times 10^2 \times Cr_2^2 - 7.49 \times Cr_2^3 \tag{20}$$

$$Cr_2 = \% \text{ Cr} + \% \text{ Mn in steel after decarburization}$$

Prediction and control of the process also requires knowledge of the amount of metallic oxidation as well as oxygen consumed. In actual melting operations, this information is extremely difficult and impractical to obtain by direct methods which would involve weighing the slag or metal before and after decarburization is completed. Metallic

‡Gram formula weight.

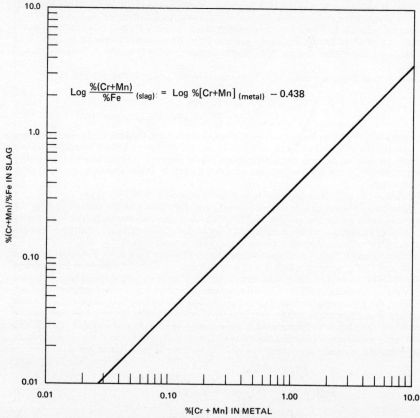

Fig. 9 Relation of ratio of chromium plus manganese to iron in slag to chromium plus manganese content of metal. *(Data of Hilty, Healy, and Crafts[13] revised by Hilty.)*

oxidation can be estimated with rather good precision, however, by means of Eq. (21), modified from Ref. 13:

$$W = \frac{1,000(Cr_1 - Cr_2)}{100S/(1+S) - Cr_2} \tag{21}$$

where W = weight of Cr + Mn + Fe oxidized in kg per metric ton of steel
Cr_1 = % Cr + % Mn in the metal before decarburization
Cr_2 = % Cr + % Mn in the metal after decarburization
$S = \dfrac{\% \ Cr + \% \ Mn}{\% \ Fe}$ in the slag after decarburization

S may be calculated by Eq. (19) or read directly from Fig. 9.

TABLE 3   Oxidation Energy

Term in Eq. (13)	kcal/(1% element oxidized)(metric ton steel)
ΔH_C (no CO_2 formation)	21,900
ΔH_C (CO formed by injected oxygen burned by air inside furnace to CO_2)	50,558
ΔH_{Si}	64,347
ΔH_M	$\Delta H_M = 44,900 - 3.60 \times 10^3 (Cr_2) + 2.87 \times 10^2 (Cr_2)^2 - 7.49 (Cr_2)^3$
	Cr_2 = % Cr + % Mn in steel after decarburization

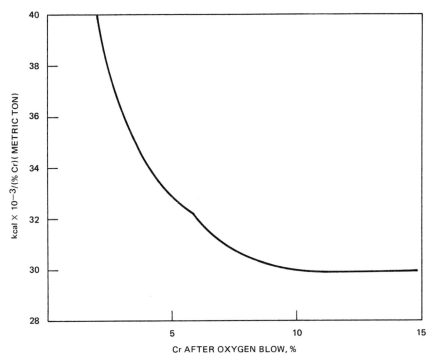

Fig. 10   Heat of oxidation of chromium and iron.

Equations (19) and (21) make possible the development of a number of relations among the individual components of metallic oxidation, oxygen use, and metal composition. Two of the more useful of these are shown in Figs. 11 and 12. As has already been emphasized, maximization of chromium retained in the steel after decarburization is the primary objective of all the processes. Figure 11 relates the amount of metal oxidized to the chromium plus manganese content of the bath after decarburization. Figure 12 gives the similar relationship for oxygen consumption.

Summary of Chemical Energy Inputs. For quick reference in making calculations of the energy balance, the various heats of oxidation are summarized in Table 3.

Electrical Energy   In the early days of decarburization of stainless steel by oxygen injection, the positive advantages of high rates of oxygen input were neither recognized nor understood. In most instances, oxygen supply systems were inadequate or operators tended to use oxygen at low rates because of a mistaken notion that injecting oxygen would make the final steel "dirty" as well as make for poor chromium recovery. Consequently, much of the energy input during carbon oxidation was supplied by electric arcs. Ultimately, development and application of the energy balance being discussed here demonstrated that high rates of oxygen input are essential to the economy and control of the process. Moreover, actual production experience proved that fears of "dirty" steel were unfounded. In fact, operators learned that lower-cost stainless steels of more consistently high quality could be produced this way.

As will become clear later in this chapter, adequate rates of oxygen input eliminate any requirements for energy input during decarburization beyond the chemical energy of oxidation. E in Eq. (13) is therefore usually zero in modern practice. In case electrical energy is to be considered, E should be expressed in terms of 860 kcal/kWh.

Apparent Heat Capacity   Heat generated during decarburization of a stainless steel bath Q_i, is dissipated in (1) raising the temperature of the molten bath Q_b, (2) increasing the sensible heat content of the furnace refractory system Q_r, and (3) supplying external heat losses Q_x. Thus,

$$Q_i = Q_b + Q_r + Q_x \tag{22}$$

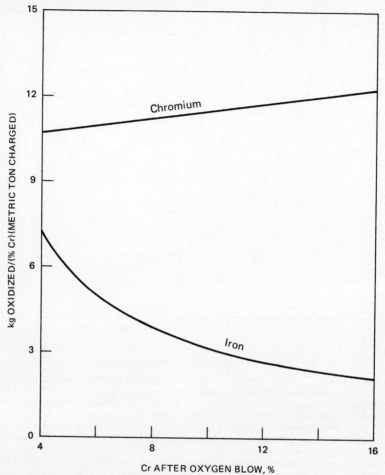

Fig. 11 Relation between the chromium (plus manganese) content of steel after oxygen injection to the amount of chromium (plus manganese) and iron oxidized. *(After Healy.[14])*

Because the heat is generated directly in the steel bath and the specific heat of the liquid steel–slag system can be considered constant within the temperature range of interest, Q_b depends solely on the temperature change induced. Q_r and Q_x, on the other hand, are functions of the rates of heat flow into the refractories and of heat radiation from the entire system. This distribution of heat for a given temperature increase is illustrated schematically by Fig. 13.

The external heat-loss rate consists of the steady-state heat-loss rate q_0, plus the amount by which that rate increases because of the temperature change. Thus,

$$Q_x = (q_0 + f\Delta T)t \tag{23}$$

where f is a constant denoting the change in q_0 with temperature.

Equation (22) can therefore be rewritten as follows:

$$Q_i = C_{p(b)}\,\Delta T + q_0 t + ft\Delta T + Q_r \tag{24}$$

in which $C_{p(b)}$ is the true heat capacity of the bath (plus slag). Collecting terms,

$$Q_i = \left(C_{p(b)} + ft + \frac{Q_r}{\Delta T}\right)\Delta T + q_0 t \tag{25}$$

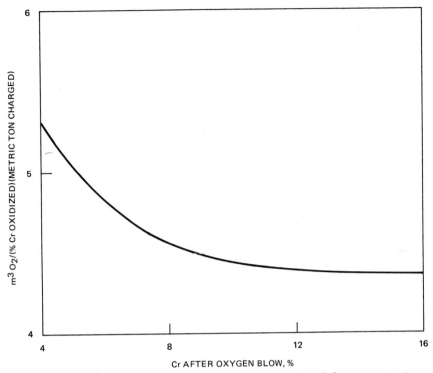

Fig. 12 Relation between the chromium (plus manganese) content of steel after oxygen injection to the amount of oxygen consumed in oxidizing chromium, manganese, and iron. (*After Healy.*[14])

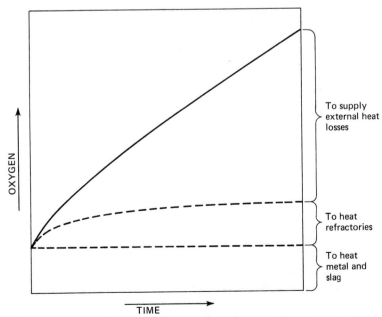

Fig. 13 Effect of time on the amount of oxygen required for a prescribed temperature increase.[11]

The expression $C_{p(b)} + ft + \dfrac{Q_r}{\Delta T}$ has the dimensions of a heat capacity. It is therefore the apparent heat capacity C_p' of Eq. (13).

The components f and Q_r of C_p' are influenced by furnace design, type and mass of the refractory lining, amount of water cooling, number of openings, etc. Broadly speaking, they are functions of the size of the furnace: as furnace size increases, the ratios of refractory mass and radiant surface area to the mass of the metal bath decrease, so that their relative effects on apparent heat capacity become less. An estimation of C_p' in terms of furnace holding capacity and duration of the decarburization period for more or less typical arc furnaces is given by Fig. 14. These relationships can also be expressed mathematically by Eq. (26), derived by the authors from Fig. 14:

$$C_p' = \text{kcal/(°C)(metric ton of charge)} = 180.12 + 948.00 \exp. \; (-3.7274 -$$
$$0.0253t + 0.5153\sqrt{t} + 3.1180 \times 10^{-5}t^2 - 0.7474 \log R) \quad (26)$$

where R = holding capacity of furnace in metric tons.

While Fig. 14 and Eq. (26) have demonstrated their utility for evaluating the relative economics of stainless steel melting processes,[10] they are strictly approximations from generalized data and may not apply directly to a particular melting unit. Moreover, they refer specifically to conventional arc furnace practice. They should therefore be used principally as guides. For more precise evaluation of the decarburization energy balance in a specific melting vessel (most especially BOF or reduced pressure vessels) C_p' must

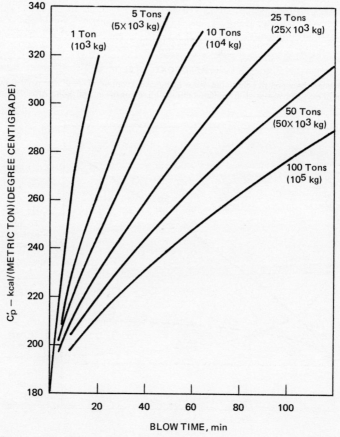

Fig. 14   Effect of time and furnace size on apparent specific heat. *(After Healy.[14])*

be determined by direct observation under operating conditions. More complete information on estimating C_p' may be found in Ref. 9 and 11.

Steady-State External Heat-Loss Rate   The steady-state heat-loss rate q_0 of Eqs. (13), (23) to (25), is essentially the rate at which heat is radiated from the complete furnace–steel bath system at constant temperature of the bath. It is thus a function of radiating surface area and therefore of furnace size. A general approximation of q_0 for arc furnaces is given by Fig. 15 and by Eq. (27):

$$q_0 = \text{kcal/(min)(metric ton)} = 24.09 - 0.19R + 8.40 \times 10^{-4}R^2 + \frac{76.24}{R} + \frac{15.43}{R^2} \quad (27)$$

While Fig. 15 and Eq. (27) are useful guides for estimating q_0, they are subject to the same limitations as Fig. 14 and Eq. (26) for apparent heat capacity. For evaluation of the energy balance in a specific melting unit, determination of the steady-state heat-loss rate by direct measurement is recommended.

Other Considerations in Heat Dissipation   As noted in the previous discussion of carbon oxidation, injection of oxygen into a steel bath in conventional arc furnace practice is accompanied by a flow of air through the furnace. The oxygen in this infiltrated air may react with the CO being generated and possibly with the metal itself. In this sense, it contributes to the total energy input. The nitrogen, however, absorbs heat, the amount of which must be considered in the total energy balance.

The heat absorbed by the nitrogen in a cubic meter of air raised from ambient to steelmaking temperatures is on the order of 1913 kcal. If the rate of infiltration of oxygen in air in cubic meters per minute per metric ton of furnace charge be assigned the symbol V_a, the heat absorbed by the nitrogen in the air passing through the furnace during an oxygen blow of t minutes is on the order of $1913 V_a t$ kcal/metric ton of charge.

The rate of air infiltration is obviously a function of a variety of factors: furnace size, geometry, tightness of construction, size and number of openings, design and operation of exhaust systems, etc., all have major influence. An illustration of the effect of furnace size on V_a is given by Fig. 16. However, Fig. 16 applies only to older arc furnaces not equipped with fume-collection systems. It is useful principally as a guide for approximating the effect of air infiltration in the energy balance. For quantitative evaluation of the

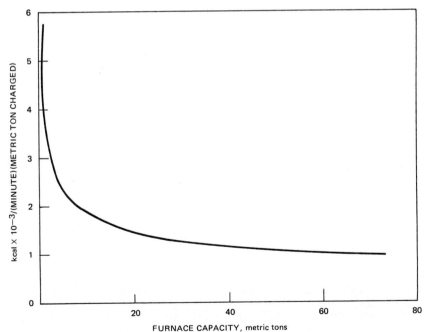

Fig. 15 Effect of furnace size on the approximate rate of heat loss. *(After Healy and Hilty.[11])*

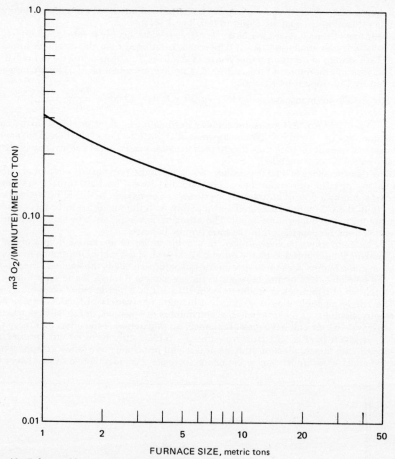

Fig. 16   Relation of furnace size and infiltration rate of atmospheric oxygen. *(After Healy and Hilty.[11])*

energy balance in any of the modern stainless steel processes, V_a should be estimated specifically for the particular furnace of interest.

Another consideration of considerable importance to the overall economy of a stainless steel process is commencement of decarburization before the charge is completely melted. In this case, a portion of the energy generated by the oxygen blow is utilized to melt the remainder of the charge. The heat of fusion of 1 metric ton of steel scrap is on the order of 67,425 kcal. For a stainless steel heat in which n tons are not yet melted at the start of decarburization, the energy dissipated in completion of melting is therefore $67,425n$ kcal.

Complete Energy Balance   By incorporating the factors for air infiltration and any unmelted charge materials, Eq. (13) becomes

$$\Delta H_c + \Delta H_{Si} + \Delta H_M + E = C_p' \, \Delta T + q_0 t + 1{,}913 V_a t + 67{,}425n \tag{28}$$

Equation (28) is the full statement of the energy balance for the decarburization period of a stainless steel heat. By means of the data given earlier in this section, including the requisite graphs and auxiliary equations, it can be evaluated for any of the commercial stainless steel processes.

Application of Data   An example of the way the data discussed can be used to predict results of blowing oxygen into a high-chromium bath is given below, after the procedures outlined in Ref. 14. The decarburization takes place in a conventional arc furnace. A straight chrome heat is used for the example.

Assumptions

Furnace size	100 metric tons
Cr at start of blow (Cr_1)	14%
Cr at end of blow (Cr_2)	Variable
Si at start of blow (Si_1)	0.25%
Si at end of blow (Si_2)	0
C at start of blow (C_1)	0.50%
C at end of blow (C_2)	0.05%
CO burned to CO_2	0
Temperature of metal at start	1500°C
Percent of bath molten	90%
Oxygen injection rate	Variable
Air infiltration rate	0.08 m³/min

Calculations

1. Assumed final temperature, °C	1850	1875
2. Cr_2 (from Fig. 6)	9.6	11.1
3. $Cr_1 - Cr_2$	4.4	2.9
4. Factor from Fig. 10, kcal	30.1×10^3	29.9×10^3
5. Heat from metallic oxidation (step 3 × step 4)	132.4×10^3	86.7×10^3
6. Heat from C ($0.45 \times 21.9 \times 10^3$)	9.9×10^3	9.9×10^3
7. Heat from Si ($0.25 \times 64.3 \times 10^3$)	16.1×10^3	16.1×10^3
8. Heat to melt 10% of charge	-6.7×10^3	-6.7×10^3
Net heat generation, kcal	151.7×10^3	106.0×10^3
9. Temperature change, °C	350	375
Heat-loss rate (Fig. 15)	900	900
Air infiltration rate (Fig. 16)	0.08	0.08
Estimated C_p' (Fig. 14) (195 + 0.87t) in 20–70 min range:		
Heat input = $(195 + 0.87t)\Delta T + 900t + 1913 \times 0.08 \times t$		
Time (first cut), min	61.5	23.8
Reestimate of C_p' (Fig. 14)	249	214
10. Time	61.3	24.5
11. m³ O_2/1% Cr ox (Fig. 12)	4.5	4.4
12. O_2 for metal ox (step 3 × step 11)	19.8	12.8
13. O_2 to oxidize C (0.45×10.05)	4.5	4.5
14. O_2 to oxidize Si (0.25×8.61)	2.15	2.15
15. Net O_2 needed × m³	26.5	19.5
16. Rate of infiltrated O_2, m³ (Fig. 16)	0.08	0.08
17. Total infiltrated O_2 (step 10 × step 16)	4.9	2.0
18. Lanced O_2 (step 15–step 17) × m³	21.6	17.5
19. O_2 input rate:		
60 min × line18/line 10 × m³/h/metric ton	21.1	42.9

Plotting blow rate (line 19) against other factors yields the results in Fig. 17. From this it can be estimated that had the blow rate used on the heat in question been 26 m³/(h)(metric ton), the temperature attained would have been 1856°C (3373°F) and Cr_2 would have been 9.93%. Blow time would have been 53 min.

Manipulation of the data in other ways can lead to other comparisons.

Calculation of the thermal and analytical changes involved in blowing steel is amenable to treatment on a computer. Reports on such work are to be found in the literature.[10]

Slag Reduction   In the electric furnace steelmaking process, the oxidation of a substantial amount of chromium during carbon removal would add considerably to the cost of stainless steel unless a means of recovering this metal was employed. In the reduced-pressure practices, while less chromium is oxidized, its reduction is still important to overall economics. In a purely mechanical sense, reduction of metallic oxides from postoxidation slags is required since these are highly viscous and even solid and cannot easily be removed. Reduction improves fluidity of these slags and thus expedites their removal.

An element more negative in the electrochemical series than chromium or iron can be used to reduce the slags; but silicon is the near-universal choice because of cost, compatibility with the stainless analysis, and because other available materials (e.g., aluminum) may have undesirable effects on inclusion formation.

As experience broadened in stainless steel manufacture, there was general recognition that the reduction of chromium from the slag after oxidation was enhanced by high

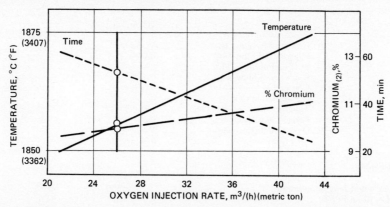

Fig. 17 Graphical solution to calculations for blow time, temperature attained, and chromium retained after decarburization.

basicity of the slag and relatively high silicon content in the metal. Data indicating the general magnitude of the effects of these two variables are shown in Fig. 18.[15,16]

The fundamental reaction for reduction of chromium from slag is

$$Cr_3O_{4(slag)} + 2Si_{(metal)} = 3Cr_{(metal)} + 2SiO_{2(slag)} \tag{29}$$

$$K = \frac{a_{Cr}^3 \, a_{SiO_2}^2}{a_{Si}^2 \, a_{Cr_3O_4}} \tag{30}$$

The silicon and chromium contents of liquid iron in equilibrium with a slag saturated with SiO_2 is shown in Fig. 19.[17] According to Fig. 19, the equilibrium constant for reaction (29) in terms of concentrations of Cr and Si in weight percent is approximately

$$K' = \frac{(\% \, Cr)^3 a_{SiO_2}^2}{(\% \, Si)^{1.75} a_{Cr_3O_4}} \tag{31}$$

over the range of Si and Cr of interest. By assuming the activity of Cr_3O_4 is a direct exponential function of % Cr in the slag and the activity of SiO_2 is an inverse function of the slag basicity V, Eq. (31) becomes

$$K'' = \frac{(\% \, Cr)^3_{metal}}{(\% \, Si)^{1.75}_{metal}(\% \, Cr)^x_{slag}V^2} \tag{32}$$

where $V = (\% \, CaO + \% \, MgO)/\% \, SiO_2$ in the slag. Solving this equation for % Cr in the slag, we have

$$\% \, Cr_{(slag)} = \frac{(\% \, Cr)^C_{metal}}{(\% \, Si)^D_{metal}V^E K''} \tag{33}$$

Expressing K''' in terms of the free energy of the reaction,

$$\log \% \, Cr_{(slag)} = C \log \% \, Cr_{(metal)} - D \log \% Si_{(metal)} - E \log V + A + \frac{B}{T} \tag{34}$$

in which A, B, C, D, and E are constants and T is the absolute temperature.

A laboratory evaluation of Eq. (34) gave the following results:[18]

$$\log \% \, Cr_{(slag)} = 4.887 - \frac{9966}{T} + 0.340 \log \% \, Cr_{(metal)}$$
$$- 0.178 \log \% Si_{(metal)} - 1.721V \tag{35}$$

Data for slag reduction taken from a 73 metric ton furnace show a considerably higher level of chromium than would be true at equilibrium (Fig. 20). The mathematical

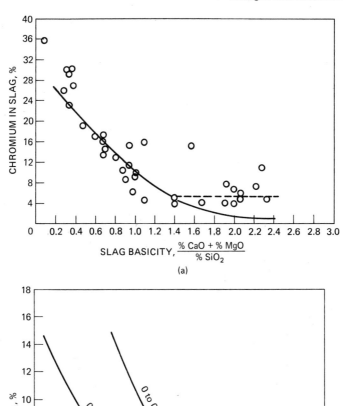

Fig. 18 Effect of slag basicity (V ratio) and bath silicon on the retention of chromium in a reduced slag. [(*a*) *Rassbach and Saunders*[15], (*b*) *Taylor.*[16]]

expression of the commercial data, Eq. (36), indicates a relatively small effect of temperature. Unlike the equilibrium equation, however, this effect is toward more complete reduction at higher temperature:[18]

$$\log \% \, Cr_{(slag)} = 1.118 + \frac{949}{T} - 0.550 \log \% \, Cr_{(metal)}$$
$$- 0.154 \log \% \, Si_{(metal)} - 0.508 \log V \quad (36)$$

Since the temperature effect is small, it may be omitted for practical purposes. For

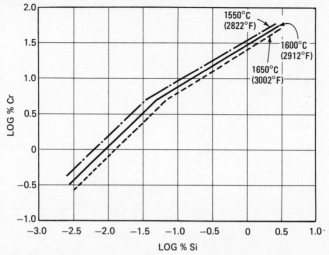

Fig. 19 Chromium and silicon contents of liquid iron in equilibrium with silica-saturated slags.[17]

general application, therefore, another expression has been developed statistically from heats of widely ranging size:[19]

$$\log \% \, Cr_{(slag)} = 1.283 \log \% \, Cr_{(metal)} - 0.748 \log \% Si_{(metal)} - 1.709 \log V - 0.923 \quad (37)$$

The wide disparity between the level to which chromium in a slag can be reduced (and sometimes is in small furnaces) and that level which actually occurs in larger units suggests the importance of mechanical factors in slag reduction, particularly mixing of metal and slag.

Perhaps the most effective stirring normally used in air-melt practice is refurnacing which was discussed earlier in this chapter. An illustration of the pronounced improvement and closer approach to equilibrium produced by refurnacing is shown in the table below:[20]

The Effect of Refurnacing on the Chromium Content of the Slag

Before refurnacing	After refurnacing
6.28–15.19%	3.64–6.69%

A word or so about temperature at reduction is warranted. The reduction of chromium by silicon is exothermic and thus might be expected to be improved by low temperature. Indeed, this was observed and is explicit in Eq. (35). Of course, the slag must be fluid for good mixing and separation so that in a practical sense a low temperature is not an unqualified benefit. Perhaps, this is what is reflected in Eq. (36) where a low temperature slightly increases the amount of unreduced chromium, and in the statistical analysis resulting in Eq. (37) which ignores the influence of temperature.

In another sense, the reduction period must be used for cooling. The temperature of the bath after oxidation is generally well above the softening temperature of the refractory and unless exposure at these temperatures is limited, severe furnace-lining wear will occur. In most large furnace practices, a considerable amount of high quality cold scrap (generally about 10% of tap weight) is added to the steel at the start of reduction to cool the metal. Very frequently, a substantial amount of the low-carbon ferrochromium that is anticipated to be needed is also added at this point, both to cool the bath and to use the excess heat efficiently to melt alloy.

Paradoxically, power is generally needed during reduction to fuse a slag and get reduction started. While the overall heat content of the furnace system may be sufficient to do the job, the transfer of this heat to the slag in a relatively motionless system is slow.

In most wrought steelmaking practices, the slag after reduction is removed and discarded.

While Eqs. (35) to (37) and Fig. 19 demonstrate the *concentrations* to which chromium in the slag can be reduced, they do not necessarily imply that greatest economy in the process is achieved by reducing the percentage of chromium in the slag to the lowest possible level. In fact, the opposite is true. Achievement of a basic slag requires addition of lime, which, in turn, increases slag *volume*. Unless the percentage of chromium unreduced in the slag decreases with increasing basicity at a greater rate than slag volume increases, additions of lime to produce a very high-basicity slag can be self-defeating. The high-basicity slag, while having a low concentration of chromium, may actually contain more weight of chromium than if reduction had been stopped at a lower basicity level with a higher *concentration* of chromium.

While this discussion of slag reduction has focused on the removal of oxidized chromium from the slag after decarburization, one should note that such slags also contain significant quantities of oxidized iron and manganese [see Fig. 9 and Eq. (19)] which are reduced concurrently with chromium. When the amount of silicon-bearing reducing agent to be added for slag reduction is being estimated, consideration of the iron and manganese contents of the slag is therefore important.

The relations among chromium, iron, manganese, silicon, and slag basicity are similar to those for chromium alone and can be developed in the same manner as was done for Eqs. (35) to (37). A general expression[19] that has proved quite useful as a guide for commercial application is

$$\log (\% \text{ Cr} + \% \text{ Mn} + \% \text{ Fe})_{slag} = 1.100 \log (\% \text{ Cr} + \% \text{ Mn})_{metal}$$
$$- 0.641 \log \% \text{ Si}_{metal} - 1.468 \log V - 0.417 \quad (38)$$

Otherwise, the slag volume–basicity relations are the same as described above for chromium alone, and the same optimum basicity range applies.

As in the discussion on oxidation, the data presented have seemed to emphasize the electric furnace and ignore the BOF practice, or the fast-growing reduced pressure practices. This has been done because the basic data developed over the years have generally been in reference to the arc furnace. Again, as in the oxidation discussion, the principles described apply to these other units.

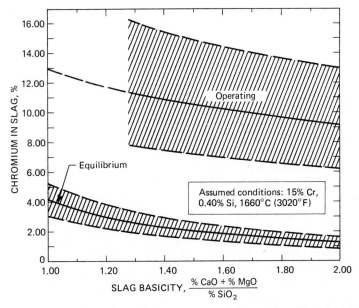

Fig. 20 Operating and equilibrium chromium contents of slags as affected by slag basicity.[18]

Published information on commercial practice emphasizes the use of silicon for reduction, the need for cooling after the blow, the desirability of slag-metal mixing in BOF practice.[1] The principles applied are no different from those presented above.

Slag reduction in the reduced pressure decarburization processes (argon-oxygen or vacuum) runs parallel to that described earlier. Refurnacing is not practiced since alternate methods of stirring inherent in those processes achieve outstanding slag-metal mixing. Also, cooling may not be desirable since the temperature after oxidation is kept low by the nature of the process. In other respects, basicity of the slag and silicon and chromium concentrations in the metal affect the process in the same way as they do the reduction in the arc furnace. In fact, slag reduction in an AOD or VOD unit probably comes much closer to equilibrium than it does in the electric furnace because of the excellent slag-metal contact caused by argon bubbling.

Phosphorus Removal   A fact that must be appreciated in approaching stainless melting by any process is that phosphorus cannot be removed from a heat containing a substantial amount of chromium. Two factors combine to make this true: the presence of a substantial amount of chromium, the oxidation of which has a greater free energy change than does the oxidation of phosphorus and the high temperature attained in stainless melting.

This one fact influences the selection of scrap and alloy and has exerted a negative influence on the production of stainless steel in the BOF if normal hot metal must be used.

Occasionally there are specifications for stainless steel calling for abnormally low phosphorus levels. These are met by melting carbon-steel scrap (and nickel if the specification so requires) and removing phosphorus from this bath. The resulting slag is discarded and only then is chromium alloy of known phosphorus content introduced. Such alloy may be charge chrome (in which case the heat must be decarburized by one of the methods discussed in earlier paragraphs) or it may be low-carbon FeCr. The important thing is that the phosphorus added stays in the metal.

Sulfur Removal   Sulfur removal from stainless steel follows the basic tenets for sulfur removal from any steel made in a basic furnace. These require adherence to various factors:

1. A basic slag
2. A low oxygen content in the slag
3. A deoxidized bath, otherwise the oxide content in the slag cannot be kept low
4. A fluid slag
5. Use of agents such as fluorspar, calcium-silicon, aluminum, etc., which promote sulfur removal beyond their effects on slag fluidity
6. Thorough mixing of slag and metal

As a rule, a lime-silica slag is used on stainless steel. Sometimes the slag is maintained in a deoxidized condition by treating (dressing) it with crushed FeSi or CaSi. If very low sulfur is needed and if the analysis or product is such that aluminum deoxidation can be tolerated, then an aluminum-dressed slag is employed. A carbonaceous slag is rarely used because of the low carbon content of most stainless grades.

The argon-oxygen process has special capabilities for desulfurization. All of the six factors listed above are readily attainable. In particular, the mixing of slag and metal produced by gaseous agitation is quite thorough. In the argon-oxygen vessel, heats can be desulfurized from about 0.03% to less than 0.010% in a matter of minutes. Unfortunately, such agitation and thorough slag mixing seldom, if ever, occurs in air-melt practices.

Fourth-hole dust removal systems affect a number of steelmaking operations. Sulfur removal can be added to the list since the fourth hole tends to draw oxygen past the slag, removing deoxidizers present to maintain a low state of slag oxidation.

Alloying Additions   Making alloy additions to stainless steel introduces few unusual problems. Unless added in extremely large quantities, sufficient to chill the bath, alloys dissolve readily. An exception would be an alloy such as ferrocolumbium which, because of a high melting point, is slow to dissolve. Consequently, care must be taken when adding this material.

Another exception, although for a different reason, is nitrogen. Stainless steels have limited solubility for nitrogen in the liquid state, depending on the alloy content. Such elements as chromium and manganese enhance nitrogen solubility while nickel and carbon detract from it. The level of solubility can be calculated from known chemistry by means of Fig. 21[21] by the technique described there.

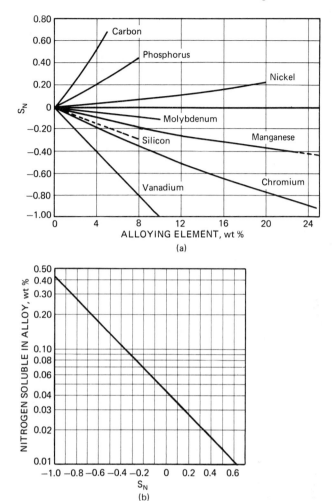

Fig. 21 Method for estimating limit of nitrogen solubility in stainless steel.[21] (a) Solubility index S_N of nitrogen in iron at 1600°C as a function of alloying elements. (b) Chart for converting S_N into % N soluble in steel alloy at 1600°C and 1 atm nitrogen pressure.

On the above graphs, S_N, the nitrogen solubility index, is actually the logarithm of the activity coefficient of nitrogen f_N. To estimate the nitrogen solubility limit in a given steel composition, use Fig. 21a to determine the nitrogen solubility index. The elements above the line $S_N = 0$, i.e., those which decrease N solubility, are treated separately from those below the line which increase N solubility. For each group of elements, begin with the line nearest the horizontal and work in sequence to the left. First a value of S_N is found on the molybdenum line for the percent of that element present in the alloy. By moving left horizontally to the manganese line, the % Mn having the same S_N is determined. To this is added the actual % Mn and for this total an S_N value is found on the Mn line. Again, move horizontally to the silicon line, find the equivalent % Si, add this to the actual % Si and locate a new S_N on the Si line. Repeat these steps moving to the left in sequence to a final S_N (which will be negative).

The operation is performed similarly on the element above the line $S_N = 0$ starting at nickel and moving to phosphorus and carbon. Determine a value of S_N (which will be positive for these elements).

Add the two values of S_N algebraically and from this determine the nitrogen solubility limit in % N from Fig. 21b.

In air-melt practice, nitrogen is added either as a Cr-N alloy or a Mn-N alloy.

When adding nitrogen, several precautions are observed in order to improve the level and consistency of nitrogen recovery. The composition of the steel is kept as rich as the specification permits in those elements which enhance nitrogen solubility. Also active stirring is employed to prevent segregation of nitrogen at the point of addition. Control of temperature is also important. A low temperature improves the solubility and hence, the recovery of nitrogen.[22]

In the argon-oxygen practice, nitrogen can be added as a gas through the tuyeres. Recovery is quite consistent and the addition is made largely by timing the period during which the gas is used.

Producing Extra-Low Carbon Levels The manufacture of stainless steel with carbon specifications of 0.030% or less by an air-melt practice requires special mention. Reference to Fig. 6 shows that attainment of carbon levels as low as 0.020 to 0.025% (to meet a final shipping specification of 0.030% maximum) requires either an extremely high temperature or a low chromium content. The very fact of trying to get a high temperature introduces complications with respect to slag generation and consistency, refractory wear, etc. As a result, most steelmakers have adopted a more or less "virgin" practice, i.e., they charge little chromium-bearing materials before decarburization. In these practices, a charge of carbon-steel scrap plus nickel is melted down and decarburized to the required level. Some steelmakers use a little stainless scrap in their practice, but the amount is limited and dictated more by a need for nickel than chromium.

After decarburization, practices diverge. In some cases, slag reduction with silicon is employed and after partial slag-off an addition of low-carbon FeCr, sufficient to bring the analysis to the required specification, is made. Generally, the chromium is added in three or four batches in order to minimize the possibility of its freezing on the bottom of the furnace. When all the necessary material is added, the heat is slagged-off and finished in the normal way. In this practice, a high-silicon, low-carbon ferrochromium is preferred. If it is not available, FeSi may be added before or with the ferrochromium. It was found that these types of practices improved chromium recovery, probably by buffering the chromium against the oxidizing potential of the relatively high FeO slag.

An alternate practice to the above is to add a substantial amount of silicon to the bath with the first batch of chromium. As each subsequent batch of chromium is added, the bath is blown with oxygen. The heat created by the oxidation of silicon causes rapid melt-in of the chromium addition. This practice minimizes the use of power for chromium melting and as a result, tends to prevent any carbon pickup from inadvertent electrode dipping.

In regard to slags on 0.03% C heats, the likelihood of carbon pickup is increased by a very basic slag. Some evidence of this is presented in Fig. 22. As a result of these findings, slags on air-melt 0.030% C steels tend toward a 1:1 basicity ratio.

Producing extra-low carbon requires extreme care, because a very small carbon pickup (as little as 0.1 lb [0.045 kg]C per ton) could cause a lost heat. As a result, successful production requires considerable attention to small details, e.g., burn off of rabble rods, care in split ends of electrodes, etc. The heats are expensive to begin with because of virgin alloy, and while offgrade steels can still be sold as conventional stainless steels, doing so requires writing off the additional cost of producing to the 0.03% C level.

The problems of producing 0.030% C levels in air-melt operations are such that extra-low carbon grades were among the first stainless steels to be adapted to argon-oxygen production. Here, while some extra blowing is required, the practice is the same as when producing the normal carbon levels, and consistency of meeting the specification is excellent.

Acid Stainless Steel Practice A small amount of stainless steel is made by an acid practice. Generally, such operation is carried out in foundries where the principle product is carbon steel with only an occasional stainless heat. Once a substantial tonnage of stainless is involved, it pays to adopt a basic slag practice.

The meltdown and oxidation practices and results when melting on a silica hearth are no different than those involved in basic practice. Salient differences appear in the reduction practice. As noted in Figs. 18 and 20 effective reduction of chromium from a slag requires a relatively high basicity and, of course, this is impossible to achieve on a silica lining without gross wear. Because of this, little chromium is recovered once it has been oxidized, hence, the high cost of acid operations.

It is possible, of course, to adopt aluminum rather than silicon for slag reduction, but

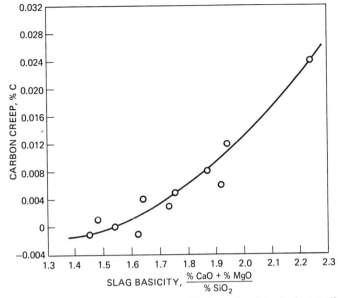

Fig. 22   Carbon pickup in a stainless steel bath as affected by slag basicity.[23]

this practice is somewhat costly, causes some reduction of silicon which may not be desirable, and may lead to an undesirably high aluminum residual.

REFERENCES

1. Carlson, R. F., and R. B. Shaw: Stainless Steel Melting by Two Low-Cost Processes; Part 1—The BOF Process, *AISI General Meeting*, May 1972.
2. Schmidt, Etterich, Bauer, and Fleischer: Production of High-Alloy Superrefined Steels in the Basic Oxygen Converter, *Stahl Eisen*, vol. 88, pp. 153–168, 1968.
3. Ardito, V. P., and R. B. Shaw: Stainless Steel Melting by Two Low-Cost Processes; Part II—The AVR (Allegheny Vacuum Refining) Process, *AISI General Meeting*, May 1972.
4. Hilty, D. C., W. D. Forgeng, and R. L. Folkman: Oxygen Solubility and Oxide Phases in the Fe-Cr-O System, *Trans. Am. Inst. Min. Metall. Pet. Eng.*, vol. 203, pp. 253–268, 1955.
5. Hilty, D. C.: Relation Between Chromium and Carbon in Chromium Steel Refining, *Electr. Furn. Conf. Proc.*, vol. 6, pp. 140–148, 1948.
6. Richardson, F. D., and W. E. Dennis: Effect of Chromium on the Thermodynamic Activity of Carbon in Liquid Iron, *J. Iron Steel Inst. London*, vol. 175, pp. 257–263, 1953.
7. Hilty, D. C., H. P. Rassbach, and W. Crafts: Observations of Stainless Steel Melting Practice, *J. Iron Steel Inst. London*, vol. 180, pp. 116–128, 1955.
8. Simkovich, A., and C. W. McCoy: The Effect of Nickel on the Chromium and Carbon Relationship in Stainless Steel Refining, *Trans. Am. Inst. Min. Metall. Pet. Eng.*, vol. 221, pp. 416–417, 1961.
9. Physical Chemistry of Steelmaking Committee, AIME: "Electric Furnace Steelmaking," vol. II, chap. 19, Wiley, New York, 1963.
10. Hilty, D. C., and T. F. Kaveney: Economic Considerations of Various Charges for Stainless Steel Production, *Electr. Furn. Conf. Proc.*, vol. 25, pp. 110–122, 1967.
11. Healy, G. W., and D. C. Hilty: Effect of Oxygen Input Rates in the Decarburization of Chromium Steel, *Trans. Am. Inst. Min. Metall. Pet. Eng.*, vol. 205, pp. 695–707, 1957.
12. Chipman, J.: Atomic Interaction in Molten Alloy Steel, *J. Iron Steel Inst. London*, vol. 180, pp. 97–106, 1955.
13. Hilty, D. C., G. W. Healy, and W. Crafts: Metallic Oxidation in Chromium Steel Melting, *Trans. Am. Inst. Min. Metall. Pet Eng.*, vol. 197, pp. 649–653, 1953.
14. Healy, G. W.: Simplified Calculation of Effects of Oxygen Blowing Rates, *Electr. Furn. Conf. Proc.*, vol. 16, pp. 252–258, 1958.
15. Rassbach, H. P., and E. R. Saunders: Reducing Period in Stainless Steel Melting, *Trans. Am. Inst. Min. Metall. Pet. Eng.*, vol. 197, pp. 1009–1016, 1953.
16. Taylor, C. R.: Some Observations on the Metallurgy of Electric Furnace Melting, *Electr. Furn. Conf. Proc.*, vol. 8, pp. 91–97, 1950.

17. Hilty, D. C.: Previously unpublished work.
18. McCoy, C. W., and F. C. Langenberg: Slag-Metal Equilibrium During Stainless Steel Melting, *Electr. Furn. Conf. Proc.*, vol. 21, pp. 17–26, 1963.
19. Hilty, D. C.: Previously unpublished work based on data from ref. 7.
20. Filar, K. J., J. P. Bartos, and G. H. Geiger: Chromium Recovery During the Manufacture of Stainless Steels, *Electr. Furn. Conf. Proc.*, vol. 25, pp. 95–99, 1967.
21. Langenberg, F. C., and M. J. Day: Application of Nitrogen Solubility Data to Alloy Steelmaking, *Electr. Furn. Conf. Proc.*, vol. 15, pp. 7–15, 1957.
22. Rassbach, H. P., E. R. Saunders, and W. L. Harbrecht: Nitrogen in Stainless Steel, *Electr. Furn. Conf. Proc.*, vol. 11, pp. 244–256, 1953.
23. Crafts, W., and H. P. Rassbach: Melting Low Carbon Stainless Steels, *Electr. Furn. Conf. Proc.*, vol. 9, pp. 95–104, 1951.
24. Fulton, J. C., and S. Ramachandran: Decarburization of Stainless Steels, *Electr. Furn. Conf. Proc.*, vol. 30, pp. 43–50, 1972.
25. Bingel, C. J., and C. B. Griffith: Production of Low Carbon Stainless Steel by the VOD Process, *Electr. Furn. Conf. Proc.*, vol. 30, pp. 51–54, 1972.

SUGGESTED SUPPLEMENTARY READING

Although not specifically cited as source material for this chapter, the following references are suggested to readers desiring further information on melting of stainless steels.

General Principles

1. Turner, T. W., and G. H. Geiger: The Chromium-Carbon-Temperature Relationship in Nickel Base Alloys, *Electr. Furn. Conf. Proc.*, vol. 26, pp. 114–118, 1968.
2. McCoy, C. W., A. F. Kolek, F. C. Langenberg: Application of Thermo-Chemical Data During Stainless Steel Melting, "Applications of Fundamental Thermodynamics to Metallurgical Processes," pp. 249–280, Gordon and Breach, New York, 1967.
3. Barnhardt, L. F.: The Parallel Oxidation of Carbon and Chromium in Liquid Iron (1600°C), Ph.D. thesis, Massachusetts Institute of Technology, Cambridge, 1965.

Air Melt

1. Physical Chemistry of Steelmaking Committee, AIME: "Electric Furnace Steelmaking," vol. I, chap. 12, Wiley, New York, 1963.
2. Melting of Stainless Steel, *Electr. Furn. Conf. Proc.*, vol. 13, pp. 166–205, 1955.

BOF

1. Method and System for the Production of Stainless Steel, French Patent 1,430,516, Jan. 24, 1966.
2. Langenberg, F. C., and E. L. Kern: The Manufacture of Stainless Steel in the Top Blown Oxygen Converter, *Iron Steel Eng.*, vol. 44, pp. 116–121, 1967.
3. Shaw, R. B.: Process for Producing Corrosion Resistant Steel, U.S. Patent 3,507,642, Apr. 21, 1970.

VOD

1. Post, C. B., R. C. Lunbach, and M. D. Sullivan: Stainless Steelmaking Utilizing Vacuum Treatment. *Philadelphia Regional Technical Meeting, AISI*, Nov. 1, 1967.
2. Stavehaug, L.: Operational Experience with Asea-SKF Ladle Furnace in Stainless Steelmaking, *Electr. Furn. Conf. Proc.*, vol. 28, pp. 52–56, 1970.
3. Yokota, K., T. Watanabe, and T. Tonge: The Study of the Mechanisms of Decarburization for Liquid Stainless Steel Under Reduced Pressure, *4th Int. Conf. Vacuum Metall.*, Tokyo, Jun. 4–8, 1973.
4. Tanoue, T., T. Ikeda, T. Fukui, M. Okada, and T. Takahashi: Reactions During the Oxygen Top Blowing of Stainless and Carbon Steel Under Vacuum, *4th Int. Conf. Vacuum Metall.*, Tokyo, Jun. 4–8, 1973.
5. Berue, J: Vacuum Refining of Stainless Steels by the B-V Process, *4th Int. Conf. Vacuum Metall.*, Tokyo, Jun. 4–8, 1973.

AOD

1. Aucott, R. B., D. W. Gray, and C. G. Holland: The Theory and Practice of the Argon-Oxygen Decarburizing Process, *J. West Scotl. Iron Steel Inst.*, vol. 79, pp. 97–127, 1971–1972.
2. Choulet, R. J., F. S. Death, and R. N. Dokken: Argon-Oxygen Refining of Stainless Steel, *Can. Metall. Qu.*, vol. 10, pp. 129–136, 1971.
3. Koontz, C. W., and D. E. Moritz: Operation of 50-Ton Argon-Oxygen Vessel at Eastern Stainless Steel Co., *Iron Steel Eng.*, vol. 48, pp. 65–70, 1968.
4. Moffitt, R. B., and J. M. Saccamano: Use of Gaseous Nitrogen in the Argon-Oxygen Process, *Electr. Furn. Conf. Proc.*, vol. 30, pp. 59–63, 1972.

5. Fabbri, S.: Argon-Oxygen Decarburization Process for Stainless Steel Production at Ilssa Viola, *Electr. Furn. Conf. Proc.*, vol. 28, pp. 41–46, 1970.
6. Hodgess, E. E., and R. L. Chapple: Quality Aspects of Argon-Oxygen Refining, *Electr. Furn. Conf. Proc.*, vol. 28, pp. 47–50, 1970.
7. Ellis, J. D., and J. M. Saccamano: Recent Developments in Argon-Oxygen Reactor Stainless Melting at Josyln, *Electr. Furn. Conf. Proc.*, vol. 27, pp. 76–79, 1969.
8. Saccamano, J. M., R. J. Choulet, and J. D. Ellis: Making Stainless Steel in the Argon-Oxygen Reactor at Josyln, *Electr. Furn. Conf. Proc.*, vol. 26, pp. 119–123, 1968.

Part **2**

Metallurgy of Stainless Steels

Chapter 4

Structure and Constitution of Wrought Austenitic Stainless Steels

CHARLES J. NOVAK

Project Manager, The International Nickel Company, New York,
New York

INTRODUCTION

The austenitic stainless steels represent the largest group of stainless steels in use, making up 65 to 70% of the total for the past several years.[1] The austenitic alloys used most often are those of the AISI 300 series. Collectively, these enjoy their dominant position because of a general high level of fabricability and corrosion resistance and because of the varied specific combinations of properties that can be obtained by different compositions within the group, providing useful material choices for a vast number of applications.

The alloys within this group are very different from one another. For perspective, a brief review of the range of these alloys begins with the leanest composition, Type 301, which is employed in applications requiring formability, particularly where stretching is involved. Also, Type 301 (17Cr-7Ni) is readily amenable to strengthening by cold-work. These uses rely on the transformation characteristics of the alloy. Type 301 is confined primarily to use at ambient temperature. Types 302 and 304 represent the "bread and butter" alloys, having somewhat greater stability and improved corrosion resistance. Type 304 is the most widely produced stainless steel and is used considerably at elevated temperatures. Type 305, with its increased nickel content, is employed where even greater stability is required. The addition of molybdenum to an essentially Type 304 base, represented by Types 316 and 317, imparts greater corrosion resistance and significantly enhanced elevated temperature strength. Alloys with greatly increased alloy contents, such as Types 309, 310, and 314, find their use primarily in elevated temperature applications.

These alloys are all based on the Fe-Cr-Ni ternary system. Their behavior depends on where they lie within the system. The phases possible in this system are numerous.

BINARY SYSTEM EQUILIBRIA

The most basic of the phases derive from the allotropic forms of iron, which can be seen by examining the Fe-Cr binary system in Fig. 1.[2] Between 1400 and 1539°C (2540 and 2800°F), pure iron exists crystallographically as body-centered cubic (bcc) *ferrite*. This highest temperature allotrope is often termed *delta ferrite*, δ. Between 910 and 1400°C (1650 and 2540°F), iron is face-centered cubic (fcc), called *gamma phase* or *austenite*, γ. Below 910°C (1650°F), iron once again becomes bcc and its structure is identified as *alpha ferrite*, α. The delta and alpha ferrites are physically indistinguishable. The nomenclature serves to identify the conditions of formation when one or both of these constituents occur. The chemistries of these phases may also differ.

The dashed line in Fig. 1 represents a third transformation point in iron. This is the *magnetic (Curie) transformation point* above which iron is paramagnetic and below which it is ferromagnetic. A rigorous discussion of these terms can be found elsewhere.[3,4]

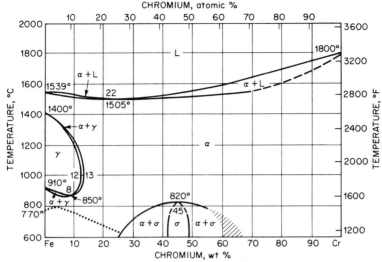

Fig. 1 Iron-chromium equilibrium diagram.[2]

Paramagnetic iron is nonmagnetic, with a permeability of 1.00. Ferromagnetic iron is magnetic with permeability greater than unity, the exact magnitude depending on composition. In this connection, it should be noted that if the fcc (γ) austenite structure is maintained to lower temperatures, the alloy will remain paramagnetic (nonmagnetic). Thus, γ austenite (fcc) is nonmagnetic at ambient temperature, while α ferrite (bcc) is magnetic. This has been shown by Hoselitz and Sucksmith[5] for the Fe-Ni binary system (Fig. 2). It may be seen that the Curie temperature of low nickel content γ is much below that of α of the same composition. The same γ versus α effect applies to Fe-Cr-Ni alloys within the scope of this book but should not be casually extrapolated to vastly different alloys within the system or to other systems. The addition of chromium in stainless steel further depresses Curie temperature.[3]

In Fig. 1, attention is directed to the left-hand side of the diagram. (The phase field, σ, in the center, will be discussed in a later section.) The addition of chromium up to about 7% reduces the temperature of both bcc $\rightleftarrows$ fcc transformation points. Above 7%, the temperature interval over which austenite exists gradually decreases until, above about 13% chromium, no transformation occurs, and ferrite exists at all temperatures. Thus, chromium is said to be a ferrite-forming element. Other elements commonly present in stainless steels exhibiting this behavior are molybdenum and silicon. Their binary equilibria with iron are shown in Fig. 3[6] and Fig. 4.[7] Aluminum, titanium, and columbium behave similarly.[8-11]

Austenitic stainless steels all contain more than 16% chromium. From Fig. 1, it is apparent that chromium contents of this magnitude would render the alloys totally ferritic (α). This effect is counteracted primarily by nickel. The binary Fe-Ni phase equilibrium is shown in Fig. 5.[12] The behavior contrasts sharply with that of chromium. The austenite (γ) field is broadened by increasing additions of nickel. Logically, nickel is termed an austenite-forming element. Manganese, like nickel, also generates extended γ field (Fig. 6[13,14]) although in *ternary* Fe-Cr-Mn alloys, manganese

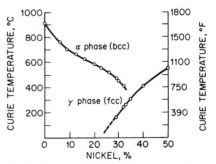

Fig. 2 Magnetic transformation (Curie) temperatures for α and γ in binary iron-nickel alloys.[5]

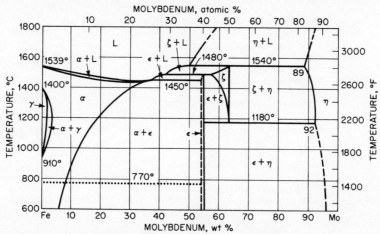

Fig. 3   Fe-Mo equilibrium diagram.[6]

behaves differently. Hochmann and Colombier[14] point out the upper gamma-field boundary is not displaced to higher temperatures, but the austenitizing effect is one of stabilizing the fcc structure upon cooling from the annealing temperature.

Miller[16] has summarized the effect of most elements on the gamma-phase field in binary alloys with iron. His summary, organized according to the periodic table of the elements, is shown in Fig. 7.

Fig. 5 is an *equilibrium* diagram for the Fe-Ni system. In actual practice, particularly at lower temperatures, equilibrium constituents do not form as predicted. This happens because large, substitutional atoms, like nickel, diffuse very slowly in iron. Normal times and/or cooling rates are insufficient to permit the diffusion necessary to achieve equilibrium.

The *transformation* diagram for the Fe-Ni system is shown in Fig. 8[17] for comparison with Fig. 5. Upon cooling, the temperature for the $\gamma \rightarrow \alpha$ transformation is depressed below that indicated under equilibrium conditions. In place of equilibrium decomposition of γ, transformation to *martensite* occurs. In low-nickel and low-carbon-content alloys, this transformation product is bcc, in contrast to the distorted tetragonal structure common to carbon steel metallurgy. It is often called α' to differentiate it from equilibrium bcc ferrite. Since the product is still bcc, other metallurgists refer to it simply as α ferrite.

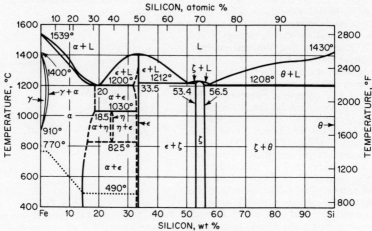

Fig. 4   Fe-Si equilibrium diagram.[7]

When this bcc constituent, whatever it is called, is reheated, the reverse transformation to austenite (γ) is displaced to higher temperatures, as shown in Fig. 8. Thus, the *metastable, nonequilibrium* transformations assume a temperature hysteresis below the $\gamma \rightarrow \alpha$ or above the $\alpha \rightarrow \gamma$ transformation temperatures indicated for equilibrium conditions. This same effect exists in the Fe-Mn system (Fig. 9) and more complicated Fe-Cr-Ni-based commercial austenitic stainless steel from which later consideration of martensite transformation temperatures (M_s, M_d) arises.

Instead of considering the effect of a particular element when added to iron, the ferrite-forming or austenite-forming tendency of a particular element has often been represented by examining what happens when a third element is added to a binary system. Many references have used pseudobinary diagrams based on ternary additions to Fe-C alloys and examined the effect of the addition on the size of the gamma (γ) field. The references to some of these diagrams are listed in Table 1, together with notations as to the effect.

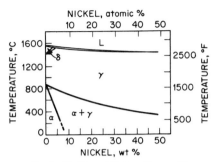

Fig. 5   Fe-Ni equilibrium diagram.[12]

IRON-CHROMIUM-NICKEL SYSTEM

Ternary Diagrams   Before reviewing phase equilibria, it should be noted that these are only approximations of the phases that may be found in a stainless steel of a particular chemistry. Normal commercial levels of other elements besides iron, chromium, and nickel are not, in general, the same as those present in the alloys used in determining the diagrams. Also, the heating times employed in experimental determinations of phase equilibria are much longer than those used in commercial practice. Despite these limitations, the diagrams are useful for describing how the alloy system behaves and thus enable prediction of the effect of changes (composition or heat treatment) within the system.

A ternary diagram for the Fe-Cr-Ni system just below the solidus temperature is shown in Fig. 10.[23] [For alloys of interest, the solidus temperatures are about 1400 to 1450°C

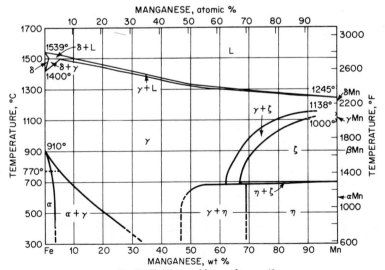

Fig. 6   Fe-Mn equilibrium diagram.[13]

PERIODIC SYSTEM OF THE ELEMENTS

Adapted Primarily for Ferrous Metallurgists

Atomic size factors (in parentheses) are % smaller (−) or larger (+) than gamma (fcc) iron at 75°F(24°C). Lattice environment (Coordination No.) is taken into account; CN is 12 except 6 for interstitials H, B, C, N, and O. Groups VI, VIb, VII, and VIIb form ionic compounds with the metals. Atomic size is based largely on work of W. Hume-Rothery and associates and L. Pauling. (Some values, such as those for H and O, are approximate.) Alloying valences are those of Pauling.

Upper table (Groups 0, I, II, III, IV, V, VI, VII)

0	I	II	III	IV	V	VI	VII
H-1 (−58) ▲ XX ⊗							
He-2 FCC (Others)	Li-3 (+23) BCC* HCP†	Be-4 (−11) ● HCP* BCC	B-5 (−29) ⊗ XX	C-6 (−34) ▲ ⊗ XX	N-7 (−36) ▲ XX	O-8 (−33) ▲ ⊗ XX	F-9
Ne-10 FCC	Na-11 (+50) BCC* HCP	Mg-12 (+27) ● HCP	Al-13 (+14) ● FCC	Si-14 (+7) ● XX	P-15 (+2) XX	S-16 (+1) XX	Cl-17 XX

Main table

0	Ia	IIa	IIIa	IVa	Va	VIa	VIIa	VIII	VIII	VIII	Ib	IIb	IIIb	IVb	Vb	VIb	VIIb
Ar-18 FCC	K-19 (+86) ⊗ BCC	Ca-20 (+56) ⊗ FCC* BCC	Sc-21 (+29) ⊗ HCP* BCC	Ti-22 (+16) ● HCP* BCC	V-23 (+6) ● BCC	Cr-24 (+1) ● BCC	Mn-25 (+1) ● XX* FCC†	Fe-26 (0) ● BCC* FCC	Co-27 (−1) ● HCP* FCC	Ni-28 (−1) ● FCC	Cu-29 (+1) ● FCC	Zn-30 (+6) ● HCP	Ga-31 (+12) ● XX	Ge-32 (+9) ● XX	As-33 (+11) XX	Se-34 (+11) XX	Br-35 XX
Kr-36 FCC	Rb-37 (+97) ⊗ BCC	Sr-38 (+71) ⊗ FCC* HCP†	Y-39 (+42) ⊗ HCP* BCC	Zr-40 (+27) ● HCP* BCC	Cb-41 (+15) ● BCC	Mo-42 (+10) ● BCC	Tc-43 (+8) HCP	Ru-44 (+6) HCP	Rh-45 (+6) FCC	Pd-46 (+9) ● FCC	Ag-47 (+14) ● FCC	Cd-48 (+20) ⊗ HCP	In-49 (+25) ⊗ XX	Sn-50 (+23) ⊗ XX	Sb-51 (+27) XX	Te-52 (+27) XX	I-53 XX
Xe-54 FCC	Cs-55 (+112) ⊗ BCC	Ba-56 (+76) ⊗ BCC	La-57 (+48) ⊗ HCP* FCC†	Hf-72 (+26) ● HCP* BCC	Ta-73 (+16) ● BCC	W-74 (+11) ● BCC	Re-75 (+9) HCP	Os-76 (+7) HCP	Ir-77 (+8) FCC	Pt-78 (+10) FCC	Au-79 (+14) ● FCC	Hg-80 (+25) ⊗ XX	Tl-81 (+36) ⊗ HCP* BCC	Pb-82 (+39) ● FCC	Bi-83 (+35) ⊗ XX	Po-84 (+40) XX	At-85
Rn-86	Fr-87	Ra-88	Ac-89 (+49) ⊗ FCC														
Alloying Valence 1	2	3	4	5	6	6	6	6	6	5.56	4.56	3.56	2.56 Note 2	1.56 Note 2	(2) Note 3	(1) Note 3	

Note 1: The rare-earth (lanthanide, 58-71) and actinide (90-103) series are omitted.
Note 2: Valence is 4 for C; 3 for N and P.
Note 3: (1) and (2) are not alloying valences.

Substitutional Solid Solutions
● Favorable size factor: 0 to ± 13%
◐ Borderline size factor: ± 14 to ± 16%
⊗ Unfavorable size factor: > ± 16%

Interstitial Solid Solutions
▲ Favorable size factor: >(−40%)
◭ Borderline size factor: (−30) to (−40%)
▲ Unfavorable size factor: <(−30%)

Structure
BCC – Body-centered cubic
FCC – Face-centered cubic
HCP – Hexagonal close-packed
XX – Not BCC, FCC, or HCP usually more complex
* Structure at 75°F(24°C)
† Also FCC   ‡ Also BCC

Type of Gamma Iron (FCC) Field if Alloyed With Iron
◤ Gamma loop, like Cr
◣ Limited gamma loop, like B
◥ Open gamma region, like Ni
◢ Limited gamma region, like C

Fig. 7 Periodic chart of the elements showing effect on gamma-phase field in binary alloys.[16]

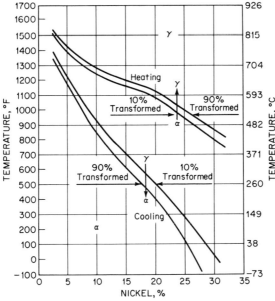

Fig. 8 Fe-Ni transformation diagram.[17]

(2550 to 2640°F).] Compositions approximating the leaner AISI 300-series stainless steels (16 to 19Cr-6 to 12Ni) would be predicted to fall either within the $\alpha + \gamma$ field or just outside of it, depending on the specific composition. Although, as noted above, Fig. 10 is an approximation and does not take into account other elements, it does reasonably represent the situation observed in practice. The leaner 300-series alloys do usually contain high-temperature ferrite α (δ) as a second constituent at very high temperatures. The exact amount of ferrite will depend on the particular composition, the degree of

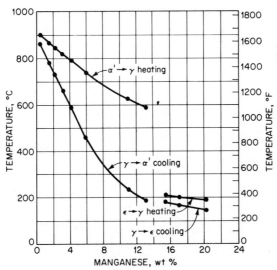

Fig. 9 Fe-Mn transformation diagram.[18]

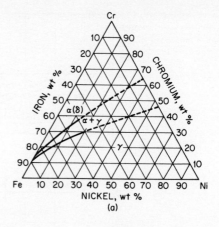

(a)

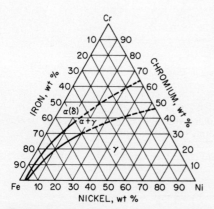

Fig. 10 Fe-Cr-Ni system just below the solidus temperature.[23]

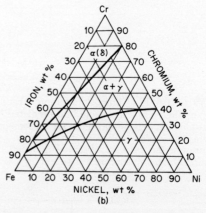

(b)

Fig. 11 Fe-Cr-Ni system at 900 to 1300°C (1650 to 2370°F). (a) Phases in the temperature range for maximum γ [900 to 1300°C (1650–2370°F)].[23] (b) Phases at 1100°C (2010°F).[26]

homogeneity, and how closely thermal history has allowed equilibrium to be approached. Highly alloyed AISI 300-series steels, to use Type 310 as an example, are shifted far enough to the right so that a fully austenitic structure is normally obtained.

The recommended annealing temperature ranges[24,25] for the austenitic stainless steels are shown in Table 2. As shown, austenitic stainless steels are usually annealed at 1008 to 1120°C (1850 to 2050°F). A major intent is to dissolve, as nearly as possible, any constituents that may be present. The ternary-phase equilibria in this temperature range, according to Bain and Aborn[23] and Pugh and Nisbet[26], are shown in Fig. 11. The diagrams differ

TABLE 1   Effect of Various Ternary Additions on Fe-C Alloys

Element	Effect on austenite field	References
Cr	Shrinks	Crafts,[19] cites Bain[20]
Cr	Shrinks	Colombier and Hockmann,[11] cites Bungart et al.[15]
Mo	Shrinks	Herzig,[21] cites Bain[20]
Si	Shrinks	Greiner,[22] cites Bain[20]
Ni	Expands	Colombier and Hochmann[11]

for several reasons, among them temperature, alloy purity, and experimental technique. They are, however, quite similar in the region of interest (lower left-hand corner). As seen by comparing Figs. 10 and 11, reducing temperature expands the austenite (γ) field near the iron-rich corner. Alloys containing 16 to 19% chromium and 6 to 12% nickel now fall clearly within the γ field.

In practice also, the ternary-based AISI Type 300-series alloys are fully austenitic.

TABLE 2   Recommended Annealing Temperatures for Austenitic Stainless Steels[24,25]

AISI type	Temperature	
	°F	°C
Unstabilized grades:		
201, 202	1850–2050	1008–1120
203	1950	1063
301, 302, 302B, 303, 303Se	1850–2050	1008–1120
304, 304N	1850–2050	1008–1120
308	1850–2050	1008–1120
309, 309S	1900–2050	1036–1120
310, 310S	1900–2100	1036–1149
314	2100	1149
316, 316N	1850–2050	1008–1120
316F	2000	1093
317	1850–2050	1008–1120
330	1950–2150	1063–1176
384	1900–2100	1036–1149
Stabilized grades:		
321	1750–2050	953–1120
347	1850–2050	1008–1120
Low-carbon grades:		
304L, S30430	1850–2050	1008–1120
316L, 317L	1900–2000	1036–1093

When ferrite is encountered, it quite often results from prior exposure at higher temperatures perhaps combined with some residual heterogeneity from the original cast structure. The base ternary chemistry is close enough to the $\gamma/(\alpha + \gamma)$ phase boundary so that modification of the base can readily result in delta (δ) ferrite. Specific variations in the AISI 300 series such as higher chromium contents (Type 309) or the addition of silicon

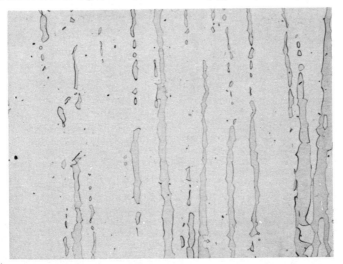

Fig. 12   Structure of annealed Type 309 stainless steel. Elongated islands are ferrite in an austenitic matrix. 100×.

(Type 302B), molybdenum (Types 316, 317), titanium (Type 321), or columbium (Type 347) will all strongly favor ferrite formation. Reduction of carbon content (as represented by Types 304L, 316L, and 317L) also will make ferrite formation more likely. The structure of annealed Type 309 stainless steel is shown in Fig. 12. The elongated constituent is ferrite in an austenite matrix. This appearance is typical of the morphology normally encountered.

Figures 10 and 11 show in another way the austenite- and ferrite-forming tendencies of

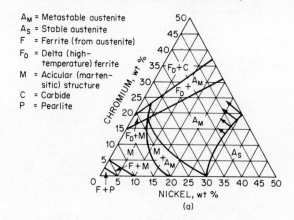

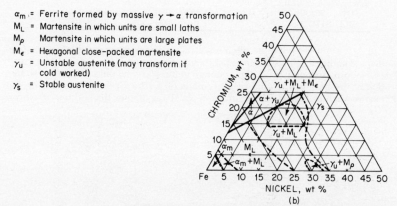

Fig. 13 Fe-Cr-Ni system at room temperature. (a) Phases after rapid cooling from temperatures of maximum γ (0.1% C).[23] A_M = metastable austenite, A_S = stable austenite, F = ferrite (from austenite), F_D = delta (high-temperature) ferrite, M = acicular (martensitic) structure, C = carbide, and P = pearlite. (b) Structure of alloys quenched from 1100°C (2012°F).[27] α_m = ferrite formed by massive $\gamma \rightarrow \alpha$ transformation, M_L = martensite in which units are small laths, M_ρ = martensite in which units are large plates, M_ϵ = hexagonal close-packed martensite, γ_u = unstable austenite (may transform if cold-worked), and γ_s = stable austenite.

nickel and chromium, respectively. The γ-field boundary shifts to higher chromium contents as nickel content is increased. When fourth elements like silicon, molybdenum, titanium, or columbium are added, nickel content is normally increased to compensate for the ferrite-forming tendency. The low-carbon grades tend to have higher nickel contents for the same reason.

Figure 13 shows the phases present in annealed materials quenched to room temperature.[23,27] Unlike previous ternary diagrams, Fig. 13 does not represent phase equilibrium.

It is analogous to Figs. 8 and 9, which depict binary systems transformation. The austenite retained upon cooling to ambient temperature is termed metastable or unstable because it is not the equilibrium constituent and can be caused to transform, either by cold-work or by cooling to lower temperatures. The austenite field is bounded on the chromium-rich (upper) side by the original $\alpha + \gamma$ field. Restricting the field on the lean-nickel, lean-chromium side are transformation boundaries.

The range of austenite stability presented in the two diagrams differ. Commercial alloys containing 16 to 19Cr-6 to 12Ni normally remain austenitic to room temperature, consistent with Fig. 13a. The more recent diagram in Fig. 13b shows transformation in such alloys. This later diagram was constructed from work where very detailed examination of

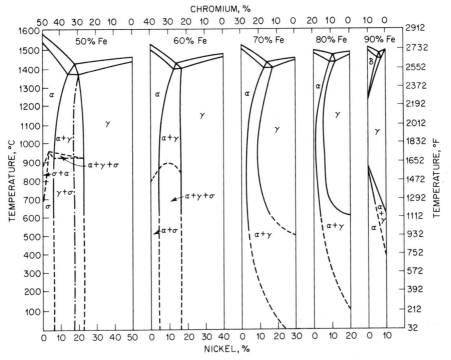

Fig. 14 Cross sections of Fe-Cr-Ni ternary.[26]

specimens was conducted on low-carbon-content alloys. Thus, Fig. 13b indicates transformation if the slightest trace of transformation product was found. Carbon also accounts for part of the difference. (The different transformation products noted in Fig. 13b will be discussed in a later section.)

Although Fig. 13a is a reasonable representation of what is normally observed in leaner AISI 300-series stainless steels, its representation of higher alloy materials is inaccurate, as reflected by the arrows marking the A_m-A_s boundary. Speich's diagram (Fig. 13b) is a much better representation. For example, alloys containing 20Cr-25Ni are exceedingly stable at room temperature.

Regardless of the exact location of the transformation boundaries, it is clear that the alloys on which the AISI 300 series is based are quite close to being other than totally austenitic. This fact is always considered in arriving at chemistry balance in alloy design. Although precipitation-hardened stainless steels are discussed elsewhere, it should be noted that not only do the direct effects of alloy additions have to be considered, but also that the changing of matrix chemistry by precipitation processes involving chromium or nickel can greatly alter the constitution of alloys. Consideration of balance is a factor in determining the composition of the widely used AISI austenitic steels also.

Pseudobinary Sections   An alternative for visualizing phase relationships is the use of cross sections through the ternary diagram, such that one of the elements is constant. Figure 14 shows sections for constant iron contents of 50, 60, 70, 80, and 90% as constructed by Pugh and Nisbet.[26]

These are equilibrium diagrams. The dashed lines used to separate the phase fields at lower temperatures mean that the transformations are not observed under practical

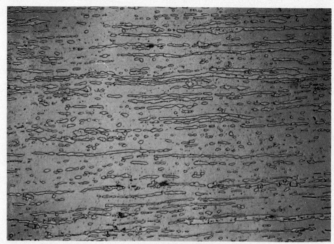

Fig. 15 Structure of annealed Type 329 stainless steel. The elongated islands are austenite in a ferrite matrix. 100×.

conditions. An alloy cooled from the γ field across dashed lines will remain austenitic. This shows in another way why the austenite is called metastable.

Figure 14 reveals how the shape of the austenite (γ) field changes with increasing total nickel plus chromium contents. At 70, 80, and 90% iron, the $\gamma/(\alpha + \gamma)$ boundary slants backward such that a fully austenitic alloy close to boundary at 1000°C (1832°F) can contain some ferrite when heated. The presence of some ferrite can be helpful in practical concerns like weld-metal integrity. In this connection, it should be noted that the established AISI composition ranges are not and should not be considered melting inaccuracy allowances. Stainless steel producers can and do control to much closer limits.

At lower iron contents, 50 and 60%, the $\alpha/(\alpha + \gamma)$ boundary does not curve, so that an austenitic alloy tends to remain so at all temperatures. This behavior is responsible in part for making very highly alloyed steels, like Type 310, more difficult to hot-work.[23]

As iron content decreases, the $\alpha + \gamma$ field also broadens, so that it is possible to have present, in alloys that are not fully austenitic, total chromium and nickel contents sufficient to impart good corrosion resistance. Such alloys are produced commercially, usually with a molybdenum addition. AISI Type 329 is one such steel. The structure of this alloy is shown in Fig. 15. The similarity to Fig. 12 is striking except that the matrix is now ferrite. There are also several proprietary alloys of this type. Because of their equilibrium two-phase constitution, such alloys are termed *duplex*. Since the ferrite is usually the predominant phase, these alloys tend to be difficult to fabricate and more expensive. Because of their corrosion and stress-corrosion resistance, they do provide an effective solution to some application problems.

Effect of Molybdenum in Fe-Cr-Ni Alloys   Molybdenum in austenitic stainless steel greatly enhances corrosion resistance and increases elevated temperature strength. Type 316 is the most common example. The ferrite-promoting characteristic of molybdenum on phase equilibria is shown in Fig. 16.[29] Significant adjustments in chromium or nickel are required to compensate for changes in molybdenum content.

Effect of Interstitials in Fe-Cr-Ni Alloys   Carbon and nitrogen are present to a functional degree in all steels. Both are austenite-forming elements.[11,15] The effect of nitrogen on Fe-Cr-Ni alloys is shown in Fig. 17.[14] Although carbon affects equilibrium phase boundaries, it is more often examined in terms of carbide precipitation and effect on transformation behavior.

The development and rapid adoption of argon-oxygen refining in stainless steel melting has brought about the use of nitrogen to control alloy constitution within the AISI ranges. Nitrogen, substituted in part for argon during refining, increases the nitrogen content of

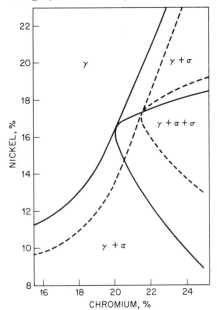

Fig. 16 Effect of molybdenum on equilibrium phases for Fe-Cr-Ni steels air-cooled from 1100 to 1150°C (2010 to 2100°F). Dashed lines = steels with 2% Mo; solid lines = steels with 3% Mo.[29]

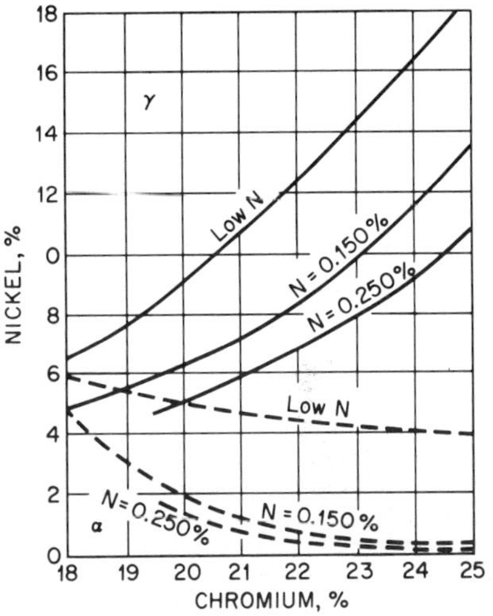

Fig. 17 The effect of nitrogen on $\gamma \rightarrow \alpha$ phase boundaries in Fe-Cr-Ni alloys.[14]

the steel. It is equally important that the nitrogen content can also be controlled adequately. Whereas nitrogen contents of 0.03 to 0.06% have been customary in the past, levels of 0.06 to 0.09% are now being produced routinely. The resulting increased austenite-forming tendency can be used to replace some nickel (on the order of a few tenths of a percent). There is a double incremental economic advantage since nitrogen is less costly than either argon or nickel. Applied judiciously, this practice has no particular adverse effect.

Previously, nitrogen was a deliberate alloying element added only in larger amounts. Between 0.10 and 0.16% nitrogen is present in Types 304N and 316N stainless steels, where it is introduced to impart increased strength.

The best known application of nitrogen as an alloying element was the development of AISI Types 201 and 202 in the 1950s. In these alloys, manganese and nitrogen were both used to partially replace nickel. In addition to assisting the stabilization of austenite, manganese serves to increase nitrogen solubility. The AISI 200-series alloys have never found the wide acceptance anticipated at the time of their development.

In recent years, combined manganese and nitrogen additions have been applied to a number of proprietary alloy systems; Tenelon (United States Steel); the Nitronic series (Armco Steel Corp.); and the 216, 217 alloys (Allegheny-Ludlum Steel Corp.).

IRON-CHROMIUM-MANGANESE SYSTEM

Manganese-nitrogen augmented steels are, as noted above, of some interest. A good description of this system has been presented by Heger.[30]

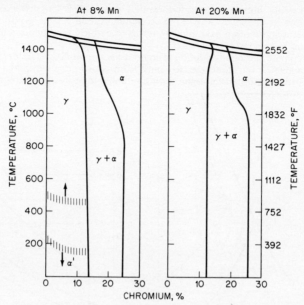

Fig. 18   Cross sections of Fe-Cr-Mn ternary.[31]

Ternary Alloys   Figure 18 shows constant manganese pseudobinary sections of the system.[31] The fact that even with 20% manganese, no more than about 12% chromium can be added while retaining an austenitic structure is significant. More chromium than this is required to provide enough corrosion resistance for most applications. Therefore, austenitic stainless steels cannot be based solely on this ternary system. The $\gamma/(\alpha + \gamma)$ phase boundaries are nearly vertical. An austenitic alloy, when heated, will remain austenitic.

Effect of Nickel and Nitrogen   Nickel or nitrogen additions will generate an austenitic structure even at 18% chromium (Fig. 19).[32] Nitrogen significantly reduces the amount of nickel necessary to assure austenite. An interesting aspect of Fig. 19 is the effect shown by manganese, normally considered to be an austenite former. As manganese is added, *more* austenite-forming nickel is required to preserve the austenitic structure. At least concerning the high-temperature $\gamma / (\alpha + \gamma)$ boundary, manganese can behave as a ferrite former. Behavior consistent with conventional wisdom is observed in the case of the low-temperature transformation. The interaction among chromium, manganese, and nickel is shown in Fig. 20.[32]

The chemistries of the various commercial alloys incorporating significant amounts of manganese and nitrogen are adjusted to provide the desired balance between the properties of greatest interest (normally corrosion resistance and strength). Nitrogen solubility must also be considered to avoid undesirable ingot effects (porosity, "bleeding"). The solubility of nitrogen in conventional types of steels has been reviewed by Turkdogan and Ignatowicz.[33] Carney[34] has

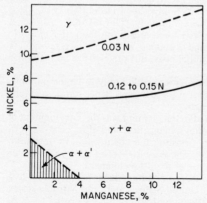

Fig. 19   Effect of nickel, manganese, and nitrogen on alloys containing 18.5% chromium at 0.05–0.08% carbon. Structure after cooling from 1075°C (1967°F).[32]

discussed solubility effects in alloys having very high manganese and very low nickel contents.

EFFECT OF ELEMENTS

Ferrite Formation The preceding constitution diagrams all concerned systems with up to only five elements. In fact, many more elements are mutually present in austenitic stainless steels.

Several studies to define the effect of combined alloy additions have been conducted.

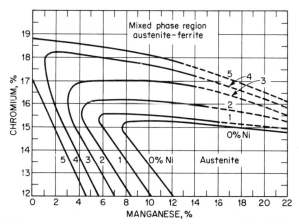

Fig. 20 Effect of chromium, manganese, and nickel on alloys containing 0.12 to 0.15% carbon and 0.08 to 0.15% nitrogen. Structure after cooling from 1075°C (1967°F).[32]

The first of these was by Schaeffler.[35] His work, as well as further work by DeLong[36] which incorporated the effect of nitrogen, was intended to define the effect of composition on weld-metal constitution. Both diagrams are shown in Fig. 21. Since they apply to weld metal, these diagrams should not be used to define precisely the phases present in wrought stainless steels. They do, however, provide some indication of the relative potency of the respective austenite stabilizers and ferrite formers.

Pryce and Andrews[37] developed equivalence coefficients for stainless steels at the hot-rolling temperature [1150°C (2102°F)]. Their diagram is shown in Fig. 22. Pryce and Andrews introduced the added refinement of allowing for the presence of titanium and columbium and the interaction of these with carbon and nitrogen. (Effective titanium = Ti − 4[(C − 0.03) + N] and effective columbium = Cb − 8[(C − 0.03) + N].)

It is interesting to note that the Pryce and Andrews silicon coefficient is twice that employed by Schaeffler and DeLong. Also, the austenitizing effects attributed to carbon and nitrogen are not as great.

Hammond,[38] citing unpublished work by J. A. Ferree, presented the diagram shown in Fig. 23. This is based on the amount of ferrite present in wrought steels at ambient temperature. Hammond's study included alloys with significant amounts of cobalt (5 to 15%). Using Ferree's work as a basis, he empirically determined the equivalence of cobalt to be 0.64 (as referenced to nickel).

Relying on equivalence formulas derived from the work of Schaeffler and Pryce and Andrews, Stokowiec et al.,[39] correlated a "ferrite factor" with magnetically measured ferrite in 5-in. (12.7 cm) square ingots of six heats of 18Cr-8Ni steel with molybdenum and titanium. The results are summarized in Fig. 24. This indicates very clearly the difficulty inherent in translating one set of results to a different set of conditions and attempting to make close predictions. (In fairness to the authors, it should be noted they were reasonably successful in rationalizing the hot-working behavior of commercial ingots from several hundred heats, based on their ferrite factor.)

Irvine et al.[40] have individually studied the effect of various elements on the delta ferrite content of stainless steel at 1050°C (1922°F). Their results showing the effect of various austenitizing elements on 0.1C-17Cr-bal Fe alloys are shown in Fig. 25. This generally confirms previous conclusions. Note the relatively modest effect of copper and manganese up to 3 to 4%, with no effect at all at higher concentrations.

The effects of substitutional elements added to 17Cr-8Ni-bal Fe alloys are shown in Fig. 26. In this case, the effects of copper, cobalt, and manganese are masked because of the small amount of ferrite initially present.

Eichelman and Hull[41] prepared the tabulation given by Table 3, summarizing still other work on defining the effects of various elements on ferrite-forming tendency.

Considerable work has been done recently to refine the ferrite predictions in welding technology. Although absolute ferrite contents are still somewhat of a problem, reproducibility is sufficient for functional utility. This work has been described by Campbell.[45] No such coordinated effort has been expended to refine the situation with regard to ingot

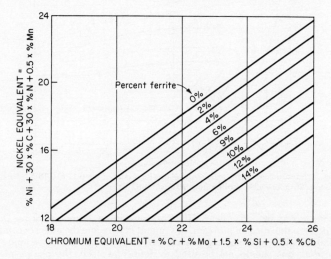

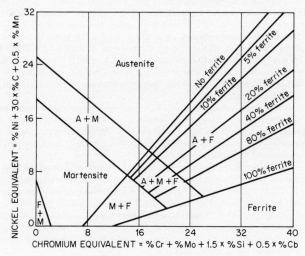

Fig. 21 Constitution of stainless steel weld deposits.[36,35]

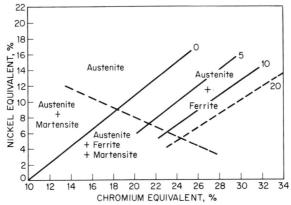

Fig. 22 Constitution of stainless steels at 1150°C (2102°F). (Cr equivalent = Cr + 3Si + Mo; Ni equivalent = Ni + 0.5Mn + 21C + 11.5N.)[37]

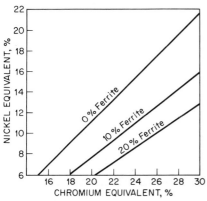

Fig. 23 Constitution of stainless steels at ambient temperature. [Cr equivalent = %Cr + 1.5Si + %Mo; Ni equivalent = %Ni + 30(%C + N) + 0.5%Mn.][38]

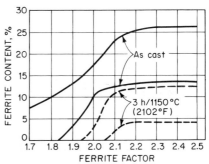

Fig. 24 Comparison between measured ferrite content in ingots and calculated "ferrite factors." Upper and lower lines are ingot center and surface, respectively.[39]

$$\text{Ferrite factor} = \text{Cr/Ni}$$
$$\text{where Cr} = \%\text{Cr} + \%\text{Mo} + 3\text{Si} + 10\,[\%\text{Ti} - (4\%\text{C})]$$
$$\text{Ni} = \%\text{Ni} + 0.5\%\text{Mn} + 21(\%\text{C} - 0.25\%\text{Ti})$$

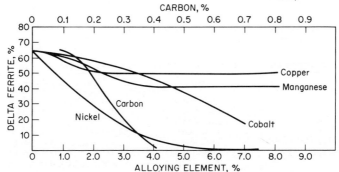

Fig. 25 Effects of various elements on constitution of 0.1C-17Cr alloys at 1050°C (1922°F).[40]

structures or wrought alloys. Therefore, the constitution diagrams and related equivalence factors should be viewed as general and approximate indications of expected trends.

Lattice Parameters Lattice parameters (or lattice constants) are the dimensions of the crystallographic unit cell. They are of interest to metallurgists because of their relationship to density, density changes occurring during precipitation, diffusion, solubility, and coherency effects with second-phase precipitation in age-hardening materials.

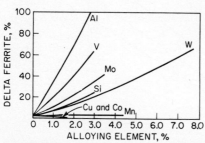

Fig. 26 Effects of various elements on constitution of 17Cr – 4Ni alloys at 1050°C (1922°F).[40]

Ridley[46] has discussed the difficulty of obtaining reliable lattice-parameter measurements in austenite because of the transformation propensity of some of the alloys. The measurement preparation techniques tend to promote transformation. To cite an example, published values for pure γ iron range from 3.572 to 3.580 Å with an additional 0.031 to 0.044 Å to be added for each percentage of carbon present. Lattice parameters for Fe-Ni-Cr austenites are given in Table 4.

The effect of elements on the lattice parameter as tabulated by Irvine et al.,[51] are presented in Table 5. As shown, the interstitial elements have large coefficients. Of the substitutional elements, those which promote ferrite tend to have the greatest effect. The austenitizing elements do not have much influence. Irvine et al.[52] previously suggested a loose correlation between lattice-parameter increment and atom size.

Solution Strengthening The strengthening effects of elements, as determined by Irvine et al.,[51] are shown in Table 6. The coefficients were derived from statistical correlation analysis, with effects of secondary variables such as ferrite content and microstructural parameters taken into account.

The effects on strengthening very generally parallel those observed for lattice-parameter changes. The interstitial elements have the largest coefficients, followed by the ferrite-forming substitutional elements.

The strength coefficients for yield strength (proof stress) and tensile strength differ. In

TABLE 3 Relative Tendency of Elements to Form Delta Ferrite

Element	Thielemann[42]	Newell and Fleischman[43]	Binder, Brown, and Franks[44]
C	−40	−30	−23
N			−20
Ni	−3	−1	−0.8
Mn	−2	−0.5	
Ti	+7.2		
Si	+5.2		
Cb	+4.5		
Mo	+4.2	+2 × Cr	+1.4
Cr	+1		1.0

+, increases ferrite; −, decreases ferrite.

TABLE 4 Reported Lattice Parameters for Austenitic Stainless Steels

Reference	Alloy	Lattice parameter, Å
Otte[47]	18Cr-9Ni	3.593
Cina[48]	18Cr-8Ni	3.591
Fiedler, et al.[49]	18Cr-8Ni	3.588
Reed[91]	Type 304	3.589
Spitznagel and Stickler[50]	Type 304	3.588 + A(%C), 0 ≤ A ≤ 17
Spitznagel and Stickler[50]	Type 316	3.588 + A(%C), 0 ≤ A ≤ 17
	Type 316L	3.588 + A(%C), 0 ≤ A ≤ 17, B(%Mo), 0 ≤ B ≤ 1.186

general, the tensile coefficients are higher, but the relative increments also change. It would be reasonable to assume a general correlation between strength increment and atomic size. Columbium and titanium, the two largest atoms listed in Table 6, do result in the greatest strengthening. Beyond this, correlations break down.

Irvine et al. suggest that the irregular pattern is due to other secondary differences such

TABLE 5   Effect of Alloying Elements on Lattice Parameter of Alloys Approximating AISI Type 302 Stainless Steel[51]

Solute	Type	Change in lattice parameter per atomic %, Å
C	Interstitial, Austenite Stabilizer	+0.0060
N		+0.0084
Si	Substitutional, Ferrite Stabilizer	−0.005
V		+0.0015
W		+0.0030
Mo		+0.0033
Ni	Substitutional, Ferrite Stabilizer	−0.0002
Mn		+0.0002
Cu		+0.0023
Co		−0.0004

as stacking-fault energy, which is not included in the statistical correlation. This could influence the amount of strain-induced transformation occurring during testing, and thus the apparent strengthening increment. Available stacking-fault energy (SFE) data are too incomplete to permit quantitative analysis of the effect of stacking-fault energy.

The alloys investigated were quenched from 1150°C (2102°F). This may not have been high enough to dissolve all dispersed carbides and nitrides. This could alter the apparent strengthening effect.

TRANSFORMATION

Stacking Faults As noted in the previous section and shown in Fig. 13, many of the austenitic AISI stainless steels could properly be termed metastable austenitic steels. Figure 13b shows several possible transformation products, after the nomenclature given by Krauss and Marder[53] and Reed and Breedis.[54]

TABLE 6   Effect of Elements on Strength of Austenite in Alloys Approximating AISI Type 302 Stainless Steel[51]

The numbers shown are coefficients for the respective elements in the following formulas, where d and t are grain diameter and twin mean-free path, respectively, in millimeters.

$$0.2\% \text{ PS (tons/in.}^2) = 4.1 + \Sigma \text{ (element coefficient) (wt \% element)} + 0.16 \text{ (\% ferrite)} + 0.46 \ (d^{-\frac{1}{2}})$$
$$\text{TS (tons/in.}^2) = 29 + \Sigma \text{ (element coefficient) (wt \% element)} + 0.14 \text{ (\% ferrite)} + 0.82 \ (t^{-\frac{1}{2}})$$

Solute	Type	Strength coefficients	
		For 0.2% proof stress	For tensile strength
N	Interstitial	32	55
C		23	35
Cb	Substitutional, Ferrite Stabilizer	2.6	5.0
Ti		1.7	3.0
Al		.8	2.4
Si		1.3	1.2
V		1.2	0
Mo		0.9	0
W		0.3	0
Cr		0.2	0
Ni	Substitutional, Austenite Stabilizer	0	−0.1
Mn		0	0
Cu		0	0
Co		0	

Some of these products arise from the different types of lattice discontinuities possible in fcc austenite. A detailed discussion is beyond the scope of this chapter, but a brief description follows. The close-packed planes in the fcc lattice are the cell diagonal (111) planes. The atoms in one such plane are shown in Fig. 27, using the representation of Quarrell[55] and Cottrell.[56] In the fcc lattice, atoms in successive planes are in the positions marked $ABCABC$.... A hexagonal-close-packed (hcp) structure is very similar, but the stacking arrangement is $ACACA$ ... instead.

The favored slip direction in the fcc lattice is [110]. Producing such slip is not easy, so slip is usually visualized as occurring in a zig-zag fashion as shown by b_2 and b_3 in Fig. 27.

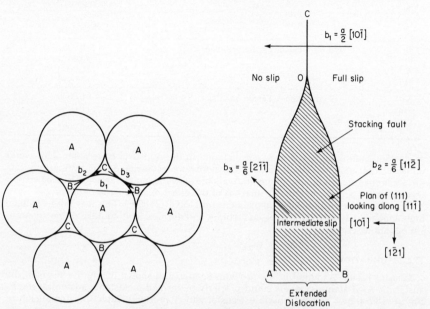

Fig. 27 Close-packed plane in fcc lattice.[55]

Fig. 28 Representation of stacking fault and dislocation dissociation.[55]

If the net slip between the (111) fcc planes is from B to C instead of B to B, the $ABCABC$ stacking sequence will be disrupted. It then becomes $ABCA/CAB$, thus generating an hcp sequence. Depending on the frequency of faulting, either an hcp structure (fault on every other plane) or a twin (fault on every plane) can result.[57-60] A metastable austenite, when cooled or deformed, can fault or undergo transformation to bcc martensite. As will be seen, a combination of these processes can also occur.

The energy associated with faulting is often considered in terms of dislocation theory. A common representation (Fig. 28) shows a dislocation split into two partial dislocations with faulted material between them.[55] A film analogy is commonly used: faulted material is considered to have "surface tension" which tends to pull the partial dislocations together. This configuration is one of relatively high energy. Its formation and stability will depend on the magnitude of the "surface tension" or stacking-fault energy.

Deformation processes involve dislocation slip or, particularly at higher temperatures, climb. Extended dislocations, such as those represented in Fig. 28, cannot readily slip past each other or climb from one plane to another.[56,59-61] In this way work-hardening behavior or strength of the material can be increased. These areas of crystallographic discontinuity or their interaction can facilitate formation of other transformation products. (This will be discussed later.) Precipitation of second phases (such as carbides) can also occur on stacking faults and precipitation on such sites is also often more advantageous.

Stacking-Fault Energy Schramm and Reed[62] recently surveyed published stacking-fault-energy (SFE) data obtained from Fe-Ni-Cr alloys. Their tabulation is shown in

TABLE 7   Stacking-Fault Energy of Fe-Cr-Ni Alloys[62]

Reference	Stacking-fault energy, mJ/m²	Composition, %				
		Cr	Ni	C	N	
Whelan et al.[63]	15–20	18–20	8–11	<0.08		(AISI 304)
Whelan[64]	30	18–20	8–11	<0.08		(AISI 304)
Swann[65]	14	17.9	7.1	0.06	0.11	
	16	17.6	7.9	0.06	0.04	
	30	18.1	12.8	0.02	0.12	
	36	17.6	12.7	0.02	0.004	
	44	17.8	17.8	0.03	0.004	
Breedis[58]	29.2	19.3	11.2			
	40.7	17.3	11.0			
	51.1	16.0	12.1			
	76.1	13.0	14.2			
	98.0	10.4	16.2			
Douglass et al.[66]	28–41	18.74	9.43	0.07		(AISI 304)
	58	20	20	0.013		
	131	20	40	0.012	0.006	
Dulieu and Nutting[67]	~50	8.5	11.84	0.05		
	23–28	18.3	10.28	0.079	0.02	
	28–32	22	9.87	0.079		
	23–28	18	9.87			
	20–25	16	9.87			
	30	18	8			(Probably
	>46	22.0	34.0	0.014		AISI 304)
Silcock et al.[68]	53	15.3	15.9	0.02		
	64	15.8	23.0	0.007	0.006	
	48	15.9	15.8	0.017	0.004	
	70.2	15.4	24.7	0.011	0.007	
Clement et al.[69]	19	16.6	9.5	0.028		
Thomas and Henry[70] and Thomas[71]	53	17.8	14.1	0.01		
Vingsbro[72]	~8	18	13	0.02		
Fawley et al.[73]	23	20	10	0.006	0.005	
	32	20	15	0.018	0.003	
	40	20	20	0.015	0.006	
	38	20	25	0.009	0.006	
	34	20	30	0.011	0.006	
	53	10	20	0.012	0.004	
	40	15	20	0.019	0.005	
	45	25	20	0.022	0.005	
	57	30	20	0.036	0.005	
	23	20	10	0.012	0.044	
	34	20	15	0.010	0.035	
	38	20	20	0.018	0.051	
	38	20	25	0.009	0.033	
	34	20	30	0.010	0.029	
	48	10	20	0.012	0.013	
	44	15	20	0.012	0.011	
	47	25	20	0.017	0.047	
	43	20	20	0.027	0.003	
	47	20	30	0.050	0.010	
Latanision and Ruff[74]	23.1 ±1.7	18.7	15.9			
Murr[75]	21	18.43	9.52	0.058		(AISI 304)

TABLE 7   Stacking-Fault Energy of Fe-Cr-Ni Alloys[62] (continued)

Reference	Stacking-fault energy, mJ/m²	Composition, %			
		Cr	Ni	C	N
LeCroisey and Thomas[76]	45	17.8	14.1	0.01	
	24	15.9	12.5	<0.01	
Latanision and Ruff[77]	16.4 ±1.1	18.3	10.7	0.005	
	23.6 ±0.9	18.7	15.9	0.005	
Butakova et al.[78]	60	5	20	0.04	
	30	10	15	0.04	
	20	15	10	0.04	
	16	18	8	0.04	

Table 7. The four-dimensional linear-regression analysis equations given in Fig. 29 were obtained by using the data in Table 6. (Silicon and manganese contents, though not listed in Table 7, were included in the analysis.)

Schramm and Reed also independently determined the stacking-fault energy of eight commercial austenitic steels, with the results shown in Table 8. These results conflict with some of those given in Fig. 29. Chromium is shown to either decrease or increase stacking-fault energy. In either case, the coefficients are small relative to some other elements. The quantitative effects of other elements also differ. Among the elements, the observed effect of nickel in increasing stacking-fault energy has been most consistent.

Cobalt as an element has a low stacking-fault energy and is recognized as reducing stacking-fault energy in Fe-Ni-Cr austenitic alloys. Results of Dulieu and Nutting[67] are presented in Table 9. Qualitative considerations suggest that the relative effect of cobalt should perhaps be greater than that indicated by Dulieu and Nutting. Cobalt has been utilized in alloys like the TRIP (transformation induced plasticity) steels[79,80] and Multi-

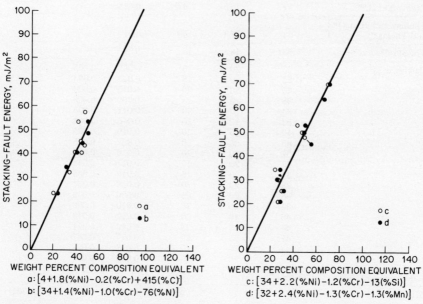

a: [4+1.8(%Ni)−0.2(%Cr)+415(%C)]
b: [34+1.4(%Ni)−1.0(%Cr)−76(%N)]

c: [34+2.2(%Ni)−1.2(%Cr)−13(%Si)]
d: [32+2.4(%Ni)−1.3(%Cr)−1.3(%Mn)]

Fig. 29   Linear-regression analysis results from data in Table 7.[62] Left: Fe-Ni-Cr-C and Fe-Ni-Cr-N. Right: Fe-Ni-Cr-Si and Fe-Ni-Cr-Mn.

phase* alloys.[81] Rationalization of its role in such alloys strongly implies significant reduction of stacking-fault energy.[79-83]

The conflicts in the various studies originate from the differences and uncertainties associated with the experimental techniques. Measurement of stacking-fault dimensions using transmission electron microscopy has often been used. X-ray diffraction techniques utilizing line broadening and shifts also have been applied.

Fe-Ni-Cr austenites are, as a class, relatively low stacking-fault-energy materials. Ener-

TABLE 8   Stacking-Fault Energy of Several Commercial Austenitic Alloys[62]

Alloy	Composition, wt %									Stacking-fault energy,* mJ/m²
	Ni	Cr	Mn	Mo	C	Si	P	S	N	
AISI 304L	8.28	18.31	0.82	0.02	0.025	0.30	0.010	0.007	0.0183	18
AISI 305	11.85	18.02	1.64	0.10	0.074	0.32	0.13	0.002		34
AISI 310S	18.8	24.7	1.73	0.44	0.047	0.56	0.022	0.005		94
AISI 316	13.01	17.15	1.40	2.09	0.055	0.53	0.027	0.008		78
21-6-9 (melt 1)†	7.11	21.00	8.75	0.03	0.027	0.43	0.011	0.003	0.31	65
21-6-9 (melt 2) †	6.48	20.30	9.55		0.034	0.13	0.022	0.012	0.26	41
22-13-5†	12.34	21.57	5.17	2.20	0.041	0.40	0.020	0.004		64
Hadfield	4.1		15.7		0.91	1.29	0.009	0.017		21

*Stacking-fault energy γ, mJ/m² = 53 + 6.2(%Ni) + 0.7(%Cr) + 3.2(%Mn) + 9.3(%Mo)
†Proprietary alloys of the Nitronic series, Armco Steel Corp.

getically, they are borderline at room temperature. They do not ordinarily spontaneously fault extensively, but can be induced to do so with the observed effects being sensitive to specific alloy chemistry and/or temperature. Stacking-fault energy varies approximately linearly with temperature in the vicinity of room temperature.[84]

Martensite Transformations   The transformation of Fe-Ni-Cr stainless steels is a complicated subject and has received a great deal of attention. It has been known for a very long time that the leaner fcc austenites (γ) transform to bcc martensite (α') at or below room temperature. As mentioned previously and as noted in Fig. 13b, there are distinctions to be drawn between the types of martensite formed. Considerable effort and discussion has been directed toward defining these types with regard to morphology and modes of formation.[47,53,54,58,85-89]

The types of martensite are chemistry-related, as shown in Fig. 13b. The large plate morphology falls close to the Fe-Ni binary system in alloys not represented by the AISI 300 series of alloys.

A characteristic of Fe-Ni-Cr alloy transformations attracting considerable attention is the appearance of an hcp phase, ϵ. Interest in this hcp constituent has increased in recent years partly because techniques for studying such constituents have progressed and partly because of recent research and development work on cobalt-bearing low-stacking-fault-energy materials like TRIP steels.[79,80] The ϵ martensite is closely related to stacking faults discussed in the previous section. Since ϵ martensite is commonly found in conjunction with α' martensite, researchers have tried to determine if ϵ is an intermediate to formation of α' martensite or a separate constituent which could form as a result of strain generated by the $\gamma \rightarrow \alpha'$ transformation. Since ϵ martensite is nonmagnetic and is difficult to define clearly by light microscopy, its identification requires diffraction techniques.

TABLE 9   Effects of Elements on Stacking-Fault Energy[67]

Element	Effect on stacking-fault energy ergs/(cm²)(atomic %)
Cr	+0.5
Ni	+1.4
Si	−3.4
Co	−0.55
Cu	+3.6
Cb	+3.2
Mo	+0.1

*Trademark, Standard Pressed Steel Co., Jenkintown, Pa.

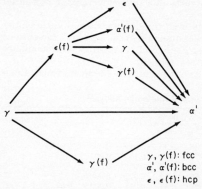

Fig. 30 Various hypothetical paths for formation of α' martensite from γ.[88]

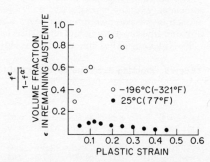

Fig. 31 Effect of temperature on formation of ϵ martensite in deformed Type 304 stainless steel.[89]

Venables[85] and Olson and Cohen[89] have shown formation of α' needles at intersections of ϵ martensite plates. Cina,[48,90] Reed,[91] and Breedis and Robertson[92] also reported the hcp structure to be an intermediate phase in the formation of α' martensite. Dash and Otte[88] reported instances of independent formation of the two phases and summarized the various possibilities as shown in Fig. 30. From subsequent work it appears ϵ is usually involved in the transformation process to α'.

As discussed by Christian[93] and others, there also has been speculation that the hcp structure could be a transition phase; this possibility is also noted in Fig. 31. The peaking nature of the data in Fig. 31 (see next paragraph) would appear to support this notion at least at large strains.

The formation of ϵ martensite should depend on temperature and composition. One example of this is shown in Fig. 31, which compares the volume fraction of ϵ in Type 304 austenite deformed at 25°C (77°F) and −196°C (−321°F).[89] Olson and Cohen[89] have described formation of transformation products by correlating austenite plastic strain and martensite formation by an expression which includes separate terms related principally to either shear-band energy (stacking-fault-energy dependent) or chemical driving force. Figure 31 is illustrative of the temperature dependence of the shear-band-energy term. It should be noted that the material described in Fig. 31 is also undergoing appreciable transformation to α', which is not included in the figure. The absolute ϵ contents are much lower than the values shown. The Olson and Cohen treatment[89] represents a generalization where α' nucleation is related to deformation zones which may or may not contain ϵ martensite.

The temperature-composition dependence of transformation is also shown in Fig. 32.[47]

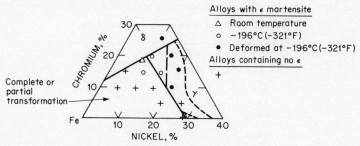

Fig. 32 Extent of ϵ martensite formation as influenced by temperature and deformation.[47] Approximate $\gamma \rightarrow \alpha$ transformation boundaries: solid line = room temperature, dashed line = −196°C (−321°F), dotted line = deformation at −196°C (−321°F).

The appearance of ϵ roughly follows the shifting of the alloy transformation/stable austenite boundary. No ϵ was found in alloys containing 10 percent or less chromium. It is also interesting to note that no ϵ was observed in the alloy containing 15Cr-5Ni, indicating an exception to the general correlation that propensity to ϵ formation should be related to stacking-fault energy. Alloys which failed to transform at $-196°C$ ($-321°F$) were further cooled to 4°K, and no transformation took place.

Schumann[114] studied the formation of ϵ and α' in series of alloys with varying manganese, nickel, and chromium contents with the results shown in Fig. 33. Alloy 1, an Fe-Mn binary, formed only ϵ except when cold-worked at $-196°C$. (For comparison with the binary diagram, see Fig. 9.) As nickel and chromium were added, the amount of ϵ formed with only cooling diminished rapidly. In alloys 7 and 8, which approximated conventional AISI composition ranges, no transformation at all occurred upon cooling. Working the alloys at ambient temperature produced some ϵ.

The transformation behavior of Fe-Cr-Co-Ni-Mo austenites has been examined by deBarbadillo.[83] Although not specifically determined, these alloys should have lower stacking-fault energies than normal AISI austenitic grades. Transformation resulting from cold-rolling at various temperatures is shown in Fig. 34. Alloys with higher nickel equivalent contents exhibited less transformation and the ϵ formation was reduced, especially at the higher rolling temperatures.

The trends observed with respect to ϵ martensite are also apparent when only α' martensite is considered. Angel's results from an 18Cr-8Ni stainless steel is shown in Fig. 35.[94] Increasing strain and decreasing temperature both cause increased transformation. (The balance of this discussion will concern effects on formation of bcc α' martensite. The ϵ martensite has not been considered in most of the past work. This does not impair the value of such work, as the contribution of this constituent to the properties of cold-worked AISI austenitic grades is still uncertain. It is sufficient to remember that strengthening effects not directly attributable to α' martensite may be due in part to the formation of hcp constituent.)

Angel's curves (Fig. 35) fit the following autocatalytic-type equation:

$$\ln (f/1 - f) = n \ln (\text{true strain}) + k \quad (1)$$

ALLOY IDENTIFICATION

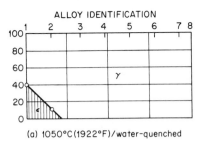

(a) 1050°C(1922°F)/water-quenched

(b) 1050°C(1922°F)/water-quenched; 10 min $-196°C(-321°F)$

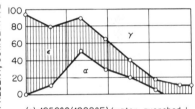

(c) 1050°C(1922°F)/water-quenched + 40% cold-work at 20°C(68°F)

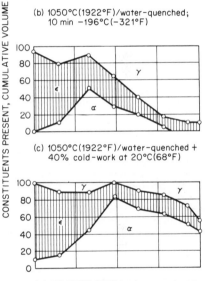

(d) 1050°C(1922°F)/water-quenched + 40% cold-work at $-196°C(-321°F)$

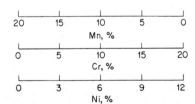

Fig. 33 Transformation products in Fe-Ni-Cr-Mn alloys. Composition of alloys is shown at the bottom of the figure, balance iron with approximately 0.03C-0.01 to 0.03Si-0.006 to 0.019N-0.012 to 0.10Al.[114]

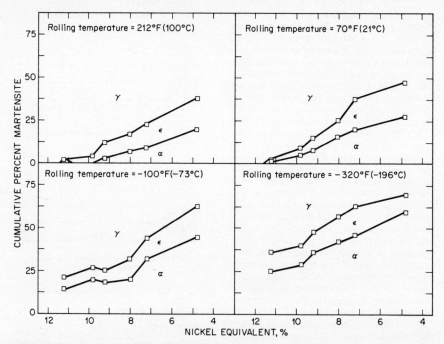

Fig. 34 The effect of composition and rolling temperature on transformation of Fe-Cr-Co-Ni-Mo austenites. (*a*) Alloys cold-rolled 30%. (*b*) Nickel equivalent = %Ni + 0.15(%Co) + 0.5(%Mn) + 30(%C).[83]

where f is the fraction transformed and n and k are constants. By studying a series of alloys, Angel found the value of n to be about 3 and independent of both alloy composition and temperature. The value of k, on the other hand, depended on both composition and temperature.

In addition to austenite composition, strain, and temperature, strain-rate effects have been examined. The results of Bressanelli and Moscowitz[95] are shown in Fig. 36. The absolute martensite contents were not determined, but the reduced transformation at higher strain rates is obvious. These authors point out that this effect is largely influenced by specimen heating at high strain rates, where temperatures of 200°F (93°C) can be reached. The effect of preventing specimen heating by use of a water bath is shown in Fig. 37. Thus, it can be seen that the primary influence is still one of temperature dependence. This effect is likely to be operative any time high-strain-rate deformation is applied to metastable austenitic steels and attempts are made to correlate observed effects with probable transformation.

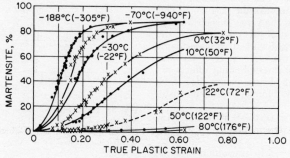

Fig. 35 Formation of α' (bcc) martensite in 18-8 stainless steel.[94]

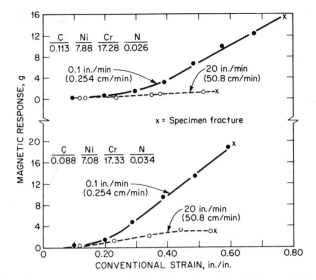

Fig. 36 Effect of strain rate on α' martensite formation in Type 304 stainless steel deformed in air.[95]

Approximate Relationship	
(g)	Percent of α'
1	20
4	50
9	70
16	90

Austenite Stabilization The preceding discussions have concerned material initially cooled from normal austenitizing temperatures. Under some circumstances transformation can be suppressed, a phenomenon which has been called *austenite stabilization*. This term refers to changes in behavior different than bulk composition effects, to be discussed in a later section.

One obvious instance of stabilization is the effect of existing α' martensite on further $\gamma \rightarrow \alpha'$ transformation. In Fig. 35, it can be seen that transformation proceeds to a "saturation" value of less than 100% α'. This is typical of Fe-Ni-Cr alloys. Angel[94] analyzed curves of the type shown in Fig. 35 and found that the rate of reaction per unit of austenite as a function of martensite content passes through a maximum at intermediate martensite contents. This behavior (Fig. 38) clearly shows a stabilizing effect during the late stages of

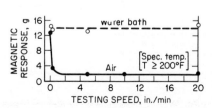

Fig. 37 Effect of test medium and resultant temperature on martensite formation in Type 301 deformed in ambient temperature bath.[95]

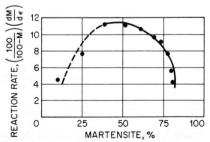

Fig. 38 Rate of reaction per unit of austenite as a function of martensite content at −70°C [−94°F].[94]

transformation. Angel attributes this stabilization to an increase in the surface energy of the martensite such that it finally exceeds the effect of externally applied stress. He also shows that the deformation energy per increment of martensite volume increases with temperature, thus rationalizing why the "saturation" volume fraction of martensite decreases with increasing temperature.

Increasing austenitizing temperature also can result in an apparent stabilization of austenite. Otte[47] and Cina[48] reported that alloys which normally transform do not do so

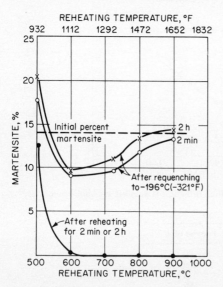

Fig. 39 Effect of reheating a previously transformed 16Ni-12Cr alloy on austenite reversion and subsequent transformation.[96]

when quenched from extraordinarily high temperatures. In Otte's case, austenitizing a 15Cr-15Ni alloy at 1320°C (2408°F) completely suppressed transformation all the way to 4°K. When quenched from 1050 to 1150°C (1922 to 2102°F), the same alloy exhibited both α' and ϵ at $-196°C$ ($-321°F$). While it is known that increasing grain size reduces M_s somewhat,[41] this effect is more pronounced.

Breedis[96] has examined the effect of reheating a high-purity 16Cr-12Ni alloy after it was quenched to $-196°C$ ($-321°F$), which then initially formed 14% α' martensite. His results are shown in Fig. 39. Specimens reheated at 500°C (932°F) and then requenched formed more martensite, whereas alloys reheated at 600, 700, and 800°C (1112, 1292, and 1472°F) generated less martensite. The increased martensite after 500°C (932°F) exposure was attributed to the relief of internal strains. Reheating to higher temperatures partially stabilizes austenite because, it is postulated, the remaining more-altered defect structure is such that it hinders subsequent development of martensite laths. Using transmission microscopy, Breedis reported the prior martensitic areas were still identifiable even after they had become austenitic.

Volumes have been written concerning austenite stabilization in other related iron-based systems, i.e., Fe-C, Fe-Ni, Fe-Ni-C. An important aspect of stabilization mechanisms in some of these other systems is solute redistribution (especially carbon). Review of these very numerous references has been entirely eliminated because, as discussed previously, the martensite in the Fe-Ni-Cr alloys of interest here is different. In addition, the carbon contents of Fe-Ni-Cr austenitic stainless steels, while not so low that the role in transformation processes is unequivocally nonfunctional, are generally low enough to make meaningful comparisons with results on related systems uncertain.

Composition and Austenite Stability Austenite in metastable alloys can transform spontaneously to martensite either on cooling or as a result of deformation. The temperature at which transformation to α' martensite occurs on cooling is called the M_s (martensite start) temperature. The temperature below which α' martensite will form under deformation conditions is called the M_d temperature. More uncommon are E_d and E_s temperatures. E_d is defined as the maximum temperature at which transformation to ϵ

TABLE 10   Transformation Temperatures for an Fe-18Cr-7Ni-0.18C Stainless Steel[97]

	Transformation temperature, °K
E_d	420
M_d	360
E_s	$\geqslant 300$
M_s	190

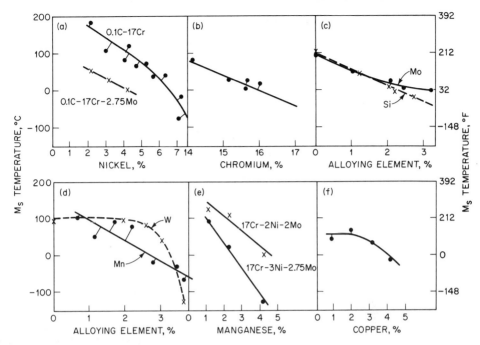

Fig. 40 Effect of alloying elements of M_s temperature.[40] (*a*) Ni on 17% Cr. (*b*) Cr on 0.14C-4Ni-2.75Mo. (*c*) Si and Mo on 17Cr-4Ni. (*d*) Mn and W on 17Cr-4Ni. (*e*) Mn on 17Cr-2.75Mo alloys containing 2 and 3% nickel. (*f*) Cu on 17Cr-2Ni-2Mo.

martensite can be deformation-induced. E_s is defined as the temperature where $\gamma \rightarrow \epsilon$ occurs spontaneously. The relative relationship between these various transformation temperatures is shown by the Remy and Pineau data given in Table 10.[97]

Several expressions relating austenite stability and chemistry have been developed. These are given in Table 11. Irvine, et al.,[40] presented their results graphically, as shown in Fig. 40. These relationships pertain to stability in terms of the $\gamma \rightarrow \alpha'$ martensite transformation. All elements cause increased stability, thus lowering transformation temperatures. An exception to this trend would probably be observed for cobalt if there were similar relationships for E_d and E_s.

Post and Eberly[98] developed their Δ factor to indicate when an alloy would resist

TABLE 11   Expressions Relating Austenite Stability and Alloy Chemistry

Reference	Quantity computed	Relationship (elements in weight %)
Post and Eberly[98]	Stability factor Δ	$Ni - \left[\dfrac{(Cr + 1.5Mo - 20)^2}{12} - 0.5Mn - 35C + 15 \right]$
Griffiths and Wright[99]	Stability factor Δ modified to include copper and nitrogen	$Ni - \left[\dfrac{(Cr + 1.5Mo - 20)^2}{12} - 0.5Mn - 35C - Cu - 27N + 15 \right]$
Eichelman and Hull[41]	M_s (°F)	$75(14.6 - Cr) + 110(8.9 - Ni) + 60(1.33 - Mn) + 50(0.47 - Si) + 3000$ $[0.068 - (C + N)]$
Monkman et al.[100]	M_s (°F)	$2160 - 66(Cr) - 102(Ni) - 2620(C + N)$
Angel[94]	M_{d30} (°C)	$413 - 462(C + N) - 9.2Si - 8.1Mn - 13.7Cr - 9.5Ni - 18.5Mo$
Floreen and Mihalisin[101] from Irvine et al.[40] and Eichelman and Hull[41]	Stability factor S	$Ni + 0.68Cr + 0.55Mn + 0.45Si + 27(C + N)$
Floreen and Mayne[103] from Irvine et al.,[40] Eichelman and Hull,[41] and Coutsouradis[102]	Stability factor S	$Ni + 0.68Cr + 0.55Mn + 0.45Si + 27(C + N) + Mo + 0.2Co$

transformation at cold reductions up to 80%. Modifying this expression to include copper and nitrogen, Griffiths and Wright[99] showed that the stability factor adequately described trends in composition versus work-hardening behavior. Also, as shown in Fig. 41, the onset of α' martensite formation seemed to correlate with the modified factor.

Using the data shown in Fig. 42, Angel[94] pointed out that M_d temperature is somewhat ambiguous. For very large strains the onset of transformation is fairly abrupt. The M_d temperature is not at all well defined for small strains. For this reason, his expression was defined for transformation at 30% strain, hence M_{d30}.

Relationships of the type shown in Table 11 have often served well in characterizing the behavior of stainless steels. However, it should be remembered that they are approximations since possible interactions are not taken into account. Figure 43, for example, shows that the effect of copper or carbon on work-hardening behavior (or stability) depends on the nickel content.[104]

Work Hardening The AISI austenitic stainless steels are only strengthened by cold-working. The effect of cold-working on room-temperature properties is shown in Fig. 44.[105]

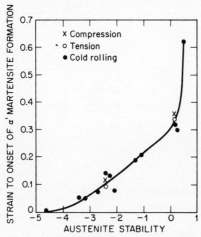

Fig. 41 Effect of austenite stability on threshold strains for α' martensite formation.[99]

The primary cause of work hardening is the transformation to martensite. Figure 45 shows the increase in α' content concurrent with strengthening in Type 301.[106] The effects of deformation and temperature are consistent with the earlier discussions of transformations. The effect of rolling temperature has been further explored by Floreen and Mihalisin.[101] As shown in Fig. 46, much higher strengths were obtained by rolling at subzero temperatures. The yield strengths obtained generally correlated with the amount of α' martensite formed.

The strength of subzero-rolled steel is further enhanced by heat treatment at 427°C (800°F). This is a general effect, defined by previous investigators.[107,108]

Figure 47 compares the effect of cold-working on the properties of Types 301 and 305 stainless steels. The much more stable Type 305 exhibits a small strengthening increment compared with metastable Type 301. That very limited transformation occurs in Type 305 is demonstrated by the permeability data of Table 12. It can also be seen that some work hardening is obtained from lattice deformation processes which precede the $\gamma \rightarrow \alpha'$ transformation.

Work hardening can also be considered from the standpoint of processes occurring during tensile testing. The behavior of a tensile specimen is determined to a considerable

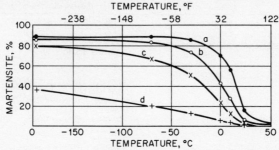

Fig. 42 Temperature dependence of martensite formation at true plastic strains of (a) 0.50, (b) 0.30, (c) 0.20, (d) 0.10.[94]

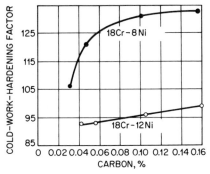 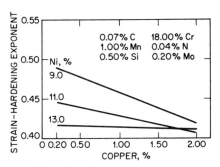

Fig. 43   Examples of interactions affecting stability of stainless steels.[104]

degree by the work-hardening behavior of the material. A simple representation of the true-stress–true-strain curve is given by

$$s = k\epsilon^n \tag{2}$$

where s = true stress
ϵ = true strain
n = work-hardening exponent

This expression defines the straight-line segment at the beginning of the true-stress–true-strain curve. Figure 48 (from Barclay[110]) shows that the point of departure from the initial straight line and the subsequent increased strengthening coincide fairly closely with the onset of measurable martensite formation. Figure 48 also shows the stabilizing effect of nickel.

In order to define the full stress-strain curve, Griffiths and Wright[99] developed a more complicated quadratic equation:

$$\log s = C_1 + C_2 \log \epsilon + C_3 (\log \epsilon)^2 \tag{3}$$

They found all the constants were influenced by austenite stability as expressed by the modified Post and Eberly stability factor (Table 11). This is shown in Fig. 49.

Bressanelli and Moscowitz[95] examined a number of Type 301 stainless steel heats and examined the relationship between apparent martensite formed during test and tensile characteristics. Those alloys developing the most martensite also exhibited the greatest work hardening (Fig. 50). The variations in chemistry were well within those defined by the AISI range for Type 301, indicating why metastable alloys for critical forming applications are often very tightly controlled in chemistry.

As has been shown, the $\gamma \rightarrow \alpha'$ transformation contributes significantly to work hardening. Since lower temperatures favor transformation, difficult forming operations are sometimes performed at subzero temperatures. The role of the transformation also explains why cold-worked stainless steel does not subsequently work harden as much as annealed material. True-stress–true-strain curves for a 17.5Cr-7Ni alloy are shown in Fig. 51.[99]

TABLE 12   Permeability of Stainless Steels as Affected by Cold-Working[109]

AISI type	Cold reduction, %	Magnetic permeability	
		$H = 50$	$H = 200$
301	0	1.0027	1.0028
	19.5	1.148	1.257
	55	14.8	19.0
305	0	1.0032	1.0044
	18.5	1.0040	1.0054
	34.5	1.017	1.020
	52.5	1.049	1.063
	84.0	1.093	1.142

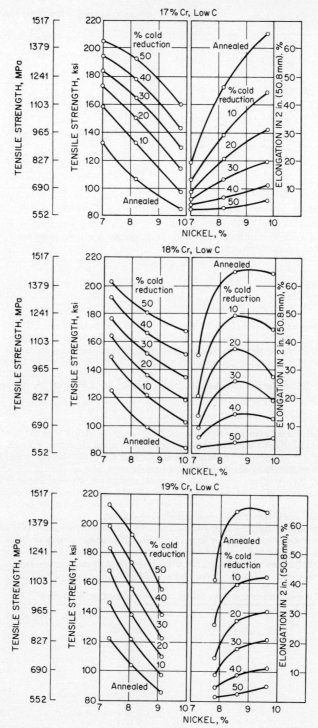

Fig. 44 Effect of chromium and nickel on tensile strength and elongation of cold-rolled steels containing 0.05% carbon.[105]

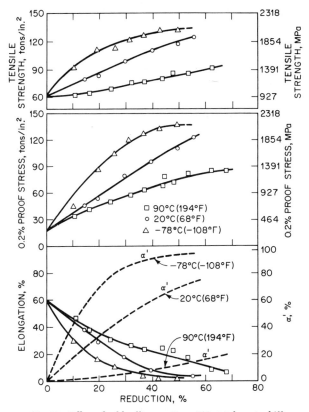

Fig. 45 Effect of cold-rolling on Type 301 stainless steel.[106]

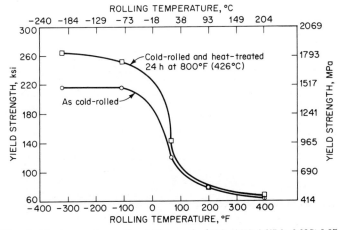

Fig. 46 Effect of rolling temperature on the yield strength of 18Cr-7.6Ni-0.95Mn-0.09Si-0.05C alloy.[108]

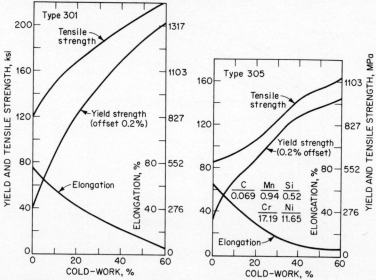

Fig. 47 Effect of cold-working on the mechanical properties of Types 301 and 305 stainless steels.[109]

Texture Crystallographic preferred orientation is often an important consideration in fcc metals. In hcp or fcc alloys, texture can cause striking effects on mechanical behavior. Also, transformation can influence texture development and vice versa. While it is true that property anisotropy is sometimes observed in the transformed less-stable austenitic stainless steels, this often has been most commonly related to the mode of transformation and the nature of the transformation product, rather than texture per se. Commercially produced flat-rolled stainless steel apparently has a very weak texture.

Strong textures do not exist because the sequences known to generate significant texture in these alloys (very extensive deformation, intermediate-to-elevated-temperature

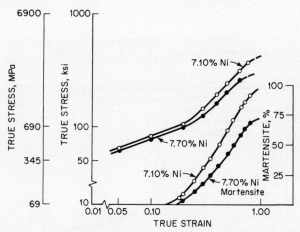

Fig. 48 Relationship between alloy stability, strain-hardening, and martensite formation in Type 301 stainless steel.[110]

deformation, and very specific heat treatments) are not applied in commercial practice.[111-113]

Stainless steel wire may quite often be strongly textured, but this does not appear to have been studied to any great extent.

The paper by Dillamore et al.[111] is a good review of the subject.

CARBIDE PRECIPITATION

Numerous constituents besides those discussed previously can occur in austenitic stainless steels. Many of these can influence behavior in a significant way.

Austenitic stainless steels may contain up to 0.08 or 0.15% carbon. The solid solubility curve for carbon in 18Cr-10Ni-bal Fe is shown in Fig. 52a.[115] The diagram indicates that at the annealing temperatures, i.e., 1000°C (1832°F) or above, substantial amounts of carbon can be dissolved.

Figure 52b shows data over a wider carbon range and also incorporates the effect of nickel. At carbon contents in the ranges present in AISI austenitic steels, the carbide is $M_{23}C_6$. At very high carbon contents a second carbide, M_7C_3, also appears. Note that nickel alters the shape of the solvus surface.

If the alloys are rapidly cooled from the anneal (for instance, by quenching), the dissolved carbon will remain in solution. This is the reason austenitic stainless steels are cooled rapidly after annealing. It is preferable to water-quench heavier section product.

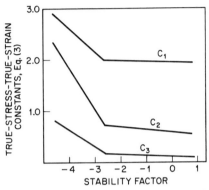

Fig. 49   Relationship between alloy stability and true-stress–true-strain equation constants.[99]

If a properly annealed and sufficiently rapidly cooled alloy is then maintained at room temperature, the alloy will remain supersaturated, and there will be no undesirable carbide precipitation effects.

In practical applications, situations arise where stainless steels cannot be handled in this way. The alloys are exposed to elevated temperatures, where precipitation then occurs as would be expected from the sloping solvus line in Fig. 52. The obvious and frequent practical example is the welding of stainless steel. During the welding process, parts of the heat-affected zone become reheated into a temperature range where carbides will precipitate. Also, stainless steels are often used at temperatures where precipitation occurs. Thus, carbide precipitation phenomena are of great significance.

$M_{23}C_6$ Carbide   The ubiquitous carbide in iron-based austenitic alloys is $M_{23}C_6$. In the absence of any strong carbide forming element, $M_{23}C_6$ is *the* carbide formed. If strong carbide formers are present, $M_{23}C_6$ will often be found in combination with other carbides. This constituent is fundamentally chromium carbide, so the designation $Cr_{23}C_6$ is used very frequently. However, since other elements can partially substitute for the chromium, $M_{23}C_6$ or other nomenclature, i.e., $(Cr,Fe)_{23}C_6$ or $(Cr,Fe,Mo)_{23}C_6$, is applied too. Since it is the most general designation, $M_{23}C_6$ will be used in this chapter.

The principal practical consequence of $M_{23}C_6$ precipitation is degradation of intergranular corrosion resistance. Classic weld-heat-affected-zone, grain-boundary sensitization is the well-known example. Because of this, $M_{23}C_6$ precipitation has been studied most extensively in conjunction with corrosion behavior. Corrosion effects have often been used to delineate precipitation conditions, particularly in early references to the phenomenon. With the advent of continually more refined electron microscopy techniques, better definition of the process has occurred.

$M_{23}C_6$ precipitation takes place in the temperature range from about 500 to 950°C (932 to 1742°F). The specific kinetics of precipitation depend on the chemistry of the alloy, the prior condition, and the precipitation sites. Usually, the kinetics are examined by annealing the alloy, cooling rapidly enough to prevent precipitation, and reheating to the temperature of interest.

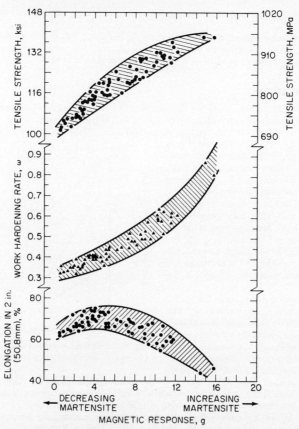

Fig. 50 Variations in tensile strength, work-hardening rate, and tensile elongation with martensite content of Type 301. Heats tested at room temperature.[95]

The precipitation kinetics in 18Cr-9Ni stainless steels (Type 304) are shown in Fig. 53. Both investigations employed higher-than-normal annealing temperatures, with resultant coarse grain size. The two results are similar, except that Cihal (Fig. 53a) did not examine ferrite-austenite boundaries and Stickler and Vinckier (Fig. 53b) did not observe precipitation within grains.

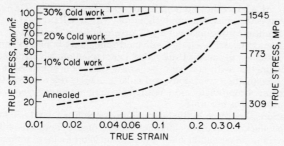

Fig. 51 True-stress–true-strain curves for a 17.5Cr-7Ni stainless steel with varying degrees of prior cold-work.[99]

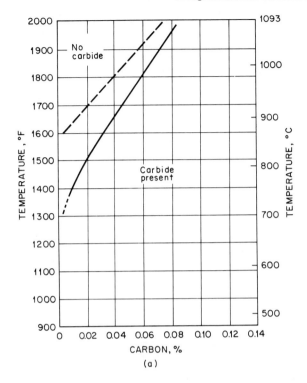

(a)

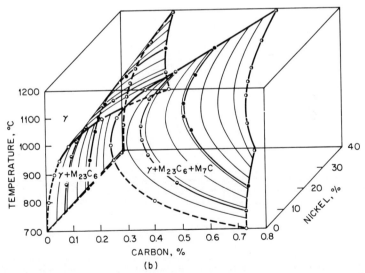

(b)

Fig. 52 Solid solubility of carbon in Fe-Cr-Ni alloys. (a) Solubility in 18Cr-10Ni.[115] (b) Effect of nickel on Fe-18Cr.[168]

Precipitation occurs very rapidly on the ferrite-austenite interfaces, followed very quickly by precipitation on other noncoherent boundaries (grain boundaries and twins). Considerably later precipitation occurs on coherent twin boundaries. This delayed precipitation on coherent boundaries was also observed by Wolff[125] on studies of higher nickel Fe-Ni-Cr alloys. The final precipitation sites are intragranular. $M_{23}C_6$ will also

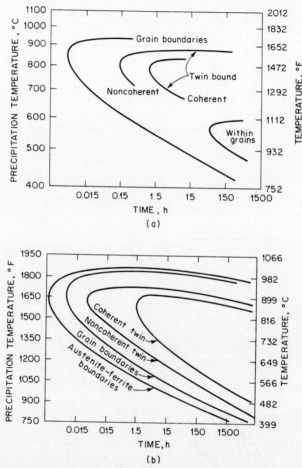

Fig. 53 Precipitation kinetics of $M_{23}C_6$ carbide in 18Cr-9%Ni stainless steels (Type 304). (*a*) Alloy containing 0.05% carbon originally quenched from 1250°C (2282°F).[116] (*b*) Alloy containing 0.038% carbon originally quenched from 1260°C (2300°F) (grain size ASTM 1).[120]

precipitate around nonmetallic inclusions in about the same time period as in noncoherent twin boundaries.[124]

Note that the temperatures for this progression of precipitation on various sites shift progressively downward, following energy considerations associated with each of these sites. The carbide forms initially in locations where it is easiest for the process to occur. For less "easy" sites, the chemical driving force must be larger. As will be shown later, this same trend exists when other more stable carbides also precipitate because of the presence of stronger carbide formers; e.g., columbium or titanium. When $M_{23}C_6$ precipitation occurs under these conditions, it tends to be delayed and is observed at the lower temperatures. Carbides having higher free energy of formation usually form first and at the higher temperatures. If critical element concentration (enhanced by segregation or diminished by prior precipitation) and diffusion considerations are added to this previous conceptualization, many precipitation processes in complex alloys can be qualitatively rationalized.

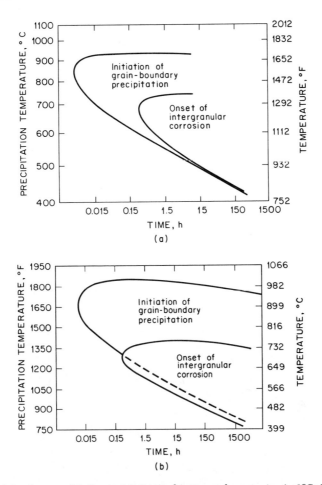

Fig. 54 Relation between $M_{23}C_6$ precipitation and intergranular corrosion in 18Cr-9Ni stainless steel (Type 304). (Intergranular corrosion detected by H_2SO_4-Cu_2SO_4 tests.) (a) Alloy containing 0.05% carbon originally quenched from 1250°C (2282°F).[116] (b) Alloy containing 0.038% carbon originally quenched from 1260°C (2300°F).[120]

The two precipitation curves in Fig. 53 do not agree precisely. These curves were derived from x-ray and electron microscopy examination on two alloys which were not precisely the same. Such differences are to be expected. C curves for alloys differing from these have been presented by many others, including Binder et al.[117] and Irvine et al.[118] The precipitation kinetics of grain boundary $M_{23}C_6$ in molybdenum-bearing Type 316 are similar to those shown for Type 304 in Fig. 53b, except that the times are slightly shorter.[124]

The precipitation of $M_{23}C_6$ carbide does not necessarily correlate directly with effects resulting from such precipitation. Intergranular corrosion behavior is the most sensitive characteristic. The results of Cihal[116] and Stickler and Vinckier,[120] comparing the initiation of grain-boundary precipitation with the onset of intergranular attack, are shown in Fig. 54. The intergranular corrosion lags considerably behind the initiation of precipitation. Differences in the corrosion test sensitivity are apparent.

The "nose" of the intergranular corrosion curve occurs at 650 to 700°C (1202 to 1292°F), the temperature range which is the one often cited as being most critical in a practical sense.

The reason the corrosion curve does not follow that for precipitation is related to the morphology of the $M_{23}C_6$ formed under different conditions. The susceptibility to intergranular corrosion will also depend on how it is determined and may even be detected under some circumstances when there is no carbide present, as in the solute segregation effect in highly oxidizing media studied and discussed by Aust et al.[121,123] However, when carbide is present, there are some very general correlations with carbide morphology. These have been reviewed by Henthorne.[127]

One of the earliest systematic investigations of $M_{23}C_6$ morphology took place in the late 1930s, as organized by ASTM Committee A-10.[128] The structure of Type 304 exposed for 6 days at various temperatures is shown in Fig. 55. The carbides are visible in all the pictures, but appear coarser after exposure at higher temperatures.

At the lowest $M_{23}C_6$ precipitation temperatures, the grain-boundary carbide assumes a virtually continuous thin sheetlike morphology.[120] As temperature is increased through 600 to 700°C (1112 to 1292°F), the particles are feathery dendrites, which form initially at boundary intersections and grow from those points.[119-126] These morphologies introduce the greatest sensitivity to intergranular corrosion, accounting for the relative positions of the curves in Fig. 54. With increasing time, the feathery dendrite structure gradually thickens and coarsens, as shown by the high-contrast "shadows" in Fig. 56.[120]

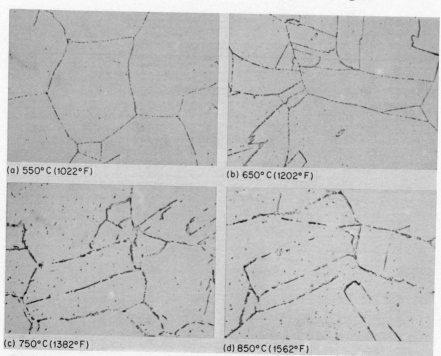

Fig. 55 Appearance of Type 304 stainless steel (0.065% carbon) sensitized for 6 days (144 h) at various temperatures. Specimens etched electrolytically in 10% oxalic acid.[128] (a) 550°C (1022°F). 750x. (b) 650°C (1202°F). 750x. (c) 750°C (1382°F). 750x (d) 850°C (1562°F). 750x.

At higher temperatures, the grain-boundary carbides are discrete geometric particles, their shape depending on the orientation of the boundary, the degree of misfit, and the particular temperature.[120,124-126,129] Stickler and Vinckier summarized the formation modes as shown in Fig. 57.

The appearance of annealed and sensitized Type 304, as revealed by transmission microscopy, is shown in Fig. 58.[130]

The $M_{23}C_6$ carbide is structurally related to the matrix, which influences its shape. In the case of the grain-boundary carbide, the cubic lattices (carbide and matrix) are parallel on one side of the boundary. The carbide thickens by growing into the parallel grain.[120,125,126,131] Wolff[125] notes that this orientation should be energetically favorable and should be enhanced by high vacancy concentration in the austenite. The other side of the boundary develops serrations composed of [111]-type interfaces.[120,129]

Noncoherent twin-boundary carbides have been reported to be lamellar[129] or rod-like.[125] The mechanism whereby lamellae form on such boundaries has been the subject of some discussion, with suggestions including the early formation of some transitional carbide, possibly Cr_7C_3.[129,132,133] The Cr_7C_3 carbide is not normally found in alloys of the AISI austenitic series.

Precipitation of $M_{23}C_6$ on coherent twins is platelike, also bearing a parallel orientation to the austenite. The shape is triangular, reflecting threefold symmetry of (111) austenite planes.[125,126,129]

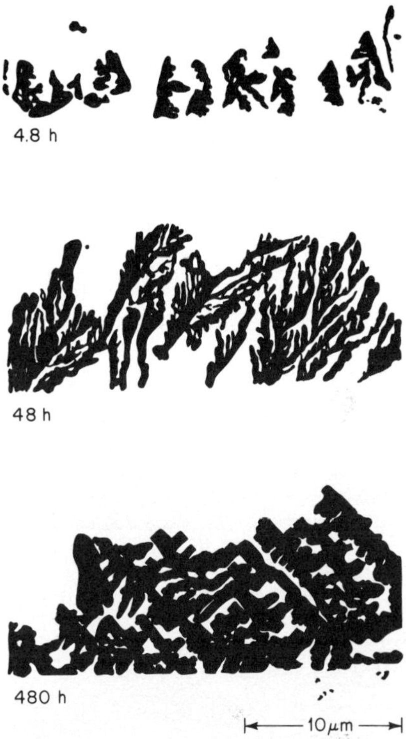

Intragranular $M_{23}C_6$ precipitation on dislocations also follows a parallel relationship to the matrix. An analysis of the planar atomic relationships of (111) planes in austenite and $M_{23}C_6$ as constructed by Lewis and Hattersley[129] is shown in Fig. 59. (These relationships will also exist partially in the case of noncoherent boundary precipitation.) Lattice parameter data for $M_{23}C_6$ is given in Table 13. The lattice parameter of $M_{23}C_6$ is roughly three times that of austenite. The unit cell contains 92 metal atoms and 24 carbon atoms. Lewis and Hattersley note that the mismatch between the A_1 planes in $M_{23}C_6$ and (111) planes in the austenite is roughly 1.3%, which would represent a low-energy interface.[129]

4.8 h

48 h

480 h

|← 10 μm →|

Fig. 56 Growth and coarsening of $M_{23}C_6$ dendrites in Type 304 stainless steel held for increasing times at 732°C (1350°F).[120]

As mentioned previously, $M_{23}C_6$ is primarily chromium carbide in which iron (or molybdenum) may substitute partially for chromium. The extent of substitution has been observed to depend on the alloy and precipitation conditions. Results of DaCasa et al.[136] showing the effect of precipitation time in different heats are given in Fig. 60. The effect of precipitation temperature is shown in Fig. 61. During initial stages of $M_{23}C_6$ carbide precipitation, the iron content is quite high. With increasing precipitation, the chromium content increases. It appears the equilibrium concentration of chromium increases at higher temperatures.

DaCasa et al.[136] cite Goldschmidt's work[135] which states that iron should not be able to substitute for more than 35% of the chromium. The fact that substitution of almost 50% has been observed at the initial stages of precipitation suggests perhaps the earliest carbide form might be something other than $M_{23}C_6$. No other carbide, however, has been specifically identified to support this speculation.

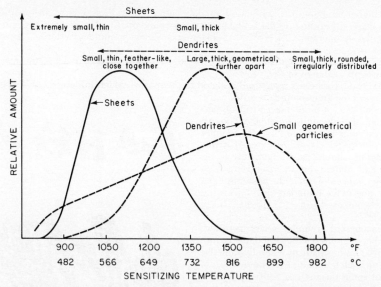

Fig. 57 The morphology of grain boundary $M_{23}C_6$ as a function of sensitizing temperature.[120]

In molybdenum-containing steels (Types 316 and 316L), the carbide, after long precipitation periods, was reported to be $(Cr_{17}Fe_{4.5}Mo_{1.5})C_6$ or $(Cr_{16}Fe_5Mo_2)C_6$.[134,124]

Some data suggests nitrogen can substitute for some of the carbon in $M_{23}C_6$, although there is no uniformity of opinion on this subject. DaCasa et al.[136] found 2% nitrogen in carbide extracts from Type 304 containing 230 ppm nitrogen. The effect of nitrogen on $M_{23}C_6$ percipitation in a more complex alloy is shown in Fig. 62.[172]

Increasing the original annealing temperature and grain size accelerates precipitation of $M_{23}C_6$, as shown in Fig. 63. This is attibuted to higher vacancy concentration and solute

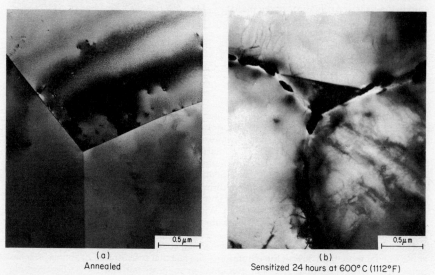

Fig. 58 Transmission micrographs of annealed and sensitized Type 304 stainless steel.[130] (a) Annealed. (b) Sensitized 24 h at 600°C (1112°F). (*Courtesy of David Vermilyea.*)

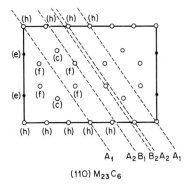

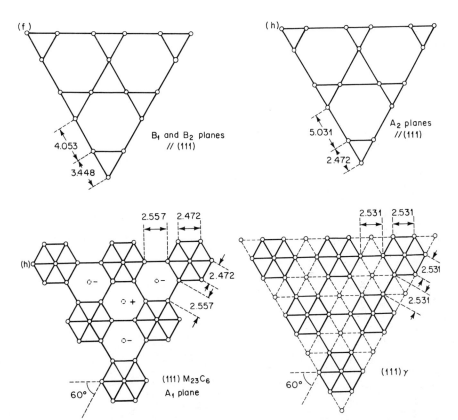

Fig. 59 Comparison of (111) atom planes in austenite and $M_{23}C_6$ carbide.[129]

segregation coupled with reduced grain-boundary area.[124] This effect persists when material is cold-worked prior to sensitization. The same relative difference exists except that both curves are moved to the left because of the cold-work, which accelerates most precipitation reactions.

One measure adopted to control $M_{23}C_6$ precipitation is to reduce the carbon content. Figures 64 and 65 show the effect of carbon on precipitation in Fe-Ni-Cr and Fe-Ni-Cr-

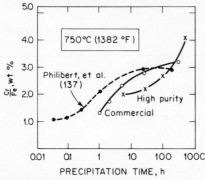

Fig. 60 Effect of precipitation time on composition of $M_{23}C_6$ in Type 304 stainless steel.[136]

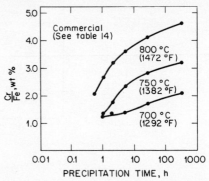

Fig. 61 Effect of precipitation conditions on composition of $M_{23}C_6$ in Type 304 stainless steel.[136]

TABLE 13   Lattice Parameter of $M_{23}C_6$ Carbide

Reference	Alloy type	Lattice parameter, Å
Lewis and Hattersley[129]	Fe-Ni-Cr	10.615
Goldschmidt[135]	Fe-Ni-Cr	10.638
DaCasa et al.[136]	Fe-Ni-Cr	10.61, 10.62*
Williams and Talks[156]	Fe-Ni-Cr	10.63–10.64
Kautz and Gerlach[134]	Fe-Ni-Cr-Mo	10.68
Weiss and Sticker[124]	Fe-Ni-Cr-Mo	10.569–10.676†

*High-purity and commercial-purity alloy, respectively.

†Varies with precipitation time and temperature. Higher temperatures and longer times increase lattice parameter.

Mo alloys, respectively. Reduced carbon contents suppress the precipitation reaction sufficiently to minimize difficulties in weld fabrication procedures not involving protracted heating periods. Extended exposure in the sensitizing range will result in precipitation.

Other compositional effects can also influence the kinetics of carbide precipitation. Increasing the content of the austenitizing elements (cobalt, manganese, or nickel) has been reported to increase the activity and diffusivity of carbon and tendency for precipitation.[116,138–142] Chromium has the opposite effect.[142]

DaCasa et al., reported precipitation retardation in their high-purity alloy (see Table 14

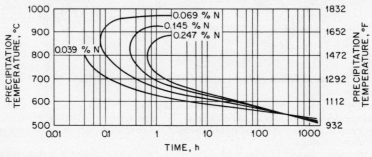

Fig. 62 Effect of nitrogen on precipitation of $M_{23}C_6$ in 0.05C-17Cr-13Ni-5Mo stainless steel.[172]

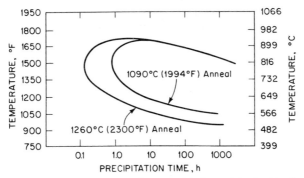

Fig. 63 Effect of annealing temperature on subsequent $M_{23}C_6$ precipitation kinetics in Type 316L (0.023% carbon) stainless steel. [ASTM grain sizes of materials annealed at 1090°C and 1260°C (1994°F and 2300°F) were 3 to 4 and greater than 1, respectively.][124]

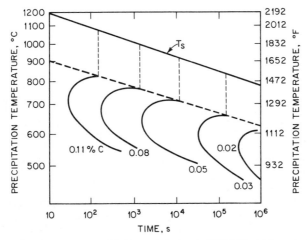

Fig. 64 Effect of carbon content on $M_{23}C_6$ precipitation in 18Cr-9Ni stainless steel, as detected by integranular corrosion tests (H_2SO_4-Cu_2SO_4). The solution temperature for each of the alloys is obtained from the T_s line.[116]

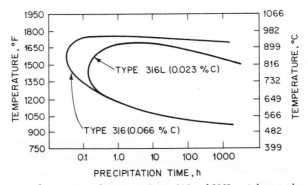

Fig. 65 Comparison of precipitation kinetics in Types 316 and 316L stainless steels, as determined by electron microscopy techniques. (Constructed from plots of Weiss and Stickler.[124])

for composition). Also, the feathery dendrite morphology was not observed. From structural considerations, there were no obvious reasons for this. The carbide found was $M_{23}C_6$.[136] Qualitatively at least, this behavior parallels reported observations that high-purity alloys are more resistant to intergranular corrosion in strong oxidizing media.[127,143,144] However, the situation is different since the reported purity effects exist

TABLE 14   Composition of Alloys Described in Figs. 60 and 61

| | Composition | | | | | | | | | |
| | Weight % | | | | | | | ppm | | |
Reference	C	Cr	Ni	Si	Mn	P	S	O	N	B
DaCasa et al.,[136] high-purity	0.065	18.2	10.0	0.17	0.08	0.008	0.019	35	80	20
DaCasa et al.,[136] commercial-purity	0.070	18.6	9.7	0.40	1.54	0.024	0.026	99	230	10
Philibert et al.[137]	0.090	18.3	9.5	0.48	0.94					

even in the absence of any $M_{23}C_6$. The similarities concern the fact that solute elements are concentrated at the grain boundaries and are available to influence precipitation. Precipitation could be altered by one or more of the elements affecting vacancy concentration or by direct participation in the $M_{23}C_6$ precipitate. Phosphorus has been shown to influence $M_{23}C_6$ precipitation. This has led to speculation that it may replace some of the carbon.[145]

Boron can affect $M_{23}C_6$ in several possible ways. Boron is well known for its beneficial effect on the elevated-temperature strength of austenitic stainless steel by delaying grain-boundary fissuring.[145-149] When boron is present in very small amounts, suppression of grain boundary $M_{23}C_6$ has been observed in connection with this phenomenon. Some question exists whether boron acts by changing vacancy concentration, lowering carbon diffusivity and solubility, or by participating directly in the carbide.[147,150-153] Boron could act in any of these modes. Boron has an intermediate size atom (see Fig. 7) which would tend to locate it at grain boundaries. In addition, its solubility is very low.

The solubility of boron in Fe-Ni-Cr alloys is shown in Fig. 66.[155] The low solubility in Fe-Ni-Cr-Mo alloys is demonstrated by the data in Table 15.[134] At low concentrations, boron can behave as an interstitial element replacing some carbon, resulting in $M_{23}(C,B)_6$. The lattice parameter of the carbide may be increased, thereby providing a better fit between parallel planes in the carbide and austenite matrix.[154,156] Using very high boron

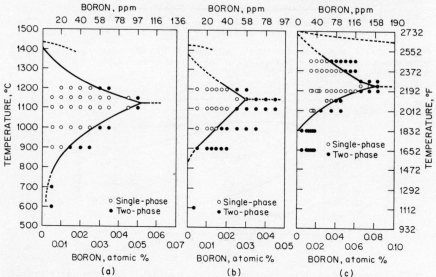

Fig. 66   Solubility of boron in high-purity Fe-Ni-Cr alloys containing less than 0.01% C.[155] (*a*) 18Cr-15Ni. (*b*) 20Cr-25Ni. (*c*) 20Cr-25Ni + 0.6Nb + 0.6Mn + 0.6Si.

concentrations (far above those normally found in stainless steels), Goldschmidt found the equilibrium boron constituent to be orthorhombic M_2B containing 30–50Cr-30–50Fe-1.5–2.0Ni. The exact composition depends upon the alloy and conditions of formation.[155]

The effect of boron on precipitation kinetics can be different, depending on the alloy chemistry and the particular conditions. Its role, however, can be profound. Application of

TABLE 15   Solubility of Boron in 16Cr-16Ni-2Mo Stainless Steel[134]

Heat-treatment temperature		Boron content of steel present in extracted residues (precipitates)	
°C	°F	Heat 4 (total B = 0.0071%)	Heat 5 (total B = 0.0077%)
1000	1832	0.006	0.004
1050	1922	0.007	0.005
1100	2012	0.001	0.004
1150	2102	0.0001	
1200	2192	0.0001	
1250	2282	0.0001	0.0001

this role in austenitic stainless steel has been restricted because of the possibility of the formation of low-melting-temperature [1150 to 1225°C (2102 to 2237°F)] eutectic. This can cause hot-shortness difficulty in hot-working and welding.

If enough $M_{23}C_6$ carbide precipitation takes place, the matrix chemistry may be sufficiently depleted of carbon and chromium that transformation of an otherwise stable alloy can occur upon cooling. Figure 67 shows this effect in Type 304 stainless steel. This principle, applied to leaner chemistries, can result in very extensive transformation. Some of the precipitation-hardening stainless steels utilize this principle. The transformation "nose" in Fig. 67 reflects the *amount* of $M_{23}C_6$ precipitation, confirming that the lower-temperature intergranular-corrosion curves are due to morphology, not carbide quantity.

In reviewing the effect of $M_{23}C_6$ morphology on intergranular corrosion, it was noted that the lower-temperature morphologies were most harmful. On this basis, there has been study and discussion of the role of deliberate precipitation of $M_{23}C_6$ in the more innocuous (high-temperature) form. In general, this approach does not work, which may be seen by referring to Fig. 52. Whatever pre-precipitation treatment is adopted, still more carbon will precipitate in the most critical range. Notwithstanding the work of Aust and coworkers[123,143,157] with a highly oxidizing corrosion medium, the normally desired microstructure in unstabilized alloys is one in which there is no $M_{23}C_6$ precipitate. Such a structure is obtained by annealing at the temperatures shown in Table 2 and cooling rapidly enough to prevent precipitation. Low carbon contents may also be applied to suppress precipitation. If this is not sufficient, then a "stabilized" grade must be applied.

MC Carbides   Types 321 and 347 stainless steels contain either Ti or Nb which form

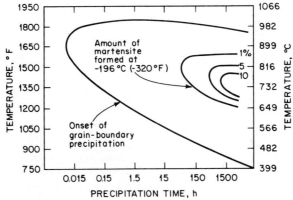

Fig. 67   Effect of $M_{23}C_6$ precipitation on austenite stability of Type 304 stainless steel.[120]

TiC or NbC, respectively. These alloy additions can be viewed in two ways. Accordingly, heat treatments may take two extremes in addition to the conventional annealing treatment in Table 2. When the alloys are employed primarily as "stabilized" grades to prevent subsequent intergranular corrosion, they are often given a "stabilizing" heat treatment which precipitates the TiC or NbC in an innocuous form, effectively reducing the matrix carbon content and thus protecting against deleterious $M_{23}C_6$ precipitation.

These stabilizing treatments are conducted at 842 to 898°C (1550 to 1650°F) and may last for several hours. The importance of the stabilizing treatment depends upon later service. They are more often applied to Type 321 than Type 347.

Alternately, the alloys may be annealed to dissolve as much of the TiC or NbC as possible, and then placed in service at some temperature within the precipitation range. The subsequent intragranular precipitation of MC during creep increases strength.[146,158-163] The MC may precipitate on dislocations,[161,163] on stacking faults,[140,158] or on both within the matrix.[164,166] Although not normally a deliberate alloying element, tantalum will also form intragranular MC.[167]

To obtain maximum strengthening effect from precipitation of MC, the annealing temperature should be very high so as to dissolve as much titanium or niobium (columbium) carbide as possible.[159,168] Use of extremely high annealing temperatures has other ramifications, so the temperatures used represent a compromise. Specially heat-treated H grades utilize the added strengthening provided by higher-than-normal annealing temperatures. For Types 321 and 347, these are 1050°C (1925°F) minimum to 1149°C (2100°F) maximum. (See, for example, Sec. II of *ASME Boiler and Pressure Vessel Code*, SA403 or ASTM A403). These temperature ranges are 10 to 24°C (18 to 43°F) above the (usual) annealing temperatures shown in Table 2.

The MC carbides usually precipitate intragranularly. However, under some conditions, precipitation at grain boundaries can occur. The best example of this is after exposure to extraordinarily high austenitizing temperatures [i.e., 1300°C (2372°F) or above] when dendritic-form TiC or CbC will subsequently precipitate. This phenomenon, occuring at weld fusion areas, can lead to a special type of corrosion decay known as *knife-edge attack*. Fortunately, such attack is not a problem in most corrosive media.

The solubility of titanium carbide in Type 321 stainless steel, as determined by White and Freeman,[159] is shown in Fig. 68. Comparison of Fig. 68 with Fig. 52 reveals that the solubility of carbon is considerably reduced in the presence of titanium. The complete solution of TiC depends on the carbon content of the alloy and the specific annealing temperature. In actual practice, some undissolved TiC is found in annealed titanium-stabilized austenitic stainless steels. Referring to Fig. 68, it can be seen that although precipitation of TiC will drastically reduce matrix carbon content, under most circumstances, some carbon will remain available for later further precipitation. $M_{23}C_6$ can still form in Type 321 stainless steel. Such precipitation, however, is delayed.

Based upon consideration of the relative atomic weights of titanium and carbon, the amount of titanium generally considered necessary for effective stabilization is four times the carbon concentration (both expressed as weight percent). However, this represents an oversimplification. Titanium carbide and titanium nitride are structurally identical. Both are face-centered-cubic, with the carbon or nitrogen occupying octahedral positions in the lattice. Nitrogen can replace carbon in the carbide and vice versa. Thus, the constituent is often called titanium carbonitride, Ti(CN).

Assuming the broadest possible circumstances, TiC or TiC plus TiN or Ti(CN) may occur in austenitic alloys. The precipitates which form depend on the concentrations of

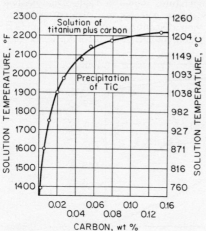

Fig. 68 The solubility of TiC in Type 321 stainless steel.[159]

titanium, carbon, and nitrogen, as well as the alloy base chemistry, which will affect the relative chemical activities of carbon and nitrogen. The nitride will apparently accept more carbon than vice versa. TiN, very common in high-nickel-content austenitic alloys, is often observed as very-well-defined bright yellow cubic particles. With the addition of carbon, a maize color develops. TiC is grey, with a less well-defined shape. Ti(CN) has an appearance between grey and yellow, depending on the carbon/nitrogen ratio.

The lattice parameters for TiN and TiC are 4.24 and 4.33 Å, respectively.[169] Observed constituents usually have intermediate parameters, reflecting nitrogen-for-carbon substitution. Grot and Spruiell,[170] studying precipitates in aged Type 321 stainless steel, found both Ti(CN) with a lattice parameter of 4.32 Å and Ti(NC) with a lattice parameter of 4.25 Å. Beattie and Hagel[171] found Ti(CN) with a lattice parameter very close to that of TiC in an Fe-Ni-Cr superalloy (A-286).

The minimum titanium content required to stabilize carbon can be related to a "combined-carbon" content, which would be related to the titanium by the ratio of atomic weights:

$$\text{Combined carbon} = \frac{\text{Ti}}{4} \tag{4}$$

In principle, it is desired to have sufficient titanium so that all the carbon is "combined-carbon." As noted above, the presence of nitrogen and the effect of heat treatment are not taken into account in this simple representation. There are many ways to refine the situation, one proposed by Cihal[116] being:

$$\text{Combined carbon} = f \left(\frac{\text{Ti-3.43(N-0.001)}}{4} \right) \tag{5}$$

where f is a factor which depends on the heat treatment. For material given a stabilizing heat treatment, $f = 1.0$. (The 3.43 coefficient for the nitrogen term is the stoichiometric relation between Ti and N.)

Columbium (niobium) carbide-stabilizing additions are normally eight to ten times the carbon content. The solubility of columbium carbide, as related to columbium in solution, is given in Fig. 69.[161] Bungardt and Lennartz[141] examined solubility in terms of the amount of columbium in the precipitated fraction as shown in Fig. 70. Relating these data to columbium carbide solubility is not rigorously correct, as other columbium-bearing phases can and do precipitate in such alloys. However, providing that the alloys do not contain very large amounts of columbium (i.e., are not vastly "overstabilized"), most of the precipitate will be CbC. As shown in Figs. 69 and 70, the solubility is quite low and annealed alloys are likely to contain some undissolved CbC. Figure 70 shows the effect of nickel on increasing the solubility, whereas 1% molybdenum had very little effect. Table 16 gives the compositions of the steels in Fig. 70.

In many respects CbC is similar to TiC. It, too, can dissolve nitrogen and is sometimes

TABLE 16   Base Compositions of Steels Described in Fig. 70[141]

Steel number	Composition, %								
	C	Si	Mn	P	S	Cr	Mo	Ni	N
A0	0.075	0.50	1.18	0.012	0.008	16.31	0.09	15.96	0.023
A1	0.078	0.48	1.13	0.012	0.010	16.02	1.19	15.86	0.023
B0	0.054	0.62	1.23	0.012	0.011	16.34	0.08	24.22	0.022
B1	0.074	0.53	1.08	0.012	0.011	16.50	1.06	25.11	0.020

referred to as carbonitride, Cb(CN). The lattice parameters reported for Cb(CN) vary from 3.379 Å (nitride) to 4.47 Å (carbide) depending on carbon/nitrogen ratio.[140,153,173] Silcock,[140] studying lattice parameters of precipitates in an 18Cr-12Ni-1Cb alloy, found that undissolved particles apparently contained relatively more nitrogen than those which appeared during subsequent aging treatments.

M₆C Carbide M_6C carbide may be found in stainless steels containing molybdenum or columbium. M_6C occurs in alloys where there are also other major precipitating constituents, and its appearance or disappearance is often related to that of the other constituents. Indeed, it would be equally proper to discuss M_6C in a later section on intermediate compounds. Precipitation is usually intragranular although intergranular formation has been reported.

In Type 316 stainless steel, M_6C occurred only after very long (1500 h) aging and then formed in a limited temperature range around 649°C (1200°F).[124] There is evidence to

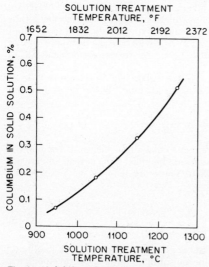

Fig. 69 Solubility of columbium in a steel containing 16.8Cr-13.25Ni-0.07C-0.94Cb.[161]

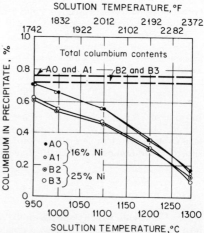

Fig. 70 Solubility of columbium. Composition of alloys is given in Table 16. Alloys were heated for 1 h and water-quenched.[141]

suggest that M_6C forms from $M_{23}C_6$ as originally suggested by Goldschmidt[135] and reinforced by Weiss and Stickler.[124] The sequence suggested is

$$M_{23}C_6 \xrightarrow[650°C\ (1202°F)]{+\ Mo} (Fe,Cr)_{21}Mo_2C_6 \xrightarrow{+\ Mo} M_6C$$

In 17Cr-13Ni-5Mo-0.05C alloys with varying nitrogen contents, Thier et al.[172] found no M_6C would form in an alloy containing 0.039% nitrogen. At nitrogen contents of 0.069% or above, M_6C precipitated in less than 1 h at 900 to 950°C (1652 to 1742°F). The overall precipitation range extended down to 700°C (1292°F), where precipitation was far behind that of $M_{23}C_6$. This primarily high-temperature mode is distinctly different precipitation behavior from that in lower molybdenum content Type 316. Figure 71 shows the variation in M_6C lattice parameter with steel nitrogen content. This shows partial substitution of nitrogen for carbon, although the kinetics of M_6C precipitation did not change as nitrogen content was increased from 0.069 to 0.247%. The appearance of M_6C in these alloys coincided with delayed precipitation of $M_{23}C_6$ and intermetallic compounds, chi and Laves phase (see Fig. 93).

Studying an 18Cr-9Ni-0.09C-1Cb alloy, Cihal and Jezek[174] found no M_6C. The predominant carbide was CbC, with some $M_{23}C_6$ also present under some precipitation conditions. (Their aging times were no longer than 500 h.) When the columbium content was raised to 2%, M_6C formed under virtually all precipitating conditions at the expense of $M_{23}C_6$, which was not found. Laves phase formed also. Additional lines were observed in the diffraction patterns of M_6C precipitated at lower temperatures, which was attributed to the presence of chromium.

Bungardt and Lennartz,[141] studying 16Cr-0.7Cb alloys with either 16 or 25% nickel, found M_6C only in the 25% Ni alloys and then only when more than 3% Mo was also present. The M_6C formed at 850°C (1566°F) but not at 650°C (1202°F). Precipitation was rapid, in 1 h.

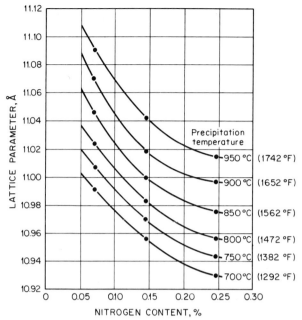

Fig. 71 Effect of alloy nitrogen content on lattice parameter of M_6C carbide in 17Cr-13Ni-5Mo-0.05C alloys.[172]

Studying a 20Cr-33Ni-2.3Mo-3.25Cu-0.04C-0.8Cb alloy (Carpenter 20Cb3*), Scharfstein and Maniar[139] found M_6C precipitated rapidly at around 950°C (1742°F) but not below that. Much less M_6C formed in a 28% Ni alloy. M_6C went into solution above 1050°C (1922°F).

From the foregoing, it is seen that M_6C precipitates rapidly (in conjunction with one or more intermetallics) in alloys containing large amounts of molybdenum or columbium or a combination of both. The precipitation occurs primarily at higher temperatures. Higher nickel contents in the matrix tend to favor the formation of M_6C.

An alternate mode is formation of M_6C after very long times at lower temperatures, where it has been postulated the M_6C forms from $M_{23}C_6$. This has been observed in Type 316 stainless steel.

Table 17 gives reported lattice parameters and suggested formulas for M_6C. Note that

TABLE 17   Some Lattice Parameters and Formulas of M_6C Carbide

Reference	Alloy investigated	Lattice parameter, Å	Suggested carbide formula
Weiss and Stickler[124]	Type 316	10.95	
Citing Koch[175]	Fe-Ni-Cr-Mo	11.11	Fe_3Mo_3C
Thier et al.[172]	Fe-Ni-Cr-Mo	See Fig. 71	
Cihal and Jezek[174]	18Cr-9Ni-2Cb	11.28	Fe_3Cb_3C
	18Cr-9Ni-2Cb (low-temperature precipitation)		$(Fe,Cr)_3Cb_3C$
Jenkinson et al.[176]	18Cr-12Ni-Cb		$FeCr_2-2Nb_4C_3$†
Scharfstein and Maniar[139]	20Cr-33Ni-3.25Cu-2.25Mo-0.8Cb		$(Mo,Cb)_3(Fe,Ni,Cr)_3C$

†Constructed from chemical analysis of residue. Interpreted in Cihal and Jezek[174] to be $(Fe,Cr)_3Nb_3C + 5CbC$.

*Trademark of Carpenter Technology Corp.

many of the formulas involve significant amounts of columbium or molybdenum. Chromium has been found or suggested in lower-temperature forms, which is consistent with the $M_{23}C_6$ precursor theory.

Other Carbides and Related Compounds   Figure 53b shows that M_7C_3 is a possible carbide in Fe-Cr-C or Fe-Cr-Ni-C alloys. This carbide, however, should exist only in materials having carbon contents above those represented by the AISI austenitic alloys. In the previous section on $M_{23}C_6$, reference was made to published speculation that M_7C_3 carbide might be a very early intermediate to the formation of $M_{23}C_6$. More direct evidence for such a sequence in nickel-rich Ni-Co-Cr-Al-Ti-C alloys has been presented by Mihalisin.[177] In terms of the key factors influencing precipitated phases, nickel- and iron-based alloys are quite different,[178] and it is not valid to transfer processes automatically from one alloy to another. There remains no definitive evidence that M_7C_3 does occur in AISI-type austenitic stainless steels. However, the speculation is noted here since not all published observations dovetail exactly, and M_7C_3 is one possible explanation.

Vanadium is not an alloying element in the AISI 300-series stainless steels. It has been studied experimentally and employed in some proprietary high-temperature alloys. When present in large quantities (1 to 1.5%), vanadium can precipitate as V_4C_3. This precipitation usually occurs on dislocations and stacking faults, somewhat similar to MC carbides.[164,165]

In titanium-bearing alloys, sulfur can combine with titanium to form complex hexagonal compounds which also incorporate carbon. These compounds are found as primary platelike particles, as well as thin intergranular precipitated platelets. They are often intimately associated with Ti(CN) particles from which they are difficult to separate in residue analysis. This has created uncertainty in identifying the precise structure and chemistry. In situ analysis, for instance, by microprobe techniques, has improved the situation.

Various sulfides or carbosulfides have been identified, as summarized in Table 18. In addition, Beattie and Hagel[178] refer to Y or τ as Ti_2SC, whereas Grot and Spruiell[170] report finding $Ti_4C_2S_2$ in Type 321. In their work on Type 321, DaCasa and Nileshwar[179] confirmed Y phase as previously reported by Gemill.[180]

TABLE 18   Summary of Chemical and Crystallographic Data on Titanium Sulfides-Carbosulfides[179]

Designation	Structure	Composition	Remarks	Reference
Y phase	Unit cell hexagonal, $a = 3.206$ Å, $c = 11.19$ Å	Not determined but believed to be a second nitride of titanium	Originally observed in 9% Cr steel containing titanium later identified in Type 321 stainless steel	Gemill[180]
τ phase	As above	69Ti-9.7N-5.7C-4.4S	Eliminating carbon and nitrogen as TiC and TiN, residual Ti and S found to correspond precisely to compound Ti_2S	Brown[181]
τ phase	Unit cell tetragonal, $a = 3.92$ Å, $b = 7.43$ Å	Not determined	From the reanalysis of the patterns reported for Y and τ phase, suggested that the two bases may not be the same	Knop[182]
Ti_2S	Unit cell hexagonal, $a = 3.22$ Å, $b = 7.64$ Å	Not determined but argue that it must be Ti_2S		Wetzler et al.[183]
Y phase	Unit cell hexagonal, $a = 3.20$ Å, $c = 11.2$ Å	60Ti-29S-11C	In Type 321	This work

Nitride Precipitation The equilibrium diagram for Fe-18Cr-Ni-N alloys at 900°C (1652°F) is shown in Fig. 72. This applies to alloys where there are no significant quantities of strong carbide-formers such as Al, V, Ti, Cb. In the absence of such elements, the equilibrium in AISI austenitic steels is between austenite and Cr_2N. Since the AISI 300-series steels contain less than 0.15% nitrogen, nitrogen is fully

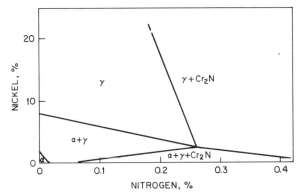

Fig. 72 Equilibrium diagram for 18Cr-Fe-Ni-N system at 900°C (1652°F).[184]

dissolved. Figure 72 shows that nickel reduces the nitrogen solubility. Manganese and chromium have the opposite effect.[30]

The solubility of nitrogen as a function of temperature is shown in Fig. 73.[185] (The discontinuity in the Eckel and Cox data arises from uncertainty caused by carbide precipitation.) It is apparent why Cr_2N precipitation is not generally a factor in AISI austenitic stainless steels. The solubility is high to begin with and, as noted previously, some nitrogen replaces carbon in carbides, further reducing the net nitrogen content. When strong nitride-forming elements are present, nitrogen does precipitate.

The participation of nitrogen in $M_{23}C_6$, MC, and M_6C precipitation has been reviewed previously. As noted, nitrogen will form Ti(CN) or TiN, and for this reason titanium is not added to nitrogen-alloyed steels. Nitrogen will also react with columbium, as mentioned previously.

Vanadium has been employed in some cases as an alloying element in conjunction with nitrogen, where deliberate precipitation of vanadium nitride during creep conditions is intended.[151,189,190] The vanadium additions, normally about 0.5%, result in creep-induced precipitation of VN_{1-x} in the matrix and on dislocations.

INTERMEDIATE PHASES

Sigma, Chi, and Laves Phases Alloy systems based on B transition elements such as manganese, iron, cobalt, and nickel, which also contain A subgroup elements like titanium, vanadium, and chromium, can form a number of intermediate phases. Nevitt[191] has reviewed formation on these phases in detail. Nevitt's summary, as modified by Decker and Floreen[192] to show only those phases occurring in iron-based alloys, is shown in Fig. 74. Of these phases, sigma (σ), chi (χ), and Laves (η) do form in the more important AISI austenitic stainless steels. These are the thermodynamically stable phases in Fe-Ni-Cr-(Mo) alloys. These phases plus gamma prime (γ'), beta (β), and mu (μ) are more likely in highly alloyed precipitation-hardening iron-based superalloy-type materials. Still another constituent, G phase ($A_6B_{16}C_7$), can form in very highly alloyed steels. Silicon is the C atom.

Some of the phases adhere very strictly to fixed stoichiometric ratios, whereas others can vary quite widely. Sigma, for example, can range from B_4A to BA_4. The factors which influence the occurrence of these phases are electron/atom ratio (e/a), atomic size, and compressibility. The situations in which a particular phase will form are quite complex. They are further confounded by the fact that the phases rarely form singularly. Thus,

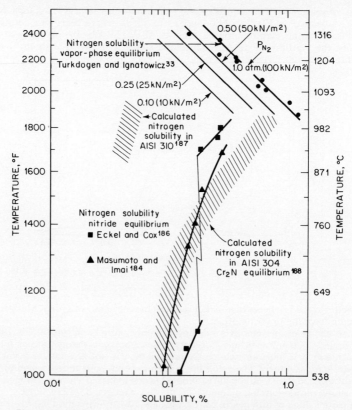

Fig. 73   Solubility of nitrogen in 18Cr-10Ni and 25Cr-20Ni alloys.[185]

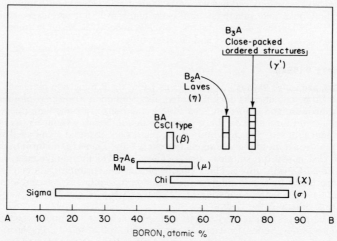

Fig. 74   Summary of possible transition element phases in iron-based alloys. The A group includes elements such as Ti, V, Cr, Cb, Mo. The B group elements are Fe, Ni, Mn, Co. (*From Nevitt*[191] *as modified by Decker and Floreen*[192].)

TABLE 19 Occurrence of Phases in Iron-based Transition Element Systems[192]

| B transition element | A elements | | | | | | | | |
	Group IV (4 e/a)			Group V (5 e/a)			Group VI (6 e/a)		
	Ti	Zr	Hf	V	Cb	Ta	Cr	Mo	W
Mn (7 e/a)	B_2A Chi Sigma	B_2A Chi	B_2A Chi	BA Chi Sigma	B_2A Chi	B_2A Chi	Sigma Chi	Sigma Chi	Chi
Fe (8 e/a)	B_2A BA Chi(Cr)	B_2A	B_2A	BA Chi(Si) Sigma	Sigma B_2A	B_2A	Sigma	Mu Sigma B_2A Chi(Cr)	B_2A Mu
Co (9 e/a)	B_2A BA	B_2A BA	B_2A BA	B_3A Sigma	B_2A	B_2A	Sigma	Mu Sigma B_3A	B_3A Mu
Ni (10 e/a)	$B_3A[\gamma]$* $B_3A[\eta]$ BA G(Si)	G(Si)	B_2A BA G(Si)	B_3A Chi(Si) Sigma G(Si)	B_3A Mu G(Si)	G(Si)	Sigma(Si)	B_3A	

Atomic size of A increases ←
e/a increases ↑
Compressibility of R increases ↑
[ ] Type of B_3A compound
( ) Stabilized by ternary addition of Si or Cr
*Transition phase

competition for a principal atom specie can be a factor. Where it can be accommodated, carbon can be important by contributing electrons.

Difficult as it is to make absolute predictions, it is useful to have some sort of reference framework with which observed occurrences can be compared. The representation shown in Table 19 is from Decker.[192] This is useful for visualizing what effects changing alloy chemistry should have. For example, if an alloy has a tendency to form sigma, increasing the nickel content should decrease the tendency. Likewise, columbium and titanium are relatively more likely to form Laves phase (B_2A) than chi or sigma.

These phases collectively precipitate over the general temperature range from 600°C (1112°F) to, in extreme cases, as high as 1150°C (2100°F). Precipitation observed in specific alloys will be discussed in the next section. Reported structures, lattice parameters, compositions, and formulas for sigma, chi, and Laves phase are given in Tables 20 to 22.

The analyses and formulas for chi from Fe-Cr-Ni alloys with 2 to 3% molybdenum are not all mutually consistent. In addition to real possible variation, analysis of residues can lead to discrepancies if other phases are also present and their quantities are estimated inaccurately. For example, sigma included with chi could lower the apparent molybdenum content of the chi. Conversely, accidental inclusion of Laves phase would attribute erroneous high molybdenum contents to either sigma or chi.

Sigma-Phase Equilibria in Fe-Ni-Cr Alloys   Because of its wide occurrence in alloys used at elevated temperatures, sigma has been studied very extensively. The presence of this hard, brittle, nonmagnetic phase in stainless steel was first noted in Fe-Cr alloys by Bain and Griffiths[199] in 1927, who referred to it as B phase.

The first study of sigma in ternary Fe-Ni-Cr alloys was by Schafmeister and Ergang.[200] They employed alloys with carbon contents from 0.02 to 0.14% and commercial levels of silicon and manganese. Later work indicated some of their boundaries were inaccurate due to the variation in carbon content. Also, some of the compositions may not have reached equilibrium.

Bradley and Goldschmidt[201] showed somewhat broader compositional limits. Rees, Burns, and Cook[202] performed very careful work on material prepared from high-purity powders (carbon and nitrogen contents below 0.01%) where they employed thorough homogenization and extremely long isothermal exposure times. Their 650°C (1200°F) data are compared with the Schafmeister and Ergang results in Fig. 75.

Nicholson, Samans, and Shortsleeve[203] and Talbot and Furman[204] later studied alloys having carbon, silicon, manganese, and nitrogen contents approximating commercially produced material. Alloy-to-alloy variation was controlled closely. Their results agreed very closely with those of Rees et al., as shown in Fig. 76. Bechtoldt and Vacher[197] constructed a pseudobinary diagram for alloys containing 70% iron; it is shown in Fig. 77.

The equilibrium diagrams presented show that the leaner AISI austenitic alloys should be relatively free from sigma formation, which agrees with usual observations. Exceptions are materials containing some residual ferrite, a constituent which will transform to sigma. Another variation would be Type 302B which contains 2 to 3% silicon in an otherwise stable base. Silicon is a notorious sigma promoter and does render Type 302B susceptible to its formation. Sigma phase exists within 5.6 to 7.6 electron/atom (e/a) ratio limits. The conventional theory is that silicon broadens the stable composition range with respect to chromium by acting as a supplemental electron acceptor.[191,193] Sigma phase, in addition to requiring the correct e/a range, will not tolerate very great differences in atomic radii. Enough silicon can be accommodated to allow significant effects.

The equilibrium diagrams also show that the higher alloy AISI Fe-Ni-Cr steels, such as 25Cr-20Ni (Type 310), should be susceptible to sigma-phase formation. This, too, is in agreement with actual experience.

A number of alloys of the Fe-18Cr-10 to 12Ni type with fourth element additions (Types 316, 317, 321, 347) appear close to the boundary at 650°C (1200°F) and quite safe at 800°C (1475°F). Of the fourth element additions represented in these alloys, molybdenum, and to a lesser extent titanium, significantly promote sigma. In these iron-rich alloys, titanium and columbium tend to participate more in other intermediate phases.

Sigma-Phase Equilibria in Fe-Cr-Ni-Mo Alloys   Molybdenum-bearing alloys (Type 316, 317) are employed at elevated temperature and also exhibit sigma-forming propensity. Phase equilibria for Fe-Ni-Cr-Mo alloys containing 70% iron have been developed by Bechtoldt and Vacher.[197] The results are shown in Fig. 78. This shows that alloys in the

TABLE 20 Lattice Parameter and Composition of Sigma Phase (Tetragonal Structure)

Reference	Alloy	Lattice parameter, Å	Composition of phase Wt %					Formula
			Fe	Cr	Ni	Mo	Si	
Hall and Algie[193]	Fe-Cr	a_o = 8.799 c_o = 4.544						Fe-Cr
	Fe-Mo	a_o = 9.188 c_o = 4.812						Fe-Mo
Weigand and Doruk[194]	17Cr-11Ni-2Mo-0.4Ti	—	—	30	4.3	9	0.8	
	17Cr-11Ni-0.9Mo-0.5Ti	—	—	33	4.5	5.4	0.7	
Weiss and Stickler[124]	Type 316	a_o = 8.28-8.38 c_o = 4.597-4.599	55	29	5	11	—	$(FeNi)_x(CrMo)_y$
Blenkinsop and Nutting[215]	Type 316L	a_o = 9.21 c_o = 4.78						
Pitea[210] and Kane[211]	20Cr-25-34Ni-6.5-8Mo	a_o = 8.87 c_o = 4.61	35/37	17/26	15/21	21/28	*	
Morley and Kirkby[198]	25Cr-20Ni		40	46	9.4	—	3	

*Approximate average compositions. Ranges observed as shown.

TABLE 21 Lattice Parameter and Composition of Chi Phase (bcc-αMn Structure)

Reference	Alloy	Lattice parameter, Å	Composition of phase Wt %				Formula
			Fe	Cr	Ni	Mo	
Kasper[195]	56Fe-17Cr-27Mo	8.920					$Fe_{36}Cr_{12}Mo_{10}$
Koh[196]	67Fe-23Cr-10Mo	8.89	62	17	. . .	18	
	Type 317*	. . . .	58	25	4	10	
Kautz and Gerlach[134]	16Cr-16Ni-2Mo	8.862					$(FeNi)_{36}Cr_{18}Mo_4$
Weiss and Stickler[124]	Type 316	8.878	52	21	5	22	

*Residue analyses, said to be "mostly" chi, balance sigma.

TABLE 22 Structure and Composition of Laves Phase (Hexagonal Structure)

Reference	Alloy	Lattice parameter, Å	Composition of phase In wt. %				Formula
			Fe	Ni	Cr	Mo	
Bechtoldt and Vacher[197]	80%Fe 20%Mo	$a_0 = 4.744$ $c_0 = 7.257$	56	—	—	44	Fe_2Mo
Bechtoldt and Vacher[197]	70%Fe 4–9%Cr 9–18%Ni 8–12%Mo	—	46	4	3–6	44	
Weiss and Stickler[124]	Type 316	$a_0 = 4.73$ $c_0 = 7.72$	38	6	11	45	
Cihal and Jezek[174]	18%Cr 9%Ni 2%Cb	$a_0 = 4.824$ $c_0 = 7.855$	—	—	—	—	

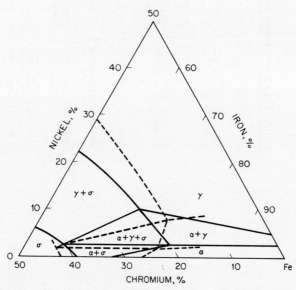

Fig. 75 Comparison of iron-rich corner of the Fe-Cr-Ni system at 650°C (1200°F) as defined by Schafmeister and Ergang[200] (solid lines) and Rees, et al.[202]

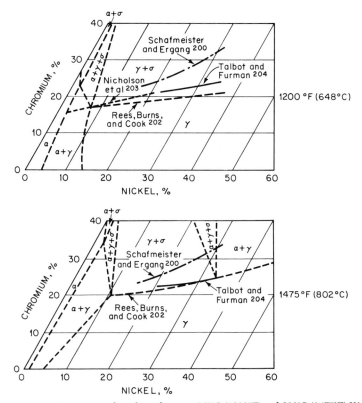

Fig. 76 Sigma-phase boundaries at 650°C (1200°F) and 800°C (1475°F).[204]

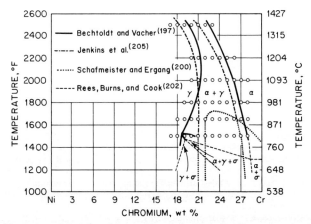

Fig. 77 Pseudobinary sigma-phase equilibrium diagram for Fe-Ni-Cr alloys containing 70% iron.[197]

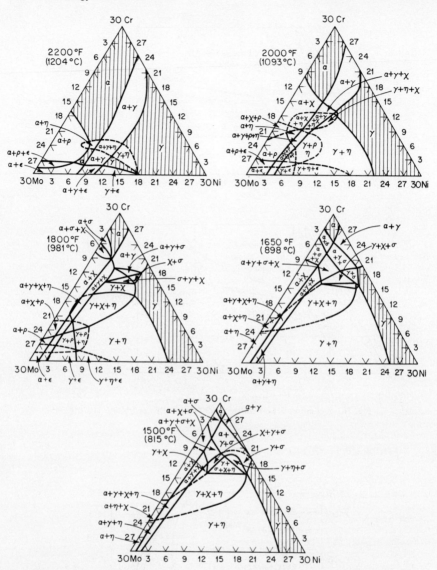

Fig. 78   Phase equilibrium for high-purity Fe-Cr-Ni-Mo alloys containing 70% iron.[197]

general Type 316-317 area can form sigma and chi, which will tend to give way to chi and Laves at higher molybdenum contents. The high-temperature diagrams in Fig. 78 show two phases not mentioned previously, ϵ (Fe$_3$Mo$_2$) and ρ. These occur in alloys with high-molybdenum and low-chromium contents and are not expected in austenitic stainless steels.

Quantitative Estimation of Sigma-Forming Tendency   In a manner analogous to estimating ferrite-austenite balance, attempts have been made to calculate the sigma-forming tendency of austenitic alloys.

The earliest computation relationship was by Gow and Harder.[206] They employed a simple relationship to estimate sigma-forming tendency:

$$\text{Ratio factor} = \frac{\%Cr - 16(\%C)}{\%Ni} \tag{6}$$

If the ratio factor was above 1.7, the alloys would form sigma. In view of its simplicity, this relationship is not much help with commercial alloys containing other elements. Note that it does take into account the effect of carbon, which is intended to suppress sigma formation.

In complex nickel-based austenitic superalloys, computation of an electron vacancy number $\bar{N}_v$ has been used to estimate sigma-forming tendency. This involves multiplying the electron vacancy for each element by its *atomic percent*. According to Woodyatt et al.,[207]

$$\bar{N}_v = 0.66Ni + 1.71Co + 2.66Fe + 4.66(Cr+Mo+W) + 5.66V + 6.66Zr + 10.66Cb \tag{7}$$

If $\bar{N}_v$ is above 2.52, the alloy should form sigma. Woodyatt et al. calculated $\bar{N}_v$ for Type 310 stainless steel to be 2.88, which agrees with the sigma-forming behavior of the alloy.

The computation of $\bar{N}_v$ is not as straightforward as it seems since the atomic percentages employed are those in the matrix. Changes in matrix concentration caused by preceding precipitation of other phases must be estimated accurately and accounted for, which may not be an easy task. Interstitial elements do not appear in Eq. (7) because it is presumed they will have precipitated. The same is true of titanium. In any stainless steels where such pre-sigma precipitation is not necessarily expected, some inaccuracy would be introduced. Some modification of the coefficients has been suggested. Mihalisin et al.[208] suggest a coefficient of 9.66 for molybdenum and tungsten.

This technique has not been used to any great extent to predict sigma in austenitic stainless steels. Recently, deBarbadillo[83] studied some experimental Fe-Cr-Co-Ni-Mo alloys which had $\bar{N}_v$ numbers in the range 2.95 to 3.05. As suggested by these numbers, the alloys formed sigma. The electron vacancy numbers (using a coefficient of 9.66 for molybdenum) correlated reasonably well with the resolution temperatures of the sigma. Although $\bar{N}_v$ originally was intended only to indicate if sigma would form, in this case it also provided a reasonable indication of sigma stability.

The most recent quantitative expression for sigma is that determined by Hull.[209] Hull related an "equivalent Cr" number to the loss in notched-impact bend ductility resulting from long-time exposure at 816°C (1500°F). Hull's alloys were based on 16Cr-20Ni-10Mn-0.25Mo, referred to as Kromarc* stainless steels. These alloys form both sigma and chi. Hull studied chill-cast samples of various alloys and developed the element coefficients by multiple regression analysis. His expression is

$$\text{Equivalent Cr} = Cr + 0.31Mn + 1.76Mo + 0.97W + 2.02V + 1.58Si + 2.44Ti$$
$$+ 1.70Cb + 1.22Ta - 0.266Ni - 0.177Co \tag{8}$$

As noted previously, the conditions for intermediate phase formation are restricted by dual constraints of either electron/atom ratio or atom size effects, or both. The matrix chemistry will have an effect, therefore expressions for one base chemistry may not translate well into another. However, the coefficients do give an indication of the relative effects of the various elements.

The Effect of Sigma   The most notorious effect of sigma is reduction of toughness. The effect on ambient-temperature toughness is shown in Fig. 79. Elevated-temperature toughness may also suffer, depending on morphology. However, this adverse effect is usually considered to be a problem only below 595°C (1000°F) or 650°C (1200°F).

Chemically, sigma is not resistant to strongly oxidizing media like hot concentrated nitric acid. In such a medium, an alloy with intergranular sigma will undergo intergranular corrosion.[127]

If conditions of formation are such that the sigma is finely dispersed within the grains, an increase in both ambient- and elevated-temperature strength can result. At very low strain rates, however, this effect may not be realized. The apparent strength may be reduced instead.[193,212]

Metallurgical Factors Affecting Sigma Formation   Cold-working tends to accelerate most precipitation reactions in austenitic stainless steels. This is also true in the case of sigma

*Trademark of Westinghouse Electric Corp.

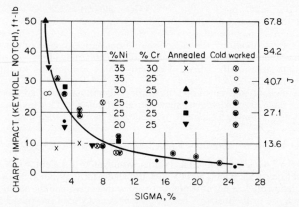

Fig. 79 Effect of sigma-phase formation on ambient-temperature impact strength of Fe-Ni-Cr alloy.[204]

formation. Data from Emmanuel[213] is shown in Fig. 80. However, it has been noted that the effect of cold-work is not straightforward. Sigma nucleates first at triple points and then at grain boundaries. The accelerating effect of cold-work has been specifically related to recrystallization to a fine grain size during the sigma-forming exposure.[124,214,215] Thus, fairly significant deformation would be expected before an effect would be observed.

Prior deformation usually also accelerates later intragranular sigma formation. Blenkinsop and Nutting[215] have suggested that this effect is related to the deformation stability and stacking-fault energy of the alloy, with more stable materials requiring greater deformation before the effect is observed. Deformation during exposure, as under creep conditions, also can promote intragranular sigma. The intragranular sigma is often plate-like, giving the appearance of needles.

Prior annealing temperature also influences the kinetics of sigma formation. Higher annealing temperatures usually retard sigma formation, an effect which is related to increased grain size and associated longer diffusion paths.[124,198] An exception would be if the constitution of the alloy is such that increasing the annealing temperature leads to the formation of delta ferrite, from which sigma will form more rapidly.[194] In fact, it was long believed that sigma could form only from ferrite. Because of the higher chromium content of ferrite, the sigma kinetics are enhanced considerably. Figure 81 shows formation of sigma phase in an island of delta ferrite. It is now well accepted that sigma can nucleate from austenite as well. The current debate is whether such nucleation is direct or

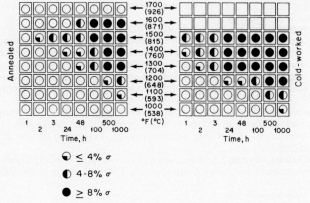

Fig. 80 Effect of 40% cold-work on rate of formation of sigma phase in 25Cr-20Ni stainless steel.[213]

requires previous $M_{23}C_6$ precipitation. There is ample evidence that either can occur, depending on the alloy and precipitation conditions.

Sigma formation from austenite can assume many forms. Figure 82 shows both intergranular sigma (and some other intermediate phase) and carbide in Type 314 stainless steel which had been in service at 871 to 927°C (1600°F to 1700°F) for 3500 h. This is

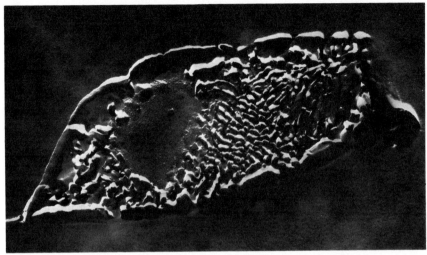

Fig. 81   Replica electron micrograph showing sigma formation in delta ferrite.

particularly heavy grain-boundary precipitation. Less severe cases will have an appearance very similar to $M_{23}C_6$ sensitized stainless steel.

Figure 83 shows very gross sigma formation in a 30Cr-25Ni-Fe alloy, which resulted from exposure at 800°C (1475°F) for 3000 h. A lower chromium alloy, 25%, exposed at 650°C (1200°F) for 3000 h developed much less sigma, as shown in Fig. 84. Precipitation of carbide on deformation planes caused by prior cold-working is also visable.

In alloys based primarily on Fe-Ni-Cr, sigma phase takes some time to form. Once formed, it can usually be redissolved at normal annealing temperatures (Table 2). In alloys containing large amounts of other elements, the pattern can be quite different. For example, in alloys containing 20Cr-24 to 32Ni-6.5 to 8Mo, sigma phase can precipitate even during hot-rolling cycles. A typical structure is shown in Fig. 85. This sigma is quite stable, and resolution does not occur below 1177°C (2150°F) or 1216°C (2200°F). This increased stability agrees with the apparent correlation between stability and N_r discussed previously.

Another way to consider the increased sigma stability caused by molybdenum is through examination of Fig. 78. Although these diagrams actually apply to alloys containing 70% iron, we can generalize an alloy of interest as being located somewhere near the top corner. As temperature is increased, intermediate phase fields can be visualized as receding toward the lower left corner. Higher molybdenum contents will place the alloy closer to the lower left corner, so that higher temperatures are required before the alloy will be left outside the intermediate phase fields. Addition of either nickel or chromium will move an alloy away from the lower left corner. Chromium, however, will do this at the expense of rendering the alloy ferritic or duplex at high temperatures.

TIME-TEMPERATURE-PRECIPITATION STUDIES IN STAINLESS STEELS

Understanding of the numerous precipitation processes in stainless steels is enhanced by reviewing specific published data.

Fe-Ni-Cr Alloys   The leaner alloys (Types 301, 302, 304) have been discussed ade-

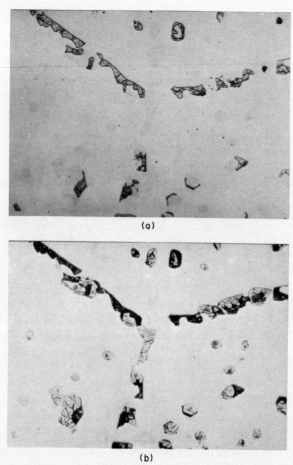

(a)

(b)

Fig. 82 Structure of Type 314 stainless steel after 3500 h at 871 to 927°C (1600° to 1700°F). (a) Etched to reveal intermediate phases. (b) Etched to darken intermediate phases and reveal carbide.

quately in the previous section on $M_{23}C_6$ precipitation, since $M_{23}C_6$ is usually the precipitating constituent.

Sigma phase in alloys of the Type 310 class has been studied extensively because of the well-known sigma-forming tendency of these alloys and also because they are used primarily at elevated temperatures. Work by White and LeMay[216] is summarized in Fig. 86. Their results concerning sigma phase agree fairly well with those of Emmanuel,[213] (Fig. 80) except that Fig. 86 also shows early carbide precipitation and late formation of ferrite. Transient transformation of sigma to ferrite had previously been reported by Dulis and Smith[217] and Morley and Kirkby[198] in connection with resolution of sigma phase at annealing temperatures.

Fe-Ni-Cr-Ti Alloys   Precipitation in Type 321 stainless steel, as observed by Grot and Spruiell,[170] is shown in Fig. 87. They did not find sigma phase, and cold-working 20% did not alter kinetics appreciably. This is consistent with previous discussion, although sigma formation would not be entirely unexpected. Weigand and Doruk[194] (Fig. 88) did report sigma in a similar alloy. This difference could be due to analytical technique.

Figures 88a and b show the effect of ferrite. Raising the annealing temperature (Fig. 88b) formed large amounts of ferrite, which accelerated subsequent precipitation.

Fe-Ni-Cr-Cb Alloys   Bungardt and Lennartz[141] represented precipitation in Fe-18Cr-16Ni-0.8Cb as shown in Fig. 89. At the lower temperature, 650°C (1200°F), only $M_{23}C_6$

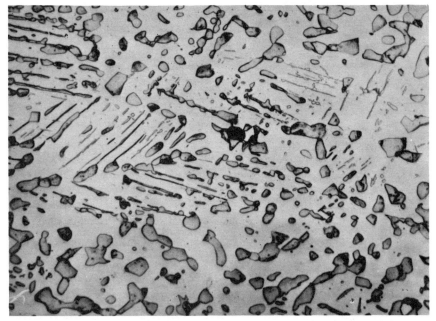

Fig. 83   Cold-worked Fe-30Cr-25Ni alloy after heating 3000 h at 800°C (1475°F).

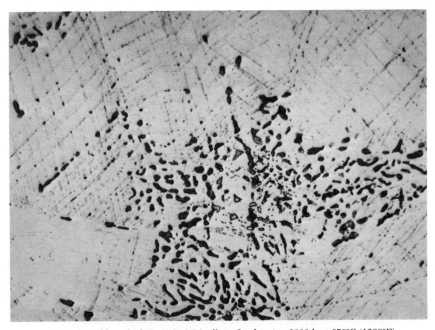

Fig. 84   Cold-worked Fe-25Cr-25Ni alloy after heating 3000 h at 650°C (1200°F).

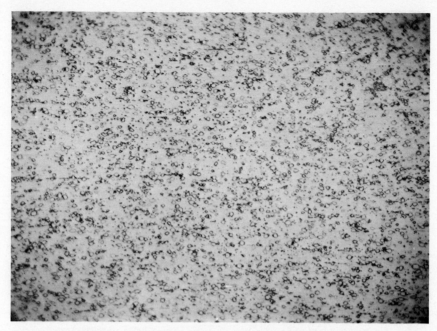

Fig. 85   Structure of hot-rolled alloy containing 20Cr-24Ni-6.5Mo.

and CbC formed. At the higher temperature, 800°C (1472°F), $M_{23}C_6$ was suppressed. When Bungardt and Lennartz increased nickel content to 25%, G phase formed after long times at 800°C (1473°F). This is consistent with the trend predicted by Table 19 as observed by looking down the columbium column.

These results agree fairly well with those of Cihal and Jezek[174] who studied 18Cr-9Ni-1Cb, except that Cihal and Jezek found sigma phase after aging at 750°C (1382°F). Cihal and Jezek's results are shown in Table 23. When Cb content was raised to 2%, both Laves phase and M_6C precipitated. They found Laves phase could be redissolved above 1000°C (1832°F), whereas the M_6C was stable to at least 1200°C (2192°F). This M_6C solution temperature is higher than that reported by Scharfstein and Maniar[139] in a 33% Ni alloy.

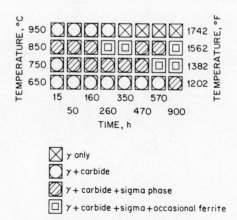

Fig. 86   Time-temperature-precipitation diagram for Type 310 stainless steel.[216]

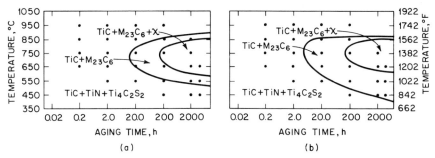

Fig. 87 Time-temperature-precipitation diagrams for Type 321 stainless steel containing 0.06C-0.5Ti.[170] (a) Annealed 1093°C (2000°F). (b) 20% cold-work.

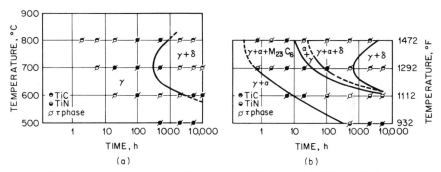

Fig. 88 Time-temperature-precipitation diagrams for 0.09C-18Cr-11Ni-0.52Ti alloy.[194] (a) Annealed at 1050°C (1922°F). (b) Annealed at 1400°C (2552°F).

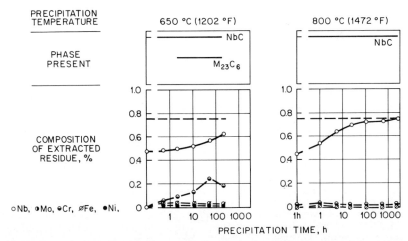

Fig. 89 Precipitation in Fe-16Cr-16Ni-0.8Cb alloy exposed at 650°C (1200°F) and 800°C (1472°F) after annealing at 1200°C (2192°F). The horizontal dashed line represents the percent of columbium present in steel.[141]

TABLE 23   Precipitates in Fe-18Cr-9Ni-Cb Alloys[174]

Solution treatment	Aging, °C/h (°F/h)	1%Cb	2%Cb
1050°C/30 min (1922°F/30 min)		NbC	$NbC + L + M_6C$
	550/32 (1022/32)	NbC	$NbC + L + M_6C$
	850/4 (1562/4)	NbC	$NbC + L + M_6C$
1250°C/1 h (2282°F/1 h)		NbC	NbC
	550/72 (1022/72)	$NbC + Cr_{23}C_6$	$NbC + Cr_{23}C_6 + M_6C'$ vw
	650/0.5 (1202/0.5)	n	$NbC + M_6C'$ w
	650/4 (1202/4)	$NbC + Cr_{23}C_6$	$NbC + M_6C'$ w
	650/32 (1202/32)	$NbC + Cr_{23}C_6$	$NbC + M_6C'$ w + σ
	650/72 (1202/72)	$NbC + Cr_{23}C_6$ w	$NbC + M_6C'$ w + σw + L vw
	650/500 (1202/500)	n	$NbC + M_6C'$ w + σ + L
	750/72 (1382/72)	$NbC + \sigma$	$NbC + M_6C + L$
	750/500 (1382/500)	$NbC + \sigma$	$NbC + M_6C + L$
	850/48 (1562/48)	NbC	$NbC + M_6C + L$
	850/500 (1562/500)	n	$NbC + M_6C + L$
	950/72 (1742/72)	n	$NbC + M_6C + L$
1320°C/10 min (2408°F/10 min)		NbC	NbC + L w
	475/500 (487/500)	n	NbC
	550/4 (1022/4)	$NbC + Cr_{23}C_6$ w	NbC + L w
	550/72 (1022/72)	$NbC + Cr_{23}C_6$ w	NbC + L w
	650/4 (1202/4)	$NbC + Cr_{23}C_6$	$NbC + M_6C'$
	650/32 (1202/32)	n	$NbC + M_6C' + \sigma$
	650/72 (1202/72)	$NbC + Cr_{23}C_6$	$NbC + M_6C' + \sigma$
	750/4 (1382/4)	n	$NbC + L$ w $+ M_6C$ w $+ \sigma$
	750/72 (1382/72)	$NbC + \sigma + Cr_{23}C_6$ vw	$NbC + L + M_6C + \sigma$
	750/500 (1382/500)	$NbC + \sigma$	$NbC + L + M_6C + \sigma$
	850/4 (1562/4)	n	$NbC + L + M_6C$
	850/48 (1562/48)	$NbC + \sigma + L$	$NbC + L + M_6C$
	850/500 (1562/500)	n	$NbC + L + M_6C$
	1150/16 (2102/16)	n	$NbC + M_6C$

L—Laves phase $[Fe,Cr]_2Nb$
M_6C carbide—Fe_3Nb_3C
M_6C' carbide $[Fe,Cr]_3Nb_3C$
n—no test
w—weak
vw—very weak diffraction lines

Fe-Ni-Cr-Mo Alloys Precipitation-time-temperature diagrams for Type 316L (0.023%C) stainless steel are shown in Fig. 90. (Although the graphs are taken from two different references, the material is the same.) Figure 90 reflects an effect mentioned previously, the acceleration of precipitation reactions by cold-work, here most noticeable in the case of $M_{23}C_6$ and sigma phase. Not as obvious is the retarding effect of higher annealing temperature on sigma-phase formation.

Weiss and Stickler[124] also studied Type 316 (0.06%C) stainless steel. The results are shown in Fig. 91. If these data are compared with Fig. 90a, it can be seen that raising the carbon content increased the kinetics of $M_{23}C_6$ precipitation but suppressed formation of M_6C and the intermediate phases sigma, chi, and Laves (eta). Results of Blenkinsop and Nutting[215] differ some from those of Figs. 90 and 91, in that the relative kinetics of the intermediate phases and $M_{23}C_6$ are different. Blenkinsop and Nutting, who studied Type 316L, reported that $M_{23}C_6$ precipitation precedes sigma only at high precipitation temperatures. White and LeMay,[218] using only metallographic techniques, reported both ferrite and $M_{23}C_6$ formed prior to sigma phase. They also reported sigma nucleated from carbide, not from the ferrite. Weigand and Doruk's data are shown in Fig. 92.[194] With 2% molybdenum, $M_{23}C_6$ was found only at precipitation temperatures below those where the intermediate phases form. This discrepancy could be related to the small amount of titanium present. Weigand and Doruk's results agree fairly well with those of Weiss and

Stickler. Figure 92 shows the effect of increasing molybdenum on promoting Laves phase (eta).

This tendency is more evident in the 5% Mo alloys investigated by Thier and Baumel,[172] as shown in Fig. 93. Thier and Baumel investigated the effect of nitrogen (0.039, 0.069, 0.145, and 0.247%) and found the relative kinetics shifted with increasing nitrogen content. As shown, nitrogen suppressed sigma, chi, and particularly Laves phase in favor of M_6C formation. This pattern is complicated by the fact that the alloys contained ferrite which affected precipitation, particularly at the lower nitrogen contents.

The trends expressed in Figs. 92 and 93 that high-molybdenum-content steels tend to precipitate chi and Laves phases at the expense of sigma phase are an apparent contradiction to Fig. 85, which showed a phase identified as sigma in an alloy containing 20Cr-24Ni-6.5Mo. The sigma in higher-nickel-content alloys is described in Table 20; the composition is considerably different. Clearly, precipitation in higher-nickel alloys is different, and more work will be required for thorough understanding. It could be that there are other phases involved in the precipitation sequence.

Fe-Ni-Cr-Mo Alloys With Other Additions Grot and Spruiell[170] investigated a Type 316 stainless steel modified with 0.29% titanium. $M_{23}C_6$ precipitation was retarded and sigma-chi formation was slightly accelerated, as compared with Type 316.

Bungardt and Lennartz[141] investigated molybdenum additions to base chemistries containing 0.06C-16Cr-16 or 25Ni-0.8Cb. They found addition of molybdenum (up to 6%) to the 16% Ni alloy promoted the formation of chi and Laves phase and eliminated $M_{23}C_6$ precipitation. Their alloys were aged at 650°C (1200°F) and 850°C (1562°F). Although chi

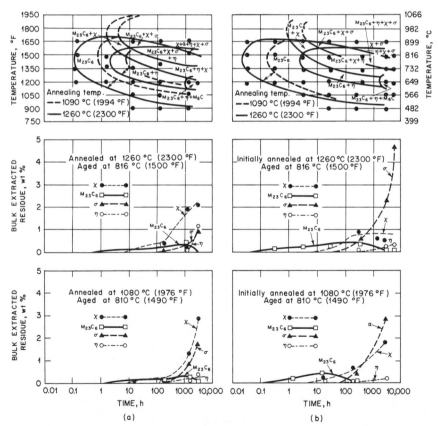

Fig. 90 Time-temperature-precipitation diagrams for Type 316L stainless steel.[124,50] (a) Annealed. (b) Cold-worked 20%.

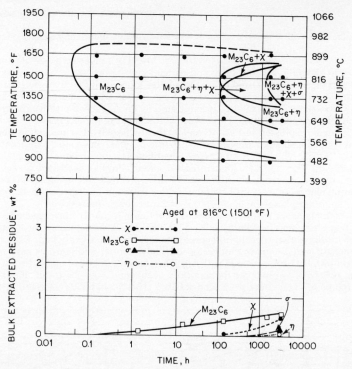

Fig. 91 Time-temperature-precipitation diagram for Type 316 stainless steel initially annealed at 1260°C (2300°F).[124]

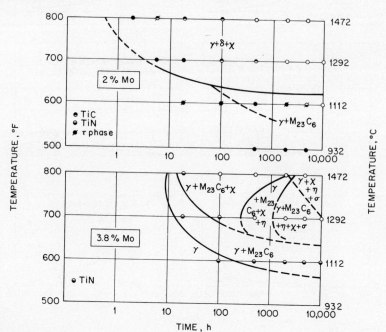

Fig. 92 Effect of molybdenum on time-temperature-precipitation diagrams for 17Cr-13Ni-Mo-0.06C alloys initially annealed at 1050 to 1070°C (1922 to 1958°F). The alloys contain 0.02 to 0.04% titanium.[194]

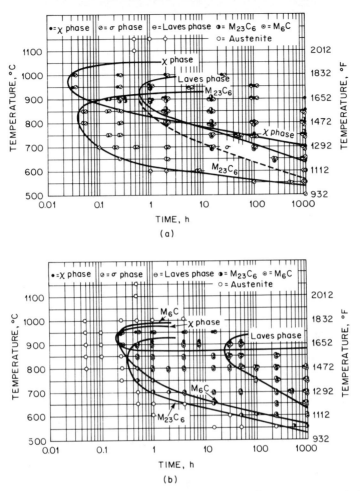

Fig. 93 Time-temperature-precipitation diagrams for 0.05C-17Cr-13Ni-5Mo alloys with different nitrogen contents.[172] (*a*) 0.039% nitrogen annealed at 1100°C (2012°F). (*b*) 0.145% nitrogen annealed at 1150°C (2102°F).

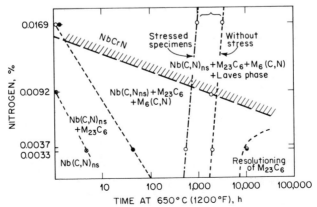

Fig. 94 Precipitation in 0.1C-16Cr-16Ni-2Mo-0.5Cb stainless steel.[219] (ns = not solutioned).

TABLE 24 Stress-Relief Heat Treatments for Austenitic Stainless Steels[220]

Anticipated service environment, or other reason for treatment	Suggested thermal treatment[a] (entered in order of decreasing preference)		
	Extra-low-carbon grades, such as Types 304L and 316L	Stabilized grades, such as Types 318, 321, and 347	Unstabilized grades, such as Types 304 and 316
Severe stress corrosion	A, B	B, A	[b]
Moderate stress corrosion	A, B, C	B, A, C	C[b]
Mild stress corrosion	A, B, C, E, F	B, A, C, E, F	C, F
Remove peak stresses only	F	F	F
No stress corrosion	None required	None required	None required
Intergranular corrosion	A, C[c]	A, C, B[c]	C
Stress relief after severe forming	A, C	A, C	C
Relief between forming operations	A, B, C	B, A, C	C[d]
Structural soundness[e]	A, C, B	A, C, B	C
Dimensional stability	G	G	G

[a]Key to letter designations of treatments:
A—Anneal at 1950 to 2050°F (1063 to 1120°C) slow cool.
B—Stress relieve at 1650°F (898°C) slow cool.
C—Anneal at 1950 to 2050°F (1063 to 1120°C) quench[f]
D—Stress relieve at 1650°F (898°C) quench[f]
E—Stress relieve at 900 to 1200°F (482 to 648°C) slow cool.
F—Stress relieve at below 900°F (482°C) slow cool.
G—Stress relieve at 400 to 900°F (204 to 482°C) slow cool.
(Usual time, 4 h/in. (25.4 mm) of section.)
[b]To allow the optimum stress-relieving treatment, the use of stabilized or extra-low-carbon grades is recommended.
[c]In most instances, no heat treatment is required, but where fabrication procedures may have sensitized the stainless steel the heat treatments noted may be employed.
[d]Treatment A, B or D also may be used, if followed by treatment C when forming is completed.
[e]Where severe fabricating stresses coupled with high service loading may cause cracking. Also, after welding heavy sections.
[f]Or cool rapidly.

and Laves phases were formed at both temperatures, chi phase was favored at 650°C (1200°F) whereas Laves was predominant at 850°C (1562°F). In the 25% Ni alloys, Laves phase formation at 850°C (1562°F) was suppressed in favor of M_6C precipitation. This trend is consistent with the trends in Table 19. In the higher-nickel alloys, precipitation of $M_{23}C_6$ at 650°C (1200°F) was more persistent. This effect of nickel agrees with that reported by Scharfstein and Maniar[139] for higher-nickel-content alloys. Bungardt and Lennartz found no sigma in any of their alloys.

Gerlach[219] has summarized precipitation in 0.1C-16Cr-16Ni-0.5Cb as shown in Fig. 94. He correlated precipitation at 650°C (1200°F) with nitrogen content. The greater stability of M_6C with increasing nitrogen content is attributed to previously noted solubility in M_6C, here referred to as $M_6(CN)$. The NbCrN shaded line represents a "double nitride" or Z phase which forms from Cb(CN) in high-nitrogen steels. Again, no sigma is reported. Sigma in such Fe-Cr-Ni-Mo-Cb steels might be expected if nickel or carbon contents were significantly reduced.

SUMMARY OF CONSTITUTION EFFECTS ON HEAT TREATMENT

The usual annealing treatments were described in Table 2. In order to avoid undesirable carbide precipitation, steels are rapidly cooled after annealing, the cooling medium depending on the section size and distortion considerations which may exist. Rapid cooling of the stabilized grades is not critical.

The purpose of the anneal may be to eliminate prior work or to dissolve any carbides which may be present, or both. The temperature ranges shown in Table 2 are employed for either intermediate or final annealing. The specific time-temperature combinations represent a compromise between achieving the primary purpose and avoiding excessive grain growth. Thin sections are commonly annealed 3 to 5 min. per 0.1 in. [2.54 mm] of thickness.

As noted in the section on carbide precipitation, the resistance of the stabilized grades to intergranular $M_{23}C_6$ precipitation can be improved by a lower temperature stabilizing heat treatment. This is more commonly applied to titanium-stabilized Type 321 than to columbium-stabilized Type 347.

Also discussed in the section on carbide precipitation was the fact that the creep behavior of the stabilized grades can be enhanced by utilizing higher-than-usual annealing treatments. This has received formal recognition with H category steels (see Chapter 21 for further details).

TABLE 25   Effect of Stress-Relief Treatments[221]

		Stress-relief heat treatment			
Material	Condition	200–400°C (392–752°F) ~ 40% peak†	550–650°C (1022–1202°F) ~ 35%†	850–900°C (1562–1652°F) ~ 85%†	950–1050°C (1742–1922°F) ~ 95%†
Type 304	SHT, SA*	NME	IGP	IGP	IGP(C)
	Weldments*	NME	IGP and SIP	IGP and SIP	IGP(C) and SIP(H)
Type 321	SHT, SA	NME	NME	NME	NME
	Weldments		SIP	SIP	SIP(H)
Type 304L	SHT, SA and weldments	NME	NME	NME	NME
Type 316	SHT, SA* and weldments*	NME	IGP	IGP	IGP(C)
Type 316 + Ti	SHT, SA, and weldments	NME	NME	NME	NME
Type 316L	SHT, SA, and weldments	NME	NME	NME	NME

SHT— Solution heat treatment, rapidly cooled from ~1050°C (1922°F).
SA— Solution annealed, slowly cooled from ~1050°C (1922°F).
IGP— Intergranular precipitation of chromium carbide (sensitization).
NME— No metallurgical effect.
SIP— Strain-induced precipitation of carbides, in weldments over 0.75 in. (19 mm).
(H)— During heating.
(C)— During cooling (assumed always to be slow).
*Likely to be sensitized prior to stress relief, unless of small section size and/or low carbon content.
†Degree of stress reduction.

In actual stainless steel structures, residual stresses are sometimes introduced which may reduce the performance of the structure. These residual stresses can arise from either welding or forming operations. These stresses can be harmful from the standpoint of stress-corrosion behavior, fatigue performance, or dimensional stability. Because of this, there is often an interest in applying stress-relieving treatments.

As discussed in this chapter, a great many metallurgical processes can occur in austenitic stainless steels. This means that any final heat treatment should be considered very carefully. The decision whether or not to stress-relieve will depend on the particular service conditions. Sangdahl[220] has summarized the various types of treatment that can be employed (Table 24). Cole and Jones[221] have listed the effects which can occur (Table 25). Stress-relief treatments must be carefully considered, and if they can be anticipated, low-carbon grades are preferable.

REFERENCES

1. American Iron and Steel Institute Statistics.
2. Bain, E. C., and R. H. Aborn: in "Metals Handbook," p. 1194, American Society for Metals, Metals Park, Ohio, 1948.
3. Bozorth, A.: "Ferromagnetism," Van Nostrand, New York, 1968.
4. Hume-Rothery, W., J. W. Christian, and W. B. Pearson: "Metallurgical Equilibrium Diagrams," pp. 237–240, The Institute of Physics, London, 1952.
5. Hoselitz, K., and W. Sucksmith: *Proc. Roy. Soc. London*, vol. 181, p. 303, 1943.
6. Sykes, W. P.: in "Metals Handbook," p. 1210, American Society for Metals, Metals Park, Ohio, 1948.
7. Rickett, R. L.: *ibid.*, p. 1217.
8. Fink, W. L., and W. E. Willey: *ibid.*, p. 1161.
9. Comstock, G. F., and J. C. Southard: *ibid.*, p. 1219.
10. Parke, R. M.: *ibid.*, p. 1186.
11. Colombier, L., and J. Hochmann: "Stainless and Heat Resisting Steel," St. Martins, London, pp. 1–24, 1968.
12. Owens, E. A., and Y. H. Liu: *J. Iron Steel Inst., London*, vol. 163, p. 132, 1949.
13. McGuire, F. T., and A. R. Troiano: in "Metals Handbook," p. 1210, American Society for Metals, Metals Park, Ohio, 1948.
14. Colombier, L., and J. Hochmann: *loc. cit.*, pp. 99–101.
15. Bungart, E., E. Junze, and E. Horn: *Arch. Eisenhuettenwes.*, vol. 29, p. 193, 1950.
16. Miller, O. O.: "Nickel Alloy Steel Data Book," sec. 8, app. B, p. 15, The International Nickel Co., New York, 1967.
17. Jones, F. W., and W. I. Pumphrey: *J. Iron Steel Inst., London*, vol. 163, p. 121, 1949.
18. Troiano, A. R., and F. T. McGuire: *Trans Am. Soc. Met.*, vol. 31, p. 340, 1943.
19. Crafts, W.: in "Metals Handbook," p. 459, American Society for Metals, Metals Park, Ohio, 1948.
20. Bain, E. C.: "Functions of the Alloying Elements in Steel," American Society for Metals, Metals Park, Ohio, 1939.
21. Herzig, A. J.: in "Metals Handbook," p. 469, American Society for Metals, Metals Park, Ohio, 1948.
22. Greiner, E. S.: *ibid.*, p. 477.
23. Bain, E. C., and R. H. Aborn: *ibid.*, p. 1261.
24. "Metals Handbook," vol. 2, p. 244, American Society for Metals, Metals Park, Ohio, 1964.
25. "Steel Products Manual, "Stainless and Heat Resisting Steels," American Iron and Steel Institute, New York, 1974.
26. Pugh, J. W., and J. D. Nisbet: *Trans. Am. Inst. Min. Metall. Pet. Eng.*, vol. 188, p. 273, 1950.
27. Speich, G. R.: in "Metals Handbook," vol. 8, p. 425, American Society for Metals, Metals Park, Ohio, 1973.
28. Kane, R. H.: Unpublished research, The International Nickel Co., Inc., New York, 1974.
29. Franks, R., W. O. Binder, and C. R. Bishop: *Trans. Am. Soc. Met.*, vol. 29, 1941.
30. Heger, J. J.: *ASTM Spec. Tech. Publ. 369*, p. 54, 1965.
31. Kinzel, A. B., and R. Franks: "Alloys of Iron and Chromium," vol. II, p. 277, McGraw-Hill, New York, 1940.
32. Binder, W. O., R. Franks, and J. Thompson: *Trans. Am. Soc. Met.*, vol. 47, pp. 231–266, 1955.
33. Turkdogan, E. T., and S. Ignatowicz: "The Physical Chemistry of Metallic Solutions and Intermetallic Compounds Symposium," vol. 2, pp. 192–198, Chemical Publishing Co., New York, 1960.
34. Carney, D. J.: "Regional Technical Meetings," pp. 103–113, Am. Iron Steel Inst., 1955.
35. Schaeffler, A. L.: *Met. Prog.*, vol. 56, p. 680, November 1969.
36. DeLong, W. B.: *Met. Prog.*, vol. 77, p. 98, February 1960.
37. Pryce, L., and K. W. Andrews: *J. Iron Steel Inst., London*, vol. 195, p. 145, 1960.

38. Hammond, C. M.: *ASTM Spec. Tech. Publ. 369,* p. 48, 1965.
39. Stokowiec, Z., C. G. Holland, A. H. Dean, and A. C. Everill: *Iron Steel Inst. London Publ. 117,* pp. 19–21, 1969.
40. Irvine, K. J., D. T. Llewellyn, and F. B. Pickering: *J. Iron Steel Inst., London,* vol. 192, pp. 227–228, 1959.
41. Eichelman, G. H., and F. C. Hull: *Trans. Am. Soc. Met.,* vol. 45, pp. 77–95, 1953.
42. Thielemann, R. H.: *Am. Soc. Test. Mater. Proc.,* vol. 40, p. 788, 1940.
43. Newell, W. D., and M. Fleischman: U. S. Patent 2,118,683, 1938.
44. Binder, W. D., C. M. Brown, and R. Franks: *Trans. Am. Soc. Met.,* vol. 41, p. 1301, 1949.
45. Campbell, H.: *Weld J.,* vol. 54, no. 12, pp. 867–871, 1975.
46. Ridley, N.: *J. Iron Steel Inst., London,* vol. 209, pt. 5, p. 396, 1971.
47. Otte, H. M.: *Acta Metall.,* vol. 5, p. 614, 1957.
48. Cina, J.: *J. Iron Steel Inst., London,* vol. 177, p. 406, 1954.
49. Fiedler, H. C., B. L. Averbach, and M. Cohen: *Trans. Am. Soc. Met.,* vol. 47, p. 267, 1955.
50. Spitznagel, J. A., and R. Stickler: *Metall. Trans.,* vol. 5, p. 1363, 1974.
51. Irvine, K. J., T. Gladman, and F. B. Pickering: *J. Iron Steel Inst., London,* p. 1017, 1969.
52. Irvine, K. J., D. T. Llewellyn, and F. B. Pickering: *J. Iron Steel Inst., London,* vol. 199, p. 153, 1961.
53. Krauss, G., and A. R. Marder: *Metall. Trans.,* vol. 2, p. 2343, 1971.
54. Reed, R. P., and F. J. Breedis: *ASTM Spec. Tech. Publ. 387,* pp. 60–132, 1966.
55. Quarrell, A. G.: "The Structure of Metals," p. 75, Institution of Metallurgists, London, 1959.
56. Cottrell, A. H.: "Dislocations and Plastic Flow in Crystals," Clarendon Press, London, 1953.
57. Dieter, G. E.: "Mechanical Metallurgy," pp. 108–109, McGraw-Hill, New York, 1961.
58. Breedis, J. F.: *Trans. Am. Inst. Min. Metall. Pet. Eng.,* vol. 230, p. 1583, 1964.
59. Friedel, J.: "Dislocations," p. 139, Addison-Wesley, New York, 1964.
60. Christian, J. W.: "The Theory of Transformations in Metals and Alloys," p. 122, Pergamon, New York, 1965.
61. Read, W. T.: "Dislocations in Crystals," McGraw-Hill, New York, 1953.
62. Schramm, R. E., and R. P. Reed: *Metall. Trans.,* vol. 6A, p. 1345, 1975.
63. Whelan, M. J., P. B. Hirsch, R. W. Horne, and W. Bollmann: *Proc. Roy. Soc. London, Ser. A,* vol. 240, pp. 524–538, 1957.
64. Whelan, M. J.: *Proc. Roy. Soc. London, Ser. A,* vol. 249, p. 114, 1959.
65. Swann, P. R.: *Corrosion,* vol. 19, pp. 102t–112t, 1963.
66. Douglass, D. L., G. Thomas, and W. R. Roser: *Corrosion,* vol. 20, pp. 15t–28t, 1964.
67. Dulieu, D., and J. Nutting: *Iron Steel Inst., London, Spec. Rept. 86,* pp. 140–145, The Iron and Steel Institute, London, 1964.
68. Silcock, J. M., R. W. Rookes, and J. Barford: *J. Iron Steel Inst., London,* vol. 204, pp. 623–627, 1966.
69. Clement, A., N. Clement, and P. Coulomb: *Phys. Status Solidi,* vol. 21, pp. K97–K98, 1967.
70. Thomas, B., and G. Henry: *Mem. Sci. Rev. Metall.,* vol. 64, pp. 625–636, 1967.
71. Thomas, B. J.: *Met. Corros.-Ind.,* no. 532, pp. 405–438, 1969.
72. Vingsbro, O.: *Acta Metall.,* vol. 15, pp. 615–621, 1967.
73. Fawley, R., M. A. Quader, and R. A. Dodd: *Trans. Am. Inst. Min. Metall. Pet. Eng.,* vol. 242, pp. 771–776, 1968.
74. Latanision, R. M., and A. W. Ruff, Jr.: *J. Appl. Phys.,* vol. 40, pp. 2716–2720, 1969.
75. Murr, L. E.: *Thin Solid Films,* vol. 4, pp. 389–412, 1969.
76. LeCroisey, F., and B. Thomas: *Phys. Status Solidi A,* vol. 2, pp. K217–K220, 1970.
77. Latanision, R. M., and A. W. Ruff, Jr.: *Metall. Trans,* vol. 2, pp. 505–509, 1971.
78. Butakova, E. D., K. A. Malyshev, and N. I. Noskova: *Fiz. Met. Metalloved.,* vol. 35, no. 3, pp. 662–664, 1973.
79. Zackay, V. F., E. R. Parker, D. Fahr, and R. Busch: *Trans. Am. Soc. Met.,* vol. 60, p. 252, 1967.
80. Chanani, G. R., V. F. Zackay, E. R. Parker: *Metall. Trans.,* vol. 2, p. 133.
81. Drapier, J. M., P. Viatour, D. Coutsouradis, and L. Habraken: *Cobalt,* no. 41, p. 171–184, 1970.
82. Tisinai, G. F., and C. H. Samans: *Trans. Am. Soc. Met.,* vol. 51, p. 589, 1959.
83. deBarbadillo, J. J.: Unpublished research, The International Nickel Co., Inc., New York, 1969.
84. Lecroisey, F., and A. Pineau: *Metall. Trans.,* vol. 3, p. 387, 1972.
85. Venables, J. A.: *Philos. Mag.,* vol. 7, p. 35, 1962.
86. Ludwigson, D. C. and K. G. Brickner: *Sheet Met. Ind.,* vol. 42, p. 245, 1965.
87. Gunter, C. J., and R. P. Reed: *Trans. Am. Soc. Met.,* vol. 55, p. 399, 1962.
88. Dash, J., and H. M. Otte: *Acta Metall.,* vol. 11, p. 1169, 1963.
89. Olson, G. B., and M. Cohen: *Metall. Trans.,* vol. 6A, p. 791, 1975.
90. Cina, B.: *Acta Metall.,* vol. 6, p. 748, 1958.
91. Reed, R. P.: *Acta Metall.,* vol. 10, p. 865, 1962.
92. Breedis, J. F., and W. D. Robertson: *Acta Metall.,* vol. 10, p. 1077, 1962.
93. Christian, J. W., *loc. cit.,* p. 910.
94. Angel, T.: *J. Iron Steel Inst., London,* vol. 177, p. 165, 1954.
95. Bressanelli, J. P., and A. Moscowitz: *Trans. Am. Soc. Met.,* vol. 59, p. 233, 1966.

96. Breedis, J. F.: *Trans. Am. Inst. Min. Metall. Pet. Eng.* vol. 236, p. 218, 1966.
97. Remy, L., and A. Pineau: *Metall. Trans.*, vol. 5, p. 963, 1973.
98. Post, C. B., and W. S. Eberly: *Trans. Am. Soc. Met.*, vol. 39, p. 868, 1947.
99. Griffiths, A.J., and J.C. Wright: *Iron Steel Inst. London Publ. 117*, p. 52, 1969.
100. Monkman, F. C., F. B. Cuff, and N. J. Grant: *Met. Prog.*, vol. 73, p. 95, April 1957.
101. Floreen, S., and J. R. Mihalisin: *ASTM Spec. Tech. Publ. 369*, p. 17, 1965.
102. Coutsouradis, D.: *Rev. Metall.* (Paris), vol. 58, p. 503, 1961.
103. Floreen, S., and C. R. Mayne: *ASTM Spec. Tech. Publ. 370*, p. 47, 1965.
104. Brickner, K. G.: "Selection of Stainless Steels," p. 1, American Society for Metals, Metals Park, Ohio, 1968.
105. Krivobok, V. N., and R. A. Lincoln: *Trans. Am. Soc. Met.*, vol. 25, p. 637, 1937.
106. Llewellyn, D. T., and J. D. Murry: *Iron Steel Inst. London Rept. no. 86*, p. 197, 1964.
107. Ziegler, N. A., and P. H. Brace: *Am. Soc. Test. Mater. Proc.*, vol. 50, p. 860, 1950.
108. Powell, G. W., E. R. Marshall, and W. A. Backofen: *Trans. Am. Soc. Test. Mater.*, vol. 50, p. 478, 1958.
109. The International Nickel Co., Inc.: "Chromium-Nickel Stainless Steel Data," Sec. 1, Bull. A, pp. 20, 22, 41, 1963.
110. Barclay, W. F.: *ASTM Spec. Tech. Publ. 369*, p. 26, 1965.
111. Dillamore, I. L., W. T. Roberts, and D. V. Wilson: *Iron Steel Inst. London Publ. 117*, p. 37, 1969.
112. Goodman, S. R., and H. Hu: *Trans. Am. Inst. Min. Metall. Pet. Eng.*, vol. 230, p. 1143, 1964.
113. Hu, H., and S. R. Goodman: *Trans. Am. Inst. Min. Metall. Pet. Eng.*, vol. 227, p. 1454, 1963.
114. Schumann, H.: *Arch. Eisenhuettenwes.*, vol. 12, p. 1170, 1970.
115. Rosenberg, S. J., and C. R. Irish: *J. Res. Nat. Bar. Stand.*, vol. 48, p. 40, 1952.
116. Cihal, V.: *Prot. Met.* (USSR), vol. 4, no. 6, p. 563, 1968.
117. Binder, W., C. Brown, and R. Franks: *Trans. Am. Soc. Met.*, vol. 41, p. 1301, 1949.
118. Irvine, K. J., D. T. Llewellyn, and F. B. Pickering: *J. Iron Steel Inst., London*, vol. 192, p. 218, 1959.
119. Kinzel, A. B.: *J. Met.*, vol. 4, p. 469, 1952.
120. Stickler, R., and A. Vinckier: *Trans. Am. Soc. Met.*, vol. 54, p. 362, 1961.
121. Aust, K. T., J. S. Armijo, and J. H. Westbrook: *Trans. Am. Soc. Met.*, vol. 59, p. 544, 1966.
122. Stickler, R., and A. Vinckier: *Trans. Am. Inst. Min. Metall. Pet. Eng.*, vol. 224, p. 1021, 1962.
123. Aust, K. T., J. S. Armijo, E. F. Koch, and J. H. Westbrook: *Trans. Am. Soc. Met.*, vol. 60, p. 360, 1967.
124. Weiss, B., and R. Stickler: *Metall. Trans.*, vol. 3, p. 851, 1972.
125. Wolff, V. E.: *Trans. Am. Inst. Min. Metall. Pet. Eng.*, vol. 236, p. 19, 1966.
126. Wilson, F. G.: *J. Iron Steel Inst., London*, vol. 209, p. 126, 1971.
127. Henthorne, M.: *ASTM Spec. Tech. Publ. 516*, p. 66, 1972.
128. ASTM Committee A-10, Subcommittee VI, *Am. Soc. Test. Mater. Proc.*, vol. 39, p. 203, 1939.
129. Lewis, M. H., and B. Hattersley: *Acta Metall.*, vol. 13, p. 1159, 1965.
130. Vermilyea, D. A., C. S. Tedmon, D. E. Broecker: *Corrosion*, vol. 31, no. 4, p. 140, 1975.
131. Singhal, K., and J. W. Martin: *Trans. Am. Inst. Min. Metall. Pet. Eng.*, vol. 242, p. 814, 1968.
132. Hattersley, B., and M. H. Lewis: *Philos. Mag.*, vol. 10, p. 1075, 1964.
133. Sleeswyck, A. W., J. N. Helle, and A. P. von Rosentiel: *Philos. Mag.*, vol. 9, p. 891, 1964.
134. Kautz, H. R., and H. Gerlach: *Arch. Eisenhuettenwes.*, vol. 39, no. 2, p. 151, 1968.
135. Goldschmidt, H.: "Interstitial Alloys," Plenum, New York, 1967.
136. DaCasa, C., V. B. Nileshwar, and D. A. Melford: *J. Iron Steel Inst., London*, vol. 207, pt. 10, p. 1325, 1969.
137. Philibert, J., G. Henry, M. Robert, and J. Plateau: *Mem. Sci. Rev. Met.*, vol. 58, p. 557, 1961.
138. Chandhok, V. K., J. P. Hirth, and E. J. Dulis: *Trans. Am. Inst. Min. Metall. Pet. Eng.*, vol. 224, p. 858, 1962.
139. Scharfstein, L. R., and G. N. Maniar: *Brit. Corros. J.*, vol. 1, p. 40, 1965.
140. Silcock, J. M.: *J. Iron Steel Inst., London*, vol. 201, p. 409, 1963.
141. Bungardt, K., and G. Lennartz: *Arch. Eisenhuettenwes.*, vol. 33, no. 4, p. 251, 1962.
142. Perkins, R. A., and P. T. Carlson: *Metall. Trans.*, vol. 5, p. 1511, 1974.
143. Armijo, J. S.: *Corrosion*, vol. 24, p. 24, 1968.
144. Desestret, A., I. Epelboin, M. Froment, and P. Guiraldeng: *Corros. Sci.*, vol. 8, p. 225, 1968.
145. Froes, F. H., M. G. H. Wells, and B. R. Banerjec: *Met. Sci. J.*, vol. 2, p. 232, 1968.
146. Mercier, A., and J. Hochman: *Rev. Metall.* (Paris), vol. 59, p. 651, 1962.
147. Crussard, C., J. Plateau, and G. Henry: *Proc. Joint Int. Conf. Creep*, Inst. Mech. Eng. (London), vol. 1, p. 98, 1963.
148. Stone, P. G.: *Iron Steel Inst. London Spec. Rept. 97*, p. 33, 1966.
149. Novak, C. J., and R. A. Kozlik: *Am. Soc. Test. Mater. Ann. Mtg.*, Paper 22, June 1966.
150. Bloom, F. K., and E. E. Denhard: *J. Met.*, p. 908, 1961.
151. Hull, F. C., and R. Stickler: *Proc. Joint Inst. Conf. Creep*, Inst. Mech. Eng. (London), vol. 1, 1963.
152. Levitin, V. V.: *Phys. Met. and Metallogr.*, vol. 11, no. 3, p. 67.
153. Ziemanski, J. P., and G. N. Aggen: *Am. Iron Steel Inst. Mtg.*, Nov. 11, 1965.
154. Williams, T. M., D. R. Harries, and J. Furnival: *J. Iron Steel Inst. London*, vol. 210, p. 351, 1972.

155. Goldschmidt, H. J.: *J. Iron Steel Inst., London*, vol. 209, no. 11, pp. 900 and 910, 1971.
156. Williams, T. M., and M. G. Talks: *J. Iron Steel Inst., London*, vol. 210, no. 11, p. 870, 1972.
157. Aust, K. T.: *Trans. Am. Inst. Min. Metall. Pet. Eng.*, vol. 245, p. 2117, 1969.
158. Van Aswegen, J. S. T., R. K. W. Honeycombe, and D. H. Warrington: *Acta Metall.*, vol. 12, p. 1, 1964.
159. White, J. E., and J. W. Freeman: *Trans. ASME, J. Eng. Power*, vol. 85, p. 108, 1963.
160. Heeley, E. J., A. T. Little, and D. F. Derbyshire: *J. Iron Steel Inst., London*, vol. 200, p. 943, 1962.
161. Irvine, K. J., J. D. Murray, and F. B. Pickering: *J. Iron Steel Inst., London*, vol. 196, p. 166, 1960.
162. Garofalo, F., F. von Gemmingen, and W. F. Domis: *Trans. Am. Soc. Met.*, vol. 54, p. 430, 1961.
163. Nutting, J., and J. M. Arrowsmith: *Symp. Structural Processes in Creep*, Iron Steel Inst. (London), p. 147, 1961.
164. Harding, H. J., and R. W. K. Honeycombe: *J. Iron Steel Inst., London*, vol. 204, p. 259, 1966.
165. Silcock, J. M.: *Acta Metall.*, vol. 14, p. 287, 1966.
166. Froes, F. H., R. W. K. Honeycombe, and D. H. Warrington: *Acta Metall.*, vol. 15, p. 157, 1967.
167. Froes, F. H., and D. H. Warrington: *Trans. Am. Inst. Min. Metall. Pet. Eng.*, vol. 245, p. 1969, 1969.
168. Tuma, H., M. Vyklicky, and K. Lobl: *Arch. Eisenhuettenwes.*, vol. 41, no. 10, p. 983, 1976.
169. ASTM Powder Diffraction Cards 6-0614, 6-0642.
170. Grot, A. S., and J. E. Spruiell: *Metall. Trans.*, vol. 6A, p. 2023, 1975.
171. Beattie, H. J., and W. C. Hagel: *J. Met.*, vol. 209, p. 911, 1957.
172. Thier, H., A. Baumel, and E. Schmidtmann: *Arch. Eisenhuettenwes.*, vol. 40, no. 4, p. 333, 1969.
173. Duwez, P., and J. O'Dell: *J. Electrochem. Soc.*, vol. 97, p. 299, 1950.
174. Cihal, V., and J. Jezek: *J. Iron Steel Inst., London*, vol. 202, p. 124, 1964.
175. Koch, W.: Metallundliche Analyze, *Stahl Eisen*, 1965.
176. Jenkinson, et al., *J. Iron Steel Inst., London*, vol. 200, p. 1011, 1962.
177. Mihalisin, J. R.: *Trans. Am. Inst. Min. Metall. Pet. Eng.*, vol. 239, p. 180, 1967.
178. Beattie, H. J., and W. C. Hagel: *Trans. Am. Inst. Min. Metall. Pet. Eng.*, vol. 233, p. 277, 1965.
179. DaCasa, C., and V. B. Nileshwar: *J. Iron Steel Inst., London*, vol. 207, p. 1003, 1969.
180. Gemill, M. G.: *J. Iron Steel Inst., London*, vol. 184, p. 122, 1956.
181. Brown, J. F.: *Metallurgia*, vol. 56, p. 215, 1957.
182. Knop, O.: *Metallurgia*, vol. 57, p. 137, 1958.
183. Wetzler, K., and G. Lennartz: *DEW Tech. Ber.*, vol. 1, p. 1, 1961.
184. Masumoto, T., and Y. Imai: *J. Jpn. Inst. Met.*, vol. 33, p. 1364, 1969.
185. Forbes-Jones, R. M.: Unpublished work, International Nickel Company, Inc., New York, 1971.
186. Eckel, J. F., and T. B. Cox: *J. Mater.*, vol. 3, p. 605, 1968.
187. Goodell, P. D., and R. H. Kane: Unpublished work, The International Nickel Company, Inc., New York, 1971.
188. Goodell, P. D.: Ph.D. thesis, University of Michigan, Ann Arbor, 1971.
189. Murray, J. D., J. Hacon, and P. H. Wanell: *Iron Steel Inst. London Spec. Rept.* 97, p. 403, 1966.
190. Liljestrand, L. G., and A. Omsen: *Metall. Trans.*, vol. 6A, p. 279, 1975.
191. Nevitt, M. V.: "Electronic Structure and Alloy Chemistry of the Transition Elements," p. 101, Interscience Publishers, New York, 1963.
192. Decker, R. F., and S. Floreen: *Am. Inst. Min. Metall. Pet. Eng. Conf. Proc.*, vol. 28, p. 69, 1965.
193. Hall, E. O., and S. H. Algie: *Metall. Rev.*, vol. 11, p. 61, 1966.
194. Weigand, H., and M. Doruk: *Arch. Eisenhuettenwes.*, vol. 33, no. 8, p. 559, 1962.
195. Kasper, J. S.: *Acta Metall.*, vol. 2, p. 456, 1954.
196. Koh, P. K.: *J. Met.*, vol. 197, p. 339, 1953.
197. Bechtoldt, C. J., and H. C. Vacher: *J. Res., Nat. Bur. Stand.*, vol. 58, no. 1, p. 7, 1953.
198. Morley, J. I., and H. W. Kirkby: *J. Iron Steel Inst., London*, vol. 172, p. 129, 1952.
199. Bain, E. C., and W. E. Griffiths: *Trans. Am. Inst. Min. Metall. Pet. Eng.*, vol. 75, p. 166, 1927.
200. Schafmeister, P., and R. Ergang: *Arch. Eisenhuettenwes.*, vol. 12, p. 459, 1939.
201. Bradley, A. J., and H. J. Goldschmidt: *J. Iron Steel Inst., London*, vol. 140, no. 11, p. 273, 1941.
202. Rees, W. P., B. D. Burns, and A. J. Cook: *J. Iron Steel Inst., London*, vol. 162, pt. 3, pp. 325–336, 1949.
203. Nicholson, M. E., C. H. Samans, and F. J. Shortsleeve: *Trans. Am. Soc. Met.*, vol. 44, p. 603, 1952.
204. Talbot, A. M., and D. E. Furman: *Trans. Am. Soc. Met.*, vol. 45, p. 429, 1953.
205. Jenkins, C. H. M., E. H. Bucknall, C. R. Austin, and G. A. Mellor: *J. Iron Steel Inst., London*, vol. 136, p. 187, 1937.
206. Gow, J. T., and O. E. Harder: *Trans. Am. Soc. Met.*, vol. 30, p. 855, 1942.
207. Woodyatt, L. R., C. T. Sims, and H. J. Beattie: *Trans. Am. Inst. Min. Metall. Pet. Eng.*, vol. 236, p. 519, 1964.
208. Mihalisin, J. R., C. G. Bieber, and R. T. Grant: *Trans. Am. Inst. Min. Metall. Pet. Eng.*, vol. 242, p. 2399, 1968.
209. Hull, F. C.: *Weld. J. (London)*, vol. 52, p. 104s, 1973.
210. Pitea, N. S.: Unpublished work, International Nickel Co., Inc., New York, 1970.
211. Kane, R. H.: Unpublished work, International Nickel Co., Inc., New York, 1971.
212. Lena, A.: *Met. Prog.*, vol. 66, p. 86, 1954.

213. Emmanuel, G. N.: The Nature, Occurence, and Effects of Sigma Phase, *ASTM Spec. Tech. Publ.* *110*, p. 82, 1950.
214. Duhaj, P., P. Ivan, and E. Makovicky: *J. Iron Steel Inst., London*, vol. 206, p. 1245, 1968.
215. Blenkinsop, P. A., and J. Nutting: *J. Iron Steel Inst., London*, vol. 205, p. 953, 1967.
216. White, W. E., and I. LeMay: *Metallography*, vol. 3, p. 35, 1970.
217. Dulis, E. J., and G. V. Smith: p. 3, *ASTM Spec. Tech. Publ.* 110, 1950.
218. White, W. E., and I. LeMay: *Metallography*, vol. 3, p. 51, 1970.
219. Gerlach, H.: *Iron Steel Inst. London Spec. Rept.* 97, p. 517, 1966. (Discussion of Stone.[148])
220. Sangdahl, G. S.: "Metals Handbook," vol. 2, p. 254, Amer. Soc. for Metals, Metals Park, Ohio, 1964.
221. Cole, C. L., and J. D. Jones: *Iron Steel Inst. London Spec. Pub.* *117*, p. 74, 1969.

Chapter 5

Structure and Constitution of Wrought Ferritic Stainless Steels

JOSEPH J. DEMO
**Senior Consultant, Materials Engineering, Engineering Department,
E. I. Du Pont De Nemours & Co., Wilmington, Delaware**

INTRODUCTION

The high chromium-iron Cr-Fe steels represent the third class of alloys in the family of stainless steels; the other two classes being austenitic and martensitic alloys. Ferritic stainless steels are iron-based alloys containing from about 12 to 30% chromium. The high chromium limit is arbitrary and is meant simply to include all commercially produced alloys. Ferritic stainless steels, though known for more than 40 years, have had more restricted use than the austenitic stainless steels. The reasons for this include: lack of the ductility characteristic of austenitic stainless steels, susceptibility to embrittlement, notch sensitivity, and poor weldability—all factors contributing to poor fabricability. However, with the increasing cost of nickel, the high resistance of the ferritics to stress-corrosion cracking and their excellent corrosion and oxidation resistance, intensive research over the decade 1960 to 1970 has resulted in ferritic alloy compositions which have good weldability and fabricability.

STRUCTURE AND CONSTITUTION

In theory, the ferritic stainless steels are structurally simple. At room temperature they consist of Cr-Fe alpha (α) solid solution having a body-centered cubic (bcc) crystal structure. The alloys contain very little dissolved carbon; the majority of the carbon present appears in the form of more or less finely divided chromium carbide precipitates. They remain essentially ferritic or bcc up to the melting point. A typical constitution diagram as published by the American Society for Metals[1] is reproduced in Fig. 1. Attention is directed to the lower chromium end of the phase diagram at the region of intermediate temperatures about which several points can be stated:

1. Chromium is a member of a group of elements called ferrite formers which extend the alpha (α) phase field and narrow down and suppress the gamma (γ) phase field. This property results in the so-called gamma loop extending in a temperature range from 850 to 1400°C.

2. As shown in Fig. 1, the transformation in chromium-free iron from α to γ phase occurs at about 910°C. As chromium is added, the transition temperature is depressed to about 850°C at 8% chromium and then rapidly increased so that at 12 to 13% chromium the transition temperature is about 1000°C.

3. The transformation from γ to α which occurs at about 1400°C for pure iron is depressed with increasing chromium to about 1000°C at 12 to 13% chromium. At this point, the upper and lower temperature curves for transformation join up to close off and form the gamma loop. Beyond 12 to 13% chromium, transformation to γ is no longer possible and an alloy would remain ferritic or bcc all the way from below room temperature to the melting point. It will be seen below that this maximum limit for the existence of γ phase is very much a function of austenitizing elements and can be moved to higher

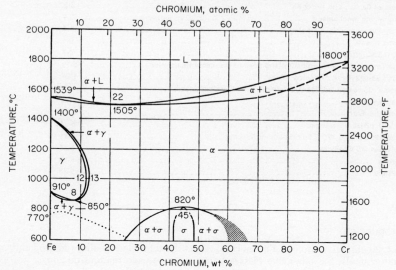

Fig. 1 Cr-Fe phase diagram.[1]

chromium levels in the presence of these elements, particularly the interstitials carbon and nitrogen. For alloys with less than about 12% chromium, an α to γ transformation occurs on heating into the γ range just as in pure iron. Ferritic stainless steels cannot normally undergo this transformation upon heating and cooling.

4. Between the γ loop and α-phase field there is a narrow transition region where an alloy at temperature will have both α and γ phases which, depending on the quench rate, may or may not be retained at room temperature.

Effect of Carbon and Nitrogen The location of the γ loop in the Fe-Cr phase diagram has been carefully studied recently by Baerlecken, Fischer, and Lorenz.[2] These investigators used magnetic measurements at elevated temperatures to determine the effect of carbon and nitrogen (and nickel) on the formation of austenite. The detailed α and γ regions these workers developed for pure iron and chromium alloys are shown in Fig. 2. The lowest point in the gamma loop occurs at 840°C and 6.5% chromium. The greatest width of the two-phase field is at about 1075°C and the complete enclosure is reached at about 11.5% chromium. Since the greatest expansion of the γ region is to about 10.6% chromium, the two-phase $\gamma +$ α region is very narrow in this high-purity alloy.

Additions of austenitizing elements, particularly carbon and nitrogen cause the outside boundary of the $\gamma + \alpha$ two-phase field to shift to higher chromium levels. The powerful effects of carbon and nitrogen in this regard are shown in Fig. 3a and b taken from Baerlecken's work.[2] Two effects are observed; namely, an expansion of the two-phase region to higher chromium contents and the shifting of the maximum extension of the $\gamma + \alpha$ phase field to higher temperatures. For example, it is seen in Fig. 3a that 0.013% carbon and 0.015% nitrogen shift

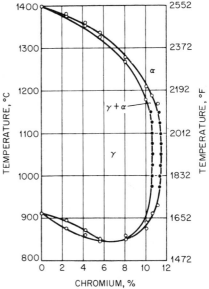

Fig. 2 The iron loop of the Cr-Fe phase diagram for alloys with about 0.004% C and 0.002% N.[2]

the maximum expansion of the $\gamma + \alpha$ from 11.5 to 17.0% chromium while 0.04% carbon and 0.03% nitrogen shift it to about 21% chromium. At still higher carbon levels, for example 0.2%, an expansion to 26% chromium is observed. In addition, the point of greatest expansion of the two-phase region is shifted to higher temperatures; from about 1075°C for the pure alloy to about 1300°C for an alloy containing 0.2% carbon. The expansion of the two-phase region to even higher temperatures is limited by the solidus temperatures of the alloys. As evident from Fig. 3b, nitrogen acts similar to carbon as a powerful expander of the two-phase $\gamma + \alpha$ field. In an alloy containing 0.25% nitrogen, the point of greatest width of the two-phase field is shifted from 11.5% chromium for the pure alloy to 28% chromium and to higher temperatures, from 1075 to about 1250°C.

Besides its effect on extending the two-phase $\gamma + \alpha$ region, carbon, because of its low solubility in the α matrix, is rejected from solid solution as the complex carbides $(Cr,Fe)_7C_3$ and $(Cr,Fe)_{23}C_6$ which precipitate predominantly at the grain boundaries. When an alloy is heated to temperatures of 1100 to 1200°C and the carbon level exceeds about 0.01%, the carbon cannot be held in solid solution even with rapid quenching and the complex carbides are formed, drastically affecting the properties of the alloys.

It is at once obvious from the above that whether or not an alloy remains completely bcc depends very much on the chromium level and the interstitial level. At low chromium levels, even alloys with relatively low interstitial levels may have a duplex structure when heated to temperatures around 1100°C. Alloys at the higher chromium levels can only have a duplex structure if they also contain high interstitial levels; otherwise these alloys

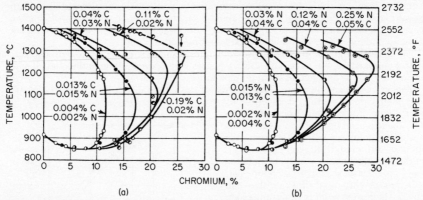

Fig. 3   Shifting of the boundary line $(\gamma + \alpha)/\alpha$ in the Cr-Fe system through increasing additions of carbon or nitrogen.[2]

are fully ferritic at all temperatures. In general, beyond about a 13% Cr content, heating to high temperatures no longer produces massive transformation of α to γ. Therefore, grain refinement and hardening by heat treatment and quenching are no longer possible.

STRENGTHENING MECHANISMS

As described above, the ferritic stainless steels are characterized by the essential absence of the α to γ transition upon heating to high temperatures. Consequently, hardening by the gamma-to-martensite transition upon cooling will not normally occur. This transformation mechanism is utilized in carbon and alloy steels and martensitic Cr-Fe alloys for achieving high hardness and strengths. The influence of heat-treatment temperature on hardness for two ferritic stainless steels and a martensitic stainless steel is depicted in Fig. 4, based on data from Newell[5] and Thielsch.[6] In contrast to the 13% martensitic steel which undergoes the $\alpha \rightarrow \gamma \rightarrow M_s$ transition, the hardness on an 18 and 20% Cr steel varies little with temperature. Some hardening occurs because of the small amount of austenite formed at temperature which depends on the chromium content and interstitial levels. For ferritic stainless steels, the hardening effect is strongest at the lower chromium ranges, but it can occur even at higher chromium levels if the carbon content is increased so as to expand the $\alpha - \gamma$ two-phase region as shown in Fig. 3a and b.

In summary, it is not possible to significantly harden or strengthen ferritic stainless steels by heating them to high temperatures and then rapidly cooling. In these alloys, the slight increases in hardness or strength when the alloys are heated above 850°C are related to an increase in grain size (through grain growth) and the presence of small volumes of austenite which revert to martensite upon cooling.

Strengthening by Heat Treatment   Though a ferritic Cr-Fe stainless cannot be strengthened or hardened by the classical $\alpha \rightarrow \gamma \rightarrow M_s$ mechanism, the alloys are susceptible to significant strengthening by heat treatment. In general, the strengthening mechanisms that do occur are not desirable because the alloys are embrittled and ductility and toughness at room temperature are severely reduced. Distinction will be made between three separate and distinct forms of embrittling mechanisms:

1. Sigma-phase precipitation
2. 475°C embrittlement
3. High-temperature embrittlement

Surveys by Thielsch,[6] Rajkay,[7] Kaltenhauser,[8] and Demo and Bond[9] have summarized the extensive literature describing these embrittling phenomena. These effects have been major deterrents to the use of ferritic stainless steels as engineering materials. Because of their importance to engineering properties, a summary of each of these embrittling effects is given here with details as to the nature and cure of each.

1. *Sigma phase* occurs in Cr-Fe alloys containing between 15 to 20% and 70% chromium exposed to temperatures from about 500 to 800°C.

2. *475°C embrittlement* occurs when a ferritic Cr-Fe stainless steel is heated between 400 and 540°C. An increase in hardness and tensile strength is observed concurrent with a substantial decrease in ductility and impact resistance.

3. *High-temperature embrittlement* derives its name from the fact that ferritic alloys with moderate-to-high carbon and nitrogen levels are brittle at room temperature following exposure of the alloys to temperatures above about 1000°C.

While all these embrittling phenomena can severely affect the mechanical properties of a ferritic Cr-Fe stainless steel in an engineering application, high-temperature embrittlement is particularly serious. This effect is serious because a useful engineering material must be capable of being welded and heat-treated while maintaining ductility, toughness, and corrosion resistance.

Sigma Phase Examination of the phase diagram in Fig. 1 shows, in addition to the gamma loop, a second zone at lower temperatures centered about 45% chromium. A detailed part of the sigma (σ) portion of the Cr-Fe phase diagram by Cook and Jones[10] is shown in Fig. 5. Pure sigma forms between 42 and 50% chromium while a duplex structure of both alpha and sigma phases has been found to form in alloys with as little as 20 and as much as 70% chromium when they are exposed to temperatures between 500 and 800°C. The existence of a compound in the Cr-Fe system at about 50% chromium was suggested as early as 1927.[11,12] It was not until 1936 that the intermetallic compound, Fe-Cr, was definitely identified as sigma phase.[13,14] Sigma phase is an intermetallic compound containing one atom of iron with one atom of chromium which is hard, nonmagnetic, and consists of a tetragonal unit cell. Extensive research has been reported describing the effort to establish the structure and transformation characteris-

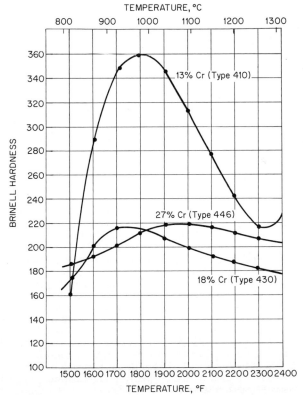

Fig. 4 Relative hardening of ferritic and martensitic Cr-Fe alloys after water quenching from indicated temperature.[5,6]

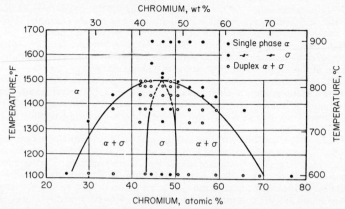

Fig. 5 Cr-Fe phase diagram in binary alloys of high purity; 25 to 76% chromium. This diagram shows pure sigma phase from 44 to 50% chromium and mixed alpha and sigma phase from about 25 to 44% and from 50 to 70% chromium with phase boundaries for temperature interval of 1100 to 1500°F (595 to 815°C).[10]

tic of this Fe-Cr compound.[15-20] Sigma phase forms in other alloy systems when two metals with a body-centered cubic and face-centered cubic (fcc) structure are alloyed together and have atomic radii not differing by more than 8%. Elements like molybdenum, silicon, nickel, and manganese shift the sigma-forming range to lower chromium content.[3,13,14,20,21] Sigma phase forms readily on heating alloys containing 25 to 30% chromium to 600°C, but only after a relatively long-time exposure. In alloys containing less than about 20% chromium, sigma phase is difficult to form.[3] Cold-work enhances the rate of sigma-phase precipitation.[14,19,21-23,25] The formation of sigma phase is accompanied by an increase in hardness and a severe reduction in ductility and toughness,[24] especially when these properties are measured at ambient temperatures. An important consideration is that in most Cr-Fe alloys, sigma requires hundreds of hours to form. This is shown by the data in Fig. 6 from Shortsleeve and Nicholson[20]

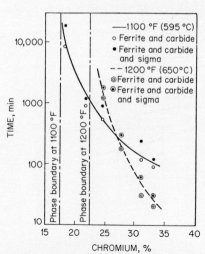

Fig. 6 Effect of chromium content on the threshold times of sigma formation at 1100 and 1200°F (595 and 650°C).[20]

describing the threshold times of sigma formation at 595 and 650°C as a function of chromium content. Based on these data, weld deposits and castings would normally not have sufficient time in the appropriate temperature ranges for sigma to form in alloys, especially those containing 15 to 33% chromium.[6] Only with long isothermal holds can sigma phase form to severely reduce the ductility and toughness of Cr-Fe alloys. A representative microstructure[24] of a 27% Cr alloy exposed for 3144 h at about 540 to 565°C shows a structure composed of ferrite, spheroidized carbides, and sigma phase (see Fig. 7). The sigma phase has been precipitated as an essentially continuous series of islands around the ferrite grain boundaries. Under some exposure conditions, these islands are preferentially attacked (see Fig. 7c) indicating that the presence of sigma phase is also detrimental to the corrosion resistance of Cr-Fe alloys. Fortunately sigma phase developed in an alloy may be brought into solution with relatively short holding periods of 1 h or more by heating at temperatures over

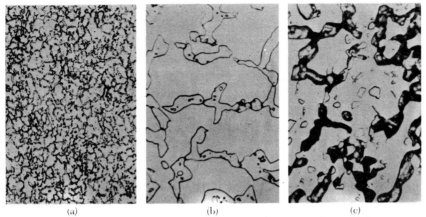

(a)   (b)   (c)

Fig. 7 (a) 27Cr-Fe alloy (air-melted) showing ferrite, carbides and intergranular sigma-phase constituent formed after heating 131 days at approximately 1050°F (565°C) (200 ×). (b) This photograph shows sigma phase with some small spheroids of carbides around which the sigma phase has formed (1000 ×). (c) Etched 10 s in aqua regia during which the sigma phase is blackened and eaten out. Carbides appear mainly in center of ferrite grains (1000 ×).[24]

800°C. Alloys containing nickel, molybdenum, and manganese may require longer holding periods or higher temperatures to dissolve sigma phase.

475°C Embrittlement   When Cr-Fe alloys containing 15 to 70% chromium are subjected to prolonged heating at temperatures between 400 and 540°C, the alloys harden and a drastic loss in ductility is observed. The hardening phenomenon is referred to as 475°C (885°F) embrittlement because peak hardness on aging occurs at this temperature as illustrated in Fig. 8[6,24] for Cr-Fe stainless steels heated for long times at specific temperatures. The effect of prolonged heating at 475°C on increasing the strength and decreasing the ductility in a 27Cr-Fe alloy is shown in Fig. 9 from the work of Newell.[24] As suggested by these data, hours of exposure at 475°C are required before noticeable changes in hardness and tensile properties are observed. However, notched specimens may reveal this embrittlement in much shorter time. Zapffe et al.,[25,26] using a 26% Cr stainless steel, were able to show embrittlement on notch samples in a bend test after only the first half hour of exposure at 475°C.

Large reductions in impact strength may also be noticed after only short-time exposure to embrittling temperature. Data taken from Colombier's book (Ref. 3, p. 50) are summarized below to illustrate this point for a steel with 0.08C-0.4Si-16.9Cr.

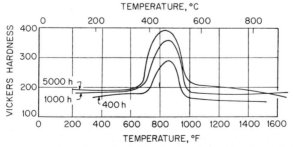

Fig. 8   Hardness surveys on bars after prolonged heating in a temperature gradient. Analysis: 0.20% max. C, 1.50% max. Mn, 0.025% max. S and P, 0.75% max. Si, 26 to 30% Cr, 1.00% max. Ni, 0.12 to 0.25% N.[24]

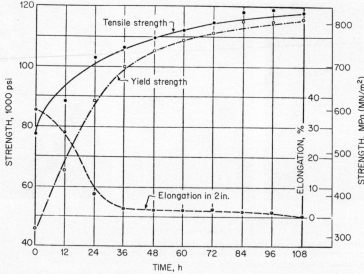

Fig. 9 Graph showing the effect of aging time at 885°F (475°C) on the room-temperature tensile properties of 27Cr-Fe alloy, air-melted.[24]

	Annealed	Heated 4 h at 450°C
Tensile strength, tons/in.^{2} (MN/m^2) ..	37.0 (571.7)	38.0 (587.1)
Yield point, tons/in.^{2} (MN/m^2)	21.0 (144.8)	25.4 (175.1)
Elongation, %	22.8	23.6
Impact values, kg-m/cm^2 (J)........	12.0 (94.5)	1.4 (11)

The mechanical properties (tensile strength, yield strength, and elongation) show essentially no effect of the embrittling treatment, but a drastic loss in impact strength is recorded. As noted by Colombier after repeated heating in the range of 450 to 500°C, the elongation starts to decrease and after a few hundred hours may be virtually zero, while an increase in tensile of some 7 to 8 tons/in.^{2} (108 to 124 MN/m^2) occurs.

The cause for the increase in strength and hardness and drastic reduction in ductility was unexplained for a long time. X-ray diffraction analysis by Becket,[27] Riedrich and Loib,[28] and Bandel and Tofaute,[29] on samples embrittled by heating in the neighborhood of 475°C showed no changes in lattice parameter. Newell,[24] while reporting no changes in lattice parameters, did note that an atomic disturbance was occurring because the diffraction lines in back-reflection spectra of an embrittled sample were diffuse and broad. Early investigators could detect no significant change in metallographic features, although Riedrich and Loib[28] and Newell[24] did report a grain-boundary widening. Based on this observation, Riedrich and Loib concluded that the embrittlement was caused by a precipitate along the grain boundary. In separate work, Bandel and Tofaute[29] discovered that an embrittled 18% Cr alloy had a lamellar precipitate. Prior to 1951, 475°C embrittlement was considered to be related to sigma-phase formation and received the attention of many studies. Newell[24] in 1946 showed that the embrittlement would occur in practically carbon-free alloys as well as in those of moderate carbon content. Bandel and Tofaute,[29] Riedrich and Loib,[28] and Newell[5] showed that the degree of hardening as a function of temperature exposure was proportional to chromium content. The data from Riedrich's and Loib's work using experimental low-carbon alloys are reproduced in Table 1. The alloys in the annealed condition at the start all measured about 145 BHN. The hardnesses after a 1000-h exposure at 475°C are given in Table 1. Newell's[5] data (reproduced in Fig. 10) also show the relationship of chromium content in commercial alloys to hardness increases. Rapid increases in hardness with exposure times were noted for Types 446 and 430 stainless steel with little change noted for a Type 410 and 405 stainless steel (12%

TABLE 1   Hardnesses* of Cr-Fe Alloys After
1000-h Exposure at 885°F (475°C) as a Function
of Chromium Contents[5,28]

Cr, wt %	Brinell hardness
14.5	150
15.9	195
17.0	223
19.4	252
20.1	260
21.9	270
23.7	290
28.7	320

*The hardness of annealed alloys at the start was about 145 Brinell.

chromium). These data indicate that the hardening occurs in alloys containing over about 15% chromium, increases with chromium content, and is particularly pronounced for a commercial Type 446 stainless steel containing 26% chromium.

In 1951 Heger[30] emphasized the suggestion first made by Bandel and Tofaute[29] and Newell[5] that the embrittlement was due to a precipitation-hardening process involved in the early stages of formation of sigma phase. This was in contrast to the theory of a minor impurity precipitation which was rendered untenable because alloy additions[30] and prior heat treatment[29] did not improve resistance to the embrittlement and even the purest Cr-Fe alloys embrittled.[27] The cause (as put forth by Heger[30] and Newell[5,24]) was the precipitation of some phase which is inherent in the Cr-Fe alloy system itself and not an impurity. Heger postulated that 475°C embrittlement occurred when a Cr-Fe alloy heated in the embrittling range undergoes the reaction:

$$\alpha \text{ phase} \rightarrow \text{transition phase} \rightarrow \sigma \text{ phase}$$

The transitory phase that precedes sigma formation at higher temperature was said to cause 475°C embrittlement. Newell described the embrittlement phenomenon as being related first to an initial lattice change or distortion in the alpha matrix leading subsequently to gross precipitation of sigma phase when the atomic mobility is increased at but slightly higher temperatures. As Heger pointed out, the transition phase is intermediate in structure between alpha and sigma and is coherent with the matrix alpha phase. The presence of this coherency between the two different structures causes large resistance to dislocation motion typical of a precipitation-hardening mechanism.[31] The generated stresses then increase the hardness and cause other property changes. While both Heger and Newell felt 475°C embrittlement was related to a transition state before sigma phase is formed, Heger pointed out a very serious contradiction of this hypothesis. Houdremont's[6,32] data (reproduced in Fig. 11) illustrate this problem. The alloys containing 17

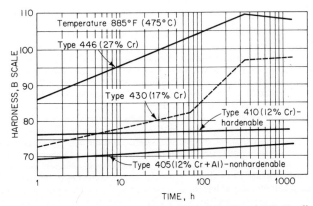

Fig. 10   Age-hardening tendencies at 885°F (475°C) of 12, 17, and 27Cr-Fe alloys.[5]

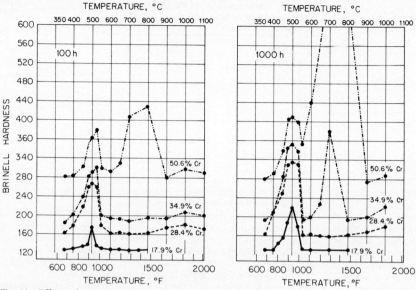

Fig. 11 Effects of temperature and aging time on the hardness increase caused by 885°F (475°C) brittleness and sigma-phase precipitation in several Cr-Fe alloys.[6,32]

and 28.4% chromium did not reveal any hardening because of sigma-phase formation (600 to 900°C). However, significant hardening in the 475°C embrittlement range (400 to 550°C) did occur. It thus appeared that 475°C embrittlement phenomenon is definitely inherent to the Cr-Fe binary system as suggested by Heger and Newell, but it is not directly related to the formation of sigma phase as postulated.

Based on extensive research work from 1951 to 1964, two hypotheses have been suggested to describe the mechanism of 475°C embrittlement. One school (Masumota, Saito and Sugihara,[33] Pomey and Bastien[34]) has attributed the changes in physical properties of alloys with aging at about 475°C to atomic ordering. In fact, Takeda and Nagai[35] claimed to have found x-ray verification for superlattices corresponding to Fe_3Cr, FeCr, and $FeCr_3$. However, all published attempts to observe superlattices in Cr-Fe alpha alloys using more sensitive neutron diffraction have been unsuccessful.[36-38] The second and more prevalent school of thought for the occurrence of 475°C embrittlement attributes the effect to the formation of a coherent precipitate due to the presence of a miscibility gap in the Cr-Fe system below about 550°C, in a chromium range where sigma phase can form at higher temperatures. The data published by Fisher, Dulis, and Carroll[39] in 1953 gave the first indication of the presence of a coherent precipitate. These investigations were able to extract fine particles about 200 Å in diameter from a 28.5% Cr alloy aged for 1 to 3 years at 475°C. The material was found to be nonmagnetic, to have a bcc structure with a lattice parameter $a = 2.877$ Å which is between that of iron and chromium, and to contain chromium in the range from 61 to 83%. Williams and Paxton[40] and Williams[37] confirmed these results and first explicitly proposed the existence of a miscibility gap below the sigma-forming region in the equilibrium diagram of Fig. 1. The extent of the miscibility gap is shown in Fig. 12 as published by Williams.[37] Alloys aged within the gap would separate into chromium-rich ferrite α^1 and iron-rich ferrite α. Reversion to the unaged condition occurs when the specimens are heated above 550°C in agreement with all experimental data. The mechanism of age-hardening by $\alpha - \alpha^1$ precipitation in the Cr-Fe alloy system has been studied in detail by Marcinkowski, Fisher, and Szirmae[41] who analyzed the influence of the formation of a chromium-rich precipitate α^1 on the deformation markings in the vicinity of hardness impressions. In addition, using extraction-replica and thin-foil transmission electron microscopy, these workers were able to show the existence of a coherent chromium-rich precipitate in an iron-rich matrix in a 46 wt % Cr-Fe alloy heated for thousands of hours at 500°C (see Fig. 13).

In more recent work on lower chromium-content alloys, Grobner[42] established the critical temperature range as well as the kinetics of the embrittling process in Cr-Fe alloys containing 14 and 18% chromium. He showed for an 18% Cr alloy that 475°C embrittlement occurs in a temperature range from 400 to 500°C for both a commercial purity alloy and a low interstitial alloy. However, the vacuum-melted alloy of higher purity requires a longer exposure time to embrittle as shown by Grobner's data on impact strength (reproduced in Fig. 14). In addition to drastic changes in toughness, embrittled alloys, whether high-purity vacuum-melted, or air-melted, show increases in yield and tensile strength and drastic reduction in elongation as shown in Table 2. Finally, Grobner showed that even steels with chromium contents as low as 14% show embrittlement when exposed in the temperature range of 370 to 485°C, but only after much longer exposure times as compared to the 18% Cr steels.

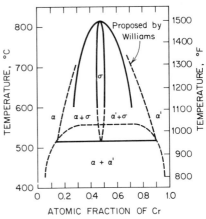

Fig. 12 Phase diagram of the Fe-Cr system according to Williams.[37]

Many investigators have studied the effect of additives on 475°C embrittlement in Cr-Fe steels.[3,6,27,29,30,42] Heger[30] noted that, in general, the addition of alloying elements offered little or no improvement in preventing the embrittlement. The effects of additives on 475°C embrittlement, taken from Heger,[30] are summarized in Table 3. While not an additive, cold-work[6] intensifies the rate of 475°C embrittlement. In addition to drastic reduction in toughness and ductility, embrittled Cr-Fe alloys show a severe reduction in corrosion resistance.[24,29] Data from Newell's article[24] tabulated in Table 4 show that an embrittled alloy corrodes about 4 to 12 times more rapidly in boiling 65% nitric acid than

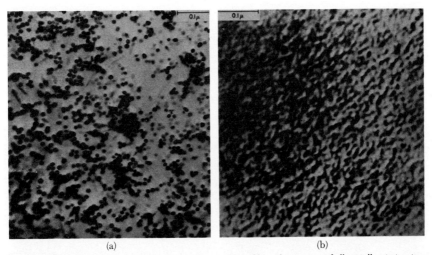

Fig. 13 (a) Electron micrograph of an extraction replica of bcc chromium-rich "zones" existing in a 47.8 atomic % Cr-Fe alloy after annealing 9650 h at 500°C (932°F). (b) Transmission electron micrograph showing structure existing in a 47.8 atomic % Cr-Fe alloy after annealing 3743 h at 500°C (932°F).[41]

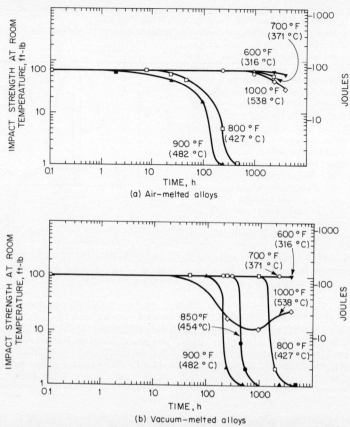

Fig. 14 Impact strength at room temperature of half-size Charpy V-notch specimens after aging at indicated times and temperatures—air-melted vs. vacuum-melted alloys—18% chromium.[42]

TABLE 2   Tensile Properties at Room Temperature of a Vacuum-melted and Air-melted Alloy After Indicated Aging Treatments[42]

			Wt. %		
			Cr	C	N
Alloy 1, vacuum-melted:			17.4	0.002	0.003
Alloy 2, air-melted:			18.0	0.044	0.091

Alloy type	Aged		0.2% offset yield strength		Tensile strength		Elongation, % (50.8-mm gage)
	Temp., °C	Time, h	ksi	MPa	ksi	MPa	
1		0	30.9	213	49.9	344	32.5
1	316	4000	31.6	217	50.8	350	38.3
1	427	4800	69.8	481	84.1	579	13.0
1	482	2400	73.4	505	100.3	690	11.5
2		0	43.0	296	69.8	481	22.5
2	316	4000	38.5	265	69.1	476	25.5
2	427	960	73.7	508	95.8	660	17.0
2	482	2400	83.4	540	104.0	717	12.5

TABLE 3   Effects of Composition on 475°C Embrittlement in Cr-Fe Alloys[6,30,42]

Element	Effect on 475°C embrittlement*
Cr	Intensifies
C	No effect;* intensifies†
Ti, Cb	Intensifies
Mn	Lowers slightly
Si	Intensifies
Al	Intensifies
Ni	Low amounts intensify, large amounts decrease
N	Very slight;* intensifies†
P	Intensifies
Mo	Intensifies
Severe cold work	Intensifies‡

*Heger.
†Grobner.
‡Thielsch.

does an annealed sample. The accelerated corrosion on embrittled alloys is probably due to the selective corrosion of the iron-rich ferrite formed because of the miscibility gap or, as suggested by Hodges,[43] due to formation of chromium-rich carbide precipitates.

The 475°C embrittlement may be alleviated and toughness and corrosion resistance restored by heating embrittled alloys at temperatures of 550°C and higher for a long enough time. As pointed out by Newell,[24] 1 h suffices to remove the embrittlement at 593°C or higher, while 5 h are required at 582°C and over 1000 h at 538°C. For compositions susceptible to σ-phase precipitation in relatively short time as indicated in Fig. 12, the 475°C embrittled alloy can be heated to temperatures above about 800°C (i.e., above the σ-forming region) and rapidly cooled to remove the embrittlement.[6]

Summary 475°C Embrittlement. Holding Cr-Fe alloys in the temperature range of 400 to 540°C causes the alloys to become brittle and to lose corrosion resistance. The embrittlement is caused by formation of a coherent chromium-rich precipitate in the iron-rich matrix as a result of a miscibility gap in the Cr-Fe phase diagram below about 550°C in the chromium range from about 15 to 70%. The 475°C embrittlement phenomenon and sigma-phase embrittlement are not related metallurgically. Significantly shorter exposure times can cause 475°C embrittlement as compared to sigma-phase embrittlement. As with sigma phase, it is unlikely that welding or a high-temperature heat treatment can produce 475°C embrittlement even if the alloy experiences a relatively slow cool through the embrittling temperature ranges. A very heavy section may suffer 475°C embrittlement during cooling. The fact that 475°C embrittlement or sigma-phase embrittlement will not normally occur in alloys welded or annealed at high temperatures and then cooled makes these embrittling problems less serious. However, alloys with more than about 16% chromium should not be used for extended service between 370 and 540°C, especially if the alloy is cycled from room temperature to the operating temperature during process shutdowns or excursions.

High-Temperature Embrittlement and Loss of Corrosion Resistance   When high-chromium stainless steels of intermediate and high interstitial content are heated above about 950°C and cooled to room temperature, they may show a severe embrittlement[31] and loss of corrosion resistance.[44] The effects can occur during welding, isothermal heat

TABLE 4   Average Rate of Corrosion in Boiling 65% Nitric Acid for 27Cr-Fe Alloy After Aging at 475°C[24]

Condition	Corrosion rates	
	mils/yr	mm/yr
Annealed	8.9	0.23
Embrittled 500 h at 475°C	31	0.79
Embrittled 6000 h at 475°C	109	2.77

treatments above 950°C, and casting operations. The effect on ductility and corrosion resistance is shown in Fig. 15[45] for a commercial AISI Type 446 stainless steel after it is welded. Of all the detrimental effects which can occur in high-chromium ferritic stainless steels following heat treatment, the so-called high-temperature embrittlement is most damaging because operations such as welding, heat treatment, and casting—all operations necessary for a material of construction—can cause serious loss in ductility and corrosion resistance. Not surprisingly, this problem has been a severe deterrent and has limited extensive use of air-melted ferritic stainless steel for commercial construction.

Background. Exceptionally thorough survey articles by Thielsch[6] and Rajkay[7] summarize all the research done up to about 1966 on the causes of the severe loss of corrosion resistance and ductility when high-chromium steels of moderate interstitial contents are heated to high temperatures. Most early investigators studied either the embrittlement

Ductility   Corrosion resistance

Fig. 15 Effect of welding on the ductility and corrosion resistance of AISI Type 446 steel; 26Cr-0.095C-0.077N; corrosion tested in boiling ferric sulfate—50% sulfuric acid solution.[45]

phenomenon or the corrosion-loss phenomenon, although as later investigators showed, the property losses are related to a single mechanism. Up to the 1960s, two theories were offered to explain the severe embrittlement:

1. The segregation or coherent state theory[6] postulated that embrittlement resulted from a clustering or segregation of carbon atoms in the ferrite matrix. During rapid cooling, most of the dissolved carbon in solid solution does not reprecipitate as carbides. Instead, the carbon atoms in the supersaturated ferrite phase group as coherent clusters which harden (i.e., embrittles) the matrix, much in the manner of certain age-hardening alloys. Annealing affected alloys between 700 and 800°C causes the carbon to precipitate as carbides, thereby removing the carbon atom clusters and the embrittlement.

2. In the martensitic mechanism first described by Pruger,[46] regions in the alloy of relatively high carbon content transform to austenite at elevated temperature. During subsequent cooling, these regions transform to brittle martensite. Annealing in a temperature range of 700 to 800°C removes the embrittlement by transforming the martensite to ferrite and chromium carbides.

The theories proposed (up to about 1960) to explain the severe intergranular attack on high-chromium ferritic alloys following high-temperature exposure are summarized below:

1. Houdremont and Tofaute[47] postulated that a carbon-rich austenite forms at the sensitizing temperature. When cooled, easily dissolved iron carbide precipitates at the grain boundaries between the austenite and ferrite phases. By annealing at about 750°C, the iron carbides are converted to chromium carbides which resist chemical dissolution and therefore the material becomes resistant to intergranular attack.

2. Hochmann[44] also proposed the necessity for austenite formation at temperature, but suggested that intergranular corrosion occurs by preferential attack on the grain-boundary austenite phase itself because of its low chromium and high carbon content.

3. Lula, Lena, and Kiefer[48] reject any mechanism of intergranular attack that requires the formation of austenite. As they pointed out, operations aimed at preventing austenite

formation following high-temperature exposure did not prevent intergranular corrosion. These workers proposed that the stress surrounding the carbide or nitride precipitates formed during cooling are the cause of rapid corrosion on the matrix adjacent to the precipitates. Annealing between 650 and 815°C annealed out the stresses caused by the precipitated phases, thus restoring corrosion resistance.

An interesting point is the lack of any suggestion by the early investigators that the high-temperature loss in corrosion resistance was due to chromium depletion adjacent to chromium carbide precipitates. This mechanism, proposed by Bain et al.[49] in 1933, and detailed by Ebling et al.,[50] has generally been accepted as the cause of intergranular attack in 18Cr-8Ni austenitic stainless steels. Application of this phenomenon to explain intergranular corrosion in a ferritic stainless steel was difficult because the effects of heat treatment on the austenitic and the ferritic stainless steels were opposite. It was known that an austenitic stainless steel would sensitize by holding in a temperature range from 400 to 800°C and that the corrosion resistance of a sensitized specimen could be restored by heating to temperatures above about 950°C which dissolved the chromium carbide precipitates. In direct contrast, an air-melted ferritic stainless steel is sensitized whenever it is heated above about 950°C. Further, the corrosion resistance of a sensitized ferritic specimen can be recovered by annealing in a temperature range from 700 to 850°C which corresponds to a part of the range where an austenitic stainless steel is sensitized. In light of these contrasting effects, attribution of the chromium depletion theory as the mechanism for corrosion loss in ferritic stainless steel did not appear possible.

High-Temperature Loss of Corrosion Resistance. In the early and mid-1960s, a renewed interest in ferritic stainless steels resulted in research studies into the mechanism for the high-temperature embrittlement and corrosion-loss phenomenon. It was Baumel[51] in 1963 who discussed the application of the chromium depletion theory to ferritic stainless steels. During the 1960s, investigations by Bond and Lizlovs,[52] Bond,[53] Baerlecken et al.,[2] Demo,[45,54] Hodge,[43,55] and Streicher[56] have confirmed that the chromium depletion theory is the most plausible explanation for the severe intergranular attack which occurs when alloys of moderate carbon and nitrogen content are heated above about 950°C and then cooled to room temperature. Henthorne[57] has compiled an extensive summary on the factors causing intergranular attack in iron- and nickel-based alloys.

Demo[54] described in 1968 the curious effects of heat treatment on the corrosion resistance of a commercial AISI Type 446 stainless steel exposed to Streicher's ferric sulfate–sulfuric acid test (ASTM A 229-58, ASTM A 262-70, Part 3 and Ref. 56). In a series of tests summarized in Table 5, he showed the poor corrosion resistance of samples water-quenched or air-cooled from 1100°C and the recovery when the sensitized samples were reheated to 850°C. However, samples, which were slowly cooled in the furnace from 1100°C to temperatures below 1000°C and then quenched, displayed corrosion resistance equivalent to the annealed sample. Based on these data and metallographic examination,

TABLE 5   Effects of Thermal Treatment on the Corrosion Resistance of AISI Type 446 Stainless Steel[54]

Sample†		Corrosion rate *		
designation	Condition	mils/yr	mm/yr	Exposure, h
1	As-received	30	0.76	120
2	30 min, 1100°C, water-quenched	780	19.8	24
3	30 min, 1100°C, air-cooled	800	20.32	24
5	30 min, 1100°C, water-quenched +			
	30 min, 850°C, water-quenched	42	1.07	120
4	30 min, 1100°C, slow cool to:‡			
	1000°C, water-quenched	767	19.48	120
	900°C, water-quenched	27	0.69	120
	800°C, water-quenched	20	0.51	120
	700°C, water-quenched	18	0.46	120
	600°C, water-quenched	25	0.64	120

*Exposed to boiling ferric sulfate—50% sulfuric acid solution. (ASTM A-262-70, Part 3, Ref. 56.)
†See Fig. 16 for microstructure of designated samples.
‡2.5°C/min in furnace.

Demo proposed two hypotheses, but favored the one describing the existence of a chromium-carbide-nitride precipitation range in the temperature region from 500 to 900°C similar to that observed for an austenitic stainless steel. Bond[53] in 1968 described the effects of carbon and nitrogen level on the sensitization of ferritic stainless steels containing 17% chromium. He concluded that intergranular corrosion of ferritic stainless steel is caused by the depletion of chromium in areas adjacent to where chromium-rich carbides and nitrides precipitate. A portion of Bond's data is given in Table 6 and shows the effects of interstitial levels on the intergranular corrosion resistance of a series of 17% Cr alloys in boiling 65% HNO_3. Based on these and other data, Bond concluded that a 17% Cr ferritic alloy containing 0.0095% nitrogen and 0.0021% carbon was resistant to intergranular corrosion after sensitizing heat treatment in the range of 900 to 1150°C. He also pointed out that alloys containing more than 0.022% nitrogen and more than 0.012% carbon were quite susceptible to intergranular corrosion after sensitizing heat treatments at temperatures higher than about 926°C (1700°F). The low interstitial requirement for resisting sensitization needs to be emphasized in contrast to the interstitial levels of about 0.06% carbon and 0.03% nitrogen in a typical air-melted 17% Cr Type 430 stainless steel. Bond also showed, through electron microscopic examination of the alloys susceptible to intergranular corrosion, grain-boundary precipitates which were absent in alloys not susceptible to such corrosion.

Demo[45] in 1971 showed that a 26% Cr alloy containing 0.014% carbon and 0.004% nitrogen after heating to 1000°C had excellent intergranular corrosion resistance if quenched and poor resistance if cooled in air or even more slowly. These results by Bond and Demo showed that ferritic stainless could be subjected to high temperature without a resulting loss of corrosion resistance provided low maximum interstitial levels were maintained in the alloys—obviously much below levels for air-melted alloys. For these low interstitial ferritic alloys, the response to heat treatment is remarkably similar to that observed for austenitic Cr-Ni stainless steels. If heated above 1000°C and water-quenched, the intergranular corrosion resistance is excellent and no grain-boundary precipitates of chromium carbides are observed; upon slow cooling, severe intergranular attack may be observed along with grain-boundary precipitates of chromium carbides.[49,58] A clear relationship between heat treatment, the presence of an intergranular precipitate and corrosion resistance exists for a low interstitial ferritic alloy.

For a commercial air-melted Type 446 (26% Cr) stainless steel, Demo[45] showed there is not a one-to-one correlation between loss of corrosion resistance and the presence of a continuous grain-boundary precipitate in contrast to austenitic stainless steels and low interstitial ferritic stainless steels. These results are shown in Fig. 16 for samples whose corrosion resistance is summarized in Table 5. For example, sample 2 (water-quenched from 1100°C) and sample 3 (air-cooled) had poor intergranular corrosion resistance consistent with the continuous chromium-rich precipitates observed in the grain boundaries. Sample 1 (as-received) and sample 4 (slowly cooled from 1100°C) showed excellent intergranular corrosion resistance consistent with the essential lack of any grain-boundary precipitate. However, sample 5 (reheated at 850°C) showed excellent intergranular corrosion resistance but also a heavy grain-boundary precipitate usually indicative of poor corrosion resistance. It is lack of correlation between corrosion resistance and grain-boundary precipitate and the fact that commercial alloys become sensitized when heated above about 1000°C that has held back the acceptance that the high-tempera-

TABLE 6   Results of the Boiling 65% Nitric Acid Test on Selected 17% Chromium Alloys Containing Carbon and Nitrogen[53]

Carbon, %	Nitrogen, %	Corrosion rate, mdd (mm/yr), for the average of five successive 48-h periods after 1-h heat treatment at indicated temperature, water-quenched			
		1450°F (788°C)	1700°F (926°C)	1900°F (1038°C)	2100°F (1150°C)
0.0021	0.0095	167 (4.24)	185 (4.70)	148 (3.76)	326 (8.28)
0.0025	0.022	164 (4.17)	944 (23.98)		761 (19.33)
0.0044	0.057	186 (4.72)		577 (14.66)	357 (9.07)
0.012	0.0089	126 (3.20)	824 (20.93)	1817 (46.15)	
0.061	0.0071	147 (3.73)	619 (15.72)	1574 (39.98)	

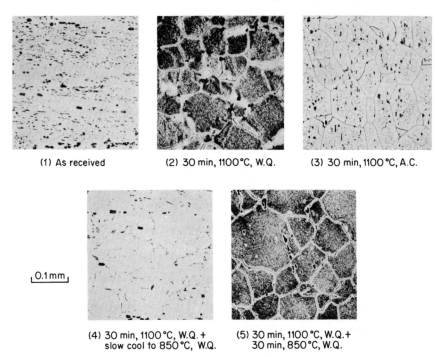

(1) As received   (2) 30 min, 1100 °C, W.Q.   (3) 30 min, 1100 °C, A.C.

0.1 mm

(4) 30 min, 1100 °C, W.Q. +   (5) 30 min, 1100 °C, W.Q. +
    slow cool to 850 °C, W.Q.   30 min, 850 °C, W.Q.

Fig. 16 Relationship between thermal treatments and microstructure on an AISI Type 446 steel; 26Cr-0.095C-0.077N; see corrosion rates for samples in table 5.[45]

ture sensitization problem in ferritic stainless steel is caused by chromium-rich precipitates formed at grain boundaries when the alloys are cooled through a temperature from about 400 to 900°C.

Using selected Fe-26Cr alloys of reduced interstitial levels, Demo[45] defined the sensitization range for Fe-26Cr alloys (0.1 in. (2.5 mm) thick). To do this he used alloys which had excellent corrosion resistance when quenched from 1100°C, but poor corrosion resistance if air-cooled such that the quenched alloys were supersaturated in carbon and nitrogen at room temperature. The water-quenched alloys were then subjected to a second heat treatment at selected times and temperatures between 400 and 1000°C. The alloys were corrosion tested and microstructurally examined. From the corrosion data, Demo constructed a time-temperature-sensitization (TTS) envelope for Fe-26Cr ferritic stainless steel as shown in Fig. 17. The microstructure of selected examples (whose positions are marked on Fig. 17) and their corrosion resistance are tabulated in Fig. 18. Sample 1, heated at 1100°C and water-quenched, had good corrosion resistance consistent with the absence of grain-boundary precipitates. Sample 2, on the other hand, air-cooled from 1100°C, had poor corrosion resistance consistent with the grain-boundary precipitates of chromium-rich carbides and nitrides. Sample 3, water-quenched from 1100°C, then reheated at 900°C, had good corrosion resistance and a harmless discontinuous intergranular precipitate. Comparing micrographs of samples 3 and 1 offers very strong evidence that chromium-rich materials precipitate even at 900°C, followed by agglomeration and growth of the precipitates. Sample 4, reheated for a short time at 700°C, exhibited good corrosion resistance, but the presence of a continuous intergranular precipitate is evident. At this temperature, the rapid precipitation of chromium-rich carbides and nitrides to relieve supersaturation was compensated for by almost simultaneous diffusion of chromium which healed the initial chromium-depleted areas adjacent to the precipitate. On the other hand, sample 5, heated for the same time as sample 4 but at 600°C, showed severe intergranular corrosion as well as a continuous grain-boundary precipitate. Under this condition of time and temperature, the rapid precipitation of chromium-rich precipi-

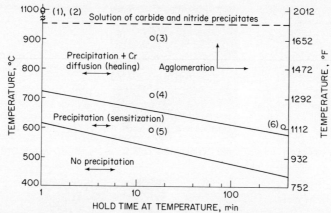

Fig. 17 TTS diagram for Fe-26Cr alloys treated initially at 1100°C (2012°F), 30 min, water-quenched, then reheated at selected lower temperatures for different times; corrosion tested in boiling ferric sulfate—50% sulfuric acid solution; (C + N) = 180 ppm.[45]

tates occurred to relieve supersaturation, but with reduced diffusion rates, chromium atoms did not have time to diffuse into the depleted areas. This fact is demonstrated by sample 6, also exposed at 600°C, but for a long time (6 h). Sample 6 had a continuous grain-boundary precipitate, but unlike sample 5, it had good corrosion resistance. The longer holding time allowed the chromium atoms to diffuse into the chromium-depleted areas adjacent to the grain-boundary precipitate restoring the alloy's corrosion resistance. In

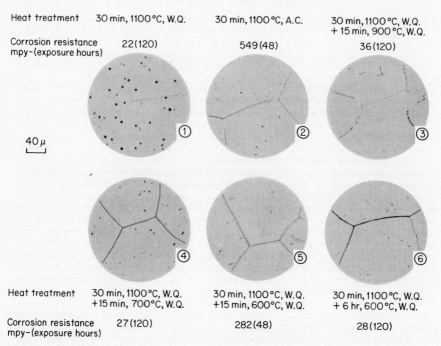

Fig. 18 Microstructure and corrosion resistance of alloys treated as indicated by the numbered positions on the TTS diagram in Fig. 17; corrosion tested in boiling ferric sulfate—50% sulfuric acid solution.[45]

consideration of Fig. 17, the line marking the low-temperature side of the TTS band reflects the minimum time and temperature required for chromium-rich carbides and nitrides to precipitate from a supersaturated solid solution and to form chromium-depleted zones. The line marking the high-temperature side of the sensitization zone represents, for 0.1 in. (2.5 mm) material, minimum conditions of time and temperature necessary for chromium diffusion to occur and heal the depleted areas after the matrix supersaturation in interstitial has been relieved by precipitation of chromium-rich carbides and nitrides.

These data are consistent with the chromium depletion theory for intergranular corrosion. When ferritic stainless steels are heated above about 950°C, the chromium-rich carbide and nitride precipitates are dissolved in solid solution. If the interstitial levels are very low, they will be maintained in solid solution if the sample is rapidly cooled. For these quenched-alloy compositions, the corrosion resistance is good. If these alloys now supersaturated in carbon and nitrogen are subjected to temperatures from about 500 to 950°C, chromium-rich carbides and nitrides rapidly precipitate to relieve supersaturation. In the temperature range of about 700 to 950°C, almost as fast as precipitation occurs, chromium diffuses into the chromium-depleted areas formed when precipitation first occurred, increasing the chromium content of these areas. Consequently intergranular corrosion resistance is good despite the observed presence of an intergranular precipitate. In the temperature range of 500 to 700°C where chromium-rich carbides and nitrides rapidly precipitate, the resulting chromium-depleted zones are not healed except during long holding times because the diffusion rate of chromium is markedly lower at these lower temperatures.

The chromium depletion theory in light of the above description can also explain the effects of heat treatment on the corrosion resistance and microstructure on the high interstitial alloys like AISI Type 430 and 446 stainless steels. For these alloys, in contrast with the low interstitial alloys, even rapid quenching from temperatures above 950°C is not fast enough to prevent precipitation of chromium-rich carbides and nitrides and chromium depletion results. This behavior is produced by the high driving force for precipitation in the intermediate temperature ranges caused by a combination of high interstitial supersaturation, rapid diffusion of carbon and nitrogen as compared to chromium and high rates of precipitation in the ferritic matrix. The corrosion resistance of a sensitized high interstitial alloy can also be restored by heating in the temperature range of about 700 to 950°C. This heat treatment permits chromium to diffuse into the depleted areas, raising the chromium content and restoring corrosion resistance even though a grain-boundary precipitate may still be observed in the microstructure (sample 5, Fig. 16). A long-time heat treatment in this temperature range as used in commercial annealing practices may even allow sufficient time for the fine grain-boundary precipitates to agglomerate into large, discontinuous precipitates which are thermodynamically more stable and often observed for long-time heat treatments (samples 1 and 4, Fig. 16).

In 1970, Hodges[43,55] demonstrated that high-purity alloys from 17 to 26% chromium were highly resistant to intergranular corrosion following exposures to temperatures above about 950°C. Based on his work, he concluded that sensitization in ferritic stainless steels could be explained best on the basis of the chromium depletion theory. Hodges noted that the sensitization-desensitization behavior of ferritic stainless steels containing moderately low interstitial levels could be described by the same type of TTS curve as reported for austenitic stainless steels—the difference being that the time sequence for sensitization-desensitization for austenitic stainless steels is minutes and hours, but only seconds and minutes for ferritic stainless steels. Hodges also showed that molybdenum as an alloying element in high-purity ferritic stainless steels shifts the sensitizing envelope to longer times, thereby delaying sensitization and loss of intergranular corrosion resistance. Streicher[59] showed for high-purity ferritic alloys that the interstitial levels tolerable without sensitization occurring are increased when molybdenum additions up to 6%, and preferably 4%, are made.

Streicher[56] has studied in detail the effects of carbon and nitrogen level and heat treatment on the microstructure and corrosion resistance of Cr-Fe alloys. In particular, he has carefully documented the regions of attack in samples which are either fully ferritic or a mixture of ferrite and austenite, depending on where the alloy composition was located according to the phase diagrams in Fig. 3 when it was exposed to high temperatures. As an example taken from his work, a commercial Type 446 steel (26% chromium) containing

0.098% carbon and 0.21% nitrogen contains up to about 40% austenite when water-quenched from a heat treatment at 1150°C. As shown in Fig. 19*a* from Streicher's work, no chromium-rich precipitates of carbon and nitrogen are formed at the boundary between austenite grains or in the austenite grains themselves because of the high solubility of carbon and nitrogen in austenite. When this sample was subjected to the ferric sulfate–sulfuric acid corrosion test, (Fig. 19*b*) severe intergranular attack occurred at the ferrite-ferrite and ferrite-austenite boundaries because carbon and nitrogen were rejected due to

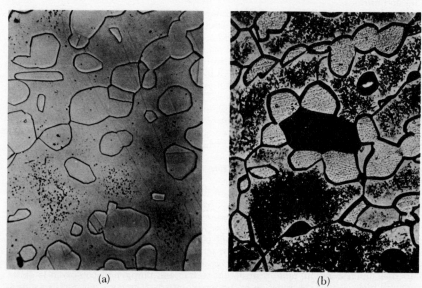

(a) (b)

Fig. 19 (*a*) Structure of Type 446 steel heated at 1150°C (500 ×). Etched surface shows "dot" precipitate in ferrite matrix, but not near austenite grains, which have absorbed carbon and nitrogen from adjacent ferrite. (*b*) Initial attack of ferric sulfate solution on Type 446 steel heated at 1150°C (2102°F), water-quenched (500 ×). Intergranular attack on ferrite-ferrite and ferrite-austenite boundaries. No intergranular attack on austenite-austenite boundaries. Localized attack on dot precipitates which are absent in zones near austenite grains, but not at ferrite-ferrite boundaries; exposed 14 h in boiling ferric sulfate—50% sulfuric acid solution.[56]

the low interstitial solubility in ferrite. However, no attack is observed at the austenite-austenite boundaries because the interstitials are maintained in solid solution due to their high solubility in austenite. Streicher[56] also showed that heat treatments have no detrimental affects on the intergranular corrosion susceptibility of high-purity 16% and 25% Cr-Fe stainless steels (carbon ≤ 0.0086%, nitrogen ≤ 0.0025%). From his work, he also concludes that the chromium depletion theory can adequately explain intergranular corrosion and other forms of localized attack occurring in Cr-Fe stainless steels.

Based on the work of a number of investigators, the high-temperature loss of corrosion resistance observed when ferritic alloys of high interstitial contents are heated above about 950°C may be explained by the chromium depletion theory which is widely accepted as the cause for sensitization in austenitic stainless steels. No support for alternate theories proposed to explain the high-temperature corrosion loss phenomenon can be found. These alternate theories were based on (1) the preferential dissolution of iron carbides, (2) accelerated corrosion due to stresses surrounding chromium-rich precipitates, (3) the presence of austenite or its decomposition products at grain boundaries, and (4) galvanic action between the precipitate and the surrounding metal matrix.

High-Temperature Embrittlement. Whenever commercial high-chromium–iron ferritic stainless steels containing moderate-to-high interstitial levels are heated above about 1000°C, the alloys at room temperature show an extreme loss in toughness and ductility. If an embrittled alloy is reheated in a temperature range of 750 to 850°C, the ductility of the alloy is restored. Two early theories, coherent state and the martensitic mechanism, proposed to explain this high-temperature embrittling phenomenon were described earlier. Baerlecken et al.,[2] Demo,[45] Semchyshen et al.,[60] and Plumtree et al.[61] through their work have shown that high-temperature embrittlement was related to interstitial levels in the alloy just as is loss of intergranular corrosion resistance.

Baerlecken et al.[2] studied the effects of heat treatment on the toughness (impact

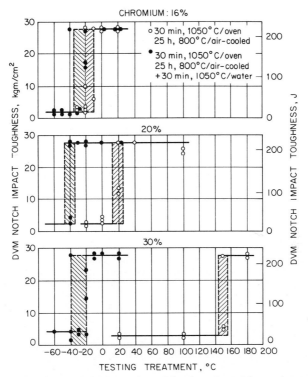

Fig. 20 Effect of heat treatment on the position of the sharp drop of the notch impact toughness-temperature curve of vacuum-melted chromium steels with 16 to 30% chromium.[2]

strength) of air-melted steels containing moderate levels of carbon and nitrogen and vacuum-melted steel containing very low interstitial levels. These workers, using air-melted steel, concluded that the variable toughness as a function of heat treatment and chromium content was connected with the structure and morphology of the carbide precipitates. Using high-purity vacuum-melted alloys given a two-stage heat treatment (30 min at 1050°C, cooled to 800°C for 25 h), these workers showed that the impact transition temperature was shifted to higher temperatures as the chromium content increased. However, if these same low interstitial alloys were given a second high-temperature heat treatment by reheating to 1050°C which would normally embrittle a high interstitial alloy they discovered that excellent low-temperature impact values were observed for alloys at all chromium levels. These results are shown in Fig. 20 from their work. They explained this effect of heat treatment on toughness by the fact that the solubility of the interstitials in the alpha solid solution decreases with increasing chromium content. Therefore, the initial two-stage heat treatment on samples of the same interstitial levels produces more precipitates of carbides and nitrides the higher the chromium content of the alloy is, with a resulting decrease in toughness (i.e., increase in the transition temperature). On the other hand, by a second-solution heat treatment and rapid quenching, it is possible, even with steels of high chromium content (and reduced carbon and nitrogen solubility), to keep the very low interstitial levels of vacuum-melted alloys in solid solution. Therefore, carbides and nitrides do not precipitate and their deleterious effects on notch impact toughness do not occur. Another important conclusion from their work is that grain size has little effect on notch impact behavior because high-chromium vacuum-melted alloys even with grain size ASTM 1-3 displayed transformation temperature of about $-40°C$.

Demo[45] studied the effect of thermal treatment on the ductility of high and low interstitial-purity alloys containing 26% chromium. As shown in Table 7, loss of ductility is observed only when the commercial AISI Type 446 stainless steel containing high interstitial levels is heated to 1100°C and water-quenched. Importantly, the same alloy more slowly cooled from the high-temperature exposure (i.e., air or slow cooled) shows excellent ductility as does the embrittled alloy when it is annealed by a second heat treatment at 850°C. In contrast, the ductility of the low interstitial 26% Cr steel is not adversely affected by heat treatment. These observations suggested to Demo that loss of ductility (i.e., tensile elongation) in Cr-Fe alloys when heated to high temperature as in welding or isothermal heat treatment was also related to interstitial content as suggested by Baerlecken et al., and cooling rate. Demo also examined in cross section the fractured edges of the heat-treated air-melted Type 446 stainless steels as shown in Fig. 21. The water-quenched sample (brittle) shows intragranular cleavage. The air-cooled sample (ductile) shows intergranular cleavage with some localized deformation and elongation of the grains. The slowly cooled sample (ductile) shows a fibrous shear structure with considerable localized deformation and elongation of the grains. Based on these observations, Demo concluded that precipitation of carbides and nitrides in the grain boundaries does not grossly affect ductility because both air-cooled and water-quenched samples had intergranular precipitates, but the failure mode in the brittle sample was predominantly intragranular. Moreover, an embrittled sample reheated to 850°C shows restored ductility despite the presence of a heavy intergranular precipitate as shown in Fig. 16 (sample 5). Finally, as shown in Table 7, an 18Cr-8Ni austenitic stainless steel which has been sensitized by heating at 677°C to cause grain-boundary precipitation of chromium carbides, retains excellent ductility.

Using thin-film electron microscopy examination, Demo has shown structural difference between embrittled and ductile alloys. Transmission micrographs of the water-quenched sample (brittle) and the air-cooled sample (ductile) are shown in Fig. 22. For the water-quenched samples, precipitates are noted not only in the grain boundaries as expected from the optical micrographs, but also on nearly all dislocations. On the other hand, no precipitates are observed on the dislocations of the air-cooled samples although grain-boundary precipitation is shown in the optical micrograph. Unrestrained motion of the dislocations in the water-quenched sample is blocked by the precipitate with a resulting increase in strength and reduction in ductility and toughness.

Demo proposed that precipitation of chromium-rich carbides and nitrides on dislocations in the grain body, and not on grain-boundary surfaces, is responsible for the severe loss in ductility when ferritic alloys are heated to high temperature. Demo suggests two possibilities to explain why chromium-rich precipitates form on dislocations in rapidly cooled samples and not in more slowly cooled samples, even though both contain

TABLE 7   Effect of Thermal Treatments on the Ductility of Stainless Alloys[45]

Condition	Elongation (in 25.4 mm) for the indicated stainless steels after heat treatment		
	AISI Type 446	High purity* 26% Cr	AISI Type 304
Annealed	25	30	78
30 min, 1100°C, water-quenched	2	30	84
30 min, 1100°C, air-cooled	27	32	85
30 min, 1100°C, slow cool† to 850°C, water-quenched	33	30	
30 min, 1100°C, water-quenched + 30 min, 850°C, water-quenched	27	29	
120 min, 677°C, air-cooled‡			84

*0.014% carbon, 0.004% nitrogen.
†Cooled in furnace at 2.5°C/min.
‡A heat treatment known to cause sensitization in AISI Type 304.

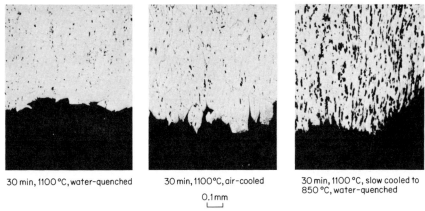

30 min, 1100 °C, water-quenched   30 min, 1100°C, air-cooled   30 min, 1100 °C, slow cooled to
850 °C, water-quenched

0.1mm
L__I

Fig. 21 Effect of cooling rate on the morphology of the fracture edges of a tensile sample made of an AISI Type 446 stainless steel heated to 1100°C (2012°F); 0.095C-0.077N. Furnace slow cool about 2.5°C (4.5°F) min.[45]

chromium-rich precipitates in the grain boundaries. First, the high interstitial contents of the air-melted alloys combined with the high interstitial supersaturation serves as a strong driving force during quenching for rapid precipitation on all high-energy surfaces such as grain boundaries and dislocations. During a slower cool, the longer relative time available to relieve supersaturation may allow diffusion of carbon and nitrogen to grain-boundary areas where the supersaturation is relieved by precipitation on the more preferred higher energy surfaces of the grain boundary. An alternate explanation is that dislocation nucleation during the rapid quench occurs simultaneously with rejection of carbon and nitrogen as chromium-rich carbides and nitrides precipitate to relieve the supersaturation. With a slower cool and therefore reduced thermal stresses, relief of supersaturation by precipita-

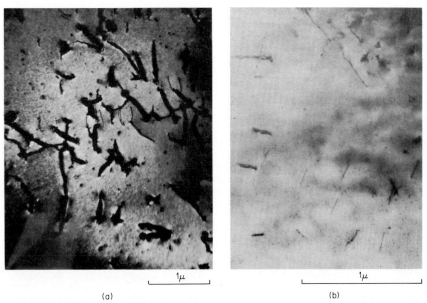

1μ   1μ

(a)   (b)

Fig. 22 Transmission electron micrographs of an AISI Type 446 stainless steel heated to 1100°C (2012°F) and (a) water-quenched; (b) air-cooled; 0.095C-0.077N.[54]

tion on high-energy surfaces may occur before dislocations are nucleated by the effects of thermal stresses. No matter, Demo associates the poor ductility of Cr-Fe alloys subjected to high-temperature exposure to fine, dispersed precipitates in the matrix preventing easy movement of dislocations similar to a hardening mechanism in a precipitation-hardened alloy.[62] An increase in strength is observed with a concomitant tremendous reduction in ductility and toughness.

Semchyshen, Bond, and Dundas[60] have reported the effects of chromium, carbon, and nitrogen levels and heat treatment on the toughness (impact resistance) of Cr-Fe alloys

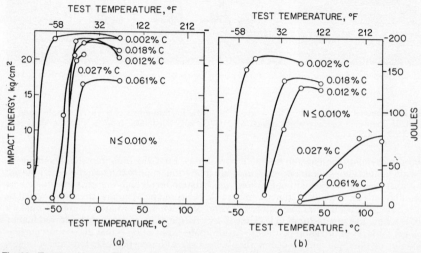

Fig. 23 Transition curves for quarter-size Charpy V-notch impact specimens of 17 Cr-0.002 to 0.061C ferritic stainless steels heat-treated at (a) 815°C for 1 h and water-quenched; (b) 815°C + 1150°C for 1 h and water-quenched.[60]

containing from about 14 to 28% chromium. The impact resistance of a 17% Cr steel in the annealed condition as a function of carbon content is shown in Fig. 23a. Note the relatively low transition temperatures even at carbon levels of 0.061%. These data may be contrasted with impact energy absorbed for the same samples sensitized by heating to 1150°C as shown in Fig. 23b. When the carbon content of the alloys exceeds about 0.018%, a large increase in transition temperature is observed. As noted, these alloys contain low levels of nitrogen (less than 0.0010%). These same workers repeated this work on a series of alloys containing increasing levels of nitrogen with carbon being held to low levels (below 0.004%). The impact data for the annealed samples and those annealed plus heated at 1150°C are shown in Fig. 24a and b. The annealed samples containing nitrogen up to 0.057% displayed excellent impact resistance. However, when the nitrogen content in the 17% Cr alloys exceeded about 0.022% nitrogen, the impact transition temperature was shifted to high temperatures following a thermal treatment at 1150°C. The same effects between carbon, nitrogen, heat treatment, and impact resistance were found for alloys containing 26% chromium. Semchyshen et al. also showed that a 17% Cr alloy containing 0.01% carbon or 0.02% nitrogen contained grain-boundary precipitates while alloys of higher purity remained free of grain-boundary precipitate after quenching from temperatures above about 925°C. Based on these data and observations, they conclude that high-temperature embrittlement (i.e., the observed increase in transition temperature when ferritic alloys are quenched from temperatures above about 1000°C) is caused by precipitates of chromium-rich carbonitrides mainly on the grain boundaries.

Plumtree et al.[61] in recent work showed that the impact transition temperature increased linearly with the total interstitial content for 25Cr-Fe alloys annealed and water-quenched. The data show a change in transition temperature from below room temperature to above in the range from 350 to 450 ppm total carbon + nitrogen + oxygen. These workers also showed that the impact transition temperature increases with the second-phase content. They proposed that increasing amounts of second phase inhomogeneously distributed throughout the matrix, particularly at the grain boundaries, lower the effective surface energy of a crack to promote cleavage failure and brittleness.

Baerlecken et al.,[2] Demo,[54] Semchyshen et al.,[60] and Plumtree et al.[61] all conclude from their data that the so-called high-temperature embrittlement phenomenon of high-chromium ferritic stainless steels is due to precipitation of chromium-rich carbides and nitrides caused by relief of supersaturation when the alloys are exposed to high temperatures. Baerlecken et al. and Semchyshen et al. find that embrittlement occurs because the

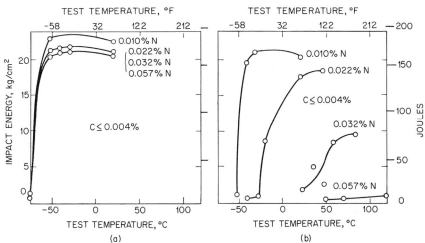

Fig. 24   Transition curves for quarter-size Charpy V-notch impact specimens of 17Cr-0.010 to 0.057N ferritic stainless steels heat-treated at (a) 815°C (1499°F) for 1 h and water-quenched; (b) 815°C (1499°F) + 1150°C (2102°F) for 1 h and water-quenched.[60]

chromium-rich precipitate forms on grain boundaries while Demo and Plumtree claim the embrittlement occurs because a finely dispersed precipitate in the grain matrix hinders dislocation motion and precipitates in the grain boundaries do not necessarily indicate alloy embrittlement. Perhaps the difference in thought resides in testing severity. A grain-boundary precipitate may be detrimental to the high-rate-energy absorbing requirement of the impact test, but perhaps not detrimental to the slow-rate-energy absorbing requirement of the tensile or slow bend test. The important point, however, is the general agreement that the high-temperature embrittlement phenomenon observed in ferritic stainless steels depends on the levels of carbon and nitrogen in the alloys. The embrittlement problem in Cr-Fe alloys will manifest itself whenever alloys containing moderate or high interstitial levels are heated to temperatures above about 950°C. The embrittlement is caused by precipitation of chromium-rich carbides and nitrides on grain boundaries and/or on dislocations. It is at once apparent that the same precipitation mechanism causing embrittlement also produces the serious loss of corrosion resistance when ferritic alloys are heated to high temperatures.

Notch Sensitivity in Annealed Alloys   Unlike the austenitic stainless steels, annealed Cr-Fe stainless steels are highly notch-sensitive in a manner similar to mild- and low-alloy steels.[24,63,64] Krivobok[65] showed in 1935 that the room-temperature impact resistance of Cr-Fe alloys in the presence of a notch sharply declined when the chromium content exceeded about 15%, and this decline in properties was independent of carbon content in the range of 0.01 to 0.20%. These data are shown in Fig. 25. Heger[66] did a comprehensive study of the effects of notching on the tensile and impact strength of annealed air-melted 27Cr-Fe alloys measured at room temperature and at elevated temperatures. These data were reported by Newell[24] in 1946. Looking first at the effect of a notch on tensile properties, Heger showed that the tensile strength increased and the elongation decreased in the presence of a notch. These effects are shown in Fig. 26 for short-time tests run from room to elevated temperature. The difference in tensile

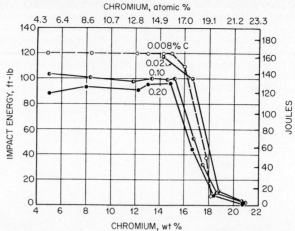

Fig. 25 Effect of variation in chromium and carbon content on the notch impact toughness of commercial chromium stainless steels.[65]

and elongation properties between notched and unnotched samples remained, even up to temperatures of 426 to 538°C. When Heger considered the effect of a notch on the impact resistance of a 27Cr-Fe alloy, he found a surprising difference in the impact energy absorbed between the notched and unnotched specimens. Similar to Krivobok's data, the notched specimen showed low impact energy absorption, but the unnotched specimen had high impact energy absorption. These data from Heger's work are shown in Fig. 27 along with the effect of testing temperature. There is a wide difference in the energy absorbed between the unnotched and notched specimen at room temperature which persists up to about 870°C testing temperature. However, the magnitude of the difference in impact absorption energy between the two types of specimens decreases as temperature increases because the impact absorption energy for the unnotched

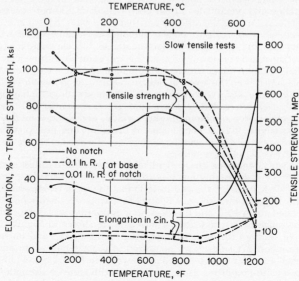

Fig. 26 Effect of a notch on the short-time, high-temperature, tensile properties of 27Cr-Fe air-melted alloy.[24,66]

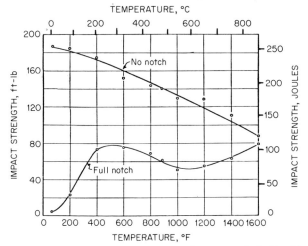

Fig. 27 Effect of temperature on the impact properties of 27% air-melted alloy. No notch vs. full notch.[24,66]

specimen declines and for the notched specimen, increases. At temperatures of 870°C and above, the alloy was no longer notch-sensitive. These data indicate the value of preheating air-melted chromium-iron alloys to reduce notch sensitivity in severe forming operations.

Based on data such as from Krivobok and Heger, it was generally believed into the late 1940s that notch sensitivity occurred independent of carbon and nitrogen content[63,67] and in fact was associated with the high chromium content of the alloys per se. Later work by Hochmann[68] and Binder and Spendelow[69] showed that notch sensitivity in annealed Cr-Fe alloys with high chromium levels was again basically caused by the presence of critical levels of interstitial elements, particularly carbon, nitrogen, and oxygen. The dramatic effects of interstitial level on the impact behavior of annealed Cr-Fe alloys were discovered when vacuum-melting techniques were developed and used to produce alloys with extremely low interstitial levels.

The impact strength measured at room temperature of vacuum-melted Cr-Fe alloys as a function of chromium content is shown in Fig. 28 from Binder et al.[69] The maximum interstitial content of the alloys used to generate these data include 0.015C-0.01N-0.04O. As shown in Fig. 28, the toughness of these high-purity alloys increases as chromium content is raised, reaching a maximum at about 26% chromium, where unheard-of impact strength values of 100 ft-lb (136 J) are apparent. In contrast to Krivobok's data (Ref. 65, Fig. 25) which showed a sharp drop in impact strength for alloys containing more than about 16% chromium, use of the vacuum-melting process has raised the level of chromium for which excellent impact toughness may be obtained in the presence of a notch from 16% to somewhat greater than 35%. The key to this difference in impact performance between normal air-melted steels and vacuum-melted alloys is primarily in their carbon and nitrogen contents. The relationship between interstitial content and chromium content on toughness was determined in a very comprehensive investigation by Binder and Spendelow[69] as shown in Fig. 29. At chromium levels above about 15 to 18%, there is a drastic decrease in the carbon and nitrogen levels tolerable in a high-chromium alloy for high room-temperature impact resistance. For an

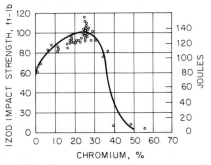

Fig. 28 Impact strength of vacuum-melted Cr-Fe alloys.[69]

air-melted steel with carbon and nitrogen contents up to about 0.12 and 0.05 %,[69] respectively, these data would predict good room-temperature impact resistance is possible only if the alloys contain chromium levels below 15 to 18%. The agreement with Krivobok's early data[65] on air-melted alloys is excellent, but the conclusion that poor impact resistance was due to chromium content per se was incorrect. The low impact resistance of Krivobok's

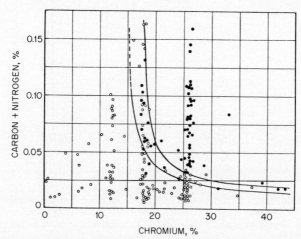

Fig. 29 Influence of carbon and nitrogen on toughness of Cr-Fe alloys. Open circles, high-impact-strength alloys; solid circles, low-impact-strength alloys.[69]

alloys containing more than 15 to 18% chromium was not caused by the chromium level, but was due to the high interstitial levels characteristic of air-melted steels.

Binder and Spendelow in their comprehensive investigation also determined the individual effects of carbon and nitrogen on impact resistance of annealed alloys at two levels of chromium, 18 and 25%. These data are tabulated in Figs. 30 and 31, respectively. Both illustrations show

1. That a straight line of a 45° slope may be drawn to separate the areas of high and low toughness

2. That there is an equivalency in the effect by carbon and nitrogen on toughness

3. That the carbon plus nitrogen sum is critical rather than the absolute value of each separately

4. That the maximum sum of carbon plus nitrogen tolerable for good room-temperature toughness is 0.055% for 18% chromium and 0.035% for 25% chromium

The achievement of levels of 0.035% and lower was possible only in the laboratory in the late 1960s. With the development of economical vacuum melting and vacuum- and gas-refining techniques, commercial production of high Cr-Fe steel became feasible and a reality. These alloys, to be described later, show excellent toughness at room temperature in the presence of notches. However, for available air-melted alloys such as AISI Type 430 (18% chromium), Type 442 (20% chromium) and Type 446 (26% chromium) notch sensitivity is a factor of major importance which must be carefully considered in application of these alloys. Good engineering practice requires avoiding surface scratches and reentrant angles, notches or other forms of stress raisers when these air-melted alloys are used under shock-loading conditions.

WELDABLE, CORROSION-RESISTANT, DUCTILE FERRITIC STAINLESS STEELS

The largest single drawback to the use of ferritic stainless steels has been the loss of corrosion resistance and ductility following exposure to high temperatures as in welding and isothermal heat treatments. The other problems with ferritic stainless steel (475°C

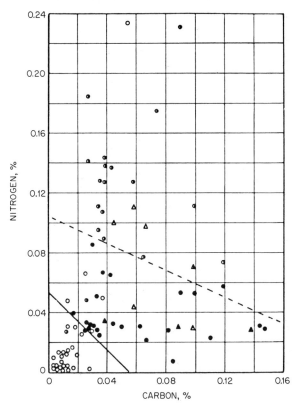

Fig. 30 Effects of carbon and nitrogen on the toughness of 17 to 19 Cr-Fe alloys. Open circles, high-impact-strength alloys; solid circles, low-impact-strength alloys; semisolid circles, intermediate-impact-strength alloys; triangles, commercial arc-melted steels.[69]

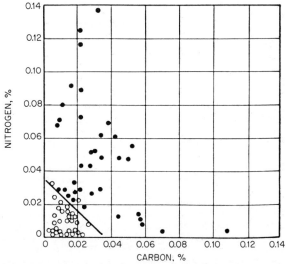

Fig. 31 Effects of carbon and nitrogen on the toughness of 24 to 26 Cr-Fe alloys. Open circles high-impact-strength alloys; solid circles, low-impact-strength alloys.[69]

and sigma-phase embrittlements) can be tolerated because relatively long exposure times at moderate temperatures are required to cause these other embrittling problems. However, unless a material has good corrosion resistance and ductility in the as-welded condition, its usefulness as a material of construction is severely limited. As described above, the cause for the serious loss in ductility and corrosion resistance when ferritic stainless steels are exposed to high temperatures, and for the notch sensitivity of annealed alloys, is related to the interstitial content of the alloys. After research in the early and mid-1960s had shown this fact, the research effort in the late 1960s saw development and commercialization of weldable, corrosion-resistant Cr-Fe alloys. Three routes to achieve interstitial control were researched and developed. Demo[70] has summarized and described these methods.

Low Interstitials By reducing the interstitial levels below certain minimum values, weldability and corrosion resistance can be produced as shown in the works of Hochmann,[68] Demo,[70] Bond,[53] Streicher,[56,59] and Hodges.[43,55] Binder's (Ref. 69, Fig. 29) early work showed how the impact resistance of annealed ferritic stainless steels varied with interstitial and chromium content. A similar type of study by Demo[70] showed the relationship of interstitial level and chromium content on the ductility and corrosion resistance of as-welded alloys. These data are summarized in Fig. 32 and include a comparison to Binder's data for impact resistance on annealed samples. The carbon and nitrogen levels which can be present without affecting the weldability of a Cr-Fe alloy are low and decrease rapidly with increasing chromium content. As can be seen from the data in Fig. 32, the interstitial tolerance level for a "good" as-welded sample at a given chromium level is lower than that needed for impact resistance of an annealed sample. Demo further studies the variation in the properties of weld ductility and weld corrosion resistance as functions of chromium content and interstitial sum level. These data are given in Table 8. As chromium content increases from 19 to 35%, the amount of carbon plus nitrogen that can be tolerated for intergranular corrosion resistance increases somewhat. Conversely, for as-welded ductility, the sum of tolerable interstitials is reduced drastically. At low chromium levels, as-welded corrosion resistance is the factor controlling whether an alloy has good weldability; at high chromium levels, as-welded ductility is the limiting factor. At the 26% chromium level, intergranular corrosion resistance is more sensitive to the interstitial sum level than is ductility while at 35% chromium, the as-welded ductility is more critically dependent on the interstitial sum than is corrosion resistance.

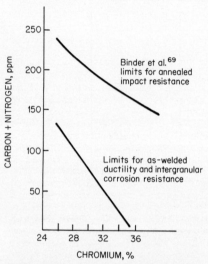

Fig. 32 Effects of carbon and nitrogen level and chromium content on the as-welded ductility and intergranular corrosion resistance of Cr-Fe ferritic stainless steels. Comparison to Binder's limit for impact resistance of annealed samples.[70]

To produce weldable and corrosion-resistant Cr-Fe alloys by this means, it is evident that very low levels of carbon and nitrogen are needed. Until recently, such low levels could only be produced in a laboratory or by using high-purity raw materials. However, technological advances in steelmaking practices have made the concept of low interstitial ferritic alloys possible through the development of such techniques as oxygen-argon melting, vacuum refining and electron-beam refining. Of particular note is the electron-beam continuous-hearth refining technique developed by Airco Vacuum Metals and described by Knoth.[71] This process has the advantage of achieving the lowest carbon and nitrogen levels by exposing a high surface-to-volume ratio of molten metal to a high vacuum for extended periods of time. As the molten metal flows down a series of water-cooled copper hearths, electron-beam heat sources provide localized regions of intense heat in the molten metal causing volatilization and removal of tramp impurity elements.

TABLE 8   Carbon plus Nitrogen Limits for As-welded Properties of Intergranular Corrosion Resistance and Ductility as a Function of Chromium Content[70]

Chromium level, wt %	Limit for sum of C + N (ppm) to have the indicated property in an as-welded alloy*	
	Intergranular† corrosion resistance	Ductility‡
19	60–80	>700
26	100–130	200–500
30	130–200	80–100
35	~ 250	<20

*Sample thickness: 0.1 in. (2.54 mm) thick.
†Intergranular corrosion resistance in boiling ferric sulfate–50% sulfuric acid solution.
‡No cracks as determined by bending around a 0.2-in. (5.08-mm) mandrel.

The process is currently being used to commercially produce a high-purity ferritic stainless containing nominally 26Cr-1Mo-bal Fe. By maintaining the carbon plus nitrogen level below 250 ppm, it is reported[72,73] that this commercially available alloy is ductile and corrosion-resistant following welding, has good toughness and combines resistance to stress-corrosion cracking with good general corrosion and pitting resistance. However, for a weldment to be resistant to intergranular attack, a carbon plus nitrogen sum level at or near 250 ppm is too high. Demo[45] reports intergranular attack on a high-purity 26% chromium alloy containing 180 ppm carbon plus nitrogen, while Streicher (Ref. 59, Table 2) shows grain dropping in the weld and heat-affected zone of two high-purity 26Cr-1Mo alloys containing, respectively, 105 and 230 ppm carbon plus nitrogen. For complete resistance to intergranular attack following welding or isothermal heat treatment, it appears that the carbon plus nitrogen levels in 26Cr and 26Cr-1Mo high-purity alloy systems must be maintained below about 100 to 120 ppm[70] with nitrogen[59] less than 90 ppm. The high impact values at and below room temperature for an electron-beam refined 26Cr-1Mo alloy as compared to a 26Cr-1Mo alloy containing 0.08% carbon is remarkable as shown in Fig. 33.[60,72] The scatter band in the E-Brite 26Cr-1Mo alloy data is the result of specimen orientation, variations in thermal treatments and cooling rates.

Interstitial Stabilization   A second means to control interstitials is to add elements to the alloy which form stronger carbides and nitrides than does chromium. Such elements include titanium, niobium, zirconium, and tantalum. The early work by Lula, Lena, and Kiefer[48] describes a comprehensive effort to study the intergranular corrosion behavior of ferritic stainless steel including the effects of titanium and niobium additions. These investigators showed that titanium and niobium additions were not completely effective in preventing sensitization when the alloys were subjected to high temperature. This result was caused by not considering the need to tie up nitrogen as well as carbon and also by the fact, unknown at the time, that TiC itself is dissolved in highly oxidizing

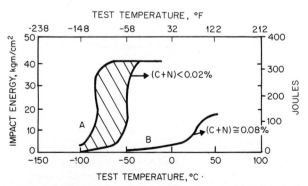

Fig. 33   (a) Charpy V-notch transition temperature range for commercially produced, electron-beam-melted ferritic steel containing 26Cr-1Mo.[72] (b) Transition curve for quarter-size V-notch impact specimens of an air-melted steel containing 26Cr-1Mo.[60]

TABLE 9   Effect of Stabilizer Additions on the Tensile Ductility of Annealed vs. Welded Samples Containing 18Cr-2Mo[60]

| C + N, wt % | Ti or Nb, wt % | % elongation in 2 in. (50 mm) | |
		Annealed	As-welded
0.005	0	33	31
0.03	0	31	8
0.07	0.5	34	30
0.06	0.6	28	21

solutions such as the boiling nitric acid solution used in the study.

More recent work by Baumel,[74] Bond and Lizlovs,[52] and Demo[75,76] has shown that niobium and titanium additions were effective in preventing intergranular corrosion following exposure of ferritic stainless steels to high temperatures such as isothermal heat treatments and welding. To resist intergranular corrosion, titanium additions of about 6 to 10 times the combined carbon and nitrogen level are necessary; for niobium, additions of 8 to 11 times are required. The relationship of interstitial content, chromium level, and titanium level for intergranular corrosion resistance and ductility after welding has been extensively studied by Demo.[75,76] Bond et al.,[52] Lula et al.,[48] Herbsleb,[77] Baumel,[74] and Cowling et al.[78] have shown that titanium-stabilized alloys may show intergranular attack when exposed to a highly oxidizing solution such as boiling nitric acid because of the dissolution of titanium carbonitrides; however, niobium-stabilized alloys resist intergranular attack even in highly oxidizing solutions.

Demo,[75,76] Semchyshen et al.,[60] Wright,[79] and Pollard[80] have reported the effects of stabilizing additions on the weld ductility of ferritic stainless steels. By introducing titanium or niobium in the ferritic alloy, the level of interstitial which can be present in the matrix without adversely affecting the room-temperature ductility after welding is significantly increased. These data are shown in Table 9 by the tensile ductility measurements on welded 18Cr-2Mo samples[60] and in Table 10 by slow bend tests on welded 26 to 30% Cr alloys.[75,76,79] With stabilizer additions, the interstitial elements are effectively tied up as stable carbides and nitrides so that their effective level in solid solution is reduced. Consequently, stabilized alloys at relatively high levels of carbon and nitrogen act similarly to the very low interstitial alloys described above in having excellent corrosion resistance and ductility (tensile or bend) following exposure to high temperatures which, without stabilization, would cause loss of corrosion resistance and ductility.

The effects of stabilizing additions on the impact properties of Cr-Fe alloys in comparison to the impact properties of low interstitial alloys, however, presents another story. The effects of stabilizing additives on impact properties have been studied and described by Semchyshen et al.[60] and Wright.[79] Two aspects have been studied, namely the effect of Ti content and interstitial level on the impact resistance of (1) annealed samples and (2) samples heated to high temperatures by welding or isothermal heat treatments. In the annealed condition, the Ti-modified steels exhibit transition temperatures commensurate with their interstitial levels; i.e., whatever the impact transition temperature is for the

TABLE 10   Effect of Titanium on the As-welded Bend Ductility for Cr-Fe Ferritic Stainless Steels Containing 26 to 30% Chromium[75,76,79]

C + N, ppm	Ti, wt %	Bend test ductility As-welded
113	0	Passed 180°, 2t*
310	0	Passed 180°, ½t†
362	0	Failed 90°, 2t*
450	0	Failed 90°, 2t*
900	0	Failed 135°, 1t†
300	0.22	Passed 180°, ½t*
387	0.24	Passed 180°, 2t*
488	0.47	Passed 180°, 2t*
850	0.45	Passed 180°, ½t†

*0.1-in. (2.54-mm) thick samples.
†0.06-in. (1.524-mm) thick samples.

unstabilized, annealed alloy as a function of interstitial level (see Fig. 29) remains about the same or is slightly reduced when the alloy is stabilized.

Stabilizing additions of titanium, however, are useful in reducing the detrimental effects of high-temperature treatments on the impact resistance of high interstitial alloys. These effects of stabilizing additions taken from Semchyshen et al.[60] are shown in Fig. 34 for air-melted commercial purity (0.07% carbon plus nitrogen) 18Cr-2Mo alloy. Increases in titanium content from 0 to 0.8% show little affect on the impact transition temperature of annealed (815°C) samples. However, increases in titanium content from zero up to

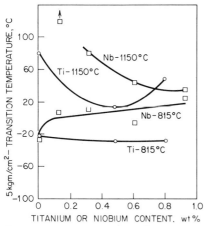

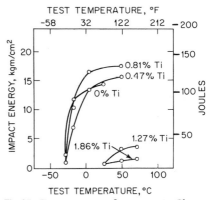

Fig. 34 Transition temperatures for quarter-size Charpy V-notch specimens air-melted commercial-purity 18Cr-2Mo steels water-quenched from 1150°C (2102°F) (sensitized) and 815°C (1499°F) (annealed) as a function of titanium or niobium content.[60]

Fig. 35 Transition curves for quarter-size Charpy V-notch impact specimens of air-melted 18Cr-2Mo-0 to 1.86Ti ferritic stainless steels heat-treated at 815°C (1499°F) for 1 h and water-quenched.[60]

about 0.5% improves (lowers) the transition temperature when the alloys are subjected to a high-temperature treatment (1150°C). These data also show that niobium additions, though effective in lowering the transition temperature for alloys subjected to high temperature, were somewhat harmful to the impact resistance of the alloys in the annealed condition. Semchyshen et al.[60] also showed that titanium additions beyond about 10 times the combined carbon and nitrogen content could affect (increase) the impact transition temperature of annealed 18Cr-2Mo alloys (0.07% carbon plus nitrogen) as shown in Fig. 35. A precipitation of an intermetallic phase markedly increased impact transition temperatures.

Superimposed on the effects of titanium and interstitial content on the ductility and impact resistance of Cr-Fe alloys is the marked affect of thickness on these properties, particularly impact resistance. This point is shown by the data in Table 11 taken from Wright's work.[79] In order to have acceptable properties (weldability and toughness) at plate gages as heavy as 0.5 in. (12.7 mm), the interstitial sum level in a 26% Cr alloy must be as low or lower than about 100 to 125 ppm. For alloys containing about 300 to 900 ppm total carbon and nitrogen, toughness may be poor at gages above about 0.13 in. (3.3 mm) and weldability poor at all gage thicknesses. The addition of titanium increases the thickness or gage level at which an alloy will have good weldability. For example, as Wright notes, a 26Cr-1Mo alloy containing 300 ppm total carbon and nitrogen and 0.22% titanium has excellent toughness and weldability (i.e., as-welded ductility and corrosion resistance) up to a gage thickness of about 0.13 in. (3.3 mm).

In summary, adding a stabilizer to an alloy of moderate carbon and nitrogen will not significantly improve the annealed impact behavior but may tremendously improve the as-welded ductility and corrosion resistance. This point is a most important difference between stabilized alloys and low interstitial alloys. The high-purity material will have

TABLE 11   Impact Transition Temperatures as a Function of Gage and Added Titanium for Annealed 26Cr-1Mo Alloys[79]

C + N, wt %	Charpy V-notch, ductile-to-brittle temperature, °C		
	Gage thickness, in. (mm)		
	0.5 (12.7)*	0.12–0.14 (3.05–3.56)*	0.06 (1.52)†
0.0065	−57		−73
0.0310	149	38	−73
0.0900	162	38	−18
0.0300 + 0.22Ti	121	−1	−46
0.0850 + 0.45Ti	107	38	−46

*Water-quenched after anneal.
†Air-cooled after anneal.

excellent toughness and as-welded corrosion resistance and ductility. The stabilized material will also have excellent as-welded corrosion resistance and ductility but may not have high room-temperature impact resistance. These effects as shown by Wright[79] are particularly magnified at section thicknesses greater than about ⅛ in. (3.18 mm). Therefore, for thick plate sections where high room-temperature toughness is an absolute requirement, the low interstitial alloys would be acceptable, but the stabilized grades would not be. On the other hand, for thin material, as required in heat-exchanger tubing, the titanium-stabilized alloys and the low interstitial alloys have similar toughness and weldability properties so that either alloy system may be used.

Weld Ductilizing Additions   A third method to produce high Cr-Fe ferritic stainless steels with good as-welded ductility is by the addition of low concentrations of selected elements with atomic radius within 15% of the alpha matrix. This method was developed and extensively investigated by R. F. Steigerwald et al.[81] As noted in Fig. 32, the carbon and nitrogen level for as-welded ductility is drastically reduced as chromium content increases. At 35% chromium, an impossibly low interstitial level of about 10 to 15 ppm is necessary for as-welded ductility. Steigerwald et al. found that in the presence of low amounts of copper, aluminum, vanadium, and combinations of these elements, alloys with good as-welded ductility could be produced at high interstitial levels. A summary of this work is shown in Fig. 36. With selective additives, an alloy containing 35% chromium can be produced with both as-welded ductility and corrosion resistance at interstitial levels of 250 ppm versus the 10 to 15 ppm level needed at this chromium level when the additives are absent. It is remarkable that a ferritic stainless steel containing 35% chromium can be made with as-welded ductility at intermediate interstitial levels.

Sigma-Phase and 475°C Embrittlement Susceptibility   By the techniques of interstitial control, Cr-Fe alloys can be produced which resist the damaging loss of corrosion resistance and ductility following high-temperature exposures as in welding or isothermal heat treatments. In addition, some alloys can be produced to also have high room-temperature impact toughness in thick sections. Therefore, by interstitial control methods, the high-temperature exposure and notch-sensitivity problems which previously have severely limited the usefulness of ferritic stainless steels have been removed. However, though not as serious as embrittling problems described

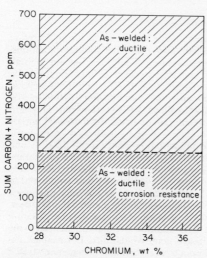

Fig. 36   Effect of weld ductilizing additives on the as-welded ductility and corrosion resistance of high Cr-Fe stainless steels; additives, singly or in combination include Al, Cu, V, Pt, Pd, Ag in a range 0.1 to 1.3%.[81]

earlier, the 475°C and sigma-phase embrittling phenomenon will still occur in alloy compositions made resistant to high-temperature exposure effects. This point has been shown by the work of Grobner[42] and Hochmann[44] and in reported data for E-Brite 26-I.[72]

Molybdenum Additions   For improving the general corrosion and pitting resistance of Cr-Fe stainless steels, the effects of molybdenum additions have been extensively studied or reported on by Bond,[82] Demo,[70] Streicher,[59] and Steigerwald[83–85] and are described in some detail in Chapter 13. Of particular note here is the effect of molybdenum additions on embrittling a Cr-Fe stainless steel. Semchyshen et al.[60] have summarized the data describing the effect molybdenum level has on the toughness of 18 and 25%

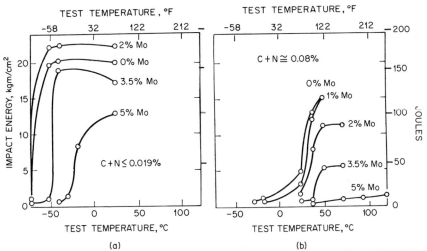

Fig. 37   Effects of molybdenum additions on the impact transition temperatures of annealed 25Cr-Fe stainless steels. (a) Vacuum-melted stainless steels heat-treated at 980°C (1796°F) for 1 h and water-quenched. (b) Air-melted stainless steels heat-treated at 815°C (1499°F) for 1 h and water-quenched. Quarter-size Charpy V-notch impact specimens.[60]

Cr alloys. The effects of molybdenum level on the impact transition temperature of annealed 25% Cr alloy containing high interstitials and low interstitials are shown in Fig. 37. There is considerable difference in the impact transition temperature of the high-purity alloys (−50°C) and the high interstitial alloys (+50°C) without a molybdenum addition, as described earlier. The point, however, is that molybdenum additions up to about 2 to 3% have little effect on toughness, but have an adverse effect when the molybdenum level exceeds about 3 to 4%. This decrease in toughness associated with high molybdenum content is caused by the formation of chi (χ) phase, a brittle inter-metallic compound of iron, chromium, and molybdenum.

Streicher[86] has reported on a study of the affects of heat treatment on the microstructure and formation of chi and sigma phase in two low interstitial alloys containing 28Cr-4Mo and 28Cr-4Mo-2Ni. Heat treatment in the range of 700 to 925°C for 1 h produced only a small amount of sigma at the grain boundaries. The largest amounts of sigma are formed by heating at 815°C. Heating for 100 h at 815°C caused sigma and large amounts of chi phase to form at grain boundaries and within the grains. The complex relationship between Cr, Mo, and Fe levels on the formation of chi and sigma phases has been described in detail by the work of McMullin et al.[87] The ternary phase diagram for the Fe-Cr-Mo system at 898°C isotherm as defined by McMullin et al. is shown in Fig. 38.[87] Chi phase is stable over a wider temperature range than sigma phase,[87] so annealing above 980°C is required to eliminate it in steels with 18% Cr and over 3.5% Mo[60] and in steels containing 28Cr-4Mo.[86]

For 26Cr-Fe alloys containing 1% molybdenum and stabilized with titanium, Aggen[88] and Demo[89] have shown that a corrosion-damaging second phase occurs in the alloy when

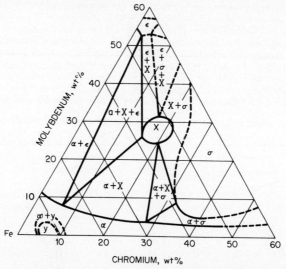

Fig. 38   Constitution of Fe-Cr-Mo alloys at 898°C (1650°F). σ, sigma; χ chi; ε, Fe₇Mo₆.[87]

a slight excess of titanium beyond that needed to tie up the interstitials is present. This phase, believed also to be chi, is richer than the matrix in titanium, molybdenum, and silicon and forms by isothermal holds for extended periods in the temperature range from 595 to 850°C. Before it has grown large enough to be seen by an optical microscope, the intergranular corrosion resistance of a susceptible alloy will be deleteriously affected when it is exposed to highly oxidizing solutions. The effect only appears in alloys containing molybdenum and excess titanium and can be removed by short annealing treatments at temperatures above about 900°C.

SUMMARY

Chromium-iron alloys are body-centered cubic up to the melting point. Therefore, hardening by the ferrite-austenite mechanism upon heating and quenching cannot occur. Ferritic Cr-Fe alloys can be embrittled by the phenomenon of 475°C embrittlement, sigma-phase embrittlement, or chi-phase embrittlement for those alloys containing

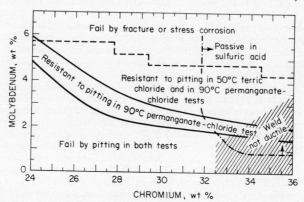

Fig. 39   Properties of Fe-Cr-Mo alloys. Pitting tests: 10% FeCl₃·6H₂O at 50°C (122°F) (with crevices, 2% KMnO₄-2% NaCl at 90°C (194°F). Stress corrosion test: 45% boiling [155°C (311°F)] MgCl₂ on welded U-bend specimens. Sulfuric acid: boiling 10% by weight. C, < 100 ppm; N, < 200 ppm; C + N, < 250 ppm.[59]

molybdenum. These embrittling mechanisms generally require a long-time isothermal treatment or very slow cool through the intermediate temperature regions such that they do not normally constitute a threat to the weldability and processing of ferritic stainless steels. The serious loss of ductility and corrosion resistance when ferritic stainless steels are subjected to high-temperature exposures as in welding or isothermal treatment and the problem of notch sensitivity have been shown to be related to interstitial levels in the alloys. By development of interstitial control techniques, it is now possible to produce high-chromium ferritic stainless steels which are corrosion-resistant and ductile following a high-temperature exposure as in welding or an isothermal heat treatment. Further, depending on the interstitial levels, high-chromium–iron alloys can be produced having excellent toughness and impact transition temperatures below room temperature. By making Cr-Fe stainless steels weldable and tough, and combining this property with stress-corrosion resistance and good general corrosion resistance, attractive new materials of construction are and will be available to compete with austenitic 18Cr-8Ni stainless steels.

Several organizations throughout the world are engaged in commercial development of ferritic stainless steels. An 18Cr-2Mo alloy stabilized with niobium or titanium is being produced in Europe. A comprehensive review article on the properties of 18% chromium ferritic alloys has been published by Schmidt and Jarleborg.[90] Where greater corrosion resistance is desired, several new compositions are either in commercial production or are actively being developed. These include a 26Cr-1Mo alloy produced either with extremely low interstitial levels by electron-beam melting techniques or with moderate interstitial levels stabilized with titanium and, to a lesser extent, with niobium. In commercial development are low interstitial alloys of the composition 26Cr-2Mo, 21Cr-3Mo, 28Cr-2Mo, 28Cr-4Mo, and 28Cr-4Mo-2Ni. These alloys have better general corrosion resistance than Type 316 stainless steel. Those like the 28Cr-4Mo and 28Cr-4Mo-2Ni alloys have been shown by Streicher[59] to have corrosion resistance in a variety of aggressive environments comparable or better than the highly alloyed nickel-based alloys. The complex relationship between Cr and Mo content on pitting resistance, ductility, and weld ductility as studied by Streicher[59] is shown in Fig. 39. As shown by these data, the 28Cr-4Mo alloys have better resistance to pitting than any other types of Cr-Mo-Fe alloys now under development. With a variety of desirable properties available, including good weldability and resistance to stress-corrosion cracking, a family of ferritic stainless steel compositions is becoming available for use as materials of construction and will replace the austenitic and nickel-based alloys in many applications.

REFERENCES

1. Bain, E. C., and R. H. Aborn: Chromium-Iron Phase Diagram, p. 1194, "Metals Handbook," American Society for Metals, Metals Park, Ohio, 1948.
2. Baerlecken, E., W. A. Fischer, and K. Lorenz: Studies of the Transformation Behavior, the Notch Impact Toughness and the Tendency Toward Intercrystalline Corrosion in Iron-Chromium Alloys with Chromium Contents up to 30%, *Stahl Eisen*, vol. 81, no. 12, pp. 768–778, 1961.
3. Colombier, L. and J. Hochmann: "Stainless and Heat-resisting Steels," Edward Arnold, England, 1967.
4. Nehrenberg, A. E. and P. Lillys: High Temperature Transformations in Ferritic Stainless Steels Containing 17 to 25% Chromium, *Trans. Am. Soc. Met.*, vol. 46, pp. 1177–1213, 1954.
5. Newell, H. D.: High Chromium-Irons, *Met. Prog.*, April, 1947, pp. 617–626.
6. Thielsch, H.: Physical and Welding Metallurgy of Chromium Stainless Steels, *Weld. J. Res. Suppl.*, vol. 30, pp. 209-s–250-s, 1951.
7. Rajkay, L.: The Thermal Embrittlement of Medium and High-Chromium Ferritic Steels, *Am. Soc. Test. Mater. Proc.*, vol. 67, pp. 158–169, 1967.
8. Kaltenhauser, R. H.: Improving the Engineering Properties of Ferritic Stainless Steels, *Met. Eng. Q.*, vol. 11, pp. 41–47, May, 1971.
9. Demo, J. J. and A. P. Bond: Intergranular Corrosion and Embrittlement of Ferritic Stainless Steels, *Corrosion*, vol. 31, no. 1, pp. 21–22, January, 1975.
10. Cook, A. J. and F. W. Jones: The Brittle Constituent of the Iron Chromium System (Sigma Phase), *J. Iron Steel Inst. London*, vol. 148, pp. 217–223, 1943.
11. Chevenard, P.: Recherches Experimentales Sur Les Alliages der Fer, de Nickel et de Chrome, *Trav. Mem. Bur. Int. Poids Mes.*, vol. 17, p. 90, 1927.
12. Bain, E. C. and W. E. Griffiths: An Introduction to the Iron-Chromium Nickel Alloys, *Trans. Am. Inst. Min. Metall. Pet. Engs.*, vol. 75, pp. 166–213, 1927.

13. Anderson, A. G. H. and E. R. Jette: X-Ray Investigation of the Iron-Chromium-Silicon Phase Diagram, *Trans. Am. Soc. Met.*, vol. 24, pp. 375–419, 1936.
14. Jette, E. R. and F. Foote: The Fe-Cr Alloy System, *Met. Alloys*, vol. 7, pp. 207–210, 1936.
15. Smith, G. V.: Sigma Phase in Stainless Steel, *Iron Age*, vol. 166, no. 22, pp. 63–68, 1950; vol. 166, no. 23, pp. 127–132, 1950.
16. Duwez, P. and S. R. Baen: *Symp. Nature, Occurrence and Effects of Sigma Phase*, ASTM, pp. 48–54, 1951.
17. Menezes, L., J. K. Roros, and T. A. Read: *Symp. Nature, Occurrence and Effects of Sigma Phase*, ASTM, pp. 71–74, 1951.
18. Dickens, G. J., A. M. B. Douglas, and W. H. Taylor: Structure of Sigma Phase in the Iron-Chromium and Cobalt-Chromium Systems, *Nature*, vol. 167, p. 192, 1951.
19. Heger, J. J.: Development of Sigma Phase in 27% Cr-Fe, *Met. Prog.*, vol. 49, p. 976B, 1946.
20. Shortsleeve, F. J., and M. E. Nicholson: Transformation in Ferritic Chromium Steels between 1100 and 1500°F (595 and 815°C), *Trans. Am. Soc. Met.*, vol. 43, pp. 142–156, 1951.
21. Olzak, Z. E.: The Effect of Alloy Composition on Sigma Phase Precipitation in 27% Chromium-Iron Catalyst Tubes, First Step Dehydrogenation, Plains Plant, The Babcock and Wilcox Tube Co., Beaver Falls, Pa., Rept. PR-4-2, Aug. 25, 1944.
22. Heger, J. J.: *Symp. Nature, Occurrence and Effects of Sigma Phase*, ASTM, pp. 75–78, 1951.
23. Gilman, J. J.: Hardening of High-Chromium Steels by Sigma Phase Formation, *Trans. Am. Soc. Met.*, vol. 43, pp. 101–187, 1951.
24. Newell, H. D.: Properties and Characteristics of 27% Chromium-Iron, *Met. Prog.*, May, 1946, pp. 977–1028.
25. Zapffe, C. A., and C. O. Worden: A Notch Bend Test, *Weld. J., Res. Suppl.*, vol. 30, pp. 47-s–54-s, 1951.
26. Zapffe, C. A., C. O. Worden, and R. L. Phebus: The Embrittlement of Ferritic Stainless Steels at 475°C, *Stahl Eisen*, vol. 71, pp. 109–119, 1951.
27. Becket, F. M.: On the Allotropy of Stainless Steels, *Trans. Am. Inst. Min. Metall. Pet. Eng.*, vol. 131, pp. 15–36, 1938.
28. Riedrich, G., and F. Loib: Embrittlement of High-Chromium Steels in Temperature Range of 570–1110°F, *Arch. Eisenhuettenwes.*, vol. 15, no. 7, pp. 175–182, 1941–1942.
29. Bandel, G., and W. Tofaute: Brittleness of Chromium Rich Steels at Temperatures Around 930°F, *Arch. Eisenhuettenwes.*, vol. 15, no. 7, pp. 307–319, 1941–1942. (Brutcher trans. no. 1893).
30. Heger, J. J.: 885°F Embrittlement of the Ferritic Chromium-Iron Alloys, *Met. Prog.*, August, 1951, pp. 55–61.
31. Thielsch, H.: Weld Embrittlement in Chromium Stainless Steels, *Weld. J., Res. Suppl.*, vol. 29, pp. 126-s–132-s, 1950.
32. Houdremont, E.: "Handbuch der Sonderstahlkunde," Springer Verlag, Berlin, 1943.
33. Masumoto, H., H. Saito, and M. Sugihara: *Sci. Rept. Res. Inst., Tohoku Univ., Ser. A*, vol. 5, p. 203, 1953.
34. Pomey, G., and P. Bastien: Les Transformation des Alliages Fer-Chrome au Voisinage de la Composition Equiatomique, *Rev. Metall. Paris*, vol. 53, pp. 147–160, 1956.
35. Takeda, S., and N. Nagai, *Mem. Fac. Eng., Nagoya Univ.*, vol. 8, p. 1, 1956.
36. Shull, C. G., E. O. Wollan, W. C. Koehler, and W. A. Strauser: *U.S. AEC Pub.*, *ORNL-728*, 1950.
37. Williams, R. O.: Further Studies of the Iron-Chromium System, *Trans. Metall. Soc. AIME*, vol. 212, pp. 497–502, 1958.
38. Tisinai, G. F., and C. H. Samans: Some Observations on 885°F Embrittlement, *J. Met.*, October, 1957, pp. 1221–1226.
39. Fisher, R. M., E. J. Dulis, and K. G. Carroll: Identification of Precipitates Accompanying 885°F Embrittlement in Chromium Steels, *Trans. Am. Inst. Min. Metall. Pet. Eng.*, vol. 197, pp. 690–695, 1953.
40. Williams, R. O., and H. W. Paxton: The Nature of Aging of Binary Iron-Chromium Alloys Around 500°C, *J. Iron Steel Inst. London*, vol. 185, pp. 358–374, 1957.
41. Marcinkowski, M. J., R. M. Fisher, and A. Szirmae: Effect of 500°C Aging on the Deformation Behavior of an Iron-Chromium Alloy, *Trans. Am. Inst. Min. Metall. Pet. Eng.*, vol. 230, pp. 676–689, 1964.
42. Grobner, P. J.: The 885°F (475°C) Embrittlement of Ferritic Stainless Steels, *Metall. Trans.*, vol. 4, pp. 251–260, 1973.
43. Hodges, R. J.: Intergranular Corrosion in High Purity Ferritic Stainless Steels: Isothermal Time-Temperature Sensitization Measurements, *Corrosion*, vol. 27, pp. 164–167, 1971.
44. Hochmann, J.: Properties of Vacuum-melted Steels Containing 25% Chromium, *Rev. Metall.*, vol. 48, pp. 734–758, 1951. (Brutcher trans. no. 2981).
45. Demo, J. J.: Mechanism of High Temperature Embrittlement and Loss of Corrosion Resistance in AISI Type 446 Stainless Steel, *Corrosion*, vol. 27, pp. 531–544, 1971.
46. Pruger, T. A.: Flow to Get Better Welding Results with 17% Chromium Steel, *Steel Horiz.*, vol. 13, pp. 10–12, 1951.
47. Houdremont, E., and W. Tofaute: Resistance In Intergranular Corrosion of Ferritic and Martensitic Chromium Steels, *Stahl Eisen*, vol. 72, pp. 539–545, 1952.

48. Lula, R. A., A. J. Lena, and G. C. Kiefer: Intergranular Corrosion of Ferritic Stainless Steels, *Trans. Am. Soc. Met.*, vol. 46, pp. 197–230, 1954.
49. Bain, E. C., R. H. Aborn, and J. J. B. Rutherford: The Nature and Prevention of Intergranular Corrosion in Austenitic Stainless Steels, *Trans. Am. Soc. Steel Treat.*, vol. 21, pp. 481–509, 1933.
50. Ebling, H. F., and M. A. Scheil: *ASTM STP No. 369*, p. 275, 1965.
51. Bäumel, A.: Zusammenhang Zwischender Wärmebehandlung und dem Korrosionsverhalten Nichtrostender Stähle mit rd. 17.9% Cr. in Siedener Konzentrierter Salpetersäure, *Arch. Eisenhuettenwes.*, vol. 34, pp. 135–149, 1963. Brit. Iron Steel Ind. trans. no. 3287, Iron and Steel Inst., London, 1963.
52. Bond, A. P., and E. A. Lizlovs: Intergranular Corrosion of Ferritic Stainless Steels, *J. Electrochem Soc.*, vol. 116, pp. 1305–1311, 1969.
53. Bond, A. P.: Mechanism of Intergranular Corrosion in Ferritic Stainless Steels, *Trans. Metall. Soc. AIME*, vol. 245, pp. 2127–2134, 1969.
54. Demo, J. J.: Effect of High Temperature Exposure on the Corrosion Resistance and Ductility of AISI 446 Stainless Steel, *NACE reprint no. 23, 1968 Conf. Nat. Assoc. Corrosion Engineers*, Cleveland.
55. Hodges, R. J.: Intergranular Corrosion in High Purity Ferritic Stainless Steels: Effect of Cooling Rate and Alloy Composition, *Corrosion*, vol. 27, pp. 119–127, 1971.
56. Streicher, M. A.: The Role of Carbon, Nitrogen and Heat Treatment in the Dissolution of Iron-Chromium Alloys In Acids, *Corrosion*, vol. 29, pp. 337–360, 1973.
57. Henthorne, M.: Intergranular Corrosion in Iron and Nickel Base Alloys, *ASTM STP No. 516*, pp. 66–119, 1972.
58. Mahla, E. M., and N. A. Nielsen: Carbide Precipitation in Type 304 Stainless Steels—An Electron Microscope Study, *Trans. Am. Soc. Met.*, vol. 43, pp. 290–322, 1951.
59. Streicher, M. A.: Development of Pitting Resistant Fe-Cr-Mo Alloys, *Corrosion*, vol. 30, pp. 77–82, 1974.
60. Semchyshen, M., A. P. Bond, and H. J. Dundas: Effects of Composition on Ductility and Toughness of Ferritic Stainless Steel, *Symp. Toward Improved Ductility and Toughness*, Kyoto, Japan, pp. 239–253, Climax Molybdenum Co., Greenwich, Conn., 1971.
61. Plumtree, A., and R. Gullberg: The Influence of Interstitial Content on the Ductile-Brittle Temperature of Fe-25 Cr Ferritic Stainless Steels, *J. Test. Eval.*, vol. 2, no. 5, pp. 331–336, 1974.
62. Gleiter, H., and E. Hornbogen: Precipitation Hardening by Coherent Particles, *Mater. Sci. Eng.*, vol. 2, pp. 285–302, 1967/1968.
63. Kinzel, A. B., and R. Franks: "The Alloys of Iron and Chromium, Vol. II—High Chromium Alloys," McGraw-Hill, New York, 1940.
64. Legat, H.: Investigation of 18-9 Chromium-Manganese Steels, *Metallwirtsch. Metallwiss. Metalltech.*, vol. 17, pp. 509–513, 1938. (Brutcher trans. no. 654).
65. Krivobok, V. N.: Alloys of Iron and Chromium, *Trans. Am. Soc. Met.*, vol. 23, pp. 1–56, 1935.
66. Heger, J. J.: The Effect of Notching on the Tensile and Impact Strength of Annealed 27% Chromium-Iron Alloy at Room and Elevated Temperatures, The Babcock and Wilcox Tube Co., Beaver Falls, Pa., Rept. no. RR-3-6, Mar. 28, 1945.
67. Lincoln, R. A.: Dissertation, Carnegie Institute of Technology, Pittsburgh, Pa., 1935.
68. Hochmann, J.: Sur L'Amelioration des Valeurs, de la Resilience des Alliages Ferritiques a 25% de Chrome par la Methode de Fusion Sous Vide, *Compt. Rend.*, vol. 226, pp. 2150–2151, 1948.
69. Binder, W. O., and H. R. Spendelow: Influence of Chromium on the Mechanical Properties of Plain Chromium Steels, *Trans. Am. Soc. Met.*, vol. 43, pp. 759–777, 1951.
70. Demo, J. J.: Weldable and Corrosion Resistance Ferritic Stainless Steels, AIME Meeting, New Developments in Ferritic and Duplex Steels, October 1972; *Trans. TMS-AIME*, vol. 5, pp. 2253–2256, 1974.
71. Knoth, R. J.: Electron Beam Continuous Hearth Refining and Its Place in the Specialty Steel Industry, presented at the *Specialty Steel Seminar*, Pittsburgh, Pa., 1969.
72. E-Brite 26-1, Brochure no. AV110-3-71, Airco Vacuum Metals, Div. of Air Reduction Co., Inc., Berkeley, Calif.
73. Knoth, R. J., G. E. Lakso, and W. A. Matejka: New Ni-free Stainless Bids to Oust Austenitic, *Chem. Eng.*, vol. 77, no. 11, pp. 170–176, May 1970.
74. Bäumel, A.: *Stahl Eisen*, vol. 84, pp. 798–802, 1964.
75. Demo, J. J.: Ferritic Iron-Chromium Alloys, Canadian Patent no. 939,936, Jan. 15, 1974.
76. Demo, J. J.: Ductile Chromium-containing Ferritic Alloy, Canadian Patent no. 952,741, Aug. 13, 1974. Patent applied for in United States.
77. Hersleb, G.: Investigation of the Effect of Heat Treatment on the Corrosion of Titanium-Stabilized Ferritic Chromium Steels in Boiling Concentrated Nitric Acid, *Werkst. Korros.*, vol. 19, no. 5, pp. 406–412, 1968.
78. Cowling, R. D., and H. E. Hintermann: The Corrosion of Titanium Carbide, *J. Electrochem. Soc.*, vol. 117, no. 11, pp. 1447–1449, 1970.
79. Wright, R. N.: Mechanical Behavior and Weldability of a High Chromium Ferritic Stainless Steel as a Function of Purity, *Weld. J., Res. Suppl.*, vol. 50, pp. 434-s–440-s, October 1971.

80. Pollard, B.: Effect of Titanium on the Ductility of 26% Chromium Low Interstitial Ferritic Stainless Steel, *Met. Tech.*, January 1974, pp. 31–36.

81. Sipos, D. J., R. F. Steigerwald, and N. E. Whitcomb: Ductile Corrosion-resistant Ferrous Alloys Containing Chromium, U.S. Patent no. 3,672,876, Jun. 27, 1972.

82. Bond, A. P.: Effects of Molybdenum on the Pitting Potentials of Ferritic Stainless Steels at Various Temperatures, *J. Electrochem. Soc.*, vol. 120, no. 5, pp. 603–613, 1973.

83. Steigerwald, R. F.: Low Interstitial Fe-Cr-Mo Ferritic Stainless Steels, *Soviet-American Symp. New Developments in the Field of Molybdenum-alloyed Cast Iron and Steel*, Moscow, January 1973. Climax Molybdenum Co., Greenwich, Conn.

84. Steigerwald, R. F.: New Ferritic Stainless Steels to Resist Chlorides and Stress Corrosion Cracking, *Tappi*, vol. 56, no. 4, pp. 129–133, 1973.

85. Steigerwald, R. F.: New Molybdenum Steels and Alloys for Corrosion Resistance, *NACE preprint no. 44, 1974 Conf. Nat. Assoc. Corrosion Engineers*, Chicago.

86. Streicher, M. A.: Microstructures and Some Properties of Fe-28%Cr-4%Mo Alloys, *Corrosion*, vol. 30, no. 4, pp. 115–124, 1974.

87. McMullin, J. G., S. F. Reiter, and D. G. Ebeling: Equilibrium Structure in Fe-Cr-Mo Alloys, *Trans. Am. Soc. Met.*, vol. 46, pp. 799–811, 1954.

88. Aggen, G.: Unpublished work, Allegheny Ludlum Industries, Inc., Pittsburgh, Pa.

89. Demo, J. J.: Unpublished work, E. I. du Pont de Nemours & Co., Inc., Wilmington, Delaware.

90. Schmidt, W., and O. Jarleborg: Ferritic Stainless Steels With 17% Cr, Climax Molybdenum GmbH, Düsseldorf, Germany—An Affiliate of American Metal Climax, Inc., 1974.

Chapter 6

Structure and Constitution of Wrought Martensitic Stainless Steels

PAUL T. LOVEJOY
Research Metallurgist, Research Center, Allegheny Ludlum Steel
Corporation. Brackenridge, Pennsylvania

CONSTITUTION

An austenitic field in the equilibrium diagram is one of the basic necessities for a martensitic stainless steel. The other necessity is that the chromium content be at or above about 10.5 wt % so that the alloy can develop a "passive film" and display the good corrosion resistance expected of a stainless steel.

The extent of the gamma loop in the binary Fe-Cr system is seen in Fig. 1 developed by Baerlecken.[1] This indicates that some additonal element or combination of elements will be necessary to expand the austenitic field to usable stainless chromium levels. Figures 2 to 4 show the extent to which several austenite formers (carbon, nitrogen, nickel) expand the gamma loop. These latter diagrams do not indicate the extent of the two-phase α plus γ field.

The extent of the two-phase region and carbide types is indicated in Figs. 5 to 7 attributed to Bungardt, Kunze, and Horne.[2] In these diagrams, the outer extent of the two-phase region is expanded but the single-phase field, necessary to achieve a uniform martensitic structure, is seen as not greatly changed.

Sections through the Fe-Cr carbon fields are shown in Fig. 8.[22] These show that as chromium increases, the single-phase austenite field decreases in area to the point where some primary carbides must be anticipated in several of the high-chromium— high-carbon alloys. Conversely, without carbon, the high-chromium steels could not be hardened.

For a specific 16Cr-2Ni alloy (Type 431), a phase diagram has been experimentally constructed as shown in Fig. 9.[3] This is compared with the theoretical diagram which was constructed from literature sources, Fig. 10. Comparisons indicate that the range for uniform hardening is considerably restricted in the real case. In order to ensure equilibrium it was found necessary in developing the diagram to use soaking times varying from ½ h at 2700°F (1468°C) to 500 h at 1200°F (634°C). This is due to the sluggish reaction kinetics in the Fe-Cr system.

Although specific phase boundaries are not presented, several authors[4,5] have shown that the austenite field may be expanded to alloys containing over 20% chromium if

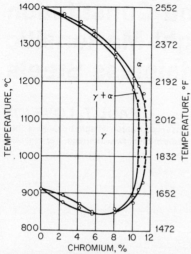

Fig. 1 The iron corner of the Fe-Cr phase diagram for alloys with approximately 0.004% C and 0.002% N.[1]

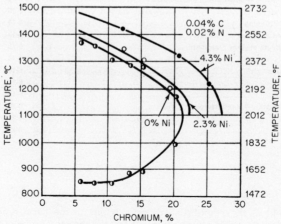

Fig. 2 Shift of gamma loop with nickel.[1]

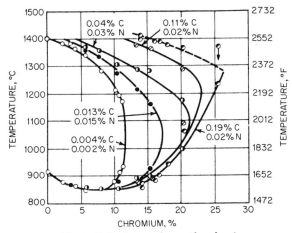

Fig. 3 Shift of gamma loop with carbon.[1]

sufficient nitrogen can be taken into solution. Dependent on heat treatment and chemistry, the austenite may be transformed or retained upon cooling. Lower temperature treatments may precipitate some carbides permitting martensite formation. The mechanism is depletion of matrix alloy content which raises the M_s temperature* for transformation.

Pseudo phase diagrams for a titanium stabilized martensitic steel have been presented by Kaltenhauser in Fig. 11.[6] These explain the behavior of a new type of maraging titanium-stabilized martensitic steel which does not require any tempering to achieve usable ductility levels at martensitic strength levels. Since the major portion of carbon is combined as a stable titanium carbide, there is no need for subsequent tempering.

Numerical Equivalents Useful engineering alloys usually contain more components than are represented on an equilibrium diagram. Thus for evaluation of structures in complex alloys various equivalent procedures have been developed. These are either equivalent procedures relating the effect of one element to that for a fixed amount of the

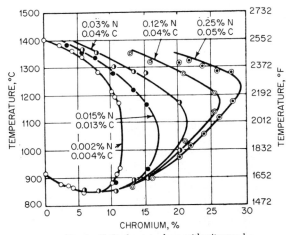

Fig. 4 Shift of gamma loop with nitrogen.[1]

*M_s means martensitic start.

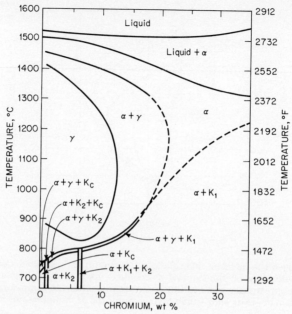

Fig. 5 Constant section at 0.05% carbon through Fe-Cr-C diagram.[2] $K_c = Fe_3C$; $K_1 = (Fe,Cr)_{23}C_6$; $K_2 = (Fe,Cr)_7C_3$.

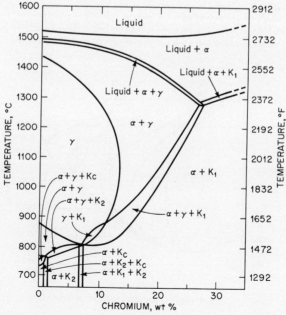

Fig. 6 Constant section at 0.10% carbon through Fe-Cr-C diagram.[2] $K_c = Fe_3C$; $K_1 = (Fe,Cr)_{23}C_6$; $K_2 = (Fe,Cr)_7C_3$.

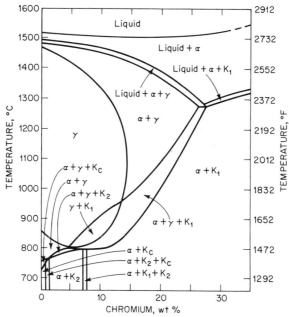

Fig. 7 Constant section at 0.20% carbon through Fe-Cr-C diagram.[2] $K_c = Fe_3C$; $K_1 = (Fe,Cr)_{23}C_6$; $K_2 = (Fe,Cr)_7C_3$.

standard or are relative potency factors. The utility is for general understanding and should not be solely relied on in specific cases.

Thielemann[7] provided one of the first formulations based on the ability of a particular element to close off the austenite field in an iron-based system. The applicable equation is

$$Cr_{Eq} = Cr + 2.1W + 2.8Ta + 4.2Mo + 4.5Cb + 5.2Si + 7.2Ti + 11V + 12Al - 40(C + N) - 3Ni - 2Mn$$

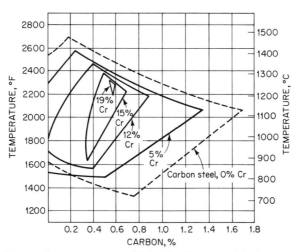

Fig. 8 Effect of several chromium contents on the carbon limitations for pure austenite at elevated temperatures.[22]

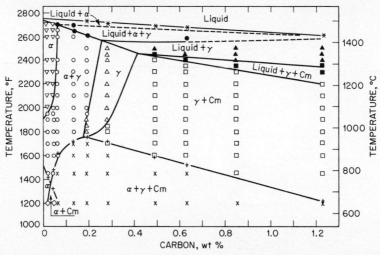

Fig. 9 Constitution diagram for 16Cr-2Ni stainless steel.[3] Symbol "Cm" indicates $(Cr,Fe)_{23}C_6$ and $(Cr,Fe)_7C_3$. Code: + = data derived from dilatometry;* = data derived from thermal analysis; all other data derived by metallographic examination.

These coefficients have been reestimated by Aggen[8] to include a 10 to 12% chromium base. This formulation is more applicable to martensitic stainless alloys:

$$Cr_{Eq} = Cr + 1.5Si + 7.2Ti + 2.5Al + 3Cb + 10Zr$$
$$+ 2V - 40(C + N) - 3Ni - 2(Mn + Cu)$$

Delta Ferrite The generally undesirable high-temperature bcc phase can occur in many martensitic stainless grades. The cause may be variation in chemistry or excessively high heat treatment.

The effects of chemistry on delta ferrite have been estimated by Irving.[9] For a fixed temperature of 1050°C, in a 12% Cr alloy having about 20% delta ferrite, the following factors were determined:

Change in Delta Ferrite, % per % Element	
N −220	Si +6
C −210	Mo +5
Ni −20	Cr +14
Co −7	V +18
Cu −7	Al +54
Mn −6	

Study of these effects in a 17Cr-4Ni base produced similar values. The carbide and nitride formers Ti and Cb were not evaluated but are known to be inherent ferrite formers and able to lessen the effects of carbon and nitrogen.

The effect of elevated temperature on delta ferrite is predicted by the phase diagram. Using a base composition of:

C	Mn	Si	Cr	N
0.1	0.5	0.25	12	0.02

Irving developed the following percentages of delta ferrite:

Temperature, °C	1050	1300	1350
% delta ferrite	0	50	100

Hence, delta ferrite may be dissolved or formed by heat treatment.

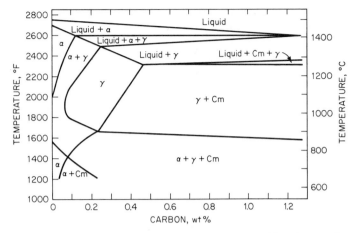

Fig. 10 16Cr-2Ni constitution diagram as extrapolated from literature.[3]

Decomposition of Delta Ferrite In simple Fe-Cr alloys delta ferrite will dissolve by the usual diffusional processes on first entering the austenite field. If retained to lower temperature, however, other phases may precipitate.

A. E. Nehrenberg and P. Lillys[4] have reported a study of the high-temperature transformations in 17 to 25% Cr steels. At high temperatures, delta ferrite transforms to austenite with all carbon taken into solution. At lower temperatures, however, they observed an aggregate of carbides in austenite. A lamellar microstructure is formed by the simultaneous growth of carbide and austenite into the delta ferrite. The temperature range for this transformation was found to bracket the A_3 from approximately 50°F (28°C) below to 200 to 300°F (111 to 166°C) above over a 17 to 25% chromium range.

The mechanism for the lamellar structure is given as initial carbide precipitation depleting the adjacent matrix of both chromium and carbon. While the carbon will diffuse quickly, a chromium gradient is formed which adjusts the local chemistry to the left, into a stable austenite region. This austenite is then either stable or unstable during cooling depending on its M_s temperatures.

As an interesting aside, Tisinai and Samans[5] have shown that lamellar ferrite may form from austenite decomposition in high chromium, carbon, and nitrogen alloys through the precipitation of carbides and nitrides.

Other work on delta ferrite decomposition in a more complex alloy (AM-350, AM-355) has been reported by Aggen.[10] This alloy, which contains Mo in addition to Fe, Ni, Cr, C, and N, demonstrates a sequence of delta ferrite dissolution as shown in Figs. 12 to 14. These photomicrographs indicate that the precipitation of austenite, carbides, and chi phase may all be encountered.

The dissolution of the delta ferrite depends on the matrix. If quenched directly into the carbide precipitation range, the decomposition proceeds mainly through the formation of austenite and carbides. The particles first form at the ferrite-austenite boundary. Later there is cellular growth of both austenite and carbide plates into the delta ferrite particles.

If the austenite is first transformed to martensite, the availability of carbon is diminished by precipitation in the matrix.

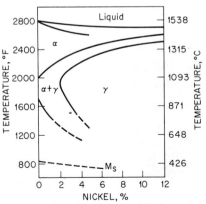

Fig. 11 Fe + 11.5Cr + 0.3Ti:Ni diagram.[6]

The ferrite is then decomposed as seen in Figs. 12 to 14. At lower temperatures of 1100 and 1250°F (580 to 662°C), distributed fine particles of austenite appear within the delta ferrite grains. There may also be carbide films formed at the austenite-ferrite boundary.

In the range of 1425 to 1600°F (761 to 857°C) decomposition proceeds mainly through the formation of austenite and massive particles of chi phase at the boundaries. Small amounts of sigma are also observed. At higher temperatures of 1750 to 1800°F (908 to 968°C), less chi and more sigma is formed. If the molybdenum were absent, the molybdenum-rich chi phase would likely be replaced by sigma phase.

Under unusual circumstances delta ferrite has been observed to transform at temperatures as low as 500 to 700°F (260 to 371°C). Dulis[11] has observed that Type 410 with 20% delta ferrite had better fatigue strength at 500°F (260°C) than at room temperature. This was attributed to precipitation of a finely distributed dispersion of alpha prime. The necessary enhanced precipitation rate is attributed to the vacancies and dislocations generated during the reversed plastic deformation.

Sigma Phase   The low chromium of the martensitic stainless grades generally ensures that sigma phase does not form during elevated temperature exposure. At lower temperatures, however, the Fe-Cr miscibility gap can result in the precipitation of alpha prime which is given as the cause of 885°F embrittlement.

If severe cold-work (95%) is utilized to enhance the reaction, sigma has been identified in 14% Cr steels heated for 10,000 hr at 900°F (471°C).[12] At 5000 hr, there was no sigma present so that in most real situations sigma is not a credible consideration for martensitic steels. Long before sigma the utility would be lost due to 885°F (474°C) or temper embrittlement.

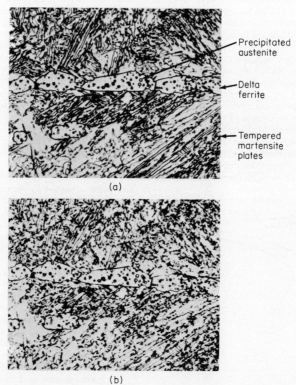

Precipitated austenite

Delta ferrite

Tempered martensite plates

(a)

(b)

Fig. 12   Delta ferrite microstructure in AM-355 following 1950°F (1063°C) + water quench + subzero cooled + 1250°F (675°C), 16 h. Shows precipitation of austenite in ferrite. (a) Sodium hydroxide etchant. (b) Reetched in oxalic acid. 2000X.[10]

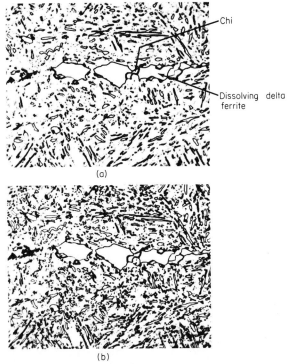

Fig. 13   Delta ferrite microstructure in AM-355 following 1950°F (1063°C) + water quench + subzero cooled + 1425°F (774°C), 16 h. Shows precipitation of austenite + chi in ferrite. (*a*) Sodium hydroxide etchant. (*b*) Reetched in oxalic acid. 2000X.[10]

STRENGTHENING MECHANISMS

In martensitic stainless steels strength implies not only the conventional flow stress for plastic deformation, but also hardness or abrasion resistance. These strength properties are determined by both the chemical makeup and the prior heat treatment.

Chemical Analysis   The most obvious strengthening mechanism is the martensite reaction. The two main chemical factors which are important are the stability of delta ferrite at the hardening temperature and the carbon content. The delta ferrite equilibrium has already been discussed.

TABLE 1   Approximate Maximum Hardness

Alloy AISI	Carbon %	Hardening temperature	As-quenched hardness, R_c
410	0.115	1700°F (927°C) ½ h	44
		1850°F (1010°C) ½ h	44.5
414	0.13	1700°F (927°C) ½ h	44
		1900°F (1038°C) ½ h	44
431	0.14	1700°F (927°C) ½ h	42
		1900°F (1038°C) ½ h	41
420	0.31	1700°F (927°C) ½ h	49
		1875°F (1024°C) ½ h	52
440C	1.0	1700°F (927°C) 1 h	52
		1900°F (1038°C) 2 h	55

Carbon Content   The trend of strength versus carbon content can be observed in the preceding table which lists the approximate maximum hardness versus alloy and carbon content.

These values indicate that higher carbon produces greater hardness until a saturation is reached at about the 0.60 carbon level in Type 440A. At this level, the austenite is saturated in carbon and further carbon is precipitated from the melt as primary carbides. These larger carbides do not enter into the hardening process, but do provide additional abrasion resistance.

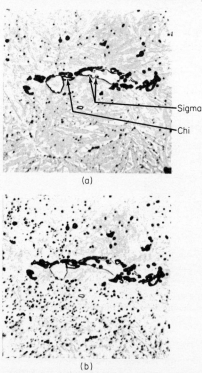

(a)

(b)

Fig. 14   Delta ferrite microstructure in AM-355 following 1950°F (1063°C) + water quench + sub-zero cooled + 1800°F (981°C), 16 h. Shows precipitation of austenite and sigma in ferrite. *(a)* Sodium hydroxide etchant. *(b)* Reetched in oxalic acid. 2000X.[10]

Other elements which are added to martensitic steels do not have the direct effect on strength that can be attributed to carbon. Their influence is usually indirect through control over phase stability, that is, relative austenite-ferrite stability at elevated temperature and the stability of austenite on cooling.

Cold-Working   The deformation of annealed martensitic stainless steels will raise strength but the data presented in Table 2 suggest that heat treatment is a more effective method to raise strength. Note the precipitous drop in elongation with only small reductions.

Although cold reduction is not suitable as a final process for Type 410, the data do indicate that considerable deformation can be utilized in fabrication with final properties developed by heat treatment.

Hardenability   The element chromium is known to greatly increase the hardenability of martensitic steels. This effect is used in many low-alloy steels. At the chromium levels necessary for a steel to be labeled stainless, the effect has saturated such that a Jominy End-Quench Hardenability Test will show no variation in hardness. Figure 15 shows TTT and E-Q curves for Type 410.

These diagrams suggest that it will be difficult to anneal these stainless steels to a soft ferrite plus carbides. Most softening attempts are better approached as over-

TABLE 2   The Effect of Cold-Work on Annealed Type 410

COMPOSITION:	C	Mn	Si	S	P	Cr	Ni
	0.10	0.44	0.349	0.016	0.017	12.18	0.405

Reduction	Yield strength MN/m²	ksi	Ultimate tensile strength MN/m²	ksi	Elongation in 2 in. (50.8 mm), %	Hardness, R_b
0	256.5	37.2	493	71.5	30	72
15	634.3	92.0	648.1	94.0	6.5	95
30	724	105.0	751.6	109.0	2.5	99
45	758.5	110.0	806.7	117.0	1.0	100
60	827.4	120.0	882.6	128.0	1.0	100

tempering operations. This is particularly true in those martensitic steels containing nickel. Figure 16 shows the retarding that can occur with nickel in Type 414. The additional nickel stabilizes austenite up to one day at temperature.

Martempering   There is sufficient hardenability in all martensitic stainless steels to permit martempering as a means to avoid cracking in complex heat-treated parts. The M_s measurements may be consulted to select appropriate quenching temperatures.

A typical martempering cycle could be constructed on Fig. 15 by cooling at a rate sufficient so as not to intersect the nose of the ferrite transformation curve, that is, 1300°F (704°C) at 200 s and not below the M_s of 680°F (360°C). This could be accomplished by quenching into a salt pot at the appropriate temperature. When the part reached a uniform temperature above the M_s, it could be cooled through the transformation range to martensite. This procedure greatly reduces the thermal strains and the danger of cracking.

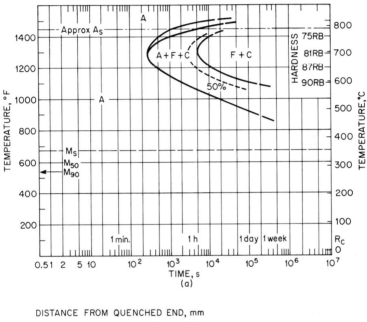

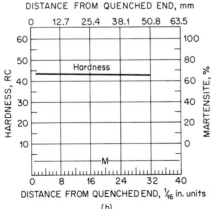

Fig. 15 (a) TTT diagram. (b) End-quench hardenability diagram for Type 410 stainless steel. Type 410 contains 0.11C-0.44Mn-0.37Si-0.16Ni-12.18Cr. Austenitized at 1800°F (981°C); grain size, 6–7. A, austenite; F, ferrite; C, carbide; M, martensite; B, bainite; P, pearlite.[20]

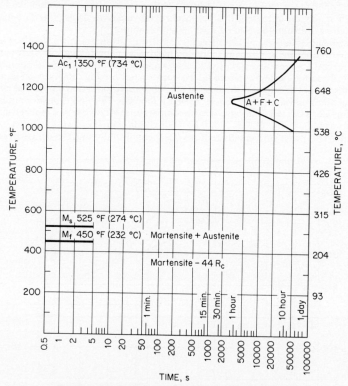

Fig. 16   TTT diagram for Type 414 stainless steel.[21]

Ausworking   Deformation of metastable austenite prior to transformation produces significant improvement in the strength and toughness of many steels. These techniques are not, however, greatly utilized in martensitic stainless steels. The lower carbon grades have only a minimal response due to the minor carbide reaction while the higher grades are generally employed where high hardness and abrasion resistance are of primary concern. As a result, there is little information available. In the precipitation-hardening grades, ausworking can be utilized to improve strength and toughness.[13,14] A typical ausworking cycle would be much like the martempering cycle previously discussed. That is, the part is cooled to below the nose of the ferrite transformation as shown in Fig. 15. The metastable austenite is then worked or deformed at this lower temperature where more time is necessary for ferrite transformation. The austenite is then strengthened prior to martensite transformation. The martensite transformation is allowed to occur by cooling after the plastic deformation.

The effect of ausworking Type 410 at 800°F (427°C) is shown in Figs. 17 and 18.[15] These show that strength properties can be raised with some attendant loss in ductility values.

If plastic working is continued after the martensite transformation, then, as the values in Fig. 19[15] show, there can be a substantial increase in strength but a greater loss in ductility levels.

STRENGTHENING MECHANISMS IN LOW-CARBON MARTENSITES

Residual stress, solid-solution hardening, and prior austenite grain size are all factors in determining the strength of a martensite structure. These have been discussed using low-carbon nickel and chromium martensites.[16]

Residual Stress   The level of residual stress is strongly related to the M_s temperature for two basic reasons. First, the volume discrepancy between austenite and ferrite increases as the metastable temperature range increases. Secondly, as the M_s decreases, there is less opportunity for autotempering.

These effects are demonstrated in Fig. 20[16] where the lower M_s steels show the greatest rise in proportional limit with tempering at 797°F (425°C). Note that the effect is stronger at lower temperatures.

Solid-Solution Strengthening   Using the same alloys, the solid-solution strengthening due to nickel and chromium has been demonstrated as shown in Fig. 21.[16] Again, note that lower temperatures are necessary to demonstrate the effect. These rates are much less than those normally associated with solid-solution strengthening in a ferritic lattice.

Prior Austenite Grain Size   The low carbon content of Floreen's alloys permits an estimate of grain-size effects obtained through heat treatment without corresponding variations in carbide solutioning. These values are shown in Fig. 22.[16]

The results follow the expected Petch relationship. Note, however, that the slope, or Petch constant, k_f is less than normally associated with ferritic steels.

MICROSTRUCTURE AND EFFECTS OF HEAT TREATMENT

Metallography   The carbon content may be utilized to separate microstructures of martensitic steels into three categories:

- Class I, Low Carbon: Needlelike structure
- Class II, Medium Carbon: Very fine needlelike structure
- Class III, High Carbon: Ultra fine structure, contains primary carbides

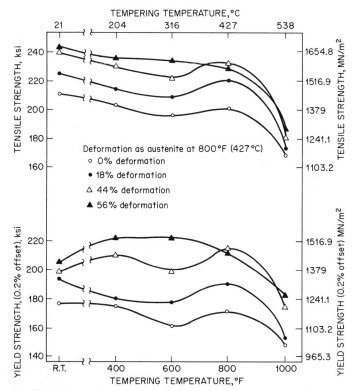

Fig. 17   The effect of tempering temperature on the tensile and yield strengths of Type 410 stainless steel deformed in the metastable austenitic condition.[15]

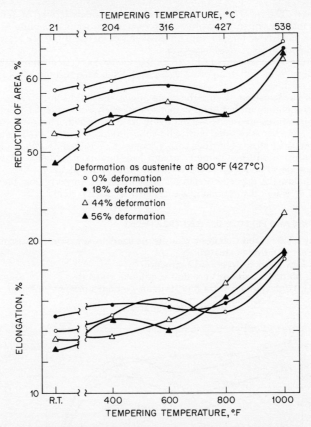

Fig. 18 The effect of tempering temperature on the reduction of area and elongation of Type 410 stainless steel deformed in the metastable austenitic condition.[15]

Structures representative of these three classes are shown in Fig. 23 in the hardened and tempered condition. In the first column the needlelike characteristic is visible. During a subcritical anneal, the needlelike structure is eliminated and visible carbides are precipitated, mostly in grain boundaries.

In the Type 420, the hardened structures have a similar appearance at low magnification.

Primary undissolved carbides are the principal constituents seen in the microstructures of the Type 440A high-carbon grades. In the annealed condition, both primary and secondary carbides can be observed as seen in Fig. 24. When hardened, the secondary carbides are taken into solution with a smaller percentage left to precipitate on grain boundaries as seen in Figs. 25 and 26.

Note the importance of the etching medium. The ammonium persulfate clearly outlines the carbide matrix boundaries, while the mixed acid etch develops additional matrix structure.

Hardening Treatments Forming an austenitic structure is the first prerequisite to achieving satisfactory properties. The factors of concern are the rate of heating and cooling, maximum temperature, and atmosphere.

The rate of heating is usually designed so that the part may be brought to a uniform temperature prior to the allotropic transformation. This is most important with heavy sections in the higher carbon grades. Occasionally a lower temperature hold at 1100°F (593°C) may be employed to further reduce strains.

The maximum temperature is determined by the need for maximum hardness. The data

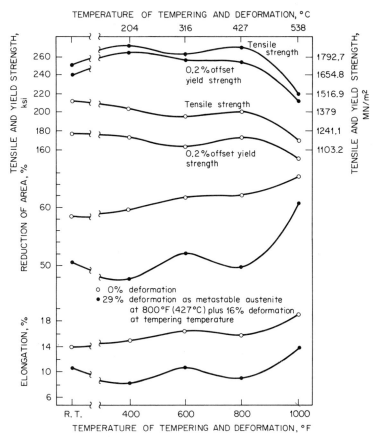

Fig. 19 The effect of deformation before and after martensite transformation on the tensile properties of Type 410 stainless steel. Steels deformed as metastable austenite to the indicated degree at 800°F (426°C), and worked as stated at the indicated temperatures after transformation.[15]

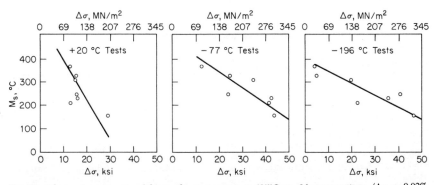

Fig. 20 Change in proportional limit after tempering at 425°C vs. M_s temperature. ($\Delta\sigma$ = 0.02% offset stress as tempered minus 0.02% offset stress as annealed.)[16]

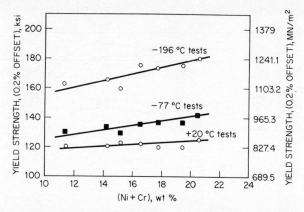

Fig. 21   Yield strength vs. total nickel plus chromium contents. Specimens tempered at 425°C.[16]

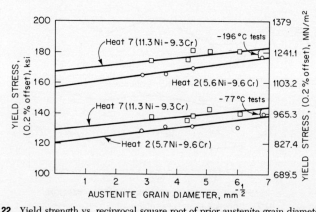

Fig. 22   Yield strength vs. reciprocal square root of prior austenite grain diameter.[16]

previously shown for Types 410, 420, and 440A illustrate the role of higher temperatures as well as the role of carbon in the attainment of greater hardness.

Heating in air can lead to surface decarburizing as shown by carbon content versus time and temperature in Table 3. The drop in bulk carbon depends on gage but note in these data the greatly reduced hardness in light-gage cutlery stock.

TABLE 3   Decarburization During Hardening

| | Atmosphere | | | |
| | Air | | Nitrogen | |
Heat treatment	% C	Hardness, R_c	% C	Hardness, R_c
Type 410, gage 0.033 in. (0.84 mm):				
1900°F (1036°C) for 10 min, air-cooled	0.14	45.0	0.13	45.5
1900°F for 60 min, air-cooled	0.059	33.0	0.14	45.5
2100°F (1149°C) for 10 min, air-cooled	0.076	40.5	0.14	46.0
2100°F for 60 min, air-cooled	0.006	97.5R_b	0.12	45.0
Type 420, gage 0.066 in. (1.68 mm):				
1900°F for 10 min, air-cooled	0.39	57.0		
1900°F for 60 min, air-cooled	0.26	48.0		
2100°F for 10 min, air-cooled	0.33	56.5		

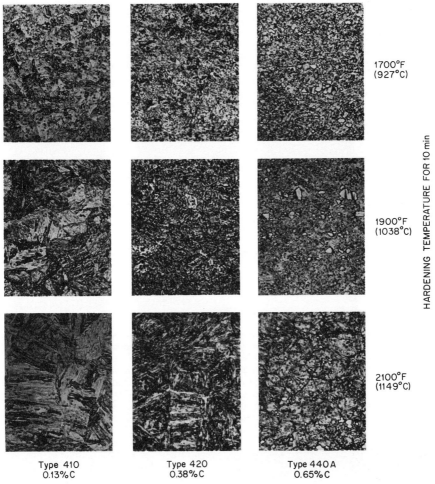

HARDENING TEMPERATURE FOR 10 min

1700°F
(927°C)

1900°F
(1038°C)

2100°F
(1149°C)

Type 410   Type 420   Type 440A
0.13%C   0.38%C   0.65%C

Tempered 7h at 400°F (204°C)

Fig. 23 Microstructures of hardened and tempered martensitic stainless steels as a function of carbon content. 500X.

The carbon loss may be reduced by heating in a nitrogen atmosphere. Note, however, that nitrogen may be absorbed and stabilize the austenite against transformation. Type 440A overheated to 2100°F (1149°C) for 10 min in nitrogen contained 94% retained austenite.

The $M_{23}C_6$ carbide begins to nucleate about 900°F (482°C) and becomes predominant above 1000°F (538°C). These carbides tend to be too large to influence strength and, additionally, are stable enough to significantly reduce the matrix carbon content which remained high during the lower temperature temper treatments. The net effect is the observed drop in hardness seen in all grades.

The chromium content of the precipitates may be followed in Fig. 28a. Note that chromium content is low until the more complex carbide types begin to form.

Rate of Cooling The great hardenability contributed by chromium removes the need to quench to avoid the formation of softer transformation products. It is possible, however, to precipitate sufficient carbide on cooling that both the M_s and the as-quenched hardness are influenced.

Data in Fig. 27 show that the cooling rate influences M_s only at higher carbon levels

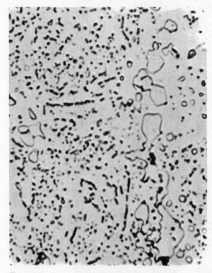

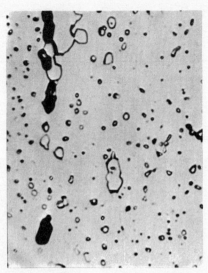

Fig. 24 Ammonium persulfate, 1500X, box annealed, Type 440A, R_b 95.

Fig. 25 Ammonium persulfate, 1500X, box annealed, +1950/2000°F (1063/1093°C), ½ h, + −125°F (−81°C), 1½ h, + 350°F (177°C), 2 h, R_c 60.

above 0.20. Note that absolute hardening temperature becomes a factor before quench rate. That is, the higher hardening temperature dissolves a greater amount of carbide into the austenite structure. This carbide may reprecipitate before martensite transformation if the cooling is sufficiently slow and the already-precipitated carbon would not be available to depress the M_s or raise hardness. The effect is minor in most practical cases. The maximum observed hardness variation is from 50 to 45 R_c for holding times of 1 h.

Tempering In the as-hardened condition, martensitic stainless grades do not have sufficient toughness for engineering utility. For this reason, as with less-alloyed martensitic steels, a lower temperature heat treatment is utilized to restore toughness.

With stainless steel there is an additional requirement to maintain corrosion resistance. Hence, it is necessary to discriminate between the higher chromium steels such as 440(ABC) and 420 and the remaining lower chromium varieties.

The higher chromium grades are usually selected with corrosion resistance in mind. This property would be adversely affected by high-temperature tempering (chromium carbide precipitation) and so these grades are usually stress-relieved at a lower temperature. Other stainless grades may be stress-relieved or tempered depending on the desired final properties.

Several reactions occur during tempering of martensitic steels. These are stress relief, previously mentioned, and a progression of carbide types tending toward more complex formulations. In the precipitation-hardenable grades there is additional precipitation of a fine dispersion of intermetallic carbides which provides additional strength.

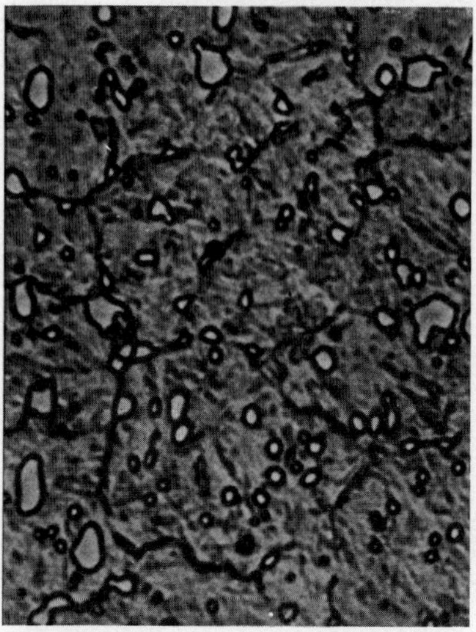

Fig. 26 Mixed acid etch, 2000X, hardened and tempered Type 440A.

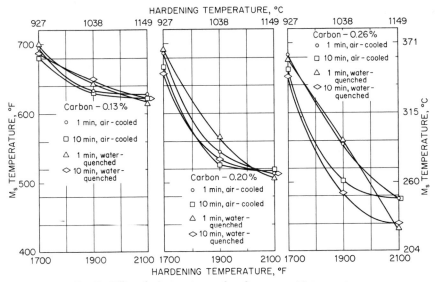

Fig. 27 Effect of solution, time, and cooling rate on M_s temperature.

The sequence of carbide reactions has been determined in Type 410 as seen in Fig. 28.[17] As-quenched, there is a fine dispersion of M_3C cementite-type carbides. These grow until at 600°F (315°C) the morphology changes from dendritic to platey-Widmanstätten distribution. At this temperature there is a slight contraction in length.

At higher temperatures, near 900°F (482°C), the M_7C_3 carbide becomes stable. These carbides may originally precipitate or may develop from favorably disposed elemental carbides. The maximum chromium in M_7C_3 is near 50% as opposed to the 18% maximum chromium in M_3C, hence the reduced corrosion resistance of martensitic grades tempered at this temperature is likely the result of a 3XX chromium-depletion mechanism.

The effect of tempering on hardness may be followed through the construction of a

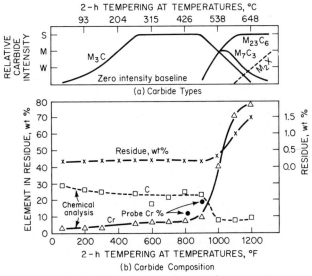

Fig. 28 Carbide analyses as a function of tempering.[17]

master tempering curve as shown in Fig. 29.[9] These show that the principal drop in hardness is associated with the precipitation of the $M_{23}C_6$ carbide. If a secondary hardening reaction exists, then the hardness would be expected to diverge from this master curve.

In practice the tempering range around 885°F (475 to 550°C) is not utilized due to the poor toughness of all martensitic stainless steels treated in this region. The reasons for the

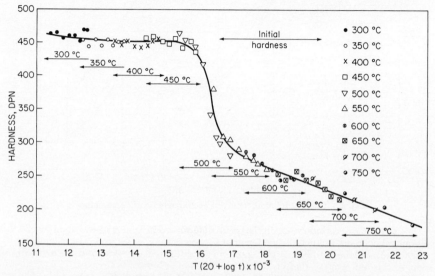

Fig. 29   Tempering curve for 0.14C-12Cr base steel.[9]

trough in toughness shown in Fig. 30[20] can be associated with the microstructural changes that are occurring in this region and with the possibility of temper embrittlement.

The principal microstructural changes are secondary hardening due to coherency strains from precipitates forming in the grain boundaries and overaging at the grain boundaries. This produces a structure which would be expected to be susceptible to brittle fracture. Additions of molybdenum or columbium,[18] the latter as shown in Fig. 31, can improve the toughness of martensitic steels in this area but the basic detrimental mechanisms remain.

Martensite Transformation Temperatures   The heat treatment of highly alloyed stainless steels requires more consideration of the martensite transformation temperature (M_s) than is necessary in other martensitic steels. In many of the precipitation and semiaustenitic grades a subzero treatment is necessary to complete transformation. In the martensitic stainless grades, the formation of enriched and therefore retained austenite in high-temperature tempering operations is a phenomenon that occurs through depressing the M_s temperature with greater alloy content.

The effects of several elements on both the A_{c1} and M_s temperatures have been given by Irving.[9] For a 12% chromium base these are given by Table 4.

Another calculation for the A_{c1} temperature is offered by Tricot and Castro[19] as follows:

$$A_1 \;(°C) = 310 + 35Cr + 3.5(Cr-17)^2 + 60Mo + 73Si + 170Cb + 290V + 620Ti \\ + 750Al + 1400B - 250C - 280N - 115Ni - 66Mn - 18Cu$$

The difference in coefficients is due to using a 17% chromium base point.

The range of martensite transformation is about 150°C (270°F) or less. Hence, it is obvious that the minimum desirable M_s would be in the order of 200°C (392°F) to assume transformation on cooling to room temperatures.

One effect of the low M_s temperatures of the stainless grades is the small autotempering that can occur as the transformed martensite cools to room temperature. Hence, at

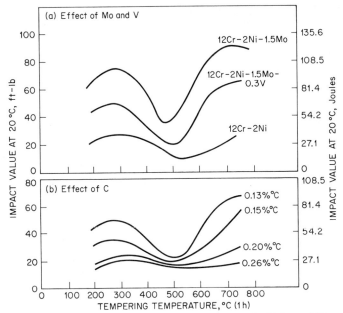

Fig. 30   Effect of tempering on impact properties of 12% Cr steels.[20]

equivalent carbon content, stainless grades may be slightly harder than corresponding carbon steels.

Retained Austenite   The austenitic structure can be retained in any operation that may lead to enrichment of the matrix with any element capable of reducing the M_s temperature. This may occur either through external contamination prior to heat treatment or by improper heat treatment leading to internal segregation. Typical mechanisms are listed below.

Higher-than-recommended hardening temperatures may dissolve an excessive amount

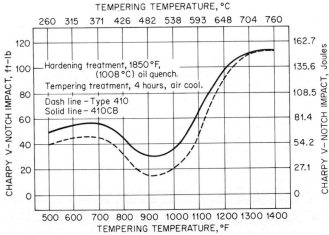

Fig. 31   Notch impact strengths of Types 410 and 410Cb stainless steels.[18]

TABLE 4

A_{c1} depression, °C per % alloy		M_s depression, °C per % alloy	
		(From 300°C)	
Nickel	−30	Carbon	−474
Manganese	−25	Manganese	−33
Cobalt	−5	Nickel	−17
Silicon	+20 −30	Chromium	−17
Aluminum	+30	Molybdenum	−21
Molybdenum	+25	Tungsten	−11
Vanadium	+50	Silicon	−11

of carbon and nitrogen. When done in air, surface decarburization is also possible. This could lead to unhardenable delta ferrite formation.

Over tempering, particularly with the nickel-containing grades, may result in nickel partitioning, forming reverted and enriched austenite which will be retained on cooling.

The last mechanism is the contamination of the surface with carbonaceous material which may be locally absorbed in heat treatment. This reemphasizes the usual stainless rule that the stock to be heat-treated must be clean.

The effect of retained austenite depends on percentage. The typical inadvertent amount encountered may range up to 25 to 30%. This amount may significantly reduce yield strengths to the austenitic level. Another potentially serious reaction can be the later martensitic transformation following tempering. This volume change could lead to cracking. The second of a double tempering is intended to temper any martensite formed in this manner. The use of a double temper is common in tool steel technology.

REFERENCES

1. Baerlecken, E., et al.: Investigations Concerning the Transformation Behavior, the Notched Impact Toughness and The Susceptibility to Intercrystalline Corrosion of Iron-Chromium Alloys with Chromium Contents to 30%, *Stahl Eisen*, vol. 81, no. 12, pp. 768–778, Jun. 8, 1961.
2. Bungardt, K., E. Kunze, and E. Horne: Structure of the System Fe-Cr-C, *Archiv Eisenhuettenwes.*, vol. 29, pp. 193–203, March 1958.
3. Johnson, C. R., and S. J. Rosenberg: Constitution Diagram for 16% Cr-2% Ni Stainless Steel, *Trans. Am. Soc. Met.*, vol. 55, pp. 277–286, 1962.
4. Nehrenberg, A. E., and P. Lillys: High Temperature Transformations in Ferritic Stainless Steels Containing 17-25% Chromium, *Trans. Am. Soc. Met.*, vol. 46, pp. 1176–1203, 1954.
5. Tisinai, G. F., and C. H. Samans: Phase Relationships and Mechanical Properties of Some Iron-Chromium Carbon-Nitrogen Alloys, *Trans. Am. Soc. Met.*, vol. 49, pp. 747–758, 1957.
6. Kaltenhauser, R. H.: Welding Maraging Stainless Steels, *Weld J., Res. Suppl.*, vol. 44, pp. 1–4, September, 1965.
7. Thielemann, R. H.: Some Effects of Composition and Heat Treatment on the High Temperature Rupture Properties of Ferrous Alloys, *Am. Soc. Test Mater. Proc.*, vol. 40, pp. 788–804, 1940.
8. Aggen, G.: U.S. Patent 3,650,731.
9. Irvine, K. J., D. J. Crowe, and F. B. Pickering: The Physical Metallurgy of 12% Chromium Steels, *J. Iron Steel Inst. London*, vol. 195, pp. 386–405, August, 1960.
10. Aggen, G.: Phase Transformations and Heat Treatment Studies of a Controlled-Transformation Stainless Steel Alloy, thesis submitted to Faculty of the Department of Metallurgical Engineering, Rensselaer Polytechnic Institute, August, 1963.
11. Dulis, E. J., et al.: Relationship Between Fatigue and Damping Characteristics and Microstructure of 12% Cr Steels, *Trans. Am. Soc. Met.*, vol. 54, pp. 456–465, 1961.
12. Link, H. S., and P. W. Marshall: The Formation of Sigma Phase in 13%-16% Chromium Steels, *Trans. Am. Soc. Met.*, vol. 44, pp. 549–559, 1952.
13. Banerjee, B. R., et al.: Ausworking T422 Stainless Steel, *Trans. Am. Soc. Met.*, vol. 56, pp. 629–642, 1963.
14. Westgren, R. C., and E. J. Dulis: Effects of Ausrolling on the Properties of Crucible 422 Stainless Steel, *ASTM STP 369*, pp. 8–15, 1963.
15. Hosoi, Y., and K. E. Pinnow: The Tensile Properties of Type 410 Stainless Steel Deformed Before and After Martensite Transformation, *Trans. Am. Soc. Met.*, vol. 53, pp. 591–602, 1961.
16. Floreen, S.: The Properties of Low Carbon Iron-Nickel Chromium Martensites, *Trans. Am. Inst. Min. Metall. Pet. Eng.*, vol. 236, pp. 1429–1440, 1966.
17. Hauser, J. J., et al.: Submicroscopic Structures in Tempering 410 Stainless Steel, *Trans. Am. Soc. Met.*, vol. 54, pp. 514–525, 1961.

18. Tanczyn, H.: Properties of 12% Chromium Alloys Modified With Small Columbium Additions, *ASTM STP 369*, pp. 80–87, 1963.
19. Tricot, R., and R. Castro: Study of the Isothermal Transformations in 17% Chromium Stainless Steels, *Met. Treat. London*, pp. 299–310, August, 1966.
20. McGannon, H. E. (ed.): "The Making, Shaping and Treating of Steel," 9th ed., pp. 1170, 1178, United States Steel Corp., Pittsburgh, Pa., 1969 (Copyright 1971, United States Steel Corp.)
21. "Republic Enduro Stainless Steels," p. 130, Republic Steel Corp., Cleveland, Ohio, 1951.
22. Roberts, G. A., J. C. Hamaker, Jr., and A. R. Johnson, "Tool Steels," p. 200, American Society for Metals, Metals Park, Ohio, 1962.

Chapter 7

Structure and Constitution of Wrought Precipitation-hardenable Stainless Steels

D. CAMERON PERRY
Manager, Special Metals Research

JOSEPH C. JASPER
Senior Research Engineer, Special Metals Research,
Research Center, Armco Steel Corporation, Middletown, Ohio

INTRODUCTION

The precipitation-hardenable stainless steels were first developed in the 1940s. Stainless W, developed by the United States Steel Corporation, is generally credited as being the first alloy of this class. Since then, three classes of precipitation-hardenable stainless steels have been developed with uses ranging from sophisticated aerospace hardware to hard nonmagnetic balls for pinball machines. They have established a permanent niche for themselves in the designer's repertoire of materials because of their unique ability to develop high strength with relatively simple heat treatments, without the loss of ductility and corrosion resistance associated with other steels of comparable strength levels. This is made possible by the use of one or both of the hardening mechanisms: martensite formation and precipitation hardening.

Over the years three basic classes of precipitation-hardenable stainless steels have evolved: austenitic, martensitic, and semiaustenitic. The final hardening mechanism in all three classes is precipitation hardening.

The precipitation-hardening mechanism is probably most familiar in the aluminum-alloy system and involves the formation of second-phase particles from a supersaturated solid solution which induces strain and thereby strengthens the metal crystal lattice. Maximum strengthening occurs before visible particles are produced in what is known as the pre-precipitation stage. During this time like atoms of precipitate tend to accumulate in clusters which are continuous or coherent with the matrix phase. Maximum strain and therefore maximum strengthening occur during this time. As the precipitate clusters grow, they reach a critical size and form a surface or grain boundary between the two phases. This loss of coherency reduces the strain in the lattice, lowers strength, and produces the phenomenon known as overaging.

Like most metallurgical processes, precipitation hardening is both time- and temperature-dependent. Higher temperatures produce maximum strengthening more quickly than lower temperatures but achieve a lower overall strength level.

The precipitation-hardening reaction in these steels is quite complex, and we shall not attempt to discuss it in great detail except to point out that several elements, either singly or in combination, have been used to obtain the precipitation-hardening reaction. They are aluminum, copper, titanium, and sometimes, molybdenum.

As mentioned above, there are three classes of these steels. Each of these classes will be described in some detail in the following sections.

SEMIAUSTENITIC PRECIPITATION-HARDENABLE STAINLESS STEELS

These semiaustenitic precipitation-hardenable stainless steels are so named because in their solution-treated or annealed condition they are essentially austenitic although they do have 5 to 20% delta ferrite present in their microstructures. This delta ferrite remains there through the various heat-treating sequences. Although these steels are austenitic in the annealed or solution-treated condition they can be transformed to martensite through a series of relatively simple thermal or thermomechanical treatments. At this point, they are much like the martensitic precipitation-hardenable stainless steels (sometimes called maraging stainless steels) in that they can be further hardened by an aging treatment to their final strength level.

The semiaustenitics are by far the most complex and challenging to a stainless steel metallurgist. They are perhaps the most critical from the standpoint of chemistry control since their analyses have to be carefully controlled so that the steel is austenitic in the annealed or solution-treated condition and remains so during shipment to the customer's plant, even in subzero temperatures. Yet this austenite must be unstable enough so that the alloy balance can be disrupted by a series of simple

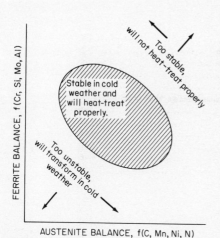

Fig. 1 Schematic representation of alloy balance to characteristics of semiaustenitic precipitation-hardenable stainless steels.

thermal treatments to achieve a substantially complete transformation to martensite. This martensite can then be subsequently age-hardened to the final strength levels.

The secret behind these steels is the very careful control of the interrelationship of austenite and ferrite formers and their relationship to the total chemical balance of the system. This is illustrated schematically in Fig. 1. When the alloy balance falls within the shaded area, proper heat-treat response will be obtained when standard heat-treating sequences are used. When the austenite and/or ferrite balances are too high, the austenite is too stable to be transformed to martensite by normal austenite conditioning treatments, and acceptable mechanical properties cannot be obtained. When the austenite and/or ferrite balances are too low, a stable austenite in the annealed condition that resists complete or partial transformation to martensite in cold weather shipments cannot be obtained. If the austenite and/or ferrite balances are even lower, an austenitic structure cannot be retained even at room temperature. Steels which have this characteristic are called martensitic precipitation-hardenable and will be discussed later.

The semiaustenitic stainless steels can be produced in all product forms but are used mostly in flat rolled sheet and strip products. In the mill-supplied condition, condition A, they are readily formable with forming characteristics similar to AISI Type 301. Then

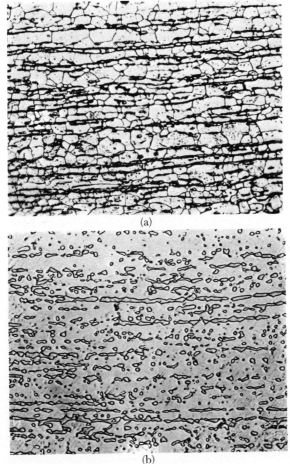

(a)

(b)

Fig. 2 (a) Austenite matrix with ferrite stringers. Etchant: (1) nitric-acetic, electrolytic; (2) 10% oxalic, electrolytic. (1000×, optical). (b) Delineation of ferrite stringers in austenite matrix. Etchant: 10% NaCN, electrolytic. (1000×, optical.)

after fabrication, through a series of relatively simple low-temperature heat treatments, they can be heat-treated to a variety of strength levels depending on the design requirements. The heat treatment consists of three basic steps: (1) austenitic conditioning, (2) martensitic transformation, and (3) precipitation or age-hardening. Each of these three steps will be discussed in some detail. As will readily be apparent, the heat-treatment temperatures can be varied over a relatively wide range depending on the end result desired.

Austenite Conditioning and Martensitic Transformation The microstructure of a semiaustenitic stainless steel in condition A (annealed or solution-treated) is shown in Fig. 2a and b. Note that the matrix is austenite with the delta ferrite stringers. The ASTM grain

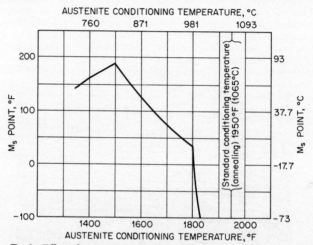

Fig. 3 Effect of austenite conditioning temperature on the M_s point.

size is approximately 10 to 14. After fabrication, the austenite must be conditioned to permit subsequent transformation to martensite.

Austenite conditioning can occur over a wide range in temperature as shown in Fig. 3. The M_s temperature of about 150 to 200°F (65 to 93°C) is obtained when the conditioning temperature is of the order of 1300 to 1500°F (704 to 815°C). Increasing the austenite conditioning temperature above 1500°F (815°C) results in a decrease in the M_s temperature so that at a conditioning temperature of about 1750°F (953°C), the M_s temperature is about room temperature. The M_f temperature, the temperature at which transformation is substantially complete, is about 150°F (83°C) below the M_s temperature shown in Fig. 3. Accompanying this phase transformation from austenite to martensite is a substantial increase in magnetic permeability and a dimensional expansion of about 0.0045 in./in. (0.045 mm/cm).

Metallurgically, heating the condition A material in the austenite conditioning range results in removing carbon from solution in the form of chromium carbides ($Cr_{23}C_6$). This occurs first at the ferrite stringer–austenite interface. If the carbon content is on the high side of the specification, carbides also will form in the grain boundaries. Removal of the carbon and chromium from the austenite matrix makes the austenite unstable and, upon cooling, results in transformation to martensite. When the austenite conditioning is accomplished at the low side of the conditioning range, that is, around 1400°F (760°C), a continuous carbide film forms around the ferrite stringers (Fig. 4). As the austenite conditioning temperature increases, say toward 1700 or 1750°F (926 or 953°C), fewer carbides are removed (Fig. 5). In this latter condition, the M_s temperature is of the order of room temperature necessitating cooling to about −100°F (−73°C) to effect complete transformation. In the former case, that is when conditioning was accomplished at about 1400°F (760°C) resulting in a M_s of about 150 to 200°F (65 to 93°C), transformation is substantially complete at about +60°F (16°C). Intermediate conditioning temperatures would result in different amounts of carbides being precipitated which would produce

Fig. 4 Condition T (transformed) showing carbides at ferrite-martensite interface. Condition R-100 is similar with fewer carbides. Etchant: Vilella's. (18,000×, electron micrograph, plastic replica technique.)

intermediate M_s and M_f temperatures from those previously described. In any event, the final transformed product would have essentially the same properties and would produce the same dimensional expansion of about 0.0045 in./in. (0.045 mm/cm).

Precipitation Hardening   The final step in heat-treating the semiaustenitics is precipitation hardening. Theoretically, precipitation hardening takes place in a temperature range of 250 to 1250°F (121 to 675°C) as shown in Fig. 6. The practical useful range, however, is from 900 to 1200°F (482 to 648°C). Specific data on the effect of precipitation-hardening temperature on mechanical properties are shown later.

The precipitation-hardening treatment has two functions: (1) it stress relieves the martensite for increased toughness, ductility, and corrosion resistance; and (2) it provides additional hardening by precipitation of an intermetallic compound.

The effect of precipitation-hardening cannot be detected by optical microscopy. Figure 7 is an optical micrograph which represents both the transformed and transformed plus hardened microstructure. However, electron microscope techniques show considerable

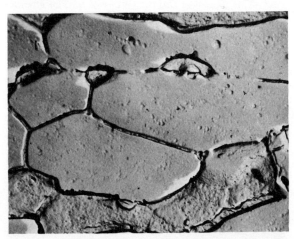

Fig. 5 Condition R-100 (transformed) showing carbides and grain boundaries. More heavily etched than Fig. 4. Note fewer carbides. Etchant: (1) nitric-acetic, electrolytic; (2) 10% oxalic, electrolytic. (18,000×, electron micrograph, plastic replica technique.)

veining through the matrix. Figure 8 shows the veining typical in the fully heat-treated conditions. This is evidence of precipitation and compositional changes in the martensitic matrix.

The mechanism of precipitation hardening in these steels is not fully understood. However, the following is a reasonable explanation of what occurs during a precipitation-hardening treatment. In the martensitic condition, the aluminum in these steels is in supersaturated solid solution. Upon heating for precipitation hardening, the aluminum in the martensite is precipitated as a Ni-Al intermetallic compound. The amount of precipitation depends on the time and temperatures at which the reaction takes place. Electron diffraction studies have identified the precipitate as a Ni-Al compound.

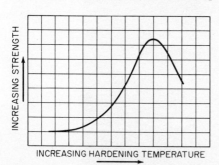

INCREASING HARDENING TEMPERATURE

Fig. 6 Effect of variation of precipitation-hardening temperature on strength.

It should be pointed out, however, that the aging of these steels is much more complex than a simple precipitation-hardening reaction, particularly when these steels are overaged at a temperature of, say, 1050°F (565°C). Upon aging at 1050°F (565°C), three separate and distinct reactions occur simultaneously. First, the precipitation reaction just described; second, the tempering of the martensitic matrix; and third, partial reversion of the matrix to form austenite. The amount of austenite formed is a function of both the aging temperature and time. The longer the time and/or the higher the temperature, the more austenite that will be reformed. The properties of the overaged material will be a summation of these three reactions. The result of the precipitation hardening will be a contraction of approximately 0.0005 in./in. (0.005 mm/cm). This amount will vary somewhat depending on the aging temperature and the amount of austenite that is reformed. This then results in a net dimensional change from condition A through the final heat-treated condition of about 0.004 in./in. (0.04 mm/cm).

In addition to the multiple thermal treatments used to develop the properties in the semiaustenitic precipitation-hardenable alloys, a thermomechanical-hardening mechanism is available. Because of the careful chemical balance, cold-work will also produce the martensitic reaction in the semiaustenitic alloys. Usually, large amounts of cold-work are required (60%) for maximum strength. Following the cold-work, only the aging step need be performed. (This process is also shown in Fig. 9.) The final properties can be

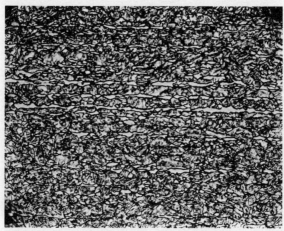

Fig. 7 Austenite transformed to martensite. Representative conditions T, R-100, TH-1050 and RH-950. Etchant: (1) nitric-acetic, electrolytic; (2) 10% oxalic, electrolytic. (1000×, optical.)

varied by using different amounts of cold-work. Because of the cold-work involved, alloys hardened using the cold-work and aging process (CH) are limited to relatively simple shapes such as flat springs.

Special Considerations During Heat Treatment When the condition A part is subjected to severe forming, significant amounts of martensite may develop in the highly formed area. Since this martensite is not taken into solution until a temperature of about 1650°F (898°C) is reached, austenite conditioning at lower temperatures (for example the

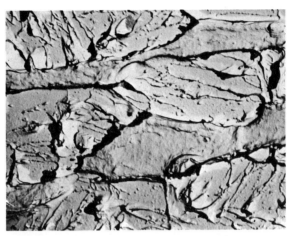

Fig. 8 Transformed and precipitation-hardened conditions TH-1050 and RH-950. Note veining throughout the martensite. Etchant: (1) nitric-acetic, electrolytic; (2) 10% oxalic, electrolytic. (18,000×, electron micrograph, plastic replica technique.)

standard 1400°F (760°C) conditioning) will result in lowered mechanical properties in those cold-worked areas. When full retention of mechanical properties is desired, there are several courses of action open to the user. First, a complete solution treatment at 1950°F (1063°C) can be employed before the standard 1400°F (760°C) conditioning treatment, or second, the 1750°F (953°C) conditioning treatment can be used. This treatment will remove the strain, take the martensite back into solution and at the same time condition the austenite so that full transformation can be obtained by cooling to −100°F (−73°C) and thus full properties can be developed upon subsequent age-hardening. This is another example of the extreme flexibility of heat treatments that can be used with these steels once the basic metallurgical principles are understood.

Now that the basic principles behind the metallurgy of the semiaustenitic stainless steels have been described, we will describe some of the basic heat treatments and mechanical properties that result from the heat treatments on several commercially available semiaustenitic stainless steels.

Commercial Semiaustenitic Precipitation-hardenable Stainless Steels, Their Chemistry, Properties, and Heat Treatment The nominal chemistry of five semiaustentic precipitation-hardenable stainless steels is given in Table 1, and the typical mechanical properties in their most widely used heat-treated condition are given in Table 2. The true precipitation-hardenable stainless steels are: 17-7PH, PH 15-7Mo, and PH 14-8Mo alloys. Types AM-350 and AM-355 are normally classed as semiaustenitic stainless steels although they do not truly have a precipitation-hardening reaction.

To describe the effect of the various heat-treating sequences on the mechanical properties of this class of steels, we shall limit our discussion to 17-7PH and PH 15-7Mo stainless steels. Figure 9 gives a schematic of the standard heat-treating sequences that are normally used for these steels. As will be observed from the following figures, a reasonably wide latitude in the times and temperatures of these three steps is possible while still enabling the user to obtain usable mechanical properties. However, for the sake of standardization and for specification purposes, the listed times and temperatures are rigidly adhered to. Normally, properties developed as a result of these treatments are

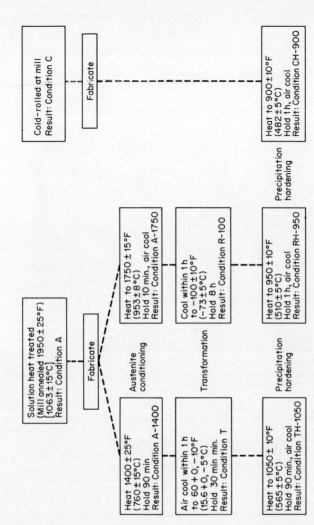

Fig. 9 Standard heat treatments for Armco 17-7PH and PH 15-7Mo.

Cold-rolled at mill
Result: Condition C

Fabricate

Heat to 900 ± 10°F
(482 ± 5°C)
Hold 1 h, air cool
Result: Condition CH-900

Solution heat treated
(Mill annealed 1950 ± 25°F)
[1063 ± 15°C]
Result: Condition A

Fabricate

Austenite
conditioning

Heat to 1750 ± 15°F
(953 ± 8°C)
Hold 10 min., air cool
Result: Condition A-1750

Transformation

Cool within 1 h
to −100 ± 10°F
(−73 ± 5°C)
Hold 8 h
Result: Condition R-100

Precipitation
hardening

Heat to 950 ± 10°F
(510 ± 5°C)
Hold 1 h, air cool
Result: Condition RH-950

Heat 1400 ± 25°F
(760 ± 15°C)
Hold 90 min
Result: Condition A-1400

Air cool within 1 h
to 60 + 0, − 10°F
(15.6 + 0, − 5°C)
Hold 30 min. min.
Result: Condition T

Heat to 1050 ± 10°F
(565 ± 5°C)
Hold 90 min, air cool
Result: Condition TH-1050

TABLE 1   Nominal Chemistry of Selected Semiaustenitic Precipitation-hardenable Stainless Steels

Grade	C	Mn	Si	Cr	Ni	Mo	Al	N
17-7PH*	0.07	0.50	0.30	17.0	7.1		1.2	0.04
PH 15-7Mo*	0.07	0.50	0.30	15.2	7.1	2.2	1.2	0.04
PH 14-8Mo†	0.04	0.02	0.02	15.1	8.2	2.2	1.2	0.005
AM-350‡	0.10	0.75	0.35	16.5	4.25	2.75		0.10
AM-355‡	0.13	0.85	0.35	15.5	4.25	2.75		0.12

*17-7PH and PH 15-7Mo are registered trademarks of the Armco Steel Corporation.
†PH 14-8Mo is a trademark of the Armco Steel Corporation.
‡AM 350 and AM 355 are trademarks of the Allegheny Ludlum Steel Corporation.

considered to be representative types of properties since many manufacturers vary the times and temperatures to fit their own particular manufacturing process.

The effect of the solution-treatment temperature on the annealed or condition A properties is shown in Fig. 10 for both 17-7PH and PH 15-7Mo alloys. The effects of the solution-treatment temperature on the final heat-treated properties are shown in Fig. 11

TABLE 2   Typical Mechanical Properties of Selected Semiaustenitic Precipitation-hardenable Stainless Steels

Grade	Condition	Form	0.2% yield strength		Ultimate tensile strength		Elongation in 2 in. (50.8 mm), %	Hardness, R_c
			ksi	MPa	ksi	MPa		
17-7PH	TH-1050	Sheet	185	1276	200	1379	9	43
PH 15-7Mo	RH-950	Sheet	225	1551	240	1655	6	48
PH 15-7Mo	CH-900	Sheet	260	1793	265	1827	2	49
PH 14-8Mo	SRH-950	Sheet	215	1482	230	1586	6	48
AM-350	SCT-850	Sheet	175	1207	206	1420	12	46
AM-355	SCT-850	Sheet	181	1248	219	1510	13	48

for both the TH-1050 and the RH-950 condition. The effect of the austenite conditioning temperature and the effect of time at the austenite conditioning temperature on the conditioned RH-950 mechanical properties for both alloys are shown in Fig. 12 and 13, respectively. The effect of refrigeration time and temperature on the tensile strength of 17-7PH conditioned RH-950 is shown in Fig. 14. PH 15-7Mo alloy responds in a similar manner. The effect of hardening time and temperature on mechanical properties is shown

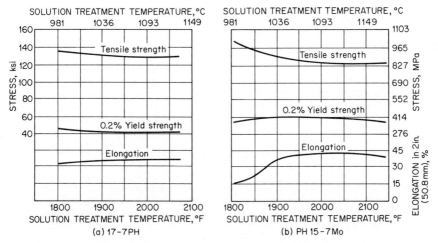

Fig. 10   Effect of solution-treatment temperature on condition A properties.

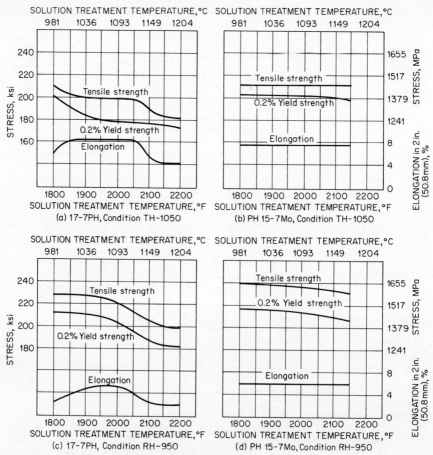

Fig. 11 Effect of solution-treatment temperatures on hardened properties.

in Fig. 15. From these curves, one can appreciate that a great deal of flexibility is available in the heat treatments of these stainless steels. Perhaps the most critical part of the heat treatment is the time delay between the austenite conditioning temperature and the refrigeration temperature.

Data similar to that shown in Fig. 16 has been developed which indicates that if maximum strength is to be obtained on any given treatment, the 1-h maximum time delay between the start of transformation and the completion of transformation must be rigidly adhered to. Otherwise the martensite tends to stabilize the remaining austenite so that full martensitic transformation cannot be obtained and thus full mechanical properties cannot be obtained on subsequent age-hardening. Time delays above the M_s temperature have no effect on the final properties, but once transformation has begun, it must be rapidly brought to conclusion by continuously cooling down to the appropriate temperature. Delays or temperature cycling will result in lowered properties.

As indicated above, all of the semiaustenitic stainless steels are capable of developing approximately the same tensile strength. However, the fracture toughness of all the steels is not the same (see Tables 3 and 4). In Table 3, three of the semiaustenitic stainless steels are shown, all heat-treated to approximately the same tensile strength level. Note that the fracture toughness as measured by the sharp notch strength to ultimate strength ratio varies from a low of 0.44 to a high of 0.93. In Table 4, the same three steels are compared

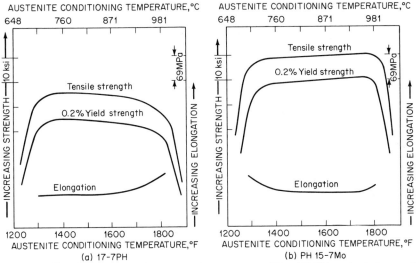

Fig. 12 Effect of austenite conditioning temperature on condition RH-950 mechanical properties.

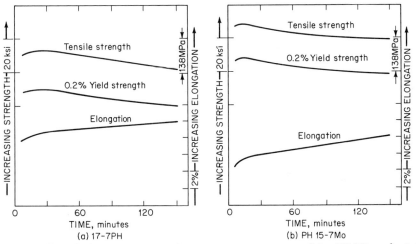

Fig. 13 Effect of time at austenite conditioning temperatures on condition RH-950 mechanical properties.

TABLE 3   Notch Toughness of Several Semiaustenitic Precipitation-hardenable Stainless Steels in Highest Strength Condition

Grade	Condition	Ultimate tensile strength		Notch strength		Notch strength/ Ultimate tensile strength ratio
		ksi	MPa	ksi	MPa	
17-7PH (air arc)	RH-950	236	1627	120	827	0.51
PH 15-7Mo (air arc)	RH-950	247	1703	108	745	0.44
PH 14-8Mo (vim)	SRH-950	240	1655	225	1551	0.93

SOURCE: NASA-Lewis Labs. Samples tested in the transverse direction. NASA edge notch specimens, 0.0007 in. (0.018 mm) max. root radius.

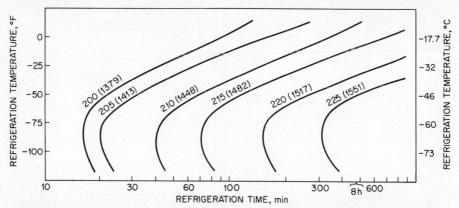

Fig. 14 Effect of variation in refrigeration cycle on tensile strength of 17-7PH in condition RH-950. Held 10 min at 1750°F (953°C), air-cooled to room temperature, liquid-cooled to temperature shown, held for time shown, hardened at 950°F (510°C) for 1 h. Curves indicate tensile strength in ksi (MPa).

at a constant sharp notch to ultimate tensile strength ratio. Note that the usable tensile strength ranges from a low of 175,000 psi (1206.6 MPa) in 17-7PH alloy to a high of 240,000 psi (1654.8 MPa) for the vacuum induction melting method PH 14-8Mo alloy. Note also that in a comparison of 17-7PH and PH 15-7Mo alloys, both heat-treated to the same RH-1100 condition, the usable tensile strength and the usable notch strength of PH 15-7Mo are approximately 20,000 psi (138 MPa) higher than that of 17-7PH. It has also been determined that the fracture toughness is an excellent indicator of the stress-corrosion cracking resistance of these steels when exposed in a marine atmosphere. The higher the toughness, the longer the life, or the higher stress that can be applied without failure.

Elevated Temperature Stability All of the precipitation-hardenable stainless steels tend to become embrittled when exposed for thousands of hours at temperatures above

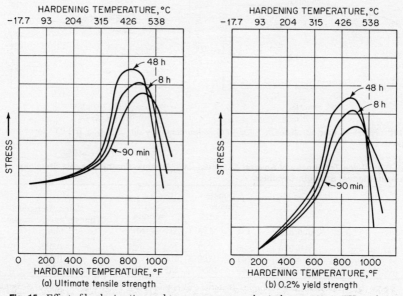

Fig. 15 Effect of hardening time and temperature on mechanical properties in TH conditions.

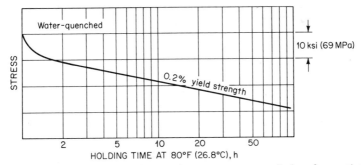

Fig. 16 Effect of time delay before transformation treatment on final aged properties.

about 550°F (288°C). The degree to which embrittlement occurs depends somewhat on the specific alloy. In general, however, long-time exposures in the 700 to 800°F (371 to 426°C) range result in sharply increased tensile and yield strengths and reduced fracture toughness. For this reason, these steels generally are limited to a maximum temperature of about 600°F (315°C) when long-time exposure in service is anticipated. The metallurgical phenomenon that is responsible for this condition is a summation of two reactions: first, continued precipitation of the intermetallic compound which causes the age-hardening reaction; and second, the mechanism analogous to the 885°F (474°C) embrittlement which is commonly experienced in the high-chromium ferritic stainless steels (such as Type 430, 446, etc.).

General Summary and Typical Uses   In view of the rather wide range of heat-treating conditions available for this class of materials, it is not too surprising to find that most users have developed their own particular set of heat-treating parameters to fit their own particular end use. Perhaps the foremost example of this is the use of these steels in brazed stainless steel honeycomb panels used in many of our military aircraft. Here, by the selection of appropriate silver-based brazing alloys, the brazing operation and the austenite conditioning treatment have been combined in one operation. Sometimes a shelving at a slightly lower temperature than the brazing temperature is required to develop the full austenite conditioning treatment. Subsequent transformation and age-hardening then result in the completed panel. Panels of all shapes have been manufactured ranging from flat panels to web-shaped panels used on military aircraft to the complex curved panels found on the Apollo Command Module.

MARTENSITIC PRECIPITATION-HARDENABLE STAINLESS STEELS

From a tonnage standpoint, the martensitic precipitation-hardenable stainless steels (or maraging stainless steels) are perhaps the most popular of this class of steels. They are used primarily in bar, rods, wire, and heavy forgings and to a minor extent in sheet form.

TABLE 4   Usable Tensile Strength of Several Semiaustenitic Precipitation-hardenable Stainless Steels at Constant Notch Strength/Ultimate Tensile Strength Ratio

Grade	Condition	Ultimate tensile strength		Notch strength		Notch strength/ ultimate tensile strength ratio
		ksi	MPa	ksi	MPa	
17-7PH (air arc)	RH-1100	175	1207	157	1083	0.90
PH 15-7Mo (air arc)	RH-1100	192	1324	174	1200	0.91
PH 14-8Mo (vim)	SRH-950	240	1655	225	1551	0.93

SOURCE: NASA-Lewis Labs. Samples tested in the transverse direction. NASA edge notch specimen, 0.0007 in. (0.018 mm) max. root radius.

TABLE 5   Nominal Chemistry of Selected Martensitic Precipitation-hardenable Stainless Steels

Grade	C	Mn	Si	Cr	Ni	Mo	Al	Cu	Ti	Cb
				MODERATE STRENGTH						
17-4PH*	0.04	0.30	0.60	16.0	4.2			3.4		0.25
15-5PH*	0.04	0.30	0.40	15.0	4.5			3.4		0.25
Custom 450†	0.03	0.25	0.25	15.0	6.0	0.8		1.5		0.3
Stainless W‡	0.06	0.50	0.50	16.75	6.25		0.2		0.8	
				HIGH STRENGTH						
PH 13-8Mo*	0.04	0.03	0.03	12.7	8.2	2.2	1.1			
Custom 455†	0.03	0.25	0.25	11.75	8.5			2.5	1.2	0.3

*17-4PH 13-8Mo, and 15-5PH are registered trademarks of the Armco Steel Corporation.
†Custom 450 and Custom 455 are trademarks of the Carpenter Technology Corporation.
‡Stainless W is a trademark of the United States Steel Corporation.

Their chemistry is so balanced that at room temperature after solution treatment they are always in the martensitic condition. They never can retain their austenitic structure at normal room temperatures.

Starting with Stainless W in the 1940s, a whole series of martensitic precipitation-hardenable stainless steels have been developed. Generally they can be classified as moderate strength [tensile strengths less than 200,000 psi (1379 MPa)] and high strength [tensile strength above 200,000 psi (1379 MPa)]. Nominal chemical analyses of representative steels of this class are given in Table 5 for both the moderate- and high-strength types. Representative mechanical properties for the moderate- and high-strength steels are given in Table 6. Metallurgically these steels are all very similar, that is, the structure is martensitic after the high-temperature solution treatment, followed by an age-hardening at temperatures ranging from 800 to 850°F (426 to 454°C) up to about 1250°F (675°C) depending on the properties desired.

The older grades in this family (Stainless W and 17-4PH) have a two-phase structure like the semiaustenitic precipitation-hardenable stainless steels, that is, stringers of ferrite in a martensitic matrix. The ferrite level generally is lower than that found in the semiaustenitics, being generally less than 10%. This ferrite results in poor through-thickness properties at all heat-treated strength levels, particularly in heavy sections. The newer steels (15-5PH, Custom 450, PH 13-8Mo, and Custom 455) are essentially ferrite-free, resulting in improved through-thickness properties in heavy sections.

The age-hardening mechanisms in these alloys are identical to those discussed for the semiaustenitics except that the actual precipitate composition may be somewhat different depending on the precipitation-hardening elements used in a particular steel. Just as for the semiaustenitics, a wide range of mechanical properties can be developed depending on the specific aging temperature used. Let us consider the mechanical properties of one of the high-strength martensitic precipitation-hardenable stainless steels, PH 13-8Mo. Table 7 gives the conventional mechanical properties for 1- to 3-in.-diameter (2.54- to 7.62-cm) bar. Note that the tensile strength can be varied from a low of 130,000 psi

TABLE 6   Typical Mechanical Properties of Selected Precipitation-hardenable Stainless Steels

Name	Condition	Form	0.2% yield strength		Ultimate tensile strength		Elongation in 2 in. (50.8 mm) or 4D, %	Reduction of area, %	Hardness, R_c
			ksi	MPa	ksi	MPa			
			MODERATE STRENGTH						
17-4PH	H-925	Bar	175	1207	190	1310	14	54	42
15-5PH	H-925	Bar	175	1207	190	1310	14	54	42
Custom 450	H-900	Bar	184	1269	196	1351	14	60	42
Stainless W	H-950	Bar	180	1241	195	1345	10		42
			HIGH STRENGTH						
PH 13-8Mo	H-950	Bar	210	1448	225	1551	12	50	47
Custom 455	H-900	Bar	235	1620	245	1689	10	45	49

TABLE 7   PH 13-8Mo, Typical Mechanical Properties [1- to 3-in. diameter (2.54- to 7.62-cm) bar]

Condition	0.2% yield strength		Ultimate tensile strength		Elongation in 2 in. (50.8 m) or 4D, %	Reduction of area, %	Hardness		
								Charpy V notch	
	ksi	MPa	ksi	MPa			R_c	ft-lb	J
A	120	827	160	1103	17	65		60	81.4
RH-950	215	1482	235	1620	12	45	48	20	27
H-950	210	1448	225	1551	12	50	47	20	27
H-1000	205	1413	215	1482	13	55	45	30	40.7
H-1050	180	1241	190	1310	15	55	43	50	67.8
H-1100	150	1034	160	1103	18	60	35	60	81.4
H-1150	105	724	145	1000	20	63	33	80	108.5
H-1150M	85	586	130	896	22	70	32	120	162.7

(896.4 MPa) to a high of 235,000 psi (1620.3 MPa), with corresponding impact energies ranging from 120 to 20 ft-lb (162.7 to 27.1 J) at the 235,000-psi (1620.3 Mpa) tensile strength level. The important plane-strain fracture toughness K_{IC}, can also be varied with heat treatment as shown in Table 8.

Heat treatments for the martensitic precipitation-hardenable steels generally follow the designation and heat treatments given in Table 9. It is of interest to note that at the lowest aging temperature, in this case 900°F (482°C), the microstructure is essentially completely martensitic. As the aging temperature increases, so does the amount of reformed austenite according to the mechanism previously discussed. The H-1150-M condition (the softest for these steels) has a rather complex microstructure. Heating to 1400°F (760°C) results in much of the martensite going into solution at that temperature. Upon cooling to room temperature some of the austenite is transformed to untempered martensite. The rest of the austenite remains as austenite and the balance is highly overaged martensite. The 1150°F

TABLE 8   PH 13-8Mo, Typical Plane-Strain Fracture Toughness

Condition	K_{Ic}		0.2% yield strength		Ultimate tensile strength	
	ksi $\sqrt{\text{in.}}$	MPa $\sqrt{\text{m}}$	ksi	MPa	ksi	MPa
H-950	75	82.4	210	1448	225	1551
H-1000	100	110	205	1413	215	1482
H-1025	125	137	195	1345	205	1413
H-1050	150	165	180	1241	190	1310
H-1000 tested at −110°F (−79°C)	50	54.9	230	1586	240	1655

TABLE 9   Heat Treatments for Martensitic Precipitation-hardenable Stainless Steels
All steels in condition A (solution treated) prior to heat treatment

Condition	Hardening temperature, °F (°C)		Hardening time, h	Type of cooling
	(±15°F)	(±8°C)		
H-900	900	(482)	1	Air
H-925	925	(496)	4	Air
H-950	950	(510)	4	Air
H-975	975	(528)	4	Air
H-1000	1000	(538)	4	Air
H-1025	1025	(552)	4	Air
H-1050	1050	(565)	4	Air
H-1075	1075	(579)	4	Air
H-1100	1100	(593)	4	Air
H-1125	1125	(607)	4	Air
H-1150	1150	(620)	4	Air
H-1150-M	1400	(760)	2	Air
(double overaged)	1150	(620)	followed by 4	Air

TABLE 10   PH 13-8Mo Bar, Typical Charpy V Notch Impact Strength at Sub-Zero Temperature

Test temperature, °F (°C)	Condition H-950, ft-lb (J)	Condition H-1000, ft-lb (J)	Condition H-1050, ft-lb (J)	Condition H-1100, ft-lb (J)	Condition H-1150M, ft-lb (J)
Room temperature	24 (32.5)	30 (40.7)	40 (54.2)	50 (67.8)	120+ (162.7+)
32 (0)	11 (14.9)	20 (27.1)	35 (47.5)	46 (62.4)	
−65 (−54)	7 (9.5)	12 (16.3)	22 (29.8)	38 (51.5)	
−110 (−79)	5 (6.8)	8 (10.8)	13 (17.6)	32 (43.4)	88 (119.3)
−175 (−115)	3 (4.1)	6 (8.1)			71 (96.3)
−220 (−140)	2 (2.7)	5 (6.8)	6 (8.1)	14 (19)	
−320 (−196)	2 (2.7)	4 (5.4)	4 (5.4)	5 (6.8)	30 (40.7)

(620°C) aging then ages the martensite that was formed as a result of the cooling from 1400°F (760°C) together with some additional reformed austenite. Therefore, the final microstructure consists of highly overaged martensite, normal overaged martensite, and reformed austenite which is completely thermally stable. This results in a heat-treated stainless steel with reasonably good impact strength at temperatures as low as the −320°F (−196°C) shown in Table 10.

As a class, the martensitic precipitation-hardenable stainless steels have corrosion resistance comparable to the more common austenitic stainless steels in most media. They have found wide use in both military and nonmilitary components for a variety of applications. They are superior in all respects to the quenched and tempered martensitic stainless steels. In many cases, because of the low dimensional change due to heat treatment [nominally a contraction of about 0.0005 in./in. (0.005 mm/cm)] and the low aging temperature, they can be machined nearly to net size prior to heat treatment with no quenching and no distortion resulting therefrom. Consequently, in many cases, they are cost effective and often cheaper for a given part than the conventional quench and tempered low-alloy steels, such as SAE 4340.

AUSTENITIC PRECIPITATION-HARDENABLE STAINLESS STEELS

Of the three classes of precipitation-hardenable stainless steels, perhaps the austenitic precipitation-hardenable stainless steels have the lowest usage. Yet these steels are considered by many to be the forerunners of the more popular nickel- and cobalt-based superalloys. Metallurgically, these steels are a very stable austenite, even after high amounts of cold-work. Precipitation-hardening elements (such as aluminum, titanium or phosphorus) are added so that upon long-time aging at about 1300°F (704°C) an interme-tallic compound is precipitated which significantly increases the strength of the steels over their solution-treated strengths. Table 11 gives the typical composition of two of the austenitic precipitation-hardenable stainless steels. Typical mechanical properties of these steels are given in Table 12. Of these, only A-286 has received much commercial acceptance.

Type A-286 has been used in all product forms, primarily in high-temperature applica-tions in jet engines, turbine wheels, fans, frames, fasteners, etc. It has also had a limited application in the cold-worked condition in cryogenic or oil field application. Being austenitic even after high degrees of cold-work, A-286 offers attractive properties even at temperatures as low as the temperature of liquid hydrogen. Some of these properties are shown in Table 13. The high strength and good ductility for fasteners which is available even at liquid hydrogen temperatures is obvious.

The corrosion resistance of these austenitic precipitation-hardenable stainless steels is

TABLE 11   Typical Composition of Austenitic Precipitation-hardenable Stainless Steels

Alloy	C	Mn	P	S	Si	Cr	Ni	Mo	Al	V	T
A−286*	0.05	1.45	0.030	0.020	0.50	14.75	25.25	1.30	0.15	0.30	2.
17-10P	0.10	0.60	0.30	0.04 max.	0.50	17.0	11.0				

*Also contains 0.005 B.

TABLE 12 Typical Heat Treatments and Mechanical Properties for Austenitic Precipitation-hardenable Stainless Steels

Alloy	Heat treatment
A-286	Solution treated at 1800°F (981°C), for 1 h, water-quenched, + aged at 1350°F (734°C) for 16 h, air-cooled.
17-10P	Solution treated at 2050°F (1120°C) for ½ h, water-quenched, + aged at 1300°F (704°C) for 12 h, water-quenched, + aged at 1200°F (648°C) for 24 h, water-quenched or air-cooled

| | Mechanical properties | | | | | | |
| | Ultimate tensile strength | | 0.2% yield strength | | Elongation in 2 in. | Reduction of | |
Alloy	ksi	MPa	ksi	MPa	(50.8 mm), %	area, %	Hardness, R_c
A-286 (bar)	150	1034	100	690	25	40	34
17-10P	143	986	98	676	20	32	31

TABLE 13 Low-Temperature Mechanical Properties of A-286 Tensile Specimens
[0.125-in. (0.317-cm) dia] cold-worked 53 percent and aged*

| Test temperature | | Ultimate tensile strength | | 0.2% Offset yield strength | | Elongation in ½ in. (1.27 cm), | Reduction of area, | Number of |
°F	°C	ksi	MPa	ksi	MPa	% in 4 × D	%	tests
75	24	208.2	1435	193.4	1333	14.0	42.3	2
−100	−73	222.2	1532	212.4	1464	14.0	41.3	2
−200	−129	230.6	1590	219.0	1510	18.3	41.8	3
−320	−196	258.3	1781	229.5	1582	21.0	41.4	3
−423	−253	285.4	1968	247.8	1708	23.3	38.9	3

*Data provided by NASA.

TABLE 14 Precipitation-hardening Stainless Steels: Developer and/or Principal Producer*

| Alloy name | Developer and/or principal producer | Nominal analysis, % | | | | | | | | |
		C	Mn	Cr	Ni	Mo	Cu	Al	Ti	Other
A-286	Allegheny-Ludlum	0.05	1.45	14.75	25.25	1.30		0.15	2.15	V 0.30; B 0.005
Almar 362		0.03		14.5	6.5				0.8	
AM-350		0.10	0.75	16.5	4.25	2.75				N 0.10
AM-355		0.13	0.85	15.5	4.25	2.75				N 0.12
AM-736		0.02		10.0	10.0	2.0		0.3	0.2	
17-4PH	Armco Steel	0.04	0.30	16.0	4.2		3.4			Cb 0.25
15-5PH		0.04	0.30	15.0	4.5		3.4			Cb 0.25
PH13-8Mo		0.04	0.03	12.7	8.2	2.2		1.1		
17-7PH		0.07	0.50	17.0	7.1			1.2		
PH15-7Mo		0.07	0.50	15.2	7.1	2.2		1.2		
PH14-8Mo		0.04	0.02	15.1	8.2	2.2		1.2		N 0.005
17-10P		0.10	0.60	17.0	11.0					P 0.30
Custom 450	Carpenter Technology	0.03	0.25	15.0	6.0	0.8	1.5			Cb 0.3
Custom 455		0.03	0.25	11.75	8.5		2.5		1.2	Cb 0.3
AFC-77	Crucible Steel	0.15		14.5		5.0				Co 13.0, V 0.4
CD-4MCu†	Cooper Alloy	0.04		26.0	5.0		3.0			
PH55A†		0.04		20.0	8.8	4.0				
Croloy 16-6PH	Babcock & Wilcox	0.035	0.80	15.75	7.5			0.40	0.60	
Illium P†	Stainless Foundry & Eng.	0.20		28.0	8.0	2.0	3.0			
Illium PD†		0.08		27.0	5.0	2.0				Co 7.0
14-6Ti	Republic Steel	0.05		14.5	6.5				0.75	
Stainless W	U.S. Steel	0.06	0.50	16.75	6.25			0.2	0.8	
Unimar CR-1	Universal Cyclops	0.01		11.5	10.25			1.15	0.3	

*Other alloys have been developed. This table reflects only those alloys currently in commercial production.
†Castings only.

comparable to the standard 300-series stainless steels in most media. While the mechanical properties of A-286 and 17-10P alloy are in many instances comparable, the high phosphorus content of 17-10P makes weldability a practical impossibility. The weldability of A-286 is quite good under most conditions, hence its more ready acceptance in the marketplace.

GENERAL SUMMARY

As a class, the precipitation-hardenable stainless steels shown in Table 14 offer the designer a unique combination of fabricability, strength, ease of heat treatment, and corrosion resistance not found in any other class of material. The austenitic precipitation-hardenable alloys have, to a large extent, been replaced by the more sophisticated and higher strength superalloys. The martensitic precipitation-hardenable stainless steels are really the workhorse of this family. While designed primarily as a material to be used for bar, rods, wire, forgings, etc., martensitic precipitation-hardenable alloys are beginning to find more use in the flat-rolled form. While the semiaustenitic precipitation-hardenable stainless steels were primarily designed as a sheet and strip product, they have found many applications in other product forms. Developed primarily as aerospace materials, many of these steels are gaining commercial acceptance as truly cost-effective materials in many applications.

Chapter 8

Structure and Constitution of Wrought Microduplex Stainless Steels

ROBERT GIBSON

**Supervisor, Nickel Alloys Research Section, Paul D. Merica
Research Laboratory, The International Nickel Company, Sterling
Forest, Suffern, New York**

INTRODUCTION

The invention of microduplex stainless steels had its genesis in a study of the phenomenon of superplasticity. Superplasticity is the occurrence of large amounts of neck-free elongation at a relatively high homologous temperature. Deformation of this type has been described in a number of alloy systems and detailed studies of its mechanism have been carried out by many workers.[1-7] Superplasticity results from a very fine-grain structure[2] which is stabilized at the deformation temperature. The presence of a second phase can most readily be employed to develop and stabilize such fine-grain structures.[5] The austenite-ferrite stainless steels were observed to be especially suitable for this purpose. The fine-grain two-phase structure of these steels was termed *microduplex*.

These stainless steels are in a range of composition centered about a 26Cr-6.5Ni alloy which is designated IN-744. Processing cycles which produce the finest grain microduplex structures result both in the greatest amount of superplasticity and the best associated

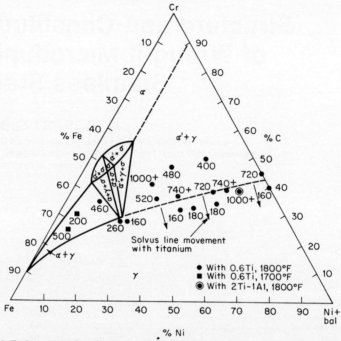

Fig. 1   Ni-Fe-Cr ternary plot of 0.2 min^{-1} hot tensile elongations of alloys. Superimposed diagram of phases present in titanium-free alloys at 1000°C.[5]

mechanical properties. This is because the fine grain size is important to strength and toughness at temperatures below those for hot deformation. Moreover, the alloys are easily hot-worked by forging, rolling, and extrusion. They are also readily cold-worked by rolling or drawing.

Because of their relatively high strength and good corrosion resistance, the microduplex stainless steels are useful engineering materials. In the sections to follow, the constitution, structure, and mechanical properties of these steels will be described.

CONSTITUTION

Microduplex Structure   The phenomenon of elevated temperature superplasticity in many two-phase Ni-Fe-Cr alloys was described by Hayden et al.[5] and Gibson et al.[11]

A 1000°C section of the Ni-Fe-Cr ternary system is shown in Fig. 1.[5] The alloys displaying superplasticity are those located in two-phase regions $\alpha' + \gamma$ (nickel- and iron-nickel-based alloys) and $\alpha + \gamma$ (stainless steels). The $\gamma - \gamma + \alpha'$ solvus line is moved to lower chromium and iron contents by titanium, which is present in most of the alloys. At temperatures around 1000°C, nickel-based alloy structures consist of a dispersion of body-centered-cubic (bcc), chromium-rich α' phase in a face-centered-cubic (fcc) γ matrix. In this same temperature range, the stainless steel alloy structures are a dispersion of fcc γ (austenite) in a matrix of bcc α (ferrite). The relative size and distribution of second-phase particles in the structures are determined by their history of thermomechanical treatment.

The several thermomechanical treatments necessary to obtain the microduplex structure in IN-744 were shown by Gibson and Brophy.[12] These treatments are depicted schematically in Fig. 2. In the hot-work cycle, the second phase is first dissolved. It then precipitates during working and stabilizes the grain size of the recrystallizing matrix. In the cold-work cycle the second phase precipitates upon reheating the cold-worked single-phase matrix, thereby minimizing grain growth. The microduplex structure results only if precipitation accompanies or precedes recrystallization. A structural size of <10 μm results from both thermomechanical treatments. Examples of the structures developed by both treatments are shown in Fig. 3[11] for a microduplex 25Cr-6Ni-0.6Ti-<0.02C-bal Fe alloy. As will be shown later, the working and heating schedules are simple and easily conducted on conventional equipment.

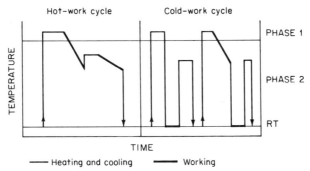

Fig. 2 Processing schedules for producing a microduplex structure in IN-744 stainless steel.[12]

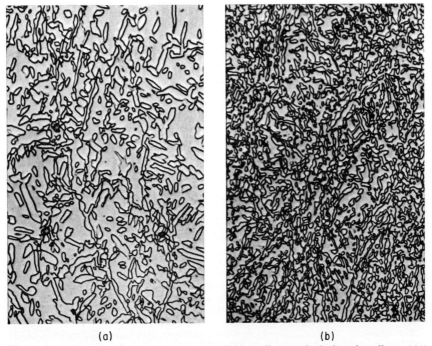

(a)   (b)

Fig. 3 Microstructures of 25Cr-6Ni-0.6Ti-<0.02C-bal Fe alloys. Etched electrolytically in 10% HCl.[11] (a) Hot-rolled from 1204°C and reheated to 927°C mfp = 3.61 μm. (b) Hot-rolled from 1204°C, cold-rolled 80% and reheated to 927°C, mfp = 2.19 μm. (750×).

Lindinger et al.[13] determined the quantitative effect of the second-phase distribution on the grain size of the matrix and also the effect of matrix grain size on superplastic deformation parameters. Grain sizes were measured on deformed specimens, and it was shown that grain size increased approximately linearly with hot tensile test time regardless of strain rate or elongation. Quantitative metallography revealed that the Zener relation for limiting grain size[14] as modified by McLean[15] describes the matrix grain size

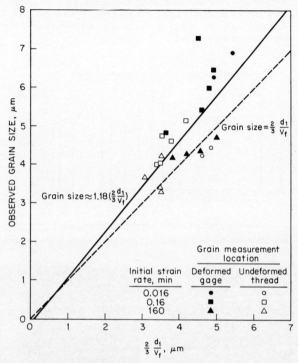

Fig. 4 Observed grain size of deformed gage and undeformed threaded sections of 982°C tensile specimens vs. Zener's predicted grain size.[13]

inhibiting action of the second phase in the microduplex structure. The broken line in Fig. 4[13] is a plot of the Zener-McLean relation

$$GS = \frac{2}{3} \frac{d_1}{V_f}$$

versus observed grain size in a microduplex 38Cr-18Fe-0.6Ti-bal Ni alloy. In this plot grain diameter is denoted by GS, d_1 is average particle diameter, and V_f is the volume fraction of second phase (here bcc chromium-rich α' phase). The least-squares fit (solid line) of the data agreed quite well with the broken line, thus supporting the conclusion that the dispersed phase inhibits matrix grain growth.

Production of the microduplex structure in scaled-up commercial heats up to ingots as large as 11,793 kg (13 tons) presented no problems. In fact, smaller grain sizes were produced in 0.51-mm (0.02-in.) cold-rolled annealed sheet from large ingots than from small laboratory heats. It was noted that no special practice was required on commercial hot-strip rolling mills to produce the microduplex structure in a wide range of product sizes.

Superplasticity Table 1 presents high-temperature tensile test results on two of the stainless steel compositions shown in Fig. 3.[12] The alloys were tested in two conditions. The first group was from 15.8-mm (0.62-in.) square bar stock which had been hot-worked starting at 1204°C. The second group was from similarly hot-worked bar stock

TABLE 1   Elevated Temperature Tensile Properties of Microduplex Stainless Steels

Alloy	Prior condition	Test temperature °F	°C	Gage length in.	mm	Strain rate, min⁻¹	Ultimate tensile strength ksi	MN/m²	% Elongation	Mean austenite spacing, μm
1		1600	871	1.25	31.8	0.160	10.8	74.5	304	
1	As-hot-worked	1700	927	1.25	31.8	0.160	7.3	50.3	304	3.61
2	from 2200°F (1204°C)	1600	871	1.25	31.8	0.160	10.5	72.4	160	
2		1700	927	1.25	31.8	0.160	6.9	47.6	208	
1		1600	871	0.75	19.1	0.266	10.5	72.4	433	
1	Hot-worked	1700	927	0.75	19.1	0.266	7.6	52.3	600	2.19
1	from 2200°F (1204°C)	1800	982	0.75	19.1	0.266	5.4	37.2	500	
2	then cold-worked	1600	871	0.75	19.1	0.266	11.8	81.3	300	
2	80%	1700	927	0.75	19.1	0.266	8.4	57.9	200	
2		1800	982	0.75	19.1	0.266	5.2	35.8	200	

Alloy 1: 25Cr-5.7Ni-0.69Ti-0.1Al-0.02C-bal Fe.
Alloy 2: 29.6Cr-6.0Ni-0.70Ti-0.16Al-0.02C-Bal Fe.

which was later cold-rolled to 9.5-mm (0.37-in.) square. In the as-hot-worked condition the microstructure was essentially ferritic, but on heating to the temperature for tensile testing, there was appreciable austenite precipitation. Figure 3 shows the microstructures resulting from heating this material to 927°C. It is evident from Fig. 3 and Table 1[11] that the sample which had been subjected to the cold-work cycle (cold-worked prior to reheating) has a finer microstructure, and that the finer structure enhanced the amount of superplastic elongation. In Table 1 it can also be seen that finer structure reduced the hot tensile strength. The materials with finer structures were deformed at a higher strain rate which should tend to increase strength. However, they exhibited about the same strength values as the somewhat coarser hot-worked samples tested at the same temperature. The necessary structure results from the fine distribution of one phase impeding grain growth in the other as shown earlier.[11]

Smith, Norgate, and Ridley[8] using the theory of Ashby and Verral[9] predicted stress-strain rate relationships for microduplex IN-744 stainless steel. The Ashby-Verral model essentially states that large strains can be obtained by grain-boundary sliding, accommodation being provided by diffusion-controlled dislocation creep. Smith et al. found some departure from the model in their experiments with IN-744 but agreement in general was good. Hayden et al.[10] reported similar relationships between grain-boundary sliding and dislocation creep, but also found that the dependence of strain rate on stress and grain size should be different in materials having fine elongated structures (such as IN-744) than in materials having fine equiaxed structures (such as microduplex nickel-based alloys). They observed, as shown in Fig. 5, that with increasing strain, the slope of the log stress–log

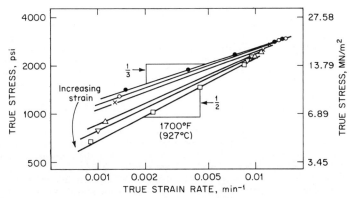

Fig. 5 The change in deformation behavior with increasing strain of a sample of IN-744 having an originally elongated grain structure.[10]

strain rate plot progressed from ⅛ to ½. Spheroidization of the structure occurred also and equiaxed structures were established at about the level of strain where the strain rate exponent reached ½.

Deformability During Hot-Working The hot workability of microduplex alloys in relatively high-strain-rate deformation processes seems to reflect their superplastic tendencies. Hot-working of IN-744 stainless steel is readily accomplished.[11] Rolling mill and extrusion press operations have shown that the material deforms easily and with a large amount of spreading in rolling. Mill loads during commercial hot-band rolling were observed to be less than those for Type 430 stainless. A plot of extrusion pressure versus temperature for IN-744, Type 304, and Type 430 stainless steels is shown in Fig. 6.[11]

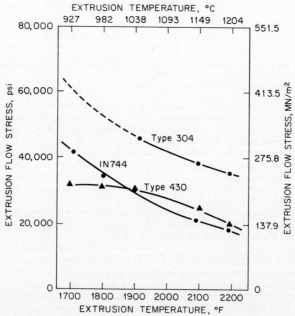

Fig. 6 Extrusion flow stress for reduction from 87.6 to 22.2-mm (3.45- to 0.87-in.) round for several stainless steels, including Type 304, Type 430 and IN-744 as-forged from 1204°C.[11,12]

Extrusion reduction was from 87.6 to 22.2-mm (3.45 to 0.87-in.) diameter bar. Each steel was in a hot-worked condition prior to extrusion. It can be seen that the flow stress of IN-744 at all temperatures between 927 and 1204°C is comparable to the lean ferritic steel and much less than that of the austenitic stainless steel. Semicommercial billets of IN-744 have been extruded to complex shapes and showed excellent die-filling ability and low extrusion pressures. Examples of these extruded shapes are shown in Fig. 7.[12]

Riedl[16] measured torsional deformation of IN-744 and a 25Cr-4Ni stainless steel. The tests were run at a test temperature of 1010°C and a rotation speed of 200 rev/min. The data plotted in Fig. 8[12] show that the 25Cr-4Ni steel reached maximum torque after a few twists whereas the maximum torque for IN-744 is achieved much sooner and is lower. The difference between the two alloys is that the IN-744 possessed a microduplex structure and the 25Cr-4Ni steel did not.

The utilization of superplasticity for low-strain-rate forming processes has been considered in several systems. Davis[17] investigated the 22Al-Zn eutectoid alloy and showed that a wide range of shapes was possible. Petersen et al.[18] illustrated the results of an internal pressure forming process he has developed for forming IN-744 sheet. Several formed parts showing results of this work are presented in Fig. 9. These are interesting and useful demonstrations, however, in the last analysis, the utility of an alloy depends largely on its engineering properties. These will be discussed in later sections.

Hot-Working of Ingots Early in the production and rolling of certain heats of IN-744, it was found[19] that beginning working in the temperature range where both austenite and ferrite are stable (below about 1050°C) resulted in cracking. Cracking during rolling was found to begin at the austenite-ferrite interfaces. A replica electron micrograph of a precipitate at the interfaces and subsequent electron diffraction analysis of extracted residues revealed $M_{23}C_6$ carbide to be present (Fig. 10). Apparently, cellular austenite plus carbide was formed by decomposition of the ferrite phase. This mechanism has been described by Nehrenberg and Lillys[20] and Kuo.[21-25]

It was later found that if a stabilizing addition of titanium was made to the alloy when

Fig. 7   Extrusions of IN-744 showing excellent die filling.[12]

more than about 0.03% carbon was contained, cracking during working begun in the two-phase temperature range was prevented. Excellent workability is possible in the steel, whether carbon is stabilized by titanium or not, when working is started in the single-phase (ferrite) temperature range.

Relationship of Microstructure and Mechanical Properties   As is widely known, finer grain sizes are expected to result in higher yield strength, fatigue strength, and toughness. Room-temperature tensile yield strength of annealed IN-744 bar, plate, and sheet ranges from 482.6 to 620.5 MN/m² depending on annealing treatment and prior process-

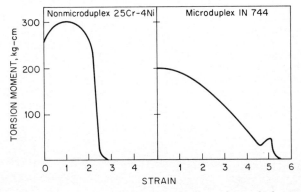

Fig. 8   Torsion test results on nonmicroduplex 25Cr-4Ni alloy and microduplex IN-744. Tests conducted at 1010°C.[12]

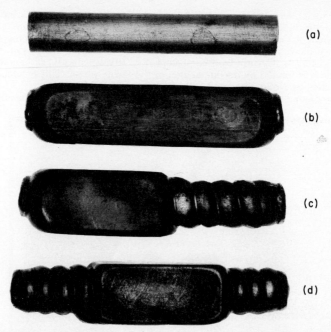

Fig. 9   Internal-pressure formed IN-744. (*a*) Starting tube. (*b*) Tube ends welded closed, pressurizing compound inserted, tube formed into die at 927°C. (*c*) Same as (b) but one end of tube wire-wrapped. (*d*) Both ends of tube wire wrapped.[18]

Fig. 10   Surface replica electron micrograph of the interphase precipitate.[11] (20,000×)

ing history. Grain size plays an important role in determining tensile properties, as shown in Fig. 11.[12] The increase in yield strength from 482.6 to 848 MN/m² was brought about by structural refinement to a 0.6-μm ferrite grain size in 0.51-mm (0.02-in.) sheet rolled from a 45,359-kg (50-ton) ingot. The form of the plot in Fig. 11 follows the Hall-Petch equation:

$$\sigma = \sigma_0 + k_y d^{-\frac{1}{2}}$$

where σ is stress and d is ferrite grain size. The apparent slope of the plot, k_y, is 1.45 kg-mm$^{-3/2}$ which is higher than the corresponding property of either of the two component phases in the microduplex structure: 0.67 for the ferrite and 1.01 for the austenite in IN-744.[26]

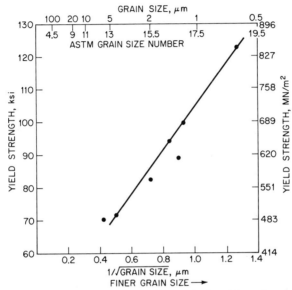

Fig. 11   Effect of grain size on 0.2% yield strength of IN-744 stainless steel.[12]

Fatigue strength of IN-744 is not affected by grain size to as great an extent as is the yield strength. However, it is considerably higher than that of conventional ferritic and austenitic stainless steels. Table 2 shows some typical values of fatigue strength of IN-744 in the microduplex condition and also in a condition where the alloy is completely ferritic and coarse grained.[11] The fatigue strength of the microduplex structure is slightly higher in the finer grained condition and is significantly higher than that of the coarse all-ferritic structure. The fatigue strength of the all-ferritic form of IN-744 is comparable to the standard ferritic grade, Type 430.

Impact properties of IN-744 are affected by grain size as seen in Fig. 12.[26] When grain size was varied from 2 to 25 μm, ductile-to-brittle transition temperature varied from

TABLE 2   Fatigue of Stainless Steels

Alloy	Structure	Grain size		10^7 cycle Fatigue strength	
		μm	ASTM	ksi	MN/m²
IN-744	Microduplex	5.7	12.7	62.7	432.3
IN-744	Microduplex	10.3	11.0	61.2	422.0
IN-744	Microduplex	25.0	8.5	57.0	393.0
IN-744	All-ferrite	65.3	5.8	42.5	293.0
Type 430	Ferrite			40.0	275.8
Type 304	Austenite			28.0	193.1

about −130°C at 2 μm to below −45°C at 25 μm. The difference in impact properties is entirely a function of structural size, since the chemical compositions of the phases in both conditions are identical. This was assured by varying only annealing time.

IN-744 may be cold-worked readily in bar, wire, and sheet forms on the same equipment and with force requirements similar to those for conventional stainless steels. A plot of room-temperature yield strength versus percent cold reduction for IN-744, Type 430,

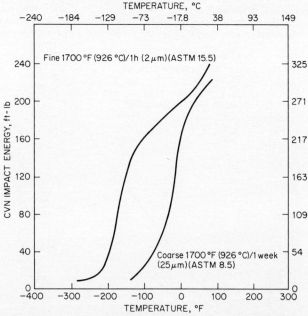

Fig. 12   Effect of grain size on ductile-to-brittle impact transition temperature of IN-744 stainless steel.[26]

and Type 304 stainless steels is presented in Fig. 13.[12] After an initial work-hardening rate similar to austenitic steel, IN-744 behaves more like the ferritic material at larger amounts of cold reduction.

Figure 14[12] shows a plot of initial grain size before wiredrawing versus strength after cold-drawing 98.8% to 0.25-mm (0.01-in.) diameter (a true strain of 4.46). Again, the

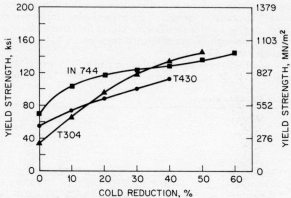

Fig. 13   Comparison of room-temperature yield strength of cold-worked IN-744 with those of cold-worked 300- and 400-series stainless steels.[11,12]

variation in grain size was obtained by varying annealing times rather than annealing temperatures prior to drawing, so that chemical composition of the phases remained constant. The increment of strengthening due to grain refinement from 6 to 0.6 μm in the annealed condition (about 414 MN/m²) is retained even after extensive cold-work. After several percent elongation, the work-hardening rate itself is insensitive to grain size. From a practical standpoint, structural refinement prior to drawing increased the strength from 1965 to 2378 MN/m² in the stainless steel wire.

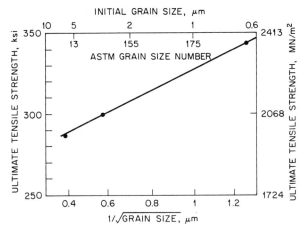

Fig. 14 Effect of starting grain size on cold-drawn strength of IN-744 wire. Wire annealed for various times at 871°C and drawn 98.8% to 0.25-mm diameter.[12]

MECHANICAL PROPERTIES OF IN-744

Several electric-furnace air-melt heats of IN-744 stainless steel have been made. The largest heat was 45,359 kg (50 tons) and the largest ingot 11,793 kg. The ingots were successfully processed into a number of product forms consisting of plate, sheet, bar, wire, and tubing. In addition, a number of extruded shapes have been made and the advantage of the lower press forces required to extrude IN-744 relative to standard 18-8 austenitic steels demonstrated.

A summary of the mechanical and physical properties of IN-744 is given in Table 3. The mechanical properties are typical of those obtained on large commercial heats when the suggested composition range shown below is employed:

Cr	25–27		25–27
Ni	6–7		6–7
C	0.06 max. (aim low)		0.06 max. (aim low)
Ti	5 times C min.		*
Mn	0.30–0.50		0.30–0.50
Si	0.30–0.65		0.30–0.65
P	0.025 max.		0.025 max.
S	0.025 max.		0.025 max.

*Severe edge cracking has been encountered in flat-rolled products when rolled in the two-phase region (under approximately 1260°C) if the carbon is not stabilized with titanium. Carbon stabilization has not been found necessary for bar products regardless of rolling temperature or for flat-rolled products if rolling initiates in the single-phase ferritic region (over approximately 1260°C). Stabilization is not required if carbon is held to 0.03% maximum.

Stability of Mechanical Properties with Elevated Temperature Exposure When exposed to temperatures in excess of 371°C and less than 538°C, an increase in strength and decrease in toughness results. Maximum effect occurs at about 482°C. Ductility (percent elongation and reduction of area) are not significantly affected. Table 4 shows the results of 5-min exposures.

TABLE 3 Mechanical and Physical Properties of IN-744 Stainless Steel

	0.2% yield strength		Tensile strength		Elongation in 2 in. (50.8 mm), %	Reduction of area, %
	ksi	MN/m²	ksi	MN/m²		
Bar:						
¾-in. (19.1-mm) diameter (as-hot-rolled)	100.2	(690.9)	114.5	(789.5)	26	57
Plate:						
1-in. (25.4-mm) (hot-rolled, annealed)	72.0	(496.5)	94.1	(648.8)	25	45
Sheet (cold-rolled, annealed):						
0.020 in. (50.8 mm) thick	92.4	(637.1)	113.1	(779.8)	20	
0.062 in. (1.57 mm) thick	91.0	(627.5)	112.0	(772.2)	22	

Fatigue strength ¾-in. (19.1-mm) diameter bar   66% of ultimate tensile strength
Density   7.72 g/cm³
Coefficient of thermal expansion, 70—800°F (21–426°C) 7.6×10^{-6} in./(in.)/(°F) (4.22×10^{-6}/°C)
Electrical resistivity, 75°F 78.0×10^{6} ohm-cm
Thermal conductivity, 100°F   9.8 Btu/hr/ft/°F (5.3 W/m/°C)
Modulus of elasticity:
Static method   0.062-in. (1.57-mm) sheet
Tension 29.6×10^{6} psi (204,092 MN/m²)
Compression 31.2×10^{6} psi (215,124 MN/m²)
Compressive yield strength $85 \times$ ksi (586.1 MN/m²)

TABLE 4   Effect of Short-Time Elevated Temperature Exposure on Mechanical Properties of IN-744 [¾-in. (19.1-mm) Diameter Bar]

COMPOSITION:	Cr	Ni	C	Ti	Mn	Si	P	S
	26.5	6.62	0.06	0.20	0.42	0.50	0.013	0.007

	0.2% yield strength		Tensile strength		Elongation in 4D,	Reduction of area,	Impact energy Charpy V 70°F (21°C)	
Exposure	ksi	MN/m²	ksi	MN/m²	%	%	ft-lb	J
1500°F (816°C)—1 h AC	76.0	524.0	106.8	736.4	30	59	40	54.2
1500°F (816°C)—1 h WQ	72.9	502.6	104.6	721.2	31	64	48	65.1
1500°F (816°C)—1 h WQ plus 5 min at temperature indicated below:								
700°F (371°C)—5 min. WQ	71.0	489.5	101.0	696.4	28	58	51	69.1
800°F (426°C)—5 min. WQ	75.7	522.0	104.7	721.9	28	59	34	46.1
850°F (454°C)—5 min. WQ	78.9	544.0	106.6	735.0	27	56	33	44.7
900°F (482°C)—5 min. WQ	83.8	577.8	110.1	759.1	27	56	20	27.1
950°F (510°C)—5 min. WQ	81.6	562.6	108.8	750.2	27	58	33	44.7

AC = air-cooled, WQ = water-quenched.

Sigma phase will form in IN-744 after exposure to certain conditions of time and temperature. Figs. 15 to 17 show the effects of time and temperature on hot-rolled, cold-worked 50% and cold-worked 90% sheet. The data relate the time-temperature dependencies to prior processing and the conditions under which sigma can be avoided.

Beetge et al.[28] concluded that transformation to sigma phase in IN-744 is an extremely slow process with significant hardness increase in hot-rolled material not occurring until after 32 h heating at 700°C. It was suggested that some sigma formation might be observed in bars or plates located in the center of bundles during cooling from annealing. However, it would not form in quantities which would have adverse effects on properties.

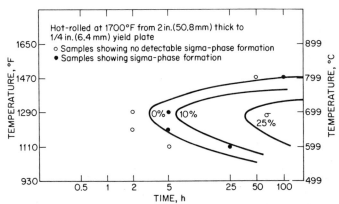

Fig. 15   Effect of time and temperature on sigma-phase formation in IN-744 stainless steel 6.4-mm hot-rolled plate.

Properties of Commercially Produced Product Forms

Sheet. Properties of 0.51-mm (0.02-in.) and 1.57-mm (0.06-in.) sheet are shown in Table 5. The CRA condition represents the prior mill condition of cold-rolling and annealing at 871°C. The other treatments were performed in the laboratory on the cold-rolled, annealed material received from the mill. The 1.57-mm (0.06-in.) sheet was cold-rolled from annealed 3.18-mm (0.13-in.) sheet and the 0.51-mm (0.02-in.) sheet from the annealed 1.57-mm (0.06-in.) sheet. Strength is reduced as the annealing temperature is raised. This ability to adjust strength level by annealing temperature would be of particular significance where forming operations are contemplated.

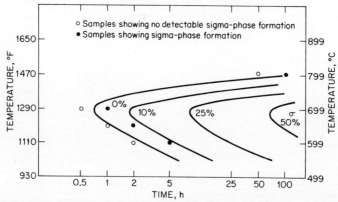

Fig. 16 Effect of time and temperature on sigma-phase formation in IN-744 stainless steel 6.4-mm plate cold-rolled 50%.

Effect of Cold-rolling on Properties of Sheet. IN-744 has a lower work-hardening rate than Type 304 but higher than that of Type 430. Table 6 shows the effect of cold-rolling 15.8-mm plate at various amounts. A tensile strength of 1227 MN/m² was attained with 80% cold reduction. Figure 18 compares the work-hardening rate of IN-744 to Types 304 and 430.

Plate. Table 7 shows the tensile and impact properties of 1-in. and ½-in. plate.

Bar. Properties of hot-rolled, water-quenched bars varying in size from 19.1- to 76.2-mm (¾- to 3-in.) diameter are shown in Table 8. Highest strength, ductility, and toughness were obtained in the hot-rolled, quenched condition.

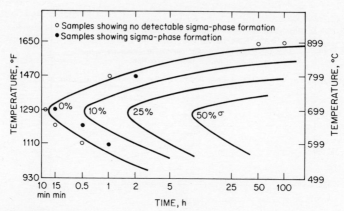

Fig. 17 Effect of time and temperature on sigma-phase formation in IN-744 stainless steel 6.4-mm plate cold-rolled 90%.

TABLE 5   Effect of Annealing Temperature on Mechanical Properties of IN-744 Stainless Steel 0.020-in. (0.51-mm) and 0.062-in. (1.57-mm) Sheet

COMPOSITION:	Cr	Ni	C	Ti	Mn	Si	P	S
	26.5	6.62	0.06	0.20	0.42	0.50	0.013	0.007

0.020-IN. (0.51-MM) SHEET						
		0.2% yield strength		Tensile strength		Elongation in 2 in. (50.8 mm),
Condition	Test direction	ksi	MN/m²	ksi	MN/m²	%
CRA	L	118.1	814.3	124.4	857.6	17
	T	134.8	929.4	135.1	931.4	14
1500°F (816°C), 2 min	L	112.3	774.3	122.2	842.4	19
	T	126.3	870.8	130.2	897.6	18
1600°F (871°C), 2 min	L	102.7	708.1	118.8	819.0	21
	T	119.7	825.3	126.8	874.2	19
1700°F (927°C), 2 min	L	94.6	652.3	113.7	784.0	22
	T	106.9	737.1	122.3	843.3	21
1800°F (982°C), 2 min	L	88.6	610.9	113.8	784.7	22
	T	99.7	687.4	119.5	824.0	21
1900°F (1038°C), 2 min	L	77.1	531.6	109.0	751.6	22
	T	88.4	609.5	117.3	808.8	21
2000°F (1093°C), 2 min	L	73.7	508.2	108.4	747.4	22
	T	80.0	551.6	114.3	788.1	22

0.062-IN. (1.57-MM) SHEET						
CRA	L	87.8	605.4	112.2	773.6	21
	T	105.2	725.4	120.3	829.4	18
1500°F (816°C), 10 min	L	86.2	594.4	108.7	749.5	24
	T	92.5	637.8	116.5	803.3	21
1600°F (871°C), 10 min	L	82.5	575.7	107.5	741.2	24
	T	88.7	611.6	114.0	786.0	22
1700°F (927°C), 10 min	L	83.5	575.7	106.9	737.1	24

CRA = cold-rolled, annealed 1600°F (871°C)—4 min AC, 30-s descale at 850°F (454°C), L = longitudinal, T = transverse.

Wire. Table 9 shows the effect of increasing amounts of cold reduction in the drawing of wire.

Tubing. Tubing was produced by hot piercing followed by cold tube reducing. Mechanical properties under various conditions are shown in Table 10. A yield strength of 935 MN/m² was attained with a 50% reduction in cross-sectional area.

Fatigue Properties Table 11 shows the smooth- and notched-rotating-beam fatigue properties of plate and bar. Smooth-bar runout is approximately 65% of tensile strength compared to approximately 35% experienced with the 18-8 austenitic steels. Limited testing to date on 0.51-mm (0.02-in.) sheet indicates a tension/tension fatigue ratio of 73%.

TABLE 6   Mechanical Properties of Cold-Rolled IN-744 Stainless Steel Sheet

COMPOSITION:	Cr	Ni	C	Ti	Mn	Si	P	S
	25.5	6.05	0.02	0.23	0.48	0.65	0.014	0.003

Cold-rolled size		Cold reduction,	0.2% yield strength		Tensile strength		Elongation in 1 (25.4 mm),
in.	mm	%	ksi	MN/m²	ksi	MN/m²	%
0.125–0.112	3.18–2.84	10	97.8	674.3	110.6	762.6	15
0.125–0.100	3.18–2.54	20	119.9	826.7	130.1	897.0	11
0.125–0.075	3.18–1.91	60	135.9	937.0	144.4	995.5	7
0.625–0.125	15.80–3.18	80	158.9	1095.6	177.7	1225.2	6

TABLE 7 Mechanical Properties of IN-744 Stainless Steel Plate

COMPOSITION:	Cr	Ni	C	Ti	Mn	Si	P	S
	25.3	6.85	0.04	0.09	0.42	0.45	0.011	0.013

CONDITION: Hot-rolled, mill-annealed 1600°F (871°C), water-quenched

Plate thickness		Test direction	0.2% yield strength		Tensile strength		Elongation in 4D, %	Reduction of area, %	Impact energy Charpy V 70°F (21°C)	
in.	mm		ksi	MN/m²	ksi	MN/m²			ft-lb	J
1	25.4	L	72.0	496.5	94.1	648.8	25	45	95	128.8
		T	79.0	544.7	96.2	663.3	21	34	71	96.3
½	12.7	L	71.3	491.6	99.4	685.4	31	57	104	141.0
		T	72.9	502.7	101.1	697.1	30	54	88	119.3

Tensiles—average of 2, CVN—average of 4 from 27,000-lb (12,247-kg) ingot.
L = longitudinal, T = transverse.

TABLE 8 Mechanical Properties of IN-744 Stainless Steel Bars

COMPOSITION:	Cr	Ni	C	Ti	Mn	Si	P	S
	26.5	6.62	0.06	0.20	0.42	0.50	0.013	0.007

CONDITION: Hot-rolled, water-quenched

Bar diameter		Test location	0.2% yield strength		Tensile strength		Elongation in 4D, %	Reduction of area, %	Impact energy Charpy V 70°F (21°C)	
in.	mm		ksi	MN/m²	ksi	MN/m²			ft-lb	J
3	76.2	L-C	73.1	504.0	90.4	623.3	25	47	65	88.1
		L-MR	73.5	506.8	92.0	634.3	29	58	79	107.1
		T-C	77.7	535.7	89.1	614.4	16	31	48	65.1
2⅛	53.9	L-C	69.3	477.8	89.8	619.2	29	55	65	88.1
		L-MR	69.9	482.0	90.1	621.2	29	56		
		L-T	73.2	504.7	93.1	641.9	21	39	42	56.9
¾	19.1	L-C	81.8	564.0	103.6	714.3	28	62	70	94.9

L = longitudinal, C = center, T = transverse, MR = midradius.

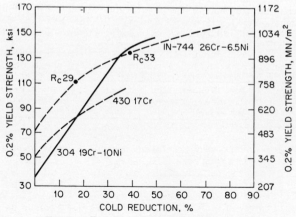

Fig. 18 Effect of cold reduction on yield strength.

TABLE 9   Mechanical Properties of Cold-Drawn IN-744 Stainless Steel Wire

COMPOSITION:	Cr	Ni	C	Ti	Mn	Si	P	S
	25.3	6.5	0.06	0.25	0.45	0.30	0.014	0.028

Wire diameter		Cold-draw, %	0.2% yield strength		Tensile strength		Elongation 2 in. (50.8 mm), %	Reduction of area, %
in.	mm		ksi	MN/m²	ksi	MN/m²		
0.098	2.49*	0	69.9	482.0	110.5	761.9	29.0	70.5
0.089	2.26	17	126.0	868.8	139.4	961.2	5.2	66.5
0.076	1.93	40	146.2	1008.1	161.3	1112.2	5.0	60.0
0.070	1.78	49	147.9	1019.8	171.8	1184.6	5.7	57.0
0.062	1.57	60	158.5	1092.9	181.3	1250.1	4.0	54.0
0.054	1.37	70	166.7	1149.4	185.5	1279.0	4.0	55.5
0.045	1.14	80	180.5	1244.5	190.2	1311.4	2.5	49.0
0.030	0.76	90	214.5	1479.0	226.8	1563.8	1.5	36.0
0.020	0.51	95	226.8	1563.8	265.5	1830.6	0.5	28.0
0.010	0.25	98			315.0	2171.9		

*Annealed 1700°F (927°C), 10 min air-cooled.
Average of two tests. 50-lb (22.7-kg) air induction melt.

TABLE 10   Mechanical Properties of IN-744 Stainless Steel Tubing

COMPOSITION:	Cr	Ni	C	Ti	Mn	Si	P	S
	25.3	6.85	0.042	0.09	0.42	0.45	0.011	0.013

Condition	0.2% yield strength		Tensile strength		Elongation in 2 in. (50.8 mm), %
	ksi	MN/m²	ksi	MN/m²	
Pierced and rolled	96.8	667.4	109.0	751.6	29
As above + 1600°F (871°C), WQ	64.3	443.3	97.4	671.6	36
As above + 1600°F (871°C), AC	74.9	516.4	103.4	712.9	35
As tube reduced*	135.6	935.0	143.7	990.8	20

*4 in. (101.6 mm) × 0.312 in. (7.92 mm) wall tube reduced to 2.875 in. (73.0 mm) OD × 0.217 in. (5.51) wall (50% reduction).
AC = air-cooled, WQ = water-quenched.

Aqueous Corrosion   Welded panels of IN-744 were exposed to marine atmosphere at the 800-ft (244-m) lot of the Francis L. LaQue Corrosion Laboratory at Kure Beach, North Carolina. Behavior at this site showed that panels welded with matching and Type 312 stainless steel filler metals had no preferential corrosion of the weld or heat-affected zones (HAZ) after 5 years exposure. General atmospheric corrosion resistance of IN-744 was judged to be comparable to that of Type 304 stainless steel.

Petersen et al.[29] however, reporting on the work of Goodell,[31] mention evidence for chloride stress-corrosion cracking in heat-affected zones. This results when composition balance is such that structure of the heat-affected zone is completely ferritic. Goodell found that proper control of structure through chemical composition, to eliminate completely ferritic heat-affected zones, provides for resistance to heat-affected zone cracking in most chloride-containing environments.

Results of general-corrosion and stress-corrosion tests of unwelded IN-744 specimens in various media are shown in Table 12. These findings indicate that IN-744 is more resistant to stress-corrosion cracking in chlorides than Type 304 stainless steel.

Data showing the acid resistance of IN-744 in several conditions are shown in Table 13. As can be seen, the microduplex material has greater resistance in these media than does Type 304 stainless steel.

Hot Corrosion   Schultz and McCarron[32] indicate that the microduplex stainless steel IN-744 is about equivalent to Types 446 and 310 stainless steels in its resistance to high-temperature oxidizing, sulfidizing, and carburizing environments. Their data are

TABLE 11 Fatigue Properties of IN-744 Stainless Steel

COMPOSITION:	Cr	Ni	C	Ti	Mn	Si	P	S
A:	26.5	6.62	0.06	0.20	0.42	0.50	0.013	0.007
B:	25.3	6.85	0.04	0.09	0.42	0.45	0.011	0.013

Heat	Product tested	Condition	0.2% yield strength		Tensile strength		Runout stress		Type test[†]
			ksi	MN/m²	ksi	MN/m²	ksi	MN/m²	
A	¾-in. (19.1-mm) bar	As-hot-rolled	100.5	692.9	112.8	777.8	66.1	455.8*	Smooth
		As-hot-rolled					31.5	217.2*	Notched
		1600°F (871°C) 1 h, AC	69.7	480.5	102.5	706.7	62.5	430.9*	Smooth
		1600°F (871°C) 1 h, AC					30.0	206.9*	Notched
B	½-in. (12.7-mm) plate	1600°F (871°C), WQ	72.9	502.6	101.5	699.8	58.5	403.4*	Smooth
		1600°F (871°C), WQ					25.0	172.4*	Notched
B	1-in. (25.4-mm) plate	1600°F (871°C), WQ	79.0	544.7	96.2	663.3	64.6	445.5*	Smooth
							26.0	179.3*	Notched
A	0.020-in. (0.51-mm) sheet	Cold-rolled + 1600°F (871°C)	118.1	814.3	124.4	857.7	95.0	655.0‡	Smooth

*Rotating beam tests.
†Notched bar K_t = 2.2.
‡Tension-tension test, R = 0.2.
Plate tests: transverse.
0.020-in. (0.51-mm) sheet: longitudinal.
AC = air-cooled, WQ = water-quenched.

TABLE 12   Corrosion Behavior of IN-744

Test medium*	Temp., °C	Atmosphere	Corrosion rate	
			in./yr	mm/yr
10%HCl	26	Nitrogen	0.162	4.11
28% HCl	52	Nitrogen	0.352	8.94
28% HCl	26	Air	0.995	25.3
5% H_2SO_4	26	Nitrogen	0.269	6.82
40% H_2SO_4	52	Nitrogen	28.2	716.28

STRESS CORROSION

Test solution	Concentration, %	Temperature, °C	Cracking time, days duplicate U-bends
$CaCl_2$	36	Boiling	OK
NaCl vapor	3	95	OK
NaCl vapor	28	95	OK
NaCl solution	3	95	OK
NaCl solution	28	95	OK
NaOH (autoclave)	90	300	OK

*Duplicate samples, no agitation.
OK = no cracks in 30 days (15 days for autoclave tests).

TABLE 13   Corrosion of IN-744 Stainless Steel in Nitric, Oxalic, and Lactic Acids
0.062 in. (1.57 mm) Cold Rolled, Annealed Sheet

COMPOSITION:	Cr	Ni	C	Ti	Mn	Si	P	S
	26.5	6.62	0.05	0.20	0.42	0.50	0.013	0.007

Five 48-h periods
average corrosion rate, in./month (mm/month)

Condition	Boiling nitric acid			Boiling 10% oxalic acid	Boiling 50% lact acid
	10%	50%	65%		
CRA	0.0000	0.0001 (0.0025)	0.0003 (0.0076)	0.0000	0.0000
TIG weld*	0.0000	0.0001 (0.0025)	0.0003 (0.0076)	0.0000	0.0000
CRA + 900°F (482°C) 1 h	0.0000	0.0001 (0.0025)	0.0004 (0.0102)	0.0008 (0.0203)	0.0000
CRA + 1200°F (649°C) 1 h	0.0000	0.0001 (0.0025)	0.0004 (0.0102)	0.0005 (0.0127)	0.0000
T-304 welded		0.0003 (0.0076)			
T-304 annealed		0.0002 (0.0051)		0.0020 (0.0508)	

*Autogenous weld.
†Average of three 48-h periods.
CRA = cold-rolled, annealed.

presented for cyclic oxidation at 871, 1038, and 1149°C in Table 14. Also shown in Table 14 is a comparison of the carburization resistance, in an H_2-2% CH_4 atmosphere at 1000°C, of IN-744, Type 446 stainless steel, and Type 310 stainless steel. As in the case of oxidation resistance the three materials are comparable.

Welding   Petersen et al.[29] reported on welding of IN-744. In their work it was found that IN-744 can readily be welded using TIG (tungsten inert gas), MIG (metal inert gas), or manual-shielded metal-arc (coated electrode) welding process. IN-744 is not susceptible to base-metal cracking and the hardness and toughness of the heat-affected zone are not adversely affected by welding. Both matching composition and Type 312 fillers were used for TIG and coated electrode welding. A matching composition filler wire was used for MIG welding. Weld properties appear in Table 15. The significantly lower percent elongation measured on the welded 1.57-mm (0.06-in.) and 0.51-mm (0.02-in.) sheet is attributed to the higher tensile strength of the base metal over that of the weld which tended to localize the elongation in the weld area.

Petersen[30] discovered that fine-grained weld structures can be produced in IN-744 with conventional welding procedures using filler metals having controlled amounts of alumi-

TABLE 14   Summary of Cyclic Oxidation Test Results in Air-H$_2$O (Cycled to Room Temperature Every 100 h)

| | Total weight change, mg/cm² | | | | | |
| | 1600°F (871°C)/1000 h* | | 1900°F (1038°C)/500 h† | | 2100°F (1149°C)/500 h‡ | |
Alloy	Undescaled	Descaled	Undescaled	Descaled	Undescaled	Descaled
446 SS	1.2	−3.4	−20	−37	−49	−80
IN-744	1.1	−3.7	−28	−42	−103	−131
310 SS	.6	−2.7	−11	−22	−101	−109

SUMMARY OF CARBURIZATION TEST RESULTS IN H$_2$-2.0% CH$_4$

| | Carburization attack 1832°F (1000°C)/100 h | |
Alloy	Weight gain, mg/cm²	Penetration, mm
446 SS	17.8	3.82
IN-744	17.1	2.57
310 SS	21.3	2.96

COMPOSITION AND CONDITION OF ALLOYS

Alloy	Condition	Fe	Ni	Cr	Mn	Si	Al	Ti	C
446 SS	1 h/1950°F (1066°C)/AC	Bal	0.30	26.6	1.27	0.60	<0.1	<0.05	0.10
IN-744	1 h/2300°F (1260°C)/AC	Bal	6.4	26.1	0.46	0.60	0.03	0.20	0.04
310 SS	1 h/1950°F (1066°C)/AC	Bal	19.4	23.9	1.50	0.48	<0.1	<0.05	0.05

*Dew point, −40°F (−40.0°C).
†Dew point, 90°F (32.2°C).
‡Dew point, 76°F (24.4°C).
AC = air-cooled.

TABLE 15   Mechanical Properties of IN-744 Stainless Steel Welds*

| Material thickness | | Condition of base metal | Filler metal† | 0.2% yield strength | | Tensile strength | | Elongation in,‡ % | Reduction of area, % | Location of fracture |
in.	mm			ksi	MN/m²	ksi	MN/m²			
0.500	12.70	HRA	None§	71	489.5	99	682.6	31	60	
		HRA	E312-16	77	530.9	101	696.4	21	53	Plate
		HRA	Matching	78	537.8	102	703.3	28	45	
0.500	12.70	HR	Matching	83	572.3	95	655.0	12	34	HAZ/weld
0.140	3.66	CRA	None§	89	613.7	106	730.9	22		
			Matching	82	565.4	96	661.9	13		Weld
			ER312	82	565.4	99	682.6	15		HAZ/weld
0.062	1.57	CRA	None§	87	600.0	112	772.2	21		
			Matching	82	565.4	94	648.1	5		Weld
			Autogenous	87	600.0	99	682.6	4		Weld
0.020	0.51	CRA	None§	89	613.7	111	765.3	17		Weld
			Autogenous	85	586.1	92	634.3	2		Weld

*As-welded with weld reinforcement removed.
†0.500-in. (12.70-mm) HRA-plate welded using coated electrode − 0.500-in. (12.70-mm) HR-plate weld using MIG. All other welds were automatic TIG process.
‡Gage length in 0.50-in. (12.7-mm) plate was 1 in. (25.4 mm) [0.250 in. (6.4 mm) diam.]; all others 2-in. (50.8-mm) gage length.
§Base metal properties: HRA = hot-rolled, annealed; HR = hot-rolled; CRA = cold-rolled, annealed.

num and nitrogen. The results of hot tensile tests on all-weld-metal tensile specimens of aluminum-containing and aluminum-free filler metals are shown in Fig. 19. Note the greatly increased tensile elongation in the fine-grained (aluminum-containing) weld. Etched weld cross sections in Fig. 20 show columnar structure in the aluminum-free weld and fine-grained structure in the weld to which 0.05% aluminum has been added.

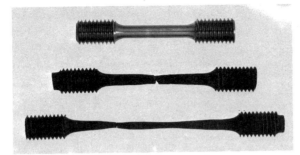

Fig. 19 Tensile specimens of all-weld-metal IN-744 stainless steel. *Top,* untested; *middle,* aluminum-free tested at 927°C; *bottom,* aluminum-containing tested at 927°C.[30]

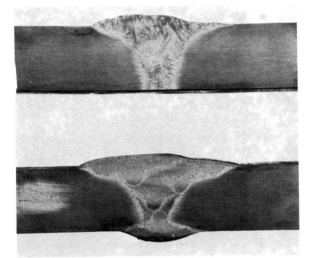

Fig. 20 Etched cross sections from aluminum-free (top) and aluminum-containing (bottom) 26Cr-6Ni-bal Fe welds made under identical conditions with the gas-metal-arc welding process. Note the columnar structure in the upper weld and fine-grained structure in the lower weld.[30] Lepito's etchant.

REFERENCES

1. Backofen, W. A., I. R. Turner, and D. H. Avery: Superplasticity in an Al-Zn Alloy, *ASM Trans. Q.,* vol. 57, no. 4, pp. 980–990, December 1964.
2. Avery, D. H., and W. A. Backofen: A Structural Basis for Superplasticity, *ASM Trans. Q.,* vol. 48, pp. 551–562, December 1965.
3. Holt, D. L., and W. A. Backofen: Superplasticity in the Al-Cu Eutectic Alloy, *ASM Trans. Q.,* vol. 59, pp. 755–768, December 1964.
4. Alden, T. H.: Superplastic Behavior of a Solid Solution Sn-1 Pct Bi Alloy, *Trans. Am. Inst. Min. Metall. Pet. Eng.,* vol. 236, pp. 1633–1634, November 1966.
5. Hayden, H. W., R. C. Gibson, H. F. Merrick, and J. H. Brophy: Superplasticity in the Ni-Fe-Cr System, *ASM Trans. Q.,* vol. 60, pp. 3–14, March 1967.
6. Packer, C. M., and O. D. Sherby: An Interpretation of the Superplasticity Phenomenon in Two-Phase Alloys, *ASM Trans. Q.,* vol. 60, pp. 21–28, March 1967.
7. Alden, T. H.: Origin of Superplasticity in the Sn 5% Bi Alloy, *Acta Metall.,* vol. 15, p. 469, March 1967.
8. Smith, C. I., D. Norgate, and N. Ridley: An Examination of the Ashby-Verral Model for Superplastic Flow as Applied to a Duplex Stainless Steel, *Scripta Metall.,* vol. 8, pp. 159–164, 1974.
9. Ashby, M. F., and R. A. Verral: Diffusion Accommodated Flow and Superplasticity, *Acta Metall.,* vol. 21, pp. 149–163, April 1973.

10. Hayden, H. W., S. Floreen, and P. D. Goodell: The Deformation Mechanisms of Superplasticity, *Metall. Trans.*, vol. 3, pp. 833–842, April 1972.
11. Gibson, R. C., H. W. Hayden, and J. H. Brophy: Properties of Stainless Steels with a Microduplex Structure, *ASM Trans. Q.*, vol. 61, p. 85, 1968.
12. Gibson, R. C., and J. H. Brophy: Microduplex Nickel-Iron-Chromium Alloys in J. J. Burke and V. Weiss (eds.), *"Ultrafine-Grain Metals,"* Proc. 16th Sagamore Army Mater. Res. Conf.," pp. 377–394, Syracuse University Press, 1969.
13. Lindinger, R. J., R. C. Gibson, and J. H. Brophy: Quantitative Metallography of Microduplex Structures After Superplastic Deformation, *ASM Trans. Q.*, vol. 62, p. 230, 1969.
14. Smith, C. S.: Grain Phases and Interfaces, *ASM Trans. Q.*, vol. 175, p. 15, 1948.
15. McLean, D.: "Grain Boundaries in Metals," p. 240, Oxford University Press, New York, 1957.
16. Riedl, J.: Investigation of a Semi-Austenitic Chromium-Nickel Steel Exhibiting Superplasticity at Elevated Temperatures, *Proc. Iron Steel Inst. Austria*, vol. 113, pp. 388–395, November 1968.
17. Fields, D. M., Jr.: oral presentation at Metal Science Forum on Superplasticity, ASM Annual Meeting, October 17, 1967, Cleveland, Ohio.
18. Petersen, W. A., and F. H. Lang: Internal Pressure Forming Process, to be published.
19. Merrick, H. F., H. W. Hayden, and R. C. Gibson: Hot Workability of Two-Phase Stainless Steels, *Metall. Trans.*, vol. 4, pp. 828–831, 1973.
20. Nehrenberg, A. E., and P. Lillys: High Temperature Transformations in Ferritic Stainless Steels Containing 17 to 25% Chromium, *Trans. Am. Soc. Met.*, vol. 46, pp. 1176–1213, 1954.
21. Kuo, K.: Metallography of Delta-Ferrite, Part I—Eutectoid Decomposition of Delta Ferrite, *J. Iron Steel Inst. London*, vol. 176, pp. 433–441, 1954.
22. Kuo, K.: Metallography of Delta-Ferrite, Part II—Formation of Delta Eutectoid in 18-4-1 Type High Speed Steels, *J. Iron Steel Inst. London*, vol. 181, pp. 128–134, 1955.
23. Kuo, K.: Metallography of Delta-Ferrite, Part III—Isothermal Transformation of Delta-Ferrite in a Low Carbon 27-5-1.5 Cr-Ni-Mo Corrosion-Resistant Steel, *J. Iron Steel Inst. London*, vol. 181, pp. 134–137, 1955.
24. Kuo, K.: Metallography of Delta-Ferrite, Part IV—Decomposition of Delta-Ferrite Between 650 and 1000°C in a Low-Carbon 18/10/3 Cr-Ni-Mo Corrosion Resisting Steel, *J. Iron Steel Inst. London*, vol. 181, pp. 213–218, 1955.
25. Kuo, K.: Metallography of Delta-Ferrite, Part V—Delta Eutectoid and the Constitution Diagram of the Fe-M-C System, *J. Iron Steel Inst. London*, vol. 181, pp. 218–227, 1955.
26. Floreen, S., and H. W. Hayden: The Influence of Austenite and Ferrite on the Mechanical Properties of Two-Phase Stainless Steels, *ASM Trans. Q.*, vol. 61, p. 489, 1968.
27. Hayden, H. W., and S. Floreen: The Deformation and Fracture of Stainless Steels Having Microduplex Structures, *ASM Trans. Q.*, vol. 61, p. 474, 1968.
28. Beetge, F. G. E., and F. P. A. Robinson: Formation of Sigma Phase in 26 Chromium-6 Nickel Stainless Steel, *Met. Mater.*, p. 408, 1973.
29. Petersen, W. A., and F. H. Lang: Welding of a High Strength Stainless Steel—IN-744, *Weld. J., Res. Suppl.*, vol. 49, no. 6, pp. 267-s–271-s, 1970.
30. Petersen, W. A.: Fine Grained Weld Structures, *Weld. J., Res. Suppl.*, vol. 52, no. 2, pp. 74-s–79-s, 1973.
31. Goodell, P. D.: unpublished work at The International Nickel Company, Inc., 1970.
32. Schultz, J. W., and R. L. McCarron: unpublished work at The International Nickel Company, Inc., 1971.

Chapter 9

Structure and Constitution of Cast Iron–Chromium Alloys

PETER F. WIESER

Research Director, Steel Founders' Society of America,
Rocky River, Ohio

INTRODUCTION

The first practical application of chromium in iron and steel was probably made by Julius Baur in 1869 following his patent of 1865.[1] Mining tools comprised the bulk of the early product. Higher chromium contents, sufficient to impart the stainless quality to steel, were investigated at the turn of the century. In England, in 1892, Hadfield[2] reported on 16% Cr alloys with upwards of 2% carbon while Strauss and Maurer investigated low-carbon chromium alloys at Krupp in Germany between 1909 and 1912. Chromium stainless steels have since been developed for specific applications to fit the special requirements ranging from welding characteristics and mechanical properties to resistance against different corrosive environments and elevated temperatures.

GENERAL CONSIDERATIONS

Strengthening   The martensite transformation is the most commonly used process of hardening. The steel casting is heated to the temperature at which the structure converts to austenite. The casting is then cooled at a rate adapted to its composition and thickness so that austenite transforms to martensite. Another process of hardening which has been gaining in popularity is age-hardening. Age-hardening is activated by first cooling the casting from an elevated temperature sufficiently rapidly so that phases that would normally develop at a slower cooling rate cannot precipitate. The casting is then heated to an intermediate temperature at which the precipitation reaction can occur under controlled conditions until the desired combination of hardness and other properties is achieved. In certain commercial cast chromium stainless steels, the combination of rapid cooling and aging leads to martensitic age-hardened steels.

Microstructure   The microstructure of cast stainless steels can be ferritic, austenitic, or martensitic, or it may be of a mixed ferritic-austenitic type, depending on composition and heat treatment. Certain hardenable chromium stainless steels can be heat-treated to exhibit either a ferritic or a martensitic structure, depending on end-use requirements. The composition of other steels is formulated to yield ferrite or austenite that is stable over a wide range of temperatures. The terms ferritic and martensitic therefore frequently indicate only the microstructure of the steel in its end-use condition.

Commercial chromium stainless steels, containing at least 17 to 20% chromium, may exhibit sigma phase on long time exposure to the temperature range of 540 to 870°C (1000 to 1600°F). Heating above 900°C (1650°F) can redissolve sigma phase.[3,4] The sigma phase is a hard, brittle constituent with a crystallographic structure characteristic of the 50 atomic % Fe-Cr alloy (Fig. 1). Elevated temperature tensile strength and wear resistance may be enhanced by the presence of sigma phase. Some commercial valve alloys, in fact, are deliberately formulated to contain appreciable amounts of sigma. In general, however, the presence of sigma phase in steel is not desired because it reduces room-temperature ductility and toughness.

Molybdenum and silicon promote sigma phase as does cold-working. Sigma phase forms more slowly in cast materials than in wrought materials unless free ferrite is present. Chromium by itself is, of course, a major factor in sigma formation. Alloy HD, for instance, contains 26 to 30% chromium, 4 to 7% nickel and is sensitive to sigma on exposure between 680 to 870°C (1200 to 1600°F),[5] while 17% Cr steel was found not to exhibit sigma phase even on holding for 10,000 h at 480, 570, and 650°C (900, 1050, 1200°F). Ninety-five percent cold-work of 17% Cr steel was required to demonstrate the presence of sigma after 5000 h at 480 and 570°C (900 and 1050°F).*

Classification   Chromium stainless steels can be grouped first, by hardenability and second, by the microstructure present in the final heat-treated condition (Table 1). The hardenable chromium stainless steels are either ferritic or martensitic and vary in chromium content between 8 and 17%. The lower level represents the limit below which the "stainless" quality can no longer be achieved. The upper level represents the approximate limit, in conjunction with the associated carbon and nickel, at which the hardening martensite transformation can be realized. The 13% Cr steels, type CA-15 and its related type CA-6NM, represent the most common of the cast chromium stainless steels which are hardenable by the martensite reaction. Both alloys are commonly air-cooled from the austenitizing temperature to develop the martensitic matrix. Annealing of alloy CA-15 at high temperatures, however, can be used to develop an essentially ferritic matrix with carbide particles. The addition of an element of limited solubility, such as copper, has been used to develop additional hardness by the age-hardening process. Alloy CB-7Cu contains about 3% copper and exemplifies this type of steel. CB-7Cu exhibits a martensitic matrix from which particles precipitate upon aging at intermediate temperatures to provide a controlled increase in strength and hardness. Another recently developed age-hardenable steel is the ferritic-austenitic alloy IN-744[6] (see Chap. 8). The aging reaction of this steel has not yet been fully investigated.

*See Ref. 3, pp. 75–78.

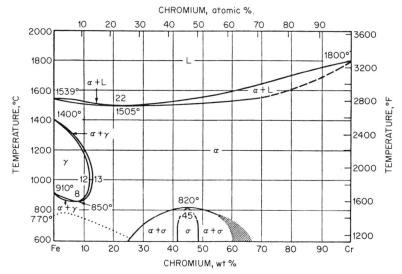

Fig. 1 The Fe-Cr constitutional diagram as reported in the *ASM* "Metals Handbook", 1948.

Most cast, nonhardenable chromium stainless steels used in the United States are ferritic and range in chromium content from 18 to 30%. Two alloys in this group, CC-50 and HC-50, cannot be hardened by heat treatment. Alloy CB-30 is essentially nonhardenable. This alloy contains less chromium than CC-50 and HC-50 (Table 1) which results in somewhat lower stability of ferrite and only a marginal degree of hardenability.

The listing in Table 1 of cast chromium steels commonly produced in the United States reveals a composition range of 8 to 30% chromium and up to 0.50% carbon. Nickel contents of chromium steels are generally below 4%. Steels with nickel levels above 7% are partially or completely austenitic and are discussed in Chap. 10. A more extensive overview regarding chromium and carbon contents of chromium stainless steels is provided by Fig. 2. The maximum contents of chromium and carbon are shown for United States, English, German, Japanese, and Russian specifications on cast steels.[7-10]

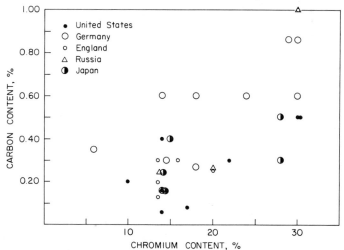

Fig. 2 The upper specification limits of chromium and carbon ranges in commercial, cast chromium steel grades.

TABLE 1 Commercial Cast Chromium Steels

Grade*	Approximate wrought alloy equivalent†	Most common structure	Hardening mechanism	Composition, %				
				Cr	C	Ni	Si	Other†
HARDENABLE CAST CHROMIUM STEELS								
HA		Ferritic + carbides	Martensite transformation	8–10	0.20 max.	1.0 max.	1 max.	0.5 max. Mo
CA-15	410	Ferritic + carbides or martensite	Martensite transformation	11.5–14.0	0.15 max.	1.0 max.	1.5 max.	0.5 max. Mo
CA-40	420	Ferritic + carbides or martensite	Martensite transformation	11.5–14.0	0.20–.40	1.0 max.	1.5 max.	0.4–1.0 Mo
CA-6NM		Martensite	Martensite transformation	11.5–14.0	0.06 max.	3.5–4.5	1 max	2.3–3.3 Cu
CB-7Cu	17-4PH	Martensite	Martensite + age hardening	15.5–17.0	0.07 max.	3.6–4.6	1.5 max.	
NONHARDENABLE CAST CHROMIUM STEELS								
CB-30		Ferritic – essentially	Marginally by martensite transformation	18–22	0.30 max.	2.0 max.	1.5 max.	
CC-50	446	Ferritic + carbides	None, ferrite is stable	26–30	0.50 max.	4.0 max.	1.5 max.	
HC	446	Ferritic + carbides	None, ferrite is stable	26–30	0.50 max.	4.0 max.	2.0 max.	

*Alloy Casting Institute (ACI) designations. The prefixes H and C signify heat- and corrosion-resistant grades, respectively.

†The equivalent AISI designations for wrought steels are approximate; wrought equivalents may differ in composition and microstructure.

‡S = 0.04 max., P = 0.04 max.

The range of chromium contents is similar for these countries but differences exist with respect to carbon. German and Russian specifications include higher carbon grades than comparable American, British, or Japanese specifications. Several German and Russian high-chromium alloys have carbon contents of 1.4 to 2.2% and are not included in Fig. 2. High-carbon, 20 to 30% Cr stainless steels are also cast in the United States as high-temperature abrasion-resistant tools. Seamless-tube-piercer points and rolling mill guides of 28Cr-2.50C steel are some examples.

Constitution   The Fe-Cr-C phase diagram provides important guidelines for processing, heat-treating, and the development of chromium stainless steels. The earliest studies of the Fe-Cr-C system were concerned with the melting point.[11] Detailed information has since been gained regarding the type of phases present and their stability as influenced by temperature. Sections through the Fe-Cr-C system are shown in Fig. 3 for several carbon contents up to 1%.[12]

Chromium limits the stability of gamma austenite, γ, in favor of alpha ferrite, α. Carbon has the opposite effect and stabilizes austenite up to at least 0.4% carbon. Increasing the carbon beyond some level above 0.4% lowers the austenite stability as seen by the reduced size of the austenite field in 1% C alloys of Fig. 3f. These trends are important to questions on heat treatment. To harden a chromium stainless steel by the martensite transformation, the steel must transform to austenite upon heating to the austenitizing temperature. For instance, a 28% Cr stainless steel such as HC-50 with 0.5% maximum carbon will consist of ferrite and carbides even at 1200°C (2192°F) (Fig. 3e). A 13% Cr steel, however, will be austenitic at 1100°C (2012°F) if the carbon content is between 0.10 and 0.40% (Fig. 3c and d). Alloy CA-15 with 0.15% C max. can therefore transform to martensite upon cooling from the austenitizing temperature (Fig. 4). A 13% Cr stainless steel with less than 0.05% C would be expected to contain substantial quantities of ferrite under the same conditions (Fig. 3a and b). Substantial amounts of carbides would be predicted, however, if the carbon content of a 13% Cr stainless steel were raised to 1% (Fig. 3f).

COMMERCIAL CAST CHROMIUM STEELS

HA Alloy   Alloy HA is a cast chromium stainless steel containing 8 to 10Cr-0.20C max. which is employed in applications requiring elevated temperature corrosion resistance in various environments (e.g., air, flue gases, and petroleum). This steel is hardenable and, like other heat-resistant cast grades, does not require any heat treatment except a thermal stress relief. Grade HA can be annealed at 885°C (1625°F) for maximum softness followed by slow cooling. For higher strength, it can be normalized by heating to 995°C (1825°F) followed by tempering at about 680°C (1250°F).

The as-cast microstructure consists of acicular ferrite containing globular carbides. Like all castings, it exhibits a finer structure near the casting surface. The microstructure after normalizing and tempering consists of carbides dispersed in a ferrite matrix.

CA-15 Alloy   Alloy CA-15 is the principal grade of cast chromium stainless steel in terms of tonnage produced. This steel contains 11.5 to 14Cr-0.15C max.-0.5Mo max.-1Ni max. and traces its development back to the turn of the century. Krupp and Mannesmann are said to have made 12% Cr steels with molybdenum additions, presumably for corrosion resistance.[13] The growth of these steels was stimulated by the steam turbine field. Applications of these steels have expanded to many other fields and given rise to numerous modifications to suit special requirements.

The principal hardening mechanism is the martensite transformation from austenite upon cooling in air (normalizing) or oil (quenching). CA-15 is commonly austenitized at 980 to 1000°C (1800 to 1850°F). Deviations from this temperature and the presence of alloying elements may lead to ferrite formation (Fig. 5). The effect of alloying elements on the stability of austenite and ferrite has been investigated repeatedly. Schneider's diagram (Fig. 5) represents a modification of the Schaeffler diagram[14] and predicts the maximum amount of ferrite that can be expected, depending on alloy content. Alloying elements either favor the stability of ferrite, e.g., chromium, or that of austenite, e.g., nickel. The ferrite- and austenite-forming tendencies relative to chromium and nickel, respectively, can therefore be expressed mathematically[14] as

$$\text{Ni equivalent} = \%\text{Ni} + \%\text{Co} + 0.5\text{Mn} + 30 \times \%\text{C} \qquad (1)$$
$$\text{Cr equivalent} = \%\text{Cr} + 2 \times \%\text{Si} + 1.5 \times \%\text{Mo} + 5 \times \%\text{V} \qquad (2)$$

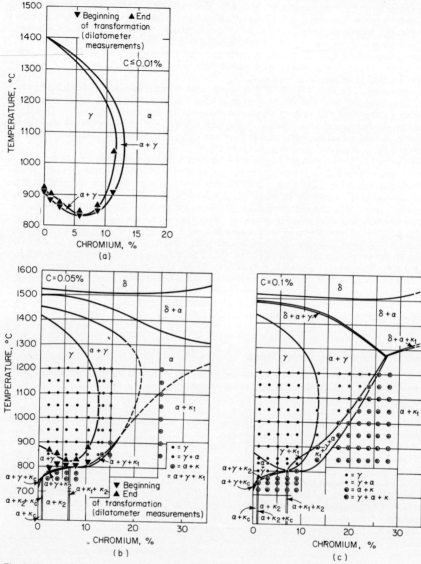

Fig. 3 Sections through the iron-rich corner of the Fe-Cr-C system.[12] (a) C ≤ 0.01%; (b) C = 0.05%; (c) C = 0.1%; (d) C = 0.2%; (e) C = 0.4%; (f) C = 1%.

Two recent publications provide additional insight into the effects of elements. Hull[15] evaluated chill cast chromium stainless steels (Cr = 12 to 24%) while E. A. Schoefer discussed Cr-Ni stainless steel castings.[16] A summary of their findings is presented in Table 2 along with that of others. Several of these authors[16-24] developed coefficients for V, Cb, Ti, etc. Cast steels, however, do not normally contain significant quantities of these elements.

The extent of the martensite transformation is also influenced by alloying elements which affect the temperature, M_s, at which austenite transforms to martensite upon cooling. Retained austenite may be present in 12% Cr steels and lower impact toughness,

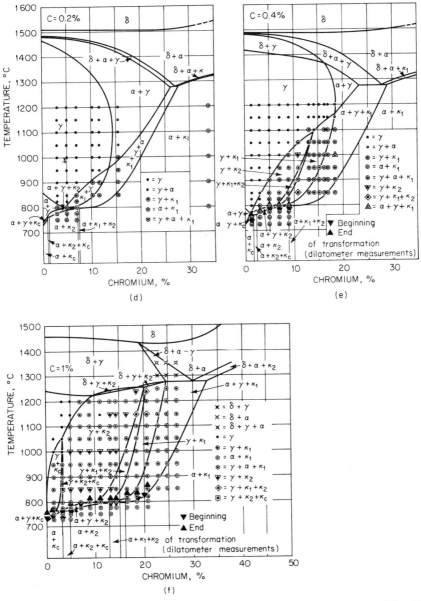

(d)

(e)

(f)

particularly if the M_s temperature is below 200°C (390°F). The depression of the M_s temperature can be estimated. The published coefficients (Table 3) vary by a factor of 2 to 3 and nearly 5 in the case of carbon.

CA-15 castings are tempered at 310°C maximum (600°F) or in the range of 600 to 800°C (1100 to 1500°F). Tempering at 480°C (900°F) must be avoided to maintain toughness. This temperature range for embrittlement corresponds approximately to that at which Fe_3C dissolves and Cr_7C_3 precipitates. Tempering above 600°C (1100°F) yields improved ductility and toughness.

Molybdenum-bearing 12% Cr stainless steels cast as ingots are sensitive to cracking

TABLE 2 Nickel and Chromium Equivalents of Alloying Elements in Stainless Steels with Respect to Delta-Ferrite Formation

	Avery[17] (cast heat-resistant alloys)	Field, Bloom, and Linnert[18] (20-10 weld metal)	Campbell and Thomas[19] (25-20 weld metal)	Henry, Clausson, and Linnert[20] (Cr-Ni weld metal)	Schaeffler[21] Cr-Ni (weld metal)	Ferree[22]	Runov[23] (Cr-Ni welds)	DeLong[24] (welds)	Guiraldenq[25] (castings)	Potak and Sagalevich[26] (castings)	Hull[15] (chill castings*)	Schoefer[16] (castings†)
Austenite formers:												
C	17	30		30	30	30			30	27	24.5	30
N	11					30		30	20	27	18.4	26(N-0.02)
Ni	1	1		1	1	1	1	1	1	1	1	1
Mn		0.5		0.5	0.5	0.5				0.5	11 Mn-0.0086Mn^2	0.5
Cu						0.3				0.33	0.44	
Co										0.4	0.41	
Ferrite formers:												
Al										4	2.48	
V									3	1.5	2.27	
Ti	1.6			5					4	4	2.20	
Si	2.8			1	1.5	1.5	3.5		1.5	2	0.48	
Cb			2	2	0.5					0.9	0.14	
Mo		2	1.5	2	1				2	1	1.21	1.5
Ta											0.21	
W											0.72	
Cr	1	1	1	1	1	1	1		1	0.5	1	1
Mn						1			0.45	1	1	1

*Range investigated: 12–24Cr, 0–22Ni, 0–20Mn, 0–6Mo, 0–4Si, 0–4V, 0–5W, 0–2Ti, 0–4Cb, 0–4Ta, 0–2Al, 0–6Co, 0–4Cu, 0–1C, 0–0.15N.

†Values applicable to: 16–26Cr, 6–14Ni, 0–4Mo, 0–1Cb, 0.30C max., 0.15N, 2Mn, 2Si.

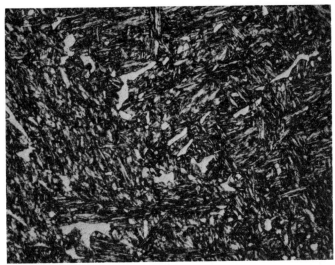

Fig. 4 Martensite with traces of ferrite in an approximately 1-in. (25-mm) section of CA-15, tempered at 1125°F (607°C). (200X) *(Certified Alloy Products, Inc.)*

and, owing to long solidification times, to segregation of nonmetallics, massive carbides, and ferrite-carbide aggregates.[13] These segregates produce low ductility and toughness and may cause hot-working difficulties.

Precision investment castings, centrifugally cast pipe, and sand castings are made of CA-15 steels. Ship propellers and turbine castings, for instance, are cast in static sand molds. Increasing section sizes of castings requires a longer time to solidify and cool. Coarser structures therefore result, as shown by Figs. 4 and 6. Delta ferrite may accentuate the susceptibility to cracking of 12% Cr stainless steel castings and contribute to loss of impact toughness.

CA-40 Alloy   The Fe-Cr alloy CA-40 is similar to type CA-15; its higher carbon content permits hardening this grade to a maximum of about 500 BHN.

The modified phase diagram (Fig. 7) suggests a fully austenitic structure at the commonly employed austenitizing temperature of 980 to 1000°C (1800 to 1850°F). Cooling from the austenitizing temperature and tempering practices are the same as those described for CA-15. Maximum softness of CA-40 is achieved by annealing at 840 to 900°C (1550 to 1650°F).

CA-6NM Alloy   Alloy CA-6NM is a casting grade developed from 12% Cr stainless steels. The principal difference with respect to CA-15 lies in the lower carbon content (0.06C versus 0.15C max.) and the higher nickel level (3.5 to 4.5Ni versus 1Ni max.). The low carbon content by itself would result in a partially ferritic structure at the austenitizing temperature (Fig. 3b to d) and thus lower the amount of martensite formed upon cooling. Nickel is therefore added since it has the effect of shifting the ferrite-gamma loop (Fig. 3a and b) to a higher chromium content, thus ensuring a fully austenitic structure at the normalizing temperature.

The microstructure is essentially 100% low-carbon martensite which provides improved weldability and impact toughness. This steel is commonly

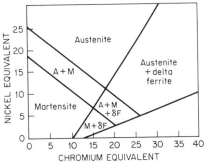

Fig. 5 The effect of composition, expressed as nickel and chromium equivalents, on structure. Schneider modification[14] of Schaeffler diagram.

TABLE 3   Depression of M_s Temperature* by 1% Alloying Element (°C)

Element	Ref. 13	Ref. 15
Carbon	474	2388
Manganese	33	54
Molybdenum	21	55
Chromium	17	47
Nickel	17	59
Silicon	11	37
Tungsten	11	43
Vanadium		127
Titanium		180
Columbium		50
Tantalum		75
Nitrogen		3222
Cobalt		13
Copper		85
Aluminum		306

*Approximately 300°C (570°F) for base 12% Cr steel.[13]

hardened by heating to 1040 to 1065°C (1900 to 1950°F) and cooling in air or oil. Tempering is performed at 315°C (600°F) or in the range of 590 to 620°C (1100 to 1150°F). Tempering at 480°C (900°F) is to be avoided because low impact toughness will result. Austenite may form from martensite if the tempering temperature exceeds 650°C (1200°F) as indicated in Fig. 8. The formation of such austenite and its transformation, upon cooling from the tempering temperature, to untempered austenite is undesirable from the standpoint of toughness and machining (hard spots).

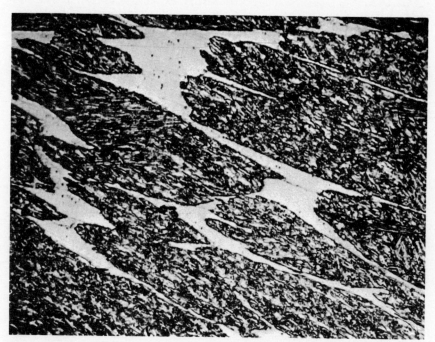

Fig. 6 Tempered martensite with islands of ferrite in a 6-in. section of CA-15. Compare to Fig. 4. (200X) (*Atlas Foundry & Machine Company.*)

The effects of heat treatment and section size on the structure of CA-6NM are illustrated in Fig. 9*a* to *c*. Chromium carbides in the ferrite structure with some martensite of as-cast 3-in. (76.2-mm) sections are dissolved by the austenitizing heat treatment and transformed to martensite during air cooling. Heavier, 6-in. (152.4-mm) sections solidify and cool more slowly giving rise to segregation and incomplete metallurgical transformation during heat treating. Ferrite pools may therefore be present as shown in Fig. 9*c*.

CB-7Cu Alloy   CB-7Cu is a martensitic, precipitation-hardenable alloy roughly analogous to 17-4PH. Compared to CA-15 the chromium content is higher and the carbon

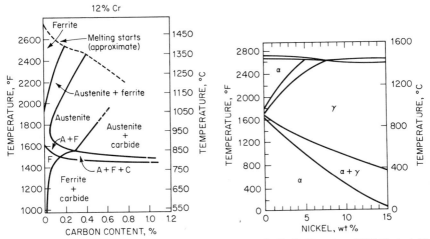

Fig. 7   The Fe-Cr section of 12% Cr steels.[28-30]   **Fig. 8**   The Fe-Cr-Ni section of 12% Cr steels.[27]

content lower. These ferrite-stabilizing factors are, however, balanced by a higher nickel content in order to obtain the desired martensitic structure upon cooling from the austenitizing temperature. The important precipitation-hardening characteristic is imparted to CB-7Cu by a copper content of 2.3 to 3.3%. The lower carbon content and the age-hardening mechanism thus provide a superior combination of strength and corrosion resistance. Another benefit of precipitation hardening is its independence of rapid cooling rates, which promotes dimensional stability and uniform hardness in heavier sections. The precipitation-hardening process takes place at intermediate temperatures, thereby reducing the need for a subsequent stress relief.

The chemical composition range of CB-7Cu is rather wide (Table 1) and some experts prefer separation into two grades: 17Cr-4Ni and 15Cr-5Ni. Higher impact values are obtained with the 15-5 steel because the lower chromium and higher nickel contents favor a more completely martensitic structure as discussed in the preceding section on CA-15.

The as-cast structure of CB-7Cu is martensitic and may contain ferrite pools. Homogenization temperatures of at least 1150°C (2100°F) are employed. Solutionizing is accomplished by heating to 1040 to 1070°C (1900 to 1950°F) followed by air cooling or quenching in oil. The choice of the precipitation-hardening temperature depends on the desired strength and toughness level. This temperature range extends from 482 to 648°C (900 to 1200°F), with higher strength and lower toughness being obtained at lower temperatures.

CB-30, CC-50, and HC Alloys   The higher chromium content of CB-30, CC-50, and HC (~20% for CB-30, ~28% for CC-50 and HC) stabilizes ferrite at all temperatures—even at the higher carbon levels in each grade. CC-50 and HC steels are therefore not hardenable by quenching, while CB-30 exhibits only a very small degree of hardenability.

CB-30 and CC-50 castings are normally supplied in the annealed condition while the heat-resisting grade HC is supplied in the as-cast condition. Annealing heat treatments consist of heating to 790°C (1450°F). CB-30 castings are furnace-cooled to 540°C (1000°F)

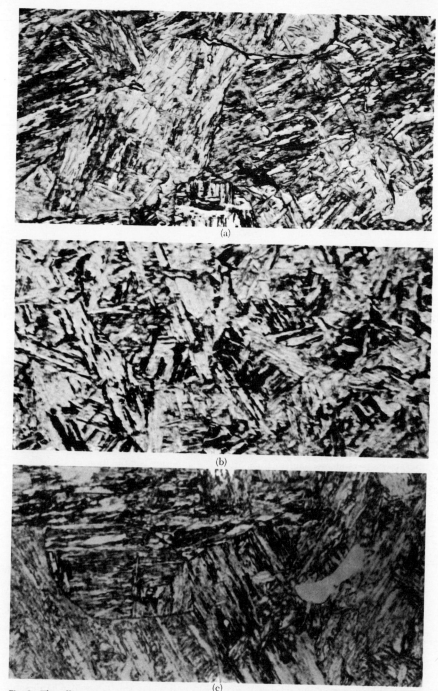

Fig. 9 The effect of heat treatment and section size on the structure of CA-6NM castings. (*a*) As-cast 3-in. (76.2-mm) section (200X). (*b*) Same as (*a*) but austenitized at 1040°C (1900°F), air-cooled and tempered at 635°C (1175°F), ferrite-free, tempered martensite (500X). (*c*) Same as (*a*) and (*b*) but 6-in. (152.4-mm) section. Note ferrite pools in tempered martensite (500X). [(*a*) and (*b*) *Atlas Foundry & Machine Company.*]

then cooled in air. CC-50 castings are cooled in air directly from the annealing temperature. The limited hardenability of CB-30 arises from the fact that a small amount of ferrite transforms to austenite at elevated temperatures, which can further be transformed to martensite upon rapid cooling. The small degree of hardenability normally present in CB-30 can be increased by balancing the composition to a low level of ferrite stabilizers (Cr, Si) and to a high level of austenite formers (Ni, C). When this is done, an austenitizing heat treatment followed by rapid cooling may be selected in favor of the conventional annealing heat treatment.

The ferritic structure of the other two grades, CC-50 and HC, is not hardenable as stated earlier. Nevertheless, the hardness, strength, and toughness of these grades may be substantially improved[31] by structural (compositional) control. The highly alloyed ferrite of these steels has a Charpy V-notch impact transition temperature above room temperature. Nickel additions in excess of 2% therefore result in substantial improvements. Significantly higher strength and toughness values are obtained by controlling the composition to 2 to 4% nickel and nitrogen contents in excess of 0.15%. Nickel and nitrogen are austenite stabilizers and modify the ferritic structure of 28% Cr steels to a mixed ferritic-austenitic type. Higher toughness results from these mixed structures because austenite, unlike ferrite, does not exhibit the temperature-dependent toughness loss.

REFERENCES

1. U.S. Patent 49,495, August 22, 1865.
2. Hadfield, R. A.: Alloys of Iron and Chromium, Including a Report by F. Osmond, *J. Iron Steel Inst. London*, vol. 2, pp. 49–175, 1892.
3. Symposium on the Nature, Occurrence and Effect of Sigma Phase, *Spec. ASTM Publ. 110*, 1950.
4. "Metals Handbook," vol. 1, 8th ed., American Society for Metals, Metals Park, Ohio, 1961.
5. Avery, H. S.: Cast Heat Resistant Alloys for High Temperature Weldments, *Welding Res. Council Bull. 143*, August, 1963.
6. Church, N. L.: Properties of Cast 26.9% Cr-6-8% Ni Stainless Steel, *Trans. Am. Foundrymen's Soc.*, vol. 79, p. 361, 1971.
7. "Steel Castings Handbook," 4th ed., Steel Founders' Society of America, Rocky River, Ohio, 1970.
8. ASTM Specifications A296 and A297.
9. "British and Foreign Specifications for Steel Castings," 3d ed., Steel Castings Research and Trade Association, Sheffield, England, 1968.
10. "British and Foreign Specifications for Steel Castings," Part 2, Steel Castings Research and Trade Association, Sheffield, England, 1962.
11. Treitschke, W., and G. Tammann: Uber die Legierungen des Eisens mit Chrom, *Z. Anorg. Chemie*, vol. 55, pp. 402–411, 1907.
12. Bungardt, K., et al.: Untersuchen über den Aufbau des Systems Eisen-Chrom-Kohlenstoff, *Arch. Eisenhuettenwes.*, vol. 29, no. 3, p. 193, March, 1958.
13. Briggs, J. Z., and T. D. Parker: "The Super 12% Cr Steels," Climax Molybdenum Company, New York, 1965.
14. Schneider, H.: Investment Casting of High-Hot-Strength 12% Chrome Steel, *Foundry Trade J.*, vol. 108, pp. 562–563, 1960.
15. Hull, F. C.: "Delta Ferrite and Martensite Formation in Stainless Steels," *Weld. J., Res. Suppl.*, May, 1973.
16. Schwarzendruber, L. J., L. H. Bennet, E. A. Schoefer, W. T. DeLong, and H. C. Campbell: Mössbauer Effect Examination of Ferrite in Stainless Steel Welds and Castings, *Weld. J., Res. Suppl.*, January, 1974.
17. Avery, H. S.: Heat Resistant Alloys, U.S. Patent 2,465,780, January 1974.
18. Feild, A. L., F. K. Bloom, and G. E. Linnert: The Effect of Variations in Chromium-Nickel Ratio and Molybdenum Content of Austenite (20Cr-10Ni) Electrodes on Properties of Armour Weldments, *NDRC Rept., OSRD no. 3034*, Dec. 14, 1943.
19. Campbell, H. C., and R. D. Thomas, Jr.: Effect of Alloying Elements on the Tensile Properties of 25-20 Weld Metal, *Weld. J., Res. Suppl.*, vol. 25, pp. 760-s–768-s, 1946.
20. Henry, O. H., G. E. Claussen, and G. E. Linnert: "Welding Metallurgy," 2d ed., American Welding Society, New York, 1949.
21. Schaeffler, A. L.: Constitutional Diagram for Stainless Steel Weld Metal, *Met. Prog.*, vol. 56, pp. 680–680B, 1949.
22. Ferree, J. A.: Free Machining Austenitic Stainless Steel, U.S. Patent 3,460,939, Aug. 12, 1969.
23. Runov, A. E.: Selection of Efficient Compositions of Cr-Ni Austenitic Steel for Welded Structures, *Autom. Weld. (USSR)*, vol. 20, no. 2, pp. 74–76, 1967.
24. DeLong, W. T.: A Modified Phase Diagram for Stainless Steel Weld Metals, *Met. Prog.*, vol. 77, pp. 98–100, 1960.

25. Guiraldenq, P.: Ferrite and Austenite Forming Tendencies of the Principal Alloying Elements in 18Cr-10Ni Stainless Steels, *Rev. Metall. (Paris), Part 1,* vol. 64, no. 11, pp. 907–939, 1967.
26. Potak, M., and E. A. Sagalevich: Structural Diagram for Stainless Steels as Applied to Cast Metal and Metal Deposited during Welding, *Avtom. Svarka,* no. 5, pp. 10–13, 1972.
27. Grobner, P. J.: *Climax Molybdenum Co. Rept. L-306-03,* Apr. 21, 1972.
28. Rickett, R. L., W. F. White, C. S. Walton, and J. C. Butler: Isothermal Transformation, Hardening, and Tempering of 12% Chromium Steel, *Trans. Am. Soc. Met.,* vol. 44, p. 138, 1952.
29. Tofaute, Sponheuer, and Bennek: Transformation, Hardening, and Tempering of Steels Containing Carbon up to 1% and Chromium up to 12%, *Arch. Eisenhuettenwes.,* vol. 9, p. 499, 1934–1935.
30. Tofaute, Kuttner, and Buttinghaus: The Iron-Chromium-Chromium Carbide-Cementite System, *Arch. Eisenhuettenwes.,* vol. 9, pp. 606–616, 1936.
31. Schoefer, E. A.: "High Alloy Data Sheets," Alloy Casting Institute Div., Steel Founders' Society of America, August, 1973.

Chapter 10

Structure and Constitution of Cast Iron-Chromium-Nickel Alloys

WILLIAM H. HERRNSTEIN

Technical Director-Metallurgical, The Duriron Company, Inc.,
Dayton, Ohio

INTRODUCTION

The Fe-Cr-Ni alloys have grown steadily in technical and commercial importance as special materials over the past half-century. Today these stainless alloys are basic materials of construction in a great variety of industrially important applications requiring a high degree of corrosion resistance with strength in aqueous environments at lower temperatures and also in oxidizing and reducing corrosive gases at higher temperatures. Guillet[1] is credited[2] with discovery of the Fe-Cr-Ni alloys based on his pioneering exploration of the metallurgy and mechanical properties of these alloys in 1906. Later, in 1909, Giesen[3] published work which added significantly to the understanding of austenitic Fe-Cr-Ni alloys. The discovery of the "stainlessness" of stainless steels, i.e., passivation, and the important role which carbon plays in corrosion resistance are credited to Monnartz[4] in 1911. In the period 1909 to 1912 the austenitic stainless steels, including the cornerstone 18Cr-8Ni alloys, were patented and first produced commercially by Maurer and Strauss.[5] Chevenard was the original investigator, in 1917 and 1918, of the high-chromium—high-nickel alloys resistant to high temperatures.[6] In the period 1931 to 1934, austenitic stainless steels having high resistance to intergranular corrosion as a result of very low carbon contents (0.03%) and duplex ferrite-in-austenite microstructures were first produced commercially in France.[6] From 1920 onward the range of Fe-Cr-Ni alloys has been extended greatly to meet specific applications involving special corrosion resistance and mechanical property requirements.

GENERAL CONSIDERATIONS

Strengthening   Strengthening in the cast Fe-Cr-Ni alloys is limited basically to three types: solid-solution hardening, precipitation hardening, and that which results when ferrite in some amount is distributed in austenite in a duplex microstructure. Of these the latter two are most significant for these corrosion-resistant alloys at elevated temperatures (above 650°C) and lower temperatures (below 315°C), respectively.

Solid-solution hardening contributes in limited fashion to the overall strength of Fe-Cr-Ni alloys and, as a consequence, is sometimes overlooked. It is recognized, however, that large additions of the substitutional solutes chromium and nickel, and smaller additions of silicon and molybdenum in many of these alloys, do act to strengthen the solid solution relative to a pure α or γ iron matrix. Likewise, carbon, even at low levels as an interstitial solute, contributes measurably to strengthening. Within the normal range of variation of chromium, nickel, molybdenum, silicon, and carbon contents embraced by the commercially important Fe-Cr-Ni alloys, solid-solution hardening may be disregarded as a significant means for strengthening.

Precipitation of carbides is a significant source of strengthening in Fe-Cr-Ni alloys for elevated temperature service. Unlike the corrosion-resistant casting alloys, in which carbon contents are purposefully held low (usually less than 0.08%) to avoid carbide precipitation and concomitant degradation of corrosion resistance, heat-resistant casting alloys have relatively high carbon contents in the range 0.20 to 0.75%. At the elevated service temperatures (above 650°C) at which these alloys are used, fine chromium-rich carbide particles of the $M_{23}C_6$ type are precipitated in the austenite or duplex matrix which strengthen the alloy, i.e., confer resistance to creep deformation and rupture. On prolonged exposure at elevated temperatures these fine precipitated carbides may over-age, i.e., spheroidize or agglomerate, leading to loss of creep resistance.[7] Formation of sigma, an Fe-Cr intermetallic phase, can occur in duplex or austenitic alloys on prolonged heating in the temperature range 650 to 870°C with resultant sharp loss in room-temperature ductility and impact toughness and milder reductions in these same properties at elevated temperatures.[8]

The nominally austenitic Fe-Cr-Ni cast alloys cannot be strengthened by thermal treatment, as can the cast Fe-Cr alloys, nor by hot- or cold-working, obviously, as can the wrought austenitic alloys. They are strengthened quite effectively, however, by balancing the alloy composition to produce a duplex microstructure consisting of ferrite phase (up to approximately 35% by volume) distributed in the austenite matrix. Whereas strengthening carbide precipitates are generally detrimental to corrosion resistance in aqueous media, the presence of ferrite in austenite not only strengthens but also improves the resistance of these alloys to stress-corrosion cracking[9] and to sensitization to intergranular corrosion attack.[10] Work by Beck, et al.[11] on 19Cr-9Ni cast steels showed that incorporation of 20 to 30% ferrite in the structure improved strength substantially without detrimental loss of ductility or impact toughness at temperatures below 425°C. The magnitude of the strengthening increase was found to depend on ferrite content as shown in Fig. 1.

Microstructures   The Fe-Cr-Ni cast stainless steels are nominally considered austenitic even though duplex ferrite-in-austenite microstructures are predominant in these alloys in the end-use condition. Depending principally on composition, but also on thermal history to a lesser extent, microstructures ranging from fully austenitic in the higher nickel grades to duplex ferrite-in-austenite to duplex austenite-in-ferrite in the higher chromium grades are included in this alloy group. Microstructures typical of this range are shown in Figs. 2 to 4. Generally speaking, the microstructures of Fe-Cr-Ni cast alloys are stable over a wide range of temperatures and the balance between austenite and ferrite phases is not radically altered between the as-cast and heat-treated conditions.

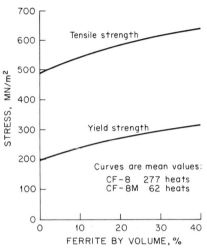

Fig. 1   Yield strength (0.2% offset) and tensile strength at room temperature as a function of ferrite content for CF-8 and CF-8M alloys. *(Adapted from Beck et al.[11])*

Carbides of several types are common constituents in Fe-Cr-Ni alloy microstructures. Both the higher and lower carbon cast alloys are hypoeutectic in composition. Thus, during solidification, any delta ferrite would be formed first, followed by austenite and then last by eutectic carbide at austenite grain boundaries, provided carbon content is sufficiently high. The amount of carbide precipitated depends on both the carbon content and the cooling rate of the casting following solidification. Morphology of these precipitated carbides in as-cast microstructures can range from discrete small particles in lower carbon alloys (see Fig. 5) to massive colonies outlining austenite grains in higher carbon alloys (see Fig 6). Of the several types of carbide which precipitate, the chromium-rich $M_{23}C_6$ type (where M (metal) represents the sum of carbide-forming elements involved) is predominant. It occurs most commonly as fine particles but may also occur in the form of lamellae, platelets, and grain-boundary films.[7] A lamellar constituent, in which carbide lamellae of the M_6C type alternate with lamellae of austenite in a structure resembling pearlite,[12] and carbides of M_7C_3 and M_3C types may also be observed in the higher carbon Fe-Cr-Ni alloys.

Much of the carbon which remains in solid solution in Fe-Cr-Ni alloys in the as-cast or solution-heat-treated conditions precipitates as a fine secondary carbide, usually of the $M_{23}C_6$ type, upon reheating of the alloy in the temperature range 650 to 1060°C. Such reheating might occur, for example, under service conditions (see Fig. 7) or during repair or fabrication welding. These secondary carbides are undesirable for optimum corrosion resistance in the low carbon (less than 0.08% C) alloys and are eliminated by subsequent solution heat treatment. In the higher carbon (0.20% to 0.75% C) alloys for heat-resisting applications, these dispersed fine carbides are desirable constituents which confer resistance to creep rupture at service temperatures.

In addition to austenite, ferrite, and carbides, sigma (σ) phase is another microstructural constituent of importance in commercial Fe-Cr-Ni cast alloys. Sigma is a hard, brittle, predominately iron-chromium intermetallic which forms most readily in austenitic or duplex alloys on prolonged heating in the temperature range 650 to 870°C. Sigma formation is time- and temperature-dependent and can be described on a transformation diagram by a typical "C" curve.[8] The formation of sigma is enhanced by addition of ferrite-stabilizing elements (such as chromium, molybdenum, and silicon). Although the phase forms most rapidly from ferrite, it can also form from austenite.[13] Sigma occurs both intergranularly in association with eutectic carbides (see Fig. 8) and intragranularly as needles or platelets (see Fig. 9). Higher aging temperatures favor the former, lower temperatures the latter. The presence of sigma phase is generally undesirable because it severely impairs room-temperature ductility and impact toughness.

Another phase, chi (χ), may be encountered in cast Fe-Cr-Ni alloys containing molybdenum. Like sigma, this phase is hard and brittle and coexists with sigma.[14] The composition of chi has been identified as Fe_3CrMo,[15] but it has been suggested that the phase also can contain considerable carbon.[16]

Classification   The cast Fe-Cr-Ni alloys usually are classified on the basis of three factors: end-use application, composition, and microstructure in the end-use condition. It should be noted that these three bases for classification are not fully independent in

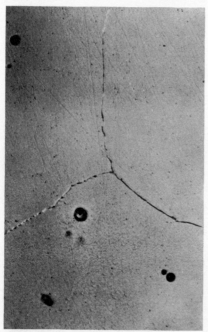

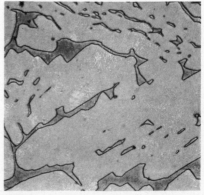

Fig. 2 Fully austenitic CN-7M alloy in solution-heat-treated and water-quenched condition. Small etch pits in grain boundary and matrix. Large particles are inclusions. Electrolytic oxalic acid etch. (500X) *(The Duriron Company.)*

Fig. 3 Duplex ferrite-in-austenite CF-8 alloy in solution-heat-treated and water-quenched condition. Electrolytic potassium hydroxide etch. (800X) *(The Duriron Company.)*

most instances. That is, classification by major end-use application also involves compositional and microstructural distinctions, for example. Nevertheless, the bases for classification are considered separately here.

A useful and convenient classification of the cast Fe-Cr-Ni alloys can be made on the basis of end-use application. More specifically, these alloys are employed most frequently in one of two major types of service:

1. Corrosion service in aqueous or liquid-vapor environments at temperatures normally below 315°C

2. Elevated temperature service at temperatures above 650°C in corrosive atmospheres of both oxidizing and reducing types

Hence, the distinction in end-use application is made between corrosion-resistant alloys and heat-resistant alloys. Classification of the cast Fe-Cr-Ni alloys as to corrosion resistant versus heat resistant is used as the basis for discussion of the individual commercial alloys in a later section of this chapter.

The commercial cast alloy designations in these two categories are listed in Table 1. In general, the resistance of the alloy to various types of corrosion attack is the paramount consideration in selection of a corrosion-resistant alloy for a particular environment and the mechanical and physical properties are normally secondary considerations. On the other hand, strength and other mechanical properties at elevated service temperatures as well as resistance to oxidation or other corrosion attack in the environment are usually equally important considerations in selection of heat-resistant alloys. From the standpoint of composition, heat-resistant alloys are generally more highly alloyed with chromium and nickel and contain substantially more carbon than the corrosion-resistant alloys. In addition, heat-resistant alloy castings are usually placed in service in the as-cast condition whereas corrosion-resistant alloy castings are normally solution heat-treated before being placed in service. Microstructurally, the heat-resistant alloys are predominately fully

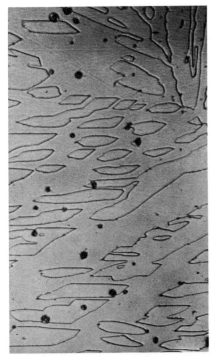

Fig. 4 Duplex austenite-in-ferrite CD-4MCu alloy in solution-heat-treated and water-quenched condition. Particles are inclusions. Electrolytic oxalic acid etch. (500X) *(The Duriron Company.)*

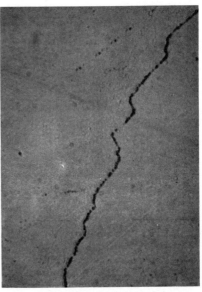

Fig. 5 Alloy CN-7M in as-cast condition. Discrete carbide particles at grain boundaries. Electrolytic oxalic acid etch. (1250X) *(The Duriron Company.)*

austenitic and contain carbide precipitates of various types whereas the corrosion-resistant alloys are predominately duplex ferrite-in-austenite without carbide precipitates.

Classification of the commercial cast Fe-Cr-Ni alloys by composition normally is made on the basis of chromium, nickel, and carbon contents. It can be seen with reference to Table 1 that both the corrosion-resistant and heat-resistant alloys may be grouped on the basis of chromium and nickel contents as Fe-Cr-Ni alloys, in which chromium content exceeds nickel content, or as Fe-Ni-Cr alloys, in which nickel exceeds chromium.

The corrosion-resistant Fe-Cr-Ni alloy group is comprised mainly of the CF alloys. As the cast counterparts of the important 18Cr-8Ni wrought stainless steels, the 19Cr-9Ni CF grades are the most widely used of the cast corrosion-resistant alloys. The principal application of the Fe-Cr-Ni alloy group is in acid services which are strongly oxidizing. Their corrosion resistance in such service is the result of their ability to passivate which, in turn, is attributable mainly to high chromium content. Of the remaining alloys in this group, CD-4MCu is unique as a higher strength alloy which can be precipitation-hardened. Alloy CE-30, CH-20, and CK-20 compositions are distinguished by their higher carbon contents in comparison with the other corrosion-resistant grades.

Alloy CN-7M is the only corrosion-resistant alloy of importance in the Fe-Ni-Cr alloy group. The higher nickel content (29%) in this alloy in combination with high chromium confers corrosion resistance superior to that of the 19Cr-9Ni stainless steels in both

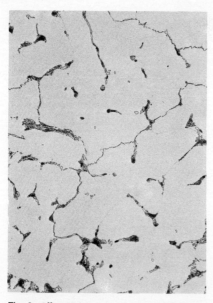

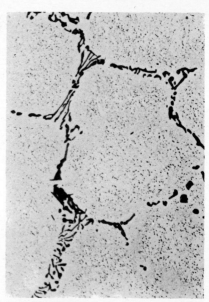

Fig. 6 Alloy HN in as-cast condition. Colonies of carbide precipitated at grain boundaries. Glyceregia etch. (250X) *(From L. Dillinger et al., "Microstructures of Heat Resistant Alloys," Alloy Casting Institute, Steel Founders Society of America, Rocky River, Ohio.)*

Fig. 7 Alloy HT-56 after creep testing for 1002 h at 760°C and 68.9 MN/m² (10 ksi). Large eutectic carbides at grain boundaries and fine secondary carbide precipitates within grains. Hot alkaline potassium ferricyanide etch. (250X) *(From H. S. Avery and N. A. Matthews, Tran. Am. Soc. Met., vol. 38, p. 1007, 1947.)*

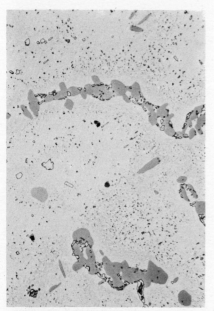

Fig. 8 Alloy HH after creep testing 9850 h at 871°C and 15.1 MN/m² (2 ksi). Large, gray masses are sigma phase associated with eutectic carbides. Electrolytic sodium cyanide etch. (500X) *(From L. Dillinger et al., op. cit.)*

Fig. 9 Alloy HH after creep testing 10,270 h at 760°C and 27.6 MN/m² (4 ksi). Gray platelets and islands are sigma phase formed within grains. Electrolytic sodium cyanide etch. (500X) *(From L. Dillinger et al., op. cit.)*

TABLE 1   Chemical Composition of Corrosion-resistant and Heat-resistant Cast Fe-Cr-Ni Alloys*

Alloy	Element concentration, wt % (m denotes maximum)									
	Cr	Ni	Mo	Si	Mn	P	S	C	Fe	Other
CORROSION-RESISTANT ALLOYS										
Fe-Cr-Ni group:										
CD-4MCu	25.0–26.5	4.75– 6.0	1.75–2.25	1.00m	1.00m	0.04m	0.04m	0.04m	Bal	2.75–3.25Cu
CE-30	26.0–30.0	8.0 –11.0		2.00m	1.50m	0.04m	0.04m	0.30m	Bal	
CF-3	17.0–21.0	8.0 –12.0		2.00m	1.50m	0.04m	0.04m	0.03m	Bal	
CF-8	18.0–21.0	8.0 –11.0		2.00m	1.50m	0.04m	0.04m	0.08m	Bal	
CF-20	18.0–21.0	8.0 –11.0		2.00m	1.50m	0.04m	0.04m	0.20m	Bal	
CF-3M	17.0–21.0	9.0 –13.0	2.0–3.0	1.50m	1.50m	0.04m	0.04m	0.03m	Bal	
CF-8M	18.0–21.0	9.0 –12.0	2.0–3.0	1.50m	1.50m	0.04m	0.04m	0.08m	Bal	
CF-12M	18.0–21.0	9.0 –12.0	2.0–3.0	2.00m	1.50m	0.04m	0.04m	0.12m	Bal	
CF-8C	18.0–21.0	9.0 –12.0		2.00m	1.50m	0.04m	0.04m	0.08m	Bal	1.0Cbm
CF-16F	18.0–21.0	9.0 –12.0	1.50m	2.00m	1.50m	0.17m	0.04m	0.16m	Bal	0.20–0.35Se
CG-8M	18.0–21.0	9.0 –13.0	3.0–4.0	1.50m	1.50m	0.04m	0.04m	0.08m	Bal	
CH-20	22.0–26.0	12.0 –15.0		2.00m	1.50m	0.04m	0.04m	0.20m	Bal	
CK-20	23.0–27.0	19.0 –22.0		1.75m	1.50m	0.04m	0.04m	0.20m	Bal	
Fe-Ni-Cr group:										
CN-7M	19.0–22.0	27.5 –30.5	2.0–3.0	1.50m	1.50m	0.04m	0.04m	0.07m	Bal	3.0–4.0Cu
HEAT-RESISTANT ALLOYS										
Fe-Cr-Ni group:										
HD	26.0–30.0	4.0– 7.0	0.5m	2.00m	1.50m	0.04m	0.04m	0.50m	Bal	
HE	26.0–30.0	8.0–11.0	0.5m	2.00m	2.00m	0.04m	0.04m	0.20–0.50	Bal	
HF	19.0–23.0	9.0–12.0	0.5m	2.00m	2.00m	0.04m	0.04m	0.20–0.40	Bal	
HH	24.0–28.0	11.0–14.0	0.5m	2.00m	2.00m	0.04m	0.04m	0.20–0.50	Bal	0.2Nm
HI	26.0–30.0	14.0–18.0	0.5m	2.00m	2.00m	0.04m	0.04m	0.20–0.50	Bal	
HK	24.0–28.0	18.0–22.0	0.5m	2.00m	2.00m	0.04m	0.04m	0.20–0.60	Bal	
HL	28.0–32.0	18.0–22.0	0.5m	2.00m	2.00m	0.04m	0.04m	0.20–0.60	Bal	
Fe-Ni-Cr group:										
HN	19.0–23.0	23.0–27.0	0.5m	2.00m	2.00m	0.04m	0.04m	0.20–0.50	Bal	
HP	24.0–28.0	33.0–37.0	0.5m	2.00m	2.00m	0.04m	0.04m	0.35–0.75	Bal	
HT	15.0–19.0	33.0–37.0	0.5m	2.50m	2.00m	0.04m	0.04m	0.35–0.75	Bal	
HU	17.0–21.0	37.0–41.0	0.5m	2.50m	2.00m	0.04m	0.04m	0.35–0.75	Bal	
HW	10.0–14.0	58.0–62.0	0.5m	2.50m	2.00m	0.04m	0.04m	0.35–0.75	Bal	
HX	15.0–19.0	64.0–68.0	0.5m	2.50m	2.00m	0.04m	0.04m	0.35–0.75	Bal	

*Compiled from E. Schoefer,[10] and E. Schoefer and T. Shields.[21]

oxidizing and reducing environments. Alloy CN-7M is particularly suited for service in sulfuric acid solutions.

The heat-resistant Fe-Cr-Ni alloy group comprises about half of the commercial heat-resistant alloys listed in Table 1, including the widely used HH and HK grades. It should be noted that nickel is present in quantity in each of these grades in addition to chromium. Good resistance to oxidation, sulfidation, and abrasion at temperatures above 650°C is afforded by the high chromium content in these alloys. In general, the higher the chromium content, the greater is the oxidation resistance of the alloy and the higher is its maximum use temperature in service. The high carbon contents in these alloys contribute significantly to high strength (i.e., resistance to creep rupture) through carbide precipitation at elevated service temperatures. The heat-resistant Fe-Cr-Ni alloys are applied successfully in oxidizing, reducing, and sulfurous atmospheres at temperatures up to 1175°C.

The Fe-Ni-Cr group of heat-resistant alloys includes only one grade, HN, which properly is classified as a stainless steel. The remaining alloys in this group contain less than 50% iron and two, HW and HX, are nickel-base alloys. High strength and resistance to thermal shock, carburization and corrosion at elevated service temperatures are afforded by the high nickel content in these alloys. Their high carbon content contributes to stress-rupture resistance via carbide precipitation as in the Fe-Cr-Ni alloys. The heat-resistant Fe-Ni-Cr alloys are used most frequently in applications involving reactive atmospheres and thermal shock at temperatures up to 1150°C.

A third basis frequently used in classifying cast Fe-Cr-Ni alloys is that of microstructure. Specifically, the distinction is made between fully austenitic alloys and duplex alloys, i.e., those which are predominately austenitic but contain some ferrite. Whether an alloy is austenitic or duplex is determined principally by the alloy composition. As discussed in detail in the next section, the chromium, nickel, and carbon contents are particularly significant compositional variables in this regard. In general terms it can be stated that the chromium-predominant Fe-Cr-Ni alloys tend to be duplex whereas the nickel-predominant Fe-Cr-Ni alloys tend to be fully austenitic. Higher carbon in the alloy composition also promotes fully austenitic microstructures. With specific reference to the commercial cast alloys listed in Table 1, it is relevant to note that the corrosion-resistant alloys are normally duplex as used except for the CF-20, CK-20, and CN-7M grades. The CD-4MCu alloy is unique in that, while duplex, the predominant and continuous phase in the microstructure is ferrite rather than austenite. With regard to the heat-resistant alloys, those in the Fe-Cr-Ni group are more frequently fully austenitic as used but may be made duplex if desired. Like the corrosion-resistant CD-4MCu alloy, alloy HD is unique in this group as a predominately ferritic alloy. On the other hand, the Fe-Ni-Cr heat-resistant group is comprised entirely of fully austenitic alloys.

Constitution   It is convenient to initiate discussion of the constitution of Fe-Cr-Ni alloys with the Fe-Cr binary phase diagram in Fig. 10. The pronounced effect of chromium in stabilizing the ferrite (α) phase in iron is obvious from the diagram. As chromium content is increased, the temperature range over which the austenite (γ) phase is stable diminishes until, at chromium contents higher than about 12%, austenite is not present in the alloy at any temperature up to the melting point.

Since carbon is present to some degree in all commercial Fe-Cr-Ni alloys, it is pertinent to consider the effect of this element on phase equilibria in the Fe-Cr system. As indicated in Fig. 10, the addition of carbon significantly expands the field of austenite phase stability, termed the gamma loop on the diagram. With increasing carbon, the austenite phase field is expanded until it reaches a maximum chromium content with approximately 0.60% carbon added.[2] It is obvious, therefore, that carbon is a potent austenite stabilizer. Further increase in carbon above about 0.60% produces carbides but no expansion of the austenite phase field. The cross-hatched band to the right of the expanded field with carbon present represents the two-phase field in which ferrite and austenite are both stable. This field extends to approximately 26% chromium beyond which austenite is no longer present at any temperature.

Having considered the effects of chromium and carbon on constitution, it is left to consider nickel as the remaining basic elemental component of the Fe-Cr-Ni alloys. This may be done with reference to Fig. 11 which depicts the effect of increasing nickel content on phase equilibria in an 18% Cr steel containing negligible carbon. It is apparent from the figure that nickel, like carbon, is a very effective austenite stabilizer. Austenite begins to appear with nickel additions of less than 2%. With increasing nickel content, austenite becomes stable over a progressively larger temperature range until, above about 13% nickel, it is a stable phase at all temperatures up to the melting point of the alloy.

From the foregoing it is apparent that the microstructures of the Fe-Cr-Ni alloys fundamentally depend on composition and that the major elemental components of these alloys are in competition in promoting austenite or ferrite phases in the alloy microstructure. In preceding sections of this chapter it has been stated that the commercial Fe-Cr-Ni alloys are either fully austenitic or duplex ferrite-in-austenite with few exceptions. The property advantages associated with each type of microstructure in the corrosion-resistant and heat-resistant alloys have been described in general terms. In cast corrosion-resistant alloys, for example, the presence of ferrite in amounts ranging up to 35% in the austenite matrix is useful in providing increased strength and substantially improved resistance to stress-corrosion cracking. It is appropriate, then, to consider empirically developed relationships between composition and microstructure which permit the founder to control microstructure and resultant properties in the cast Fe-Cr-Ni alloys.

Schoefer[17] has developed a one-line constitution diagram for cast Fe-Cr-Ni alloys with which the ferrite content of the alloy can be estimated accurately knowing only the alloy composition. The Schoefer diagram was derived from an earlier diagram developed by Schaeffler[18] for weld metal. Use of the Schoefer diagram requires that all ferrite-stabilizing elements in the composition be converted into "chromium equivalents" and that all austenite-stabilizing elements be converted into "nickel equivalents" through the use of coefficients representing the ferritizing or austenitizing power of each element. A total chromium equivalent Cr_e and total nickel equivalent Ni_e are calculated for the alloy composition according to the following expressions:

$$Cr_e = \%Cr + 1.5(\%Si) + \%Mo + \%Cb - 4.99$$
$$Ni_e = \%Ni + 30(\%C) + 0.5(\%Mn) + 26(\%N - 0.02) + 2.77$$

where the elemental concentrations are percent by weight. Other investigators[19] have developed similar expressions which encompass additional alloying elements and different compositional ranges within the Fe-Cr-Ni alloy system.

With total chromium and nickel equivalents determined from the above, reference is

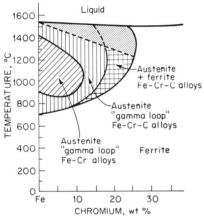

Fig. 10 Fe-Cr constitution diagram. The dotted overlap region between the liquid and solid fields for pure Fe-Cr alloys indicates the lowering of the freezing point caused by additions of carbon. (*Adapted from Zapffe.*[2])

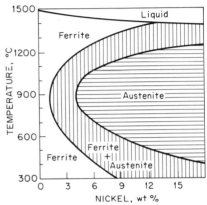

Fig. 11 Constitution diagram showing effect of nickel on phase equilibria in an Fe-Cr alloy containing 18% chromium with negligible carbon. Iron is replaced with nickel toward the right in the diagram. (*Adapted from C. Zapffe.*[2])

made to the Schoefer diagram in Fig. 12 which relates the ratio Cr_e/Ni_e to ferrite number for the specific composition involved. The ferrite number so obtained has been adopted as the accepted index which quantifies the ferrite content of the composition. Although closely related to actual ferrite content, particularly at lower ferrite contents, the ferrite number does not correspond precisely to percent of ferrite over the entire range of the Schoefer diagram.

The utility of the Schoefer diagram is apparent. It is useful for estimation of ferrite content, if the composition of an alloy is known, and for setting aim values for individual elements in calculating the charge for an alloy in which a specified ferrite range is desired.

COMMERCIAL CAST IRON-CHROMIUM-NICKEL ALLOYS

It is convenient for consideration of individual alloys to group the cast Fe-Cr-Ni alloys by end-use application, i.e., corrosion-resistant alloys and heat-resistant alloys.

Corrosion-Resistant Alloys

Corrosion-resistant-alloy compositions are distinguished from heat-resistant-alloy compositions principally by lower carbon contents and, in some grades, by the purposeful addition of molybdenum and copper. In general, corrosion-resistant-alloy compositions are balanced to result in a fully austenitic or a duplex ferrite-in-austenite microstructure. Strengthening in the corrosion-resistant alloys generally is related to the amount of ferrite phase in the duplex microstructure. These alloys are normally utilized in the solution-heat-treated condition to minimize the presence of carbide and sigma phases, thereby maximizing corrosion resistance. For further information on properties and application of individual corrosion-resistant alloys beyond that summarized here, the reader is referred to the data compilations of the Steel Founders' Society of America (SFSA).[10.20]

CF Alloys The CF alloys comprise the most widely used of the corrosion-resistant alloys. In the solution-heat-treated condition these stainless steels are resistant to a wide variety of corrosives. Their corrosion resistance is generally superior to that of the

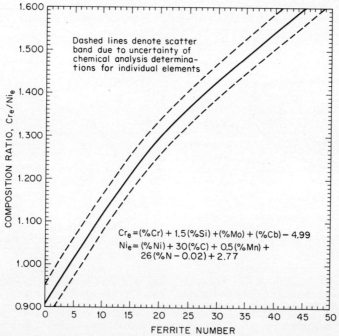

Fig. 12 Constitution diagram for estimation of ferrite content in stainless steel castings within the composition range of 16 to 26Cr-6 to 14Ni-0 to 4Mo-0 to 1Cb-up to 0.30C-0.15N-2.00Mn-2.00Si. *(Adapted from E. Schoefer.[17])*

martensitic, ferritic, and precipitation-hardenable grades. The CF alloys are nominally 19Cr-9Ni in composition with controlled lower carbon contents. The composition is normally balanced between ferrite- and austenite-stabilizing elements to produce a duplex microstructure, that is, 5 to 25% ferrite in an austenite matrix. A controlled amount of ferrite is desirable in the microstructure of these alloys because it improves strength, weldability, and resistance to stress-corrosion cracking and to sensitization to intergranular corrosion attack.

All but the lowest carbon CF alloys contain intergranular, predominately chromium carbide precipitates in the duplex structure in the as-cast condition, or whenever slowly cooled from high temperatures, as after welding. This carbide precipitation effectively depletes the matrix adjacent to the grain boundaries in chromium, the element most responsible for the "stainless" properties of the alloy, and thereby renders the alloy susceptible to rapid intergranular attack in certain severe corrosives. The alloy is described as sensitized when in this condition. For this reason the CF alloys are used in the solution-heat-treated condition for optimum corrosion resistance. The carbide precipitates are dissolved on solution treatment at 1040 to 1150°C and precipitation does not recur when the alloy is rapidly cooled from this temperature, especially through the critical precipitation temperature range between 425 and 870°C. The CF alloys are not hardenable by heat treatment. Strengthening in these alloys is confined to that brought about by solid-solution hardening and controlling the fraction of ferrite phase in the duplex microstructure.

CF-8 Alloy. Alloy CF-8 is one of the more widely used of the CF grades. The wrought counterpart of CF-8 is AISI Type 304. Composition of the alloy is 19Cr-9Ni with 0.08C max. Microstructure of the alloy as-cast consists of austenite containing dispersed ferrite, typically about 10%, and precipitated carbides. For maximum corrosion resistance CF-8 is solution heat-treated in the range 1040 to 1120°C and then quenched in water, oil, or air to ensure no reprecipitation of carbides on cooling to room temperature. Holding time at the solution temperature and quenching medium needed to avoid carbide precipitation depend on casting section thickness.

The microstructure of properly solution heat-treated CF-8 consists of ferrite dispersed in austenite with no visible carbide precipitation. If the heat-treated material is subsequently exposed to temperatures in the range 425 to 870°C, as in welding, it is sensitized. Castings in this condition must be reheat-treated to be made fully corrosion-resistant. Alloy CF-8 has excellent corrosion resistance in a great variety of media and is widely used in corrosion services, especially in strongly oxidizing acid solutions such as nitric acid.

CF-3 Alloy. Alloy CF-3 is quite similar in composition to CF-8 except that the carbon content of CF-3 is limited to 0.03% maximum. Its wrought counterpart is AISI Type 304L. By virtue of its lower carbon content CF-3 possesses somewhat better general corrosion resistance than CF-8, but the two alloys are used in similar applications. However, the lower carbon content of CF-3 permits the alloy to be field welded without rendering the material susceptible to intergranular corrosion attack through sensitization, i.e., carbide precipitation at the grain boundaries. Hence, alloy CF-3 is suited particularly to applications where warm- or hot-forming or repair welding must be performed in the field without subsequent heat treatment.

The as-cast microstructure of CF-3 consists of austenite containing dispersed ferrite, typically 10 to 20%, with little or no precipitated carbides. As a consequence, the alloy can be applied in some corrosive environments in the as-cast condition. For maximum corrosion resistance, however, the alloy should be solution heat-treated and quenched as described for CF-8. If the heat-treated material is subsequently exposed to temperatures in the range 425 to 870°C, precipitation of carbides will be quite limited to none. Moreover, any carbides which might form would be located within the ferrite phase rather than at grain boundaries so that susceptibility to intergranular attack is not increased significantly.

CF-8M and CF-3M Alloys. The CF-8M and CF-3M alloys are quite similar in composition to the CF-8 and CF-3 alloys, respectively, except for the addition of 2.0 to 3.0% molybdenum and slightly higher nickel contents in each alloy. Wrought counterparts of the CF-8M and CF-3M alloys are AISI Types 316 and 316L, respectively. The higher nickel content in these alloys is needed to offset the ferrite-stabilizing influence of the molybdenum addition in order that the composition may be balanced to produce the desired duplex microstructure in CF-8M and CF-3M castings. Addition of molybdenum to the 19Cr-9Ni alloy improves general corrosion resistance in weakly oxidizing and reducing corrosive media, e.g., dilute sulfuric acid, and significantly increases resistance of the material to pitting corrosion attack.

Alloy CF-8M and CF-3M microstructures are duplex as normally produced, consisting typically of 15 to 25% ferrite in an austenite matrix. As in the CF-8 and CF-3 alloys, the ferrite phase provides a preferred location for precipitation of carbides, thereby lessening the potential for intergranular corrosion susceptibility resulting from carbide precipitation at austenite grain boundaries. The CF-3M alloy, by virtue of its lower carbon content, does not require postweld heat treatment in analogous fashion to alloy CF-3. For maximum corrosion resistance, both CF-8M and CF-3M should be solution heat-treated in the temperature range 1065 to 1150°C and quenched to ensure the absence of carbide precipitates in the microstructure.

CF-12M Alloy. Alloy CF-12M is basically a higher carbon (0.12% maximum) version of alloy CF-8M. The alloy is useful in the same types of corrosion services as CF-8M, but by virtue of its higher carbon content, CF-12M possesses somewhat lower overall corrosion resistance at temperatures below 540°C. The higher carbon content of CF-12M, however, permits the alloy to be balanced readily to a fully austenitic microstructure. This is advantageous in services with operating temperatures exceeding 650°C where ferrite may transform on holding to brittle sigma phase. By suitable balancing of the composition, CF-12M can be made duplex or fully austenitic in microstructure. For maximum corrosion resistance CF-12M should be solution heat-treated in the range 1095 to 1150°C and quenched to ensure the absence of carbide precipitates in the microstructure.

CF-8C Alloy. Alloy CF-8C is a modified CF-8 composition containing an addition of columbium (niobium) or columbium and tantalum to prevent precipitation of chromium carbides at grain boundaries when the material is heated in the range 425 to 870°C. The wrought counterpart of CF-8C is AISI Type 347. By heat-treating at 870 to 900°C after the customary solution heat treatment at 1065 to 1120°C to dissolve any chromium carbides present in the as-cast alloy, preferential general precipitation of columbium carbides is induced. This characteristic of the alloy eliminates the possibility that it will be sensitized to intergranular attack by depletion of chromium adjacent to grain boundaries through precipitation of predominantly chromium carbides when the alloy is subsequently heated in the 425 to 870°C range for limited times, as in welding, or for longer times, as in service at elevated temperatures. Thus, alloy CF-8C has advantages compared with CF-8 in instances where castings cannot be solution heat-treated conveniently following welding or where service temperatures will exceed 425°C. Alloy CF-8C provides nominally equivalent corrosion resistance to CF-8 and is applied in the same types of services. The alloy as normally produced has a duplex microstructure containing typically 5 to 20% ferrite in the austenite matrix.

CF-20 Alloy. Alloy CF-20 is similar in composition to CF-8 but has a higher carbon content, 0.20% maximum. Its wrought counterpart is AISI Type 302. The alloy possesses corrosion resistance superior to that of the Fe-Cr alloys, e.g., CA-15, but inferior to that of the lower carbon Fe-Cr-Ni alloys, e.g., CF-8. Consequently, CF-20 is normally applied in less severely oxidizing corrosion services than CF-8. The as-cast microstructure of CF-20 consists of austenite containing carbide precipitates. For maximum corrosion resistance the alloy is solution heat-treated in the range 1095 to 1150°C and quenched. Selection of holding time at temperature and type of quench depends on casting section thickness.

CF-16F Alloy. Alloy CF-16F is a free-machining 19Cr-9Ni alloy containing 0.16C max. The wrought counterpart of this alloy is AISI Type 303. It is similar in composition to alloys CF-8 and CF-20 but with small additions of selenium and phosphorus to improve machinability. The complex selenides which are formed and are present in the material as-cast and as-heat-treated act as chipbreakers during machining and are responsible for the free-machining quality of the alloy. Microstructure of the alloy in the as-cast condition is normally duplex, containing up to 15% ferrite, with carbide and selenide precipitates. For maximum corrosion resistance, the alloy is solution heat-treated at 1065 to 1120°C and quenched to remove carbide precipitates. Solution heat treatment is also required after welding to avoid sensitization to intergranular corrosion attack. The corrosion resistance of CF-16F is similar to but somewhat inferior to that of alloy CF-20.

Controlled Ferrite Grades. Although the CF alloys cannot be strengthened by heat treatment, they are strengthened effectively by increasing the percentage of ferrite phase at the expense of the austenite phase in their duplex microstructures. This fact has led to the adoption of "controlled ferrite" grades, designated with an A suffix, in some CF alloys, i.e., CF-8A, CF-3A, and CF-3MA, for applications where higher strength is desired. Minimum yield strength and ultimate tensile strength specification requirements for these controlled ferrite grades are 5 to 7 ksi (34.5 to 48.3 MN/m²) and 7 to 10 ksi (48.3 to 68.9 MN/m²) higher, respectively, than for the regular grades. These higher strengths are obtained by adjusting the balance between austenite- and ferrite-stabilizing elements within the normal chemical range limits specified for the alloy to increase the volume fraction of ferrite in the microstructure. The higher ferrite contents so produced generally improve the resistance of the alloy to stress-corrosion cracking as well as increase its strength. Because of the thermal instability of these higher ferrite microstructures, the controlled ferrite grades are not considered suitable for service at temperatures above 340°C (CF-3A) or 425°C (CF-8A and CF-3MA).

CD-4MCu Alloy Alloy CD-4MCu is nominally a 26Cr-6Ni alloy with 0.04C max. and additions of molybdenum and copper. The alloy has no wrought counterpart. Alloy CD-4MCu in the as-cast condition has a duplex microstructure consisting of austenite in a ferrite matrix. Carbide precipitates, although limited by the low maximum carbon content of the alloy, are also dispersed in the ferrite matrix and degrade corrosion resistance if not removed by solution heat treatment. For complete solution of carbides and maximum corrosion resistance, CD-4MCu is solution heat-treated at 1120°C minimum for 2 h to assure uniform temperature, cooled slowly to the range 1010 to 1065°C, held for ½ h and quenched. Holding at the lower temperature is required in order to avoid cracking the castings on quenching, particularly in thicker sections. Microstructure of the alloy in the heat-treated condition is also duplex, consisting of 35 to 40% austenite in a ferrite matrix.

Alloy CD-4MCu is basically ferritic and possesses a yield strength about double that of the 19Cr-9Ni austenitic alloys with high hardness, good tensile ductility, and satisfactory impact toughness. The high strength and hardness of the alloy in combination with its excellent corrosion resistance are particularly advantageous in corrosion services involving abrasion or erosion-corrosion. Alloy CD-4MCu has corrosion resistance superior to that of the CF alloys in many corrosive media. It is widely applied in severe acid services under both oxidizing and reducing conditions and has exceptional resistance to stress-corrosion cracking in chloride environments.

The CD-4MCu alloy may be further strengthened by aging to induce precipitation hardening in the temperature range 480 to 510°C following solution heat treatment. The extent of this aging response and overall properties of the alloy in the aged condition, including corrosion resistance, strength, impact ductility, and quench-cracking propensity, are dependent in complex fashion on the upper and lower solution-heat-treat temperatures, aging temperature, and time at aging temperature. Because the alloy possesses adequate strength for most applications and excellent corrosion resistance in the solution-heat-treated condition, it is seldom used in the aged condition.

CE-30 Alloy   Alloy CE-30 is nominally a 30Cr-10Ni alloy containing 0.30C max. The wrought counterpart of CE-30 is AISI Type 312. The microstructure of the alloy as-cast is duplex ferrite-in-austenite with carbide precipitates. Although the carbon content of the alloy is high for a corrosion-resistant grade, impairment of its intergranular corrosion resistance by chromium depletion through carbide precipitation in the temperature range 425 to 870°C is limited by its higher chromium content and duplex microstructure. Thus, the alloy is useful in applications where heat treatment of castings before or after welding is not feasible. Exposure to temperatures near 840°C for long periods will result in formation of sigma phase which embrittles the alloy at room temperature.

Alloy CE-30 should be solution heat-treated in the temperature range 1095 to 1120°C and quenched to maximize corrosion resistance and ductility. The alloy is resistant to dilute sulfuric, sulfurous, and sulfite media and is applied widely in such services in the pulp and paper industry. A controlled ferrite grade of the alloy, designated CE-30A, with composition balanced to obtain 5 to 20% ferrite in the microstructure is applied in stress-corrosion cracking environments within the oil-refining industry.

CG-8M Alloy   Alloy CG-8M is nominally a 19Cr-9Ni alloy containing 0.08C max. and 3.0 to 4.0Mo. The wrought counterpart of CG-8M is AISI Type 317. The alloy is quite similar in composition to CF-8M except that it possesses additional molybdenum to increase corrosion resistance in reducing and pitting environments. Alloy CG-8M is solution heat-treated in the range 1040 to 1120°C and quenched to maximize corrosion resistance. Microstructure of the alloy in the heat-treated condition is duplex, consisting typically of 15 to 35% ferrite in an austenite matrix. The alloy is useful in applications involving reducing corrosive media (e.g., sulfurous and sulfuric acids) and pitting agents (e.g., halogen salts). The high ferrite content of CG-8M confers considerable resistance to stress-corrosion cracking. Exposure of the alloy for extended periods to temperatures above 650°C should be avoided to prevent embrittlement from ferrite transformation to sigma phase.

CH-20 Alloy   Alloy CH-20 is nominally a 25Cr-12Ni alloy containing 0.20C max. It is similar in composition to alloy CE-30 but has lower chromium and carbon contents and a higher nickel content. The wrought counterpart of CH-20 is AISI Type 309. The microstructure of the alloy as-cast is duplex, consisting of small amounts of ferrite in an austenite matrix, with carbides present. For maximum corrosion resistance CH-20 is solution heat-treated in the temperature range 1095 to 1150°C and quenched to ensure the absence of carbides in the microstructure. Postweld solution heat treatment is recommended to prevent sensitization to intergranular corrosion attack.

Like all austenitic cast stainless steels, CH-20 is not hardenable by heat treatment. The mechanical properties of the alloy are intermediate between those of the CE-30 and CF-8 types; i.e., it possesses more ductility than CE-30 and higher strength than CF-8. Alloy CH-20 is substantially more corrosion-resistant than CF-8 in some corrosion environments. The alloy is applied most frequently in hot dilute sulfuric acid service. It is sometimes made with a 0.10% maximum carbon content (CH-10) and also with an addition of molybdenum (CH-10M) to further its corrosion resistance over the CF-8 and CF-8M alloys.

CK-20 Alloy   Alloy CK-20 is nominally a 25Cr-20Ni alloy containing 0.20C max. The wrought counterpart of CK-20 is AISI Type 310. Although similar in composition to alloy CH-20, the substantially higher nickel content of CK-20 imparts additional corrosion resistance at higher temperatures in the same types of media for which alloy CH-20 is generally applied. It is these special service requirements at higher temperatures which justify the application of CK-20 despite its higher nickel content and associated higher cost. The microstructure of CK-20 as-cast is austenitic with precipitated carbides dispersed in the matrix.

For maximum corrosion resistance and improved ductility the alloy is solution heat-treated in the range 1095 to 1175°C and quenched to ensure the absence of carbide precipitates in the microstructure. Alloy CK-20 is more susceptible than higher chromium CE-30, and less susceptible than lower chromium CF-8, to sensitization to intergranular attack on heating to temperatures in the range 425 to 870°C following solution heat treatment. Intergranular corrosion resistance of the alloy is not impaired significantly by such elevated temperature exposure provided that the duration of exposure is short. Alloy CK-20, as an austenitic alloy, is not hardenable by heat treatment.

CN-7M Alloy   Alloy CN-7M is nominally a 29Ni-20Cr alloy with copper and molybdenum additions and 0.07C max. which, although it is less than 50% iron, is nevertheless considered a stainless steel. The alloy has no counterpart AISI wrought designation. Alloy CN-7M is a fully austenitic alloy in the solution-heat-treated condition and is not hardenable by heat treatment. As for the 19Cr-9Ni steels, solution heat treatment is required to maximize corrosion resistance. The alloy is solution heat-treated at 1120°C minimum and then quenched to ensure the absence of precipitated carbides in the microstructure. Postweld solution heat treatment is recommended. Attention to control of composition and heat treatment are necessary with CN-7M, as with other fully austenitic cast stainless steels, to avoid cracking on thermal stressing as encountered in casting cut off and repair welding. To minimize cracking potential and maximize corrosion resistance, it is desirable that the carbon content of the alloy be well below the maximum permitted, for example, 0.03%. Alloy CN-7M possesses the best overall corrosion resistance of all of the corrosion-resistant alloys discussed here. It is widely used in severe corrosion services, including sulfuric, nitric, phosphoric, fluoboric, and dilute hydrochloric acids, caustic media, seawater, and hot chloride salt solutions.

Heat-Resistant Alloys

The heat-resistant Fe-Cr-Ni cast alloys comprise those which are employed for their resistance to corrosive oxidizing or reducing gases at temperatures above 650°C. The primary requirements for heat-resistant alloys are (1) that the alloy be resistant to the specific atmosphere of interest, and (2) that the mechanical properties and microstructure of the alloy remain relatively stable with long exposure times at elevated service temperatures. In general, heat-resistant alloys are more highly alloyed than the corrosion-resistant alloys and have substantially higher carbon contents which, via carbide precipitation, confer superior mechanical properties at elevated temperatures. Oxidation, abrasion, and sulfidation resistance in these alloys are imparted by their high chromium contents whereas corrosion and thermal shock resistance and creep strength are imparted by their high nickel contents. The service atmospheres of most importance for heat-resistant alloys are air and flue gases of sulfur-bearing and non-sulfur-bearing types. For further information on properties and application of individual heat-resistant alloys beyond that summarized here, the reader is referred to the data compilations of the SFSA.[20,21]

Heat-resistant alloys are classified in three compositional groups for convenience: Fe-Cr alloys, Fe-Cr-Ni alloys, and Fe-Ni-Cr alloys. The Fe-Cr group, consisting of HA and HC alloys, is treated in Chap. 9. The latter two groups are considered here.

Fe-Cr-Ni Alloys   The Fe-Cr-Ni group comprises alloys HD, HE, HF, HH, HK, and HL. These alloys contain 19 to 32Cr-4 to 22Ni-0.20 to 0.60C and are predominately or fully austenitic in microstructure, except for alloy HD. They properly may be considered stainless steels inasmuch as they are iron-based alloys. They are not hardenable by heat treatment and are usually, but not always, applied in the as-cast condition in oxidizing, reducing, and sulfur-bearing atmospheres.

HD Alloy. Alloy HD is nominally 29Cr-6Ni with 0.50C max. Its wrought counterpart is AISI Type 327. Alloy HD is similar to Fe-Cr alloy HC in composition except for its higher nickel content which confers added strength at elevated service temperatures. The alloy is suitable for use in sulfur-bearing atmospheres because of its high chromium content. It is normally applied in the as-cast condition.

Alloy HD is predominantly ferritic like the Fe-Cr alloys. Its microstructure as-cast is duplex austenite-in-ferrite with chromium-rich carbide precipitates. The alloy is strengthened and embrittled at room temperature by sigma-phase formation when exposed to temperatures in the range 700 to 815°C for extended periods. Once embrittled, ductility may be restored to the alloy by heating at 980°C minimum followed by rapid cooling to below 650°C.

HE Alloy. Alloy HE is nominally 29Cr-9Ni with 0.20 to 0.50C. Its wrought counterpart is AISI Type 312. The high chromium content of the alloy makes it quite serviceable in high sulfur atmospheres. The alloy has excellent corrosion resistance, moderate strength and good ductility at elevated temperatures. Alloy HE castings are normally applied in the as-cast condition.

The microstructure of the alloy as-cast is duplex ferrite-in-austenite with chromium-rich carbide precipitates. Although alloy HE is not hardenable by heat treatment, its ductility can be improved to some degree by solution heat treatment at 1095°C followed by quenching. The alloy is quite prone to room-temperature embrittlement by sigma-phase formation when exposed for long periods to temperatures in the 650 to 870°C range.

HF Alloy. Alloy HF is nominally 22Cr-10Ni with 0.20 to 0.50C. The wrought counterpart of HF is AISI Type 302B. The composition of this alloy is similar to that of the 19Cr-9Ni corrosion-resistant alloys except for a significantly higher carbon content and slightly higher chromium and nickel contents. Alloy HF is applied under conditions where high strength in combination with corrosion resistance are required in the 650 to 870°C temperature range. The higher chromium content in comparison with the 19Cr-9Ni steels is desired for improved oxidation resistance at service temperatures. The higher nickel and carbon contents are needed to offset the ferrite-stabilizing effect of the additional chromium in order that the as-cast microstructure of the alloy be fully austenitic. Any ferrite present in the microstructure would transform to sigma phase with consequent embrittlement of the alloy in service. The as-cast microstructure of alloy HF consists of eutectic, and occasionally lamellar, chromium-rich carbides in an austenite matrix. Upon aging in service, additional finely dispersed carbides are usually precipitated. The alloy is not hardenable by heat treatment. Thus, HF castings are normally utilized in the as-cast condition.

HH Alloy. Alloy HH is nominally 27Cr-12Ni with 0.20 to 0.50C. The wrought counterpart of HF is AISI Type 309. Alloy HH possesses high strength and excellent resistance to oxidation at temperatures up to 1095°C and, as a consequence, is the most widely used of the heat-resistant alloys. The alloy is suitable for application in oxidizing environments involving air or normal combustion gases. It is generally unsuitable, however, in strongly carburizing applications where significant absorption of carbon from the service environment is probable. The ductility and thermal shock resistance of the alloy are seriously impaired under these circumstances.

Although HH is essentially an austenitic alloy, its compositional balance of austenite- and ferrite-stabilizing elements is borderline such that the alloy may be partially ferritic (Type I) or fully austenitic (Type II) in the as-cast condition as desired. The alloy is used in both conditions depending on strength and ductility requirements in service. For optimum ductility with lower strength near 980°C, for example, the partially ferritic Type I microstructure is desired. For higher strength, with less ductility, the fully austenitic Type II structure is preferred. At lower service temperatures, i.e., near 870°C, the partially ferritic alloys are subject to embrittlement by sigma-phase formation and at still lower service temperatures, i.e., near 760°C, to comparable ductility loss by carbide precipitation. Generally, the partially ferritic HH alloy is considered best suited for applications which involve changing temperature or applied stress levels in service, whereas the fully austenitic HH alloy is preferred for applications which require optimum creep strength or which involve temperature cycles extending into the sigma-phase formation range.

The microstructure of alloy HH is basically austenitic as-cast but may be partially ferritic as stated. Chromium-rich carbides and sigma phase may also be present in the microstructure in amounts depending on the composition and thermal history of the sample under consideration. Alloy HH cannot be hardened by heat treatment and castings in this alloy normally are supplied in the as-cast condition. Where increased resistance to thermal fatigue from temperature cycling is desired, it is recommended that alloy HH be held at 1040°C for 12 h and furnace-cooled before placing in service.

HI Alloy. Alloy HI is nominally 29Cr-15Ni with 0.20 to 0.50C. The alloy has no wrought counterpart. Compared with alloy HH, HI contains additional increments of both chromium and nickel. The greater chromium content makes this grade more resistant to oxidation than HH such that HI is suitable for use at temperatures up to 1175°C. In addition to compositional similarity, alloy HI is also similar to HH in mechanical properties and in sensitivity of microstructure to composition. The alloy may be balanced so as to be partially ferritic or fully austenitic, but it is usually produced with the latter microstructure. Thus, the as-cast microstructure of alloy HI normally consists of eutectic chromium-rich carbides in an austenite matrix. On aging in the temperature range 760 to 870°C, finely dispersed predominately chromium carbides are precipitated which increase the strength and reduce the ductility of the alloy at room temperature. Since these carbides are dissolved and remain in solution at service temperatures above 1095°C, room-temperature ductility generally is not degraded when the alloy is used near the upper limit of its service temperature range. Alloy HI castings are not hardenable by heat treatment and are normally furnished in the as-cast condition.

HK Alloy. Alloy HK is nominally 27Cr-19Ni with 0.20 to 0.60C. The wrought counterpart of HK is AISI Type 310. The chromium content of HK is sufficiently high to confer corrosion resistance to hot gases, including both sulfur-bearing and non-sulfur-bearing types, under oxidizing and reducing conditions at temperatures up to 1150°C. Since the higher nickel content of HK confers high resistance to creep deformation, the alloy is widely applied in structural applications requiring high strength at temperatures above 1040°C. Alloy HK is not recommended, however, for services involving severe thermal shock.

It is desirable that HK be fully austenitic in microstructure and the alloy is usually so produced. Partially ferritic microstructures are possible, however, within the chemical composition ranges specified for the alloy. The as-cast microstructure of HK normally consists of an austenite matrix containing massive eutectic carbides at austenite grain boundaries. Upon aging in service, fine chromium-rich carbides are precipitated within the austenite which contribute to the creep strength of the alloy and which may, at higher service temperatures, agglomerate with time at temperature. Lamellar carbides, which alternate with austenite lamellae in a structure resembling pearlite, can also be observed in the HK alloy. Formation of brittle sigma phase occurs rapidly in ferrite-containing HK at temperatures near 815°C and can also form directly from the austenite on holding in the temperature range 760 to 870°C. Since silicon confers resistance to carburization of HK alloy, it is usually placed near the upper limit (2.00%) of the alloy specification range for applications where carburization may be a factor.

The creep resistance and stress-rupture life of HK are strongly dependent on the carbon content of the alloy. The higher the carbon content within the 0.20 to 0.60% specification range, the greater the creep resistance and the longer the rupture life but the lower the residual room-temperature ductility after aging. As a consequence of this strong property dependence on carbon content, commercial HK alloy is subdivided into three different grades: HK-30, HK-40, and HK-50, for which the number suffix denotes the midvalue of a ±0.05% carbon range in the composition. Of the three grades, HK-40 is the most widely used. Alloy HK castings cannot be hardened by heat treatment and are usually furnished in the as-cast condition.

HL Alloy. Alloy HL is nominally 31Cr-21Ni with 0.20 to 0.60C. The alloy, which has no wrought counterpart, is similar to alloy HK but has higher chromium content. As a consequence HL has greater resistance to corrosion by hot gases and is the most resistant of the Fe-Cr-Ni alloys to corrosion in high sulfur atmospheres up to 980°C. Alloy HL possesses high-temperature strength equivalent to that of HK and is useful in place of that alloy in more severe oxidizing environments. Alloy HL is normally fully austenitic. The microstructures of the alloy as-cast and aged at service temperatures are quite like those of HK alloy. Castings of HL alloy are not hardenable by heat treatment and are normally applied in the as-cast condition.

Fe-Ni-Cr Alloys   The Fe-Ni-Cr group comprises alloys HN, HP, HT, HU, HW, and HX. These alloys contain 23 to 68Ni-10 to 28Cr-0.20 to 0.75C and are all fully austenitic in microstructure. The alloys in this group are not stainless steels inasmuch as they contain less than 50% iron. In each alloy nickel is either the predominant element or the base metal. These alloys are suitable for application in most services at temperatures up to 1150°C but, because of their high nickel contents, are not suitable for use in high sulfur-bearing atmospheres. The Fe-Ni-Cr alloys are not hardenable by heat treatment and are normally applied in the as-cast condition.

HN Alloy. Alloy HN is nominally 22Cr-26Ni with 0.20 to 0.50C. The alloy has no wrought counterpart. Alloy HN possesses high-temperature strength equivalent to, and ductility superior to, that of the more widely used HT alloy. It is applied most frequently in applications requiring high strength in the 980 to 1095°C temperature range. Alloy HN is fully austenitic at room and elevated temperatures. Because the nickel content of the alloy is greater than its chromium content it is not susceptible to sigma-phase formation when exposed to temperatures in the 650 to 870°C range. The microstructure of HN as-cast consists of austenite containing chromium-rich eutectic carbides. Secondary precipitation of finely dispersed carbides occurs within the austenite upon aging at service temperatures. Alloy HN castings are not hardenable by heat treatment and are normally furnished in the as-cast condition.

HP Alloy. Alloy HP is nominally 27Cr-34Ni with 0.35 to 0.75C. The alloy has no wrought counterpart. The composition of HP is related to that of the HN and HT alloys in that it possesses a higher chromium content like HN, and a higher nickel content like HT. By virtue of its high alloy content, HP alloy is resistant to both oxidizing and carburizing environments at elevated temperatures. The alloy is fully austenitic and is utilized for its good creep-rupture resistance in the 980 to 1095°C temperature range. The microstructure of HP as-cast consists of austenite containing massive intergranular eutectic carbide precipitates. Secondary precipitation of fine chromium-rich carbides occurs within the austenite upon aging at service temperatures. Alloy HP castings are not hardenable by heat treatment and are normally furnished in the as-cast condition.

HT Alloy. Alloy HT is nominally 17Cr-34Ni with 0.35 to 0.75C. The wrought counterpart of HT alloy is AISI Type 330. The alloy possesses good resistance to oxidation and carburization and is applied satisfactorily in oxidizing environments up to 1150°C and in reducing environments up to 1095°C where high strength and thermal shock resistance are desired. Alloy HT is not well suited for use in high sulfur-bearing atmospheres. Because increased carbon content does not impair the high-temperature ductility of HT, the alloy is particularly useful in carburizing services. Since silicon confers added resistance to carburization in the alloy, it is recommended that HT castings intended for carburizing service contain a minimum 1.5%.

Alloy HT is fully austenitic. The microstructure of the alloy as-cast consists of austenite containing sizeable amounts of eutectic carbides at the grain boundaries. Fine, secondary carbides are precipitated within the austenite upon aging at service temperatures. Alloy HT castings are not hardenable by heat treatment and are normally furnished in the as-cast condition. However, improved resistance to thermal fatigue may be obtained by holding castings at 1040°C for 12 h and furnace cooling prior to placing in service.

HU Alloy. Alloy HU is nominally 20Cr-38Ni with 0.35 to 0.75C. The alloy has no wrought counterpart. The additional chromium and nickel in the HU composition, compared with alloy HT, confer additional corrosion resistance at high temperatures in both oxidizing and reducing atmospheres, including those of the sulfur-bearing type. The alloy is resistant to carburization and possesses high-temperature strength and resistance to thermal fatigue equivalent to that of the HT alloy. Alloy HU is fully austenitic. Its microstructures in the as-cast and aged conditions are quite like those of the HT alloy as described previously. Alloy HU castings are not hardenable by heat treatment and are normally furnished in the as-cast condition. Improved resistance to thermal fatigue may be obtained, however, by heat treatment as described for alloy HT.

HW Alloy. Alloy HW is a nickel-base alloy nominally containing 13Cr-59Ni-0.35 to 0.75C. The alloy has no wrought counterpart. The high nickel content of HW confers excellent resistance to carburization, thermal shock, and thermal fatigue. Although not as strong as alloy HT, HW alloy possesses satisfactory strength with excellent oxidation resistance in strongly oxidizing atmospheres up to 1040°C. The alloy is particularly suited for use in construction of heat-treating fixtures which must experience severe thermal shock and thermal fatigue.

The microstructure of alloy HW is austenitic with varying amounts of carbides depending on carbon content and thermal history of the sample. As-cast, the microstructure consists of austenite containing massive intergranular carbides of the eutectic type. Upon aging at service temperatures, secondary chromium-rich carbides are precipitated in a fine dispersion within the austenite except in areas immediately adjacent to the eutectic carbides. This secondary precipitation results in an increase in the room-temperature strength of the alloy with no significant change in ductility. Alloy HW castings are not hardenable by heat treatment and are normally applied in the as-cast condition.

HX Alloy. Alloy HX is a nickel-base alloy nominally containing 18Cr-65Ni-0.35 to 0.75C. The alloy has no wrought counterpart. Alloy HX is more resistant to hot-gas corrosion than alloy HW at elevated temperatures up to 1150°C by virtue of its higher chromium and nickel contents. The additional chromium in the HX composition also confers resistance to sulfur-bearing reducing gases at high temperatures. In addition to greater corrosion resistance, alloy HX possesses high-temperature strength and resistance to carburization and thermal fatigue equivalent to those of the HW alloy. The microstructures of alloy HX in the as-cast and aged conditions are quite like those of alloy HW. Alloy HX castings are not hardenable by heat treatment and are normally furnished in the as-cast condition.

REFERENCES

1. Guillet, L.: Nickel-Chrome Steels, *Rev. Metall.*, (Paris) vol. 3, pt. 1, p. 332, 1906.
2. Zapffe, C.: "Stainless Steels," American Society for Metals, Cleveland, 1949.
3. Giesen, W.: The Special Steels in Theory and Practice, *Iron and Steel Inst.*, *Carnegie Scholarship Mem.*, vol. 1, p. 1, 1901.
4. Monnartz, P.: The Study of Iron-Chromium Alloys With Special Consideration of Their Resistance to Acids, *Metallurgie* (Paris), vol. 8, p. 161, 1911.
5. Maurer, E., and B. Strauss: German Patent 304,126, October, 1912; 304,159, December, 1912; British Patents 15,414 and 15,415, June, 1913.
6. Colombier, L., and J. Hochmann: "Stainless and Heat Resisting Steels," St Martin's Press, New York, 1968.
7. Avery, H.: Metallographic Technique for Fe-Cr-Ni Heat Resisting Casting Alloys, "Metals Handbook," vol. 8, p. 104, American Society for Metals, Metals Park, Ohio, 1973.
8. Blower, R., and G. Cox: Formation of σ Phase in Cast Austenitic Steels and Its Effect on Room- and Elevated-Temperature Mechanical Properties, *J. Iron Steel Inst. London*, p. 769, 1970.
9. Fontana, M., and N. Greene: "Corrosion Engineering," McGraw-Hill, New York, 1967.
10. Schoefer, E.: "High Alloy Data Sheets, Corrosion Series," Alloy Casting Institute Div., Steel Founders' Society of America, Cleveland, 1973.
11. Beck, F., E. Schoefer, J. Flowers, and M. Fontana: New Cast High-Strength Alloy Grades by Structure Control, in "Advances in the Technology of Stainless Steels and Related Alloys," *ASTM Spec. Tech. Publ. 369*, p. 159, 1965.
12. Microstructure of Fe-Cr-Ni Heat-resistant Casting Alloys, "Metals Handbook," vol. 7, p. 177, American Society for Metals, Metals Park, Ohio, 1972.
13. Spaeder, C., and K. Brickner: Modified Type 316 Stainless Steel With Low Tendency To Form Sigma, in "Advances in the Technology of Stainless Steels and Related Alloys," *ASTM Spec. Tech. Publ. 369*, p. 143, 1965.
14. Andrews, K.: A New Intermetallic Phase in Alloy Steels, *Nature*, vol. 164, p. 1015, 1949.
15. McMullin, J., S. Reiter, and D. Ebeling: Equilibrium Structures in Fe-Cr-Mo Alloys, *Trans. Am. Soc. Met.*, vol. 46, p. 799, 1954.
16. Goldschmidt, H.: *Trans. Am. Soc. Met.*, vol. 46, p. 807, 1954.
17. Schoefer, E.: Appendix to Mössbauer-Effect Examination of Ferrite in Stainless Steel Welds and Castings, *Weld. Res.*, vol. 39, p. 10-s, January 1974.
18. Schaeffler, A.: Constitution Diagram for Stainless Steel Weld Metal, *Met. Prog.*, p. 68-B, November, 1949.
19. Hull, F.: Delta Ferrite and Martensite Formation in Stainless Steels, *Weld. Res.*, vol. 38, p. 193-s, May, 1973.
20. Briggs, C. (ed.): "Steel Castings Handbook," Steel Founders' Society of America, Cleveland, 1970.
21. Schoefer, E., and T. Shields: "High Alloy Data Sheets, Heat Series," Alloy Casting Institute Div., Steel Founders' Society of America, Cleveland, 1973.

Chapter **11**

Effect of Chromium on the Structure and Properties of Stainless Steels

LEWIS P. MYERS

Supervisor, Stainless Steel Research, Carpenter Technology
Corporation, Reading, Pennsylvania

INTRODUCTION

Stainless steels are a broad class of alloys characterized by their resistance to corrosion at ambient temperature and resistance to scaling at high temperature. Stated another way, stainless steels show a degree of passivity which can approach noble behavior and which renders them suitable for use unprotected in environments that reduce more ordinary steels to a worthless state. The characteristics which identify a steel as stainless are imparted by chromium more so than by any other element. In some stainless steels, stainlessness or passivity is imparted solely by the addition of chromium. Other alloying elements, however, enhance the effect of chromium in many environments and impart many of the special properties which can be found among the scores of commercial stainless steels. Of the large number of factors which influence passivity Zapffe[1] has listed seven as having principal importance:

1. Chromium content
2. Oxidizing conditions
3. Chloride ion susceptibility (pitting)
4. Nickel content
5. Heat treatment (sensitization)
6. Carbon content
7. Molybdenum content

By and large the corrosion and oxidation resistance of stainless steels increases with increasing chromium content. The manner in which chromium imparts these characteristics has been the basis for both considerable speculation and work in the laboratory. The popular concept, which also has considerable scientific support,[42] is that chromium forms a thin adherent oxide which retards or effectively prevents further oxidation or corrosion. Environments which are oxidizing strengthen this film while those which are reducing tend to break down the film.

EFFECT ON MICROSTRUCTURE

Iron-Chromium System   Any attempt to show the broad effects of chromium on the constitution of stainless steels in a limited way must necessarily take a qualitative approach. These effects might best be illustrated by examining the influence of chromium in the absence of the austenite formers, on one hand, and in the presence of appreciable amounts of austenite formers on the other hand.

The influence of chromium on the structure of iron is shown by the constitution diagram in Fig. 1 which was prepared by Hansen[3] using data from numerous sources. Supplements by Elliot[4] and Shunk[5] to Hansen's work[3] show additional data on the Fe-Cr system. It is seen in Fig. 1 that increasing chromium decreases the range of temperature over which austenite exists until, at approximately 12% chromium, ferrite is stable at all temperatures to the solidus. The boundaries of the liquidus and solidus meet at 22% chromium and 1507°C (2744°F). In the Fe-Cr system austenite does not exist above 1390°C (2534°F) or below 830°C (1526°F).

Although iron containing in excess of 12% chromium is ferritic at all temperatures, commercial ferritic stainless steels containing up to as much as 27% chromium may contain some austenite at elevated temperatures because of the presence of carbon and nitrogen in small to moderate amounts.

The influence of chromium on the structure of iron containing 8% nickel, the third most common alloying element in stainless steels (after carbon), is seen in Fig. 2. The presence of 8% nickel has extended the austenite field to approximately 22% chromium and decreased the lowest temperature of the field to approximately 550°C (1022°F). Further increases in the nickel content or the addition of other austenite-stabilizing elements further expands the austenite field to higher chromium and higher and lower temperatures.

Iron-Chromium-Nickel System   The Fe-Cr-Ni system is known only semiquantitatively. However, precise information for a system composed of several pure elements and in a true state of equilibrium would seem to be of no increased usefulness with respect to identifying the structure of commercial alloys. A comprehensive review of the Fe-Cr-Ni system was made by Bain and Aborn.[25] Their study resulted in a series of semiquantitative diagrams which show the effect of nickel and temperature on structure at constant chromium content ranging from 0 to 24% as noted in Fig. 3.

Stabilization of Austenite   Figure 4 shows the influence of chromium on the minimum nickel content required for a stable austenitic structure in steels containing about 0.1% carbon. The decreasing nickel as chromium increases to about 18% and the subsequent rise in nickel with further increases in chromium has been noted to be the result of the formation of two conjugate solutions, one being ferrite and the other austenite. In this system the ferrite contains more chromium and less nickel than the average amount of these two elements in the steel whereas the austenite contains more nickel and less chromium.

The effect of chromium on the extent of the austenite in Fe-C alloys is seen in Fig. 5. The range of carbon and temperature within which austenite free of ferrite is obtained is diminished by chromium. In steels containing more than about 12% chromium, ferrite will be a permanent constituent in the absence of some significant amount of carbon.

Austenite–Austenite Plus Ferrite Boundary   In a study on the sensitization of austenitic stainless steels[58] the following relationship was found to express the boundary between the austenite and austenite plus ferrite fields for steels with a composition within the range of 18 to 25% chromium, 9 to 25% nickel, up to 0.05% carbon and up to 0.15% nitrogen:

$$30(\%C) + 26(\%N) + (\%Ni) - 1.3(\%Cr) + 11.1 = 0$$

EFFECT ON EMBRITTLEMENT

Sigma Phase   Hall and Algie[15] have presented a most extensive review of the sigma phase. Sigma phase was discovered by Bain and Griffiths in 1927,[41] but its structure was not identified until 1954. Since that time sigma phase has been shown to have a

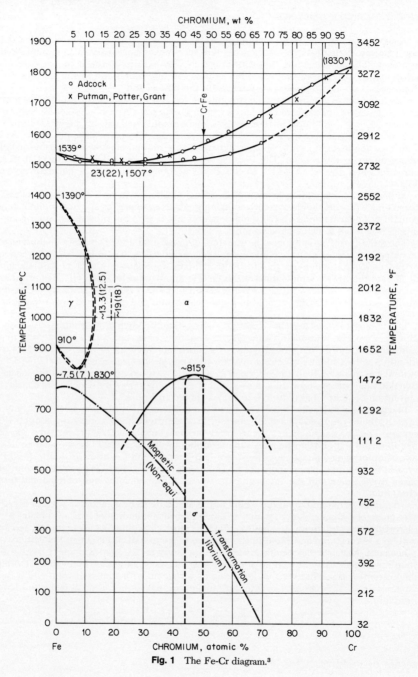

Fig. 1 The Fe-Cr diagram.[3]

complex tetragonal structure which reveals a degree of order in some alloys in that certain crystallographic sites are preferred by some elements.

Sigma phase forms in transition-alloy systems and is important primarily because of its deleterious effects on mechanical and corrosion properties. Significant effort has been made to determine the chromium limits of the sigma-phase field and the exact structure of component phase or phases. There is conflicting evidence regarding these. The commonly accepted diagram for sigma phase in the Fe-Cr system is that shown in Fig. 1.

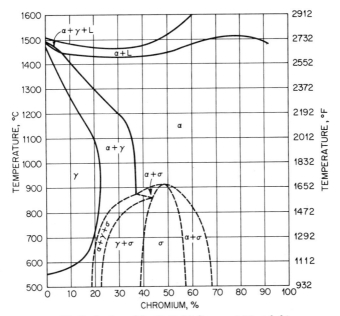

Fig. 2 Section of the Fe-Cr-Ni diagram at 8% nickel.[6]

Modifications of this diagram have been proposed wherein α and a chromium-rich precipitate designated α' are shown to exist below approximately 520°C (968°F).[9,43] In commercial ferritic stainless steels small amounts of other elements, particularly the ferrite stabilizers and notably silicon, widely expand the chromium range over which sigma will form.

Many of the common AISI austenitic stainless steels containing more than 17% chromium can develop sigma. In those steels which contain both austenite and ferrite sigma formation occurs within the ferrite, usually limiting its growth to the confines of the ferrite. In the completely austenitic steels, such as Type 310, sigma forms directly from the austenite usually along grain boundaries. In commercial stainless steels the occurrence of sigma phase and its extent is found to be favored by decreasing nickel-chromium ratios and increasing ferrite content.

For suitably heat-treated Cr-Ni-Fe alloys containing about 0.1% carbon, sigma phase can be expected for chromium contents above the curve *ABCD* in Fig. 6. The addition of molybdenum, silicon, niobium, titanium, and probably aluminum and tungsten, will shift curve *ABCD* to lower chromium levels. Between approximately 15 to 30% nickel, Fig. 6 also marks the approximate boundary between austenite and duplex structures of ferrite and austenite. The coincidence between this boundary and the sigma-phase boundary has been attributed to the fact that sigma forms more readily from ferrite than austenite.

Embrittlement of Chromium Steels (885°F-475°C)   Brittleness can occur in plain chromium stainless steels containing more than about 15% chromium during exposure to temperatures in the range of about 370 to 540°C (700 to 1000°F) with maximum embrittlement occurring at 475°C (885°F). The propensity for embrittlement increases with increasing chromium and time at temperature. Embrittlement of this nature is stated to be due to the formation of a body-centered cubic (bcc) compound of iron and chromium containing 70 to 80% chromium. Embrittlement which occurs on heating to a higher temperature, 605 to 799°C (1120 to 1470°F), is due to the precipitation of sigma phase.[10]

It has been noted that changes in impact and bend ductility representing a degree of

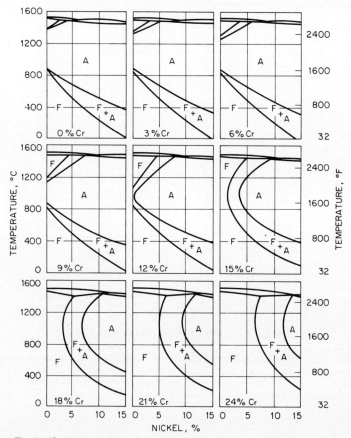

Fig. 3   The Fe-Cr-Ni diagram at constant chromium.[25] A = austenite, F = ferrite.

embrittlement have been observed for a 27% Cr steel after 1 h at 475°C (885°F) while severe embrittlement existed after 50 h. Changes in electrical resistivity, specific gravity, and magnetic coercive force have been noted to accompany embrittlement. Decreased resistance to acid attack (Fig. 7), increased grain-boundary attack, and the darkening of ferrite have also been observed as a result of 475°C (885°F) embrittlement.[52] The formation of a bcc chromium-rich precipitate has been noted to accompany embrittlement and provides the basis for an explanation for changes in structure and properties associated with the embrittlement.

Figure 8 shows the effect of long-time exposure to 482, 566, and 649°C (900, 1050, and 1200°F) on the impact strength of Types 410 (12Cr), 430 (17Cr), and 304 (18Cr-9Ni). The Type 430 was embrittled at the lower temperatures whereas the Type 410 was not appreciably affected. This difference between the two alloys is to be expected because of the higher chromium content and ferritic structure of the 430 alloy. Embrittlement occurred for the Type 304 with the higher exposure temperatures having the greater effect.

EFFECT ON TRANSFORMATION AND HARDENING

Transformation When cooled from the austenitizing temperature, chromium decreases the rate of transformation of the austenite to ferrite and carbides resulting in increased hardenability and air-hardening response. This effect of chromium is seen by comparing the isothermal transformation diagrams for a hardenable stainless steel against a carbon steel of similar carbon content (note Figs. 9 and 10, respectively).[38] The increase in hardenability results from the increased incubation time for the precipitation of carbides and ferrite and is seen as a shift to the right of the nose of the $A+F+C$ curve for the 12% Cr steel compared to the SAE 1008 steel.

Hardening Chromium increases the hardening temperature required for maximum quenched hardness from about 975°C (1787°F) for 12% chromium to 1100°C (2012°F) for 20% chromium.[31]

The effect of chromium on the constitution of 1-in.-diameter (25.4-mm) bar in the normalized condition is seen in Fig. 11. It is seen that there is a critical relationship between carbon content, chromium content, and air-hardening response, i.e., transformation to martensite on cooling from the normalizing temperature.

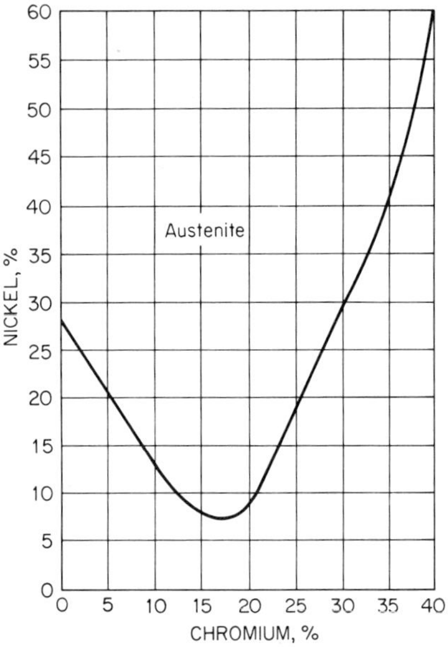

M_s **Temperature** The influence of chromium on M_s is dependent to a large extent on other elements present and no single equation describing the effect of chromium is applicable over a range of alloy systems.

In a base analysis containing 12% chromium, 0.1% carbon, and having an M_s of 300°C, Irvine, Crowe, and Pickering[12] stated that chromium depresses the M_s by 17°C for each 1%. However, this value along with the values given for other elements was regarded to be only indicative because of the influence of variations in the base composition.

Based on dilatometric measurements for 25 heats of stainless steels of selected composition, Eichelman and Hull[50] determined the effects of various alloying elements including chromium on M_s to be approximately as follows:

$$M_s\,(°F) = 75(14.6 - Cr) + 110(8.9 - Ni) + 60(1.33 - Mn) + 50(0.47 - Si) + 3000(0.068 - [C + N])$$

In listing the nickel equivalents of silicon, manganese, chromium, carbon, and nitrogen, chromium was given a value of 0.68. These conclusions were limited to alloys with the following compositional limits by weight percent:

10 – 18 chromium	0.3 – 2.6 silicon
6 – 12 nickel	0.004 – 0.12 carbon
0.6 – 5.0 manganese	0.01 – 0.06 nitrogen
	(Balance iron)

Fig. 4 The effect of chromium on the minimum nickel content required for a stable austenitic structure in steels containing about 0.1% carbon.[26]

EFFECT ON PHYSICAL PROPERTIES

Lattice Constants The effect of chromium on the lattice constant of Fe-Cr alloys rapidly quenched to prevent the precipitation of sigma phase has been reported by several researchers.[16,17] Independently determined results are in good agreement and show an increasing parameter with increasing chromium. In the range of 12 to 25%

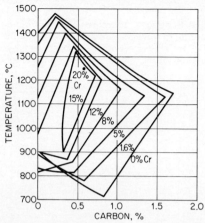

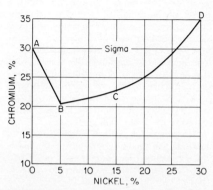

Fig. 5 The effect of chromium on the extent of austenite in Fe-Cr alloys.[32]

Fig. 6 Approximate Cr-Ni boundary for susceptibility to sigma formation in steels containing 0.1% carbon.[28]

chromium the rate of increase is relatively constant at approximately 1.5×10^{-4} Å per 1% chromium.

Specific Volume Adcock[18] observed that the specific volume of Fe-Cr alloys increases linearly with increasing chromium from 0 to 100%.

Thermal Expansion Over the chromium range found in stainless steels increasing chromium decreases the coefficient of thermal expansion for Fe-Cr alloys at a nearly constant rate at temperatures in the ferromagnetic range.[19] At higher temperatures which result in a nonferromagnetic condition, the coefficient was found to increase at a steady rate with increasing chromium.

Thermal Conductivity Shelton and Swanger[20] have shown that chromium markedly

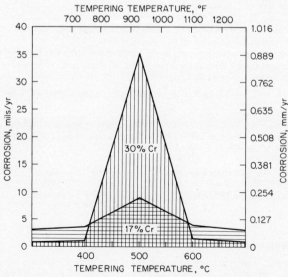

Fig. 7 Effect of 475°C (885°F) embrittlement on the corrosion resistance of 17 and 30% Cr steels in boiling 50% hydrochloric acid; steels tempered 1 h at the indicated temperature.[11]

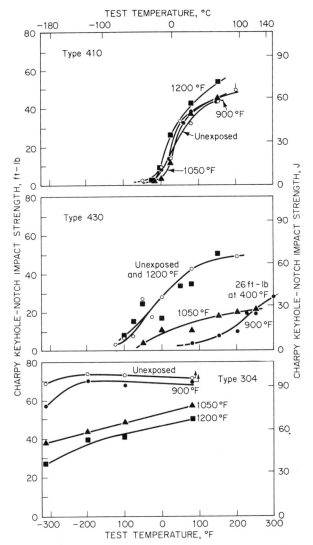

Fig. 8 Effect of 10,000 h at 482°C (900°F), 566°C (1050°F) and 649°C (1200°F) on the impact characteristics of Type 410 (12% Cr), 430 (17% Cr) and 304 (18Cr-8Ni).[40]

decreases the thermal conductivity of Fe-Cr alloys with the rate of decrease rapidly diminishing above about 12 to 15% chromium.

Electrical Resistivity Zapffe[2] reported that chromium increases the electrical resistivity of all stainless steels with the resistivity of the hardenable grades being four to six times that of mild steel.

Kinzel and Franks[8] stated that on the basis of care exercised in the preparation of test material, Adcock's data[18] for Fe-Cr alloys should be the most reliable of several investigators listed.

Modulus of Elasticity Chromium apparently lowers the modulus of elasticity from a typical value of 30×10^6 psi (206,843 MN/m^2) for mild steel to 28 to 29×10^6 psi (193,053 to 199,948 MN/m^2) for most quench-hardenable stainless steels.[2]

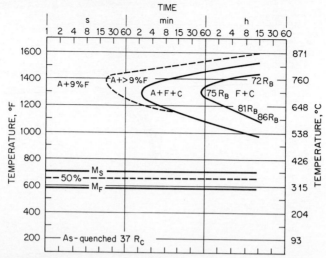

Fig. 9 Isothermal transformation diagram for 0.06C-12.5Cr stainless steel.[38]

EFFECT ON WORK HARDENING

In ferritic and hardenable stainless steels chromium has but a small effect on the rate of work hardening, i.e., a slight increase with increasing chromium, which results from the mild solid-solution effects[21] (strengthening) exerted by chromium.

In austenitic stainless steels Bloom, Goller, and Mabus[22] observed a large effect of chromium on cold-work-hardening rate depending on nickel content as illustrated in Fig. 12.

In combination with 12 to 18% nickel, greater than about 12% chromium was observed to have no more than a small effect as measured after 62.5% cold reduction by upsetting. At lower levels of nickel, increasing chromium markedly decreased the work-hardening factor as a result of its stabilizing effect on austenite, which was not a significant factor at the higher nickel level.

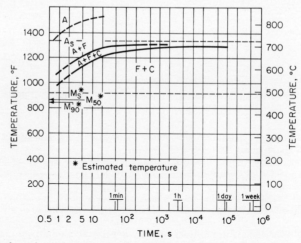

Fig. 10 Isothermal transformation diagram for SAE 1008 (0.06% carbon) rimmed steel.[38]

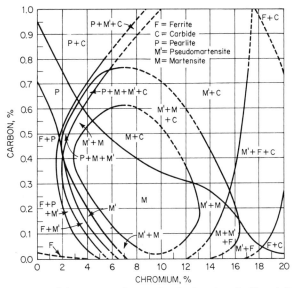

Fig. 11   Structure of chromium steels normalized in bars 1-in. (~25-mm) diameter.[13]

EFFECT ON CORROSION AND ATTACK BY GASES

Corrosion by H₂S   Data reported by Naumann[23] for chromium and chromium-nickel stainless steels indicate that the resistance of these steels to corrosion by hydrogen sulfide at elevated temperatures increases with increasing amounts of chromium up to approximately 25% (Table 1).

The laboratory results from a series of tests by Schafmeister and Naumann[33] on stainless steels showed that chromium increases the resistance of these steels, both with and without nickel, to attack by hot sulfuretted hydrogen. The increased resistance resulting

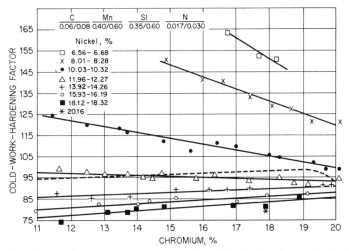

Fig. 12   The influence of chromium content on the cold-work hardening of austenitic stainless steels containing less than 0.08% carbon.[22]

TABLE 1   The Corrosion Rate of Chromium and Cr-Ni
Steels During 120 h in 100% H_2S at Atmospheric
Pressure[23]

| Material, % | Corrosion Rate, mils/yr (mm/yr) | |
	344°C (651°F)	500°C (932°F)
5Cr	240 (6.10)	1000 (25.40)
9Cr	200 (5.08)	700 (17.78)
12Cr	130 (3.30)	400 (10.16)
17Cr	90 (2.29)	200 (5.08)
25Cr		100 (2.54)
18Cr-9Ni	80 (2.03)	200 (6.10)
26Cr-20Ni	60 (1.52)	100 (2.54)

from increasing chromium in excess of about 14 to 16% is small but may be crucial at service temperatures in the vicinity of 500°C (932°F) or somewhat higher.

Carburization   Martin and Weir[24] showed that increasing the chromium content of a 9% Ni steel from 11 to 28% chromium increases the resistance of the steel to carburization by carbon dioxide at 776°C (1428°F) with the incremental effect of chromium in excess of 20% being quite small.

Resistance to Sulfur in Flue and Process Gases   Chromium increases the resistance of both ferritic and austenitic stainless steels to attack by combustion gases at elevated temperatures. Increased resistance in austenitic stainless steels to attack by sulfur vapor at elevated temperatures is obtained by increasing chromium to a level greater than 20%.

Oxidation Resistance   Binder and Brown[35] have shown that increasing chromium increases resistance to atmospheric corrosion with the amount of atmospheric corrosion by an industrial environment being minimal at about 13% chromium. Chromium increases resistance to oxidation at 1000°C (1832°F) in the manner shown in Fig. 13. According to McKay and Worthington,[37] steels with 18% chromium will retain most of their brightness during long exposure to average rural and urban atmospheres, are slightly stained in mild industrial atmospheres, and probably will be pitted by strongly sulfurous industrial and marine atmospheres.

The maximum temperatures resulting in no more than limited scaling after prolonged service as a function of chromium are shown in Table 2. These data are for medium-to-low carbon steels containing no appreciable amount of any alloying element other than chromium.

Monypenny[30] has noted that the effect of chromium on oxidation resistance may not be appreciably affected by nickel sufficient to result in an austenitic structure. In fact, an austenitic steel might show greater oxidation than a ferritic alloy with similar chromium because of the higher thermal expansion of the austenitic structure and the attendant spalling of the initially formed protective oxide.

A plot of the chromium content of a number of commercial steels against the maximum temperature without excessive scaling produces the curve in Fig. 14. The influence of chromium on resistance to high-temperature steam has been reported to be similar to that noted for high-temperature oxidation.[54]

Corrosion Resistance in Aqueous Solutions   The resistance to corrosion imparted by chromium is due to a state of passivity resulting from a protective chromium oxide. Chromium increases resistance to attack under conditions favorable to the formation of the protective film and can be deleterious in a reducing environment. Mason[39] has shown (Fig. 15) that the resistance of Cr-Fe alloys to corrosion by dilute nitric acid, an oxidizing environment, increases with increasing chromium while

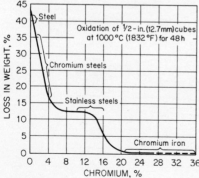

Fig. 13 Oxidation of chromium steels at 1000°C (1832°F).[14]

TABLE 2 The Influence of Chromium in Chromium Steels on the Maximum Temperature Without Appreciable Scaling in Air for Either Continuous or Intermittent Exposure[29]

Chromium, %	Maximum temperature without appreciable scaling	
	°C	°F
12	700–750	1292–1382
16	800–850	1482–1530
20	950–1000	1742–1832
25	1050–1100	1922–2012
30	1100–1150	2012–2102

in dilute sulfuric acid, a reducing environment, chromium decreases resistance to attack. When used for the handling of nitric acid, stainless steels generally contain 17 to 18 or possibly 20% chromium. Larger amounts may be required for special purposes or in high-temperature service.

Passivity Uhlig and Wulff [51] have presented a concept of passivity which states that the passive alloys and the transition and pretransition elements like chromium and nickel are passive and become more so if in contact with an oxidizing or electron-absorbing agent like nitric acid, or an adsorbed layer of oxygen atoms. On the other hand, these metals and alloys lose passivity if charged with hydrogen. The hydrogen, which tends to dissolve in the metal lattice as protons and electrons, is thought to fill in electronic energy levels of the lattice normally responsible, when unoccupied, for passivity. Removal of the hydrogen through exposure of the metal to air or an oxidizing medium causes the metal to change from an active to a passive state.

Resistance to Pitting Corrosion Monypenny[27] has concluded from an assemblage of data that raising the chromium from 12% or so to 16 to 18% is at least as effective in imparting resistance to corrosion by contaminated steam in turbines as adding 35% nickel at the lower level of chromium.

Corrosion by Molten Salt The influence of chromium in high carbon cast Fe-Ni-Cr alloys in molten salts is to decrease resistance to surface and intergranular corrosion, particularly when chromium is increased from 11% to the 20 or 30% level.[59]

Stress Corrosion The mechanism responsible for stress-corrosion cracking in Fe-Cr-Ni alloys has been extensively studied but as yet there seems to be little agreement as to the process responsible for the propagation of stress-corrosion cracks in these alloys. At the lower levels of chromium in stainless steels, chromium appears to increase resis-

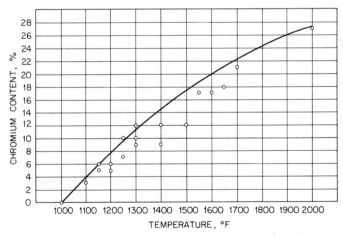

Fig. 14 Chromium required for freedom from significant oxidation at elevated temperatures.[54]

tance to stress-corrosion cracking. At higher levels of chromium (15 to 25%) resistance shows a decline. Latanision and Staehle[48] concluded that for Fe-Ni alloys containing 10 to 20% nickel, minimum resistance to stress-corrosion cracking lies somewhere in the range of 12 to 25% chromium. Despite some conflicting evidence, it is widely held that martensitic and ferritic alloys which do not contain nickel do not suffer to any significant extent from stress-corrosion cracking;[36] however, all martensitic steels at hardness levels above about Rockwell C 20 to 24 are susceptible to hydrogen cracking. In environments where hydrogen is thought to be liberated by cathodic corrosion, increasing chromium would be expected to impart increased resistance to hydrogen cracking through increased corrosion resistance.

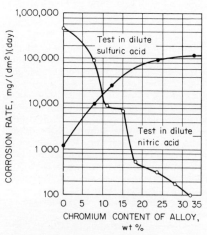

Fig. 15 The corrosion of Cr-Fe alloys in dilute sulfuric and nitric acids.[39]

Intergranular Corrosion The influence of chromium content is to increase the tolerance for carbon, i.e., the amount which will not result in appreciable intergranular attack after exposure of the steel to the sensitizing temperature range. For instance, tests on specimens sensitized 1 h at 650°C (1200°F) in boiling acidified copper sulfate solution indicated that increasing chromium from 18 to 25% in austenitic stainless steels containing 7 to 25Ni-0.015 to 0.05C-0.05N max. will increase the tolerance for carbon by a factor of approximately 3.[58]

Intergranular Corrosion After Welding Lula, Lena, and Keifer[62] noted that strips of ferritic stainless steels containing 16 to 28% chromium, principally Types 430, 442, and 446, showed no effect of chromium content on the influence of intergranular corrosion in the welded condition. Corrosion behavior was evaluated in two solutions: (1) 10% sulfuric acid plus 10% copper sulfate and (2) 65% boiling nitric acid.

Low-Carbon Steels Containing 10 to 18% Chromium Low-carbon (i.e., up to about 0.12%) chromium stainless steels are identified as belonging to one of two groups. The first, containing 10 to 14% chromium, responds to quench hardening. The second group, containing 15 to 18% chromium, is used as-annealed because it lacks a hardening response. In a broad sense, Type 410 represents the first group and Type 430 the second. The first provides limited corrosion and oxidation resistance in combination with high tensile strength [up to 200,000 psi (1379 MN/m²)] whereas the second provides higher corrosion and oxidation resistance but affords limited strength [70,000 to 90,000 psi (483 to 621 MN/m²) tensile].

Higher Chromium and Nickel Percentages Where corrosion and oxidation resistance, exceeding that of the 18Cr-8Ni steels are required, higher chromium-nickel steels are used. The higher alloy steels generally fall into one of two groups: the first contains 22 to 25% chromium plus 10 to 14% nickel and the second, 20 to 25% chromium plus 20 to 22% nickel. Carbon may be present up to 0.20 to 0.25% in the wrought condition and up to 0.50% in castings. In the annealed condition tensile and yield strengths of these alloys generally are somewhat higher than those of the 18-8 steels.[7]

EFFECT ON HOT-WORKING

The hot-working of stainless steels requires considerable care, particularly with respect to the choice of temperature. For the hardenable chromium stainless steels a suitable initial temperature is about 1175°C (2147°F). A lower initial temperature of 1038 to 1093°C (1900 to 2000°F) should be used for the ferritic stainless steels irrespective of chromium content because of the softness and excessive grain growth of these steels at high temperatures. Austenitic stainless steels are, in general, hot-worked from about the same temperatures as the hardenable steels. To a large degree, the hot-working temperature of stainless steels is predicated by the microstructure of the steel at the hot-working temperature.

Hot Workability of Austenitic Stainless Steels In a study on the effect of nickel, chromium, trace elements, ferrite, and ferrite factor (given below) on the hot workability of austenitic stainless steels, one of several conclusions listed was that chromium has a marked effect on the rollability of all grades of austenitic stainless steels, with the critical limits appearing to be 19% for 18-8 steels and 18% for 18Cr-10Ni-Mo and 18Cr-8Ni-Ti steels. When chromium exceeded these amounts, cracking was found to increase rapidly.[55] Ferrite factor was listed as Cr^1/Ni^1 where

$$Cr^1 = \%Cr + \%Mo + 3(\%Si) + 10(Ti)$$

where $Ti = \%Ti - 4(\%C)$

$$Ni^1 = \%Ni + \tfrac{1}{2}(\%Mn) + 21(\%C)$$

where $C = \%C - \tfrac{1}{4}(\%Ti)$.

EFFECT ON HEAT TREATMENT

Heat treatment of chromium stainless steels can be considered from three levels of chromium, i.e., 12, 15 to 21, and 21 to 27%.

In general, the 12% steels are hardenable depending on carbon content and are typically used in the hardened and tempered condition. Oil- or air-quenching from the hardening temperature is commonly used, with the oil producing higher hardness and the air minimizing the chance for cracking and warping. Full annealing of the hardenable stainless steels is accomplished by heating above the lower critical transformation temperature followed by slow cooling to 538 to 593°C (1000 to 1100°F) then air cooling to room temperature.

Stainless steels containing 15 to 21% chromium and low carbon are, to a large degree, ferritic at the low chromium end and totally ferritic at the higher chromium end. Being nonhardenable or only moderately so, heat treatment of the intermediate level chromium steels is generally limited to an anneal consisting of heating to 760 to 816°C (1400 to 1500°F) for a limited time followed by a moderate rate of cooling to room temperature.

Heat treatment of the higher chromium ferritic steels, i.e., over 21%, is similarly limited to an anneal. However, these steels are especially susceptible to embrittlement in the range of 427 to 760°C (800 to 1400°F). For this reason high-chromium stainless steels are annealed in the range of 760 to 927°C (1400 to 1700°F) followed by oil- or water-quenching. In some steels, such as Type 446 (27% chromium), nitrogen additions are used to overcome excessive grain growth.

Except in special instances heat treatment of the austenitic stainless steels, irrespective of the chromium content, is limited to annealing. For these grades annealing consists of heating to a temperature high enough to place the carbides in solution, except for the stabilized grades, but low enough to prevent extended grain growth, followed by cooling fast enough to prevent reprecipitation of carbides.[53]

Tempering. Chromium has been observed to increase resistance to tempering by decreasing the kinetics of the precipitation and growth of carbides in the matrix.

EFFECT ON STRENGTH

Fatigue Strength   Chromium is thought to have no effect on fatigue strength of steel.[38]

Wear Resistance   Chromium is reported to increase the wear resistance of martensitic stainless steels. In addition, a slight beneficial effect in ferritic and austenitic stainless steels can be expected due to solid-solution hardening.

Creep Strength   Reportedly, additions of chromium have little effect on creep strength.

Impact Strength   In general, the ferritic stainless steels have low impact strength and are relatively notch-sensitive at ambient temperature, especially when chromium is over about 20 to 21%. At 26 to 27% chromium, impact strength is no more than 2 to 3 ft-lb (2.7 to 4.1 J) at room temperature.

Binder and Spendelow[44] have shown that Cr-Fe alloys containing up to at least 35% chromium can achieve high room-temperature impact strength if carbon and nitrogen are decreased to critical low levels which are predicated by chromium content.

Small amounts of ferrite in martensitic stainless steels, due to either slightly increased chromium or decreased carbon, enhance impact strength but may be deleterious to fatigue strength. The common commercial ferritic stainless steels, however, show a decrease in impact strength with increasing chromium. For example, annealed Type 430 (17% chromium) has Charpy V-notch (CVN) transition temperature near room temperature, whereas Type 446 (27% chromium) has a CVN transition temperature of about 149°C (300°F).[53]

Strengthening Effects Chromium in the range of 12 to 22% has only a small, but important, strengthening effect on low-carbon chromium steels. Lacy and Gensamer[49] have listed the strengthening coefficient for chromium in iron as 1400 psi (9653 kN/m²) per 1% chromium up to 42% chromium content.

In the quenched and tempered condition, increases in chromium resulting in stable ferrite decrease hardness and tensile strength. Adcock[46] has shown that the hardness of low-carbon Fe-Cr alloys increases continuously with increasing chromium to about 70%. The influence of chromium on the tensile properties and hardness of annealed chromium steels containing 0.10% carbon is seen in Fig. 16.

It is reported[45] that the hardness and tensile strength of Cr-Fe alloys of high purity

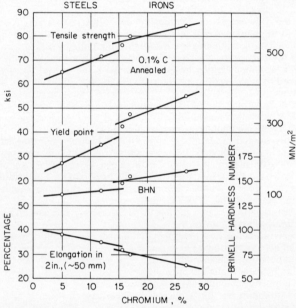

Fig. 16 The influence of chromium on the mechanical properties of annealed chromium steels containing 0.10% carbon.[47]

increase, while elongation decreases, with increasing chromium content to at least 55%. In the chromium range of most commercial stainless steels, i.e., 12 to 25 or 30%, the rate of change in these properties is approximately linear at about 0.9 points Rockwell B and 1100 psi (7584 kN/m²) per 1% chromium.

Elevated Temperature Properties The increased resistance to tempering imparted by chromium acts to enhance the elevated temperature strength of the martensitic stainless steels. In the nonhardenable grades, chromium contributes little to strength at the higher elevated temperatures. In high-temperature service the primary effect of chromium is to maintain the integrity of the steel by imparting resistance to oxidation.

In evaluating the effects of variations in chromium, nickel, and carbon plus nitrogen on the stress-rupture strength of 1093°C (2000°F) solution treated 18 Cr-8 Ni steels, it was observed that increases in the amount of chromium in solid solution (chromium ranging from about 11 to about 19%) had an important strengthening effect at temperatures of 538 to 704°C (1000 to 1300°F). Chromium, however, was found to be detrimental to high-temperature strength when the formation of sigma phase was promoted.[60]

EFFECT ON WELDING

The increase in hardenability attendant to the addition of chromium to carbon steel increases the susceptibility to hydrogen-induced cold cracking in the heat-affected zone (HAZ) of martensitic stainless steels.[56] In principle, ferritic stainless steels are easier to weld than the martensitics due to the absence of gross structural changes, but in reality, ferritics are susceptible to embrittlement because of grain growth at high temperatures and coarse columnar grains in the cast structure of the weld. The effect of grain growth is most pronounced in the high-chromium alloys, i.e., those with chromium content greater than 17%.

Microfissuring, which is found to occur in the welding of austenitic stainless steels, is effectively reduced or eliminated by the introduction of ferrite in the weld deposit through the use of higher chromium-containing filler metals such as Type 309.

CHROMIUM-NICKEL-MANGANESE AUSTENITIC STAINLESS STEELS

Renshaw and Lula[34] conducted a study of the influence of alloying elements on the corrosion properties of a series of Cr-Ni-Mn austenitic steels including AISI Types 201, 202, 204, 204L, and 20Cr-6Ni-8Mn and found that increasing chromium has a beneficial effect, as might be expected. A steel containing nominally 20Cr-5.5Ni-9Mn-0.2 to 0.4 N and low carbon was noted to resist boiling 65 wt % nitric acid in a manner comparable to Type 304. There was no marked effect of chromium between 17 and 20% in boiling glacial acetic acid and room-temperature sulfurous acid. In mild environments, such as citric and phosphoric acids, Types 201 and 202 are reportedly equal to Types 301 and 302. In strong organic acids such as boiling 50% lactic, corrosion resistance appeared to be a function of chromium content. A chromium content of 20% was inadequate to obtain satisfactory resistance to 10% oxalic acid at 93°C (200°F). Salt spray tests showed a significant beneficial effect of increasing chromium from about 15% to the 20% level. It was further concluded that the Cr-Ni-Mn austenitic stainless steels are subject to stress-corrosion cracking like the Cr-Ni steels and that stress-corrosion resistance does not appear to be influenced by chromium, nickel, or manganese provided the structure is austenitic.

PRECIPITATION-HARDENABLE STAINLESS STEELS

Chromium in precipitation-hardenable (PH) stainless steels imparts resistance to oxidizing and chloride environments and can have some beneficial effect in mildly reducing environments depending on the alloy content of nickel, copper, and molybdenum. Increased resistance to hydrogen embrittlement can be expected for increased levels of chromium, resulting in decreased cathodic corrosion.

Chromium content has a major influence on the PH stainless steels and must be controlled in conjunction with overall alloy levels to a greater extent than with most other martensitic and austenitic stainless steels. For instance, a review of a number of the recent developments reveals that chromium plus nickel or nickel equivalent is usually maintained in the range of 20 to 23 with chromium ranging from about 10 to 16%. Increases in chromium at the 10 to 14% level without an adjustment in the nickel content will result in excess stable austenite while increases at the 15 to 16% level will result in ferrite or ferrite plus stable austenite.

Chromium has little direct influence on the aging response and strength of these steels in the normal heat-treated conditions.

Precipitation-hardenable stainless steels may show thermal instability, i.e., increased strength and decreased toughness and ductility, when held for long periods in the range of 315 to 480°C (600 to 900°F). This type of aging behavior is generally considered to increase with increasing chromium. Susceptibility to thermal instability can be controlled to a large degree, however, by careful selection of the initial heat treatment.

REFERENCES

1. Zapffe, C. A.: "Stainless Steels," p. 36, American Society for Metals, Cleveland, 1949.
2. *Ibid.*, pp. 147–188.

3. Hansen, P. M.: "Constitution of Binary Alloys," 2d ed., pp 525–532, McGraw-Hill, New York, 1958.
4. Elliott, R. P.: "Constitution of Binary Alloys, First Supplement," pp. 345–346, McGraw-Hill, New York, 1965.
5. Shunk, F. A.: "Constitution of Binary Alloys, Second Supplement," pp. 269–270, McGraw-Hill, New York, 1969.
6. Kinzel, A. B., and R. Franks: "Alloys of Iron and Chromium," p. 274, vol. II, McGraw-Hill, New York, 1940.
7. Ibid., pp. 302–360.
8. Ibid., pp. 94–96.
9. Williams, R. O.: "Further Studies of the Iron-Chromium System," Trans. Am. Inst. Min. Metall. Pet. Eng., vol. 212, pp. 497–502, 1958.
10. "The Making, Shaping and Treating of Steel," 8th ed., pp. 1131–1140, United States Steel Corp., Pittsburgh, Pa., 1964.
11. Bandel, G., and W. Tofaute: Brittleness of High Chromium Steels Near 500°C, Techn. Mitt. Krupp Forschungsber., vol. 4, 1941.
12. Irvine, K. I., D. J. Crowe, and F. B. Pickering: The Physical Metallurgy of 12% Chromium Steels, J. Iron Steel Inst. London, vol. 195, pp. 386–405, August 1960.
13. Crafts, W.: Chromium in Steel, p. 460, "Metals Handbook," American Society For Metals, Cleveland, Ohio, 1948.
14. Ibid., p. 461, Fig. 10, (after MacQuigg).
15. Hall, E. O., and S. H. Algie: The Sigma Phase, Metall. Rev., vol. 11, pp. 61–88, 1966.
16. Preston, G. D.: X-ray Examination of Chromium Iron Alloys, Appendix I to paper by F. Adcock, J. Iron Steel Inst. London, vol. 124, pp. 139–141, 1931.
17. Andersen, A. G. H., and E. R. Jette: X-ray Investigation of the Iron-Chromium-Silicon Phase Diagram, Trans. Am. Soc. Met., vol. 24, pp. 375–419, 1936.
18. Adcock, F.: The Chromium-Iron Constitutional Diagram (Part X of Alloys of Iron Research), J. Iron Steel Inst. London, vol. 124, pp. 99–149, 1931.
19. Chevenard, P.: Experimental Investigation of Iron-Nickel-Chromium Alloys, Trav. Mem. Bur. Int. Poids Mes., vol. 17, p. 144, 1927.
20. Shelton, S. M., and W. H. Swanger: Thermal Conductivity of Irons and Steels and Some Other Metals in the Temperature Range 0 to 600°C, Trans. Am. Soc. Steel Treat, vol. 21, pp. 1061–1078, 1933.
21. Gensamer, M., and C. E. Lacy: The Tensile Properties of Alloy Ferrites, Trans. Am. Spc. Met., vol. 32, pp. 88–104, 1944.
22. Bloom, F. K., G. N. Goller, and P. G. Mabus: The Cold Work Hardening Properties of Stainless Steel in Compression, Trans. Am. Soc. Met., vol. 39, pp. 843–867, 1947.
23. Naumann, F. K.: Chem. Fabr., vol. 11, p. 365, 1938.
24. Martin, W. R., and J. R. Weir: J. Nucl. Mater., vol. 16, 1965.
25. Bain, E. C., and R. H. Aborn: The Iron-Nickel-Chromium System, "Metals Handbook," pp. 418–422, American Society for Metals, Cleveland, Ohio, 1939.
26. Monypenny, J. H. G.: "Stainless Iron and Steel," vol. I, 3d ed. rev., p. 69, Chapman and Hall, London, 1951.
27. Ibid., pp. 447–448.
28. Ibid., p. 90, Fig. 20.
29. Ibid., p. 367.
30. Ibid., p. 380.
31. Monypenny, J. H. G.: "Stainless Iron and Steel," vol. I, 2d ed. rev., p. 575, Wiley, New York, 1931.
32. Monypenny, J. H. G.: "Stainless Iron and Steel," vol. 2, 3d ed. rev., p. 36, Chapman and Hall, London, 1954.
33. Schafmeister and Naumann: Tech. Mitt. Krupp, p. 100, June, 1935.
34. Renshaw, W. G., and R. A. Lula: The Corrosion Properties of Chromium-Nickel-Manganese Austenitic Stainless Steels, Am. Soc. Test. Mater. Proc., vol. 56, pp. 866–889, 1956.
35. Binder, W. O., and C. M. Brown: Atmospheric Corrosion Tests on High-Chromium Steels, Am. Soc. Test. Mater. Proc., vol. 46, pp. 593–608, 1946.
36. Lillys, P., and A. E. Nehrenberg: Effect of Tempering Temperature on Stress-Corrosion Cracking and Hydrogen Embrittlement of Martensitic Stainless Steels, Trans. Am. Soc. Met., vol. 48, pp. 327–355, 1956.
37. McKay, R. J., and R. Worthington: "Corrosion Resistance of Metals and Alloys," p. 492, Reinhold, New York, 1936.
38. Brickner, K. G.: Stainless Steels for Room and Cryogenic Temperatures, in "Selection of Stainless Steels," pp. 1–29, American Society for Metals, Metals Park, Ohio, 1968.
39. Mason, J. F., Jr.: Corrosion Resistance of Stainless Steels in Aqueous Solutions, in "Selection of Stainless Steels," p. 67, American Society for Metals, Metals Park, Ohio, 1968.
40. Parker, T. D.: Strength of Stainless Steels at Elevated Temperature, in "Selection of Stainless Steels," p. 57, American Society for Metals, Metals Park, Ohio, 1968.

41. Bain, E. C., and W. E. Griffiths: An Introduction to the Iron-Chromium-Nickel Alloys, *Trans. Am. Inst. Min. Metall. Pet. Eng.*, vol. 75, pp. 166–211, 1927.
42. Rhodin, T. N.: Oxide Films Composition Studies, *Ann. NY Acad. Sci.*, vol. 58, pp. 855–872, 1954.
43. Williams, R. O., and H. W. Paxton: The Nature of Aging of Binary Iron-Chromium Alloys Around 500°C, *J. Iron Steel Inst. London*, vol. 185, p. 358, 1957.
44. Binder, W. O., and H. R. Spendelow, Jr.: The Influence of Chromium on the Mechanical Properties of Plain Chromium Steels, *Trans. Am. Soc. Met.*, vol. 43, pp. 759–777, 1951.
45. *Ibid.*, p. 763, Fig. 2.
46. Adcock, F.: The Chromium-Iron Constitutional Diagram, *J. Iron and Steel Inst. London*, vol. 124, no. II, pp. 99–146, 1931.
47. Thum, E. E.: Corrosion Resisting Steels for High Strength, *Met. Prog.*, vol. 6, pp. 49–57, June 1936.
48. Latanision, R. M., and R. W. Staehle: *Proc. Conf. Fundamental Aspects of Stress-Corrosion Cracking*, NACE, Houston, Texas, 1969.
49. Lacy, C. E., and M. Gensamer: Properties of Alloyed Ferrites, *Trans. Am. Soc. Met.*, vol. 32, pp. 88–110, 1944.
50. Eichelman, G. H., Jr., and F. C. Hull: The Effect of Composition on the Temperature of Spontaneous Transformation of Austenite to Martensite in 18-8 Type Stainless Steel, *Trans. Am. Soc. Met.*, vol. 45, pp. 77–104, 1953.
51. Uhlig, H. H., and J. Wulff: The Nature of Passivity in Stainless Steels and Other Alloys, I and II, *Trans. Am. Inst. Min. Metall. Pet. Eng.*, vol. 135, pp. 494–521, 1939.
52. Fisher, R. M., E. J. Dulis, and K. G. Carroll: Identification of the Precipitate Accompanying 885°F Embrittlement in Chromium Steel, *Trans. Am. Inst. Min. Metall. Pet. Eng.*, vol. 197, pp. 690–695, May 1953.
53. "The Making, Shaping and Treating of Steel," 9th ed., chap. 46, pp. 1163–1191, United States Steel Corp., Pittsburgh, Pa., 1971.
54. *Ibid.*, p. 1196.
55. Stokowiec, Z., C. G. Holland, A. H. Dean, and A. C. Everill: Effect of Composition Balance and Trace Elements on the Hot Workability of Austenitic Stainless Steels, in "Stainless Steels," pp. 17–23, *Iron Steel Inst. London Publ. 117*, 1969.
56. Gooch, T. G.: Welding Metallurgy of Stainless Steel, in "Stainless Steels," pp. 77–84, *Iron Steel Inst. London Publ. 117*, 1969.
57. Marsh, A. E.: Role of High-Alloy Steels in Elevated Temperature Environments, in "Stainless Steels," pp. 167–188, *Iron Steel Inst. London Publ. 117*, 1969.
58. Binder, W. O., C. M. Brown, and R. Franks: Resistance to Sensitization of Austenitic Chromium-Nickel Steels of 0.03% Max. Carbon Content, *Trans. Am. Soc. Met.*, vol. 41, pp. 1301–1346, 1949.
59. Jackson, J. H., and M. H. LaChance: Resistance of Cast Fe-Ni-Cr Alloys to Corrosion in Molten Neutral Heat Treating Salts, *Trans. Am. Soc. Met.*, vol. 46, pp. 157–183, 1954.
60. Monkman, F. C., P. E. Price, and N. J. Grant: The Effect of Composition and Structure on the Creep Rupture Properties of 18-8 Stainless Steels, *Trans. Am. Soc. Met.*, vol. 48, pp. 418–445, 1956.
61. Uhlig, H. H.: "Corrosion Handbook," pp. 663–664, Wiley, New York, Chapman and Hall, London, 1948.
62. Lula, R. A., A. J. Lena, and G. C. Kiefer: Intergranular Corrosion of Ferritic Stainless Steels, *Trans. Am. Soc. Met.*, vol. 46, pp. 197–230, 1954.
63. Kinzel, A. B., and R. Franks: "Alloys of Iron and Chromium," pp. 228–260, vol. II, McGraw-Hill, New York, 1940.

Chapter **12**

Effect of Nickel on the Structure and Properties of Wrought and Cast Stainless Steels

EDWIN SNAPE
Research Manager, Paul D. Merica Research Laboratory, The
International Nickel Company, Sterling Forest, Suffern, New York

INTRODUCTION

Twenty years ago Monypenny[1] made the observation that nickel was the most important metal deliberately added to high-chromium steels to improve properties. In the ensuing years, nickel has assumed even greater importance. In 1969 alone, nickel stainless steel ingot production in the United States exceeded 1 million tons. Nickel contained in the stainless steel was well over 200 million lb. Because nickel is such an important ingredient in stainless steels, there is a wealth of information on its effects on properties. For ease of reference the effects of nickel in ferritic, martensitic, austenitic, and duplex stainless steels will be treated separately here after a general discussion of the effects of nickel on microstructure.

EFFECT OF NICKEL ON MICROSTRUCTURE

Austenite–Austenite plus Ferrite Phase Boundary The presence of other major and minor elements in commercial stainless steels which influence the position of the austenite–austenite plus ferrite phase boundary makes accurate predictions of the effect of nickel per se on microstructure very difficult. As shown in Figs. 1 and 2, the influence of nickel can be qualitatively depicted by comparing diagrams corresponding to a given chromium content and increasing nickel content.

Progressive additions of nickel displace the delta ferrite zone to higher temperatures and increase the amount of austenite formed at higher temperatures. The stability of the austenite is also increased by nickel so that at about 8% nickel an austenitic structure persists at room temperature. As shown in Fig. 3, with chromium contents above or below about 18%, increasing amounts of nickel are required to ensure that fully austenitic structures are obtained at room temperature.

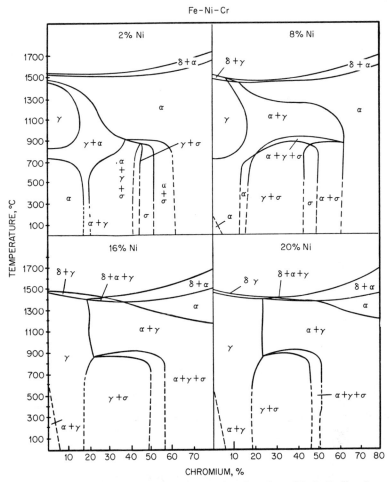

Fig. 1   Effect of nickel content on the gamma-phase boundary of Fe-Cr-Ni alloys.[2]

Figure 4 shows a diagram constructed from several phase analyses[5-9] of wrought stainless steels subjected to conventional annealing treatments. This diagram shows the nickel level required to give a fully austenitic structure (curve *AB*) and the nickel level required for stable austenite (curve *AC*). The data were obtained from steels with carbon contents up to about 0.1%, nickel contents ranging from 0 to 35%, and chromium contents from 15 to 35%. Thus, Fig. 4 should serve as an approximate guide to the effect of nickel on the microstructure of commercial stainless steels subjected to conventional processing. The amount of nickel required to stabilize austenite (curve *AC*) decreases to about 4.5% at 25% chromium. Curve *AC* passes through a minimum because as chromium content increases to about 25%, the amount of nickel needed to provide a duplex (as opposed to a fully ferritic) structure increases slightly. At 30% chromium, more than 5% nickel is required to provide a duplex structure.

In an attempt to account for the presence of alloying elements commonly found in stainless steels, various investigators have proposed empirical equations to determine the nickel level required to develop a fully austenitic structure at room temperature. For example, Post and Eberly[10] proposed an equation of the form

$$Ni = \frac{(Cr + 1.5Mo - 20)^2}{12} - \frac{Mn}{2} - 35C + 15$$

This equation was thought to be valid for the following range of compositions:

C 0.03–0.2%
Mn 0.4–4.0%
Si 0.3–0.5%
Cr 14–25%
Ni 7.5–21%
Mo 0–3%

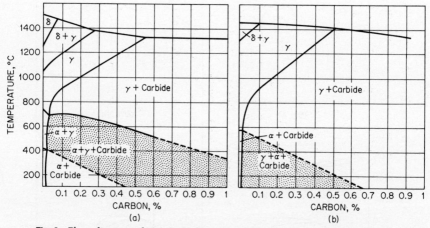

Fig. 2 Phase diagrams of 18% Cr steels containing *(a)* 4% nickel and *(b)* 8% nickel.[3]

If the nickel content is greater than the summation of the elements on the right-hand side of the equation, the homogenized alloy could be expected to be fully austenitic.

Binder, Brown, and Franks[7] proposed the following alternative equation for determining the minimum nickel content to obtain a fully austenitic structure in steels containing appreciable nitrogen:

$$\%Ni = 1.3(\%Cr) - 30(\%C) - 26(\%N_2) - 11.1$$

This equation was found to be valid within the following composition limits:

C 0–0.05%
N$_2$ 0–0.15%
Cr 18–25%
Ni 9–25%

Since castings are less homogeneous than wrought alloys, different equations have been developed to predict the nickel content needed for a completely austenitic structure. For weld deposits, Thomas[11] proposed the following equation:

$$Ni = 1.1(Cr + Mo + 1.5Si + 0.5Cb) - \frac{Mn}{2} - 30C - 8.2$$

Sigma Phase Colombier and Hochmann[3] concluded that nickel displaces the sigma-forming range to lower chromium contents and higher temperatures. Schafmeister and Ergang[12] speculated that this was due to the ability of the sigma phase to absorb as much as 10% nickel. Oliver[13] claimed that nickel raised the temperature range for sigma formation from 1500 to 1700°F (815 to 926°C). Nickel does not promote sigma formation to the same degree as does manganese or the strong ferrite-forming elements such as molybdenum, silicon, and aluminum. In fact, it is generally felt that sigma formation becomes increasingly difficult as the nickel content exceeds about 30%.[12,14] Pryce and Andrews[8] suggested that nickel reduces the tendency for sigma formation under some conditions.

M_s Temperature   In carbon-hardened, martensitic stainless steels the effect of nickel on the temperature of transformation of austenite to martensite can have important practical consequences. For example, nickel additions have been used to intensify the hardening capacity of cutlery steels and to enhance corrosion resistance. The presence of too much nickel in such steels would result in the retention of soft austenite. In studies of 18Cr-8Ni and 12Cr-10Ni stainless steels, Eichelman and Hull[15] found that nickel influenced M_s temperature according to the following relationship:

$$M_S = 75(14.6 - Cr) + 110(8.9 - Ni) + 60(1.33 - Mn) + 50(0.47 - Si) + 3000[0.068 - (C + N)]$$

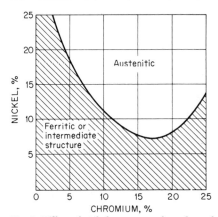

Fig. 3   Effect of nickel content on boundary of metastable austenite for 0.1% C steels rapidly cooled from 1100°C (2012°F).[4]

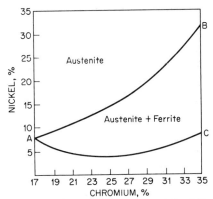

Fig. 4   Nickel content required to provide a fully austenitic structure (curve *AB*) and stable austenite (curve *AC*) in stainless steels subjected to conventional hot-working and annealing schedules. (Constructed from data in Ref. 5 to 9.)

Figure 5 shows the effect of increasing nickel content from 4 to 12% on the M_s temperature of an 18Cr-0.04C carbon steel.[3] Nickel is more potent than chromium or manganese in decreasing M_s temperature.

EFFECT OF NICKEL ON PROPERTIES OF FERRITIC STAINLESS STEELS

Melting   Besabrasow and Samarin[16] determined oxygen solubility in Fe-Cr-Ni baths containing 20% chromium and 30% chromium at 1520°F (826°C) and 1620°F (881°C) as a function of iron and nickel content (Fig. 6). Their results indicate that as nickel is substituted for iron, oxygen solubility decreases.

Hot Workability   Nickel has little effect on hot workability, provided a completely ferritic structure persists at the hot-working temperature. However, as exemplified by work on microduplex stainless steels,[17] when nickel content is increased to the point where austenite is formed at the hot-working temperature, the power required to produce a given amount of deformation is increased and, in the absence of titanium, edge cracking may occur.

High-Temperature Corrosion and Scaling Temperature   Data on the effect of nickel on oxidation behavior are inconclusive. In reviewing the oxidation behavior of Fe-Cr alloys, Wood[18] claimed that relatively small amounts of nickel (<0.5%) increase oxidation resistance. This was attributed to restricted diffusion of iron or chromium to the alloy-scale interface due to segregation of nickel in the subscale. He further stated that in those cases where oxidation resistance is due to a Cr_2O_3 film, the presence of Ni^{2+} would be expected to reduce oxidation rate. Other workers claim that nickel has no effect on high-temperature corrosion[19] or scaling resistance unless a fully austenitic structure is obtained. Sharp[20] found that addition of as little as 0.14% nickel to an 18% Cr steel actually doubled the oxidation rate. However, since base compositions were not given, this may not be the effect of nickel per se. Oxidation resistance was further reduced as the nickel content was in-

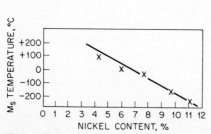

Fig 5   Effect of nickel on M_s temperature of an 18Cr–0.04C steel.[3]

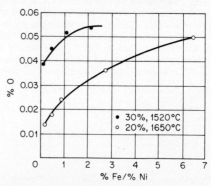

Fig. 6   Effect of nickel on oxygen solubility in molten 30% Cr and 20% Cr steels at 1520 and 1650°C (2768 and 3002°F) respectively.[16]

creased to about 8% (Table 1). Similarly, the corrosion of commercial ferritic steels in oil-fired power stations has been reported by Jackson[21] to increase as small amounts of nickel are added.

TABLE 1   Oxidation of Fe-Cr-Ni Alloys at 1123° K[20]

| Alloy | | Oxidation weight gain, mg/m² | | | | | |
| Ni | Cr | 5 h | | 10 h | | 40 h | |
		Mean	Range	Mean	Range	Mean	Range
<0.005	19.30	1.31	0.42	2.36	1.62	2.60	1.34
0.14	18.25	4.00	2.95	4.99	1.95	7.43	2.22
7.95*	18.2	8.84	2.88	10.34	1.22	11.92	0.64
13.85*	17.8	10.11	0.63	13.46	1.91	20.41	1.81

*Austenitic at 1123°K (850°C).

Room-Temperature Mechanical Properties   The potent toughening influence of nickel in ferritic stainless steels has not gone unnoticed. Several steel companies in Europe have exploited this beneficial effect of nickel for at least 30 years. For example, a 26Cr-0.08C-0.2Mn-0.6Si-4Ni-2Mo steel was developed in Sweden for use in the paper industry.[22] Improved bending properties and impact toughness were cited as advantages over straight chromium steels with similar chromium content. More recent accounts of the effect of nickel on toughness of high-chromium ferrite can be found in the work of Floreen and Hayden[5] and MacDonald.[23] Addition of 6% nickel to a vacuum-melted 25% Cr steel lowered the ductile-brittle transition temperature by more than 200°F (93°C) (Fig. 7). Since the effect of nickel was more pronounced than is commonly observed in low-alloy steel ferrites, the authors speculated that nickel reduced susceptibility to embrittlement during cooling from the annealing temperature. A similar effect of nickel on the ductile-brittle transition temperature was observed by MacDonald[23] in the case of vacuum-induction-melted and electron-beam-melted 30% Cr steel (Fig. 8). He found that an addition of 2% nickel to a vacuum-induction-melted 30% Cr steel had the same effect on room-temperature toughness and the brittle-to-ductile transition temperature as electron-beam refining of a nickel-free 30% Cr steel. Church[24] studied the effect of manganese, cobalt, and nickel on the toughness of cast, air-melted 26% Cr steel. Only nickel significantly improved toughness (Fig. 9).

Regarding the effect of nickel on strength, Snape[25] noted that nickel significantly increased room-temperature strength of electron-beam-melted 26Cr-1Mo steel. Addition of 2.5% nickel increased yield strength from about 48 to 65 ksi (331 to 448 MN/m²). This data (Table 2) contradicts speculation by Thielsch[26] that nickel would have little effect on room-temperature strength. The use of nickel to promote intermetallic precipitation in ferritic stainless steels has been discussed by Aronsson and Manenc,[27] Hughes,[28] Hopkin,[29] and Pickering.[30] Age-hardening of 25% Cr steels by nickel, aluminum, and titanium produced hardness values greater than R$_c$ 50.[30] However, impact toughness was very low.

TABLE 2   Effect of Nickel on Yield Strength of EB Melted Ferritic Stainless Steels[25]

Steel	Yield stress, (0.2% offset)		Ultimate tensile strength		Elongation, %	Reduction of area, %
	ksi	MN/m²	ksi	MN/m²		
27Cr-0.7Mo-0Ni	48.5	334.4	56.7	390.8	44	67
27Cr-0.7Mo-2.5Ni	66.3*	457.1	77.0	530.8	37	68
	61.3	422.6				

*Yield point.

Fatigue Strength   A comparison of handbook data on Type 446 stainless steel[31] with data obtained by Gibson et al.[17] suggests that nickel has little influence on fatigue properties.

Elevated Temperature Mechanical Properties   A patent by Wylie[32] discussed the use of nickel in conjunction with molybdenum and/or copper to increase the high-temperature strength of steels containing 14 to 17% chromium and 0.03% carbon. Although the steels were described as ferritic, it is probable that they had a room-temperature structure consisting of ferrite and a low-carbon martensite. Results obtained by Coffin and Swisher,[33] in terms of stress for a flow rate of 1% per 100,000 h at 840°F (448°C), showed that nickel had no effect on creep strength of 12% Cr steels.

Regarding 885°F (473°C) embrittlement, Colombier and Hochmann[3] stated that nickel is harmful but gave no supporting evidence. However, Guyaev et al.[34] demonstrated that nickel accelerated 885°F (473°C) embrittlement of 21% Cr steels when the steels were in a completely ferritic state. They speculated that nickel reduced the temperature at which precipitation processes occur and that ordering reactions and precipitation occurred simultaneously in the presence of nickel. The embrittling effect of nickel was apparently

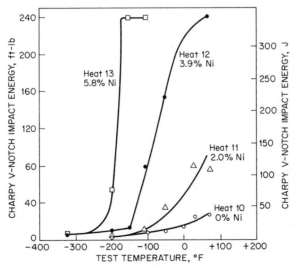

Fig. 7   Effect of nickel on Charpy V-notch (CVN) impact toughness of vacuum-melted 25% Cr steels.[5]

less pronounced when austenite was present in the microstructure. Bandel and Tofaute[35] also claimed that nickel increased 885°F (473°C) embrittlement.

Cold Fabricability The potent effect of nickel in lowering the ductile-to-brittle transition temperature is manifest in cold-working. For example, a 32Cr-4Ni-2Mo steel studied by Bieber[36] was cold-workable by virtue of the nickel content. However, in view of the effect of nickel in increasing annealed strength and increasing work-hardening rate, nickel probably increases the power requirements for a given amount of cold reduction.

With regard to formability, Waxweiler[37] claimed that the tendency to ridging in steels

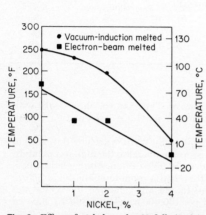

Fig. 8 Effect of nickel on the 60 ft-lb (81.3J) brittle-to-ductile transition temperature of 30% Cr steels.[23]

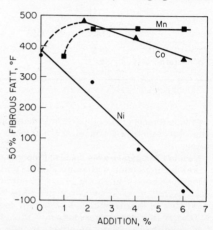

Fig. 9 The effect of nickel, manganese, and cobalt on the impact transition temperature of 26% Cr ferritic stainless steel. All specimens water-quenched after 2 h at 2100°F (1148°C) (Ni series) or 2200°F (1203°C) (Mn and Co series).[24]

containing 14 to 18% chromium could be diminished by increasing a parameter termed *austenite potential* above 35% according to the formula:

$$\% \text{ austenite} = 288C + 350N + 22Ni + 7.5Mn - 18.75Cr - 54Si + 388.5$$

This indicates that increasing nickel content should be beneficial although the effects of carbon and nitrogen are clearly more pronounced. Snape[25] also noted that the addition of 2.5% nickel to an electron-beam-melted 25Cr-1Mo steel resulted in a modest improvement in stretchability and drawability.

Welding Arness[38] claimed that addition of 0.3 to 3% nickel to steels containing 8 to 15% chromium and less than 0.07% carbon promoted strong, tough welds. He further noted that nickel produced a fine grain structure and improved the resistance of welds to certain corrosive agents. In applications where stress-relieving is impractical, Arness recommended addition of about 1% nickel.

Eberle[39] noted that nickel reduced the impact properties of 28% Cr steels after prolonged exposure at 1300°F (704°C). This was attributed to sigma formation. However, as shown in Table 3, the effect of nickel on sigma formation in weld deposits is relatively slight.

TABLE 3   Effect of Nickel on Sigma Formation in Weld Deposits of Ferritic Stainless Steels[39]

| | CVN impact toughness at 300°F (149°C), ft-lb(J) | |
Nominal composition	As-welded	Welded and held 100 h at 1300°F (704°C)
0.15C-23Cr-0.2Ni-0.2N	22.0 (29.8)	24.0 (32.5)
0.14C-23Cr-1.8Ni-0.15N	22.6 (30.6)	18.7 (25.4)
0.14C-25Cr-0.2Ni-0.2N	21.3 (28.8)	10.2 (13.8)
0.15C-26Cr-1.3Ni-0.2N	30.3 (42.2)	7.2 (9.8)

General Corrosion Resistance   Studies of the effect of nickel on the passivating tendency[40,41] and pitting resistance of ferritic stainless steels[42,43] indicate that nickel should improve atmospheric corrosion resistance.

Chernova and Tomashov[40] found that 0.5% nickel increased the tendency of a 25% Cr steel to become passive in 1 N H_2SO_4 at room temperature. They also noted that nickel reduced the anodic dissolution rate. Binder[41] also claimed that nickel increased the tendency of chromium steels to become passive, at least up to 22% chromium. More recently, Lizlovs and Bond[42] demonstrated that additions of up to 1% nickel to 18Cr-2Mo-0.03C steels depressed the critical current density in 0.1 N HCl to the point where no active region was displayed. An increase in nickel content from 0.11 to 0.62% resulted in complete suppression of the active region indicating that nickel promotes passivation.

Using immersion tests, Langer et al.[43] found that nickel increased the pitting resistance of 21% Cr steels in a 0.5 N solution of iron chloride. Potentiostatic studies by the same authors showed that nickel increased the potential at which the protective film is broken down during anodic polarization in 3% NaCl. On the other hand, Lizlovs and Bond[42] found that addition of up to 1% nickel in 18Cr-2Mo-0.03C steels did not change pitting potential significantly in 0.1 N HCl in comparison with titanium (Table 4). These authors suggest that the sharp increase in pitting potential with titanium additions is probably due to the fact that titanium ties up the carbon and nitrogen and thus prevents the formation of zones depleted in chromium and molybdenum.

TABLE 4   Comparison of the Effect of Nickel and Titanium on Average Pitting Potentials in 0.1 N HCl[44]

Alloy	Average pitting potential vs. SCE,* V
18Cr-2Mo-<0.05C-0.11Ni	0.31
18Cr-2Mo-<0.05C-0.62Ni	0.35
18Cr-2Mo-0.031C-1.08Ni	0.34
18Cr-2Mo-0.034C-0.47Ti	<0.8

*SCE = saturated calomel electrode.

Very recently, Lizlovs and Bond[44] developed potentiodynamic polarization curves in 1 N H_2SO_4 and 1 N HCl for 25% Cr ferritic stainless steels containing 0 to 5Mo-0 to 4Ni. The critical current density was decreased by molybdenum and molybdenum plus nickel additions in both acids. In 25Cr-3.5Mo steels, increasing the nickel content from 1 to 2.5% decreased the critical current density in 1 N H_2SO_4 to such an extent that local action cathodic current was larger than the critical current and, as a result, the critical behavior could not be observed (Fig. 10). Figure 11 shows the marked effect of nickel on the critical current density of the 25Cr-3.5Mo steel in 1 N HCl.

Colbeck and Garner[45] found that the addition of 1% nickel to a 25% Cr steel improved corrosion resistance in boiling 25% ammonium chloride. However, as shown in Table 5, nitrogen content varied significantly. Kuscynski and Weiss[46] observed that addition of 3.8% nickel to a 26Cr-1.8Mo-0.08C steel also improved corrosion resistance in saltwater and nitric acid. A steel of similar composition was also highly resistant to zinc chloride solutions.[46] Maxwell[47] found that the rate of corrosion of chromium steels in organic acids and alkalies was significantly reduced by alloying with nickel. Addition of 4.5% nickel and 1.5% molybdenum to steels containing 25 to 30% chromium was said to be particularly effective in increasing corrosion resistance.

TABLE 5   Effect of Nickel on Corrosion Resistance of Ferritic Stainless Steels in Boiling Ammonium Chloride[45]

Composition	Weight loss, g/(m²) (24 h)
Fe-0.13C-25Cr-0.11N	0.8287
Fe-0.11C-25.2Cr-0.24N-1.1Ni	0.5320

With regard to intercrystalline corrosion, Baerlecken et al.[48] investigated the behavior of steels containing 12 to 35% chromium and 2 to 5% nickel. The steels were vacuum-melted and contained less than 0.1% (C+N) and corrosion tests were conducted in a boiling copper sulfate–sulfuric acid solution containing metallic copper. They found that nickel had no effect on intercrystalline corrosion of completely ferritic steels. However, when nickel promoted austenite formation, resistance to intercrystalline corrosion was found to be greatly improved.

Stress-Corrosion-Cracking Resistance There is some evidence which indicates that nickel may be detrimental to stress-corrosion-cracking (SCC) resistance. For example, it has been shown that ferritic stainless steels free of nickel and certain other elements are

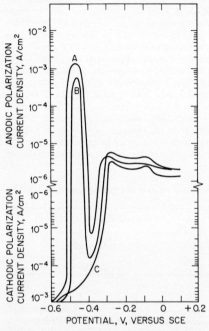

Fig. 10 Potentiodynamic polarization curve for high-purity 25Cr–3.5Mo stainless steels in 1 N H₂SO₄ at 29.8°C (85.6°F). Curve A, 25Cr–3.5Mo; curve B, 25Cr–3.5Mo–1Ni; curve C, 25Cr–3.5Mo–2.5Ni.[44]

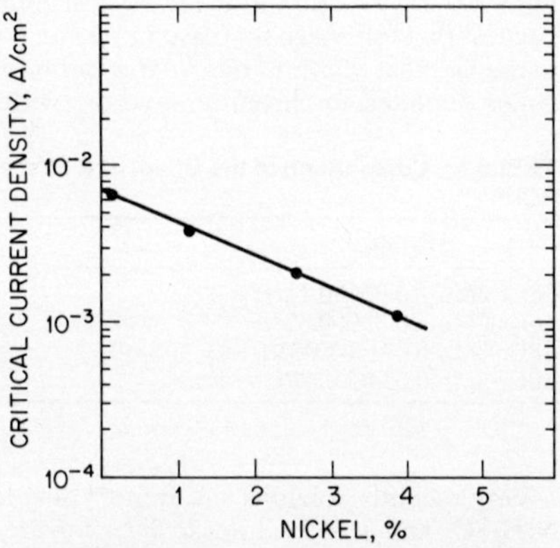

Fig. 11 Dependence of critical current density on nickel content for high-purity 25Cr–3.5Mo stainless steels in 1 N HCl at 29.8°C (85.6°F).[44]

not susceptible[49] while addition of nickel causes susceptibility.[45,50] A number of theories have been advanced in attempts to explain the apparent adverse effect of nickel.[51,52] For example, Graf[52] associated stress-corrosion-cracking susceptibility with the addition of alloying elements more noble than the matrix and concluded that susceptibility should pass through a maximum as the concentration of the noble element is increased. This is supported by the work of Latanision and Staehle[53] and Copson.[54] Latanision and Staehle found that absolute resistance is not achieved until about 50% nickel for an Fe-20Cr base.

In recent studies on 18% Cr and 25% Cr steels, it has been shown that nickel can produce susceptibility regardless of wide differences in the amounts of carbon, nitrogen, and other residual elements.[49] It was shown that up to 1.5% nickel could be tolerated, except in the case of cold-worked material. A cold-worked 1.5% Ni steel cracked, whereas a cold-worked 1% Ni steel did not. Apparent interactions between nickel and copper and nickel and molybdenum were also shown by the latter investigators (Figs. 12 and 13). However, recent work showed that an electron-beam-melted 26Cr-1Mo steel containing 2.6% nickel was not susceptible to stress-corrosion cracking in boiling MgCl₂.[25] In this case, the level of interstitials was very low. Thus the effect of nickel on stress-corrosion cracking is influenced by interstitial content, at least in high-purity material.

There are at least two other independent observations which suggest that nickel either has no influence or actually has a beneficial influence on stress-corrosion-cracking resistance. Wylie[32] patented a steel containing 14 to 17% chromium and 1 to 1.5% nickel with or without molybdenum or copper which was claimed to have excellent stress-corrosion-cracking resistance in a variety of chloride media. More recently, Truman[55] described a ferritic stainless steel developed by Firth Vickers Stainless Steel Ltd. which reportedly had good stress-corrosion-cracking resistance. The steel contained 16Cr-2.5Ni-1Mo (Table 6). Further, in tests in flowing seawater,[56] U-bend specimens of 12 ferritic stainless steels containing 0.5 to 6% nickel survived a 2-year exposure with no visible cracking or corrosion (Table 7).

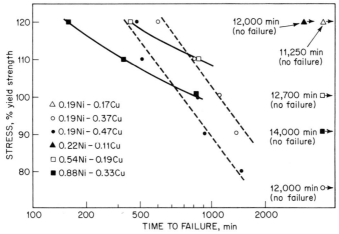

Fig. 12   Time to failure at various stresses for tensile specimens of 18Cr–2Mo stainless steels containing copper and nickel.[49]

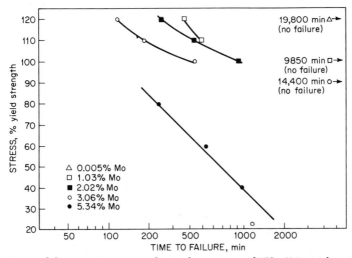

Fig. 13   Time to failure at various stresses for tensile specimens of 17Cr–2Mo stainless steels containing copper and nickel.[49]

TABLE 6   Stress-Corrosion-Cracking Resistance of Smooth Tension Specimens of Fe-0.03C-0.5Si-0.6Mn-15.7Cr-2.5Ni-1Mo-0.5Cb Steel Exposed to Various Chloride Media[55]

Corrodent	Results
42% boiling MgCl$_2$	No failure at 500 h
3% NaCl at 250°C	No failure at 500 h
Specimen coated with NaCl and held at 330°C in steam	No cracking at 3250 h
Specimen form simulated crevice in heat-transfer surface. Water contained 1000 ppm NaCl and metal temperature was 330°C	No cracking at 1152 h

Corrosion by Liquid Metals   The presence of nickel in ferritic stainless steels greatly enhances the rate of dissolution in molten lead.[57] This is because nickel is readily soluble in lead and selective attack of the nickel occurs.

Electrical Resistivity and Thermal Conductivity   A comprehensive study of the effect of nickel on electrical properties of ferritic stainless steels was conducted by Masumoto and Nakamura.[58] They found that the resistivity increased considerably with increasing nickel content. The mean temperature coefficient of electrical resistivity and the mean thermo-emf relative to copper decreased with increasing nickel content. Further, the strain gage factor

$$K = \frac{\delta R}{R} \cdot \frac{l}{\delta l}$$

decreased with increasing nickel or cobalt content.

TABLE 7   Corrosion of Ferritic Stainless Steel U-Bends in Flowing Seawater[56]

EXPOSURE PERIODS: Group 1: 1/17/69 to 1/19/71, 732 days
Group 2: 1/17/69 to 2/26/71, 770 days
U-bends formed from 6 × 0.75 × 0.4 in. (152.4 × 19.1 × 10.2 mm) blanks

Composition, wt %					Group 1		Group 2	
Cr	Ni	Mo	Si	Fe	Stress-corrosion cracking	Localized attack, mil (mm)	Stress-corrosion cracking	Localized attack, mil (mm)
20	4	4	1.5	Bal	None	Perforated	None	Nil
20	4	5		Bal	None	Nil	None	6 (0.152)
20	2	6		Bal	None	Nil	None	Nil
20	6	6		Bal	None	Nil	None	Nil
20	4	8		Bal	None	Nil	None	Nil
20	6	8		Bal	None	Nil	None	Nil
20	6	10		Bal	None	Nil	None	Nil
24	4	4		Bal	None	Nil	None	Nil
32	4			Bal	None	Nil	None	Perforated
32	4	1		Bal	None	Nil	None	Nil
32	4	2		Bal	None	Nil	None	Nil
32	6	2		Bal	None	Nil	None	Nil
32	4	3		Bal	None	Nil	None	Nil
32	4	4		Bal	None	Nil	None	Nil
36	4			Bal	None	5 (0.127)	None	Nil
40	0.5			Bal	None	Nil	None	Nil

Magnetic Properties   According to Bozorth,[60] the only Fe-Cr-Ni alloys which are useful for magnetic purposes are those having a face-centered cubic (fcc) structure. This is because the ferritic stainless steels have intermediate coercivity and are therefore not useful either as hard magnetic materials or as high-permeability materials. For this reason little is known about the effect of nickel on magnetic properties. Work by Houdremont[61] does, however, indicate that increasing nickel from about 2 to 12% in a 20Cr-0.5Ti-0.05C steel progressively decreases the saturation magnetic induction of the steel.

Adherence of Coatings Such as Porcelain Enamel   The observation that nickel forms a spinel with Cr_2O_3 and thereby increases the tenacity of mill scale[62] suggests that nickel should promote adherence of many oxide coatings including porcelain enamel.

EFFECT OF NICKEL IN MARTENSITIC STAINLESS STEELS INCLUDING PRECIPITATION-HARDENABLE STEELS

Room-Temperature Mechanical Properties   Depending on carbon content, as the chromium content of stainless steels is increased for greater corrosion resistance, they lose their hardening capacity and transform to ferrite on cooling to room temperature. The addition of nickel restores the ability of the steel to transform to martensite on quenching or air cooling.[1,63] This is illustrated by the data in Fig. 14 and Tables 8 to 10. This beneficial effect of nickel on the mechanical properties of steels containing about 0.1% carbon and 10 to 20% chromium has been the basis of development of a number of commercial stainless steels, including AISI Type 431.

Nickel is an important ingredient of precipitation-hardenable steels. For example, Moll et al.[64] showed that the optimum properties of a Cr-Mo-Co precipitation-hardenable steel are obtained with 1.80 to 1.90% nickel. Increasing nickel content significantly decreased yield strength (Fig. 15) while decreasing nickel content below 1.80% decreased the tensile elongation in the solution-annealed condition. These effects were attributed to the influence of nickel on the compositionally induced austenite stability of these steels.

Elevated Temperature Mechanical Properties   Nickel is added to valve steels with chromium contents on the order of 20 to 22% and about 2% silicon to avoid the formation of delta ferrite. Thus, nickel indirectly benefits the high-temperature scaling resistance of martensitic stainless steels by permitting the use of higher chromium and silicon contents.[65]

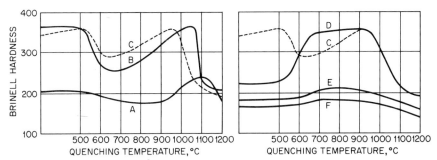

Fig. 14   Influence of nickel on the quenching behavior of steels with 20% chromium.[1] Steel A: 0.23C−19.9Cr−0.27Ni, as-rolled. Steel B: 0.23C−19.2Cr−2.16Ni, oil-quenched from 1000°C (1832°F). Steel C: 0.21C−19.8Cr−4.40Ni, oil-quenched from 800°C (1472°F). Steel D: 0.21C−19.8Cr−4.40Ni, water-quenched from 1100°C (2012°F). Steel E: 0.23C−20.5Cr−6.64Ni, water-quenched from 1100°C (2012°F). Steel F: 0.24C−20.2Cr−8.40Ni, water-quenched from 1100°C (2012°F).

General Corrosion Resistance   Tests in the 80 and 800 ft (24.4 and 244 m) lots at the Kure Beach, North Carolina, corrosion test station of the International Nickel Company, indicated that increasing the nickel content of 12% Cr steels from about 2.5 to 4.5% improves marine atmosphere corrosion resistance.[66] Cold-rolled, annealed, and pickled test panels of 4.5% Ni steels showed significantly less rust staining than panels of a 2.5% Ni steel after a 7-month exposure.

Castings   Nickel is generally added to martensitic stainless steel castings to improve strength, ductility, and corrosion resistance. For example, Souresny and Sauer[67] developed a nickel-containing 13% Cr cast steel for highly stressed components of hydraulic power plants. They found that increasing nickel from 1.25 to 4% improved cavitation resistance, sand erosion resistance, and alternating bend fatigue strength in the wet and dry state when tested using notched and smooth bar specimens. They also noted that nickel improved welding behavior.

Venturi tube and vibration test techniques have confirmed the beneficial effect of nickel on cavitation resistance of cast martensitic stainless steels and weld deposits.[68] Figure 16 shows the effect of nickel on cast 14% Cr steels with 0.05 to 0.08% carbon.

In 17Cr-4Ni PH stainless steel castings, nickel must be controlled within the range 3.6 to 4.6% to avoid the formation of too much delta ferrite or to avoid producing austenite which is too stable to be transformed during refrigeration.[69]

A cast, age-hardened 10.5 to 12.5% Cr stainless steel recently developed by Floreen[70] utilizes 6 to 8% nickel to ensure a fully martensitic structure after normalizing. Table 11 shows the effect of increasing nickel content from about 5 to 12% on strength and toughness. At 5% nickel, toughness is relatively low. Increasing nickel content improves toughness but as nickel content increases above 8%, strength and toughness are reduced due to the formation of a mixed martensitic-austenitic structure.

TABLE 8 Effect of About 2% Nickel on the Mechanical Properties of 10% Cr Steel[1]

(Bars 1¼-in. (32-mm) diameter, oil hardened 900°C, and then tempered as indicated)

Steel	%C	%Si	%Mn	%Cr	%Ni
A	0.39	0.08	0.10	10.0	0.42
B	0.39	0.12	0.32	10.5	2.24

Steel	Tempered at, °C	Yield point		Tensile strength		Elongation, % on 2 in. (50 mm)	Reduction of area, %	Brinell value	Izod impact					
		tons/in.²	MN/m²	tons/in.²	MN/m²				ft-lb			J		
A	600	49.0	675.6	64.2	885.2	15.0	45.9	302	22	19	20	29.8	25.7	27.1
	650	39.6	546	55.8	769.4	18.5	54.6	262	28	28	26	37.9	27.9	35.2
	700	31.2	430.2	49.6	683.9	24.5	58.6	235	75	66	72	101.5	89.5	97.5
B	600	53.2	733.5	62.7	864.5	17.0	48.5	293	16	18		21.7	24.4	
	650	46.4	641.1	59.0	813.5	20.0	52.2	277	30	29	26	40.6	39.3	35.2
	700	45.2	623.2	58.4	805.2	21.0	51.0	269	32	34	33	43.4	46.0	44.7

TABLE 9 Influence of Nickel on Low-Carbon 13% Cr Steel, Air-hardened from 950°C (1740°F) and Water-quenched from 700°C (1290°F)[1]

Composition, %			Tensile strength		Yield strength		Elongation in 2 in. (50 mm), %	Reduction of area, %	Brinell hardness		Izod impact	
C	Cr	Ni	psi	MN/m²	psi	MN/m²			Hardened	Tempered	ft-lb	J
0.09	13.7	0.10	83,000	572.2	66,400	457.8	32.5	68.8	241	179	100 96 106	135.6 130.2 143
0.08	13.3	0.46	91,200	628.7	77,000	530.8	32.0	68.8	340	217	98 98 101	132.5 132.5 137
0.08	13.6	0.80	100,200	690.8	87,500	603.2	29.0	63.7	351	241	86 86 88	116.5 116.5 119.2
0.10	14.1	1.23	104,500	720.4	89,900	619.8	25.5	55.8	418	255	65 62 65	87.7 87.7 87.7

TABLE 10 Effect of Nickel on Mechanical Properties of 18% Cr Steels[63]

Chemical composition, %	Treatment, °C		Yield point		Maximum stress		Elongation in 2 in. (50 mm), %	Reduction of area, %	Izod impact						Brinell hardness
	Air-hardened	Tempered	tons/in.²	MN/m²	tons/in.²	MN/m²			ft-lb			J			
C 0.10 Cr 17.0 Ni 0.28	950 950	500 600	22 22	303.3 303.3	31 29	427.4 399.8	32 37	62 66	3 5			4.12 6.77			166 156
C 0.09 Cr 17.8 Ni 2.08	950 950	500 600	46 34	634.2 468.8	58 43	799.7 592.8	22 28	59 62	96 88 88 86 75 94	130 119 119 116.5 105.5 127					265 225

EFFECT OF NICKEL IN DUPLEX STAINLESS STEELS

Hot Workability   In the hot-working of 21Cr-5Ni steels, Cherkashina et al.[71] recommended that nickel should be maintained with the range 4.8 to 5.3% to avoid cracking. This level of nickel was apparently necessary to avoid excessive formation of coarse-grained ferrite. However, provided enough titanium is present to tie up carbon and nitrogen, nickel content is not critical for good hot workability.

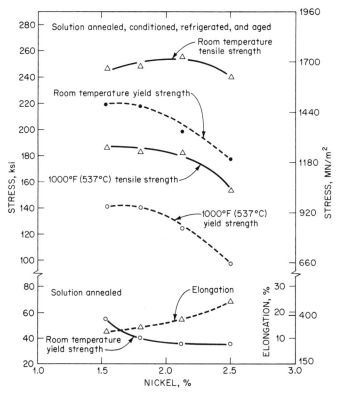

Fig. 15   Effect of nickel content on annealed and hardened properties of the C-50 type steels.[64]

High-Temperature Corrosion and Scaling Resistance   Brasunas et al.[72] showed that nickel improved scaling resistance of ferritic-martensitic or ferritic-austenitic stainless steels in air at 100°F (532°C). This beneficial effect of nickel was noted over a wide chromium range (11 to 31%).

Room-Temperature Mechanical Properties   Figure 17 shows results of a study by Houdremont[61] on the effect of increasing nickel content of stainless steels containing 20Cr-0.5Ti-0.05C on strength and ductility. Properties vary as the structure changes from ferrite to ferrite plus martensite to ferrite plus austenite. These property changes have been analyzed in great detail by Gibson[73] and by Floreen and Hayden.[5] They varied the percentage of ferrite in duplex ferritic-martensitic and ferritic-austenitic steels by varying chromium and nickel content. Increasing nickel content in ferritic-martensitic steels from about 2.8 to 5.5% and decreasing chromium content from about 24 to 16.5%, progressively increased martensite content. As a result, strength was increased and the impact energy was increased with a lowering of the ductile-to-brittle impact transition temperature on the order of 500°F (257°C) for air-cooled samples and 300°F (147°C) for water-quenched samples.

In ferritic-austenitic steels, increasing nickel content from about 3 to 9% and reducing

TABLE 11 Effect of Nickel on Properties of High-Strength Age-hardening Stainless Steel in 1-in. (25.4-mm) Section[70]

Composition				Heat treatment, °F	Yield strength, 0.2% offset		Ultimate tensile strength		Elongation, %	Reduction of area, %	CVN	
Ni	Cr	Si	C		psi	MN/m²	psi	MN/m²			ft-lb	J
5.0	11.3	0.55	0.023	1900*/1 h + 850†/3 h	129,000	889.3	147,000	1013.4	15	57	16.0	21.6
5.8	12.0	0.60	0.016	1900/1 h + 850/3 h	131,000	903.1	143,000	985.8	14	51	33.2	45
6.9	11.4	0.47	0.023	1900/1 h + 850/3 h	137,000	944.5	147,000	1013.4	15	55	36.2	49
7.0	10.8	0.69	0.014	1900/1 h + 850/3 h	136,000	937.6	158,000	1089.2	18	59	36.2	49
8.0	12.0	0.77	0.016	1900/1 h + 850/3 h	135,000	930.7	155,000	1068.6	16	52	26.0	35.2
9.7	11.6	0.57	0.026	1900/1 h + 850/3 h	121,000	834.2	138,000	951.4	20	54	19.5	26.4
11.8	11.1	0.59	0.026	1900/1 h + 850/3 h	91,000	627.3	129,000	889.3	21	52	23.0	31.2

*1036.7°C.
†454°C.

chromium content from about 32 to 19.5% increased austenite content from 0 to 85% and reduced yield strength and increased impact toughness.

Gibson[73] found that the effect of nickel content depended on chromium content and annealing temperature. At 26% chromium, increasing nickel from about 5 to 8% had little effect on strength but significantly improved ductility after annealing ¼-in. (6.35-mm) plate at 1500, 1600, or 1700°F (807, 862, or 917°C). At 28% chromium, increasing nickel content from about 6 to 9% again had little effect on strength after annealing at 1500 and 1600°F (807 and 862°C) but increased ductility. However, after annealing at 1700°F (917°C), the 6% Ni steel had a yield strength of about 80 ksi (558.7 MN/m²) and an elongation of about 11% whereas the 9% Ni steel had a yield strength of about 69 ksi (475.7 MN/m²) and an elongation of about 32%. This emphasizes the importance of considering processing conditions when attempting to explain compositional effects.

Fatigue Strength Gibson[73] observed that increasing nickel content of a 26% Cr steel from about 5 to 7% increased the 10⁷ cycle fatigue strength from about 52 to 65 ksi (363.2 to 453.9 MN/m²). Similar beneficial effects of nickel were noted in steels with nominally 28 and 30% chromium.

Elevated Temperature Mechanical Properties Gulyaev et al.[74] plotted phase diagrams for 21% Cr steels with 0 to 6% nickel, 0.04 or 0.1% carbon, with and without titanium. They concluded that nickel reduced 885°F (473°C) embrittlement in duplex steels.

Cold Fabricability Although there are no data on the effect of nickel on cold fabricability or duplex stainless steels, the beneficial effect of nickel on room-temperature ductility would suggest that nickel would have a beneficial effect on stretch formability.

General Corrosion Resistance and Stress-Corrosion-Cracking Resistance Jackson[75] exposed stress-corrosion specimens (U bends) of cold-worked and annealed martensitic-ferritic and ferritic-austenitic stainless steels to a 5% sodium chloride solution acidified with 0.5% acetic acid and saturated with hydrogen sulfide at room temperature. General corrosion resistance and stress-corrosion-cracking resistance improved as nickel content increased. All steels with greater than 7% nickel were uncracked after a 30-day exposure.

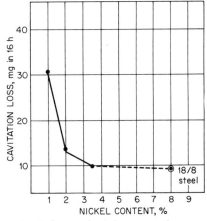

Fig. 16 Influence of nickel content on the cavitation resistance of cast stainless steels with 14% chromium and 0.05–0.08% carbon.[68]

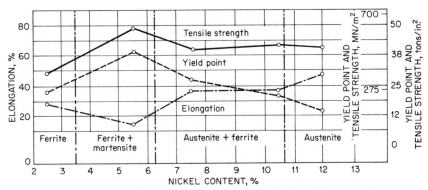

Fig. 17 Effect of nickel on mechanical properties of duplex stainless steels.[61]

Magnetic Properties As shown in Fig. 18, increasing nickel content in duplex 20% Cr steels results in a pronounced decrease in saturation magnetic induction corresponding to an increase in the percentage of austenite in the steel.

EFFECT OF NICKEL IN AUSTENITIC STAINLESS STEELS

Melting Nickel lowers the melting point by about 9°F (4.4°C) per percent nickel.[76] While the effect of nickel is not as potent as elements such as carbon and boron, it nevertheless has an important bearing on the melting and casting behavior of austenitic stainless steels since lower melting and pouring temperatures contribute to improved refractory and mold life.

Hot Workability In hot-working of austenitic stainless steels, the presence of a small amount of delta ferrite can produce edge cracking. For this reason, nickel content is

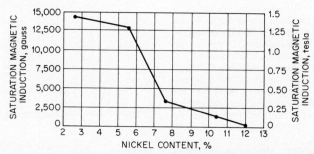

Fig. 18 Effect of nickel on magnetic properties of duplex stainless steels.[61]

usually adjusted to prevent delta ferrite formation. The extent to which delta ferrite formation can be overcome by nickel depends on the composition of the steel. For example, in steels containing 28Cr-8Mo, increasing nickel content from about 28 to 34% did not completely eliminate delta ferrite.[77]

Ludwigson and Brickner[78] found that the beneficial effect of nickel on hot workability of Type 201 steel was maximized by low levels of carbon and nitrogen. They developed

TABLE 12   Equation Relating Number of Twists Withstood to Temperature and Composition of Type 201 Steel[78]

Number of twists withstood = −34.91
$$+78.74 \ (\%C)$$
$$-5.739 \ (\%Mn)$$
$$+5.386 \ (\%Ni)$$
$$-6.118 \ (\%Cr)$$
$$+24.71 \ (\%N)$$
$$+0.08356 \ (T)$$
$$-1292 \ (\%C - 0.11)^2$$
$$+105.8 \ (\%C - 0.11) \ (\%Mn - 6.5)$$
$$-47.12 \ (\%C - 0.11) \ (\%Ni - 5.1)$$
$$-2.134 \ (\%Ni - 5.1)^2$$
$$-47.65 \ (\%Ni - 5.1) \ (\%N - 0.09)$$
$$-2.493 \ (\%Cr - 16.4)^2$$
$$+79.27 \ (\%Cr - 16.4) \ (\%N - 0.09)$$
$$+0.2828 \ (\%C - 0.11) \ (T - 2150)$$
$$-0.02492 \ (\%Mn - 6.5) \ (T - 2150)$$
$$+0.01493 \ (\%Ni - 5.1) \ (T - 2150)$$
$$-0.02589 \ (\%Cr - 16.4) \ (T - 2150)$$
$$+0.1621 \ (\%N - 0.09) \ (T - 2150)$$
$$+0.4981 \ (\%C - 0.11) \ (\%Mn - 6.5) \ (T - 2150)$$
$$-0.3386 \ (\%Ni - 5.1) \ (\%N - 0.09) \ (T - 2150)$$
$$+0.2043 \ (\%Cr - 16.4) \ (\%N - 0.09) \ (T - 2150)$$

Standard error of estimate (SE) = 8.3
Coefficient of determination (R^2) = 0.827

an equation based on hot torsion tests relating hot workability to temperature and composition (Table 12). Figure 19 shows the results of their studies of the effect of nickel content. As nickel content increases, the number of twists to failure increases indicating improved hot workability.

The beneficial effect of nickel and its relation to nitrogen content was confirmed by Janzon[79] in more highly alloyed austenitic stainless steels. He found that increasing nickel content from about 10.5 to 13.5% in a 17.5Cr-2.8Mo steel eliminated delta ferrite and improved hot workability. However, in higher nitrogen steels containing no delta ferrite at the hot-working temperature, increasing nickel content can give rise to a grain-boundary eutectic which impairs hot workability (Fig. 20).

High-Temperature Corrosion and Scaling Resistance   As shown in Fig. 21, up to a certain nickel level, nickel improves the scaling resistance of austenitic stainless steels at any given chromium level.[72] Up to 20% chromium, scaling resistance improves progressively with increasing nickel content. At higher chromium contents, the optimum nickel level appears to be between 10 and 20%. These results are borne out by the fact that two of the most popular types of stainless steel in use, the 25Cr-12Ni and 25Cr-20Ni grades, constitute the most economical alloy combinations for high scaling resistance in air.

Hobby and Wood[80] studied the oxidation behavior of several Fe-Cr-Ni and Fe-Cr alloys in 1 atm (0.101 MPa) oxygen and 800 to 1200°C (1472 to 2192°F). They found that nickel reduced the growth rate of oxide scales. They concluded that nickel and iron ions doped the chromium oxide scale more effectively together than singly.

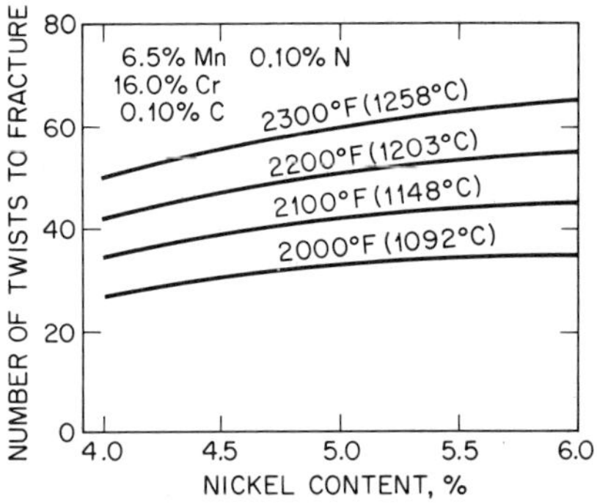

Fig. 19 Effect of nickel content on number of twists sustained in hot torsion tests.[78]

Room-temperature Mechanical Properties Nickel influences mechanical properties chiefly through its effect on austenite stability. In the nickel range where transformation of austenite to martensite can occur, increasing nickel content reduces strength and increases ductility. This is illustrated by the data in Table 13, which also shows that the effect of nickel becomes less pronounced as carbon content, and hence austenite stability, increases.[81]

Regarding fracture toughness, nickel has a beneficial effect on toughness of age-hardened austenitic stainless steels.[82]

Cryogenic Properties   Ul'yanin et al.[83] found that increasing nickel content of a 17% Cr steel from 10 to 20% had no effect on yield or ultimate strengths over the temperature range +20 to −253°F (−6.6 to −157°C) but improved ductility and fracture toughness. The same authors found that additions up to about 4% nickel reduced yield strength and increased tensile strength at −320°F (−196°C). This effect of nickel on strength was thought to be due to the increased ductility at higher nickel contents permitting more strain hardening to occur before fracture. There is some evidence that at −253°F (−157°C) toughness goes through a maximum at about 25% nickel.[84] Data by Spaeder and Brickner[85] shown in Fig. 22 illustrate the beneficial effect of nickel on low-temperature toughness of 18Cr-15Mn-0.4N steels. Since the base composition is, in this instance, extremely stable, these data suggest that the beneficial effect of nickel on toughness cannot be entirely ascribed to the influence of nickel on austenite stability.

Fatigue Strength   Data on endurance limits in bending fatigue for a variety of stainless steels with nickel contents ranging from 6 to 20% indicate that nickel has little effect on fatigue strength of conventional austenitic stainless steels.[86] Work by Koversistyi et al.[87] indicates that nickel increases fatigue strength of age-hardened austenitic stainless steels.

Elevated Temperature Mechanical Properties   The effect of nickel on high-temperature strength depends on base composition. As shown in Table 14, for steels of the 18Cr-8Ni type, short-term tensile strength is increased by nickel over the temperature range 1200 to 1800°F (649 to 972°C).[88] On the other hand, nickel has no effect on short-term

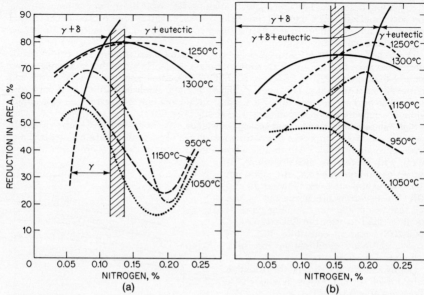

Fig. 20 Effect of nitrogen and nickel content on hot ductility of 17.5Cr–2.8Mo steels. *(a)* 10% nickel; *(b)* 13% nickel.[79]

elevated temperature tensile strength or on creep strength of 25% Cr steels containing about 0.2 to 0.5% nitrogen over the temperature range 70 to 1650°F (21 to 870°C).[89]

Cold Fabricability   Of all the elements in stainless steel, nickel is the one element which can most conveniently be adjusted to provide a wide range of forming characteristics.

Nickel exerts its influence on cold fabricability of stainless steel sheet primarily through

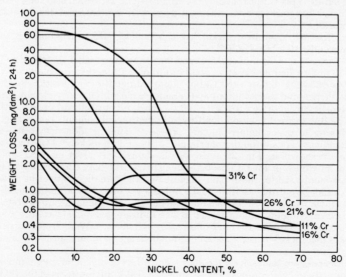

Fig. 21 Influence of nickel on the scaling rates at 1000°C (1832°F) for ternary Fe-Ni-Cr alloys with chromium contents between 11 and 31%.[72]

TABLE 13 Effect of Nickel on the Properties of Softened and Cold-rolled High-Chromium–Nickel Steel Strip[81]

Composition, %			Softened		Cold-rolled 30%		Cold-rolled 50%	
C	Cr	Ni	Tensile strength, psi (MN/m²)	Elongation in 2 in. (50 mm), %	Tensile strength, psi (MN/m²)	Elongation in 2 in. (50 mm), %	Tensile strength, psi (MN/m²)	Elongation in 2 in., %
0.053	17.13	7.07	132,000 (910)	20	183,000 (1261.6)	6	205,000 (1413.3)	1.5
0.050	16.83	9.79	86,000 (592.9)	65	129,000 (889.3)	20	160,000 (1103)	5.5
0.056	18.68	7.33	122,000 (841.1)	41	183,000 (1261.6)	8	213,000 (1468.4)	1.5
0.051	18.22	9.14	86,000 (592.9)	65	122,000 (841.1)	21	156,000 (1075.5)	5.0
0.140	17.26	7.07	128,000 (882.4)	80	206,000 (1420.2)	20	255,000 (1757.9)	6
0.130	17.08	9.65	94,000 (648)	70	140,000 (965.2)	20	175,000 (1206.4)	7
0.160	19.68	6.68	102,000 (703.2)	72	156,000 (1075.5)	37	194,000 (1337.4)	9
0.160	18.88	8.78	98,000 (675.6)	63	142,000 (978.9)	33	176,000 (1213.3)	8

TABLE 14 Effect of Increased Nickel on the Short-Time Tensile Properties of Low-Carbon 18-8[88]

COMPOSITION:	C	Cr	Ni
Steel A:	0.07	18.98	8.46
Steel B:	0.07	18.78	14.66

Temperature		Steel A			Steel B		
°C	°F	Tensile strength, psi (MN/m²)	Elongation in 2 in. (50 mm), %	Reduction of area, %	Tensile strength, psi (MN/m²)	Elongation in 2 in. (50 mm), %	Reduction of area, %
20	70	100,000 (758.3)	58	60	85,000 (585.9)		
425	800	66,000 (455)	46	70	66,000 (455)		
540	1000	60,000 (413.6)	40	68	60,000 (413.6)		
650	1200	50,000 (344.7)	48	65	53,000 (365.4)	40	63
760	1400	25,000 (172.3)	53	55	38,000 (261.9)	46	60
870	1600	13,000 (89.6)	55	43	25,000 (172.3)	38	54
980	1800	7,000 (48.3)	70	50	10,000 (68.9)	50	65

control of structure and, in particular, through its effect on austenitic stability. As nickel content is reduced, austenite stability decreases and work-hardening tendency increases (Fig. 23).

Figure 24 shows the effect of nickel content on the true-stress–true-strain curve of 17% Cr steels containing less than 0.1% carbon. At strain values above about 15%, nickel reduces flow stress. Increasing nickel content from 8 to 10% increases the maximum uniform strain and total strain, i.e., ductility (Fig. 25). A further increase in nickel content decreases ductility. Fracture stress decreases with increasing nickel. Holmes and Gladman[91] suggest that these effects are consistent with the effect of nickel in increasing stacking-fault energy of the austenite thereby reducing the tendency to deform by transformation to martensite, by mechanical twinning, and by movement of dissociated dislocations.

In practical terms, the effect of increasing nickel on tensile ductility is manifest as a reduction in stretch formability and a reduction in stretching force as measured qualitatively by Erickson cupping tests (Fig. 26).

In deep drawing, die force and die energy decrease linearly with a logarithmic increase in nickel content. Funke et al.[92] found that the drawing force for an 18% Cr steel containing 13.5% nickel increased

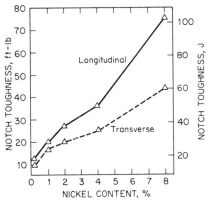

Fig. 22   Effect of nickel content on the $-320°F$ ($-196°C$) Charpy V-notch impact properties of high-strength Cr-Mn-N steels.[85]

more slowly than that for a 7.6% Ni steel. The limiting drawing ratio, which is a quantitative measure of drawability, representing the balance between the force of deformation and tearing strength of stainless steel decreased with increasing nickel content.

From the above it can be deduced that nickel has two principal effects on cold

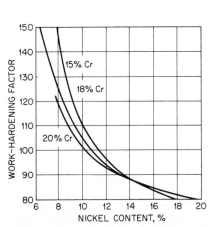

Fig. 23   Influence of nickel content on the work-hardening tendency of austenitic Cr-Ni steels with 0.08% carbon.[90]

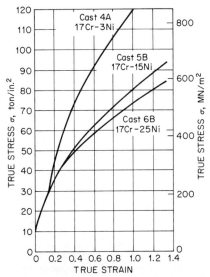

Fig. 24   Effect of nickel content on the true-stress—true-strain curve of 17% Cr steels solution-treated at 1150°C (2102°F) and water-quenched.[91]

fabricability of stainless steel sheet. Increasing nickel above about 10% reduces the energy needed to deform 18% Cr stainless steel either in stretching or drawing modes, but also reduces the total amount of deformation attainable in a given part. The nickel level desired for a given part will therefore depend largely on the capability of the forming equipment and the dimensions of the part being formed.

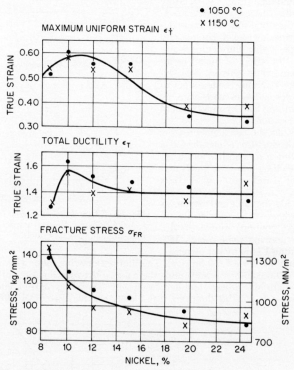

Fig. 25 Effect of nickel content on maximum uniform strain, total strain, and fracture stress of 17% Cr steel.[91]

In the production of fasteners, the reduction of work hardening by increasing nickel content can have substantial benefits on thread rollability.[93] Thus, Type 305 stainless steel (10 to 13% nickel) has substantially better thread rollability than Type 301 stainless steel (6 to 8% nickel). Similar comments apply to cold headability.[94] Figure 27 shows that for compressions up to 10%, the load required to compress a 20% Cr stainless steel different amounts decreases as nickel content increases above about 4 to 5%.

Welding   The coefficient of linear expansion of weld metal decreases markedly as nickel content increases up to 60%.[95] Figure 28 shows the effect of nickel on the mean coefficient of expansion of steels containing 18 to 22% chromium over the temperature ranges 20 to 300°C (68 to 572°F) and 20 to 600°C (68 to 1112°F). These temperatures represent the lower and upper limits of the temperature range to which joints between austenitic and nonaustenitic steels are likely to be subjected, and in which the diffusional processes take place on an appreciable scale. Gotal'skii and Vasil'ev[95] suggest that this reduction in coefficient of expansion with increasing nickel is responsible for reducing stresses in welded joints. Nickel also reduces carbide stability in austenitic steels.[96] This increases the amount of carbon dissolved in the weld metal and reduces welding stresses by reducing the activities of carbon in weld metal and baseplate.[95] Nickel appreciably reduces the rate at which interlayers developed in the fusion zone between austenitic stainless steel weld deposits and pearlitic steels.[97] It raises the lower working temperature for joints by 100 to 150°C (212 to 302°F) without danger of diffusion processes developing. In addition to the interlayer thicknesses being reduced by nickel, increasing nickel in the weld metal reduces the degree to which the heat-affected zone (HAZ) is decarburized (Figs. 29 and 30).

Sadowski investigated the effects of nickel between 17 and 21% on cracking of a CK-20 type alloy (25Cr-1Mn-bal Fe) using the shielded-metal-arc (SMAW) process and the gas-tungsten-arc (GTAW) process with matching filler composition. Nickel increased crack sensitivity in the GTAW deposit and was slightly beneficial in the SMAW weld metal.

General Corrosion Resistance Increasing nickel content of 18% Cr steel from about 8 to about 12% has little effect on pitting corrosion resistance or general corrosion resistance in marine atmospheres.[99]

Nickel increases the ability of stainless steel to passivate in sulfuric acid although at nickel levels on the order of 10% or higher, this effect of nickel is overshadowed by the fact that nickel raises the passivating potential.[100] Padget et al.[101] tested 23 steels varying in nickel content from 6 to 25% in 10% H_2SO_4. They found that nickel increased the rest potential, critical corrosion potential, and flade potential, the latter effect depending on chromium level (Fig. 31). The rest potential current density was decreased by nickel up to about 16% nickel (Fig. 32). The critical corrosion current density was also decreased by nickel but there was little benefit above about 18% nickel (Fig. 33).

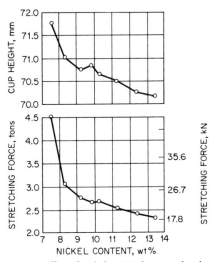

Fig. 26 Effect of nickel on Erickson cup height and stretching force.[92]

Figure 34 shows the major beneficial effect of nickel on room-temperature corrosion resistance in 5% H_2SO_4. Table 15 shows the beneficial effect of nickel content on corrosion resistance of boiling 3 and 6% sulfuric acid. Such observations have been

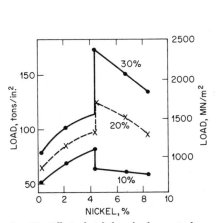

Fig. 27 Effect of nickel on loads required to compress a 20% Cr steel to stated amounts.[1]

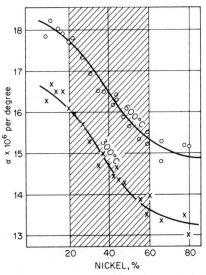

Fig. 28 Effect of nickel on the coefficient of linear expansion of Cr-Ni austenite (18 to 22% chromium).[95]

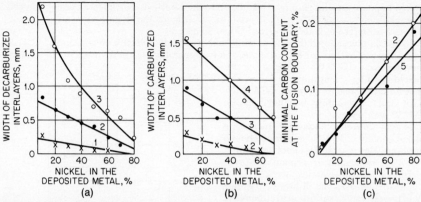

Fig. 29 Effects of the nickel content of deposited metal on the width of (a) the decarburized interlayers, (b) the carburized interlayers, and (c) the concentration of carbon in the decarburized interlayers in specimens heat-treated as under (1) 450°C (842°F), 1000 h; (2) 550°C (1022°F), 1000 h; (3) 650°C (1202°F), 1000 h; (4) 750°C (1382°F), 1000 h; and (5) 650°C (1202°F), 20 h.[97]

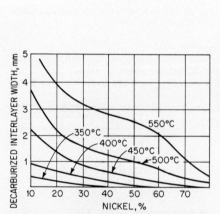

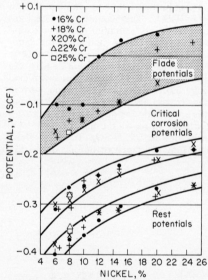

Fig. 30 Composite graph of variation in the width of the decarburized interlayers in fusion zones between medium-carbon steel and austenitic welds with different nickel contents after aging for 10^5 h at 350 to 550°C (662 to 1022°F).[97]

Fig. 31 Effect of nickel on rest potential, critical corrosion potential, and flade potentials of Ni-Cr stainless steels in 10% H_2SO_4 at 20°C (68°F).[101]

TABLE 15 **Influence of Nickel Content on Attack by Boiling H_2SO_4[3]**

Steel composition, %			Loss in weight, mg/(dm²) (24 h)	
Cr	Ni	Mo	3% acid	6% acid
20	8	2.5	3000	60,000
20	15	2.5	1200	1500
20	25	2.5	700	800

confirmed repeatedly. In general, a sudden improvement in corrosion resistance has been noted beyond a certain nickel content. Thus, in 0.5% sulfuric acid at room temperature this level is 13 to 15%[3] whereas in boiling 29.8% sulfuric acid, the level is 25 to 35%.

There is conflicting evidence concerning the effect of nickel on the passivation behavior in hydrochloric acid. Tomashov found that nickel increased the potential for break-

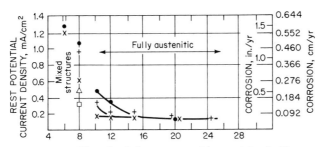

Fig. 32   Effect of nickel on rest potential current density.[101]

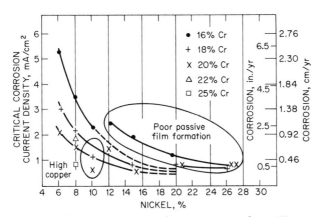

Fig. 33   Effect of nickel on critical corrosion current density.[101]

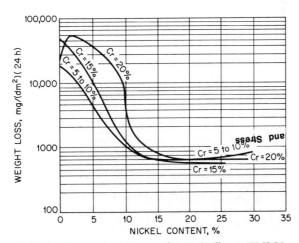

Fig. 34   Influence of nickel on the corrosion resistance of Fe-Ni-Cr alloys in 5% H_2SO_4 at 30°C (86°F).[3]

down of passivity[102] whereas Troselius[100] claimed that nickel had the reverse effect. In actual corrosion tests, nickel has a significant beneficial effect on corrosion resistance in hydrochloric acid of all concentrations at room temperature (Fig. 35).

In boiling nitric acid, nickel is considerably more effective than manganese in reducing corrosion rate (Table 16). Brunet et al.[103] developed cathodic polarization curves in 1 N nitric acid at 20°C (68°F) which showed that nickel increased corrosion rate of 17% Cr steel (Fig. 36).

The harmful effect of chromium on corrosion resistance in aqueous sodium hydroxide and molten sodium hydroxide is counteracted by increasing nickel content.[104]

Figure 37 provides a convenient summary of the effects of nickel on corrosion resistance in various media and provides some indication of why nickel stainless steels and alloys find such widespread applications as container materials for many aggressive media.

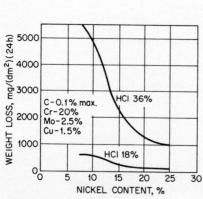

Fig. 35 Influence of nickel content on the corrosion rates for steels with 20Cr–2½Mo–1½Cu in cold 36 and 18% HCl.[3]

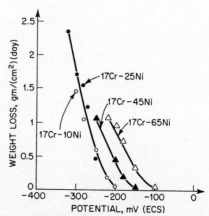

Fig. 36 Influence of nickel content of a 17% Cr steel on cathodic corrosion after 4 h at constant potential in 1 N nitric acid at 20°C (68°F).[103]

By permitting the incorporation of higher levels of molybdenum while maintaining an essentially austenitic structure, nickel indirectly increases resistance to corrosion in a variety of aggressive media. For example, in acid mixtures containing sulfuric acid and nitric acid resistance is improved as nickel and molybdenum contents are increased.

Stress-Corrosion Resistance   The beneficial effect of nickel on the resistance of austenitic stainless steels to transcrystalline stress corrosion is well known. With normal purity heats, about 40% nickel is required to avoid stress-corrosion cracking (Fig. 38). However, high-purity steels are resistant to stress corrosion at low nickel levels.[106–108] For example, Lee and Uhlig[108] found that a high-purity 30.8% Ni steel made from electrolytic iron and carbonyl nickel was not susceptible to stress-corrosion cracking in $MgCl_2$ at 130°C (266°F) for times up to and including 200 h (Fig. 39).

In addition to the effect of impurities, Figs. 40 and 41 show how the nickel level needed for complete resistance also depends on the presence of interstitials.[107–110] A 20% nickel, low nitrogen steel, for example, does not crack in $MgCl_2$ at 130°C (266°F) despite anodic polarization whereas a high nitrogen heat fails whether polarized or not.[108]

Regarding the mechanism by which nickel improves stress-corrosion-cracking resistance of stainless steels, Lee and Uhlig[108] concluded that nickel shifts the critical cracking potential in the noble direction so that when the corrosion potential is exceeded, cracking no longer occurs (Fig. 42).

Based on studies of 15% Cr steels in 10% Na_2SO_4 at 50°C (122°F), 1% NaCl at 90°C (194°F) and boiling 42% $MgCl_2$, Ryabchenkov and Sidorov[111] also concluded that nickel improved stress-corrosion-cracking resistance through its effect on electrochemical properties.

Harston and Scully[112] found that addition of nickel to Type 304 stainless steel reduced

TABLE 16 Tests in Boiling 65% Nitric Acid[131]

Composition, %					First 48-h period		Second 48-h period		Third 48-h period	
C	Cr	Mn	Ni	Cu	Penetration, in./month (mm/month)	Weight loss, mg/(dm²) (day)	Penetration, in./month (mm/month)	Weight loss, mg/(dm²) (day)	Penetration, in./month (mm/month)	Weight loss, mg/(dm²) (day)
0.07	17.60	9.12		0.89	0.0041 (0.104)	264	0.0042 (0.107)	278	0.0044 (0.112)	288
0.09	18.21	7.91	2.37		0.0029 (0.074)	193	0.0029 (0.074)	193	0.0029 (0.074)	193
0.08	18.24	5.88	4.37		0.0020 (0.051)	132	0.0022 (0.056)	146	0.0022 (0.056)	146
0.08	18.80	6.06	4.72	0.89	0.0017 (0.043)	113	0.0018 (0.046)	119	0.0016 (0.041)	106
0.07	18.61	0.41	9.04		0.0010 (0.025)	66	0.0011 (0.028)	73	0.0014 (0.090)	93

multiple crack nucleation in boiling 42% magnesium chloride. They speculated that nickel might lower the reactivity of the freshly created metal surface at the crack tip and that the role of nickel in controlling nucleation of attack can be related to its corrosion resistance in magnesium chloride and its hydrogen overpotential.

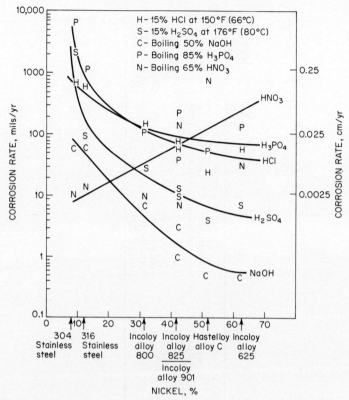

Fig. 37   Effect of nickel content on corrosion rate in a variety of aggressive media.[105]

Douglass et al.[113] attributed the beneficial effects of nickel, particularly in the absence of nitrogen, to an increase in stacking-fault energy (SFE) and enhanced cross slip and dislocation tangling with increasing nickel content.

The effect of nickel on intergranular stress-corrosion cracking of austenitic stainless steels is not clearcut. There is some controversy concerning the mechanism of intergranular failure and the precise effects of nickel. For example, Mel'kumov and Topilin[114] claimed that a 25Cr-0.35N steel was resistant to intergranular corrosion under the most severe conditions. Also, work by The International Nickel Company, Inc.,[115] has shown that an alloy of the nominal composition 60Ni-30Cr-10Fe is resistant to intergranular cracking for periods up to 48 weeks in 600°F (312°C) contaminated water. These observations conflict with those of Coriou et al.[116,117] in which it is claimed that alloys containing between about 10 and 70% nickel are susceptible to intergranular stress-corrosion cracking in pure and contaminated high-temperature water.

There is a sizable body of evidence which shows a relationship between nickel and the interstitial elements carbon and nitrogen and intergranular cracking. As shown in Fig. 43, if the nickel content of an 18% Cr steel is raised from 9 to 13%, carbon content must be reduced from 0.025 to 0.016% to maintain absolute immunity. Increasing nitrogen content also increases the nickel level at which intergranular cracking is observed.[118] Gulyaev and Tokareva[119] found that steels with 9 to 12% nickel were resistant to intergranular stress-corrosion cracking provided carbon content did not exceed 0.02% and steels with 19 to 40% nickel were resistant provided carbon content did not exceed 0.006%.

A recent paper by Cordovi[115] provides the most comprehensive state-of-the-art review of the environment and compositional factors influencing intergranular stress-corrosion cracking.

Nuclear Properties Table 17 shows the principal helium generators in stainless steels.[120] Nickel has a mean cross section about 10 times smaller than nitrogen and about 10 times larger than iron. The effect of nickel on helium generation is, however, about twice that of iron.[121]

Corrosion by Liquid Metals Corrosion tests by Roy et al.[122] of Types 304, 316, and 347 stainless steels and Incoloy alloy 800 in 1300°F (704°C) sodium flowing at 17 ft/s (5.2 m/s) showed the corrosion rate of Incoloy alloy 800 (32% nickel) to be about twice that of the stainless steels (Fig. 44). This was believed to be due to a selective dissolution of nickel.

Magnetic Properties Figure 45 shows a plot of nickel content versus Neel temperature determined from several independent investigations. Flansburg and Hershkowitz[123] found that line broadening occurred below the Neel Temperature for Type 316 stainless steel (13.3 atomic % nickel) and above the Neel temperature for Type 301 and 304 stainless steels (7.5 and 8.8 atomic % nickel). They considered the line broadening was due to short-range ordering.

The permeability of cold-worked austenitic stainless steels is reduced by increasing nickel content.[124] For example, in Fig. 46 the top curve shows a hundredfold increase of maximum permeability at 90% reduction for an alloy containing 9.3% nickel while with 10.6% nickel, permeability was increased only from 1.2 to 1.4 by the same amount of cold work.

Electrical Properties Electrical resistivity increases and the temperature coefficient of resistance decreases as nickel content increases (Fig. 47). In Silcock's work,[125] the difference between resistivity at 30 and 600°C (86 and 1112°F) shows less scatter and decreased linearly with rise in nickel content.

Coefficient of Thermal Expansion and Thermal Conductivity The coefficients of thermal expansion of Types 301 and 304 stainless steel are identical at 0 and 70°F (21 and −17°C) suggesting that nickel has little effect on 18% Cr steels over the approximate

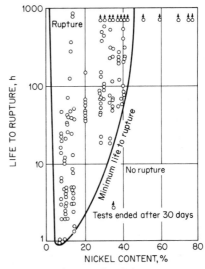

Fig. 38 Influence of nickel content on resistance to stress corrosion.[106]

TABLE 17 Principal Helium Generators in Stainless Steels[120]

Mean (n, α) cross section of natural elements in fast fission flux, measured in barns	
Matrix elements	Elements in nonmetallic inclusions
B 0.119*	S 0.014
N 0.041	Ca 0.0065
Ni 0.0042	O 0.006
Ti 0.0029	Mg 0.0029
Fe 0.00040	
Cr 0.00034	
V 0.00004	
Nb 0.00004	

*755 barn in thermal flux.

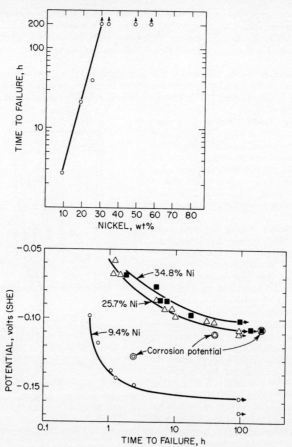

Fig. 39 Stress-corrosion cracking of 20% Cr stainless steels in $MgCl_2$ at 130°C as a function of nickel content.[108]

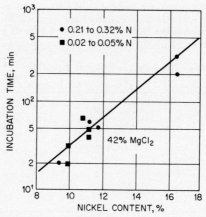

Fig. 40 Effect of nickel and nitrogen content on incubation time for onset of cracking of 17 to 19Cr-0.03 to 0.06C steels.[109]

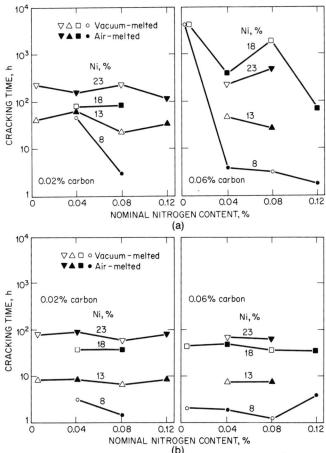

Fig. 41 Effect of nickel, nitrogen, and carbon on stress corrosion of *(a)* annealed and *(b)* cold-worked austenitic stainless steel in boiling 42% MgC1₂.[110]

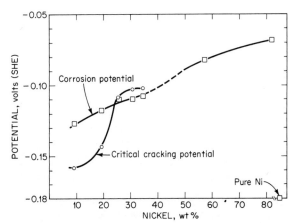

Fig 42 Effect of alloyed nickel on critical cracking and corrosion potentials of 20% Cr stainless steels in MgCl₂ at 130°C (266°F).[108]

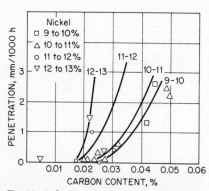

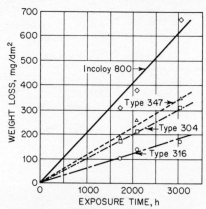

Fig. 43 Influence of carbon and nickel content on the depth of intergranular corrosion in boiling copper sulfate. Steels cooled in air from 1075°C (1967°F) and reheated 100 h at 550°C (1022°F).[3]

Fig. 44 Corrosion behavior of annealed LMFBR materials in sodium at 1300°F (704°C) with less than 10 ppm oxygen and a velocity of 17 ft/s (5.2 m/s).[122]

range 6 to 12% nickel.[126] Similarly, nickel has little effect on thermal conductivity over the temperature range 0 to 900°F (−17 to 477°C).

Stacking-Fault Energy   A systematic study by Dulieu and Nutting[127] has shown a well-defined increase in stacking-fault energy of 18% Cr steels with increasing nickel content (Fig. 48). They showed an increase in stacking-fault energy of about 1.4 ergs/cm² (1.4 × 10⁻⁷ J/cm²) for every atomic percent of nickel added. Silcock et al.[128] examined steels with chromium contents in the range 15 to 16% and found an increase of 0.7 to 0.95 erg/cm² (7 × 10⁻⁸ to 9.5 × 10⁻⁸ J/cm²) for every atomic percent of nickel added.

Castings   Beckius[129] studied the effect of nickel on density and solidification shrinkage of a 17.7Cr-0.04C steel. He observed a sharp increase in density from about 7.62 to about 7.77 g/cm³ as nickel content increased from about 4.5 to 8% as the structure changes from ferritic to austenitic. Increasing nickel content from 0 to 15% progressively increased solidification shrinkage. Shrinkage of the 15% Ni steel was almost twice that of the nickel-free steel.

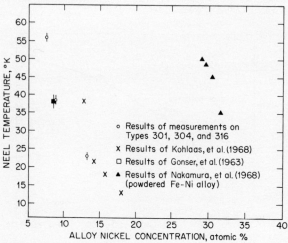

Fig. 45   Plot of Neel temperature vs. nickel content of several Fe−Ni and Fe−Cr−Ni alloys.[123]

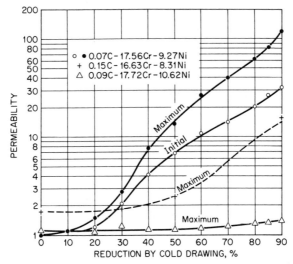

Fig. 46   Effect of cold-work on the permeability of 18-8 stainless steel.[124]

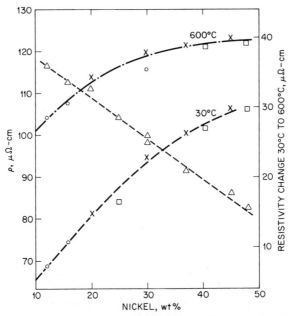

X Alloys prepared by British Steel Corp.
□ Alloys prepared by Central Electricity Generating Board
o Alloys containing NbC
△ Change in resistivity from 30 to 600°C (303 to 873 K)

Fig. 47   Resistivity of Fe–16Cr–Ni alloys with varying nickel content.[125]

Regarding the effect of nickel on room-temperature properties of austenitic stainless steel castings, data by Franson[130] on the effect of increasing nickel content on CF-3M (19Cr-12Ni-2.5Mo) and CF-3 (19Cr-11Ni) alloys indicated that sigma-phase embrittlement in as-cast, air-cooled 8-in. (20.32-cm) sections could be eliminated by increasing

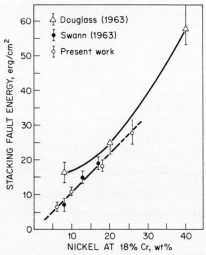

Fig. 48   Influence of nickel content on stacking-fault energy of Fe–18Cr alloys.[127]

nickel content to 18%. Impact values were increased from 6 to 9 ft-lb (8.1 to 12.2 J) to 200 ft-lb (271.2 J). No advantage was gained by increasing the nickel content of the CF-3 alloy.

REFERENCES

1. Monypenny, J. H. G.: in F. C. Thompson (ed.), "Stainless Iron and Steel, Vol. 2, Microstructure and Constitution," 3d ed. rev., p. 113, Chapman and Hall, London, 1954.
2. "Chromium-Nickel Stainless Steels," p. 7, Dev. and Res. Dept., The International Nickel Company, Ltd., 1962.
3. Colombier, L., and J. Hochmann: "Stainless and Heat Resisting Steels," p. 16, translated by Scripta Technica Ltd., Edward Arnold, St Martin's Press, New York, 1968.
4. Keating, F. H.: "Chromium-Nickel Austenitic Steels," Butterworths Scientific Publications and Imperial Chemical Industries, London, 1956.
5. Floreen, S., and H. W. Hayden: *Trans. Am. Soc. Met.*, vol. 61, p. 489, 1968.
6. Hayden, H. W., and S. Floreen: *Metall. Trans.*, vol. 1, p. 1955, 1970.
7. Binder, W. O., C. M. Brown, and R. Franks: *Trans. Am. Soc. Met.*, vol. 41, p. 1301, 1949.
8. Pryce, L., and K. W. Andrews: *J. Iron Steel Inst. London*, vol. 195, p. 145, 1960.
9. Scherer, G., G. Riedrich, and G. Hoch: *Arch. Eisenhuettenwes.*, vol. 7, p. 187, 1933.
10. Post, C. B., and W. S. Eberly: *Trans. Am. Soc. Met.*, vol. 39, p. 868, 1947.
11. Thomas, R. O., Jr.: Private communication from H. Thielsch referenced in *Weld. J., Res. Suppl.*, vol. 30, p. 209, 1951.
12. Schafmeister, P., and R. Ergang: *Arch. Eisenhuettenwes.*, vol. 12, p. 459, 1938–1939.
13. Oliver, D. A.: *Met. Prog.*, vol. 55, p. 665, 1949.
14. Nicholson, M. E., C. H. Samans, and F. J. Shortsleeve: *Trans. Am. Soc. Met.*, vol. 44, p. 601, 1952.
15. Eichelman, A. H., Jr., and F. C. Hull: *Trans. Am. Soc. Met.*, vol. 45, p. 77, 1953.
16. Besabrasow, S. W., and A. M. Samarin: *Izv. Akad. Nauk. SSSR, Otd. Tekh. Nauk.*, no. 12, p. 1790, 1953.
17. Gibson, R. C., H. W. Hayden, and J. H. Brophy: *Trans. Am. Soc. Met.*, vol. 61, p. 85, 1968.
18. Wood, G. C.: *Corros. Sci.*, vol. 2, p. 173, 1962.
19. Properties of Carbon and Alloy Seamless Steel Tubing for High-Temperature and High-Pressure Service, *Tech. Bull. no. 6-E*, The Babcock and Wilcox Tube Co., 1948.
20. Sharp, W. B. A.: *Corros. Sci.*, vol. 8, p. 717, 1968.
21. Jackson, P.: *J. Inst. Fuel*, p. 315, 1967.
22. "Acid and Heat Resisting Steels," Bulletin, Uddeholm Corrosion, Uddeholm Aktiebolog, Uddeholm, Sweden, 1947.

23. MacDonald, D. F.: Unpublished work at The International Nickel Company, Inc., May 1970.
24. Church, N. L.: Unpublished work at The International Nickel Company, Inc., October 1970.
25. Snape, E.: Unpublished work at The International Nickel Company, Inc., February 1971.
26. Thielsch, H.: *Weld. J., Res. Suppl.*, p. 577, December 1950.
27. Aronsson, B., and J. Manenc: *Mem. Sci. Rev. Metall.*, vol. 64, p. 1037, 1967.
28. Hughes, H.: *J. Iron Steel Inst. London*, vol. 203, p. 1019, 1965.
29. Hopkin, L. M. T.: *Prog. Appl. Mater. Res.*, vol. 7, p. 33, 1967.
30. Pickering, F. B.: *Iron Steel Inst. London Spec. Rept.* no. 114, p. 131, 1968.
31. "Metals Handbook," 8th ed., vol. 1, p. 418, American Society for Metals, Metals Park, Ohio, 1961.
32. Wylie, R. D.: "Low Carbon Ferritic Stainless Steel," U.S. Patent 3,023,098, Feb. 27, 1962.
33. Coffin, F. P., and T. H. Swisher: *Trans. ASME*, vol. 54, p. 59, 1932.
34. Gulyaev, A. P., Z. G. Fel'dgandler, and L. Ya Savkina: *Met. Sci. Heat Treat.*, nos. 3–4, p. 181, March–April 1965.
35. Bandel, B., and W. Tofaute: *Arch. Eisenhuettenwes.*, vol. 15, p. 307, 1941.
36. Bieber, C. G.: Unpublished work at The International Nickel Company, Inc., 1969.
37. Waxweiler, J. H.: U.S. Patent 2,851,384, Sept. 9, 1958.
38. Arness, W. B.: U.S.Patent 2,310,341, Feb. 9, 1943.
39. Eberle, F.: *Babcock and Wilcox Tube Company Rept. no. 2786*, October 1942.
40. Chernova, G. P., and N. D. Tomashov: *Corros. Met. Alloys*, no. 5, p. 1, 1965.
41. Binder, W. O.: "Corrosion of Metals," p. 56, American Society for Metals, Cleveland, Ohio, 1946.
42. Lizlovs, E. A., and A. P. Bond: *J. Electrochem. Soc.*, vol. 116, p. 574, 1969.
43. Langer, N. A., N. N. Yagupol'skaya, N. I. Kakhovskii, Y. A. Yushchenko, V. G. Fartushnyi, and G. I. Chalyuk: *Met. Sci. Heat Treat.*, nos. 1–2, p. 121, 1966.
44. Lizlovs, E. A., and A. P. Bond: *J. Electrochem. Soc.*, vol. 118, p. 22, 1971.
45. Colbeck, E. W., and R. P. Garner: *J. Iron Steel Inst. London*, vol. 139, p. 99, 1939.
46. Kuczynski, W., and M. H. Weiss: *Przem. Chem.*, vol. 17, p. 175, 1933.
47. Maxwell, H. L.: in H. H. Uhlig (ed.), "Corrosion Handbook," p. 148, Wiley, New York, 1948.
48. Baerlecken, E., W. A. Fischer, and K. Lorenz: *Stahl Eisen*, vol. 81, p. 768, 1961.
49. Bond, A. P., and H. J. Dundas: *Corrosion*, vol. 24, p. 344, 1968.
50. Scheil, M. A.: "Symposium on Stress Corrosion Cracking of Metals," p. 395, ASTM-AIME, 1944.
51. Schreir, L. L.: "Corrosion of Metals and Alloys," vol. 1, George Neimes, London, 1963.
52. Graf, L.: in W. D. Robertson (ed.), "Stress-Corrosion Cracking and Embrittlement," p. 48, Wiley, New York, 1956.
53. Latanision, R. M., and R. W. Staehle: *Proc. Conf. Fund. Aspects Stress Corrosion Cracking*, p. 214, NACE, Houston, Texas, 1967.
54. Copson, H. R.: in T. N. Rhodin (ed.), "Physical Metallurgy of Stress-Corrosion Fracture," p. 126, Interscience, New York, 1959.
55. Truman, J. E.: "Metals and Materials," vol. 2, p. 208, 1968.
56. Anderson, D. B.: Unpublished work by The International Nickel Company, Inc., Mar. 31, 1971.
57. Gurinsky, D. H.: *AIME Nuclear Metallurgy Symp.*, p. 1, 1956.
58. Masumoto, H., and N. Nakamura: *Nippon Kinzoku Gakkaishi*, vol. 32, no. 9, p. 852, 1968.
59. Shelton, S. M., and W. H. Swanger: *Trans. Am. Soc. Steel Treat.*, vol. 21, p. 127, 1933.
60. Bozorth, R. M.: "Ferromagnetism," Van Nostrand, New York, 1951.
61. Houdremont, E.: "Handbuch der Sonderstahlkunde," 3d ed., Springer, Berlin, 1963.
62. Edstrom, J. O.: *J. Iron Steel Inst. London*, vol. 185, p. 450, 1957.
63. Colbeck, E. W.: *Trans. Manchester Assoc. Eng.*, vol. 1, 1949–1950.
64. Moll, J. H., W. Stasko, and A. Kasak: *Tech. Rept. AFML-TR-67-286*, September 1967.
65. Cameron, J.: *Met. Treat. London*, p. 149, 1953.
66. Taylor, V. G.: Unpublished work at The International Nickel Company, Inc., November 1967.
67. Souresny, H., and H. Sauer: *Giesserei-Rundschau*, vol. 15, no. 12, p. 29, 1968.
68. Mousson, J. M.: *Edison Electr. Inst. Bull.*, vol. 5, p. 373, 1937.
69. Dvorak, R. J., and J. C. Fritz: *Met. Prog.*, vol. 86, no. 2, p. 174, 1964.
70. Floreen, S.: *Trans. Am. Foundrymen's Soc.*, vol. 79, p. 25, 1971.
71. Cherkashina, N. P., V. V. Barzii, and A. A. Babakov: *Met. Sci. Heat Treat.*, p. 191, April 1965.
72. Brasunas, A. de S, J. T. Gow, and D. E. Harder: *Symp. Materials Gas Turbines*, ASTM, 1946.
73. Gibson, R. C.: Unpublished work at The International Nickel Company, Inc., June 1969.
74. Gulyaev, A. P., A. G. Fel'dgandler, and L-Ya. Savkina: *Met. Sci. Heat Treat.*, p. 181, April 1965.
75. Jackson, R. P.: Unpublished work at The International Nickel Company, Inc., September 1968.
76. Forbes Jones, R. M.: Paper presented at 76th Am. Foundrymen's Soc. Casting Cong., Philadelphia, 1972.
77. Kane, R. H.: Private communication, The International Nickel Company, Inc.
78. Ludwigson, D. C., and K. G. Brickner: "Mechanical Working and Steel Processing VI," p. 71, 1969.
79. Janzon, B.: *J. Iron and Steel Inst. London*, p. 826, October 1971.
80. Hobby, M. G., and G. C. Wood: *Oxid. Met.*, vol. 1, no 1, p. 23, 1969.
81. Krovobok, V. N., et al.: *Trans. Am. Soc. Met.*, vol. 25, p. 637, 1937.
82. Kovneristyi, Y. K., and V. M. Blinov: *Met. Sci. Heat Treat.*, no. 1, p. 52, 1971.
83. Ul'yanin, E. A., N. A. Sorokina, and Y. M. Zaretskii: *Met. Sci. Heat Treat.*, no. 9, p. 8, 1969.

84. Ul'yanin, E.A., and B.M. Ovsyannikov: *Met. Sci. Heat Treat.*, no. 5–6, p. 467, 1970.
85. Spaeder, C. E., and K. G. Brickner: Paper presented at Pet. Mech. Eng. Pressure Vessels Piping Conf., Denver, Colo., September 1970.
86. "Chromium-Nickel Stainless Steel Data," *Sec. I, Bull. B*, Dev. and Res. Dept., The International Nickel Company, Inc., 1963.
87. Kovnersistyi, S. E., et al.: *Met. Sci. Heat Treat.*, no. 4, p. 30, 1971.
88. Pilling, N. B., and R. Worthington: *Symp. Effect Temp. Property of Metals, ASTM Spec. Tech. Publ. STP 12*, p. 495, 1931.
89. Mel'kumov, I. N., and V. V. Topilin: *Met. Sci. Heat Treat.*, no. 3, p. 47, 1969.
90. Zapffe, C. A.: *Trans. Am. Soc. Met.*, vol. 34, p. 71, 1945.
91. Holmes, B., and T. Gladman: *British Steel Corp. Publ. SF 732*, May 1970, 5 pp.
92. Funke, P., K. Bungardt, and W. Küppers: *DEW Tech. Ber.*, vol. 9, p. 370, 1969.
93. Griffin, D. F.: *Am. Mach.*, p. 115, Jun. 22, 1964.
94. Centi, G., and A. Masi: *Assoc. Ital. Chem. Eng. Symp.*, Nazionale Cogne Spa, Milan, May 4–27, 1971, 6 pp.
95. Gotal'skii, Yu. N., and V. G. Vasil'ev: *Autom. Weld.* (USSR), no. 5, p. 8, 1969.
96. Zemzin, V. N.: *Mashinostroenie*, Moscow, 1966.
97. Ignatov, V. A., V. N. Zemzin, and G. L. Petrov: *Autom. Weld. (USSR)*, no. 8, p. 1, 1967.
98. Sadowski, E. P.: Paper presented at 54th Ann. Meeting Am. Weld. Soc., Chicago, Apr. 6, 1973.
99. Dautovich, D. P.: Unpublished work at The International Nickel Company, Inc., 1972.
100. Troselius, L.: *Corros. Sci.*, vol. 11, p. 473, 1971.
101. Padget, G., J. S. Wilde, and A. Edwards: *British Steel Corp. Publ. SF 729*, May 1970.
102. Tomashov, M. D.: *Prot. Met. (USSR)*, vol. 3, p. 1, 1968.
103. Brunet, S., et al: *Mem. Sci. Rev. Metall.*, vol. 67, p. 781, 1970.
104. Zitter, H., and F. Matzer: *Nickel-Ber.*, vol. 26, p. 129, 1968.
105. Scarberry, R. C., D. L. Graver, and C. D. Stephens: *CEBELCOR Tech. Rept. RT. 153*, January 1969.
106. Copson, H.: "Physical Metallurgy of Stress Corrosion Fracture," p. 247, Interscience Publishers, New York, 1959.
107. Dautovich, D. P.: Unpublished work at The International Nickel Company, Inc., 1972.
108. Lee, H. H., and H. H. Uhlig: *J. Electrochem. Soc.*, vol. 117, no. 1, p. 18, 1970.
109. Wiegand, H., F. W. Hirth, R. Naumann, and H. Speckhardt: *Werkst. Korros.*, vol. 22, p. 612, July 1971.
110. Loginow, A. W., and J. F. Bates: *Corrosion*, vol. 25, no. 1, p. 15, 1969.
111. Ryabchenkov, A. V., and V. P. Sidorov: *Zashch. Met.*, vol. 5, no. 4, p. 376, 1969.
112. Harston, J. D., and J. C. Scully: *Corrosion*, vol. 26, no. 9, p. 387, 1970.
113. Douglass, D. L., G. Thomas, and W. R. Roser: *Atomic Power Equip. Dept. Rept. APED-4239*, General Electric Co., April 1963.
114. Mel'kumov, I. N., and V. V. Topilin: *Met. Sci. Heat Treat.*, no. 3, p. 47, 1969.
115. Cordovi, M. A.: Paper no. 7 presented at The International Nickel Power Conf., Kyoto, Japan, 1972.
116. Coriou, H., L. Grall, P. Olivier, and H. Willermoz: *Fundamental Aspects Stress Corrosion*, NACE Proc., p. 352, 1969.
117. Coriou, Grall, and Pelras: Extended Abstract 4th *Int. Cong. Metallic Corros.*, Amsterdam, p. 94, September 1969.
118. Medvedev, Y. S., and T. D. Tomilina: *Zashch. Met.*, vol. 5, no. 4, p. 394, 1969.
119. Gulyaev, A. P., and T. B. Tokareva: *Met. Sci. Heat Treat.*, no. 2, p. 29, 1971.
120. Lagerberg, G., and L. Egnell: *Nucl. Eng. Int.*, p. 203, March 1970.
121. Ljungberg, L.: AES—384 Paper presented at the ASTM 71st Ann. Meeting, San Francisco, June 1968.
122. Roy, P., G. P. Wozaldo, and F. A. Comprelli: *Proc. Int. Conf. Sodium Tech. Large Fast Reactor Des.*, p. 131, Nov. 7–9, 1968.
123. Flansburg, L. D., and N. Hershkowitz: *J. Appl. Phys.*, vol. 41, no. 10, p. 4082, 1970.
124. Horwedel, C. R.: "Magnetic Characteristics of Some Cold-worked Austenitic Iron-Chromium-Nickel Alloy Wires," thesis, Ohio State University, 1935.
125. Silcock, J. M.: *Met. Sci. J.*, vol. 5, p. 182, 1971.
126. Furman, D. E.: *Trans. Am. Inst. Min. Metall. Pet. Eng.*, vol. 188, p. 688, 1950.
127. Dulieu, D., and J. Nutting: *Iron Steel Inst. Spec. Rept.* no. 86, p. 140, 1964.
128. Silcock, J. M., R. W. Rookes, and J. Barford: *J. Iron Steel Inst. London*, vol. 196, p. 623, June 1966.
129. Beckius, K.: *Proc. 35th Int. Foundry Cong.*, p. 19, Kyoto, Japan, October 1968.
130. Franson, I. A.: Unpublished work at The International Nickel Company, Inc., October 1966.
131. Kinzel, A. B., and R. Franks: "Alloys of Iron and Chromium," vol. 2, McGraw-Hill, New York, 1940.

Chapter **13**

Effect of Molybdenum on the Structure and Properties of Wrought and Cast Stainless Steels

ROBERT O. CARSON
Senior Research Metallurgist

RALPH G. GRAHAM
Development Metallurgist

**Atlas Steels, A Division of Rio Algom
Limited, Welland, Ontario, Canada**

The principal functions of molybdenum as an alloying element in stainless steels are:

- Improvement of the corrosion resistance of austenitic and ferritic stainless steels
- Improvement of the elevated temperature mechanical properties of austenitic stainless steels
- Improvement of the strength and resistance to tempering of martensitic stainless steels

EFFECTS OF MOLYBDENUM ON THE CORROSION RESISTANCE OF WROUGHT AUSTENITIC AND FERRITIC STAINLESS STEELS

In Seawater The significantly improved resistance to corrosion in seawater of the molybdenum-bearing AISI Types 316 and 317 austenitic stainless steels over that of the molybdenum-free Types 302, 304, and 309 is illustrated by the data presented in Table 1.[1]

The corrosion behavior of commercial high-nickel alloys in quiet or low-velocity (0.305

TABLE 1   Corrosion of Stainless Steels by Seawater Under Fouling and Nonfouling Conditions[1]

	Corrosion Rate,* mils/yr (mm/yr)	
Type	Kure Beach, N.C. (active fouling)‡	Duxbury, Mass. (nonfouling)§
302	1.1† (0.028)	0.2 (0.005)
304	1.5† (0.038)	<0.1 (0.003)
309	0.7 (0.018)	0.3 (0.008)
316	<0.1 (0.003)	<0.1 (0.003)
317	<0.1 (0.003)	<0.1 (0.003)

*Based on 160-day exposure between May and November.
†Pits completely perforated specimens.
‡Active fouling conditions refer to very low water velocities in which barnacles and other marine organisms have the opportunity to become attached to the exposed material.
§Nonfouling conditions occur when water velocities are high enough to prevent such attachment.

to 0.610 m/s or 1 to 2 ft/s) is shown in Table 2.[2] Samples were evaluated after a 2-year exposure in seawater at Wrightsville Beach, North Carolina. The Ni-Cr-Mo alloys exhibited superior resistance to corrosion when compared to the molybdenum-free alloys. In seawater at such low velocities, Type 316 stainless steel would exhibit appreciable pitting. It is generally agreed that, in order to avoid corrosion in Type 316 tubular condensers handling seawater, the flow rate through them should exceed 1.5 m/s (5 ft/s).

In Acids Molybdenum-bearing austenitic stainless steels are well-suited for applications involving contact with a variety of acids, such as phosphoric, acetic, and sulfuric. The effect of molybdenum content on the corrosion rates of a series of austenitic stainless steels in phosphoric, sulfuric, and hydrochloric acid solutions is shown in Figs. 1 to 3, respectively. The compositions of the steels used in the tests are given in Table 3 (alloys A to I, inclusive).[3]

The effect of increasing molybdenum content in improving the corrosion resistance of the steels to boiling 50 and 65% phosphoric acid solutions is very pronounced up to about 1% molybdenum (Fig. 1). Little improvement appears to have resulted from increasing molybdenum content beyond 1%.

The corrosion rates of Types 304 and 316 stainless steels in 85% phosphoric acid over the temperature range from 80 to 130°C (176 to 266°F) are compared in Table 4.[4] The transition from the passive to the active state in Type 304 occurs between 105 and 107°C (221 to 225°F). Therefore, above 107°C, there is a marked increase in the corrosion rate for that grade. Type 316 remains in the passive state up to about 130°C (266°F), at which temperature its corrosion rate becomes quite high. The corrosion rate for Type 316 at 130°C (266°F), can be reduced by a factor of 10 by anodic protection. Type 304 can be anodically protected with similar effectiveness. However, failure of the anodic coating through mechanical damage or other cause will result in localized catastrophic corrosion, if the passive/active transition temperature for the grade is exceeded.

TABLE 2 **Corrosion Rating of Nickel Alloys[2]**

Rating group	Corrosion behavior	Alloy	Major alloy content
	NO GENERAL CORROSION		
1A	No attack	N	54Ni-19Cr-10Mo-11Co
		R	62Ni-22Cr-9Mo-2Fe
		T	56Ni-16Cr-16Mo-6Fe-4W
1B	Little or no pitting on boldly exposed areas, minor attack in crevices	O	47Ni-22Cr-9Mo-18Fe
		P	69Ni-7Cr-16Mo-4Fe
		Q	42Ni-21Cr-3Mo-30Fe
		S	66Ni-20Cr-5Mo-6Fe
1C	Little or no pitting on boldly exposed surfaces, moderate to severe attack in crevices	U	53Ni-18Cr-3Mo-18Fe
		V	42Ni-12Cr-6Mo-35Fe
1D	Moderate to severe attack in boldly exposed surfaces and in crevices	G	63Ni-35Cr-2Fe
		1	76Ni-20Cr-3Fe
		J	73Ni-15Cr-7Fe
		K	30Ni-20Cr-47Fe
1E	Consistently severe attack by pitting and crevice corrosion	F	77Ni-16Cr-7Fe
		H	60Ni-19Cr-17Co
		L	32Ni-20Cr-47Fe
		A	97Ni-2Be

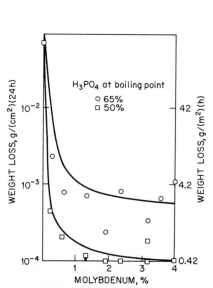

Fig. 1 Effect of molybdenum content on the corrosion rate in boiling phosphoric acid of alloys A to I (Table 3).[3]

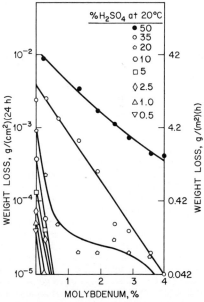

Fig. 2 Effect of molybdenum content on the corrosion rate in sulfuric acid solutions at 20°C of alloys A to I (Table 3).[3]

Corrosion rate in sulfuric acid solutions at 20°C (68°F) is reduced by increasing molybdenum content (Fig. 2). Even though the general corrosion rate is increased by increasing H_2SO_4 concentration, the beneficial effect of increasing molybdenum is still quite marked at 50% H_2SO_4.

Molybdenum does not appear to be particularly effective in reducing corrosion of austenitic stainless steels immersed in hydrochloric acid solutions at ambient temperature (Fig. 3). There does appear to be some slight reduction in corrosion rate with increasing molybdenum content in fairly dilute solutions of the acid (0.5 to 1.0% HCl).

Pitting and Crevice Corrosion   The considerable beneficial effects of molybdenum in improving the resistance of stainless steels to pitting and crevice corrosion have been determined experimentally by several investigators.

Brigham[5] has expressed critical pitting temperature (CPT) as a function of molybdenum content (Fig. 4). His work indicates that, the higher the molybdenum content (up to about

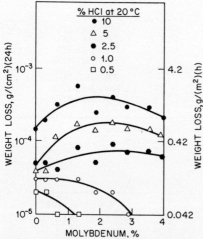

Fig. 3 Effect of molybdenum content on corrosion rate in hydrochloric acid solutions at 20°C of alloys A to I (Table 3).[3]

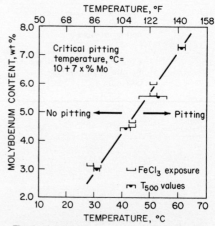

Fig. 4 Critical pitting temperature as a function of molybdenum content for experimental and commercial stainless steels. 24-h exposure in 10% $FeCl_3$ solution. Exposed in 3.5% NaCl solution, pH 3 at 500 mV_{SCE} progressively increasing temperature until pitting indicated. (SCE = saturated calomel electrode.)[4]

7%), the higher is the temperature required to produce pitting in a 10% $FeCl_3$ solution. Experimental alloys used in this work contained about 18Cr-20Ni-0.2N and up to 7% Mo. Results on commercial steels and alloys (e.g., Type 317L stainless steel) were generally similar to those of the experimental alloys having the same molybdenum contents. With combinations of temperature and molybdenum to the left of and above the line, no pitting will occur, while with those to the right of and below the line, pitting can be expected.

Bond and Lizlovs[6] demonstrated that as little as 0.5% molybdenum significantly reduced pitting in austenitic stainless steels containing 17.6Cr-13.5Ni and 20Cr-39Ni. Pitting resistance improved as molybdenum was increased from 0 to 0.5%. As could be expected, the pitting resistance of the 39% Ni steel was generally better than that of the steel containing only 13.5% nickel. In addition, these investigators found that high-purity, i.e., low-interstitial, alloys were generally superior in pitting resistance to those containing appreciable amounts of carbon and nickel. Their findings could help to explain the variations in pitting resistance observed between commercial heats of Type 304 stainless steel, in which molybdenum can vary from 0.1 to 0.6%.

Figure 5[3] illustrates the beneficial effect of increasing molybdenum content on the breakdown potentials in a 0.6% NaCl solution of the alloys listed in Table 3. The higher

TABLE 3 Steel Compositions Used for Corrosion Tests by Truman et al.[3]

Alloy origin	C	Si	Mn	Cr	Ni	Mo	N	S	P	Co	V	Ti	Nb	W	Cu	Si
A lab.*	0.055	0.47	0.96	18.51	10.00	0.01	0.013	0.014	0.024	0.25	0.04	0.02	0.02	0.13	0.20	0.024
B lab.*	0.055	0.49	0.94	18.44	10.05	0.29	0.015	0.015	0.024	0.27	0.05	0.02	0.02	0.13	0.21	0.026
C lab.*	0.06	0.48	0.91	18.40	9.98	0.70	0.015	0.015	0.025	0.27	0.05	0.02	0.02	0.14	0.22	0.024
D lab.*	0.055	0.53	1.14	17.93	10.01	1.26	0.013	0.016	0.026	0.25	0.04	0.02	0.02	0.13	0.23	0.025
E lab.*	0.05	0.49	1.18	17.56	11.50	1.90	0.012	0.014	0.022	0.24	0.04	0.02	0.02	0.14	0.20	0.020
F lab.*	0.05	0.51	1.17	17.61	11.76	2.42	0.013	0.015	0.023	0.24	0.04	0.02	0.02	0.14	0.21	0.018
G lab.*	0.055	0.54	1.45	18.55	13.94	2.92	0.011	0.016	0.023	0.25	0.04	0.02	0.02	0.13	0.21	0.020
H lab.*	0.06	0.47	1.44	18.58	13.90	3.56	0.012	0.017	0.025	0.25	0.04	0.02	0.02	0.13	0.22	0.018
I lab.*	0.05	0.51	1.41	18.48	14.95	3.98	0.012	0.016	0.023	0.24	0.05	0.02	0.02	0.14	0.22	0.020
J lab.†	0.043	0.50	0.74	18.22	14.80	0.02	0.034	0.009	0.007	0.01	0.03			0.03		
K lab.†	0.046	0.46	0.71	18.26	15.03	0.99	0.035	0.006	0.007	0.07						
L lab.†	0.056	0.56	0.73	18.24	15.05	2.31	0.030	0.008	0.006							
M lab.†	0.051	0.54	0.73	18.20	15.00	3.96	0.033	0.009	0.008	0.08						
Q comm.	0.06	0.58	1.64	18.81	10.20	0.17		0.007	0.028							
R comm.	0.06	0.37	1.51	17.84	9.90	2.98		0.006	0.022			0.007	0.002		0.10	
S comm.	0.05	0.32	0.38	18.40	9.20	2.75		0.012	0.013							
T comm.	0.06	0.58	1.64	18.81	10.20	0.32		0.007	0.030							
U comm.	0.07	0.49	1.57	18.65	9.42	1.25		0.008	0.030							
V comm.	0.05	0.43	1.56	17.47	11.41	2.80		0.015	0.023							

*Iron, nickel, ferromolybdenum, ferrochromium.
†Iron, nickel, ferromolybdenum, ferrochromium + added base elements.

TABLE 4   Corrosion Rates of Types 304 and 316 Stainless Steel in 85% Phosphoric Acid[4]

Temperature, °C	Corrosion rate, mg/(dm²)(day) [g/(m²)(h)]	
	Type 304	Type 316
80	3 (0.013)	2 (0.008)
100	19 (0.08)	53 (0.223)
113	2,600 (10.92)	205 (0.861)
130	10,600 (44.52)	1,850 (7.77)

the breakdown potential (the potential required to produce a current of 0.1 A/m²) the greater is the resistance to pitting.

The resistances of 10 different metals and alloys to pitting corrosion in a ClO_2 solution simulating that used in wood-pulp bleaching operations are compared in Table 5.[7] The reference metal (No. 7 in the table) was Type 316 stainless steel to which a corrosion rate of 1 was assigned. The corrosion rates of all the other materials were compared thereto. Disregarding the metals tantalum, titanium, and pure lead, the marked improvement in corrosion resistance with increasing molybdenum content is evident.

Table 6 compares the relative corrosion, appearing as pits, of the same 10 metals and alloys, plus Inconel, in a solution which simulates the chloride-bearing waters of pulp-bleaching plants.[8] Insofar as is practicable, it is general practice to protect the metal parts in the chlorinating stage with rubber coverings. However, some metal parts must remain exposed to the corroding environment, and the use of corrosion-resistant steels and alloys is therefore mandatory in their manufacture.

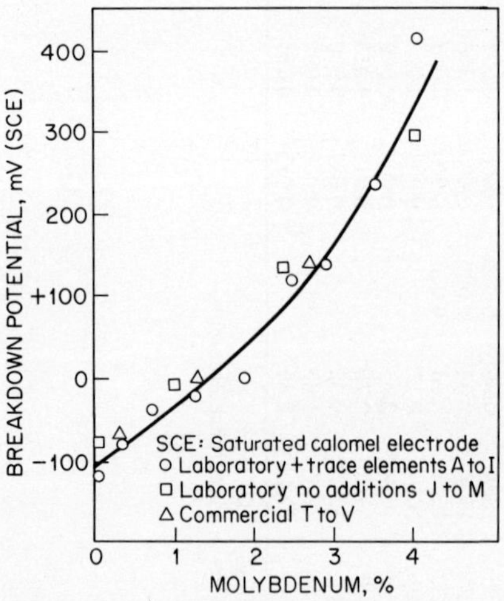

Fig. 5 Effect of molybdenum content on breakdown potential of alloys A to I, J to M, T to V (Table 3) in a 0.6 M NaCl + 0.1 M NaClCO₃ solution.[3]

The corrosion resistance of the 18% Cr stainless steels is also improved by molybdenum additions. The most commonly used molybdenum-bearing ferritic stainless steel is AISI Type 434 (18Cr-1Mo), which exhibits superior corrosion resistance to the molybdenum-free 18% Cr grade, AISI Type 430. Increasing the molybdenum content to 2% further improves corrosion resistance. The composition limits of the 18Cr-2Mo grade are given in Table 7.[9] It is noted that, as well as controlling interstitials (carbon plus nitrogen) to a low total level, the steel is stabilized to avoid sensitization to intergranular corrosion in weldments by either a titanium or columbium (niobium) addition.

Table 8 shows that 18Cr-2Mo exhibits superior pitting corrosion resistance to that of either Type 304 or Type 430. The limited data on Type 316 suggests that the pitting corrosion resistance of it and 18Cr-2Mo are similar. Crevice corrosion resistance of the 18Cr-2Mo grade appears to be similar or slightly superior to that of Type 316 (Table 9).[9]

The effect of molybdenum in increasing the pitting potential and, hence, resistance to pitting corrosion of 17 to 18% Cr ferritic stainless steels in a 0.1 N HCl solution is illustrated in Table 10.[10] All the ferritic stainless steels studied in this investigation, i.e., those listed in Table 10, were very sensitive to crevice corrosion in HCl solutions.

Lizlovs and Bond also studied the effects of molybdenum additions to 25% Cr ferritic steels (similar to AISI Type 442) on their corrosion resistance.[11] Their findings are summarized in Tables 11 and 12. Table 11 shows that increasing molybdenum content up to 3.5 to 5.0% improves the corrosion resistance of high-purity (low-interstitial) 25% Cr steels in both oxygen-saturated 1 N H_2SO_4 and nitrogen-saturated 1 N HCl solutions. In Table 12, the resistance to pitting corrosion of high-purity and commercial-purity 25% Cr

TABLE 5 Comparison of the Corrosion Rates of Different Metals and Alloys in a ClO₂ Solution[7]

SOLUTION CONDITIONS: ClO_2 concentration: 0.05 g of active Cl per liter
Chloride concentration: 0.05 mols/liter as NaCl
Temperature, 50°C (132°F), pH = 1.2

Material	Composition, %				Relative corrosion rate
	Cr	Ni	Mo	Other	
1. Tantalum					0.000
2. Titanium					0.003
3. Hastelloy C	17	51	19		0.04
4. Acid-proof steel	18	15	4.3		0.20
5. Lead, chemically pure					0.45
6. Incoloy 825	About 20	About 40	About 3	Cu about 2	0.8
7. Reference metal*	17	13	2.4		1
8. Stainless steel	18	9			1.7
9. Aluminum				0.01Cu	24
10. Carbon steel				0.03–0.06C	32

*Corrosion rate of reference metal, Type 316 stainless steel (No. 7): 0.75 g/(m²)(h).

TABLE 6 Comparison of Corrosion Rates of Different Metals and Alloys in a Cl₂ Solution[8]

COMPOSITION: Chloride = 0.2 mols/liter, pH = 1.2, Cl_2 concentration = 0.5 g active Cl/liter.
TEST TIME: 100 h, except for carbon steel and aluminum which were removed after 2 h

Material	Composition %				Relative corrosion rate
	Cr	Ni	Mo	Others	
1. Titanium					0.00
2. Tantalum					0.01
3. Incoloy 825	About 20	About 40	About 3	Cu about 2	0.02
4. Hastelloy C	17	51	19		0.03
5. Acid-proof steel	18	15	4.3		0.31
6. Acid-proof steel*	17	13	2.4		1.0
7. Lead, chemically pure					1.1
8. Stainless steel	18	9			2.0
9. Inconel					3.7
10. Aluminum				0.01Cu	54
11. Carbon steel				0.03–0.06C	165

*Corrosion rate of reference metal Type 316 stainless steel (No. 6), assigned relative rate of 1.0, was 0.1 g/(m²)(h).

TABLE 7 Composition Limits for 18Cr-2Mo Ferritic Stainless Steel[9]

%C + %N	0.04 max.
%Cr	18/20
%Mo	1.75/2.25
%Ti	0.25 min. [5 × (%C + %N) min.]
or	
%Cb	9 × (%C + %N) min.
%Mn	1.0 max.
%Si	1.0 max.
%S	0.03 max.
%P	0.04 max.
%Cu	0.2 max. ⎫ %Cu + %Ni, 0.5 max.
%Ni	0.4 max. ⎭

TABLE 8   Comparison of Resistance to Pitting Corrosion of Four Stainless Steels in Oxygen-saturated NaCl Solutions at 90°C[9]

Solution, ppm			Weight loss, mg/(dm²)(day) [g/(m²)(h)]			
Cl⁻	Cu²⁺	Zn²⁺	18Cr-2Mo	Type 430	Type 304	Type 316
18,200			0	46 (0.19)	0	
1200	400		180 (0.76)	900 (3.78)	190 (0.8)	
600	1	5	0.4 (0.002)		6.1 (0.026)	
600	5		3.3 (0.014)		14 (0.059)	1.4 (0.006)
600	20		6.0 (0.025)		84 (0.35)	9.0 (0.038)
180	60		0.9 (0.004)	40 (0.17)	5 (0.02)	

TABLE 9   Comparison of Crevice* Corrosion Rates for Three Stainless Steels in Oxygen-saturated NaCl Solutions[9]

Solution, ppm		Weight loss, mg/(dm²)(day) [g/(m²)(h)]		
Cl⁻	Cu²⁺	18Cr-2Mo	Type 304	Type 316
600	1	0.8 (0.003)	12 (0.05)	3.5 (0.01)
200	1	0.2 (0.0008)	15 (0.06)	2.6 (0.01)

*Crevices artificially formed by use of rubber bands and plastic spacers during exposure.

TABLE 10   Average Pitting Potentials of Some Ferritic Stainless Steels in 0.1 N Hydrochloric Acid[10]

Alloy	Average pitting potential vs. SCE,* V
Type 430	0.18
Type 434	0.19
17Cr	0.26
17Cr-1Mo	0.32
17Cr-3Mo	>0.80
18Cr-2Mo-0.11Ni	0.31
18Cr-2Mo-0.62Ni	0.35
18Cr-2Mo-1.08Ni	0.34
18Cr-2Mo-0.47Ti	>0.8
18Cr-2Mo-1.86Ti	0.63
18Cr-2Mo-0.91Ti-0.57Ni	>0.8
18Cr-2Mo-1.75Ti-2.08Ni	0.62

*SCE = saturated calomel electrode.

TABLE 11   Corrosion Rates of High-Purity 25% Cr Ferritic Stainless Steels at 25°C[11]

	Corrosion rate, mg/(dm²)(day) [g/(m²)(h)] after 24-h exposure	
Steel	1N H₂SO₄ O₂-saturated	1N HCl N₂-saturated
25Cr	20,000 (84)	39,400 (165.5)
25Cr-2Mo	2,450 (10.3)	1,260 (5.3)
25Cr-3.5Mo	Nil*	556 (2.3)
25Cr-5Mo	Nil*	307 (1.3)

*Six-day exposure.

steels are compared. The levels of the interstitials, carbon and nitrogen, in the commercial steels were found to be detrimental to pitting corrosion resistance in acidified 0.33 M $FeCl_3$ solutions even when molybdenum content was raised to 5.0%. The high-purity 25% Cr steel containing no molybdenum did not pit but exhibited only uniform corrosion in the same medium.

A commercially available ferritic stainless steel containing 26% chromium and 1% molybdenum exhibits better resistance to both pitting and crevice corrosion than does Type 316 stainless steel. This grade, known commercially as E-Brite 26:1, is electron-beam melted to achieve very low interstitial levels (0.005% maximum carbon, 0.015% maximum nitrogen) in order to prevent embrittlement and also to achieve its outstanding corrosion resistance. However, the costly melting operation, together with rather stringent licensing requirements, have precluded wide commercial application of the grade up to this time.

Stress Corrosion   The 18Cr-8Ni austenitic stainless steels are susceptible to stress-corrosion failures under high stresses in chloride environments. Truman et al.[3] found no difference in rupture time for Type 304 and Type 316 specimens stressed to the same level in boiling 42% $MgCl_2$ solutions. Type 316 exhibited a slightly longer rupture time in a boiling 30% NaCl solution than did Type 304 under the same conditions of stress. It is therefore evident that molybdenum has no appreciable beneficial effect on stress-corrosion failures in chloride environments. In order to overcome stress-corrosion failures in austenitic stainless steels, nickel contents of 35% or more are required. The ferritic stainless grades (AISI Types 430 and 434, 18Cr-2Mo and E-Brite 26:1) are immune to stress-corrosion cracking in chloride environments.

EFFECTS OF MOLYBDENUM ON THE STRUCTURE AND PROPERTIES OF STAINLESS STEELS

Structure Effects in Austenitic Stainless Steels   Molybdenum is known as a *ferrite former* in stainless steels, i.e., it tends to promote ferrite formation and to restrict austenite formation. In the Cr-Ni austenitic stainless steels, the tendency of molybdenum is therefore to promote a duplex structure which is prone to tearing during deformation at hot-working temperatures. In addition, the ferrite tends to transform to the brittle sigma and/or chi phases (depending on molybdenum content) during holding in or slow cooling through the temperature range of 750 to 870°C (about 1380 to 1600°F). To minimize the formation of the undesirable ferrite, sigma or chi phases, compositions are "balanced" to compensate for the molybdenum addition. This is usually accomplished by increasing nickel (austenite-former) content and reducing chromium (ferrite-former) content. This "balancing" is seen in the compositions of AISI Types 304 and 316 (see Appendix 1, United States).

Mechanical Properties of Austenitic Stainless Steels   The room-temperature mechanical properties of austenitic stainless steels are not appreciably altered by additions of 2 to 4% molybdenum. Typical annealed properties of Type 304 and Type 316 stainless steels at room temperature are, for all practical purposes, identical and of the following order:

> Ultimate tensile strength . . . .   568 MPa (82.4 ksi)
> 0.2% offset yield strength . . . . . .   276 MPa (40 ksi)
> Elongation 50%
> Hardness . . . .   149 Brinell
> Impact strength (standard Izod) .   110 ft-lb (149J)
> Modulus of elasticity in tension .   193,000 MPa (28×10^6 psi)

However, elevated temperature ultimate tensile and yield strengths are increased by molybdenum additions. (See comparison for Types 304 and 316 in Table 13.) Resistance to creep at elevated temperatures of Type 316 is also superior to that of Type 304. A stress of 171 MPa is necessary to produce 1% creep in Type 316 in 10,000 h at 538°C (1000°F). To produce the same amount of creep in Type 304 under the same temperature and time conditions, the stress required is only 119 MPa. High-temperature oxidation resistance of the austenitic stainless steels does not appear to be affected appreciably by molybdenum content.

TABLE 12   Comparison of Corrosion Rates of High-Purity and Commercial-Purity 25% Cr Ferritic Stainless Steels in Acidified 0.33 M FeCl₃ Solutions at 25°C[11]

Steel	High-purity alloys*		Commercial-purity alloys†	
	Exposure, days	Corrosion rate, mg/(dm²)(day) [g/(m²)(h)]	Exposure, days	Corrosion rate, mg/(dm²)(day) [g/(m²)(h)]
25Cr	7	40 (0.17)	1	1,224 (5.14)
25Cr-1Mo			1	3,112 (13.07)
25Cr-2Mo	31	Nil		
25Cr-2.5Mo			1	855 (3.59)
25Cr-3.5Mo	31	Nil	1	558 (2.34)
25Cr-5Mo	31	Nil	1	324 (1.36)

*Tested at pH 1.
†Tested at pH 2.

Hot Workability   Increasing the molybdenum content of the Cr-Ni austenitic stainless steels contributes to hot-working difficulties. Since Type 316 is stronger than Type 304 at hot-working temperatures (1100 to 1300°C), greater force is required to produce the same amount of deformation. This problem is further accentuated with Type 317, which contains about 1% more molybdenum than Type 316. Furthermore, the hot ductility of the molybdenum-bearing austenitic stainless steels is generally lower than that of the molybdenum-free grades. Therefore more frequent reheats are often necessary when hot-working the molybdenum-bearing grades. Consequently, yields from cast to wrought product can be somewhat lower than for the molybdenum-free steels. This is particularly true if the combination of lower hot ductility and higher ferrite content leads to hot tearing, and thus, to increased conditioning losses. Therefore careful control of composition balance during steelmaking, in order to minimize ferrite in the cast product, is an important aspect in the manufacture of molybdenum-bearing austenitic stainless steels.

The contribution of increasing molybdenum content to higher hot strength and lower hot ductility is probably the principal reason why relatively few austenitic stainless steel grades containing more than 6% molybdenum are produced commercially. The increased tendency to sigma- and/or chi-phase embrittlement as molybdenum content is increased may also be an important consideration.

Martensitic Stainless Steels   The martensitic stainless steels (nominally containing about 12% chromium, e.g., AISI Type 410) are employed in applications requiring a combination of high strength plus a limited degree of corrosion resistance. The corrosion resistance of such grades is generally quite inferior to that of the ferritic Type 430

TABLE 13   Comparison of Ultimate Tensile and Yield Strengths of Types 304 and 316 Stainless Steel at Room and Elevated Temperatures

Temperature			Ultimate tensile strength		0.2% offset yield strength	
°C	°F	Type	ksi	MPa	ksi	MPa
20	68	304	85	586	35	241
		316	85	586	38	262
316	600	304	64	441	25	172
		316	78	538	35	241
538	1000	304	55	379	18	124
		316	66	455	28	193
760	1400	304	29	200	14	96.5
		316	40	276	20	138
871	1600	304	17	117	10	68.9
		316	25	172	15	103

but ultimate tensile strengths in excess of 1379 MPa (200,000 psi) can be developed by heat treatment.

Molybdenum additions (0.5 to 4.0%) increase the tempering resistance (Fig. 6) and intensify the secondary hardening reaction of the 12% Cr martensitic stainless steels. Molybdenum also improves room-temperature ultimate and yield strengths (Fig. 7) and

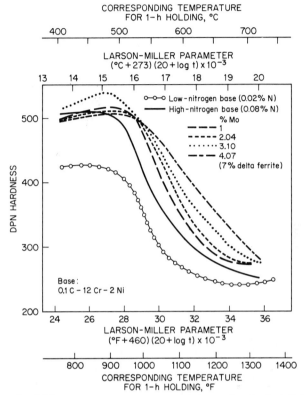

Fig. 6 Effect of molybdenum on tempering resistance and secondary hardening of a 12% Cr martensitic stainless steel.[12]

resistance to deformation at elevated temperatures (Fig. 8). It should be noted that a possibly detrimental effect from retention of delta ferrite results when molybdenum contents get too high. Note retention of 7% delta ferrite with 4% molybdenum (Fig. 7).

The martensitic stainless steels are widely used in steam power plants for such components as turbine blades. Molybdenum additions increase the maximum permissible operating temperatures for such parts.

Precipitation-hardenable Stainless Steels Molybdenum is added as an alloying element to some precipitation-hardenable stainless steels, such as Armco PH15-7Mo (15Cr-7Ni-2Mo-1Al) and AM-350 (16Cr-4Ni-3Mo). The general benefits arising from the presence of molybdenum are improved corrosion resistance, ambient-temperature mechanical properties, and high-temperature strengths as compared to the molybdenum-free precipitation-hardenable grades.

Stainless Steel Castings Molybdenum, added to Cr-Ni austenitic stainless steels for cast components, has similar effects to those exhibited in the wrought steel equivalents. It improves pitting resistance in seawater and other chloride environments and general corrosion resistance to solutions of acids such as sulfuric and phosphoric. In addition, molybdenum improves resistance to deformation in castings at elevated temperatures. Table 14 compares the room and elevated temperature strengths of CF-8 and CF-8M, the cast steel equivalents of the wrought AISI Types 304 and 316, respectively.

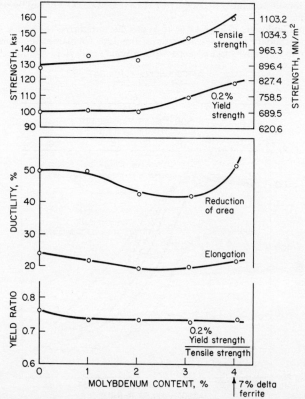

Fig. 7 Effects of molybdenum content on the room-temperature tensile properties of a quenched and tempered 12% Cr martensitic stainless steel. Base steel: same as for Fig. 6. Heat treatment: quenched 1050°C (1920°F), tempered 1h at 650°C (1200°F).[12]

Ideally, the cast structure of CF-8M consists of an austenite matrix with 5 to 20% ferrite distributed as discrete islands throughout the matrix. Molybdenum-bearing austenitic stainless steel castings are not recommended for service above 650°C (1200°F). Should the ferrite occur as a continuous, or even partly continuous, network, transformation to the brittle sigma and/or chi phase during operations at temperatures above that limit could lead to catastrophic service failures.

A molybdenum-bearing martensitic stainless steel casting grade, CA-6NM (13Cr-4Ni-0.7Mo) can be heat-treated to achieve a 0.2% offset yield strength of 695 MPa (100,000 psi) at room temperature. It also exhibits better corrosion resistance and is less sensitive to cracking during casting than the CA-15 (12% Cr) grade.

APPLICATIONS AND CASE HISTORIES

AISI Types 316 and 317 Austenitic Stainless Steels   Corrosion of equipment contributes substantially to operational costs in the chemical process industries. Molybdenum-free Cr-Ni austenitic stainless steels (such as Type 304) are used successfully for many applications in mildly and moderately corrosive environments. However, under more severely corrosive conditions, use of the molybdenum-bearing Types 316 and 317 often becomes mandatory.

Many instances of equipment failure due to excessive corrosion in the chemical processing industries have been traced to the use of Type 304 stainless steel instead of the preferred Types 316 or 317. Furthermore, low molybdenum levels in Type 316 can lead to corrosion problems. Tikkanen[13] cites an example of differential corrosion in components of fatty-acid distillation columns manufactured from Type 316 stainless steel. Some parts were found to be severely pitted while others were unattacked. Some parts rendered completely unserviceable by very severe pitting were found to contain only 1.5% molybdenum, which is less than the AISI minimum. Severe pitting was found in parts containing the AISI minimum of 2.0% molybdenum.

Parts containing 2.2% molybdenum exhibited only minor pitting. The molybdenum content of the unattacked parts was 2.7%. Also cited was the experience of a large Finnish cellulose sulfite mill. Seven digesters, lined with an austenitic stainless steel containing 4% molybdenum, were found to be corrosion-free after 10 years of service.

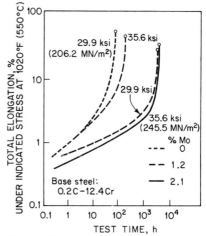

Fig. 8 Effect of molybdenum content on the resistance to hot deformation of a 12% Cr martensitic stainless steel.[12]

Type 316 stainless steel has performed satisfactorily as turbine and reheat piping in steam power-generating plants. Operating temperatures in those applications were in 540 to 650°C (1000 to 1200°F) range.[14]

Long-time exposure at elevated temperatures can reduce the toughness of Type 316 stainless steel.[15] Apparently, this results from the precipitation of carbides and sigma phase. Table 15 gives results of Charpy V-notch impact tests on specimens of welded Type 316 piping before and after cycling to simulate service in a steam power plant. The results show that a gradual decrease in impact strength, more evident in the room-temperature tests, occurred as the exposure progressed. However, impact strength at the design operating temperature of 650°C (1200°F) was still quite adequate. The total time of exposure at 665°C (1225°F) during 251 weekly cycles was 28,000 h.

Heat-affected-zone cracking has been a problem with weldments in Type 347 stainless steel, the columbium (niobium) stabilized 18Cr-8Ni grade. The same problem does not occur with weldments in Type 316 because of its higher hot ductility as compared to that of Type 347.

Fourdrinier wire for the pulp and paper industry is produced from Type 317 stainless steel by many wire manufacturers. However, in order to ensure optimum corrosion resistance, it is common practice to specify molybdenum content in the upper half of the 3 to 4% range for that application.

Other Austenitic Stainless Steels and Alloys Austenitic stainless steels with higher molybdenum contents (up to 6 to 7%) are being developed experimentally. Steels

TABLE 14   Comparison of Ultimate Tensile and Yield Strengths of CF-8 and CF-8M Austenitic Stainless Steel Castings

Temperature		Type	Ultimate tensile strength		0.2% offset yield strength	
°C	°F		ksi	MPa	ksi	MPa
20	68	CF-8	78	538	34	234
		CF-8M	79	545	37	255
538	1000	CF-8	55	379	17	117
		CF-8M	56	386	21	145
648	1200	CF-8	44	303	16	110
		CF-8M	40	276	18	124
760	1400	CF-8	26	179	15	103
		CF-8M	26	179	15	103

TABLE 15   Effects of Cyclic Variations of Stress and Temperature on the Room and Elevated Temperature Notch Toughness of Type 316 Stainless Steel Welded Piping[15]

Weekly cycles*	Charpy V-notch impact tests energy absorbed, ft-lb(J) †					
	Center of weld		Fusion line		Base metal	
	72°F	1200°F	72°F	1200°F	72°F	1200°F
0	120 (163)‡	120 (163)‡	120 (163)‡	120 (163)‡	120 (163)‡	120 (163)‡
4	89 (121)	110 (149)	80 (108)	120 (163)‡		
30	40 (54)	86 (117)	43 (58)	118 (160)		
56	46 (62)	81 (110)	25 (34)	95 (129)		
83	43 (58)	118 (160)	2 9(39)	112 (152)		
135	40 (54)	75 (102)	27 (37)	101 (137)		
251	33/38 (45/52)	80 (108)	25 (34)	70/77 (95/104)		
251	No additional heat treatment				22/32 (30/43)	62/74 (84/100)
251	Heat-treated 1 h at 1650°F, air-cooled				44	
251	Heat-treated 1 h at 1750°F, air-cooled				120 (163)‡	
251	Heat-treated, 1 h at 1850°F, air-cooled				120 (163)‡	
251	Heat-treated 1 h at 1950°F, air-cooled				120 (163)‡	

*Weekly cycle: 19 h at room temperature with maximum bending load. 118 h at 1225°F with 5000 psi (34.5 MN/m²) stress and no bending load. Time at 1225°F (650°C) during 251 weekly cycles was approximately 28,000 h.

†1 ft-lb force = 1.355818 J. Cross-sectional area of Charpy specimen at root of V is 80 mm². Therefore, impact strength equivalent of 1 ft-lb force is 16.9 kJ/m².

‡Capacity of machine, specimen did not break.

containing 4.5% molybdenum are becoming popular for use in highly corrosive environments. For instance, an austenitic stainless steel containing 18Cr-24Ni-4.5Mo, with or without 1.5% copper, exhibited good resistance to corrosion in the highly corrosive conditions encountered in sulfuric acid production and in the production of acetic acid by the butane and naphtha processes. It also performed excellently as piping for handling seawater.

A heavy-oil cooler in an ethylene plant[16] operated under the following conditions:

- Tube side: seawater, allowed to evaporate intermittently
- Shell side: hot oil with an inlet temperature of about 225°C (435°F)

Carbon steel tubes failed in 6 months due to general corrosion. Pitting and stress-corrosion cracking caused failures in 1 to 2 weeks in both Type 304 and Type 316 stainless steel tubes. Tubes manufactured from an 18Cr-24Ni-4.7Mo austenitic stainless steel exhibited no attack after 1.5 years of service.

Excellent resistance to corrosion in all concentrations of H_2SO_4 at temperatures up to 60°C (140°F) is exhibited by wrought Stainless 20 (20Cr-28.5Ni-2.5Mo-3.5Cu), Incoloy 825 (42Ni-21.5Cr-3Mo-2Cu-0.9Ti), and cast CN-7M (20Cr-29Ni-2Mo-3Cu). However, these grades do not resist attack by all concentrations of the acid at all temperatures. For instance, the upper limit of concentration for no attack at the boiling point is 10% H_2SO_4. The above-mentioned alloys are also recommended for service in seawater or phosphoric acid environments.

A recently developed austenitic stainless steel grade, containing 22Cr-13Ni-5Mn-2Mo plus a nitrogen addition (commercially designated 22:13:5) possesses room-temperature ultimate and yield strengths of 930 and 516 MPa, respectively. It is reported to have excellent crevice-corrosion resistance in 10% $FeCl_3$ and is expected to be well-suited for service in marine environments.

Ferritic Stainless Steels   AISI Type 434, the 1% molybdenum modification of Type 430 ferritic stainless steel, possesses a resistance to corrosion in chloride environments superior to the basic grade. Its consequent ability to combat the corrosive action of road salts has resulted in its extensive use for automobile trim.

The additional 1% molybdenum in the 18Cr-2Mo grade results in further improvement of corrosion resistance over that of Type 434, particularly resistance to chlorides and to stress-corrosion cracking. Applications for the 18Cr-2Mo grade include heat-exchanger, feedwater, heater, and condenser tubing.

REFERENCES

1. La Que, F. L., and H. R. Copson: "Corrosion Resistance of Metals and Alloys," 2d ed., chap. 15, Reinhold, 1963.
2. Niederberger, R. B., R. J. Ferrara, and F. A. Plummer: Corrosion Resistance of Nickel Alloys in Quiet and Low Velocity Sea Water, *Mater. Prot. Perform.*, vol. 9, no. 8, pp. 18–22, August 1970.
3. Truman, J. E., G. P. Sanderson, and P. M. Haigh: The Effects of Alloying with Molybdenum on the Resistance to Corrosion of 18% Chromium Austenitic Stainless Steels, "Molybdenum 1973," proceedings of a symposium organized by the Noranda Sales Group, Apr. 12–13, 1973, Copenhagen, Denmark, pp. 1–11.
4. Lizlovs, E. A.: Corrosion Behavior of Types 304 and 316 Stainless Steel in Hot 85% Phosphoric Acid, *Corrosion*, vol. 25, no. 9, pp. 389–393, September 1969.
5. Brigham, R. J.: Pitting and Crevice Corrosion Resistance of Molybdenum-bearing Austenitic Stainless Steel, "Molybdenum 1973," proceedings of a symposium organized by the Noranda Sales Group, Apr. 12–13, 1973, Copenhagen, Denmark, pp. 19–27.
6. Bond, A. P., and E. A. Lizlovs: Anodic Polarization of Austenitic Stainless Steels in Chloride Media, *J. Electrochem. Soc.*, vol. 115, no. 11, pp. 1130–1135, November 1968.
7. Passienen, K., and P. E. Ahlers: Corrosion of Acid-proof Steel in ClO_2 Solutions, *Pap. Puu*, vol. 48, no. 9, pp. 549–560, 1966.
8. Passienen, K., and P. E. Ahlers: Corrosion of Acid-proof Steel in Cl_2 Solutions, *Pap. Puu*, vol. 50, no. 8, pp. 467–472, 1968.
9. "18Cr-2Mo," *Brochure M254 25M 573*, Climax Molybdenum Co., Greenwich, Conn.
10. Lizlovs, E. A., and A. P. Bond: Anodic Polarization of Some Ferritic Stainless Steels in Chloride Media, *J. Electrochem. Soc.*, vol. 116, no. 5, pp. 574–579, May 1969.
11. Lizlovs, E. A., and A. P. Bond: Anodic Polarization Behavior of 25% Chromium Ferritic Stainless Steels, *J. Electrochem. Soc.*, vol. 118, no. 1, pp. 22–28, January 1971.
12. Briggs, J. Z., and T. D. Parker: "The Super 12% Cr Steels," Climax Molybdenum Co., Greenwich, Conn.
13. Tikkanen, M. H.: Corrosion Resistance of Molybdenum-bearing Steels in Industry, "Molybdenum 1973," proceedings of a symposium organized by the Noranda Sales Group, Apr. 12–13, 1973, Copenhagen, Denmark, pp. 29–34.
14. Blumberg, H. S.: "Type 316 for Elevated Temperature Power Plant Applications," Climax Molybdenum Co., Greenwich, Conn., 1965.
15. Mochel, N. L., C. W. Ahlman, G. C. Wiedersum, and R. H. Zong: Performance of Type 316 Stainless Steel Piping at 5000 psi and 1200°F, *Proc. Am. Power Conf.*, vol. XXVIII, 1966.
16. Blom, Uno: Two Austenitic Stainless, 4.5% Molybdenum, Steels—Properties and Experience from Their Use, "Molybdenum 1973," proceedings of a symposium organized by the Noranda Sales Group, Apr. 12–13, 1973, Copenhagen, Denmark, pp. 35–42.
17. *Met. Prog.*, vol. 104, no. 4, pp. 112, 130, and 166, September 1973.

Chapter 14

Residual and Minor Elements in Stainless Steels

R. A. LULA
Assistant to the Vice President—Technical Director, Advanced Technology Planning, Research Center, Allegheny Ludlum Steel Corp., Brackenridge, Pennsylvania

I. M. BERNSTEIN
Metallurgy and Materials Science Department, Carnegie-Mellon University, Pittsburgh, Pennsylvania

There are two general classes of elements which are present in small amounts in stainless steels. Those which are not intentionally added are referred to as *residual, or tramp, elements* and their concentrations are controlled by either selection of raw materials or by melting practice. Harmful ones are kept at a very low level, while those shown to be innocuous can be tolerated to higher concentrations. The other class of elements present in small quantities, when deliberately added to impart specific properties, are referred to as *minor elements*.

RESIDUAL ELEMENTS

Type and Quantity of Residual Elements   There are four major sources for residuals in stainless steels:

1. Residual elements from iron stainless steel scrap. This is the main source of impurities in steel and includes the elements sulfur, phosphorus, tin, lead, zinc, antimony, bismuth, copper, tungsten, vanadium, etc. Some of these can also be deliberate minor additions. The amount of residuals normally present in austenitic stainless steels is shown in Table 1,[1] and can be considered representative for all types of stainless steel.

2. Residuals from alloying materials. When alloying elements are added to the steel bath, either in elemental form or as ferroalloys, they can contribute the following resid-

TABLE 1   Typical Amounts of Residual Elements in Austenite Stainless Steels[1]

Element	Typical amount, %
Pb	0.002
Sn	>0.01
Co	0.20
Cu	0.15
Zn	0.01
Cb	0.01
As	0.01
Al	0.01
Mo	0.05
B	>0.0005
Ti	>0.05
V	>0.05
Se	>0.02
Sb	>0.01
N	0.04
O_2	0.015
P	0.020
S	0.015
Si	0.60
Mn	1.25
H_2	0.0007 (7 ppm)

uals: aluminum, cobalt, tantalum, lead, carbon, and silicon. This is seldom considered to be a serious source of residuals.

3. Impurities from deoxidizers or other melt practice additions. Deoxidizers, or elements with a high affinity for oxygen, are added at the end of the melting cycle to decrease the oxygen content of the steel bath. Elements used for this purpose are manganese, silicon, aluminum, titanium, magnesium, and calcium. While the attempt is made to incorporate the products of deoxidation in the slag, small amounts of these elements can be retained in the steel.

A special case is when rare-earth metals and boron are used to improve hot workability of the higher-alloyed austenitic stainless steels. These are intentionally added, and thus do not strictly conform to the working definition of residual elements, except for the fact that in special cases their presence is undesirable.

4. Residuals from the atmosphere. During melting and finishing operations, nitrogen, oxygen, and hydrogen can be picked up from the atmosphere. The solubility of nitrogen in stainless steels is much higher than in carbon steel but is normally kept within the relatively narrow and tolerable range of 0.025 to 0.045%, unless intentionally added. The oxygen content is controlled by deoxidizers, as mentioned previously. The hydrogen has to be limited to below 3 ppm and this is accomplished by minimizing the amount of moisture in the scrap, and by the melting practice.

TABLE 2   Classification of Residual Elements[2]

Set I, substantially absorbed in slag	Set II, distributed between slag and metal	Set III, substantially absorbed by metal	Set IV, substantially driven from metal and slag
Ca, Mg, Ce, La, Ti, Zr, Al, Si	Mn, P, S, Se, Cb, Ta, V, B	Cu, Mo, Co, W, Sn, As, Sb, Ag	Cd, Zn, Bi, Pb

The behavior of the residual elements which originate from either raw materials or melting additives in austenitic stainless steels (previously described in groups 2 and 3) has been further classified by the Open Hearth Group, as shown in Table 2.[2] The elements are classified in four subsets. Those in the first set are completely oxidized and will thus be found in the slag, except when they are added as deoxidizers just before tapping. In this latter case, a small amount could be retained in the steel. The elements in the second set are only partially oxidized and transferred to the slag. In carbon or low-alloy-steel melting practice, these elements can be substantially eliminated by "slagging-off." In the case of stainless steel, however, this is not economically feasible since a high percentage of the chromium also is oxidized into the slag and subsequently has to be returned to the metal bath during a reduction period, in which silicon is added to the slag. Many of the residuals listed in Set II, particularly phosphorus, are then returned to the metal bath. Fortunately, sulfur and selenium, which also are part of this set, can be reduced to very low levels with adequate slag practice, and will not redissolve with the chromium. The elements in the third set are retained in the steel since their oxides are not stable. The elements in the fourth set have high vapor pressure at the steel melting temperature and should vaporize from both the molten steel and the slag. Exceptions to this last prediction are occasionally found with lead and bismuth, and their presence can seriously impair hot workability.

With proper controls and melting practice the amount of residuals in the AISI-type stainless steels can be limited to the strict specifications shown in Table 3. The AMS specifications also limit copper and molybdenum to 0.50% maximum.

Influence of Residuals on Hot Workability   Some residual elements can, under certain circumstances, improve the hot workability of stainless steels. More often, however,

TABLE 3   Residuals in AISI Stainless Steels

Type steel	P, %	S, %	Si, %	Mn, %
200 series	0.060 max.	0.030 max.	1.0 max.	
300 series	0.045 max.	0.030 max.	1.0 max.	2.0 max.
Type 303	0.20 max.	0.15 min.	1.0 max.	2.0 max.
400 series	0.040 max.	0.03 max.	1.0 max.	1.0 max.
Types 416 and 430T	0.06 max.	0.15 min.	1.0 max.	1.25 max.

they are harmful due to the formation of low-melting eutectics and a lowering of the melting point of steel. Table 4 shows the eutectic formation temperature of iron with additions of antimony, arsenic, copper, boron, phosphorus, and sulfur, as taken from binary phase diagrams.[3] While in most cases a substantial amount of the residual element is needed to reach the eutectic composition, the melting temperature drops

TABLE 4   Eutectic Temperatures of Fe-Sb, Fe-As, Fe-Cu, Fe-B, Fe-P, Fe-S[3]

Alloy system	Eutectic temperature		Eutectic minimum concentration
	°C	°F	
Fe-Sb	1000	1828	8.0% Sb
Fe-As	832	1528	7.0% As
Fe-Cu	1095	2001	6.0% Cu
Fe-B	1175	2145	0.1% B
Fe-P	1050	1922	2.5% P
Fe-S	989	1810	

precipitously with even minute additions of the second element. The only exception is the Fe-Cu system.

Since copper does not produce a rapid decrease in melting temperature, additions of up to about 2%, or even more, can be tolerated without impairing hot workability, although the AMS maximum allowable is only 0.50%.

The multi-elements of stainless steels have more complex phase diagrams than the binaries; nevertheless it can be assumed that the strong influence of these residuals on the melting temperature is the same in the sense that their presence will result in a drastic reduction in the melting temperature. Since it is well known that even very small amounts of a liquid phase produce hot shortness during hot-working, it becomes mandatory to limit the amounts of antimony, arsenic, boron, phosphorus, and sulfur to very low levels. Sulfur is a simple residual to control since the formation of a low-melting iron sulfate phase can be avoided when the common additions (manganese and chromium) are present. Sulfur, however, is in general deleterious to other properties, and its level should be kept low, even if it can be present in combined form.

Similar difficulties are encountered with lead and tin additions; the allowable tolerances for these are shown in Table 5 [4-7]

TABLE 5   Tolerance Levels for Lead and Tin

	Tolerable limit, %		
Alloy	Pb	Sn	Reference
T310	0.004	0.04	Lynch[4]
T304	0.008	0.10	
T302	....	>0.20	Mitchell[5]
T410	....	>0.20	
T430	....	>0.20	
18-8	0.005		Bergh[6]
18-8 Mo	0.005		
T310	0.005		
T310	0.010		Ravizza and Nicodemi[7]

Tolerances for lead, in agreement with those in Table 5, are reported by Stokowiec,[8] but the levels for tin were found to be lower, although they are not specified. Ravizza,[7] in a study of Type 310, found that lead over 0.01% is deleterious to workability, while below 0.01% its presence is not important.

The influence of some residuals on hot workability can be quite complex, as is the case with boron,[9] reported to improve hot workability of austenitic stainless steels up to 1300 to 1400°C (2375 to 2550°F) in amounts less than about 0.009%. Higher amounts are deleterious. This is illustrated in Fig. 1 showing the ductility, as measured by the reduction in area, as a function of temperature for several heats of Type 316 stainless steel, with boron contents of 0.0009, 0.004, 0.009 and 0.017%. The ductility is improved by boron up to 0.009%, but is drastically reduced above approximately 1150°C (2100°F), due to lowering of the melting point of steel. However, the use of boron in the steel industry for the hot-working of stainless steel is limited.

The rare-earth metals have been used for many years to improve the hot workability of the higher-alloyed stainless steels, in particular Type 316. Since their addition is deliberate, they qualify more as minor elements than as residuals.

Influence of Residuals on Weldability   The welding behavior of stainless steel has some similarities with hot-working or high-temperature tensile properties, and it might be expected that the role of residuals would be comparable for all three. Welding, however, is a much more complex process and although numerous investigations have been carried out, the role of residuals in that process is not well understood.[10]

A major concern with residuals is their influence on crack susceptibility in the weld or heat-affected zone. A survey of the literature[11] cites several papers dealing with the influence of sulfur and phosphorus on hot cracking of welds or associated structures in austenitic stainless steels. These all show that sulfur and phosphorus in excess of a particular value enhance hot cracking, with the critical value being a function of composition and welding condition. Thielsch[12] gives 0.030 to 0.035% as the maximum tolerable amount of phosphorus for a fully austenitic stainless steel and 0.025% sulfur when using covered electrodes and 0.015% sulfur for gas-shielded-arc welding. Bernstein[13] found that the phosphorus content of Type 310 bare filler metal should be 0.015% maximum to prevent cracking, while for ferritic-containing welds, the maximum is 0.03%. He found, however, that the sulfur content should not exceed 0.015% for any kind of austenitic weld. According to Linnert,[10] aluminum, calcium, magnesium, titanium, and zirconium residuals could promote slag formation during fusion welding. Hydrogen and, occasionally, high nitrogen can lead to weld porosity.

Influence of Residuals on Mechanical Properties   The influence of residuals on the mechanical properties depends on the form in which these are found in the alloy. Elements like sulfur are normally present in nonmetallic inclusions and can promote a degradation in mechanical properties in amounts exceeding the allowable maximum limit, generally 0.03%. In applications for which the through-thickness properties, especially ductility, of the steels are important, it becomes necessary to further reduce the maximum allowable sulfur to 0.020% or even lower, since sulfide inclusions, elongated in the hot-rolling direction, are a source of gross mechanical anisotropy. An example is martensitic stainless steels, especially Type 403, which are used in rela-

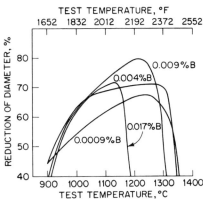

Fig. 1 The effect of boron on Type 316L austenitic stainless steel, tested by tensile deformation at a strain rate of 6/s.[9]

tively heavy sections in steam turbines, and require a sulfur level lower than usual to ensure adequate transverse properties. For most other stainless steels, especially austenitic stainless steels, the standard sulfur levels are satisfactory.

The majority of those residual elements which are present in solid solution in austenitic or ferritic stainless steels do not significantly change mechanical properties. They can have, however, an indirect influence inasmuch as they affect the phase balance of stainless steel. The behavior of various elements in this regard is shown in Table 6.

Nickel has been included as a possible residual since, in ferritic or martensitic stainless steels, it could be present in the scrap.

The residuals may play a role in modifying crystal structure of the steels for compositions located close to the austenite-ferrite phase boundary. This is illustrated by the

TABLE 6   Influence of Residuals on Stainless Steel Structure

Austenitizers	Cu, Co, Ni, N, C
Ferritizers	Si, Mo, Al, P, V, Ti, Cb, W, Zr
Carbide and Nitride Formers	Ti, Cb, Ta, W, Zr, V

DeLong constitution diagram[14] for stainless steel (Fig. 2). The cross-hatched area in Fig. 2 represents the AISI composition range for Type 316. It can be seen that in this range the structure can be completely austenitic, or it can form increasing amounts of delta ferrite as the chromium equivalent increases and the nickel equivalent decreases. The formation of delta ferrite should be prevented or at least minimized since it is known to impair the hot workability. Since residuals such as silicon and manganese are factored in the chromium and nickel equivalents, they can influence the high-temperature structure and impair the hot workability of these steels. Control of the residual elements has to be exercised.

Control of residuals becomes particularly important in metastable austenitic stainless steels. Type 301, for instance, owes its strength, when temper-rolled, both to work hardening of the austenite and to the strain-induced partial transformation of the austenite to martensite. The amount of martensite formed in this way, all other conditions kept constant, depends on how the specific composition can modify the M_s temperature. Such a relation between composition and M_s temperature has been determined empirically.

One of the formulas[15] uses M_{D30}, defined as the temperature at which 50% martensite is formed by 30% true strain in tension:

$$M_{D30}\,(^\circ\text{C}) = 413 - 462(\text{C}+\text{N}) - 9.2(\text{Si}) - 8.1(\text{Mn}) - 13.7(\text{Cr}) - 9.5(\text{Ni}) - 18.5(\text{Mo})$$

This equation illustrates that the elements manganese, silicon, molybdenum, carbon, and nitrogen, which can be present as residuals, play an important role in determining the M_s temperature and subsequent strength characteristics of cold-rolled metastable austenites.

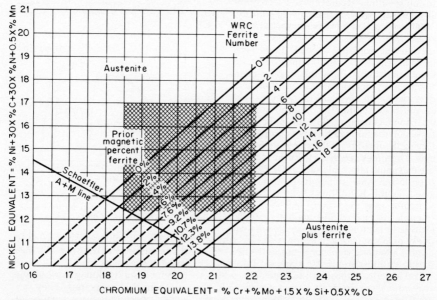

Fig. 2 The DeLong constitution diagram, revised January 1973, to convert it to the WRC Ferrite Number System for weld metals.[14]

Residual carbon and nitrogen are of special importance in all ferritic stainless steels since they influence the brittle-to-ductile transition temperature. Binder[16] established the relationship between carbon content and transition temperature and showed that acceptable toughness in ferritic stainless steels requires the carbon content to be reduced to very low levels. Figure 3[17] illustrates the effect of carbon content on the transition temperature of 17% Cr steel.

Influence of Residuals on Corrosion Resistance   Residual elements can have both beneficial and harmful effects on the corrosion properties of stainless steels. Variations can be found even for the same element since its role depends on whether it is present as a precipitate or in solid solution.

Moskowitz[18] has reviewed the literature and characterized the influence of residuals on the pitting resistance of austenitic stainless steel. He classifies the behavior of elements into three categories:

1. Elements present in solid solution which, in general, have no substantial effect. Cobalt, copper, lead, phosphorus, tantalum, tin, tungsten, and zirconium fall into this category. Some elements in solid solution promote passivity and, hence, are beneficial. These include molybdenum, boron (in solution), nitrogen, silicon, silver, rhenium, and vanadium.

2. Elements which when present as a metallic second phase (as with lead) are, in general, neutral in their behavior. An exception may be the case of silver, which is considered beneficial.

3. Elements which form nonmetallic second phases and are detrimental, e.g., columbium, boron (precipitate), carbon (as carbides), selenium, sulfur, tellurium, and titanium.

Scharfstein[19] reviewed the literature and has presented some new information on the influence of residuals on the general corrosion resistance of austenitic stainless steels. He concludes that residual copper, cobalt, and molybdenum are beneficial to general corrosion resistance. Boron is beneficial in amounts less than 0.007% and harmful at higher percentages. Aluminum, columbium, titanium, sulfur, carbon, and silicon can be detrimental above certain concentrations. These trends are also found to depend on the specific heat treatment imposed on the alloy.

Since carbon is a ubiquitous and unique residual, its effect on corrosion will be considered separately. In properly annealed austenitic stainless steels, carbon is present in solid solution. When present in amounts greater than 0.03%, carbon can be precipitated

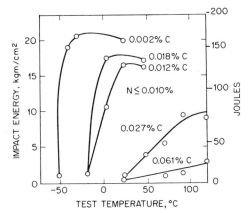

Fig. 3 Transition curves for quarter-size Charpy V-notch impact specimens of 17Cr-0.002 to 0.061C ferritic stainless steels heat-treated at 815°C + 1150°C (1499°F + 2102°F) for 1 h and water-quenched.[17]

at grain boundaries as chromium carbides, if the steel is exposed to temperatures in the range 538 to 815°C (1000 to 1500°F). This precipitation (also called sensitization) renders the material susceptible to intergranular corrosion[20] in certain corrosive environments. Sensitization can be avoided either by reducing the carbon content to a level below 0.03% or by using titanium or columbium to form stable carbides, thereby preventing chromium depletion. This point will be reconsidered in a later section. In ferritic stainless steels, intergranular corrosion due to precipitation of chromium carbides[21] can result from fast cooling from temperatures above approximately 927°C (1700°F). In this case, carbon (and nitrogen) has to be lowered to less than 100 ppm[22] in order to avoid intergranular corrosion. Titanium additions have been found to reduce this susceptibility, but only in some corrosive environments.

MINOR ELEMENTS

The structure, mechanical properties, and corrosion resistance of stainless steels are determined by the major alloying elements—iron, chromium, nickel, and molybdenum. Various improvements or modifications of the properties of stainless steels can be accomplished by intentional addition of small quantities of minor elements. Those elements added most often are carbon, nitrogen, vanadium, tungsten, boron, titanium, columbium, tantalum, sulfur, selenium, and lead.

Carbon and Nitrogen   These are present as solid-solution interstitial elements in both austenite or ferrite. Their behavior has previously been discussed in the residual section since their presence cannot be avoided during melting. Carbon and nitrogen are also deliberately added to certain stainless steels, primarily for strengthening. In martensitic stainless steels, for example, carbon is added for both strength and hardness in amounts varying from 0.15% maximum in AISI Types 403 and 410 to more than 0.15% in Type 420 and to 0.60 to 1.2% in Types 440A, 440B, and 440C.

Since the maximum amount of carbon that can be retained in solid solution during austenization is about 0.5%, steels with more carbon will contain eutectic chromium carbides which form during solidification, as well as the usual other carbides. The presence of such carbides is useful for wear resistance and, for this reason, the high-carbon martensitic stainless steels find application in cutlery and other such products.

The effect of carbon content on the maximum hardness of 12% Cr steels[23] and the tempering response[24] is shown in Figs. 4 and 5, respectively. On tempering 12% Cr steels, carbon will form the following carbides: Fe_3C, Cr_7C_3, M_2X (where M is primarily chromium and X can be carbon or nitrogen), $M_{23}C_6$. When other alloying elements are present (Mo, W, V), M_6C carbide is also found.

Another important function of carbon in 12% martensitic steels results from its ability to stabilize austenite, thereby helping to avoid formation of delta ferrite; about 0.10% carbon is needed for this in plain 12% Cr steels and about 0.20% in 12% Cr steels containing molybdenum, tungsten, vanadium, or columbium, all elements which stabilize ferrite.

Carbon is not as widely used in austenitic stainless steels, although it (and nitrogen) is the most potent solid-solution strengthening element in austenite as shown in Fig. 6.[25] The two interstitial elements increase the proof strength more than the substitutional elements on an atomic percent basis. The influence of carbon on the tensile properties of austenitic steels is illustrated in Table 7.[26] A difference in carbon content of 0.03% maximum in Type 304L versus 0.04 to 0.08% in Type 304 results in a 10-ksi (68.95-MPa) difference in tensile strength and 2 to 7 ksi (13.79 to 48.27MPa) difference in 0.2% offset yield strength. As a result of this, the "ASME Boiler and Pressure Vessel Code"[27] lists 75 ksi (517 MPa) minimum tensile strength for Type 304 and 70 ksi (482.65 MPa) for Type 304L; the maximum allowable stresses are lower at all temperatures listed for Type 304L. The main reason, of course, why carbon is not used extensively to increase the strength of austenitic stainless steels is the danger of sensitization. It is considered wiser to strengthen with other alloying elements.

Nitrogen, as mentioned, also increases the strength of austenitic steels. This is shown in Fig. 7[28] for Type 304 containing up to 0.30% nitrogen. Nitrogen, since it does not promote sensitization, is used more than carbon as a means of increasing the strength, particularly

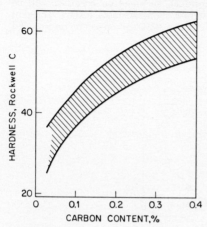

Fig. 4 The effect of carbon content on the maximum hardness of 12% Cr steels.[23]

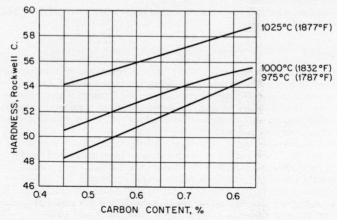

Fig. 5 Hardness of tempered 15.5 to 16% Cr steel as a function of temperature and carbon content.[24]

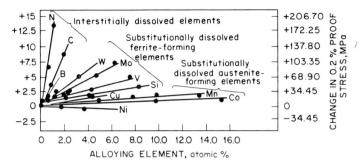

Fig. 6 The effect of solid-solution hardening in austenite (adequately solution-treated).[25]

the yield strength. Examples of nitrogen-bearing stainless steels and their corresponding strengths are shown in Table 8.

The high-manganese austenitic steels, represented by the AISI 200 series, were initially developed to conserve nickel by replacing it partially with manganese and nitrogen. Since the high manganese increases the steel's solubility for nitrogen, these steels are

TABLE 7   Typical Tensile Properties of Annealed Type 304 Stainless Steel[26]

Type	Form	Tensile strength ksi	Tensile strength MPa	Yield strength, 0.2% offset ksi	Yield strength, 0.2% offset MPa	Elongation 2 in. (50.8 mm), %	Reduction of area, %	Hardness Brinell	Hardness Rockwell B
304	Sheet and strip	85	586	35	241	50			80
	Plate	85	586	30	207	60	70	150	
	Bars	85	586	30	207	60	70	150	
304L	Sheet and strip	75	517	28	193	50			70
	Plate	75	517	28	193	50		140	

more amenable to solid-solution strengthening by nitrogen. As a result, the AISI 200 series and several proprietary alloys with high manganese and nitrogen have higher strength in the solution-annealed condition than conventional Cr-Ni austenitic steels.

Sulfur, Selenium and Lead for Free-machining   These three elements are commonly found as trace residuals in most stainless steels. They qualify also as minor elements since they are added to some grades of stainless steel to improve machinability. Alloying with sulfur, selenium, and lead has been found to result in prolonged tool life, reduced power requirements, and greater machining speeds. On the negative side, they can decrease the corrosion resistance and mechanical properties, especially the ductility perpendicular to the hot-rolling direction. Free-machining stainless steels rely primarily on sulfur, with selenium used only in large forging stock, or when surface finish is an important requisite. Lead is used only infrequently, primarily because of the difficulties of introducing it into the steel in a uniform well-dispersed form, and because lead-bearing scrap is undesirable. The free-machining grades and their respective alloy contents are:

Type 416: 0.30 to 0.40 S or 0.15 to 0.25 Se

Type 430F: 0.40 to 0.50 S

Type 303: 0.30 to 0.40 S

Type 203: 0.30 to 0.40 S

Sulfur can be added to any stainless steel

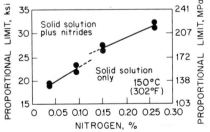

Fig. 7 Effect of nitrogen on the proportional limit of Type 304 stainless steel.[28]

TABLE 8   Nitrogen-bearing Austenitic Stainless Steels

| | | Typical tensile properties | | | |
| | | Tensile strength | | 0.2% yield strength | |
Alloy	N, %	ksi	MPa	ksi	MPa
304N	0.10	85	586.1	42	289.6
201	0.14	115	792.9	50	344.7
204	0.24	105	724.0	56	386.1
205*	0.35	125	861.8	70	482.6
219†	0.25	115	792.9	60	413.7

*Proprietary Allegheny Ludlum Steel Corporation commercial steel: 17Cr-1.25Ni-15Mn-0.15C-0.35N.

†Proprietary Allegheny Ludlum Steel Corporation commercial steel: 21Cr-6Ni-9Mn-0.03C-0.25N.

grade when improved machinability is desired, but its effect is less pronounced in grades containing hard particles such as titanium, columbium carbides, or chromium carbides. The presence of oxide inclusions also impairs sulfur's effect on machinability. The influence of sulfur on machinability of stainless steel is illustrated in Fig. 8.[29]

Sulfur can be present in stainless steel as manganese or chromium sulfides. When the manganese content is low (under 0.4%), sulfur is found as chromium sulfide and chromium-rich manganese sulfide.[30] With intermediate manganese content (0.40 to 1.80%)

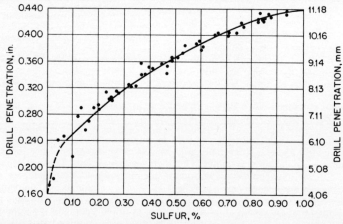

Fig. 8 Machinability (as measured by drill penetration) of stainless steels can be improved by additions of sulfur (or selenium) to the metal.[29]

only chromium-rich manganese sulfide is present. At high manganese content (>1.80%), only relatively pure manganese sulfide forms. From a machinability point of view, a high manganese/sulfur ratio is desirable since the manganese sulfide is soft and provides internal lubrication during cutting. This is illustrated in Fig. 9.[30]

When corrosion resistance takes precedence (often encountered in stainless steels), a low Mn/S ratio is preferred since the chromium sulfides or chromium-rich manganese sulfides have superior corrosion resistance.[31,32]

The shape of the sulfide inclusions also has a strong influence on machinability. Short,

TABLE 9   High-Temperature Properties of Types 304 and 347[36]

| Type | Tensile strength, ksi (MPa) | | 0.2% Yield strength, ksi (MPa) | | Stress for rupture, ksi (MPa), 1000 h | |
	650°C(1202°F)	815°C(1499°F)	650°C(1202°F)	815°C(1499°F)	650°C(1202°F)	815°C(1499°F)
304	45(310.3)	22(151.7)	16(110.3)	12(82.74)	15(103.4)	3.7(25.5)
347	52(358.5)	25(172.4)	20(137.9)	17(117.2)	22(151.7)	4.8(33.1)

heavy-shaped inclusions are preferred to long, thin inclusions, [33,34] with the shape of the sulfide inclusions being influenced by the oxygen content of the steel.[35]

Titanium, Columbium, and Tantalum   Titanium and columbium, as previously discussed, are added to austenitic stainless steels to eliminate susceptibility to intergranular corrosion (caused by the precipitation of chromium carbides) and the associated chromium depletion adjacent to the grain-boundary carbides. The reason for this is that both titanium and columbium form more stable carbides than does chromium. They resist solutionizing at the annealing temperature [above 1038°C (1900°F)], and thus prevent harmful chromium carbide precipitation if the steel is subsequently exposed to the sensitizing temperature range [593 to 816°C (1100 to 1500°F)], as might be the case, for example, during welding.

Two standard AISI steels, Types 321 and 347, are stabilized with titanium and columbium, respectively; other austenitic steels can also be stabilized by the addition of these elements. The amount of stabilizing element is related to carbon content as follows:

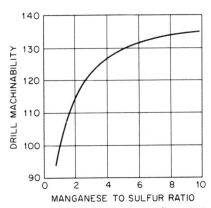

$$Ti \geq 4 \times C \%$$
$$Cb \geq 8 \times C \%$$
$$Ta \geq 16 \times C \%$$

Fig. 9 As manganese-sulfur ratios of Type 416 stainless rise, drill machinability ratings (based on time required to drill a hole of standard depth) increase appreciably. The "100" rating was obtained on conventional Type 416 with 0.32% S and BHN 200.[30]

Tantalum is not generally used alone but is present in conjunction with columbium (generally from the ferroalloy addition). Because of its lower atomic weight, about twice as much tantalum as columbium is needed.

Besides being used as a stabilizing element in austenitic stainless steel, columbium also imparts superior high-temperature strength for both short-time as well as long-time testing. Table 9[36] shows the 649°C (1200°F) and 816°C (1500°F) short-time tensile and stress-rupture properties of Types 304 and 347. The superior strength of the latter is attributed to the presence of columbium.

Both titanium and columbium can also be used in ferritic steels to reduce susceptibility to intergranular corrosion. The minimum Ti/C ratio is about 8.

Precipitation-hardening Elements: Aluminum, Titanium, Copper, and Phosphorus   The basic requirement for precipitation hardening in an alloy system is a decrease in solid solubility with decreasing temperature. This is illustrated in Fig. 10[37] showing the iron-rich corner of the Fe-Ti phase diagram. The maximum solubility for titanium is about 7% at 710°C (1310°F), and decreases gradually to 3% at 483°C (900°F). While there are many elements that meet this general requirement, only titanium, copper, and aluminum are used in commercial alloys to enhance the mechanical properties. Beryllium also has interesting precipitation-hardening properties, but commercialization has not been possible because its toxicity creates melting and fabrication problems.

The precipitation-hardening potential of titanium in the iron system has been known for a long time;[38] the precipitated phase formed is Fe_2Ti. Wasmuth also shows the precipitation possibility of copper in ferrite, with the precipitation in this case being almost pure copper.

The solubility for copper in austenite is much higher than in ferrite (approximately 8% versus 1.4%). It is thus possible to achieve a high degree of supersaturation in ferrite by solutionizing in austenite and cooling fast enough to prevent precipitation when the austenite transforms to ferrite or martensite.

Aluminum precipitation-hardening was first observed in the Fe-Ni-Al permanent magnets.

There are several precipitation-hardening stainless steels which have gained extensive commercial acceptance because of a favorable combination of mechanical and corrosion properties and because of convenient fabrication characteristics. Only a few of these

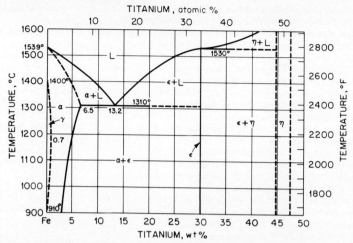

Fig. 10 Iron-rich corner of the iron-titanium phase diagram.[37]

steels, representative of the precipitation hardening type, are considered here (the reader is referred to Chapter 7 for a more detailed discussion). These can be divided into two groups:

1. Martensitic precipitation-hardening steels: 17-4PH, 17-7PH, AM-362
2. Austenitic precipitation-hardening steel: A-286

The steels in group 1 are always martensitic at room temperature, and since the precipitation-hardening reaction occurs in the martensite, we will refer to them as *martensitic.* The second group, represented by A-286, is an austenitic steel with the precipitation occurring in the austenite. The composition of these steels is shown in Appendix B. The precipitation hardening reaction in 17-4PH is attributed to copper, which is taken into solution in austenite during a high-temperature annealing treatment. The material transforms to martensite (which has low solubility for copper) upon cooling to room temperature. A subsequent aging treatment at relatively low temperature [425 to 595°C(800 to 1100°F)] results in precipitation of a copper-rich phase. The hardness and mechanical

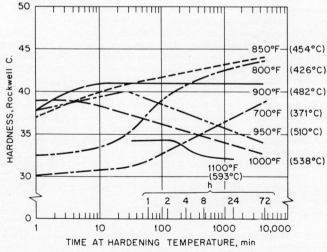

Fig. 11 Effect of aging temperature and time on the hardness of 17-4PH.[39]

properties change with the aging temperature. Figure 11[39] shows aging and overaging hardness curves as a function of aging temperature and time. The precipitation reaction in AM-362 is due to a Ti-Ni compound; in 17-7PH it is due to an Al-Ni compound. In both cases, precipitation occurs in the martensite.

The alloy A-286 consists, in the annealed condition, of a supersaturated solid solution of austenite with about 2% titanium. Aging in the 650 to 760°C (1200 to 1400°F) range will result in the precipitation of a transition γ' phase, Ni_3Ti, with an fcc lattice and coherent with the matrix. This structure produces the maximum hardening possible in this alloy. Overaging leads to coalescence of the γ' phase and the formation of the stable Ni_3Ti hexagonal phase.

Other Alloying Elements   Other alloying elements are used for specific purposes in stainless steels. In martensitic steels, tungsten, molybdenum, and vanadium are used to increase the high-temperature strength [425 to 650°C(800 to 1200°F)], primarily by increasing the resistance to tempering. Small amounts of boron and nitrogen are also used in the martensitic steels for high-temperature strength.

In austenitic steels, molybdenum and tungsten enhance high-temperature strength by solid-solution strengthening. Silicon, also in solid solution in austenite, is used to increase the resistance to carburizing. Two AISI steels, Types 302B and 314, have 2 to 3% and 1.50 to 3% silicon, respectively. Aluminum is used in some proprietary stainless steels to improve oxidation resistance.

REFERENCES

1. Heger, J. J.: Effects of Residual Elements on Properties of Austenitic Stainless Steels, *ASTM Spec. Tech. Publ. 418*, p. 122, 1966.
2. Derge, G. (Ed.): "Basic Open Hearth Steel Making," vol. III, pp. 160–163, American Institute of Mining, Metallurgical, and Petroleum Engineers, New York, 1964.
3. "Metals Handbook," American Society for Metals, Metals Park, Ohio, 1948.
4. Lynch, D. W. P.: *AIME Proc. Elec. Fur. Conf.*, vol. 19, pp. 220–223, 1961.
5. Mitchell, J. R., et al.: *AIME Proc. Elec. Fur. Conf.*, vol. 19, pp. 233–234, 1961.
6. Bergh, S.: *Iron Age*, vol. 164, no. 2, pp. 96–99, 1949.
7. Ravizza, P., and W. Nicodemi: *Rev. Metall. (Paris)*, pp. 351–357, April 1965.
8. Stokowiec, Z., et al.: *Iron Steel Inst. London Publ.* 117, pp. 17–23, 1969.
9. Keown, S. R.: *Scand. J. Metall.*, vol. 2, pp. 59–63, 1973.
10. Linnert, G. E.: "Effects of Residual Elements on Properties of Austenitic Stainless Steels," *ASTM Spec. Tech. Publ. 418*, pp. 105–119, 1966.
11. Borland, J. C., et al.: *Report B5/1/59*, British Welding Research Association, London, 1959.
12. Thielsch, H.: *Weld. J., Res. Suppl.*, vol. 29, no. 2, pp. 361–404, 1950.
13. Berenstein, A., et al.: *Weld. J., Res. Suppl*, pp. 504S–508S, November 1965.
14. Delong, W. T.: Ferrite in Austenitic Stainless Steel Weld Metal, *Weld. J., Suppl.*, July 1974.
15. Angel, T.: *J. Iron Steel Inst. London*, vol. 177, pp. 165–174, May 1959.
16. Binder, W. O., et al.: *Trans. Am. Soc. Met.*, vol. 43, pp. 759–777, 1951.
17. Semchyshen, M., et al.: Effects of Composition on Ductility and Toughness of Ferritic Stainless Steels, "Symposium: Toward Improved Ductility and Toughness," Kyoto, Japan, Oct. 25–26, 1971, Climax Molybdenum Co., Greenwich, Conn., 1972.
18. Moskowitz, A., et al.: *ASTM Spec. Tech. Publ. 418*, pp. 3–213, July 1966.
19. Scharfstein, L. R.: *ASTM Spec. Tech. Publ. 418*, pp. 90–104, July 1966.
20. Aborn, R., and E. Bain: *Trans. Am. Soc. Steel Treat.*, vol. 18, pp. 837–893, 1930.
21. Lula, R. A., et al.: *Trans. Am. Soc. Met.*, vol. 46, p. 197, 1954.
22. Steigerwald, R. F.: New Ferritic Stainless Steels to Resist Chlorides and Stress-Corrosion Cracking, *Tappi*, vol. 56, no. 4, April 1973.
23. Briggs, J. Z., and T. D. Parker: "The Super 12 Percent Cr Steels," p. 159, Climax Molybdenum Company, Greenwich, Conn., 1965.
24. Colombier, L., and J. Hochmann: "Aciers Inoxidables-Aciers Refractaires," p. 42, Dunod, Paris, 1955.
25. Irvine, J. J., et al.: *J. Iron Steel Inst. London*, vol. 199, pp. 153–175, October 1961.
26. "Mechanical and Physical Properties of Austenitic Chromium-Nickel at Ambient Temperatures," Sec. 1, *Bulletin A*, The International Nickel Company, New York, 1963.
27. "ASME Boiler and Pressure Vessel Code," Section VIII, Table UHA-23, p. 148, 1965.
28. Ferry, B. N., and J. T. Eckel: *J. Mater.*, vol. 5, no. 1, pp. 99–107, March 1970.
29. "Machining of stainless Steels," p. 21, American Society for Metals, Materials and Process Engineering Bookshelf, 1968.
30. Kovach, C. W., and A. Moskowitz: *Met. Prog.*, vol. 91, pp. 173–180, August 1967.

31. Garvin, H. W., and R. M. Larrimore, Jr.: *Trans. Am. Inst. Min. Metall. Pet. Engl., vol. 233, pp. 133–150*, 1965.
32. Henthorne, M.: *Corrosion*, vol. 26, no. 10, pp. 511–528, 1970.
33. Kiessling, R.: "Nonmetallic Inclusions in Steel," *Iron Steel Inst. London Publ. 115*, part III, 1968.
34. Kiessling, R.: *J. Met.*, vol. 21, no. 10, p. 48, October 1969.
35. Sims, C. E., and F. B. Dahle: *Trans. Am. Foundrymen's Soc.*, vol. 46, p. 65, 1938.
36. "Chromium-Nickel Stainless Data," sec. 1, *Bulletin B*, The International Nickel Company, New York, 1963.
37. "Metals Handbook," p. 1219, American Society for Metals, Metals Park, Ohio, 1948.
38. Wasmuth, R.: *Arch. Eisenhuettenwes.* vol. 5, p. 45, 1931.
39. Goller, G. N., and W. C. Clarke, Jr.: *Iron Age*, vol. 165, p. 86, Mar. 2, 1950.

Part **3**

Corrosion Resistance

Effects of Composition, Structure, and Heat Treatment on the Corrosion Resistance of Stainless Steel

LAWRENCE R. SCHARFSTEIN

Director, Nuclear Materials, Carpenter Technology Corporation, Steel Division, Reading, Pennsylvania

The corrosion resistance of the stainless steels varies considerably with composition, structure, and heat treatment. Since the stainless steels are categorized by a structure nomenclature (austenitic, ferritic, etc.), it is possible to rank the general corrosion resistance of the alloys as: austenitic, best, and martensitic, worst. Ranking this way is possible since structure depends on composition and heat treatment.

AUSTENITIC STAINLESS STEELS

Composition All stainless steels contain iron and chromium, in addition to incidental elements due either to manufacturing or specific additions. The austenitic stainless steels contain a minimum of 8% nickel (or a substitute, such as Mn or Mn + N) and at least 17% chromium. Other alloying elements which may be added for strength or corrosion resistance are: copper, carbon, nitrogen, molybdenum, columbium, titanium, and aluminum.

General Corrosion The austenitic stainless alloys are considered to be the steels most resistant to industrial atmospheres and acid media. Bright-polished surfaces, maintained free of accumulated grime, will remain bright under most ambient conditions. As conditions become more severe (higher temperatures, stronger acids, etc.) more alloying content (over that of AISI Type 304 stainless steel) is required.

Pitting Corrosion The addition of molybdenum (over 2%) promotes resistance to pitting.[1,2] AISI Type 316 is the most popular alloy with added molybdenum. High chloride content (over 1000 ppm) or lack of circulation will pit Type 316. For aggressive pitting media, higher nickel content and higher molybdenum content are required. The most resistant alloys are actually nickel-based with added chromium and molybdenum.

Another variable to be considered when discussing pitting is the microcleanliness of the alloy. Everything else being equal, the cleaner the steel (fewer inclusions, precipitates, etc.), the better the pitting resistance. Cleaner steels are the result of pure melting stock and remelting.

Intergranular Corrosion A major disadvantage to using the austenitic stainless steels is that certain heat treatments, in the so-called "sensitizing range," cause the alloys to become more susceptible to intergranular corrosion. The sensitizing temperature range is between 1100 and 1600°F (593 to 871°C). The degree of susceptibility after heating in this range is a function of time, temperature, and composition.[3] Type 304 stainless steel is readily susceptible after 1 h at 1250°F (677°C) but probably not too badly affected in 1 h at either 1100°F (593°C) or 1500°F (871°C). By lowering the carbon content to below the saturation value for the solid-solution alloy, sensitization is largely avoided. An AISI series of alloys with lower carbon (below 0.03%) is available and identified by the suffix L; for example, AISI Type 304L is the lower carbon version of Type 304.

The deleterious effect of carbon generally is explained by the chromium-depletion theory. Sensitization leads to the formation and precipitation of a chromium-rich carbide, with the formula $M_{23}C_6$, along the grain boundaries. The areas immediately adjacent to the precipitate are depleted in chromium since the diffusion rate of chromium is lower than carbon, and the $M_{23}C_6$ precipitate is richer in chromium in proportion to carbon, although M may contain some nickel and/or molybdenum. At a temperature of 1500°F (816°C) or higher, recovery is obtained through increased diffusion of chromium to the depleted areas.

In addition to lower carbon, a series of "stabilized" stainless steels containing Cb or Ti are also available to resist sensitization. The stabilizing element preferentially ties up the excess solid-solution carbon thereby preventing its precipitation as $M_{23}C_6$. In order to obtain satisfactory stabilization, the stabilizing element must be present in a minimum ratio to carbon (weight percent) as follows: Cb, at least $8 \times$ C minimum, and Ti, at least $5 \times$ C minimum. If substantial nitrogen is present, more stabilizing element content is required since Cb and Ti also readily form nitrogen compounds, diminishing their effectiveness.

Accelerated intergranular attack of sensitized steel will occur primarily in oxidizing acid media. Accelerated laboratory test solutions, for example, are nitric acid, nitric plus hydrofluoric acid, sulfuric acid plus ferric sulfate, or sulfuric acid plus copper sulfate. Besides nitric acid, attack often reported from the field is in solutions containing concentrated acetic acid, chromates, and strong organic acids.

Stress Corrosion   Many austenitic stainless steels are susceptible to stress-corrosion cracking in chloride-containing solutions especially at pH 2 to 10 and temperatures over 150°F (303°C). Concentrated caustic solutions (over 10 wt %) are also known to cause stress-corrosion cracking. There are many other media and conditions which could lead to stress-corrosion cracking, but they are not as frequently documented in the literature. A great deal of care must be exercised, therefore, when specifying austenitic stainless steel in the highly stressed condition. Through proper selection, heat treatment, etc., some specific stainless steels can be used under conditions wherein stress-corrosion cracking would be likely with AISI Type 304. Austenitic alloys, with high nickel content (over 30%) are relatively immune in many industrial (as contrasted to accelerated test) media. Other alloys, such as high-chromium ferritic-austenitic, and straight ferritic (low nickel–low copper) stainless steels are available from several manufacturers for replacement of 18-8 stainless alloys when stress-corrosion cracking is a possibility with 18-8.

Stress-corrosion cracking of the austenitic stainless steels is a subject exceedingly widely discussed and written about. For that reason the reader is referred to Chapter 16, the bibliography, and a good metallurgical library if information on this subject is desired (also see Ref. 4).

Crevice Corrosion   The behavior of a particular stainless steel in a pitting test is a good indication of its crevice corrosion behavior. Crevice corrosion refers to accelerated attack occurring between tightly fitting surfaces such as a bushing—sleeve, flange, gasket, etc. The cause of attack is a concentration cell (gradient) in the solution between the areas exposed to the tightly fitting faces and the more accessible surface areas. The crevice is depleted in oxygen while enriched in metal ions, thereby polarizing the steel towards the active potential. Preventive or corrective actions, besides opening the crevice, are alloying with molybdenum, chromium, and nickel.

Galvanic Corrosion   The austenitic stainless steels can be passive or active (sometimes alternately both) in an aqueous environment. When passive, stainless steels are relatively noble. Therefore, all metals more active in that environment will behave as an anode when galvanic contact is made. On the other hand, when active, the stainless steels behave similarly to iron and they, in turn, will be the anode in a galvanic cell if the other metal is more noble. The austenitic stainless alloys, in comparison to martensitic and some ferritic stainless steels, aluminum, and copper are generally more passive in aqueous acidic media (except under strongly reducing conditions).

Erosion-Corrosion   The austenitic stainless steels are good alloys to select for erosion-corrosion resistance. Generally, the higher chromium, higher hardness alloys resist this form of corrosive attack best. Therefore, certain ferritic stainless alloys may be a better choice than the austenitic, especially if pitting and crevice attack are also possible. Temperature is an important variable. The higher the temperature, the more difficult to resist erosion-corrosion attack.

Heat Treatment   As was discussed earlier, the austenitic stainless steels have excellent corrosion resistance in the solution-annealed condition. The annealing temperature range is 1650 to 2000°F (899 to 1093°C). The alloys should be cooled rapidly after annealing to avoid sensitization. Grain growth begins to occur at approximately 1800°F (982°C), depending on composition and cleanliness. The annealing practice usually specified is 1850 to 1950°F (1010 to 1066°C) for a period of 1 h per inch (25.4 mm) of thickness followed by rapid cooling, such as a water quench.

FERRITIC STAINLESS STEELS

Composition The ferritic stainless steels contain at least 12% chromium with less than 0.10% carbon. The alloys are nonhardenable (see Chapter 5 for details) and exhibit the best corrosion resistance in the annealed condition. Alloying with chromium and molybdenum may improve corrosion resistance but complex chromium-rich carbides (and nitrides) can precipitate during welding or stress relief with consequential deterioration in general or intergranular corrosion resistance.

General Corrosion As the chromium increases so does the general corrosion resistance of the ferritic stainless steels. Groups of alloys are available with chromium in the following ranges: 12 to 16, 16 to 20, 23 to 29%. For best general corrosion resistance, the highest chromium content is preferable, assuming a good solution-annealed structure.

Pitting Corrosion The pitting resistance of the ferritic alloys improves somewhat with chromium but alloying with molybdenum is much more effective.[2] To provide pitting resistance, the alloy should contain at least 23 to 24% chromium and over 2% molybdenum. The precipitation of complex carbides as a result of welding or heat treatment decreases pitting resistance. To avoid this, some new alloys have recently become available with controlled low levels of carbon and nitrogen (<0.015% C + N).

Intergranular Corrosion Until recently, the ferritic stainless alloys were not considered to be too susceptible to intergranular corrosion. It appears that our knowledge was merely inadequate.[2] The alloys can be sensitized and are susceptible to intergranular attack. The sensitizing temperature is 600 to 650°C (1112 to 1202°F). Complex chromium carbides and nitrides precipitate in the grain boundaries and in this condition, strongly oxidizing acids will cause intergranular attack. As with the austenitic stainless alloys, preventative measures are: postweld annealing [approximately 760°C (1400°F)], stabilization with titanium and columbium (niobium), or lowering of the carbon and/or nitrogen. Since most of the better corrosion-resistant ferritic alloys contain over 23% chromium, the chromium carbides are easily precipitated. A carbon content of less than 0.02% is required to prevent precipitation and intergranular attack. Recently a few ferritic alloys have become available which are stabilized or contain very low levels of carbon and nitrogen. These alloys should be considered when good corrosion resistance, regardless of heat-treat condition, is required.

Stress Corrosion Many ferritic stainless alloys are resistant to chloride stress corrosion (SC) in environments conducive to such attack in the austenitic stainless steels. At least 20% chromium plus 1% or more of molybdenum are required to have adequate general resistance to the chloride-bearing environments. Bond and Dundas[5] surprised many metallurgists when they reported that small quantities (less than 1%) of nickel and/or copper promoted susceptibility to stress-corrosion cracking (SCC). For this reason, higher purity melting stock is required to prevent stress-corrosion cracking in the ferritic series. One other drawback is the greater susceptibility to hydrogen embrittlement observed with cold-worked or aged ferritic stainless steels as compared to the austenitic alloys.

Crevice Corrosion The situation as related to crevice corrosion is similar to that described for pitting corrosion. Higher chromium and molybdenum contents are beneficial; sensitization, lack of circulation, etc., are detrimental.

Galvanic Corrosion The active-passive behavior of the stainless alloys, depending on environment, composition, and heat treatment, repeats with the ferritic stainless alloys although passivity may be slightly more difficult to achieve than with the austenitic alloys. As a rule, the alloys will be passive in media with pH in excess of 3.0 and an oxidizing environment. In oxidizing acids, the solution-annealed alloys (with higher chromium content) will probably be passive. On the other hand, sensitized ferritics will probably be active in the same environment. The above information should serve merely as a guide when considering galvanic coupling or galvanic corrosion possibilities between ferritic stainless and other alloys.

Erosion-Corrosion Since resistance to erosion-corrosion is related to surface hardness and corrosion resistance, some of the high-chromium, high-molybdenum ferritic stainless alloys are good choices for this application. Cold-working would enhance their resistance. Most of the alloys can be hardened somewhat by cold-working. In general, stainless steels perform satisfactorily in service where erosion-corrosion is a possibility.

The explanation lies in the assumption that high velocity causes agitation, mixing, and aeration, all of which are considered beneficial for preventing localized attack.

PRECIPITATION-HARDENABLE AND TWO-PHASE STAINLESS STEELS

Composition   The precipitation-hardenable alloys primarily are specified where strength or hardness, in excess of properties obtainable with ferritic or austenitic stainless steels, are needed. Corrosion resistance is of secondary importance. Many precipitation-hardenable stainless alloys are proprietary. One popular alloy, whose patent has expired, is known as ASTM Type 630 or 17-4, composed of 17Cr-4Ni-4Cu-Cb-bal Fe. The alloy exhibits good corrosion resistance in the annealed or soft-temper condition. Corrosion behavior for these alloys is, however, strongly dependent on heat treatment and structure.

The two-phase alloys, such as AISI Type 329, contain a mixed structure consisting of ferrite and austenite. The alloys are usually high in chromium content (over 22%) with insufficient nickel (less than 8%) to promote a fully austenitic structure. Many of the stainless alloys falling into this category are proprietary. These alloys offer excellent corrosion resistance at reasonable prices but problems are encountered in fabrication. Properties vary with heat treatment.

General Corrosion   With relatively high chromium content, the alloys exhibit good general corrosion resistance. But heat treatment and structure play an important role. Precipitation or aging reactions deleteriously affect corrosion. Therefore, it is preferable to avoid maximum precipitation, if possible, when corrosion resistance is of major concern. Very little data are published on corrosion resistance as a function of heat treatment. It is therefore recommended that potential users write to the suppliers for data if none are available.

Pitting Corrosion   The pitting resistance of most precipitation-hardened alloys in the aged condition is poor. On the other hand, pitting resistance of most two-phased alloys, with over 20% chromium, is good. One major exception to the last statement applies to aged sigma or hardened martensitic phases, if they are present.

Intergranular Corrosion   Precipitation-hardened stainless alloys normally contain chromium carbides among the precipitated phases. As a result, highly oxidizing acids, such as boiling nitric, attack the chromium-depleted zones. Ferritic-austenitic two-phase stainless alloys resist sensitization by precipitating chromium carbides preferentially around the ferrite (high-chromium) phase rather than in the grain boundaries of the austenite. The relatively richer chromium ferrite is only negligibly affected. Several European stainless steel suppliers promote the use of the lower cost ferritic-austenitic stainless steels (in lieu of low-carbon or stabilized grades) to resist intergranular corrosion.

Stress Corrosion   The precipitation-hardened grades are susceptible to cracking (SCC) when loaded in tension in several corrosive environments. The higher the strength (or hardness), the greater the degree of susceptibility. On the other hand, dual-phase alloys, such as ferrite-austenite, appear to have a crack-arrest capability (as the crack reaches a new phase, propagation ceases) and are resistant to stress corrosion in a wide range of environments.

Crevice Corrosion   Precipitation-hardened stainless steels are not recommended if crevice corrosion is a possibility. Several forms of localized attack are prevalent in the crevice when hardened stainless alloys are used, namely: stress corrosion, pitting, and intergranular attack. A high-chromium (over 20%) ferritic-austenitic stainless should perform much better in a crevice in the solution-annealed condition.

Galvanic Corrosion   Previous statements made concerning active-passive electrode potential behavior are applicable to these alloys. The precipitation-hardened alloys may be more difficult to passivate than the austenitic or ferritic stainless steels. The dual-structure alloys' electrode behavior is more like their counterpart austenitic or ferritic alloys.

Erosion-Corrosion   Resistance to erosion is a function of hardness. Therefore the precipitation-hardened grades are likely to show improved resistance to the erosive effects of velocity. However, their reduced corrosion resistance may offset this advantage resulting in essentially no improvement over austenitic stainless steels. It is recommended that each alloy, heat treatment, and environment be evaluated under service conditions. Erosion-corrosion resistance of high-chromium duplex alloys, such as AISI Type 329, should be good.

MARTENSITIC STAINLESS STEELS

Composition   The martensitic stainless alloys contain the minimum chromium content to impart passivity in moist air, namely, 12%. Additional chromium would promote ferrite and prevent the austenite-to-martensite transformation upon cooling from the austenitizing temperature. For this reason, chromium is kept to approximately 14% maximum in martensitic stainless alloys. Nickel promotes austenite formation and its retention upon cooling and is therefore another restricted element. On chemical balance, the corrosion resistance of the martensitic stainless steels is poor. The composition is strictly aimed for strength and hardness. The alloys should not be selected for use in severe corrosive media.

Corrosion Resistance   As mentioned above, limitations on chromium and nickel result in poor corrosion resistance. In addition, for extreme hardness, higher carbon is added which also decreases the corrosion resistance either through local precipitates or interstitial carbon. Some writers suggest that the general corrosion resistance of the martensite is best immediately upon quenching from the austenitizing treatment. Although this may be true, the alloys are so brittle and unmanageable that they must be stress-relieved (tempered) for most practical purposes. Fortunately, the corrosion requirements for cutlery and turbine blades are not too demanding, and quenched and tempered AISI 410 stainless is quite suitable in these applications.

Concerning specific forms of corrosion such as intergranular, pitting, stress, etc., one must realize that the usual martensitic stainless alloys are not chosen for their corrosion resistance to these types of attack. Galvanic corrosion may still be a problem, however. If a martensitic stainless, such as Type 410, is galvanically coupled to an austenitic stainless, such as Type 316, in a weak acid, moist steam, etc., the polarization between the dissimilar metals may act deleteriously against the 410. Hydrogen embrittlement, perhaps really a specialized case of stress-corrosion cracking, is always a possibility with the martensitic stainless steels when used either electrically coupled or uncoupled.

REFERENCES

1. Brigham, R. J., and E. W. Tozer: *Corrosion*, vol. 30, no. 5, pp. 161–166, May 1974.
2. Streicher, M. A.: *Corrosion*, vol. 30, no. 3, pp. 77–91, March 1974.
3. Savkins, L. Ya., and E. G. Fel'dgandler: *Metalloved. Term. Obra. Met.*, vol. 11, pp. 10–13, November 1968.
4. Fundamental Aspects of Stress Corrosion Cracking, *Proc. Conf. Nat. Assoc. Corrosion Eng.*, 1969.
5. Bond, A. P., and H. J. Dundas: *Corrosion*, vol. 24, no. 10, pp. 344–352, October 1968.

Chapter **16**

Corrosion Resistance in Aqueous Media

BENGT WALLÉN
Head, Corrosion Laboratory

JAN OLSSON
Metallurgical Engineer, Corrosion Laboratory, Avesta Jernverks
AB, Avesta, Sweden

PASSIVITY

The good resistance of stainless steels to corrosion is a consequence of their capacity for becoming passivated. Passivity is a highly complex concept and a clearcut definition is difficult to give. In simple terms, passivity implies that under special circumstances a metal or alloy will lose its chemical reactivity and behave as an inert metal.

The nature of passivity is in dispute and there are several schools with their own explanations of the phenomenon. Most scientists embrace the "oxide film theory," and this theory will be applied in the following discussion. According to the oxide film theory, the metal in the passive state is covered by a very thin, invisible film of oxide, formed by the metal reacting with the ambient medium. This protective film acts as a barrier between the metal and its environment and thereby reduces its rate of dissolution.

Electrochemical Significance of Passivity   When a metal is exposed to an aqueous solution containing ions of the metal, both an oxidation of metal atoms into metal ions

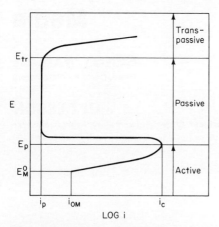

Fig. 1   Relationship between corrosion rate and the electrode potential of a metal capable of being passivated.

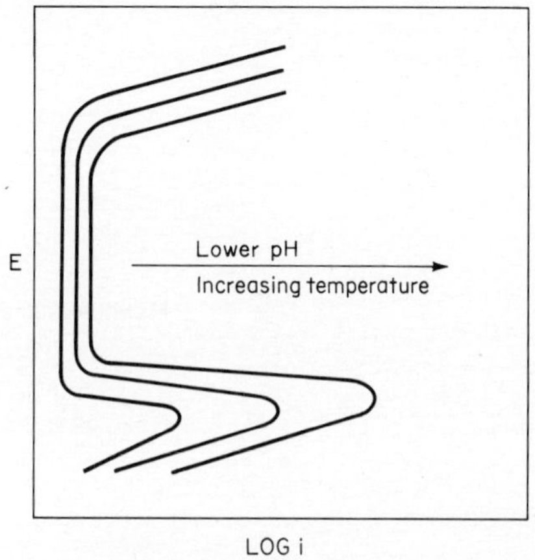

Fig. 2   Effect of pH and temperature on the corrosion rate of a metal capable of being passivated.

and a reduction of metal ions into metal atoms occur at the surface of the metal. These reactions occur at the equilibrium potential E_M^0 of the metal and at a rate which is determined by the exchange current density i_{OM}. If a current is passed through the metal electrode, the electrode potential will change: the electrode is polarized. At the same time the magnitude of the subcurrents will change and they will no longer be identical. The relationship between potential E and current density i is known as the polarization curve of the metal.

Figure 1 presents a schematic anodic polarization curve for a metal which can be passivated. The anodic current density is proportional to the corrosion rate of the metal. At low potentials, the metal will corrode, and if the potential is increased, the rate of corrosion will rise rapidly. This is the active range of the metal. If the potential is raised further, the corrosion will drop suddenly to a very low value i_p, which then will remain constant over a very wide potential range. This is the passive range. Passivation of the metal requires that passivation potential E_p be attained, i.e., that a current density higher than the critical current density i_c be passed through the metal electrode. If the potential is increased above the transpassivation potential E_{tr}, the corrosion rate will rise again since the passive film will be dissolved. This is the transpassive range.

The critical values E_p, i_c, i_p, and E_{tr} are affected by such factors as the temperature and pH of the corrosive medium. As shown in Fig. 2, a higher temperature as well as a lower pH will cause i_c to increase and the width of the passive range to shrink. On the other hand, the passivation potential E_p and the passivation potential i_p in the passive range will normally be only very slightly affected.

Conditions for Passivity   Two electrode processes occur on a corroding metal surface. The corrosion of the metal is the anodic process and this is balanced by a cathodic process. The latter is a reduction of an oxidizing agent such as atmospheric oxygen, dissolved in the electrolyte, Fe^{3+} ions or nitric acid. If the polarization curves for the two processes are plotted on the same graph, the points of intersection of the curves will indicate both the corrosion potential and the rate of corrosion of the metal.

Figure 3 shows a few different situations which may occur when a metal capable of being passivated is exposed to an acid. Besides the anodic polarization curve of the metal, the figure includes four cathodic polarization curves representing different concentrations of the oxidizing agent. When the content of oxidizing agent is low (curve 1), the point of intersection A will lie within the active range of the metal and corrosion will thus be heavy. At a slightly higher concentration of oxidizing agent (curve 2), there are three points of intersection, of which only two, B and C, are electrically stable. In this case the metal exhibits unstable passivity and the rate of corrosion can vary from very low (point C) to very high (point B). Curve 3 represents a more highly oxidizing electrolyte. The single point of intersection D lies well within the passive range. In an excessively oxidizing electrolyte (curve 4) the metal will corrode in the transpassive state.

When the cathodic process has attained a certain rate, more oxidizing agent will not be able to diffuse toward the metal surface per unit time. This rate is often referred to as the diffusion limit current density i_l. In Fig. 3, i_l has only been plotted on curve 3, but it exists on all cathode curves. If the passivity at point D is to be stable, i_l must be greater than i_c. The diffusion limit current density rises sharply if agitation or the flow rate of the electrolyte is increased.

The examples cited above show that a metal is passivated spontaneously only if the electrolyte contains an oxidizing agent which is capable of raising the corrosion of the metal up to the critical current density, i_c. It is possible, however, for the metal to be kept passive without an oxidizing agent in the electrolyte. This requires that the

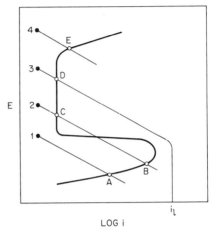

Fig. 3   Effect of an oxidizing agent on the corrosion rate of a metal capable of being passivated.

metal be oxidized anodically, the metal being made the anode in an electric circuit. This procedure is known as anodic protection and involves the use of a special power source, a potentiostat, to maintain the potential of the metal at, say point D in Fig. 3. In this case, the cathodic process occurs on an auxiliary electrode immersed in the electrolyte.

As pointed out in the preceding section, passivity is only ensured when the concentration of oxidizing agent is correct, i.e., corresponding to curve 3 in Fig. 3. If the composition, temperature, or degree of agitation of the electrolyte is changed, both the cathodic and the anodic curves may take on a different appearance. Should the oxidizing agent be used up, for instance, curve 2 may be reached, rendering the passivity unstable. Under certain conditions, only minor mechanical damage to the passive film would then be required to activate the entire metal surface. Another example is that the temperature rises or the electrolyte becomes more acidic. As shown in Fig. 2, i_c is then increased so that even a concentration of oxidizing agent corresponding to curve 3 in Fig. 3 may produce unstable passivity.

It follows from the above that a metal which has been passivated in a certain electrolyte will not necessarily maintain this passivity if the metal is subsequently exposed to another electrolyte of a completely different composition. On the other hand, if anodic protection is employed, the passivity will be maintained as long as the potentiostat delivers the correct current.

Stainless Steels   In connection with Fig. 1, it was shown that the passivity of a metal can be characterized by means of electrochemical parameters. The size of the passivation potential E_p and the magnitude of the critical current density i_c determine how easily the metal can be rendered passive. The current density i_p indicates the rate of corrosion in the passive condition and the transpassive potential E_{tr} determines the strength of the oxidizing agents which the metal can resist.

Figure 4 shows schematically the anodic polarization curves for iron and chromium in an acid. Iron is passivated only at highly positive potentials and also requires a high critical current density. However, the transpassive potential lies at very high values.

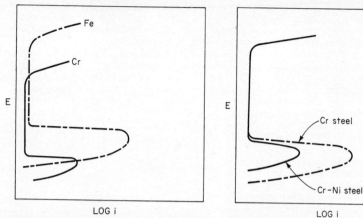

Fig. 4. Relationship between the corrosion rate and the electrode potential of iron and chromium.

Fig. 5 Relationship between corrosion rate and the electrode potential of a chromium steel and a Cr-Ni steel.

Chromium is much easier to passivate, since E_p is considerably lower, approximately 0.5 V, and i_c is several orders of magnitude lower.

Alloying iron with chromium considerably facilitates passivation since the polarization curve of the chromium steel will be very similar to that of pure chromium. However, a certain minimum content of chromium is required to achieve this effect. In neutral aqueous solutions, the minimum is approximately 12% chromium.

Effect of Alloying Elements on the Passivity of Stainless Steels Increasing the *chromium* content beyond 12% will yield steels which can be passivated in more aggressive electrolytes. Alloying the steel with both chromium and *nickel* will markedly facilitate passivation, as shown diagrammatically in Fig. 5.

As a result of the admixture of nickel, i_c is reduced, and the active range is contracted. The passivation potential E_p is shifted slightly toward the more electropositive direction. In all, this means that Cr-Ni steels are easier to passivate than plain chromium steels and that their corrosion rate in the active range will be lower.

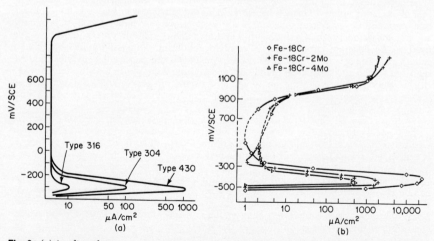

Fig. 6 (*a*) Anodic polarization curves for AISI Types 430, 304, and 316 in 5% sulfuric acid at 25°C (78°F). (*b*) Anodic polarization curves for Fe-18Cr stainless steels with varying molybdenum contents in 1 N sulfuric acid at 25°C (78°F). (*b*) from Rockel, M. B.: The Effect of Molybdenum on the Corrosion Behavior of Iron-Chromium Alloys, *Corrosion*, vol. 29, no. 10, pp. 393–396, Oct. 1973.

Alloying the austenitic Cr-Ni steels with small amounts of *molybdenum* will further reduce i_c. These steels are therefore very easily passivated, even in nonoxidizing acids. Figure 6 indicates the approximate magnitude of the critical current density i_c of a few different steel grades when exposed to 5% sulfuric acid at room temperature.

The oxidizing agent in this acid is dissolved atmospheric oxygen which, at saturation, yields a diffusion limit current density i_l, of approximately 100 μA/cm². This means that AISI Type 430 Cr steel cannot be passivated, Type 304 Cr-Ni steel is on the borderline, while Type 316 Cr-Ni-Mo steel can readily be passivated, even if the acid is not fully air-saturated. Alloying plain chromium steels with molybdenum will also have the same effect, as illustrated in Fig. 6b.

However, the molybdenum-bearing Cr-Ni steels have poor properties in the transpas-

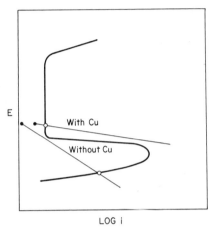

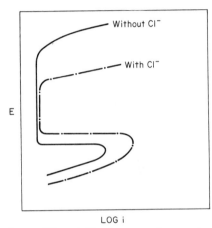

Fig. 7 Importance of the cathodic process for the corrosion rate of a metal capable of being passivated.

Fig. 8 Effect of chloride ions on the corrosion rate of a stainless steel.

sive range and, consequently, are not very suitable for highly oxidizing electrolytes. Replacing molybdenum with *silicon* in Cr-Ni steels will improve their properties in the transpassive range.

The alloying elements discussed so far produce their effect by shifting the anodic polarization curve of the steel in a favorable direction. Adding a small amount of *copper* to the steels will not appreciably affect the polarization curve of the steel but will instead facilitate the cathodic process, i.e., the reduction of the oxidizing agent. Figure 7 shows how the admixture of copper reduces the polarization of the cathodic reaction so that the steel can be passivated instead of corroding in the active state.

Protective Capacity of Passive Films   The passive films of stainless steels are very thin, being 10 to 50 Å thick, and are generally described as hydrous oxides. As compared with the composition of the matrix, the films are enriched primarily with chromium, silicon, and molybdenum. Normally the films are virtually free of pores, but their stability may be weakened considerably locally.

The structure of the film corresponds to that of the underlying metal, and it will therefore have different properties in areas where the steel surface is disturbed. The passivity will thus be impaired over discrete inclusions such as intermetallic compounds or chromium carbides and at grain-boundary precipitates. Other defects may exist where the metal lattice is exposed to mechanical stresses or where slip bands reach the surface.

In some electrolytes, generally those containing halogen ions such as chlorides, the stability of the passive films may be considerably reduced. Figure 8 illustrates schematically how an admixture of chloride affects an anodic polarization curve for a steel in contact with an acid. The chloride reduces the width of the passive range as the result of a widening of the active range and an earlier rise in current at electropositive potentials. The latter phenomenon is caused by the chloride ions at a certain potential (the pitting or breakthrough potential) being capable of penetrating the passive films and destroying them. This occurs chiefly in such areas where the films have been weakened for reasons discussed above.

Passivation of a metal surface requires that the entire surface be reached by a sufficient quantity of oxidizing agent. Should any part of the surface be shielded, such as by a foreign object on the surface, concentration gradients may arise. The content of oxidizing agent may then be sufficient to keep the free-metal surface passive, but beneath the

Fig. 9   General corrosion on a tube (heating coil) of Type 304 inadvertently exposed to diluted sulfuric acid.

foreign object, the content will be so low that the passivity there may become unstable. It is thus important that the surface of the metal be kept clean and free from mill scale, deposits, and the like.

CORROSION

Their capacity for being passivated is the strength of the stainless steels. Paradoxically, it is also their weakness. In the great majority of cases, passivity gives the steels excellent resistance to general corrosion and galvanic corrosion. On the other hand, under special conditions, passivity may break down locally and a large cathodic area (the passive area) will then accelerate the corrosion of a very small anodic area (the small activated spots). This is a contributory cause of crevice corrosion, pitting, intergranular corrosion, and stress-corrosion cracking.

However, each of the above-mentioned types of corrosion has its own explanation and occurs in most cases under its own special conditions. The different types of corrosion will be dealt with individually here, but mainly with the austenitic steels in mind, since these dominate in stainless steel structures which must withstand wet corrosion.

The corrosion resistance of ferritic stainless steels is chiefly determined by the amount of chromium and molybdenum. Their resistance is approximately the same as for austenitic stainless steels with the same amount of these alloying elements.

For martensitic and precipitation-hardenable stainless steels it is more difficult to predict the corrosion rate on the basis of composition because the fabrication of such steels involves a heat treatment in order to optimize mechanical properties and corrosion resistance. Such heat treatment causes precipitation of phases which almost always contain chromium and molybdenum, and the consequence is depletion of these elements in the matrix, which reduces the corrosion resistance. In general, however, such steels show a corrosion resistance corresponding to that for AISI Types 410 to 430 but better resistance is sometimes reported.

General Corrosion

In general corrosion, the entire surface of the steel which is exposed to the electrolyte is attacked uniformly (Fig. 9). This type of corrosion sometimes causes heavy material losses, but is nevertheless the least dangerous type of corrosion, since the attack is uniform over the entire steel surface and the corrosion damage can generally be predicted.

The extent of general corrosion is entirely determined by the properties of the electro-

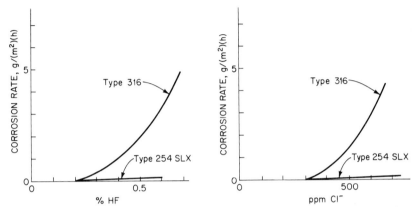

Fig. 10   Corrosion rate for Types 316L and 254SLX in a specific 73% phosphoric acid, technical grade, at 50°C (122°F).

lyte and the steel. If the combination is such that the steel is passive, corrosion will be modest as illustrated by the following example. In an oxidizing electrolyte, such as 20% HNO_3 up to 90°C (194°F), chromium steel Type 430, Cr-Ni steel Type 304, and Cr-Ni-Mo steel Type 316 are passive. In this case, which may be represented by point D in Fig. 3, the corrosion rate is below 0.1 mm/yr.

In a very heavily oxidizing electrolyte, such as highly concentrated nitric acid (99% HNO_3) at 40°C (104°F), the corrosion potential of the three types of steel mentioned above will lie within the transpassive range. This case is represented by point E in Fig. 3, and the corrosion rate is above 1 mm/yr.

As a third example, let us consider a case where certain steel grades are passive while others corrode in the active state, such as in nonoxidizing acid. As discussed in connection with Fig. 1, in 5% H_2SO_4 at room temperature the molybdenum-bearing Type 316 is passive, and the corrosion rate is less than 0.1 mm/yr. The passivity and corrosion rate of Type 304 is entirely determined by the aeration of the acid, and the loss of metal is somewhere between 0.1 and 1.0 mm/yr. Finally, Type 430 chromium steel will corrode in the active state at a rate exceeding 1 mm/yr.

One factor which has a strong influence on the rate of corrosion is the purity of the corrosive medium. It was shown above how chloride ions in the solution affect the appearance of the anodic polarization curve and Figs. 10 to 14 show how the corrosion rate of two different steel grades is altered by the admixture of chloride and fluoride ions in phosphoric acid. Certain additives can also reduce the corrosion rate by reducing the required passivation current density. Examples of such additives are aluminum oxide (Al_2O_3) and silicon dioxide (SiO_2), both of which form complexes with the fluoride ions.

Other additives affect the cathodic polarization curve and can thereby shift the potential of the steel to the stable passive range. This applies to oxidizing agents of various types. A practical example is a sulfuric acid bath for pickling copper alloys in which the sulfuric acid's content of Cu^{2+} ions permits the use of stainless steel under conditions which would otherwise render such use unthinkable. The isocorrosion chart in Fig. 15 shows the influence of various levels of copper in the sulfuric acid on the corrosion rate of Type 316 and Fig. 16 shows the influence of iron sulfate.

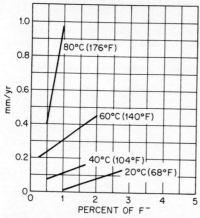

Fig. 11 Corrosion rate for 832 SK steel in 76% phosphoric acid with varying amounts of fluoride additives.

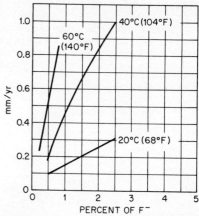

Fig. 12 Corrosion rate of 832 SK steel in 41.4% phosphoric acid with varying amounts of fluoride additives.

In general, corrosion resistance can be augmented by increasing the amount of alloying elements, especially chromium and molybdenum. However, molybdenum has a negative effect if the ambient environment is heavily oxidizing (e.g., nitric acid), so molybdenum-bearing steels can, in some cases, corrode at a faster rate than steels without molybdenum. Silicon and copper are added to steels intended for use in special ambient conditions, e.g., highly oxidizing solutions such as 99% nitric acid (18Cr-15Ni-4Si) or dilute sulfuric acid (20Cr-25Ni-4Mo-2Cu). The usability of stainless steels in different electrolytes may be reported in many different ways, i.e., by explicitly reporting the corrosion rate in graphs or tables, by plotting isocorrosion graphs for the corrosion rate of 0.1 mm/yr, or by symbolizing the corrosion rate in tabular form as is done in Table 1.

The corrosion rate is expressed as weight reduction per surface unit and time unit, e.g., grams per square meter per hour [$g/(m^2)(h)$]. It can also be expressed as thickness reduction per time unit, e.g., millimeters per year (mm/yr). The former expression is used

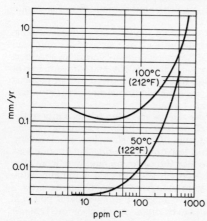

Fig. 13 Corrosion rate for 832 SK steel in 85% phosphoric acid with varying amounts of chloride additives.

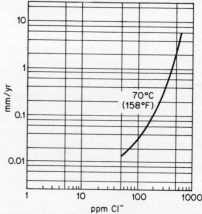

Fig. 14 Effect of varying amounts of chloride additives on the corrosion rate of 832 SK steel in technical grade phosphoric acid having the following chemical composition: 76% H_3PO_4-4.1SO_4^{2-}-0.005 (50 ppm) Cl^--0.1F^--0.3Al-0.3Mg-0.2Fe.

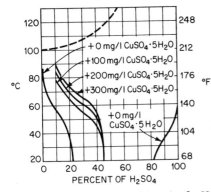

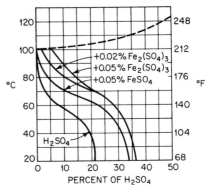

Fig. 15   Isocorrosion curves, 0.1 mm/yr, for 832 SK steel in pure sulfuric acid and in sulfuric acid to which different amounts of copper sulfate have been added. Broken-line curve represents the boiling point.

Fig. 16   Isocorrosion curves, 0.1 mm/yr, for 832 SK steel in pure sulfuric acid and in sulfuric acid to which different amounts of iron sulfate have been added. Broken-line curve represents the boiling point.

in connection with laboratory experiments, while the latter is more easily understandable for practical evaluations. Many corrosion tables based on laboratory experiments use the unit g/(m²)(h). However, with regard to stainless steel, this unit is in virtual agreement with mm/yr, i.e., 1 g/(m²)(h) = 1.1 mm/yr. A generally accepted practical limit for full resistance to general corrosion is 0.1 mm/yr. The designations used in Table 1 to describe the corrosion rate in the many media listed are shown below. Throughout Table 1, *B* in the temperature column represents a boiling solution, all concentrations in the table are given in weight percent and, unless otherwise specified, the solvent is water.

Designation	Corrosion rate, mm/yr	Usability of the material
0	<0.1	Fully resistant
1	0.1–1.0	Not resistant; usable in certain cases
2	>1.0	Severe corrosion; not usable
P as in 0ᴾ	Represented by numerical designa-	Risk of pitting
S as in ˢ0	tions which indicate the average corrosion rate and not the depth of local corrosion	Risk of stress-corrosion cracking

In many cases the information in Table 1 is supplemented with curves: isocorrosion curves on which every point corresponds to a corrosion rate of 0.1 mm/yr (Figs. 17 to 25), and curves for three-component systems comprising nitric acid, sulfuric acid, and water (Figs. 26 and 27). On these latter curves the concentration of sulfuric acid (wt % H_2SO_4) appears on the ordinate and the concentration of nitric acid (wt % HNO_3) on the abscissa. The remainder, i.e., 100% minus the sum of the percentage contents of the acids, is water. Within unshaded areas, the corrosion rate is less than 0.1 mm/yr and the material in question is fully resistant. It should be pointed out that much of these corrosion data are based on laboratory experiments, in other words, on ideal, controlled corrosion conditions involving pure chemicals. Consequently, minor deviations in behavior under practical operating conditions are unavoidable. The tables and curves are thus only intended to provide *initial guidelines* when materials are to be selected. Before the final decision concerning a material is made, corrosion specialists should be contacted. To solve the problem of material selection, it is vital that as many facts as possible about the actual corrosion conditions be gathered. Information about the behavior of previously used materials also facilitates material selection.

The corrosion table and curves are based primarily on laboratory experiments conducted at the Avesta Jernverk laboratory and on practical experience. However, in order to provide a wider base for data acquisition, the Avesta data have been supplemented by

TABLE 1 Corrosion Table

Corrosive medium	Temp., °C (°F)	Degree of attack on							
		Plain carbon steel	393 M(SIS-14-2301)*	249 MV (SIS-14-2320)*	832 MV (SIS-14-2333)*	453 S (SIS-14-2324)*	832 SK (SIS-14-2343)*	832 SL†	254 SLX†
Acetic acid, CH$_3$COOH:									
1%	90 (194)	2	0	0	0	0	0	0	0
1%	B‡	2	1	0	0	0	0	0	0
5%	20 (68)	1	1	0	0	0	0	0	0
5%	50 (122)	2	2	1	0	0	0	0	0
5%	75–90 (167–194)	2	2	2	0	0	0	0	0
5%	B	1	1	1	1	0	0	0	0
10%	20 (68)	2	2	2	0	0	0	0	0
10%	75–80 (167–176)	2	2	2	0	0	0	0	0
10%	90–B (194–B)	2	1	1	1	0	0	0	0
20%	20 (68)	2	2	2	0	0	0	0	0
20%	80 (176)	2	2	2	0	0	0	0	0
20%	85 (185)	2	2	2	1	0	0	0	0
20%	B	2	2	1	2	0	0	0	0
50%	20–50 (68–122)	2	2	2	0	0	0	0	0
50%	80 (176)	2	2	2	0	0	0	0	0
50%	90 (194)	2	2	2	1	0	0	0	0
50%	100–B (212–B)	2	2	1	2	0	0	0	0
80%	20 (68)	2	2	2	0	0	0	0	0
80%	40–80 (104–176)	2	2	2	0	0	0	0	0
80%	85–B (185–B)	2	2	2^P	2^P	0	0	0	0
99.5%	200 (392)	2	2	2	2	0	0	0	0
100%	20–75 (68–167)	2	1	0	0	0	1	0	0
100%	80–90 (176–194)	2	2	0	0	0	0	0	0
100%	100 (212)	2	2	1^P	0	1	0	0	0
100%	B	2	2	2^P	2^P	0	0	0	0

See Fig. 17 for further information about risk of pitting in 80–100% acid.

Medium	Temp. °C (°F)						
Acetic acid + acetic anhydride + sulfuric acid, see under Sulfuric acid							
Acetic acid + formalin + formic acid, see under Formic acid							
Acetic acid + formic acid, see under Formic acid							
Acetic acid + nitric acid, see under Nitric acid							
Acetic acid + potassium permanganate $CH_3COOH + KMnO_4$							
99% 1%	B			0	0	0	0
Acetic acid + sodium chloride: $CH_3COOH+NaCl$							
1% 1%	70–B (158–B)	2	2^P	$s0^P$	$s0^P$	$s0^P$	$s0^P$
1% 5%	50 (122)		1^P	0^P	0^P	0^P	0^P
3% 4%	B						
4% 1%	70–B (158–B)	2^P	2^P	$s0^P$	$s0^P$	$s0^P$	$s0^P$
7% 5%	70 (158)			$s1^P$	$s1^P$	$s1^P$	$s1^P$
7–10% 8.5%	80 (176)			$s1^P$	$s1^P$	$s1^P$	$s1^P$
10% 5%	B			$s1^P$	$s1^P$	$s1^P$	$s1^P$
10% 26%	B		1^P	1^P	$s1^P$	$s1^P$	$s1^P$
25% 26%	B		1^P	1^P	$s1^P$	$s1^P$	$s1^P$
Acetic acid + sulfuric acid, see under Sulfuric acid							
Acetic anhydride, $(CH_3CO)_2O$:							
100%	20–80 (68–176)	2	1	0	0	0	0
100%	B	2	2	1	1	1	0
Acetic anhydride + acetic acid + sulfuric acid, see under Sulfuric acid							
Acetone, $(CH_3)_2CO$	20–B (68–B)	2	1	0	0	0	0
Acetyl chloride, CH_3COCl	B	2^P	1^P	1^P	0^P	0^P	0^P
			Risk of pitting only in presence of moisture.				
Adipic acid, $(C_2H_4COOH)_2$, all conc.	100 (212)	0	0	0	0	0	0
	200 (392)	0	0	0	0	0	0
Agfa glycine, see Developers							

*Avesta proprietary grade designation plus Swedish standard designation. See Appendix 1, Sweden, for composition and Table 1, Chap. 1, for comparison of Swedish standard with other specification standards.

†Avesta proprietary grade designation. See Appendix 2 for composition.

‡B = boiling point.

TABLE 1 Corrosion Table (Continued)

Corrosive medium	Temp., °C (°F)	Plain carbon steel	393 M (SIS-14-2301)*	249 MV (SIS-14-2320)*	832 MV (SIS-14-2333)*	453 S (SIS-14-2324)*	832 SK (SIS-14-2343)*	832 SL†	254 SLX†
					Degree of attack on				
Alum, potassium aluminum sulfate, KAl(SO₄)₂:									
2.5%	90 (194)	2	1	1	0	0	0	0	0
2.5%	B	2	2	2	1	0	0	0	0
5.5%	20–90 (68–194)	2	2	1	0	0	0	0	0
5.5%	B	2	2	2	1	1	1	1	0
10%	20 (68)	2	2	0	0	0	0	0	0
10%	50 (122)	2	2	1	0	0	0	0	0
10%	80 (176)	2	2	1	1	0	0	0	0
10%	B	2	2	2	1	1	1	0	0
15%	50 (122)	2	2	1	0	0	0	0	0
15%	80 (176)	2	2	2	1	1	1	0	0
15%	B	2	2	2	2	2	2	0	0
Hot saturated	B	2	2	2	2	2	2	1	0
Aluminum, Al, melted	700 (1292)	2	2	2	2	2	2	2	2
	750 (1382)	2	2	2	2	2	2	2	2
Aluminum acetate, Al(CH₃COO)₃:									
Saturated at 20°C	20 (68)		0	0	0	0	0	0	0
at 20°C	B			0	0	0	0	0	0
at B	B			0	0	0	0	0	0
Aluminum chloride, AlCl₃:									
5%	50 (122)	2		0[P]	0[P]	0[P]	0[P]	0[P]	0[P]
5%	100 (212)	2		2	2[P]	2[P]	2[P]	0[P]	0[P]
10%	100 (212)	2	2	2	2	2	2	2	2
10%	150 (302)		2	2	2	2	2	2	2
20%	100 (212)		2	2	2	2	2	2	2

Substance	Temp, °C (°F)	1	2	3	4	5	6	7	8
20%	150 (302)	2	2	2	2	2	2	2	2
25%	20 (68)	2	2	2	2	2	2	1ᴾ	1ᴾ
25%	60 (140)	2	2	2	2	2	2	2	2
27.5%	110 (230)	2	2	2	2	2	2	2	2
Aluminum chloride + hydrochloric acid + iron chloride, see under Hydrochloric acid									
Aluminum nitrate, Al(NO₃)₃, all conc.	20 (68)	0	0	0	0	0	0	0	0
Aluminum nitrate + nitric acid + potassium nitrate, see under Nitric acid									
Aluminum sulfate, Al₂(SO₄)₃:									
0.5%	50 (122)	2	0	0	0	0	0	0	0
1.0%	20 (68)	2	0	0	0	0	0	0	0
2.3%	B	2	2	2	0	0	0	0	0
5%	B	2	2	2	0	0	0	0	0
10%	20 (68)	2	0	0	0	0	0	0	0
10%	50 (122)	2	0	0	1	1	1	0	0
10%	B	2	2	2	0	0	0	0	0
23%	20 (68)	2	2	2	0	1	1	0	0
23%	100 (212)	2	2	2	1	0	0	0	0
27%	20 (68)	2	2	2	0	1	1	0	0
27%	B	2	2	2	1	1	1	1	0
Saturated	B	2	2	2	2	2	2	2	0
Aluminum sulfate + sulfuric acid, see under Sulfuric acid									
Ammonium acetate + potassium bichromate: NH₄OOC CH₃ + K₂Cr₂O₇ 3% 2.5%	B	2	2	0	0	0	0	0	0
Ammonium alum, (NH₄)Al(SO₄)₂·12H₂O, 10%	B	2	2	2	2	0	2	0	0
Ammonium aluminum sulfate, see Ammonium alum									
Ammonium bicarbonate, NH₄HCO₃, all conc.	20 (68)	0	0	0	0	0	0	0	0
	25 (77)	2	2	2	2	1	1	1	1
Ammonium bifluoride, NH₄HF₂, 10%		1	1	1	1	1	0	0	0
Ammonium bisulfite, NH₄HSO₃: 10%	20 (68)	2	2	1	0	0	0	0	0
10%	B	2	2	1	1	0	0	0	0

The above values are for the liquid phase and the air-free gaseous phase. If air is present, attacks by sulfu-

TABLE 1 Corrosion Table (Continued)

Corrosive medium	Temp, °C (°F)	Plain carbon steel	393 M(SIS-14-2301)*	249 MV (SIS-14-2320)*	832 MV (SIS-14-2333)*	453 S (SIS-14-2324)*	832 SK (SIS-14-2343)*	832 SL4	254 SLX4
					Degree of attack on				
Ammonium bromide, NH₄Br, 1–5%	20–50 (68–122)	2	2^P	0^P	0^P	0^P	0^P	0^P	0
Ammonium carbonate, (NH₄)₂CO₃ : H₂O, all conc.	20 (68)	0	0	0	0	0	0	0	0
	100 (212)			0	0	0	0	0	0
Ammonium chloride, NH₄Cl:									
1%	20 (68)		0^P	0^P	0^P	0^P	0^P	0^P	0^P
1%	100 (212)		1^P	1^P	$s0^P$	0^P	$s0^P$	$s0^P$	$s0^P$
5%	B	2	0^P	0^P	$s0^P$	0^P	$s0^P$	$s0^P$	$s0^P$
10%	20–50 (68–122)		1^P	1^P	$s0^P$	0^P	$s0^P$	$s0^P$	$s0^P$
10%	90–100 (194–212)		1^P	1^P	$s1^P$	$s0^P$	$s0^P$	$s0^P$	$s0^P$
10%	B		1^P	1^P	0^P	0^P	0^P	0^P	0^P
10%	135 (275)			0^P	$s1^P$	$s1^P$	$s0^P$	$s0^P$	$s0^P$
20%	20–50 (68–122)		1^P	1^P	$s1^P$	$s0^P$	$s1^P$	$s1^P$	$s0^P$
20%	90 (194)		2^P	2^P	$s1^P$	$s0^P$	$s1^P$	$s1^P$	$s1^P$
50%	B	2	2^P	2^P	$s2^P$	$s1^P$	$s0^P$	$s0^P$	$s0^P$
50%	115 (239)	2				$s0^P$	$s0^P$	$s0^P$	$s0^P$
Ammonium chloride + sodium phosphate NH₄Cl + Na₃PO₄ 40% 1.2%	100 (212)				$s0^P$	0^P	$s0^P$	$s0^P$	$s0^P$
Ammonium chloride + zinc chloride NH₄Cl + ZnCl₂ 20% 20%	65 (149)		1^P		$s1^P$	$s0^P$	$s0^P$	$s0^P$	$s0^P$

	Temp. °C (°F)							
Ammonium chlorostannate, pink salt, (NH₄)₂SnCl₆ saturated at 20°C	20 (68)	2	2^P	1^P	2^P	0^P	0^P	0^P
	60 (140)	2	2^P	2^P	2^P	2^P	1^P	1^P
Ammonium fluoride, NH₄F, 10%	25 (77)	0	1	1	0	0	0	0
Ammonium hydroxide, NH₄OH, all conc.	0–B (32–B)	0						
Ammonium nitrate + ammonium sulfate, NH₄NO₃ + (NH₄)₂SO₄, all proportions	60 (140)		0	0	0	0	0	0
	120 (248)		2	1	1	1	0	0
Ammonium nitrate + ammonium sulfate + nitric acid + phosphoric acid, see under Phosphoric acid								
Ammonium nitrate + phosphoric acid, see under Phosphoric acid								
Ammonium oxalate, (NH₄)₂C₂O₄:								
1–8%	20 (68)			0	0	0	0	0
5–20%	100 (212)			1	0	1	⅓0	0
Ammonium perchlorate, NH₄ClO₄:								
10%	20 (68)		2^P	0^P	0^P	0^P	0^P	0^P
10%	B			1^P	S0^P	S0^P	S0^P	S0^P
20%	30 (86)			0^P	0^P	0^P	0^P	0^P

Risk of stress-corrosion cracking and pitting only in presence of Cl⁻ ions.

	Temp. °C (°F)						
Ammonium persulfate, (NH₄)₂S₂O₈, all conc.	20 (68)	0	0	0	0	0	0
	70 (158)	0	0	0	0	0	0
Ammonium phosphate, mono-, di- and tri- NH₄H₂PO₄, (NH₄)₂HPO₄, (NH₄)₃PO₄, all conc.							
Ammonium sulfate, (NH₄)₂SO₄, all conc.	20–100 (68–212)	0	0	0	0	0	0
	20–B (68–B)	2	1	1	0	0	0
Ammonium sulfate + ammonium nitrate, see under Ammonium nitrate							
Ammonium sulfate + ammonium nitrate + nitric acid + phosphoric acid, see under Phosphoric acid							
Ammonium sulfate + nitric acid, see under Nitric acid							
Ammonium sulfate + phosphoric acid + sulfuric acid, see under Phosphoric acid							
Ammonium sulfate + sulfuric acid, see under Sulfuric acid							

TABLE 1 Corrosion Table (Continued)

Corrosive medium	Temp, °C (°F)	Plain carbon steel	393 M(SIS-14-2301)*	249 MV (SIS-14-2320)*	832 MV (SIS-14-2333)*	453 S (SIS-14-2324)*	832 SK (SIS-14-2343)*	832 SL†	254 SLX†
			Degree of attack on						
Ammonium sulfide, (NH₄)₂S, all conc.	20 (68)		1	0	0	0	0	0	0
Ammonium sulfite, (NH₄)₂SO₃, saturated	20–B (68–B)		0	0	0	0	0	0	0
Ammonium thiocyanate, NH₄SCN, all conc.	100 (212)		0	0	0	0	0	0	0
Amyl alcohol, C₅H₁₁OH	20–100 (68–212)		0	0	0	0	0	0	0
Amyl chloride, CH₃(CH₂)₃CH₂Cl, all conc.	20 (68)				0[p]	0[p]	0[p]	0[p]	0[p]
Aniline, C₆H₅NH₂ Tech. grade, concentrated	20 (68)		0	0	0	0	0	0	0
Aniline hydrochloride, C₆H₅NH₂ · HCl: All conc.	20 (68)		2[p]	2[p]	2[p]	2[p]	2[p]	s2[p]	s1[p]
5%	100 (212)		2[p]	2[p]	s2[p]	0[p]	s2[p]	2	2
Antimony, Sb, melted	650 (1202)		2	2	0[p]	0[p]	0[p]	0[p]	0[p]
Antimony chloride, SbCl₃, all conc.	20 (68)	2							
Bagasse + sulfuric acid 48%	180 (356)							0	0
2%	180 (356)							0	0
Gaseous phase of above									
Barium chloride, BaCl₂ · 2H₂O: 6%	100 (212)		0[p]	0[p]	0[p]	0[p]	0[p]	0[p]	0[p]
23%	100 (212)		1[p]	0[p]	0[p]	0[p]	0[p]	0[p]	0[p]
Melted	B		2	2	2	2	2	2	2
Barium hydroxide, Ba(OH)₂, all conc.	0–B (32–B)	0	0	0	0	0	0	0	0
Barium nitrate, Ba(NO₃)₂, all conc.	B		0	0	0	0	0	0	0
Barium peroxide, BaO₂, 10%	95 (203)			0	0	0	0	0	0
Beer	20–70 (68–158)			0	0	0	0	0	0

Substance	°C (°F)								
Benzaldehyde, C_6H_5CHO	100 (212)			2	0	0[p]	0[p]	0	0
Benzalkonium chloride, 1%	60 (140)			2	0	0	0[p]	0[p]	0
Benzene, C_6H_6	20–B (68–B)			2	0	0	0	0	0
Benzenesulfonic acid, $C_6H_5SO_2OH$:									
5%	40 (104)	2	1	0	0	0	0	0	0
5%	50 (122)	2	2	0	0	1	0	0	0
5%	60 (140)	2	2	0	1	2	0	0	0
10%	40 (104)	2	1	0	0	0	0	0	0
10%	50 (122)	2	2	0	0	1	0	0	0
10%	80 (176)	2	2	2	1	2	0	0	0
10%	100 (212)	2	2	2	2	2	1	2	2
20%	50 (122)	2	2	2	2	2	1	2	1
100%	20 (68)	2	2	0	0	0	0	0	0
Benzoic acid, C_6H_5COOH, all conc.	20–B	2	0	0	0	0	0	0	0
Benzyl chloride, $C_6H_5CH_2Cl$, all conc.	100 (212)				so[p]	so[p]	so[p]	so[p]	so[p]
Beryllium chloride, $BeCl_2$, all conc.	100 (212)				so[p]	so[p]	so[p]	so[p]	so[p]
Bismuth, Bi, melted	500 (932)				0	0	0	0	0
	550 (1022)				1	1	1	2	1
	650 (1202)				2	1	1	2	1
Bleaching baths, bleaching agents, see under Calcium hypochlorite, Sodium hypochlorite, Potassium hypochlorite, Chloride of lime and Sodium dithionite									
Blood, meat juices, body tissues	20 (68)	0	0[p]	0[p]	0	0	0[p]	0	0
	37 (99)	2	0[p]	0[p]	0[p]	0[p]	0[p]	0	0
Borax, sodium tetraborate, $Na_2B_4O_7 \cdot 10H_2O$:									
All conc.	20–B (68–B)	0	0	0	0	0	0	0	0
Melted		2	2	2	2	2	2	2	2
Boric acid, H_3BO_3:									
Cold saturated, approx. 4%	B	2	0	0	0	0	0	0	0
Hot saturated, approx. 20%	B	2	1	0	0	1	0	0	0
Boric acid + hydrochloric acid + nickel sulfate:									
H_3BO_3 + HCl + $NiSO_4$	80 (176)		so[p]	so[p]	so[p]	so[p]	so[p]	so[p]	so[p]
1.5% 0.2% 25%									
Boric acid + nickel chloride + nickel sulfate + sulfuric acid									
H_3BO_3 + $NiCl_2$ + $NiSO_4$ + H_2SO_4 pH 2.9	70 (158)	2	0	0	0	0	0	0	0
40 g/l 60 g/l 300 g/l 1 ml/l									
Boron trichloride, BCl_3, 100%	20 (68)	2	0	0	0	0	0	0	0

Risk of pitting in presence of moisture.

TABLE 1 Corrosion Table (Continued)

Corrosive medium	Temp, °C (°F)	Plain carbon steel	393 M(SIS-14-2301)*	249 MV (SIS-14-2320)*	832 MV (SIS-14-2333)*	453 S (SIS-14-2324)*	832 SK (SIS-14-2343)*	832 SL†	254 SLX†
					Degree of attack on				
Bromine, Br$_2$:									
Pure, water-free 100%	20 (68)	2^P	2^P	2^P	2^P	2^P	2^P	2^P	1^P
Aqueous solution 0.03%	20 (68)	2^P	2^P	0^P	0^P	0^P	0^P	0^P	0^P
Aqueous solution 0.15–0.3%	20 (68)	2^P	2^P	1^P	1^P	1^P	1^P	1^P	0^P
Aqueous solution 1%	20 (68)	2^P	2^P	2^P	2^P	0	0	0	1^P
Butyl acetate, CH$_3$COOC$_4$H$_9$	25–B	0	0	0	0	0	0	0	0
Butyl alcohol, C$_4$H$_9$OH	20–B (68–B)			0	0	0	0	0	0
Butyric acid, C$_3$H$_7$COOH:									
100%	20 (68)	2	2	2	0	0	0	0	0
100%	B	2	2	2	1	0	0	0	0
Calcium arsenate, Ca$_3$(AsO$_4$)$_2$, all conc.	B		0	0	0	0	0	0	0
Calcium bisulfite, Ca(HSO$_3$)$_2$:									
10%	20 (68)	2	1	1	0	0	0	0	0
10%	B	2	2	1	1	0	0	0	0
		The above values are for the liquid phase and the air-free gaseous phase. If air is present, attacks by sulfurous and sulfuric acid can occur in the gaseous phase.							
Calcium bisulfite + sulfurous acid, see under Sulfurous acid									
Calcium chloride, CaCl$_2$:									
5%	20 (68)	2	0^P	0^P	0^P	0^P	0^P	0^P	0^P
5%	50 (122)	2	1^P	0^P	0^P	0^P	0^P	0^P	0^P
5%	100 (212)	2	1^P	1^P	$^{s}0^P$	0^P	$^{s}0^P$	$^{s}0^P$	$^{s}0^P$
10%	20 (68)	2	1^P	1^P	0^P	0^P	0^P	0^P	0^P
10%	50 (122)	2	1^P	1^P	0^P	0^P	0^P	0^P	0^P
10%	100–B (212–B)	2	1^P	1^P	$^{s}0^P$	0^P	$^{s}0^P$	$^{s}0^P$	$^{s}0^P$

Corrosion resistance table (ratings: 0 = resistant, 1 = fairly resistant, 2 = not resistant; superscript markers [P] = pitting, [s] = stress-corrosion cracking)

Substance	Temp °C (°F)								
10%	135 (275)	2	1[P]	1[P]			1[s,P]	0[s,P]	0[s,P]	0[s,P]
25%	100 (212)	2	2[P]	1[P]			0[P]	0[s,P]	0[s,P]	0[s,P]
40%	100 (212)									
62%	155 (311)									
73%	176 (349)									
Calcium chloride + calcium hydroxide, see under Calcium hydroxide										
Calcium hydroxide, Ca(OH)₂, all conc.	0–B (32–B)	0	0	0	0	0	0	0	0	0
Calcium hydroxide + calcium chloride: Ca(OH)₂ + CaCl₂										
1%	B									
1%	B	0[P]		0[P]	0[s,P]	0[s,P]	0[s,P]	0[s,P]	0[s,P]	0[s,P]
Calcium hypochlorite, Ca(ClO)₂:										
1%	20 (68)	2	2[P]	1[P]	1[P]	1[P]	0[P]	0[P]	0[P]	0[P]
2%	100 (212)	2	2[P]	2[P]	1[s,P]	1[s,P]	1[P]	1[s,P]	0[s,P]	0[s,P]
6%	20 (68)	2	2[P]	2[P]	2[P]	1[P]	1[P]	1[P]	0[P]	0[P]
6%	100 (212)	2	2[P]	2[P]	2[s,P]	1[s,P]	1[s,P]	1[s,P]	1[s,P]	0
Calcium hypophosphite, (CaH₂PO₂)₂, 5%	B	0	0	0	0	0	0	0	0	0
Calcium nitrate, Ca(NO₃)₂: All conc.	100 (212)	0	0	0	0	0	0	0	0	0
Melted	148 (298)									
Calcium sulfate, CaSO₄, all conc.	100 (212)	2	0	0	0	0	0	0	0	0
Calcium sulfate + phosphoric acid + sulfuric acid, see under Phosphoric acid										
Calcium sulfide, CaS, all conc.	100 (212)	0	0	0	0	0	0	0	0	0
Camphor, C₁₀H₁₆O	20 (68)	0	0	0	0	0	0	0	0	0
Carbon disulfide, CS₂ 100%	20–46 (68–115)	2	0	0	0	0	0	0	0	0
Carbon disulfide + hydrogen sulfide + sodium hydroxide: CS₂ + H₂S + NaOH 0.1% Saturated 0.5%	B									
Carbon monoxide, CO, aqueous solution	100 (212)	0	0	0	0	0	0	0	0	0
Carbon tetrachloride, CCl₄: 100%	20 (68)	0	0	0	0	0	0	0	0	0
100%	B	0	0	0	0	0	0	0	0	0

Risk of pitting and stress-corrosion cracking in presence of moisture.

Substance	Temp °C (°F)								
Carnallite, KCl · MgCl₂: Saturated	20 (68)	2	2[P]	2[P]	0[P]	0[P]	0[P]	0[P]	0[P]	0[P]
Saturated at 20°C	B	2	2[P]	2[P]	1[s,P]	1[s,P]	0[s,P]	0[s,P]	0[s,P]	0[s,P]
Celluloid, dissolved in acetone	All	2	1	1	0	0	0	0	0	0
Cellulose acetate, dissolved in acetone, 20%	20 (68)	2	1	1	0	0	0	0	0	0

TABLE 1 Corrosion Table (Continued)

Corrosive medium	Temp., °C (°F)	Plain carbon steel	393 M (SIS-14-2301)*	249 MV (SIS-14-2320)*	832 MV (SIS-14-2333)*	453 S (SIS-14-2324)*	832 SK (SIS-14-2343)*	832 SL†	254 SLX†
Chloramine, NH₂Cl:									
Dilute	20 (68)				0[P]	0[P]	0[P]	0[P]	0[P]
15%	50 (122)				0[P]	0[P]	0[P]	0[P]	0[P]
Chloric acid, HClO₃:									
1.0%	20 (68)	2	2[P]	2[P]					
100%	20 (68)		2[P]	2[P]	2[P]	2[P]	2[P]	1[P]	1[P]
Chloride of lime, CaOCl₂:									
Active chlorine, 0.8%	20 (68)		2[P]	2[P]	1[P]	0[P]	0[P]	0[P]	0[P]
1.0 %	B						0[s,P]	0[s,P]	0[s,P]
20%	35 (95)		2	2	1	1	0[P]	0[P]	0[P]
30%	20 (68)					1	1	1	1
Chlorine, Cl₂:									
Dry gas, 100%	70 (158)	0	0	0	0	0	0	0	0
Moist gas	20–60 (68–140)	2[P]	2[P]	2[P]	2[P]	2[P]	2[P]	2[P]	1[P]
	60–100 (140–212)	2[P]	2[P]	2[P]	2[s,P]	2[s,P]	2[s,P]	2[s,P]	2[s,P]
Moist gas, >0.4% H₂O	20–60 (68–140)	1[P]	0[P]	0	0	0	0	0	0
Aqueous solution, 1 mg/l	20 (68)				1[P]	0[P]	0[P]	0[P]	0[P]
Aqueous solution, pH = 2, 0.5 g/l	20 (68)				1[P]	1[P]	1[P]	0[P]	0[P]
Aqueous solution, pH = 2, 1.0 g/l	20 (68)				1[P]	2[P]	1[P]	1[P]	0[P]
Aqueous solution, 1.3 g/l	50 (122)								
Chlorine + hydrochloric acid, see under Hydrochloric acid									
Chlorine + sodium chloride:									
Cl₂ + NaCl									
Saturated Saturated	80 (176)	2	2[P]	2[P]	2[s,P]	2[P]	2[s,P]	2[s,P]	1[s,P]

Risk of stress-corrosion cracking and pitting in presence of moisture.

Chemical	Temp °C (°F)								
Chlorine + sulfuric acid, see under Sulfuric acid									
Chlorine dioxide, ClO₂:									
Dry gas	20 (68)					0	0	0	0
Moist gas	20 (68)					2ᴾ	2ᴾ	2ᴾ	2ᴾ
Aqueous solution with 0.1–0.5 g/l active chlorine and 1.8 g/l Cl⁻, pH=1.2	50 (122)			2ᴾ	2ᴾ	2ᴾ	2ᴾ	1ᴾ	0ᴾ
Aqueous solution with 2 g/l active chlorine	70 (158)			2ᴾ	2ᴾ	s2ᴾ	s2ᴾ	s2ᴾ	s2ᴾ
Chloroacetic acid:									
mono- CH₂ClCOOH 30%	80 (176)	2	2	2	2	2	2	2	2
50%	20 (68)	2	2	2	2	2	2	2	2
di- CHCl₂COOH 100%	100 (212)	2	2	2	2	2	2	2	2
tri- CCl₃COOH 100%	100 (212)	2	2	2	2	2	2	2	2
Chlorobenzene, C₆H₅Cl:									
100%	20 (68)	2	0	0	0	0	0	0	0
100%	B	2	1	0	0	0	0	0	0
Chloroform, CHCl₃:									
All conc.	20 (68)	1	0ᴾ	0ᴾ	0ᴾ	0ᴾ	0ᴾ	0ᴾ	0ᴾ
	B	0ᴾ	s0ᴾ	s0ᴾ	s0ᴾ	s0ᴾ	s0ᴾ	s0ᴾ	0ᴾ
Dry, 100%	B	0	0	0	0	0	0	0	0
Chlorohydrin, CH₂ClCHOH · CH₂OH:									
All conc.	B	0ᴾ	0ᴾ	0ᴾ	s0ᴾ	s0ᴾ	s0ᴾ	s0ᴾ	s0ᴾ
Dry, 100%	B	0	0	0	0	0	0	0	0
Chlorohydrin + hydrochloric acid CH₂ClCHOH · CH₂OH + HCl 4%	95 (203)	2	2	2	2	2	2	2	2
Chlorosulfonic acid, HOClSO₂:									
0.5%	20 (68)	2ᴾ	2ᴾ	1ᴾ	0ᴾ	0ᴾ	0ᴾ	0ᴾ	0ᴾ
10%	25 (77)	2ᴾ	2ᴾ	2ᴾ	2ᴾ	2ᴾ	s0ᴾ	2ᴾ	1ᴾ
100%	25 (77)	2ᴾ	2ᴾ	1ᴾ	0ᴾ	0ᴾ	0ᴾ	0ᴾ	0ᴾ
Chlorotoluene, ClC₆H₄CH₃:									
Dry, 100%	B	0	0	0	0	0	0	0	0
Moist, 100%	B	2ᴾ	2ᴾ	2ᴾ	s2ᴾ	s2ᴾ	s2ᴾ	s1ᴾ	s1ᴾ
Choline chloride, C₅H₁₄NCl, 70%	25 (77)	2ᴾ	0	0	0	0	0	0	0
Chrome alum, see Potassium chromium sulfate									

TABLE 1 Corrosion Table (Continued)

Corrosive medium	Temp, °C (°F)	Plain carbon steel	393 M(SIS-14-2301)*	249 MV (SIS-14-2320)*	832 MV (SIS-14-2333)*	453 S (SIS-14-2324)*	832 SK (SIS-14-2343)*	832 SL†	254 SLX†
					Degree of attack on				
Chromic acid, CrO_3									
5%	80 (176)	2			0	0	0	1	0
5%	B	2	2	2	2	2	2	2	2
10%	40 (104)	0	0	0	0	0	0	0	0
10%	B	2	2	2	2	2	2	2	2
20%	20 (68)	2			0	0	0		0
20%	50 (122)	0	2	1	1	1	1	1	0
20%	B	1	2	2	2	2	2	2	2
40%	20 (68)	1	2	2	1	1	1	2	2
40%	40 (104)	1	2	2	2	2	2	2	2
50%	20 (68)	2	2	2	2	2	2	2	2
50%	50–B (122–B)				2		2		
Chromic acid + nitric acid: CrO_3 + HNO_3									
1%	80 (176)			0	0	0	0	0	0
1%									
Chromic acid + phosphoric acid, see under Phosphoric acid									
Chromic acid + phosphoric acid + sulfuric acid, see under Phosphoric acid									
Chromic acid + sulfuric acid, see under Sulfuric acid									
Citric acid, $C_3H_4(OH)(COOH)_3$:									
1%	20 (68)	2	1	0	0	0	0	0	0
1%	B	2	2	1	0	0	0	0	0

Medium	Conc.	Temp. °C (°F)	1	2	3	4	5	6	7	8
	5%	20–50 (68–122)	2	2	1	0	1	0	0	0
	5%	85–B (185–B)	2	2	2	0	0	0	0	0
	5%	140 (284)		2	2	1	1	0	0	0
	10%	20–40 (68–104)	2	2	1	0	0	0	0	0
	10%	85–B (185–B)	2	2	2	1	1	0	0	0
	25%	20 (68)	2	2	1	0	0	0	0	0
	25%	40 (104)	2	2	2	1	1	0	0	0
	25%	85 (185)	2	2	2	0	0	0	0	0
	25%	100 (212)	2	2	2	1	1	0	0	0
	25%	B	2	2	2	2	2	0	0	0
	50%	20 (68)	2	2	1	2	0	0	0	0
	50%	40 (104)	2	2	2	0	0	0	0	0
	50%	100 (212)	2	2	2	0	0	0	0	0
	50%	B	2	2	2	2	2	1	1	1
	67%	B	2	2	2	2	2	1	1	1
Citric acid + ferric chloride + sodium chloride:										
$C_3H_4(OH)(COOH)_3$ + $FeCl_3$ + NaCl 8% 1g/l 4.5%		pH 1.52 B	2	2P	2P	s1P	s1P	s1P	s1P	s0P
Coal gas, town gas				0	0	0	0	0	0	0
Cobalt sulfate, $CoSO_4$, 3%		65 (149)								
Cobalt sulfate + sodium chloride:										
$CoSO_4$ + NaCl 3% 0.1%		85 (185)	1			s0P	s0P	s0P	s0P	s0P
Cod-liver oil		B								
Coffee, aqueous extract		20–B (68–B)	2	0	0	0	0	0	0	0
Common salt, see Sodium chloride										
Copper acetate, $Cu(C_2H_3O_2)_2$, all conc.		B								
Copper carbonate, basic, $CuCO_3 \cdot Cu(OH)_2$, saturated in 50% ammonia solution		20 (68)	2	0	0	0	0	0	0	0
Copper chloride, $CuCl_2$:										
	1%	20 (68)	2			0P	0P	0P	0P	0P
	1%	60 (140)	2			s1P	1P	s1P	s1P	s1P
	1%	75 (167)	2			s2P	2P	s2P	s2P	s1P
	2–5%	60 (140)	2			s2P	1P	s1P	s1P	s1P
	8%	20 (68)	2			0P	0P	0P	0P	0P
	8%	B	2	2P	2P	s2P	2P	s2P	s2P	s2P
	8%	135 (275)	2	2P	2P	s2P	s2P	s2P	s2P	s2P
Copper chloride + hydrochloric acid, see under Hydrochloric acid										

TABLE 1 Corrosion Table (Continued)

Corrosive medium	Temp., °C (°F)	Plain carbon steel	393 M(SIS-14-2301)*	249 MV (SIS-14-2320)*	832 MV (SIS-14-2333)*	453 S (SIS-14-2324)*	832 SK (SIS-14-2343)*	832 SL†	254 SLX†
Copper cyanide, Cu(CN)₂ saturated at 100°C	B	2	2	0	0	0	0	0	0
Copper nitrate, Cu(NO₃)₂ all conc.	20–B (68–B)		0	0	0	0	0	0	0
Copper sulfate, CuSO₄ all conc.	20–B (68–B)		0	0	0	0	0	0	0
Copper sulfate + hydrochloric acid, see under Hydrochloric acid									
Copper sulfate + sulfuric acid, see under Sulfuric acid									
Creosote oil	20 (68)	1	1	1	0	0	0	0	0
	B	2	2	1	0	0	0	0	0
Creosote + sodium chloride:									
Creosote + NaCl 97% 3%	20 (68)	1	2^P	1^P	0^P	0^P	0^P	0^P	0^P
Crude oils, see Oils									
Cup grease	20 (68)			0	0	0	0	0	0
Cycloserine mash	25 (77)				0	0	0	0	0
Detergents, alkaline or neutral, chloride-free, 1%	80 (176)		0	0	0	0	0	0	0
Developers:									
Methol developer	20 (68)	2	0	0	0	0	0	0	0
Methol hydroquinine developer	20 (68)	2	0	0	0	0	0	0	0
Pyrogallol developer	20 (68)	2	2	0	0	0	0	0	0
Agfa glycine	20 (68)		1						0
Dextrose and starch syrup, pure	20 (68)								0
Dichlorethane, see Ethylene chloride									
Dichlorethylene, C₂H₂Cl₂ 100%	20–B (68–B)		0	0	0	0	0	0	0

Substance	Temp. °C (°F)							
Digallic acid, see Tannic acid								
Digester gases, see Sulfite gas								
Diphyl	350 (662)	0	0	0	0	0	0	0

Risk of stress-corrosion cracking and pitting in presence of moisture.

Drinking water, 200 mg/l Cl⁻	20–100 (68–212)	0	0	0	0	0		

Warning: stress-corrosion cracking possible in presence of Cl⁻ as impurity.

Ether, ethyl, $(C_2H_5)_2O$	20–B (68–B)	0	0	0	0	0	0	

Risk of pitting and stress-corrosion cracking can be present on hot walls during boiling. Application in question determines which grade should be selected.

Ethyl alcohol, C_2H_5OH, all conc.	20–B (68–B)	0	0	0	0	0		
Ethyl alcohol + iodine + sodium iodide, see under Iodine.								
Ethyl alcohol + nitric acid + sulfuric acid, see under Nitric acid								
Ethyl chloride, C_2H_5Cl, 100%	20–B (68–B)	0	0	0	0	0	0	

Risk of stress-corrosion cracking and pitting in presence of moisture.

Ethyl nitrate, $C_2H_5NO_2$	20 (68)	2	0	0	0	0		
Ethylene bromide, $C_2H_4Br_2$, 100%	20 (68)	0	0					

Risk of pitting in presence of moisture.

Ethylene chloride, dichloroethane, $C_2H_4Cl_2$, 100%	20–B (68–B)	0	0	0	0	0		

Risk of stress-corrosion cracking and pitting in presence of moisture.

Ethylene glycol, see Glycol								
Fatty acids, oleic acid, stearic acid:								
100%	20 (68)	0	0	0	0	0		
100%	80–130 (176–266)	1	0	0	0	0		
100%	150 (302)	2	1	1	0	0		
100%	180 (356)	2	2	2	0	0		
100%	235 (455)	2	2	1	1	0		
100%	300 (572)	2	2	2	2	0		
Ferric chloride, see Iron(3)chloride								
Ferric chloride + citric acid + sodium chloride, see under Citric acid								
Ferric nitrate, see Iron(3)nitrate								
Ferric sulfate, see Iron(3)sulfate								
Ferrous chloride, see Iron(2)chloride								

16-25

TABLE 1 Corrosion Table (Continued)

Corrosive medium	Temp., °C (°F)	Plain carbon steel	393 M(SIS-14-2301)*	249 MV (SIS-14-2320)*	832 MV (SIS-14-2333)*	453 S (SIS-14-2324)*	832 SK (SIS-14-2343)	832 SL†	254 SLX†
						Degree of attack on			
Ferrous sulfate, see Iron(2)sulfate									
Fixing, salt, acid:									
40% sodium thiosulfate, $Na_2S_2O_3$ + 2.5% potassium dithionite, $K_2S_2O_4$	20 (68)	2	2[P]	0[P]	0[P]	0	0	0	0
19% sodium thiosulfate, $Na_2S_2O_3$ + 4.7% sodium sulfite, Na_2SO_3 + 0.5% sulfuric acid, H_2SO_4	20 (68)			0[P]	0[P]	0[P]	0[P]	0[P]	0[P]
Kodak F 24 Amfix (contains Cl^-)	20 (68)			0[P]	0[P]	0[P]	0[P]	0[P]	0[P]
Pitting is encountered more frequently in the gaseous phase. If the bath contains chlorides, pitting can also occur in the liquid phase.									
Fluorine, F_2:									
Dry gas	20 (68)	0	0	0	0	0	0	0	0
Moist gas	20 (68)	2	2	2	2	2	2	1	1
Fluosilicic acid, H_2SiF_6:									
22%	60 (140)	2	2	2	1	1	1	1	1
Vapor	100 (212)	2	2	2	1	1	1	1	1
Fluosilicic acid + phosphoric acid + sulfuric acid, see under Phosphoric acid									
Formaldehyde, formalin, HCHO, pure, all conc.	20–B (68–B)	2	0	0	0	0	0	0	0
Formalin, see Formaldehyde									
Formalin + formic acid + acetic acid, see under Formic acid									

Formic acid, HCOOH (see Fig. 18):

Conc.	Temp. °C (°F)	1	2	3	4	5	6	7	8
0.5%	70 (158)	0	0	0	0	0	0	0	2
1%	20 (68)	0	0	0	0	0	2	2	2
1%	40–B (104–B)	0	0	0	0	1	1	2	2
2%	20 (68)	0	0	0	0	0	2	2	2
2%	40–60 (104–140)	0	0	0	0	1	1	2	2
2%	100 (212)	0	0	0	0	2	2	2	2
5%	20–60 (68–140)	0	0	0	0	1	2	2	2
5%	80 (176)	0	1	1	1	2	2	2	2
5%	100 (212)	0	0	0	0	2	2	2	2
5%	B	0	0	0	0	2	2	2	2
10%	20–40 (68–104)	0	0	0	1	1	1	2	2
10%	60–70 (140–158)	0	1	1	1	2	2	2	2
10%	100 (212)	0	0	0	0	2	2	2	2
10%	B	0	0	0	0	2	2	2	2
25%	20 (68)	0	0	1	1	1	2	2	2
25%	80 (176)	0	1	1	1	2	2	2	2
25%	90 (194)	0	0	0	0	2	2	2	2
25%	100–B (212–B)	0	0	0	1	2	2	2	2
50%	20 (68)	0	0	0	1	1	2	2	2
50%	50 (122)	1	1	1	1	2	2	2	2
50%	70 (158)	0	0	0	1	2	2	2	2
50%	80 (176)	0	0	1	1	2	2	2	2
50%	100–B (212–B)	0	0	0	0	2	2	2	2
65%	60–80 (140–176)	0	1	1	1	1	2	1	2
65%	100 (212)	1	0	0	0	2	2	2	2
80%	20 (68)	0	1	1	1	1	1	2	1
80%	B	1	0	0	0	2	2	2	2
90%	20 (68)	0	1	0	1	1	2	2	2
90%	40 (104)	1	0	0	0	2	2	2	2
90%	60 (140)	0	1	1	1	2	2	2	2
90%	80 (176)	1	0	2	2	2	2	2	2
90%	100 (212)	0	0	0	0	2	2	2	2
90%	B	0	0	0	0	2	2	2	2
100%	20 (68)	0	1	1	1	1	1	1	2
100%	60 (140)	0	1	2	2	2	2	2	2
100%	100–B (212–B)	0	0	0	0	2	2	2	2

Formic acid + acetic acid:

HCOOH	+ CH₃COOH	1	2	3	4	5	6	7	8
1%	99% B	0	0	0	0	0			
2%	8% B	0	0	0	0				
2%	98% B	0	1	1	1				

TABLE 1 Corrosion Table (Continued)

Corrosive medium	Temp., °C (°F)	Degree of attack on							
		Plain carbon steel	393 M(SIS-14-2301)*	249 MV (SIS-14-2320)*	832 MV (SIS-14-2333)*	453 S (SIS-14-2324)*	832 SK (SIS-14-2343)*	832 SL†	254 SLX†
3%	7%	B						0	0	0
5%	5%	B			1		1	1	1
5%	10%	B			1		1	1	1
5%	25%	B					1	1	1
5%	95%	B		2		0	0	0	0
6%	30%	200 (392)	2	2	2	2	2	2	2
10%	50%	B					1	1	1
10%	90%	B					0	0	0
20%	80%	B					0	0	0
Formic acid + formalin + acetic acid HCOOH + HCHO + CH₃COOH									
1% 40% 0.1%	B				1		0	0	0
Formic acid + potassium bichromate HCOOH + K₂Cr₂O₇									
2% 2.5%	B	2					0	0	0
French turpentine, see Turpentine									
Freon	<200 (<392)	1	0	0	0	0	0	0	0
Fruit juices, wines	20 (68)	2	0	0	0	0	0	0	0
	B		1		0	0	0	0	0
Furfural, C₄H₃OCHO:									
100%	B	2	0	0	0	0	0	0	0
Vapor	200 (392)	2	0	0	0	0	0	0	0
Gallic acid, trihydroxybenzoic acid, C₆H₂(OH)₃COOH 25% (saturated at 100°C)	B		0	0	0	0	0	0	0

If SO₂ is used as preservative, molybdenum-containing steel should be used.

Substance	Temp. °C (°F)								
Gasoline, see under Petrol									
Gelatine, all conc.	All			0	0	0	0	0	0
Glucose, all conc.	20 (68)								0
Glycerine, $C_3H_5(OH)_3$, all conc.	All			0	0	0	0	0	0
Glycol, ethylene glycol, $C_2H_4(OH)_2$, all conc.	20 (68)					0	0	0	0
Guano, dry or moist	20 (68)	2		0	0	0	0	0	0
Hydrobromic acid, HBr:									
30%	25 (77)	2	2^P	2^P	2^P	2^P	2^P	2^P	1^P
100%	25 (77)	0	0	0	0	0	0	0	0
Hydrochloric acid, HCl:									
0.1%	20–50 (68–122)	1	1^P	1^P	1^P	1^P	0^P	0^P	0^P
0.1%	B	2	1^P	${}_S1^P$	${}_S1^P$	${}_S1^P$	${}_S0^P$	${}_S0^P$	${}_S0^P$
0.2%	20 (68)	1	1^P	1^P	1^P	1^P	0^P	0^P	0^P
0.2%	50 (122)	2	2	1^P	1^P	1^P	0^P	0^P	0^P
0.5%	20 (68)	2	1^P	1^P	1^P	1^P	0^P	0^P	0^P
0.5%	50 (122)	2	2	2	2	2	2	2	2
0.5%	B	2	2	2	2	1^P	0^P	0^P	0^P
1%	20 (68)	2	2	2	2	2	1^P	1^P	1^P
1%	50 (122)	2	2	2	2	1^P	2	1^P	${}_S1^P$
1%	60 (140)	2	2	2	2	2	2	2	2
1%	80 (176)	2	2	2	2	2	2	1^P	0^P
1%	B	2	2	2	2	1^P	1^P	2	2
2%	20 (68)	2	2	2	2	2	2	2	0^P
2%	60 (140)	2	2	2	2	2	2	1^P	1^P
2%	100 (212)	2	2	2	2	2	2	2	1^P
3%	20 (68)	2	2	2	2	2	2	1^P	2
3%	60 (140)	2	2	2	2	2	2	2	0^P
3%	70 (158)	2	2	2	2	2	2	1^P	1^P
3%	80 (176)	2	2	2	2	2	2	1^P	1^P
3%	100 (212)	2	2	2	2	2	2	2	2
3%	B	2	2	2	2	2	2	2	2
5%	20–70 (68–158)	2	2	2	2	2	2	2	2
5%	B	2	2	2	2	2	2	2	2
8%	60 (140)	2	2	2	2	2	2	2	2
10%	20–35 (68–95)	2	2	2	2	2	2	2	2
10%	60 (140)	2	2	2	2	2	2	2	2
20%	20–35 (68–95)	2	2	2	2	2	2	2	2
30–37%	20 (68)	2	2	2	2	2	2	2	2

TABLE 1 Corrosion Table (Continued)

Corrosive medium	Temp., °C (°F)	Plain carbon steel	393 M(SIS-14-2301)*	249 MV (SIS-14-2320)*	832 MV (SIS-14-2333)*	453 S (SIS-14-2324)*	832 SK (SIS-14-2343)*	832 SL†	254 SLX†
Hydrochloric acid + aluminum chloride + iron chloride									
HCl + AlCl₃ + FeCl₂ + FeCl₃ 1.8% 1.0% 8.8% 6.0%	100 (212)	2	2^P	2^P	$s2^P$	2^P	$s2^P$	$s2^P$	$s2^P$
Hydrochloric acid + boric acid + nickel sulfate, see under Boric acid									
Hydrochloric acid + chlorine:									
HCl + Cl₂									
5% Saturated	100 (212)	2	2	2	2	2	2	2	2
10% Saturated	90 (194)	2	2	2	2	2	2	2	2
15% Saturated	80 (176)	2	2	2	2	2	2	2	2
20% Saturated	60 (140)	2	2	2	2	2	2	2	2
37% Saturated	25 (77)	2	2	2	2	2	2	2	2
Hydrochloric acid + chlorohydrin, see under Chlorohydrin									
Hydrochloric acid + copper chloride or copper sulfate:									
HCl + CuCl₂ or CuSO₄									
10% 0.05%	80 (176)	2	2	2	2	2	2	2	2
10% 1.5%	B	2	2	2	2	2	2	2	2
25% 0.05%	25 (77)	2	2	2	2	2	2	2	2
25% 0.05%	50 (122)	2	2	2	2	2	2	2	2
37% 0.05%	25 (77)	2	2	2	2	2	2	2	2

Degree of attack on

Hydrochloric acid + iron chloride:
HCl + FeCl₂ or FeCl₃

Substance	°C (°F)								
HCl + FeCl₂ or FeCl₃ 10% 0.06%	80 (176)	2	2	2	2	2	2	2	2
25% 0.06%	50 (122)	2	2	2	2	2	2	2	2
25% 0.06%	70 (158)	2	2	2	2	2	2	2	2
Hydrochloric acid + nitric acid, see under Nitric acid									
Hydrochloric acid + sodium chloride: HCl + NaCl 1% 30%	40 (104)	1[P]	2[P]	2[P]	2[P]	2[P]	2	2	2
Hydrocyanic acid, prussic acid, HCN, 100%	20 (68)	0	0	0	0	0	2	2	2
Hydrofluoric acid, HF: 1%	20 (68)	0	1	1	1	1	2	2	2
10%	20 (68)	2	2	2	2	2	2	2	2
75%	30 (86)	2	2	2	2	2	2	2	2
100%	20 (68)	1	1	1	1	1	1	1	1
Hydrofluoric acid + iron(2)sulfate: HF + FeSO₄ 1.5% 6%	70 (158)	1	1	1	1	2	2	2	2
Hydrofluoric acid + nitric acid, see under Nitric acid									
Hydrofluoric acid + nitric acid + phosphoric acid, see under Phosphoric acid									
Hydrofluoric acid + nitric acid + phosphoric acid + sulfuric acid, see under Phosphoric acid									
Hydrofluoric acid + phosphoric acid, see under Phosphoric acid									
Hydrofluoric acid + phosphoric acid + sulfuric acid, see under Phosphoric acid									
Hydrofluoric acid + potassium chlorate + sulfuric acid: HF + KClO₃ + H₂SO₄ 1% 3% 9%	60 (140)	0	0	s1	0	s1[P]	2[P]	2[P]	2[P]
Hydrogen chloride, anhydrous, HCl, dry	20–40 (68–104)			0	0	0	0	0	0
	100 (212)			1	1	1	1	1	1
	250 (482)			1	1	1	2	2	2
	400–500 (752–932)	0	1	2	2	2	2	2	2

TABLE 1 Corrosion Table (Continued)

Corrosive medium	Temp., °C (°F)	Degree of attack on							
		Plain carbon steel	393 M(SIS-14-2301)*	249 MV (SIS-14-2320)*	832 MV (SIS-14-2333)*	453 S (SIS-14-2324)*	832 SK (SIS-14-2343)*	832 SL†	254 SLX†
Hydrogen iodide, HI:									
10%	20 (68)	2	2	2	2	1	1	1	1
100%	20 (68)	0	0	0	0	0	0	0	0
			Some risk of pitting.						
Hydrogen peroxide, H₂O₂:									
1–2%	50 (122)	0	0	0	0	0	0	0	0
5%	20 (68)	0	0	0	0	0	0	0	0
5%	40–50 (104–122)	0		0	0	0	0	0	0
10%	23 (73)		0	0	0	0	0	0	0
10%	40 (104)	0		0	0	0	0	0	0
10%	60–80 (140–176)			0	0	0	0	0	0
15%	22 (72)	0	0	0	0	0	0	0	0
15%	30–40 (86–104)			0	0	0	0	0	0
15%	50–80 (122–176)			0	0	0	0	0	0
30%	27 (81)			0	0	0	0	0	0
30%	40–80 (104–176)			0	0	0	0	0	0
50%	40 (104)			0	0	0	0	0	0
			A slow decomposition of unstabilized H₂O₂ occurs in contact with all stainless steels.						
Hydrogen peroxide + sodium chloride, see under Sodium chloride									
Hydrogen sulfide, H₂S:									
	100 (212)	1	0	0	0	0	0	0	0
	200 (392)	2	0	0	0	0	0	0	0
Moist gas or saturated aqueous solution	20 (68)	2^P	2^P	2^P	1^P	0	0	0	0

	Temp. °C (°F)								
Hydrogen sulfide + carbon disulfide + sodium hydroxide, see under Carbon disulfide									
Ink, iron tannate ink	20–B (68–B)	1^P	1^P	2^P	2^P	0^P	0^P	0^P	0^P
Ink, synthetic, chloride-free	20–B (68–B)	0	0	0	0	0	0	0	0
Iodine, I$_2$:									
Dry	20 (68)	0	0	0	0	0	0	0	0
Moist	20 (68)	2	2^P	2^P	2^P	2^P	2^P	1^P	1^P
1% aqueous solution	20 (68)	2^P	1^P	0^P	0^P	0^P	0^P	0^P	0^P
2% aqueous solution + 1% KI	20 (68)	2^P	1^P	0^P	0^P	0^P	0^P	0^P	0^P
Iodine + ethyl alcohol + sodium iodide:									
I$_2$ + C$_2$H$_5$OH + NaI 2% 47% 2.4%	44 (111)	2	1^P	0^P	0^P	0^P	0^P	0^P	0^P
Iodoform, CHI$_3$:									
Crystallized	20 (68)		0^P	0^P	0^P	0^P	0^P	0^P	0^P
Vapor	50 (122)								
Iron(2)chloride, ferrous chloride, FeCl$_2$, 10%	20 (68)		0^P	0^P	0^P	0^P	0^P	0^P	0^P
Iron(3)chloride, ferric chloride, FeCl$_3$:									
1%	20 (68)	2	2^P	1^P	0^P	0^P	0^P	0^P	0^P
5–50%	20 (68)	2	2^P	2^P	2^P	2^P	1^P	1^P	1^P
10%	50 (122)	2	2^P	2^P	2^P	2^P	2^P	2^P	1^P
Iron chloride + aluminum chloride + hydrochloric acid, see under Hydrochloric acid									
Iron chloride + citric acid + sodium chloride, see under Citric acid									
Iron chloride + hydrochloric acid, see under Hydrochloric acid									
Iron(3)chloride + nitric acid, see under Nitric acid									
Iron(3)chloride + sodium chloride:									
FeCl$_3$ + NaCl 5% 10%	25 (77)	2	2^P	2^P	2^P	2^P	2^P	1^P	1^P
	50 (122)	2	2^P	2^P	2^P	2^P	2^P	2^P	1^P
Iron(3)nitrate, ferric nitrate, Fe(NO$_3$)$_3$, all conc.	20 (68)	2	0	0	0	0	0	0	0
Iron(2)sulfate, ferrous sulfate, FeSO$_4$:									
10%	20 (68)	0	0	0	0	0	0	0	0
10%	90–B (194–B)	1	1	1	0	0	0	0	0

TABLE 1 Corrosion Table (Continued)

Corrosive medium	Temp, °C (°F)	Degree of attack on							
		Plain carbon steel	393 M(SIS-14-2301)*	249 MV (SIS-14-2320)*	832 MV (SIS-14-2333)*	453 S (SIS-14-2324)*	832 SK (SIS-14-2343)*	832 SL†	254 SLX†
Iron(2)sulfate + hydrofluoric acid, see under Hydrofluoric acid									
Iron(2)sulfate + sulfuric acid, see under Sulfuric acid									
Iron(3)sulfate, ferric sulfate, $Fe_2(SO_4)_3$									
10%	20–B (68–B)			0	0	0	0	0	0
Iron(3)sulfate + sulfuric acid, see under Sulfuric acid									
Iron tannate, see Ink									
Lactic acid, $C_2H_4(OH)COOH$:									
1%	20–50 (68–122)	1	1	1	0	0	0	0	0
1.5%	20 (68)	1	1	1	1	0	0	0	0
1.5%	B	2	2	2	2	0	0	0	0
5%	20–80 (68–176)	2	2	2	0	0	0	0	0
5%	90 (194)	2	2	2	1	0	0	0	0
5%	B	2	2	2	2	0	0	0	0
10%	20–75 (68–167)	2	2	2	0	0	0	0	0
10%	90–100 (194–212)	2	2	2	1	0	0	0	0
10%	B	2	2	2	2	0	0	0	0
25%	20–50 (68–122)	2	2	2	0	0	0	0	0
25%	75–90 (167–194)	2	2	2	1	0	0	0	0
25%	100 (212)	2	2	2	2	1	1	0	0
25%	B	2	2	2	2	1	1	1	0
50%	20–50 (68–122)	2	2	2	0	0	0	0	0
50%	80–90 (176–194)	2	2	2	1	0	0	0	0
50%	100 (212)	2	2	2	2	1	1	1	0

Medium	Temp. °C (°F)								
50%	B	0	1	1	1	2	2	2	2
75%	20–50 (68–122)	0	0	0	0	0	2	2	2
75%	75 (167)	0	0	0	0	1	2	2	2
75%	100 (212)	0	0	0	0	2	2	2	2
80%	20 (68)	0	0	0	0	0	2	2	2
80%	75 (167)	0	0	0	0	1	2	2	2
Approx. 90%	B	0	1	1	1	2	2	2	2
Approx. 90%	20 (68)	0	0	0	0	0	2	2	2
Approx. 90%	40 (104)	0	0	0	0	1	2	2	2
Approx. 90%	50–100 (122–212)	0	1	1	1	2	2	2	2
Lactic acid + potassium bichromate: $C_2H_4(OH)COOH + K_2Cr_2O_7$ 2.5% / 3%	B	0	0	0	0	0	1	1	2
Lactic acid + sodium chloride: $C_2H_4(OH)COOH + NaCl$ 1.5–2%	B	s0[P]	s0[P]	s0[P]		s2[P]	2[P]		
Lactic acid + sulfuric acid: $C_2H_4(OH)COOH + H_2SO_4$ 10% / 25%	B	1	2	2	2	2	2	2	2
25% / 50%	B	1	2	2	2	2	2	2	2
Lead, Pb. Melted with oxidation-inhibiting surface layer of charcoal. Without this protection there will be heavy oxidation at the surface of the molten lead	400 (752)	0	0	0	0	1	2	2	2
	600 (1112)	0	0	0	0	1	2	2	2
	900 (1652)	2	2	2	2	2	2	2	2
Lead acetate, $Pb(CH_3COO)_2 \cdot 3H_2O$, all conc.	20–90 (68–194)	0	0	0	0	0	0	0	0
	B	0	0	0	0	0	0	0	1
	B	0	0	0	0	0	0	1	
Lead nitrate, $Pb(NO_3)_2$, all conc.	B	s0[P]	s0[P]	s0[P]	0[P]	s0[P]	1[P]	2[P]	2
Lithium chloride, LiCl: 10%	B	s0[P]	s0[P]	s0[P]	s0[P]	s1[P]	1[P]	2[P]	2
10%	135 (275)	s0	s0[P]	s1[P]	s1[P]	s1[P]	2[P]	2[P]	2
40%	115 (239)	0	s0	s1	s1	s1	1	2	2
Lithium hydroxide, LiOH, 2.5%	220 (428)			0	0	0			
Lithographic oil									
Lubricating oils, see Oils									
Lysol: 2%	20 (68)	0	0	0	0	0	0	0	1
Concentrated	20–B (68–B)	0	0	0	0	0	0	0	2

TABLE 1 Corrosion Table (Continued)

Corrosive medium	Temp., °C (°F)	Plain carbon steel	393 M(SIS-14-2301)*	249 MV (SIS-14-2320)*	832 MV (SIS-14-2333)*	453 S (SIS-14-2324)*	832 SK (SIS-14-2343)*	832 SL†	254 SLX†
Magnesium bisulfite, $Mg(HSO_3)_2$:									
10%	20 (68)	2	1	1	0	0	0	0	0
10%	B	2	2	1	1	0	0	0	0
Magnesium carbonate, $MgCO_3$, all conc.	20 (68)	The above values are for the liquid phase and the air-free gaseous phase. If air is present, attacks by sulfurous and sulfuric acid can occur in the gaseous phase.							
Magnesium chloride, $MgCl_2$:									
2.5%	20 (68)	2	0^P	0^P	0^P	0^P	0^P	0^P	0^P
5%	B	2	1^P	0^P	$s0^P$	$s0^P$	$s0^P$	$s0^P$	$s0^P$
5%	135 (275)	2	2^P	1^P	$s0^P$	0^P	$s0^P$	$s0^P$	$s0^P$
10–20%	20 (68)	2	2^P	1^P	0^P	$s0^P$	0^P	0^P	0^P
20–45%	B	2	2^P	1^P	$s0^P$	$s0^P$	$s0^P$	$s0^P$	$s0^P$
Magnesium sulfate, $MgSO_4$:									
5%	20 (68)	1	0	0	0	0	0	0	0
5%	60 (140)	2	1	0	0	0	0	0	0
10%	20 (68)	2	0	0	0	0	0	0	0
10%	60 (140)	2	1	1	0	0	0	0	0
20%	20 (68)	2	1	1	0	0	0	0	0
26%	B	2	2	1	0	0	0	0	0
26%	20 (68)	2	2	2	0	0	0	0	0
Malic acid, $C_2H_3(OH)(COOH)_2$:									
1%	20 (68)	1	0	0	0	0	0	0	0
5–50%	100 (212)	2	2	0	0	0	0	0	0
Manganese chloride, $MnCl_2$:									
5%	100 (212)	2	1^P	0^P	$s0^P$	0^P	$s0^P$	$s0^P$	$s0^P$

Degree of attack on

Medium	Temp °C (°F)								
10%	B								
10%	135 (275)								
20%	100 (212)								
50%	B	2	2^P	2^P	s0^P	s0^P	s0^P	s0^P	s0^P
Manganese dioxide + sulfuric acid, see under Sulfuric acid									
Manganese sulfate, MnSO₄:									
All conc.	20 (68)		0	0	0	0	0	0	0
23%	100 (212)		0	0	0	0	0	s0^P	s0^P
Mayonnaise	B								
Meat juices, see Blood									
Mercuric chloride, sublimate, HgCl₂:									
0.1%	20 (68)	2	2^P	2^P	1^P	1^P	0^P	0^P	0
0.1%	B		2^P	2^P	s1^P	s1^P	s0^P	s0^P	s0^P
0.7%	20 (68)		2^P	2^P	1^P	1^P	0^P	0^P	0
0.7%	B		2^P	2^P	s2^P	s2^P	s2^P	s1^P	s1^P
1–10%	100 (212)								
1–10%	135 (275)								
Mercuric cyanide, Hg(CN)₂, 5%	20 (68)	2	2	0	0	0	0	0	0
Mercuric nitrate, Hg(NO₃)₂, 5%	20 (68)	0	0	0	0	0	0	0	0
Mercury, Hg	20–400 (68–752)		0	0	0	0	0	0	0
Methanol, see Methyl alcohol									
Methol developer, see Developers									
Methol hydroquinine developer, see Developers									
Methyl alcohol, methanol, CH₃OH, 100%	B	0	0	0	0	0	0	0	0
Methyl chloride, CH₃Cl:									
100%	20 (68)	0	0	0	0	0	0	0	0
100%	B	0	0	0	0	0	0	0	0

Risk of stress-corrosion cracking and pitting in presence of moisture.

Medium	Temp °C (°F)								
Methylene chloride, CH₂Cl₂:									
All conc.	B	0^P	0^P	0^P	0^P	s0^P	s0^P	s0^P	s0^P
Dry, 100%	B	0	0	0	0	0	0	0	0
Milk:									
Fresh	20 (68)	1	0	0	0	0	0	0	0
	B	2	1	1	0	0	0	0	0
Sour	20 (68)	2	1	1	0	0	0	0	0
Mineral oils, see Oils									
Mustard	20 (68)	2	1^P	0^P	0^P	0^P	0^P	0^P	0^P

Risk of pitting becomes higher with increasing

TABLE 1   Corrosion Table (Continued)

Corrosive medium	Temp., °C (°F)	Degree of attack on							
		Plain carbon steel	393 M(SIS-14-2301)*	249 MV (SIS-14-2320)*	832 MV (SIS-14-2333)*	453 S (SIS-14-2324)*	832 SK (SIS-14-2343)*	832 SL†	254 SLX†
Naphthalene, $C_{10}H_8$	25 (77)								
Nickel chloride, $NiCl_2$:									
10%	20 (68)	2	1^P	0^P	0^P	0^P	0	0	0
10%	100 (212)	2	1^P	1^P	0^P	0^P	0^P	0^P	0^P
Nickel chloride + boric acid + nickel sulfate + sulfuric acid, see under Boric acid									
Nickel nitrate, $Ni(NO_3)_2$, 5–10%	20 (68)	2	0	0	0	0		0	0
Nickel sulfate, $NiSO_4$, all conc.	B	2	2	0	0	0		0	0
Nickel sulfate + boric acid + hydrochloric acid, see under Boric acid									
Nickel sulfate + boric acid + nickel chloride + sulfuric acid, see under Boric acid									
Nitric acid, HNO_3 (see Fig. 19):									
0.5%	250 (482)	2	0	0	0	0	0	0	0
1%	20–50 (68–122)	2	0	0	0	0	0	0	0
1%	80–90 (176–194)	2	1	0	0	0	0	0	0
5%	20–50 (68–122)	2	0	0	0	0	0	0	0
5%	85–B (185–B)	2	1	0	0	0	0	0	0
5%	130 (266)	2	2	2	2	2	2	2	2
5%	290 (554)	2	2	2	2	2	2	2	2
7%	20–50 (68–122)	2	0	0	0	0	0	0	0

... amounts of salt and vinegar in mustard. 832 SK can be used for mustard-making equipment if it is cleaned at regular intervals.

1	2	3	4	5	6	7	8		
0	0	0	0	0	0	1	2	B	7%
0	0	0	0	0	0	0	2	20–50 (68–122)	10%
0	0	0	0	0	0	1	2	75–B (167–B)	10%
2	2	2	2	2	2	2	2	145 (293)	10%
0	0	0	0	0	0	0	2	20–50 (68–122)	20%
0	0	0	0	0	0	1	2	90 (194)	20%
0	0	0	0	0	1	2	2	B	20%
0	0	0	0	0	0	0	2	20 (68)	30%
0	0	0	0	0	0	0	2	50–70 (122–158)	30%
0	0	0	0	0	0	1	2	90–100 (194–212)	30%
0	0	0	0	0	1	2	2	B	30%
0	0	0	0	0	0	0	2	50 (122)	40%
0	0	0	0	0	1	1	2	90 (194)	40%
0	0	0	0	0	1	2	2	100–B (212–B)	40%
0	0	0	0	0	0	0	2	20–50 (68–122)	50%
0	0	0	0	0	0	1	2	80 (176)	50%
0	0	0	0	0	1	1	2	90 (194)	50%
0	0	0	0	0	1	2	2	100 (212)	50%
0	0	0	0	0	1	2	2	B	50%
0	0	0	0	0	0	0	2	50 (122)	60%
0	0	0	0	0	1	1	2	60–90 (140–194)	60%
0	0	0	0	0	1	2	2	100 (212)	60%
0	0	0	0	0	1	2	2	B	60%
1	1	1	1	1	0	0	2	20–50 (68–122)	65%
0	0	0	0	0	1	1	2	80 (176)	65%
0	0	0	0	0	1	2	2	100 (212)	65%
1	1	1	1	1	1	2	2	B	65%
1	1	1	1	1	0	0	2	175 (347)	65%
0	0	0	0	0	1	1	2	100 (212)	70%
0	0	0	0	0	1	2	2	30–50 (86–122)	80%
1	1	1	1	1	2	2	2	60 (140)	80%
1	1	1	1	1	2	2	2	80 (176)	80%
1	1	1	1	1	0	1	2	B	80%
0	0	0	0	0	1	1	2	20 (68)	90%
0	0	0	0	0	1	1	2	80 (176)	90%
1	1	1	1	1	2	2	2	B	90%
1	1	1	1	1	2	2	2	30 (86)	94%
0	0	0	0	0	0	0	2	25 (77)	97%
2	2	2	2	2	2	2	2	25 (77)	99%
2	2	2	2	2	2	2	2	40 (104)	99%
0	2	2	2	2	2	2	2	B	99%

TABLE 1 Corrosion Table (Continued)

Corrosive medium	Temp., °C (°F)	Degree of attack on							
		Plain carbon steel	393 M(SIS-14-2301)*	249 MV (SIS-14-2320)*	832 MV (SIS-14-2333)*	453 S (SIS-14-2324)*	832 SK (SIS-14-2343)	832 SL†	254 SLX†
Nitric acid, red, fuming: $HNO_3 + N_2O_4 + H_2O$ 72.7% 26.4% 0.9% Specific gravity 1.615	25 (77)				0	0	1		
	40 (104)				1	1	1		
Nitric acid + acetic acid: $HNO_3 + CH_3COOH$ 10–40% 20%	20 (68)	2	1	1	0	0	0	0	0
Nitric acid + aluminum nitrate + potassium nitrate: $HNO_3 + Al(NO_3)_3 + KNO_3$									
15% 0% Saturated	90 (194)				0	0	0	0	0
15% 30% 13%	90 (194)				0	0	0	0	0
60% 0% Saturated	70 (158)				0	0	0	0	0
60% 9–30% 1%	70 (158)				0	0	0	0	0
65–67% 15–20% 8–11%	60 (140)				0	0	0	0	0
88% 10% 0%	B				1	1	1	1	1
88% 0% 10%	B				1	1	1	1	1
Nitric acid + ammonium nitrate + ammonium sulfate + phosphoric acid, see under Phosphoric acid									
Nitric acid + ammonium sulfate: $HNO_3 + (NH_4)_2SO_4$ 26% 30%	80 (176)				0	0	0	0	0
Nitric acid + chromic acid, see under Chromic acid									

Nitric acid + ethyl alcohol + sulfuric acid:

Material	°C (°F)								
HNO₃ + C₂H₅OH + H₂SO₄									
0% 33% 61%	130 (266)	2	2	2	2	2	2	2	2
0% 7% 65%	130 (266)	2	2	2	2	2	2	2	2
1% 33% 61%	130 (266)	2	2	2	2	2	2	2	2
5% 7% 65%	130 (266)	2	2	2	2	2	2	2	2
Nitric acid + hydrochloric acid:									
HNO₃ + HCl									
9% 18%	90 (194)	2	2	2	2	2	2	2	2
17% 28%	20 (68)	2	2	2	2	2	2	2	2
Nitric acid + hydrofluoric acid:									
HNO₃ + HF									
1.5% 0.5%	80 (176)	2	2	2	2	2	2	2	1
10% 3%	70 (158)	2	2	2	2	2	2	2	2
20% 4%	25 (77)	2	2	2	2	2	2	2	1
20% 4%	65 (149)	2	2	2	2	2	2	2	2
Nitric acid + hydrofluoric acid + phosphoric acid, see under Phosphoric acid									
Nitric acid + hydrofluoric acid + phosphoric acid + sulfuric acid, see under Phosphoric acid									
Nitric acid + iron(3)chloride:									
HNO₃ + FeCl₃									
10% 6%	20 (68)	2^P	2^P	1^P	1^P	0^P	0^P	0*^{R}	0^P
Nitric acid + oxalic acid:									
HNO₃ + (COOH)₂									
50% 300 g/l	70 (158)	2	1	1	0	0	0	0	0
Nitric acid + oxalic acid + sulfuric acid, see under Oxalic acid									
Nitric acid + phosphoric acid + sulfuric acid, see under Phosphoric acid									
Nitric acid + sodium chloride:									
HNO₃ + NaCl									
55% 1%	80 (176)	2	2	2	s1^P	1^P	s1^P	s1^P	s1^P
Nitric acid + sodium fluoride:									
HNO₃ + NaF									
10% 1%	60 (140)	2	2	2	2	2	2	1	1

TABLE 1 Corrosion Table (*Continued*)

Corrosive medium		Temp., °C (°F)	Degree of attack on							
			Plain carbon steel	393 M(SIS-14-2301)*	249 MV (SIS-14-2320)*	832 MV (SIS-14-2333)*	453 S (SIS-14-2324)*	832 SK (SIS-14-2343)*	832 SL†	254 SLX‡
Nitric acid + sulfuric acid (see Figs. 26–27):										
HNO_3	+ H_2SO_4									
1%	5%	25 (77)				0	0	0	0	0
1%	5%	50 (122)				0	0	0	0	0
1%	10%	25 (77)				0	0	0	0	0
1%	10%	80 (176)				1	0	0	0	0
1%	95%	50 (122)				1	0	0	0	0
1%	99%	35 (95)				0	0	0	0	0
3%	10%	25 (77)				0	0	0	0	0
3%	10%	80 (176)				1	0	0	0	0
3%	50%	25 (77)				0	0	0	0	0
5%	20%	25–50 (77–122)				0	0	0	0	0
5%	60%	25–50 (77–122)				0	0	0	0	0
5%	60%	80 (176)					1	1	1	1
10%	60%	60 (140)	2	2		0	0	0	0	0
10%	60%	80 (176)	2	2		1	1	1	1	1
10%	80%	50 (122)				0	0	0	0	0
10%	80%	80 (176)				1	1	1	1	1
10%	90%	35 (95)				0	0	0	0	0
20%	80%	20 (68)	0	0	0	0	0	0	0	0
20%	80%	60 (140)		1	1	1	0	0	0	0
20%	80%	100 (212)				1	1	1	1	1
30%	20%	80 (176)				1	0	0	0	0
30%	40%	80 (176)				1	1	1	1	1
30%	70%	35 (95)				0	0	0	0	0
50%	20%	80 (176)				1	1	1	1	0

Material	Temperature °C (°F)								
50% 50%	60 (140)	0	0	0	1	1	1	1	2
65% 35%	35 (95)	0	0	0	0	0	0	0	0
90% 10%	35 (95)	0	0	0	0	0	0	0	0
Nitro cellulose:									
Pure	20 (68)	0	0	0	0	0	0	0	0
With traces of acid	20 (68)	0	0	0	0	0	1	1	1
Nitrous acid, HNO_2, all conc.	20 (68)	0	0	0	0	0	2	2	2
Oils: Crude oils, mineral oils, lubricating oils, vegetable oils, etc.	B	0	0	0	0	0	0	0	0
Oleic acid, see Fatty acids									
Oxalic acid, $(COOH)_2$ (see Fig. 20):									
0.5%	20 (68)	0	0	0	0	1	1	1	1
0.5%	35 (95)	0	0	0	0	1	1	1	1
0.5%	60 (140)	0	0	0	0	1	2	2	2
0.5%	80 (176)	1	1	2	2	2	2	2	2
0.5%	B	2	2	2	2	2	2	2	2
1%	35 (95)	0	0	0	0	1	1	1	1
1%	60 (140)	0	0	0	0	2	2	2	2
1%	B	1	1	2	2	2	2	2	2
2.5%	20 (68)	0	0	0	0	1	1	1	1
2.5%	40 (104)	0	0	0	0	2	2	2	2
2.5%	60 (140)	0	0	0	0	2	2	2	2
2.5%	80 (176)	0	0	0	0	2	2	2	2
2.5%	B	1	1	1	1	1	2	2	2
5%	20 (68)	0	0	0	0	2	2	2	2
5%	35 (95)	0	0	0	0	2	2	2	2
5%	60 (140)	0	0	0	0	2	2	2	2
5%	85 (185)	0	0	0	0	2	2	2	2
5%	100 (212)	1	1	1	1	2	2	2	2
5%	B	1	1	2	2	2	2	2	2
10%	20–35 (68–95)	0	0	0	0	2	2	2	2
10%	50 (122)	0	0	0	0	2	2	2	2
10%	60 (140)	0	0	0	0	2	2	2	2
10%	80 (176)	0	0	0	0	2	2	2	2
10%	100–B (212–B)	1	1	1	1	2	2	2	2
25%	60 (140)	0	0	1	1	2	2	2	2
25%	75 (167)	0	0	2	2	2	2	2	2
25%	100 (212)	1	0	0	1	1	1	2	2
25%	B	1	2	2	2	2	2	2	2

TABLE 1 Corrosion Table (Continued)

Corrosive medium	Temp., °C (°F)	Degree of attack on							
		Plain carbon steel	393 M(SIS-14-2301)*	249 MV (SIS-14-2320)*	832 MV (SIS-14-2333)*	453 S (SIS-14-2324)*	832 SK (SIS-14-2343)*	832 SL†	254 SLX†
Oxalic acid + nitric acid, see under Nitric acid									
Oxalic acid + nitric acid + sulfuric acid: (COOH)₂ + HNO₃ + H₂SO₄									
20 g/l 0 g/l 50 g/l	60 (140)	2					2	2	
20 g/l 5 g/l 50 g/l	60 (140)	2					0	0	0
20 g/l 10 g/l 50 g/l	60 (140)						0	0	0
Paraffin	0–100 (32–212)	0	0	0	0	0	0	0	0
Pectin	100 (212)	2			0	0		0	0
Perchloric acid, HClO₄:									
10%	25 (77)	0	2	2	2	2	2	1	1
100%	20 (68)	2	2	2	2	2	2	2	2
		Risk of pitting in presence of Cl⁻ ions.							
Perchloroethylene, see figures for Trichloroethylene									
Petrol	20–B (68–B)	0	0	0	0	0	0	0	0
Phenol, C₆H₅OH:									
All conc.	20–50 (68–122)	0	0	0	0	0	0	0	0
70–100%	B	2	2	1	1	0	0	0	0
Phosphoric acid, H₃PO₄, chem. purity (see Fig. 21):									
1%	20 (68)	2	0	0	0	0	0	0	0
1%	B	2	2	1	0	0	0	0	0
1%	140 (284)	2	2	1	0	0	0	0	0
3%	100 (212)	2	2	0	0	0	0	0	0
5%	20–60 (68–140)	2	0	0	0	0	0	0	0
5%	85 (185)	2	0	0	0	0	0	0	0
5%	B	2	2	0	0	0		0	0

Conc.	Temp °C (°F)								
10%	40 (104)	2	2	2	0	0	0	0	0
10%	60 (140)	2	2	2	0	0	0	0	0
10%	80 (176)	2	2	2	0	0	0	0	0
10%	100 (212)	2	2	2	0	0	0	0	0
10%	B	2	2	2	0	0	0	0	0
20%	35 (95)	2	2	2	0	0	0	0	0
20%	60 (140)	2	2	2	0	0	0	0	0
20%	B	2	2	2	0	0	0	0	0
30%	20–35 (68–95)	2	2	2	0	0	0	0	0
30%	60 (140)	2	2	2	0	0	0	0	0
30%	100 (212)	2	2	2	1	0	0	0	0
40%	35 (95)	2	2	2	0	0	0	0	0
40%	50 (122)	2	2	2	0	0	0	0	0
40%	100 (212)	2	2	2	1	0	0	0	0
40%	B	2	2	2	2	0	0	0	0
50%	20 (68)	2	2	2	0	0	0	0	0
50%	35 (95)	2	2	2	0	0	0	0	0
50%	50 (122)	2	2	2	1	0	0	0	0
50%	85 (185)	2	2	2	2	0	0	0	0
50%	100 (212)	2	2	2	2	0	0	0	0
50%	B	2	2	2	2	1	0	0	0
60%	20 (68)	2	2	2	0	0	0	0	0
60%	35 (95)	2	2	2	1	0	0	0	0
60%	100 (212)	2	2	2	2	1	0	0	0
60%	B	2	2	2	2	2	0	0	0
70%	35 (95)	2	2	2	1	0	0	0	0
70%	90 (194)	2	2	2	2	1	0	0	0
70%	B	2	2	2	2	2	1	0	0
80%	20 (68)	2	2	2	1	0	0	0	0
80%	35 (95)	2	2	2	2	1	0	0	0
80%	80 (176)	2	2	2	2	2	0	0	0
80%	100 (212)	2	2	2	2	2	1	0	0
80%	B	2	2	2	2	2	2	0	0
85%	20 (68)	2	2	2	1	1	0	0	0
85%	50 (122)	2	2	2	2	2	0	0	0
85%	95 (203)	2	2	2	2	2	2	0	0
85%	B	2	2	2	2	2	2	2	0
Phosphoric acid, technical grade: 29.4% P_2O_5 + 1.8% SO_4^{2-} + 0.03–0.06% Cl^- + 1.3% F^-, acid value 3.15, 40%	25 (77)	2	2	2	1	0	0	0	0

TABLE 1 Corrosion Table (Continued)

Corrosive medium	Temp., °C (°F)	Degree of attack on							
		Plain carbon steel	393 M(SIS-14-2301)*	249 MV (SIS-14-2320)*	832 MV (SIS-14-2333)*	453 S (SIS-14-2324)*	832 SK (SIS-14-2343)*	832 SL†	254 SLX†
30.5% P_2O_5 + 1.8% SO_4^{2-} + 1.5% F^- + 0.02% Cl^-, acid value 3.22, 42.1%	75 (167)	2	2	2	2	1	1	0	0
53.9% P_2O_5 + 3% SO_4^{2-} + 0.5% F^- + 0.03% Cl^- acid value 2.87, 75%	20 (68) 75 (167)	2 2	2 2	2 2	2 2	0 1	0 1	0 0	0 0
55% P_2O_5 + 3% SO_4^{2-} + 0.7% F^- + 0% Cl^-, acid value 2.88, 76.5%	50 (122)	2	2	2	2	0	0	0	0
55.2% P_2O_5 + 4.1% SO_4^{2-} + 0.1% F^- + 0.005–0.020% Cl^-, acid value 3.09, 76.5%	50 (122)	2	2	2	2	0	0	0	0
55.2% P_2O_5 + 4.1% SO_4^{2-} + 0.1% F^- + 0.035% Cl^-, 76.5%	70 (158)	2	2	2	2	0	0	0	0
55.2% P_2O_5 + 4.1% SO_4^{2-} + 0.01% F^- + 0.075% Cl^-, 76.5%	70 (158)	2	2	2	2	2	2	0	0
Superphosphoric acid: 74.6% P_2O_5 + 1% SO_4^{2-} + 0.3% F^- + 0% Cl^-, 103%	70 (158)	2	2	2	2	2	2	1	1
Phosphoric acid + ammonium nitrate: H_3PO_4 + NH_4NO_3 10% 30%	120 (248) 150 (302)		1				0 1	0 1	0 1
Phosphoric acid + ammonium nitrate + ammonium sulfate + nitric acid: H_3PO_4 + NH_4NO_3 + $(NH_4)_2SO_4$ + HNO_3 4% 15% 9% 9%	80 (176) 100 (212)	2	1 0	0 0	0 0	0 0	0 0	0 0	0 0

Phosphoric acid + ammonium sulfate + sulfuric acid:

H_3PO_4	$(NH_4)_2SO_4$	$+ H_2SO_4$	°C (°F)								
10%	25%	1.5%	90 (194)	0	0	0	0	2			
15%	25%	1.0%	100 (212)	0	0	0		2			
15%	25%	3.0%	100 (212)	0	0	0		2			
15%	30%	3.0%	90 (194)	0	0	0		2			
15%	20%	20.0%	20 (68)	0	0	0	0	2			
16%	9%	1.0%	80 (176)	0	0	0	0	0			

Phosphoric acid + calcium sulfate + sulfuric acid:

H_3PO_4	$+ CaSO_4$	$+ H_2SO_4$	°C (°F)								
4%	50%	2%	50 (122)	0	0	0	0	1	2	2	2
22%	traces	1%	70 (158)	0	0	0	0	1	1	2	2

Phosphoric acid + chromic acid:

H_3PO_4	$+ CrO_3$		°C (°F)								
80%	10%		20 (68)	0	0	0	0	0			
80%	10%		60 (140)	1	2	2	2	2			

Phosphoric acid + chromic acid + sulfuric acid:

H_3PO_4	$+ CrO_3$	$+ H_2SO_4$	°C (°F)								
57%	9%	14%	80 (176)		2	2					

Phosphoric acid + fluosilicic acid + sulfuric acid:

H_3PO_4	$+ H_2SiF_6$	$+ H_2SO_4$	°C (°F)								
30%	1%	3%	70 (158)	0	0	0	1	2	2	2	2
55%	1%	1%	90 (194)	1	1	1	2	2	2	2	2

Phosphoric acid + hydrofluoric acid:

H_3PO_4	$+ HF$		°C (°F)								
1.5%	1.0%		50 (122)	1	1	2	2	2	2	2	2
41.4%	0.5%		20 (68)	0	0	0	0	1	1	2	2
41.4%	0.5%		40 (104)	0	0	1	1	2	2	2	2
41.4%	0.5%		60 (140)	0	1	1	1	2	2	2	2
41.4%	1.0%		20 (68)	0	0	1	1	2	2	2	2
41.4%	1.0%		40 (104)	0	1	1	1	2	2	2	2
41.4%	1.0%		60 (140)	1	1	2	2	2	2	2	2
41.4%	2.5%		20–40 (68–104)	0	1	1	1	2	2	2	2
41.4%	2.5%		60 (140)	1	1	2	2	2	2	2	2
76.0%	0.5%		20 (68)	0	0	0	0	1	1	2	2
76.0%	0.5%		40 (104)	0	0	0	0	1	2	2	2
76.0%	0.5%		60 (140)	0	0	1	1	2	2	2	2

TABLE 1 Corrosion Table (Continued)

Corrosive medium		Temp., °C (°F)	Degree of attack on							
			Plain carbon steel	393 M (SIS-14-2301)*	249 MV (SIS-14-2320)*	832 MV (SIS-14-2333)*	453 S (SIS-14-2324)*	832 SK (SIS-14-2343)*	832 SL†	254 SLX†
76.0%	0.5%	80 (176)	2	2	2	2	1	1	1	1
76.0%	1.0%	20 (68)	2	2	2	1	0	0	0	0
76.0%	1.0%	40 (104)	2	2	2	2	1	0	0	0
76.0%	1.0%	60 (140)	2	2	2	2	1	1	1	0
76.0%	1.0%	80 (176)	2	2	2	2	2	1	1	1
76.0%	2.0%	20 (68)	2	2	2	2	1	0	0	0
76.0%	2.5%	20 (68)	2	2	2	2	1	1	0	0
80.0%	1.0%	120 (248)	2	2	2	2	2	2	2	2
Phosphoric acid + hydrofluoric acid + nitric acid: H_3PO_4 + HF + HNO_3										
18.0% 0.2% 28.0%		65 (149)	2	2	2	2	1	1	1	1
19.3% 0.1% 31.2%		65 (149)	2	2	2	2	1	0	0	0
19.3% 0.1% 31.2%		90 (194)	2	2	2	2	1	1	1	1
Phosphoric acid + hydrofluoric acid + nitric acid + sulfuric acid: H_3PO_4 + HF + HNO_3 + H_2SO_4										
7.9% 0.1% 12% 25.8%		90 (194)	2	2	2	2	1	1	1	1
Phosphoric acid + hydrofluoric acid + sulfuric acid: H_3PO_4 + HF + H_2SO_4										
25.0% 1% 2%		80 (176)	2	2	2	2	2	2	2	1
41.4% 1% 2%		40 (104)	2	2	2	2	2	2	1	0
Phosphoric acid + nitric acid + sulfuric acid: H_3PO_4 + HNO_3 + H_2SO_4										
43% 2.0% 45.0%		100 (212)				1	1	1	1	

Chemical	Temp. °C (°F)	C1	C2	C3	C4	C5	C6	C7	C8
43% 2.2% 45.0%	105 (221)					2	1	1	1
64% 1.9% 23.0%	90 (194)				0	1	0	0	0
66% 7.2% 10.5%	100 (212)					1	1	1	1
78% 3.0% 18.0%	95 (203)					1	1	1	0
Phosphoric acid + sulfuric acid:									
$H_3PO_4 + H_2SO_4$									
40.0% 2.0%	B					2	2	2	2
41.4% 2.0%	80 (176)	2	2	2	2	1	0	0	0
41.4% 3.5%	80 (176)	2	2	2	2	1	1	0	0
43.0% 47.0%	70 (158)	2	2	2	2	2	1	1	1
53.0% 15.0%	60 (140)	2	2	2	2	2	2	2	1
76.0% 3.5%	80 (176)	2	2	2	2	1	1	0	0
Phosphoric anhydride, phosphorus pentoxide, P_2O_5:									
Dry	20 (68)	0			0	0	0	0	0
Moist	20 (68)	0			1	0	0	0	0
Phosphorus pentachloride, PCl_5, 100%	20 (68)	0	0		0	0	0	0	0
Phosphorus pentoxide, see under Phosphoric anhydride									
Picric acid, trinitrophenol, $C_6H_2(NO_2)_3OH$:									
1%	B	2	2						
All conc.	20 (68)	2	2	1	0				
Potassium, K, melted	540–600 (1004–1112)	2		2		0			
Potassium acetate, $KOOCCH_3$:									
All conc.	100 (212)					0	0	0	0
Melted	292 (558)		2			0	0	0	0
Potassium acetate + sodium acetate:									
$KOOCCH_3 + NaOOCCH_3$									
70% 30%	300 (572)					0	0	0	0
Potassium aluminum sulfate, see Alum									
Potassium bicarbonate, $KHCO_3$, all conc.	100 (212)					0	0	0	0
Potassium bichromate, $K_2Cr_2O_7$:									
20%	90 (194)	0	0			0	0	0	0
25%	20 (68)	0	0			0	0	0	0
25%	B	2	2	2		0	0	0	0
Potassium bichromate + ammonium acetate, see under Ammonium acetate									
Potassium bichromate + formic acid, see under Formic acid									

Risk of pitting in presence of moisture.

TABLE 1 Corrosion Table (*Continued*)

Corrosive medium	Temp., °C (°F)	Plain carbon steel	393 M(SIS-14-2301)*	249 MV (SIS-14-2320)*	832 MV (SIS-14-2333)*	453 S (SIS-14-2324)*	832 SK (SIS-14-2343)*	832 SL†	254 SLX†
									Degree of attack on
Potassium bichromate + lactic acid, see under Lactic acid									
Potassium bichromate + sulfuric acid, see under Sulfuric acid									
Potassium bisulfate, KHSO₄:									
2%	90 (194)	2	2	2	2	0	0	0	0
5%	20 (68)	2	2	2	1	0	0	0	0
5%	50 (122)	2	2	2	1	0	0	0	0
5%	90 (194)	2	2	2	2	0	1	1	0
10%	20 (68)	2	2	2	1	0	0	0	0
10%	90 (194)	2	2	2	2	1	1	1	1
10%	100 (212)	2	2	2	2	2	2	1	1
15%	90 (194)	2	2	2	2	2	2	2	1
Potassium bisulfite, KHSO₃:									
10%	20 (68)	2	1	1	0	0	0	0	0
10%	B	2	2	1		0	0	0	0
Potassium bitartrate, KH(CHOHCOO)₂:									
Saturated at 100°C	B	2	2	2	1	0	0	0	0
Potassium bromide, KB, all conc.	20 (68)	2	2ᴾ	0ᴾ	0ᴾ	0ᴾ	0ᴾ	0	0
	50 (122)	2	2ᴾ	0ᴾ	0ᴾ	0ᴾ	0ᴾ	0	0
Potassium bromide + potassium ferricyanide:									
KBr + K₃Fe(CN)₆ 2.3% 1.5%	20 (68)		0ᴾ		0ᴾ	0ᴾ	0ᴾ	0ᴾ	0ᴾ

The above values are for the liquid phase and the air-free gaseous phase. If air is present, attacks by sulfurous and sulfuric acid can occur in the gaseous phase.

Chemical	Temp., °C (°F)								
Potassium carbonate, K₂CO₃:									
All conc.	B	2	0	0	0	0	0	0	0
Melted	900–1000 (1652–1832)	2	2	2	2	2	2	2	2
Potassium chlorate, KClO₃:									
7–10%	50 (122)	2	0	0	0	0	0	0	0
10%	100 (212)		0	0	0	0	0	0	0
36%	B		1	1	0	0	0	0	0
Potassium chlorate + hydrofluoric acid + sulfuric acid, see under Hydrofluoric acid									
Potassium chloride, KCl:									
10%	50 (122)	2	1ᴾ	1ᴾ	0ᴾ	0ᴾ	0ᴾ	0ᴾ	0ᴾ
35%	B	2	2	1ᴾ	s1ᴾ	0ᴾ	0ᴾ	s0ᴾ	s0ᴾ
Potassium chromate, K₂CrO₄, all conc.	B	2	0	0	0	0	0	0	0
Potassium chromium sulfate, chrome alum, KCr(SO₄)₂:									
6%	20–90 (68–194)	2	2	2	2	0	0	0	0
17%	20 (68)	2	2	2	2	0	0	0	0
20%	B	2	2	2	2	2	1	0	0
40%	20 (68)	2	2	2	2	2	1	0	0
Potassium cyanide, KCN, all conc.	B	2	0	0	0	0	0	0	0
Potassium dithionite + sodium thiosulfate, see Fixing salt									
Potassium ferricyanide, K₃Fe(CN)₆, all conc.	20 (68)	2	0	0	0	0	0	0	0
	B		2	0	0	0	0	0	0
Potassium ferricyanide + potassium bromide, see under Potassium bromide									
Potassium ferrocyanide, K₄Fe(CN)₆, all conc.	20 (68)	2	0	0	0	0	0	0	0
	B		2	0	0	0	0	0	0
Potassium hydroxide, KOH:									
10%	B		0	0	0	0	0	0	0
20%	20 (68)		0	0	0	0	0	0	0
25%	B		2	1	0	0	0	0	0
50%	20 (68)		1	0	s1	s1	s1	s1	s1
50%	B		2	2	s1	s1	s1	s1	s1

There is risk of pitting and stress-corrosion cracking of stainless steels in the presence of Cl⁻ ions.

TABLE 1 Corrosion Table (Continued)

Corrosive medium	Temp., °C (°F)	Degree of attack on							
		Plain carbon steel	393 M(SIS-14-2301)*	249 MV (SIS-14-2320)*	832 MV (SIS-14-2333)*	453 S (SIS-14-2324)*	832 SK (SIS-14-2343)*	832 SL†	254 SLX†
70%	120	2	2	2	1[s]	1[s]	1[s]	1[s]	1[s]
Melted	300–365 (572–689)		2	2	2[s]	2[s]	2[s]	2[s]	2[s]
Potassium hypochlorite, KClO:									
<2%	20 (68)				1[P]	0[P]	0[P]	0[P]	0[P]
>2%	20 (68)				2[P]	1[P]	1[P]	0[P]	0[P]
Potassium iodide, KI, all conc.	B		2[P]	1[P]	0[P]	0[P]	0[P]	0[P]	0[P]
			Risk of pitting, particularly in alkaline solutions.						
Potassium nitrate, KNO₃:									
All conc.	20–B (68–B)		0	0	0	0	0	0	0
Melted	550 (1022)		2	0	0	1	1	0	
	780 (1436)								
Potassium nitrate + aluminum nitrate + nitric acid, see under Nitric acid									
Potassium oxalate, K₂C₂O₄, all conc.	20 (68)	2	0	0	0	0	0	0	0
	B	2	2	0	0	0	0	0	0
Potassium permanganate, KMnO₄:									
5–10%	20 (68)		0	0	0	0	0	0	0
10%	B		1	0	0	0	0	0	0
Potassium permanganate + acetic acid, see under Acetic acid									
Potassium peroxide, K₂O₂, 10%	20–90 (68–194)		0	0	0	0	0	0	0
Potassium persulfate, K₂S₂O₈:									
4%	20 (68)	2	2	1	0	0	0	0	0
Saturated	20 (68)	2	2	2	2	1	1	0	0
Potassium sulfate, K₂SO₄, all conc.	B		0	0	0	0	0	0	0
Potassium sulfide, K₂S, 1%	20 (68)	2	0	0	0	0	0	0	0

Medium	Temp. °C (°F)							
Propylene dichloride, $CH_2ClCHClCH_3$ 100%	20 (68)			0	0	0	0	0
Risk of pitting in presence of moisture.								
Prussic acid, see Hydrocyanic acid								
Pyridine, C_5H_5N	100 (212)			0	0	0	0	0
Pyrogallic acid, pyrogallol, trihydroxybenzene, $C_6H_3(OH)_3$, all conc.	20–B (68–B)	2		0	0	0	0	0
Pyrogallol developer, see Developers								
Quinine bisulfate, all conc.	20 (68)	2	2	2	2	0	0	0
Quinine solution, ammoniacal	20 (68)	2	0	0	0	0	0	0
Quinine sulfate, all conc.	20 (68)	2	2	0	0	0	0	0
Quinosol, $C_9H_6NOSO_3K \cdot H_2O$, 0.2–0.5%	20 (68)			0	0	0	0	0
Saccharin, all conc.	100 (212)			0	0	0	0	0
Salicylic acid, $C_6H_4(OH)COOH$: 5%	20–85 (68–185)		0	0	0	0	0	0
20%	100 (212)		0	0	0	0	0	0
Seawater, natural or synthetic	20–50 (68–122)	1^P	1^P	1^P	s_1^P	0^P	0^P	0^P
	B	2^P	2^P	s_1^P	0^P	s_0^P	s_0^P	s_0^P
The molybdenum-containing steels can be used at temperatures up to 50°C at constant water velocities constantly exceeding 1.5 m/s (4.9 ft/s) if crevices can be avoided.								
Silver bromide, AgBr, all conc.	20–B (68–B)	2^P	0^P	0^P	0	0	0	0
Little risk of pitting because the salt is difficult to dissolve.								
Silver bromide + silver iodide: AgBr + AgI All conc. 0–2%	B	0^P	s_0^P	0	0	0	0	0
Little risk of pitting and stress-corrosion cracking because the salts are difficult to dissolve.								
Silver nitrate, $AgNO_3$: All conc.	20–B (68–B)	2	0	0	0	0	0	0
Melted	250 (482)	2	2	0	0	0		
Soap, see also Soft soap Sodium, Na, melted	540–600 (1004–1112) 800 (1472)			0	0	0	0	0
Sodium acetate, $NaOOCCH_3$, all conc.	20–340 (68–644)	0	0	0	0	0	0	0
Sodium acetate + potassium acetate, see under Potassium acetate								

TABLE 1 Corrosion Table (Continued)

Corrosive medium	Temp., °C (°F)	Degree of attack on							
		Plain carbon steel	393 M(SIS-14-2301)*	249 MV (SIS-14-2320)*	832 MV (SIS-14-2333)*	453 S (SIS-14-2324)*	832 SK (SIS-14-2343)*	832 SL†	254 SLX†
Sodium aluminate, NaAlO₂, all conc.	20 (68)		0	0	0	0	0	0	0
Sodium bicarbonate, NaHCO₃, all conc.	20–100 (68–212)		0	0	0	0	0	0	0
Sodium bichromate + sodium chlorate + sodium chloride + sodium hypochlorite, see under Sodium chloride									
Sodium bichromate + sulfuric acid, see under Sulfuric acid									
Sodium bisulfate, NaHSO₄:									
1%	85 (185)								0
2%	20 (68)								0
2%	85 (185)	2	2	2	1			0	0
4%	20 (68)	2	2		0			0	0
4%	B	2	2	2	1	0	0	0	0
5%	20 (68)	2	2	2	2	0	0	0	0
5%	85 (185)	2	2	2	1	0	0	0	0
10%	20 (68)	2	2	2	1	0	0	0	0
10%	50 (122)	2	2	2	2	0	0	0	0
10%	B	2	2	2	2	1	1	1	0
15%	85 (185)	2	2	2	2	2	2	1	0
Sodium bisulfite, NaHSO₃:									
10%	20 (68)	2	1	1	0	0	0	0	0
10%	B	2	2	1	1	0	0	0	0

The above values are for the liquid phase and the air-free gaseous phase. If air is present, attacks by sulfurous and sulfuric acid can occur in the gaseous phase.

Sodium bromide, NaBr:									
5–10%	20 (68)	2			0^P	0^P	0^P	0^P	0^P
20%	80 (176)				${}^S0^P$	0^P	${}^S0^P$	${}^S0^P$	${}^S0^P$
Sodium carbonate, Na_2CO_3:									
All conc.	20–B (68–B)		0	0	0	0	0	0	0
Melted	900 (1652)	2	2	2	2	2	2	2	
Sodium carbonate + sodium chloride:									
Na_2CO_3 + NaCl									
1% 25%	20 (68)				0	0	0	0	0
Sodium chlorate, $NaClO_3$:									
10–20%	B				0	0	0	0	0
30%	20 (68)				0	0	0	0	0
30%	B				1	0	0	0	0
		Risk of stress-corrosion cracking and pitting in presence of Cl^- ions.							
Sodium chlorate + sodium bichromate + sodium chloride + sodium hypochlorite, see under Sodium chloride									
Sodium chlorate + sodium chloride:									
$NaClO_3$ + NaCl									
30% 5%	B				${}^S1^P$	${}^S0^P$	${}^S0^P$	${}^S0^P$	${}^S0^P$
35% Saturated	120 (248)	2	2^P	2^P	${}^S2^P$	${}^S0^P$	${}^S0^P$	${}^S0^P$	${}^S0^P$
70% Saturated	120 (248)	2	2^P	2^P	${}^S1^P$	${}^S0^P$	${}^S0^P$	${}^S0^P$	${}^S0^P$
Sodium chloride, common salt, NaCl:									
0.01%	B	2	1^P	0^P	0^P	0	0	0	0
0.01%	150 (302)	2	1^P	0^P	${}^S0^P$	${}^S0^P$	${}^S0^P$	${}^S0^P$	${}^S0^P$
1%	135 (275)	2	2^P	1^P	${}^S0^P$	${}^S0^P$	${}^S0^P$	${}^S0^P$	${}^S0^P$
3%	20–60 (68–140)	2	1^P	1^P	1^P	0^P	0^P	0^P	0^P
26%	25 (77)	2	1^P	0^P	0^P	0^P	0^P	0^P	0^P
Sodium chloride + acetic acid, see under Acetic acid									
Sodium chloride + chlorine, see under Chlorine									
Sodium chloride + citric acid + ferric chloride, see under Citric acid									
Sodium chloride + cobalt sulfate, see under Cobalt sulfate									
Sodium chloride + creosote, see under Creosote									

TABLE 1 Corrosion Table (Continued)

Corrosive medium	Temp., °C (°F)	Plain carbon steel	393 M(SIS-14-2301)*	249 MV (SIS-14-2320)*	832 MV (SIS-14-2333)*	453 S (SIS-14-2324)*	832 SK (SIS-14-2343)*	832 SL†	254 SLX†
					Degree of attack on				
Sodium chloride + hydrochloric acid, see under Hydrochloric acid									
Sodium chloride + hydrogen peroxide:									
$NaCl + H_2O_2$									
1% 3%	80 (176)				0[S,P]	0[P]	0[S,P]	0[S,P]	0[S,P]
10% 1%	20 (68)				0[P]	0[P]	0[P]	0[P]	0[P]
Sodium chloride + iron(3)chloride, see under Iron(3)chloride									
Sodium chloride + lactic acid, see under Lactic acid									
Sodium chloride + nitric acid, see under Nitric acid									
Sodium chloride + sodium bichromate + sodium hypochlorite + sodium chlorate:									
$NaCl + Na_2Cr_2O_7 + NaClO + NaClO_3$									
10% 0.15% 0.12% 40%	60 (140)				1[P]	0[P]	0[P]	0[P]	0[P]
Sodium chloride + sodium carbonate, see under Sodium carbonate									
Sodium chloride + sodium chlorate, see under Sodium chlorate									
Sodium chloride + sodium hydroxide, see under Sodium hydroxide									
Sodium chloride + sulfuric acid, see under Sulfuric acid									
Sodium chlorite, $NaClO_2$:									
5%	20 (68)				2	2	2	1	0

Risk of stress-corrosion cracking and pitting in presence of Cl⁻ ions.

	2	2	2	2	2	1
B						

5%

	B	2	2	2	2	2	1
Sodium chlorite + sodium pyrophosphate: NaClO₂ + Na₄P₂O₇, 0.6% active Cl₂ 0.2%	80 (176)				80^P	80^P	80^P
Sodium citrate, Na₃C₆H₅O₇:							
3.5%	20–100 (68–212)	2	0	0	0	0	0
35%	100 (212)	2	0	0	0	0	0
Sodium cyanide, NaCN, all conc.	B	0	0	0^P	0	0	0
Sodium dithionite, Na₂S₂O₄, 2%	70 (158)	0	0	0^P	0	0	0

Risk of pitting is encountered more frequently in the gaseous phase.

	B	2	2	2	2	2	1
Sodium fluoride, NaF, 5%	20 (68)	1	1	0	0	0	0
Sodium fluoride + nitric acid, see under Nitric acid							
Sodium hydroxide, NaOH (see Fig. 22):							
10%	21 (70)	0	0	0	0	0	0
10%	90 (194)	0	0	0	0	0	0
10%	B	1	1	0	0	0	0
20%	20–50 (68–122)	0	0	0	0	0	0
20%	90–B (194–B)	1	1	0	0	0	0
25%	20 (68)	0	0	0	0	0	0
25%	B	2	2	1	0	0	0
30%	20 (68)	1	1	0	0	0	0
30%	100 (212)	1	1	0	0	0	0
30%	B	2	2	$s1$	$s0$	$s0$	$s0$
40%	80 (176)	1	1	0	1	0	0
40%	90 (194)	1	1	0	0	0	0
40%	100 (212)	1	1	0	1	1	1
50%	60 (140)	1	0	0	0	0	0
50%	90 (194)	2	1	0	0	0	0
50%	100 (212)	2	1	1	0	1	0
50%	120 (248)	2	2	1	1	1	$s0$
50%	B	2	2	$s1$	$s1$	$s1$	$s1$
60%	90 (194)	1	1	0	0	0	0
60%	120 (248)	2	1	1	1	1	1
60%	B	2	$s2$	$s2$	$s2$	$s2$	$s2$
70%	90 (194)	1	0	0	0	0	0
70%	130 (266)	2	1	1	1	1	1

TABLE 1   Corrosion Table (Continued)

Corrosive medium	Temp., °C (°F)	Plain carbon steel	393 M(SIS-14-2301)*	249 MV (SIS-14-2320)*	832 MV (SIS-14-2333)*	453 S (SIS-14-2324)*	832 SK (SIS-14-2343)*	832 SL†	254 SLX†
					Degree of attack on				
70%	B	2	2	2	s1	s2	s2	s2	s2
78%	120 (248)	2	2	1	1	0	0	0	0
90%	300 (572)	2	2	2	s2	s1	s1	s1	s1
Melted	320 (608)	2	2	2	s2	s2	s2	s2	s2
Sodium hydroxide + carbon disulfide + hydrogen sulfide, see under Carbon disulfide									
Sodium hydroxide + sodium chloride:									
NaOH + NaCl									
1% 1–25%	50 (122)				0	0	0	0	0
5% 20%	108 (226)				0	0	0	0	0
5% 40%	80 (176)				0	0	0	0	0
5% 40%	108 (226)				0	0	0	0	0
10% 20–25%	108 (226)				0	0	0	0	0
20% 10–20%	108 (226)				0	0	0	0	0
20% 40%	80 (176)				0	0	0	0	0
40% 1–20%	80 (176)				0	0	0	0	0
40% 1–20%	108 (226)				1	1	1	0	0
60% 2%	100 (212)				1	1	1	1	0
90% 10%	525 (977)				s1	s1	s1	s1	s1
Sodium hydroxide + sodium phosphate, see under Sodium phosphate									
Sodium hydroxide + sodium sulfide:									
NaOH + Na₂S									
2.5% 1%	B		0	0	0	0	0	0	0
65% 10%	165 (329)	2	2	2	s2	s2	s2	s2	s1

Chemical	°C (°F)	1	2	3	4	5	6	7	8
Sodium hypochlorite, NaClO:									
5%	20 (68)	2	2^P	2^P	1^P	1^P	0^P	0^P	0^P
5%	B	2	2^P	s1^P	1^P	s1^P	s1^P	s1^P	s1^P
Sodium hypochlorite + sodium bichromate + sodium chlorate + sodium chloride, see under Sodium chloride									
Sodium iodide + ethyl alcohol + iodine, see under Iodine									
Sodium metaborate, NaBO$_2$ · 4H$_2$O, melted	100 (212)			0	0	0	0	0	0
Sodium nitrate, NaNO$_3$:									
All conc.	20–B (68–B)	2		0	0	0	0	0	0
Melted	360 (680)								
Sodium nitrite, NaNO$_2$, all conc.	B	2		0	0	0	0	0	0
Sodium oleate, see also Soap, NaC$_{18}$H$_{33}$O$_2$, all conc.	20 (68)			0	0	0	0	0	0
Sodium perborate, NaBO$_3$ · H$_2$O$_2$ · H$_2$O, all conc.	20 (68)	2		0	0	0	0	0	0
Sodium perchlorate, NaClO$_4$ · H$_2$O, 10%	B	2	2	0	0	0	0	0	0
Sodium peroxide, Na$_2$O$_2$:									
10%	20 (68)	2	1	0	0	0	0	0	0
10%	100 (212)	2	2	0	0	0	0	0	0
Sodium phosphate, Na$_3$PO$_4$, all conc.	B			0	0	0	0	0	0
Sodium phosphate + ammonium chloride, see under Ammonium chloride									
Sodium phosphate + sodium hydroxide:									
Na$_3$PO$_4$ + NaOH									
0.2% 0.5%	B			0	0	0	0	0	0
0.2% 0.7%	B			0	0	0	0	0	0
1% 5%	80 (176)	2		0	0	0	0	0	0
Sodium pyrophosphate + sodium chlorite, see under Sodium chlorite									
Sodium salicylate, NaC$_7$H$_5$O$_3$, all conc.	20 (68)			0	0	0	0	0	0
Sodium silicate, Na$_2$SiO$_3$, all conc.	100 (212)			0	0	0	0	0	0
Sodium sulfate, Na$_2$SO$_4$, all conc.	20 (68)	1		0	0	0	0	0	0
Sodium sulfate + sulfuric acid, see under Sulfuric acid									
Sulfuric acid									

Risk of pitting and stress-corrosion cracking in presence of Cl^- ions.

TABLE 1   Corrosion Table (Continued)

		Degree of attack on							
Corrosive medium	Temp., °C (°F)	Plain carbon steel	393 M(SIS-14-2301)*	249 MV (SIS-14-2320)*	832 MV (SIS-14-2333)*	453 S (SIS-14-2324)*	832 SK (SIS-14-2343)*	832 SL†	254 SLX†
Sodium sulfate + sulfuric acid + zinc sulfate, see under Sulfuric acid									
Sodium sulfide, Na₂S:									
5%	B	2	0	0	0	0	0	0	0
10%	20 (68)	2	0	0	0	0	0	0	0
10–50%	B	2	2	2	0	0	0	0	0
Sodium sulfide + sodium hydroxide, see under Sodium hydroxide									
Sodium sulfite, Na₂SO₃:									
50%	20 (68)	2	1	1	0	0	0	0	0
50%	B	2	2	2	0	0	0	0	0
Sodium sulfide + sodium thiosulfate + sulfuric acid, see Fixing salt									
Sodium tetraborate, see Borax									
Sodium thiosulfate, Na₂S₂O₃ 16–25%	20–B (68–B)	2	0[P]	0[P]	0[P]	0	0	0	0
Sodium thiosulfate + potassium dithionite, see Fixing salt									
Sodium thiosulfate + sodium sulfite + sulfuric acid, see Fixing salt									
Soft soap, solid or in solution	20 (68)	2	0	0	0	0	0	0	0
Spinning baths, see Sulfuric acid + sodium sulfate + zinc sulfate									

[P] Risk of pitting encountered more frequently in the gaseous phase. If the salt is contaminated with Cl⁻ ions, there is also risk of pitting in the liquid phase.

Substance	Temp. °C (°F)									
Stannic chloride, SnCl₄:										
5–24%	20 (68)	2	2^P	2^P	1^P	1^P	1^P	1^P	1^P	1^P
18–25%	B	2	2^P	2^P	1^P	1^P	2^P	2^P	2^P	2^P
Stannous chloride, SnCl₂:										
5%	20 (68)	2	2^P	2^P	1^P	1^P	0^P	0^P	0^P	0^P
5%	50 (122)	2	2^P	2^P	1^P	0^P	0^P	0^P	0^P	0^P
5%	B	2	2^P	2^P	$S2^P$	1^P	$S0^P$	$S0^P$	$S0^P$	$S0^P$
Starch solution, see also Dextrose:										
Starch, pure, all conc.	60 (140)			0	0	0	0	0	0	0
Starch + hydrochloric acid, pH 1.9, 31.5%	150 (302)	2	2	2	2	2	2	2	2	1
Stearic acid, see Fatty acids										
Strontium nitrate, Sr(NO₃)₂, all conc.	100 (212)	2		0	0	0	0	0	0	0
Sublimate, see Mercuric chloride										
Sugar, see Syrup and sugar										
Sulfamic acid, NH₂SO₃H:										
1%	75 (167)	2		0		0	0	0	0	0
2%	50 (122)	2		0		0	0	0	0	0
2%	75 (167)	2		1		1	1	1	0	0
3–5%	75 (167)	2		2		0	1	0	0	0
5%	50 (122)	2		0		0	0	0	0	0
6–10%	60 (140)	2		1		1	1	1	1	0
10%	75 (167)	2		2		2	2	1	1	0

Carbon steel requires inhibitors for example when cleaning with sulfamic acid.

Substance	Temp. °C (°F)								
Sulfate cellulose, see White liquor									
Sulfite gas (containing SO₂):									
Digester gases, 6 atg.	140–150 (284–302)	2	2	2	1	0	0	0	0
Gas given off by waste liquor	80 (176)	2	2	2		0	0	0	0

Oxidation to H₂SO₄ can occur in the presence of air, thus resulting in general corrosion.

Substance	Temp. °C (°F)								
Sulfite liquor, see Calcium, potassium, magnesium and ammonium bisulfite									
Sulfur, S:									
Melted	240 (464)	2	0	0	0	0	0	0	0
Melted	B (445) (833)	2	2	2	2	1	1	1	1
Sulfur vap.	570 (1058)	2	2	2	2	2	2	2	2
Sulfur dichloride, SCl₂:									
100%	20 (68)	2	1	0	0	0	0	0	0
100%	B	2	2	2	0	0	2	2	2

Risk of stress-corrosion cracking and pitting in presence of moisture.

TABLE 1 Corrosion Table (Continued)

Corrosive medium	Temp., °C (°F)	Plain carbon steel	393 M(SIS-14-2301)*	249 MV (SIS-14-2320)*	832 MV (SIS-14-2333)*	453 S (SIS-14-2324)*	832 SK (SIS-14-2343)*	832 SL†	254 SLX†
Sulfur dioxide, see Sulfurous acid									
Sulfur dioxide + sulfuric acid, see under Sulfuric acid									
Sulfur monochloride, S₂Cl₂:									
Dry, 100%	20 (68)	2	1	1	0	0	0	0	0
	B	2	2	2	0	0	0	0	0
Moist, 100%	20 (68)	2	2P	1P	1P	1P	1P	1P	1P
Sulfuric acid, H₂SO₄ (see Fig. 23):									
0.1%	100 (212)	2	2	2	2	0	0	0	0
0.5%	20 (68)	2	2	1	0	0	0	0	0
0.5%	50 (122)	2	2	2	0	0	0	0	0
0.5%	100 (212)	2	2	2	2	1	1	1	1
1%	20 (68)	2	2	2	0	0	0	0	0
1%	50–60 (122–140)	2	2	2	1	0	0	0	0
1%	70 (158)	2	2	2	1	0	0	0	0
1%	85 (185)	2	2	2	2	0	0	0	0
1%	100 (212)	2	2	2	2	1	1	1	1
2%	20 (68)	2	2	2	0	0	0	0	0
2%	50 (122)	2	2	2	1	0	0	0	0
2%	60 (140)	2	2	2	1	0	0	0	0
3%	20 (68)	2	2	2	0	0	0	0	0
3%	35 (95)	2	2	2	1	0	0	0	0
3%	50 (122)	2	2	2	1	0	0	0	0
3%	85 (185)	2	2	2	2	0	0	0	0
3%	100 (212)	2	2	2	2	1	1	1	1
5%	20 (68)	2	2	2	1	2	2	2	0
5%	35 (95)	2	2	2	1	0	0	0	0

%	Value (unit)	1	2	3	4	5	6	7	8
5%	60 (140)	0	0	0	0	2	2	2	2
5%	75 (167)	0	1	1	1	2	2	2	2
5%	85 (185)	0	2	2	2	2	2	2	2
5%	3	2	2	2	2	2	2	2	2
10%	20–35 (68–95)	0	0	0	0	2	2	2	2
10%	50 (122)	0	0	0	1	2	2	2	2
10%	60 (140)	0	0	1	1	2	2	2	2
10%	80 (176)	1	1	2	2	2	2	2	2
10%	3	2	2	2	2	2	2	2	2
20%	20 (68)	0	0	0	0	2	2	2	2
20%	40 (104)	0	0	1	1	2	2	2	2
20%	50 (122)	0	1	1	1	2	2	2	2
20%	60 (140)	0	1	2	2	2	2	2	2
20%	70 (158)	0	2	2	2	2	2	2	2
20%	100 (212)	1	2	2	2	2	2	2	2
30%	20 (68)	0	0	1	1	2	2	2	2
30%	40 (104)	0	1	2	2	2	2	2	2
30%	60 (140)	0	2	2	2	2	2	2	2
30%	70 (158)	1	2	2	2	2	2	2	2
40%	20 (68)	0	2	2	2	2	2	2	2
40%	30–50 (86–122)	0	2	2	2	2	2	2	2
40%	60 (140)	1	2	2	2	2	2	2	2
40%	90 (194)	2	2	2	2	2	2	2	2
50%	20–30 (68–86)	0	2	2	2	2	2	2	2
50%	40 (104)	0	2	2	2	2	2	2	2
50%	50 (122)	1	2	2	2	2	2	2	2
50%	70 (158)	2	2	2	2	2	2	2	2
60%	20–35 (68–95)	0	2	2	2	2	2	2	2

TABLE 1 Corrosion Table *(Continued)*

Corrosive medium	Temp, °C (°F)	Degree of attack on							
		Plain carbon steel	393 M(SIS-14-2301)*	249 MV (SIS-14-2320)*	832 MV (SIS-14-2333)*	453 S (SIS-14-2324)*	832 SK (SIS-14-2343)*	832 SL†	254 SLX†
60%	40 (104)	2	2	2	2	2	2	2	2
60%	70 (158)	2	2	2	2	2	2	2	2
70%	20–35 (68–95)	2	2	2	2	2	2	2	0
70%	40 (104)	2	2	2	2	2	2	2	1
70%	70 (158)	2	2	2	2	2	2	2	2
80%	20 (68)	2	2	1	1	1	1	1	0
80%	40 (104)	2	2	2	2	1	1	1	0
80%	50 (122)	2	2	2	2	2	2	2	1
80%	60 (104)	2	2	2	2	2	2	2	2
85%	20 (68)	1	1	1	0	0	0	0	0
85%	40 (104)	2	2	2	1	1	1	1	0
85%	50 (122)	2	2	2	2	2	2	2	1
90%	20 (68)	1	1	1	0	0	0	0	0
90%	40 (104)	2	2	2	1	1	1	1	0
90%	70 (158)	2	2	2	2	2	2	2	1
94%	40 (104)	2	2	2	1	1	0	1	0
94%	50 (122)	2	2	2	1	1	1	1	1
96.4%	35 (95)	1	1	1	0	0	0	0	0
96.4%	40 (104)	1	1	1	1	0	0	1	0
96.4%	50 (122)	2	2	2	1	1	1	2	1

Sulfuric acid (continued)

Concentration	Temp. °C (°F)								
98%	30 (86)	0	0	0	0	0	1	1	1
98%	40 (104)	0	1	0	0	1	1	1	1
98%	50 (122)	1	1	0	1	2	2	2	2
98%	80 (176)	2	2	2	2	2	2	2	2
100%	70 (158)			0	0	0			2

Sulfuric acid, SO₃, fuming (oleum):

Concentration	Temp. °C (°F)								
7% 100%	60 (140)	0	0	0	0	0	0	0	0
11% 100%	60 (140)	0	0	0	0	0	0	0	0
11% 100%	100 (212)	1	0	0	0	1	2	2	2
60% 100%	20–70 (68–158)	2	2	2		2	2	2	2
60% 100%	80 (176)			0	0	0	2		

Sulfuric acid + acetic acid:
$H_2SO_4 + CH_3COOH$

Concentration	Temp. °C (°F)								
1% 1%	20 (68)			0	0	0	0		
1% 1%	3			1	1	1	2		
1% 25%	3			1	1	2	2	2	2
1% 30%	140 (284)	2	1	2	2	2	2	2	2
2% 0.5%	3			1	1	1	2	2	2
2% 25%	80 (176)			2	2	2	2	2	2
3% 0.2%	120 (248)	2	1	0	0	1	2	2	2
5% 90%	20 (68)			2	2	2	2	2	2
10% 2%	3	2	0	0	0	2	2	2	2
10% 90%	20 (68)	2		0	0	0	2	2	2

Sulfuric acid + acetic acid + acetic anhydride:
$H_2SO_4 + CH_3COOH + (CH_3CO)_2O$

Concentration	Temp. °C (°F)								
0.36% 71.3% 28.34%	135 (275)	2	2	1	1	2	2	2	2
5% 47.5% 47.5%	20–40 (68–104)	2	2	0	0	0	2	2	2
5% 47.5% 47.5%	80 (176)	2	2	1	1	2	2	2	2

Sulfuric acid + aluminum sulfate:
$H_2SO_4 + Al_2(SO_4)_3$

Concentration	Temp. °C (°F)								
42% 1.5%	45 (113)	2	2	2	2	2	2	2	1

Sulfuric acid + ammonium sulfate:
$H_2SO_4 + (NH_4)_2SO_4$

Concentration	Temp. °C (°F)								
0.2% 42%	100 (212)	2	2	0	0	1	2	0	0
1% 20%	3	2	2	0	1	1	2	0	0
1% 40%	80 (176)	2	2	0	1	1	2	0	0
1% 40%	3	2	2	1	2	2	2	1	0
2% 40%	80 (176)	2	2	0	1	1	2	0	0
2% 40%	3	2	2	1	2	2	2	1	1

TABLE 1 Corrosion Table (Continued)

		Temp., °C (°F)	Degree of attack on							
			Plain carbon steel	393 M(SIS-14-2301)*	249 MV (SIS-14-2320)*	832 MV (SIS-14-2333)*	453 S (SIS-14-2324)*	832 SK (SIS-14-2343)*	832 SL†	254 SLX†
5%	10%	40 (104)	2	2	1	0	0	0	0	0
5%	20%	40 (104)	2	2	1	0	0	0	0	0
5%	20%	60 (140)	2	2	2	1	0	0	0	0
5%	20%	80 (176)	2	2	2	2	2	1	1	0
5%	20%	3	2	2	2	2	0	0	1	1
5%	40%	60 (140)	2	2	2	1	0	0	0	0
5%	40%	3	2	2	2	2	2	1	1	1
10%	20%	40 (104)	2	2	2	1	0	0	0	0
10%	20%	80 (176)	2	2	2	2	2	1	1	0
10%	20%	3	2	2	2	1	0	1	1	1
10%	40%	40 (104)	2	2	2	2	1	0	0	0
10%	40%	80 (176)	2	2	2	2	2	1	1	1
10%	51%	100 (212)	2	2	2	2	2	1	1	1

Sulfuric acid + ammonium sulfate + phosphoric acid, see under Phosphoric acid.

Sulfuric acid + bagasse, see under Bagasse

Sulfuric acid + boric acid + nickel chloride + nickel sulfate, see under Boric acid

Sulfuric acid + calcium sulfate + phosphoric acid, see under Phosphoric acid

Sulfuric acid + chlorine:

H_2SO_4 +	Cl_2	Temp., °C (°F)	Plain carbon steel	393 M	249 MV	832 MV	453 S	832 SK	832 SL	254 SLX
40–50%	Saturated	25 (77)	2	2	2	2^P	2^P	2^P	2^P	2^P

Conc.		Temp °C (°F)							
60%	Saturated	40 (104)	2			2[P]	2[P]	2[P]	2[P]
82%	Saturated	50 (122)	2			2[P]	1[P]	1[P]	1[P]
85%	Saturated	50 (122)	2			1[P]	1[P]	1[P]	1[P]
96%	Saturated	50 (122)	2[P]			1[P]	1[P]	1[P]	1[P]
Sulfuric acid + chromic acid, see Figs. 24 and 25; compare Sulfuric acid + potassium or sodium bichromate:									
1% $K_2Cr_2O_7$ = 0.682% CrO_3									
1% $Na_2Cr_2O_7$ = 0.795% CrO_3									
Sulfuric acid + chromic acid + phosphoric acid, see under Phosphoric acid									
Sulfuric acid + copper sulfate, see Fig. 15			2						
H_2SO_4 + $CuSO_4$									
4%	1%	20 (68)	2	2	0	0	0	0	0
4–5%	5% saturated	20 (68)	0	0	0	0	0	0	0
8%	0.05%	80 (176)	2	2	2	1	0	0	0
8%	1%	20 (68)	1	1	0	0	0	0	0
8%	5%	20 (68)	1	2	0	0	0	0	0
10%	10%	B					0	0	0
13%	1.3%	40 (104)					0	0	0
14%	1.5%	40 (104)					0	0	0
16%	12%	120 (248)					1	1	1
16%	13%	90 (194)					0	0	0
65%	0.05%	38 (100)					0	0	0
65%	1%	38 (100)					0	0	0
Sulfuric acid + ethyl alcohol + nitric acid, see under Nitric acid									
Sulfuric acid + fluosilicic acid + phosphoric acid, see under Phosphoric acid									
Sulfuric acid + hydrofluoric acid + nitric acid + phosphoric acid, see under Phosphoric acid									
Sulfuric acid + hydrofluoric acid + phosphoric acid, see under Phosphoric acid									
Sulfuric acid + hydrofluoric acid + potassium chlorate, see under Hydrofluoric acid									

TABLE 1 Corrosion Table (Continued)

Corrosive medium	Temp, °C (°F)	Plain carbon steel	393 M (SIS-14-2301)*	249 MV (SIS-14-2320)*	832 MV (SIS-14-2333)*	453 S (SIS-14-2324)*	832 SK (SIS-14-2343)*	832 SL†	254 SLX†
Sulfuric acid + iron(2)sulfate:									
H_2SO_4 + $FeSO_4$									
5% 0.05%	70 (158)	2	2	2	2	0	0	0	0
5% 5%	40 (104)	2	2	2	0	0	0	0	0
8% 20%	20 (68)	2	2	0	0	0	0	0	0
10% 0.2%	B	2	2	2	2	2	2	2	1
17% 7%	60 (140)	2	2	2	1	0	0	0	0
25% Saturated at 25°C	B	2	2	2	2	2	2	2	2
Sulfuric acid + iron(3)sulfate (see Fig. 16):									
H_2SO_4 + $Fe_2(SO_4)_3$									
2% 0.02%	B				1	0	0	0	0
2% 10%	100 (212)				0	0	0	0	0
7% 0.05%	80 (176)				0	0	0	0	0
7% 10%	80 (176)				0	0	0	0	0
8% 0.05%	80 (176)		2	2	0	0	0	0	0
10% 2%	B	2	2	2	2	2	2	2	0
Sulfuric acid + lactic acid, see under Lactic acid									
Sulfuric acid + manganese dioxide:									
H_2SO_4 + MnO_2									
40% 0.5%	20 (68)			1	1	1	1	1	0
Sulfuric acid + nitric acid, see under Nitric acid									
Sulfuric acid + nitric acid + phosphoric acid, see under Phosphoric acid									
Sulfuric acid + oxalic acid + nitric acid, see under Oxalic acid									

Sulfuric acid + phosphoric acid, see under Phosphoric acid

Sulfuric acid + potassium bichromate:

$H_2SO_4 + K_2Cr_2O_7$

			Temp °C (°F)	1	2	3	4	5	6	7	8
1%	5%		35 (95)	0	0	0	0	0	0	0	0
1.5%	2.5%		B	0	0	0	0	0	1	2	2
5–10%	5%		35 (95)	0	0	0	0	0	0	0	2
51%	6%		70 (158)	2	2	2	2	2	2	2	2
80%	8%		25 (77)			0		0			

See also Sulfuric acid + chromic acid:
1% $K_2Cr_2O_7$ = 0.682% CrO_3

Sulfuric acid + sodium bichromate:

$H_2SO_4 + Na_2Cr_2O_7$

			Temp °C (°F)	1	2	3	4	5	6	7	8
10%	9%		50 (122)	0	0	0	0	0			
20%	2.6%		50 (122)	0	0	0	0	0			
25%	30%		108 (226)	2	2	2	2	2	2	2	2
32%	26%		90 (194)	2	2	2	2	2	2	2	2
46%	23%		100 (212)	2	2	2	2	2	2	2	2

See also Sulfuric acid + chromic acid:
1% $Na_2Cr_2O_7$ = 0.795% CrO_3

Sulfuric acid + sodium chloride:

$H_2SO_4 + NaCl$

			Temp °C (°F)	1	2	3	4	5	6	7	8
0.5%	1%		B	2	2	2	2	2	2	2	2
10%	5%		80 (176)	2	2	2	2	2	2	2	2

Sulfuric acid + sodium sulfate:

$H_2SO_4 + Na_2SO_4$

			Temp °C (°F)	1	2	3	4	5	6	7	8
0.5%	1%		B	0	1	1	1	1	2	2	2
0.5%	4%		B	0	1	1	1	1	2	2	2
3%	2%		B	1	2	2	2	2	2	2	2
5%	15%		95 (203)	1	2	2	2	2	2	2	2
13%	20%		50 (122)	0	1	1	1	2	2	2	2
25%	24%		30 (86)	0	0	0	0	2	2	2	2

Sulfuric acid + sodium sulfate + zinc sulfate (spinning bath):

$H_2SO_4 + Na_2SO_4 + ZnSO_4$

			Temp °C (°F)	1	2	3	4	5	6	7	8
10%	20%	1%	50 (122)	0	0	1					
10%	20%	3%	B	2	2	2					
12%	10%	3%	60 (140)	0	0	1	2	2	2	2	2
12%	21%	0.3% + H_2S	60 (140)	1	2	2					
15%	11%	3%	B	2	2	2					

Technical spinning bath with 7–8% H_2SO_4

	Temp °C (°F)	1	2	3	4	5	6	7	8
H_2SO_4	45–60 (113–140)	0	0	0	2	2	2	2	2

TABLE 1 Corrosion Table (Continued)

Corrosive medium	Temp., °C (°F)	Degree of attack on							
		Plain carbon steel	393 M(SIS-14-2301)*	249 MV (SIS-14-2320)*	832 MV (SIS-14-2333)*	453 S (SIS-14-2324)*	832 SK (SIS-14-2343)*	832 SL†	254 SLX†
Same bath saturated with H₂S	45 (113)						1	0	0
	60 (140)						1	1	0
Technical spinning bath with 11% H₂SO₄	60 (140)						1	0	0
Same bath saturated with H₂S	45 (113)						1	0	0
	60 (140)						2	2	1
Sulfuric acid + sodium sulfite + sodium thiosulfate, see Fixing salt									
Sulfuric acid + sulfur dioxide:									
$H_2SO_4 + SO_2$									
0.5% Saturated	90 (194)	2	2	2	2	1	1	0	0
0.5% Saturated	B	2	2	2	2	2	2	2	1
10% Saturated	50 (122)	2	2	2	2	2	1	1	0
20% Saturated	40 (104)	2	2	2	2	2	1	1	0
20% Saturated	60 (140)	2	2	2	2	2	2	2	2
30% Saturated	20 (68)	2	2	2	2	2	1	1	0
30% Saturated	80 (176)	2	2	2	2	2	2	2	2
50% Saturated	20 (68)	2	2	2	2	2	2	1	0
60% Saturated	20 (68)				1	1	1	2	0
96% Saturated	55 (131)				1	1	1	1	1
98% 0.02%	80 (176)	2			1			1	1
Sulfuric acid + zinc sulfate:									
$H_2SO_4 + ZnSO_4$									
0.5% 30%	B	2	2	2	2	1	1	1	0
1% 1%	65 (149)	2	2	2	1	0	0	0	0
2% 30–45%	80 (176)	2	2	2	2	1	1	0	0
10% 5%	50 (122)	2	2	2	2	1	1	0	0

Sulfurous acid, H_2SO_3:

Substance	Temp. °C (°F)									
Sulfur dioxide in aqueous solution,										
2% SO_2	50 (122)	2	2	1	0	0	0	0	0	0
5% SO_2	20 (68)	2	2	1	0	0	0	0	0	0
10% SO_2	160 (320)	2	2	1	0	0	0	0	0	0
20% SO_2	20 (68)	2	2	1	0	0	0	0	0	0
Saturated	20 (68)	2	2	1	0	0	0	0	0	0
Saturated	135 (275)	2	2	2	1	1	0	0	0	0
Saturated	200 (392)	2	2	1	1	0	0	0	0	0
Moist SO_2 gas, air-free, 100%	20 (68)	2	2	1	0	0	0	0	0	0
	100 (212)	2	2	1	0	0	0	0	0	0

Oxidation to H_2SO_4 can occur in the presence of air, thus resulting in general corrosion. Grade 254 SLX is best suited for such conditions.

Substance	Temp. °C (°F)								
Dry SO_2 gas, 100%	300 (572)	0	0	0	0	0	0	0	
Dry SO_2, liquid, 100%	25 (77)	0	0	0	0	0	0	0	
Sulfurous acid + calcium bisulfite:									
H_2SO_3 + $Ca(HSO_3)_2$									
or $Mg(HSO_3)_2$									
or $NaHSO_3$									
or NH_4HSO_3									
1–2% 1–5%	140 (284)	2	2	2	1	0	0	0	0

The above values are for the liquid phase and the air-free gaseous phase. If air is present, attacks by sulfurous and sulfuric acid can occur in the gaseous phase.

Superphosphoric acid, see Phosphoric acid, technical grade

Synthetic ink, see Ink

Substance	Temp. °C (°F)							
Syrup and sugar:								
All conc.	All	0	0	0	0	0	0	0
+Cl⁻, 500 mg/l	90 (194)		0	0ᵖ	0ᵖ	0ᵖ	0ᵖ	
Tall oil	100 (212)	0	2	SOᵖ	0ᵖ	0	0	
	300 (572)	2	1	0	0	0	0	

254 SLX is recommended for crude tall oil containing traces of H_2SO_4.

Substance	Temp. °C (°F)							
Tannic acid, tannin, digallic acid, $C_{14}H_{10}O_9$:								
5%	20 (68)	1	0	0	0	0	0	0
5%	B	2	1	0	0	0	0	0
10%	20 (68)	1	0	0	0	0	0	0
10%	80 (176)	2	2	0	0	0	0	0

TABLE 1 Corrosion Table (Continued)

Corrosive medium	Temp., °C (°F)	Plain carbon steel	393 M(SIS-14-2301)*	249 MV (SIS-14-2320)*	832 MV (SIS-14-2333)*	453 S (SIS-14-2324)*	832 SK (SIS-14-2343)*	832 SL†	254 SLX†
10%	B	2	2	0	0	0	0	0	0
25%	100 (212)	2	2	1	0	0	0	0	0
50%	20 (68)	2	1	1	0	0	0	0	0
50%	65 (149)	2	1	1	0	0	0	0	0
50%	B	2	2	1	0	0	0	0	0
Tar, pure	All	2	0	0	0	0	0	0	0
Tartaric acid, $C_2H_2(OH)_2(COOH)_2$:									
1%	90 (194)	2	2	0	0	0	0	0	0
1%	B	2	2	0	0	0	0	0	0
20%	70 (158)	2	2	1	0	0	0	0	0
20%	100 (212)	2	2	2	1	0	0	0	0
30%	60 (140)	2	2	2	0	0	0	0	0
30%	90–B (194–B)	2	2	2	1	0	0	0	0
50%	50 (122)	2	2	2	0	0	0	0	0
50%	70 (158)	2	2	2	0	0	0	0	0
50%	90 (194)	2	2	2	1	1	1	1	1
50%	B	2	2	2	2	1	1	0	0
60%	80 (176)	2	2	2	1	1	1	1	1
60%	100 (212)	2	2	2	2	1	1	0	0
75%	100 (212)	2	2	2	1	1	1	1	1
75%	B	2	2	2	1	1	1	0	0
Textile dyes, basic, neutral and acid	B	2	0	0	0	0	0	0	0
Thionyl chloride, $SOCl_2$ 100%	20–40 (68–104)	2	1	0	0	0	0	0	0
Tin, Sn, Melted									
	300 (572)	2	2	2	0	0	0	0	0
	350 (662)	2	2	2	1	1	1	1	1
	400 (752)	2	2	2	1	1	1	1	1

Risk of pitting in presence of moisture.

Substance	Temp °C (°F)							
[continued]	500–700 (932–1292)	2	2	2	2	2	0^P	0
Tincture of iodine, 10% ethanol solution of I_2	20 (68)	1^P	0	0^P	0	0^P	0^P	0
Toluene, $C_6H_5CH_3$, 100%	B							
Town gas, see Coal gas								
Trichloroethylene, CCl_2CHCl, technical grade	20 (68)	2	0	0	0	0	0	0
	B	2	1	0	0	0	0	0

Risk of stress-corrosion cracking and pitting in presence of moisture.

Substance	Temp °C (°F)							
Trihydroxybenzene, see Pyrogallic acid								
Trihydroxybenzoic acid, see Gallic acid								
Trinitrophenol, see Picric acid								
Turpentine, turpentine oil								
Urea, $CO(NH_2)_2$	20 (68)	0	0	0	0	0	0	0
	180 (356)	0	0	0	0	0	0	0

Grade 832 SKR with lower ferrite content than standard is recommended here.

Substance	Temp °C (°F)							
Urine	0–60 (32–140)	0^P	0^P	0^P	0^P	0^P	0^P	0^P

No risk of pitting if continuous or periodic water rinse is provided.

Substance	Temp °C (°F)							
Vegetable oils, see Oils								
Vinegar:								
Without H_2SO_4, 4–5%	20 (68)	2	0	0	0	0	0	0
With H_2SO_4, 4–5%	B	2	2	1	1	0	0	0
Water, H_2O, see Drinking water, Seawater								
Water glass, see Sodium silicate								
White liquor (Sulfate cellulose): Degree of causticity, 84.1% Sulfidity, 31.4% Na_2S Active alkali, 132.4 g/l Total alkali, 149.6 g/l NaOH 90.8 g/l, Na_2S 41.6 g/l Na_2CO_3 17.2 g/l, Cl^- 206 mg/l	180 (356)	0	0	0	0	0	0	0
White liquor to which has been added 1% NaCl	180 (356)	0	s_1	s_1	0	0	0	0
Same, evaporated to 1/4	180 (356)	0	0	0	0	0	0	0
Wines, see Fruit juices								
Xylene, $C_6H_4(CH_3)_2$, all conc.	B	0	0	0	0	0	0	0
Yeast	All	0	0	0	0	0	0	0

TABLE 1 Corrosion Table (Continued)

Corrosive medium	Temp., °C (°F)	Plain carbon steel	Degree of attack on						
			393 M(SIS-14-2301)*	249 MV (SIS-14-2320)*	832 MV (SIS-14-2333)*	453 S (SIS-14-2324)*	832 SK (SIS-14-2343)*	832 SL†	254 SLX†
Zinc, Zn, melted	425 (797)	2	2	2	2	2	2	2	2
	500 (932)		0	0	0	0	0	0	0
Zinc carbonate, ZnCO₃, all conc.	20 (68)								
Zinc chloride, ZnCl₂:									
5–20%	20 (68)		0^p	0^p	0^p	0^p	0^p	0^p	0^p
5–20%	B	2	1^p	1^p	$s1^p$	0^p	$s0^p$	$s0^p$	$s0^p$
20–70%	150 (302)	2	2^p	2^p	$s2^p$	$s0^p$	$s0^p$	$s0^p$	$s0^p$
75%	200 (392)	2	2^p	2^p	$s2^p$	$s1^p$	$s1^p$	$s0^p$	$s0^p$
80%	150 (302)	2				$s1^p$	$s1^p$	$s0^p$	$s0^p$
Zinc chloride + ammonium chloride, see under Ammonium chloride									
Zinc cyanide, Zn(CN)₂, all conc.	20 (68)		0	0	0	0	0	0	0
Zinc nitrate, Zn(NO₃)₂, 75%	175 (347)		0	0	0	0	0	0	0
Zinc sulfate, ZnSO₄:									
20%	20–B (68–B)	2	2	2	0	0	0	0	0
40%	B		2	2	1	0	0	0	0
Zinc sulfate + sodium sulfate + sulfuric acid, see under Sulphuric acid									
Zinc sulfate + sulfuric acid, see under Sulfuric acid									
Zirconium oxychloride, ZrOCl₂:									
11%	80 (176)		2^p	2^p	$s2^p$	1^p	$s1^p$	$s1^p$	$s0^p$
11%	100 (212)		2^p	2^p	$s2^p$	2^p	$s2^p$	$s2^p$	$s1^p$
20%	80 (176)		2^p	2^p	$s2^p$	2^p	$s1^p$	$s1^p$	$s0^p$
20%	100 (212)		2^p	2^p	$s2^p$	$s2^p$	$s2^p$	$s2^p$	$s1^p$

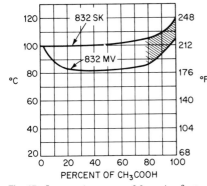

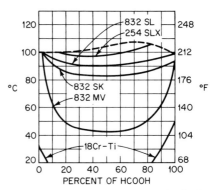

Fig. 17 Isocorrosion curves, 0.1 mm/yr, for two grades of steel in pure acetic acid at different concentrations and temperatures. The top curve coincides with the boiling point. The shaded area represents a risk of pitting attack on 832 MV steel.

Fig. 18 Isocorrosion curves, 0.1 mm/yr, for the steels shown, in chemically pure formic acid. Broken-line curve represents the boiling point.

certain values taken from corrosion handbooks issued by the following companies: Deutsche Edelstahlwerke, Fagersta Bruks AB, Imperial Metal Industries, The International Nickel Company, Mannesmann AG, Nyby Bruk AB, Sandvikens Jernverks AB, and Uddeholms AB. The corrosive media in Table 1 are arranged in alphabetical order with suitable cross-references.

For the purpose of testing the usability of various steel grades in certain ambient conditions, steel manufacturers usually provide test samples which can then be placed in a reactor, in a pipeline, or in another suitable place and tested for corrosion resistance by weighing the sample before and after the test. Electrochemical measurements may also be made to determine the instantaneous corrosion rate of the material in a pipeline or reactor, etc. Such measurements are made in accordance with the so-called polarization resistance method. It is also possible to get an idea of the corrosion rate by measuring the corrosion potential of the material in the process solution, provided that the anodic polarization curve of the material in the same solution is available.

Intergranular Corrosion

This is a type of corrosion which is localized at the grain boundaries of the steel while the steel surface elsewhere remains comparatively intact (see Fig. 28). However, since the

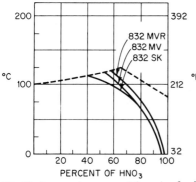

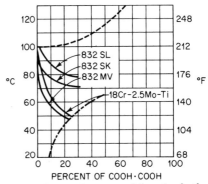

Fig. 19 Isocorrosion curves, 0.1 mm/yr, for the steels shown, in pure nitric acid at different concentrations and temperatures. Broken-line curve represents the boiling point.

Fig. 20 Isocorrosion curves, 0.1 mm/yr, for the steels shown, in chemically pure oxalic acid. Broken-line curve represents the boiling point and chain-line curve represents solubility.

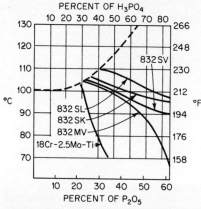

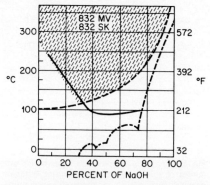

Fig. 21 Isocorrosion curves, 0.1 mm/yr, for the steels shown, in pure phosphoric acid at different concentrations and temperatures. Broken-line curve represents the boiling point.

Fig. 22 Isocorrosion curves, 0.1 mm/yr, for 832 MV and 832 SK steels, in pure sodium hydroxide at different concentrations and temperatures. The shaded field represents application areas in which the risk of stress-corrosion cracking is present. The broken-line curve represents the boiling point and the chain-line curve represents the melting point.

nature and causes of this type of corrosion are well-known, it can usually be prevented by selecting the right grade of steel for the ambient conditions at hand.

If a stainless steel is heated to 500 to 850°C (932 to 1562°F) or is allowed to cool slowly through this temperature range, the carbon in the vicinity of the grain boundaries will diffuse toward the boundaries and there combine with chromium to produce chromium carbides. These carbides bind considerable quantities of chromium, thereby depleting the base metal of chromium close to the grain boundaries. Since the passivation capacity of the steel declines along with the chromium content, it is possible that an electrolyte may be aggressive enough to activate the low-chromium zone but not the unaffected surface of the grains, which remain passive. It is primarily acids that are dangerous in this respect, but attack has also been observed in seawater. This galvanic cell has a small anodic area and a large cathodic area, thus introducing the risk of rapid, selective dissolution of the metal at the grain boundaries.

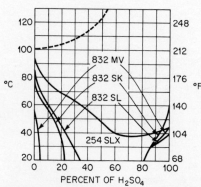

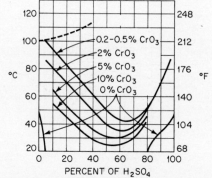

Fig. 23 Isocorrosion curves, 0.1 mm/yr, for the steels shown, in pure sulfuric acid at different concentrations and temperatures. Broken-line curve represents the boiling point.

Fig. 24 Isocorrosion curves, 0.1 mm/yr, for 832 MV steel in sulfuric acid with different amounts of chromium trioxide additives. Broken-line curve represents the boiling point.

The severity of the attack is determined by the extent to which the continuity of the carbide precipitates, and thereby also the sensitive zone, has had time to develop. For a given steel composition and temperature, it is primarily the time spent in the dangerous temperature range which is decisive. Besides chromium carbides, other phases rich in chromium (such as sigma phase) may concentrate at the grain boundaries. The chromium content of these compounds is lower than that of the chromium carbides, however, and the depletion of chromium from the adjacent metal will thus not be as severe. In this case, more aggressive electrolytes (such as hot concentrated nitric acid or acid mixtures containing hydrogen fluoride) are required in order to provoke attack.

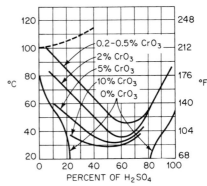

Fig. 25 Isocorrosion curves, 0.1 mm/yr, for 832 SK steel in sulfuric acid with different amounts of chromium trioxide additives. Broken-line curve represents the boiling point.

The austenitic and ferritic stainless steels are generally supplied heat-treated such that they are free of carbides. However, when the steel is welded, the dangerous carbide-precipitation temperature range will always exist at a distance of a few millimeters from the weld bead. A zone with carbide precipitates, and thus with a propensity towards intergranular corrosion, will therefore run parallel to the weld (see Fig. 29). At a given temperature, the sensitivity of this zone is determined by the carbon content and heating time of the steel. An austenitic steel with a relatively high carbon content, such as 0.08% carbon, thus becomes sensitive after only a few seconds, while a steel with a low carbon content, such as 0.02%, will withstand a few hours' heating. The ferritic steels are more sensitive than the austenitic and require considerably lower carbon contents to ensure acceptable protection against intercrystalline (intergranular) corrosion. This is true because the diffusion rate for carbon is higher in ferrite than in austenite and because ferrite possesses much lower solubility for carbon, which also increases the tendency of carbide precipitates to form.

Thus, one way of reducing the risk of chromium carbide precipitation and resultant intergranular corrosion is to use a steel with a low carbon content. Normally, a steel with a maximum carbon content of about 0.05% is sufficient to prevent intercrystalline corrosion in austenitic steels, but steels with 0.030% C max. or even 0.020% C max. are required in some aggressive media. The effect of the carbon content can be illustrated in a TTS (time-temperature-sensitization) graph (see Fig. 30).

Another way of reducing the risk of intercrystalline corrosion is to stabilize the steel with titanium or niobium. These elements have a greater affinity for carbon than chromium, binding the carbon as titanium or niobium carbides and suppressing the formation of chromium carbides. However, when stabilized steels (especially titanium-stabilized steels) are welded, the carbides near the weld dissolve due to the high temperature there. A subsequent heating to the sensitization temperature in connection with stress-relieving or an additional welding pass may then give rise to precipitation of chromium carbide. [Chromium carbides precipitate faster than titanium carbides reform at temperatures below about 850°C (1562°F).] Such chromium carbide precipitates may give rise to a type of intercrystalline corrosion known as "knife-line attack" because it appears in a narrow zone right next to the weld. However, this type of corrosion is rare, although it has been observed in nitric acid when the corrosion resistance of the material has otherwise been "on the borderline."

Stabilized steels possess greater strength than low-carbon steels and are especially preferable at elevated temperatures. Under long-term exposure to temperatures over 450 to 500°C (842 to 932°F), carbides may precipitate even in low-carbon steels; in such cases, stabilized steel should be used. Stabilization raises the content of oxidic slags in the steel, leading to a deterioration of the surfaces. Stabilized steels should therefore not be used in cases where a high finish is desired; in such cases, low-carbon stainless steels are

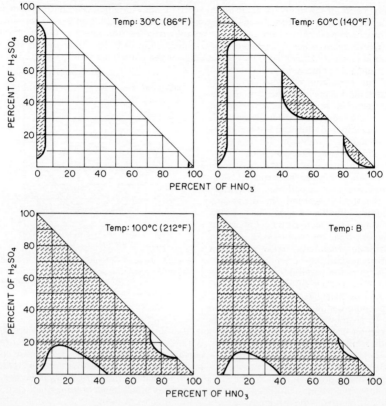

Fig. 26 Corrosion rates for 832 MV steel in mixtures of sulfuric acid, nitric acid, and water at varying temperatures. Shaded fields represent corrosion rates greater than 0.1 mm/yr; unshaded areas represent corrosion rates lower than 0.1 mm/yr.

preferable. Low-carbon steels may also be endowed with a strength comparable to that of stabilized steels by means of nitrogen alloying or moderate cold deformation.

Pitting Corrosion

Pitting is an extremely localized attack resulting in holes in the metal (Fig. 31). This type of corrosion is very dangerous, since the steel may quickly be fully penetrated despite the fact that its general corrosion rate is often very low.

We have described how certain halogens (chiefly chloride ions) can penetrate the passive film at a certain potential and destroy it at weak points. This produces very small anodes of active steel surrounded by a large cathodic area consisting of the passivated surface. This provides the conditions necessary for a rapid dissolution of the metal in the microanodes, provided that the chloride ions are able to remain in the anodes and prevent repassivation and that the electrolyte contains a sufficient quantity of oxidizing agent to maintain the passivity of the cathodic surface.

The increased corrosion of the steel surface inside the corrosion pit gives the electrolyte there a high concentration of positively charged metal ions. These positive ions are balanced out by negatively charged ions which migrate down into the pit under the influence of the galvanic current. If the electrolyte contains chloride ions, these will make up the greater portion of the migration, owing to their high mobility. The electrolyte in the

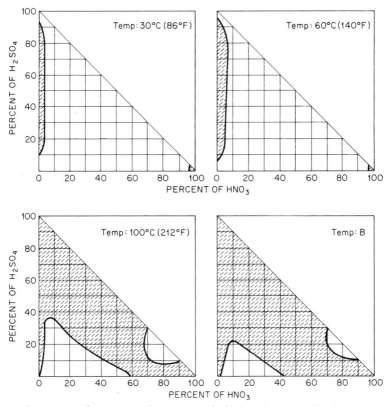

Fig. 27   Corrosion rate for 832 SK steel in mixtures of sulfuric acid, nitric acid, and water at varying temperatures. Shaded fields represent corrosion rates higher than 0.1 mm/yr; unshaded areas represent corrosion rates lower than 0.1 mm/yr.

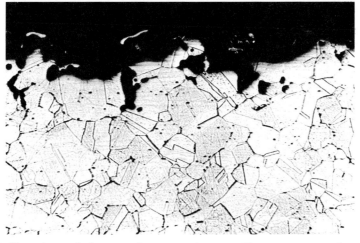

Fig. 28   Photomicrograph of intergranular corrosion close to a weld in an austenitic stainless steel. (800X)

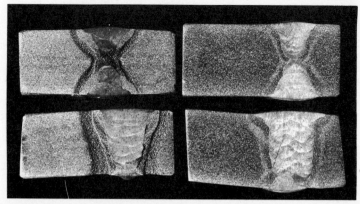

Fig. 29   Sensitized zone in welded 832 MV (left) and 832 SK plates. Carbon content of both steels is 0.054%. The plates were etched in a nitric acid—hydrofluoric acid solution.

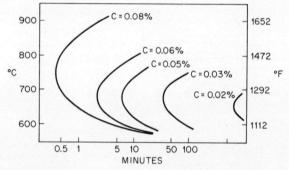

Fig. 30   TTS diagrams for five 18Cr-9Ni steels with different carbon contents.

Fig. 31   Type 304 pipe pitted in brackish water.

pit will therefore consist of a concentrated metal chloride solution which is hydrolyzed to insoluble hydroxide and free hydrochloric acid. Since the rate of corrosion in the active region is increased by both the elevated chloride content and the lowered pH (cf. Figs. 2 and 8), the rate of migration of chloride ions into the corrosion pits also increases, resulting in a rapidly accelerating autocatalytic process. The corrosion pits usually grow in the downward direction under the influence of gravity, since the heavy, concentrated solution inside the pit is necessary for its activity. This means that pitting is more likely to occur on horizontal than on vertical surfaces and that the metal will often be undermined if the surfaces form an angle with the vertical plane.

A prerequisite for the development of pitting is the presence in the electrolyte of ions capable of destroying passivity. In practice, this means chlorides and chloride-bearing ions such as hypochlorites; fluorides and iodides are less dangerous. An additional condition is the presence of an oxidizing agent capable of maintaining the corrosion potential of the steel at a sufficiently high level in the passive range (cf. Fig. 8). The most common oxidizing agent is dissolved oxygen, but Fe^{3+} and Cu^{2+} also have a high pitting effect. Pitting can occur at all pH levels, except the very highest. The attacks on high-alloy austenitic steels, however, are most severe in acid solutions, although when conditions are excessively acidic, general corrosion takes over. Elevated temperatures lead to heavier attack, but if the oxidizing agent is oxygen, a maximum will be reached at approximately 80°C (176°F), since the solubility of the oxygen in the electrolyte is too low at higher temperatures.

Pitting is more severe in still chloride solutions and diminishes in severity with the rising flow rate of the electrolyte. For the practical use of stainless steel in chloride solutions, 1.5 to 2 m/s (4.9 to 6.5 ft/s) is usually specified as the minimum permissible flow rate, while an upper limit is normally unnecessary, since stainless steel possesses excellent resistance to erosion-corrosion and may, according to information in the literature, be used at flow rates of up to 40 m/s (131 ft/s). The favorable effect of high flow rate is attributed to the fact that it prevents the sedimentation of solid particles which could otherwise give rise to aerating elements and that it results in a constant renewal of the electrolyte in a new pit, preventing a drop in the pH and permitting repassivation.

As far as the composition of the steel is concerned, resistance to pitting increases with rising levels of chromium and molybdenum, the latter being the most effective (see Fig. 32).

When stainless steel is welded, a discoloration almost always occurs on the steel surface in a zone extending some 5 to 15 mm (0.2 to 0.6 in.) on both sides of the weld—even when

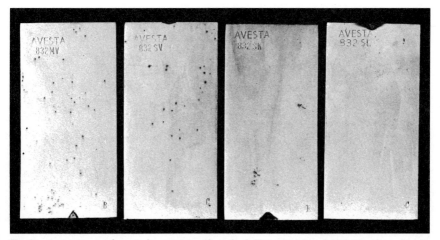

Fig. 32 Austenitic stainless steels containing (from the left) 0, 1.5, 2.7, and 4.5% Mo after a 20-min test in 4% NaCl + 0.1% $K_3Fe(CN)_6$ at room temperature. The pits, which are actually blue, indicate susceptibility to pitting.

an inert gas shield is used during welding. This brown or brown-black oxide film has a very negative effect on the steel's resistance to pitting and should be removed by pickling or grinding.

A common way of indicating the resistance of a material to pitting is to report its pitting potential (see Fig. 33). However, the value which is obtained from laboratory trials is heavily dependent on the testing method used, and it is virtually impossible to compare the absolute values obtained in one laboratory to those obtained in another. On the other

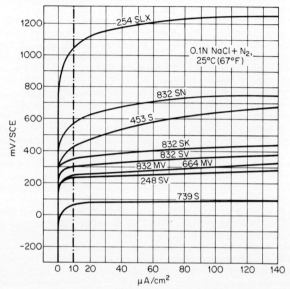

Fig. 33 Anodic polarization curves for 9 stainless steels (composition noted in Appendix 2). Breakthrough potential is defined as the potential at which the current density has reached 10 μA/cm² and is represented by the chain line. Resistance to pitting increases as the breakthrough potential increases and is highest for 254 SLX steel.

hand, agreement with actual practice is good to the extent that a stainless steel which exhibits a higher pitting potential than another steel also exhibits higher resistance in, for example, seawater.

Crevice Corrosion

This type of corrosion occurs inside crevices and under shielded areas on a metal surface where a stagnant solution may develop. Examples are shown in Figs. 34 and 35.

If a stainless steel surface containing a crevice is immersed in an air-saturated solution, the electrolyte inside the crevice will initially be identical to that outside. We assume that the oxygen content of the electrolyte is sufficient to passivate the steel and thus provide conditions equivalent to those prevailing at point D in Fig. 3 both inside and outside the crevice.

Oxygen is now consumed to maintain the passivity. The transport of oxygen to the free surface of the steel creates no problems, but the diffusion of oxygen through the electrolyte in the narrow crevice is sluggish. Gradually, the oxygen in the electrolyte inside the crevice will therefore become depleted, and in the end, the oxygen content will be so low that passivity can no longer be maintained. The situation inside the crevice may now be considered equivalent to the one at point A in Fig. 3. There has now developed a galvanic cell with a small anode inside the crevice and a large cathode on the passivated free surface of the steel.

Crevice corrosion can occur in many media but attacks are most severe in chloride solutions. The crevices may be created by deposits on the steel surface, such as sand and dirt, or by corrosion products and other solids in the electrolyte. Natural crevices are

Fig. 34   Crevice corrosion beneath rubber gasket in stainless steel plate-type heat exchanger operating in polluted harbor water.

always present in flanged joints, threaded pipe connections, and poorly-executed welded joints.

The risk of crevice corrosion can, of course, be reduced if crevices are avoided by using welded joints in place of riveted or bolted joints, by frequent removal of deposits from the steel surface or by the application of water-repellent sealant compound in flanged joints.

The initiation of crevice corrosion in chloride solutions displays striking similarities with the initiation of pitting, and it is the destructive effect of the chloride ions on the passive film which starts the attack in both cases. The propagation of the attack in the two types of corrosion also takes the same course—an autocatalytic process which lowers the pH and accelerates the migration of chloride ions to the corrosion site; consequently, the same alloying elements may be used to raise the resistance of stainless steels to these two

Fig. 35   Crevice corrosion on contact surface between cover and body on Type 316 gate valve after 4 years in cold seawater.

types of corrosion. Molybdenum-alloyed Cr-Ni steels possess much better resistance to crevice corrosion than other stainless steels, due partly to the low active corrosion of these steels.

Stress-Corrosion Cracking

A great deal of research has been directed toward the understanding of this phenomenon. Much of this research attempted to determine a general mechanism by which stress-corrosion cracking (SCC) causes alloys to fail, in the hope that an understanding of the general mechanism would lead to solutions to the problem. The fact that no single mechanism has been developed, despite considerable effort over several decades, is testimony to the complexity of the problem. The consensus at this time is that the possibility of evolving a general mechanism is remote.

The initial stage of stress-corrosion cracking is very similar to the pitting process. The first step is that the passive film, under the action of specific ions, such as chlorides, is destroyed at isolated points where microanodes are formed. If local stress concentrations are present at these points, the stresses which were earlier unable to crack the steel will be fully concentrated at the weak spots formed by the small pits and there give rise to primary cracks. This initial stage may take a very long time, partly as a result of the repassivation of the pits, although the time is shortened if the temperature is high.

The cracks now propagate as a result of interaction between the tensile stresses, which may be very high at the tips of the cracks, and electrochemical corrosion. As in pitting, the driving force for electrochemical corrosion is the potential difference between the large passive steel surface and the active metal in the bottom of the crack, where conditions are acidic because of the presence of hydrolyzed corrosion products. At the bottom of the crack, new metal layers are continuously exposed and activated both electrochemically by the acid environment and mechanically by the tensile stresses. The combined activation has the effect that corrosion proceeds virtually without activation polarization, which explains the high rate—up to a few millimeters per hour—at which the cracks may propagate through the steel.

Stress-corrosion cracking is influenced by a number of interrelated variables which are briefly discussed below.

Tensile Stresses   Tensile stress can either be residual stresses caused by structural work (i.e., welding, bending, machining, etc.) or operational factors (i.e., pressure and temperature). Susceptibility to stress-corrosion cracking increases with increasing tensile stress. It is difficult to specify the lowest stress that causes stress-corrosion cracking since susceptibility is also controlled by other factors. If severe corrosive conditions are present, a stress corresponding to one-half the yield strength at the temperature in question will be sufficient to initiate stress-corrosion cracking.

Compressive stresses do not cause stress-corrosion cracking. One approach, then, is to reduce the residual tensile stresses adjacent to welds, for example, by applying compressive stresses by means of shot blasting.

Corrosive Media   The most common agents that cause stress-corrosion cracking are chlorides, caustic solutions, and hydrogen sulfide.

Chlorides. Chlorides such as KCl, NaCl, $CaCl_2$, and $MgCl_2$ are encountered in various amounts both in potable water and plant-operating water. The risk of stress-corrosion cracking increases as chloride content increases. However, no threshold value beneath which the various steel grades are resistant to stress-corrosion cracking can be specified since there is considerable risk that the chloride content will increase. The coffee boiler shown in Fig. 36 offers an example. Originally, the chloride content of the water in the heating jacket was less than 50 mg/l, but it increased sharply because of evaporation. Susceptibility to stress-corrosion cracking caused by chlorides is greatest within the pH range of 3 to 8. Chloride-induced stress-corrosion cracking is transcrystalline in nature. The photomicrograph in Fig. 37 shows a typical crack of this type.

Caustic Solutions. Stress-corrosion cracking caused by caustic solutions (such as KOH, NaOH, and LiOH) can be both transcrystalline and intercrystalline. This form of stress-corrosion cracking occurs at concentrations of about 20% and at high temperatures.

Hydrogen Sulfide. Aqueous solutions containing large amounts of H_2S cause a form of stress-corrosion cracking in 18Cr-8Ni steel at low pH levels, especially below 4. Damage of this type is very seldom encountered in molybdenum-bearing austenitic steels. Stress-corrosion cracking caused by H_2S is characteristically transcrystalline in nature.

Temperature   Stress-corrosion cracking caused by chlorides is very seldom encountered below 60°C (140°F). However, susceptibility increases sharply as temperature increases above that point. Stress-corrosion cracking caused by caustic solutions occurs at very high temperatures, approximately 130°C (266°F), as shown in Fig. 22. In H_2S solutions, stress-corrosion cracking takes place primarily at low temperatures. At higher temperatures the solubility of H_2S in water decreases in open systems. Oddly enough, this susceptibility is also lower in closed, pressurized systems at, for example, 120°C (248°F). One possible explanation is that protective sulfide films are formed on the steel surface.

Redox Potential of the Solution   Laboratory experiments at Avesta have shown that the potential assumed by a steel in a chloride solution, which depends on the redox potential of the solution, is of vital importance with regard to stress-corrosion cracking. The oxidizing ions Fe^{3+} and Cu^{2+}, for example, cause pitting rather than stress-corrosion cracking. This same phenomenon has been observed when the potential of a sample is raised using a potentiostat. Actually, stress-corrosion cracking seems to occur within a relatively narrow potential range, approximately 30 mV, which is characteristic of each steel grade. The more highly alloyed (nobler) the steel is, the higher the range. Below this potential interval, the steel is cathodically protected against stress-corrosion cracking. For example, one 18Cr-8Ni steel tested in 40% $CaCl_2$ at 100°C (212°F), at a load corresponding to two-thirds of the yield strength at temperature, proved to have

Fig. 36   Stress-corrosion cracking in coffee boiler made of 18Cr-9Ni stainless steel. Chloride content of the water in the heating jacket originally was less than 50 mg/l but it increased sharply because of evaporation.

cathodic protection at −360 mV/SCE.* The shortest time to fracture was obtained at −340 mV/SCE, and pitting commenced at −320 mV/SCE.

In practice, the same effect as that obtained by cathodic protection from a base sacrificial anode (Zn, Fe, Al), or an external d-c source can be obtained by the quantitative reduction of all oxidizing agents (usually oxygen) in the solution. This can occur, for example, by adding excessive hydrazine to a closed cooling system and reducing the redox potential to a risk-free value.

Stress-corrosion cracking caused by caustic solutions is not considered potential-dependent. In H_2S-saturated solutions, it occurs under strongly reducing conditions. Oxygen or other oxidizing agents are virtually absent.

Chemical and Structural Composition of the Steel   Stress-corrosion cracking has sometimes been called the "Achilles' heel of stainless steels," but there are ways of coming to grips with the problem by altering the composition of the materials. Nickel is the alloying element which has the strongest reducing effect on the susceptibility to stress-corrosion cracking in chloride solutions. However, about 35 to 40% is needed to fully prevent this type of corrosion.

A decrease in susceptibility to stress-corrosion cracking can be achieved if the nickel content is reduced enough to form delta ferrite, which is less susceptible to stress-corrosion cracking. Consequently, a steel such as one containing 26Cr-5Ni-1.5Mo, with a structure of about 70% delta ferrite, is relatively immune to stress-corrosion cracking caused by chlorides up to about 100°C (212°F).

Silicon and molybdenum also improve resistance to stress-corrosion cracking, probably because these elements promote passivation. Carbon, nitrogen, phosphorus, and sulfur have very little effect on material that has been annealed and quenched, within the

*SCE = Saturated Calomel Electrode.

chemical composition limits encountered in ordinary Cr-Ni and Cr-Ni-Mo steels. Sulfur in concentrations used in the free-machining grades (approx. 0.2%) will impair corrosion resistance. Carbon, in the form of grain-boundary carbides, can increase susceptibility. Vacuum-melted ferritic steels, with extremely low nitrogen and phosphorus contents, are better able to resist stress-corrosion cracking than the standard ferritic grades.

Two common media used to determine susceptibility to stress-corrosion cracking in stainless steels are: 40% $CaCl_2$, pH = 6, 100°C (212°F) and 44.7% $MgCl_2$, boiling 154°C

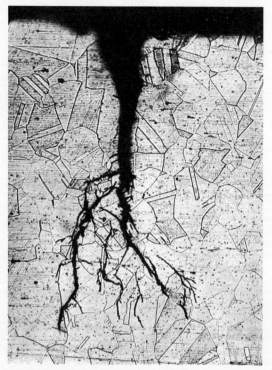

Fig. 37 Transcrystalline stress-corrosion cracking in 18Cr-9Ni stainless steel. (800X)

(309°F). Table 2 presents the average time to fracture under uniaxial testing in these two solutions for several frequently used Avesta steels. The load in all tests was two-thirds of the yield strength at test temperature.

Galvanic Corrosion

In galvanic corrosion, the corrosion rate of a metal is increased by its contact with another metal whose corrosion potential is higher in the electrolyte in question. This type of corrosion may be envisioned as a short-circuited galvanic cell where the more electroposi-tive metal forms the positive pole and the less electropositive metal forms the negative pole. The metal-to-metal contact gives the metals the same potential, and the short-circuit current is generated by a cathodic reaction, usually oxygen reduction, on the more electropositive metal and an anodic reaction involving increased corrosion on the less electropositive metal. The corrosion rate of the more electropositive metal is generally somewhat lower than when the metal does not form part of a galvanic couple.

The extent of the corrosion naturally depends on how large the difference is between the corrosion potentials of the two elements of metal couple when not short-circuited. This difference varies, however, according to the corrosive medium involved. The corro-sion potentials of different metals and alloys in a given medium are usually presented in a galvanic series. However, such tables may be somewhat misleading, since many factors other than the potential difference are of great importance. A large potential difference

TABLE 2   Average Time to Fracture

Steel grade		Average time to fracture, h	
Swedish Standard,* SIS-14-	Avesta†	CaCl₂	MgCl₂
	248 SV	No fracture	3
2324	453 S	No fracture	3
2333	832 MV	110	4
2343	832 SK	450	5
	832 SN	750	8
	832 SL	900	9
	254 SLX	>1000	70

*For composition, see Appendix 1, Sweden. †For composition, see Appendix 2.

does not always mean that galvanic corrosion will be severe, since a high polarization of one of the electrode reactions may reduce the current of the galvanic cell to harmless values. The ratio between the anodic and cathodic areas plays a decisive role. A small anodic area and a large cathodic area, as in the case of a carbon steel rivet in a stainless steel plate, is of course much more dangerous than the reverse situation. The conductivity of the electrolyte must also be taken into consideration. High conductivity means that the attack on the less electropositive metal may extend far beyond the point of contact, but when conductivity is low (e.g., in fresh water), the attack will occur close to the point of contact and is therefore more dangerous. On the other hand, where the distance between anode and cathode is greater, the danger will increase if the electrolyte has good conductivity.

Passive stainless steels display comparatively electropositive corrosion potentials and, in consequence, they generally form the electropositive component in a metal couple. In seawater Type 316L steels (molybdenum alloyed) thus strongly increase corrosion on cast iron and carbon steel (see Fig. 38) and can, in some cases, even increase the rate of corrosion of some different bronzes and brasses. Among common structural materials only graphite and titanium are capable of giving rise to galvanic corrosion on Type 316L.

In order to avoid galvanic corrosion, the first thing to do is to select materials which are close to each other in the galvanic series or to prevent metal-to-metal contact by means of insulation. Another means of reducing the risk is to paint the metal surfaces, but never the less electropositive surface alone, since defects in the paint can give rise to very severe corrosion due to the unfavorable ratio of small anodic areas to large cathodic areas.

Erosion-Corrosion

Erosion-corrosion is a form of corrosion which occurs at high relative metal-liquid velocities. The relative motion results in an accelerated supply of the corrosive agent to the corroding metal surface and the removal of corrosion products from the corroding site. The concept of erosion-corrosion also includes a mechanical wearing-away of corrosion products which have been deposited on the metal surface. If the solution contains solid particles (such as precipitated salt crystals or sand), the corrosion rate is naturally greater.

Stainless steel possesses very good resistance to erosion-corrosion, thanks to the stability of the passive surface film. In practice, however, stainless steels can be attacked, especially when the composition and temperature of the electrolyte are such that the passivity of the stainless steels is not fully stable. Thus, erosion-corrosion can occur on, for example, pump impellers made of stainless steel which are exposed to sulfuric acid or pipelines in which sulfuric acid is pumped at great speed.

The form of erosion-corrosion which arises when the solution contains solid particles is known in practice from urea manufacture, where carbamate crystals contribute to heavy attacks on valves (see Fig. 39) and pumps, and from phosphoric acid manufacture, where gypsum can give rise to erosion-corrosion on agitators, pump impellers, pipelines, and valves.

The resistance of stainless steels to erosion-corrosion is generally increased by the same alloying elements as those which increase resistance to general corrosion in the electrolyte in question. In practice, this means that steels such as Types 316 and 317 often possess better resistance than steels such as Type 304. Another factor of importance is the

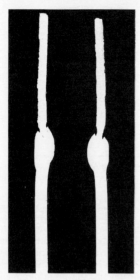

Fig. 38 Galvanic corrosion on unalloyed steel (top) in contact with stainless steel after exposure in cold seawater.

Fig. 39 Spindle of Type 329 pressure-reduction valve attacked by erosion-corrosion in a urea plant.

hardness of the surface. However, materials possessing high hardness (such as martensitic steels or precipitation-hardenable steels) generally exhibit insufficient corrosion resistance to offer an alternative to fully austenitic steels. They are preferable only when resistance to general corrosion is fully adequate, especially in situations where much of the erosion-corrosion can be attributed to abrasion by solid particles.

REFERENCES

Because the authors have chosen to write an unannotated chapter based principally on the data and practical observations developed at Avesta Jernverks, the references which follow are appended as a guide to the literature.

General Texts

Uhlig, H. H.: "Corrosion and Corrosion Control," Wiley, New York, 1963.
Tomashov, N. D.: "Theory of Corrosion and Protection of Metals," Macmillan, New York, 1966.
Fontana, M. G., and N. D. Greene: "Corrosion Engineering," McGraw-Hill, New York, 1967.
Wranglén, G.: "An Introduction to Corrosion and Protection of Metals," Institut för Metallskydd, Stockholm, 1972.

Passivation

Steigerwald, R. F.: Electrochemistry of Corrosion, *Corrosion*, vol. 24, pp. 1–10, 1968.
Greene, N. D.: The Classical Potentiostat: Its Application to the Study of Passivity, *Corrosion*, vol. 15, pp. 369t–372t, 1959.
West, J. M.: Applications of Potentiostats in Corrosion Studies, *Br. Corros. J.*, vol. 5, pp. 65–71, 1970.
Lizlovs, E. A., and A. P. Bond: Anodic Polarization of Some Ferritic Stainless Steels in Chloride Media, *J. Electrochem. Soc.*, vol. 117, pp. 775–779, 1970.
Greene, N. D.: Predicting Behavior of Corrosion-resistant Alloys by Potentiostatic Polarization Methods, *Corrosion*, vol. 18, pp. 136t–142t, 1962.

Intergranular Corrosion

Henthorne, M.: "Localized Corrosion—Cause of Metal Failure," pp. 66–119, *ASTM Spec. Tech. Publ. 516*, 1972.
Intergranular Corrosion of Chromium-Nickel Stainless Steels—Final Report, *Welding Res. Counc. Bull. No. 138*, February 1969.
Mason, J. F., Jr.: "Selection of Stainless Steels," p. 71, American Society for Metals, Metals Park, Ohio, 1968.

Brown, M. H.: Behavior of Austenitic Stainless Steels in Evaluation Tests for the Detection of Susceptibility to Intergranular Corrosion, *Corrosion*, vol. 30, no. 1, pp. 1–12, January 1974.

Pitting and Crevice Corrosion

Szklarska-Smialowska, Z.: Review of Literature on Pitting Corrosion Published Since 1960, *Corrosion*, vol. 27, no. 6, pp. 223–233, June 1971.

Uhlig, H. H.: Distinguishing Characteristics of Pitting and Crevice Corrosion, *Mater. Prot. Perform.*, vol. 12, no. 2, pp. 42–44, February 1973.

Lizlovs, E. A.: "Localized Corrosion—Cause of Metal Failure," pp. 201–209, *ASTM Spec. Tech. Publ. 516*, 1972.

Brigham, R. J.: Pitting and Crevice Corrosion Resistance of Commercial 18% Cr Stainless Steels, *Mater. Perform*, vol. 13, no. 11, pp. 29–31, November 1974.

Stress-Corrosion Cracking

Staehle, R. W.: Comments on the History, Engineering and Science of Stress Corrosion Cracking, pp. 3–14, *Proc. Nat. Assoc. Corros. Eng. Symp. Fundamental Aspects of Stress Corrosion Cracking*, 1969.

Copson, H. R.: Effect of Composition on Stress Corrosion Cracking of Some Alloys Containing Nickel, pp. 247–272, "Physical Metallurgy of Stress Corrosion Fracture," Interscience, New York, 1959.

Sedriks, A. J.: Stress-Corrosion Cracking of Stainless Steels and Nickel Alloys, *J. Inst. Met.*, vol. 101, pp. 225–231, 1973.

Kowaka, M., and H. Fujikawa: Effects of Several Elements on Stress Corrosion Cracking of Austenitic Stainless Steels in Boiling Mg Cl_2 Solution, *J. Japan Inst. Met.*, vol. 34, no. 10, pp. 1054–1062, 1970.

Cunha-Belo, M., and J. Montuelle: Resistance of High Purity Stainless Steels to Stress Corrosion, *Corros. Trait. Prot. Finition*, vol. 20, no. 2, pp. 105–112, March 1972.

Uhlig, H. H., and J. Lincoln: Chemical Factors Affecting Stress Corrosion Cracking of 18-8 Stainless Steels, *J. Electrochem. Soc.*, vol. 105, pp. 325–332, June 1958.

McGuire, M. F., A. R. Troiano, and R. F. Hehemann: Stress Corrosion of Ferritic and Martensitic Stainless Steels in Saline Solutions, *Corrosion*, vol. 29, no. 7, pp. 268–271, July 1973.

Bloom, F. K.: Stress Corrosion Cracking of Hardenable Stainless Steels, *Corrosion*, vol. 11, no. 8, pp. 351t–361t, August 1955.

Hart, A. C.: Stress-Corrosion Cracking of Cast Iron-Nickel-Chromium Alloys, *Br. Corros. J.*, vol. 6, pp. 164–169, July 1971.

Chapter **17**

Resistance to Corrosion in Gaseous Atmospheres

L. A. MORRIS
Manager, Physical Metallurgy, Metallurgical Laboratories,
Falconbridge Nickel Mines Ltd.,
Thornhill, Ontario, Canada

INTRODUCTION

Stainless steels are among the most popular construction materials for elevated temperature process systems. There are numerous standard wrought and cast grades and proprietary grades available to the materials specialist. Proper selection of the optimum grade for particular environmental conditions presents numerous problems to the materials engineer. Consideration must be given to the high-temperature strength and structural stability of the various grades; adequate corrosion resistance is necessary for efficient operation of process equipment; the economics of the final selection must be feasible on a cost-to-performance basis. Although it is recognized that all facets must be considered, the following sections will be limited to the subject of corrosion resistance in elevated temperature gaseous environments [temperatures greater than approximately 1000°F (538°C)]. Furthermore, since the selection of a material commonly is made from a series of readily available products and the bulk of the information reported is based on experience and fundamental studies on these products, emphasis will be placed on the gaseous corrosion resistance of the standard American Iron and Steel Institute (AISI) (wrought) and Alloy Casting Institute (ACI) (cast) grades of stainless steels.

Much attention has been given to the compatibility of stainless steels with air or oxygen. However, recent trends in nuclear reactor design and chemical process and steam-generation equipment have resulted in renewed interest in stainless steel oxidation in carbon monoxide, carbon dioxide, and water vapor. Other gases, such as sulfur dioxide, hydrogen sulfide, hydrocarbons, ammonia, hydrogen, and the halogens may be present in variable proportions and may strongly affect corrosive conditions. Information concerning the practical limits of operation of stainless steels is available for the simpler gaseous environments. However, it is exceedingly more difficult to predict service lives for the complex, multicomponent environments without the aid of controlled field testing. A considerable amount of data has been generated concerning the reaction mechanisms between stainless steels and simple gas atmospheres but, even here, considerable disagreement exists.

This chapter is intended to be a summary of the practical information available with respect to the compatibility of stainless steels with the environments mentioned above; wherever possible, the significant details of reaction mechanisms are presented. In order to clarify the information related to scaling mechanisms for the materials specialist and provide background for the failure analyst, a brief general review of oxidation theory precedes the discussion of stainless steel corrosion. A detailed description of oxidation theory and mechanisms may be had by consulting several excellent monographs.[1-5]

OXIDATION OF METALS AND ALLOYS

Oxide Structures   Practically all oxides are semiconductors, and electrical conduction may occur either through electron holes (p-type semiconduction) or through electrons (n-type semiconduction). Oxide semiconductors are not of exact stoichiometric composition, but may contain an excess of either cations or anions. This excess is accomplished by having cation or anion vacancies or ions in interstitial positions in the lattice. Thus, the model for a p-type semiconducting oxide is one in which the cation lattice contains vacant sites, and electrical neutrality is maintained by the formation of cations of higher valency or electron holes. Electrical conductivity occurs by the movement of electron holes and of ions via cation vacancies. The model for a metal excess or n-type oxide is one in which there are metal ions and electrons in interstitial positions or anion vacancies in the lattice.

The oxides formed on alloys are ternary semiconducting layers and the dissolution of solute metal ions into the oxide layer of the solvent element affects the concentration of defects. The rate of growth of these compounds depends on the defect concentration; therefore, reaction kinetics may be increased or decreased by the addition of solute ions.

The variable composition range of oxides is one of the most important factors when considering oxidation reactions. The nature of the defect structure of an oxide which thickens by a diffusion mechanism determines the oxidation rate. For an oxide layer growing on a metal, an oxygen pressure gradient and a defect gradient exist across the oxide. A concentration gradient within a single, solid phase causes diffusion of ions via interstitial, or vacant, lattice sites. Therefore, a knowledge of the defect structure and nature of the diffusing species is necessary in order to understand the oxidation mechanism.

Oxidation Rates and Mechanisms   Although compact oxides grow by a diffusion mechanism, other processes may be rate controlling, giving rise to a number of rate laws. A major consideration of gas-metal reaction studies is the determination of an empirical rate equation and, if possible, theoretical rate equations based on physical theory to explain the kinetics of the reaction.

The simplest rate expression is the linear equation, where the thickness of the oxide film has no influence on the rate of uptake of oxygen and is directly proportional to time. If an oxide is nonprotective, offering no barrier between the gas phase and metal surface, the linear law is expected to hold. Porous or cracked oxides are formed on a number of metals which show a strong tendency to oxidize at a linear rate. These metals generally have a low or high volume ratio of oxide to metal consumed. A low volume ratio suggests that the metal is always exposed to the gas phase.

Under special conditions, the growth of a compact pore-free scale may follow a linear rate law. For example, owing to the exceptionally high concentration of vacant lattice sites in some oxides, ions can diffuse rapidly to the oxide-gas interface, and a surface reaction becomes rate controlling when the oxidizing potential of the gas phase is low.

The parabolic rate has been observed in numerous cases and is based on rate control by either cation or anion diffusion across a barrier film. The oxidation rate is inversely proportional to the film thickness, and therefore, oxide growth decreases with increasing time. Wagner has described the mechanism for scale growth on a pure metal according to this law.[6] The rate of oxidation is controlled by the diffusion of reactants on a concentration gradient existing across the scale. An expression for the rate of oxidation in terms of the specific conductivity of the oxide, the transport numbers of ions and electrons and the free energy decrease of the oxidation reaction was derived. Experimental verification was obtained for several metals.

Kinetic data for thin-film formation have been found to obey cubic and logarithmic rate laws. It has been suggested that thin films ($<10^{-4}$ cm) form by ion migration under the influence of a strong electric field across the oxide, whereas thick films are formed by thermally activated diffusion in an electrically neutral oxide.

The oxidation rates of alloys rarely agree with a given rate law over a range of conditions. Deviations often occur and a combination of rate equations is required to describe the reaction kinetics. Therefore, it is not possible to predict the effects to be expected from the addition of an alloying element to a pure metal by a unified theory. Numerous factors must be considered; for example, the affinity of the alloy constituents for the components of the reactant gas, the solubility limits of the phases, the diffusion rates of atoms in alloys and in the oxides, the formation of ternary compounds, the relative volumes of the various phases, all of which may be functions of temperature and pressure. Several limiting cases of alloy oxidation have been theoretically treated, and it is hoped that advancements in knowledge will permit the derivation of a more universal theory.

Oxide Morphologies   Moreau and Bénard[7] have presented a general classification of the different scale morphologies which may occur on an alloy A-B based on experimental observations. The classes are illustrated diagrammatically in Fig. 1. Class I refers to the case of selective oxidation (preferential oxidation of a single element). This classification can be divided into two subgroups, I_A and I_B, where the former concerns the selective oxidation of the minor addition and the latter the major component. In each case, there appear two possibilities. The oxide of the minor, more reactive, element may be nucleated and precipitate within the matrix of the major element. The formation process is called internal oxidation (I_A^1). Another possibility is the formation of an oxide film of the minor element (I_A^2).

Again two possibilities exist in the case of the selective oxidation of the major element. A thick oxide layer may be formed on the alloy surface, which contains entrapped globules of the addition element (I_B^1), or the more noble element may concentrate at the metal-oxide interface, and subsequently diffuse back into the metal phase (I_B^2).

Class II deals with the simultaneous oxidation of both elements. Again, it is possible to subgroup the various modes of oxidation. In Class II_A, the oxides are insoluble, and either the minor or the major element has a greater affinity for oxygen. If the minor element has a higher affinity, its oxide may nucleate on the surface or precipitate as internal oxide. Since the oxide of the major element can form, it will entrap these nuclei or precipitate as the metal-oxide interface recedes. The end result is a dispersion of one oxide in the other and internal precipitates of the former in the metal phase (II_A^1). If the major element has a greater affinity for oxygen, internal oxidation does not occur as above. Therefore, the reaction product consists of a dispersion of oxide particles in the oxide of the major element (II_A^2).

The second subgroup refers to mixed oxides, that is, oxides in which the two alloying

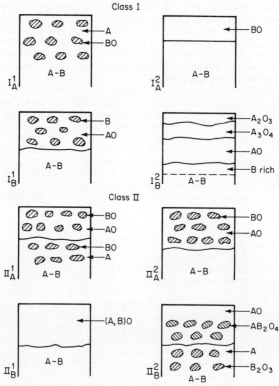

Fig. 1 Oxidation modes of alloys.[7]

elements are associated. These oxides occur most frequently at high temperatures and oxygen potentials. The simplest case to describe is the formation of a solid solution of the oxide of one element in the oxide of the other (II_B^1). The other case concerns the formation of oxides which approach stoichiometric composition (II_B^2). This reaction often gives rise to a spinel oxide, AB_2O_4.

The above classification is quite general, and introduces some clarity to the complex problem of alloy oxidation. It is unfortunate that variations from these simple cases may occur as a result of mechanical stresses, coalescence of oxides, and other factors often characteristic of a particular system.

In the above classification, the possible formation of multilayered scales was also considered. If a metal exhibits several stable oxides, they may appear in various proportions, depending on conditions of temperature and pressure. The oxide richest in metal will be located adjacent to the metal phase, whereas that richest in oxygen will be nearest the gas phase. Even under conditions of high oxidation potentials, where only the appearance of the most stable oxide is expected, the potential at the metal-oxide interface favors the formation of the lower oxides, and these will grow. Examples illustrating these characteristics are copper, which forms cuprous and cupric oxides, and iron, which forms wustite, magnetite, and hematite.

HIGH-TEMPERATURE CORROSION OF STAINLESS STEELS

Reaction with Oxidizing Gases

Oxidation reactions are the more frequent causes of high-temperature corrosion of stainless steels. This is not surprising because most environments are either air, oxygen, carbon dioxide or steam, or complex atmospheres containing one or more of these gases (sulfur dioxide may also be included but has been deferred to the following section on sulfur-bearing gases). Most studies have been associated with air or oxygen (dry and damp), and a considerable amount of fundamental and practical data has been recorded. Rapid accumulation is presently occurring with respect to corrosion by carbon dioxide and steam at temperatures up to 2200°F (1204°C). Nevertheless, the oxidation behavior of stainless steels still defies description by a unified mechanism partly because of the complex nature of the problem, and partly because of disagreement and lack of re-producibility concerning scale structure and kinetic data. The large number of combinations that exist in gaseous and alloy compositions adds further complications. However, with the information at hand, it is usually possible to specify the most suitable grade of stainless steel for mildly corrosive conditions: when operating conditions become severe, it is often necessary to test coupons in actual or carefully simulated service conditions.[8]

Reaction Kinetics Most of the empirical rate expressions have been observed with chromium and chromium-nickel stainless steels and, therefore, it is difficult to discuss any particular rate equation. A general formulation of rate data has been presented by Wood[9] and is illustrated in Fig. 2. Under mild conditions, a protective film grows according to curve OAD and the rate of oxidation decreases with time (the parabolic rate may be closely approximated in

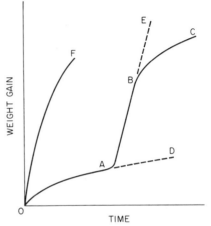

Fig. 2 Typical rate data for the oxidation of chromium and Ni-Cr stainless steels at elevated temperatures.[9]

this range). For severe environments, an initial (induction) period OA is followed, then a sudden increase in rate, curve AB, occurs (film breakthrough). Depending on alloy composition and oxidizing conditions, either self-healing of the oxide will occur and curve BC is followed for some time after which breaks of the type AB are repeated, or a nonprotective oxide is maintained and BE is followed. Under extreme conditions, OF is followed directly and the oxide is nonprotective. The actual geometry of the curves and the occurrence of "breakthrough" are dependent on time, alloy composition, and environment. Reproducibility with standard conditions is often poor. For these reasons, and the fact that corrosion data are reported in a variety of ways (weight gain per unit area, weight loss per unit area, penetration rate or scale thickness), it is difficult to precisely compare the performance of the different grades under the same conditions. Nevertheless, general trends can be indicated.

Oxidation Mechanisms When iron is heated in highly oxidizing gases at temperatures greater than 1000°F (538°C), a multilayered scale is formed consisting of wustite at the metal-oxide interface, an intermediate layer of magnetite, and hematite at the oxide-gas interface. Oxidation proceeds at a rapid rate, and this has been attributed to the occurrence of the wustite phase. This oxide contains an inordinate number of cation vacancies and a large composition range, which are conducive to rapid diffusion of iron ions across the scale. Thus, the oxide thickens rapidly at the expense of the metallic phase. It has been established that additions of chromium and nickel to iron impart oxidation resistance by removal of wustite as a stable phase. Chromium additions are much more effective than nickel in this respect and quantities greater than approximately 13% promote the formation of oxides rich in chromium. The excellent oxidation resistance of the ferritic chromium and austenitic chromium-nickel stainless steels to mildly oxidizing conditions is attributed to the protective barrier films formed by chromium-rich compounds.

In general, when wrought or cast chromium and Cr-Ni stainless steels are heated to elevated temperatures in an oxidizing gas, chromium is selectively oxidized producing a thin film of chromic oxide, "Cr_2O_3". (The quotation marks indicate that the oxide is doped with small quantities of iron or iron and nickel, depending on the base composition of the alloy.) Oxidation occurs at a slow rate (according to curve OA in Fig. 2) since cation diffusion through this oxide is extremely slow. This film is referred to as a Type A scale by some investigators,[10-14] and its formation leads to low oxidation rates. It is possible after a period of time, depending on alloy composition and temperature, for film breakdown to occur and a rapid period of oxidation, typified by curve AB in Fig. 2, is experienced. This period corresponds with the formation of a Type B scale which is a duplex structure consisting of an inner layer of spinel oxide, $FeFe_{2-x}Cr_xO_4$ where $0 < x < 2$ and may contain nickel, manganese, and silicon in solution, and an outer layer of ferric oxide, "Fe_2O_3", containing chromium and other alloying elements in solution.

The breakdown of the Type A to the Type B scale is classified as a Type I break.[10-14] The mechanism and morphological developments of breakthrough are not clearly understood. It appears that breakthrough occurs at highly localized sites randomly distributed over the specimen surface; this results in the production of warts or nodules of stratified Type B scale.[12,13] Depending on alloy composition and oxidizing conditions, the nodules may expand laterally until the entire surface is covered with stratified scale.[9] In some cases, breakthrough remains localized, and the protective oxide, "Cr_2O_3", persists for long periods of time.[15]

Two theories have been presented to account for the Type A to Type B scale change. It has been suggested that either a chemical mechanism is operative, whereby the protective scale is penetrated by iron ions causing transformation to the spinel oxide and producing iron (ferric) oxide at the outer surface,[12-14] or scale cracking occurs and the underlying alloy (depleted in chromium) reacts directly with the atmosphere producing the spinel oxide and outer iron oxides. In either case, a stratified scale is generated over the whole or part of the surface; the scale may again become protective, establishing kinetics according to curve BC, or remain nonprotective and follow BE. Only one Type I break will occur per sample and indeed may never occur for alloys of high chromium content particularly at low service temperatures.[12,16]

If kinetics are established according to curve BC in Fig. 2, subsequent breaks of similar geometry to AB may occur. These have been classified as Type II breaks and are characterized by cracks in scales which are thicker than about 10 μm.[12] After the break, the scale becomes protective and rates are re-established according to the BC geometry. Oxidation continues, and this pattern may be repeated. At temperatures greater than 1600°F (871°C), the occurrence of Type II breaks appears to be the general rule rather than the exception particularly with steels containing less than about 20% chromium. It has been suggested that accumulation of voids and silica at the metal-oxide interface contributes to scale breaks.[17]

Internal oxidation of the alloy phase also occurs when the metal is in contact with the spinel oxide. If localized breakdown occurs, subscale precipitation is only noted below the nodular growths. The oxide particles are "Cr_2O_3" or spinel of higher chromium content than the spinel phase in the scale. Subscale formation is not observed beneath "Cr_2O_3" films except in alloys containing high nickel concentrations,[18] but, a silica subscale has been reported for commercial steels.[15]

The surface reactions which occur on stainless steels in oxidizing gases are extremely complex. In addition, impurities in commercial materials generate further complications and many investigators are confining their research to pure binary alloys in an attempt to clarify some of the discrepancies of stainless steel oxidation.

Practical Considerations   Good oxidation resistance of stainless steels requires that the scale formed should be chromic oxide, "Cr_2O_3". It is apparent from the above discussion that when stainless steels are exposed to an oxidizing atmosphere, chromium is selectively oxidized to form "Cr_2O_3" scales. During scale formation, chromium is depleted and iron or iron and nickel are enriched in the metal at the metal-oxide interface. It is imperative that the extent of chromium depletion does not fall below the values required to stabilize "Cr_2O_3" scales. Internal oxidation should not occur since the formation of oxide precipitates further depletes the alloy surface of chromium. Croll and Wallwork[18] recently showed in a comprehensive study on the oxidation of ternary Fe-Cr-Ni alloys at 1832°F (1000°C) that the minimum chromium interface concentration required to maintain "Cr_2O_3" scales is 14 atomic % in binary Fe-Cr alloys and is dependent on the nickel concentration for ternary alloys. The variation in the chromium interface content with alloy composition is shown in Fig. 3. The minimum chromium interface content required to stabilize "Cr_2O_3" in ternary alloys was determined to occur at a concentration of 7 atomic % Cr, 70 atomic % Ni, and 23 atomic % Fe. These

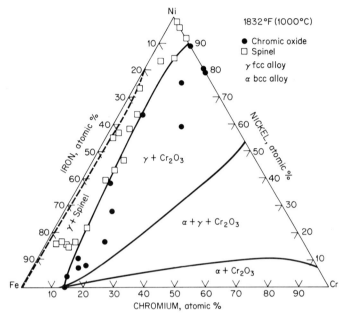

Fig. 3 The section of the Fe-Ni-Cr-O phase diagram at 1832°F (1000°C) and a constant oxygen concentration approximating the limit of oxygen solubility in the alloy matrix, showing the oxides in equilibrium with the various alloy compositions.[18]

investigators also examined the occurrence of internal oxidation in the alloys at 1832°F (1000°C). The bulk compositions of alloys which showed chromic oxide stability and no internal oxide are given in Fig. 4. It is also known that alloys which form "Cr_2O_3" scales oxidize at different rates presumably related to the extent of doping of the chromic oxide scale. Investigations have shown that good oxidation resistance is obtained with binary Fe-Cr and ternary Fe-Cr-Ni alloys containing 20 to 25Cr, 25Cr-20Ni, and 20Cr-70Ni-bal Fe.[19,20] Many commercial stainless steels approach these compositions.

It should be pointed out that much of the experimental data reported for stainless steels is based on short-term tests and caution must be taken when applying the data to field service. Vyklický and Měřička demonstrated that increased oxidation rates of steels approximating Types 430, 446, 304, and 310 were observed during long-term testing (~6000 h) in air and that the increased rates could substantially affect estimated service lives based on short-term tests.[20] It was proposed that the increased rates resulted from the absorption of nitrogren from the atmosphere and the eventual precipitation of chromium carbonitride in the metal at the metal-oxide interface. The precipitation reaction further depleted the alloy surfaces of chromium, lowering the stability of protective scales.

Experimental data of the type reported above, and years of experience with commercial wrought and cast stainless steels, have shown that as the chromium and nickel contents in iron are increased, the oxidation rate is greatly reduced. The information available permits one to assign upper service temperature limits for most of the commercial steels exposed in air. Table 1 indicates the maximum recommended temperatures in air to prevent excessive scaling of wrought stainless steels and Table 2 gives corresponding data for the

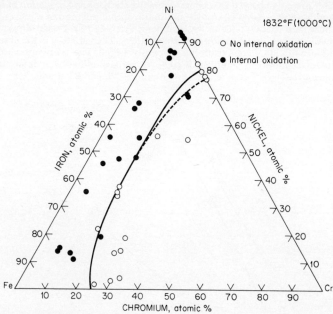

Fig. 4   The section of the Fe-Cr-Ni-O system at 1832°F (1000°C) and constant oxygen content, showing the boundaries defining the limit of stability of chromic oxide (solid line) and the appearance of internal oxide in these alloys (broken line).[18]

TABLE 1   Recommended Maximum Service Temperatures in Air for Wrought Stainless Steels

Material type	Intermittent service		Continuous service	
	°C	°F	°C	°F
201	815	1500	845	1550
202	815	1500	845	1550
301	840	1550	900	1650
302	870	1600	925	1700
304	870	1600	925	1700
308	925	1700	980	1800
309	980	1800	1095	2000
310	1035	1900	1150	2100
316	870	1600	925	1700
317	870	1600	925	1700
321	870	1600	925	1700
330	1035	1900	1150	2100
347	870	1600	925	1700
406	815	1500	1035	1900
410	815	1500	705	1300
416	760	1400	675	1250
420	735	1350	620	1150
440	815	1500	760	1400
405	815	1500	705	1300
430	870	1600	815	1500
442	1035	1900	980	1800
446	1175	2150	1095	2000

TABLE 2   Approximate Maximum Recommended Service Temperatures in Air for Cast Stainless Steels

Material type	Compositions preferred for cyclic service	Continuous service °C	Continuous service °F
HA		650	1200
HC	Good	1120	2050
HD		1065	1950
HE		1065	1950
HF		900	1650
HH		1065	1950
HI		1120	2000
HK		1095	2000
HL		1150	2100
HN	Good	1095	2000
HT	Very good	1035	1900
HU	Very good	1095	2000
HW	Excellent	1095	2000
HX	Excellent	1150	2100

cast stainless steels. All alloys would give excellent service at lower temperatures [1000 to 1300°F (538 to 704°C)] and, at higher service temperatures, the alloys containing greater quantities of chromium and nickel would be selected. The maximum service temperatures given reflect the beneficial effect of increasing chromium contents on oxidation resistance. Isolating the steels with an approximately constant chromium content shows the beneficial effect of higher nickel additions on oxidation resistance. Although nickel has a small affinity for oxygen, it influences the composition, adhesion, and possibly, the mechanical properties of the scale, thereby improving the long-term oxidation resistance of nickel-bearing steels.[16] It has been suggested that even a small amount of nickel dissolved in "Cr_2O_3" scales reduces the rate of cation diffusion and the rate of oxidation.[9] Furthermore, it appears that nickel retards the transformation of Type A ("Cr_2O_3") to Type B scales (spinel and ferric oxide).[17]

The data in Table 2 on upper service temperature limits for cast steels are based on limited reported information and practical experience and can only be considered approximate. For cast alloys of similar composition to wrought grades, the upper service temperatures might be slightly lower since the matrix chromium content is generally less than comparable wrought grades owing to the higher carbon content and subsequent formation of secondary chromium-rich carbides in the cast steels at temperature.

In many processes, isothermal conditions are not maintained and thermal cycling prevails. Upper operating temperatures must be lowered for the wrought and cast stainless steels to avoid excessive scaling. The temperature limits for cyclic conditions are shown in the column "Intermittent Service" in Table 1. The specific limits for the cast steels are not well documented, but preferred compositions can be indicated based on practical experience. Expansion and contraction differences between the alloys and scales during heating and cooling cause cracking or spalling of the protective scales which allows the oxidizing media to attack the exposed metal surface. The expansion characteristics of the straight-chromium grades are more compatible than those of the wrought austenitic Cr-Ni steels and this is reflected in the temperature limits in Table 1. Vylický and Měřička reported in their studies on the long-term cyclic oxidation resistance of Types 442, 446, 304, and 310 steels that thermal cycling decreases the oxidation rate of ferritic steels and increases the rate for austenitic steels relative to isothermal exposure.[20]

The spalling resistance of the Cr-Ni steels is greatly improved at higher nickel levels and is illustrated in Fig. 5.[94] Nickel reduces the differential thermal expansion between alloy and oxide and thereby reduces stresses at the alloy-oxide interface during cooling. Furthermore, it has been postulated that improved scale adhesion and lower sensitivity to cracking may be due to the doping of chromic oxide with nickel and the better mechanical properties of doped scales. Type 446 steel was reported to be superior to Type 310 steel during long-term cyclic tests,[20] but Grodner has shown that Types 309 and 310 steels are equivalent or slightly superior as shown in Fig. 6.[21] The high-nickel cast steels (HW, HX) however, can be considered superior to the best ferritic grades for thermal cycling applications. The outstanding cyclic oxidation resistance of these grades can be attributed to the conditions noted above and also to the scale keying effect of internal oxide particles reported by Croll and Wallwork in high-nickel alloys with "Cr_2O_3"-rich scales[18] (see Fig. 4). The high-nickel grades are often specified at intermediate and high temperatures since they are resistant to brittle sigma-phase formation and have much better load-bearing capacity than the ferritic steels.

Some preliminary studies have been conducted on the effects of rare earth additions, particularly cerium, and yttrium and thorium on the isothermal and cyclic oxidation resistance of stainless steels. The results indicate that these additions greatly increase cyclic oxidation resistance of the alloys investigated. It has been suggested that internal oxide particles of the added elements act as vacancy sinks and prevent the formation of voids at the metal-oxide interface.[22] Also addition metal ions may enter external scales and alter the mechanical properties of the oxide, or internal oxide particles could key the external scale to the alloy similar to high-nickel steels noted above.[18]

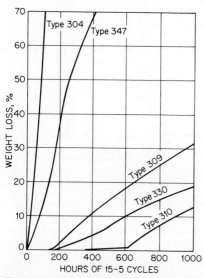

Fig. 5 Resistance of austenitic stainless steels to cyclic conditions at 1800°F (980°C) (cycle consists of 15 min at temperature and 5 min in air).[94]

Effects of Oxidizing Atmosphere and Minor Addition Elements The data presented in the previous section pertain basically to oxidation of commercial and high-purity stainless steels in air. The effects of minor elements normally found in stainless steels (such as carbon, silicon, manganese, titanium, niobium, aluminum, and molybdenum) on oxidation resistance were not discussed. Some of these elements strongly influence the gas corrosion resistance of stainless steels and their presence at various levels in commercial steels accounts for some of the ambiguity between service lives of similar grades. In this section, the effects of oxidizing gases other than air and minor elements on the oxidation resistance of stainless steels will be presented. Surface condition of the steels can also influence oxidation behavior and these effects will be elucidated wherever possible.

Effect of Atmosphere Although reaction mechanisms are probably similar in air, oxygen, water vapor, and carbon dioxide (formation and breakdown of protective oxides) reaction rates may vary considerably. For example, similar scaling behavior has been observed for chromium and Cr-Ni steels in air and oxygen; however, the reaction rates are greater in the initial stages in pure oxygen and scale breakdown occurs more rapidly as the oxygen potential (in oxygen-nitrogen atmospheres) is increased.[23] Results obtained in air should be applied with care when considering service in pure oxygen. Nitrogen in air may substitute for oxygen ions in the protective "Cr_2O_3" scale and assist in reducing oxidation rates.[9] At very high temperatures approaching the upper service limits for stainless steels, oxidation rates in pure oxygen and air would probably be equivalent since it has been observed that chromium depletion in the alloy is increased by carbonitride precipitation at high service temperatures.[20]

In almost all cases considered, an increase in corrosion rate is observed for chromium and Cr-Ni steels in the presence of large or small amounts of water vapor.[12,24,26] Exceptional behavior was noted for Type 446: corrosion was less in moist air than in dry air.[12]

Figure 7 illustrates the effect of moist air on the oxidation of Types 302 and 330. Type 302 undergoes rapid corrosion in wet air at 2000°F (1093°C), whereas a protective film is formed in dry air. The higher nickel Type 330 is less sensitive to the effects of moisture. In a literature survey,[27] it was illustrated that increasing chromium and nickel contents permit higher operating temperatures in moist air. Type 446 is usable at temperatures approaching 2000°F (1093°C). Types 309 and 310 are superior at temperatures greater

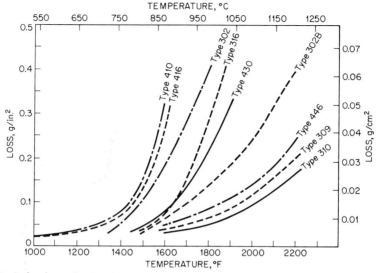

Fig. 6 Scaling losses developed on a 12-period intermittent heating and cooling cycle for various types of stainless steel.[21]

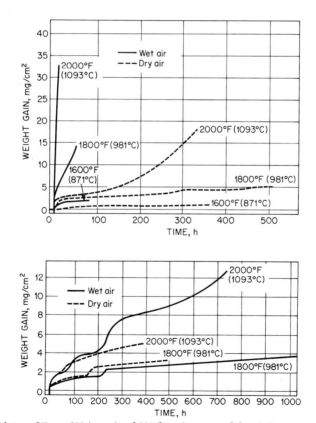

Fig. 7 Oxidation of Types 302 (upper) and 330 (lower) in wet and dry air.[12]

TABLE 3   Defilmed Metal Weight Losses of Stainless Steel Tested at 1200°F (648°C) for 7 Days in Oxygen[28]

Sample	Surface preparation	Defilmed metal weight loss, mg/cm²	
		Dry O_2	Wet O_2
304	Wet ground	0.19	3.6
	Electropolished	0.16	5.9
321	Wet ground	0.27	1.2
	Electropolished	0.16	6.5
316	Wet ground	0.15	1.8
	Electropolished		6.6
347	Wet ground	0.24	2.3
	Electropolished	0.36	6.4

than 1800°F (981°C). Ruther and Greenberg have shown that additions of moisture to oxygen significantly increase the corrosion rates of Types 304, 316, 321, and 347 steels as shown in Table 3.[28] Thus, for the lower chromium and nickel grades listed in Tables 1 and 2, the temperature limits for service in moist air should be adjusted downwards by approximately 100 to 150°F (38 to 65°C).

The application of stainless steels in steam-generating plants has been of interest for many years. Incorporation of steam superheaters in nuclear reactor applications, the consequences of thermal overshoots during loss-of-coolant accidents in reactors and the increase in current steam superheater temperatures in generating plants have stimulated investigations on the corrosive effects of high-temperature steam.[28-33] The main features of steam oxidation of stainless steels are that oxidation rates are significantly higher in steam than in air and that the oxidation behavior of the steels is very sensitive to surface condition prior to exposure. Furthermore, it appears that chromium is lost from external scales formed in steam and protective high-chromium scales are more difficult to form.[33]

Ruther and Greenberg studied the effects of steam temperature, pressure, oxygen and hydrogen content, and velocity on the corrosion of Types 304 and 406 steels and conducted limited tests on other 300- and 400-series steels.[28] The results of this study for oxidation tests carried out in 600 psig (4137 kPa) steam containing 30 ppm oxygen are given in Table 4. It can be seen that the corrosion rates are extremely sensitive to the method of surface preparation. Treatments which introduced surface cold-work resulted in a substantial decrease in corrosion rate persisting for times up to at least 2000 h. The effect of cold-work is reflected in the data reported in Table 4 for the austenitic steels. The total corrosion of mechanically treated (MT) and electropolished (EP) Type 304 with increasing temperature is shown in Fig. 8. It can be seen that as the service temperature exceeds approximately 700°F (371°C), the effect of surface preparation becomes significant and more pronounced at higher temperatures. Caplan has reported that cold-work improves the resistance of binary Fe-Cr alloys similar to Type 446 stainless steel to

TABLE 4   Defilmed Metal Weight Losses of Stainless Steel Tested at 1200°F (648°C) for 7 Days in Steam at 600 psig (4137 kPa): 30 ppm O_2[28]

Sample	Surface preparation	Defilmed metal weight loss, mg/cm²
304	Wet ground	6.6
	Electropolished	7.5
321	Wet ground	1.8
	Electropolished	9.2
316	Wet ground	0.34
	Electropolished	9.0
347	Wet ground	3.9
	Electropolished	11.2
405	Electropolished	18.9
406	Electropolished	2.0
410	Electropolished	11.4
430	Electropolished	5.0
446	Electropolished	0.34

oxidation in damp argon at 1112°F (600°C).[35] The beneficial effect of surface cold-work was still evident after long exposure time even though the metal is stress-relieved at temperature.

Board et al. observed the beneficial effect of cold-work on the oxidation resistance of Types 304, 321, and 347 steels and a 20Cr-25Ni-Nb steel in steam at atmospheric pressure over the temperature range 1022 to 1382°F (550 to 750°C).[32] It was pointed out that the oxidation resistance of austenitic stainless steels in steam was dependent on (surface) structural features which affected the rate of chromium diffusion to the alloy surface. Features which promoted the rapid diffusion of chromium to the surface assisted with the formation of protective chromium-rich oxides and good oxidation resistance. The features cited were fine grain size and a heavily cold-worked structure, which are reported to increase the rate of diffusion of chromium in the alloy. It was also observed that chromium depletion by volatilization during prior heat-treatment schedules resulted in increased oxidation rates upon subsequent exposure of samples to super-heated steam.

Oxidation kinetic and mechanistic studies have been complicated by the sensitive dependence of oxidation mechanism to microstructure. However, some general observations can be noted so that a knowledge of the practical limits of stainless steels in steam service can be indicated. At 1112°F (600°C) flowing steam (30 to 91

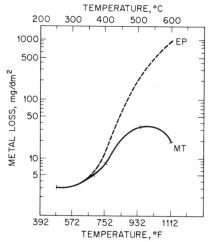

Fig. 8   Total corrosion of Type 304 in superheated steam after 1000 h; MT = mechanically treated; EP = electropolished.[31]

m/s) was observed to be approximately 1.5 times more corrosive to Type 304 than static gas; oxygen contents up to 30 ppm have no effect.[28] Flaking and loss of the outer corrosion products were severe in the dynamic (flowing steam) tests.

Comparative oxidation tests on Types 304, 316, and 347 stainless steels in superheated steam and air have shown that the steels oxidize about two to three times more in steam than in air over a wide temperature range.[33,34] Figures 9a and b show the results of comparative studies on oxidation kinetics on Types 316 and 347 steels at 1112 to 1292°F (600 to 700°C). Bittel et al. showed that the parabolic rate constants for Type 304L in steam were greater than those determined in air by a factor of 10^3.[34] Type 316 steel has been reported to be superior to Types 321, 347, and 304.[23,33,34] These grades are comparable in oxidation resistance in steam to Type 430 and are superior to Type 410. The 400 series exhibits improved corrosion resistance as the chromium content is increased, and a dramatic increase is observed as the chromium level exceeds about 16% in Types 430 and 446 (see Table 4). Type 406 has a high resistance to steam and it was assumed that the high aluminum content was responsible for reduced corrosion rates.[28]

The oxides and oxide morphologies produced on stainless steels in steam and simulated steam (water vapor-argon atmospheres) have not been clearly established. Several investigators have reported scale structures similar to the Type B scales found on alloys oxidized in air, namely, an inner spinel layer and an outer ferric oxide layer.[29,30,35] This structure was noted for Types 304 and 406 in superheated steam and on an Fe-24Cr alloy in simulated steam (Ar saturated at 77°F [25°C]). Only the spinel layer was observed on Types 316 and 347 in one atmosphere steam in the temperature range 1110 to 1290°F (598 to 697°C).[25,33] Large amounts of wustite occur on Fe-Cr alloys in simulated steam (0.1 H_2O, 0.9 Ar) at 1290 to 2010°F (697 to 1098°C) for alloys containing less than 15% chromium.[36] A characteristic scale consisting of an outer layer of wustite and a porous inner layer of wustite and Fe-Cr spinel is produced. At temperatures below 1650°F (898°C), a layer of higher oxides of iron is formed on the outer wustite scale. At 1470°F (798°C), the layer is magnetite (Fe_3O_4) and at 1290°F (697°C) hematite (Fe_2O_3) is produced on magnetite. The authors postulated that the outer wustite scale grows by cation migration and the porous inner scale by a dissociative mechanism (vapor transport mechanism). This mechanism may be important in cases where porous scales are formed on steels.

Summarizing scaling kinetics and mechanisms and oxide structures on stainless steels in steam, it appears that chromium-rich scales only grow on high-chromium steels or alloys which have received heavy surface cold-work. An Fe-Cr spinel preferentially grows on low-chromium steels and oxidation rates are controlled by diffusion of ions through this oxide. Oxidation rates may be two to three times greater in steam than in air due to the

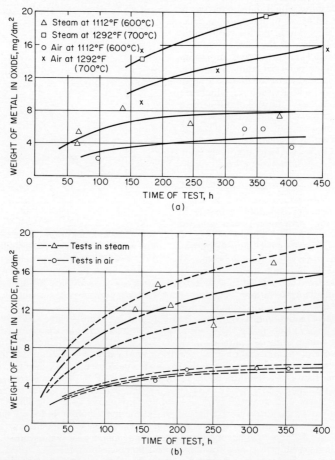

Fig. 9   (a) Oxidation of Type 316 steel in air and steam. (b) Oxidation of Type 347 steel in air and steam at 1112°F (600°C).[33]

inhibition of the growth of "Cr_2O_3" scales. In cold-worked or high-chromium steels, the formation of "Cr_2O_3" scales is promoted and oxidation rates are reduced, and, in favorable circumstances, could approach rates similar to oxidation rates in air. Wustite may occur as a major reaction product on steels of marginal chromium content (<15%) at high temperatures. Layers of magnetite and hematite atop the wustite scale are favored at lower temperatures. Oxidation rates would be substantial if wustite occurs as a major reaction product.

It is difficult to indicate uniquely the maximum service temperatures for stainless steels in steam service, especially in view of the sensitivity of corrosion rate to surface condition. It has been stated that the austenitic 18Cr-8Ni grades may be used up to 1500 to 1600°F (815 to 871°C) and Types 309, 310, and 446 at high temperatures.[28,30,31,36,37] Type 316 is superior to Types 304, 321, and 347[28,33,34] and comparable to Type 430. Types 304, 321, and 347 are being used to produce low-pressure steam at temperatures approaching 1400°F (760°C).[26] Scales on Types 304, 347, and 316 tend to exfoliate at higher temperatures (1500°F [815°C]).[38] The data reported herein suggest that the maximum service temperatures for stainless steels in steam should be reduced by 100 to 300°F (38 to 149°C) compared with the temperatures given for service in air in Tables 1 and 2. The temperatures for the lower chromium grades (Types 410, 430, 304, 316, 321, 347, and HA and HF alloys) should be reduced by the greatest amounts, i.e., 200 to 300°F (93 to 149°C) and smaller reductions (100°F [38°C]) can be tolerated for the higher chromium grades such as Types 309, 310, 446, and most of the high-chromium and high-chromium–nickel cast grades. Type 316 stainless would be preferred over Types 304, 321, and 347 of the lower chromium, austenitic grades. Type 406 might be an economical choice for some applications.

Interest in the oxidation of stainless steel in carbon dioxide and carbon dioxide/carbon

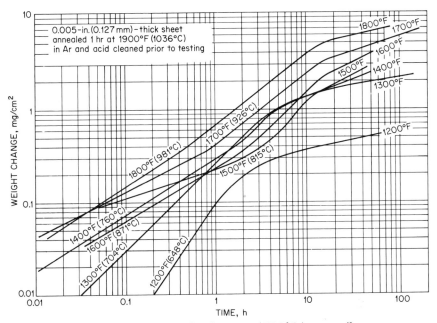

Fig. 10 Oxidation of Type 304 in carbon dioxide at 1 atm (101.3 kPa) pressure.[40]

monoxide atmospheres in the temperature range 1100 to 1800°F (593 to 981°C) has been stimulated since austenitic steels are scheduled for use in gas-cooled nuclear reactors.[39–42] Little detailed work has been conducted on the 400 series steels or binary Fe-Cr alloys except for some investigations on the effects of aluminum and yttrium additions.[22,40]

McCoy conducted a comprehensive study on the oxidation of Type 304 in carbon dioxide over the temperature range 1200 to 1800°F (648 to 981°C). The reaction kinetics were very complex demonstrating essentially protective behavior although several transitions occurred which were approximately linear. The results of the kinetic studies for one atmosphere carbon dioxide are given in Fig. 10. It was also determined that the oxidation rate of Type 304 depended on the carbon dioxide pressure over the range 40 to 200 torr (5.3 to 26.7 kPa). The effect of carbon dioxide pressure on the total corrosion of Type 304 at 1500°F (815°C) is shown in Fig. 11. A rapid increase in scaling rate occurs at approximately 40 torr (5.3 kPa) and rates are insensitive to pressure above about 200 torr (26.7 kPa). The steel is carburized in carbon dioxide at these temperatures and the effect of pressure is also noted in Fig. 11 (carburization will be discussed below in a later section).

McCoy found in his tests that the oxide scale was primarily ferric oxide, "Fe_2O_3", at 1200°F (648°C). At 1300 to 1800°F (704 to 981°C) the major oxides were spinel and "Fe_2O_3". These scales are similar to the Type B scales observed in air oxidation (see above). Oxidation rates were less for cold-worked material, however, the rates were similar to annealed material after 100 h at temperature. Draycott and Smith noted the formation of chromic oxide "Cr_2O_3" on cold-worked surfaces of Type 321 steel oxidized at 1020 to 1290°F (549 to 697°C) in carbon dioxide; cold-worked surfaces were more resistant than etched surfaces. A multilayered scale was formed in the latter case.[43] Board and Winterborne also observed significantly lower oxidation rates for cold-worked surfaces of Types 316 and 347 steels oxidized for long terms in carbon dioxide: 1 vol % carbon

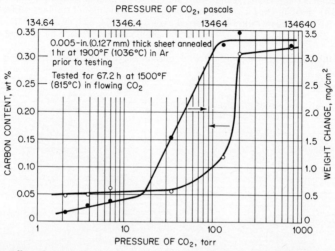

Fig. 11   Effect of carbon dioxide pressure on the carburization and oxidation of Type 304 at 1500°F (815°C).[40]

monoxide at 1202°F (650°C) and 1292°F (700°C) and 400 and 600 psig (2758 and 4137 kPa).[44] They noted that there were essentially no differences in weight gains in wet and dry gas and at pressures of 400 and 600 psig (2758 and 4137 kPa). The latter observation agrees with the high-pressure work of McCoy in carbon dioxide at 1500°F (815°C).[40] The weight gain data of Board and Winterborne were also similar when the results for cold-worked and solution-treated steels were taken into account. The oxidation of cold-worked Types 316 and 347 in carbon dioxide resulted in the formation of protective "Cr_2O_3" scales.[44] Less protective spinel oxide was formed on solution-treated material and an iron-rich oxide grew atop this scale, similar to the Type B scales noted above.

Protective scales of "Cr_2O_3" and spinel oxides are formed on 20Cr-25Ni steels in carbon dioxide over the range 1280 to 1560°F (692 to 849°C).[39-41] Weight gains were very low (0.1 and 0.2 mg/cm² after 100 h at 1380°F (748°C) and 1560°F (849°C), respectively). The better resistance compared with Type 304 steel was attributed to the formation of protective "Cr_2O_3" films. It appears that the higher nickel concentration promoted the formation of protective "Cr_2O_3" scales.

Type 406 stainless steel is highly resistant to carbon dioxide at 1700°F (926°C); a protective "Al_2O_3" film was the only oxide observed.[40] Francis and Jutson observed that a Fe-15Cr-4Al-1Y alloy (essentially Type 406 with 1% Y) had outstanding resistance to carbon dioxide as shown in Fig. 12. The authors noted external scales of "Al_2O_3" and an Fe-Cr spinel ($FeCr_2O_4$). The yttrium was considered to form Y_2O_3 only and probably existed as internal oxide. It was concluded that oxidation rates were low due to the slow diffusion of aluminum ions through the "Al_2O_3" film.

The available data on the oxidation kinetics of stainless steels in carbon dioxide atmospheres indicate that oxidation rates are slightly greater than in air.[40] The higher Cr-Ni steels tend to form highly protective "Cr_2O_3" scales rather than less protective spinel-ferric oxide scales. Thus, it would appear that the service temperature limits reported in Tables 1 and 2 should be revised slightly downwards by 100 to 200°F (38 to 93°C) for the low-chromium and Cr-Ni steels (e.g., Types 410, 430, 302, 321, 316, and 347). The high-chromium and Cr-Ni steels could be used close to their listed service temperature (Types

309, 310, 330, and most of the cast steels). High-aluminum-bearing steels give good service in carbon dioxide.

Effects of Impurities   In most studies on the oxidation properties of commercial stainless steels, the effects of trace or minor elements are often overlooked. These elements may affect the rate-controlling reactions producing important changes in corrosion behavior. Solution of trace elements in protective scales may influence film breakdown or the mechanical properties of the scale.

The effect of silicon on oxidation resistance has been studied under a variety of

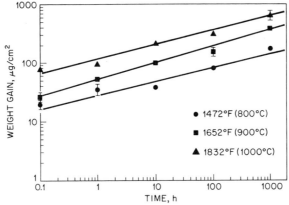

Fig. 12   Oxidation of an Fe-15Cr-4Al-1Y alloy in 1 atm (101.3 kPa) CO_2.[22]

conditions; the protective nature and subsequent breakdown of scales formed on a Type 446 steel containing 0.44% silicon has been attributed to the formation of silica films at the metal-oxide interface.[10,12,13] In a recent note, Caplan and Cohen illustrated that 0.5% silicon in pure Fe-26Cr alloys does not improve oxidation resistance.[45] Francis,[46] however, found a sharp increase in oxidation rate in carbon dioxide when silicon was removed from a 20Cr-25Ni steel; this investigator postulated that silicon assisted in the growth of a chromium-rich oxide film.

Mangone et al. indicated that the presence of 1% silicon in an experimental cast stainless steel, containing nominally 25Cr-30Ni with the balance essentially iron, did not significantly affect oxidation rate. However, when manganese was added to the alloy system, the presence of silicon was beneficial.[47] The improved cyclic oxidation resistance of the higher silicon-bearing Type 302B steel compared with Type 302 is evident in Fig. 6. In general, it appears that higher silicon contents are beneficial in commercial stainless steels when held within the ranges specified for the different grades.

Manganese has been found to be a deleterious element in Type 446[45] and in a 20Cr-25Ni steel.[46] A pure Fe-26Cr-1Mn alloy oxidized at the same rate as a Type 446 steel containing 0.75% manganese; both rates were greater than the pure binary (Fe-Cr) alloy. A spinel oxide ($MnO \cdot Cr_2O_3$) occurs at the expense of the protective "Cr_2O_3" film.

The additions of 0.8 and 5% manganese to the experimental cast stainless steel noted above containing nominally 0.5C-25Cr-30Ni-bal Fe, and referred to below as "cast experimental stainless steel," also caused a significant increase in alloy oxidation rate.[47] The lower recommended service temperatures given for Types 201 and 303 in Table 1 further indicate the detrimental effect of manganese on oxidation behavior. Therefore, it can be concluded that manganese additions to stainless steels cannot be recommended for good oxidation resistance and should be controlled to the lowest level possible.

Small quantities of molybdenum are not deleterious; however, large additions can lead to catastrophic failure of the oxide.[48,49] Extreme conditions depend on the molybdenum and chromium contents and temperature. Studies of the effect of molybdenum additions to a cast experimental stainless steel showed that additions of up to 4% molybdenum only slightly lowered the oxidation resistance of the alloy at 2200°F (1204°C). In addition, the temperature limits suggested for molybdenum-bearing Types 316 and 317 compare favorably with those given for Type 304. The information available indicates that molybdenum additions of up to 5% can be tolerated in commercial stainless steels without undue sacrifice in oxidation resistance.

Mangone et al. studied the effects of 1.5 and 2.5% Ti and 2% Nb additions on the oxidation resistance of a cast experimental stainless steel at 2200°F (1204°C).[47] Oxidation resistance was reduced by these additions, and niobium additions were more detrimental than titanium additions. These data and the temperature limits noted in Table 1 for Types 302, 304, 321, and 347 point out that while small additions of niobium and titanium (<1%) do not impair the oxidation resistance of stainless steels in general, larger additions should be avoided. A summary of the test results on the effects of manganese, silicon, molybdenum, titanium, and niobium on the oxidation resistance of the cast experimental stainless steel is given in Table 5.

Aluminum additions significantly improve the oxidation resistance of stainless steels when present in sufficient quantities to form aluminum-rich films (Al_2O_3 or aluminum-bearing spinels). Ruther and Greenburg showed that Type 406 stainless steel containing about 4.5% aluminum was considerably more resistant to superheated steam than other steels with similar chromium contents.[29] As noted above, McCoy demonstrated that this steel was also highly resistant to oxidation in carbon dioxide at 1700°F (926°C) owing to the formation of an "Al_2O_3" film.[40] Chalk has reported the outstanding oxidation resistance of a proprietary stainless steel containing, typically, 0.04C-0.3Mn-0.02P-0.01S-1.0Si-18.0Cr-0.3Ni-0.4Ti-2.0Al-bal Fe, for 100-h tests in static air over the temperature range 1400 to 2400°F (760 to 1315°C). This steel oxidized much less than Types 304, 430, 442, and 446 particularly at temperatures exceeding 1800 to 2000°F (981 to 1093°C).[50] Mangone et al.[47] also reported improved oxidation resistance of their "experimental cast stainless steel" after aluminum additions were made. However, Krainer et al.[51] noted that "Cr_2O_3" scales are preferred when cyclic conditions are encountered.

It can be positively concluded that aluminum additions to wrought and cast stainless steels improve general oxidation resistance particularly for isothermal conditions.[48] The highest additions possible without seriously degrading other properties should be considered. Additions of 1 to 3% could be made to most wrought alloys and higher levels could be considered for cast alloys not required to meet specifications other than corrosion resistance.

The additions of small quantities of rare earth elements and yttrium improve the oxidation of binary Fe-Cr alloys[52] and rare earth additions to ternary alloys also increase oxidation resistance.[51,53] Cyclic oxidation resistance in particular is improved because of the external scale keying effect of rare earth or yttrium oxide subscale precipitates. It is suggested that greater advantage be taken of rare earth additions to stainless steels for improved oxidation resistance.

Reaction with Sulfidizing Gases

Reaction with sulfur-bearing gases is another common form of high-temperature corrosion. Alloys react with sulfur in the form of hydrogen sulfide, sulfur dioxide, or sulfur vapor to produce sulfides, oxides, or sulfur-oxygen compounds with one or more of the alloying elements. Complex reaction products may form on a steel during high-temperature corrosion in sulfur dioxide since two competing reactions may occur:

$$SO_2 + M \rightarrow MS + O_2$$
$$SO_2 + 2M \rightarrow 2MO + S$$

In hydrogen sulfide atmospheres, hydrogen is evolved, and reaction takes place in a

TABLE 5   Effect of Various Minor Elements on the Oxidation Resistance of a Cast Stainless Steel[47]

| | Intended composition, wt % | | | | | | | Average metal loss, g* |
C	Cr	Ni	Si	Mn	Mo	Nb	Ti	
0.5	25	30	1	0.8				0.1147
0.5	25	30	2	0.8				0.1060
0.5	25	30	1	0.8	2			0.1285
0.5	25	30	1	0.8	4		1.5	0.1459
0.5	25	30	1	5				0.1569
0.5	25	30	1	0.8		2		0.1577

*Based on descaled metal weight loss after exposure of coupons for 100 h in air at 2200°F (1204°C).

reducing environment. Fundamentally, the same features described above for alloy oxidation apply to the formation of sulfide scales.[95]

Reaction Kinetics   It is sufficient to note that the empirical rate equations noted above for oxidation reactions apply equally well to the formation of sulfide scales. Often the linear rate equation holds due to the porous nature of many metal sulfide scales. In some cases, the parabolic law is obeyed when compact scales are formed. It is generally observed that sulfide scales formed on metals and alloys contain much higher defect concentrations compared with oxides, and therefore, corrosion rates are much greater for similar thermal conditions.[95]

Sulfidation Mechanisms   The mechanisms of sulfidation of metals and alloys have yet to be explored in detail. Most studies have been confined to pure metals.[1,2] Fundamental investigations have been hampered because the number of stable sulfides is much greater than that of oxides; the low melting points of metal sulfides and metal-sulfide eutectics have complicated matters. In sulfur dioxide, metal sulfates, sulfides, and oxides may be formed. Sulfides formed by reaction with sulfur or hydrogen sulfide are usually more voluminous than corresponding oxides, and porous or cracked scales are generated.

The scales formed on stainless steels in sulfur-bearing oxidizing gases (SO_2) are generally oxides. "Cr_2O_3" is formed if the oxygen potential and steel chromium content are high whereas duplex scales are formed under other conditions. One general feature characteristic of the oxidation of stainless steels in sulfur dioxide is the formation of internal chromium sulfide precipitates in the alloy at the metal-scale interface. Internal sulfidation further reduces the chromium content of the steel at the interface and oxidation rates are, in general, increased compared with reaction in air.

The sulfide scale formed in reducing atmospheres on stainless steels containing less than 20% chromium (Types 304, 410, 430) is primarily iron sulfide ("FeS").[54-56] At low chromium contents, the scale may be duplex, consisting of an inner layer of iron sulfide containing appreciable amounts of dissolved chromium and an outer layer of "pure" iron sulfide. Higher chromium contents approaching the 20% level promote the formation of the single-layered scale of iron sulfide containing chromium in solution.[56] The development of chromium sulfides is promoted on alloys containing more than 20% chromium. These sulfides may give rise to complex stratified scales containing layers of CrS, Cr_2S_3, FeS, and FeS_2.[57,59] It is generally accepted that the transport of iron or chromium ions through the sulfide layers is the rate-controlling step. The low-melting-point nickel–nickel sulfide eutectic may form on the austenitic steels containing greater than 25% nickel unless chromium is present in high concentrations. The occurrence of molten phases during high-temperature service leads to catastrophic destruction of the alloy. It is impossible to present a section of the modes of sulfide scale formation on stainless steels since the details of sulfidation mechanisms are few. Most data refer to practical situations and are discussed in the following sections.

Practical Considerations

Reaction with Sulfur Dioxide   Stainless steels containing more than 18 to 20% chromium are resistant to dry sulfur dioxide. However, reaction rates are higher than in air.[59-62] In 24-h tests over the temperature range 1100 to 1600°F (593 to 871°C), only a heavy (tarnish) film was formed on Type 316 in atmospheres varying from 100% oxygen to 100% sulfur dioxide.[63] Moist sulfur dioxide is more corrosive than dry gas and the effect is illustrated by the data given in Table 6 for the oxidation of Type 302 stainless steel in sulfur dioxide at 1650°F (898°C) for 24 h. The recommended upper service temperatures for a number of wrought stainless steels are shown in Table 7. The effectiveness of higher chromium content on increasing the service temperatures is apparent. The cast stainless steels of comparable composition can be used at the service temperatures indicated. It should be noted that the high-nickel cast stainless steels (HT, HU, HW, HX) are not recommended for oxidizing atmospheres containing large concentrations of sulfur, and therefore, should not be used in atmospheres containing large amounts of sulfur dioxide.

Reaction with Hydrogen Sulfide   Much of the recent data concerning high-temperature corrosion of stainless steels by hydrogen sulfide has stemmed from the use of these steels in catalytic reformers and desulfurizers; therefore, published information is given for hydrogen–hydrogen sulfide atmospheres. However, it was shown in an earlier

TABLE 6   Oxidation of Type 302 Stainless Steel in Sulfur Dioxide at 1650°F (898°C) for 24 h[64]

Condition	Weight gain, mg/cm²
Atmosphere	46
Atmosphere + 2% SO_2	113
Atmosphere + 5% SO_2 + 5% H_2O	358

study[65] that chromium and Cr-Ni stainless steels are rapidly corroded at high temperatures in 100% hydrogen sulfide, as reported in Table 8. The data indicate the beneficial effect of increasing the chromium content of steels to values greater than 12 to 15%. Incremental additions of chromium up to approximately 25% impart progressively greater resistance. Nickel contents up to 20% do not appear to be detrimental in the presence of high chromium contents (20 to 25%); experience has shown that higher nickel contents are deleterious (unless the chromium concentration is raised to 50 to 60%) and that the high-nickel cast stainless steels (namely, HT, HU, HW, and HX) should definitely not be used in hydrogen sulfide atmospheres. The data in Table 9 for corrosion studies on three austenitic steels in a 50 vol % H_2–50 vol % H_2S atmosphere show that the service temperatures can be raised slightly as the hydrogen sulfide concentration in the gas is reduced (compare with data in Table 8 for 100% H_2S). The beneficial effect of aluminum diffusion coatings (which greatly enrich the sample surface in aluminum) is also noted in Table 9. The results show that the upper limit for stainless steels in 50% H_2S atmospheres is approximately 950°F (510°C) and that Type 310 stainless steel is the favored grade. Aluminum diffusion coatings would permit service temperatures to be increased to 1300°F (704°C). Further reductions in hydrogen sulfide content would give rise to lower corrosion rates. The data in Table 10 show that for only 2 vol % H_2S in hydrogen at one atmosphere pressure, corrosion rates are very low over the temperature range 650 to 850°F (343 to 454°C).

Backensto et al.[68] and Sorell and Hoyt[54] have reported data for a wide range of operating conditions which might be encountered in catalytic reformers and desulfurizers. Table 11 gives a comparison of the performance of the 400- and 300-series stainless steels over the temperature range 950 to 1390°F (510 to 752°C) and hydrogen sulfide contents of 0.05 to 0.80 vol % based on laboratory data. At 1390°F (752°C) none of the steels has sufficient corrosion resistance for practical use except at very low hydrogen sulfide contents. At approximately 1000°F (538°C), the 16% Cr, 26% Cr, and the austenitic Cr-Ni steels corrode at approximately the same rate. At higher temperatures, the straight-chromium steels are corroded at considerably higher rates.

Tests on manganese-modified steels (Type 202) revealed that hydrogen sulfide corrosion rates were equivalent to the conventional austenitic steels up to 900°F (482°C), but higher above this temperature.[68] Merrick and Mantell[69] inferred that Types 201 and 202 would not be more resistant than the conventional austenitic steels.

The 18Cr-8Ni stainless steels have been used extensively in industry to combat hydrogen–hydrogen sulfide atmospheres at high pressures.[54] Figure 13 demonstrates the effect of hydrogen sulfide content and temperature on the corrosion rate of austenitic Cr-Ni steels in general.

It is apparent from the data presented that stainless steels are limited for service in hydrogen sulfide atmospheres. Temperatures must be restricted to 1000 to 1100°F (538 to

TABLE 7   Recommended Maximum Service Temperatures in Sulfur Dioxide for Selected Stainless Steels

Material	Temperature	
type	°C	°F
304	800	1472
321	800	1472
347	800	1472
310	1050	1922
410	700	1292
430	800	1472
446	1025	1875

TABLE 8   Corrosion Rates of Chromium and Chromium-Nickel Steels in 100% H₂S at Atmospheric Pressure (120-h Test)[65]

| | Corrosion rate, mils/yr (mm/yr) | |
Material	400°C	500°C
5% Cr steel	240 (6.1)	1000 (25.4)
9% Cr steel	200 (5.08)	700 (17.8)
410	130 (3.30)	400 (10.2)
430	90 (2.29)	200 (5.08)
446		100 (2.54)
304	80 (2.03)	200 (5.08)
310	60 (1.52)	100 (2.54)

TABLE 9   Sulfidation Rates of Austenitic Stainless Steels in 50 vol % H₂—50 vol % H₂S at Atmospheric Pressure (150-h Tests)[66]

| Material type | Corrosion rate, mils/yr (mm/yr) | | | |
	500°C (932°F)	550°C (1022°F)	600°C (1112°F)	700°C (1292°F)
304	44 (1.13)	62 (1.58)	116 (2.95)	400 (10.16)
310	36 (0.91)	57 (1.45)	110 (2.79)	352 (8.94)
316	59 (1.5)	96 (2.44)	175 (4.45)	424 (10.77)
	ALUMINUM DIFFUSION-COATED SAMPLES			
304			7 (0.18)	33 (0.84)
310			3 (0.08)	27 (0.69)
316			4 (0.10)	29 (0.74)

593°C) unless the hydrogen sulfide content of the gas is controlled to very low levels, in which case, service temperatures could be increased to 1300 to 1400°F (704 to 760°C). The high-chromium-bearing grades are preferred for hydrogen sulfide service, and nickel contents up to 20% are favorable in the presence of high chromium content (25 to 30%). The high-nickel cast stainless steels should not be used in hydrogen sulfide.

Reaction with Sulfur Vapor   Chromium and Cr-Ni stainless steels are attacked readily by sulfur vapor at temperatures approaching 1000°F (538°C) as shown in Tables 12 and 13. Increased resistance is obtained by increasing the chromium content to more than 20%. The higher Cr-Ni grades (310, 314) give good service around 1000 to 1200°F (538 to 648°C). Use of the high-nickel cast steels (HT, HU, HW, HX) should again be avoided. The high silicon content of Type 314 stainless steel seems to be beneficial (Table 12). West[72] has indicated that Type 310 is the best selection of the austenitic steels for sulfur vapor service up to 1300°F (704°C). Krebs[26] has reported that Type 310 tubes have been used in chemical plants for heating sulfur to about 1100°F (593°C).

Reaction in Flue and Process Gases
Effect of Sulfur in Flue and Process Gases. It is extremely difficult to generalize corrosion rates in flue and process gases. The gas composition and temperature may vary

TABLE 10   Corrosion Rates of Alloys Exposed on Hydrotreating Test Rack [2 vol % H₂S; 0.5 to 1.0 vol % NH₃, balance H₂; 2254 h at 650 to 850°F (343 to 454°C)][67]

Material type	Corrosion rate, mils/yr (mm/yr)
410	86.9 (2.31)
430	21.9 (0.56)
446	8.7 (0.22)
304	4.8 (0.12)
316	1.7 (0.04)
321	1.7 (0.04)
347	2.1 (0.05)
309	4.2 (0.11)
310	2.3 (0.06)

TABLE 11 Corrosion Rates of 300- and 400-Series Stainless Steels in Hydrogen–Hydrogen Sulfide Atmospheres[68]

Test Conditions:

Temperature, °F	950	960	970	985	1120	1390	1390
(°C)	(510)	(515)	(520)	(530)	(604)	(752)	(752)
H$_2$ pressure, psig	175	845	485	485	485	185	185
(kPa)	(1207)	(5826)	(3344)	(3344)	(3344)	(1276)	(1276)
H$_2$S conc, vol %	0.10	0.80	0.75	0.05	0.05	0.05	0.15
Time, h	598	461	234	222	415	458	468

Material type	Corrosion rate, mils/yr (mm/yr)						
405(12Cr)	75 (1.91)						180 (4.57)
410(12Cr)		220 (5.59)	190 (4.83)	300 (7.62)	100 (2.54)	13 (0.33)	160 (4.06)
430(16Cr)		39 (0.99)	30 (0.76)	60 (1.52)		16 (0.41)	240 (6.10)
446(26Cr)	10 (0.25)	15 (0.38)	16 (0.41)	42 (1.07)	41 (1.04)	76 (1.93)	230 (5.84)
Cr-Ni steels	7 (0.18)	23 (0.58)	27 (0.69)	40 (1.02)	12	5 (0.13)	65 (1.65)

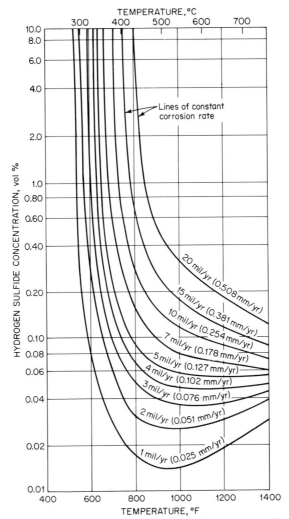

Fig. 13 Effect of temperature and hydrogen sulfide content on the corrosion rate of austenitic stainless steels (pressure range is 175 to 500 psig [1207 to 3447 kPa], exposure times greater than 150).[70]

TABLE 12   Corrosion of Stainless Steels in Sulfur Vapor at 1060°F (571°C)

Material type	Corrosion rate* mils/yr (mm/yr)
314	16.9 (0.43)
310	18.9 (0.48)
309	22.3 (0.57)
304	27.0 (0.69)
302B	29.8 (0.76)
316	31.1 (0.79)
321	54.8 (1.39)

*Corrosion rates based on 1295-h tests, International Nickel Company data.

TABLE 13   Effect of Temperature on the Corrosion Resistance of High-Chromium Steel (Type 446) to Sulfur Vapor (24-h Tests)[71]

Temperature		Corrosion rate	
°C	°F	mils/yr	mm/yr
295	560	9	0.23
360	680	9	0.23
455	850	28	0.71
575	1070	46	1.17
700	1290	102	2.59
820	1510	310	7.87
880	1620	580	14.73

considerably in the same process unit. White[8] and Collins[73] have expressed the necessity for field tests.

Combustion gases normally contain sulfur compounds and will generate approximately 0.0016 vol % SO_2 or H_2S for each grain (65 mg) of sulfur per 100 ft³ (2.83 m³) of flue gas. Combustion gases of a fuel oil containing 0.7 wt % S would have, for example, 60 grains (3900 mg) of sulfur per 100 ft³ (2.83 m³). Hydrogen sulfide and sulfur dioxide levels would rarely exceed 0.5 vol % in flue gases. Sulfur dioxide is present in an oxidizing gas along with carbon dioxide, nitrogen, water vapor, and excess oxygen. Protective oxides are generally formed, and depending on exact conditions and sulfur content, the corrosion rate may be approximately the same as in air[74] or slightly greater. This refers to clean oxidizing combustion atmospheres in the absence of corrosive fuel-ash products. The resistance of stainless steels to normal combustion gases is increased by successive increments in chromium content, as shown in Fig. 14. Table 14 indicates the beneficial effect of chromium and the influence of fuel source. Corrosion rates of 1 to 2 mils/yr (0.025 to 0.051 mm/yr) have been reported for Types 304, 321, 347, and 316 in the temperature range 1200 to 1400°F (648 to 760°C). High-nickel–chromium steels, such as Types 309 and 310, are often used in more aggressive atmospheres.

Reducing flue gases contain various amounts of hydrogen sulfide, hydrogen, water vapor, carbon monoxide, carbon dioxide, and nitrogen but no free oxygen. The corrosion rates encountered in these environments are sensitive to hydrogen sulfide content and temperature, and satisfactory material selection often necessitates service tests. For example, Guthrie and Merrick[75] reported that commercial steam-reforming tubes of Type 310 steel could accept feed stocks containing about 2.5 wt % sulfur even though hydrogen

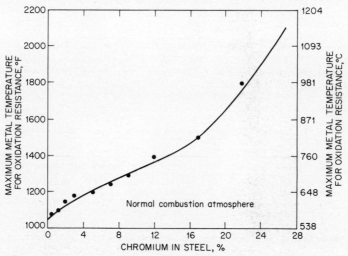

Fig. 14   Effect of chromium on the oxidation resistance of steel in a normal combustion atmosphere.[26]

TABLE 14   Corrosion Rate of Stainless Steels in Flue Gases (Exposure 3 months)[8]

Material type	Corrosion rate, mils/yr (mm/yr)		
	Coke oven gas [1500°F (815°C)]	Coke oven gas [1800°F (981°C)]	Natural gas [1500°F (815°C)]
430	91 (2.31)	236 (5.99)†	12 (0.30)
446(26 Cr)	30 (0.76)	40 (1.02)	4 (0.10)
446(28 Cr)	27 (0.69)	14 (0.36)	3 (0.07)
302B	104 (2.64)	225 (5.72)	
309S	37 (0.94)*	45 (1.14)	3 (0.07)
310S	38 (0.97)*	25 (0.64)	3 (0.07)
314	23 (0.58)*	94 (2.39)	3 (0.07)

*Pitted specimens, average pit depth.
†Specimens destroyed.

sulfide was present in the effluent gas. These investigators concluded that either the steam in the feed gas maintained oxidizing conditions in the high-temperature zone or a protective coke film formed a barrier between the tube and feed. Thus, corrosion rates for stainless steels in reducing, hydrogen sulfide-bearing flue gases are not expected to be as high for hydrogen sulfide–hydrogen atmospheres at equivalent hydrogen sulfide contents because of the presence of oxidizing species (CO_2/H_2O) in the former.

Jackson et al.[76] conducted an extensive study on the corrosion resistance of cast stainless steel in oxidizing and reducing flue gases containing various sulfur levels and the work has been summarized by Schoefer.[77] In reducing flue gas (no free oxygen) up to 100 gS (6500 mg) (grains of sulfur per 100 ft³ (2.83 m³) of gas) did not affect corrosion rates at 1800°F (981°C) until the alloy nickel content exceeded 20%. Higher chromium contents were required to maintain low corrosion rates until the nickel content approached 65% where a smaller amount of chromium was required. Thus, HC, HD, HE, HF, HH, HK and the higher nickel HU and HX alloys performed well. HT and HW would be poor choices. When the sulfur content was adjusted to 300 to 500 gS (19,500 to 32,500 mg), only the HL, HD, HE, and HH alloys offered reasonable scaling resistance and the high-nickel alloys were rapidly attacked. At 500 gS (32,500 mg) only the HC, HD, and HE alloys can be considered. However, the resistance to attack by these alloys at 1800°F (981°C) is limited.

The oxidation behavior of cast stainless steels at 1800°F (981°C) in an oxidizing flue gas containing up to 100 gS (6500 mg) is similar to air. In a 300 gS (19,500 mg) atmosphere, HC, HD, HE, HH and HK alloys would give good service.

The corrosion rates for several of the cast stainless steels for service in air and oxidizing and reducing flue gases containing 5 and 100 gS (325 and 6500 mg) are given in Table 15. The high corrosion rates of the low-chromium–high-nickel HT and HW alloys in the 100 gS (6500 mg) reducing flue gas should be noted. The high rates are attributed to the formation of a low-melting-point metal-metal sulfide eutectic.

Jackson et al.[76] also studied the effects of cyclic temperature and various alloy additions to cast stainless steels on flue-gas corrosion. Cyclic temperature did not seriously affect corrosion rates for alloys containing more than 20% nickel in an oxidizing atmosphere containing 100 gS (6500 mg). Cyclic temperatures under reducing conditions caused more metal loss in the higher nickel alloys. Higher silicon levels (1.5 to 2.5%) and aluminum additions of about 1% were beneficial in reducing corrosion rates. Vanadium and molybdenum additions increased the rate of attack slightly.

Reaction with Other Gases

Carburizing Gases   Stainless steels will react with hydrocarbon or carbonaceous gases at elevated temperature. Carbon is absorbed, and subsequently diffuses into the alloy interior. Carbides of the most reactive alloying additions (Cr, Nb, Ti) are precipitated in the steel matrix and grain boundaries. The reaction is broadly termed carburization and the usual effects are reductions in ductility and impact properties depending on the degree and distribution of absorbed carbon. Also, subsequent exposure of a severely chromium-depleted steel to an oxidizing gas results in very high oxidation rates. The extent of carburization is a function of the alloy content, temperature, service time, and the chemistry of the environment. Carburization has been observed to occur in hydro-

TABLE 15 Oxidation Resistance of Cast Stainless Steels in Air, Oxidizing and Reducing Flue Gases at 2000°F[8]
(Expressed as mils per year [millimeters per year] metal loss) (gS = grains of S [mg] per 100 ft³ [2.83 m³])

ACI grade	Cr-Ni	In air	Oxidizing flue gas		Reducing flue gas	
			5 gS (325)	100 gS (6500)	5 gS (325)	100 gS (6500)
HH	26-12	40–90 (1.016–2.286)	50–70 (1.270–1.778)	40–100 (1.016–2.54)	20–50 (0.508–1.270)	30 (0.762)
HI	28-15	30–50 (0.762–1.270)	20–50 (0.508–1.270)	40 (1.016)	20 (0.508)	30 (0.762)
HK	26-20	40 (1.016)	50 (1.270)	40 (1.016)	20–50 (0.508–1.270)	30 (0.762)
HL	30-20	40 (1.016)	50 (1.270)	40–50 (1.016–1.270)	20 (0.508)	30 (0.762)
HT	15-35	50 (1.270)	60–300 (1.524–7.62)	100–500 (2.54–12.70)	50–200 (1.270–5.08)	300–800 (7.62–20.32)
HU	18-38	40–50 (1.016–1.270)	40–60 (1.016–1.524)	40–100 (1.016–2.54)	20–50 (0.508–1.270)	20–30 (0.508–0.762)
HW	12-60	30–50 (0.762–1.270)	40–60 (1.016–1.524)	30–70 (0.762–1.778)	20–30 (0.508–0.762)	100–700 (2.54–17.78)
HX	18-65	30 (0.762)	30 (0.762)	30–40 (0.762–1.016)	20 (0.508)	20–50 (0.508–1.270)

TABLE 16   Pack Carburization Tests*,[74]

Material type	Composition	Si content, %	Increase in bulk carbon content, %
330	15Cr-35Ni	0.47	0.23
330	15Cr-35Ni + Si	1.00	0.08
310	25Cr-20Ni	0.38	0.02
314	25Cr-20Ni + Si	2.25	0.03
309	25Cr-12Ni	0.25	0.12
347	18Cr-8Ni + Nb	0.74	0.57
321	18Cr-8Ni + Ti	0.49	0.59
304	18Cr-8Ni	0.39	1.40
302B	18Cr-8Ni + Si	2.54	0.22
446	28Cr	0.34	0.07
430	16Cr	0.36	1.03

*40 cycles of 25 h at 1800°F (981°C).

carbons, carbon monoxide–carbon dioxide atmospheres, pure carbon dioxide and molten metals containing dissolved carbon.

Of the elements present in stainless steels, field experience and laboratory tests have demonstrated that carburization resistance depends on chromium content. Carburization is reduced as chromium is progressively increased. Table 16 indicates the increase in carbon content of wrought chromium and Cr-Ni steels obtained in pack carburizing tests at 1800°F (981°C). Comparison of Types 430 and 446 illustrates the effectiveness of chromium. Minor alloying additions also influence the degree of carbon absorption. Silicon, titanium, and niobium retard carburization as shown in Table 16. Increasing quantities of nickel are advantageous in carburizing systems. The effect of nickel is illustrated in Table 16 (see Type 330) and in Fig. 15. Common selections for high-temperature service in carburizing atmospheres are Types 309, 310, and 330. Type 321 is reported to be slightly more resistant than Types 304, 316, and 347.[79]

Chromium is also beneficial in reducing the rate of carburization of cast stainless steels. However, high nickel contents are preferred, as shown by the data for HC, HH, HK, HT, and HW alloys in Fig. 16. The results of an Alloy Casting Institute (Division of Steel Founders' Society of America) survey showed, for alloy coupons exposed for 1000 h at 1700°F (926°C) in a carrier gas with 2% methane, that HH and HK alloys were extensively carburized whereas the higher nickel alloys (HN, HT, HU, HW and HX) were little affected.[80] The beneficial effect of increased silicon content was also noted. Industry has generally recognized that the HT, HU, HW, and HX alloys in increasing order of resistance are the best selections for combating severe carburizing conditions; and high silicon contents are preferred.

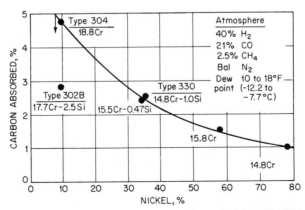

Fig. 15 Effect of nickel on gas carburization of 15% Cr steels at 1785°F (975°C), 1500 h. (*International Nickel Co.*)

Little work has been done to determine the effects of microstructure on carburization resistance parallel to the findings on the effects of grain size and cold-work on oxidation resistance noted above. English[81] has reported on the effect of grain structure on the carburization resistance of centrifugally cast HK alloys at 1922°F (1050°C). Figure 17 shows that after long exposure times, alloys with a columnar grain structure are more resistant to carburization than those with an equiaxed grain structure.

Carburization of stainless steels oxidized in carbon monoxide–carbon dioxide atmospheres and pure carbon dioxide has been reported.[39,40,42,62] These gases are normally

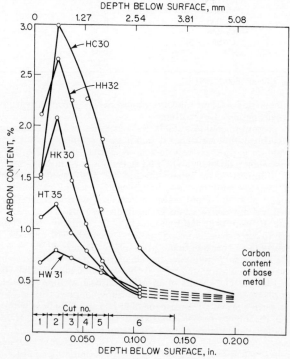

Fig. 16   Heat-resistant-alloy—carbon penetration after pack carburizing at 1800°F (981°C) for 100 h. (*Adapted from Avery.*[78])

considered noncarburizing. Two mechanisms have been presented to account for the occurrence of carburization. Jepson et al.[83] suggested that carbon is deposited on compact oxide surfaces and then is transferred through the oxide to the alloy by a diffusion mechanism. There is some doubt as to the origin of carbon deposition. On the other hand, McCoy[40] has postulated that a porous oxide in the outer scale provides pockets for accumulation of carbon monoxide. Conditions near the metal surface become reducing as well as oxidizing and carburization occurs. Both mechanisms may be valid, since the oxide is compact in one case and porous in the other.

The nature of the oxide formed in carbon-oxygen atmospheres definitely influences the tendency for stainless steel to carburize. Martin and Weir[84] have shown that the formation of oxides rich in "Cr_2O_3" impedes carburization. Figure 18 illustrates the effect of chromium content on the carburization of a 9% Ni steel in carbon dioxide. When the chromium content exceeds approximately 11%, "Cr_2O_3" is established as the primary oxide and carburization decreases. McCoy[70] noted that no detectable carburization occurred in Type 406 steel due to the formation of a very protective "Al_2O_3" film. This author also concluded that more than 25% chromium would be required in the absence of aluminum to suppress carburization, in agreement with Fig. 18.

Another form of metal deterioration encountered in carburizing gases (with or without

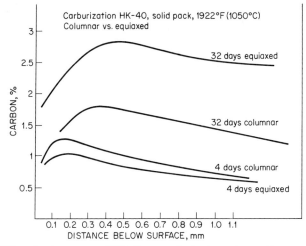

Fig. 17 Effect of grain structure of HK alloy on carburization resistance.[81]

oxygen-bearing components) at elevated temperature occurs by the metal-dusting phenomenon.[85,86] Corrosion is generally limited to the temperature range 800 to 1500°F (426 to 815°C) and alloy attack occurs by localized pitting or overall surface wastage. The corrosion products consist of dust or powder containing metal carbides, metal oxides, and graphite. Carburization of the surfaces from which the metal is lost is usually observed. Of a number of stainless steels exposed to atmospheres which cause metal dusting, none was found to be immune to this type of attack over long exposure times.[86] Prange[87] has noted that under similar metal-dusting conditions Types 310, 316, and 302B steels are more resistant than Types 304, 321, and 347.

Several mechanisms have been proposed to explain metal dusting. Hoyt and Caughey proposed that carbon, produced by catalytic decomposition of carbon monoxide at iron- or nickel-rich sites on the alloy surface, enters the steel forming chromium carbide initially at grain-boundary sites and eventually in the matrix.[85] An appreciable density change occurs so that the surface grains are either disintegrated or detached from the steel at grain boundaries. Mechanisms based on volatile carbonyl formation[88] and alternate cycles of carburization and oxidation[89] have been proposed.

Hydrogen Attack by hydrogen may be encountered in ammonia synthesis, hydrodesulfurization, hydrogenation, and oil refining equipment (see Chap. 44). Carbon steels are inadequate for high-pressure hydrogen systems at temperatures exceeding approximately 450°F (232°C). Although the mechanism is not fully understood, various authorities believe that hydrogen diffuses into the steel and reacts with iron carbide at grain-boundary sites or pearlite colonies, producing methane gas. The methane gas, which cannot diffuse out of the steel, collects to form blisters and/or cracks in the material.[90,91] To prevent methane formation, cementite (Fe_3C) must be replaced by more stable carbides. Elements such as chromium, vanadium, titanium, or niobium are added to steels to form stable carbides. Nelson,[92] in a compre-

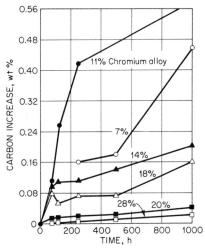

Fig. 18 Effect of chromium content on the carburization of a 9% Ni steel in carbon dioxide at 1428°F (775°C).[84]

TABLE 17   Corrosion Rates of Stainless Steels in Ammonia Converter and Plant Line[93]

Material type	Nominal Ni content %	Corrosion rate, mils/yr (mm/yr)	
		Ammonia* converter	Ammonia† plant line
446		1.12 (0.028)	164.5 (4.07)
430		0.9 (0.023)	
302B	10	0.73 (0.019)	
304	9	0.59 (0.015)	99.5 (2.53)
316	13	0.47 (0.012)	>520 (13.21)
321	11	0.47 (0.012)	
309	14	0.23 (0.006)	95 (2.41)
314	20	0.1 (0.003)	
330	34	0.06 (0.002)	
330	36	0.02 (0.001)	

*5 to 6% NH_3:29,164 h at 915 to 1024°F (490 to 550°C).
†99.1% NH_3:1540 h at 935°F (500°C).

hensive survey of all available service data, demonstrated that increasing chromium contents in steel permit higher operating temperatures and hydrogen partial pressures. Chromium carbide forms in these steels and is stable in the presence of hydrogen. Under severe conditions of operation [temperatures greater than 1100°F (593°C)] steels containing greater than 12% chromium are resistant to attack in all known applications. Thus, stainless steels are considered to be immune to hydrogen attack.

Nitrogen, Ammonia   Most metals and alloys are inert in molecular nitrogen at elevated temperatures. However, atomic nitrogen will react with and penetrate many steels, producing hard brittle nitride surface layers. Iron and aluminum, titanium, chromium, and other alloying elements may take part in these reactions. Two of the main sources of atomic nitrogen are the dissociation of ammonia in converters, plant lines, and heaters which operate in the temperature range of 700 to 1100°F (371 to 593°C) at pressures varying from atmospheric to 15 ksi (103.4 MPa), and nitriding furnaces. In these atmospheres (atomic nitrogen and hydrogen), the chromium carbide present in low-chromium steels, Cr_7C_3, may be attacked by atomic nitrogen to produce chromium nitride (more stable than Cr_7C_3) and release carbon to react with hydrogen, forming methane gas.[90] Either blistering or cracking or both can occur as described above. However, with chromium contents in excess of 12%, it appears that the carbide in these steels, $Cr_{23}C_6$, is more stable than chromium nitride and reaction does not occur. Hence, the stainless steels are employed for high-temperature service in hot ammonia atmospheres.

The behavior of stainless steels in ammonia depends on temperature, pressure, gas concentration, and the chromium and nickel contents of the steel. Results from field tests have demonstrated that the corrosion rates (depth of altered metal or case) for chromium stainless steels are greater than those for the austenitic grades. In the latter case, alloys with higher nickel contents have better resistance to corrosion.[90,93] Higher corrosion rates are experienced at increased ammonia contents. Corrosion rates for several stainless steels exposed in an ammonia converter and plant line are given in Table 17.

The high corrosion rate for the Type 316 steel in the ammonia plant line in Table 17

TABLE 18   Nitriding Kinetics of Chromium and Chromium-Nickel Stainless Steels in Ammonia Atmospheres*[90]

Material type	Nitriding kinetics, mils/yr (mm/yr) (depth of nitriding)
410	120 (3.048)
430	80 (2.032)
446	40 (1.016)
321	25 (0.064)
347	15 (0.038)
310	30 (0.762)

*3 to 15% NH_3: 840 to 970°F (449 to 520°C): 96 to 4380 h.

suggests that rapid nitriding of the alloy occurs because of the high molybdenum content. The rapid corrosion rates of the straight-chromium grades in high ammonia environments should also be noted. Cihäl has also reported that the austenitic stainless steels give better performance than the chromium steels in ammonia service.[90] Table 18 gives the nitriding kinetics for a number of chromium and Cr-Ni steels in test-plant runs.

It is apparent that chromium steels are unsuitable for service in atomic nitrogen or cracked ammonia at temperatures exceeding approximately 950°F (510°C) and that Cr-Ni steels should be selected. The lower alloyed steels (such as Types 304, 321, 347) would be selected for mild conditions and the high-alloy steels (Types 310, 330, HK, HT, HU, HW, HX) for more severe conditions. Figure 19 shows that Fe-Cr-Ni alloys containing between 20 and 80% Ni give the best resistance to high ammonia atmospheres.

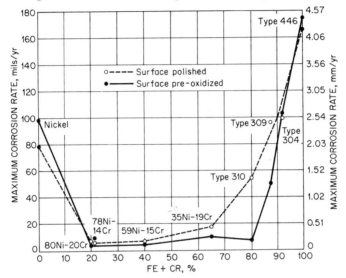

Fig. 19 Corrosion of Fe-Cr-Ni alloys by anhydrous ammonia at 932°F (500°C). (Based on 1540-h exposure.) *(Adapted from Krebs.[26])*

Halogens Stainless steels are severely attacked by halogen gases at elevated temperatures. Fluorine is more corrosive than chlorine, and the upper temperature limits for dry gases are approximately 480°F (249°C) and 600°F (315°C) respectively, for the wrought high chromium-nickel grades.[37] Hydrogen chloride gas is not as corrosive and the service temperature could be raised to 750 to 800°F (399 to 426°C). Alloys with high nickel content are preferred for chlorine and hydrogen chloride service and the cast HW and HX steels might be considered for use at temperatures up to 850 to 950°F (454 to 510°C).

SUMMARY

A considerable amount of fundamental and practical data concerning the corrosion resistance of stainless steels at elevated temperatures has been reported. However, from the present discussion, it is apparent that much remains to be done in both areas. Operating experience has to a great extent documented the uses and limitations of stainless steels in many cases; nevertheless, due to the urgency of practical problems, compatibility tests in numerous industrial environments are often required. Future advances in fundamental research may eliminate the need for many field tests and permit higher operating limits for the present and/or slightly modified grades through a knowledge of the detailed corrosion mechanisms. Comprehensive reports of practical operating experience can contribute to basic studies. The effects of thermal cycling, high gas pressures, surface preparation (industrial finishes), surface geometry and stress on service life may provide important data. Fundamental studies on the defect structure of oxides and sulfides, the effects of impurities on corrosion rate and the plastic and adherence properties of oxides and sulfides are some areas that would provide beneficial data to the industrial field.

It is hoped that the present discussion will assist the engineer in understanding the nature of high-temperature corrosion problems and in the selection of stainless steels for particular corrosive conditions.

REFERENCES

1. Hauffe, K.: "Oxidation of Metals," Plenum, New York, 1965.
2. Kubaschewski, O., and B. E. Hopkins: "Oxidation of Metals and Alloys," Butterworths, London, 1962.
3. Bénard, J.: "Oxidation des Metaux," (2 vols.), Gauthier-Villars, Paris, 1962–1964.
4. Kofstad, P.: "High Temperature Oxidation of Metals," Wiley, New York, 1966.
5. Rapp, R. A.: *Corrosion*, vol. 21, p. 382, 1965.
6. Wagner, C.: "Atom Movements," p. 153, American Society for Metals, Metals Park, Ohio, 1953.
7. Moreau, J., and J. Bénard: *Rev. Metall. (Paris)*, vol. 59, p. 161, 1962.
8. White, W. F.: *Mater. Prot.*, vol. 2, p. 47, 1963.
9. Wood, G. C.: *Corros. Sci.*, vol. 2, p. 173, 1962.
10. Yearian, H. J., E. C. Randell, and T. A. Longo: *Corrosion*, vol. 12, p. 515t, 1956.
11. Yearian, H. J., W. Derbyshire, and J. F. Radavich: *Corrosion*, vol. 13, p. 597, 1957.
12. Caplan, D., and M. Cohen: *Corrosion*, vol. 15, p. 141t, 1959.
13. Caplan, D., and M. Cohen: *J. Met.*, vol. 4, p. 1057, 1952.
14. Edstrom, J. O.: *J. Iron Steel Inst. London*, vol. 185, p. 450, 1957.
15. Wood, G. C., and M. G. Hobby: *J. Iron Steel Inst. London*, vol. 203, p. 54, 1965.
16. Hobby, M. G., and G. C. Wood: *Oxid. Met.*, vol. 1, p. 23, 1969.
17. Yearian, H. J., H. E. Boren, Jr., and R. E. Warr: *Corrosion*, vol. 12, p. 561t, 1956.
18. Croll, J. E., and G. R. Wallwork: *Oxid. Metals*, vol. 1, p. 55, 1969.
19. Brasunas, A. DeS., J. T. Gow, and O. E. Harder: Symposium on Materials for Gas Turbines, *Am. Soc. Test. Mater. Proc.*, vol. 46, p. 870, 1946.
20. Vyklický, M., and M. Měřička: *Br. Corros. J.*, vol. 5, p. 162, 1970.
21. Grodner, A.: *Weld. Res. Counc. Bull.*, no. 31, 1956.
22. Francis, J. M., and J. A. Jutson: *Corros. Sci.*, vol. 8, p. 445, 1968.
23. McCullough, H. M., M. G. Fontana, and F. H. Beck: *Trans. Am. Soc. Met.*, vol. 43, p. 404, 1951.
24. Eberle, F., F. G. Ely, and J. A. Dillon: *Trans. ASME*, vol. 76, p. 64, 1954.
25. LeMay, I.: Paper presented at Conference of Metallurgists, Montreal, Canada, 1964.
26. Krebs, T. M.: *Process Industry Corrosion Notes*, Ohio State University, September, 1960.
27. Jones, D. A.: *AEC Res. Dev. Rep.*, HW-76952, 1963.
28. Ruther, W. E., and S. Greenberg: *J. Electrochem. Soc.*, vol. 111, p. 1116, 1964.
29. Ruther, W. E., R. R. Schleuter, R. H. Lee, and R. K. Hart: *Corrosion*, vol. 12, p. 147, 1966.
30. Wozaldo, G. P., and W. L. Pearl: *Corrosion*, vol. 21, p. 355, 1965.
31. Warzee, M., J. Hannaut, M. Maurice, C. Sonnen, J. Waty, and P. Berge: *J. Electrochem. Soc.*, vol. 112, p. 670, 1965.
32. Board, J., G. Holyfield, and J. Dalley: *Metallurgie (Berlin)*, vol. 8, p. 23, 1968.
33. Le May, I.: Paper presented at the 3rd Int. Cong. Met. Corros., 1965.
34. Bittel, J. T., L. H. Sjodahl, and J. F. White: *Corrosion*, vol. 25, p. 7, 1969.
35. Caplan, D.: *Corros. Sci.*, vol. 6, p. 509, 1966.
36. Fujii, C. T., and R. A. Meussner: *J. Electrochem. Soc.*, vol. 111, p. 1215, 1964; vol. 110, p. 1195, 1963.
37. Corrosion Resistance of the Austenitic Chromium-Nickel Stainless Steels in High Temperature Environments, *Inco Bull.*, 1963.
38. Eberle, F., and C. H. Anderson: Paper No. 61-Pur-3, ASME, 1961.
39. Daniel, H. T., J. E. Antill, and K. A. Peakall: *J. Iron Steel Inst. London*, vol. 201, p. 154, 1963.
40. McCoy, H. E.: *Corrosion*, vol. 21, p. 84, 1965.
41. Francis, J. M., and W. H. Whitlow: *J. Iron Steel Inst. London*, vol. 203, p. 468, 1965.
42. Fujii, C. T., and R. A. Meussner: *J. Electrochem. Soc.*, vol. 114, p. 435, 1967.
43. Draycott, A., and R. Smith: Australian Atomic Energy Commission, Report E-52, March, 1960.
44. Board, J., and R. Winterborne: *Br. Corros. J.*, vol. 4, p. 86, 1969.
45. Caplan, D., and M. Cohen: *Nature*, vol. 205, p. 690, 1965.
46. Francis, J. M.: *J. Iron Steel Inst. London*, vol. 204, p. 910, 1966.
47. Mangone, R. J., C. J. Slunder, and A. M. Hall: *Summary Rept.*, ACI Project no. 32, Battelle Memorial Institute, Jul. 15, 1958.
48. Brasunas, A. DeS., and N.J. Grant: *Trans. Am. Soc. Met.*, vol. 44, p. 1117, 1952.
49. Brenner, S. S.: *J. Electrochem. Soc.*, vol. 102, p. 16, 1955.
50. Chalk, D. L.: *Met. Prog.*, vol. 102, p. 57, 1972.
51. Krainer, H., L. Wetternick, and C. Carius: *Arch. Eisenhuettenwes.*, vol. 22, p. 103, 1951.

52. Felton, E. J.: *J. Electrochem. Soc.*, vol. 108, p. 490, 1961.
53. Eiselstein, H. L., and J. C. Hosier: U.S. Patent No. 3,729,308, 1973.
54. Sorell, G., and W. B. Hoyt: *NACE Tech. Comm. Rept.*, Publication 56-7, 1956.
55. "Inspection of Catalytic Reforming Units," D-X Sunray Oil Co., Tulsa, Okla., 1955.
56. Bruns, F. J.: *NACE Tech. Comm. Rept.*, Publication 57-2, 1957.
57. Davin, A., and D. Coutsouradis: *Corros. Anticorros.*, vol. 11, p. 347, 1963.
58. Davin, A., D. Coutsouradis, M. Urbain, and L. Hobroken: *Belg. Chem. Ind.*, vol. 30, p. 340, 1965.
59. Farber, M., and D. M. Ehrenberg: *J. Electrochem. Soc.*, vol. 99, p. 427, 1952.
60. Wellman, E.: *Z. Elektrochem.*, vol. 37, p. 142, 1931.
61. Hallett, M. M.: *J. Iron Steel Inst. London*, vol. 170, p. 321, 1952.
62. Iparic, H.: *Her Vakuumschmelze*, p. 290, 1923–1933.
63. Nicholson, J. H., and E. J. Kwasney: *Trans. Electrochem. Soc.*, vol. 91, p. 681, 1947.
64. Hatfield, W. H.: *J. Iron Steel Inst. London*, vol. 115, p. 483, 1927.
65. Naumann, F. K.: *Chem. Fabr.*, vol. 11, p. 365, 1938.
66. Morris, L. A., and W. Engel: Unpublished research, Falconbridge Metallurgical Laboratories, Thornhill, Ontario, Canada.
67. Jones, J. F., and R. D. McMunn: Paper No. 18 presented at NACE Annual Meeting, Mar. 19–23, 1973, Anaheim, California, (*Mater. Prot. Perform.*, vol. 12, p. 22, 1973.)
68. Backensto, E. B., R. D. Drew, J. E. Prior, and J. W. Sjoberg: *NACE Tech. Comm. Rept.*, Publication 58-3, 1958.
69. Merrick, R. D., and C. L. Mantell: *Chem. Eng.*, vol. 72, p. 144, 1965.
70. Backensto, E. B., and J. W. Sjoberg: *Corrosion*, vol. 15, p. 125t, 1959.
71. Kinzel, A. B., and R. Franks: "Alloys of Iron and Chromium," vol. 11, McGraw-Hill, New York, 1940.
72. West, J. R.: *Chem. Eng.*, vol. 58, p. 276, 1951.
73. Collins, W. J.: *Prod. Eng.*, p. 88, Nov. 25, 1963.
74. Mason, J. F., J. J. Moran, and E. N. Skinner: *Corrosion*, vol. 16, p. 593t, 1960.
75. Guthrie, J. E., and R. D. Merrick: *Mater. Prot.*, vol. 3, p. 32, 1964.
76. Jackson, J. H., C. J. Slunder, O. E. Harder, and J. T. Gow: *Trans. ASME*, vol. 75, p. 1021, 1953.
77. Schoefer, E. A.: *Ind. Heat.*, p. 1917, October, 1967.
78. Avery, H. S.: in C. Edeleanu (ed.), "Materials Technology in Steam Reforming Processes," Chap. 13, Pergamon, New York, 1966.
79. Stanley, J. K.: *J. Mater.*, vol. 5, p. 957, 1970.
80. Report No. 46 to Alloy Casting Institute, Battelle Memorial Institute, Columbus, Ohio. Jan. 7, 1960.
81. English, R. H.: "Aspects of Alloy Selection and Use of Materials for Pyrolysis Furnaces," *Preprint Paper No. 46*, *NACE Ann. Meeting*, Houston, Texas, 1969.
82. Inouye, H.: *Proc. Conf. Corros. Reactor Mater.*, International Atomic Energy Authority, Vienna, Jun. 4–8, 1962.
83. Jepson, W. B., J. E. Antill, and J. B. Warburton: *Br. Corros. J.*, vol. 1, p. 15, 1965.
84. Martin, W. R., and J. R. Weir: *J. Nucl. Mater.*, vol. 16, p. 19, 1965.
85. Hoyt, W. B., and R. H. Caughey: *Corrosion*, vol. 15, p. 627t, 1959.
86. Lefrancois, P. A., and W. B. Hoyt: *Corrosion*, vol. 19, p. 360t, 1963.
87. Prange, F. A.: *Corrosion*, vol. 15, p. 619t, 1959.
88. Slunder, C. J.: *NACE Tech. Comm. Rept.*, Publication 60-6, 1960.
89. Eberle, F., and R. D. Wylie: *Corrosion*, vol. 15, p. 622t, 1959.
90. Cihǎl, V.: *Proc. 1st Int. Cong. Met. Corros.*, London, p. 591, 1961.
91. Geerlings, H. G., and J. C. Jongebreur: *Proc. 1st Int. Cong. Met. Corros.*, London, p. 573, 1961.
92. Nelson, G. A., and R. T. Effinger: *Weld. J.*, *Res. Suppl.*, vol. 34, p. 125, 1955: Shell Development Co., Emeryville, Calif., *Corrosion Data Survey*, 1950.
93. Moran, J. J., J. R. Mihalisin, and E. N. Skinner: *Corrosion*, vol. 17, p. 191t, 1961.
94. Eiselstein, H. L., and E. N. Skinner: *ASTM Spec. Tech. Publ. no.* 165, 1964.
95. Mrowec, S.: in Z. A. Foroulis (ed.), "High Temperature Metallic Corrosion of Sulphur and Its Compounds," p. 55, The Electrochemical Society, New York, 1970.

Chapter **18**

Resistance to Liquid Metals, Salts, and Fuel Ash Deposits

JOHN W. KOGER

Metallurgist, Union Carbide Corporation, Nuclear Division, Oak Ridge, Tennessee

FUEL ASH DEPOSITS

Fuel ash corrosion occurs mainly on heater and superheater tubing under relatively low-melting deposits of alkali complex sulfates resulting from alkali and sulfur contained in both solid and liquid fuels.[1-4] The effect of fuel-ash deposits is quite complicated primarily because of all the different type fuels, the different products of combustion, and the different exposure temperatures. In many combustion systems, stainless steels are not considered because of the high temperatures. However, there are many applications where consideration is given to austenitic stainless steels as superheater tubes.

Components of ash deposits resulting from boilers which burned high-alkali coal have caused accelerated corrosion in Type 321 stainless steel superheater platens.[5] The corrosion was a pitting type, accompanied by surface carburization and subsurface sulfide formation. Laboratory tests showed that MgO additions reduced the corrosivity of white-layer ash deposits. Other fixes included plating with 25-20 (Type 310) steel, reduced metal and gas temperatures, and excess air.

Oil ash with a vanadium content as low as 0.001% attacked stainless steels at temperatures over 650°C.[6] The corrosion rate increased rapidly with increasing vanadium or temperature. An addition of 0.2% organic magnesium compound to the fuel oil decreased the corrosion rate to the same level as that in vanadium-free fuels.

A 24Cr-18Ni, a 12Cr-8Ni-1Mo-1V-9Mn, and a 15Cr-37Ni-1Ti-3W steel all showed low resistance to artificial oil ash containing 41.6% V_2O_5 and 11.2% Na_2SO_4 at 730°C.[7] Magnesium sulfate or MgO additions proved to be beneficial. Generally corrosion increased rapidly with increasing temperatures, exposure time, and V_2O_5 and Na_2SO_4 content.[8]

In a study involving several corrosive variables, Type 347 stainless steel was submerged in K_2SO_4, Na_2SO_4 and in fly ash with or without 0.5 or 2% NaCl and heated in air for 336 h to 540, 630, or 760°C.[9] The weight loss was negligible in pure fly ash, K_2SO_4, and Na_2SO_4, but increased with temperature and chloride content. The attack was intergranular and the grain boundaries were chromium enriched and iron deficient. Type 316 stainless steel and 15Cr-10Ni-6Mn-1Mo steel were heated to 630, 690, and 740°C in mixtures 20 to 40% in K_2SO_4 or Na_2SO_4, fly ash, and 0, 0.5, or 1.5% NaCl in synthetic combustion gas for 200 h. The maximum weight loss was observed at 690°C. The corrosion was intergranular. The presence of Na_2SO_4 or K_2SO_4 did not accelerate the normal oxidation of steel in air whereas in sulfur-containing combustion gases, K_2SO_4 caused more attack than Na_2SO_4.

In laboratory tests on stainless steels to determine the effects of oil ash deposits, conclusions were:

1. The higher the V_2O_5/Na_2O ratio of the deposits the greater the corrosion.
2. Many deposits contained a constituent that fused at about 570°C.
3. All of the deposits were less corrosive at temperatures below 570°C.[10]

Investigation of the ash composition following high-temperature corrosion by heavy oil ashes of austenitic stainless steel superheater tubes disclosed that the deposits adjacent to the tube walls consisted principally of sodium and sulfur independent of the quantity of vanadium in the fuels.[11] Reactions with sodium sulfate compounds at high temperature were found to be responsible.

Type 321 stainless steel was exposed to synthetic flue-gas atmospheres at temperatures ranging from 316 to 538°C in the presence of various salt mixtures.[12] Addition of chloride salts to mixed sulfates greatly accelerated the corrosion. At 316°C sulfur-containing salts such as bisulfates and pyrosulfates were very corrosive.

Corrosion resulting from the action of flue gases and accumulated deposits in municipal incinerators was studied and correlated with laboratory studies.[13] Types 304 and 321 were exposed to the flue gases at temperatures ranging from 427 to 671°C and a maximum temperature of 816°C. Wastage on the Type 304 was consistently less than that on the Type 321 stainless steel. Maximum wastage was about 60 mils/month (1.5mm/month). Analysis of the deposits showed large quantities of lead as $PbSO_4$, chloride as NaCl, and zinc. Other elements such as potassium, calcium, aluminum, iron, and silicon were found in smaller amounts. In the laboratory experiments, stainless steel specimens were exposed to synthetic flue gases, fly ash, mixtures of sulfates and iron oxide with and without sodium chloride, and to lead chloride, zinc chloride, and zinc. Specimens of Type 321 stainless steel showed no accelerated attack at 540°C when the specimens were embedded in fly ash and exposed to the flue gas. Lead chloride accelerated the attack. Zinc chloride was less harmful, but zinc itself was quite corrosive. Sodium chloride additions accelerated the attack.

SALTS

Fluoride Salts The primary considered use of fluoride salts for the last 20 years has been as fuel carriers and heat-transfer fluids in molten-salt reactors. Fluoride salts are also used as salt baths.

Because the products of oxidation of metals by fluoride melts are quite soluble in the corroding media, passivation is precluded, and the corrosion rate depends on other factors, including the thermodynamic driving force of the corrosion reactions. Design of a practicable system utilizing molten fluoride salts, therefore, demands the selection of salt constituents such as LiF, BeF_2, UF_4, and ThF_4 that are not appreciably reduced by available structural metals and alloys whose components can be in near-thermodynamic equilibrium with the salt.

Free energy of formation data reveal clearly that in reactions with structural metals (M)

$$2UF_4 + M \leftrightarrow 2UF_3 + MF_2 \tag{1}$$

chromium is much more readily attacked than iron, nickel, or molybdenum.[14-16] The result of this selective attack is often void formation.

Nickel-based alloys, more specifically Hastelloy N and its modifications, are considered the most promising for use in molten salts and have received the most attention. Stainless steels, having more chromium than Hastelloy N, are more susceptible to corrosion by fluoride melts but can be considered for some applications.

Oxidation and selective attack may also result from impurities in the melt,

$$M + NiF_2 \rightarrow MF_2 + Ni \tag{2}$$
$$M + 2HF \rightarrow MF_2 + H_2 \tag{3}$$

or oxide films on the metal,

$$NiO + BeF_2 \rightarrow NiF_2 + BeO \tag{4}$$

followed by reaction of NiF_2 with M. As purification methods have been developed, corrosion rates of all alloys have decreased.

Reactions (2), (3), and (4) will proceed essentially to completion at all temperatures considered for a reactor circuit. Accordingly, such reactions can lead (if the system is poorly cleaned) to a rapid initial corrosion rate. However, these reactions do not give a sustained corrosive attack.

Reaction (1) with UF_4, on the other hand, may have an equilibrium constant which is strongly temperature-dependent; hence, when the salt is forced to circulate through a temperature gradient, a possible mechanism exists for mass transfer and continued attack. Reaction (1) is of significance mainly in the case of alloys containing relatively large amounts of chromium.

In early work with rather impure fluoride salts, certain stainless steels became magnetic after salt exposure.[17] It was found that the corrosion of the alloy by the fluoride salt resulted in chromium removal and left a magnetic Fe-Ni alloy.

In impure fluoride salts and in a nonisothermal system with a maximum temperature of 816°C, Type 316 stainless steel showed approximately the same depth of attack as some nickel-based alloys.[17] However, deposits in the cold zone were excessive. Preliminary studies in static LiF-UF_4 (76–24 mole %) at 700°C and 600 h revealed rapid attack with the following stainless steels: Types 304, 304L, 316, 316L, 321, 347, 405, 410, 430, and 446.[18]

A type 304 stainless steel thermal-convection loop with removable specimens operated for 9 years (80,000 h) with a LiF-BeF_2-ZrF_4-UF_4-ThF_4 (70-23-5-1-1 mole %) salt at a maximum temperature of 688°C and a ΔT of 100°C.[19] Examination of the hottest specimen after 5700 h exposure (Fig. 1) disclosed voids extending 75 μm (3 mils) into the surface. Microprobe analysis showed an appreciable chromium gradient for 28 μm (1.1 mils) (Fig. 2).

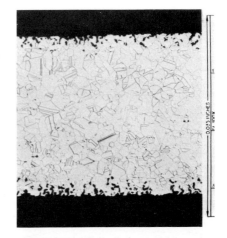

Fig. 1 Microstructure of type 304L stainless steel specimen for loop 1258 exposed to LiF-BeF_2-ZrF_4-ThF_4-UF_4 (70-23-5-1-1 mole %) for 5700 h at 688°C. (100×)

The weight changes of the hot leg specimens after 32,000 h are seen in Fig. 3. Note the dependence of weight loss with time and temperature. Voids extended for at least 250 μm (10 mils) into each specimen (Fig. 4). At loop shutdown, the specimens had been exposed to the salt for 49,000 h. The maximum weight loss was 95.9 mg/cm², equivalent to a uniform corrosion rate of 21.8 μm/yr (0.86mil/yr). For the most part, the corrosion and mass transfer was controlled by the solid-state diffusion rate of chromium.

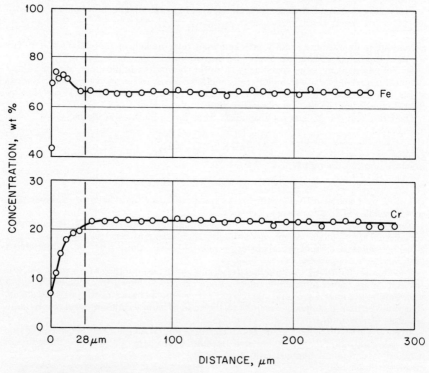

Fig. 2 Chromium and iron concentration gradient in a type 304L stainless steel specimen from loop 1258 exposed to LiF-BeF$_2$-ZrF$_4$-ThF$_4$-UF$_4$ (70-23-5-1-1 mole %) for 5700 h at 688°C.

A Type 316 stainless steel thermal-convection loop with removable specimens operated for 4490 h with a quite pure LiF-BeF$_2$–ThF$_4$-UF$_4$ (68-20-11.7-0.3 mole %) salt at a maximum temperature of 650°C and a ΔT of 110°C.[19] After 1410 h the hottest specimen showed subsurface voids for a distance of 25 μm (1 mil). After 2842 h the specimen had lost a total of 6.2 mg/cm², equivalent to a uniform corrosion rate of 24.4 μm/yr (0.96 mil/yr).

The main corrosion reaction in this system is

$$2UF_4 + Cr \longleftrightarrow CrF_2 + 2UF_3 \tag{5}$$

In order to determine if the mass transfer of the stainless steel would decrease, UF$_3$ was added to the salt after the 2842-h exposure measurements to make the salt less oxidizing. In the next 645-h time period the mass transfer was somewhat less, and the overall corrosion rate was 21.1 μm/yr (0.83 mil/yr). In the final 811-h time period, the weight loss of the hottest specimen increased such that the uniform corrosion rate was more than 25 μm/yr (more than 1 mil/yr). However, the overall mass transfer, evidenced by weight changes of other corrosion specimens, remained quite low.

The average uniform corrosion rate for the hottest specimen was 25 μm/yr (1 mil/yr) for the entire 4298-h period of loop operation. Figure 5 shows the microstructures of hottest and coldest specimens at the end of the run. Figure 5a shows a cross section of the specimen magnified 100 times with voids extending about 25 μm (1 mil) into the surface.

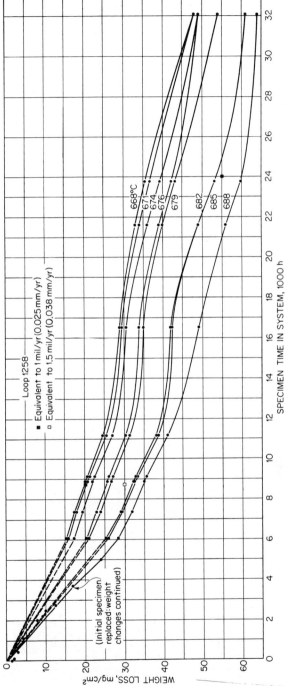

Fig. 3 Weight changes of type 304L stainless steel specimens from loop 1258 exposed to LiF-BeF$_2$-ZrF$_4$-ThF$_4$-UF$_4$ (70-23-5-1-1 mole %) for various times and temperatures.

Figure 5*b* and *c* are views magnified 500 times of as-polished and etched specimens, respectively. In Fig. 5*c* note that the etching reveals a 75-μm-wide (3 mil) affected area. This complete area is depleted of chromium. Figure 5*d* shows the specimen in the coldest position (560°C). Some deposits are seen.

Fluoride baths are used in the fused salt fluoride volatility process. Early scouting tests

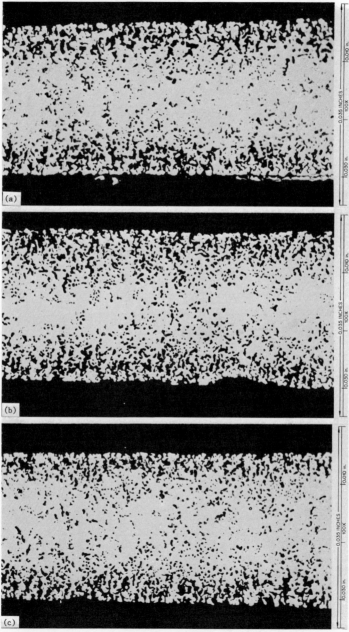

Fig. 4   Microstructures of type 304L stainless steel specimens from loop 1258 exposed to LiF-BeF$_2$-ZrF$_4$-ThF$_4$-UF$_4$ (70-23-5-1-1 mole %) for 45,724 h at (*a*) 685°C, (*b*) 679°C, and (*c*) 674°C (100×, reduced 28%.)

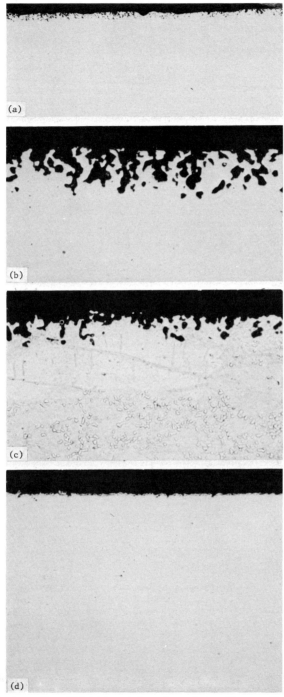

Fig. 5 Microstructures of type 316 stainless steel specimens in loop 22 exposed to LiF-BeF$_2$-ThF$_4$-UF$_4$ (68-20-11.7-0.3 mole %) after 4298 h. Hot leg, 650°C: (*a*) cross section of specimen, 100X; (*b*) as polished, 500X; (*c*) etched 500X. Cold leg, 560°C: (*d*) as polished, 500X. Reduced 24.5%.

in ZrF_4-KF-NaF (44.5-48.5-7.0 mole %) at 675°C with HF bubbled through the melt disclosed corrosion rates of austenitic stainless steels from 100 to 175 μm/h (4 to 7 mils/ h).[20] Nickel and nickel-based alloys were obviously superior.

Chloride Salts   Molten salts consisting of chlorides are also important for many different applications, although they have probably been studied less than the fluorides. The corrosion reactions previously discussed for fluoride salts generally apply in fused chloride salt systems also.

Early corrosion data was generated for some stainless steels in the NaCl-KCl-MgCl eutectic.[21,22] Static test results are given in Table 1 and nonisothermal test results are given in Table 2. A little more localized attack was noted in the nonisothermal test.

TABLE 1   Static Test of NaCl-KCl-MgCl$_2$ with and without 5% BiCl$_3$ Exposed to Stainless Steel for 1000 h at 500°C

Material type	NaCl-KCl-MgCl$_2$ eutectic			Eutectic + 5% BiCl$_3$	
	Type corrosion	Maximum penetration, μm/yr	Approx. weight change, %	Type corrosion	Approx. weight change, %
347	Intergranular	25	−0.6	Intergranular	−30
430				Intergranular	−21
446	Intergranular	25	−4.2	Intergranular	−27

TABLE 2   Tilting Furnace Test of NaCl-KCl-MgCl$_2$ Exposed to Stainless Steels for 1000 h at 500 to 450°C

Material type	NaCl-KCl-MgCl$_2$ eutectic		
	Type	Maximum penetration, μm/yr	Weight change, mg/ (cm^2)(yr)
304L	Intergranular	10	−12.1
310	None	0	−2.8
316	Intergranular	10	−2.9
347	Intergranular and transgranular	120	−4.6
410	Intergranular	25	−4.1
430	Transgranular	50	−0.8
441	Intergranular	10	+4.2

Experiments conducted on a 16Cr-7.5Ni-1Mn and a 19Cr-10Ni-2Mn low-carbon stainless steel in molten chlorides of potassium, sodium, and magnesium and in mixtures of the three at 700 to 900°C by Russian investigators[23] showed chromium depletion. In static tests at 700°C the corrosion rate fell sharply in the first 2 to 3 h and subsequently varied little with time. After 10 h, the corrosion rates were much the same for all alloys. The corrosion rate did increase with temperature, and the corrosion resistance increased with increasing nickel content. The corrosion rate of the low-carbon stainless steel was much higher in $MgCl_2$ (5 times) than in NaCl or KCl. Examination of the microstructure of specimens of that alloy showed large interconnected cavities. The number of cavities and depth of penetration increased with the increased corrosion activity of the melt and with exposure time. For 10-h exposure, the maximum depth of penetration was: 10 μm (0.4 mil) in KCl, 15 μm (0.6 mil) in NaCl, and 35 μm (1.4 mils) in $MgCl_2$. The cavities were mainly situated along grain boundaries and produced a pattern similar to that found in intergranular corrosion. Chemical analyses of the salt after test disclosed large amounts of chromium in the melt. Electrochemical studies showed that the increased rate of corrosion in the $MgCl_2$ was due to hydrogen ions, which resulted from water in the melt. This effect was worse in $MgCl_2$ because of its tendency to hydrolyze.

Other Russian investigators[24-27] have related dissolved water to gross electrochemical corrosion in the molten salts, and they feel that this electrochemical action explains the formation of cavities in the surface layer of Cr-Ni steels. A comparison of the potentials for iron, chromium, and nickel in molten chlorides[28] showed that chromium is the least noble. Thus the selective removal of chromium was responsible for the resulting corrosion behavior. The chromium removal commenced on the grain boundaries and was then accompanied by diffusion of chromium inside the grain to the boundary layer, gradually enlarging the cavities in the metal.

Edeleanu et al.[29] observed voids in an 18-8 steel that had been exposed to a 50% NaCl-50% KCl melt in the presence of air at 800°C for 100 h. These voids, which were separate from one another and from the outside of the specimen, were very similar, if not identical, to those formed by exposure of alloys to fluoride salt mixtures. Careful examination showed that the attack was not continuous at the grain boundaries and was thus not ordinary intergranular attack. When the material was exposed to an etch that should not attack 18-8 steel, a narrow region on each side of the grain boundaries and next to the surface was etched. The area etched was the chromium-depleted region (as shown with the aid of the x-ray scanning microanalyzer) and was surrounded by large and small voids. Another etching treatment showed considerable martensite formation at the grain boundaries, extending somewhat beyond the region containing the visible voids. Their explanation, like those given for fluoride corrosion, was that chromium was selectively removed by the corrosion reaction, and as it diffused outwards, vacancies moved inward and segregated to form visible voids (Kirkendall effect). The diffusion rate at the boundaries is faster than that at the grains, so that the chromium near the grain boundaries would diffuse rapidly. The void formation would probably assist the process since once the voids are formed, the chromium would diffuse outward, partially by surface diffusion, which is a faster process. The voids would grow as fresh vacancies arrive and eventually join to give the appearance of intergranular corrosion. The martensitic transformation is consistent with such an explanation since at the 8% nickel level a decrease in chromium in the alloy would raise the M_s (martensitic start) temperature to above room temperature.

Seybolt[30] studied the corrosion behavior of a Ni-20Cr alloy and a stainless steel alloy submerged in molten chlorides in the presence of oxygen from 700 to 1000°C. This experiment included the effect of both oxidation and molten chloride attack. The selective removal of chromium was accompanied sometimes by iron. The loss of alloy constituents caused a countercurrent flow of vacancies, which condensed into an interconnecting pore network (as opposed to nonconnecting voids found in fluoride salt corrosion without oxygen) filled with salt. At 1000°C the pores were larger and more spheroidized because of increased void formation. Since the salt penetrated the structure, the loss of alloying constituents did not require intermetallic diffusion over long distances, but instead corrosion products were removed by solution of alloying constituents as ions in the pore-salt network. The chromium corrosion product was Na_2CrO_4 or K_2CrO_4. Seybolt presents evidence that suggests that recrystallization occurs in the porous zone and that in the Ni-20Cr alloy, chromium diffuses down grain boundaries of the grain network to be deposited at grain boundary—pore intersections as chromium ions. The concentration gradient of chromium ions in the salt phase forces chromium to diffuse out to the bulk salt where Cr_2O_3 is formed.

Phosphate Salts   Results of screening studies made in molten sodium polyphosphate in connection with a homogeneous-reactor concept are given for various stainless steels in Table 3.[31] Nickel-based alloys were found to be superior to the stainless steels.

TABLE 3   Corrosion Rate of Stainless Steels in Molten Phosphates at 700°C After a 120-h Exposure

Material type	SHMP*, mg/(cm²)(h)	Sodium Polyphosphate, mg/(cm²)(h)
301	4.6	1.8
302	4.1	1.7
304	3.8	1.5
310	1.9	0.57
316	3.1	3.3
321	4.0	1.0
347	3.9	1.6
410	11.6	2.5
430	8.9	2.2

*Commercial grade sodium hexametaphosphate, Na_2O to P_2O_5 ratio of 1:12.

Sodium Hydroxide Stainless steels exhibit severe chemical attack at about 600°C in NaOH.[32] Table 4 gives 24-h screening tests results at 538°C for several stainless steels.

TABLE 4   Corrosion of Stainless Steels Exposed to Sodium Hydroxide for 24 h at 538°C

Material type	Depth and type of attack
304	7.6 μm, pitting
317	Intergranular
347	Oxidation, no selective attack
410	25 μm, pitting
430	4 μm, pitting
446	4 μm, pitting

The corrosion rate of 18-8-1 stainless steel is 78.4 mg/(dm²) (day) after 4 weeks at 400°C and is >1000 mg/(dm²) (day) after 1 week at 600°C.[33]

LIQUID METALS

Sodium The liquid metal of most interest at the present time to stainless steel users is sodium. This interest stems from the development of the liquid-metal (sodium) fast-breeder reactors. Stainless steels are a very important part of these reactor systems, thus extensive studies of the compatibility of stainless steel with sodium have been made.

Corrosion of metals or alloys by liquid metals is generally related to the solubilities of the constituent materials. Other corrosion mechanisms are important also. Impurities in the liquid metals may promote oxidation-reduction-type reactions and electron transfer. Because the sodium will be used as a heat-transfer fluid, many tests are run in flowing nonisothermal systems constructed to make up certain parts of a proposed reactor. Temperature-gradient mass-transfer effects on the hot and cold portions of the system are studied. Because of the temperature dependence of solubility, large amounts of materials only sparingly soluble in the liquid metal can be transferred. Also, since a large reactor system would consist of material other than stainless steels, dissimilar metal effects must be considered. For example, decarburization can occur from certain unstable ferritic alloys having higher carbon activities than other materials in the system.

Pure sodium (very low concentration of impurities) is generally not a problem to stainless steel. However, since sodium is quite reactive, it is easily contaminated and contaminants can cause problems. Of particular concern are oxygen, carbon, nitrogen, and hydrogen. Sodium contaminated with oxygen can be highly corrosive and much referenced early work which gives high corrosion rates for stainless steel used high-oxygen-containing sodium. Oxygen-exchange reactions between sodium and alloy compounds are quite important. Carbon can cause excess carburization which can significantly affect mechanical properties. Nitrogen can produce a similar effect. Hydrogen can cause embrittlement.

Iron and molybdenum are the most corrosion-resistant constituents of stainless steel in sodium containing less than 10 ppm oxygen. In pumped loops with sodium containing less than 10 ppm oxygen, where nickel and chromium are selectively removed, the initial rate of weight loss is relatively high, but it decreases to a lower steady-state rate in times that range from many weeks at about 600°C to about 300 h above 700°C.[34–38] The accompanying loss of chromium and nickel caused the surface of the stainless steel to change from the austenitic phase (gamma or fcc structure) to ferritic (alpha or bcc structure),[37–43] since austenite is not stable with less than about 8% nickel and 15% chromium. A typical range of thickness for the ferrite layer formed on stainless steel exposed to high-velocity sodium at 755°C for 2004 h in hot-trapped sodium and 521 h in sodium containing 4 ppm oxygen is 5 to 12 μm (0.2 to 0.5 mil).

At oxygen levels in the sodium above 10 ppm, the concentration of chromium on the surfaces of the stainless steel is high enough to promote the formation of surface deposits of sodium chromite ($NaCrO_2$), and initial weight gains are seen. (A similar reaction is apparently the cause of the high initial corrosion rates observed in purer sodium.) Subsequently, weight losses are measured as $NaCrO_2$ is transferred to the colder regions and as chromium is leached from the surface. Generally, as the oxygen level increases, depletion of chromium and nickel decreases.[39] Zebroski and others[39,40,43] have noted that the steady-state surface of stainless steel in sodium containing about 50 ppm oxygen is enriched in nickel and chromium because of the oxygen dependence of iron corrosion. The selective oxidation of chromium and the leaching of nickel are the dominant processes and influence grain-boundary areas more than just the dissolution of iron.[44]

Increasing oxygen content in the sodium increases the corrosion rate of iron and chromium.[42] Up to 500 ppm oxygen in sodium, the corrosion rate of nickel is not affected.[37,42,45] Thus in sodium containing 50 ppm oxygen, the surface of stainless steel will become enriched in nickel.[42]

The corrosion rate of austenitic stainless steels in low oxygen (10 ppm or less) has been reported to be from 7.5 to 40 μm/yr (0.3 to 1.5 mil/yr) in the 704°C range.[42,46] In sodium containing 25 ppm oxygen and at temperatures of 450 to 725 °C, the corrosion of stainless steel has been described by the equation[37]

$$S = 2.3 \times 10^{-6} e^{-17.500/RT}$$

A 18Cr-18Ni-2Si steel exposed in 650°C sodium averaging 30 ppm oxygen for 5060 h had a weight gain of 364 mg/dm^2 and a surface reaction layer of 50 μm (2 mils).[47] Spalling was noted and attributed to the silicon which was selectively removed from the alloy.

The corrosive attack of stainless steels at temperatures above 760°C has been excessive in some tests.[42] The mass transfer obtained for several stainless steels during 1000-h exposure in flowing sodium at 816°C cold trapped at 149°C is given in Table 5.

TABLE 5 Hot- and Cold-Zone Change of Stainless Steels Exposed to Flowing Sodium at 816°C for 1000 h

Material type	Hot-zone attack, μm	Cold-zone ($\Delta T = 150°C$) deposit, μm
304	50	25
310	225	75
316	50	125
330	50	50
347	50	25
430	25	125

In a sodium system with 3 ppm oxygen and a flow rate greater than 6 m/s the corrosion rate of Type 316 stainless steel at 704°C was 21.3 μm/yr (0.84 mil/yr).[48] Mechanical property degradation was noted and was caused by changes in chemical composition and mass transfer. Other effects of the sodium exposure were carbon, nitrogen, and boron removal, formation of sigma phase, and formation of subsurface voids.

Types 304, 316, 321, and 347 stainless steels were exposed to flowing sodium at 704 and 621°C for times up to 15,726 h.[49] Changes in chemical composition and microstructure increased with increasing exposure time. Chromium, nickel, and manganese were depleted from surface layers up to 130 μm thick. Types 304 and 316 lost carbon while Types 321 and 347 gained carbon. Ferrite layers formed at the exposed surfaces. Sigma-phase precipitation increased with exposure time.

The transport and deposition characteristics of radioactive stainless steel corrosion products have been studied in a pumped sodium loop.[50] The flow rate was 1100 kg/h and the temperature was 600°C. The iron behavior was characterized by its appearance as a deposit immediately downstream of the test section. Chromium was within the deposit and iron penetrated into the base metal. Manganese transport was characterized by preferential migration to the cold trap.

Corrosion and mass-transfer behavior of austenitic stainless steels in a natural-circulation sodium loop was studied using tracer techniques over a temperature range from 630 to 230°C for a period of 2000 h.[51] Iron and cobalt deposited by atomic diffusion and by particle formation prior to accumulation. Chromium formed chemical compounds prior to accumulation. The mechanism of the deposition of nickel and manganese could not be made clear.

Increasing sodium velocity increases the corrosion of austenitic stainless steels. In sodium with less than 10 ppm oxygen the dependence of the corrosion rate of Type 316 stainless steel on velocity is essentially linear through about 4.5 m/s (15 ft/s) and increases at a decreasing rate at higher velocities.[46] A downstream effect is observed with Type 316 stainless steel exposed to low-oxygen (less than 10 ppm) sodium at 704°C under isothermal conditions. Corrosion rates decreased downstream, all approaching the same value regardless of velocity.[46]

The downstream effect is a reduction of the steady-state corrosion rate with distance along an isothermal section of the sodium circuit. The downstream effect is attributed to the absorption of chromium and nickel that dissolved upstream of a given specimen on the active sites for dissolution of iron for the specimen.[52]

Experiments with sodium of varying oxygen content indicated that weight losses from stainless steels were prevented at oxygen levels below 0.2 ppm.[53] Corrosion rates of nickel specimens were unaffected by oxygen concentration in the range 0.2 to 5 ppm. Continuous measurements of oxygen activity in the sodium circuit demonstrated a consumption of oxygen, which is related to oxygen-consuming corrosion reactions in the high-temperature region of the loop. A mechanism has been proposed which considers the equilibrium between sodium, iron, and their dissolved oxides.[54] Rate values predicted by this mechanism compare reasonably well with those obtained experimentally.

As mentioned earlier, carbon transport to and from stainless steels occurs as the result of a difference in chemical activity of various materials in the system or the temperature dependence of this activity.[42] In a single-metal system, austenitic stainless steels exposed to low-oxygen (less than 10 ppm) sodium decarburized at 650 to 700°C and carburized in the lower temperature zones. In a mixed system, stabilized 16Cr-13Ni-Nb steel picked up carbon to a depth of 100 μm (4mils) from 18Cr-9Ni steel in 1000 h at 600 to 700°C in sodium of less than 10 ppm oxygen.[55]

Carbon has been shown to penetrate stainless steel both inter- and intragranularly producing $M_{23}C_6$ in the matrix material and, in the case of Type 316 stainless steel, M_6C carbide at the surface.[37]

In a 20,000-h loop study, the gross carbon content of Type 316 stainless steel in the hot leg doubled while the carbon content of 2¼ Cr-1Mo steel in the cold leg correspondingly decreased.[56]

Evaluation of a sodium test loop with Type 316 in the hot leg and Type 304 in the cold leg has shown that both carbon and nitrogen are lost from the high-temperature regions of the system and deposited either elementally (for carbon) or in combination with other elements in the areas of decreasing temperature and in the cold-leg regions.[57] Surface values of less than 100 ppm have been observed at a 719°C region for both carbon and nitrogen with depleted depths to up to 750 μm (30 mils). High carbon and nitrogen levels in the cold leg up to 1200 ppm are attributed to surface deposits. There is no evidence to indicate that carbon and nitrogen diffuse into cold-leg components.

A mathematical analysis to be used to evaluate and predict the carburization-decarburization behavior of Types 304 and 316 stainless steel exposed to sodium has been developed.[58]

Zirconium is often used in a hot trap to getter oxygen from sodium. In less than 1000-h exposure the carbon contents of Types 304 and 316 stainless steel exposed to zirconium-gettered sodium at 705 and 760°C were reduced by 30 to 50%.[59]

Nitriding of stainless steels has occurred when nitrogen was used as a cover gas in a sodium system.[60,61] The nitriding appears to be a function of alloy composition.[62,63]

Exposure of sodium to ambient air and subsequent refill and operation at temperature can cause intergranular attack in unstressed material and cracking in stressed austenitic stainless steel.[64,65]

Potassium   The resistance of 18Cr-8Ni grades of stainless steels to corrosion by sodium and potassium is comparable. Reported corrosion rates at temperatures to 850°C fall within the range of 0.2 to 2.0 mg/(cm²)(month) or 2.5 to 15 μm/yr (0.1 to 1.0 mil/yr).[66,67]

An 8000-h test with Type 316 stainless steel in (32 to 38 ppm oxygen) potassium flowing at 1.5 m/s (5 ft/s) and a maximum temperature of 816°C with a ΔT of 167°C resulted in a weight loss rate of 34 mg/(dm²)(month) and less than 25 μm (<1 mil) intergranular attack.[68] Under less favorable conditions, more than 100 ppm oxygen and greater than 4.5 m/s (>15 ft/s) velocity, complete grain removal occurred in 385 h.[68] In other tests with Type 316 stainless steel at 760 to 871°C in a thermal-convection loop, the penetration rate was 7.5 μm/yr (0.3 mil/yr) while in a forced-convection loop the rate was 15 μm/yr (0.6 mil/yr).[69-71] In these tests, nitrogen and carbon from the stainless steel migrated to other metallics in the system.[71]

A Type 316 stainless steel loop which operated 24,000 h circulating potassium-sodium eutectic at 593 to 760°C revealed 24 μm (1 mil) decarburization in the hotter regions and 125 μm (5 mils) carburization in the colder regions.[72]

Pitting and tunneling to a depth of 1250 μm (50 mils) was found in Type 316 stainless steel exposed to potassium at 760°C after 350 h.[73]

Lithium   Seebold et al.[74] showed that chromium was selectively removed from Type 304 stainless steel by air-contaminated lithium. High-purity lithium (no chloride, less than 100 ppm nitrogen) under helium, lithium contaminated with 0.36% air, and long-term air-contaminated lithium under air were exposed to the stainless steel at a maximum of 816°C and a minimum of 427°C. For high-purity lithium, only a small mass-transfer deposit was found after 720 h. The deposit consisted of all the constituents of the stainless steel, intergranular penetration was less than one grain diameter, and the lithium contained 0.1% Cr(VI). The mass-transfer deposit resulting from the action of the lithium contaminated with 0.36% air was ferromagnetic and almost plugged the tube in 72 h. The intergranular penetration was a little more than one grain diameter, and 4.6% chromium was found in the lithium near the mass-transfer deposit. Beyond the deposit zone, in the cooler section, 16.9% chromium was found in the lithium. The tube that contained the long-time air-contaminated lithium became completely plugged over a distance of 4 cm in 48 h. The mass-transfer deposits were strongly ferromagnetic and consisted of 85 to 86Fe-7 to 10Ni-4 to 7Mn, and up to 2% chromium. The chromium content of the lithium was 12% within the deposit zone and 25% beyond the deposit zone. Electron microprobe analysis indicated that the mass-transfer deposits consisted of a uniform mixture of iron and nickel. Analysis of the corroded tubing showed that chromium has been preferentially removed to a depth of 10 μm (0.4 mil). Almost no chromium was seen in the first 5 μm (0.2 mil). The effect of the air-contaminated lithium on the corrosion behavior of the stainless steel was due to oxygen (or nitrogen) impurities (oxidation) and was not typical of pure lithium behavior. Thus the chromium depletion was due to chromium being electrochemically less noble than nickel or iron.

Lithium can attack grain-boundary carbide precipitates and cause grain-boundary penetration in Types 430 and 446 stainless steels. Austenitic stainless steels have the additional problem of nickel removal at grain boundaries and selective removal of chromium and nickel from specimen surfaces.[75] High-carbon-content stainless steels tend to decarburize.[76]

Type 316 stainless steel exposed to 538°C lithium flowing at 0.6 m/s (2 ft/s) showed less than 12-μm (<0.5-mil) penetration after 160 h.[77] Stainless steels start to mass transfer in lithium at temperatures above 600°C.[78] At 649°C, 195°C ΔT, Type 310 stainless steel had a penetration rate of 100 μm (4 mils) in 1000 h.[79] At higher temperatures, 704 to 815°C, attack and mass transfer become more severe.

Cesium   Stainless steels, both austenitic and ferritic, exposed to liquid and gaseous cesium at temperatures from 400 to 870°C and for 500 h showed very little attack and some weight gain.[80-82] Oxygen in the cesium is apparently responsible for the weight gain as it causes the formation of a complex mixture of oxides on the stainless steel.[80] There are indications that stainless steels experience liquid-metal embrittlement in liquid cesium.[83]

Lead   Stainless steels have rather poor resistance in lead. Nickel has a rather high solubility, and chromium has a higher solubility than iron.

Type 304 stainless steel is unattacked by 400°C lead in 500 h exposure.[84] Corrosion increases as the temperature is raised. For example, the calculated corrosion rate of Type 410 stainless steel is 330 μm/yr (13 mils/yr) in 1346 h in 655°C lead with a 167°C ΔT.[85] In 1000°C lead the corrosion rate of Types 302 and 347 stainless steel was 1000 μm/yr (39 mils/yr).[86] However, in 982°C lead, Type 446 stainless steel exhibited only slight attack after 250 h.[87]

Bismuth   Bismuth can be quite aggressive to stainless steels. Bismuth is generally much more corrosive to stainless steel than lead and mercury, primarily because of the much higher solubility of stainless steel constituents in bismuth. Nickel has a very high solubility in bismuth, 3.0 wt % at 450°C and about 5.4 wt % at 550°C.[88] In general, corrosion increases with increasing temperature, thermal gradient, chromium and nickel content. Zirconium has been shown to be an effective inhibitor.[88]

The lead-bismuth eutectic (45Pb-55Bi) is less aggressive than bismuth. In general, the austenitic stainless steels exhibit good resistance at 230°C, some attack at 570°C, and poor resistance at 1000°C.[89]

Types 304 and 430 stainless steels were severely attacked at 750°C by Bi-Te mixtures with corrosion rates that increased rapidly with tellurium concentration.[90] At tellurium concentrations of less than 1 wt %, Type 304L was attacked much more than Type 430. This effect was due to the large solubility of nickel in bismuth. Type 430 can be used to approximately 275°C.

Mercury   The corrosion rates for some stainless steels in mercury are summarized in Table 6.[91-94]

TABLE 6   Corrosion of Steels in Mercury

Material type	Temperature, °C	Time, h	Corrosion rate, μm/yr
405	482	2160	28
406	482	1440	76
410	538	1440	61
	649	1440	107
304	649	460	500
347	482	720	1000
310	649	500	1200

Unalloyed and low-alloy steels are more resistant to attack by mercury than are the stainless steels primarily because of the solubility of nickel.[95]

Tin, Zinc, Aluminum, Cadmium   Austenitic and ferritic stainless steels have limited-to-poor corrosion resistance to tin, zinc, aluminum, and cadmium at their melting points and poor resistance above.[89]

Gallium   Types 430 and 347 stainless steel are resistant to gallium at 200°C but react readily at higher temperatures.[96] Exposure of the above alloys for 2 days at 350°C caused no attack.[89]

Indium   Austenitic stainless steel was not attacked by indium in static tests at 650 and 750°C.[89,97] However, Type 316 stainless steel was penetrated in 134 h in a loop test at 600 and 700°C.

A recent text by Berry[98] includes many references to molten-salt and liquid-metal corrosion of stainless steel and many different alloys and metals and is recommended for a more complete picture of the various types of corrosion.

REFERENCES

1. Nelson, W., and A. Cain: *Trans. ASME,* vol. 82, p. 1940, 1960.
2. Rahmel, A.: *Arch. Eisenhuettenwes.,* vol. 31, p. 59, 1961.
3. Rahmel, A.: *Mitt. Ver. Gross Kesselbesitzer,* vol. 74, p. 319, 1961.
4. Rahmel, A., and W. Jäger: *Z. Anorg. Allg. Chem.,* vol. 303, p. 90, 1960.
5. Sedor, P., E. K. Diehl, and D. H. Barnhart: External Corrosion of Superheaters in Boilers Firing High-Alkali Coals, *Trans. ASME,* vol. 82, pp. 181–190, 1960.
6. Mikulin, A. D., Yu. V. Mikulin, G. G. Koznov, R. M. Berezina, L. A. Aleksandrova, and B. V. Losikov: "Oil Ash Corrosion," pp. 219–227, Moskva, Mashgiz, 1962.
7. Kovalev, Ye. A.: "Oil Ash Corrosion," pp. 190–201, Moskva, Mashgiz, 1962.
8. Lipshteyn, R. A., S. E. Khaykina, E. S. Ginsburg, T. A. Blagova, and A. S. Avetisyan: Vanadium Corrosion of Heat-resistant Steel, pp. 158–171, "Corrosion Prevention in Internal Combustion Engines, and Gas Turbines," pp. 158–171, Moskva, Mashgiz, 1962.
9. Bishop, R. J., and J. A. C. Samms: Corrosion of Austenitic Superheater Steels by Alkali Sulfate-Alkali Chloride Mixtures in Air and in Combustion Gases, *Werkst. Korros.,* vol. 17, pp. 197–207, 1966.
10. Ishihara, Y.: High Temperature Corrosion of Stainless Steel by Fuel Oil Ash, *Bu. Jpn. Pet. Inst.,* vol. 10, pp. 28–33, 1968.
11. Harada, Y., and K. Abe: High Temperature Corrosion on Austenitic Stainless Superheater Tubes by Heavy Oil Ashes, *Boshoki Gijutsu,* vol. 20, pp. 516–524, 1971.
12. Miller, P. D., H. H. Krause, J. Zupan, and W. K. Boyd: Corrosive Effects of Various Salt Mixtures under Combustion Gas Atmospheres, *Corrosion,* vol. 28, p. 223, 1972.
13. Miller, P. D., and H. H. Krause: Factors Influencing the Corrosion of Boiler Steels in Municipal Incinerators, *Corrosion,* vol. 27, p. 31, 1971.
14. Baes, C. R., Jr.: The Chemistry and Thermodynamics of Molten Salt Reactor Fuels, *Reprocessing of Nuclear Fuels,* vol. 15, pp. 617–644, 1969.

15. Long, G.: *Reactor Chem. Div. Ann. Prog. Rept., Jan. 31, 1965, USAEC Rep. ORNL-3789*, p. 65, 1965.
16. Koger, J. W.: *MSR Program Semiann. Prog. Rept., Aug. 31, 1970, USAEC Rept. ORNL-4622*, p. 170, 1970.
17. Manly, W. D.: Corrosion Behavior of Fused Fuels, *Proc. 2d Fluid Fuels Dev. Conf., USAEC Rept. ORNL-CF-52-4-197*, p. 370–412, 1952.
18. Buttram, H. J., R. O. Hutchison, and P. J. Hagelston: Corrosion Test by Fluoride Salt, *USAEC Rept. Y-B15-19*, 1951.
19. Koger, J. W.: Alloy Compatibility with LiF-BeF$_2$ Salts Containing ThF$_4$ and UF$_4$, *USAEC Rept. ORNL-TM-4286*, 1972.
20. Goldman, A. E., and A. P. Litman: Corrosion Associated with Hydrofluorination in the Oak Ridge National Laboratory Fluoride Volatility Process, *USAEC Rept. ORNL-2833*, 1961.
21. Susskind, H., F. B. Hill, L. Green, S. Kalish, L. Kukacka, W. E. McNulty, and E. Wirsing, Jr.: Corrosion Studies for a Fused Salt-Liquid Metal Extraction Process for the Liquid Metal Fuel Reactor, *USAEC Rept. BNL-585*, 1960.
22. Susskind, H., F. B. Hill, L. Green, S. Kalish, L. Kukacka, W. E. McNulty, and E. Wirsing: Combating Corrosion in Molten Extraction Processes, *Chem. Eng. Prog.*, vol. 56, pp. 57–63, 1960.
23. Stepanov, S. I., E. B. Kachina-Pullo, V. N. Devyatkin, and E. A. Ukshe: Investigation of Corrosion Processes in Molten Chlorides, in A. I. Belyaev (ed.), "Surface Phenomena in Metallurgical Processes," pp. 203–210, trans. by Consultant. Bureau, New York, 1965.
24. Kochergin, V. P., A. V. Kabirov, and O. N. Skornyakova: *Zh. Prikl. Khim.*, vol. 27, p. 944, 1954, as cited in ref. 23.
25. Kochergin, V. P., M. S. Garpinenko, O. N. Skornyakova, and I. Sh. Minulina: *Zh. Prikl. Khim.*, vol. 29, p. 566, 1956, as cited in Ref. 23.
26. Kochergin, V. P., and G. I. Stolyarova: *Zh. Prikl. Khim.*, vol. 29, p. 703, 1956, as cited in Ref. 23.
27. Tomashov, N. D., and N. I. Tugarinov: *Zh. Prikl. Khim.*, vol. 30, p. 1619, 1957, as cited in Ref. 23.
28. Delimarskii, Yu. K., and B. F. Markov: Electrochemistry of Molten Salts, *Metallurgizdat*, 1960, as cited in Ref. 23.
29. Edeleanu, C., J. G. Gibson, and J. E. Meredith: Effects of Diffusion on Corrosion of Metals by Fused Salts, *Proprietes des Joints de Grains, 4th Colloque de Metallurgie*, Jun. 27–28, 1960, Saclay, France, pp. 71–74, 1961.
30. Seybolt, A. U.: *Oxid. Met.*, vol. 2, pp. 119–143, 1970.
31. Hiller, M. A., T. L. Young, L. F. Grantham, and W. S. Ginell: Molten Phosphate Reactor Fuels. II— Corrosion of Metals in Molten Sodium Polyphosphate, *USAEC Rept. NAA-SR-5926*, 1961.
32. Williams, D. D., J. A. Grand, and R. R. Miller: The Reactions of Molten Sodium Hydroxide with Various Metals, *J. Am. Chem. Soc.*, vol. 78, pp. 5150–5155, 1956.
33. Gregory, J. N., and P. F. Wave: Preliminary Work on Corrosion in Caustic Soda, *RCTC/P-33*, 1954.
34. Mottley, J. D.: *GEAP-4313*, General Electric Co., 1964.
35. Weeks, J. R., C. J. Kalmut, and D. H. Gurinsky: Corrosion by the Alkali Metals, "Alkali Metal Coolants," pp. 3–22, International Atomic Energy Agency, Vienna, 1967.
36. Thorley, A. W., and C. Tyzack: Corrosion Behavior of Steels and Nickel Alloys in High-Temperature Sodium, "Alkali Metal Coolants," pp. 97–118, International Atomic Energy Agency, Vienna, 1967.
37. Thorley, A. W., and J. A. Bardsley: *J. R. Microsc. Soc.*, vol. 88, pp. 431–447, 1968.
38. Roy, P., S. Dutina, and F. Comprelli: in J. E. Draley and J. R. Weeks (eds.), "Corrosion by Liquid Metals," pp. 1–20, Plenum, New York, 1970.
39. Romano, A. J., S. J. Watchel, and C. J. Kalmut: Preliminary Corrosion Results of Haynes 25 and Type 304 Stainless Steel with 4 and 12 ppm Oxygen in Sodium at Temperatures up to 760°C, *Proc. Int. Conf. Sodium Tech. and Large Fast Reactor Design,Part I*, pp. 151–152, *USAEC Rept. ANL-7520*, 1968.
40. Rowland, M. C., D. E. Plumlee, and R. S. Young: *GEAP-4831*, General Electric Co., 1965.
41. Whitlow, G. A., J. C. Cwynar, R. L. Miller, and S. L. Schrock: Sodium Corrosion Behavior of Alloys for Fast Reactor Application, in S. Jansson (ed.), *Chemical Aspects of Corrosion and Mass Transfer in Liquid Sodium, Proc. AIME Symp.*, Detroit, pp. 1–63, 1973.
42. Brasunas, Anton de S., and E. E. Stansbury: "Symposium on Corrosion Fundamentals," pp. 65–83, The University of Tennessee Press, 1956.
43. Zebroski, E. L., R. S. Young, F. A. Comprelli, and D. Dutina: Effects of Mass Transfer, and of Changes in Properties, on Austenitic Steels in Flowing Sodium, "Alkali Metal Coolants," pp. 195–210, International Atomic Energy Agency, Vienna, 1967.
44. Borgstedt, H. U.: Discussion of Grain Boundary Grooving of Type 304 Stainless Steel and Armco Iron due to Liquid-Sodium Corrosion, *Corrosion*, vol. 27, p. 478, 1971.
45. DeVan, J.: Corrosion of Iron-and Nickel-Base Alloys in High Temperature Sodium and NaK, "Alkali Metal Coolants," pp. 143–159, International Atomic Energy Agency, Vienna, 1967.
46. Roy, O., G. P. Wozadlo, and F. A. Comprelli: Mass Transport and Corrosion of Stainless Steels in Flowing Sodium Systems at 1300°F, *Proc. Int. Conf. Sodium Tech. and Large Fast Reactor Design, USAEC Rept. ANL-7520*, pp. 131–141, 1968.
47. Lee, W. T.: Corrosion of Type 18-18-2 Stainless Steel in 1200°F Static Sodium, *USAEC Rept. LMEC-69-11*, 1969.

48. Effects of Sodium Exposure on Corrosion and Strength of Stainless Steels, *Summary Report, Sodium Mass Transfer Program*, GEAP-10394, 1971.
49. Sandusky, D. W., J. S. Armijo, and W. J. Wagner: Influence of Long-Term Sodium Exposure on Composition and Micro-structure of Austenitic Alloys, *J. Nucl. Mater.*, vol. 46, pp. 225–243, 1973.
50. Claxton, K. T., and J. G. Collier: Mass Transport of Stainless Steel Corrosion Products in Flowing Liquid Sodium, in S. Jansson (ed.), *Chemical Aspects of Corrosion and Mass Transfer in Liquid Sodium, Proc. AIME Symp.*, Detroit, pp. 101–129, 1973.
51. Sagawa, N., H. Iba, T. Murata, and S. Kawahara: Transport and Deposition of Metals in Sodium-Stainless Steel Systems, *J. Nucl. Sci. Tech.*, vol. 10, pp. 458–469, 1973.
52. Isaacs, H. S., A. J. Romano, C. J. Klamut, and J. R. Weeks: A Model for the Downstream Effect in the Corrosion of Steels by Liquid Sodium, in S. Jansson (ed.), *Chemical Aspects of Corrosion and Mass Transfer in Liquid Sodium, Proc. AIME Symp.*, Detroit, pp. 223–231, 1973.
53. Borgstedt, H. U., and G. Grees: Relations between Corrosion Test Results and a Possible Mechanism of Liquid Sodium Corrosion, in S. Jansson (ed.), *Chemical Aspects of Corrosion and Mass Transfer in Liquid Sodium, Proc. AIME Symp.*, Detroit, pp. 265–277, 1973.
54. Blair, R. C., and Z. A. Munir: Predictions of Corrosion Rates of Stainless Steel in Flowing Liquid Sodium, *Corrosion*, vol. 26, p. 15, 1970.
55. Borgstedt, H. U.: Observations of a Transport of Carbon through Liquid Sodium from Unstabilized to Stabilized Austenitic Stainless Steel, *Corros. Sci.*, vol. 8, pp. 405–412, 1968.
56. Rowland, M. C., and D. E. Plumbee: Sodium Mass Transfer, XXII Metallurgical Examination of the Test Loops, *AEC Rept.* GEAP-4838, 1965.
57. Shiels, S. A., C. Bagnall, and S. L. Schrock: Interstitial Mass Transfer in Sodium Systems, in S. Jansson (ed.), *Chemical Aspects of Corrosion and Mass Transfer in Liquid Sodium, Proc. AIME Symp.*, Detroit, pp. 157–176, 1973.
58. Snyder, R. B., K. Nateson, T. F. Kassner: Generalized Method of Computing Carbon-Diffusion Profiles in Austenitic Stainless Steels Exposed to a Sodium Environment, *USAEC Rept. ANL-8015*, 1973.
59. Lee, W. T.: Biaxial Stress-Rupture Properties of Austenitic Stainless Steels in Zirconium-Gettered Sodium, *USAEC Rept. NAA-SR-12353*, 1967.
60. Brush, E. G., and C. R. Rodd: Preliminary Experiments on the Nitriding of Reactor Materials in Sodium, *USAEC Rept. KAPL-M-EGB-21*, 1955.
61. Gill, J. J., and J. C. Bokros: Nitriding of Type 304 Stainless Steel in a Sodium Nitrogen System, *USAEC Rept. NAA-SR-6162*, 1961.
62. Donaldson, D. M.: Compatibility Problems in Fast Reactors, in "Technology, Engineering and Safety," vol. 5, Progr. Nucl. Energy Series IV, pp. 89–121, Macmillan, New York, 1963.
63. Smith, C. S.: Grains, Faces and Interfaces: An Interpretation of Microstructure, *Trans. Am. Inst. Min. Metall. Pet. Eng.*, vol. 175, pp. 15–51, 1948.
64. Comprelli, F. A., F. J. Hetzler, and T. A. Lauriten: Clad Compatibility with Mixed Oxide Fuel and Sodium, pp. 355–373, *Proc. Conf. Safety, Fuels, and Core Design in Large Fast Power Reactors, October 11–14, 1965, USAEC Rept. ANL-7120*.
65. Smith, F. A., E. L. Kimont, and L. H. Bohne: Water Cleaning and Air Storage Effects on Sodium-exposed Fuel Clad Alloys, 304 and 304L Stainless Steel, pp. 426–436, *Proc. Int. Conf. Sodium Tech. and Large Fast Reactor Design, November 7–9, 1968, Pt. I. Sessions on Sodium Technology, USAEC Rept. ANL-7520*.
66. DeVan, J. H.: Compatibility of Structural Materials with Boiling Potassium, *USAEC Rept. ORNL-TM-1361*, 1966.
67. Harms, W. O., and A. P. Litman: Compatibility of Materials for Advanced Space Nuclear Power Systems, *USAEC Rept. ORNL-TM-1964*, 1967.
68. Walker, C. L., and H. D. Wilsted: Final Report—Investigation of Bimetallic Liquid Metal Systems, *USAEC Rept. GMAD-3643-8*, 1966.
69. Goldmann, K., and J. M. McKee: Oxygen Effects in a Type 316 Stainless Steel, Nb-1% Zr, Liquid Potassium System, *Nucl. Appl.*, vol. 6, pp. 321–331, 1969.
70. Goldmann, K., and J. M. McKee: Effects of Oxygen in a Type 316 Stainless Steel, Cb-1% Zr, Liquid Potassium System, *Trans. Am. Nucl. Soc.*, vol. 11, p. 115, 1968.
71. Hyman, N., S. Kostman, and J. McKee: MCR Liquid Metal Technology Summary Report, *USAEC Rept. GMAD-3078-32*, p. 2, 1965.
72. Hoffman, T. L.: Corrosion Experience with Type 317 Stainless Steel in Sodium-Potassium Eutectic Alloy at 1400°F, *USAEC Rept. IN-1185*, 1968.
73. Woodward, C. E., J. R. Potts, C. J. Lymperes, and G. F. Schenck: Post-Test Examinations of Type 316 Stainless Steel Pump Impeller R17C3, *Rept. no. TIM-842*, Pratt and Whitney Aircraft-CANEL, 1964.
74. Seebold, R. E., L. S. Birks, and E. J. Brooks: *Corrosion*, vol. 16, pp. 468–470, 1960.
75. Beskorovaynyy, N. M., V. K. Ivanov, and V. V. Petrashko: Corrosion of Chromium-Nickel Stainless Steel in Lithium, in V. S. Yemel'yanov and A. I. Yevstyukhin (eds.), "Metallurgy and Metallography of Pure Metals," pp. 163–172, Moscow, 1966. Joint Publ. Res. Service-37-701, pp. 33–41 (English trans.).
76. Amateau, M. F.: The Effect of Molten Alkali Metals on Containment Metals and Alloys at High Temperatures, *DMIC Rept. 169*, 1962.

77. Parkingson, W. W., and O. Sisman: Liquid Metal Loops Irradiated in the ORNL Graphite Reactor and the LITR, *USAEC Rept. ORNL-2630*, 1959.
78. DeVan, J. H., A. P. Litman, J. R. DiStefano, and C. E. Sessions: Lithium and Potassium Corrosion Studies with Refractory Metals, "Alkali Metal Coolants," pp. 675–695, International Atomic Energy, Vienna, 1967.
79. Dana, A. W., Jr., O. H. Baker, and M. Ferguson: Investigation of Large Scale Dynamic Liquid Lithium Corrosion Apparatus, *USAEC Rept. BW-5229*, 1952.
80. *Proc. NASA-AEC Liquid-Metals Corrosion Meeting*, Lewis Research Center, Cleveland, Ohio, Oct. 2–3 1963, vol. 1; pp. 243–246, Report NASA SP-41.
81. Research and Development Program of Thermionic Conversion of Heat to Electricity, *Rept. GEST-2035*, vol. 1, 1964.
82. Winslow, P. M.: Corrosivity of Cesium, *Corrosion*, vol. 21, pp. 341–349, 1965.
83. Levinson, D. W.: Stress-Dependent Interactions between Cesium and Other Materials, *Rept. no. IITRI-B215-22*, 1964.
84. Frye, J. H., W. D. Manly, and J. E. Cunningham: Metallurgy Div. Ann. Prog. Rept. for Period Ending, September 1, 1959, *USAEC Rept. ORNL-2839*, 1959.
85. Tolson, G. M., and A. Taboada: A Study of Lead and Lead Salt Corrosion in Thermal-Convection Loops, *USAEC ORNL-TM-1437*, 1966.
86. Wilkinson, W. D., E. W. Hoyt, and H. V. Rhude: Attack on Materials by Lead at 1000°C, *USAEC Rept. ANL-5449*, 1955.
87. Parkman, Ralph, and O. Cutler Shepard: Investigation of Materials for Use in a Heat Transfer System Containing Liquid Lead Alloys, *Rept. no. XII, USAEC ORO-45*, 1951.
88. Romano, A. J., C. J. Klamut, and D. H. Gurinsky: The Investigation of Container Materials for Bi and Pb Alloys, Part I, Thermal Convection Loops, *USAEC Rept. BNL-811*, 1963.
89. Miller, E. C.: Corrosion of Materials by Liquid Metals, "Liquid Metals Handbook," NAVEXOS-P-733 (Rev.), 1952.
90. Kanne, W. R., Jr.: Corrosion of Metals by Liquid Bismuth-Tellurium Solutions, *Corrosion*, vol. 29, p. 75, 1973.
91. Nuclear Metallurgy, A Symposium on Behavior of Materials in Reactor Environment, Feb. 20, 1956, *IMD Spec. Rept. Ser. no. 2*, Institute of Metals Div., 1956.
92. Nejedlik, J. F., and E. J. Vargo: Kinetics of Corrosion in a Two Phase Mercury System, *Corrosion*, vol. 20, pp. 384–390, 1964.
93. Nejedlik, James F.: The SNAP 2 Power Conversion System, *USAEC Rept. NAA-SR-6311*, 1962.
94. Fleitman, A. H., A. J. Romano, and C. J. Klamut: Corrosion of Carbon of Steel by High-Temperature Liquid Mercury, *J. Electrochem. Soc.*, vol. 110, pp. 964–969, 1963.
95. Nejedlik, J. F., and E. J. Vargo: Material Resistance to Mercury Corrosion, *Electrochem. Techn.*, vol. 3, pp. 250–258, 1965.
96. Wilkinson, W. D.: Effects of Gallium on Materials at Elevated Temperatures, *USAEC Rept. ANL-5027*, 1953.
97. Derow, H., and B. E. Farwell: SNAP-8 Materials Semi-Annual Report, January, June 1966, *Rept. NASA-CR-72156*, 1966.
98. Berry, W. E.: "Corrosion in Nuclear Application," Wiley, New York, 1971.

Part **4**

Physical and Mechanical Properties

Chapter **19**

Physical Properties
of Stainless Steels

JACK R. LEWIS

Manager, Material Properties, Rocketdyne Division, Rockwell
International, Canoga Park, California

INTRODUCTION

The following physical properties of the stainless steels are covered in this chapter:
- Melting range
- Density
- Specific heat

- Thermal conductivity
- Thermal diffusivity
- Coefficient of expansion
- Electrical resistivity
- Magnetic permeability
- Elastic modulus

Where available, these properties are presented in graphical form as a function of temperature. In addition, summary tables are included showing the room-temperature physical properties of major wrought and cast alloys.

Graphical data are presented in ascending numerical sequence for wrought alloys and in alpha numerical order for cast alloys; e.g., 15-5PH is followed by 17-4PH, Type 201, Type 202, Type 301, etc. This order of presentation was felt to be more convenient to the user than a system organized according to crystallographic structure. Within each property group, the wrought alloys are covered first, followed by the cast alloys.

The data in this chapter were drawn from a variety of sources. In many cases, data from different sources were not in complete agreement, reflecting the normal variations from heat-to-heat of alloy and differences between experimental procedures of different laboratories. In such cases, judgment was used to present a compromise curve for practical engineering use.

TABLE 1   Wrought Alloys—Nominal Room-Temperature Properties

Alloy	Density		Thermal diffusivity		Thermal conductivity		Specific heat	
	lb/in.³	kg/m³	ft²/h	m²/h	Btu/(h)(ft²)(°F/ft)	cal/(s)(cm²)(°C/cm)	Btu/(lb)(°F)	cal/(g)(°C)
201	0.28	7700			9.4*	0.039	0.12	0.39
202	0.28	7700	0.13	0.012	9.4*	0.039	0.12	0.39
301	0.28	7700	0.16	0.015	8.5	0.035	0.11	0.36
302	0.29	8000			7.0	0.029	0.12	0.39
303	0.29	8000			7.0	0.029	0.12	0.39
304	0.29	8000	0.15	0.014	8.0	0.033	0.09	0.29
305	0.29	8000			9.4	0.039	0.12	0.39
308	0.29	8000			8.8	0.036	0.12	0.39
309	0.29	8000	0.13	0.012	9.0	0.037	0.12	0.39
310	0.29	8000			7.0	0.029	0.10	0.33
316	0.29	8000	0.15	0.014	7.8	0.032	0.11	0.36
321	0.29	8000	0.14	0.013	9.3*	0.038	0.11	0.36
347	0.29	8000			8.5	0.035	0.10	0.33
403	0.28	7700			14.4*	0.059	0.11	0.36
405	0.28	7700			15.6*	0.064	0.11	0.36
409	0.28	7700			14.4*	0.059	0.11	0.36
410	0.28	7700	0.23	0.021	14.4*	0.059	0.11	0.36
414	0.28	7700			14.4*	0.059	0.11	0.36
416	0.28	7700	0.26	0.024	14.4*	0.059	0.11	0.36
420	0.28	7700			13.5	0.055	0.11	0.36
430	0.28	7700	0.23	0.021	11.9	0.049	0.11	0.36
434	0.28	7700					0.11	0.36
436	0.28	7700			13.8*	0.057	0.11	0.36
440-C	0.28	7700			14.0*	0.057	0.11	0.36
446	0.27	7500	0.21	0.020	10.5	0.043	0.11	0.36
AM350					8.2	0.034		
AM355	0.28	7700			8.2	0.034		
Custom 450	0.28	7700						
Custom 455†	0.28	7700			10.0	0.041		
PH15-7MO†	0.28	7700			9.0	0.037		
15-5 PH†	0.28	7700					0.11	0.36
17-4 PH†	0.28	7700			6.5	0.027	0.10	0.33

*Thermal conductivity at 212°F.
†Annealed.

DEFINITIONS

Coefficient of Thermal Expansion   The change in a unit measure of material occasioned by a change of one degree in temperature. Coefficient of expansion is thus the slope of the dilation-temperature curve. The instantaneous coefficient of expansion is the slope at a specific temperature; the mean coefficient is the mean slope between two designated temperatures. Coefficients of expansion may be expressed in either volumetric or linear terms, with the latter being most commonly used.

Density   The density of a material is the mass contained in a unit volume. The units are kilograms per cubic meter or pounds per cubic inch.

Elastic Modulus   The force per unit area required to cause a unit change in length of a material when applied to opposite ends of a prism of unit length. The stress required to develop unit strain; or the slope of the elastic portion of a stress-strain curve. Units are expressed as pounds per square inch or Pascals (Newtons per square meter).

Electrical Resistivity   The electrical resistance measured between opposite faces of a cube of material of unit dimensions. Resistivity is expressed in ohm-meters, microhm-centimeters, or (archaically), ohms per circular mil-foot.

Magnetic Permeability   A dimensionless parameter expressing the ease by which a material can be magnetized. The ratio of induction to magnetizing force.

Electrical resistivity, $\mu\Omega$-cm	Mean coefficient of expansion		Elastic modulus		Magnetic permeability	Melting range	
	70-800°F μin./(in.)(°F)	20-425°C μm/(m)(°C)	10^6 psi	10^4MPa		°F	°C
69	10.2	(18.4)	28	19.3	1.02	2550–2650	1398–1454
69	10.4	(18.7)	28	19.3	1.008	2550–2650	1398–1454
72	10.0	(18.0)	29	20.0	1.02	2550–2590	1398–1420
70	9.8	(17.6)	28	19.3	1.008	2550–2590	1398–1420
72	9.8	(17.6)	28	19.3	1.008	2550–2590	1398–1420
70	10.1	(18.2)	29	20.0	1.008	2550–2650	1398–1454
72	9.8	(17.6)	28	19.3	1.008	2550–2650	1398–1454
72	10.1	(18.2)	28	19.3	1.008	2550–2590	1398–1420
78	9.6	(17.3)	29	20.0	1.008	2550–2650	1398–1454
88	9.3	(16.7)	28	19.3	1.008	2550–2650	1398–1454
73	9.7	(17.5)	28	19.3	1.008	2500–2550	1371–1398
72	9.7	(17.5)	29	20.0	1.008	2550–2600	1398–1427
72	10.0	(18.0)	29	20.0	1.008	2550–2600	1398–1427
57	6.4	(11.5)	29	20.0		2700–2790	1483–1532
61	6.7	(12.1)	29	20.0		2700–2790	1483–1532
61	6.5	(11.7)	29	20.0		2700–2790	1483–1532
58	6.2	(11.2)	32	22.0	700–1000	2700–2790	1483–1532
72	6.4	(11.5)	29	20.0		2600–2700	1427–1483
57	6.3	(11.3)	29	20.0	700–1000	2700–2790	1483–1532
55	6.4	(11.5)	29	20.0		2650–2750	1454–1510
60	6.2	(11.2)	28	19.3	600–1100	2600–2750	1427–1510
60	6.6	(11.9)	29	20.0	600–1100	2600–2750	1427–1510
60			29	20.0	600–1100	2600–2750	1427–1510
	6.7	(12.1)	29	20.0		2500–2700	1371–1483
64	6.1	(11.0)	29	20.0	400–700	2600–2750	1427–1510
78	7.1	(12.8)	29	20.0			
75	7.3	(13.1)	29	20.0			
99	6.1	(11.0)	28	19.3			
90	6.6	(11.9)	29	20.0	109		
80	8.9	(16.0)	28	19.3	5.3		
98	6.3	(11.3)	28	19.3	95		
98	6.2	(11.2)	28	19.3	95		

Melting Range   The temperatures which define the solidus and liquidus of an alloy.

Specific Heat   The quantity of heat required to change by one degree the temperature of a body of material of unit mass. The numerical value of specific heat is the same in both English and CGS units, because the unit of heat (Btu or calories) is defined as the quantity of heat required to raise one unit mass of water by one degree. The numerical value of specific heat in the International System is *not* the same as in the English or CGS systems, since the unit of energy (the Joule) is defined differently. Units of specific heat are Btu/(lb)(°F) and Joules/(kg)(°K).

Thermal Conductivity   A measure of the rate at which a material transmits heat. If a thermal gradient of one degree per unit length is established over a material of unit cross-sectional area, then the thermal conductivity is defined as the quantity of heat transmitted per unit time. Thermal conductivity is expressed in units of Btu/(h)(ft^2)(°F/ft) or W/(m^2)(°K/m). These expressions are frequently abbreviated as Btu/h-ft-°F or Watts/meter-°K.

Thermal Diffusivity   A property which determines the rate at which a temperature front moves through a material. The ratio of thermal conductivity to the product of specific heat and density. Thermal diffusivity is expressed in units of square feet per hour, or square meters per second.

A summary of some physical properties of wrought alloys at room temperature is contained in Table 1. Similar data for cast alloys can be found in Chap. 2, Table 5.

THERMAL EXPANSION

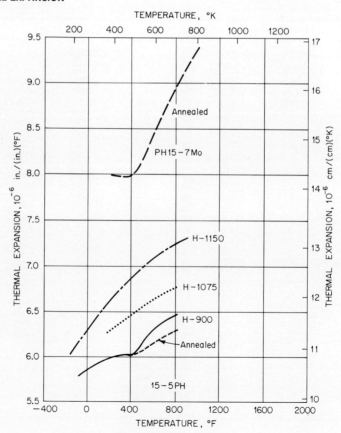

Fig. 1   (Ref. 4, 7, 13, 23.)

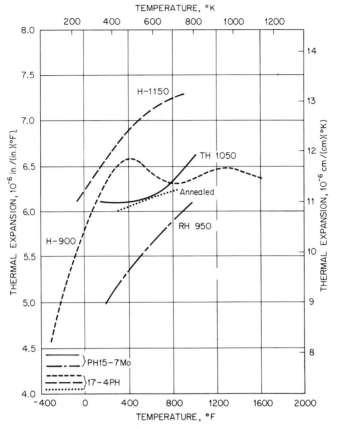

Fig. 2   (Ref. 4, 7, 8, 9, 23.)

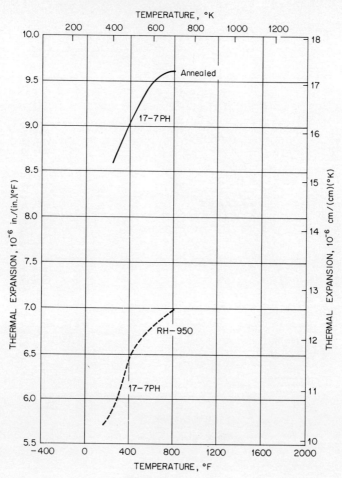

Fig. 3   (Ref. 4, 7, 23.)

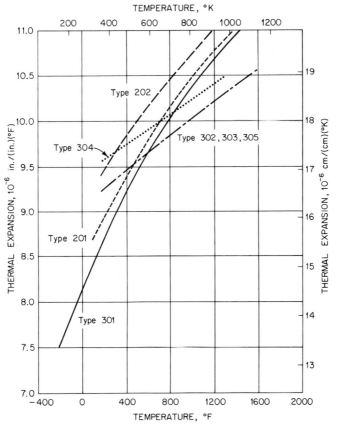

Fig. 4   (Ref. 2, 4, 5, 7, 8, 10, 15.)

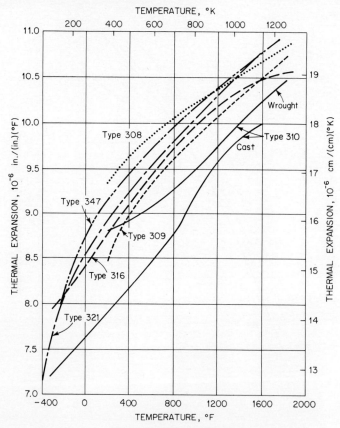

Fig. 5   (Ref. 2, 5, 7, 8, 10, 15.)

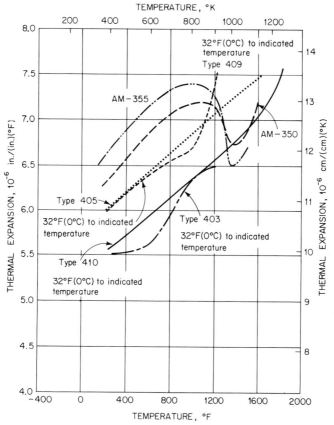

Fig. 6   (Ref. 2, 3, 4, 7, 15.)

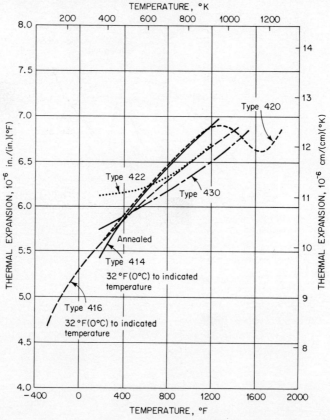

Fig. 7   (Ref. 2, 3, 7, 8, 10, 15.)

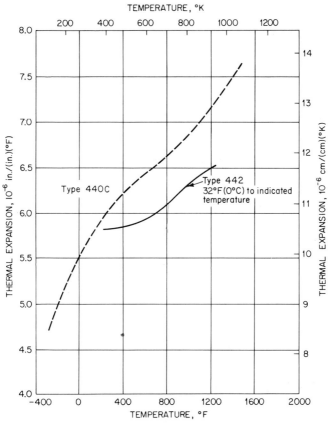

Fig. 8   (Ref. 2, 3, 4, 8, 11, 15.)

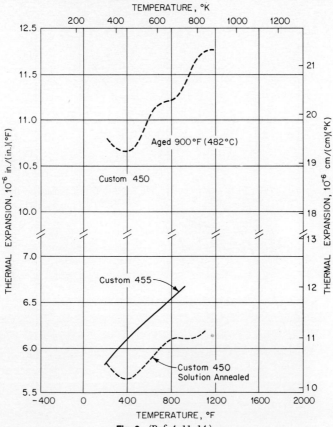

Fig. 9 (Ref. 4, 11, 14.)

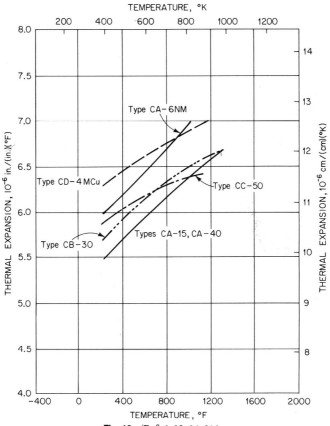

Fig. 10   (Ref. 4, 12, 14, 21.)

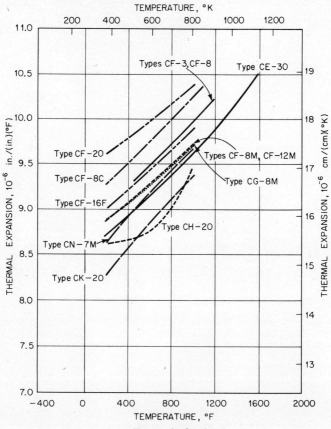

Fig. 11   (Ref. 21.)

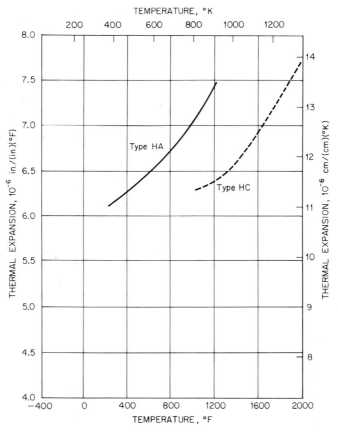

Fig. 12   (Ref. 22.)

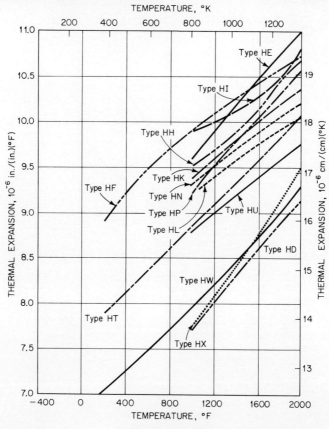

Fig. 13 (Ref. 22.)

THERMAL CONDUCTIVITY

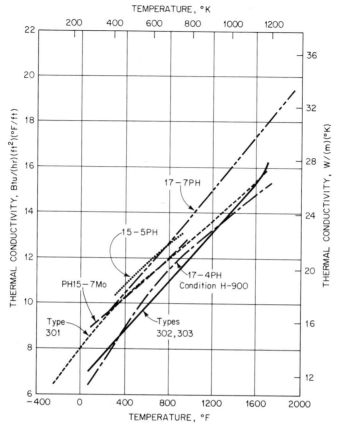

Fig. 14 (Ref. 4, 5, 13, 16, 17, 18, 23, 24, 25, 26.)

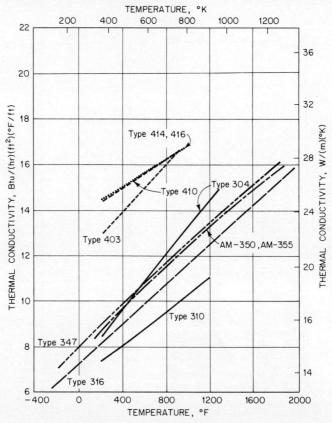

Fig. 15   (Ref. 2, 3, 4, 5, 16, 26, 27, 33.)

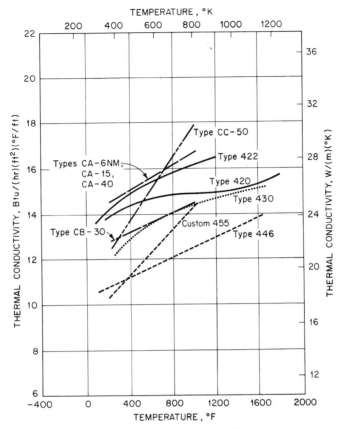

Fig. 16   (Ref. 2, 3, 4, 12, 15, 21, 26, 28.)

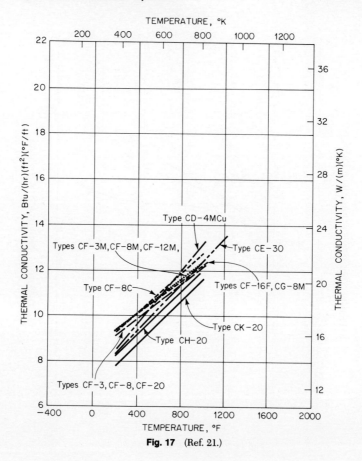

Fig. 17   (Ref. 21.)

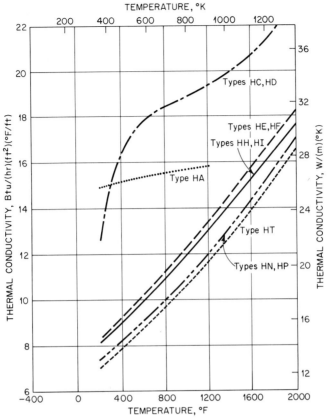

Fig. 18   (Ref. 22.)

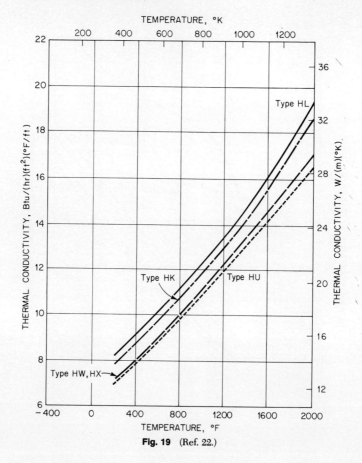

Fig. 19   (Ref. 22.)

THERMAL DIFFUSIVITY

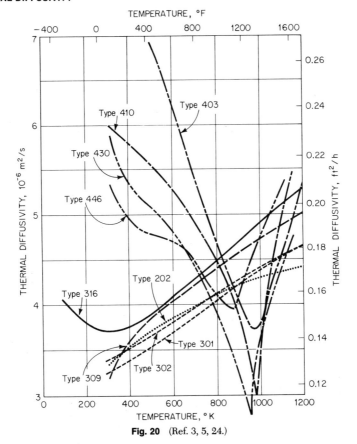

Fig. 20   (Ref. 3, 5, 24.)

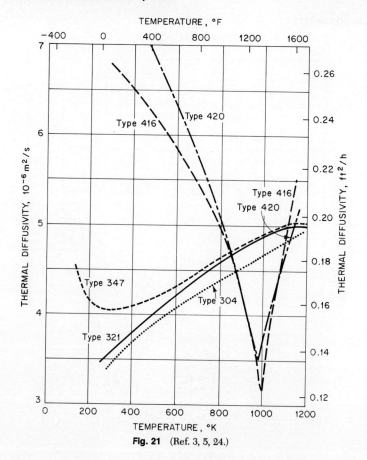

Fig. 21 (Ref. 3, 5, 24.)

SPECIFIC HEAT

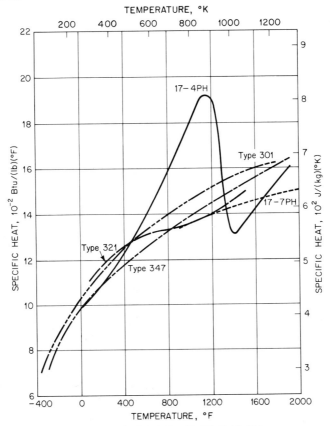

Fig. 22   (Ref. 1, 4, 5, 6, 19, 25, 26, 29, 30.)

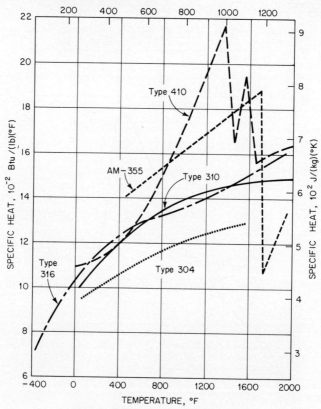

Fig. 23   (Ref. 1, 3, 5, 6, 19, 26, 29, 30, 33.)

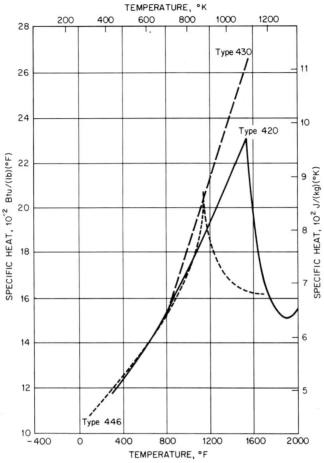

Fig. 24   (Ref. 3, 25, 26, 30, 31.)

ELECTRICAL RESISTIVITY

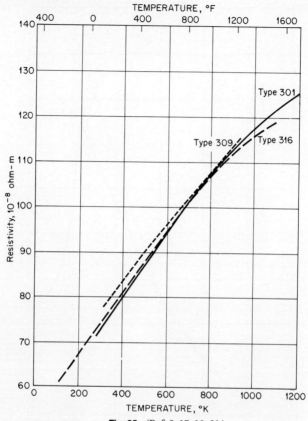

Fig. 25   (Ref. 6, 15, 16, 20.)

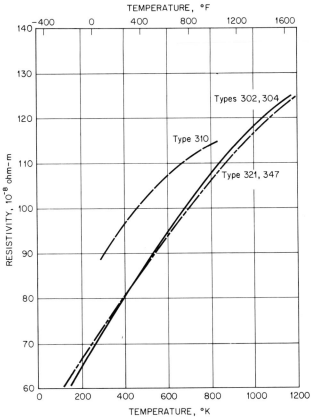

Fig. 26   (Ref. 6, 15, 20.)

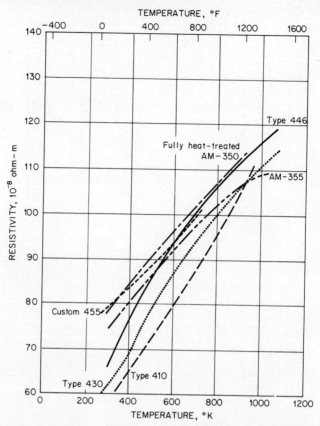

Fig. 27   (Ref. 3, 12, 15, 16.)

ELASTIC MODULUS

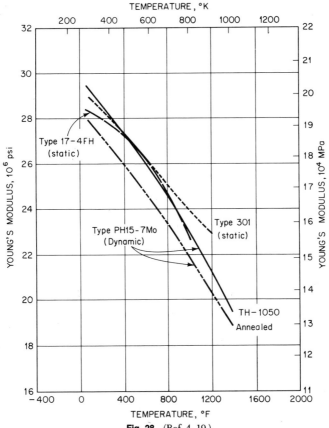

Fig. 28   (Ref. 4, 19.)

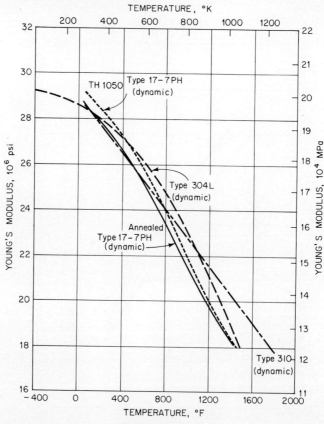

Fig. 29   (Ref. 7, 19.)

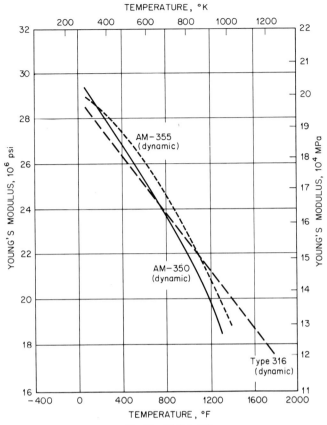

Fig. 30 (Ref. 4, 19.)

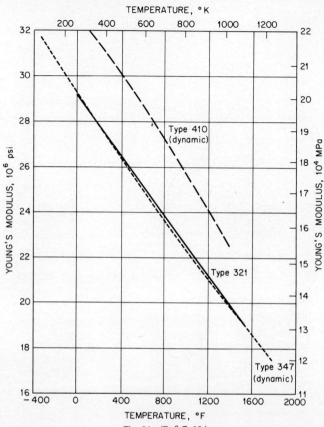

Fig. 31   (Ref. 7, 19.)

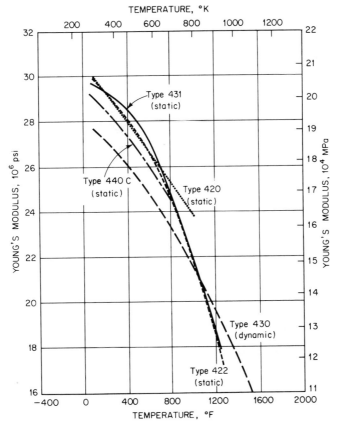

Fig. 32   (Ref. 19, 31.)

REFERENCES

1. Neel, D. S., et al.: The Thermal Properties of Thirteen Solid Materials to 5000 F or Their Destructive Temperatures, *Tech. Documentary Rep. No. WADD 60-924*, 1962.
2. "Properties of 200:300:400 Series," Republic Steel Corp., Cleveland, Ohio, 1972.
3. Haag, J. G., and D. B. Roach: Some Physical Properties of Martensitic Stainless Steels; *DMIC Memo 68*, 1960.
4. "Metallic Materials and Elements for Aerospace Vehicle Structures," MIL-HDBK-5B, Dept. of Defense, 1972.
5. Lucks, C. F., and H. W. Deem: Thermal Properties of Thirteen Metals, *ASTM Spec. Tech. Publ.* 227,1958.
6. Finch, R. A.: The Resistivity and Specific Heat of Type 310 Stainless Steel from the Apollo H-11 Heat Transfer Model, TDR AI-64-128, Atomics International Div., Rockwell International, Canoga Park, Calif., 1964.
7. Rion, W. C., Jr.: Stainless Steel Information Manual for the Savannah River Report, *DP 860, Vol. I*, U.S. Dept. of Commerce, 1964.
8. Williams, L. R., J. D. Young, and E. H. Schmidt: Design and Development Engineering Handbook of Thermal Expansion Properties of Aerospace Materials at Cryogenic and Elevated Temperatures, *Report R-6981*, Rocketdyne Div., Rockwell International, Canoga Park, Calif., 1967.
9. Deel, O. L., and H. Mindlin: Engineering Data on New Aerospace Structural Materials, *AFML-TR-72-196*, 1972.
10. *Tech. Bull.* T411, Babcock and Wilcox Company, Beaver Falls, Pa.
11. "Carpenter Custom 450," Carpenter Technology Corporation, Reading, Pa., 1971.
12. "Carpenter Custom 455," Carpenter Technology Corporation, Reading, Pa., 1971.

13. Hoenie, A. F., and D. B. Roach: New Developments in High-Strength Stainless Steels, *DMIC 223*, 1966.
14. Deel, O. L., and H. Mindlin: Engineering Data on New Aerospace Structural Materials, *AFML-TR-71-249*, 1971.
15. "Blue Sheet" Technical Bulletins, Allegheny Ludlum Steel Corp., Pittsburgh, Pa.
16. Eldridge, E. A., and H. W. Deem: Report on Physical Properties of Metals and Alloys from Cryogenic to Elevated Temperatures, *ASTM Spec. Tech. Bull. 296*, 1960.
17. Schwartzbart, F. R.: Cryogenic Materials Data Handbook, *AFML-TDR-64-280*, vol. I, U.S. Air Force Materials Laboratory, 1968.
18. Ermolaev, B. I.: Thermal Conductivity of Alloy Steels, *Metalloved. Term. Obrab. Met.*, vol. 10, p. 1, October 1971.
19. Unpublished data, Rocketdyne Div., Rockwell International, Canoga Park, Calif.
20. Clark, A. F., G. E. Childs, and G. H. Wallace: Low-Temperature Electrical Resistivity of Some Engineering Alloys, *Cryog. Eng.*, vol. 15, p. 85, 1970.
21. High Alloy Data Sheets, Corrosion Series: Alloy Casting Inst. Div., Steel Founders' Society of America, Rocky River, Ohio.
22. High Alloy Data Sheets, Heat Series: Alloy Casting Inst. Div., Steel Founders' Society of America, Rocky River, Ohio.
23. "Precipitation Hardenable Stainless Steels," Republic Steel Corp., Cleveland, Ohio, 1972.
24. Jenkins, R. J., and R. W. Westover: Thermal Diffusivity of Stainless Steel over the Temperature Range 20°C–1000°C; *USNRDL-TR-484*, 1961.
25. Fieldhouse, I. B., et al.: Thermal Properties of High Temperature Materials, *WADC Tech. Rep. 57-487*, 1958.
26. Fieldhouse, I. B., and J. I. Lang: Measurement of Thermal Properties, *WADD-TR-60-904*, Armour Research Foundation, 1961.
27. Ewing, C. T., et al.: Thermal Conductivity of Liquid Sodium and Potassium, *J. Am. Chem. Soc.*, vol. 74, p. 11, 1952.
28. Silverman, L.: Thermal Conductivity Data Presented for Various Metals and Alloys up to 900°C, *J. Met.*, vol. 5, p. 631, 1953.
29. Lewis, J. R.: Personal files.
30. Douglas, T. B., and A. C. Victor: Enthalpy and Specific Heat of Nine Corrosion-Resistant Alloys at High Temperatures; *J. Res. Nat. Bur. Stand.*, vol. 65C, no. 1, p. 65, 1961.
31. Stull, D. R., and R. A. McDonald: The Enthalpy and Heat Capacity of Magnesium and of Type 430 Stainless Steel from 700 to 1100°K, *J. Am. Chem. Soc.*, vol. 77A, p. 5293, 1955.
32. Kattus, J. R., et al.: Determination of Tensile, Compressive, Bearing, and Shear Properties of Sheet Steels at Elevated Temperatures, *WADC TR-58-365*, Southern Research Inst., Birmingham, Alabama, 1958.
33. Fieldhouse, I. B., et al.: Measurements of Thermal Properties, *WADC-TR-58-274*, Armour Research Foundation, Chicago, 1958.

Chapter **20**

Mechanical Properties of Stainless Steels at Cryogenic Temperatures and at Room Temperature

K. G. BRICKNER
and
JOSEPH D. DEFILIPPI
Research Laboratory,
United States Steel Corporation, Monroeville, Pennsylvania

AT CRYOGENIC TEMPERATURES

Introduction

Metals intended for low-temperature service must exhibit certain desirable characteristics apart from, and in addition to, satisfactory engineering properties, such as yield and tensile strengths. Experience gained from the World War II failure of ship steels by brittle fracture has shown designers that many metals which are satisfactory for room-temperature service will not perform adequately at lower service temperatures.

The danger at low temperatures is brittle fracture, which can result in catastrophic destruction of complex engineering structures and equipment. Usually, at high temperatures, constructional metals will not fail without giving warning by stretching, sagging, bulging, or otherwise indicating failure plastically. At low temperatures, however, metals, which are ordinarily ductile, may suddenly fail without any evidence of prior plastic deformation and at very low levels of stress. Failures of this type are known as brittle failures. Figure 1 shows the effect of decreasing temperature on the toughness (as determined by the Izod impact test) and on the tensile elongation of annealed AISI Type

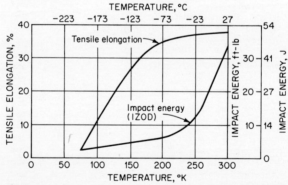

Fig. 1 Tensile elongation and impact energy of a chromium stainless steel (AISI Type 430, annealed).[1]

430 stainless steel.[1] Note the sharp decrease in toughness between room temperature and about −73°C (−100°F) and the sharp decrease in tensile elongation below about −101°C (−150°F). This steel behaves in a brittle manner at low temperatures.

To overcome the brittle-failure problem, structures and equipment are designed to minimize stress concentrations and to utilize materials that, based on tests and service experience, will exhibit a high degree of toughness under the service conditions.

Many steels perform admirably in relatively low-temperature service. However, relatively few steels are suitable for the handling, storage, or transportation of liquefied gases, such as nitrogen, oxygen, hydrogen, and helium. These liquefied gases boil at what are known as cryogenic temperatures; that is, those below about −101°C (−150°F). Within the family of stainless steels, only the austenitic stainless steels are suited for cryogenic service. The austenitic stainless steels exhibit tough behavior at cryogenic temperatures.

Although the toughness of materials at low temperatures is extremely important in the design of cryogenic equipment, other properties must also be considered. For instance, the tensile properties of a material are important because these determine the section thickness of the equipment. In addition, the thermal-expansion characteristics of a material are important because large changes in temperature, such as encountered in going from cryogenic temperatures to room temperature, can impose rather high stresses on a piece of equipment. Also, because cryogenic temperatures are relatively difficult to maintain, the thermal conductivity and the specific heat of materials are important to cryogenic-equipment designers. The physical properties of austenitic stainless steels were discussed in Chap. 19; this chapter will review the effect of cryogenic temperatures on the mechanical properties of austenitic stainless steels.

Effects of Composition and Heat Treatment

Austenitic Stability   The compositions of austenitic stainless steels have a pronounced influence on the mechanical properties at cryogenic temperatures. This effect is manifested primarily through control of austenite stability. Figure 2 shows the effect of decreasing temperature between +200 and −200°C (+392 and −364°F) on the tensile properties of a stable steel (such as AISI Type 310) and of a metastable steel (such as AISI Type 304).[2] Note the sharp increase in tensile strength and decrease in elongation with decreasing temperature in the metastable steels. Increased stability of austenitic stainless steels results primarily from an increase in the following elements, in decreasing order of potency: nitrogen, carbon, nickel, manganese, and chromium. Because nickel is a major alloying element in austenitic stainless steels, varying from about 4 to 22%, its effect is very great. Figure 3 shows the effect of nickel between 8 and 20% on tensile strength and elongation between room temperature and −200°C (−364°F).[2] That the effects shown in Fig. 3 are due to instability or transformation of austenite to martensite can be seen from Fig. 4.[2]

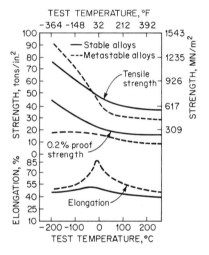

Fig. 2   Effect of alloy stability on tensile properties of austenitic steels.[2]

Nitrogen markedly affects the stability of austenitic stainless steels. Figure 5[2] shows the effect on tensile properties of adding 0.2% nitrogen to Type 304 steel as a function of decreasing temperature. Note that with decreasing temperature, the temperature dependence of the yield strength of Type 304N steel is greater than that of Type 304 steel but the temperature dependence of the tensile strengths of the two steels is about the same. Elongation, however, increases to a maximum between −90 and −100°C (−130 and −148°F) and then decreases slightly, but below −50°C (−58°F), the elongation of Type 304N steel is better than that of Type 304 steel.

The effect of decreasing the stability of Type 304N steel on low-temperature tensile properties by decreasing the nickel content of the steel is shown in Fig. 6.[2] In general, between room temperature and −200°C (−364°F), as nickel is decreased from a range of 8 to 10% to 5% yield strength and elongation decrease and tensile strength increases.

Tensile Properties   In considering the effect of cryogenic temperatures on the tensile properties of various austenitic stainless steels (Types 302, 304, 316, 321, 347, 309, and 310, Table 1[2]) note that the high ductility (elongation and reduction of area) of the austenitic stainless steels is retained at cryogenic temperatures. This behavior also holds down to −253°C (−425°F).[3] Note also that the yield and tensile strengths increase as the temperature is decreased, with the larger increase occurring in the tensile strength. The exceptions occur in Types 309 and 310 steels, which exhibit almost as great an increase in yield strength as in tensile strength. This behavior is probably due to the slightly higher amount of carbon[4] and greater austenite stability[5] in these steels as compared with the other steels listed in Table 1. Interstitial elements, such as carbon, are known to have a marked effect on the yield strength of alloys at low temperatures.

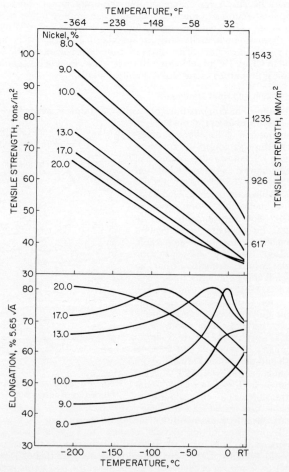

Fig. 3   Effect of nickel on the tensile strength and elongation properties at subzero test temperatures.[2]

Similarly, austenitic stainless steels containing intentional additions of nitrogen, such as Type 202 steel, exhibit higher yield strength at cryogenic temperatures than most other austenitic stainless steels. The cryogenic tensile properties of two nitrogen-containing austenitic stainless steels are shown in Table 2.

Toughness   As one might expect from the good ductility exhibited by the austenitic stainless steels, the toughness is excellent at cryogenic temperatures. Although there are differences in the energy absorbed in impact tests by the various austenitic stainless steels, these differences may not significantly affect their engineering performance. This occurs because for the relatively low yield strengths (compared with ferritic or martensitic steels) and high energy-absorption values, critical flaw sizes (calculated from fracture mechanic concepts) would generally be larger than the thicknesses at which these steels would generally be used. Therefore, these materials would yield plastically in service. The results of Charpy V-notch impact tests on Types 304, 304L, 310, and 347 steels conducted at room temperature, −196°C (−320°F), and −253°C (−425°F) are shown in Table 3.[3] The toughness of these four steels decreases somewhat as the temperature is decreased from room temperature to −196°C (−320°F), but on the

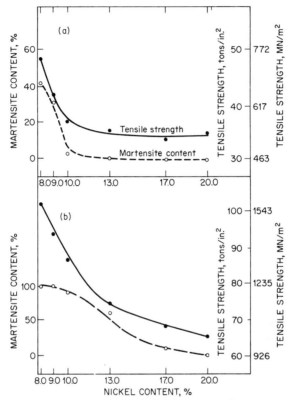

Fig. 4 Relationship between tensile strength and martensite content of austenitic steels with varying nickel content. (*a*) Room temperature. (*b*) At −196°C (−321°F).[2]

further decrease to −253°C (−425°F), the toughness remains about the same. The toughness is excellent at −253°C (−425°F) and the toughness of Types 304 and 310 is significantly higher than that of Types 304L and 347. The results of impact tests on these four steels at −196 and −253°C (−320 and −425°F) for various plate thicknesses,[3] Table 4, indicate that the toughness of the austenitic stainless steels is not markedly affected by plate thickness. Some additional toughness data for various austenitic stainless steels between room temperature and −196°C (−320°F) are shown in Table 1.[2] Inasmuch as the data were obtained from specimens machined from ¾-in.-diameter (19-mm) bar stock, the properties are not directly comparable with those from plate. Unlike the Cr-Ni austenitic stainless steels, the Cr-Mn-N austenitic stainless steels do not exhibit tough behavior at cryogenic temperatures (Fig. 7) although they are very stable.[6] Their brittle behavior at cryogenic temperatures has been attributed to deformation faulting.[6]

Fatigue Properties Another property that is important in cryogenic equipment subject to vibration is fatigue strength. Only relatively limited data are available on the fatigue properties of austenitic stainless steels at cryogenic temperatures; however, the available data indicate that the endurance limit increases as the temperature decreases (Fig. 8).[7] Also, Fig. 9 shows the fatigue properties of cold-worked Type 304 steel at several temperatures.[8] Both smooth and notched bars show increasing strength with decreasing temperatures, although the improvement in the fatigue life of the notched bars is less pronounced than in the smooth bars. This increase in fatigue strength of the austenitic

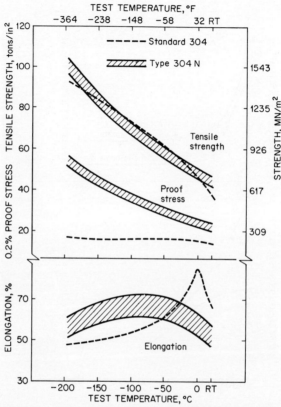

Fig. 5 Comparison of the tensile properties of Type 304N (0.2% nitrogen) and Type 304 steels at subzero temperatures.[2]

stainless steels with decreasing temperature is consistent with the increasing tensile strength noted in these steels with decreasing temperature. Most authorities believe that the fatigue strength correlates with the tensile strength of a material, the fatigue strength increasing with the tensile strength.

Some recent Russian studies[9] indicate that the fatigue limit increases monotonically with decreasing temperature for both smooth and notched samples of steels with a stable austenitic microstructure (Fig. 10). The martensitic transformation lowers the fatigue limit. A peak occurs on the curve showing the variation of the cycles to failure with temperature for an 18Cr-8Ni steel at −196°C (−320°F) (Fig. 11). If an 18Cr-10Ni steel is cold-worked to a strength of 150 kg/mm² (1468.6 MN/m²) and an 18Cr-8Ni steel to a strength of 170 kg/mm² (1664.5 MN/m²), the fatigue limit of the 18Cr-10Ni steel, with the more stable austenite, is about 55% of the ultimate strength, whereas that of the 18Cr-8Ni steel is only about 30%.

Heat Treatment   Except for the effects of sensitizing treatments, which simulate the effect of stress-relieving treatments (discussed in the next section), relatively little specific information is available concerning the effects of heat treatment on the properties of austenitic stainless steels at cryogenic temperatures. In general, as annealing temperature is raised, ductility and toughness are increased, and strength is decreased.

Effects of Fabrication

The fabrication of stainless steels involves two principal processes: forming, which imparts cold-work to the steels, and welding.

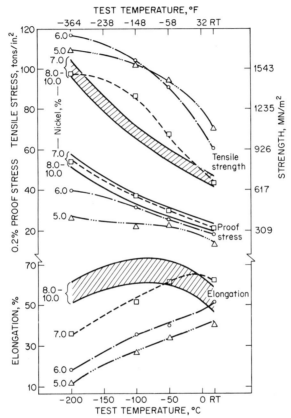

Fig. 6 Effect of nickel on tensile properties of nitrogen-bearing Type 304 steel at subzero temperatures.[2]

Properties in the Cold-Worked Condition   The effect of cold-work on the tensile properties of notched and unnotched Type 310 steel between room temperature and −252°C (−423°F) is shown in Table 5.[10] Note that, as expected, the yield and tensile strengths increase with increasing amounts of cold-work and with decreasing test temperature. Also, the elongation decreases with increasing amounts of cold-work, but, in general, the elongation at cryogenic temperatures is better than that at room temperature. The notched properties simulate the effect of stress raisers imparted during fabrication. Note that the notched (K_t of 6.3)-to-unnotched tensile ratio of the Type 310 steel is a relatively high 0.91 or higher for all test conditions. For Type 310 steel, the yield and tensile strengths increase with increasing amounts of cold-work and with decreasing temperature. The effect of cold-work on the yield and tensile strengths between room temperature and −252°C (−425°F)[8] is illustrated in Fig. 12 for Type 301 steel and in Fig. 13 for Types 304 and 304L steels.

When very high strength is required in a cold-worked austenitic stainless steel, it is

TABLE 1 Tensile and Impact Properties of Selected Austenitic Stainless Steels[2]

Steel	Property	Test temperature						
		−196°C (−320°F)	−140°C (−220°F)	−100°C (−148°F)	−50°C (−58°F)	−20°C (−4°F)	0°C (32°F)	20°C (68°F)
302	Tensile strength, ksi (MN/m²)	207.4 (1430)	175.6 (1210.8)	158.6 (1093.5)	135.7	119.2 (821.9)	104.2 (718.5)	80.6 (555.7)
	Proof stress, 0.2% offset, ksi (MN/m²)	37.2 (256.5)	35.8 (246.8)	35.2 (242.7)	41.2 (284.1)	35.8 (246.8)	33.7 (232.4)	31.2 (215.1)
	Elongation (5.65√A), %	47.8	47.2	54.1	60.2	67.1	86.2	67.0
	Reduction of area, %	59.2	72.2	71.0	74.4	75.0	79.0	76.8
	Charpy V, ft-lb (J)	152 (206.7)	139 (189)	137 (186.3)	137 (186.3)	139 (189)	148 (201.3)	133 (180.9)
	Izod, ft-lb (J)	118 (160.5)	118 (160.5)	117 (159.1)	118 (160.5)	118 (160.5)	111 (151)	107 (145.5)
304	Tensile strength, ksi (MN/m²)	233.4 (1609.3)	198.4 (1368)	185.9 (1281.8)	159.7 (1101)	141.6 (976.3)	128.4 (885.3)	89.6 (617.8)
	Proof stress, 0.2% offset, ksi (MN/m²)	33.6 (231.7)	35.8 (246.8)	32.3 (222.7)	34.3 (236.5)	34.9 (240.6)	35.2 (242.7)	32.7 (255.5)
	Elongation (5.65√A), %	38.2	41.2	42.9	50.1	55.9	64.7	70.8
	Reduction of area, %	67.0	68.0	69.0	71.0	67.0	75.0	77.4
	Charpy V, ft-lb (J)	124 (168.6)	118 (160.5)	124 (168.6)	143 (194.5)	143 (194.5)	150 (204)	160 (217.6)
	Izod, ft-lb (J)	118 (160.5)	118 (160.5)	118 (160.5)	118 (160.5)	118 (160.5)	117 (159.1)	113 (153.7)
316	Tensile strength, ksi (MN/m²)	197.3 (1360.4)	164.8 (1136.3)	145.8 (1005.3)	120.7 (832.2)	104.8 (722.6)	98.6 (679.8)	84.7 (584)
	Proof stress, 0.2% offset, ksi (MN/m²)	64.5 (444.7)	60.5 (417.1)	55.6 (383.4)	48.8 (336.5)	41.7 (287.5)	37.9 (261.3)	34.0 (234.4)
	Elongation (5.65√A), %	56.0	59.5	67.1	84.0	87.3	80.1	60.7
	Reduction of area, %	67.3	70.0	75.0	74.0	74.0	62.0	77.4
	Charpy V, ft-lb (J)	122 (165.9)	144 (155)	135 (183.6)	137 (186.3)	141 (191.8)	141 (191.8)	124 (168.6)
	Izod, ft-lb (J)	118 (160.5)	118 (160.5)	118 (160.5)	118 (160.5)	118 (160.5)	117 (159.1)	113 (153.7)
321	Tensile strength, ksi (MN/m²)	226.7 (1563.1)	189.3 (1305.2)	170.0 (1172.2)	147.6 (1017.7)	127.7 (880.5)	110.4 (761.2)	85.8 (591.6)
	Proof stress, 0.2% offset, ksi (MN/m²)	38.1 (262.7)	35.2 (242.7)	35.2 (242.7)	34.5 (237.9)	36.1 (248.9)	41.0 (282.7)	29.3 (202)

	36.2	36.9	39.7	47.6	53.5	64.2	63.8
Elongation (5.65√A), %	36.2	36.9	39.7	47.6	53.5	64.2	63.8
Reduction of area, %	57.7	67.7	67.0	70.0	71.7	75.0	77.4
Charpy V, ft-lb (J)	98 (133.3)	104 (141.4)	122 (165.9)	154 (209.4)	166 (225.8)	146 (198.6)	156 (212.2)
Izod, ft-lb (J)	118 (160.5)	118 (160.5)	118 (160.5)	118 (160.5)	118 (160.5)	113 (153.7)	113 (153.7)
347							
Tensile strength, ksi (MN/m²)	222.4 (1533.4)	188.2 (1297.6)	170.9 (1178.4)	145.6 (1003.9)	127.2 (877)	111.6 (769.5)	94.3 (650.2)
Proof stress, 0.2% offset, ksi (MN/m²)	38.8 (267.5)	43.5 (299.9)	43.2 (297.9)	44.8 (308.9)	42.8 (295.1)	40.1 (276.5)	35.2 (242.7)
Elongation (5.65 √A), %	38.4	39.5	41.6	49.5	56.2	65.2	54.6
Reduction of area, %	58.0	65.0	70.0	69.6	74.0	75.0	72.0
Charpy V, ft-lb (J)	90 (122.4)	98 (133.3)	110 (758.5)	129 (175.4)	139 (189)	127 (172.7)	124 (168.6)
Izod, ft-lb (J)	118 (160.5)	117 (159.1)	118 (160.5)	118 (160.5)	118 (160.5)	117 (159.1)	117 (159.1)
309							
Tensile strength, ksi (MN/m²)	179.2 (1235.6)	144.3 (994.9)	134.4 (926.7)	117.6 (810.9)	109.8 (757.1)	105.3 (726)	100.1 (690.2)
Proof stress, 0.2% offset, ksi (MN/m²)	93.2 (642.6)	74.1 (510.9)	65.0 (448.2)	58.0 (400)	52.9 (364.7)	52.0 (358.5)	48.4 (333.7)
Elongation (5.65√A), %	48.2	45.2	47.2	54.8	44.7	51.7	48.3
Reduction of area, %	35.0	60.5	65.0	66.0	65.0	67.0	69.6
Charpy V, ft-lb (J)	66 (89.5)	72 (97.6)	85 (115.3)	106 (143.7)	120 (162.7)	121 (164.1)	125 (169.5)
Izod, ft-lb (j)	76 (103.1)	79 (107.1)	82 (111.2)	107 (145.1)	108 (146.4)	111 (150.5)	114 (154.6)
310							
Tensile strength, ksi (MN/m²)	165.1 (1138.4)	141.1 (972.9)	138.0 (951.5)	123.0 (848.1)	114.2 (787.4)	108.9 (750.9)	98.1 (676.4)
Proof stress, 0.2% offset, ksi (MN/m²)	97.4 (671.6)	80.9 (557.8)	67.6 (466.1)	56.9 (392.3)	50.8 (350.3)	49.5 (341.3)	46.1 (317.9)
Elongation (5.65√A), %	17.4	33.0	42.7	52.7	47.3		49.7
Reduction of area, %	15.2*	25.0*	55.0	56.0	48.0		60.8
Charpy V, ft-lb (J)	38 (51.5)	41 (55.6)	46 (62.4)	69 (93.6)	73 (99)	71 (96.3)	75 (101.7)
Izod, ft-lb (J)	40 (54.2)	50 (67.8)	59 (80)	71 (96.3)	80 (108.5)	80 (108.5)	82 (111.2)

*Premature failure initiating at gage marks.

TABLE 2   Tensile Properties of Two Nitrogen-Containing Austenitic Stainless Steels

Test temperature		Yield strength (0.2% offset)		Tensile strength		Elongation in 1-in. (25.4 mm), %	Reduction of area, %
°F	°C	ksi	MN/m²	ksi	MN/m²		
TYPE 202 STEEL							
80	26.8	44.3	305.4	92.0	634.3	81	
−100	−73	65.2	449.6	162.3	1119.1	68	70
−200	−129	78.4	540.6	181.1	1248.7	60	66
−320	−196	97.7	673.6	165.0	1137.7	21*	17*
ASTM A-412 STEEL, GRADE XM-14							
80	26.8	62.6	431.6	116.8	805.3	59	69
−100	−73	92.5	637.8	155.9	1074.9	54	64
−200	−129	119.0	820.5	167.5	1154.9	40	61
−320	−196	138.5	955	238.4	1643.8	33	54

*Fracture near gage marks.
Note: ½-in. thick (12.7-mm) plate.

TABLE 3   Transverse Charpy V-Notch Impact Strength of Some Austenitic Stainless Steels[3]

AISI Type	Energy absorbed, ft-lb (J)		
	80°F (26.8°C)	−320°F (−196°C)	−425°F (−254°C)
304	154 (208.8)	87 (118)	90 (122.04)
304L	118 (160)	67 (90.9)	67 (90.9)
310	142 (192.6)	89 (120.7)	86 (116.6)
347	120 (162.7)	66 (89.5)	57 (77.3)

TABLE 4   Low-Temperature Impact Strength of Several Annealed Austenitic Stainless Steels[3]

AISI Type	Testing temperature		Specimen orientation	Type of notch	Product size	Energy absorbed,	
	°F	°C				ft-lb	J
304	−320	−196	Longitudinal	Keyhole	3-in. (76.2-mm) plate	80	108.5
	−320	−196	Transverse	Keyhole	3-in. (76.2-mm) plate	80	108.5
	−320	−196	Transverse	Keyhole	2½-in. (63.5-mm) plate	70	94.9
	−425	−254	Longitudinal	Keyhole	½-in. (12.7-mm) plate	80	108.5
	−425	−254	Longitudinal	V notch	3½-in. (88.9-mm) plate	91.5	124.1
	−425	−254	Transverse	V notch	3½-in. (88.9-mm) plate	85	115.3
304L	−320	−196	Longitudinal	Keyhole	½-in. (12.7-mm) plate	73	99
	−320	−196	Transverse	Keyhole	½-in. (12.7-mm) plate	43	58.3
	−320	−196	Longitudinal	V notch	3½-in. (88.9-mm) plate	67	90.9
	−425	−254	Longitudinal	V notch	3½-in. (88.9-mm) plate	66	89.5
310	−320	−196	Longitudinal	V notch	3½-in. (88.9-mm) plate	90	122
	−320	−196	Transverse	V notch	3½-in. (88.9-mm) plate	87	118
	−425	−254	Longitudinal	V notch	3½-in. (88.9-mm) plate	86.5	117.3
	−425	−254	Transverse	V notch	3½-in. (88.9-mm) plate	85	115.3
347	−320	−196	Longitudinal	Keyhole	½-in. (12.7-mm) plate	60	81.4
	−320	−196	Transverse	Keyhole	½-in. (12.7-mm) plate	47	63.7
	−425	−254	Longitudinal	V notch	3½-in. (88.9-mm) plate	59	80
	−425	−254	Transverse	V notch	3½-in. (88.9-mm) plate	53	71.9
	−320	−196	Longitudinal	V notch	6½-in. (165.1-mm) plate	77	104.4
	−320	−196	Transverse	V notch	6½-in. (165.1-mm) plate	58	78.6

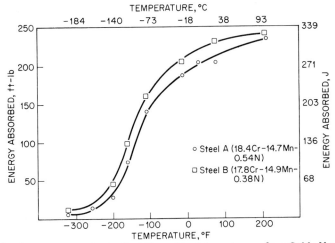

Fig. 7 Results of impact tests on longitudinal Charpy V-notch specimens of two Cr-Mn-N austenitic stainless steels.[6]

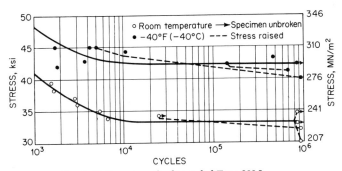

Fig. 8 Fatigue strength of annealed Type 302.[7]

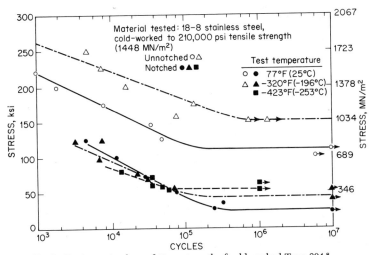

Fig. 9 Reciprocating beam fatigue strength of cold-worked Type 304.[8]

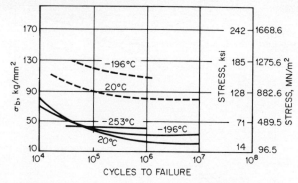

Fig. 10 Fatigue characteristics—fatigue strength of steel 0Kh18N10 (18Cr-10Ni, now designated 08Kh18N10) after cold-working [σ_b = 150 kg/mm² (1471 MN/m²)]. Dashed line-smooth samples; solid line-notched samples.

advantageous to conduct the rolling or forming at low temperatures. A practical application of this technique is the cryogenic stretch-forming of missile cases. With cryogenic stretch-forming, yield and tensile strengths of about 240 and 260 ksi (1654.9 and 1792.7 MN/m²), respectively, with good toughness have been reported.[11] An example of the effect of temperature of rolling on the properties of Type 301 stainless steel is shown in Fig. 14.[5] Note the marked increase in strength when the rolling temperature is lowered from 90 to −78°C (194 to −108°F).

As expected, cold-working results in a slight decrease in toughness, and this subject has been studied intensively by Watson and his associates. In one investigation of the notch characteristics of Type 301 steel cold-rolled various amounts and tested at temperatures to −253°C (−425°F), Watson and Christian[12] reported that the mechanical properties of Type 301 steel depend on both the original austenitic structure and the martensite induced by the combination of low temperature and plastic strain. They noted that reductions in tensile strength and elongation between −196 and −253°C (−320 and −425°F) are indicative of the occurrence of the austenite-to-martensite transformation at these low temperatures. These reductions in strength and ductility were accompanied by decreasing notched-to-unnotched tensile ratios, which they considered to be an index of

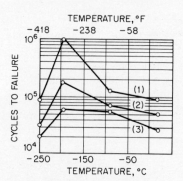

Fig. 11 Fatigue characteristics—cycles to failure as a function of temperature for steel 1Kh18N8, (18Cr-8Ni) [cold-rolled plate, σ_b = 170 kg/mm² (1667MN/m²)], under stresses: (1) 75 kg/mm² (735MN/m²); (2) 90 kg/mm² (883MN/m²); and (3) 105 kg/mm² (1030MN/m²).[9]

embrittlement. In a later investigation, Christian, Gruner, and Girton[10] demonstrated that higher toughnesses were obtained from cold-worked Type 310 steel (a stable austenitic stainless steel) than from cold-worked Type 301 steel (a metastable austenitic stainless steel). Note, for example, in Table 5 that Type 310 steel can be cold-worked as much as 85% and still have a notched-to-unnotched tensile ratio greater than unity at −253°C (−425°F).

Properties in the Welded Condition   As mentioned under the section on joining, welding produces marked changes in the microstructure of austenitic stainless steels. For instance, in the heat-affected zone (HAZ) adjacent to welds, chromium carbides will precipitate to varying degrees. This precipitation of carbides, known as sensitization, depends on the carbon content of the stainless steel and the exposure time in the range 427 to 871°C (800 to 1600°F). Because these carbides precipitate in the grain boundaries of the steels, they may be detrimental to the toughness of the steels. Figure 15 shows the results of impact tests conducted on Types

TABLE 5   Mechanical Properties of Type 310 Stainless Steel After Various Amounts of Cold-Rolling[10]*

Cold-work, %	Testing temperature °F	Testing temperature °C	Yield strength psi	Yield strength (MN/m²)	Tensile strength psi	Tensile strength (MN/m²)	Elongation, %	Notch tensile strength (K_t = 6.3) ksi	Notch tensile strength (K_t = 6.3) (MN/m²)	Notched-unnotched tensile ratio
0	78	25.5	40,300	277.9	85,000	586.1	46	93.9	647.4	1.09
	−320	−196	86,500	596.4	164,000	1130.1	71	155	1068.7	0.95
	−423	−253	113,000	779.1	196,000	1351.4	52	182	1254.9	0.93
12.5	78	25.5	87,600	604	100,000	689.5	24	115	792.9	1.15
	−320	−196	131,000	903.2	182,000	1254.9	51	186	1282.5	1.02
	−423	−253	156,000	1075.6	221,000	1523.8	43	213	1468.6	0.96
37.5	78	25.5	125,000	861.9	139,000	958.4	9	167	1151.5	1.20
	−320	−196	162,000	1117	208,000	1434.2	31	237	1634.1	1.14
	−423	−253	191,000	1316.9	243,000	1675.5	27	261	1799.6	1.07
60	78	25.5	153,000	1054.9	174,000	1199.7	3	180	1241.1	1.03
	−320	−196	205,000	1413.5	233,000	1606.5	17	248	1710	1.06
	−423	−253	232,000	1599.6	278,000	1916.8	18	296	2040.9	1.06
75†	78	25.5	160,000	1103.2	179,000	1234.2	3	197	1358.3	1.10
	−320	−196	215,000	1482.4	242,000	1668.6	13	269	1854.8	1.11
	−423	−253	254,000	1751.3	281,000	1937.5	14	312	2151.1	1.11
75†	78	25.5	157,000	1082.5	181,000	1248	2	194	1337.6	1.07
	−100	−73	190,000	1310.1	204,000	1406.6	3	220	1516.9	1.08
	−320	−196	223,000	1537.6	251,000	1730.6	10	278	1916.8	1.11
	−423	−253	261,000	1799.6	290,000	1999.6	5	329	2268.5	1.12
80	78	25.5	168,000	1158.4	189,000	1303.2	2	198	1365.2	1.05
	−320	−196	236,000	1627.2	156,000	1075.6	9	267	1841	1.05
	−423	−253	254,000	1751.3	296,000	2040.9	9	320	2206.4	1.08
85	78	25.5	167,000	1151.5	191,000	1316.9	2	197	1358.3	1.03
	−423	−253	253,000	1744.4	300,000	2068.5	7	307	2116.8	1.02
90	78	25.5	170,000	1172.2	198,000	1365.2	1	198	1365.2	1.00
	−423	−253	264,000	1820.3	308,000	2123.7	5	300	2068.5	0.97
92	78	25.5	169,000	1165.3	200,000	1379	2	196	1351.4	0.98
	−423	−253	270,000	1861.7	313,000	2158.1	5	290	1999.6	0.93

*All tests in longitudinal direction.
†Results based on two heats.

302, 304, and 304L steels in the annealed and in the sensitized conditions.[13] Note that in the relatively high-carbon (0.15% maximum) Type 302 steel, the sensitization treatment has markedly reduced the toughness of the steel at −184°C (−300°F). However, the toughness of the lower-carbon Types 304 and 304L steels remains relatively high after sensitization. Thus, for cryogenic equipment that is welded, low-carbon (0.08% maximum) austenitic stainless steels, such as Type 304, appear to be a better construction material than the high-carbon austenitic stainless steels, such as Type 302 stainless steel.

The combined effect of cold-work and sensitization on the toughness of austenitic stainless steels has been evaluated by Schmidt.[14] His results are plotted in Fig. 16. Note that with severe sensitization and substantial amounts of cold-work—a rare occurrence in actual practice—the toughness of Type 304 is still above 20 ft-lb (27.2J). Binder[15] has also shown that Type 304 steel can be cold-worked at −196°C (−320°F) up to 20% without reducing the toughness below ASME Boiler and Pressure Vessel Code requirements. Studies by Kramer and Baldwin[16] also demonstrate the significance of carbon content on the low-temperature ductility of sensitized stainless steel. The results of studies in which specimens were heated for 24 h at 1200°F and tested at −196°C (−320°F) with low rates of strain show that the loss of ductility varies inversely with the carbon content. Moreover, the results show that Type 304L exhibits no evidence of embrittlement regardless of the testing speed.

Significantly, as outlined above, the severity of sensitization is a function of carbon content and time at the sensitizing temperature. Also, because of the sensitization of austenitic stainless steels when heated in the range 800 to 1600°F (427 to 871°C), stress relieving of welded austenitic stainless steel structures is generally not recommended.[17] The information detailed above is from laboratory tests in which samples were deliberately treated to represent extreme conditions that are unusual in actual fabrication. Table

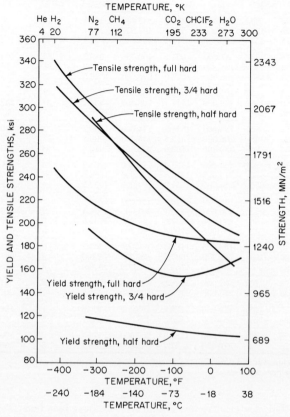

Fig. 12 Effect of decreasing temperature on the yield and tensile strengths of cold-worked Type 301.[8]

6 shows the results of impact tests at −196°C (−320°F) and −251°C (−421°F) on specimens taken from the HAZ of Types 304, 304L, and 310 steel plates that were manually metal-arc welded, gas-metal-arc welded, and submerged-arc welded (both heavy pass and light pass).[18] The results show that the toughness of the HAZ of austenitic stainless steels is not markedly affected by welding conditions.

Summary

For cryogenic-temperature applications, the austenitic stainless steels are an excellent choice because they are relatively easy to fabricate and weld, do not require heat treatment after fabrication, and exhibit relatively high strength with excellent stability and toughness at very low temperatures.

AT ROOM TEMPERATURE

Introduction

Although stainless steels were developed to obtain resistance to corrosion, their excellent mechanical properties in some applications are as important as corrosion resistance in determining the life or utility of a given structure. With so many types of stainless steels available, a wide range of mechanical properties can be obtained. In this section, the wide range of properties of the various martensitic, ferritic, austenitic, and precipitation-hardenable stainless steels are discussed along with the significance of these properties with respect to design and fabrication. Because data on the mechanical properties of

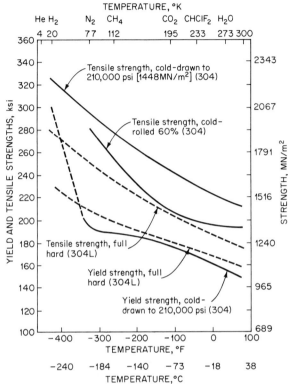

Fig. 13 Effect of decreasing temperature on the yield and tensile strengths of cold-worked Types 304 and 304L.[8]

stainless steels are too extensive to cover completely, emphasis will be placed on the mechanical properties of the standard grades of stainless steel as designated by the American Iron and Steel Institute (AISI). Additional data on the properties of stainless steels are compiled, but by no means completely, in a number of other works.[19–25]

Martensitic Stainless Steels

The martensitic stainless steels are those that contain more than about 11.5% chromium and have a predominantly austenitic microstructure at elevated temperatures that can be transformed into martensite by suitable cooling to room temperature. The chemical composition of the standard grades of martensitic stainless steels as designated by the AISI are shown in Appendix 1.

   Tensile Properties   As discussed in Chap. 6, the martensitic stainless steels are similar to the quenched and tempered alloy steels, and like these steels, they have mechanical properties that are amenable to control through heat treatment. Because of the high alloy content of the standard martensitic stainless steels, these steels are all air-hardenable. Representative tensile properties of these steels in the quenched (as air-hardened) and tempered condition and also in the annealed condition are shown in Table 7.

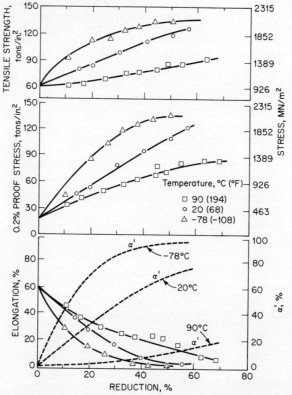

Fig. 14   Effect of rolling temperature on properties and martensite (α') content of Type 301.[5]

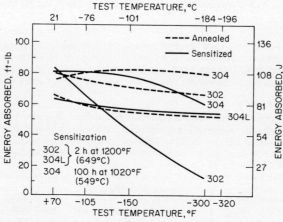

Fig. 15   Results of Charpy keyhole impact tests on Types 302, 304, and 304L in the annealed and annealed and sensitized conditions.[13]

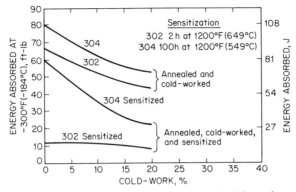

Fig. 16 Combined effect of cold-work and sensitization on Charpy-keyhole-notch toughness of Types 302 and 304.[14]

TABLE 6   Charpy V-Notch Impact Values at −320 and −421°F (−196 and −251.7°C) for AISI Types 304, 304L, and 310 Stainless Steel Welded Plates[19]

AISI Type	Welding method	Energy absorbed, ft-lb (J)*			
		Notch in weld metal	Notch in heat-affected zone at indicated distance from notch to fusion line, in. (mm)		
			1/16 (1.59)	1/8 (3.18)	1/2 (12.7)
	IMPACT VALUES AT −320°F (−196°C)				
304	Manual-covered electrode	15 (20.3)	44 (59.7)	49 (66.4)	55 (74.6)
	Gas-metal arc	38.5 (52.2)	51.5 (69.8)	63 (85.4)	64.5 (87.5)
	Submerged arc, heavy pass	12 (16.3)	56 (75.9)	68 (92.2)	†
	Submerged arc, light pass	10 (13.6)	51 (69.2)	59 (80)	57 (77.3)
304L	Manual-covered electrode	23 (31.2)	58 (78.6)	60.5 (82)	63.5 (86.1)
	Gas-metal arc	48.5 (65.8)	58.5 (79.3)	56 (75.9)	65.5 (88.8)
	Submerged arc, heavy pass	17.5 (23.7)	58.5 (79.3)	60 (81.4)	†
	Submerged arc, light pass	18 (24.4)	59 (80)	57.5 (78)	60 (81.4)
310	Manual-covered electrode	43 (58.3)	71 (96.3)	74 (100.3)	79.5 (107.8)
	IMPACT VALUES AT −421°F (−251.7°C)				
304	Manual-covered electrode	12 (16.3)	47 (63.7)	55 (74.6)	52.5 (71.2)
	Gas-metal arc	22.5 (30.5)	53 (71.9)	62 (84.1)	60 (81.4)
	Submerged arc, heavy pass	20 (27.1)	55.5 (75.3)	66 (89.5)	†
	Submerged arc, light pass	8 (10.8)	50 (67.8)	60 (81.4)	60 (81.4)
304L	Manual-covered electrode	14 (19)	59 (80)	52 (70.5)	55 (74.6)
	Gas-metal arc	45 (61)	53 (71.9)	45 (61)	64 (86.8)
	Submerged arc, heavy pass	21 (28.5)	53 (71.9)	57.5 (78)	†
	Submerged arc, light pass	16 (21.7)	52 (70.5)	56 (75.9)	62.5 (84.8)
310	Manual-covered electrode	37 (50.2)	70.5 (95.6)	71 (96.3)	73.5 (99.7)

*Values are averages of three tests for the weld metal, four tests for the notch located 1/16 and 1/8 in. from the fusion line, and two tests for the notch located 1/2 in. from the fusion line.

†Base plate was too narrow to machine specimens with the notch located 1/2 in. from the fusion line.

To obtain optimum mechanical properties in hardened martensitic stainless steels, it is necessary to austenitize these steels within a temperature range that will result in the maximum amount of austenite (in some martensitic stainless steels this amount may be less than 100%) and also to dissolve all carbide present. Figure 17 shows the effect of austenitizing temperature on the hardness of 12%Cr steels with carbon contents between 0.016 and 0.14%.[26] In general, maximum hardness occurs when the austenitizing temperature is between about 982 and 1093°C (1800 and 2000°F), and increases with increasing carbon content.

Properly austenitized and quenched 12%Cr steels must be tempered to obtain mechanical properties suitable for engineering applications. Figure 18 shows the effect of tempering temperature (2-h temper) on the hardness of 12%Cr steels that contain 0.055 to 0.14% carbon.[26] Note that these steels do not soften appreciably until the tempering temperature exceeds 482°C (900°F). Also, a secondary hardening occurs when tempering at about 427°C (800°F). Tempering between 538 and 760°C (1000 and 1400°F) decreases the hardness of these steels considerably. At 816°C (1500°F), which is slightly above the A_1

TABLE 7   Typical Tensile Properties of the AISI Standard Martensitic Stainless Steels in the Annealed and Tempered Conditions

AISI Type	Tempering temperature °F	°C	Yield strength (0.2% offset) ksi	MN/m²	Tensile strength ksi	MN/m²	Elongation in 2 in. (50.8 mm), %	Reduction of area, %
403, 410,	None (annealed)		40	275.8	75	517.1	30	65
416, 416Se	400	204	145	999.8	190	1310.1	15	55
	600	315	140	965.3	185	1275.6	15	55
	800	426	150	1034.3	195	1344.5	17	55
	1000	538	115	792.9	145	999.8	20	65
	1200	648	85	586.1	110	758.5	23	65
	1400	760	60	413.7	90	620.6	30	70
414	None (annealed)		95	655	120	827.4	17	55
	400	204	150	1034.3	200	1379	15	55
	600	315	145	999.8	190	1310.1	15	55
	800	426	150	1034.3	200	1379	16	58
	1000	538	120	827.4	145	999.8	20	60
	1200	648	105	724	120	827.4	20	70
420	None (annealed)		50	344.8	95	655	25	55
	400	204	200	1379	255	1758.2	10	35
	600	315	195	1344.5	250	1723.8	10	35
	800	426	200	1379	255	1758.2	10	35
	1000	538	145	999.8	170	1172.2	15	40
	1200	648	85	586.1	115	792.9	20	55
431	None (annealed)		95	655	125	861.9	20	60
	400	204	155	1068.7	205	1413.5	15	55
	600	315	150	1034.3	195	1344.5	15	55
	800	426	155	1068.7	205	1413.5	15	60
	1000	538	130	896.4	150	1034.3	18	60
	1200	648	95	655	125	861.9	20	60
440A	None (annealed)		60	413.7	105	724	20	45
	600	315	245	1689.3	265	1827.2	5	20
440B	None (annealed)		62	427.5	107	737.8	18	35
	600	315	270	1861.7	280	1930.6	3	15
440C	None (annealed)		70	482.7	110	758.5	13	25
	600	315	275	1896.1	285	1965.1	2	10

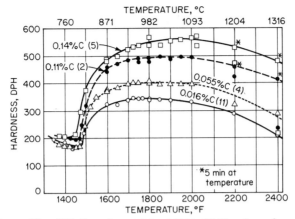

Fig. 17 Hardness of four 12% Cr steels containing 0.016 to 0.14% carbon, after quenching from a series of temperatures. Held 1 h at 1093°C (2000°F) or lower and 30 min at 1204°C (2200°F) or 5 min at 1316°C (2400°F) before quenching.[26]

critical temperature, austenite reversion with subsequent transformation to martensite on cooling results in considerable hardening. As one might expect, the steels with the higher carbon contents exhibit the higher hardness at any specific tempering temperature. Increasing the tempering time from 1 to 8 h has relatively little effect on the hardness of 12%Cr steels when tempering is conducted between 204 and 427°C (400 and 800°F).[26] However, between about 427 and 788°C (800 and 1450°F), the hardness decreases considerably as time at tempering temperature is increased. Above about 788°C (1450°F), the A_1 critical temperature, hardness increases with increasing time at tempering temperature.

The variation that occurs in the tensile properties of Type 410 steel with tempering temperature is shown in Fig. 19. The variation in yield and tensile strengths follows the same general trend as was observed with hardness.[27] Depending on the tempering temperature selected, yield strengths between about 60 and 150 ksi (413.7 and 1034.3 MN/m²) and tensile strengths between about 85 and 210 ksi (586 and 1448 MN/m²) can be obtained with Type 410 steel. As expected, ductility, as measured by elongation and reduction of area, decreases as yield and tensile strengths increase.

In general, the tensile properties of the other martensitic stainless steels vary with tempering temperature in the same manner as those of Type 410 steel. However, with the

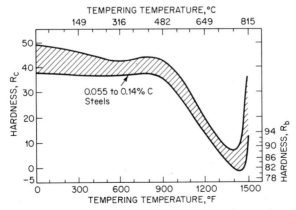

Fig. 18 Effect of tempering temperature on hardness of 12% Cr stainless steels tempered for 2 h.[26]

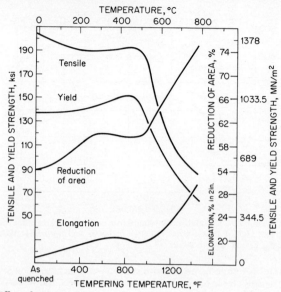

Fig. 19 Effect of tempering for 1 h on the tensile properties of hardened Type 410.[27]

same tempering temperature, the higher carbon steels and those that contain nickel exhibit somewhat higher yield and tensile strengths and lower ductility than does Type 410 steel.

Toughness The toughness or capacity of a material to yield plastically under high localized stress, such as that introduced by a notch, is an important engineering property. Industry is moving toward standardization of the Charpy V-notch impact test as an indicator of notch toughness in materials specification. However, most of the toughness data for the martensitic stainless steels was obtained in the Izod impact test, but these data are still useful. As shown in Table 8, Types 440A, 440B, and 440C exhibit relatively low toughness at room temperature compared with that of the other standard martensitic steels. For the standard martensitic stainless steels in the quenched (as air-hardened) condition or in the quenched and tempered condition, the room-temperature toughness is variable and depends on the composition and heat treatment employed for a particular heat. The toughness of these steels in the hardened condition generally increases as the carbon, nitrogen, phosphorus, sulfur, silicon, manganese, and tramp-element (Pb, Sn, Sb) contents decrease and as the nickel content increases.

Like many alloy steels, the martensitic stainless steels are susceptible to temper embrittlement. Figure 20 shows the effect of tempering temperature on the toughness of Type 410 stainless steel.[28] Compared with the toughness in the quenched condition, the

TABLE 8 Typical Room-Temperature Izod Impact Properties of Annealed AISI Standard Martensitic Stainless Steels

AISI Type	Energy absorbed	
	ft-lb	J
403, 410	90	122
414	50	67.8
416, 416Se	60	81.4
420	90	122
431	50	67.8
440A	15	20.3
440B	5	6.8
440C	5	6.8

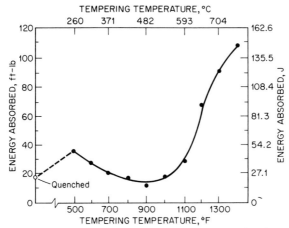

Fig. 20 Izod impact values for Type 410, quenched from 982°C (1800°F) and tempered for 3 h at indicated temperature.[28]

toughness during tempering increases significantly at about 260°C (500°F) because of precipitation of Fe_3C and the attendant decrease of carbon in solid solution and because of a slight decrease in yield and tensile strength. In general, the best combination of high strength and toughness can be obtained for the standard martensitic stainless steels by tempering at about 260°C (500°F). The trough in the toughness curve in the tempering range 371 to 593°C (700 to 1100°F) is believed to be caused by local overaging of precipitates at grain boundaries that leads to crack initiation and subsequent propagation through a microstructure that is not very crack resistant.[29] Above 593°C (1100°F), good toughness values are obtained. However, as shown in Table 7, tempering in this range results in a marked reduction in yield and tensile strengths.

Fatigue and Abrasion Resistance   The fatigue strength of metals is important in applications in which cyclic loading occurs. Because the fatigue strength of metals is usually correlated with tensile strength, the hardened martensitic stainless steels generally exhibit a higher fatigue strength than the ferritic or austenitic stainless steels, which have relatively low strengths. However, the fatigue strengths of martensitic stainless steels are not significantly different from those of the carbon and alloy steels at the same tensile-strength levels. Some fatigue data[20] for Type 410 steel with a Rockwell C hardness of 35 and with several surface conditions are shown in Fig. 21. As with other

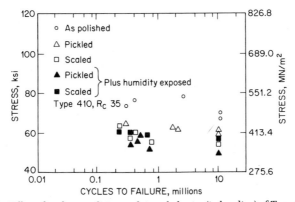

Fig. 21   Effect of surface condition on fatigue behavior (in bending) of Type 410.[20]

steels, the steel-surface condition has a marked effect on fatigue properties, and the fatigue properties of polished specimens are better than those of pickled or scaled specimens.

Another important property in the selection of materials for some applications is abrasion, or wear, resistance. In general, the harder the material, the greater its abrasion resistance. However, in applications in which corrosion occurs, this general rule does not

TABLE 9   Results of Abrasion Tests on Selected Steels

	Performance in			
	Coal-conveyor-bottom measured loss		Coal-bunker corrosion rate	
Steel	mils/million tons	mm/million kg	mils/yr	mm/yr
Type 410	8.9	0.0003	0.1	0.003
ASTM A517 (Grade F)	49.4	0.0015	4.4	0.112
Abrasion-resisting steel*	51.0	0.0015	4.1	0.104
Carbon steel	72.5	0.0022	7.1	0.180

*Nominally 0.40C-1.75Mn-0.25Si.

hold. The results of tests and service experience indicate that in certain of these applications, the martensitic stainless steels are superior to other abrasion-resistant materials. Table 9, which compares the weight loss exhibited by Type 410 steel and several other steels in two coal-handling applications, shows that Type 410 steel is much superior to the other steels.

Fabrication Effects   The martensitic stainless steels are generally used in the tempered condition, but parts are usually formed or machined from these steels in the annealed condition to take advantage of the better ductility and machinability. However, the relatively moderate ductility precludes their use in applications requiring a high degree of formability, except those in which multiple anneals and draws are tolerable.

The high-carbon standard grades such as Types 440A, 440B, and 440C are generally not recommended for applications requiring welding, although low-carbon Type 410 steel can be welded with relative ease. As explained elsewhere in the handbook, fabrication by welding is advisable only when proper procedures of preheating and postheating are used. A rather marked tendency toward temper embrittlement suggests that these steels should not be heat-treated in the range 371 to 593°C (700 to 1100°F).

Ferritic Stainless Steels

The ferritic stainless steels contain more than about 10% chromium, are not completely hardenable by heat treatment, and are used in a condition in which their microstructures consist of ferrite and carbides. The chemical compositions of the standard grades of ferritic steels, as designated by the AISI, are shown elsewhere in this handbook, and the chemical compositions of two nonstandard grades that have achieved or probably will achieve increased attention are shown in Appendix 2.

Tensile Properties   Representative tensile properties of the ferritic stainless steels are shown in Table 10. In comparison with low-carbon steels (such as SAE 1010), the ferritic stainless steels exhibit slightly higher yield and tensile strengths and lower elongations. Accordingly, more power is required to form the ferritic stainless steels than low-carbon steels.

Toughness and Fatigue Properties   Shown in Tables 11 and 12 are the Charpy V-notch impact transition temperatures and endurance limits for some of the ferritic stainless steels. In the family of stainless steels, the standard ferritic grades (such as Type 430 stainless steel) have the lowest toughness; the Charpy V-notch impact transition temperature of the standard steels, except for Type 405 stainless steel, is above room temperature. However, Binder[30] in the early 1950s showed that ferritic stainless steels with very low carbon and nitrogen contents exhibit excellent toughness (see Fig. 29, Chap. 5). In the 1960s and early 1970s, commercial methods were developed for decreasing carbon and nitrogen to low levels in ferritic stainless steels by melt pro-

TABLE 10   Typical Room-Temperature Tensile Properties of Annealed Standard and Two Nonstandard Ferritic Stainless Steels

Steel	Yield strength (0.2% offset)		Tensile strength		Elongation in 2 in. (50.8 mm), %
	ksi	MN/m²	ksi	MN/m²	
STANDARD					
405	40	275.8	65	448.2	25
409	40	275.8	68	468.9	30
429	40	275.8	70	482.7	30
430	50	344.8	75	517.1	25
430F	55	379.2	80	551.6	25
430Se	55	379.2	80	551.6	25
434	53	365.4	77	530.9	23
436	53	365.4	77	530.9	23
442	45	310.3	80	551.6	20
446	50	344.8	80	551.6	20
NONSTANDARD					
18-2	43	296.5	68	468.9	37
26-1	50	344.8	70	482.7	30

TABLE 11   Charpy V-Notch Impact Transition Temperature of Some Ferritic Stainless Steels

Steel	Transition temperature*	
	°F	°C
STANDARD		
Type 405	40	4.4
Type 409	70	21
Type 430	70–212	21–100
Type 446	250	121
NONSTANDARD		
Type 409 modified†	−70	−57
18Cr-2Mo	0	−17.7
26Cr-1Mo	0	−17.7

*Based on 25 ft-lb (33.9 J) of energy absorbed.
†Modified with up to 1% nickel.

TABLE 12   Endurance Limits in Bending of Some Ferritic Stainless Steels

Steel	10⁷-cycle endurance limit	
	ksi	MN/m²
Type 430	45	310.3
Type 446	47	324.1
26Cr-1Mo	47	324.1

cesses such as the argon-oxygen decarburization, vacuum-oxygen decarburization, and electron-beam refining.

Note that the transition temperature of the low-carbon, low-nitrogen 18Cr-2Mo and 26Cr-1Mo steels is below room temperature (20°C, 68°F), Table 11. However, the 18Cr-2Mo and 26Cr-1Mo steels must be cooled rapidly to avoid 474°C (885°F) embrittlement. The effect of cooling rate through this range on the toughness of low-carbon (0.002%), low-nitrogen (0.008%) stainless steels is shown in Table 13.

Fabrication Effects

Formability. Because ferritic stainless steels are generally used in sheet applications, the forming characteristics of these steels are of considerable importance. The average

TABLE 13   Effect of Cooling Rate on the Room-Temperature Charpy V-Notch Toughness of High-Purity Ferritic Stainless Steels

	Energy absorbed after various cooling treatments,* ft-lb (J)		
Steel	Water-quenched	Air-cooled	Furnace-cooled
12Cr	240 (325.4)	240 (325.4)	240 (325.4)
17Cr	240 (325.4)	15–240 (20.3–325.4)	22–240 (29.8–325.4)
26Cr-1Mo	240 (325.4)	130–145 (176.3–196.6)	3–4 (4.1–5.4)

*Samples heated to 1600°F (871°C) for 20 min prior to cooling.

plastic strain ratio $\bar{r}$ and the average work-hardening exponent $\bar{n}$ are measures of formability. High values for these parameters are generally desirable, though the configuration of the part and the forming method are important in determining the minimum acceptable values. Low-carbon plain carbon steels intended for forming applications exhibit an $\bar{r}$ value between 1.2 and 1.8 and an $\bar{n}$ value between 0.22 and 0.26. Table 14 exhibits representative $\bar{r}$ and $\bar{n}$ values for some ferritic stainless steels. Note that the $\bar{n}$ values are

TABLE 14   Representative $\bar{r}$ and $\bar{n}$ Values for Various Ferritic Steels

Steel	$\bar{r}$	$\bar{n}$
Low-carbon and plain carbon	1.2–1.6	0.22–0.26
Type 430	1.2	0.21
18Cr-2Mo	1.5	0.20
26Cr-1Mo	1.4	0.21

less than the range for the low-carbon steels. Although the $\bar{r}$ values represent properties that can be exhibited by these steels, much lower values are obtained if these steels are not properly processed. The drawability (low $\bar{r}$ value) will be poor when the cube-on-face texture, which is present in the hot band, is retained in annealed sheet. In general, low hot-rolling temperatures, high annealing temperatures, and a double-cold-reduction schedule are required to produce sheet with high $\bar{r}$ values.[31] The effect of cold reduction on the $\bar{r}$ value of 18Cr-2Mo stainless steel sheet is shown in Fig. 22.[32]

Ridging, or roping, is a surface defect which occurs in ferritic stainless steels that are subjected to large amounts of strain during forming. This undesirable defect occurs parallel to the direction of rolling and appears as narrow raised areas similar to corrugations on the surface of the sheet or strip. Figure 23 shows the appearance of ridging in a

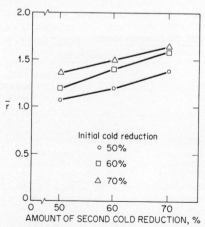

Fig. 22   Effect of double-cold-reduction schedule on the average plastic-strain ratio of 18Cr-2Mo stainless steel.[32]

Fig. 23   Deep-drawn automobile hub cap of Type 430, illustrating ridging (or roping).

TABLE 15   Representative Bend Ductility of Some As-welded Ferritic Stainless Steels

Steel	Bend-test results*
Type 430	30° (0.51 rad) bend, cracked
Type 409	180° (3.06 rad) bend, no failure
18Cr-2Mo	180° (3.06 rad) bend, no failure
26Cr-1Mo	180° (3.06 rad) bend, no failure

*1T bend radius.

deep-drawn automobile hub cap made from Type 430 stainless steel. Ridging is detrimental to the appearance of formed parts, and expensive grinding and polishing operations are required to eliminate it. Chao was the first to show that ridging is fundamentally a recrystallization problem and results from retention of a banded distribution of the cube-on-face texture in a cube-on-corner matrix texture in annealed sheet.[33] Ridging is minimized by controlling processing conditions such as by the use of low-rolling temperatures and high box-annealing temperatures and/or by additions of columbium (niobium).

Weldability. With the exception of Type 405 and Type 409 stainless steel, the standard ferritic stainless steels exhibit poor ductility in the welded condition, and, therefore, should not undergo forming operations when welded. The poor ductility is caused by a large grain size in the HAZ. In some environments localized corrosion occurs in this zone. However, Type 409, 18Cr-2Mo, and 26Cr-1Mo stainless steels exhibit good ductility and good corrosion resistance in the welded condition and can readily be formed. The bend ductility of some of the ferritic stainless steels in the as-welded condition is shown in Table 15. To ensure good ductility in the 18Cr-2Mo and 26Cr-1Mo stainless steels, care must be taken to avoid nitrogen pickup during welding. The toughness of Type 409 and modified (with up to 1% nickel) Type 409 steels in the welded condition is sufficient for their use in structural applications such as shipping containers. The toughness of these steels in the welded condition is shown in Table 16.

Austenitic Stainless Steels

The austenitic stainless steels, as their name implies, have an austenitic (face-centered-cubic) microstructure at room temperature and cannot be hardened to any great extent by heat treatment, although they can be appreciably strengthened by cold-work. For instance, at room temperature these steels can exhibit yield strengths between 30 and 200 ksi (206.9 and 1379 MN/m²), depending on the amount of cold-work and the specific composition of the steel. Furthermore, these steels exhibit good ductility and toughness, even at high-strength levels. The chemical compositions of the standard AISI austenitic stainless steels are given elsewhere in this handbook.

The austenitic stainless steels can be classified into two groups based on the stability of the austenite: stable austenitic stainless steels and metastable austenitic stainless steels. The stable austenitic stainless steels are those with microstructures that remain austenitic even after much straining. The metastable austenitic stainless steels are those with microstructures that transform readily to an acicular martensitic structure during straining. The difference between these two groups of steel is best illustrated by the stress-strain diagrams of two typical steels—one from each group (see Fig. 24). Type 310, representative of the stable austenitic stainless steels, exhibits a normal stress-strain curve for the austenitic structure. Type 301, representative of the metastable austenitic stainless steels, exhibits a stress-strain curve in which the rate of strain hardening increases markedly at the onset of the martensite transformation that usually occurs after about 10 to 15% strain.

TABLE 16   Representative Base-Metal and Heat-affected-zone Toughness of Type 409 and Nickel-modified Type 409 Stainless Steels at Room Temperature

Steel	Energy absorbed at room temperature,* ft-lb (J)	
	Base metal	Heat-affected zone
Type 409	12 (16.3)	2 (2.7)
11Cr-1Ni-0.5Ti	26 (35.3)	12 (16.3)
11Cr-1Ni	26 (35.3)	12 (16.3)

*Half-size transverse Charpy V-notch specimens.

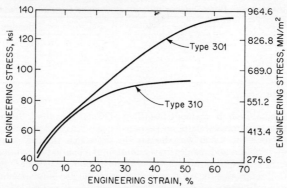

Fig. 24 Stress-strain curves for Types 301 and 310.

Tensile Properties Table 17 lists the typical room-temperature tensile properties of the standard AISI grades of stainless steels in the annealed condition, [19] and also shows some of the same effects of composition and stability on their tensile properties that were described above. A comparison of the tensile strengths of the metastable Types 201, 202, and 301 with those of the stable Types 305 and 310 shows that the metastable steels have higher tensile strengths than the stable steels. The yield strengths, however, are not affected by transformation but are primarily dependent on solid-solution hardening. Because the interstitial elements, particularly carbon and nitrogen, have the

TABLE 17 Typical Room-Temperature Tensile Properties of Annealed Standard Austenitic Stainless Steels

AISI Type	Yield strength (0.2% offset)		Tensile strength		Elongation in 2 in. (50.8 mm), %
	ksi	MN/m²	ksi	MN/m²	
201	55	379.2	115	792.9	55
202	55	379.2	105	724	55
301	40	275.8	110	758.5	60
302	40	275.8	90	620.6	50
302B	40	275.8	95	655	55
303	35	241.3	90	620.6	50
303Se	35	241.3	90	620.6	50
304	42	289.6	84	579.2	55
304L	39	268.9	81	558.5	55
305	38	262	85	586.1	50
308	35	241.3	85	586.1	50
309	45	310.3	90	620.6	45
309S	45	310.3	90	620.6	45
310	45	310.3	95	655	45
310S	45	310.3	95	655	45
314	50	344.8	100	689.5	40
316	42	289.6	84	579.2	50
316L	42	289.6	81	558.5	50
317	40	275.8	90	620.6	45
321	35	241.3	90	620.6	45
347	40	275.8	95	655	45
348	40	275.8	95	655	45
384	35	241.3	75	517.1	55
385	30	206.9	72	496.4	55

TABLE 18   Tensile-Strength Requirements at Standard Temper for Austenitic Stainless Steels

Temper	Minimum yield strength		Minimum tensile strength	
	ksi	MN/m²	ksi	MN/m²
¼-Hard	75	517.1	125	861.9
½-Hard	110	758.5	150	1034.3
¾-Hard	135	930.8	175	1206.6
Full-hard	140	965.3	185	1275.6

greatest effect on solid-solution hardening, those grades with high carbon and nitrogen contents have relatively high yield strengths. For example, compare the yield strengths of Types 201 and 202 steels with those of the lower carbon and lower nitrogen steels, such as Types 301 and 302 steels.

The austenitic stainless steels are also used in the cold-worked condition because they retain considerable ductility and toughness at very high yield and tensile strengths. The tempers to which these steels are supplied are shown in Table 18.[19,20]

Figures 25 to 30 illustrate the effect of cold-work on the tensile properties of a number of the standard austenitic stainless steels.[23] For a given amount of cold-work, the metastable austenitic stainless steels, Types 201 and 301, exhibit higher yield and tensile strengths and higher elongation than the stable austenitic steels, such as Types 305 and 310.

Significantly, within a given grade of austenitic stainless steel, composition has a twofold effect on the properties of the steel in the cold-worked condition: (1) it affects the stability of the austenite, and (2) it affects the solid-solution hardening of the austenite and of any martensite formed during cold-work. Because almost all elements in metastable

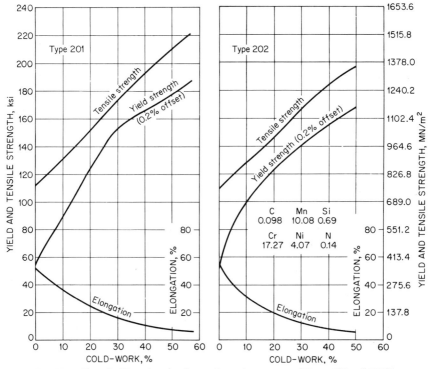

Fig. 25   Effect of cold-working on the mechanical properties of Types 201 and 202.[23]

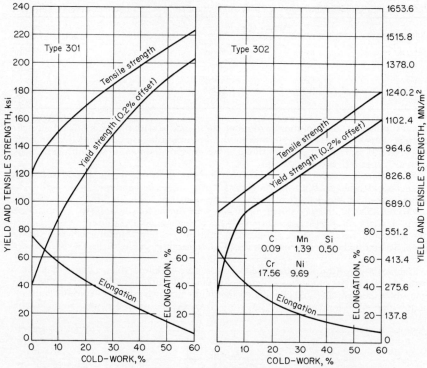

Fig. 26   Effect of cold-working on the mechanical properties of Types 301 and 302.[23]

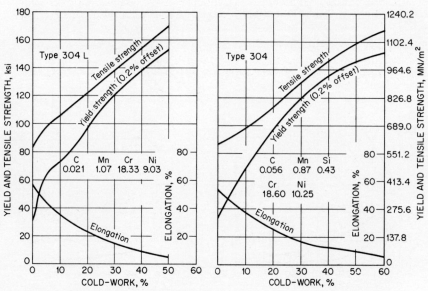

Fig. 27   Effect of cold-working on the mechanical properties of Types 304 and 304L.[23]

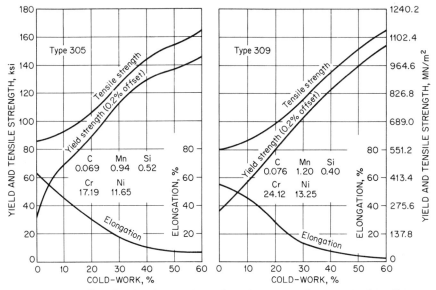

Fig. 28 Effect of cold-working on the mechanical properties of Types 305 and 309.[23]

austenitic stainless steels increase the stability of the austenite, a factor that decreases tensile strength, and because almost all elements increase the solid-solution hardening of the austenite and of any martensite formed during cold-work, the effect of composition on the tensile properties is complex. For example, additions of an element such as carbon may initially increase the strength of cold-worked austenitic stainless steels because of its contribution to the solid-solution hardening of the austenite and martensite. However, above a certain amount, its effect on the stabilization of the austenite offsets its solid-solution-hardening effect, and thereby decreases the tensile strength of the steel. The

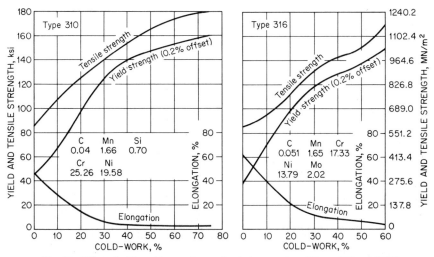

Fig. 29 Effect of cold-working on the mechanical properties of Types 310 and 316.[23]

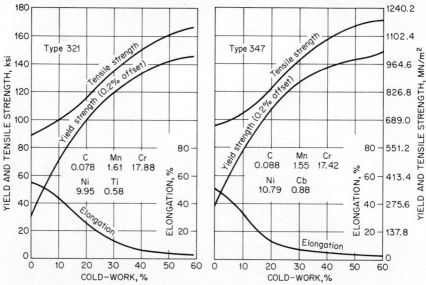

Fig. 30 Effect of cold-working on the mechanical properties of Types 321 and 347.[23]

effect of stability on the elongation of cold-worked Type 301 stainless steel is shown in Figure 31.[34]

In stable austenitic stainless steels, nickel and copper tend to decrease the work-hardening rate and tensile strength, whereas all other elements increase the work-hardening rate and tensile strength. Some effects of composition are shown in Figures 32

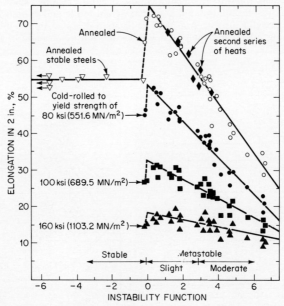

Fig. 31 Relation between elongation and instability function for metastable and stable austenitic stainless steels. This function is related to the composition of the steel and is a measure of the propensity of the austenite to transform to martensite during deformation.[34]

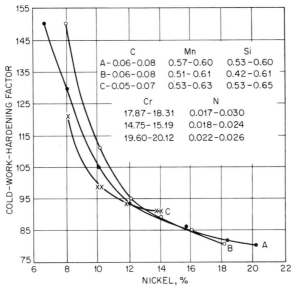

Fig. 32 Influence of nickel content on the cold-work-hardening factor of Cr-Ni stainless steels containing 15, 18, and 20% chromium.[35]

to 35; the "cold-work hardening factor" in Figures 32 to 34 is arbitrarily defined as the area under a load-reduction curve from the 0.5% offset yield strength to 62.5% reduction in height of a specimen.[35]

Toughness and Fatigue Resistance Because the austenitic stainless steels are often used for structural applications, particularly when cold-worked, the toughness and fatigue strength of these steels are of interest. At room temperature, the austenitic stainless steels in the annealed condition exhibit exceptional toughness. Charpy V-notch energy-absorption values in excess of 100 ft-lb (135.6 J) are generally obtained. The notched tensile strength is often used as a measure of toughness for cold-reduced sheet. Figure 36, which demonstrates the effect of cold reduction on the notched tensile strength of Type 301,[24] shows that the toughness of the austenitic stainless steels, even after cold-rolling reductions to high tensile strengths, is still excellent. Note that the notched tensile strength of Type 301 steel in the longitudinal direction (with a notch severity of 17 K_t) is about the same as or slightly higher than the unnotched tensile strength of the steel at 30 to 60% cold reduction [tensile strengths of 170 to 220 ksi (1172.2 to 1516.9 MN/m²)]. Moreover, the notched tensile strength in the transverse direction, although less than the unnotched tensile strength, is still relatively high, which indicates good notch toughness.

Table 19 shows the fatigue, or endurance, limits (in bending) of several annealed austenitic stainless steels.[23] These endurance limits are about one-half of the tensile strength and do not differ significantly from one another. The endurance limit will increase with increasing amounts of cold-work.

Fabrication Effects The austenitic stainless steels are readily formable. In general, steels with high work-hardening rates (such as Types 301 and 201 steels) have proper-

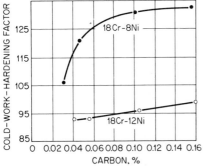

Fig. 33 Influence of carbon on the cold-work-hardening factor in stable and metastable steels. This factor is the area under a load-reduction curve from 0.5 to 62.5% reduction.[35]

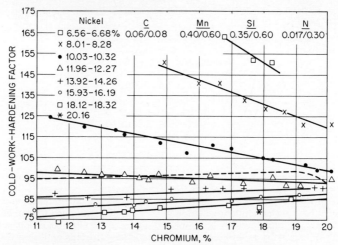

Fig. 34 Influence of chromium content on the cold-work-hardening factor of Cr-Ni stainless steels containing 6.5, 8, 10, 12, 14, 16, and 18% nickel.[35]

ties required for structural or severe stretch-forming application. The more stable steels with low work-hardening rates (such as Types 305, 384, and 385) are generally satisfactory for spinning and cold-heading applications.

The austenitic stainless steels are readily weldable in both the annealed and cold-worked conditions. Because the high strength is imparted by cold-working, fabrication operations that impart heat to a part, such as welding, have a pronounced effect on the strength remaining in the fabricated part. However, by suitable welding and joint design techniques, much of the strength in cold-worked austenitic stainless steels can be retained. Table 20 shows the effect of welding on the tensile strength of cold-worked Type 301 steel.[36] Note in particular that an appreciable portion of the strength in the 40% cold-worked Type 301 steel is retained after welding.

Precipitation-Hardenable Stainless Steels

The precipitation-hardenable stainless steels, which were developed during the latter part of World War II, probably represent one of the more significant developments in stainless steels within the last 50 years. The basic concept for the precipitation hardening of stainless steels was probably first described by Foley in 1934.[37] But it was not until the latter stages of World War II that the first practical precipitation-hardenable stainless steel

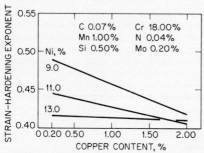

Fig. 35 Effect of copper content on the strain-hardening exponent of stable austenitic stainless steels at several nickel levels.[43]

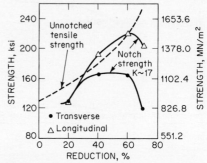

Fig. 36 Effect of reduction by cold-rolling and test direction on notch strength of Type 301 sheet.[24]

TABLE 19   Typical Endurance Limits in Bending of Annealed Cr-Ni Stainless Steel Sheet

AISI	Endurance limit	
Type	ksi	MN/m²
301	35	241.3
302	34	234.4
303	35	241.3
304	35	241.3
316	39	268.9
321	38	262
347	39	268.9

was developed. Since that time a whole family of precipitation-hardenable stainless steels has been developed.

The popular precipitation-hardenable stainless steels, the chemical compositions of which are shown elsewhere, can be divided into three classes:

1. Martensitic types, which are generally supplied by the producer in the martensitic condition, and which are precipitation-hardened by a simple aging heat treatment.

2. Semiaustenitic types, which are supplied in the austenitic condition, and for which before hardening, the austenite must be transformed to martensite by a special heat treatment and then aged.

3. Austenitic types, which are generally supplied in the austenitic condition and in which precipitation hardening occurs in the austenitic matrix during aging.

Tensile and Toughness Properties   Shown in Tables 21 through 29 are the typical room-temperature tensile and toughness properties of the precipitation-hardenable stainless steels for a variety of annealing and precipitation-hardening heat treatments.[19–24,38–41]

The martensitic precipitation-hardenable steels have the highest yield strengths, whereas the austenitic and semiaustenitic precipitation-hardenable steels have the lowest yield and tensile strengths and the highest elongation. More recent developments that involve melting these steels to low carbon, manganese, phosphorus, and nitrogen levels have improved their toughness.[42]

Fabrication Effects   Because of the low strength in the annealed condition, the austenitic and semiaustenitic stainless steels can withstand moderately severe formations. This is not true of the martensitic steels, which have much lower ductility. The high strength of the precipitation-hardenable steels cannot always be used to full advantage because at the high-strength levels, they are susceptible to stress-corrosion cracking and are also somewhat notch-sensitive. Consequently, it is often necessary to overage these steels to obtain lower strengths and better stress-corrosion and toughness characteristics.

With the exception of the steels containing phosphorus as an alloying element, the precipitation-hardenable steels can be welded satisfactorily. The weld-crack susceptibility of the phosphorus-containing steels can be reduced somewhat by the use of partially ferritic weld metals.

Nonstandard Stainless Steels

In addition to the stainless steels already mentioned, many other stainless steels have been developed for special applications. Shown in Tables 30 and 31 are the nominal composition and typical tensile properties of steels used in room-temperature applications. Of particular interest are the corrosion-resistant casting alloys, many of which are

TABLE 20   Effect of Welding on the Longitudinal Room-Temperature Tensile Strength and Elongation of Cold-worked Type 301 Stainless Steel

Amount of	Tensile strength, ksi (MN/m²)	
cold work, %	Unwelded	Welded
40	185 (1275.6)	129 (889.5)
62	224 (1544.5)	148 (1020.5)
78	298 (2054.7)	133 (917)

TABLE 21   Typical Room-Temperature Properties of 17Cr-7Ni Ti Stainless Steel

Heat treatment	Yield strength (0.2% offset)		Tensile strength		Elongation in 2 in. (50.8 mm) (or 4 × D), %	Hardness, Rockwell C
	ksi	MN/m²	ksi	MN/m²		
Annealed*	95	655	135	980.8	5	26
Hardened, 950°F (510°C)†	200	1379	210	1448	5	46
Hardened, 1000°F (538°C)†	190	1310.1	200	1379	5	42
Hardened, 1050°F (565°C)†	170	1172.2	190	1310.1	7	39

*Annealed at 1850 to 1950°F (1008 to 1063°C) and air-cooled.
†Annealed material heated to the indicated temperature for ½ h and air-cooled.

TABLE 22   Typical Room-Temperature Mechanical Properties of 17Cr-4Ni Cu Stainless Steel

Heat treatment	Yield strength (0.2% offset)		Tensile strength		Elongation in 2 in. (50.8 mm) (or 4 × D), %	Hardness, Rockwell C	Charpy V-notch energy absorbed	
	ksi	MN/m²	ksi	MN/m²			ft-lb	J
Annealed*	145	999.8	160	1103.2	5	35		
Hardened, 900†	185	1275.6	200	1379	14	44	20	27.1
Hardened, 925‡	175	1206.6	190	1310.1	14	42	25	33.9
Hardened, 1025‡	165	1137.7	170	1172.2	15	38	35	47.5
Hardened, 1075‡	150	1034.3	165	1137.7	16	36	40	54.2
Hardened, 1150‡	125	861.9	145	999.8	19	33	50	67.8

*1900°F (1036°C) for ½ h, air-cooled.
†1900°F (1036°C) for ½ h, air-cooled; 900°F (482°C) for 1 h, air-cooled.
‡1900°F (1036°C) for ½ h, air-cooled; 925 (496), 1025 (552), 1075 (579), or 1150 (620) °F (°C) for 4 h, air-cooled.
Note: Impact properties are minimum values.

TABLE 23   Typical Room-Temperature Mechanical Properties of 15Cr-5Ni Cu Stainless Steel

Heat treatment	Yield strength (0.2% offset)		Tensile strength		Elongation in 2 in. (50.8 mm) (or 4 × D), %	Hardness, Rockwell C	Charpy V-notch energy absorbed	
	ksi	MN/m²	ksi	MN/m²			ft-lb	J
Hardened, 900*	185	1275.6	200	1379	14	44	20	27.1
Hardened, 925†	175	1206.6	190	1310.1	14	42	25	33.9
Hardened, 1025†	165	1137.7	170	1172.2	15	38	35	47.5
Hardened, 1075†	150	1034.3	165	1137.7	16	36	40	54.2
Hardened, 1150†	125	861.9	145	999.8	19	33	50	67.8

*1900°F (1036°C) for ½ h, oil- or air-cooled; 900°F (482°C) for 1 h, air-cooled.
†1900°F (1036°C) for ½ h, oil- or air-cooled; 925 (496), 1025 (552), 1075 (579), or 1150 (620) °F (°C) for 4 h, air-cooled.
Note: Impact properties are minimum values.

counterparts of wrought stainless steel grades, and the high-manganese, low-nickel (or no nickel) austenitic stainless steels, which were developed to provide alternatives to the high-nickel 300 series of stainless steels in times of nickel shortages. In many applications, the high-manganese austenitic stainless steels are excellent engineering materials and should be considered on their own merits rather than just being regarded as substitutes for 300-series steels during nickel shortages. These steels are readily formable and weldable and generally exhibit higher yield and tensile strengths than do the 300-series steels.

TABLE 24   Typical Room-Temperature Mechanical Properties of 14.5Cr-6.5Ni Ti Stainless Steel

Heat treatment	Yield strength (0.2% offset)		Tensile strength		Elongation in 2 in. (50.8 mm) (or 4 × D), %	Hardness, Rockwell C	Charpy V-notch energy absorbed	
	ksi	MN/m²	ksi	MN/m²			ft-lb	J
Annealed*	108	744.7	125	861.9	16	25		
Hardened, 900†	182	1254.9	188	1296.3	13	41	6	8.1
Hardened, 950†	172	1185.9	177	1220.4	14	39	10	13.6
Hardened, 975†	167	1151.5	172	1185.9	15	38	15	20.3
Hardened, 1000†	160	1103.2	165	1137.7	16	37	30	40.7
Hardened, 1050†	144	992.9	152	1048	18	33	50	67.8
Hardened, 1150†	115	792.9	140	965.3	21	30	80	108.5

*Solution-annealed at 1500°F (815°C) for 1 h, air-cooled.
†Solution-annealed at 1500°F (815°C) for 1 h, air-cooled; 900 (482), 950 (510), 975 (524), 1000 (538), 1050 (565), or 1100 (593) °F (°C) for 8, 4, 4, 3, 2 and 1 h, respectively, air-cooled.

TABLE 25   Typical Room-Temperature Mechanical Properties of 13Cr-8Ni Mo Stainless Steel

Heat treatment	Yield strength (0.2% offset)		Tensile strength		Elongation in 2 in. (50.8 mm) (or 4 × D), %	Hardness, Rockwell C	Charpy V-notch energy absorbed	
	ksi	MN/m²	ksi	MN/m²			ft-lb	J
Annealed*	160	1103.2	100	689.5	15	35		
Hardened, 950†	214	1475.5	188	1296.3	16	46	18	24.4

*Solution-annealed at 1700°F (926°C) for ½ h, air-cooled or oil-quenched.
†1700°F (926°C) for ½ h, air-cooled or oil-quenched; 950°F (510°C) for 4 h, air-cooled.

TABLE 26   Typical Room-Temperature Mechanical Properties of 17Cr-7Ni Al and 15Cr-7Ni Mo Stainless Steels

Heat treatment	Yield strength (0.2% offset)		Tensile strength		Elongation in 2 in. (50.8 mm) (or 4 × D), %	Hardness, Rockwell
	ksi	MN/m²	ksi	MN/m²		
			17Cr-7Ni Al			
A*	40	275.8	130	896.4	35	B85
TH 1050†	185	1275.6	200	1379	9	C43
RH 950‡	220	1516.9	235	1620.3	6	C48
C§	190	1310.1	220	1516.9	5	C43
CH 900¶	260	1792.7	265	1827.2	2	C49
			15Cr-7Ni Mo			
A*	55	379.2	130	896.4	35	B88
TH 1050†	200	1379	210	1448	7	C44
RH 950‡	225	1551.4	240	1654.8	6	C48
C§	190	1310.1	220	1516.9	5	C43
CH 900¶	260	1792.7	265	1827.2	2	C49

*Annealed at 1950°F (1063°C), air-cooled.
†Annealed material hardened by heating + 1400°F (760°C) for ½ h, cooling to 60°F (15.6°C) + 0 to 10°F (0 to 6°C) within 1 h, and heating to 1050°F (565°C) for 1 h, air-cooled.
‡Annealed material heated to 1750°F (953°C) for 10 min, air-cooled, refrigerated at −100°F (−73°C) for 8 h, heated to 950°F (510°C) for 1 h, air-cooled.
§As-cold-rolled.
¶As-cold-rolled material heated to 900°F (482°C) for 1 h, air-cooled.

TABLE 27   Typical Room-Temperature Mechanical Properties of 14Cr-8Ni Mo Stainless Steel

Heat treatment	Yield strength (0.2% offset)		Tensile strength		Elongation in 2 in. (50.8 mm) (or 4 × D), %	Hardness, Rockwell	Toughness* Energy absorbed	
	ksi	MN/m²	ksi	MN/m²			in.-lb/in.²	J/m²
A†	55	379.2	125	861.9	25	B88		
SRH 950‡	220	1516.9	235	1620.3	5	C49	850	14.9
SRH 1050‡	205	1413.5	215	1482.4	5	C46	1000	17.5

*Precracked sheet Charpy specimen.
†Annealed at 1825°F (996°C), air-cooled.
‡Annealed material reheated to 1700°F (926°C) for 1 h, air-cooled, refrigerated at −100°F (−73°C) for 8 h, reheated to 950°F (510°C) or 1050°F (565°C) for 1 h, air-cooled.

TABLE 28   Typical Room-Temperature Mechanical Properties of 16.5Cr-4.5Ni Mo and 15.5Cr-4.5Ni Mo Stainless Steels

Heat treatment	Yield strength (0.2% offset)		Tensile strength		Elongation in 2 in. (50.8 mm) (or 4 × D), %	Hardness, Rockwell	Charpy V-notch energy absorbed	
	ksi	MN/m²	ksi	MN/m²			ft-lb	J
16.5Cr-4.5Ni Mo								
H*	60	413.7	145	999.8	40	C20		
DA†	149	1027.4	186	1282.5	12	C41		
SCT-850‡	173	1192.8	206	1420.4	13	C45	14	19
SCT-1000‡	148	1020.5	169	1165.3	15	C38	25	33.9
15.5Cr-4.5Ni Mo								
H*	65	448.2	175	1206.6	30	B95		
DA†	155	1068.7	195	1344.5	10	C41	10	13.6
SCT-850‡	190	1310.1	220	1516.9	13	C43	18	24.4

*Annealed at 1950°F (1063°C), air-cooled.
†Annealed material reheated to 1350°F (734°C) for 1 to 2 h, air-cooled, reheated to 850°F (454°C) for 1 to 2 h, and air-cooled.
‡Annealed material reheated to 1750°F (953°C) for 10 min, air-cooled, refrigerated at −100°F (−73°C) for 3 h, reheated to 850°F (454°C) or 1000°F (538°C) for 3 h and air-cooled.

TABLE 29   Typical Room-Temperature Mechanical Properties of Austenitic 15Cr-25Ni Ti, 17Cr-10Ni P, and 18Cr-9Ni P Stainless Steels

Heat treatment	Yield strength (0.2% offset)		Tensile strength		Elongation in 2 in. (50.8 mm) (or 4 × D), %	Hardness, Rockwell
	ksi	MN/m²	ksi	MN/m²		
15Cr-25Ni Ti						
Annealed*	37	255.1	90	620.6	77	B82
Hardened†	100	689.5	146	1006.7	25	C32
17Cr-10Ni P						
Annealed‡	38	262	89	613.7	70	B82
Hardened§	98	675.7	143	986	20	C32
18Cr-9Ni P						
Annealed‡	56	386.1	116	799.8	57	B92
Hardened¶	124	855	168	1158.4	19	C38

*1850°F (1008°C) or 1650°F (898°C), oil-quenched.
†1325°F (718°C) for 16 h, air-cooled.
‡2050°F (1120°C), oil-quenched.
§1300°F (704°C) for 24 h, water-quenched.
¶1350°F (734°C) for 16 h, water-quenched.

TABLE 30   Composition and Tensile Properties of Annealed Corrosion-resistant Stainless Steel Castings

ACI cast alloy designation	Counterpart of AISI wrought alloy type	Typical composition, %				Yield strength (0.2% offset)		Tensile strength		Elongation in 2 in. (50.8 mm), %
		C	Cr	Ni	Other	ksi	MN/m²	ksi	MN/m²	
CA-15	410	0.15	12.0	1.0*		75	517.1	100	689.5	30
CA-40	420	0.40	12.0	1.0*		65	448.2	110	758.5	18
CB-30	431	0.30	20.0	2.0*		60	413.7	95	655	15
CC-50	446	0.50	28.0	4.0*		60	413.7	95	655	15
CE-30		0.30	28.0	10.0		60	413.7	95	655	15
CF-3	304L	0.03	19.0	10.0		37	255.1	75	517.1	55
CF-3M						37	255.1	75	517.1	55
CF-8	304	0.08	19.0	9.0		37	255.1	75	517.1	55
CF-20	302	0.20	19.0	9.0		36	248.2	77	530.9	50
CF-8M	316	0.08	19.0	10.5	2.5Mo	42	289.6	80	551.6	50
CF-12M	316	0.12	19.0	10.5	2.5Mo	42	289.6	80	551.6	50
CF-8C	347	0.08	19.0	10.5	Cb, 8 × C min, 1% max.	38	262	77	530.9	39
CF-16F	303	0.16	19.0	10.5	1.5% max. Mo, 0.3Se	40	275.8	77	530.9	52
CG-8M		0.08	19.0	9.5	3.0 min. Mo	43	296.5	80	551.6	50
CH-20	309	0.20	24.0	13.0		50	344.8	88	606.7	38
CK-20	310	0.20	25.0	20.0		38	262	76	524	37

*Maximum.

TABLE 31   Composition and Tensile Properties of Some Nonstandard Stainless Steels

Steel type	C	Mn	Cr	Ni	Other	Yield strength (0.2% offset)		Tensile strength		Elongation in 2 in. (50.8 mm), %
						ksi	MN/m²	ksi	MN/m²	
AUSTENITIC										
18Cr-18Ni-2Si	0.07	1.4	18.0	18.0	2.0Si	35	241.3	80	551.6	55
26Cr-6Ni	0.05	1.0	26.0	6.5	0.25Ti	75	617.1	100	689.5	35
AUSTENITIC HIGH MANGANESE										
203EZ	0.05	6.0	17.0	6.0	2.0Cu	40	275.8	85	586.1	50
204	0.06	8.0	18.0	5.0	0.20N	55	379.2	100	689.5	50
205	0.18	15.0	17.0	1.3	0.35N	75	517.1	130	896.4	45
211	0.05	6.0	17.0	5.5	1.5Cu	40	275.8	85	586.1	60
216	0.06	8.3	20.0	6.0	2.5Mo, 0.37N	60	413.7	100	689.5	45
18Cr-2Ni Mn	0.10	12.0	18.0	1.6	0.35N	65	448.2	120	827.4	55
18Cr-3Ni Mn	0.05	13.0	18.0	3.3	0.30N	67	462	114	786	50
18Cr-5Ni Mn	0.10	15.0	17.5	5.5	0.38N	55 min.	379.2 min.	105 min.	724 min.	40 min.
18Cr-Mn	0.10	15.0	18.0	0.2	0.40N	70	482.7	125	861.9	45

REFERENCES

1. McClintock, M.: "Cryogenics," Reinhold, New York, 1964.
2. Sanderson, G. P., and D. T. Llewellyn: Mechanical Properties of Standard Austenitic Stainless Steels in the Temperature Range −196 to +800 C, *J. Iron Steel Inst. London*, vol. 207, pp. 1129–1146, August 1969.
3. McConnell, J. H., and R. R. Brady: Austenitic Stainless Steels—Thousands of Tons in −300 to −425 F Service, *Chem. Eng.*, pp. 125–128, Jul. 11, 1960.
4. Flinn, P. A.: Solid Solution Strengthening, "Strengthening Mechanisms in Solids," American Society for Metals, Metals Park, Ohio, 1962.
5. Llewellyn, D. T., and J. D. Murray: Cold-worked Stainless Steels, *High Alloy Steels Spec. Rep. No. 86*, The Iron and Steel Institute, London, 1964.
6. Defilippi, J. D., K. G. Brickner, and E. M. Gilbert: Ductile-to-Brittle Transition in Austenitic Stainless Steels, *Trans. Am. Inst. Min. Metall. Pet. Eng.*, vol. 245, pp. 2141–2148, October 1969.
7. Henke, R. H.: Low-Temperature Properties of Austenitic Stainless Steels, *Weld. J., Res. Suppl.*, vol. 37, no. 7, p. 304–5, July 1958.

8. Chromium-Nickel Stainless Steel Data, Section I, Wrought Stainless Steels, Bulletin C, "Mechanical Properties of Austenitic Chromium-Nickel Stainless Steels at Subzero Temperatures," The International Nickel Company, Inc., New York, 1963.

9. Kovneristyi, Yu. K.: Structure and Properties of Steels for Operation at Cryogenic Temperatures, *Met. Sci. Heat Treat.*, pp. 683–690, September–October 1969.

10. Christian, J. L., J. D. Gruner, and L. D. Girton: The Effects of Cold Rolling on the Mechanical Properties of Type 310 Stainless Steel at Room and Cryogenic Temperatures, *Trans. Am. Soc. Met.*, vol. 57, pp. 199–207, 1964.

11. Alper, R. A.: Cryogenically Stretch-formed Type 301 Stainless Steel for Cryogenic Service, *Mater. Res. Stand.*, vol. 4, pp. 525–532, October 1964.

12. Watson, J. F., and J. L. Christian: Mechanical Properties of High Strength Type 301 Stainless Steel at 70, −320, and −423 F in the Base Metal and Welded Joint Configuration, *ASTM Spec. Tech. Publ. 287*, 1961.

13. Krivobok, V. N.: Properties of Austenitic Stainless Steels at Low Temperature, *Nat. Bur. Stand. U.S. Circ. 520*, 1952.

14. Schmidt, E. H.: Low Temperature Impact of Annealed and Sensitized 18-8, *Met. Prog.*, vol. 54, pp. 698–704, November 1948.

15. Binder, W. O.: Effect of Cold Work at Low Temperature on Austenitic 18-8, *Met. Prog.*, vol. 58, pp. 201–207, August 1950.

16. Kramer, A., and W. Baldwin, Jr.: Carbide Precipitation and Brittleness in Austenitic Stainless Steels, *Trans. Am. Soc. Met.*, vol. 50, pp. 803–813, 1958.

17. Huseby, R. A.: Stress Relieving of Stainless Steels and the Associated Metallurgy, *Weld. J. Res. Suppl.*, vol. 37, pp. 304-s–315-s, July 1958.

18. Mishler, H. W., and H. J. Nichols: An Investigation of the Low-Temperature Impact Properties of Stainless Steel Weldments, *Weld. J. Res. Suppl.*, vol. 40, pp. 564-s–568-s, December 1961.

19. "Steel Products Manual: Stainless and Heat Resisting Steels," American Iron and Steel Institute, Washington, D.C., April 1963.

20. Wrought Stainless Steels, "*Metals Handbook*," Vol. I, 8th ed., American Society for Metals, Metals Park, Ohio, 1961.

21. "Alloy Digest, Stainless, Corrosion, and Heat Resisting Steels," No. 7, Engineering Alloys Digest, Inc., Upper Montclair, N.J., 1952.

22. Metal Progress Databook, *Met. Prog.*, vol. 104, p. 32, 1973.

23. "Chromium-Nickel Stainless-Steel Data," The International Nickel Company, Inc., New York, 1963.

24. "Aerospace Structural Metals Handbook, Vol. I, Ferrous Alloys," 3rd rev., Syracuse University Press, Syracuse, N.Y., 1966.

25. Briggs, J. Z., and T. D. Parker: "The Super 12% Cr Steels," Climax Molybdenum Company, 1965.

26. Rickett, R. L., W. F. White, C. S. Walton, and J. C. Butler: Isothermal Transformation, Hardening and Tempering of 12% Chromium Steel, *Trans. Am. Soc. Met.*, vol. 44, p. 138, 1953.

27. McGannon, H. E. (ed.): "The Making, Shaping, and Treating of Steel," 8th ed., United States Steel Corp., Pittsburgh, 1964.

28. Rion, W. C., Jr.: Properties, Stainless Steel Information Manual for the Savannah River Plant, Vol. I, *U.S. Atomic Energy Comm. DP-860*, NASA N64-33060, July 1964.

29. Irvine, K. J., D. J. Crowe, and F. B. Pickering: The Physical Metallurgy of 12% Chromium Steels, *J. Iron Steel Inst. London*, vol. 195, p. 386, 1960.

30. Binder, W. O., and H. R. Spendclow: The Influence of Chromium on the Mechanical Properties of Plain Chromium Steels, *Trans. Am. Soc. Met.*, vol. 43, p. 759, 1951.

31. Gokyu, I., K. Suzuki, and S. Ino: Drawability of 18 Cr Stainless Steels Produced by Double Cold Rolling and Annealing Process, *J. Jpn. Inst. Met.*, vol. 34, p. 516, 1970.

32. Davison, R. M.: Formability of Low-Interstitial 18pct Cr–2 pct Mo Ferritic Stainless Steel, *Metall. Trans.*, Vol. 5, pp. 2287–2294, November 1974.

33. Chao, H. C.: The Mechanism of Ridging in Ferritic Stainless Steels, *Trans. Am. Soc. Met.*, vol. 60, p. 37, 1967.

34. Brickner, K. G., and D. C. Ludwigson, U.S. Patent 3,599,320, Aug. 17, 1971.

35. Bloom, F. K., C. N. Goller, and P. G. Mabus: The Cold Work-hardening Properties of Stainless Steel in Compression, *Trans. Am. Soc. Met.*, vol. 39, p. 843, 1947.

36. Watson, J. F., and J. C. Christian: Mechanical Properties of High-Strength Type 301 Stainless Steel at 70, −320, and −423 F in the Base Metal and Welded Joint Configuration, *ASTM Spec. Tech. Publ. 287*, p. 136, 1961.

37. Foley, F. B.: U.S. Patent 1,943,595, Jan. 16, 1934.

38. Smith, R., E. H. Wyche, and W. W. Gorr: A Precipitation-hardening Stainless Steel of the 18% Chromium, 8% Nickel Type, *Trans. Am. Inst. Min. Metall. Pet. Eng.*, vol. 167, pp. 313–343, 1946.

39. Lena, A. J.: Precipitation Reactions in Iron-Base Alloys, "Precipitation From Solid Solution," p. 244, American Society for Metals, Cleveland, 1959.

40. Marshall, M. W.: The Newer Precipitation Hardening Stainless Steels, *ASM Rep. System Paper W-10-4-65*, 1965.

41. Slunder, C. J., A. F. Hoenie, and A. M. Hall: Thermal and Mechanical Treatments for Precipita-

tion-hardenable Stainless Steels and Their Effect on Mechanical Properties, *NASA Tech. Memo. X-53578,* 1967.

42. Perry, D. C., and M. W. Marshall: Alloying Precipitation-hardening Stainless Steels for Strength and Stability, *ASTM Spec. Tech. Publ. 369,* p. 285, 1965.
43. Brickner, K. G.: Stainless Steels for Room and Cryogenic Temperatures, "Selection of Stainless Steels," American Society for Metals, Metals Park, Ohio, 1968.

Chapter 21

Mechanical Properties of Stainless Steels at Elevated Temperatures

JOHN H. HOKE

Professor, Department of Materials Science, College of Earth and Mineral Sciences, The Pennsylvania State University, University Park, Pennsylvania

Metallic materials are widely used for elevated temperature applications. However, they are not particularly satisfactory for such service. In addition to a lowering of strength and elastic properties, time-dependent phenomena such as creep, oxidation, and structural instability may occur. Since metals are used successfully at high temperatures, obviously one can cope with these problems.

   The standard stainless steel alloys were not developed for high-temperature service, but rather for resistance to corrosive environments at ambient and moderate temperatures.

Since these alloys also offer good resistance to oxidation, they naturally were adopted for requirements needing strength at high temperatures.

The austenitic grades show the best combination of strength and oxidation resistance for long service at temperatures above 1000°F (538°C). For lower temperatures and shorter times, the high-strength grades (such as martensitic and precipitation hardenable) may prove more advantageous. With increasing temperature and service life requirements strengthening due to such procedures as cold-working, martensitic transformation, and precipitation hardening become increasingly ineffective. Thus, solid-solution and particle strengthening become the main mechanisms for developing high-temperature strength, and alloys are most likely to be used in the annealed or structurally stable condition. Since reactions with the environment are covered elsewhere in this handbook, this chapter will concentrate on elevated temperature mechanical properties.

Strength properties at elevated temperatures have been measured and reported for many years. Sources of such information are varied including journal articles, company and technical society publications. Unfortunately, a considerable degree of difference in results is encountered within grades and may be greater than variations from one grade to another. This is caused by variations in chemistry, melting, structure due to processing, etc. Thus, the choice of data for presentation here has been made somewhat arbitrarily.

GENERAL BEHAVIOR OF METALLIC MATERIALS UNDER STRESS AT ELEVATED TEMPERATURES

The behavior of a metal under stress at elevated temperatures is quite different from that at ordinary temperatures. Creep, a continuous, slow deformation, may occur. This can take place at a stress below the proportional limit determined by short-time tests. Creep is a thermally activated process which occurs because certain obstacles to deformation exist which can be overcome by the combined action of the applied stress and thermal fluctuations. Practically, in structural applications, this results in accumulating strains beyond the elastic, e.g., bolting stresses decrease with time due to relaxation; turbine blading may become distorted; boiler tubing may swell and rupture.

Testing programs have been developed for measuring long-time service behavior. These have also resulted in a change in attitude toward creep—not to prevent it, but to design for it. Continuing creep under tensile loading will eventually result in failure known as stress rupture or creep rupture. The important variables are temperature and stress.

In most cases testing programs are carried out by:
- Heating of specimen to temperature
- Applying load
- Measuring the increase in length periodically

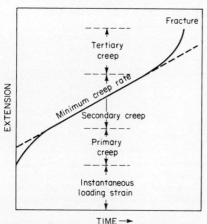

Fig. 1 Schematic creep-rupture curve in tension at constant temperature and load.

Usually, tests are run at constant load rather than at constant stress since seldom are attempts made to compensate for the change in stress with changing specimen dimensions. The information obtained from such a test can be illustrated schematically by the idealized creep curve shown in Fig. 1. Increasing temperature and stress produces an increase in creep or elongation rate and a decrease in time to failure.

We note from Fig. 1 that in addition to the initial strain produced by loading of the test specimen, the resulting curve can be divided into three portions for discussion purposes. They are:

1. Primary or first stage creep characterized by a decreasing creep rate

2. Secondary or minimum creep characterized by a constant creep rate

3. Tertiary or third stage creep characterized by an increasing creep rate and approaching rupture

Except for applications involving very short-time service life such as for rocket and missile applications, most of the exposure time of a structural part is in the secondary or minimum creep range. Thus, for practical purposes primary and tertiary creep are frequently ignored and the two main bits of information obtained from each completed test are the minimum creep rate and time to failure. Depending on the anticipated use of the resulting information, emphasis may be given to either of these two. For example, creep rate values may be determined and the test discontinued before fracture occurs. Onset of tertiary creep is usually due to increasing stress because of necking or internal void formation. It is of little importance other than to indicate that fracture is imminent.

Complete evaluation of a material involves many tests at various temperatures and stress levels. Data obtained from such tests are used for design purposes through various extrapolation and interpolation procedures. For example, information needed for a boiler being designed for 20 years service obviously cannot be obtained by a full-life test. Even so, test programs may become quite involved and time-consuming.

Log-log presentation of stress versus time to failure data at constant temperature, or stress versus minimum creep rate frequently show straight-line behavior. This is illustrated for several austenitic stainless steels in Fig. 2. This permits extrapolation and interpolation readily.

Testing programs could be further reduced significantly if results obtained at one temperature could be correlated with those obtained at another. Unfortunately, metallurgical or microstructural changes which will influence properties may also occur with

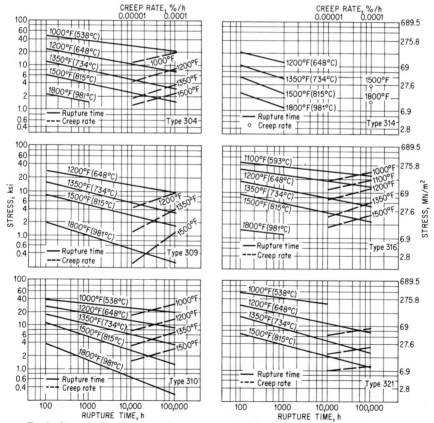

Fig. 2 Stress vs. rupture time and creep-rate curves for several austenitic stainless steels.[1]

changes in temperature. Various relations have been proposed for such correlation, such as the Larson-Miller parameter[2] for stress-rupture behavior:

$$P = T (C + \log t)$$

where P = Larson-Miller parameter
T = temperature, degrees absolute
t = time to failure
C = constant (~ 20)

We note by this equation that temperature and time have been incorporated into one number, P. Log-log presentation of stress versus P should also give straight-line behavior, thus permitting characterizations of the stress-rupture behavior as a function of stress and temperature with only several tests needed.

Frequently, interpolated and extrapolated values from raw data are presented as stress to produce rupture in a specified number of hours at various temperatures, and stress to produce a specified strain in a specified time at various temperatures, as is done frequently in this chapter. In addition, isochronous stress-strain curves sometimes are used to present short-time, high-stress, high-temperature behavior where primary creep may be predominant. Such results are usually presented graphically as stress versus total strain after various time intervals.

Other problems occurring due to elevated temperatures, but difficult to evaluate, are thermal fatigue resulting from cyclic stresses developing during thermal cycling and thermal shock or failure due to high stress produced by steep thermal gradients such as occurs during quenching or flame impingement on a cold surface. Important factors in thermal shock resistance are fatigue strength at mean temperature σ_f, thermal conductivity k, Young's modulus E, and coefficient of thermal expansion α. These have been related to a so-called thermal shock parameter P as follows:

$$P = \frac{\sigma_f k}{Ea}$$

ELEVATED TEMPERATURE MECHANICAL PROPERTIES OF STAINLESS STEELS

Short-time Properties of Standard Grades Even though time-dependent behavior at elevated temperature may be of most concern, some applications are designed on the basis of short-time test results with appropriate factors of safety. In addition, time-dependent behavior does not become of much concern at temperatures below 900°F (482°C), and certain applications may not involve exposure to high service temperatures for extended periods of time.

Austenitic Alloys. Data on yield strength and ultimate tensile strength, taken from *ASTM Data Series* DS 5S2[3] for some austenitic grades are presented in Tables 1 and 2. In these tables the strength at temperature is given as a fraction of the room-temperature strength. Thus, the rate of decrease with increasing temperature is more evident, and may be more typical than actual values that may be encountered from heat to heat. However, these ratios are converted to stress values in Tables 3 and 4 for quick reference purposes. Elastic moduli values also change with increasing temperature as given in Table 5 for certain of the austenitic grades.

Straight-Chromium Alloys. For the hardenable grades the high strengths developed by heat treatment will increasingly temper off with time as the test temperature is increased. Thus, properties are usually reported for the annealed condition. Data for some of the straight-chromium grades are presented in Tables 6 and 7. These steels, except if heat-treated when the properties are rather temporary, as just mentioned, are generally considered inferior in strength to the austenitic grades at temperatures of 1000°F (538°C) and above.

Time-dependent Properties of Standard Grades Data on creep and creep-rupture properties are frequently encountered in both tabular and graphical form. Raw data are usually presented graphically on log-log paper as stress versus secondary (minimum) creep rate, or stress versus time to rupture. Since such graphs are typically straight line, interpolation and extrapolation procedures are simple. Interpolated data are frequently presented in both graphical and tabular form.

Austenitic Alloys. The average stress to produce a minimum creep rate of 1% in 10,000

TABLE 1 Ratio of Yield Strength at Temperature to Yield Strength at Room Temperature for Wrought Austenitic Stainless Steels[3]

Temperature		Grades					
°F	°C	304	304L	316	316L	321	347
75	24	1.00	1.00	1.00	1.00	1.00	1.00
100	38	0.96	0.97	0.97	0.97	0.97	0.98
200	93	0.83	0.85	0.86	0.85	0.85	0.92
300	149	0.75	0.77	0.78	0.76	0.76	0.85
400	204	0.69	0.70	0.70	0.70	0.69	0.80
500	260	0.65	0.65	0.66	0.64	0.64	0.75
600	316	0.61	0.62	0.63	0.61	0.61	0.72
700	371	0.59	0.60	0.60	0.58	0.59	0.69
800	427	0.56	0.58	0.59	0.55	0.57	0.68
900	482	0.54	0.56	0.58	0.53	0.57	0.67
1000	538	0.52	0.53	0.57	0.50	0.56	0.67
1100	593	0.49	0.50	0.55	0.47	0.55	0.66
1200	649	0.47	0.45	0.54	0.42	0.53	0.65
1300	704	0.44		0.51		0.50	0.61
1400	760	0.39		0.48		0.47	0.54
1500	816	0.31		0.43		0.40	0.43
1600	871	0.20					

TABLE 2 Ratio of Tensile Strength at Temperature to Tensile Strength at Room Temperature for Wrought Austenitic Stainless Steels[3]

Temperature		Grades					
°F	°C	304	304L	316	316L	321	347
75	24	1.00	1.00	1.00	1.00	1.00	1.00
100	38	0.97	0.97	0.97	0.97	0.97	0.97
200	93	0.86	0.86	0.91	0.88	0.89	0.87
300	149	0.80	0.79	0.89	0.83	0.84	0.80
400	204	0.78	0.76	0.87	0.81	0.83	0.75
500	260	0.77	0.75	0.87	0.80	0.83	0.73
600	316	0.77	0.74	0.88	0.80	0.83	0.72
700	371	0.77	0.73	0.87	0.80	0.83	0.71
800	427	0.76	0.72	0.86	0.79	0.83	0.71
900	482	0.74	0.70	0.83	0.76	0.83	0.71
1000	538	0.70	0.66	0.78	0.72	0.79	0.70
1100	593	0.63	0.60	0.71	0.66	0.71	0.67
1200	649	0.55	0.53	0.62	0.59	0.61	0.62
1300	704	0.46	0.45	0.52	0.50	0.49	0.54
1400	760	0.35	0.36	0.41	0.41	0.37	0.43
1500	816	0.25	0.26	0.30	0.31	0.25	0.28

TABLE 3 Effect of Temperature on Yield Strength, ksi (MN/m²), of Wrought Austenitic Stainless Steels[3]

Temperature		Grades					
°F	°C	304	304L	316	316L	321	347
75	24	36.9 (254.4)	33.8 (233.1)	38.0 (262)	33.7 (232.4)	29.7 (204.8)	38.2(263.4)
100	38	35.4 (244.1)	32.8 (226.2)	36.9 (254.4)	32.7 (225.5)	28.8 (198.6)	37.4 (259.9)
200	93	30.6 (211)	28.7 (197.9)	32.7 (225.5)	28.6 (197.2)	25.2 (173.8)	35.1 (242)
300	149	27.7(191)	26.0 (179.3)	29.7 (204.8)	25.6 (176.5)	22.6 (155.8)	32.5 (224.1)
400	204	25.5(175.8)	23.7 (163.4)	26.6 (183.4)	23.6 (162.7)	20.5 (141.3)	30.6 (211)
500	260	24.0 (165.5)	22.0 (151.7)	25.1 (173.1)	21.6 (148.9)	19.0 (131)	28.7 (197.9)
600	316	22.5 (155.1)	21.0 (144.8)	23.9 (164.8)	20.6 (142)	18.1 (124.8)	27.5 (189.6)
700	371	21.8 (150.3)	20.3 (140)	22.8 (157.2)	19.5 (134.5)	17.5 (120.7)	26.4 (182)
800	427	20.7 (142.7)	19.6 (135.1)	22.4 (154)	18.5 (127.6)	16.9 (116.5)	26.0 (179.3)
900	482	19.9 (137.2)	18.9 (130.3)	22.0 (151.7)	17.9 (123.4)	16.9 (116.5)	25.6 (176.5)
1000	538	19.2 (132.4)	17.9 (123.4)	21.7 (148.6)	16.9 (116.5)	16.6 (114.5)	25.6 (176.5)
1100	593	18.1 (124.8)	16.9 (116.5)	20.9 (144.1)	15.8 (108.9)	16.3 (112.4)	25.2 (173.8)
1200	649	17.3 (119.3)	15.2 (104.8)	20.5 (141.3)	14.2 (97.9)	15.7 (108.3)	24.8 (171)
1300	704	16.2 (111.7)		19.4 (133.8)		14.8 (102)	23.3 (160.7)
1400	760	14.4 (99.2)		18.2 (125.5)		14.0 (96.5)	20.6 (142)
1500	816	11.4 (78.6)		16.3 (112.4)		13.7 (94.5)	16.4 (113.1)
1600	871	7.4 (51)					

TABLE 4   Effect of Temperature on Ultimate Tensile Strength, ksi (MN/m²), of Wrought Austenitic Stainless Steels[3]

Temperature		Grades					
°F	°C	304	304L	316	316L	321	347
75	24	83.9 (578.5)	79.2 (546.1)	83.3 (574.4)	78.9 (544)	81.8 (564)	87.0 (600)
100	38	81.4 (561.3)	76.8 (529.5)	80.8 (557.1)	76.5 (527.5)	79.3 (546.8)	84.4 (581.9)
200	93	72.1 (497.1)	68.1 (469.5)	75.8 (522.6)	69.4 (478.5)	72.8 (502)	75.7 (522)
300	149	87.1 (600.6)	62.6 (431.6)	74.1 (510.9)	65.5 (451.6)	68.7 (473.7)	69.6 (480)
400	204	65.4 (450.9)	60.2 (415.1)	72.5 (499.9)	63.9 (440.6)	67.9 (468.2)	65.3 (450.2)
500	260	64.6 (445.4)	59.4 (409.6)	72.5 (499.9)	63.1 (435.1)	67.9 (468.2)	63.5 (437.8)
600	316	64.6 (445.4)	58.6 (404)	73.3 (505.4)	63.1 (435.1)	67.9 (468.2)	62.7 (432.3)
700	371	64.6 (445.4)	57.8 (398.5)	72.5 (499.9)	63.1 (435.1)	67.9 (468.2)	61.8 (426.1)
800	427	63.8 (439.9)	57.0 (393)	71.6 (493.7)	62.3 (429.6)	67.9 (468.2)	61.8 (426.1)
900	482	62.1 (428.2)	55.4 (382)	69.1 (476.4)	60.0 (413.7)	67.9 (468.2)	61.8 (426.1)
1000	538	58.7 (404.7)	52.3 (360.6)	65.0 (448.2)	56.8 (391.6)	64.6 (445.4)	60.9 (419.9)
1100	593	52.9 (364.7)	47.5 (327.5)	59.1 (407.5)	52.1 (359.2)	58.1 (400.6)	58.3 (402)
1200	649	46.1 (317.9)	42.0 (289.6)	51.6 (355.8)	46.6 (321.3)	50.0 (344.8)	53.9 (371.6)
1300	704	38.6 (266.1)	35.6 (245.5)	43.3 (298.6)	39.5 (272.4)	40.1 (276.5)	47.0 (324.1)
1400	760	29.4 (202.7)	28.5 (196.5)	34.2 (235.8)	32.3 (222.7)	30.3 (208.9)	37.4 (257.9)
1500	816	21.0 (144.8)	20.6 (142)	25.0 (172.4)	24.5 (168.9)	20.5 (141.3)	24.4 (168.2)

TABLE 5   Moduli of Elasticity at Various Temperatures for Several Austenitic Stainless Steels[1]

Temperature			Grades					
°F	°C	Modulus*	302	304	310	316	321	347
200	93	E	27.9 (192.4)	27.9 (192.4)	28.2 (194.4)	28.1 (193.7)	28.0 (193.1)	28.2 (194.4)
		G	10.8 (74.5)	11.1 (76.5)	10.9 (75.2)	11.0 (75.8)	10.8 (74.5)	11.0 (75.8)
300	149	E	27.3 (188.2)	27.1 (186.9)	27.5 (189.6)	27.5 (189.6)	27.3 (188.2)	27.5 (189.6)
		G	10.4 (71.7)	10.8 (74.5)	10.6 (73.1)	10.6 (73.1)	10.6 (73.1)	10.7 (73.8)
400	204	E	26.7 (184.1)	26.6 (183.4)	26.8 (184.8)	26.9 (185.5)	26.5 (182.7)	26.8 (184.8)
		G	10.1 (69.6)	10.5 (72.4)	10.3 (71)	10.3 (71)	10.3 (71)	10.4 (71.7)
500	260	E	26.0 (179.3)	26.0 (179.3)	26.2 (180.6)	26.3 (181.3)	25.8 (177.9)	26.1 (180)
		G	9.8 (67.6)	10.2 (70.3)	10.0 (69)	10.0 (69)	9.9 (68.3)	10.1 (69.6)
600	316	E	25.4 (175.1)	25.6 (176.5)	25.5 (175.8)	25.6 (176.5)	25.3 (174.4)	25.4 (175.1)
		G	9.5 (65.5)	9.9 (68.3)	9.7 (66.9)	9.7 (66.9)	9.7 (66.9)	9.8 (67.6)
700	371	E	24.8 (171)	24.7 (170.3)	24.9 (171.7)	24.9 (171.7)	24.5 (168.9)	24.8 (171)
		G	9.3 (64.1)	9.7 (66.9)	9.4 (64.8)	9.4 (64.8)	9.4 (64.8)	9.5 (65.5)
800	427	E	24.2 (166.9)	24.1 (166.2)	24.2 (166.9)	24.2 (166.9)	23.8 (164.1)	24.1 (166.2)
		G	9.0 (62.1)	9.5 (65.5)	9.1 (62.7)	9.1 (62.7)	9.1 (62.7)	9.2 (63.4)
900	482	E	23.6 (162.7)	23.2 (160)	23.6 (162.7)	23.5 (162)	23.2 (160)	23.4 (161.3)
		G	8.8 (60.7)	9.2 (63.4)	8.8 (60.7)	8.8 (60.7)	8.8 (60.7)	8.9 (61.4)
1000	538	E	23.0 (158.6)	22.5 (155.1)	23.0 (158.6)	22.8 (157.2)	22.5 (155.1)	22.8 (157.2)
		G	8.6 (59.3)	8.9 (61.4)	8.5 (58.6)	8.5 (58.6)	8.5 (58.6)	8.6 (59.3)
1110	593	E	22.3 (153.8)	21.8 (150.3)	22.4 (154.4)	22.2 (153.1)	21.9 (151)	22.0 (151.7)
		G	8.4 (57.9)	8.6 (59.3)	8.2 (56.5)	8.3 (57.2)	8.2 (56.5)	8.3 (57.3)
1200	649	E	21.8 (150.3)	21.1 (145.5)	21.8 (150.3)	21.5 (148.2)	21.2 (146.2)	21.4 (147.6)
		G	8.2 (56.5)	8.3 (57.2)	7.9 (54.5)	8.1 (55.8)	7.9 (54.5)	8.1 (55.8)
1300	704	E	21.2 (146.2)	20.4 (140.7)	21.2 (146.2)	20.8 (143.4)	20.4 (140.7)	20.7 (142.7)
		G	7.9 (54.5)	8.0 (55.2)	7.6 (52.4)	7.9 (54.5)	7.7 (53.1)	7.8 (53.9)
1400	760	E	20.6 (142)	19.4 (133.8)	20.5 (141.3)	20.0 (137.9)	19.7 (135.8)	20.0 (137.9)
		G	7.7 (53.1)	7.7 (53.1)	7.2 (49.6)	7.7 (53.1)	7.4 (51)	7.5 (51.7)
1500	816	E	20.0 (137.9)	18.1 (124.8)	19.0 (131)	19.1 (131.7)	19.1 (131.7)	19.4 (133.8)
		G	7.5 (51.7)	7.4 (51)	6.9 (47.6)	7.5 (51.7)	7.1 (49)	7.2 (49.6)

*E, modulus of elasticity in tension × 10⁶ psi (GN/m²). G, modulus of elasticity in shear × 10⁶ psi (GN/m²).

TABLE 6   Effect of Temperature on Yield Strength, ksi (MN/m²), of Some Straight-Chromium Stainless Steels[4]

Temperature		Grades				
°F	°C	410*	409	420*	430	446
70	21	145 (999.8)	40 (275.8)	158 (1089.4)	45 (310.3)	50 (344.8)
400	204	135 (930.8)	24 (165.5)	153 (1054.9)		
600	316	125 (861.9)	22 (151.7)	148 (1020.5)		
800	427	115 (792.9)	20 (137.9)	140 (965.3)		
1000	538	95 (655)	17 (117.2)	75 (517.1)	24 (165.5)	40 (275.8)
1100	593				18 (124.1)	23 (158.6)
1200	649	40 (275.8)	13 (89.6)		12 (82.7)	12 (82.7)

*Heat-treated.

TABLE 7   Effect of Temperature on Ultimate Tensile Strength, ksi (MN/m²), of Some Straight-Chromium Stainless Steels[4]

Temperature		Grades				
°F	°C	410*	409	420*	430	446
70	21	155 (1068.7)	68 (468.9)	218 (1503.1)	77 (530.9)	85 (586.1)
400	204	150 (1034.3)	54 (372.3)	205 (1413.5)	67 (462)	84 (579.2)
600	316	145 (999.8)	51 (351.6)	200 (1379)	63 (434.4)	83 (572.3)
800	427	130 (896.4)	46 (317.2)	190 (1310.1)	56 (386.1)	78 (537.8)
1000	538	100 (689.5)	36 (248.2)	105 (724)	36 (248.2)	70 (482.7)
1100	593				27 (166.2)	35 (241.3)
1200	649	45 (310.3)	23 (158.6)		19 (131)	23 (158.6)
1300	704				13 (89.6)	16 (110.3)
1400	760	18 (124.1)			8 (55.2)	10 (69)
1500	816				6.5 (44.8)	8 (55.2)
1600	871	15 (103.4)			4.5 (31)	6 (41.4)

*Heat-treated.

TABLE 8   Average Stress, ksi (MN/m²), to Produce 1% Elongation in 10,000 h for General Austenitic Stainless Steels[5]

Grade	Temperature, °F (°C)				
	1000 (538)	1100 (593)	1200 (649)	1300 (704)	1500 (816)
301	19 (131)	12.5 (86.2)	8 (55.2)	4.5 (31)	1.8 (12.4)
302	20 (137.9)	12.5 (86.2)	7.5 (51.7)	4.3 (29.6)	1.5 (10.3)
302B			7 (48.3)	4.5 (31)	1 (6.9)
303	16.5 (113.8)	11.5 (79.3)	6.5 (44.8)	3.5 (24.1)	0.7 (4.8)
304/304L	20 (137.9)	12 (82.7)	7.5 (51.7)	4 (27.6)	1.5 (10.3)
305	19 (131)	12.5 (86.2)	8 (55.2)	4.5 (31)	2 (13.8)
309	16.5 (113.8)	12.5 (86.2)	10 (69)	6 (41.4)	3 (20.7)
310	33 (227.5)	23 (158.6)	15 (103.4)	10 (69)	3 (20.7)
314	20 (137.9)	13 (89.6)	7.5 (51.7)	5 (34.5)	2.5 (17.2)
316/316L	25 (172.4)	17.4 (120)	11.6 (80)	7.5 (51.7)	2.4 (16.5)
317	23 (158.6)	16.8 (115.8)	11.2 (77.2)	6.9 (47.6)	2 (13.8)
321	18 (124.1)	17 (117.2)	9 (62.1)	5 (34.5)	1.5 (10.3)
347/348	32 (220.6)	23 (158.6)	16 (110.3)	10 (69)	2 (13.8)

h at various temperatures for a number of the austenitic steels is given in Table 8. Similarly, average stress to produce rupture in 100, 1000, 10,000, and 100,000 h is given in Tables 9 to 11.

Some rupture data for several grades for still higher temperatures of 1600 to 2000°F (871 to 1093°C) are given in Table 12. Note that at these high temperatures the rupture strength for any appreciable period of time drops to quite low values.

Straight-Chromium Alloys. Average stress to produce 1% elongation in 10,000 h for several straight-chromium stainless steels at various temperatures is presented in Table 13, while stress for rupture in 1000 and 10,000 h is given in Table 14. The superiority of the austenitic grades is most evident when comparison of long-time strengths is made.

TABLE 9   Average Stress, ksi (MN/m²), to Produce Rupture in 100 and 1000 h for Several Austenitic Stainless Steels[4]

Time to rupture, h	Temperature		Grade					
	°F	°C	302/4	309	310	316	321	347
100	1000	538	47 (324.1)		38 (262)			54 (372.3)
	1100	593	34 (234.4)		32 (220.6)	45 (310.3)	42 (289.6)	
	1200	649	23 (158.6)	28 (193.1)	26 (179.3)	32 (220.6)	29 (200)	28 (193.1)
	1300	704	15 (103.4)	20 (137.9)	20 (137.9)	22 (151.7)	19 (131)	20 (137.9)
	1400	760	10 (69)	13 (89.6)	15 (103.4)	13 (89.6)	12 (82.7)	13 (89.6)
	1500	816	7 (48.3)	8 (55.2)	11 (75.8)	9 (62.1)	7 (48.3)	9 (62.1)
	1600	871	4 (27.6)	5 (34.5)	7 (48.3)	6 (41.4)		
1000	1000	538	37 (255.1)		32 (220.6)		42 (289.6)	49 (337.9)
	1100	593	25 (172.4)		25 (172.4)	37 (255.1)	30 (206.9)	35 (241.3)
	1200	649	17 (117.2)	19 (131)	18 (124.1)	24 (165.5)	18 (124.1)	23 (158.6)
	1300	704	10 (69)	12 (82.7)	13 (89.6)	16 (110.3)	11 (75.8)	14 (96.5)
	1400	760	7 (48.3)	8 (55.2)	8 (55.2)	10 (69)	7 (48.3)	8 (55.2)
	1500	816	4 (27.6)	4 (27.6)	6 (41.4)	7 (48.3)	4 (27.6)	4 (27.6)
	1600	871	3 (20.7)	3 (20.7)	4 (27.6)	3 (20.7)		

TABLE 10   Average Stress, ksi (MN/m²), to Produce Rupture in 10,000 h for Several Austenitic Stainless Steels[3]

Temperature		Grades					
°F	°C	304	304L	316	316L	321	347
1000	538	36 (248.2)	25 (172.4)	43 (296.5)	39 (268.9)	40 (275.8)	48 (331)
1050	566	28 (193.1)	20 (137.9)	34 (234.4)	30.5 (210.3)	31 (213.7)	36 (248.2)
1100	593	22.2 (153.1)	15.6 (107.6)	26.5 (182.7)	23.5 (162)	23.5 (162)	27.5 (189.6)
1150	621	17.3 (119.3)	12.2 (84.1)	20.8 (143.4)	18.2 (125.5)	17.3 (119.3)	20.5 (141.3)
1200	649	13.8 (95.2)	9.7 (66.9)	16.2 (111.7)	14.2 (97.9)	12.9 (88.9)	15.6 (107.6)
1250	677	10.8 (74.5)	7.6 (52.4)	12.7 (87.6)	11 (75.8)	9.7 (66.9)	11.9 (82.1)
1300	704	8.5 (58.6)	6 (41.4)	9.9 (68.3)	8.5 (58.6)	7.2 (49.6)	9 (62.1)
1350	732	6.7 (46.2)	4.7 (32.4)	7.7 (53.1)	6.6 (45.5)	5.4 (37.2)	6.8 (46.9)
1400	760	5.3 (36.5)	3.7 (25.5)	6 (41.4)	5.1 (35.2)	4 (27.6)	5.1 (35.2)
1450	788	4.15 (28.6)	2.9 (20)	4.7 (32.4)	3.95 (27.2)	3.05 (21)	3.85 (26.5)
1500	816	3.25 (22.4)	2.3 (15.9)	3.7 (25.5)	3.05 (21)	2.28 (15.7)	2.9 (20)

TABLE 11   Average Stress, ksi (MN/m²), to Produce Rupture in 100,000 h for Several Austenitic Stainless Steels[3]

Temperature		Grades					
°F	°C	304	304L	316	316L	321	347
1000	538	25.8 (177.9)	19.5 (134.5)	37 (25.5)	34.5 (237.9)	29 (200)	37.5 (258.6)
1050	566	20 (137.9)	15 (103.4)	28 (193.1)	25 (172.4)	23 (158.6)	28 (193.1)
1100	593	15.8 (108.9)	11.6 (80)	20.8 (143.4)	18.5 (127.6)	16.5 (113.8)	20.8 (143.4)
1150	621	12.5 (86.2)	8.9 (61.4)	15.1 (104.1)	13.7 (94.5)	12 (82.7)	15.3 (105.5)
1200	649	9.8 (67.6)	6.9 (47.6)	11.4 (78.6)	10.1 (69.6)	8.7 (60)	11.5 (79.3)
1250	677	7.6 (52.4)	5.3 (36.5)	8.4 (57.9)	7.4 (51)	6.3 (43.4)	8.6 (59.3)
1300	704	6 (41.4)	4.1 (28.3)	6.3 (43.4)	5.5 (37.9)	4.6 (31.7)	6.4 (44.1)
1350	732	4.7 (32.4)	3.15 (21.7)	4.7 (32.4)	4 (27.6)	3.3 (22.8)	4.7 (32.4)
1400	760	3.7 (25.5)	2.4 (16.5)	3.45 (23.8)	3 (20.7)	2.45 (16.9)	3.55 (24.5)
1450	788	2.9 (20)	1.87 (12.9)	2.6 (17.9)	2.2 (15.2)	1.75 (12.1)	2.64 (42.7)
1500	816	2.3 (15.9)	1.45 (10)	1.95 (13.4)	1.6 (11)	1.27 (8.8)	1.95 (13.4)

TABLE 12   Rupture Characteristics, ksi (MN/m²), of Five Standard Austenitic Stainless Grades at 1600–2000°F (871–1093°C)[6]

Time to rupture, h	Temperature °F	°C	Grades 302	309S	310S	314	316
100	1600	871	4.7 (32.4)	5.8 (40)	6.6 (45.5)	4.7 (32.4)	5 (34.5)
	1800	982	2.45 (16.9)	2.6 (17.9)	3.2 (22.1)	2.6 (17.9)	2.65 (18.3)
	2000	1093	1.3 (9)	1.4 (9.7)	1.5 (10.3)	1.5 (10.3)	1.12 (7.7)
1000	1600	871	2.8 (19.3)	3.2 (22.1)	4 (27.6)	3 (20.7)	2.7 (18.6)
	1800	982	1.55 (10.7)	1.65 (11.4)	2.1 (14.5)	1.7 (11.7)	1.25 (8.6)
	2000	1093	0.76 (5.2)	0.83 (5.7)	1.1 (7.6)	1.12 (7.7)	0.36 (2.5)
10,000	1600	871	1.75 (12.1)		2.5 (17.2)	1.95 (13.4)	1.4 (9.7)
	1800	982	0.96 (6.6)	1 (6.9)	1.35 (9.3)	1.1 (7.6)	0.6 (4.1)
	2000	1093	0.46 (3.2)	0.48 (3.3)	0.76 (5.2)	0.85 (5.9)	

TABLE 13   Average Stress, ksi (MN/m²), to Produce 1% Elongation in 10,000 h for Several Straight-Chromium Stainless Steels[5]

Grade	Temperature, °F (°C) 1000 (538)	1100 (593)	1200 (649)	1300 (704)	1500 (816)
430	8.5 (58.6)	4.7 (32.4)	2.6 (17.9)	1.4 (9.7)	
430FSe	8.5 (58.6)	4.6 (31.7)	1.9 (13.1)	1.3 (9)	
442	8.5 (58.6)	5 (34.5)	1.6 (11)	1 (6.9)	0.6 (4.1)
446	6.4 (44.1)	2.9 (20)	1.4 (9.7)	0.6 (4.1)	0.4 (2.8)
403	11 (75.8)	4.5 (31)	2 (13.8)	1.4 (9.7)	
410	11.5 (79.3)	4.3 (29.6)	2 (13.8)	1.5 (10.3)	
416	11 (75.8)	4.6 (31.7)	2 (13.8)	1.2 (8.3)	
420	9.2 (63.4)	4.2 (29)	2 (13.8)	1 (6.9)	
431	6.8 (46.9)	3.5 (24.1)			

TABLE 14   Average Stress, ksi (MN/m²), to Produce Rupture in 1000 and 10,000 h for Several Straight-Chromium Stainless Steels in the Annealed Condition[6]

Time to rupture, h	Temperature °F	°C	Grades 405	410	430	446
1000	900	482	25 (172.4)	34 (234.4)	30 (206.9)	
	1000	538	16 (110.3)	19 (131)	17.5 (120.7)	17.9 (123.4)
	1100	593	6.8 (46.9)	10 (69)	9.1 (62.7)	5.6 (38.6)
	1200	649	3.8 (26.2)	4.9 (33.8)	5 (34.5)	4 (27.6)
	1300	704	2.2 (15.2)	2.5 (17.2)	2.8 (19.3)	2.7 (18.6)
	1400	760	1.2 (8.3)	1.2 (8.3)	1.7 (11.7)	1.8 (12.4)
	1500	816	0.8 (5.5)		0.9 (6.2)	1.2 (8.3)
10,000	900	482	22 (151.7)	26 (179.3)	24 (165.5)	
	1000	538	12 (82.7)	13 (89.6)	13.5 (93.1)	13.5 (93.1)
	1100	593	4.7 (32.4)	6.9 (47.6)	6.5 (44.8)	3 (20.7)
	1200	649	2.5 (17.2)	3.5 (24.1)	3.4 (23.4)	2.2 (15.2)
	1300	704	1.4 (9.7)	1.5 (10.3)	2.2 (15.2)	1.6 (11)
	1400	760	0.7 (4.8)	0.6 (4.1)	0.7 (4.8)	1.1 (7.6)
	1500	816	0.4 (2.8)		0.5 (3.4)	0.8 (5.5)

Allowable Stresses. These have been established with respect to wrought products, welds, forgings, castings, and boltings in great detail in the "Boiler and Pressure Vessel Code"[7] in the sections on power boilers and unfired pressure vessels. These code values are the minima of several criteria involving tensile, yield, creep, and rupture strengths and are widely used by industry for design purposes for reliable service. Some data extracted from Section VIII for austenitic plate materials are given in Table 15. For detailed tabulations regarding published allowable stresses, see Sections I, III, and VIII of the "Boiler and Pressure Vessel Code."[7]

TABLE 15   Maximum Allowable Stress, ksi (MN/m²), Values in Tension for Austenitic Stainless Steel Unfired Pressure Vessels[7]

Temperature		Grades					
°F	°C	304	321	347	309	310	316
75*	24	75 (517.1)	75 (517.1)	75 (517.1)	75 (517.1)	75 (517.1)	75 (517.1)
75	24	18.75 (129.3)	18.75 (129.3)	18.75 (129.3)	18.75 (129.3)	18.75 (129.3)	18.75 (129.3)
200	93	16.65 (114.8)	18.75 (129.3)	18.75 (129.3)	18.75 (129.3)	18.75 (129.3)	18.75 (129.3)
300	149	15 (103.4)	17 (117.2)	17 (117.2)	17.3 (119.3)	18.5 (127.6)	17.9 (123.4)
400	204	13.65 (94.1)	15.8 (108.9)	15.8 (108.9)	16.7 (115.1)	18.2 (125.5)	17.5 (120.7)
500	260	12.5 (86.2)	15.2 (104.8)	15.2 (104.8)	16.6 (114.5)	17.7 (122)	17.2 (118.6)
600	316	11.6 (80)	14.9 (102.7)	14.9 (102.7)	16.5 (113.8)	17.2 (118.6)	17.1 (117.9)
700	371	10.8 (74.5)	14.8 (102)	14.8 (102)	16.4 (113.1)	16.6 (114.5)	17 (117.2)
800	426	10 (69)	14.55 (100.3)	14.55 (100.3)	15.7 (108.3)	15.7 (108.3)	16.75 (115.5)
900	482	9.4 (64.8)	14.1 (97.2)	14.1 (97.2)	13.8 (95.2)	13.8 (95.2)	16 (110.3)
1000	538	8.8 (60.7)	13.5 (93.1)	13.5 (93.1)	10.5 (72.4)	11 (75.8)	14 (96.5)
1100	593	7.5 (51.7)	12.5 (86.2)	12.5 (86.2)	6.5 (44.8)	5 (34.5)	10.4 (71.7)
1200	649	4.5 (31)	5 (34.5)	5 (34.5)	3.8 (26.2)	2.5 (17.2)	6.8 (46.9)
1300	704	2.42 (16.7)	2.7 (18.6)	2.7 (18.6)	2.3 (15.9)	0.75 (5.2)	4.0 (27.6)
1400	760	1.4 (9.7)	1.55 (10.7)	1.55 (10.7)	1.3 (9.0)	0.35 (2.4)	2.35 (16.2)
1500	816	0.75 (5.2)	1 (6.9)	1 (6.9)	0.75 (5.2)	0.2 (1.4)	1.5 (10.3)

*Specified room-temperature minimum tensile strength.

Austenitic Chromium-Nickel-Manganese Stainless Steels   The austenitic Cr-Ni-Mn, or 200 series, stainless steels have been developed comparatively recently and are being considered separately from the standard grades. These steels were developed primarily for the conservation of nickel, but their selection is frequently based on competitive cost-property characteristics. They are stronger and have better ductility than corresponding Cr-Ni steels at elevated temperatures.[8] However, the improvement of long-time properties is not as marked as for the short-time properties. Strength properties are presented in Tables 16 and 17.

Precipitation-hardenable Stainless Steels   The high strength of the precipitation-hardenable stainless steels is developed by intermediate temperature aging treatments. Thus, these steels in the aged condition are of limited use for high-temperature service because of overaging reactions that reduce strength properties. Tensile and rupture data for a number of the semiaustenitic precipitation-hardenable stainless steels are given in Tables 18 and 19. Some limited creep data are given in Table 20.

Casting Alloys   The stainless steels are frequently used in cast form for high-temperature applications. Since special casting grades have been developed for such service, elevated temperature properties are reported separately in Table 21[11] and in Table 4, Chap. 2. Stainless casting alloys are usually divided into two main groups: those primarily for heat resistance (H) and those for corrosion resistance (C). Some short-time, high-temperature strength properties of the corrosion-resistant grades are given in Table 22.

DEVELOPMENT OF IMPROVED HIGH-TEMPERATURE STAINLESS STEELS

As mentioned earlier, the stainless steels used for high-temperature service were developed primarily for their corrosion resistance rather than their heat resistance. Since the composition of these grades may not be optimum for creep and rupture resistance, further studies have been made emphasizing such properties.

H Grades of Austenitic Stainless Steel   In the past, testing programs have indicated considerable scatter in the creep and stress-rupture behavior within grades of various austenitic stainless steels. In particular, problems encountered with Type 321 superheater tubing led to research sponsored by ASTM-ASME. Initial observations showed a correlation of high creep rates with a fine grain size. Research indicated, however, that the heat treatment was the most important factor rather than the resulting grain size. Previously some alloys went into service in the stabilized condition to reduce sensitization problems. Such treatments reduce the creep resistance. A carbon level of 0.04%

TABLE 16   Stress, ksi (MN/m²), to Produce Rupture in 100, 1000, and 10,000 h for Ni-Cr-Mn Stainless Steels[7]

Temperature		Time to	Grades			
°F	°C	rupture, h	201	202	204	204L
1200	649	100	29 (200)	31 (213.7)	30 (206.9)	29 (200)
1350	732	100	15 (103.4)	16.2 (111.7)	17.5 (120.7)	11 (75.8)
1500	816	100	7.4 (51)	8.8 (60.7)	8.8 (60.7)	5 (34.5)
1200	649	1000	22 (151.7)	25 (172.4)	23.6 (162.7)	20.3 (140)
1350	732	1000	10 (69)	11.1 (76.5)	11.2 (77.2)	6.7 (46.2)
1500	816	1000	4 (27.6)	4.4 (30.3)	4.4 (30.3)	2.6 (17.9)
1200	649	10,000	16.5 (113.8)	20 (137.9)	18 (124.1)	14.2 (97.9)
1350	732	10,000	6.6 (45.5)	7.6 (52.4)	7.2 (49.6)	4.1 (28.3)

minimum was also found necessary to assure higher creep-rupture strength, which reduces the applicability of the ELC grades for high-temperature applications.

Thus, a modification called the H grade has been applied to most of 300 stainless steels in all product forms. These grades must have a carbon content greater than 0.04% and must be applied in the solution-annealed condition. They were introduced to establish a more positive control of the short-time creep-rupture properties and assure continuation of long-time service life. They have been found to have up to three times the service life encountered for some of the standard heats.

Nitrogen Additions to Austenitic Stainless Steel   During the course of the studies mentioned in the previous section, it was found that the high-temperature strength of Type 304 had been improving over the past 20 years. Boiler code allowable stresses have been increased from 1949 through 1969 because of demonstrated improvement in properties. Such improvements were attributed mainly to increasing nitrogen contents.

The Joint Committee (ASTM-ASME) on the Effect of Temperature on the Properties of Metals sponsored a Symposium on Elevated Temperature Properties as Influenced by Nitrogen Additions to Types 304 and 316 Stainless Steel. The papers presented at this symposium have been published as *Special Technical Publication 522*.[12] These papers report that controlled additions of nitrogen to both Types 304 and 316 stainless steel produce a consistent improvement in tensile properties. The addition of 0.10 to 0.13%

TABLE 17   Effect of Temperature on Tensile Strength, psi (MN/m²), of Ni-Cr-Mn Stainless Steels[9]

		ULTIMATE TENSILE STRENGTH			
Temperature		Grades			
°F	°C	201	202	204	204L
70	21	117275 (808.6)	108175 (745.9)	103625 (714.5)	99200 (684)
200	93	97645 (673.3)	95765 (660.3)	97785 (674.2)	85750 (591.2)
400	204	81370 (561)	85095 (586.7)	86740 (598.1)	76105 (524.7)
600	316	79040 (545)	83600 (576.4)	86345 (595.3)	74110 (511)
800	426	76530 (527.7)	77760 (536.2)	78760 (543.1)	70040 (482.9)
1000	538	69530 (479.4)	72135 (497.4)	70940 (489.1)	61630 (424.9)
1200	649	47625 (328.4)	55670 (383.8)	53710 (370.3)	46120 (318)
1400	760	27210 (187.6)	30800 (212.4)	23120 (159.4)	32125 (221.5)
1600	871	18925 (130.5)	17280 (119.1)	16690 (115.1)	17240 (118.9)
		0.2% OFFSET YIELD STRENGTH			
70	21	53050 (365.8)	51560 (355.5)	55915 (385.5)	50645 (349.2)
200	93	38890 (268.1)	43435 (299.5)	47470 (327.3)	39250 (270.6)
400	204	30895 (213)	33400 (230.3)	35485 (244.7)	31510 (217.3)
600	316	27360 (188.6)	29800 (205.5)	31245 (215.4)	27455 (189.3)
800	426	26210 (180.7)	28055 (193.4)	28875 (199.1)	23390 (161.3)
1000	538	23405 (161.4)	25000 (172.4)	25605 (176.5)	22020 (151.8)
1200	649	20480 (141.2)	22550 (155.5)	23180 (159.8)	20625 (142.2)
1400	760	18190 (125.4)	19400 (133.8)	21880 (150.9)	17775 (122.6)
1600	871	14020 (96.7)	15120 (104.3)	15415 (106.3)	13810 (95.2)

TABLE 18   Effect of Temperature on Tensile Strength of Several Semiaustenitic Precipitation-hardenable Stainless Steels[10]

Alloy	Condition	Temperature °F	°C	Ultimate tensile strength ksi	MN/m²	0.2% offset yield strength ksi	MN/m²
350	DA	75	24	174	1199.7	144	992.9
		400	204	163	1123.9	123	848.1
		500	260	164	1130.8	122	841.2
		600	316	166	1144.6	126	868.8
		700	371	172	1185.9	168	1158.4
		800	426	166	1144.6	112	772.2
		900	482	144	992.9	98	675.7
		1000	538	109	751.6	82	565.4
350	SCT	75	24	203	1399.7	170	1172.2
		400	204	188	1296.3	141	972.2
		600	316	189	1303.2	136	937.7
		700	371	190	1310.1	128	882.6
		800	426	186	1282.5	125	861.9
		900	482	166	1144.6	111	765.3
		1000	538	106	730.9	85	586.1
355	CRT	75	24	233	1606.5	215	1482.4
		400	204	209	1441.1	186	1282.5
		600	316	202	1392.8	171	1179
		800	426	186	1282.5	149	1027.4
		900	482	174	1199.7	144	992.9
		1000	538	139	958.4	116	799.8
17-7PH	TH-1050	75	24	193	1330.7	182	1254.9
		200	93	185	1275.6	175	1206.6
		400	204	174	1199.7	165	1137.7
		600	316	162	1117	155	1068.7
		700	371	155	1068.7	145	999.8
		800	426	144	992.9	130	896.4
		900	482	124	855	90	620.6
17-7PH	RH-950	75	24	221	1523.8	215	1482.4
		200	93	210	1448	200	1379
		400	204	196	1351.4	179	1234.2
		600	316	184	1268.7	164	1130.8
		700	371	175	1206.6	154	1061.8
		800	426	160	1103.2	137	944.6
		900	482	133	917	113	779.1
		1000	538	930	641.2	76	524

nitrogen to Type 304L increases the room- and elevated temperature strength of this steel to the equivalent of Type 304. Nitrogen markedly increases the creep and rupture strength at 1200°F (648°C), but less so at 1350 and 1500°F (734 and 815°C). This improvement is illustrated by the creep and rupture data in Table 23. Comparison of these data with those of standard grades can be made by referring to Tables 8, 10, and 11. A similar improvement is also noted in Type 216, which normally contains nitrogen.

After considerable effort ASME approved the use of N grades of 304 and 316; these grades must contain 0.10 to 0.16% nitrogen. Design stresses for these grades are given in Table 24, resulting from Code Case 1423-2 which was approved by the ASME Council on March 9, 1972.

Carbide-stabilizing Additions to Austenitic Stainless Steel   Many studies have been made for improving the properties of the 18-8 series heat-resisting steels by adding or optimizing various alloying elements. These elements have been divided into three categories:

1. Interstitial elements carbon, nitrogen, and boron which are soluble in the austenitic matrix as interstitials

TABLE 19   Stress-Rupture Properties of Several Semiaustenitic Precipitation-hardenable Stainless Steels[10]

Alloy	Condition	Temperature		Stress, ksi (MN/m²), to produce rupture in	
		°F	°C	100 h	1000 h
AM-350	DA	800	426	161 (1110.1)	158 (1089.4)
		900	482	105 (724)	92 (634.3)
		1000	538	58 (399.9)	50 (344.8)
AM-350	SCT	800	426	186 (1282.5)	183 (1261.8)
		900	482	118 (813.6)	95 (655)
AM-355	SCT	800	426	186 (1282.5)	180 (1241.1)
		900	482	118 (813.6)	98 (675.7)
		1000	538	70.5 (486.1)	57.5 (396.5)
AM-355	CRT	800	426	190 (1310.1)	182 (1254.9)
		900	482	135 (930.8)	116 (799.8)
		1000	538	85 (586.1)	65 (448.2)
17-7PH	TH-1050	600	316	170 (1172.2)	158 (1089.4)
		700	371	130 (896.4)	122 (841.2)
		800	426	110 (758.5)	90 (620.6)
		900	482	78 (537.8)	52 (358.5)
17-7PH	RH-950	600	316	188 (1296.3)	180 (1241.1)
		700	371	169 (1165.3)	146 (1006.7)
		800	426	113 (779.1)	92 (634.3)
		900	482	61 (420.6)	44 (303.4)
17-7PH	CH-900	600	316	220 (1516.9)	216 (1489.3)
		700	371	194 (1337.6)	180 (1241.1)
		800	426	135 (930.8)	73 (503.3)
		900	482	53 (365.4)	36 (248.2)
PH15-7Mo	TH-1050	600	316	179 (1234.2)	178 (1227.3)
		700	371	161 (1110.1)	159 (1096.3)
		800	426	139 (958.4)	137 (944.6)
		900	482	108 (744.7)	98 (675.7)
PH15-7Mo	RH-950	600	316	202 (1392.8)	200 (1379)
		700	371	193 (1330.7)	191 (1316.9)
		800	426	174 (1199.7)	171 (1179)
		900	482	125 (861.9)	108 (744.7)
PH15-7Mo	TH-1050	75	24	211 (1454.8)	204 (1406.6)
		200	93	205 (1413.5)	200 (1379)
		400	204	195 (1344.5)	187 (1289.4)
		600	316	182 (1254.9)	171 (1179)
		700	371	175 (1206.6)	162 (1117)
		800	426	165 (1137.7)	150 (1034.3)
		900	482	143 (986)	127 (875.7)
		1000	538	114 (786)	97 (668.8)
PH15-7Mo	RH-950	75	24	238 (1641)	220 (1516.9)
		200	93	227 (1565.2)	208 (1434.2)
		400	204	211 (1454.8)	190 (1310.1)
		600	316	203 (1399.7)	170 (1172.2)
		700	371	195 (1344.5)	160 (1103.2)
		800	426	182 (1254.9)	149 (1027.4)
		900	482	161 (1110.1)	128 (882.6)
		1000	538	130 (896.4)	101 (696.4)

TABLE 20   Creep Properties of Certain Semiaustenitic Precipitation-hardenable Stainless Steels[10]

| Alloy | Condition | Temperature | | Stress, ksi (MN/m²), to produce a creep rate of | |
		°F	°C	0.001%/h	0.0001%/h
AM-350	SCT	800	426	107 (737.8)	
17-7PH	TH-1050	600	316	135 (930.8)	125 (861.9)
		700	371	105 (724)	100 (689.5)
		800	426	60 (413.7)	45 (310.3)
		900	482	23 (158.6)	
17-7PH	RH-950	600	316	105 (724)	126 (868.8)
		700	371	60 (413.7)	87 (599.9)
		800	426	31 (213.7)	36 (248.2)
		900	482	12.5 (86.2)	14 (96.5)
PH15-7Mo	RH-950	600	316	131.5 (906.7)	150 (1034.3)
		700	371	120.5 (830.8)	142 (979.1)
		800	426	95 (655)	109 (751.6)
		900	482	36 (248.2)	40.5 (279.2)

2. Carbide-stabilizing elements which form carbides that are less soluble in the austenitic matrix

3. Substitutionally soluble elements, e.g., molybdenum and copper, which may or may not form carbides, being soluble in austenite as substitutionals

Effects of carbon and nitrogen have been discussed in the previous sections. Boron

TABLE 21   Short-Time High-Temperature Properties of Heat-resistant Stainless Steel Casting Grades[11]

| Grade | Temperature | | Tensile strength | | Yield strength (0.2% offset) | |
	°F	°C	ksi	MN/m²	ksi	MN/m²
HA (9Cr)	1000	538	67	462	42	289.6
	1100	593	44	303.4	32	220.6
HD (327)	1400	760	36	248.2		
	1600	871	23	158.6		
	1800	982	15	103.4		
HF (302B)	1200	649	57	393		
	1400	760	35	241.3	21.55	148.6
	1600	871	22	151.7		
HH-1 (309)	1400	760	33	227.5	17	117.2
	1600	871	18.5	127.6	13.5	93.1
	1800	982	9	62.1	6.3	43.4
HH-2 (309)	1400	760	35	241.3	18	124.1
	1600	871	22	151.7	14	96.5
	1800	982	11	75.8	7	48.3
HI (28Cr-15Ni)	1400	760	38	262		
	1600	871	26	179.3		
HL (30Cr-20Ni)	1400	760	50	344.8		
	1600	871	30.4	209.6		
	1800	982	18.7	128.9		
HT (330)	1200	649	42.4	292.3	28	193.1
	1400	760	35	241.3	26	179.3
	1600	871	18.8	129.6	15	103.4
	1800	982	11	75.8	8	55.2
	2000	1093	6	41.4		

TABLE 22   Short-Time High-Temperature Properties of Corrosion-resistant Stainless Steel Casting Grades[1]

Grade	Temperature		Tensile strength		Yield strength (0.2% offset)	
	°F	°C	ksi	MN/m²	ksi	MN/m²
CF-8 (304)	75	24	78	537.8	34	234.4
	1000	538	55	379.2	17	117.2
	1200	649	44	303.4	16	110.3
	1400	760	26	179.3	15	103.4
CF-20 (302)	75	24	80	551.6	35	241.3
	1000	538	58	399.9	17	117.2
	1200	649	46	317.2	16	110.3
	1400	760	29	200	18	124.1
CF-8C (347)	75	24	78	537.8	34	234.4
	1000	538	58	399.9	22	151.7
	1200	649	47	324.1	20	137.9
	1400	760	26	179.3	18	124.1
CF-8M (316)	75	24	79	544.7	37	255.1
	1000	538	56	386.1	21	144.8
	1200	649	40	275.8	18	124.1
	1400	760	26	179.3	15	103.4
CH-20 (309)	75	24	76	524	36	248.2
	1200	649	41	282.7	16	110.3
	1400	760	25	172.4	16	110.3
	1600	871	12	82.7	10	69
CK-20 (310)	75	24	80	551.6	33	227.5
	1200	649	54	372.3	20	137.9
	1400	760	32	220.6	19	131
	1600	871	16	110.3	13	89.6

additions apparently produce a more uniform distribution of precipitated carbides in the matrix. Titanium (Type 321) and niobium (Type 347) are added to austenitic alloys to prevent sensitization problems while molybdenum (Type 316) improves pitting resistance markedly. Molybdenum also increases the high-temperature strength by solid-solution hardening.

Types 321 and 347 are also utilized for heat-resisting applications, but the amounts of Ti and Nb added to give atomic ratios of at least 1 may not be optimum for creep-rupture resistance. Studies[13] on the effects of Ti, Nb, and V additions indicate that higher strengths developing in these alloys may be attributed to a fine distribution of $M_{23}C_6$ precipitates. The highest values of 700°C (1292°F), 10,000-h rupture strength were obtained at Ti/C and Nb/C atomic ratios of 0.8 and 0.2 to 0.4, respectively. For the vanadium, a V/C ratio of about 1 was observed for maximum properties at 700°C (1292° F) and 800°C (1472°F), but at 600°C (1112°F) the strength continued to increase with vana-

TABLE 23   Creep and Stress-Rupture Properties of Types 304N and 316N Stainless Steel[12]

Grade	Temperature		Stress, ksi (MN/m²), for rupture in		Stress, ksi (MN/m²), for a minimum creep rate of	
	°F	°C	10,000 h	100,000 h	0.0001%/h	0.00001%/h
304N (0.14N)	1050	566	34 (234.4)	27 (186.2)	31 (213.7)	25 (172.4)
	1200	649	18 (124.1)	12.5 (86.2)	15 (103.4)	10.2 (70.3)
	1350	732	8.8 (60.7)	6 (41.4)	7.5 (51.7)	5.5 (37.9)
	1500	816	4.8 (33.1)	3.3 (22.8)	4 (27.6)	
316N (0.13N)	1050	566	41.5 (286.1)	33 (227.5)	37 (255.1)	29 (200)
	1200	649	26 (179.3)	19 (131)	17 (117.2)	12.5 (86.2)
	1350	732	14 (96.5)	9.3 (64.1)	8.7 (60)	6.1 (42.1)
	1500	816	6.5 (44.8)	4 (27.6)	4 (27.6)	2.6 (17.9)

TABLE 24   Design Stresses for Grades 304N and 316N Stainless Steel[12]

Temperature		Maximum allowable stress, ksi (MN/m²)			
°F	°C	Grade 304N		Grade 316N	
75	24	20.0 (137.9)	20.0 (137.9)*	20.0 (137.9)	20.0 (137.9)*
100	38	20.0 (137.9)	20.0 (137.9)	20.0 (137.9)	20.0 (137.9)
200	93	17.9 (123.4)	20.0 (137.9)	19.4 (133.8)	20.0 (137.9)
300	149	15.7 (108.3)	19.0 (131)	17.8 (122.7)	19.2 (132.4)
400	204	14.1 (97.2)	18.3 (126.2)	16.5 (113.8)	18.8 (129.6)
500	260	13.0 (89.6)	17.8 (122.7)	15.4 (106.2)	18.6 (128.2)
600	316	12.4 (85.5)	17.4 (120)	14.6 (100.7)	18.6 (128.2)
650	343	12.2 (84.1)	17.3 (119.3)	14.2 (97.9)	18.6 (128.2)
700	371	11.9 (82)	17.15 (118.2)	13.9 (95.8)	18.6 (128.2)
750	399	11.75 (81)	16.9 (116.5)	13.6 (93.8)	18.5 (127.6)
800	427	11.55 (79.6)	16.6 (114.5)	13.3 (91.7)	18.4 (126.9)
850	454	11.3 (77.9)	16.3 (112.4)	13.1 (90.3)	18.3 (126.2)
900	482	11.05 (76.2)	15.9 (109.6)	12.8 (88.3)	18.1 (124.8)
950	510	10.8 (74.5)	15.6 (107.6)	12.6 (86.9)	17.8 (122.7)
1000	538	10.55 (72.7)	15.0 (103.4)	12.4 (85.5)	17.4 (120)
1050	566	10.3 (71)	12.4 (85.5)	12.2 (84.1)	15.8 (108.9)
1100	593	9.75 (67.2)	9.75 (67.2)	11.7 (80.7)	12.4 (85.5)
1150	621	7.7 (53.1)	7.7 (53.1)	9.8 (67.6)	9.8 (67.6)
1200	649	6.05 (41.7)	6.05 (41.7)	7.4 (51)	7.4 (51)

*The stress values in column 2 are permissible for applications where short-time tensile properties govern to permit use where slightly higher deformation is acceptable.

dium content up to 1.53%. The high strengths in the steels containing the proper amounts of Ti, Nb, and V are related mainly to the fine distribution of $M_{23}C_6$ precipitates, caused by acceleration of nucleation due to the foregoing precipitation of an MC-type carbide within the austenite grains. Solid-solution strengthening contributes to the improvement of the rupture strength of the vanadium steel at 600°C (1112°F).

Thus, the Ti/C and Nb/C ratios of 1 in commercial alloys are not optimum for best heat resistance. However, the optimum values were also found to depend on expected service temperatures and times, trending toward lower ratios with increasing temperatures and times. The beneficial effects of vanadium additions up to a ratio of 3 are not being commercially exploited. Some creep-rupture strength values are given in Table 25.

Garofalo et al.[14] have shown that prestraining of Type 316 at room temperature followed by aging leads to $M_{23}C_6$ carbide precipitation on dislocations, increasing creep and rupture resistance significantly.

The Super 12% Cr Steels   Previous data have indicated that the straight-chromium stainless steels have long-time, high-temperature strengths inferior to those of the austenitic grades. Many have investigated the possibility of improving these steels. Briggs and Parker[15] have compiled a great deal of information on modified 12% Cr alloys. In general, these alloys can be heat-treated to high strengths in large section sizes and have hot strengths greater than those of other nonaustenitic steels, even comparing favorably with those of austenitic steels in some ranges. Certain advantages

TABLE 25   Maximum Stress-Rupture Strength Values Obtained by Additions of Ti, Nb, and V to 18-10 Stainless Steel[13]

Addition	Temperature		Rupture Strength, kg/mm² [MN/m²]	
	°F	°C	1000 h	10,000 h
Ti	1202	650	16 [156.9] (1.2)*	11 [107.9]
	1292	700	11 [107.9]	7.5 [73.5] (0.8)*
Nb	1202	650	17 [166.7] (0.7)*	12 [117.7]
	1292	700	11 [107.9]	8 [78.5] (0.2–0.3)*
V	1202	650	30 [294.2] (3.0)*	
	1292	700	12 [117.7] (1.0)*	
	1472	800	7 [68.6] (1.0)*	

*Metal/carbon atomic ratio.

over austenitic stainless steels also exist, such as higher damping capacity and lower coefficients of thermal expansion, resulting in improved resistance to thermal shock and thermal fatigue.

A great many alloys have been developed by various companies that can be classified in this section. The work of Briggs and Parker[15] is suggested for detailed information with respect to composition, properties, and trade names that cannot be included here. Such steels can be divided into three classes:

- Class I—Super 12% Cr steels containing molybdenum, but no other strong carbide formers or cobalt
- Class II—Super 12% Cr steels containing molybdenum and other strong carbide-forming elements, but no cobalt
- Class III—Super 12% Cr steels containing cobalt and molybdenum

Historically, the Class I steels were developed first to give better corrosion resistance, or hot strength than standard 12% Cr steels. Class II steels were developed during World War II for better hot strength than Class I steels. Class III steels superimpose precipitation hardening on martensitic hardening for development of high strength. Short-time, elevated temperature tensile properties are summarized in Fig. 3, which indicates a wide

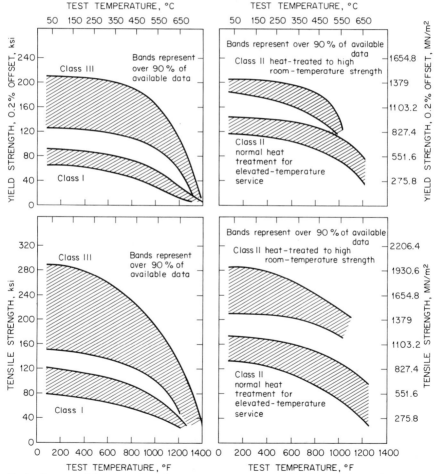

Fig. 3 Summary of short-time elevated temperature tensile strength data for three classes of Super 12% Cr steels.[15]

range in properties among the various alloys within each class. Stress for 100,000-h rupture life for a Class II alloy is given in Fig. 4.

Elevated temperature properties of certain of these 12% Cr alloys, as well as others of high chromium content, are given in ASTM *Special Technical Publication 228.*[16]

Austenitic Superalloys   Likewise, considerable developmental work has been carried out for improvement of the high-temperature strength of the austenitic alloys through further compositional modifications. For this class of stainless steels, modifications can

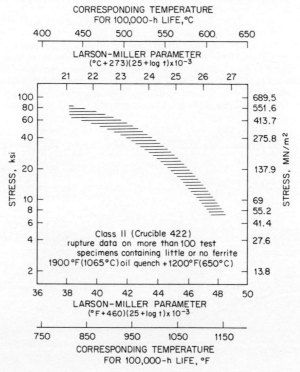

Fig. 4   Stress for 100,000-h rupture life for a Class II alloy (Crucible 422).[15]

be more extensive and frequently, the resulting alloys can hardly be considered stainless steels. Thus, nickel-based, cobalt-based, and complex-based superalloys are not considered here, though they are important materials for high-temperature applications.

Some strength data for three austenitic superalloys that can still be considered stainless steels are given in Table 26. The considerable improvement in strength of these alloys over the standard grades is quite obvious.

MICROSTRUCTURAL STABILITY

The austenitic grades are normally used in the solution-treated condition for best creep and stress-rupture resistance. However, service in the temperature range 800 to 1500°F (426 to 815°C) may result in grain-boundary carbide precipitation for grades such as 302, 310, and 316. This usually does not affect service at temperature significantly, but it may result in sensitization problems when process equipment is off-stream and exposed to corrosive environments at ambient temperatures. Such carbide precipitation may also reduce room-temperature toughness, but again probably not enough to be of concern.[19]

The use of stabilizing heat treatments reduces the creep resistance of these alloys and is not recommended. Thus, the H grades mentioned earlier require solution annealing as

TABLE 26   Elevated Temperature Properties of Three Austenitic Stainless Steel Superalloys

Property	Temperature °F	°C	Alloy 19-9DL*	16-25-6*	15-15N†
Tensile strength, ksi (MN/m²)	70	21	130 (896.4)	135 (930.8)	85 (586.1)
	1000	538	85 (586.1)	98 (675.7)	
	1100	593	79 (544.7)	95 (655)	
	1200	649	73 (503.3)	85 (586.1)	64 (441.3)
	1300	704	62 (427.5)	74 (510.2)	
	1350	732			57 (393)
	1400	760	52 (358.5)	58 (399.9)	
	1500	816	30 (206.9)	42 (289.6)	35 (241.3)
1000 h rupture strength, ksi (MN/m²)	1000	538	55 (379.2)	72 (496.4)	
	1100	593	46 (317.2)	50 (344.8)	
	1200	649	35 (241.3)	33 (227.5)	33 (227.5)
	1300	704	21 (144.8)	22 (151.7)	
	1350	732			18.5 (127.6)
	1400	760	12 (82.7)	14 (96.5)	
	1500	816	9 (62.1)	9 (62.1)	96.2 (63.4)
10,000 h rupture strength, ksi (MN/m²)	1000	538	47 (324.1)	65 (448.2)	
	1100	593	40 (275.8)	40 (275.8)	
	1200	649	31 (213.7)	24 (165.5)	26.5 (182.7)
	1300	704	17 (117.2)	14 (96.5)	
	1350	732			13 (89.6)
	1400	760	8 (55.2)	8 (55.2)	
	1500	816	4.5 (31)	5 (34.5)	6.5 (44.8)
Creep strength, 1% in 10,000 h, ksi (MN/m²)	1000	538	40 (275.8)	35 (241.3)	
	1100	593	24 (165.5)	28 (193.1)	
	1200	649	20 (137.9)	22 (151.7)	23.2 (160)
	1300	704	13 (89.6)	15 (103.4)	
	1350	732			13.5 (93.1)
	1400	760	8 (55.2)	10 (69)	
	1500	816		6 (41.4)	9.4 (64.8)
Creep strength, 1% in 100,000 h, ksi (MN/m²)	1000	538	19 (131)	24 (165.5)	
	1100	593	12 (82.7)	18 (124.1)	
	1200	649	10 (69)	13 (89.6)	15.5 (106.9)
	1300	704	6 (41.4)	9 (62.1)	
	1350	732			9 (62.1)
	1400	760		7 (48.3)	
	1500	816		4 (27.6)	5.4 (37.2)

*From Metals Progress Data Sheet.[17]
†From the Babcock & Wilcox Co.[18]

part of their specifications. Use of the extra-low-carbon grades involves the penalty of lower strengths. The stabilized grades 321 and 347 are widely used at elevated temperatures, not only because of minimization of sensitization problems, but also because of higher strength potential.

In alloys containing greater than 16.5% chromium, sigma phase may form during long-time service at temperatures between 1100 and 1700°F (593 and 926°C). Sigma phase is a complex, intermetallic Cr-Fe compound of high strength, low toughness, and low creep strength. The stabilized grades have some tendency to develop sigma phase in a grain-boundary distribution after long periods of time which leads to significant loss of toughness and ductility at ambient temperatures. This may complicate problems associated with repair and maintenance.

The amount and rate of sigma formation depend on time, temperature, composition balance, and working history of the steel. Increasing nickel content reduces tendency toward sigma while chromium, molybdenum (Type 316), silicon, etc., and the presence of free ferrite and cold-working promotes sigma formation. Thus, the more highly alloyed stainless steels may be quite prone to sigma formation, resulting in serious degradation of toughness and ductility at ambient temperatures.

More serious, however, is the reduction in long-time creep-rupture resistance. Such effects show up as breaks in the log-log plots of stress versus minimum creep rate or rupture life. Thus, extrapolation procedures (such as for 100,000-h design considerations) become unreliable unless tests have been run for sufficiently long times to determine whether such breaks are present and what is the associated change in slope of the design curves. Use of parameters, particularly for extrapolation to higher temperatures, is even more questionable since structural instability occurs more rapidly with increasing temperature.

As mentioned earlier, strengthening due to precipitation hardening, cold-working, or martensite formation in the hardenable grades decreases rapidly at temperatures above 900°F (482°C) due to overaging, recrystallization, and tempering reactions. Such strengthening mechanisms are ineffective for long-time high-temperature service applications.

REFERENCES

1. "Mechanical and Physical Properties of the Austenitic Chromium-Nickel Stainless Steels at Elevated Temperatures," The International Nickel Co. Inc., New York, 1963.
2. Larson, F., and J. Miller: A Time-Temperature Relationship for Rupture and Creep Stress, *Trans. ASME*, vol. 74, p. 765, 1952.
3. Smith, G.: An Evaluation of the Yield, Tensile, and Rupture Strengths of Wrought 304, 316, 321 and 347 Stainless Steels at Elevated Temperatures, *ASTM Data Series DS 5S2*, American Society for Testing and Materials, Philadelphia, Pa., 1969.
4. "Armco Stainless Steels," Armco Steel Corporation, Advanced Materials Div., Baltimore, Md., 1972.
5. "Stainless Steel: Concepts in Design and Fabrication," The Committee of Stainless Steel Producers, American Iron and Steel Institute, New York, 1970.
6. Parker, T.: Strength of Stainless Steels at Elevated Temperatures, in "Selection of Stainless Steels," American Society for Metals, Metals Park, Ohio, 1968.
7. "Boiler and Pressure Vessel Code," American Society for Mechanical Engineers, New York.
8. "Chromium-Nickel-Manganese Stainless Steels," Union Carbide Corporation, Ferroalloys Div., New York, 1962.
9. Allegheny-Ludlum Steel Corporation, Pittsburgh, Pa.
10. Semiaustenitic Precipitation Hardenable Stainless Steels, *Defense Metals Information Center, DMIC Rept. 164*, Battelle Memorial Institute, Columbus, Ohio, 1961.
11. "Stainless Steel and High Alloy Heat Resistant Castings, Their Engineering Properties and Applications," The International Nickel Co. Inc., New York, 1968.
12. "Elevated Temperature Properties as Influenced by Nitrogen Additions to Types 304 and 316 Austenitic Stainless Steel," *Spec. Tech. Publ.* 522, The American Society for Testing and Materials, Philadelphia, Pa., 1973.
13. Shinoda, T., T. Ishii, R. Tanake, T. Mimino, K. Kinoshita, and K. and I. Minegishi: Effect of Some Carbide Stabilizing Elements on Creep-Rupture Strength and Microstructural Changes of 18-10 Austenitic Steel, *Metall. Trans.*, vol. 4, no. 5, p. 1213, 1973.
14. Garofalo, F., F. von Gemmingen, and W. Domis: The Creep Behavior of an Austenitic Stainless Steel as Effected by Carbides Precipitated on Dislocations, *Trans. Am. Soc. Met.*, vol. 54, p. 430, 1961.
15. Briggs, J., and T. Parker: "The Super 12% Chromium Steels," Climax Molybdenum Company, New York, 1965.
16. Simmons, W., and H. Cross: Report on Elevated Temperature Properties of Chromium Steels (12–27 percent), *Spec. Tech. Publ.* 228, The American Society for Testing and Materials, Philadelphia, Pa., 1958.
17. Approximate Strength of Industrial Gas Turbine Alloys Treated for Optimum Properties, *Met. Prog.*, vol. 69, no. 2, p. 80-b, 1956.
18. Ewing, J., *Bull. TR-555*, The Babcock and Wilcox Company, Tubular Products Div., Beaver Falls, Pa., 1958.
19. Hoke, J., and F. Eberle: Experimental Superheater for Steam at 2000 psi and 1250°F—Report after 14281 Hours of Operation, *Trans. ASME*, vol. 79, no. 2, p. 307, 1957.

Part 5

Fabrication and Design Practices

Chapter **22**

Criteria for Design of Forgings*

JAMES R. BECKER
**Manager, Advanced Products Development, Cameron Iron Works,
Houston, Texas**

FRANCIS W. BOULGER
**Senior Technical Adviser, Battelle Columbus Laboratories,
Columbus, Ohio**

INTRODUCTION

The purpose of this chapter is to make available a summary on forging design technology. The information for this chapter was obtained from a review of both foreign and domestic literature. It covers published and unpublished information on the factors important in choosing the most economical forging design. Another aim of this chapter is to provide

*Adapted, with permission, from Chapter 8, "Forging Equipment, Materials and Practices," Metals and Ceramics Information Center, distributed as MCIC-HB-03 by National Technical Information Service.

realistic guidelines for designers to select candidate parts for precision forging and to provide an assessment of various approaches to precision forging.

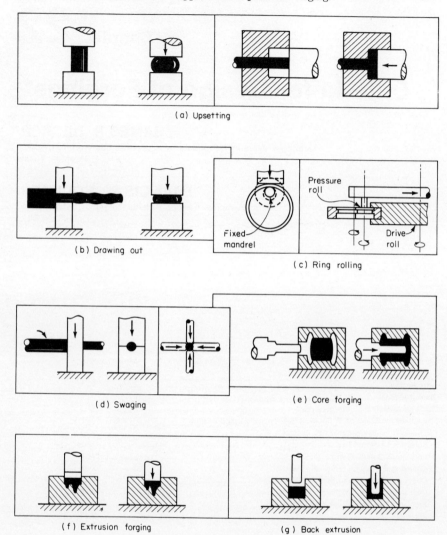

(a) Upsetting

(b) Drawing out

(c) Ring rolling

(d) Swaging

(e) Core forging

(f) Extrusion forging

(g) Back extrusion

Fig. 1 Principles of several types of forging operations.

BACKGROUND

While forging may be defined broadly as changing the shape of metals by plastic deformation, there are a number of specific types of forging operations that in many cases require specialized equipment. Descriptions of several types of forging operations and the specialized equipment needed for them are presented in Table 1 and the principles are illustrated in Fig. 1.[1] The forces required to deform metal in each of these operations differ considerably, depending on the relative amount of confinement of the workpiece by the die. With increasing confinement, friction increases rapidly. Furthermore, when workpiece temperatures are higher than that of the die, heat transfer occurs and billet surfaces are chilled. Such factors increase forging pressure. In some operations such as upsetting or ring rolling, there is considerable latitude for metal to flow freely since there is little confinement. On the other hand, during core forging, die forging, and extrusion operations the metal is so confined by the dies that there is little or no free metal flow. Extrusion forging, for example, approaches complete confinement at the end of the forging stroke. This results in considerably greater resistance to metal flow. Thus, a metal which can be deformed easily when frictional loads are small requires relatively high forging pressures during extrusion forging.

TABLE 1   Description of Machinery Used for Several Common Types of Forging Operations

Type of forging	Method of operation	Commonly used machinery
Upsetting	Compression in the longitudinal axis of the work	Single-action and counterblow hammers Upsetting machines Hydraulic, air, and mechanical presses High-energy-rate machines
Drawing out	Stretch-out of the work by a series of upsets along the length of the workpiece	Single-action hammers Hydraulic and air presses
Die forging	Compression in a closed impression die	Single-action and counterblow hammers Hydraulic and mechanical presse High-energy-rate machines Impacters
Ring rolling	Radial compression on a ring shape to increase diameter	Ring-rolling mills Hammers and presses with supported mandrel
Swaging	Circumferential compression to lengthen a workpiece	Swaging machines Single-action hammers Air and hydraulic presses
Core forging	Displacing metal with a punch to fill a die cavity	Multiple-ram presses
Extrusion forging	Forcing a metal into a die opening by restricting flow in other directions	Hydraulic and mechanical press Multiple-ram presses High-energy-rate machines
Back extrusion	Forging with a punch and forcing metal to flow opposite to the punch direction	Single-action and counterblow hammers Hydraulic and mechanical press Multiple-ram presses High-energy-rate machines

When a component of a machine takes shape on the drawing board of the design engineer, the method to be used in its manufacture may still be entirely open. The number of possible manufacturing processes is increasing day by day, and the optimum process can be found only by careful weighing of technological advantages and limitations in relation to the economy of production.[2]

Forging has much to offer in quality. In common with other plastic metalworking processes, forging yields materials of high density and fine grain with no internal cavities. It has the unique advantage of producing a continuous-grain flow pattern, a characteristic considered desirable. Some components, such as crankshafts from machine-rolled bars, exhibit a favorable fiber structure in some directions but poor structure in others because the ends of its fibers are cut.

Once the choice in favor of forging has been made, the component has to be redesigned according to the needs of the forging process. The technical success and economy of the forging depends very largely on this phase of design.

The technique selected for forging a part is largely determined by the quantity and properties of parts to be produced, since the forging cost usually increases with the severity of dimensional precision requirements. To be economical, the higher cost of precision forging must be outweighed by savings in cost of raw materials and machining that would result if open-die, blocker-type, or conventional forgings were used.

The American Society for Metals (ASM)[3] has prepared a handbook for the Air Force which is concerned with the design of forgings; therefore, this chapter is concerned primarily with the criteria for choosing the design of forgings.

After a survey on the feasibility of establishing analytical procedures for designing intermediate dies in sequences of closed dies (preform dies), Kalpakjian[4] concluded that knowledge on the subject was limited. As in many areas of materials processing, the practical knowledge and experience in forging is considerably ahead of analytical studies in the field. Closed-die forging is a complex process in which a number of factors influence the overall performance. This is why the analytical support for process design has not yet extended very far beyond the simple shapes (rounds, disks, hubs, and blades). Although considerable progress has been made since Kalpakjian's review in 1966, most forging designers still rely on experience and empirical approaches.

Each forging organization has developed its own method for designing dies for transforming a billet of material into the final shape by following certain basic rules. It is evident that there is an almost infinite variety of shapes in forging and that each geometry presents its own set of problems.

During the past few years the U.S. government has sponsored numerous programs which advanced the state of the art of forging. An Air Force–sponsored program aimed at correlating material technology with forging equipment and design[5] led to a book describing forging practices for a wide variety of materials.[1] This extensive review and analysis of the forging field revealed that, in addition to determining metallurgical variables, a detailed engineering study is necessary to analyze and establish the mechanical parameters involved in the forging processes. Since then, the U.S. government has sponsored a number of other programs concerned with process development and the forging of hardware for the aerospace industry. These programs have provided a wealth of worthwhile information concerned with forging design, materials, practices, forging tooling, and computer-aided design of preform dies.

PROCESS VARIABLES

Once the decision has been made to use a forging for a particular component, there are several process variables that must be considered. Many times, these process variables will control various aspects of a forging design. By dictating the forging designs, many of the design criteria for the tooling are also established. The following is a list of some of the variables that will effect a forging design and also the design of the die:

1. Properties desired in the forging.
2. The material selected for the forging.
3. The location of the test material.
4. Finish allowances.
5. Grain orientation.
6. Location of the parting line.
7. Part shape: ribs, webs, and bosses.
8. Draft angles.
9. Will flash be required, and if so where can it be located?
10. Does the part contain internal cavities, such as holes?
11. The quantity of parts required.

The designer decides on the shape of the forging and the properties required for the intended service. He should also keep in mind the tolerances needed because they influence some performance characteristics and, particularly, process costs. The unit die costs are influenced mainly by part quantity and the geometry specified. It is common practice for conventional-tolerance closed-die forgings to be made with excess stock which has to be removed later. That practice lowers die costs, compared with precision-tolerance forgings, and allows the designer some latitude in changing the dimensions of the finished part as experience is accumulated and design refinements appear desirable. Those advantages, which are even more pronounced for forgings made to blocker-type tolerances, are obtained at the expense of higher costs for metal removed and waste of workpiece material.

Precision forging is frequently the most economical method for producing parts in large or relatively large quantities. It is most likely to be economical for processing an expensive material that is difficult to machine. In some cases, forging closer to final dimensions results in superior mechanical and physical properties. In some cases, precision forging is impractical because of part complexity or difficulty in producing components with adequate surface integrity. Precision forgings are characterized by smaller radii, smaller draft angles, and smaller stock allowances for finishing. These factors usually result in higher die costs than for blocker- or conventional-tolerance forgings. This ordinarily requires that the die design be finalized before a commitment is made to the precision-forging approach. Otherwise, subsequent changes in design of the finished component will require modifications in the finishing die and sometimes in the blocker or preforming dies.

Locating the parting line and flash gutters (Fig. 2) is an important part of process design. The parting line is the location where the dies meet and the gutters provide space for excess material. Ordinarily, the gutters are located at the parting line. Some forging operations require no parting lines, whereas others need complicated parting lines. Flash formation can create problems, because it prevents continuous grain flow near the surface of the forging. Subsequent trimming of the flash exposes the ends

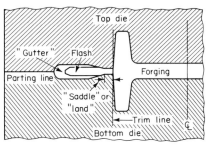

Fig. 2   Example of conventional flash gutter and parting line design.[1]

of the fibered grains and this impairs corrosion resistance. Flash dimensions also have a marked effect on forging pressures.

Design details can limit the number of applicable forging processes. Only a few processes, such as core forging, can produce parts with an internal cavity or hole. Not all tooling designs permit the use of punches.

GUIDELINES FOR SELECTION OF THE MOST ECONOMICAL FORGING DESIGN

Checklist for Selecting Design Features   Once the choice of manufacturing processes has been made in favor of forging for the component to be produced, the design of the forging takes place. Much like shopping for an automobile, a checklist for the most economical forging design is also required. Whatever the reason for selecting a forging, be it shape, properties, or quantity, the economics of the process must be considered. Many times there may be a trade-off between the process economics and the primary reason for choosing a forging, just as a trade-off is often required between the cost and a particular feature of an automobile.

The general guidelines for selecting the most economical forging design are as follows:

1. Selection of design features
2. Part shape classification
3. Choice of the design to suit the material
4. Choice of the design to suit the equipment
5. Cost comparison for different types of design

The specific factors to be considered in selecting the most economical forging design are as follows:

1. Selection of design features
   a. Material to be forged
   b. Forging process variables
   c. Quantity
   d. Delivery
   e. Property requirements
   f. Application
   g. Expected service life
   h. Degree of precision desired
2. Part shape classification (angles, draft, radii, stock allowances)

    a. Blocker-type design
    b. Commercial or conventional design
    c. Close-to-finish design
    d. Precision design
    e. Circular, disks, or cones
    f. Structural
3. Choice of the design to suit the material
4. Choice of the design to suit the equipment
    a. Hammers
    b. Hydraulic presses
    c. Mechanical presses
    d. Screw presses
    e. Upsetters
    f. Open-die forging equipment
5. Cost comparison for different designs
    a. Machining
    b. Tooling
    c. Material
    d. Quantity requirements
    e. Testing requirements

For the above checklist to be meaningful, each item should be considered in detail because they all have a bearing on the design of the forging and tooling.

Selection of Design Features

Material. Workpiece material is probably the most important single factor affecting economical forging design. The choice of the workpiece material will depend on many factors, such as intended usage, desired properties, corrosion resistance, density, availability, material cost, and elevated-temperature strength.

Sabroff, Boulger, and Henning[1] grouped different materials according to forgeability and flow strength or pressure required to produce the same forging. In this context,

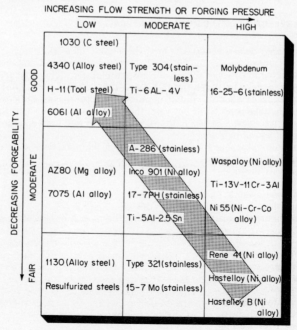

Arrow denotes increasing ease of die filling

Fig. 3 General diagram of influence of forgeability and flow strength on die filling.[1]

forgeability is the tolerance of a material for deformation without cracking. According to Fig. 3, aluminum has low flow strength and moderate-to-good forgeability, depending on the alloy grade. The stainless steels have moderate-to-high flow strengths and good-to-fair forgeability.

Gure,[6] who classified materials according to ease of forging, states that "differences in forgeability are greater between different metals than between alloys of the same material and degree of forging pressure determines the limiting size and intricacy of the part."

Sabroff, Boulger, and Henning[1] went a little further and looked at some of the alloys of steel and assigned numbers to their relative difficulty of forging in terms of load required to forge the various alloys at appropriate temperatures as shown in Table 2. It can be seen that AISI 4340, a medium-alloy steel, has been assigned number 1 and all of the AISI 440 stainless steels were assigned number 2, which means that for the same part design, twice as much load would be required to forge the part from AISI 440 stainless steel as would be required to forge AISI 4340.

TABLE 2 Comparison of Various Steel Alloys by Relative Forging Difficulty—Based on Load[2]

Alloy	Forging temperature		Relative forging load
	°F	°C	
AISI 4340	2300	1259	1.0
AISI 410	2150	1176	1.2–1.5
AISI 414	2150	1176	1.3–1.5
AISI 416	2150	1176	1.3–1.5
Greek Ascoloy	2200	1204	1.5–1.7
AISI 420	2200	1204	1.1–1.2
AISI 440A	2100	1149	2.0
AISI 440B	2100	1149	2.0
AISI 440C	2050	1120	2.0
Lapelloy C	2250	1231	2.0

Altan and Boulger[7] summarized flow stress data from a number of sources of published literature. Table 3 is a summary of that data for stainless steels. They show that forging flow stresses should be expected to vary considerably among materials and with temperature and strain rate.

TABLE 3 Summary of C and m Values Describing the Flow Stress-Strain Relationship $\bar{\sigma} = C\,(\bar{\epsilon})^m$ for 300 and 400 Series Stainless Steels[7]

Material	Strain*	Temper-ature		C		m	Strain rate range per second
		°F	°C	ksi	MN/m^2		
300 series	0.7	2200	1200	4.1–13.9	28.27–95.84	0.096–0.326	0.2–460
400 series	0.7	2200	1200	7.5–11.2	51.71–77.22	0.131–0.158	0.8–100

*True or logarithmic strain.

In most practical closed-die forging operations the workpiece material is at a higher temperature than the dies. The metal flow and die filling are largely determined by resistance of the forging materials to flow, the friction and cooling effects at the die-material interface, and the complexity of the forging shape. The forging load and energy are essentially determined by the flow stress of the forged material, friction conditions, and geometrical shapes. The flow stress increases with increasing strain rate, or ram velocity, and with decreasing temperature. The net effect of these variables depends on the specific workpiece material.[8] The flow stress of a metal is influenced by

1. Factors unrelated to the deformation process such as chemical composition, metallurgical structure, phases, grain size, segregation, and prior strain history.
2. Factors explicitly related to the deformation process including
   a. Temperature of deformation θ
   b. Degree of deformation or strain $\bar{\epsilon}$
   c. Rate of deformation or strain rate $\dot{\bar{\epsilon}}$

Thus, the flow stress $\bar{\sigma}$ which determines the resistance of a metal to deformation is expressed as follows:

$$\bar{\sigma} = F(\theta, \bar{\epsilon}, \dot{\bar{\epsilon}}) \tag{1}$$

Equation (1) illustrates that the flow stress $\bar{\sigma}$ is a function of temperature θ, strain ϵ, and strain rate $\dot{\epsilon}$.

In hot forging of metal at temperatures above the recrystallization temperature, the influence of strain on flow stress is insignificant, while the influence of strain rate (i.e., rate of deformation) becomes increasingly important. Consequently, in hot forging of most metals at temperatures above the recrystallization temperature, Eq. (1) can be reduced to

$$\bar{\sigma} = F(\theta, \dot{\bar{\epsilon}}) \tag{2}$$

Equation (2) states that at high temperatures the flow stress $\bar{\sigma}$ is influenced only by deformation temperature θ and by the deformation rate, i.e., strain rate $\dot{\bar{\epsilon}}$.

The degree of dependency of the flow stress on temperature varies largely for different metals and alloys. At room temperature, the influence of strain rates on flow stress is insignificant in most metals. It was empirically found that the effects of strain on flow stress for most materials, i.e., the strain-hardening effect, can be expressed in the following equation:

$$\bar{\sigma} = K(\bar{\epsilon})^n \tag{3}$$

where K = flow stress $\bar{\sigma}$ when strain $\bar{\epsilon} = 1$
n = strain-hardening coefficient

At high temperatures (above the recrystallization temperature) the effect of strain hardening is minimal for most materials. Consequently, at a given temperature it is possible to approximate the variation of flow stress $\bar{\sigma}$ in function of strain rate $\dot{\bar{\epsilon}}$ by

$$\bar{\sigma} = C(\dot{\bar{\epsilon}})^m \tag{4}$$

where C = flow stress $\bar{\sigma}$ when strain rate $\dot{\bar{\epsilon}} = 1$
m = strain-rate coefficient[7]

Forging Process. The forces required to deform metal in the operations mentioned in Fig. 1 and Table 1 differ considerably, depending on the relative amount of confinement of the workpiece by the dies. With increasing confinement, friction increases rapidly. Furthermore, when workpiece temperatures are higher than the dies, heat transfer occurs and billet surfaces are chilled. Both factors increase forging pressures. Obviously, the behavior of metals during forging is influenced by the time necessary to complete the plastic shaping. Thus, it is important to recognize that the basic difference between the types of equipment lies in their forging velocities or rates of deformation. Forging hammers, for instance, deform metals at rates of deformation on the order of 100 times the rates of hydraulic presses.

Metals forged in hammers and screw presses are likely to exhibit a significant temperature rise during rapid deformation. The temperature rise is usually less significant during press forging.

For forging steels and other alloys subject to scaling, the hammer has an advantage because scale is loosened by the repetitive striking action of the hammer and can be removed easily from the die cavity. In presses, the scale is frequently pressed into the workpiece surface and is difficult to remove from die recesses.

Hydraulic presses are favored for metals that have forging temperatures close to those practical for heated dies. Conversely, hammers and screw presses are preferred for forging metals that require higher workpiece temperatures. Hydraulic presses are often preferred for converting cast ingots, because it is easier to observe any cracks or ruptures that occur during forging and to correct deformation schedules.

Because of basic differences in the time required to form a particular shape, the most practical forging design for hammers or screw or mechanical presses may differ from that for hydraulic presses. The most noticeable difference is in section size for materials having forging temperatures higher than that permissible for dies. There are a few cases in which forging designs are particularly suited to one form of equipment. For example, multiple-ram hydraulic presses have advantages in shape versatility not available in screw presses, hammers, or mechanical presses. On the whole, however, the majority of shapes can be forged interchangeably with either hammers or presses. The basic comment here is that hammers, screw presses, and mechanical presses are preferred for stainless steel forgings containing thin sections. In all other cases, choice of equipment is optional. In most cases, the choice is more a matter of economics and equipment availability than of technical considerations.

Quantity. Quantity requirements have a very definite bearing on cost, part design, and choice of process techniques. This is true no matter how a part is to be produced, whether by machining, casting, or forging. There is a critical or break-even lot size which separates the number of parts which can be produced most economically by one or another alternative procedure. A cost saving can be realized by choosing the proper method of producing the part.

When a component is designed, consideration should be given to all possible methods of producing the part. It often is a mistake to assume that machining even small quantities of parts from blocks or open-die forgings will be the most economical alternative. Such a decision is often made before considering the competitive approaches in sufficient detail.

Larger part quantities result in lower unit costs because some expenses are prorated. Die costs are prorated against the number of components produced per die; setup costs are variable according to the number of parts made per lot. Some other types of costs do not change with lot size or total production quantity; charges for materials and final machining sometimes fall in that category. In general, all types of costs will vary among competing processes.

Delivery. The delivery schedule of the product is a very important requirement that must be agreed upon between vendor and buyer. Three important factors must be determined at the beginning of the manufacturing contract as follows:

- Initial delivery date and number of pieces
- Subsequent schedule (pieces per month)
- The date the order is to be completed and total number of forgings.

The total quantity ordered affects the design of the most economical dies and tooling. The initial delivery usually depends on when the parts are needed and how soon the parts can be produced. The time lag before initial delivery depends on delivery of material and the time required to produce the type of tooling needed. The existing production schedule has a definite bearing on how soon the production of a new order can be initiated.

Subsequent schedules usually depend on how soon the parts are needed along with relative costs of producing and storing forgings produced in different lot sizes.

The total number of pieces ordered and the completion date are important because they determine the per piece price, the type of tooling employed, and the precision attained. Usually, more precision can be built into the manufacturing process with a larger parts order.

Property Requirements. When shape is the only requirement, forging is just one of the many processes available. Many times, however, forging is the only process that can produce the necessary mechanical properties. To obtain all of the benefits of the forging process, the designer must advise the manufacturer of the properties desired. The property requirements should be described by the designer in the specifications furnished to the manufacturer. The specification should include both the standard requirements for the material as well as any additional requirements and/or exceptions. In addition, the designer should identify the minimum tensile properties required as well as the maximum and minimum hardness at specific locations.

Application. The service application of the part has a definite bearing on how the part should be forged. Parts requiring more ductility in some areas than in others can be forged to provide the proper grain flow. Grain flow causes specific orientation of the inhomogeneities, as described earlier. The forging company can be of valuable assistance to the designer when a critical part is being designed. The forging company can suggest designs which will guarantee that the critical area will receive additional work to improve yield strength, ductility, and toughness. Because of variations in equipment available in the individual forge shops, not all forging companies produce the same part in the same manner. Therefore, the design of the forging should give the forging producer some latitude, or the organization should be consulted during the design stages of the part. The type of equipment in a particular forging plant often dictates the location of details such as the parting line. In many forgings, the location of the parting line can be very critical.

Therefore, the forging company and the designer need to work together so that the parting line will not detrimentally affect the region in the part which has the most critical design requirements.

Expected Service Life. The designer bases the selection of material, size, and shape on a desired or expected life on consideration of service stresses and environment. The expected service life of a forging should also influence processing practices.

When service lives are expected to be short and replacement frequent, it may be wise to design forgings with a reasonably high degree of precision. This approach simplifies replacement and minimizes time delays and costs associated with finishing operations. For some applications, forging to closer tolerances produces better properties. On the other hand, processing to more precise tolerances than necessary is not always economically desirable. Building more precision into tooling can be expensive; there is less incentive to do so when

1. Service life is long or replacements are unlikely to be needed.

2. Replacement parts will probably represent a redesign based on accumulated service experience or other reasons.

3. The likelihood of shortening die life excessively is enhanced by going to greater precision.

Degree of Precision Desired. One of the first decisions made by the designer is determination of the degree of precision desired in the forging. Figure 4 illustrates four different classes of forgings known as open-die design, blocker design, conventional design, and precision, or close-to-finish, design. Forging to the precision, or close-to-finish, design results in a minimum amount of machining allowance surrounding the finished part. An open-die design is essentially a rough block; the finished part has to be machined almost completely to the desired shape. The other two designs, blocker and conventional, are modifications between these two extremes which differ in the amount of machining required to produce the finished part. Figure 5 shows the effect of the four types of forging design on the shape of a particular type of structural part.[6] As illustrated, a part produced by open-die or hand-forging techniques would weigh approximately 5 times the weight of the machined part. A precision forging for the same end use would weigh approximately 1.2 times the weight of the machined part. Blocker or conventional forging designs result in varying degrees of excess stock; for example, a blocker forging would weigh approximately 3.6 times and the conventional, or finished, design would weigh approximately 1.5 times the weight of the finish-machined part. The costs of both forging and subsequent machining vary with part design.

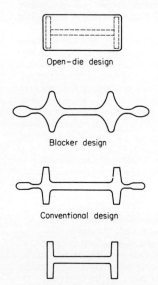

Open-die design

Blocker design

Conventional design

Precision or close-to-finish design

Fig. 4 Comparison of stock allowances for different types of designs.

Part Shape Classification

Blocker-Type Designs. There are no specific rules of thumb for the stock allowance and radii for blocker-type forgings. Like conventional-type forging designs, the stock allowance is a function of product size (weight, length, width, and thickness). In general, the stock allowance and radii are two to three times those for conventional designs.

Commercial, or Conventional, Designs. Commercial, or conventional, designs have more refined details than blocker-type designs, usually draft angles of 5 to 7°, smaller radii, smaller finish allowances, and specific dimensional tolerances that can be achieved on most commercial forging equipment.

The book on forging design by The American Society for Metals[3] gives considerable detail about the design of commercial forgings; therefore, this section is rather brief and general.

The typical stock allowances for commercial or conventional forging designs (Fig. 6) are made up of the following allowances:

- Machining
- Draft
- Thickness
- Shrinkage
- Die wear
- Mismatch

Experience with impression die forgings made in presses and hammers indicates that conventional tolerances provide adequate dimensional accuracy for most industrial applications.[10] Furthermore, the tolerances for forgings made to conventional design can be met by all producers using equipment normally available. Narrower tolerances than those

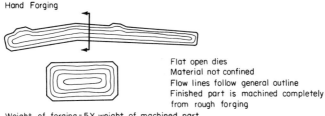

Hand Forging

Flat open dies
Material not confined
Flow lines follow general outline
Finished part is machined completely
from rough forging

Weight of forging = 5X weight of machined part

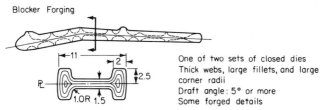

Blocker Forging

One of two sets of closed dies
Thick webs, large fillets, and large
corner radii
Draft angle: 5° or more
Some forged details

Weight of forging = 3.6 X weight of machined part

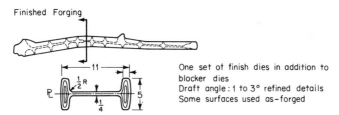

Finished Forging

One set of finish dies in addition to
blocker dies
Draft angle: 1 to 3° refined details
Some surfaces used as-forged

Weight of forging = 1.5 X weight of machined part

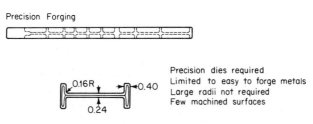

Precision Forging

Precision dies required
Limited to easy to forge metals
Large radii not required
Few machined surfaces

Weight of forging = 1.2 X weight of machined part

Fig. 5 Comparative weights of forgings and machined parts for different forging designs.[6]

discussed below can often be established by mutual agreement between producer and customer.

The standard tolerance for length and width of forgings made to conventional design is ±0.003 in./in. (±0.076 mm/mm). The value also applies to diameters. This tolerance includes allowances for shrinkage, die sinking, and die polishing variations.[10]

Die wear influences the overall length and width tolerance. The allowance varies according to the material and the shape of the forging. Consequently, die-wear tolerances for various materials are applied in addition to the length and width tolerances on

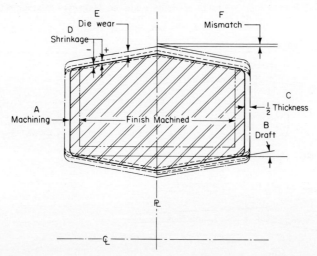

Fig. 6 Items that comprise the stock allowances for conventional types of forgings.[9] A, Machining allowance—applied to each surface which is to be machined. B, Draft allowance—applied to each surface perpendicular to the parting plane. This allowance need not be applied to surfaces showing draft as a natural contour. C, Thickness tolerance—calculated for each forging as a single figure which is then divided for application above and below the parting plane. D, Shrinkage tolerance—applied to the greatest width and the overall length dimensions in company with the die-wear tolerance. E, Die-wear tolerance—applied to the greatest width and overall length dimensions in company with the shrinkage tolerance. F, Mismatch tolerance—applied both to overall width and overall length dimensions. (*Note:* Tolerances and allowances have been exaggerated for clarity.)

dimensions pertaining to forged surfaces only. Die-wear tolerances do not apply on center-to-center dimensions.

Die-wear tolerances for all external length, width, and diameter dimensions are computed by multiplying the greatest external length or outside diameter (measured parallel with the fundamental parting line of the dies) by the appropriate factor in Table 4 and are then combined with plus values of length and width tolerances. Die-wear tolerances on external dimensions are expressed as plus values only.[10]

TABLE 4   Die-Wear Tolerance Factors for 300 and 400
Series Stainless Steels[10]

Materials	Factor (per inch)
400 series	0.006
300 series	0.007

Die-wear tolerances for all internal length, width, and diameter dimensions are computed by multiplying the greatest internal length or inside diameter and are expressed as minus values only. Die-wear tolerances per surface on both external and internal dimensions are one-half of the computed amount.

The standard thickness tolerances for conventional-type forgings increase with the weight of the forging. For example, a 15-lb (6.8-kg) steel forging would have a thickness tolerance of $+\frac{1}{16}$, $-\frac{1}{32}$ in. ($+1.59$, -0.79 mm); while a 200-lb (90.72-kg) forging would have a thickness tolerance of $+\frac{5}{32}$, $-\frac{3}{32}$ in. ($+3.97$, -2.38 mm).

Thickness and die-closure tolerances, which are equivalent terms, vary for the 300 and 400 series stainless steels, as shown in Table 5. Tolerances on extremities of forgings extending perpendicularly more than 6 in. (15.24 cm) from the parting line include the die-closure tolerance and, in addition, a length tolerance of ±0.003 in./in. (±0.076 mm/mm). This tolerance is added to that derived from Table 5 but applies only to such extremities.

Match, sometimes called mismatch, tolerances also are affected in the stock allowance for conventional-type forging designs. Match tolerance relates to displacement of a point in one die from the corresponding point in the opposite half of the die in any direction parallel with the fundamental parting line of the dies. Match tolerances are based on weight of the forging after trimming and are expressed as fractions of an inch (millimeter) according to Table 6.

Match tolerances are applied separately independent of all other tolerances. Where possible, measurements are made at areas of the forging unaffected by die wear. The method of determining the amount of match or mismatch on a forging is shown in Fig. 7.

Close-to-Finish Designs. Close-to-finish design types of forgings are similar to commercial or conventional forging designs except that the machining allowances are reduced. The other criteria of commercial designs such as thickness, length and width, die-wear tolerance, and mismatch tolerance remain essentially the same. Close-to-finish designs have slightly larger machining allowances and draft angles than precision designs.

Precision Designs. The close dimensional accuracy of precision forgings is not covered by universal standards. The tolerances are negotiated by the producer and the customer.

Choosing the Design to Suit the Material   Finish allowance (sometimes called clean-up allowance, forging envelope, or machining allowance) is the amount of excess metal surrounding the intended final shape. The finish allowance depends to a great extent on the oxidation behavior of the metal being forged. Since aluminum and magnesium alloys do not oxidize appreciably at forging temperature, they are often forged with little or no finish allowances. Most other metals, however, are subject to oxidation, contamination, or decarburization at their respective forging temperatures. Hence, a finish allowance is necessary so that affected metal can be removed by machining. The minimum finish allowance usually depends on how much surface material should be removed. Finish allowances usually increase with size because of longer heating times, added operations, and a greater chance of nicks, dents, and other defects occurring during handling. Figure 8 indicates practical finish allowances recommended for several forging alloy systems. Forgings with smaller finish allowances are obtainable, but usually at added cost.

Choosing the Design to Suit the Equipment

Hammers. Hammer dies usually consist of two blocks of hardened steel containing several impressions or shaped cavities as shown in Figure 9. Hammer forgings differ in some respects from certain types which are better adapted for production in presses. Hammer forgings must always be made with draft, a parting line, and flash. They usually are made in several sequential steps without reheating. Hammers seldom have devices for ejecting the part from the dies. Ordinarily, excess material is provided to permit holding the workpiece (a tong hold) during forging and moving it from one impression to another position.

Draft angles normally between 5 and 7° are necessary on hammer forgings in order to facilitate removing the forging from the dies. Drafts are expressed as angles from the axis of the hammer stroke. The stroke is perpendicular to the forging plane. Even when the parting line is inclined with respect to the forging plane and the principal dimensions of the forging are laid out on an inclined plane, draft angles are still referred to the stroke axis of the hammer.

Figure 9 shows a typical set of hammer dies and identifying features that are sometimes incorporated into die blocks. Some dies will not have all of the features shown in Fig. 9; but they will have many of them.

The blocking impression is used to develop the desired directional characteristics; it imparts the general shape and contour to the forging. A good blocker impression has large

TABLE 5 Thickness or Die-Closure Tolerances for Stainless Steels[10]

Tabulated values are plus values, only, expressed in inches (millimeters).

Materials	Area at the trim line—flash not included, in.² (m²)						
	10 (0.006) and under	Over 10–30 (0.006–0.019) incl.	Over 30–50 (0.019–0.032) incl.	Over 50–100 (0.032–0.006) incl.	Over 100–500 (0.06–0.32) incl.	Over 500–1000 (0.32–0.64) incl.	Over 1000 (0.64)
400 series	1/32 (0.79)	1/16 (1.59)	3/32 (2.38)	1/8 (3.18)	3/16 (4.76)	1/4 (6.35)	5/16 (7.94)
300 series	1/16 (1.59)	3/32 (2.38)	1/8 (3.18)	5/32 (3.97)	3/16 (4.76)	1/4 (6.35)	5/16 (7.94)

TABLE 6 Match Tolerances for Stainless Steels as a Function of Forging Weight[10]

Tabulated figures are amounts of displacement, expressed in inches (millimeters) of a point in one die-half from the corresponding point in the opposite die-half in any direction parallel to the parting line of the dies.

Material	Weights of forgings after trimming, lb (kg)								
	Less than 2 (0.91)	Over 2–5 (0.91–2.27) incl.	Over 5–25 (2.27–11.34) incl.	Over 25–50 (11.34–22.68) incl.	Over 50–100 (22.68–45.36) incl.	Over 100–200 (45.36–90.72) incl.	Over 200–500 (90.72–226.8) incl.	Over 500–1000 (226.8–453.6) incl.	Over 1000 (453.6)
Stainless steels	*	1/32 (0.79)	3/64 (1.19)	1/16 (1.59)	3/32 (2.38)	1/8 (3.18)	5/32 (3.97)	3/16 (4.76)	1/4 (6.35)

*Customarily negotiated with purchaser.

radii and gradual transitions between thick and thin sections. Smooth flow of metal in blocking gives a forging its structural soundness and establishes the grain flow pattern.

Edging, sometimes called drawing, fullering, or rolling, resembles open-die forging operations. The stock is elongated by working between die surfaces that have rounded edges and flat or appropriately shaped faces. Drawing reduces the cross section of the bar

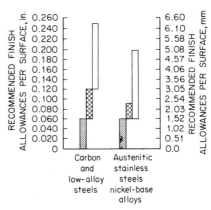

Legend

Relative forging size	Maximum dimension, in.(cm)
Small	Up to 20 (50.8)
Medium	20 to 40 (50.8 to101.6)
Large	Over 40 (101.6)

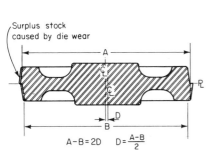

Fig. 7   Determination of match or mismatch on a forging.[10] A, Projected maximum overall dimensions measured parallel to the main parting line of the dies. B, Projected minimum overall dimensions measured parallel to the main parting line of the dies. D, Displacement.

$$A - B = 2D \qquad D = \frac{A-B}{2}$$

Fig. 8   Recommended finish allowances for die forgings of various alloy systems.[5]

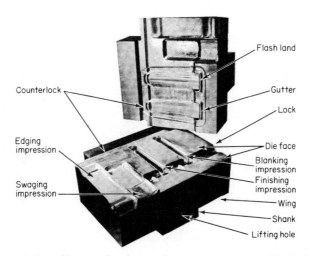

Fig. 9   A typical set of hammer dies showing the various components of the die blocks.[9]

at one or both ends, and fullering reduces a portion between the two ends. Edging is performed at any location on the bar in an impression which may vary in depth and is generally flat. The bar may be turned 90° after each blow so that every section remains rectangular. Edge rolling is like edging, except that a radius in the impression imparts a circular cross-sectional form to the piece.

Hydraulic Presses. The hydraulic press is the most versatile type of forging equipment; it is used mostly for large and complicated forgings. One of its limitations is that it operates at slower ram velocities than hammers, mechanical presses, and screw presses. Because it is slower, it is not usually recommended for small forgings where heat transfer is a problem. An example of the type of forging produced in hydraulic presses is shown in Fig. 10. Hydraulic presses are also preferred for applications where a sustained load is

(a)

(b)

Fig. 10 Examples of forgings produced on hydraulic presses. (*a*) Turbine shaft, A-286, 340 lb (154.4 kg). (*b*) Lateral fitting, Type 304 stainless steel, 1570 lb (712.8 kg). (*Cameron Iron Works.*)

required, such as for hydrostatic extrusion, isothermal forging, and cup forming, and for applications in which a long stroke is required (such as extrusion).

In general, hydraulic presses can be used for any application in which hammers, mechanical presses, or screw presses are used, while the reverse is not always true. For example, hydraulic presses are usually used for parts with long projections which require deep cavities in the dies. For forging thin parts the faster-acting forging equipment is better suited as it obtains thinner webs.[12]

The tooling for a hydraulic press can either be quite simple, like that used in hammers, or it can be rather complicated. Most hydraulic presses are equipped with ejectors for removing forgings from the dies.

An advantage of using hydraulic presses for forging parts is that the ram stroke can be controlled either through controls or by the use of positive stops either on the columns or on the tooling. Also, on many presses the load applied to the workpiece can be controlled through selective valving. The chief disadvantages of hydraulic presses are their slow ram movement and stroking rates. These characteristics cause more die chilling and limit the minimum section thicknesses that can be forged.

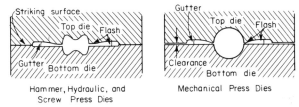

Hammer, Hydraulic, and   Mechanical Press Dies
Screw Press Dies

Fig. 11   Design differences between hammer, hydraulic, screw, and mechanical press dies.[11]

Mechanical Presses. Designing dies for use in mechanical presses more closely parallels designing for hammers than for hydraulic presses. The principal difference is that the dies for hammers and sometimes for hydraulic presses must come in contact (kiss) to control the filling of the cavity. In a mechanical press, the dies (top and bottom) should never come in contact. This is important because a mechanical press is set to produce a very positive stroke of definite length. If the stroke should be shortened inadvertently or stopped by the dies coming in contact or the cavity overfilling because of an excess amount of stock, something has to give. The press frame or the tooling may break, or at best the press will be locked closed and cannot be opened without considerable effort. Many times, in order to unlock a mechanical press it is necessary to cut the tooling out of the press with a torch. Therefore, the dies are designed to prevent contact as shown in Fig. 11. Some mechanical presses are provided with special features which simplify unlocking.

As a general rule, any part that can be made on a hammer can be made on a mechanical press. Mechanical presses are primarily used for producing small, hot forgings for which a short stroke is adequate, and they also are used for producing cold forgings. Small parts or parts requiring small amounts of ram movement that are sometimes produced on hydraulic presses can also be made on mechanical presses.

The primary advantages of mechanical presses are their high stroking and production rates and the ease with which they can be automated.

Screw Presses. Screw presses are not widely employed in the United States, although they have been used in the copper and brass industry for years. Screw presses are most widely used in European industry. Designing forgings for production in screw presses is almost identical to designing forgings for hammers, except that a screw press cannot withstand very much off-center loading. Therefore, edging or blocking is usually performed in separate equipment. Since a screw press does not operate as fast as a hammer, the flash land should be less restrictive than the type used for hammer forgings and more like the designs used for mechanical presses.

Screw presses have several advantages over hammers. First, the amount of load applied to the workpiece can be controlled by metering devices in screw presses; such energy control is more difficult in hammers. Screw presses usually provide better axial alignment. Another advantage of screw presses over hammers is that ejectors in the base of the presses facilitate removal of forgings from the dies. This permits using less draft and deeper cavities in the dies, features which increase the number of shape combinations that can be forged in a screw press.

Open-Die Forging Equipment. Open-die forging, which sometimes is called hand forging, blacksmith forging, or slab forging, is the oldest of the forging processes and is performed between simple dies. The product of the ancient hand forger depended on manual skill and the limitations of the equipment and materials available. Early methods were replaced eventually by mechanically operated hammers and presses.[13] Today, the forger has improved equipment and instrumentation for the control of the heating, handling, and working of the metal. The largest known open-die forging press in the Western world is a 10,000-metric ton hydraulic press.[14] Open-die forgings are generally produced on either hammers or hydraulic presses and range in size from less than 1 lb (0.454 kg) to 400 tons (362,800 kg).

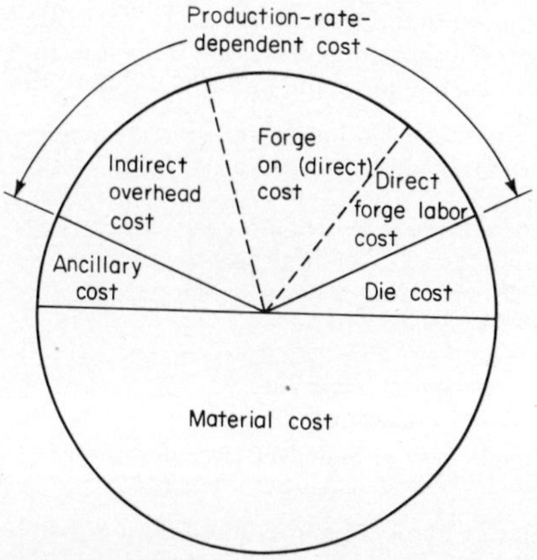

The greatest advantage of open-die forgings is that forging dies generally do not have to be made before the forging can be made. The greatest disadvantage of open-die forgings is that machining costs for producing the finished part are often high. Open-die forgings are forged with as much as 2 in. (50.8 mm) of added stock per surface.

Cost Comparison for Different Types of Designs The costs for producing forgings depend on many factors, such as material, dies, labor, use rate, testing, inspection, overhead costs, indirect costs, and profit. These charges will vary from plant to plant and also from part to part within an individual plant.

Fig. 12 Breakdown of total costs for steel forgings.[15]

Hobdel and Thomas[15] surveyed costs for several forging plants and parts and arrived at the diagram shown in Fig. 12. As can be seen in Fig. 12, the cost of raw material comprises approximately 50% of the total cost of the forging, the costs dependent on production rate comprise another 30%, and die costs and ancillary costs each amount to approximately 10%.

The yield of drop forgings from material brought into the plant is, for the industry as a whole, about 70%. This industry-wide average, however, conceals very large variations. Under optimum conditions a material yield of about 90% can be obtained for symmetrical upset forgings. At the other extreme, the yield may be less than 50%.[28]

Considering the average yield of 70% and assuming that material costs are about half the total cost, reducing the waste of scrap by 50% could reduce the total costs by about 7.5%.

To achieve a 7.5% savings by increased production would mean a production rate increase of about 25%. In many plants this is virtually impossible without drastic alterations to the plant and to the methods of working. Die costs represent about 10% of the total cost of a forging, so that a 50% reduction in die costs would add 5% to the profit on a forging which, in many cases, is equivalent to doubling the present profit.[15] The above discussion applies to conventional closed-die forging practices.

Open-Die Forging. It is obvious for open-die forging that die costs would not amount to 10% of the total forging costs. The die costs for a typical open-die forging might only be on the order of ½ to 1% of the total forging costs. On the other hand, the material yield of the material brought into the forge shop could be well below 50%, which is far less than the 70% average. Thus, the material cost would more than offset the savings that could be achieved by the reduced die costs.

When a part is produced that has a low material yield, the excess material must be removed by one practice or another. Many times it is removed as flash at the press, but in the case of open-die forgings, the excess material is removed by expensive machining operations.

Precision Forging. Precision forging results in a high material yield, sometimes on the order of 80 to 90%. In order to obtain such high yields, the tooling costs are usually higher than the 10% noted in Fig. 12. Precision forging tooling can be quite complicated, and additional tooling is often required for preforming. Preform tooling distributes the stock in such a manner that the part can be produced successfully in the final precision dies.

The design of precision finishing tooling is different than that for conventional-design forgings. This is because precision forging tooling has to withstand pressures approaching 200,000 psi (1379 MN/m²), compared with conventional forging pressures which are rarely above 100,000 to 125,000 psi (689.5 to 861.9 MN/m²). Construction to withstand the higher pressures adds to the overall die costs. The design requirements for precision forgings are discussed elsewhere in this chapter.

Because precision forgings are made closer to final dimensions, the machining requirements and costs are reduced as discussed previously.

Quantity Requirements. The cost of a forging depends on various compromises. The components can be "hogged" out by machining from a simple, cheap wrought hand-forged shape with great loss of material and expense in machining. At the other extreme, a precision-forged component can be made to save on material and machining at the expense of higher tooling costs.

Hand-forged shapes are usually considered only for prototype components. The technical need for grain flow that faithfully follows the contours of the forging may dictate the use of die forging for production components, quite apart from economic advantages. The question of whether to plan for a conventional die forging or to go for the precision approach also has to be settled. The choice depends mainly on the shape of the component, the material in which it is to be made, and the quantity involved.

Testing Requirements. The amount of testing to be performed on forgings is directly related to their property requirements and intended application. For example, many of the parts going into aerospace applications require 100% nondestructive inspection along with destructive tests on specimens taken from each forging. In addition, forgings are periodically sectioned, and specimens are taken from various locations throughout the forging. On the other hand, many of the forgings used in the automotive industry receive only nondestructive inspection for internal defects.

It is obvious that the number and types of testing to be performed on a forging have a very definite bearing on the cost and can also influence the method of forging. The part designer should specify the type and amount of testing needed. Unnecessary testing may yield information, but it adds to the overall cost of the forging. On the other hand, the cost of the additional testing is a small price to pay if it prevents a loss of life or a failure in a critical application.

Precision Forgings—Design and Selection

Checklists for Selection of Process. As for all manufacturing processes, the designer and manufacturing engineer must decide how a forging should be produced to meet the requirements most economically. Such decisions should be based on evaluating alternatives among factors on a checklist similar to the following:

1. Material to be forged
2. Property requirements
3. Finish allowances on forgings
4. Delivery schedule
5. Quantity of parts required
6. Final part dimensions
7. Expected surface requirements

The limits imposed by materials on section thickness were discussed earlier. They influence the degree of precision attainable under practical and economical conditions.

In some instances the properties required for the application will dictate that the part be made by precision forging regardless of other factors such as quantity or delivery schedule; larger quantities favor the economics of precision forging. The designer must always remember, however, that the component design must be finalized before releasing the order for the precision forging dies. Any change in design of the part after the dies are fabricated will almost always result in scrapping the dies and fabricating new ones no matter how slight the change. Precision forgings have too little excess stock to allow much shifting of a boss or rib once the dies are fabricated.

The delivery schedule for parts made by precision forging can result in longer lead times required for the initial order, due to the time necessary for fabricating the dies. After the dies are fabricated, the lead time for subsequent orders will usually be less than for conventional or open-die forgings.

Precision Forgings from Steel. Precision forging operations for steel are more difficult than those for light metals. The greater difference in die and stock temperature is one source of trouble. Chilling of the workpiece, which raises the forging pressure, can be minimized by heating the dies as much as practical, shortening transfer time from furnace to die, and shortening workpiece-die contact time. Other problems in the precision forging of steel are caused by its propensity for scaling and decarburization.

High-Energy-Rate Precision Forging. High-energy-rate forging (HERF) is characterized by high ram speeds and short deformation periods of approximately 0.003 s. Strain

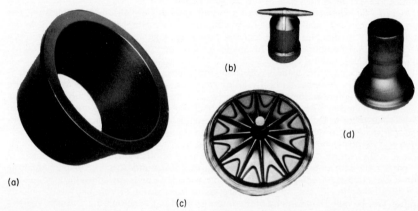

Fig. 13 Examples of high energy rate forgings produced on the Dynapak press. (*a*) Support tub, Type 304L, 60 lb (27.2 kg). (*b*) Gas inlet, Type 347 vacuum arc remelted, 4 lb (1.8 kg). (*c*) Turbine wheel (flash still to be trimmed), A-286, 20 lb (9.1 kg). (*d*) Unnamed, 15-5 PH, 18 lb (8.2 kg). *(Precision Forge Co.)*

rates on the order of 5000 to 8000 per second have been achieved.[16-18] Some examples of steel forgings produced on HERF equipment are shown in Fig. 13.

The development of die designs necessary for containment of the high die pressures encountered in HERF forging represents a giant step forward in the precision forging of steels. Basically, the tooling consists of a series of shrink rings and well-guided punches. Multiring die containers are necessary because of the large radial stresses developed during forging. The tooling designs used for forging in HERF machines are similar to those used in the cold-forging industry and successfully applied in precision forging of stainless steel.

It has been claimed that precision forging of stainless steel in HERF equipment provides the following advantages:
- Good dimensional tolerance[18]
- Improvements in fatigue life[18]
- Increase in strength and ductility[17]
- Improvements in heat-treat response[17]
- Forgings of complex configurations
- Forgings with zero draft and small fillet radii

It is unlikely that any of these advantages are a direct result of using a particular type of high-velocity equipment. Some of the disadvantages in forging on HERF machines are:
- Requirement of very accurate tooling alignment.
- Requirement of accurate location of billet; preforms sometimes are required to achieve the precise location.
- Difficulty in removing forging from dies.
- Fast deformation rates; this produces some defects which require additional stock or redesign of the part.
- Poor die life.

REFERENCES

1. Sabroff, A. M., F. W. Boulger, and H. J. Henning: "Forging Materials and Practices," Reinhold, New York, 1968.
2. Illinois Institute of Technology: "Principles of Forging Design," sponsored by Committee of Hot Rolled and Cold Finished Bar Producers, American Iron and Steel Institute, New York.
3. "Forging Design Handbook," American Society for Metals, Metals Park, Ohio, 1974.
4. Kalpakjian, S.: A Survey of the Feasibility of an Analytical Approach to Die Design in Closed-Die Forging, *DMIC Memorandum 217*, Jun. 1, 1966.
5. Henning, H. J., A. M. Sabroff, and F. W. Boulger: Study of Forging Variables, *Air Force Contract No. AF-22(600)-4293*, Battelle Memorial Institute, Final Rept. issued December 1964.
6. Gure, C.: Designing Forged Parts, *Prod. Eng., (NY)*, vol. 33, no. 9, pp. 47–52, April 1962.
7. Altan, T., and F. W. Boulger: Flow Stress of Metals and Its Application in Metal Forming Analyses, *Trans. ASME*, ser. B, vol. 95, no. 4, pp. 1009–19, Nov. 6, 1973.
8. Altan, T., A. F. Gerds, D. E. Nichols, H. J. Henning, and R. J. Fiorentino: A Study of Mechanics of Closed-Die Forging, *Contract No. DAAG 46-68-C-00111*, Battelle's Columbus Laboratories, Final Rept., August 1970.
9. "Closed-Die Forgings—Their Design and Application," Bethlehem Steel Handbook No. 2068, Bethlehem Steel Co., Bethlehem, Pa.
10. Jenson, J. E.: "Forging Industry Handbook," Forging Industry Assoc., Cleveland, Ohio, 1966.
11. "Designing for Alcoa Forging," Aluminum Company of America, Pittsburgh, 1950.
12. Lake, F. N., and D. J. Moracz: Comparison of Major Forging Systems, *Contract No. F33615-67-C1109*, TRW, Inc., Final Rept., May, 1971.
13. "Open-Die Forging Manual," Open-Die Forging Institute, New York, 1962.
14. Brochure, Japan Steel Works, printed 1970.
15. Hobdell, A. C., and A. Thomas: Approaches to Cheaper Forgings, *Met. Form.*, vol. 36, no. 1, pp. 17–25, January 1969.
16. Parkinson, F. L.: High Energy Rate Forging Development, *Contract No. AF33(600)-42523*, Western Gear Corp., Final Tech. Rept., November 1964.
17. Truelock, D. W., J. R. Russell, and C. M. Phelan: "High Velocity Forging Technology," *Contract No. AF33615-67-C-1179*, Vought Aeronautics Div., LTV Aerospace Corp., Final Rept., November 1968.
18. Headman, M. L.: "The Impact of High-Velocity Forging on Gear Technology," paper presented at the Aerospace Gearing Committee Meeting, Portsmouth, N.H., Aug. 24–25, 1968.

Chapter **23**

The Extrusion of
Stainless Steel Components

JACQUES SEJOURNET
and
HENRI THANNBERGER
International Division, CEFILAC, Paris, France

GENERAL DESCRIPTION OF EXTRUSION

Extrusion is a well-known process for producing hollow or solid bars having a great length and given inside and outside contours. It basically consists in heating a cylindrical billet of metal to its deformation temperature, inserting it into a cylindrical container capable of sustaining high pressures, and forcing the plastic metal through a passageway whose cross-sectional contour is that which is desired for the product.

Direct Extrusion The most general embodiment of the process is direct extrusion (Fig. 1) in which, during extrusion, the container is motionless and is integral with a die showing an axial aperture with the cross section corresponding to the outside contour of the desired product. A cylindrical ram designed for a sliding fit in the container is actuated by the hydraulic or mechanical force of the press, runs through the rear end of the container, and forces the metal of the billet to flow through the die aperture.

If a hollow product (e.g., a tube) is desired (Fig. 2), the billet inserted into the container is axially hollow and a mandrel protruding from the front face of the ram runs through the billet hole up to the aperture of the die, which it partly closes. The cross-sectional contour of the mandrel is that which is desired for the inside hole of the extruded product so that a properly outlined ringlike aperture is available for the metal to flow out.

The ram is stopped before coming into contact with the die so that there remains in the container a nondeformed part of the billet, called the discard, which has to be severed from the extruded product and evacuated (Fig. 3).

Forces Involved The force F' which has to be transmitted by the ram in order to cause the metal to flow out consists of two elements:

- The force F needed for the mere deformation of the metal
- The force $F' - F$ required to overcome the friction between the metal billet and the container wall and the mandrel.

The latter corresponds to a waste of energy: at the beginning of the extrusion process its dissipation generates an overheating of the container and of the billet skin, irregular redundant work in the metal and cracks on its surface. Progressively, as the friction is reduced, this force is less and less dissipated in the metal, but more and more in the

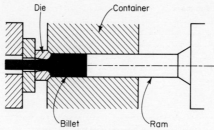

Fig. 1 Direct extrusion of a solid bar.

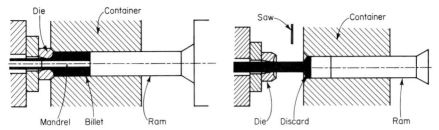

Fig. 2 Direct extrusion of a tube.   **Fig. 3** End of the extrusion process.

piping and valves, which in turn are warmed up. For this reason, and except for light alloys, this friction force has always been kept as low as possible by lubricating between the lateral surfaces of the billet and of the container, but it will be seen in the next section, "Characteristics of Glass-lubricated Extrusion of Steel," that a satisfactory extrusion has been made possible which reduces the friction force to an unnoticeable amount.

Calculation of the Force F Needed for Elongating the Metal. This elongation is defined by the extrusion ratio δ, namely the ratio between the cross-sectional areas available to the metal in the container and in the die aperture, respectively. (δ is also equal to the ratio between a given length of extruded product and the length of billet needed for producing it, provided that the billet fills up the container.)

According to Siebel's calculation[1] and to a constant practice, whenever δ roughly exceeds 10:1, the force F is in proportion with the logarithm of the extrusion ratio and with the cross-sectional area A available to the metal in the container.

$$F = KA \ln \delta \tag{1}$$

The extrusion factor K is expressed in the same unit system as a pressure and depends on the composition of the billet alloy and on its temperature when being extruded. Steel extruders commonly call it the resistance to deformation by extrusion. Figure 4 shows its values as a function of the temperature when use is made of naperian logarithms.

Calculation of the Total Force Needed Along the Extrusion. Let us assume that a solid

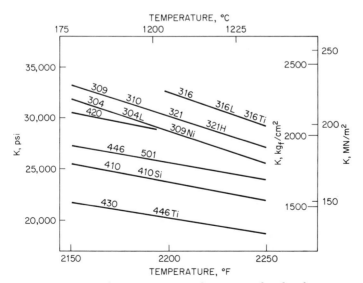

Fig. 4. K factor vs. temperature for various grades of steel.

billet is extruded from a container with an inside diameter D, that the coefficient of friction between the lateral surfaces of the billet and container is f, and that the remaining length of the billet is x.

When the front of the ram travels by dx, the force F' drops by the corresponding friction force:

$$dF' = f\,\frac{4F'}{\pi D^2}\,\pi D\,dx = \frac{4f}{D}\,F'\,dx$$

Thus, since $F' = F$ when $x = 0$,

$$F' = F e^{4fx/D} \qquad (2)$$

Figure 5 shows the values of the ratio F'/F as a function of the billet length for various values of the coefficient of friction f. The value $f = 0$, corresponding to a perfect lubricant,

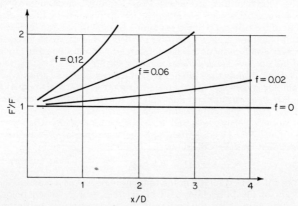

Fig. 5 Influence of friction on the required force.

can be taken into consideration only when proper lubrication is used. It entails consequences which are reported in the section on characteristics. The value $f = 0.02$ corresponds to a good, though not perfect, lubricant. In this case, if the billet length is equal to four times its diameter, the friction force already amounts to 38% of the useful force.

The value $f = 0.06$ corresponds to the use of such well-known lubricants as graphite; a ratio $x/D = 3$ is enough to cause the friction force to be equal to the useful force for a billet length equal to three times its diameter. The value $f = 0.12$ roughly corresponds to the non-lubricated friction of hot steel tools; friction force equals useful force when $x/D = 1.5$. Still larger ratios, F'/F, would be obtained when extruding with a mandrel.

Keeping in mind that the basic effect of the friction force is to adversely affect the tools and the extruded product, it is obvious that a drastic reduction of friction is the first condition for extruding sensitive alloys.

Physical Aspect of a Poorly Lubricated Extrusion The above theoretical analysis leads to the following practical consequences:

1. The temperature of the metal under deformation will be increased during the extrusion operation as the coefficient of friction increases.

2. Since the thermal insulation of the die is poor, this will cause it to warm up and to be highly sensitive to frictional wear.

3. The friction force along the lateral surface of the billet will cause the container wall to warm up and will create in the whole billet a radial gradient of stresses so that all parts in the billet will at any time be the subject of a deformation.

4. Under certain conditions of metal flow, the shear stresses in the billet may reach their ultimate value, which will cause the skin of the billet to be separated from the flowing metal and to pile up at the corner between the container wall and die, thus forming a ring, called the dead angle.

As a consequence of point 1, the extrusion of such metals as aluminum alloys has to be carried out at a very low speed, so that the generated heat can be evacuated.

Point 2 is illustrated by Fig. 6, which shows the poor surface condition of a die after the poorly lubricated extrusion of one steel bar. Additionally, the diameter of the die-bearing land may have increased because of wear or decreased because of metal creep.

Figure 7 shows the axial section of a steel billet on which a rectangular grid had initially been machined. This billet has been hot-extruded without being lubricated and its pattern clearly shows both a deformation in its whole length (point 3) and the formation of a dead angle (point 4). It will be seen in the discussion on lubrication that proper lubrication offsets or radically changes all these phenomena.

Piercing in a Press (Fig. 8) Another very frequently used step in the extrusion process is the piercing operation: the billet at deformation temperature is inserted into a blind container and, after upsetting it into close contact with the container walls, a

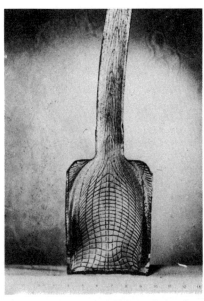

Fig. 6 Die after one push without glass lubricant.   **Fig. 7** Macrograph of a billet extruded without glass lubrication.

piercing tool is axially forced into it; the passageway available to the metal is the ringlike space between the piercing tool and the container wall. In this operation, friction occurs along the piercing tool and along the container walls. When this friction is not properly reduced, cracks appear on the outside surface of the billet. For this reason, piercing with poor lubrication is frequently carried out "by compensation": a square billet is inserted into a container with a clearance exactly equal to the cross-sectional area of the piercing tool, so that the simultaneous upsetting and piercing of the billet do not entail any change in its length.

Hydrostatic Extrusion With this special process (Fig. 9), the metal to be transformed is subject to friction only with the die. A billet with a nose matching the die entry is inserted into a container with a very large clearance. The container is filled with a lubricating liquid and a tightly fitting ram is forced into the container thus pressurizing the liquid to a sufficient extent to force the metal of the billet to flow out through the die.

This process can be used only at temperatures where appropriate fluids can be found. In the case of steel, in view of its high resistance at such temperatures, this limits the extrusion ratio to low values.

CHARACTERISTICS OF THE GLASS-LUBRICATED EXTRUSION OF STEEL

The general description just given has shown that friction and overheating of the tools were the two major obstacles to satisfactory extrusion. In fact, until a satisfactory solution

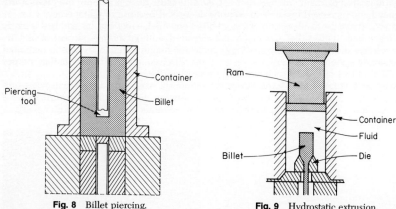

Fig. 8 Billet piercing.   **Fig. 9** Hydrostatic extrusion.

to this problem was found, the extrusion of carbon steel was limited to the transformation of short billets with a low extrusion ratio and the extrusion of stainless steel led to products with so poor a surface condition that they had to be thoroughly machined. This problem was studied by Jacques Sejournet, assisted by Louis Labataille. The first trials made in 1938 led to the conclusion that steel extrusion was possible provided that sufficient insulation and lubrication was ensured. They found that the appropriate lubricant had to be viscous within the deformation temperature range, however high these temperatures are, and that, above 1000° F (550° C), this viscous lubricant could consist of a glass, an enamel, or a mixture of metal oxides or salts.[2,3]

Glass, with several of its most commonly manufactured compositions, shows a gently decreasing viscosity within the range where it is appropriate for lubrication as a function of the temperature. Figure 10 shows this viscosity for window glass.

The lubricating power of a properly selected glasslike material is best shown by recording the force required by an extrusion versus the ram travel (according to Fig. 5). Figure 11 shows the automatically recorded graph of the glass-lubricated extrusion of a stainless steel billet about 3 diameters in length. Except for a starting peak, the record is perfectly horizontal so that the coefficient of lateral friction must be considered equal to zero.

In addition to being an excellent lubricant when hot, glass also is a very good insulator: heat leakages from the hot metal into the tools are limited. By combining this property with a fast, short-lasting extrusion operation, it is possible to maintain both a good surface

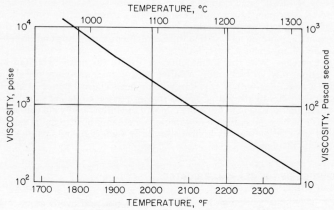

Fig. 10 Viscosity of a glass vs. its temperature.

condition and accurate dimensions in the tooling. In fact, the extrusion of steel lasts a few seconds and the runout speed of the extruded product amounts to 6 to 30 ft (1.8 to 9.1 m)/s.

The absence of lateral frictional force ensures a perfect uniformity of the pressure in nearly the whole mass of the billet, which is deformed only in the close vicinity of the die. The shearing effect always occurs within the layer of lubricant so that there is no "dead angle" and the lateral surface of the billet is transformed into the lateral surface of the

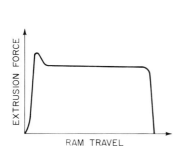

Fig. 11 Extrusion force during a glass-lubricated extrusion.

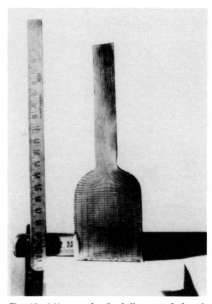

Fig. 12 Macrograph of a billet extruded with glass.

product. All this can be seen in Fig. 12, which is similar to, and should be compared with, Fig. 7.

GLASS-LUBRICATED EXTRUSION OF STAINLESS STEEL— DETAILED SEQUENCE OF OPERATIONS

Preparation of the Billets Billets are cut to the appropriate weight from cylindrical bars forged, rolled, or cast to diameters slightly smaller than the diameters of the press containers through which they will be transformed.

The surface condition of the bars must be sound. It is impossible to express a roughness requirement (e.g., in microinches) because the depth of the surface undulations is not the critical factor.

The cutting operation is carried out with rotary saws or abrasive wheels which ensure a good perpendicularity of the end faces to the axis. Then, the sharp front edge of the billet is removed. If appropriate, the billet is axially cold-bored.

Heating Since the billets have to be heated to a temperature in the vicinity of 2200° F (1200° C), i.e., above the temperature at which they begin to oxidize rapidly, steps must be taken to avoid oxidation (which would spoil their surface condition). The heated billet also must show a good temperature homogeneity. A few good solutions are in current use.

Nonoxidizing Flame Furnace. Several furnace builders have developed satisfactory solutions. For instance, an oil- or gas-fed rotary hearth furnace is fed with air in an amount far below what would be necessary to ensure complete combustion of the fuel. A continuous control of the dissociation of water and CO_2 in the various sectors of the furnace provides conditions under which the billets are neither oxidized nor carburized.

The combustion is completed outside the furnace and the heat thus generated is used to preheat the air and the fuel before they are admitted into the furnace.

Billets heated by this means show a good temperature homogeneity and a sound surface condition.

Induction Heating. The billets are pushed through a tunnel consisting of a series of coils of an appropriate diameter fed by an alternating current, generally at normal frequency. To avoid oxidation, the strictly confined atmosphere of the tunnel is composed of argon or of the gas resulting from a previous combustion. When carefully carried out, this heating process proves quite satisfactory.

Salt Bath Heating. Billets, preheated in a conventional flame furnace to about 1500° F (815° C), are dipped into a bath of barium chloride electrically heated by a Joule effect to the desired temperature. This method is nonoxidizing and removes all impurities from the billet surface. Changes in the temperature of the bath can be achieved very quickly. But this method is very expensive, so that it can be used only in pilot installations transforming a very large variety of metals and alloys in small tonnages.

Enamel Coating Prior To Heating. The billet is first dipped at room temperature into a suspension of enamel which forms a continuous protective layer, then it is heated by any conventional means: flame, induction, or an economically advantageous combination of both.

Glass Coating of the Lateral Surface   As soon as it issues from the furnace, the hot billet is rolled down a slant table covered with an appropriate glass.

Piercing   (This step is omitted when making solid sections or hollow sections with a small inside diameter.) The billet is immediately inserted into the container of a vertical piercing press and then pierced to a cross-sectional circle slightly exceeding the desired final inside contour of the product.

In view of the required concentricity, this can be achieved by two different methods.

Upsetting-Piercing a Solid Billet. If the desired billet inside diameter is large, the force of the press is first applied through an assembly of two coaxial tools: the piercing tool and an upsetting ring which completes the closing of the upper end of the container. This causes the billet to be upset until it comes into close contact with the container wall. Then, the force of the press is applied through the piercing tool, which axially penetrates through the billet by forcing its metal to laterally flow upward. When the piercing tool has nearly completed its travel, an axial plug in the bottom of the container, matching the diameter of the piercing tool is slightly withdrawn to permit a residue to be shorn off from the billet. This method is cheap, since the residue is the only metal loss.

Expanding a Cold-Bored Pilot Hole. If the desired inside billet diameter is small, the following method is often preferred. The cold preparation of the billet includes boring an axial pilot hole of small diameter. The press into which the heated billet is inserted does not need to include an upsetting ring and the means for operating it; it is equipped with a frustum-shaped so-called expanding tool designed to be guided by the pilot hole. The largest diameter of the expanding tool corresponds to the desired final inside diameter of the billet. The tool is forced through the billet and a residue is shorn off in the same manner as from an initially solid billet.[4]

In addition to the residue, this method results in waste due to the cold-boring, but it achieves a better-centered hole than the former method especially when the ratio of length to inside diameter of the expanded billet is very large.

When the desired billet inside diameter is small, an obvious extrapolation of this method consists of cold-boring the billet to its final diameter and bypassing the piercing press.

Extrusion   The billet is pushed into the container of the horizontal hydraulic extrusion press, often by the ram of the press itself. If appropriate, a mandrel protrudes from the ram through the billet bore until its front end passes through the die. Then the force of the press is applied to the ram, which forces the metal of the billet to first be upset and come into close contact with the container wall, and then to flow out through the die. The die entry facing the billet has previously been covered with cold glass.

This glass reservoir progressively melts under the heat of the billet and provides a continuous coating of the extruded product, thus avoiding friction and limiting heat exchanges between the metal and the die.

When the extrusion is nearly completed, the ram is stopped, the container is moved backward so that a rotary saw or a shearing device can separate the extruded product from the nonextruded part of the billet (the discard). The latter is ejected, the tools are inspected and the press is ready for another push.

The extruded product is cooled either in the open air on a conventional cooling bed, or quickly, by immersion in a water tank or, in some cases, very slowly, according to its metallurgical structure.

Straightening and Detwisting When cool, the extruded sections are straightened and detwisted on a stretch-straightening bench in one operation, during which the major part of the glass coating then scales off.

Tubes are straightened on a roller machine.

Pickling The straightened sections and the as-cooled tubes are dipped into molten soda or into a solution of mixed hydrofluoric and sulfuric acids, which dissolves the oxides remaining on their surfaces. They are then passivated and rinsed.

The extruded products are then ready for use as-extruded or they may be cold-drawn to smaller sizes.

LUBRICATING PROCEDURE

The lubrication procedure must be such that the flowing metal never comes into direct contact with the tools since this would cause local defects both on the product and on the tools.

Extrusion of Solid Sections The friction conditions to be avoided are of two kinds.

Friction of the Lateral Surface of the Billet Along the Container Wall. Each element of the billet surface travels longitudinally without changing its area, so that it is sufficient to have initially coated it with a thin layer of lubricant. This is easily done by causing the hot billet, before insertion into the container, to roll along a table covered with glass powder. The powder picked up by the billet immediately melts and builds up a continuous lubricating and insulating layer.

Friction of the Lateral Surface of the Generated Product Along the Die. This lateral surface is considerably larger than that of the nondeformed billet, in a proportion which depends on the extrusion ratio and the intricacy of the produced section. It is therefore necessary, all along the extrusion, to supply this rapidly increasing surface with a continuous film of molten lubricant. The most common procedure consists of placing a pad of glass powder against the flat entry face of the die. When the front face of the billet comes into contact with the pad, it causes a small layer of the pad to melt. This layer is carried along with the flowing metal and the next layer melts in turn; this procedure is repeated in a continuous manner during the entire extrusion process.

The composition of the glass used is so selected that, with the extrusion speed used for steels, the layer of glass coating the extruded product has a given, well-controlled thickness.

Extrusion of Hollow Sections For the outside surface of the product, the same lubrication problems as described for the extrusion of solid sections are faced, and they are solved in the same manner.

Additionally, it is necessary to offset the friction between the inside surface of the billet and the mandrel. During extrusion, the surface to be lubricated increases in a proportion equal to the extrusion ratio. Its lubrication is ensured by coating either the inside surface of the billet or the lateral surface of the mandrel with an amount of glass sufficient to generate an appropriate glass layer on the increased surface of the extruded product. The main part of this glass is practically coextruded with the metal of the billet.

Piercing Since the length of the billet increases when it is pierced, its lateral surface in contact with the container wall must be lubricated to reduce friction. This increase in length is small however (below 50%), so that the method just described for piercing solid sections easily applies.

The travel of the tool along the inside surface of the billet also has to be lubricated and the rate of increase of this surface is either large (expansion) or even infinite (upsetting-piercing of a solid billet). A reservoir of glass lubricant is therefore built up close to the piercing or expanding tool. It progressively melts in contact with the billet and supplies a continuous film coating the billet bore as soon as it is created.

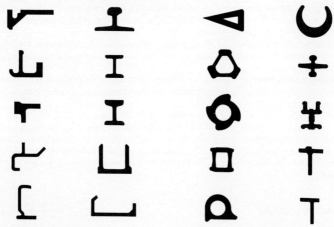

Fig. 13 Examples of extruded steel sections. These sections are commonly extruded in carbon steel and can be extruded in stainless steel.

SIZE RANGES OF PRODUCTION

With a given extrusion press, it is possible to produce a great variety of products since one has only to change the die and, for hollow sections, the mandrel. A few examples of extruded steel sections are shown in Fig. 13.

The main factors for assessing the feasibility of a given section on a given installation are:

1. Its cross-sectional area, most often represented by its weight per unit length (1 in.² corresponds to 3.4 lb/ft for steel or 1 cm² corresponds to 0.85 kg/m).

2. Its desired length.

The points to be considered are examined below.

Stress on the Ram   The running pressure to be expected for a given extrusion is

$$P = K \ln \delta \qquad (3)$$

easily derived from Eq. (1).

In the case of stainless steels, the order of magnitude of K is 20,000 to 30,000 psi (137.9 to 206.8 MN/m²) (Fig. 4). In view of the starting conditions and of the necessary clearances, the stress σ on the ram may exceed the running pressure by 25%, and it is advisable in industrial practice to keep this value below 150,000 psi [1034.3 MN/m²] (or, as an exception, below 180,000 psi [1241 MN/m²]).

This leads to

$$\ln \delta < \frac{\sigma}{1.25K} \quad \text{or} \quad \frac{150,000}{1.25 \times 30,000} \approx 4$$

with $\delta = 55{:}1$.

If the stress limit 180,000 is considered, this would lead to a limit higher than $\delta = 70{:}1$, but 70:1 is a reasonably large extrusion ratio and is often regarded as a limit.

For the same reasons, the container diameter must be large enough for its cross-sectional area, reduced when appropriate by that of the mandrel, to avoid an overstress of the ram when the nominal force of the press N (short tons) is applied to it.

$$A > \frac{2000N}{\sigma} = \frac{N}{75} \text{ in.}^2 \text{ normally} \qquad (4)$$

$$= \frac{N}{90} \text{ in.}^2 \text{ as an exception}$$

If the force of the press N is expressed in metric tons, the areas in square millimeters (mm²) and the magnitudes homogeneous to pressures in kilograms force per millimeter (kgf/mm), the formula becomes

$$A > \frac{1000N}{\sigma} = 9.5N \text{ mm}^2 \text{ normally} \tag{4a}$$

$$= 8N \text{ mm}^2 \text{ as an exception}$$

It follows that the smallest cross-sectional area which can be obtained on a press with a nominal force N (short tons) is

$$\frac{N}{75 \times 55} = 2.4 \times 10^{-4}N \text{ in.}^2$$

or in weight per unit length

$$3.4 \times 2.4 \times 10^{-4}N = 8 \times 10^{-4}N \text{ lb/ft} \tag{5}$$

As an exception, this lower limit can be reduced to

$$\frac{N}{90 \times 70} = 1.6 \times 10^{-4}N \text{ in.}^2 \text{ or } 5.4 \times 10^{-4}N \text{ lb/ft}$$

In metric units, the smallest cross-sectional area is

$$\frac{9.5N}{55} = 0.18N \text{ mm}^2 \text{ or } 1.5 \times 10^{-3}N \text{ kg/m} \tag{5a}$$

As an exception:

$$\frac{8N}{70} = 0.12N \text{ mm}^2 \text{ or, roughly, } 10^{-3}N \text{ kg/m}$$

Force Required of the Press   A container is selected with a useful cross-sectional area A consonant with Eq. (4).

The force required for extrusion

$$F = \frac{1.25KA}{2000} \ln \delta \qquad \text{short tons}$$
$$\tag{6}$$
or
$$F = \frac{1.25KA}{1000} \ln \delta \qquad \text{metric tons}$$

must be smaller than the nominal force N of the press.

Extrusion of Solid Sections   On a given press, with a given container, the smallest feasible solid section has a cross-sectional area a derived from formula (6).

$$a = A \, e^{-2000N/1.25KA}$$

or

$$a = A \, e^{-1000N/1.25KA} \qquad \text{(metric units)}$$

Figure 14 gives horizontally the unit weights of products which can be extruded from a press with the force shown vertically.

The normal limits are shown by the solid lines $\delta = 55{:}1$ and $\delta = 9{:}1$. As a still reasonable exception, the limiting ratios $\delta = 70{:}1$ and $\delta = 5{:}1$ may be considered. The corresponding container diameters are shown on curves roughly perpendicular to the limits.

Large solid sections are feasible as long as a circle centered on their center of gravity and comprising their whole contour has a diameter clearly smaller than the container diameter. Sections for cold-drawing can be slightly altered to meet this requirement.

Within these limits, the contour must additionally meet a few conditions ensuring the life of the die.

Extrusion of Tubes   It is usual to define the geometry of a tube on a graph (Fig. 15) where the abscissa x shows its wall thickness and the ordinate y shows its outside diameter.

If such a tube is extruded from a container with an inside diameter D, the useful cross-sectional area of the container will be

$$A = \frac{\pi}{4} \, [D^2 - (y - 2x)^2]$$

and the extrusion ratio

$$\delta = \frac{A}{\pi x(y - x)}$$

For each set of values of the nominal force N of the press, extrusion factor K, and the container diameter D, the range of feasible tubes is limited by a contour A, B, C, D, E, F, A, in which appear all or some of the following curves:

AB corresponding to the nominal force of the press.

Its equation in the x, y system can be shortly written

$$A \, \ln\delta = 1600 \, \frac{N}{K}$$

or, in metric units,

$$A \, \ln\delta = 800 \, \frac{N}{K}$$

BC corresponding to the smallest permissible mandrel (with a diameter m_0)

$$y = m_0 + 2x$$

CD corresponding to the lowest economically reasonable extrusion ratio δ_0

$$\delta = \delta_0$$

DE corresponding to the largest permissible mandrel

$$A = \frac{N}{75} \text{ or } \frac{N}{90}$$

or (in broken lines)

$D_1 E_1$ corresponding to the largest permissible outside diameter y_1

$$y = y_1$$

EF and FA corresponding to the smallest permissible wall thickness generally in proportion with the outside diameter

$$EF: y = nx$$

with a lower limit

$$FA: x = 0.12 \text{ in. (3.05 mm)}$$

Figure 15 shows the relative positions of ranges corresponding to a given value of the

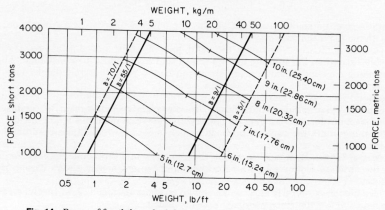

Fig. 14 Range of feasibility of solid products according to the force of the press.

ratio N/K for container diameters 7 and 9 in. (17.78 and 22.86 cm), respectively. Normal conditions are shown in solid lines and exceptional conditions in broken lines.

In actual practice, the set of container diameters is so selected as to permit tubes of the most usual steel grade with the minimum wall thickness to be made with a continuous range of outside diameters. This requires point A' of a larger container to coincide with point E of the immediately smaller one.

In the case of Fig. 15 where the container diameters 7 and 9 in. (17.78 and 22.86 cm) have been selected for the sake of clarity, this means that if a container diameter larger than 7 in. (17.78 cm) is contemplated, it will be far below 9 in. (22.86 cm), the more as the production flexibility of the latter is obviously very limited.

Extrusion of Hollow Sections   The mathematical conditions are the same as for a tube having the same unit weight and the same cross-sectional bore area. The geometrical conditions are the same as for a solid section with the same outside contour.

Generally, the shape of the inside contour does not raise any serious problem, but when the question arises, its angular positioning with reference to the outside contour may require special attention.

Length of the Extruded Product   When a product is extruded from a container C in diameter with an extrusion ratio δ, its length amounts to

$$L = \delta n C \text{ in.}$$

n, the ratio of the upset billet length (not including the extrusion discard) to the container diameter, should reasonably lie between given limits.

When very long products are desired, it may therefore be necessary to select a high extrusion ratio and, consequently, a powerful press. When very short products are desired, it may, on the contrary, be advantageous to extrude a product several times the desired length in one push and to cut it accordingly. Figure 16 shows the length of extruded product for which an appropriate press force can be selected versus its unit weight. Solid and broken lines are the admitted normal ($n = 2$, $n = 3.5$) and exceptional ($n = 1$, $n = 4$) limits. The corresponding ranges of admittedly permissible extrusion ratios are also shown (exceptional figures in parenthesis).

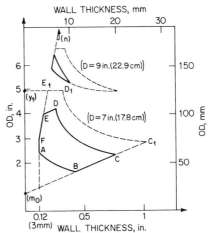

Fig. 15 Range of feasibility of tubes on a press with a given force and containers 7 in. (17.8 cm) and 9 in. (22.9 cm) in diameter.

Selection of an Extrusion Press   When selecting an extrusion press, account is taken first of the most frequently desired products. According to the data shown in this section, the force of the press and one container diameter are thus selected.

The total range of products feasible on this press is then compared with the potential market and the selected data are slightly changed to cover a part of the market consonant with the expected yearly output.

APPLICATION OF STAINLESS STEEL EXTRUDED PRODUCTS

Solid Sections   The chemical industry is one of the greatest customers of stainless steel solid sections. It mainly orders conventional shapes such as L's, T's, U's, and I's. In this field, extrusion takes advantage of its ability to produce small tonnages.

Frames for doors and windows are now produced by folding sheets, which leads neither to the most economical cost price nor to the most favorable cross section. Asymmetrical sections with a variable thickness would be more advantageous. They can easily be produced by extrusion and this market is expected to be developed for extrusion.

Rings for Jet Engines   Nearly all the rings for jet engines are made today by bending an extruded section with the appropriate contour (Fig. 17).

Tubes   Stainless steel tubing is the field where the development of glass-lubricated

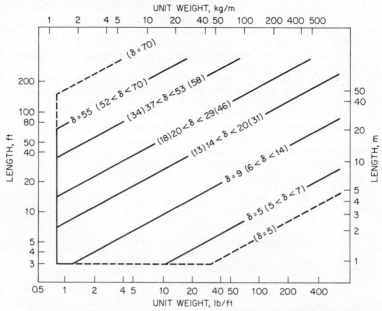

Fig. 16   Feasible length of solid sections on a 2000-short ton (17.79-MN) press.

extrusion has been the most impressive. Until 1950, a seamless tube in 18-8 stainless steel was made in a difficult and intricate manner starting from a short, thick-walled, large-diameter blank produced on a push bench, a rolling mill, or even a graphite-lubricated extrusion press. The surface was affected by the lubricating graphite and by the grains of the grinding wheels.

This blank was ground inside and outside, then, it underwent several cold-drawings with intermediate heat-treating and descaling operations.

A production improvement appeared with cold-rolling machines, but their production capacity was poor so that the produced tonnage was low and the cost high.

A few years and many efforts have been necessary to develop the extrusion process for stainless steel tubes, but the technical progress was such that, today, stainless steel tubes extruded for several purposes are used as-extruded, after pickling and straightening.

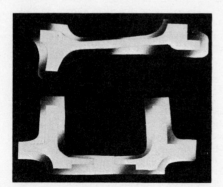

Fig. 17   Cross sections of partly as-extruded, partly cold-finished rings for jet engines.

In one plant, the hourly output has been increased by extruding a large-diameter tube and reducing its diameter on a stretch-reducing mill before cooling.

Hollow Sections   Among the various shapes thus produced, special mention should be made of stainless steel nuts for the bolt industry, where semiproducts can be supplied at request, in the desired tonnage, with practically no waste of metal.

OTHER POTENTIALITIES OF A STAINLESS STEEL EXTRUSION PLANT

An extrusion plant designed for fabricating stainless steel products is also capable of transforming other alloys, such as nickel alloys, within the same temperature range, or such exotic metals as titanium and zirconium at a lower temperature and refractory materials such as molybdenum, tungsten, columbium and their alloys at higher temperatures.

The extrusion of carbon and low-alloy steels into a great variety of solid and hollow sections is also commonly performed on extrusion presses for stainless steel (e.g., finned tubes for boilers, ball-bearing steel tubes, and hollow bars).

Extrusion presses for the massive production of plain carbon steel tubes are specific. Some of them have recently been erected and their working conditions ensure a large hourly output, which allows them to compete advantageously with the older processes already well established in this field, a competition which is practically unknown to stainless steel tubing extrusion plants since they are nearly the sole suppliers on the market.

EXISTING INSTALLATIONS

The role of glass-lubricated extrusion devoted to stainless steel, which started in 1950, can be summed up briefly as follows:

In France, the 1500-ton (13.3-MN) extrusion press on which the process has been developed is specially equipped for the pilot production of all kinds of tubes and sections among which stainless steel has an important share. More bulky products are produced on a more modern 3000-ton (26.7-MN) extrusion press.

In the United States, nine firms produce stainless steel tubes and sections in addition to nickel tubing and exotic material.

In Sweden, two firms operate four presses entirely devoted to stainless steel tubing. In Japan, Great Britain, Austria, Italy and Spain, a total of eleven firms include stainless steel tubing or sections in their production. A plant with the same purpose is now being erected in India.

REFERENCES

1. Siebel, E., and E. Fangmeier: Untersuchen über den Kraftbedarf beim Pressen und Lochen, *Mitt. Kaiser-Wilhelm-Inst. Eisenforsch. Duesseldorf*, vol. 13, p. 29, 1931. (Trans. by André Collinet, Librairie Polytechnique Paris et Liege, 1936.)
2. Sejournet, J., and L. Labataille: Extrusion of Metals, U.S. Patent 2,538,917.
3. Sejournet, J., and L. Labataille: *Machinery (London)*, vol. 85, pp. 471–480, Sept. 3, 1954.
4. Buffet, J., and J. Meriaux: Method of Boring Metals, U.S. Patent 2,956,337.

Chapter **24**

Machining Wrought and Cast Stainless Steels*

DEO M. BLOTT
**Machining Specialist, Technical Sales, Universal-Cyclops
Specialty Steel Division, Pittsburgh, Pennsylvania**

*The discussion and data on machining of cast stainless steels has been extracted, with permission, from publications of the Steel Founders' Society of America.[1-3]

INTRODUCTION

This chapter has been prepared to assist in selection of speeds and feeds, tool configurations, and type of lubricant for the most economical machining of stainless steels. These recommendations have been made as precise as possible in order to keep the amount of readjustment to a minimum.

Stainless steels are usually selected for their high strength and toughness and their unique ability to resist heat and corrosion. In many applications the machinability of one grade versus another is a deciding factor. All stainless steels are machinable, but just as their physical and mechanical properties differ significantly, they also exhibit varying degrees of machinability.

In the broad range of machine tools employed in the metalworking industry, automatic screw machines stand out for their productivity. They are used extensively to convert stainless steel bar stock into an almost endless variety of parts essential to all types of equipment.

Machining behavior of metals is a subject of continuing concern to metal producers and consumers alike. *Machinability* is the term used to denote the machining performance of a material, or the capability of being cut or machined by the appropriate tool. Figure 1 is a machinability chart showing surface feet per minute (surface ft/min) recommended when using high-speed steel tools. The ratings shown compare various stainless steels based on AISI B1112 as 100% machinable. Surface feed per minute is shown across the top of the chart while percent machinability is shown at bottom of the chart.

The term stainless steel is generally applied to iron-based alloys containing chromium in amounts greater than 11.5%. Additions of carbon, nickel, manganese, silicon, molybdenum, titanium, columbium (niobium), and other alloying elements are used to produce desired corrosion resistance and/or special mechanical properties.

Additions of greatest interest to machine-shop personnel are sulfur, selenium, and a sulfur-aluminum combination. These elements promote free-machining behavior by producing nonmetallic inclusions which act to reduce chip length and to reduce galling and seizing tendencies. In reality, this distinction—whether or not a grade has been modified for free machining—is the most important classification when considering material for extensive machining operations.

The most popular classification system for all stainless steels, based on microstructure and heat-treatment response, separates the grades into three groups: hardenable (martensitic), nonhardenable (ferritic), and austenitic. Each group contains some free-machining grades. A brief description of these three categories follows.

Hardenable Stainless Steels This class of stainless steels is composed of those grades of the 400 series which are hardenable by heat treatment. Free-machining types are 416, 420F, 420FSe, 440F, and 440FSe. Regular types are 403, 410, 414, 420, 431, 440A, 440B, and 440C. All are martensitic and therefore magnetic as-annealed. They can be hardened and tempered to various strength levels. In this class the easiest grade to machine is Type 416; the hardest to machine, because its high-carbon content is abrasive to cutting tools, is Type 440C.

Nonhardenable Stainless Steels Steels in this category are those of the 400 series which are not significantly hardenable by heat treatment. They are ferritic, and therefore magnetic as-annealed. Free-machining types are 430F and 430FSe; regular types are 405, 430, 442, 443, and 446.

Austenitic Stainless Steels   These are the so-called "chrome-nickel" grades of the 300 series. More recently, this class has been augmented with several Cr-Ni-Mn grades of

Surface ft/min

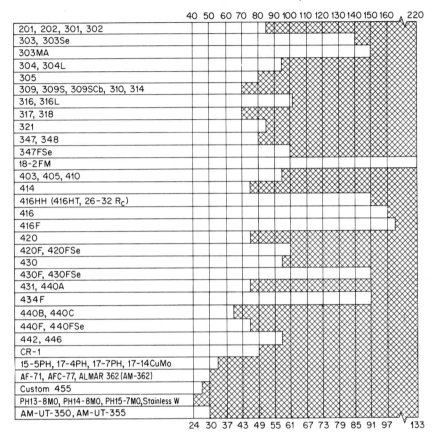

Machinability rating, %, based on 100% for AISI B1112
using high-speed steel tools

Conversion: surface ft/min × 0.3048 = surface m/min

Fig. 1   Machinability of stainless steels compared with AISI B1112.

the 200 series. As-annealed these grades are austenitic in structure and are essentially nonmagnetic. They are not hardenable by heat treatment, but most of them work harden rapidly, much more so than either the ferritic or martensitic stainless steels.

Free-machining grades are: 303, 303MA, 303Se, 316F, and 347FSe. A partial list of other standard austenitic grades includes: 201, 202, 301, 302, 304, 305, 308, 309, 310, 314, 316, 317, 318, 321, 347, and 348. Many others, not officially designated as AISI standards, are commercially available.

The austenitic grades are relatively more difficult to machine than most of the martensitic or ferritic stainless steels. The main difference is that the austenitic grades are gummy in the annealed condition, tend to machine with a stringy chip and, unless proper techniques are employed, rapid work hardening during machining can cause machining problems.

Free-Machining Additions A few words now about the most popular free-machining additions: sulfur and selenium. Improved machinability is achieved because these elements form nonmetallic inclusions which promote brittle, easily disposable chips. One side effect of these additions is decreased transverse ductility which may result in cracking during forming operations such as staking, flaring, thread rolling, and upsetting. Another is lowered corrosion resistance of the steel. These are some of the reasons why free-machining grades cannot be specified for all jobs. They are also the reasons for the considerable amount of development work to improve overall performance of free-machining grades.

A successful approach to improve the most popular Cr-Ni free-machining stainless steel, Type 303, was to lower the sulfur content and add aluminum. The resulting steel, Uniloy 303MA, has proven its merit in many applications requiring not only improved machinability, but also improved formability and improved resistance to corrosion.

Much work has also gone into improving the free-machining grades of the 400 series. Most notable is the work on 416 which has resulted in several improvements tailored to fill specific customer needs. An outstanding example is Duplex 416.

GENERAL MACHINING GUIDES

Some general hints on machining stainless steel are:

1. Machine tools should be rigid, modern, and as much "overpowered" as possible. The best practice is to use the machine up to about 75% of its rated capacity.

2. The workpiece and tool should be held rigid. Tool overhang should be minimized and extra support used when necessary.

3. Tools, either high-speed or carbide, should be kept sharp at all times, preferably being sharpened at regular intervals rather than out of necessity.

4. A good lubricant should be used such as sulfur-chlorinated petroleum oil. This is particularly useful for heavy cuts at relatively slow feeds. Thinning with paraffin oil is recommended for finish cuts at higher speeds; this blend will help keep the workpiece and tool cooler.

5. Particularly with the Cr-Ni austenitic grades, all possible care should be exercised to take positive cuts and avoid dwelling so as not to work harden and glaze the material.

The prime rule when machining stainless steels is, "get in and get out" with all tooling.

Box-Tool Turning Operations The cutting quality of stainless steel determines the rake and clearance angles required for satisfactory machining.

Generally, the tools employed on automatic machines, especially blade-type units, are arranged for tangent cutting. Lathe tools differ in that they are mounted for radial cutting. With single-point tools, the cutting angle, back rake, side rake, and front and side clearance are all ground into the tool. This is necessary because of the cutting action that takes place. With conventional box tools, balanced turning tools, and knee tools for automatic screw machines, tangential cutting simplifies tool geometry (see Fig. 2).

Box tools are standard equipment on automatic screw machines and turret lathes and are used extensively in turning all stainless steels. They have V-shaped or roller work supports and are used for roughing and finishing cuts. The V-type supports are susceptible to galling and seizing of work on some stainless steels. Roller-type rests are usually preferred.

Rollers must be set behind the cutting edge of the turning tool to eliminate the possibility of work hardening metal ahead of the box-tool blade.

Box tools are preferred to balance turning tools for machining of stainless steels as they offer a more rigid condition for cutting. Blades used in box tools should be of adequate size to eliminate chatter and help carry away heat (see Fig. 3).

Most turning blades require V grooves for chip curling or chip breaking to eliminate long stringy chips which clog the tool and mar the finish on the part being turned. The grooves should not break through the front cutting edge of the tool since a torn surface will result. This type of tool will also increase tool life and permit a heavy depth of cut (see Fig. 4).

Sometimes it is better to curl chips and let them fall to the bottom of the machine, rather than try to break them into small pieces when box turning some stainless steels. When high surface finish is a factor, a secondary operation should remove at least 0.010 to 0.020 in. (0.254 to 0.508 mm) at reduced feeds per revolution.

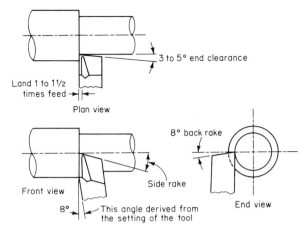

Fig. 2 Typical roller box turning tools.

High-speed steel tooling operated at conventional speeds and feeds is recommended. The use of high-cobalt steels permits increased speeds, but requires shallower depth of cut to avoid tool chipping. Carbide-insert tools are employed but usually require further reduction in depth of cut when compared with high-speed steel or cast-alloy tools when using comparable feeds. Carbides can be used to turn with extremely high speeds using 0.002 to 0.003 in. (0.051 to 0.076 mm) depth of cut and fine feeds.

Lubrication is necessary for turning operations. Sulfurized cutting oil is recommended for heavy cuts and may be thinned with paraffin oil for light feeds. Soluble oil is often used, especially with carbide tooling.

Drilling A sharp drill is an economical one. Loss of accuracy, increase in rejects, poor surface finish on the product, loss of tool materials through breakage or excessive grinding, higher tool and labor costs, and loss in output result from dull tools.

Any standard well-sharpened twist drill or oil hole drill made of high-speed steel will drill stainless steels satisfactorily. The included angle should be between 130 and 140°, with a clearance of 6 to 15° (see Fig. 5). This clearance will vary with the grade of stainless being used. It should be sufficient to prevent excessive rubbing action or work hardening at the bottom of the hole. However, it should not be so large that it weakens drill cutting edges or causes the drill to hog into the work.

Web thickness should be reduced to eliminate excessive heat generation and work hardening. A device for precision drill sharpening or measuring should be used when possible. Web thickness should normally be one-sixteenth of drill diameter (see Fig. 6).

If the cutting edges of a drill are unequal in length, the drill tends to crowd to one side.

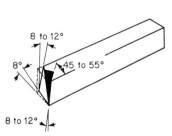

Fig. 3 Box tool blade illustrating chipbreaker. Employs a V-shaped hook for better chip handling. The narrower the hook the tighter the chip coil.

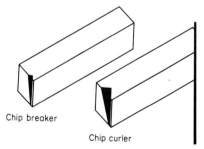

Fig. 4 Typical box tool blades.

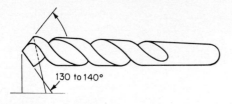

Fig. 5 Standard screw machine drill illustrating included angle.

Fig. 6 Twist drill showing thinned web.

This produces an oversize hole and the metal work hardens and glazes, making reaming and tapping extremely difficult. Honing the ground surfaces after sharpening increases drill life considerably.

When using a drill jig, bushings should be as short as possible. A clearance of at least one drill diameter between the bushing and the work will help clear chips. When drilling deep holes in excess of 5 or 6 diameters of the drill—whether on automatic screw machines or drill presses—it is recommended that crankshaft-type drills or drills with a high helix, correct cutting angle, and thinned web be used (see Fig. 7).

Should glazing or work hardening occur when using a drill press, chalk may be used on the drill cutting edges or in the hole of the workpiece to help start a cutting action through the glazed surface.

Speeds. Speeds or surface feet per minute vary with the grade of stainless being used. This variation can be from 40 to 125 surface ft/min (12 to 38 surface m/min). Factors controlling surface feet per minute are: wall thickness of the part, stainless grade, diameter of drill, and depth of hole being drilled.

Feeds. Feeds for drilling stainless also depend on drill diameter and the depth of hole; usually between 0.002 and 0.020 in. (0.051 and 0.508 mm). Normally, the larger the drill, the faster the feed. Dwells should be held to a minimum to reduce work hardening the metal, especially when drill pullouts are used.

If insufficient feed is maintained on a drill, a rubbing action dulls cutting edges causing work hardening of the metal. To prevent runout and breakage, use screw-machine-length drills whenever possible. The centering drill ahead of the drilling operation must be kept sharp and the dwell limited to minimize work hardening of metal.

Lubrication is necessary for all drilling operations. Sulfur-based oil is most normally used, either pure or diluted with paraffin oil. Soluble oil is sometimes used successfully if overheating becomes a problem.

Reaming The reaming operation is conducted on stainless steels for finishing holes requiring accuracy of dimension and smoothness of finish. This can be accomplished on holes previously machined by drilling, boring, or punching operations. It may be necessary to modify reamer styles and angles when reaming various grades of stainless because of the difference in cutting behaviors.

Standard-type reamers, either high-speed

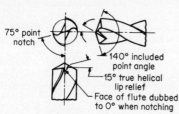

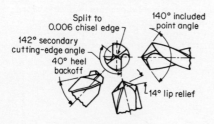

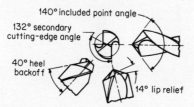

Fig. 7 Screw machine drill angles.

steel or carbide-tipped, with straight or spiral flute design, are in general use with various grades of stainless steel. Other types of reamers sometimes used are shell, adjustable, and inserted blade.

Although stainless steel can be reamed with all of the types mentioned above, those with spiral flutes usually produce better finish, are less susceptible to chattering, and can dispose of chips better when deep-hole reaming.

Stub-length screw-machine reamers are recommended for most screw-machine work. Left-hand spiral flutes and right-hand rotation for cutting is considered standard.

Due to their construction, solid reamers are the best choice in the smaller sizes since the possibility of error and deflection is reduced. They are sometimes uneconomical in larger sizes because of relatively higher costs. Some companies regrind solid reamers in the larger sizes to the next lower size if the range permits.

The quality of finish when reaming depends to a great extent on the proper width of lands and on the keen finish of the cutting edges. A polished finish on a reamer will

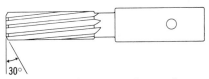

Fig. 8 Stub screw machine reamer showing clearance angle.

produce a better finish on the part. Oil stoning after grinding materially lengthens the life of the tool.

A definite cutting action is necessary in reaming stainless—otherwise burnishing or work hardening of metal may result. Reamer life is also shortened when there is an insufficient amount of stock to be removed. If the drill is too near the reamer size or cuts oversize, which they usually do, the reamer will not have enough bit and has a tendency to wedge rather than cut, resulting in excessive reamer wear or breakage.

Reamers should be mounted in a floating holder and usually remove from 0.006 to 0.016 in. (0.152 to 0.406 mm) for holes ¼ to 1 in. (6.35 to 25.4 mm) diameter. As the diameter of the hole increases, the amount allowed for reaming should be increased. Stub reamers or reamers as short as possible are used to eliminate bell-mouthed or tapered holes.

Grinding of reamers should be done in fixtures or on tool and cutter grinders to assure smooth accurate holes. For general applications, 30° lead on the chamfer angle with a clearance angle of approximately 7° is used. Reamers for machining stainless should be ordered with narrow land widths to reduce heat and rubbing in order to reduce work hardening of material (see Fig. 8).

Speeds. Speeds will vary with different grades of stainless in meeting dimensional tolerances, smooth finishes or both. On work where tolerance of hole is the main factor, higher speeds can be used. Lower speeds are recommended for smooth finishes. When using high-speed steel reamers, speeds of 35 to 50 surface ft/min (11 to 15 surface m/min) are used when finish is desired; if hole size is most important, 60 to 120 surface ft/min (18 to 37 surface m/min) is used. If the required finish is not obtained using sulfur-based oil, try thinning with paraffin oil.

Feeds. Feeds are based on type of material, depth of hole, finish required, and design of reamer being used. Feed per revolution is usually between 0.003 and 0.008 in. (0.076 and 0.203 mm) or slightly faster than the drilling feed used in the same type material.

Tapping All stainless steels may be tapped when special attention to selection of taps and equipment is followed. The free-machining types present fewer problems and are very similar to carbon steels. For all grades, a 15° hook grind has been found effective and such taps are commercially available. If taps being used do not have the recommended 15° hook, they should be reground (see Fig. 9).

Taps with thin lands should be used for deep-hole tapping to reduce bearing pressures (see Fig. 10). Rough threads are not always caused by the tap but may be the result of work hardening caused by drilling the material prior to the tapping operation.

Usually, high-speed steel taps with precision-ground threads and polished flutes are used. Use spiral-fluted taps when available since they offer better chip control and cut more freely than straight-fluted taps. Make sure taps are sharp; use taps as short in length as possible. If permissible, do not tap over 75% thread and generally, 65% is sufficient. Higher percentages of thread do not materially increase the strength of the thread and may cause breakage of the tap.

If, due to unusual requirements, specifications for minor diameters of tapped holes are especially exacting, it may be impractical to hold tolerances with a tap drill alone. Reaming after drilling may then be necessary. In such cases, the tap drill should be from 0.006 to 0.012 in. (0.152 to 0.305 mm) smaller than the minor tap diameter.

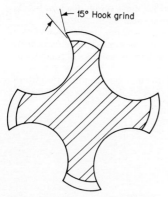

Fig. 9 Standard tap with required hook angle.

Do not attempt to grind taps freehand, especially the chamfer end, when working stainless. Gun-type taps should be avoided when tapping blind holes because of the packing of chips. Two-fluted taps are used for $\frac{1}{4}$ in. (6.35 mm) and smaller; three-fluted taps between $\frac{1}{4}$ and $\frac{1}{2}$ in. (6.35 and 12.70 mm); and four or more flutes over $\frac{1}{2}$ in. (12.70 mm) diameter.

Stainless steels may also be successfully tapped with fluteless taps.

Torn and rough threads may result from excessive tap-bearing area and may be overcome by decreasing the width of lands of tap by grinding down the heel (see Fig. 11). For the softer austenitic grades, taps with interrupted threads should be considered if torn or rough threads are a problem.

Speeds. Tapping speeds are usually slower for stainless than for carbon steels. They are controlled by the class of thread, hardness of material, wall thickness of the part, and usually fall within a range of 10 to 35 surface ft/min (3 to 11 surface m/min). Sulfur-based oils, under high pressure, are recommended for coarse threads; sulfur-based oil, cut back with paraffin oil, for fine threads. White lead is used on tapping machines when heavy cuts or full threads are required.

Threading Self-opening die heads are recommended for threading all grades of stainless steels. Solid dies are sometimes used, especially in smaller sizes below $\frac{1}{8}$-in. (3.175-mm) diameter. Larger sizes are likely to tear threads when they are backed off.

Standard high-speed steel chasers ground with about a 15° hook angle are used for

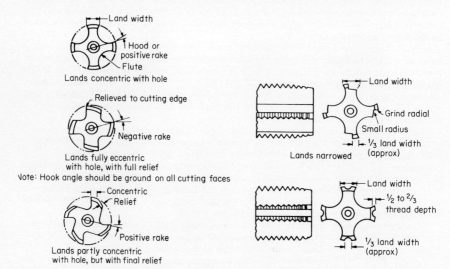

Fig. 10 Illustration of tap modified to reduce strength.

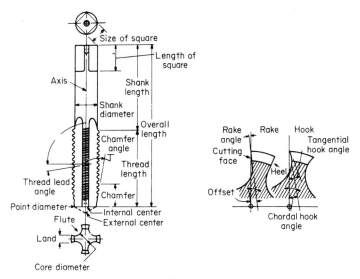

Fig. 11 Standard tap angles.

straight threads. Circular or tangent-type chasers require 20 to 25° rake angles (see Figs. 12 and 13).

Chasers should have a 1½- to 3-thread lead and must be ground by machine. A short lead or chamfer may cause chasers to chip or break and usually requires lower cutting speeds. Parts should be beveled or chamfered so that all chasers will start cutting more easily and at the same time. Normally, thread blanks should be the same diameter as the outside diameter of the threads to be cut. Oversize blanks can cause rough and ragged threads.

Speeds. Like other machining operations, threading of stainless steels depends on several factors, such as the type of stainless, thread size, finish, and speeds used. Better threads usually require lower speeds of 10 to 25 surface ft/min (3 to 8 surface m/min).

Lubrication is necessary for successful threading operations. Sulfurized cutting oil is

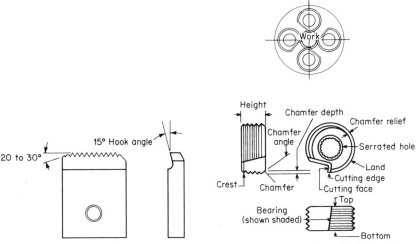

Fig. 12 Two views of a flat chaser.   **Fig. 13** Components of a circular die head chaser.

used, especially for coarse threads, and may be thinned with paraffin oil when cutting fine threads.

Because of the tremendous pressure stainless steel exerts on die heads when threading coarse threads, it is advisable to use larger die heads and chasers than are normally used. The larger chasers help carry away heat and usually retain their sharpness longer. If

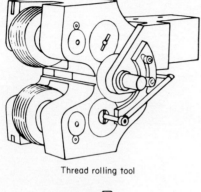

Thread rolling tool

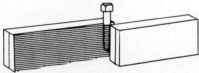

Reciprocating threading tool

Fig. 14   Typical threading tools.

Fig.   15   Typical   dovetail   form tool.

highly finished or extremely accurate threads are required, it may be necessary to produce these by thread grinding or chasing.

Thread Rolling   Tools, equipment and materials have been developed to the extent that thread rolling is accepted as a very practical method of producing precise threads on stainless steel parts. This is accomplished by several methods such as single roll or bump rolling, two-roll straddle type or tangent type, and threading the part from the end, similar to thread-cutting dies (see Fig. 14). These operations are performed on lathes and automatics.

Secondary thread-rolling operations are executed with various thread- and form-rolling principles such as cylindrical dies using two or three dies and reciprocating-type dies. Parts requiring long threads that must be rolled close to a shoulder use through-feed rolling in combination with in-feed rolling. In this type of operation, the cylindrical dies are actuated to feed to the required depth of thread at the shoulder position, then parts are automatically fed endwise to complete rolling the full length of thread required. When threads longer than the normal die widths or full-length bars must be threaded, the through-feed method is used.

Where parts are to be roll-threaded, chamfer on each end of the thread should be 30°. In case the end threads do not fill out, or where the thread rolls chip, the chamfer should be decreased and penetration time of thread rolls should also be decreased.

For roll-threading stainless steels, the diameter of blank must be held within a few ten-thousandths of an inch and is usually held slightly below the pitch diameter of the thread. Care should be exercised to prevent work hardening of the metal before thread rolling.

Speeds used when thread rolling on lathes and automatics are usually the same as for other tools. Feeds recommended when thread rolling stainless steels with the two-roll straddle-type method are usually 0.008 to 0.012 in. (0.203 to 0.305 mm) depending on diameter and threads per inch. For feed selection consult thread-rolling equipment suppliers.

Lubrication is necessary when thread rolling. Sulfurized cutting oil is normally used, especially for coarse threads, and may be thinned with paraffin oil when cutting fine threads.

Forming   The efficiency of forming tools is governed by speed, feed, width of the form tool, depth of cut, diameter of stock and design of the tool. When rough forming on multiple-spindle automatic screw machines, it is recommended, when possible, to break sharp corners and increase side clearances to the limits allowed. This requires

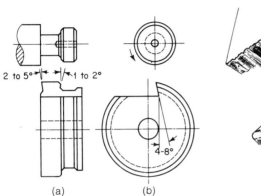

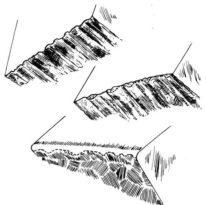

Fig. 16   Circular form tool illustrating (a) side rake angle and (b) top rake angle.

Fig. 17   Honing tool cutting edge. After a tool has been ground, minute peaks make up the cutting edge (top). During cutting these bear the brunt of pressure and break off until the whole edge is dull (center). Honing or lapping the cutting edge to a small radius by rocking the tool slightly creates a more lasting edge (bottom).

using a finish form tool, and if finish or close tolerance is a factor, a shave-tool operation should be added.

The clearance mentioned above is easily ground on simple flat form tools. However, on circular or dovetail form tools, little change can be made (see Fig. 15).

The top rake angle ground in form tools influences the finish of the formed parts. This angle should be between 4 and 10° for best results. Numerous shops use an 8° top rake angle for rough-forming operations and 4° for finish-forming operations (see Fig. 16). These angles usually extend tool life and give the best finish. The finish must be smooth on the form tool to reproduce on the formed part (see Fig. 17).

Experience has proven that the top face of the tool, where the chips pass over, should be polished to a very fine finish. If this finish has grinding marks, the chips have a tendency to telescope. This can mar the finish and interfere with the oil stream.

When insufficient feed is maintained on a form tool, a rubbing action is set up that dulls the cutting edge very rapidly. The tools should have sufficient feed, especially at the beginning of the cut, to eliminate glazing and work hardening of the metal. Dwell (the end of the form tool cut) should also be held to a minimum to prevent work hardening and glazing of the part. When glazing occurs, it is more difficult to perform satisfactory thread rolling, knurling, or secondary turning operations.

The amount of material removed with a form tool can become a factor. A part requiring turning of only 0.002 to 0.004 in. (0.051 to 0.102 mm) from the stock diameter always presents a problem. If possible, the next size larger stock should be considered.

To reduce chatter marks usually caused by vibration, it is necessary to keep machines and toolholder fixtures as rigid as possible, reduce the overhang of tools, and use steady rests on long slender parts.

If the cutting edge of a form tool chips, it is usually caused by excessive top rake. Here, the suggested remedy is to grind less top rake angle on the form tool.

If the cutting edge of a form tool burns, the cause may be excessive speed or the tool may have been burned while sharpening. The latter often can happen without being

TABLE 1 Stainless Steel Machining Data: Feeds and Speeds for Automatics with High-Speed Steel Tools

Machining operation	Width or depth, in. (mm)	Diameter of hole, in. (mm)	303MA Surface ft/min*	303MA Feed†	303 303Se Surface ft/min	303 303Se Feed
End working tools:						
Balance turning	0.250 (6.35)		150	0.0055	140	0.0055
Boring	0.005–0.010 (0.13–0.25)		100	0.0055	100	0.0055
Box tools	0.062 (1.58)		150	0.0065	140	0.0065
	0.125 (3.18)		150	0.006	140	0.006
	0.250 (6.35)		145	0.0055	135	0.0055
	0.375 (9.53)		140	0.0047	135	0.0047
	0.500 (12.7)		135	0.004	130	0.004
Chamfer and face			150	0.006	140	0.006
Counterbore and trepan	0.0935 (2.37)	½ (812.7)	100	0.003	100	0.003
Drills		⅛ (3.18)	100	0.003	100	0.003
		¼ (6.35)	100	0.004	100	0.004
		⅜ (9.53)	100	0.0045	100	0.0045
		½ (12.7)	100	0.0045	100	0.0045
		¾ (19.1)	105	0.0055	105	0.0055
		1 (25.4)	105	0.0064	105	0.0064
		1¼ (31.8)	110	0.007	110	0.007
Hollow mill	0.062 (1.58)		135	0.0085	130	0.0085
	0.125 (3.18)		125	0.0068	125	0.0068
	0.187 (4.75)		120	0.006	120	0.006
	0.250 (6.35)		115	0.0055	115	0.0055
Knurl tools—On			150	0.011	140	0.011
(Turret)—Off			150	0.022	140	0.022
Pointing and Facing			150	0.0015	140	0.0015
Reamers		Under ½ (12.7)	Sizing 90	0.006	90	0.006
		Over ½ (12.7)	90	0.0085	90	0.0085
			Finish 35	0.0035	35	0.0035
Recessing			100	0.001	90	0.001
Taps			10–25		10–25	
Threading dies			10–25		10–25	
Cross-slide tools:						
Cutoff	0.062 (1.58)		150	0.0017	140	0.0017
	0.125 (3.18)		150	0.0021	140	0.0021
	0.187 (4.75)		150	0.0022	140	0.0022
	0.250 (6.35)		150	0.0025	140	0.0025
Form (circular, flat, dovetail)	0.500 (12.7)		150	0.0021	140	0.0021
	1.000 (25.4)		145	0.0017	135	0.0017
	1.500 (38.1)		145	0.0015	135	0.0015
	2.000 (50.8)		140	0.0013	130	0.0013
	2.500 (63.5)		135	0.001	125	0.001
Knurl ⅜ in. max. width			150	0.012	140	0.012
Shave tool	0.500 (12.7)		150	0.0021	140	0.0021
	1.000 (25.4)		145	0.0017	135	0.0017
	1.500 (38.1)		145	0.0015	135	0.0015
	2.000 (50.8)		140	0.0013	130	0.0013

*Surface ft/min × 0.3048 = surface m/min.
†Feed × 25.4 = mm feed per revolution.

201 202 301 302 304		305 316 347FSe / 304L 304N 309 309S 309SCb 310 314 / 316L 317 318 347 348		416F		416		416HH 416HT (26–32R$_c$) 430F 430FSe 434		420F 420FSe	
Surface ft/min	Feed	Surface ft/min	Feed	Surface ft/min	Feed	Surface ft/min	Feed	Surface ft/min	Feed	Surface ft/min	Feed
100	0.0045	70	0.004	165	0.0057	160	0.0052	150	0.005	100	0.0045
80	0.004	60	0.0035	115	0.0057	110	0.0052	100	0.005	80	0.0045
100	0.005	70	0.004	165	0.0067	160	0.0062	150	0.006	100	0.0057
95	0.0045	70	0.003	165	0.0057	160	0.0052	150	0.005	100	0.0045
95	0.0045	65	0.003	160	0.005	155	0.005	145	0.0047	95	0.0045
90	0.004	60	0.0025	155	0.005	150	0.0045	140	0.0042	95	0.004
90	0.0035	60	0.0025	150	0.0045	145	0.004	135	0.0037	90	0.0035
100	0.0045	70	0.004	165	0.0062	160	0.0057	150	0.0055	100	0.005
65	0.002	40	0.0018	115	0.0035	110	0.003	100	0.0027	50	0.0025
65	0.002	40	0.0018	115	0.0035	110	0.003	100	0.0027	50	0.0025
70	0.0033	45	0.003	115	0.0042	110	0.0037	100	0.0035	55	0.0032
70	0.0035	45	0.0032	115	0.0045	110	0.004	100	0.0037	55	0.0035
70	0.0037	45	0.0035	115	0.0047	110	0.0042	100	0.004	55	0.0037
70	0.0042	50	0.004	120	0.0055	115	0.005	105	0.0047	60	0.0042
70	0.0052	50	0.005	120	0.006	115	0.0057	105	0.0055	60	0.005
75	0.006	50	0.0055	125	0.007	120	0.0067	110	0.0064	65	0.0055
130	0.0065	65	0.006	150	0.008	145	0.0075	135	0.0072	90	0.0065
125	0.0055	60	0.005	140	0.0065	135	0.006	125	0.0058	85	0.005
120	0.0048	55	0.0045	135	0.006	130	0.0052	120	0.005	80	0.0045
115	0.0045	55	0.004	130	0.0055	125	0.005	115	0.0047	75	0.0042
140	0.009	70	0.009	165	0.012	160	0.011	150	0.010	100	0.009
140	0.018	70	0.018	165	0.024	160	0.022	150	0.020	100	0.018
140	0.0013	70	0.0012	165	0.002	160	0.0015	150	0.0013	100	0.0012
90	0.005	60	0.0045	105	0.0057	100	0.0052	90	0.005	75	0.0045
90	0.007	60	0.0065	105	0.008	100	0.0075	90	0.0072	75	0.0062
35	0.003	35	0.003	50	0.0042	45	0.0037	35	0.0035	35	0.0035
90	0.0008	60	0.0007	115	0.0017	110	0.0012	100	0.001	75	0.0008
10–25		10–25		15–35		15–30		10–25		10–25	
10–25		10–25		15–35		15–30		10–25		10–25	
140	0.0012	70	0.001	165	0.0022	160	0.0017	150	0.0015	100	0.0013
140	0.0018	70	0.0015	165	0.0027	160	0.0022	150	0.002	100	0.0017
140	0.0018	70	0.0015	165	0.0027	160	0.0022	150	0.002	100	0.0017
140	0.002	70	0.0017	165	0.0032	160	0.0027	150	0.0024	100	0.0021
140	0.0015	70	0.0012	165	0.0025	160	0.002	150	0.0018	100	0.0017
135	0.0012	65	0.001	160	0.0022	155	0.0017	145	0.0014	95	0.0013
135	0.0012	65	0.001	160	0.002	155	0.0015	145	0.0013	95	0.0012
130	0.001	60	0.0009	155	0.0018	150	0.0013	140	0.0011	90	0.001
125	0.0008	55	0.0007	150	0.0016	145	0.0011	135	0.0009	85	0.0008
140	0.010	70	0.009	165	0.0117	160	0.0112	150	0.011	100	0.010
140	0.0015	70	0.0015	165	0.0025	160	0.002	150	0.0018	100	0.0017
135	0.0012	65	0.001	160	0.0021	155	0.0016	145	0.0014	95	0.0013
135	0.0012	65	0.001	160	0.002	155	0.0015	145	0.0013	95	0.0012
130	0.001	60	0.0009	155	0.0018	150	0.0013	140	0.0011	90	·0.001

TABLE 1   Stainless Steel Machining Data: Feeds and Speeds for Automatics with High-Speed Steel Tools (Continued)

	403 405 410 430		414 420 431 440A 440FSe		440B 440C		CR-1	260 BHN	15-5PH 17-4PH 17-7PH 17-14CuMo
							Annealed		Annealed
Machining operation	Surface ft/min	Feed	Surface ft/min	Feed	Surface ft/min	Feed	Surface ft/min	Feed	Surface ft/min
End working tools:									
Balance turning	95	0.004	75	0.0035	65	0.0035	80	0.0045	55
Boring	80	0.004	65	0.0035	55	0.0035	60	0.004	50
Box tools	95	0.0055	75	0.005	65	0.005	80	0.005	55
	90	0.0042	75	0.004	65	0.004	75	0.0045	50
	85	0.0042	75	0.004	60	0.004	75	0.0045	50
	85	0.0038	70	0.0035	60	0.0035	70	0.004	45
	80	0.0032	70	0.003	60	0.003	70	0.0035	40
Chamfer and face	95	0.0045	75	0.004	65	0.004	80	0.0045	55
Counterbore and trepan	45	0.0023	45	0.002	45	0.002	45	0.002	45
Drills	45	0.0023	45	0.002	45	0.002	50	0.0025	50
	48	0.003	48	0.0029	48	0.0027	50	0.003	50
	48	0.0032	48	0.003	48	0.003	55	0.0035	50
	48	0.0035	48	0.0032	48	0.0032	60	0.004	50
	52	0.004	52	0.0038	52	0.0038	60	0.0045	50
	52	0.0047	52	0.0042	52	0.0042	60	0.005	50
	54	0.005	54	0.0045	54	0.0045	60	0.0055	50
Hollow mill	70	0.006	70	0.0055	70	0.0055	70	0.006	60
	65	0.0045	65	0.004	65	0.004	65	0.0055	55
	60	0.0042	60	0.004	60	0.004	60	0.005	55
	60	0.004	60	0.0037	60	0.0037	60	0.005	55
Knurl tools—On (Turret)—Off	95	0.009	75	0.009	65	0.009	80	0.009	55
	95	0.018	75	0.018	65	0.018	80	0.018	55
Pointing and Facing	95	0.0011	75	0.0010	65	0.0010	80	0.0013	55
Reamers	75	0.0035	75	0.003	70	0.003	70	0.005	60
	75	0.005	75	0.0045	70	0.0045	70	0.007	55
	35	0.0035	35	0.003	35	0.003	35	0.003	35
Recessing	70	0.0007	60	0.0006	50	0.0006	70	0.001	50
Taps	10–25		10–25		10–25		10–25		10–25
Threading dies	10–25		10–25		10–25		10–25		10–25
Cross-slide tools:									
Cutoff	95	0.0011	75	0.001	65	0.001	80	0.0012	55
	95	0.0015	75	0.0012	65	0.0012	80	0.0018	55
	95	0.0015	75	0.0012	65	0.0012	80	0.0018	55
	95	0.002	75	0.0018	65	0.0018	80	0.002	55
Form (circular, flat, dovetail)	95	0.0015	75	0.0012	65	0.0012	80	0.0015	55
	90	0.0011	70	0.001	60	0.001	75	0.0012	50
	90	0.001	70	0.0009	60	0.0009	75	0.0012	50
	85	0.0009	65	0.0008	55	0.0008	70	0.001	45
	80	0.0007	60	0.0006	50	0.0006	65	0.0001	45
Knurl ⅜ in. max. width	95	0.009	75	0.008	65	0.008	80	0.010	55
Shave tool	95	0.0015	75	0.0012	65	0.0012	80	0.0015	55
	90	0.0011	70	0.001	60	0.001	75	0.0012	50
	90	0.001	70	0.009	60	0.0009	75	0.0012	50
	85	0.0009	65	0.0009	55	0.0008	70	0.001	45

Stainless Steel Type

| AF-71 AFC-77 Almar 362 (AM-362) AM-350 | | | AM-355 Custom 455 HNM | | PH 13-8Mo PH 14-8Mo PH 15-7Mo Stainless W | | 18-2FM | |
| 150 BHN 250 BHN | Hardened | 275 BHN 325 BHN | 325 BHN 375 BHN | | 375 BHN 440 BHN | | | |
Feed	Surface ft/min	Feed	Surface ft/min	Feed	Surface ft/min	Feed	Surface ft/min	Feed
0.0035	50	0.0035	45	0.003	40	0.0025	220	0.006
0.0035	50	0.0035	45	0.003	40	0.0025	165	0.006
0.0045	50	0.004	45	0.004	40	0.0035	220	0.007
0.0045	50	0.004	45	0.004	40	0.003	220	0.006
0.004	45	0.0035	40	0.0035	35	0.003	215	0.0055
0.004	40	0.0035	40	0.003	35	0.0025	210	0.005
0.0035	40	0.003	35	0.0025	30	0.002	200	0.0045
0.004	50	0.004	45	0.003	40	0.003	220	0.0065
0.002	45	0.002	40	0.002	35	0.002	165	0.004
0.0025	45	0.002	35	0.002	25	0.0015	165	0.004
0.003	45	0.0025	35	0.0025	25	0.0002	165	0.0042
0.0035	45	0.003	35	0.003	25	0.0025	165	0.0045
0.004	45	0.0035	35	0.0035	25	0.003	165	0.0047
0.0045	45	0.004	35	0.004	25	0.0035	170	0.0055
0.0055	45	0.005	35	0.005	25	0.004	170	0.006
0.0055	45	0.0055	35	0.0055	25	0.005	175	0.007
0.0045	55	0.004	50	0.0035	45	0.003	200	0.008
0.0045	55	0.004	50	0.0035	45	0.003	190	0.007
0.004	55	0.0035	50	0.003	45	0.002	175	0.0065
0.004	50	0.0035	45	0.003	45	0.002	170	0.006
0.008	50	0.008	45	0.008	40	0.008	220	0.012
0.016	50	0.016	45	0.016	40	0.016	220	0.024
0.001	55	0.001	50	0.001	45	0.001	220	0.002
0.003	55	0.0025	50	0.002	45	0.002	150	0.006
0.003	50	0.0025	45	0.002	40	0.002	150	0.008
0.003	35	0.0025	35	0.002	35	0.002		
0.001	50	0.001	45	0.0007	45	0.0007	165	0.002
	10–25		10–25		10–25		15–35	
	10–25		10–25		10–25		15–35	
0.001	50	0.001	45	0.001	40	0.001	220	0.0025
0.001	50	0.001	45	0.001	40	0.001	220	0.0027
0.0015	50	0.001	45	0.001	40	0.001	220	0.003
0.0015	50	0.001	45	0.001	40	0.001	220	0.0032
0.0012	50	0.001	45	0.0006	40	0.0005	220	0.0025
0.0012	45	0.0008	40	0.0006	35	0.0005	220	0.0022
0.001	45	0.0008	40	0.0006	35	0.0004	210	0.002
0.001	45	0.0008	40	0.0006	35	0.0004	205	0.0018
0.001	40	0.0008	35	0.0006	30	0.0004	200	0.0016
0.008	55	0.008	45	0.008	45	0.008	220	0.0117
0.0012	50	0.001	45	0.0006	40	0.0005	220	0.0025
0.0012	45	0.0008	40	0.0006	35	0.0005	215	0.0021
0.001	45	0.0008	40	0.0006	35	0.0004	210	0.002
0.001	40	0.0008	35	0.0006	30	0.0004	205	0.0018

visible, but will show up after etching in acid. Sometimes a tool material with higher red hardness or a change in cutting oil may be required to eliminate burning.

Rough finishes can be caused by dull tools, insufficient feed, excessive feeds, improper top rake angle, or a cutting oil that is not carrying away the heat. Increased surface feet per minute will sometimes eliminate a rough finish problem (see Tables 1 and 2). If possible,

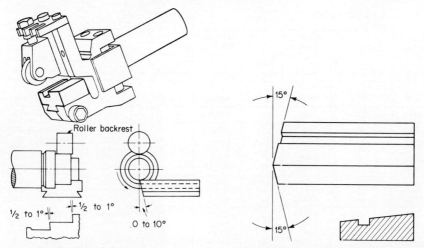

Fig. 18   Typical shaving tool.   **Fig. 19**   Skive tool illustrating clearance angle.

a turning operation preceding the forming operation will extend tool life and improve its finish.

Lubrication is necessary for all forming operations. Sulfurized cutting oil is recommended for heavy cuts and may be thinned with paraffin oil for light forming operations. Soluble oil is used occasionally when carbide-insert tools are used.

Shaving Operations   The shave tool is used for close tolerance and fine finishes on the OD of work machined on multiple-spindle automatic screw machines. Since a roller backrest is used in conjunction with a shave tool, the cutting pressures are high; therefore, only 0.005 to 0.010 in. (0.127 to 0.254 mm) material is removed.

Unlike form tools that cut radially, the shave tool is a tangent cutting tool and floats on a hinged area causing the tool and roller to seek their own centers (see Fig. 18).

Tool materials for shave tools are made of high-speed steel, cast-alloy, or carbide-tipped tools and use approximately the same feeds specified for forming operations (Table 1).

Lubrication is required for shaving operations and use of sulfurized cutting oil is recommended. This oil may be thinned with paraffin oil. Occasionally soluble oil is used on some free-machining stainless steels. Clearance angles are usually 3 to 8°; sharpening should be done with a fine-grit wheel.

Skiving   The skive tool is used for machining special-shaped stainless steel parts on automatic screw machines. This tool produces accurate sizes and fine finishes. It can be used to machine parts that might break off if a plunge cut were made with a form tool. Good examples of parts machined with a skive tool are mechanical pencil points.

Usually a skive tool is a flat tool made of either high-speed steel or carbide. The cutting angle may be from 5 to 30° depending on the diameter of stock used and diameters being turned. Normally a 15° cutting angle and 15° clearance angle will produce acceptable parts (see Fig. 19). These tools are operated at feeds and speeds used for form tools and may require steady rests or supports to eliminate breaking off of the part being machined. Best results are obtained if the skive tool removes only 0.005 or 0.010 in. (0.127 or 0.254 mm) of metal. Lubrication is required for skiving operations and sulfur-based oil is recommended. If thinning is necessary, use paraffin oil. Due to the skive-tool angle, a longer stroke is necessary, limiting its application and increasing cycle time.

Knurling   Knurling can be accomplished on all stainless steels by the screw machine and lathe method. This operation is used to raise or roughen surfaces of turned work by

TABLE 2   Conversion of Surface ft/min* to rpm

ft/min	10	15	20	25	30	40	50	60	70	80	90	100
Diam., in. (mm)							rpm					
¹⁄₁₆ (1.59)	611	917	1223	1528	1834	2445	3057	3668	4280	4891	5502	6114
⅛ (3.18)	306	459	611	764	917	1222	1528	1834	2139	2445	2750	3056
³⁄₁₆ (4.76)	204	306	408	509	611	815	1019	1222	1426	1630	1834	2038
¼ (6.35)	153	229	306	382	458	611	764	917	1070	1222	1376	1528
⁵⁄₁₆ (7.94)	122	183	245	306	367	489	611	733	856	978	1100	1222
⅜ (9.53)	102	153	204	255	306	408	509	611	713	815	916	1018
⁷⁄₁₆ (11.11)	87	131	175	218	262	349	437	524	611	699	786	874
½ (12.70)	76	115	153	191	229	306	382	459	535	611	688	764
⁹⁄₁₆ (14.29)	68	102	136	170	204	272	340	407	475	543	611	679
⅝ (15.88)	61	92	123	153	184	245	306	367	428	489	552	612
¹¹⁄₁₆ (17.46)	56	83	111	139	167	222	278	333	389	444	500	555
¾ (19.05)	51	76	102	127	153	203	254	306	357	409	458	508
¹³⁄₁₆ (20.64)	47	71	95	119	142	190	237	282	332	379	427	474
⅞ (22.23)	44	66	87	109	131	175	219	262	306	349	392	438
¹⁵⁄₁₆ (23.81)	41	61	81	101	122	163	204	244	285	326	366	407
1 (25.40)	38	57	76	96	115	153	191	229	267	306	344	382
1¹⁄₁₆ (26.99)	36	54	72	90	108	144	180	215	251	287	323	359
1⅛ (28.58)	34	51	68	85	102	136	170	204	238	272	306	340
1³⁄₁₆ (30.16)	32	48	64	81	97	129	161	193	225	258	290	322
1¼ (31.75)	31	46	61	76	92	123	153	183	214	245	274	306
1⁵⁄₁₆ (33.34)	29	44	58	73	87	116	146	175	204	233	262	291
1⅜ (34.93)	28	42	56	70	83	111	139	167	195	222	250	278
1⁷⁄₁₆ (36.51)	27	40	53	66	80	106	133	159	186	212	239	265
1½ (38.10)	25	38	51	64	76	102	127	153	178	204	230	254
1⁹⁄₁₆ (39.69)	24	37	49	61	73	98	122	146	171	195	220	244
1⅝ (41.28)	24	35	47	59	71	94	117	141	165	188	212	234
1¹¹⁄₁₆ (42.86)	23	34	45	57	68	90	113	136	158	181	203	226
1¾ (44.45)	22	33	44	55	66	87	109	131	153	175	196	218
1¹³⁄₁₆ (46.04)	21	32	42	53	63	84	106	127	148	169	190	211
1⅞ (47.63)	20	31	41	51	61	82	102	122	143	163	184	204
1¹⁵⁄₁₆ (49.21)	20	30	39	49	59	79	99	118	138	158	177	197
2 (50.80)	19	29	38	48	57	76	96	115	134	153	172	191
2⅛ (53.98)	18	27	36	45	54	72	90	108	126	144	162	180
2¼ (57.15)	17	25	34	42	51	68	86	102	119	136	153	170
2⅜ (60.33)	16	24	32	40	48	64	81	97	113	129	145	161
2½ (63.50)	15	23	31	38	46	61	76	92	107	122	138	153
2⅝ (66.68)	14	22	29	36	44	58	73	87	102	116	131	145
2¾ (69.85)	14	21	28	35	42	56	70	83	97	111	125	139
2⅞ (73.03)	13	20	26	33	40	53	66	79	92	106	119	132
3 (76.20)	13	19	26	32	38	51	64	76	89	102	114	127
3⅛ (79.38)	12	18	24	31	37	49	61	73	85	98	110	122
3¼ (82.55)	12	18	23	29	35	47	58	70	82	94	105	117
3⅜ (85.73)	12	17	23	28	34	45	57	68	79	90	102	113
3½ (88.90)	11	16	22	27	33	44	55	66	76	87	98	109
3⅝ (92.08)	11	16	21	26	32	42	52	63	74	84	95	105
3¾ (95.25)	10	15	20	26	31	41	51	61	71	82	92	102
3⅞ (98.43)	10	15	20	25	30	39	49	59	69	79	89	99
4 (101.60)	10	14	19	24	29	38	48	57	67	76	86	96

*Surface ft/min × 0.3048 = surface m/min.

TABLE 2 Conversion of Surface ft/min* to rpm (Continued)

ft/min	110	120	130	140	150	160	170	180	190	200	210
Diam., in. (mm)						rpm					
¹⁄₁₆ (1.59)	6725	7337	7948	8560	9171	9782	—	—	—	—	—
⅛ (3.18)	3362	3667	3973	4278	4584	4890	5195	5501	5806	6112	6417
³⁄₁₆ (4.76)	2242	2446	2649	2853	3055	3261	3465	3668	3872	4076	4278
¼ (6.35)	1681	1832	1986	2139	2292	2445	2598	2750	2903	3056	3209
⁵⁄₁₆ (7.94)	1344	1466	1589	1711	1833	1955	2077	2200	2322	2444	2567
⅜ (9.53)	1121	1222	1323	1425	1527	1629	1731	1832	1934	2036	2139
⁷⁄₁₆ (11.11)	961	1049	1136	1224	1311	1398	1486	1573	1661	1748	1833
½ (12.70)	840	917	993	1070	1146	1222	1299	1375	1452	1528	1604
⁹⁄₁₆ (14.29)	747	813	883	951	1019	1086	1154	1222	1290	1358	1426
⅝ (15.88)	673	736	796	857	918	979	1040	1102	1163	1224	1283
¹¹⁄₁₆ (17.46)	611	666	722	770	833	888	944	999	1054	1110	1167
¾ (19.05)	559	610	661	711	762	813	864	914	965	1016	1070
¹³⁄₁₆ (20.64)	521	569	616	664	711	758	806	853	901	948	987
⅞ (22.23)	482	526	569	613	657	701	745	788	832	876	917
¹⁵⁄₁₆ (23.81)	448	488	529	570	611	651	692	733	773	814	857
1 (25.40)	420	458	497	535	573	611	649	688	726	764	802
1¹⁄₁₆ (26.99)	395	431	467	503	539	579	610	646	682	718	755
1⅛ (28.58)	374	408	442	476	510	544	578	612	646	680	714
1³⁄₁₆ (30.16)	354	386	419	451	483	515	547	580	612	644	675
1¼ (31.75)	337	367	398	428	459	490	520	551	581	612	641
1⁵⁄₁₆ (33.34)	320	349	378	407	437	466	495	524	553	582	611
1⅜ (34.93)	306	334	361	389	417	445	472	500	528	556	584
1⁷⁄₁₆ (36.51)	292	318	345	371	398	424	451	477	504	530	558
1½ (38.10)	279	305	330	356	381	406	432	457	483	509	535
1⁹⁄₁₆ (39.69)	268	293	317	342	366	390	415	439	464	488	514
1⅝ (41.28)	257	281	304	328	351	374	398	421	445	468	493
1¹¹⁄₁₆ (42.86)	249	271	294	316	339	362	384	407	429	452	475
1¾ (44.45)	240	262	283	305	327	349	371	392	414	436	459
1¹³⁄₁₆ (46.04)	232	253	274	295	317	338	359	380	401	422	443
1⅞ (47.63)	224	244	265	286	306	326	347	367	388	408	428
1¹⁵⁄₁₆ (49.21)	217	236	256	276	296	315	335	355	374	394	414
2 (50.80)	210	229	248	267	287	306	325	344	363	382	402
2⅛ (53.98)	198	216	234	252	270	288	306	324	342	360	378
2¼ (57.15)	187	204	221	238	255	272	289	306	313	340	357
2⅜ (60.33)	177	193	209	225	242	258	274	290	306	322	338
2½ (63.50)	168	184	199	213	230	245	260	275	291	306	321
2⅝ (66.68)	160	174	189	203	218	232	247	261	276	290	306
2¾ (69.85)	153	167	181	195	209	222	236	250	264	278	292
2⅞ (73.03)	145	158	172	185	198	211	224	238	251	264	279
3 (76.20)	140	152	165	178	191	203	216	228	241	254	267
3⅛ (79.38)	134	146	159	171	183	195	207	219	232	244	257
3¼ (82.55)	129	140	152	164	176	188	199	211	222	234	247
3⅜ (85.73)	124	136	147	158	170	181	192	203	215	226	238
3½ (88.90)	120	131	142	153	164	174	186	196	207	218	229
3⅝ (92.08)	116	126	137	147	158	168	179	189	200	210	221
3¾ (95.25)	112	122	133	143	153	163	175	184	194	205	214
3⅞ (98.43)	108	118	128	138	148	158	167	177	186	197	207
4 (101.60)	105	115	124	134	143	153	163	172	182	191	201

220	230	240	250	260	270	280	290	300	325	350	375	400
—	—	—	—	—	—	—	—	—	—	—	—	—
6723	7028	7334	7639	7945	8251	8556	8862	9171	9935	10699	11463	—
4482	4686	4890	5093	5297	5501	5705	5908	6114	6623	7133	7642	8152
3361	3514	3667	3820	3972	4125	4278	4431	4584	4966	5348	5730	6112
2689	2811	2934	3056	3178	3300	3423	3545	3666	3971	4277	4582	4888
2241	2343	2445	2546	2648	2750	2852	2954	3057	3311	3566	3821	4076
1921	2008	2095	2183	2270	2357	2445	2532	2620	2838	3057	3275	3494
1681	1757	1833	1910	1986	2063	2139	2215	2292	2483	2675	2866	3057
1494	1562	1630	1698	1766	1833	1901	1969	2037	2207	2377	2547	2717
1345	1406	1467	1528	1589	1650	1711	1772	1834	1987	2139	2292	2445
1222	1278	1333	1389	1445	1500	1556	1611	1667	1806	1941	2084	2223
1120	1171	1222	1273	1324	1375	1426	1477	1528	1655	1783	1910	2038
1034	1081	1128	1175	1222	1269	1316	1363	1410	1528	1646	1763	1881
960	1004	1048	1091	1135	1179	1222	1266	1310	1419	1528	1637	1746
896	937	978	1019	1059	1100	1141	1182	1222	1324	1426	1528	1630
840	879	917	955	993	1031	1070	1108	1146	1241	1337	1432	1528
791	827	863	899	935	971	1007	1043	1078	1168	1258	1348	1438
747	781	815	849	883	917	951	985	1018	1103	1188	1273	1358
708	740	772	804	836	868	901	933	965	1045	1126	1206	1287
672	703	733	764	794	825	856	886	917	993	1069	1146	1222
640	669	698	728	757	786	815	844	873	946	1018	1091	1164
611	639	667	694	722	750	778	806	833	903	972	1042	1111
584	611	638	664	691	717	744	771	797	863	930	996	1063
560	586	611	637	662	688	713	738	764	827	891	955	1018
538	562	587	611	636	660	684	709	733	794	855	916	978
517	541	564	588	611	635	658	682	705	764	822	881	940
498	521	543	566	589	611	634	656	679	735	792	849	905
481	502	524	546	567	589	611	633	654	709	764	818	873
464	485	506	527	548	569	590	611	632	685	737	790	843
449	469	489	509	530	550	570	591	611	662	713	764	815
434	453	473	493	513	532	552	572	591	640	690	739	788
421	439	458	477	497	516	535	554	573	620	668	716	764
395	413	431	449	467	485	503	521	539	584	629	674	719
374	390	407	424	441	458	475	492	509	551	594	636	679
353	370	386	402	418	434	450	466	482	522	563	603	643
336	344	367	382	397	413	428	443	458	496	534	573	611
320	335	349	364	378	393	407	422	436	472	509	545	582
306	319	333	347	361	375	389	403	416	451	486	520	555
292	306	319	332	345	359	372	385	398	431	465	498	531
279	293	306	318	331	344	357	369	381	413	445	477	509
268	281	293	306	318	330	342	354	366	397	427	458	488
259	270	282	294	306	317	329	341	352	381	411	440	470
249	260	272	283	294	306	317	328	339	367	396	424	452
240	251	262	273	284	295	306	316	327	354	381	409	436
232	242	253	263	274	285	295	306	316	342	368	395	421
224	234	244	255	265	275	285	295	305	331	356	382	407
217	227	237	246	256	266	276	285	295	320	345	369	394
210	220	229	239	248	258	267	277	286	310	334	358	382

revolving hardened steel wheels against the work. Straight, diamond, spiral, or rope knurling are accomplished in various ways on the machines mentioned above.

Sometimes the knurl or a pair of knurls operates straight in from a cross slide or a single knurl passes over the top of the piece. Other knurling operations are performed by feeding on the end of piece with an adjustable knurl holder that carries a pair of straight knurls. If these knurls are set parallel to the axis of the work, they produce a straight-knurled surface and if set at an angle, produce either a spiral or diamond knurl.

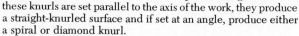

Speeds used are the same as those used for turning operations (Table 1). Feeds are considerably higher than for forming operations, usually 0.008 to 0.012 in./rev (0.203 to 0.305 mm/rev) is normal for cross-slide knurling. Feeds per revolution recommended when knurling from the end of part are 0.009 to 0.011 in. (0.229 to 0.279 mm). This is called on feed. The off feed should be double the on feed, or 0.018 to 0.022 in. (0.457 to 0.559 mm) (see Table 1). Sulfurized chlorinated oils or water-soluble oils are also used to eliminate heat and the possibility of metal flaking.

Roller Burnishing   All stainless steels that are machinable on automatic screw machines or lathes can also be roller burnished. This is a process often overlooked when surface finishing is a problem. Burnishing, properly applied, has delivered surface finishes down to 5 μin. (see Fig. 20).

To obtain such results calls for an understanding of the method used and its limitations. Roller burnishing usually does not change the workpiece diameter. This process should not be used to correct tapered dimensions or true up bell-mouthed parts on ID work.

Fig. 20 Surface created by burnishing.

The object of roller burnishing is to push the surface peaks into the surface valleys. Most turned surfaces are similar to a thread under high magnification, and if they can be smoothed out, a lower microinch finish is possible.

Tools or work are revolved at high surface feet per minute, and feeds are also very high when burnishing from the end of the part (see Fig. 21). In the latter operation, a three-roll holder is used. When burnishing from the cross slide, a single wheel can be used or double wheels, similar to knurling or thread rolling, are used.

Chips, especially on multiple-spindle automatics, can become troublesome with some types of stainless steels. Therefore, if possible, the burnishing operation should be done in one of the top spindle positions. On single-spindle work, cross-slide cuts which produce a high volume of chips should not be done while burnishing work is in progress.

A lightweight low-viscosity lubricating oil works well. Sulfurized chlorinated oils or water solubles are also being used. Roller wear and flaking of material can be minimized when using higher speeds and feeds.

Cutoff Procedures   Circular cutoff tools are sometimes preferred to straight cutoff blades since they afford a more rigid setup and can be designed to permit a minimum

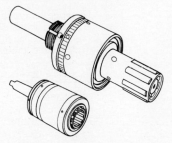

Fig. 21 Typical burnishing rollers.

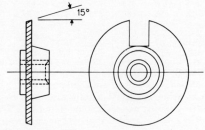

Fig. 22 Circular cutoff tool illustrating clearance angle.

amount of tool overhang. Tools should be designed slightly heavier than those used for mild steels and nonferrous metals.

For work not too large in diameter, the end cutting edge angle should be 10 to 15° and as the size of the work increases, the angle can be reduced down to 5° or less. The reduced angle reduces deflection of the tool but increases cutoff burr that may have to be removed by a secondary operation (see Fig. 22).

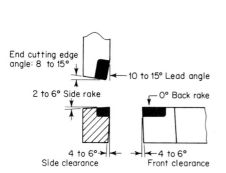

Fig. 23 Lathe turning tool with carbide insert.

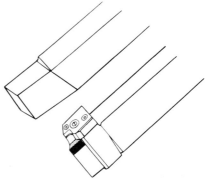

Fig. 24 Illustration of solid single-point turning tool and turning tool with replaceable insert.

Straight cutoff blades are ground with a side clearance of 2 to 3° and circular cutoff blades should be designed with the same amount of clearance. An end clearance angle of 7 to 9° is recommended and if top rake angle is needed, some operators grind a long radius on top of tool. Feeds and surface feet per minute are shown in Table 1.

Lubrication is required for cutoff operations and use of sulfurized cutting oil is recommended. This oil may be thinned with paraffin oil. Occasionally soluble oils are used with good results.

Turret Lathe Operations Turret lathe operations are usually considered single-point turning operations. Due to the types of tools used on turret lathes, most shops are able to machine at slightly higher cutting speeds than on other types of machines. Most stainless steel machining operations use tools with positive rake angles (see Fig. 23). A few martensitic grades, such as 420 and the 440 types, require negative rake angles to reduce abrasive wear of the tools.

Some stainless steel alloys, particularly the 200 and 300 series, have a tendency to work harden. Therefore, a positive feed should be maintained and tools should not be allowed to dwell in the cut. The austenitic grades require using heavy-duty lathes with rigid tooling setups (see Fig. 24). If feed loads are not high, this material causes some tools to chatter.

Speeds and Feeds. Carbide-insert tools are recommended on turret lathes because of their heavy, rigid construction.

Feeds in a range of 0.009 to 0.016 in. (0.229 to 0.406 mm) are normally used for rough turning operations and 0.003 to 0.010 in. (0.076 to 0.254 mm) for finishing operations. Speeds for straight chromium stainless steels are usually between 200 and 500 surface ft/min (61 to 152 surface m/min) and for Cr-Ni grades, between 200 and 400 surface ft/min (61 to 122 surface m/min).

A heavy mixture of soluble oil is recommended on turret lathe work, especially when using carbide tools.

Milling Usually, more rigid and heavier equipment is needed to mill stainless steels than carbon steels. This helps eliminate chatter. Climb milling is advantageous because cutting pressures are directed downward toward the machine and fixtures. To use climb milling, the machine must be in good condition and have all backlash eliminated in order to avoid cutter breakage (see Fig. 25).

It is necessary to keep milling cutters sharp to produce accuracy and smooth finish.

Work should be flooded with a good sulfurized oil diluted with paraffin oil. Where light cuts are taken at high cutting speeds, soluble oils are used. Soluble oils are particularly recommended with carbide cutters.

Cutters for stainless steel should be designed with ample space between teeth to facilitate chip control. The majority of milling operations on stainless steels are performed with high-speed steels. In general, milling cutters should be sharpened with a positive

Fig. 25   Milling operations.

rake angle of 5 to 20° for high-speed steel. Carbide rake angles are usually sharpened with less angle than those on the high-speed steel cutters.

Usually a relief angle of 5° works satisfactorily for most stainless steels.

Since austenitic stainless steel grades work harden, it is a good practice to use slow speeds and heavy, continuous cuts. If cutters are allowed to idle when cutting, glazing and work hardening occur. Feeds when using high-speed steel cutters should be about 0.005 in. (0.127 mm) per tooth for roughing and 0.003 in. (0.076 mm) per tooth for finishing.

Speeds. Approximate milling speeds when using high-speed steel cutters on free-machining stainless steels are 60 to 130 surface ft/min (18 to 41 surface m/min). Speeds for nonfree-machining stainless steels are in a range of 35 to 80 surface ft/min (11 to 24 surface m/min). Most stainless steels are milled at normal speeds required for turning operations on the same type materials.

Care of Tools   For better finishes and maximum production, tools should never be allowed to become excessively dull. Dullness results in poor work, greatly increased power requirements, and tool breakage. When tools are sharpened at predetermined intervals, less grinding is necessary, resulting in longer tool life.

Off-hand-grinding, especially for single-point tools, is preferred in some shops. If high dimensional accuracy is required, tools must be machine ground. Regardless of how tools are sharpened, the cutting edges must not show signs of burning. This can happen very easily and may not be visible unless the tool is etched in acid.

Type and condition of the grinding wheel is important. Watch for loading or glazing of the wheel since this causes the tool to overheat. Wheels that become loaded must be redressed. If tools become overheated, discontinue grinding, but do not quench a tool that has become colored. A good rule to follow is, "If the tool is too hot to hold in your hands, stop grinding for a while." After carefully grinding, hone the tools to remove all peaks and grinding wheel marks from the cutting edges.

When sharpening carbide-insert tools, excessive metal on the steel shank should be removed with a regular grinding wheel to eliminate loading of the diamond wheel. The continuous movement of a tool across the wheel face, when using a regular grinding wheel or a diamond wheel, aids in keeping the wheel open and hastens the removal of stock from the tool.

Sawing

Hack Saws. The power hack saw should be operated at 60 to 100 strokes per minute, with 0.002 to 0.003 in. (0.051 to 0.076 mm) feed per stroke. Due to work hardening of some grades, a positive feed must be used to eliminate teeth riding over the material without cutting. When rubbing occurs on the return stroke, glazing and work hardening of the metal will dull the saw and reduce saw life.

Usually saws having 6 teeth per inch give best results for bar diameters 1 in. (25.4 mm) and over. Smaller sizes require more teeth to assure that at least two teeth are cutting the material at the same time. Between 10 and 18 teeth should be used for stock under 1-in. (25.4-mm) diameter.

Band Saws. High-speed band saws work as well as power hack saws but usually require less feed. Slow speeds of 40 to 80 ft/min (12 to 24 m/min) with medium-heavy feed pressures should be used for all stainless steels.

Circular Screw Slotting Saws. The peripheral speed should vary with the degree of hardness of the material. Harder materials require slower speeds.

Most stainless steel should be sawed at 60 to 80 peripheral ft/min (18.3 to 24.4 peripheral m/min). Saws should be run slower than milling cutters and feeds should be moderate. No saw can stand up under the constant blow of a chattering cut.

A free-cut, curled chip indicates ideal feeding pressure and the fastest cutting time with greatest saw life. Sulfur-based or water-soluble oils should be used on all sawing operations.

Cutting Oils The cutting oil most commonly used when machining stainless steels is sulfur-chlorinated oil containing active sulfur that is usually diluted or blended with paraffin oil. This oil seems to have the best lubrication and antiweld properties.

When heavy cuts are made, or if tapping or threading are done, less thinning of sulfur-based oil is necessary. Operations such as deep-hole drilling and reaming can usually be accomplished best by thinning sulfur-based oil with paraffin oil.

Fig. 26 Illustration of coolant applied to drilling operation.

In spite of the lubricating and cooling action of the cutting fluid, some metal-to-metal contact always exists. Temperatures high enough to weld specks of metal to the workpiece and tool are generated in limited areas. For this reason a lubricant must be used to coat the tool with oil so particles of metal will not weld readily. This film of oil also tends to keep temperatures from rising above the welding point (see Fig. 26).

Water soluble oil may also be used when machining stainless steels. This oil has higher cooling properties and is used where light cuts and high cutting speeds are used, especially with carbide tooling.

Cutting fluids should always be maintained in a clean, fresh condition and at full strength. If no type of filtering system is used with regular oil, machines should be drained regularly and fresh oil added. Oil removed from machines can sometimes be used again if filtered properly, eliminating metal particles the oil has accumulated. For oil selection, it is recommended that oil suppliers be consulted.

Summary

1. Use sharp cutters with positive rake angles, relief angles and smooth surfaces.
2. Use sufficient cut to prevent riding, burnishing, glazing, or work hardening of metal.
3. Use adequate feeds.
4. Eliminate heat to improve tool life.
5. Always resharpen tools when changing from one type of stainless steel to another.
6. Use recommended surface feet per minute.
7. Work within 75% of machine capacity.
8. Use as large a tool as possible to carry away heat and gain rigidity.
9. Cutting oils are a must on most stainless steel machining operations. The heavier mixture is used for heavy cuts and for threading and tapping operations.

CLEANING AND PASSIVATING AFTER MACHINING

For a stainless steel part to achieve maximum resistance to corrosion, and in order to avoid discoloration, it is essential to remove all surface contaminants. A clean stainless steel surface will generate a protective oxide film in normal air. The steel is then said to be in a "passive" condition. Foreign matter such as iron filings, steel particles, and embedded grit interfere with this film formation. Furthermore, the contaminants themselves may rust and cause the stainless surface to appear streaked or otherwise discolored.

Stainless steel parts must be thoroughly degreased prior to any passivating treatment. Lubricants, grease, oil (even fingerprints) not removed from the part will prevent successful passivation. In instances where lubricants containing protein are not removed, immersion in the acid passivating bath can cause a tightly adhering brown stain to form on the part. The importance of degreasing cannot be overemphasized.

The passivation process can be speeded by immersing or otherwise contacting the part with a strong oxidizing agent; nitric acid solutions normally are used for this purpose. Solutions of nitric acid in water provide the further advantage of dissolving iron or steel particles, thus removing areas of probable corrosive attack.

The most popular solution for passivating stainless steel consists of 20 vol % nitric acid operating at 120°F (49°C). After immersion for a minimum of 30 min, the parts should be thoroughly rinsed in clean hot water.

Considerable latitude exists in the choice of acid concentration, bath temperature, and immersion time. For example, when passivating the 300 series stainless steels and those steels of the 400 series containing 17% or more chromium (except for the free-machining grades), a solution containing 20 to 40% nitric acid may be used at 130 to 160°F (54 to 71°C) for from 30 to 60 min. The same bath may be used for the 400 series steels containing less than 17% chromium and the straight-chromium free-machining grades if the temperature is lowered to 110 to 130°F (43 to 54°C).

A solution containing 15 to 30 vol % nitric acid and 2 wt % sodium dichromate operating at 110 to 130°F (43 to 54°C) is recommended for the free-machining grades and the high-carbon heat-treatable types of the 400 series. Immersion time is about 30 min. This treatment is suggested for use on material which shows evidence of etching in any of the previously mentioned solutions. A followup treatment for about 1 h in 5 wt % sodium dichromate at 140 to 160°F (60 to 71°C) is sometimes used.

MACHINING CAST STAINLESS STEELS

High-Speed Steel Tooling   Most machining operations can be performed satisfactorily on all cast high alloys but certain precautions must be observed. It is important that the tool be kept continually entering into the metal to avoid work hardening the surface from rubbing or scraping. Slow feeds, deep cuts, and powerful, rigid machines are necessary for best results. Work should be firmly mounted and supported, and tool mountings should provide maximum stiffness.

Table 3 presents data on feeds and speeds for high-speed steel tooling. In determining the most satisfactory combination of speed and feed, speed should be reduced first, then feed. For production work, it is more common to use carbide tooling with modern machine tools.

When using high-speed steel tools, it is recommended that both the work and the tool be flooded with lubricant to keep the temperature down. The low thermal conductivity of the cast stainless steels makes it essential that cooling be provided. Sulfur-chlorinated petroleum oil may be used either pure or diluted with a paraffin blending oil. For light finishing cuts at high speed, cooling is more important than lubricant, so greater dilution may be used.

Turning. Chips on many of the grades are characteristically tough and stringy. For this reason chip curlers and chipbreakers are frequently recommended whenever the size of the tool permits. They minimize friction and are especially important on the austenitic grades. Single-point high-speed steel turning tools are usually ground to 4 to 10° side and back rake, 4 to 7° side relief, 7 to 10° end relief, 8 to 15° end cutting angle, 10 to 15° side cutting edge angle and $\frac{1}{32}$- to $\frac{1}{8}$-in. (0.79 to 3.2-mm) nose radius.

Milling. Keep work hardening to a minimum by preventing spring or chatter, which causes intermittent cutting. Provide sufficient rigidity in tool frames, tables, overarms, and work supports. Use the largest diameter possible for cutter arbors, tool shanks, and toolholders and keep tools properly sharpened.

The cut must be definite and once started should not be stopped unless absolutely necessary. If the cut is stopped, back the tool off before stopping the machine, and when

TABLE 3 Machining of Cast High Alloys with High-Speed Steel Tools

ACI type	Rough turning		Finish turning		Drilling		Tapping speed, surface ft/min	Note
	Speed, surface ft/min‡	Feed, in./rev	Speed, surface ft/min	Feed, in./rev	Speed, surface ft/min	Feed, in./rev		
CA-15	40–55	0.020–0.025	80–110	0.005–0.010	35–75	*	10–25	
CA-40	30–50	0.020–0.025	60–100	0.005–0.010	30–60	*	10–20	
CB-30	35–50	0.020–0.025	70–100	0.005–0.010	40–60	*	10–25	
CB-7Cu	25–70	0.020–0.025	50–70	0.005–0.010	20–45	*	6–15	
CC-50	30–60	0.020–0.025	60–120	0.005–0.010	40–60	*	10–25	
CD-4MCu	40–50	0.020–0.025	80–100	0.005–0.010	30–50	*		
CE-30	30–40	0.020–0.025	60–80	0.005–0.010	30–60	*	10–25	†
CF-3, CF-8	25–35	0.020–0.025	50–70	0.005–0.010	20–40	*	10–20	†
CF-20	25–35	0.020–0.025	50–70	0.005–0.010	20–40	*	10–20	†
CF-3M, CF-8M	25–35	0.020–0.025	50–70	0.005–0.010	20–50	*	10–20	†
CE-8C	30–40	0.020–0.025	60–80	0.005–0.010	30–60	*	10–25	†
CF-16F	45–55	0.020–0.025	90–110	0.005–0.010	30–80	*	15–30	
CG-8M	25–35	0.020–0.025	50–70	0.005–0.010	20–50	*	10–20	†
CH-20	25–35	0.020–0.025	50–70	0.005–0.010	20–50	*	10–20	†
CK-20	25–35	0.020–0.025	50–70	0.005–0.010	20–40	*	10–20	†
CN-7M	45–55	0.020–0.025	90–110	0.005–0.010	30–60	*	10–25	
HA	40–50	0.010–0.030	80–100	0.005–0.010	35–70	*	10–25	†
HC	40–50	0.025–0.035	80–100	0.010–0.015	40–60	*	10–25	†
HD	40–50	0.025–0.035	80–100	0.010–0.015	40–60	*	10–25	†
HE	30–40	0.020–0.025	60–80	0.005–0.010	30–60	*	10–25	†
HF	25–35	0.020–0.025	50–70	0.005–0.010	20–40	*	10–20	
HH	25–35	0.015–0.020	50–70	0.005–0.010	20–40	*	10–20	
HI	25–35	0.015–0.020	50–70	0.005–0.010	20–40	*	10–20	
HK	25–35	0.020–0.025	50–70	0.005–0.010	20–40	*	10–20	
HL	30–40	0.020–0.025	60–80	0.005–0.010	20–40	*	10–20	
HN	35–45	0.020–0.025	70–90	0.005–0.010	30–60	*	10–25	
HT	40–45	0.024–0.035	80–90	0.005–0.010	40–60	*	5–15	†
HU	40–45	0.025–0.035	80–90	0.010–0.015	40–60	*	5–15	†
HW	40–45	0.025–0.035	80–90	0.010–0.015	40–60	*	5–15	†
HX	40–45	0.025–0.035	80–90	0.010–0.015	40–60	*	5–15	†

*Drilling feeds:

Drill diam., in.	Feed, in./rev
Under 1/8	0.001–0.002
1/8–1/4	0.002–0.004
1/4–1/2	0.004–0.007
1/2–1	0.007–0.015
Over 1	0.015–0.025

†Use chip curler.

‡Surface ft/min × 0.3048 = surface m/min. See Table 2 for conversion to rpm.

starting again, allow for undercut. Cutters should have sufficient space between the teeth for chip storage and clearance.

Start slowly at 30 surface ft/min (9 surface m/min) for high-speed steel cutters and increase speed until the cutters are performing at high efficiency, but without too much tool wear.

Drilling. In drilling, the work-hardening effect cannot be avoided. Therefore, the rate of feed per drill revolution must be greater than the depth of the previous work-hardened surface. Whenever possible, use plenty of coolant and flood the workpiece and the drill. A small stream of coolant may cause drills to crack. Drills should be correctly ground and sharp; large drills should be machine-ground to maintain correct angles and cutting edges. Short fluted drills give greater rigidity. Drills should be ground to an included angle of about 135 to 140° with a clearance angle of 12 to 15°. The web of the drills can be thinned at the chisel point to reduce cutting pressure and reduce the chance of splitting at the point. A good starting range would be 15 to 50 surface ft/min (5 to 15 surface m/min). Generally, 25 to 50% heavier feeds should be used than for carbon and low-alloy steels.

Tapping. Most troubles encountered in tapping holes in stainless steel castings can be eliminated by proper care in the drilling operation to ensure sharp, properly ground drills, correct alignment, rigid fixtures, etc. It is best to first ream small-diameter tap holes and work where Class 3 fits are required. Due to the tendency of stainless steel to flow or "mush out" when tapped, tap drills should be of the largest size permissible. For holes over ½-in. (12.7-mm) diameter, drills should be at least 0.005 in. (0.127 mm) larger. This is especially important when tapping fine-pitched threads. There should be sufficient clearance between the root and crest of the threads to prevent galling, torn threads, and broken taps. Threads should not be tapped more than 75%. Because of the toughness of stainless alloys, a 50% thread will hold satisfactorily and will be much easier to tap. High-speed commercially ground taps are recommended, with a 12 to 15° hook grind at the cutting edge of the flute to allow free cutting. In tapping deep or blind holes, the bearing surface of the tap should be thinned down by grinding back the heel one-third to one-half the commercially ground width to ensure cutting smoother threads and to increase tap life.

Carbide Tooling   Most of the same machining operations discussed under high-speed steel tooling can also be performed successfully, and frequently with a considerable saving in machining time, using carbide tooling, but some important differences in technique must be observed.

Because of the increased speed and depth of cut possible with carbide tooling, horse-power requirements are greater than for conventional tooling. Toolholders must be extremely rigid to prevent chattering or rubbing of the tool on the metal surface. Such action, particularly on the austenitic alloys, forms irregular work-hardened patches leading to greatly increased tool breakage.

Chips on many high-alloy grades are characteristically tough and stringy. Therefore, to protect operating personnel and reduce friction, chip curlers and chipbreakers are recommended whenever the size of the tool permits. They are especially important when machining the austenitic grades. A guide for grinding single-point carbide tools is shown in Fig. 27. Interrupted cuts should be avoided whenever possible to prevent work hardening the alloy at the point where the tool leaves or enters the casting. If it is necessary to begin a cut in an area that may have been work hardened by previous machining, a deep enough cut should be taken to get under the hardened area quickly. To provide sufficient cooling lubrication, the work must be flooded at all times. This is particularly true when a shallow cut is being made since most of the heat generated in the tool will be localized in a very small volume of material at the tip. In general, a water-soluble coolant, two to three times as heavy as that used with conventional tooling, is best. Because they tend to break down carbide cutting edges, sulfur-based oils should be avoided.

Speeds and Feeds. Suggested ranges for speeds and feeds when using carbide tooling are given in Table 4 for each of the ACI alloy grades. As recommended for high-speed steel tooling, in selecting the best combination of speed and feed, speed should be reduced first and then feed. Modifications outside these stated ranges may be required depending on individual experience and particular job requirements. For example, in rough turning a thin shaft, both depth of cut and feed may be reduced to avoid deflection. The recommended finish turning values shown in the table are satisfactory for subsequent

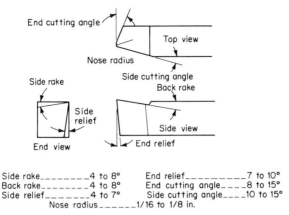

Side rake _____ 4 to 8°   End relief _____ 7 to 10°
Back rake _____ 4 to 8°   End cutting angle ____ 8 to 15°
Side relief _____ 4 to 7°   Side cutting angle ____ 10 to 15°
                Nose radius _____ 1/16 to 1/8 in.

Fig. 27   Guide for grinding single-point carbide tooling.

TABLE 4   Machining of Cast Alloys with Carbide Tools

| | Rough turning | | Finish turning | | Drilling | | |
ACI type	Speed, surface ft/min‡	Feed, in./rev	Speed, surface ft/min	Feed, in./rev	Speed, surface ft/min	Feed, in./rev	N
CA-15	150–300	0.060–0.125	200–300	0.010–0.030	50–80	*	
CA-40	150–250	0.060–0.090	200–300	0.010–0.030	40–60	*	
CB-30	150–200	0.060–0.090	200–250	0.010–0.030	40–60	*	
CB-7Cu	150–250	0.060–0.125	200–250	0.010–0.030	50–80	*	
CC-50	150–200	0.060–0.090	200–250	0.010–0.030	50–80	*	
CD-4MCu	150–250	0.060–0.125	200–300	0.010–0.020	50–80	*	
CE-30	150–200	0.060–0.090	200–250	0.005–0.020	50–80	*	
CF-3, CF-8	150–350	0.060–0.125	200–350	0.010–0.030	50–80	*	
CF-20	150–300	0.060–0.125	200–300	0.010–0.030	50–80	*	
CF-3M, CF-8M	150–300	0.060–0.090	200–300	0.005–0.020	50–80	*	
CF-8C	150–300	0.060–0.090	200–300	0.005–0.020	30–60	*	
CF-16F	150–300	0.060–0.090	200–300	0.005–0.020	30–60	*	
CG-8M	100–250	0.060–0.090	200–250	0.005–0.020	40–60	*	
CH-20	100–250	0.060–0.090	200–250	0.005–0.020	40–60	*	
CK-20	100–250	0.030–0.060	150–200	0.005–0.020	40–60	*	
CN-7M	100–200	0.030–0.060	150–250	0.005–0.020	30–60	*	
HA	150–300	0.060–0.125	200–300	0.010–0.030	50–100	*	
HC	100–200	0.030–0.060	150–250	0.005–0.010	40–60	*	
HD	100–200	0.030–0.060	150–250	0.005–0.010	40–60	*	
HE	100–150	0.020–0.050	150–200	0.005–0.010	30–60	*	
HF	100–200	0.020–0.050	150–200	0.005–0.010	30–60	*	
HH	100–150	0.020–0.050	100–200	0.005–0.010	30–40	*	
HI	100–150	0.020–0.050	100–150	0.005–0.010	20–40	*	
HK	100–150	0.020–0.090	150–250	0.005–0.015	25–50	*	
HL	90–150	0.020–0.060	150–200	0.005–0.015	25–60	*	
HN	90–150	0.015–0.060	150–200	0.005–0.015	30–60	*	
HT	100–150	0.020–0.090	150–250	0.005–0.015	30–60	*	
HU	100–150	0.020–0.060	150–200	0.005–0.015	30–60	*	
HW	80–100	0.030–0.090	100–180	0.005–0.015	25–30	*	
HX	80–100	0.030–0.090	100–180	0.005–0.015	30–60	*	

*Drilling feeds:
Drill diam., in.	Feed, in./rev
Under 1/8	0.002–0.004
1/8–1/4	0.004–0.008
1/4–1/2	0.004–0.008
1/2–1	0.007–0.015
Over 1	0.020–0.030

† Use chip curler.
‡ Surface ft(min × 0.3048 = surface m/min. See Table 2 for conversion to rpm.

grinding or polishing. If turning is the last operation, a more appropriate feed range would be approximately 0.002 (on austenitic steels at least 0.004 should be allowed because of work hardening) to 0.006 in./rev. (0.05 to 0.15 mm/rev.).

Carbide tooling is particularly recommended for turning, boring, and facing because of the much higher output it makes possible. When tools are maintained properly and the machining setup provides sufficient rigidity, enough horsepower and an adequate supply of coolant, tool breakage should not present serious problems.

Because of the greater initial expense and higher cost of retipping, drilling with carbide tooling is generally not economically justified except at fairly high production rates. To avoid breakage, holes below about 0.090 in. (2.3 mm) should be avoided whenever design considerations permit. If a hole below this diameter must be made with a carbide drill, it is best to avoid the use of automatic feed and instead use manual feed so that force can be adjusted by "feel."

Since the work-hardening effect cannot be avoided, the rate of feed must be greater than the depth of the previously hardened surface. Wherever possible, use plenty of coolant to flood the workpiece and the drill. A small stream of coolant, causing irregular cooling, may cause drills to crack. Drills should be kept sharp and, when possible, machine-ground to maintain correct angles and cutting edges. An included angle of 135 to 140° with a clearance angle of about 8 to 10° is generally best.

A good starting range for drilling speed is 30 to 60 surface ft/min (9 to 18 surface m/min) with feed rates as shown in Table 4. If multiple drilling is necessary to achieve the required final diameter, there should be a substantial size increment between each drill to prevent chipping of the drill and the work hardening of the casting. Drills should cut continuously. If at any time a clean chip does not emerge from the hole, drilling should be stopped immediately. Because carbide drills are more brittle than steel ones, they should not be used where there is sand on the casting.

Milling and Reaming. Where production runs are large enough to justify the cost of carbide tooling, milling and reaming operations can also be performed successfully. With milling, one recommended approach is to start at about 80 surface ft/min (24 surface m/min) (as opposed to 30 surface ft/min [9 surface m/min] for high-speed tooling) and then increase speed until the cutters are performing efficiently but without excessive wear. For reaming, speed is approximately the same as for drilling, and the depth of cut is generally from 0.002 to 0.004 in. (0.05 to 0.1 mm) per reamer tooth. If a cut under 0.002 in. (0.05 mm) is taken, the work surface is likely to glaze and there will be considerable wear on the reamer.

When reaming holes to a final diameter of over ¾ in. (19.05 mm), holes should be drilled ¹⁄₁₆ in. (1.6 mm) undersize to provide an adequate depth of cut for the reamer, and a proportionately larger reaming allowance should be made on holes over 2 in. (50.8 mm) in diameter.

TROUBLE CHECKLIST WHEN MACHINING STAINLESS STEEL

Broaching Troubles
A. Breakage
   1. Material too soft or too hard
   2. Teeth too thin on broaching tool
   3. Broach not properly lined up
   4. Rake angle too high
   5. Broach clogging with chips
   6. Improper coolant
B. Improper finish
   1. Material too soft
   2. Broach alignment
   3. Chip problem
   4. Improper coolant
   5. Alignment
C. Broach wear
   1. Improper coolant
   2. Excessive heat
   3. Material too hard

   4. Abrasive material
   5. Excessive feed
   6. Improper hook
D. Chatter
   1. Removing excessive metal
   2. Broaching too fast
   3. Parts not rigid
   4. Improper coolant
E. Tool marks
   1. Broach rough ground
   2. Soft material
   3. Feeding too fast
   4. Pickup on broach teeth

Counterboring Troubles
A. Breakage or chipped edges
   1. Excessive dullness
   2. Wrong size tool

3. Eccentric hole
4. Insufficient coolant
5. Tool jabbing
6. Previous tools work-hardening metal

B. Chatter
1. Excessive clearance
2. Pickup on tool
3. Chips packing
4. Worn toolholder
5. Worn spindle bearings
6. Tool margins too wide
7. Lack of rigidity

C. Tolerances not maintained
1. Dull tool
2. Wrong angles
3. Loose spindle
4. Feed too light
5. Insufficient coolant

Cutoff Troubles

A. Breakage
1. Tool too thin for stock
2. Excessive rake
3. Excessive angle
4. Tool jabbing
5. Tool dull
6. Tool not on center

B. Chatter
1. Tool too thin for stock
2. Off center
3. Play in spindle
4. Excessive front angle
5. Excessive top rake angle

C. Rough finish
1. Dull tool
2. Off center
3. Insufficient angle
4. Play in spindle
5. Excessive feed
6. Chips interfering with coolant
7. Insufficient coolant

D. Overall length varies
1. Tool too thin
2. Point angle wrong
3. Excessive feed
4. Spindle end play
5. Loose collet

Drilling Troubles

A. Drill breakage
1. Dull drill
2. Excessive feed
3. Soft material
4. Excessive web thickness
5. Drill too long
6. Too much speed
7. Drill binding in hole
8. Improper coolant
9. Drill jabbing
10. Lack lip clearance

11. Heel not properly backed off
12. Misalignment

B. Drill wear
1. Feed too light
2. Excessive speed
3. Improper coolant
4. Material too soft or too hard
5. Drill not lined up
6. Abrasive material
7. Drills soft
8. Chips clogging flute

C. Rough finish
1. Soft material
2. Too much feed
3. Loose spindle
4. Improper coolant
5. Poor chip elimination
6. Improper grind
7. Chipped lip

Form Tool Troubles

A. Chatter marks on parts
1. Bad spindle bearings
2. Loose spindle
3. Tool just sharpened
4. Tool below center
5. Too much top rake angle
6. Excessive width tool
7. Material needs steady-rest or support
8. Excessive feed or speed
9. Check cutting oil
10. Material too soft

B. Tool burns
1. Dull tools
2. Tool set above center
3. Insufficient feed
4. Excessive feed, speed, or tension
5. Tool edge buildup
6. Improper cutting oil
7. Material too hard or too soft
8. Check tool hardness
9. Insufficient top rake
10. Tool overheating during sharpening
11. Red hardness of tool low
12. Insufficient side clearance
13. Chips obstructing oil stream
14. Another tool overheating part

C. Excessive tool wear
1. Feed too low or too high
2. Speed high or low
3. Cutting edge buildup
4. Tool rubbing on cutting edge or side
5. Tool above or below center
6. Excessive top rake
7. Improper coolant
8. Tools soft
9. Tool overheating during sharpening

10. Chip disposal incorrect
11. Material too hard or too soft
12. Tools ground with coarse wheel
13. Worn toolholder
14. Excessive dwell on form cam

Milling Troubles

A. Excessive cutter wear and vibration
   1. Too much speed
   2. Improper feed
   3. Improper coolant
   4. Lands too wide
   5. Insufficient rake angle
   6. Material soft
   7. Soft cutters
   8. Loose work table

Reaming Troubles

A. Rough finish
   1. Reamer ground with rough finish
   2. Excessive feed
   3. Soft material
   4. Dull reamer
   5. Too little to ream out
   6. Reamer removing excessive material
   7. Reamer bugging up
   8. Improper coolant
   9. Chip disposal improper
   10. Reamer lands too wide
B. Burnished surface
   1. Material too hard
   2. Lands too wide
   3. Excessive speed
   4. Insufficient metal removal
   5. Hole walls work hardened by drill
   6. Slow feed
   7. Improper coolant
C. Chatter
   1. Loose spindles
   2. Excessive speeds
   3. Lands too narrow
   4. Excessive stock removal
   5. Not enough metal left for reaming
   6. Improper coolant
   7. Improper feed

Turning Troubles

A. Tools breaking down and burning
   1. Too much feed
   2. Excessive speed
   3. Improper clearance
   4. Improper size tools
   5. Insufficient coolant

6. Tools ground with rough finish
7. Tools too soft
8. Chip disposal
9. Improper tool setting
10. Material too hard
11. Dull tools
B. Tool buildup on cutting edge
   1. Not enough feed
   2. Speed too slow
   3. Improper coolant
   4. Material too soft
   5. Tools not ground with smooth finish
   6. Improper clearance
   7. Tools not set on center

Tapping Troubles

A. Tapped hole oversize
   1. Hole large before tapping
   2. Tap picking up
   3. Oversize tap
   4. Improper coolant
   5. Chips packing in flutes
B. Rough threads
   1. Material too soft
   2. Improper or dirty coolant
   3. Improper hook
   4. Flutes packing with chips
   5. Thin land by backing off heel
   6. Material work hardened before tapping
   7. Improper chamfer or lead angle
   8. Tap picking up metal
   9. Improper feed
   10. Improper speed
   11. Poor alignment or eccentric hole

Threading Troubles

A. Rough threads
   1. Dull chasers
   2. Improper grind
   3. Misalignment
   4. Chasers hitting shoulder
   5. Improper feed
   6. Chips packing
   7. Cooling inadequate
   8. Oversize blank
   9. Speed or feed too high
   10. Not sufficient hook
   11. Material too soft
   12. Chasers not cutting evenly
   13. Improper chamfer on blank
   14. Excessive face angle on chasers

REFERENCES

1. Helber, W. F.: Machining of Cast High Alloys, *8 Plus,* no. 12, 1967.
2. Schoefer, E. A.: "High Alloy Data Sheets, Corrosion Series," Alloy Casting Institute Div., Steel Founders' Society of America, 1973.
3. Schoefer, E. A., and T. A. Shields: "High Alloy Data Sheets, Heat Series," Alloy Casting Institute Div., Steel Founders' Society of America, 1973.

Chapter 25

Soldering and Brazing Stainless Steels

DONALD A. CORRIGAN
Manager of Development, Handy & Harman, Fairfield, Connecticut

SOLDERING

Definition   Soldering has been defined by the American Welding Society (AWS) as a group of processes wherein coalescence is produced by heating base metals to a suitable temperature below their solidus using a filler metal having a liquidus not exceeding 427°C (800°F). The solder is usually fed between properly fitted surfaces of the joint by capillary attraction.

A metallurgical bond is produced in soldering by a metal solvent action. A very small amount of base metal dissolves in the molten solder. The ease of wetting is related to the ease with which this solvent action occurs. Upon solidification, the joint is held together by the same type of attraction between adjacent atoms that holds a piece of solid metal together.

Principles of Soldering   To achieve a sound soldered joint, the following considerations are important:

1. Joint design
2. Surface preparation
3. Heating method
4. Solder
5. Fluxes
6. Postsoldering treatment

Joint Design. Solder joints should be designed with the requirements and limitations of soft solders in mind. The joint must be designed so that the solder is not required to contribute to the structural strength of the assembly. Solders, as structural materials, are weak when compared to stainless steel. The necessary strength can be provided by shaping the parts to be joined so that they interlock. The solder then merely seals and stiffens the assembly. A good seal can best be obtained if the joint areas are precoated (pretinned) before assembly. If mechanical joining methods cannot be employed where structural strength is required, brazing or welding must be performed.

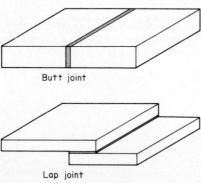

Butt joint

Lap joint

Fig. 1   Basic butt and lap joints for soldering.

There are two basic types of joint design used for soldering: the lap joint and the butt joint. Figure 1 illustrates these two basic types. All mechanical joints and edge reinforcings commonly used in soldering are combinations of the basic lap or butt joints. The lap joint should be employed wherever possible since it offers the best possibility for maximum strength. For a detailed description of many typical solder joint designs, consult the appropriate section of the "Welding Handbook."[1]

Clearance between parts being joined should be such that the solder can be drawn into the space between them by capillary action. Joint clearances of 0.006 to 0.010 cm are optimum. Capillary attraction does not function with clearances greater than about 0.025 cm.

Normally, during soldering, the solder is fed into the joint and little or no problem exists except that the joint be accessible. When automatic equipment is used, or where special feeding problems exist, the solder may be preplaced in the joint. The most common preforms are made from wire and strip.

Surface Preparation. The parts to be joined should be thoroughly cleaned of all grease, dirt, oxide, and other foreign material prior to fluxing. Since solder adheres more readily to roughened surfaces, highly polished surfaces should be rubbed with abrasives. Chemical cleaning by pickling will also provide an adequate surface. Soldering should be performed as soon after cleaning as practical.

Heating Methods. The heating method may be any of the common methods used for soldering, e.g., soldering iron, torch, resistance or induction heating. The proper application of heat is essential in any soldering operation. The heat should be supplied in a manner that allows the solder to melt, wet, and flow over the surface of the parts being jointed.

Solders. Tin-lead binary solders constitute the largest portion of solders in use. For joining most stainless steels, the solder employed should contain at least 50% tin since these solders offer the best combination of wetting properties and strength. Tin-lead solders normally used for stainless steel are shown in Table 1. The 60 grade solder is used where soldering temperatures must be minimized.

For cryogenic service, alloys containing less tin with silver additions up to 1.5% are recommended because of their greater low-temperature ductility. The wetability of these silver-containing solders is not as good as the straight tin-lead solders and often a flash electroplating of nickel or copper over the stainless steel is required to achieve a sound joint.

Specifications for solders have been published by the American Society for Testing and Materials (ASTM Designation B-32) and by the United States government (Federal Specification QQ-S-571).

TABLE 1 Tin-Lead Solders Suitable for Stainless Steel

ASTM solder classification	Nominal composition, wt %		Liquidus temperature, °C
	Tin	Lead	
50	50	50	217
60	60	40	190
70	70	30	192

Fluxes. A soldering flux must be capable of promoting or accelerating the wetting of metals and solder. The purpose of the flux is to remove and exclude small amounts of oxides and other impurities from the joint. An efficient flux removes films and oxides from the metal and solder and prevents reoxidation of the surfaces when heated. It should lower the surface tension of the molten solder to ensure adequate flow and adherence to the base metal. The flux should be readily displaced by the molten solder.

The chromium oxide surface film found on stainless steel is refractory and difficult to remove. A highly active flux must be employed. The required highly corrosive fluxes consist of inorganic acids like orthophosphoric acid, or mixed chloride-type salts. A number of commercially available fluxes will yield satisfactory results. Ordinary paste fluxes and flux-cored solders of the resin or organic type are generally not active enough for stainless soldering.

Postsoldering Treatment. The corrosive fluxes required for stainless steel soldering must be removed after soldering. The residue is chemically active and may cause severe corrosion at the joint. It is absolutely essential that all traces of flux residue be removed by neutralizing and thorough rinsing with water.

BRAZING

Definition The American Welding Society defines brazing as a group of joining processes wherein coalescence is produced by heating to a suitable temperature and by using a filler metal having a liquidus above 427°C (800°F) and below the solidus of the base metals. If filler metals with melting temperatures below 427°C (800°F) are used for joining, the process is called soldering.

In brazing, filler metal is distributed between the closely fitted surfaces of the joint by capillary attraction. Processes, like braze welding, are not technically brazing processes since capillary action is not a factor. The filler metal in braze welding is melted and deposited in grooves and fillets exactly at its point of use. Limited base metal fusion may occur in braze welding but, by definition, not in brazing.

Advantages of Brazing All of the standard wrought stainless steels can be brazed satisfactorily. The quality of brazed joints can be affected by the choice of brazing process, temperature, filler metals, and protective atmospheres or activating flux. It is important to keep in mind that the joint must be made compatible with the performance required of the assembly in service.

Brazing is most widely used for joining stainless to dissimilar metals including stainless steels of dissimilar composition, carbon and low-alloy steels, copper-based alloys and titanium. A principal advantage of brazing is that it can be used to join stainless to dissimilar metals where welding cannot be done satisfactorily. Stainless steels can be routinely brazed to all commonly used metals except aluminum and magnesium.

Other potential advantages of brazing are:

1. Economical joining of complex multicomponent assemblies.
2. The ability to preserve metallurgical characteristics of the base metals.
3. Minimum stress fabrication of large assemblies.
4. Provides a simple means for obtaining extensive and complex joints.
5. The ability to join widely different metal thicknesses.

6. Possesses the capability for precision production tolerances and reproducible joints in delicate assemblies.

7. The ability to mass produce small or medium assemblies on continuous, automated equipment.

Principles of Brazing   Capillary flow of the molten filler metal between the surfaces to be joined is the principal requirement in producing a good brazement. To obtain adequate flow, the faying surfaces must be wet by the molten filler and the joint must be properly spaced to permit capillary attraction and resultant coalescence.

Capillarity is a function of the surface tension between base metal, filler metal, flux or atmosphere, and the contact angle between filler metal and base metal. Flow characteris-

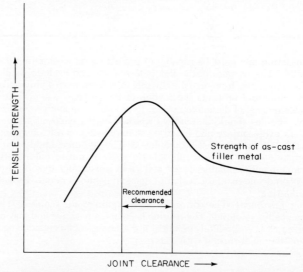

Fig. 2   Tensile strength vs. joint clearance—brazed butt joint.

tics are also affected by fluidity, viscosity, vapor pressure, gravity and any metallurgical reaction that may occur between filler and base metal. Brazed joints are made with clearances of a few thousandths of a centimeter between base metal surfaces. High brazing filler fluidity is, therefore, a desirable characteristic.

In the simplest example of brazing, the surfaces of the joint are cleaned to remove oxide and contaminants and coated with a flux. Brazing filler metal is then melted on the surface of the joint area. Capillary attraction between filler and base metal is much greater than between flux and base metal. Flux is, therefore, replaced by the filler metal. Upon cooling, the joint is filled with solid brazing alloy and the flux is found at the joint periphery.

Atmosphere furnace brazing is a preferred method for brazing stainless steels. Post-braze cleaning is eliminated. Dry hydrogen, argon, helium, dissociated ammonia, or vacuum can all be used with satisfactory results, provided proper precautions are taken.

Joint Design   Many variables must be considered in manufacturing a reliable brazement, but the most important consideration is the mechanical design of the assembly.

A properly designed brazement in stainless steel, in contrast to a soldered joint, can provide adequate strength without auxiliary mechanical interlocking. The design of a brazement should be handled like the design of any other machined or fabricated part, with proper attention being given to stress concentration, static loading, etc.

Types of Joints.   The type of joint to be employed in a brazement is influenced by many factors, e.g., ultimate service requirement, brazing process, prior fabrication techniques, etc. In general, the inherent strength of brazing filler metal is less than the stainless steel base metal. The joint strength will be influenced by a number of factors, e.g., joint clearance, defects in the brazement as well as the type of filler metal chosen.

Lap and butt joints are the two basic types of joints employed in brazing. In the lap joint, the area of overlap may be varied so that the joint will be stronger than the stainless base metal, even while employing a lower strength filler metal. Lap joints, however, have the disadvantage of increasing the metal thickness at the joint and of creating stress concentrations at each end of the joint where there is a change in cross section. Butt joints are employed where the thickness of a lap joint would be objectionable or where a completed butt joint will meet the brazement service requirements.

Joint Strength—Butt Joints. The strength of a properly executed butt joint may be sufficiently high so that failure will occur in the base metal. The strength of a butt joint depends on filler metal composition, base metal–filler metal interaction during the brazing cycle, defects and joint clearance. Joint clearance, in particular, can have a potent effect on the mechanical performance of a brazement. The influence of joint clearance is shown schematically in Figure 2. For maximum strength in a stainless steel brazement, the recommended joint clearance is typically 0.0025 to 0.0125 cm, with 0.005-cm clearance a good compromise. Testing of brazements and standard test methods for evaluation

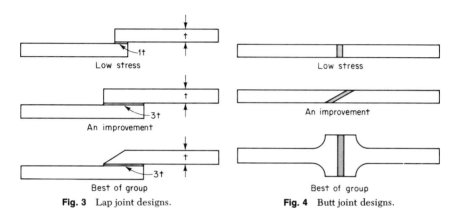

Low stress	Low stress
An improvement	An improvement
Best of group	Best of group
Fig. 3 Lap joint designs.	**Fig. 4** Butt joint designs.

of base metal-filler metal-brazing process combinations are treated in later sections of this chapter.

Stress Distribution—Lap and Butt Joints. In brazements where joints are lightly loaded, it may be most economical to employ simplified lap or butt joints. In general, however, the loading of a brazement requires the same design considerations given to other joints or changes in cross section. Good design will employ a brazement with a minimum of stress concentration and distribute the stresses to the base metal. Figures 3 and 4 illustrate various improvements that can be made in the basic lap and butt designs for critical applications. The issue of adequate brazement design has been discussed extensively in American Welding Society publications[2,3] and readers should refer to the appropriate sections for advice on critical brazement design problems.

Filler Metal Selection   The choice of filler metal depends on the kind of stainless steel being joined and the end application. Generally, silver-based, nickel-based, copper, and gold alloys are used, although, for specific applications, cobalt, platinum, palladium, and manganese-based materials have been employed. Table 2 gives the AWS designation, nominal composition, and brazing temperature range for some of the more common filler metals employed with stainless steel.

A convenient means of grouping the various filler metals is based on service temperature of the brazement. The B Cu fillers are suitable for applications up to about 260°C. The silver-based B Ag types are general-purpose filler alloys that are suitable up to a maximum of about 350°C service temperature. They are most commonly used for applications that have service temperatures below 200°C. Above 350°C, the B Ni filler metals or the B Au materials are usually required. Filler metals used for service applications above 350°C are usually employed with furnace brazing in high-purity reducing atmospheres or vacuum.

Silver-based Filler Metal. Silver-based alloys of the B Ag type and other silver brazing alloys designed specifically for stainless steel are the most widely used filler materials. Alloy B Ag-3, which contains 3% nickel, is the most widely employed filler, particularly for austenitic stainless materials. Most brazing is done with these silver-based fillers in the range 620 to 870°C, although special materials have been developed for applications like aircraft honeycomb panels which require higher brazing temperatures.

All the usually employed silver brazing alloys contain copper and many contain cadmium and zinc. Excessive brazing temperature and time can result in extensive grain-boundary penetration of the stainless, thereby embrittling the brazement. The high Cr-Ni austenitic types, like Type 310, are particularly sensitive to this type of attack. Brazing should be done on annealed material and stress buildup during silver brazing should be avoided. Zinc and cadmium-bearing silver-based alloys should not be used for components that will be exposed to high vacuum. Filler materials like B Ag-18, a Ag-Cu-Sn alloy, will provide suitable brazements for use in high vacuum.

TABLE 2   Commonly Used Filler Metals for Stainless Steel Brazing

	Nominal composition, wt %							
	SILVER-ALLOY FILLER METALS							
AWS designation	Ag	Cu	Zn	Cd	Ni	Sn	Li	Brazing temperature range, °C
B Ag-1	45	15	16	24				618–760
B Ag-1a	50	15.5	16.5	18				635–760
B Ag-3	50	15.5	15.5	16	3			688–815
B Ag-4	40	30	28		2			779–900
B Ag-7	56	22	17			5		652–760
B Ag-18	60	30				10		718–850
B Ag-19	92.5	Bal.					0.2	891–980
None	40	30	25		5			860–925
None	63	28.5			2.5	6		802–870

	NICKEL-ALLOY FILLER METALS						
AWS designation	Ni	Cr	Si	B	Fe	Other	Brazing temperature range, °C
B Ni-1	Bal.	14	4	3.5	4.5	0.75 C	1065–1200
B Ni-3	Bal.		4.5	3.1	1.5 max.		1010–1175
B Ni-7	Bal.	13				10 P	925–1035

	COPPER- AND GOLD-ALLOY FILLER METALS			
AWS designation	Cu	Au	Ni	Brazing temperature range, °C
B Cu-1	99.9 Min.			1095–1150
B Au-4		82	18	950–1000

Nickel-based Filler Metal. The B Ni group of nickel-based brazing filler materials rank next to the silver brazing materials in frequency of use when brazing stainless. Nickel brazing alloys are particularly useful where excellent corrosion resistance and high-temperature strength are required. The nickel brazing alloys, however, have the undesirable characteristics of poor ductility and flow. The nickel-based filler metal alloys with the stainless steel base metal to produce a braze metal which is less ductile than either the unalloyed filler or the base metal. The compositions formed in stainless steel brazements are higher melting alloys that block flow into the joint during brazing. Large clearances are usually necessary between the surfaces to be joined.

Copper Filler Metal. The B Cu group of copper filler metals melt at about 1080°C and flow freely at 1120°C. The high brazing temperature and the required protective atmosphere restrict the use of these fillers to furnace-brazing applications. The limited corrosion resistance of copper filler materials limit their use to environments that are not highly corrosive.

Gold-based Filler Alloys. The B Au group of gold-based brazing alloys are sometimes used for stainless brazing. The high cost of these filler metals and the high flow temperatures of these alloys restrict these materials to specialized applications where corrosion resistance and joint ductility are simultaneously required.

Metallurgical Problems Associated with Brazing

Ferritic Stainless Steel. The ferritic nonhardenable stainless steels, like Types 430 and 446, are usually brazed with silver-based filler metals. Ferritic stainless is particularly sensitive to a form of interface corrosion when flux brazed with certain B Ag fillers like B Ag-1, B Ag-1a and B Ag-2.[4] The interfacial corrosion is electrochemical in nature. The bond between base metal and filler metal can be completely destroyed by the action of tap water in as little as 1 week. Small additions of nickel to silver-based fillers minimize this interface corrosion. A special brazing alloy (63Ag-28.5Cu-6Sn-2.5Ni) has been developed for flux brazing Type 430 and is suitable for most applications.

Brazing Type 430 in the absence of flux (e.g., in dry hydrogen, argon or vacuum), tends to minimize the possibility of interface corrosion. The exception to this rule is when silver-based manganese-bearing alloys are used for fillers. Furnace brazing will not prevent the interface corrosion problem in Type 430 with this type of alloy,[5] presumably because a vulnerable manganese-rich layer is produced on the surface of the steel.

Table 3 lists applications and recommended filler, and flux or atmosphere requirements for these materials.

TABLE 3   Recommended Filler and Brazing Protection—Ferritic Nonhardenable Stainless Steel

Type	Typical application	Recommended		
		Filler	Flux	Atmosphere
430	Decorative trim	Ag-28.5Cu-2.5Ni-6Sn	AWS-3A	Dry hydrogen if no flux
	Kitchen sinks	Ag-30Cu-25Zn-5Ni	AWS-3A	None with flux
446	Resistance to high-temperature scaling	Ag-40Cu-5Zn-1Ni	AWS-3A	None
	Resistance to sulfur-bearing gasses	B Au-4	AWS-3B	Dry hydrogen

Martensitic Stainless Steel. Brazing filler materials must be compatible with the heat treatment required for these alloys. This is usually done by selecting filler metals with brazing temperatures corresponding to the austenitizing temperature of the stainless. Rapid cooling from the brazing temperature is required. Table 4 lists some applications with recommended filler metal and flux or atmosphere requirements for grades 403 and 440A.

TABLE 4   Recommended Filler and Brazing Protection—Martensitic Hardenable Stainless Steel

Type	Typical application	Recommended		
		Filler	Flux	Atmosphere
403	Turbine blades	Ag-28.5Cu-6Sn-2.5Ni	AWS-3A	Dry hydrogen (none if fluxed)
440A	Cutlery, surgical tools	Ag-28.5Cu-6Sn-2.5Ni	AWS-3A	Dry hydrogen

Austenitic Stainless Steel. The nonhardenable austenitic stainless steels, like the 200 and especially the 300 series, are widely used for both torch- and furnace-brazed assemblies. Alloys of the B Ag-3 type are commonly used for brazing these materials. Typical applications with recommended filler and protection are shown in Table 5. Caution should be exercised when brazing these materials. The unstabilized grades, such as Types 302 and 304, are subject to carbide precipitation when held in the range of 425 to 825°C. The extent of carbide precipitation and consequent loss of corrosion resistance is governed by the time the unstabilized austenitic stainless is held in the sensitizing range. Sensitization can be minimized by making the brazing thermal cycle as short as possible. When torch brazing small parts, thermal cycles are short enough so that serious loss of corrosion resistance does not occur.

The stabilized grades of austenitic stainless (e.g., Types 321 and 347) are virtually immune to the deleterious effects of carbide precipitation in brazing. Unstabilized grades in extra low carbon analysis (e.g., Type 304L) are also relatively insensitive to carbide precipitation. These can be brazed satisfactorily with the same brazing cycles as the stabilized types.

TABLE 5   Recommended Filler and Brazing Protection—Austenitic Stainless Steel

Type	Typical application	Recommended		
		Filler	Flux	Atmosphere
304	Chemical process equipment	B Ag-3	AWS-3A	None
		Ag-28.5Cu-6Sn-2.5Ni	AWS-3A	Dry hydrogen if no flux
	Cooking utensils	B Ag-4	AWS-3A	None
	Elevated temperature (to 370°C)	Ag-40Cu-5Zn-1Ni	AWS-3A	None or dry hydrogen
	Heat exchangers	B Ag-19	No	Argon or dry hydrogen
	Vacuum tubes	B Au-4	No	Argon or dry hydrogen
321 or 347	High temperature service (>370°C)	B Au-4	AWS-3B	Argon or dry hydrogen
		B Ni-1	No	Dry hydrogen
	Hydraulic tubing	Ag-40Cu-5Zn-1Ni	AWS-3A	None with flux, dry hydrogen

Precipitation-hardenable Stainless. Precipitation-hardenable steels, like Types 17-7PH and AM-350, can be brazed using a number of commercially available filler materials. As is the case with the straight martensitic grades, brazing thermal cycles must be compatible with their heat treatments. Heat treatments vary widely for these high-strength materials and specific brazing procedures are required for each. Table 6 shows typical applications of these materials with recommended filler metal and brazing atmospheres.

TABLE 6   Recommended Filler and Brazing Protection—Precipitation-Hardenable Stainless Steel

Type	Typical application	Recommended		
		Filler	Flux	Atmosphere
15-7Mo	Aircraft honeycomb panels	B Ag-19 + Ni	None	Argon
AM-350	Hydraulic tubing	Ag-28Cu-0.2Li	None	Argon

Brazing Processes   Any of the common brazing processes may be used to make brazed joints in stainless steel. Among these are torch, dip, induction, resistance, and furnace brazing. In addition, specialized heating methods have been developed for the brazing of aircraft honeycomb structures, e.g., quartz lamp, electric blanket, and luminous wall-type furnaces.

Furnace brazing is most widely used, because for many stainless applications, brazing in a prepared atmosphere or vacuum is required.

Induction heating is useful for those brazements that require extremely high heating rates to minimize oxidation of the stainless components.

As a general rule, greater process control is required with any of the above procedures than for an equivalent carbon steel brazement.

Surface Preparation, Furnace Atmospheres, and Fluxes   The chromium oxides on the surface of stainless steel are more difficult to clean than oxides found on the surface of carbon steel. Mechanical or chemical cleaning before brazing is recommended. Abrasive paper, filing, or machining can provide effective mechanical cleaning. Contaminants, such as grease and oil, must be removed prior to brazing. Pickling with a nitric-hydrofluoric acid mixture of 15 to 20% HNO_3 and 2 to 5% HF at 60 to 80°C will provide an adequate brazing surface.

Many stainless steel assemblies can be furnace-brazed in protective atmospheres without the aid of flux. The use of flux may require postbraze cleaning and its use increases the likelihood of low-strength joints because of flux entrapment.

Furnace atmosphere dew points must be below $-50°C$ to guarantee the proper metal-metal oxide equilibrium at brazing temperature. The formation of oxide films on heating will be prevented by the high purity of the atmosphere. If adequate atmospheric protection is not provided, it will be necessary to rely on high activity fluxes when brazing stainless steels.

Hydrogen, argon, helium, and dissociated ammonia can be used as furnace atmosphere protection. A precaution to observe is that certain stainless steels may be inadvertently nitrided at brazing temperatures by dissociated ammonia.

Vacuum atmospheres promote wetting by minimizing base metal oxides at brazing temperatures. Surfaces are protected from reoxidation during brazing. The level of vacuum required for satisfactory brazing will vary with a number of factors, e.g., type of equipment, heating rate, base and filler metal out-gassing, etc. Manufacturers of base and filler metals and suppliers of vacuum equipment should be consulted for specific recommendations.

There is no single universal flux for all brazing applications of stainless steel. Flux is required when torch brazing and, in some instances, in furnace-brazing operations. Table 7 lists three fluxes that are commonly used for brazing stainless steel, along with their major constituents and effective temperature range. Flux removal is often necessary after stainless brazing. Removal may be accomplished by water rinsing, chemical or mechanical cleaning, or combinations of these.

TABLE 7   Commercial Brazing Fluxes for Stainless Steel

AWS brazing flux type no.	Suitable filler metals	Effective temperature range, °C	Major constituents
3A	B Ag	570–875	Boric acid, borates, fluorides, fluoborate, wetting agent
3B	B Ag, B Cu, B Au, B Ni	735–1150	Same as 3A
5	B Cu, B Ag (8–19) B Ni, B Au	760–1200	Borax, boric acid, borates

Testing of Brazed Joints

Mechanical Properties. It is important to recognize that the mechanical properties of a brazement depend to a large extent on the design of the joint and the properties of the base metal. Specific mechanical property data for a base metal–filler combination should be treated with care as brazement strength is highly dependent on joint geometry. It is recommended that for critical brazements, preliminary data be obtained using the "Standard Method for Evaluating the Strength of Brazed Joints,"[2] developed by the American Welding Society. More detailed testing of simulated and final brazements should be carried out under service conditions to assure that required performance is attained.

Assuming good brazing procedure, the strength of a brazed stainless steel joint depends to a large extent on the strength of the steel itself. The stronger the steel, the stronger the joint that is obtainable. Strengths may range from 350 to 900MN/m² or more for higher-strength alloys. The effect of base metal strength on joint strength is shown below for 0.95-cm-diameter rod butt joints in Type 303 stainless brazed with filler B Ag-1a.

AISI Type 303	Base metal hardness	Base metal tensile strength, MN/m²	Brazement tensile strength, MN/m²
Lot 1	Rockwell B85	674	350
Lot 2	Rockwell B103	779	630

Standard Test Procedures. The importance of standardizing a method for evaluating the strength of brazed joints cannot be overemphasized. Different test specimen designs will result in different sets of data. Figure 5 illustrates the effect of varying overlap distance on the shear strength of Type 410 stainless steel, brazed in dry hydrogen using B Ni-1 filler metal. The most sensitive portion of the shear strength curve is the low overlap region where apparent joint strength is the highest. The designer should be more interested in the high overlap portion of the curve, where load capacity is the highest. Where possible, the brazement should be designed so that failure occurs in the base metal with a minimum overlap.

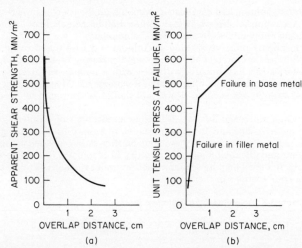

Fig. 5 (*a*) Unit shear stress vs. overlap distance. (*b*) Unit tensile strength vs. overlap distance. (Type 410 stainless lap joint brazed in dry hydrogen—B Ni-1 filler.)

Inspection of Brazed Joints. Inspection is the last step in the brazing procedure and is essential to ensure a high-quality assembly. The inspection method chosen will depend on the service requirements of the assembly. Inspection methods are often specified by regulatory codes or by the ultimate user. Tests and examinations of brazed joints may be conducted on either test specimens or the finished braze assembly, and may be either destructive or nondestructive.

Among the methods normally employed are:

1. Visual examination. The most widely used method of inspection. In critical cases, additional testing procedures are required.
2. Proof testing. Testing under loads greater than the design.
3. Helium leak testing.
4. Fluorescent and dye penetrant inspection procedure.
5. Magnetic particle inspection.
6. Electrical resistance testing.
7. Radiography.
8. Ultrasonic inspection.
9. Destructive mechanical tests—peel, tension, shear, fatigue, torsion.
10. Metallographic examination.

For a detailed description of destructive and nondestructive methods of brazement testing, consult the appropriate section of the "Welding Handbook."[6]

REFERENCES

1. "Welding Handbook," 5th ed., sec. 3, chap. 44, American Welding Society, New York, 1964.
2. "Welding Handbook," 6th ed., sec. 3B, chap. 60, American Welding Society, New York, 1971.
3. "Welding Handbook," 5th ed., sec. 3, chap. 43, American Welding Society, New York, 1964.
4. Interface Corrosion in Brazed Joints in Stainless Steel, *Tech. Bull. T-9,* Handy & Harman, New York.
5. McDonald, A. S.: Alloys for Brazing Thin Sections of Stainless Steel, *Weld. J.,* vol. 36, pp. 131-s–140-s, 1957.
6. "Welding Handbook," 6th ed., sec. 1, chap. 6, American Welding Society, New York, 1968.

Chapter 26

Welding Stainless Steels

WILLIAM E. HENSLEY

**Principal Welding Engineer, Fluor Engineers & Constructors, Inc.,
Irvine, California**

This chapter will cover the welding of stainless steels. It will include the welding of ferritic, martensitic, and austenitic grades in both the wrought and cast states. An additional breakdown will be made for flat plate and pipe. The welding of stainless steels to dissimilar metals will also be discussed. Within these breakdowns, various welding processes, joint preparation, electrode selection, heat treatment, and possible problem areas will be related.

THE WELDING PROCESSES

Shielded Metal-Arc Welding This is a manual welding process in which an arc is formed between the electrode, which is a flux-covered consumable electrode, and the part to be welded. The molten puddle is protected from atmospheric oxidation by the gas shield supplied by the decomposition of the flux coating during combustion. Additional shielding is supplied by a molten slag. The filler metal comes from the center or core of the electrode. A schematic view of this process is found in Fig. 1.

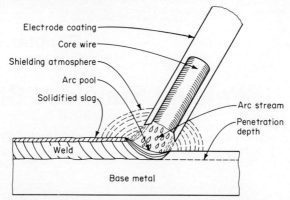

Fig. 1 Schematic of shielded metal-arc welding process.

Shielded metal-arc welding is the most versatile and widely used of all the welding processes. It can be used in nearly any position: overhead, vertical, or horizontal. It can be used in nearly every kind of joint. However, there are several disadvantages:

1. The skill needed to produce a sound weld is greater than with the gas-shielded-arc processes.
2. It is difficult to see during welding because of the slag cover.
3. The slag blanket is a source of inclusions.
4. The slag must be removed between passes.

Welding of the ferritic or martensitic stainless steels by this process is similar to welding carbon steels. They may require preheat or postweld heat treatment to prevent cracking. Austenitic steels have a higher coefficient of expansion than ferritic or martensitic steels and for this reason have more of a tendency to distort and warp. Austenitic stainless steels are welded in the annealed condition and preheating or postweld heat treatment are not commonly used. These points will be discussed in more detail.

Gas-Tungsten-Arc Welding Gas-tungsten-arc welding (GTAW) is a process that may be done either manually or automatically. In this process the heat is provided by an arc between the workpiece and a nonconsumable electrode. Filler metal may or may not be added depending on the joint configuration. Oxidation protection is provided by a stream of inert gas or mixture of gases. Since there is no flux to provide protection, the

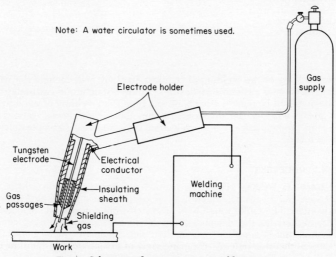

Fig. 2 Schematic of gas-tungsten-arc welding process.

TABLE 1 Nonconsumable Electrodes for Gas-Tungsten-Arc Welding

AWS	Chemical analysis
EWP	99.5% minimum tungsten
EWTh-1	98.5% tungsten + 0.8–1.2% thoria
EWTh-2	97.5% tungsten + 1.7–2.2% thoria
EWTh-3	98.95% tungsten + 0.35–0.55% thoria
EWZr	99.2% tungsten + 0.15–0.40 zirconium

shielding gas must prevent contamination since even a small amount of air will contaminate the weld. A schematic view of this process is found in Fig. 2.

Gas-tungsten-arc welding is a versatile process that can be used in all positions. It is particularly useful in welding thin sections because of the concentrated heat impact of the arc. In general, the process is not used for wall thicknesses above ¼ in. (6.35 mm) because of the relatively slow speed. However, when the welded product demands extremely clear, high-quality work (such as in the aerospace program) gas-tungsten-arc welding is used.

The shielding gases used are argon, helium, or a mixture of argon and helium. The same gases are used for backup. Which of these gases is chosen depends on many things. Argon is generally preferred for the following reasons:

1. It gives better protection at a lower flow rate.

2. It produces lower heat impact and is less likely to result in burn-through in thin sections.

3. It is less affected by variations in the arc.

4. It is less expensive than helium and the supply is more plentiful.

Since helium produces a higher heat impact and deeper penetration, it is used where thicker sections, more than $\frac{1}{16}$ in. (1.59 mm), are to be welded.

There are five types of tungsten electrodes shown in Table 1 that may be used for gas-tungsten-arc welding. The types preferred for welding stainless steels are the thoriated electrodes containing 1.7 to 2.2% thoria. They are recommended because they have better emissive properties and may be used at higher current with better arc stability than pure tungsten electrodes. Care must be taken not to contaminate the molten stainless steel puddle by allowing the end of the electrode to come in contact with the puddle. This can result in pieces of the tungsten electrode becoming embedded in the weld metal, which causes loss in ductility.

Bare stainless steel filler metals are used for GTAW. Since the gas provides the shielding, no coating is necessary. These filler materials are designated by American Welding Society Specification AWS A5.9-69. A list of filler metals and their compositions is found in Table 2. As shown in this table, there are compositions available to match the composition of most stainless steels. However, the choice of the proper filler metal is more difficult than just matching chemistry. Such things as the chemical proportions of the filler metal, as well as the diffusion of the alloying elements, from the filler metal to the weld heat-affected zone, and to the base metal, must be considered. These are discussed in more detail in the section concerned with the welding of the different classes of stainless steels.

Gas-Metal-Arc Welding Gas-metal-arc welding (GMAW) is a semiautomatic machine or automatic process in which an arc is struck between the filler metal and the workpiece which, in turn, supplies the heat. Thus, the filler metal is also the electrode.

TABLE 2 Filler Materials GTAW and GMAW Process for Welding Stainless Steels

Base metal	Filler metal
302, 304, 308	ER308
304L	ER308L
309	ER309
310	ER310
316	ER316
316L	ER316L
321	ER321
347	ER347

Since the filler metal is bare wire, the workpiece must be protected from oxidation by a gas or mixture of gases. A schematic view of this process is found in Fig. 3.

The advantages of this process are numerous. It has greater speed than shielded metal-arc welding since with gas-metal-arc welding the electrode feed is continuous and there is no slag to be removed. In addition, a smaller diameter electrode wire is used for a specific welding current, which results in a higher current density and a more rapid rate of metal deposit. Since there is no slag in this process, it is often possible to produce a more defect-free weld. (Slag is often the source of weld defects for shielded metal-arc welding.) As compared to shielded metal-arc welding, gas-metal-arc welding has a few limitations that should be recognized. In strong winds, gas-metal-arc welding is limited because the gas shield may be blown away; thus protection from strong drafts is needed. Equipment is

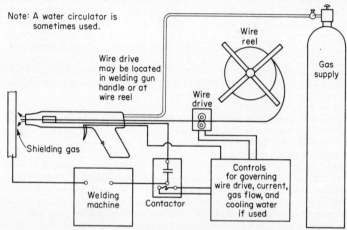

Fig. 3 Schematic of gas-metal-arc welding process.

more expensive, and since there is no slag to cool the weld metal, it cools faster and is more sensitive to weld cracking than it is when welded by shielded metal-arc welding.

Three types of gas-metal-arc welding are used to weld stainless steels: spray transfer, short-circuiting transfer, and pulse-arc transfer. To accomplish spray transfer, a high current density is needed. In this process, the metal transfers across the arc in the form of drops which range from large drops that fall from the end of the electrode to a stream of fine drops that spray from the end of the electrode. Since the voltage and current are high for this process, the puddle is very fluid, limiting the process to flat or horizontal positions. Pulse-arc transfer is a spray-type transfer welding process where the transfer occurs at regular intervals instead of at a random interval. Short-circuiting transfer uses a low current and low heat input, which makes it useful for welding thin sections. It can also be used in any position. The droplet of molten metal makes contact with the workpiece creating a short circuit and the arc is extinguished. When the molten metal bridge is broken, the arc is reignited.

Several shielding gases are used for welding stainless steels with the gas-metal-arc processes. The type of metal transfer has an effect on the type of shielding gas used. The mixture should contain at least 97.5% inert gas (argon or helium) to maintain good oxidation resistance. The gas mixture may have up to 2% oxygen for the spray-arc transfer process, while gas mixtures with up to 2.5% carbon dioxide with argon have been used for short-arc transfer. Mixtures with helium are not commonly used because of its high cost.

Electrode wires used for gas-metal-arc welding are shown in Table 2. The same precautions mentioned above with gas-tungsten-arc welding concerning the selection of filler metals apply here. The full discussion of filler metals is presented later.

Submerged-Arc Welding   The heat for welding in this process is supplied by an arc between the electrode, which is consumable, and the workpiece. In this process, the workpiece is protected from oxidation or other contamination by a layer of granular flux. The molten weld puddle made up of the molten metal and molten flux is highly

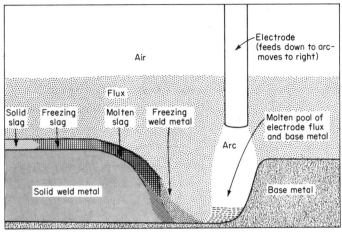

Fig. 4 Schematic of submerged-arc welding process.

conductive and conducts the electricity from the arc to the base metal. The flux has an additional function besides that of acting as a protective shield: it may supply alloying elements, deoxidizers, and scavengers which react with the weld metal. A schematic view of this process is found in Fig. 4.

Submerged-arc welding may be semi- or fully automatic. The advantages of this process are as follows: shielding is not required to protect the operator; the process can be used at high speeds and high deposition rates; the process can be used on nearly any thickness of metal; it may be used for applying a surface or buildup on flat surfaces or pipe. Some of the disadvantages are: flux may become contaminated and cause weld porosity; fixtures are required to contain the flux; the slag must be removed from the welds; the process is restricted to flat and horizontal positions to avoid runoff of the flux.

Generally, the quality of welds is high for submerged-arc welding. However, care must be taken to control the process, since the heat input is higher than found in other processes, the composition of the weld metal is difficult to control and the weld metal is slower to cool. This can affect the grain size and also the diffusion of elements from the flux and weld metal into the heat-affected zone of the base metal. This in turn can deleteriously affect the mechanical properties of the joint and cause cracking due to hot shortness. The selection of filler metal and flux is very important to help eliminate some of the problems just discussed. Table 3 lists suggested electrode wires for submerged-arc welding. It may be necessary to adjust the weld deposit to obtain the desired composition, which can be done with the flux. Alloying elements such as chromium, nickel, molybdenum, and columbium may be added through the flux. If no alloying is necessary through the flux, a neutral flux may be used.

WELDING CHARACTERISTICS OF STAINLESS STEELS

Ferritic Stainless Steels   Ferritic stainless steels are less difficult to weld than martensitic stainless steels. They, by definition, have the composition that produces a ferritic

TABLE 3   Filler Metals for Submerged-Arc Welding

Base metal	Filler metal
302, 304, 308	ER308
304L	ER308L
309	ER309
310	ER310
316	ER316
316L	ER316L
321	ER321
347	ER347

TABLE 4   Preheat and Postweld Heat Treatment of Ferritic Stainless Steels

Type	Preheat temperature, °F (°C)	Postweld annealing temperature, °F (°C)
405	150–300 (66–149)	1200–1400 (648–760), air-cooled
409	150–300 (66–149)	1200–1400 (648–760), air-cooled
430	150–300 (66–149)	1400–1550 (760–842), air-cooled
442	300–500 (149–260)	1450–1650 (787–898), rapidly cooled
446	300–500 (149–260)	

structure at room temperature (see Chap. 5). However, variation or segregation in the normal chemical composition can cause formation of small amounts of martensite after heating above the austenitic-forming temperature and cooling to room temperature. While the amount of martensite formation is small, it is located at the grain boundaries in the heat-affected zone after welding. The formation of martensite may result in lower ductility and toughness. The detrimental martensite may be removed by postweld annealing. However, if postweld heat treating is not possible, it is recommended that a ferritic stainless steel with strong ferrite formers, such as Ti, Al, Cb, be used to prevent formation of martensite.

Ductility and toughness are markedly increased with small increases in temperatures. For this reason, preheating is frequently used to prevent weld cracking. The need to preheat is determined by many parameters such as composition, type of joint, mechanical properties, and thickness of the steel being welded.

Beneficial effects from preheating are due to the reduction of shrinkage stresses by lowering the ΔT between base and weld metal and by reducing the yield strength. The exact preheat temperature is difficult to determine without knowing all of the parameters, but a temperature in the range of 150 to 550°F (66 to 288°C) is generally sufficient to prevent cracking. See Table 4 for specific temperatures.

Generally, steels less that ¼ in. (6.35 mm) thick are not preheated since they are less likely to crack than those over ¼ in. (6.35 mm) thick.

Postweld heat treating is used to accomplish two purposes: to relieve stress and to transform any martensite to ferrite. This, in turn, results in a completely ferritic structure and restores the corrosion resistance and mechanical properties to their original state. The only condition caused by the high welding temperatures that cannot be corrected is that of ferritic grain coarsening. Before the decision is made to postweld heat-treat, the increased cost of fixturing, prevention of scale, and time must be considered. Because of the brittle temperature range of 1050 to 750°F (565 to 399°C), care must be taken not to slow cool through this range. Other than that, ferritic stainless steel may be cooled either in air or by water quenching. (See Table 4 for specific temperatures.)

The filler metals used to weld the subject material are shown in Table 5. As shown in this table, both austenitic and ferritic filler metals are used. The ferritic filler metals, when used, give the weld joint essentially the same physical and mechanical properties as well as matching color, appearance, and corrosion resistance. Austenitic stainless steels are used when the design or joint configuration demands a more ductile joint in the as-welded condition. The ferritic stainless steels should be welded with the austenitic stainless steel fillers if the material is to be used in the as-welded condition. If, however, they are to be annealed after welding, a matching ferritic filler metal is used. Problems may be encountered with a postweld heat-treat cycle if austenitic stainless steel fillers are used. The normal range for postweld annealing, 1450 to 1550°F (778 to 842°C), is in the sensitizing-temperature range for austenitic steels. Therefore, the use of austenitic steel fillers in this case should be avoided.

Martensitic Stainless Steels   Martensitic stainless steels are more difficult to weld than the ferritic stainless steels because of the phase change from austenite to martensite

TABLE 5   Welding Electrodes for Ferritic Stainless Steel

Type	Electrode or rods
405	405 (Cb), 430, 308, 309, 310
430	430, 308, 309, 310
430F	430, 308, 309, 310
442	442, 308, 309, 310
446	446, 308, 309, 310

(face-centered cubic to body-centered cubic structure) that occurs during cooling after welding. Because of the change in volume, increased hardness, and accompanying loss of ductility, special care must be taken to prevent these steels from cracking. These treatments will be discussed in more detail later.

The types of martensitic stainless steels are 403, 410, 414, 416, 416 Si, 420, 431, 440A, 440B, and 440C (see Chap. 6). They derive their corrosion resistance from chromium which ranges from 11.5 to 18%. Since chromium is a ferrite former, the steels with higher chromium require more carbon to promote martensite formation during heat treatment. With the increased carbon content, the problem of preventing cracking in the heat-affected zone becomes more difficult.

The most effective way to prevent cracking is to preheat and control the interpass temperature. The usual preheat temperature range for martensitic stainless steels is 400 to 600°F (205 to 316°C). Carbon content is used to judge whether or not preheating is necessary. Below 0.10% carbon, neither preheat nor postweld heat treatment is necessary. Carbon between 0.10 and 0.20% requires a preheat up to 500°F (260°C). This class of stainless steels is always welded in the annealed condition, since the material, in the heat-treated condition, has a martensitic structure which is hard and brittle. The martensitic structures do not have the ductility to accept the stress imposed by the thermal change caused by welding and, if they were welded in this condition, severe cracking would result. Martensitic stainless steels have been designed by their chemistry to produce high strength. To obtain this strength, they must be given a postweld heat treatment after welding. This treatment consists of heating to a temperature high enough to form austenite and then rapidly quenching to room temperature. The quenching media may be air for thin sections or oil for thicker sections. Care must be taken to prevent warping and distortion during quenching. These problems can be minimized by proper fixturing and proper design. Table 6 shows the recommended postweld heat treatments for martensitic stainless steels. In addition, these steels must be protected from oxidation during heat treatment. Argon and helium gas may be used to provide this protection, but they are very expensive. Exothermic or endothermic gases are much cheaper and provide excellent protection and are, therefore, used more often.

Austenitic Stainless Steels   Austenitic stainless steels are more weldable than the other grades of stainless steels. Because they undergo no phase change, regardless of temperature, and because they have a face-centered cubic structure, the weld joints are ductile and tough even in the as-welded condition. Exceptions are the free-machining grades which contain sulfur (303) or selenium (303 Se). These elements cause severe hot-short cracking. Other grades of austenitic stainless steels are 302, 304, and 304L, which differ in their carbon content. Consequently, they differ in their weldability and performance in service because of the amount of carbon present to form carbides in the heat-affected zone after the heating and cooling cycle during welding. Other types of austenitic stainless steels, developed for increased corrosion resistance and higher creep strength, are 316, 316Cb, 316L, and 317. All of these contain molybdenum, a carbide former, which promotes carbides in the grain boundaries of the heat-affected zone during welding. The formation of carbides can be inhibited by an extra-low-carbon content, as in 316L. Stabilized austenitic stainless steels are 318, 321, 347, and 348. These grades are stabilized with columbium, columbium plus tantalum, or titanium to prevent the formation of chromium carbides where these steels are heated in the sensitizing range 800 to 1600°F (420 to 871°C) during welding or during operation after welding.

As indicated previously, the principal problem encountered with welding stainless

TABLE 6   Postweld Heat Treating of Martensitic Stainless Steels

Type	Austenitizing temperature, °F (°C)	Tempering temperature, °F (°C)
403, 410	1700–1850 (926–1008)	900–1200 (482–648)
414	1700–1925 (926–1050)	900–1200 (482–648)
416, 416 Se	1700–1850 (926–1008)	1000–1200 (538–648)
420	1800–1950 (981–1063)	400–700 (204–371)
431	1800–1950 (981–1063)	1000–1175 (538–635)
440A	1850–1950 (1008–1063)	300–700 (150–371)
440B	1850–1950 (1008–1063)	300–700 (150–371)
440C	1850–1950 (1008–1063)	375 (190)

steels is that of carbide precipitation. Unstabilized stainless steels (such as Types 302, 304, 316, and 317) are subject to carbide precipitation when heated in the 800 to 1600°F (426 to 871°C) range. This carbide precipitation is in the form of chromium carbides and occurs at the grain boundaries. This, in turn, results in a depletion of chromium in the matrix adjacent to the grain boundaries which in turn reduces corrosion resistance. As the result of high temperatures encountered during welding, this condition occurs in the heat-affected zone. The problem just described can be overcome in three ways. For Types 302, 304, 316, and 317, sensitization can be removed by solution heat treatment whereby the carbides are put back into solution and the normal corrosion resistance is restored. However, this treatment may be inconvenient and sometimes may be impossible to perform. The solution treatment temperature is very high, 1875 to 2000°F (1022 to 1093°C). At these temperatures, unless the steels are protected from the atmosphere, oxidation will occur. In addition, these sections may sag unless supported, or severe distortion may occur during rapid cooling. If these grades cannot be solution treated after welding, it is recommended that the user consider either the low-carbon grades or the stabilized grades instead.

Extra-low-carbon stainless steels (such as 304L and 316L), because of their low-carbon content, are less susceptible to carbide precipitation in the 800 to 1600°F (426 to 871°C) range. They have enough immunity to carbide precipitation to be weldable without causing loss of corrosion resistance in the heat-affected zone. However, if they are held at this temperature for prolonged periods of time, sensitization will occur. Therefore, they are used only to 800°F (426°C).

The stabilized grades, 318, 321, 347, and 348 are usable to higher temperatures in the sensitizing temperature range because they have higher strength at elevated temperatures and because they do not form intergranular chromium carbides when heated in the 800 to 1600°F (426 to 871°C) temperature range. The addition of titanium or columbium or columbium plus tantalum tie up the carbon as stable carbides in the matrix. These carbides do not go into solution during the rapid heating caused by welding. Therefore, the chromium-depleted areas are not present to contribute to corrosion problems.

Another problem that must be accounted for when welding austenitic stainless steels is that of microfissuring. Microfissuring is the intergranular cracking that occurs in the weld metal or in the heat-affected zone and is sometimes referred to as hot cracking. Weld metal that is wholly austenitic is more susceptible to hot cracking than that which contains some delta ferrite. The alloy content of the weld metal is therefore very important to the susceptibility to this problem. Thus, the filler metal must be of a suitable composition to produce a controlled amount of ferrite; 3 to 5% ferrite is the desired amount to prevent hot cracking. The Schaeffler diagram (Fig. 5) can be used to determine the amount of ferrite present in a weld of a given composition. Another way to measure the ferrite is to use a magnetic analysis device. Since ferrite is magnetic and austenite is not, the magnetic device is calibrated to show the extent of magnetic force, and thus the amount of ferrite present in the microstructure.

Preheating of austenitic stainless steels is not recommended since no benefit can be obtained. On the other hand, postweld stress relieving is recommended. Stress-relief heat treatment is generally done at a temperature high enough to be out of the sensitizing range; 1650°F (898°C) is a standard temperature used.

Filler metals recommended for austenitic stainless steel are found in Table 7. The selection of filler materials must be given careful consideration to prevent loss of corrosion and hot-short cracking. Types 310, 310Cb, 310Mo, and 330 produce a weld that is fully austenitic. Thus, other electrodes, such as 308, and 309, are used when fully restrained joints are to be welded. As discussed earlier, the Schaeffler diagram can be used to predict the amount of ferrite. Most filler metal compositions are adjusted by the manufacturers to yield a weld deposit that will contain enough ferrite to prevent problems.

Precipitation-Hardenable Stainless Steels The chemical compositions of the typical precipitation-hardening stainless steels are discussed in Chap. 7. The steels are commonly divided into three classes and will be discussed as such.

Martensitic. The martensitic stainless steels have an austenitic structure in the solution-treating temperature range, between 1900 and 1950°F (1036 to 1063°C), but undergo an austenite-to-martensite phase transformation when cooled to room temperature. When reheated to 900 to 1100°F (482 to 593°C), precipitation occurs. As the precipitation occurs, the soft martensite is strengthened (in the matrix) and hardened. The hardening is due to

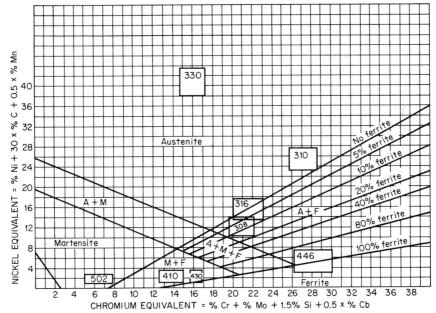

Fig. 5 Constitution diagram of stainless steel weld metal. (Chart is to be used for guidance only. Other factors such as base metal, mass effect, cooling rate, etc., will influence the results.)

the precipitation of alloying elements like copper, molybdenum, aluminum, titanium, and columbium as intermetallic compounds. These steels are usually very weldable. The filler materials generally used match the base metals being welded, although the 300 series stainless steel fillers may be used if the joint strength does not have to match the base metal strength.

Semiaustenitic. The semiaustenitic stainless steels, because of their chemical composition, do not transform to martensite when cooled to room temperature, but retain their austenitic structure. For these steels to be strengthened, they must be heated to a temperature range between 1200 and 1600°F (648 to 815°C) where precipitation occurs. This depletes the matrix of enough austenite-forming elements to permit the phase transformation from austenite to martensite as the steel is cooled again to room temperature. These steels are strengthened by heating to 800 to 1100°F (426 to 593°C) where precipitation occurs. The reaction is similar to that of the martensitic stainless steels. These steels are readily weldable and are usually welded in the soft, tough austenitic condition. They are therefore similar to the 300 series stainless steels in weldability. However, they can be welded in the as-transformed martensite condition due to the low

TABLE 7   Filler Metals Recommended for Welding Austenitic Stainless Steels

Type of steel	Electrode or rod
302, 304	308
304L	308L, 347
303, 303 Se	312
310	310
316	316
316L	318, 316L
317	317
318	318
321	347
347	347
348	347

hardness and high ductility of the martensite at that point. Like the martensitic precipitation-hardening stainless steels, these materials may be welded with the 300 filler metals if matching joint efficiency to base metal strength is not necessary. However, if high strength is needed, the filler metal should match the base metal. This grade should be fully heat-treated after welding to obtain full strength of the weld joint.

Austenitic. Austenitic precipitation-hardening stainless steels have enough alloy content to remain austenitic regardless of the heat treatment. These steels are heat-treated by solution treating at 2000 to 2050°F (1093 to 1120°C) and rapidly cooling to room temperature. This is followed by precipitation at 1200 to 1400°F (648 to 760°C). Because the matrix is austenitic, the resultant hardness is less than that of the other two types. Alloys of the austenitic group are generally welded using matching filler metals.

DISSIMILAR METAL WELDING OF STAINLESS STEELS

Ferritic and martensitic stainless steels are readily weldable to most other steels, such as carbon steels and low-alloy steels, as well as austenitic stainless steels. Generally, when dissimilar material combinations are being welded, the metallurgy of the combinations must be taken into consideration in the selection of filler metal, welding procedures, joint design, and heat treatment. Austenitic filler materials can be used to join almost any combination when welding dissimilar stainless steels. Type 309 is one of the most popular filler materials for making dissimilar metal joints. Another widely used filler is the nickel-chromium-iron material ERNiCrFe-6. The welding procedure and joint design selections will depend on many specifics that cannot be considered in this chapter, but in all cases it is best to use processes and designs to minimize residual stresses. It is good practice to "butter" surfaces of dissimilar metals with an austenitic stainless steel, such as Type 309, prior to making the weld joint. By doing this, any heat treatment that is necessary to provide strength to the base material can be done before making the weld joint. Therefore, when the weld joint is made, and high restraint is present, the actual joint is between two austenitic stainless steel materials and further heat treatment is not necessary. As discussed before, the austenitic joint is a ductile joint that can deform without cracking. Carbon-steel filler materials should never be used since they will produce a hard, brittle weld deposit that is very sensitive to cracking. As far as heat treating is concerned, any that is to be used must be designed to the different materials involved and must be related to the properties desired. The heat treatment must be based on prior experience and cannot be detailed specifically.

When welding austenitic stainless steels to carbon steels, an austenitic stainless steel filler metal should be used. Again, Type 309 filler is the most widely used. As discussed above, it is advisable to "butter" the surface of the carbon steel with a layer of 309 filler to prevent or minimize cracking. Low-carbon electrodes should be avoided. Welding of one type of austenite to another often occurs in actual practice. When this occurs, a filler metal that matches the chemistry of either base metal should be used.

JOINT DESIGN CONSIDERATIONS

Joint Configurations Welding process, welding position and material thickness must be taken into account when choosing the type of joint. The choice also depends on whether homogeneous or clad plate is to be welded. In the latter case, the type of joint must be such that the stainless layer is not melted when depositing the root bead on the carbon-steel side. If this should occur, the result may be a root bead of low-alloy content, sensitive to crack formation. In welding clad plate from the stainless side, an over-alloyed electrode (22Cr-12-14Ni-3Mo) must be used.

Ideal joint configurations for homogeneous plate are shown in Fig. 6. Fig 7 gives details for clad-plate joints.

Joint Economics. Table 8 shows the average value, for horizontal welding, of current, welding rate, welding time and electrode consumption when welding either a butt joint or V-groove joint. The data are based on electrodes with either a basic or rutile coating and include stub losses. Similar data for fillet welds and corner or lap welds are given in Table 9.

Fig. 6 Ideal joint designs for homogeneous sheet and plate. *(Avesta Jernverks Aktiebolag.)*

BUTT JOINT BETWEEN PLATES WITH RAISED EDGES

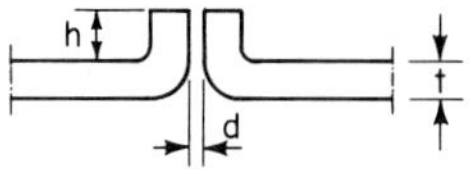

Welding process	Dimensions, mm (in.)	Remarks
TIG welding	$t \leqslant 2$ (0.08) $h = 1.5–2$ $d = 0$	The edges are melted down to form a butt weld

EDGE JOINT

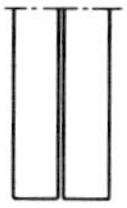

TIG welding		Normally used for light gage sheet. In the case of material thickness greater than 3 mm (0.08 in.) the weld should be regarded as a seal weld only. Carried out with or without filler wire

BUTT JOINT

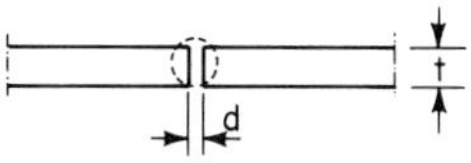

Welding process	Dimensions, mm (in.)	Remarks
Metal-arc welding	$t = 1–3$ (0.04–0.12) $d = 0–1$ (0–0.04)	Backing bar is recommended
Submerged-arc welding	$t = 2–4$ (0.08–0.16) $d = 0$	Backing bar required
Manual TIG welding	$t = 1–3$ (0.04–0.12) $d = 0–2$ (0–0.08)	Carried out with or without filler wire depending on gap width
TIG welding	$t = 1.5–3$ (0.06–0.12) $d = 0$	Carried out with or without filler wire
MIG welding	$t = 2–4$ (0.08–0.16) $d = 0–2$ (0–0.08)	Backing bar required

BUTT JOINT

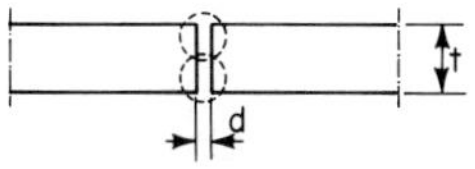

Welding process	Dimensions, mm (in.)	Remarks
Metal-arc welding	$t = 3–4$ (0.12–0.16) $d = 0–2$ (0–0.08)	
Submerged-arc welding	$t = 4–8$ (0.16–0.32) $d = 0$	Backing bar recommended

Welding process	Dimensions, mm (in.)	Remarks
Manual TIG welding	$t = 3–5$ (0.12–0.20) $d = 0–1$ (0–0.04)	Filler wire used
TIG welding	$t = 3–6$ (0.12–0.24) $d = 0$	Filler wire used
Manual MIG welding	$t = 4–8$ (0.16–0.32) $d = 0–1$ (0–0.04)	
MIG welding	$t = 3–8$ (0.12–0.32) $d = 0–1$ (0–0.04)	

SINGLE VEE JOINT

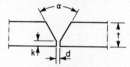

Welding process	Dimensions, mm (in.)	Remarks
Metal-arc welding	$t = 3–12$ (0.12–0.47) $d = 1–3$ (0.04–0.12) $k = 0–2$ (0–0.08) $\alpha = 60°$	Single- or double-sided weld
Submerged-arc welding	$t = 8–12$ (0.32–0.47) $d = 0–2$ (0–0.08) $k = 0–2$ (0–0.08) $\alpha = 60°$	Single- or double-sided weld. Metal-arc welded root beads as support
TIG welding	$t = 4–6$ (0.16–0.24) $d = 0–0.3$ (0–0.01) $k = 1.5–2$ (0.06–0.08) $\alpha = 90°$	Single-sided weld. Used for welding root beads where high quality is required especially as regards surface finish. Filling carried out by another process
TIG welding with filler wire	$t = 6–15$ (0.24–0.59) $d = 0–0.4$ (0–0.015) $k = 1–1.5$ (0.04–0.06) $\alpha = 70°$	
Manual MIG welding	$t = 4–12$ (0.16–0.47) $d = 0–2$ (0–0.08) $k = 2–3$ (0.08–0.12) $\alpha = 60°$	Single- or double-sided weld
MIG welding	$t = 8–12$ (0.32–0.47) $d = 0–2$ (0–0.08) $k = 0–2$ (0–0.08) $\alpha = 60°$	Single- or double-sided weld. Metal-arc welded root beads as support

SINGLE VEE JOINT FOR HORIZONTAL WELD WITH WORKPIECES VERTICAL

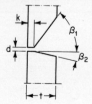

Fig. 6   *(Continued)*

Welding process	Dimensions, mm (in.)	Remarks
Metal-arc welding Manual MIG welding	$t = 8\text{--}25$ (0.32–0.98) $d = 1.5\text{--}3.5$ (0.06–0.14) $k = 1\text{--}2.5$ (0.04–0.10) $\beta_1 = 55°$ $\beta_2 \cong 10°$	The angles may be varied from the values stated but β_1 + β_2 must be $\geqslant 60°$

U JOINT

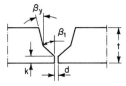

Welding process	Dimensions, mm (in.)	Remarks
Metal-arc welding Submerged-arc welding	$t = 12\text{--}20$ (0.47–0.94) $d = 0\text{--}2$ (0–0.08) $k = 2\text{--}3$ (0.08–0.12) $\beta_1 = 30\text{--}45°$ $\beta_y = 15°$	Single- or double-sided weld. Metal-arc welded root beads as support in submerged-arc welding

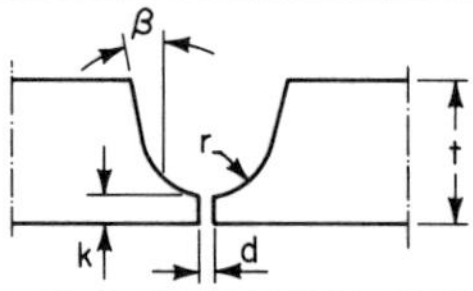

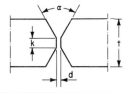

MIG welding Manual MIG welding	$t = 12\text{--}20$ (0.47–0.79) $d = 0\text{--}2$ (0–0.08) $k = 2\text{--}3$ (0.08–0.12) $r = 6$ (0.24) $\beta = 15°$	Single- or double-sided weld. Metal-arc welded root beads as support in MIG welding

DOUBLE VEE JOINT

Welding process	Dimensions, mm (in.)	Remarks
Metal-arc welding Submerged-arc welding	$t = 12\text{--}30$ (0.47–1.18) $d = 1\text{--}3$ (0.04–0.12) $k = 0\text{--}2$ (0–0.08) $\alpha = 60°$	Metal-arc welded root beads as support in submerged-arc welding
MIG welding Manual MIG welding	$t = 12\text{--}30$ (0.47–1.18) $d = 0\text{--}2$ (0–0.08) $k = 2\text{--}3$ (0.08–0.12) $\alpha = 60°$	Metal-arc welded root beads as support in MIG welding

Fig. 6   (Continued)

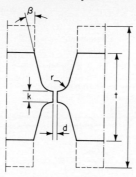

Welding process	Dimensions, mm (in.)	Remarks
Metal-arc welding	$t \geqslant 30$ (1.18) $d = 1\text{–}3$ (0.04–0.12) $k = 0\text{–}2$ (0–0.08) $r = 6\text{–}8$ (0.24–0.32) $\beta = 10\text{–}15°$	The joint may be made with straight outer edges ($\beta = 0°$) to a depth $\leqslant$ the width, for material thicknesses greater than 100 mm (3.84 in.)

Fig. 7 Ideal joint designs for clad sheet and plate. *(Avesta Jernverks Aktiebolag.)*

SINGLE VEE JOINT

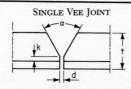

Welding process	Dimensions, mm (in.)	Remarks
Metal-arc welding	$t = 10\text{–}16$ (0.39–0.63) $d = 0\text{–}2$ (0–0.08) $k = 1.5\text{–}2$ (0.06–0.08) $\alpha = 60°$	

U JOINT

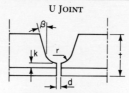

Welding process	Dimensions, mm (in.)	Remarks
Metal-arc welding Submerged-arc welding	$t = 15\text{–}25$ (0.59–0.98) $d = 0\text{–}2$ (0–0.08) $k = 1.5\text{–}2$ (0.06–0.08) $r = 6$ (0.24) $\beta = 15°$	Submerged-arc welding is supplemented by metal-arc welding for root beads and cladding

DOUBLE VEE JOINT

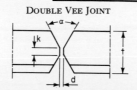

Welding process	Dimensions, mm (in.)	Remarks
Metal-arc welding Submerged-arc welding	$t = 20\text{--}40\ (0.79\text{--}1.57)$ $d = 0\text{--}3\ (0\text{--}0.12)$ $k = 0\text{--}2\ (0\text{--}0.08)$ $\alpha = 60°$	Submerged-arc welding is supplemented by metal-arc welding for root beads and cladding

DOUBLE Y JOINT

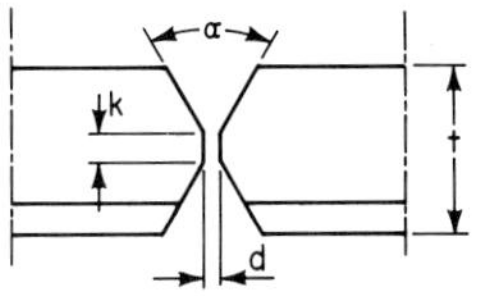

Welding process	Dimensions, mm (in.)	Remarks
Submerged-arc welding	$t = 20\text{--}40\ (0.79\text{--}1.57)$ $d = 0\text{--}0.5\ (0\text{--}0.02)$ $k = 4\text{--}6\ (0.16\text{--}0.24)$ $\alpha = 60°$	Cladding welded with covered electrodes

DOUBLE U JOINT

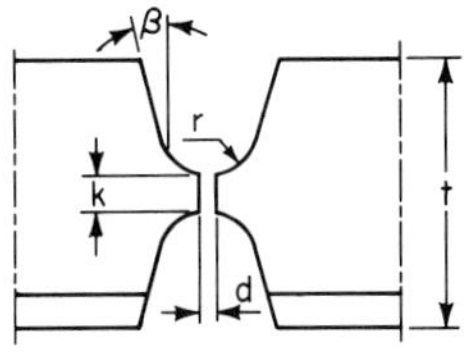

Welding process	Dimensions, mm (in.)	Remarks
Metal-arc welding	$t \geqslant 30\ (1.18)$ $d = 0\text{--}3\ (0\text{--}0.12)$ $k = 2\text{--}3\ (0.08\text{--}0.12)$ $r = 6\ (0.24)$ $\beta = 15°$	

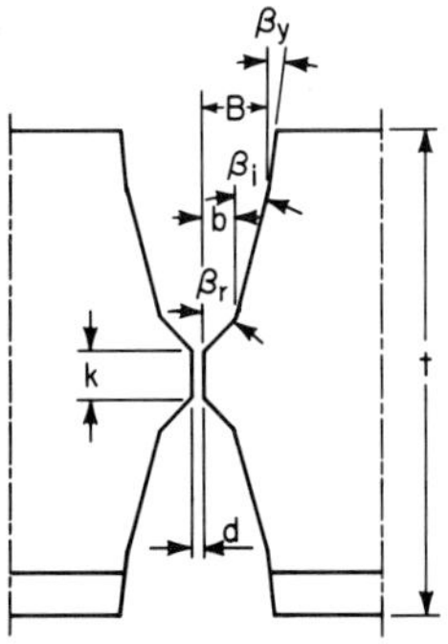

Submerged-arc welding	$t \geqslant 30\ (1.18)$ $d = 0\text{--}0.5\ (0\text{--}0.02)$ $k = 4\text{--}6\ (0.16\text{--}0.24)$ $b = 6\text{--}8\ (0.24\text{--}0.32)$ $B = 20\ (0.79)$ $\beta_r = 45°$ $\beta_i = 15°$ $\beta_y = 4°$	Cladding welded with covered electrodes. $B = 20$ mm (0.29 in.) for thicknesses $\geqslant 110$ mm (4.33 in.) other data being the same

Fig. 7 *(Continued)*

TABLE 8 Data for Welding Calculations

BUTT WELDING FROM ONE SIDE

Material thickness, t		Electrode diameter		Gap width, d		Current, A	Welding rate		Number of electrodes per meter (ft) of weld	Welding time per meter (ft) of weld min
mm	in.	mm	in.	mm	in.		cm/min	in./min		
1.5	0.06	2.0	0.08	0.5–0.7	0.02–0.03	35–45	30	11.8	3.7 (1.13)	3.3 (1.0)
2.0	0.08	2.5	0.10	0.8–1.0	0.03–0.04	55–70	32	12.6	2.9 (0.88)	3.1 (0.95)
2.5	0.10	3.25	0.13	1.0–1.2	0.04–0.05	85–105	36	14.2	2.6 (0.79)	2.8 (0.85)
3.0	0.12	3.25	0.13	1.2–1.5	0.05–0.06	90–110	34	13.4	2.9 (0.88)	2.9 (0.88)

BUTT WELDING FROM BOTH SIDES*

Material thickness, t		Bead no.	Electrode diameter		Gap width, d		Current, A	Welding rate		Number of electrodes per meter (ft) of weld	Welding time per meter (ft) of weld min
mm	in.		mm	in.	mm	in.		cm/min	in./min		
2.0	0.08	1 2	2.5	0.10	0.8–1.0	0.03–0.04	55–70	32	12.6	6.4 (2)	6.3 (1.92)
2.5	0.10	1 2	3.25	0.13	1.0–1.2	0.04–0.05	85–105	36	14.2	5.4 (1.6)	5.6 (1.7)
3.0	0.12	1 2	3.25	0.13	1.2–1.5	0.05–0.06	90–110	35	13.8	5.7 (1.7)	5.7 (1.7)

4.0	0.16	1	4.0	0.16	1.5–2.0	0.06–0.08	115–140	33	13	2.2	5.0	(0.7)	3.1	6.1	(0.9)	(1.8)
		2	3.25	0.13			90–110			2.8		(0.9)	3.0		(0.9)	
5.0	0.20	1	5.0	0.20	2.0–2.5	0.08–0.10	150–175	32	12.6	2.1	4.5	(0.6)	3.1	6.3	(0.9)	(1.9)
		2	4.0	0.16			110–135			2.4		(0.7)	3.2	(1)		

Single-V Groove Joint†

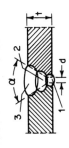

Material thickness (mm / in.)	Bead no.	Electrode diameter (mm / in.)	Gap width, d (mm / in.)	Current, A	Welding rate (cm/min / in./min)	Number of electrodes per meter (ft) of weld	Welding time per meter (ft) of weld (min)
4.0 / 0.16	1 2	2.5 0.10 3.25 0.13	1.0 / 0.04	70–80 95–110	25 / 9.8	4.6 (1.4) 3.9 (1.2) 8.5 2.6	8.0 (2.4)
5.0 / 0.20	1 2	2.5 0.10 4.0 0.16	1.0 / 0.04	65–75 110–135	24 / 9.4	4.6 (1.4) 3.1 (0.9) 7.7 2.3	8.2 (2.5)
6.0 / 0.24	1 2	3.25 0.13 4.0 0.16	1.5 / 0.06	80–100 120–140	20 / 7.9	4.0 (1.2) 4.3 (1.3) 8.3 2.5	10.0 (3.1)
7.0 / 0.28	1 2	3.25 0.13 5.0 0.20	1.5 / 0.06	90–110 150–180	18 / 7.1	4.5 (1.4) 4.1 (1.3) 8.6 2.7	11.0 (3.4)
8.0 / 0.32	1 2	4.0 0.16 5.0 0.20	2.0 / 0.08	110–130 155–190	18 / 7.1	3.5 (1.1) 4.4 (1.3) 7.9 2.4	11.2 (3.4)
9.0 / 0.35	1 2	4.0 0.16 5.0 0.20	2.0 / 0.08	110–130 160–195	15 / 5.9	4.0 (1.2) 5.8 (1.8) 9.8 3.0	13.4 (4.1)
10.0 / 0.39	1 2 3	4.0 0.16 4.0 0.16 5.0 0.20	2.0 / 0.08	110–130 120–145 160–195	17 / 6.7	4.0 (1.2) 4.5 (1.4) 5.0 (1.5) 13.5 4.1	17.9 (5.5)

TABLE 8 Data for Welding Calculations *(Continued)*

DOUBLE-V GROOVE JOINT ‡

*The root has been ground prior to applying the back weld.
†*Note:* For a back weld, the requirements per meter will be either about 5 electrodes of 2.5 mm
(0.10 in.) or about 3.5 electrodes of 3.25 mm (0.14 in.) depending on the amount ground away.
‡For calculation purposes, a double-V groove joint is regarded as two single-V groove joints.
SOURCE: Avesta Jernverks Aktiebolag.

TABLE 9 Data for Welding Calculations

FILLET WELD*

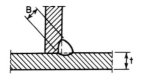

Material thickness, t		Electrode diameter		Bead thickness, B		Current, A	Welding rate		Number of electrodes per meter (ft) of weld		Welding time per meter (ft) of weld	
mm	in.	mm	in.	mm	in.		cm/min	in./min				
1.5	0.06	2.0	0.08	2.0	0.08	40–50	22	8.7	6.0	(1.8)	4.6	(1.4)
2.0	0.08	2.5	0.10	2.5	0.10	55–75	22	8.7	4.8	(1.5)	4.6	(1.4)
2.5	0.10	2.5	0.10	2.5	0.10	60–80	24	9.4	4.8	(1.5)	4.2	(1.3)
3.0	0.12	3.25	0.13	3.0	0.12	85–105	26	10.2	4.0	(1.2)	3.8	(1.2)
4.0	0.16	3.25	0.13	3.0	0.12	95–115	28	11	4.0	(1.2)	3.6	(1.1)
5.0	0.20	4.0	0.16	3.5	0.14	120–140	26	10.2	3.1	(0.9)	3.9	(1.2)
6.0	0.24	4.0	0.16	4.0	0.16	125–145	20	7.9	4.0	(1.2)	5.0	(1.5)
7.0	0.28	4.0	0.16	4.5	0.18	130–150	16	6.3	5.1	(1.6)	6.1	(1.9)
8.0	0.32	5.0	0.20	5.0	0.20	160–180	18	7.1	4.0	(1.2)	5.7	(1.7)
9.0	0.35	5.0	0.20	5.5	0.22	165–190	15	5.9	4.8	(1.5)	6.5	(2)
10.0	0.39	5.0	0.20	6.0	0.24	170–200	13	5.1	5.7	(1.7)	7.5	(2.3)

CORNER AND LAP WELDS†

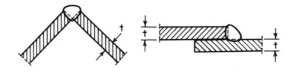

Material thickness, t		Electrode diameter		Current, A	Welding rate		Number of electrodes per meter (ft) of weld		Welding time per meter (ft) of weld	
mm	in.	mm	in.		cm/min	in./min				
1.5	0.06	2.0	0.08	45–55	50	19.7	2.9	(0.9)	2.0	(0.6)
2.0	0.08	2.5	0.10	65–75	45	17.7	2.4	(0.7)	2.2	(0.7)
2.5	0.10	2.5	0.10	70–80	42	16.5	2.6	(0.8)	2.4	(0.7)
3.0	0.12	3.25	0.14	95–105	40	15.7	2.2	(0.7)	2.5	(0.8)
4.0	0.16	3.25	0.14	100–115	33	13	3.2	(1)	3.0	(0.9)
5.0	0.20	4.0	0.16	125–140	29	11.4	2.7	(0.8)	3.4	(1)

*The data given here are valid for a bead deposited on workpieces at right angles to each other.
†The data given here are valid for one bead.
SOURCE: Avesta Jernverks Aktiebolag.

TABLE 10 Parameters for Arc Welding High-Alloy Castings

ACI alloy*	Preheat	Postheat	Electrodes/filler metals, AWS designations			Remarks
			Shielded-metal-arc (SMA) electrodes†	Gas-metal-arc (GMA) electrodes§	Gas-tungsten-arc (GTA) filler metals¶	
			CORROSION-RESISTANT TYPES			
CA-6NM	212–300°F (100–149°C)	Heat to 1100–1150°F (593–620°C), air-cool	Lime-coated of similar composition			Interpass temperature: 500–600°F (260–315°C). Preheat not required for small welds in sections not subject to high stresses. Electrodes for nonpreheated castings should have a carbon content of about 0.04%.
CA-15	400–600°F (204–315°C)	Heat to 1125–1450°F (606–787°C), air-cool	E410-15	ER410	ER410	Large or critical welds may be given a full post-weld reheat treatment to 1750°F (953°C) min, followed by a temper. Do not cool below 300°F (149°C) prior to postheat treatment.
CA-40	300–600°F (149–315°C)	Cool to 300°F (149°C) min, heat to 1100–1450°F (593–787°C), air- or furnace-cool	E410-15	ER410	ER410	
CB-7Cu	Not required (see remarks)	Harden at 900–1100°F (482–593°C); to restore heavy-section hardenability, heat at 1850–1950°F (1008–1063°C), quench	Lime-coated 17-4PH	17-4PH	17-4PH	Large welds in sections thicker than ¾ in. (19.05 cm) can be preheated to 500°F (260°C). Single-pass welds normally do not require postweld heat treatment. Noncritical fabrication welds can be made with AWS E308-15 or E312-15 (or ER308 or ER312).
CB-30	600–800°F (315–426°C)	Cool to 150°F (65°C) max, heat to 1450°F (787°C) min, air-cool	E442-15			
CC-50	400–1300°F (204–704°C)	Heat to 1550–1900°F (842–1036°C), air-cool	E446-15	Not recommended	No filler, root passes only	Low-ductility, difficult-to-weld alloy. AWS E310-15, E312-15, and E329-15 are also used to improve weld ductility.
CD-4MCu	Not required	Heat to 2050°F (1120°C) min, furnace-cool to 1900–1750°F (1036–953°C) range, quench	Lime-coated of similar composition	Not recommended	Cast rod of similar composition	
CE-30	Not required	Heat to 2000–2050°F (1093–1120°C), quench	E312-15			
CF-3	Not required (see remarks)	Not required	E308L-15	ER308L	ER308L	Postheat [1900°F (1036°C) min, quench] may be used if castings will be exposed to severely corrosive environments. Use AWS E308-15, E316-15, ER308, or ER316 if postheat specified.
CF-3M	Not required (see remarks)	Not required	E316L-15	ER316L	ER316L	
CF-8	Not required	Heat to 1900–2050°F (1036–1120°C), quench	E308-15	ER308	ER308	

Alloy	Preheat	Postweld heat treatment	Covered electrode	Bare welding rod or electrode	Bare welding rod or electrode	Remarks
CF-8C	Not required	Heat to 1950–2050°F (1063–1120°C), quench	E347-15	ER316	ER316	Postweld heat treatment may be omitted if castings will not be exposed to severely corrosive environments. If omitted, use low-carbon electrodes.
CF-8M	Not required	Heat to 1950–2100°F (1063–1149°C), quench	E316-15	ER316	ER316	
CF-12M	Not required	Heat to 1950–2100°F (1063–1149°C), quench	E316-15	ER316	ER316	
CF-16F	Not required	Heat to 2000–2100°F (1093–1149°C), quench	E309-15	ER308	ER308	
CF-20	Not required	Heat to 2000–2100°F (1093–1149°C), quench	E308-15	ER308	ER308	
CG-8M	Not required	Heat to 1900°F (1036°C) min, quench	E317-15	ER317	ER317	Postweld heat treatment may be omitted if castings will not be exposed to severely corrosive environments. If omitted, use low-carbon electrodes.
CH-20	Not required	Heat to 2000–2100°F (1093–1149°C), quench	E309-15	ER309	Not recommended	
CK-20	Not required	Heat to 2000–2150°F (1093–1176°C), quench	E310-15	ER310	Not recommended	
CN-7M	Not required (see remarks)	Heat to 2050°F (1120°C) min, quench	E320-15	ER320	ER320	Preheat at 400–600°F (204–315°C) for large restrained-section welds.
CW-12M	Not required	Heat to 2150°F (1176°C) min, quench	ENiMo-2-15	ERNiMo-5	Not recommended	
CY-40	Not required	Heat to 1900–2050°F (1036–1120°C), quench	ENiCrFe-1 Inco	ENiCrFe-1 (coating removed)	Not recommended	
CZ-100	Not required	Not required	ENi-1	Not recommended	Not recommended	Preheat of 200–300°F (93–149°C) is desirable for complex castings where high stresses may be developed in welding.
HEAT-RESISTANT TYPES						
HA	450–550°F (232–288°C)	Heat to 1200–1300°F (648–704°C), air-cool	E508-18	Not recommended	No filler, root passes only	Low-ductility, difficult-to-weld alloy. Each bead should be peened. AWS E310-15, E312-15, and E329-15 are also used to improve weld ductility.
HC	400–1300°F (204–704°C)	Heat to 1550–1900°F (842–1036°C), air- or furnace-cool	E446-15	Not recommended	No filler, root passes only	Large welds in sections thicker than 3/4 in. (19.05 mm) can be preheated to 1650–1750°F (898–953°C). Large, complex castings can be postweld heat-treated at 1900–2050°F (1036–1120°C) for 3–4 h.
HD	Not required	Stress relief only	E446-15		No filler, root passes only	
HE	Not required (see remarks)	Not required (see remarks)	E312-15 E310-15HC	ER310	No filler, root passes only	Large welds in sections thicker than 3/4 in. (19.05 mm) can be preheated to 1650–1750°F (898–953°C). Large, complex castings can be postweld heat-treated at 1900–2050°F (1036–1120°C) for 3–4 h.
HF	Not required (see remarks)	Not required (see remarks)	E308-15 E310-15 (0.30 C) E330-15	ER310 (0.30 C)	No filler, root passes only	Large welds in sections thicker than 3/4 in. (19.05 mm) can be preheated to 1100–1300°F (593–704°C). Stress relieve sections thicker than 1 in. (25.4 mm) at 1600°F (871°C).
HH	Not required (see remarks)	Not required (see remarks)	E309-15HC E310-15HC	ER309	No filler, root passes only	Large welds in sections thicker than 3/4 in. (19.05 mm) can be preheated to 1650–1750°F (898–953°C). Large complex castings can be postweld heat-treated at 1900–2050°F (1036–1120°C) for 3–4 h.

TABLE 10 Parameters for Arc Welding High-Alloy Castings *(Continued)*

ACI alloy*	Preheat	Postheat†	Shielded-metal-arc (SMA) electrodes‡	Gas metal-arc (GMA) electrodes§	Gas-tungsten-arc (GTA) filler metals¶	Remarks
			Electrodes/filler metals, AWS designations			
HK	Not required (see remarks)	Not required (see remarks)	E310-15HC	ER310HC	ER310HC	Large welds in sections thicker than ¾ in. (19.05 mm) can be preheated to 1650–1750°F (898–953°C). Similarly, a postweld stress relief of 1 h at 1600°F (871°C) min may be desirable.
HL	Not required (see remarks)	Not required (see remarks)	E310-15HC	ER310HC	ER310HC	
HN	Not required (see remarks)	Not required (see remarks)	E330-15HC	ER330HC	ER330HC	
HP	Not required (see remarks)	Not required	E310-15HC			
HT	Not required (see remarks)	Not required (see remarks)	E330-15HCHS	ER330	No filler, root passes only	Large welds in sections thicker than ¾ in. (19.05 mm) can be preheated to 1650–1750°F (898–953°C). Large welds or critical welds in complex castings may be postweld heat-treated for 3–4 h at 1900–2050°F (1036–1120°C).
HU	Not required (see remarks)	Not required (see remarks)	E330-15HCHS E310-15	ER330 ER310	ER330HC ER310	
HW	Not required (see remarks)	Not required	ENiCr-1 ENiCrFe-1 E330-15	Not recommended	Not recommended	Large or critical welds may be given a postweld stress relief at 1750°F (953°C) for 2 h.
HX	Not required	Not required	ENiCrFe-1 E309-15 E330-15HC	Not recommended	No filler, root passes only	

*ACI: Alloy Casting Institute Div., Steel Founders' Society of America.

†In many instances, the postweld heat treatment restores maximum corrosion resistance. Small welds which have been made to improve the appearance of casting surfaces that will not be exposed to corrosive attack in service often do not require postweld treatment if they are made with low-carbon electrodes.

‡SMA welding is normally done using d-c reverse polarity and lime-coated electrodes. Successful welds can be made, however, with a-c. The equivalent titania-coated electrode is then substituted.

§GMA welding electrodes are normally $\frac{1}{32}$ to $\frac{3}{32}$ in. (0.79 to 2.38 mm) in diameter. Welding current is normally d-c reverse polarity. Preferred shielding gas is 98Ar-2O$_2$ at a flow rate of 30 to 50 ft³/h (0.084 to 1.4 m³/h) (alloy HT; 100% Ar, 30 to 35 ft³/h [0.84 to 0.98 m³/h]). An alternate shielding gas is 75Ar-25CO$_2$, at 20 cfh (0.56 m³/h).

¶GTA welding electrode is AWS EWTh-2. Filler rod, if used, is normally $\frac{1}{16}$ to $\frac{3}{16}$ in. (1.59 to 4.76 mm) in diameter. Welding current is d-c straight polarity. Preferred shielding gas is 100% Ar at a flow of 20 to 50 ft³/h (0.56 to 1.4 m³/h)(alloy CB-7CU; 15 ft³/h [0.42 m³/h]; alloys CC-50 and HC, 15 to 25 ft³/h (0.42 to 0.70 m³/h). An alternate shielding gas is 100% He at 20 to 50 ft³/h (0.56 to 1.4 m³/h).

SOURCE: Steel Founders' Society of America.

WELDING STAINLESS STEEL PIPE

The information about processes, filler metals, heat treatment, and metallurgy in the preceding sections also applies to welding stainless steel pipe. However, some additional specifics are necessary. The common types of ferritic stainless steels used for pipe are 405, 430, and 446. The filler materials, heat treatment, and metallurgy are as described previously. For pipe welding, if postweld heat treatment is not possible, it is recommended that multiple pass welding be used. The use of small-diameter electrodes, low current, and stringer beads can minimize embrittlement. With this technique, after the first pass, the application of subsequent weld beads has the effect of an anneal on the prior deposited beads to reduce the embrittlement in the weld and heat-affected zone. Common martensitic stainless steel pipe materials are Types 410 and 420. Since these steels are highly susceptible to cracking, preheating is very desirable. However, in the welding of these sections, up to ⅛ in. (3.18 mm), preheating may be eliminated without fear of cracking. Postweld heat treatment is necessary to obtain full joint strength. The austenitic steels are used more often than the martensitic or ferritic grades. Nearly all of the grades of austenitic stainless steels are used to make pipe. To enumerate, Types 304, 304L, 310, 316, 316L, 321, 347, and 348 are commercially available in pipe form. To provide complete root penetration, the root pass is usually made with the gas-tungsten-arc welding process. To ensure clean inside surfaces, free from oxidation, the inside of the pipe should be purged with argon or helium while welding the root pass. For thin-walled pipe, up to ³⁄₁₆ in. (4.76 mm) thick, gas-tungsten-arc welding is used for the complete weld. With pipe of heavier wall thickness, the process is finished using either shielded metal-arc, gas-metal-arc, or submerged-arc welding.

CAST STAINLESS STEELS

In general, both the wrought and cast forms of stainless steels can be welded using the same or similar processes and techniques. Because of the differences in grain size, chemical composition (particularly chemical segregation in cast material) and microstructure between the cast and wrought material, each case must be considered separately. No definite set of rules can be given. Experience from prior work is the best guide. However, some general rules can be applied.

Cast stainless steels are readily weldable by the standard arc welding processes. They are as easy to weld as their wrought counterparts. The austenitic alloys are considered more weldable than the ferritic or martensitic grades. The low-carbon austenite is more weldable than the high-carbon austenite. Welding is used for several purposes with cast stainless steels. Primarily it is used to join complex shapes into assemblies. In these instances, castings may be joined to castings or to wrought members. Welding is also used to repair castings by improving surface finish and by replacing areas that were removed that contained cracks, shrinkage, or porosity voids. A summary of the parameters for arc welding of stainless steel castings is found in Table 10.

Dissimilar welds between low-alloy carbon steel and cast stainless steels can be made successfully, provided the proper precautions are taken. As with any other dissimilar metal joints, the effect of the filler metal on the heat-affected zone and base metal must be considered. The Schaeffler diagram can be used to predict the structure. The use of carbon or low-alloy steel filler metal on high-alloy steel is rare because of the tendency to produce brittle welds that are prone to cracking. A method of preventing martensite in the heat-affected zone under restraint that is commonly used when welding to low-alloy materials is to first butter the low-alloy steel with a layer of austenitic material (as described previously). Thus, the weld-heat-affected zone can be tempered back, or stress-relieved, without restraint, and the final weld can be made with the normal filler metal.

Chapter 27

Forming Sheet, Strip, and Plate

JOSEPH A. FERREE

**Research Metallurgist—Retired, Allegheny Ludlum Steel
Corporation, Research Center, Brackenridge, Pennsylvania**

SELECTION FOR FORMABILITY

The selection of a stainless steel grade for a specific application is usually based on end-use requirements rather than on formability alone. Corrosion resistance, oxidation resistance, strength, weldability, work hardenability and finish characteristics are among the factors which can dictate the choice. Many functional components, where only moderate corrosion resistance is required and appearance is not important, can be made of the lower chromium ferritic grades which offer an excellent combination of properties, formability, and cost. Where more specific properties are required, the higher-chromium ferritic types or one of the austenitic grades may be necessary even though the material and fabricating costs are higher.

All of the flat-rolled stainless steels are fabricated by the methods used for plain carbon and low-alloy steels. However, details of the tooling, lubrication and other practices usually have to be modified for maximum productivity.

Based on forming characteristics, the stainless steels can be divided into several broad categories:

1. The ferritic types, e.g., AISI 405, 409, 430, and 446, which are similar to low-carbon steels but have somewhat higher strength and lower ductility.
2. The martensitic grades, e.g., AISI 403, 410, 420, 431, and 440, which compare with higher carbon low-alloy steels.
3. The austenitic steels, AISI 200 and 300 series, which are characterized by high work-hardening rates.
4. Miscellaneous types including the precipitation-hardenable steels and proprietary analyses which cover a broad range of analyses and a variety of special properties.

The nominal composition ranges for the basic stainless steels most often used in production forming operations are given in Appendixes 1 and 2.

Typical mechanical property ranges for these annealed steels are given in Chap. 20, Tables 7, 10, and 17. A low-carbon deep-drawing steel, for comparison purposes, would have the following properties: tensile strength, 40 to 50 ksi (275 to 345 MPa) yield strength, 20 to 35 ksi (140 to 240 MPa); elongation in 2 in. (50.8 mm), 35 to 45%.

Compared to other ferrous alloys, the austenitic stainless steels have extremely high work-hardening rates. The ferritic stainless steels are comparable to the low-carbon steels in work-hardening characteristics. The austenitic steels retain a high level of ductility at high-strength levels. The effects of 30% cold reduction by cold-rolling on the strength and ductility of typical analyses are shown in Table 1.

TABLE 1   Mechanical Properties After 30% Cold Reduction

Material	Tensile strength		Yield strength, 0.2% offset		Elongation, % in 2 in. (50.8 mm)
	MPa	ksi	MPa	(ksi)	
301	1340	195	1100	160	18.0
304	1000	145	860	125	16.5
305	790	115	710	103	17.0
405	585	85	565	82	5.0
409	690	100	670	97	2.5
430	725	105	705	102	2.5
Low-carbon steel	565	82	520	75	12.0

Formability Factors   The usual tensile test values do not fully describe formability. The two properties of primary concern in most forming operations are stretchability and drawability, both of which can be determined from tensile test data.

Stretchability is primarily a function of the material's cold-work-hardening rate which is indicated by the work-hardening coefficient n. This coefficient is the slope of the true-stress–true-strain curve. It is also equal to the true strain at which necking begins in tensile testing (uniform elongation). In materials with high n values, localized deformation causes a rapid increase in strength with the result that the most highly strained areas resist further deformation and subsequent deformation is transferred to adjacent, weaker areas. As a result, strains are uniformly distributed over a large area. In materials with low n values, localized straining causes thinning without a sufficient increase in strength to prevent the process from continuing until ultimate failure occurs. Strains are concentrated, rather than being distributed over the area being deformed. Work hardenability is basically dependent on composition.

Drawability is related to the plastic strain ratio $\bar{r}$, which is the ratio of the strain in the plane of the sheet to the strain in the thickness direction. In practical terms, $\bar{r}$ is a measure of the resistance to thinning and is independent of the work-hardening rate. Values of $\bar{r}$ greater than 1 are indicative of a favorable crystallographic texture or orientation and are produced by controlled rolling and annealing practices. High values of $\bar{r}$ indicate that the material can be compressed comparatively easily in the flange area as it is drawn into the die, but the walls of the drawn portion are capable of sustaining relatively high drawing loads without excessive thinning and fracturing.

Simulative tests can also provide useful information on stretchability and drawability. However, mechanical variables such as lubrication, die radii and clearances, and punch speed are introduced which can lead to inconclusive results unless they are carefully standardized.

In pure stretch-forming operations, the blank flange is firmly clamped by the hold-down ring to prevent any material from being drawn into the die. Simulative tests to evaluate stretchability are the Ericksen and Olsen cupping tests and hydraulic bulge tests. In the Ericksen and Olsen tests the material is stretched through a die by a punch with a spherical nose. In the hydraulic bulge test the material is expanded through a die opening by hydraulic pressure without the use of a punch, which eliminates some of the variables associated with mechanical tooling. The criterion in these tests is either the height (or depth) of the cup or bulge at which fracturing occurs.

In contrast to stretch forming, where the blank flange is restrained, in drawing operations the flange hold-down pressure is controlled in a double-action press to allow the metal to flow into the die without stretching or wrinkling. Drawability is measured by the Swift test, from which the limiting drawing ratio (LDR) can be determined. Blanks with increasingly larger diameters are drawn into cylindrical, flat-bottomed cups to determine the maximum blank size which can be drawn successfully without fracturing. The limiting drawing ratio equals maximum blank diameter divided by punch diameter. Lubrication, die radii, and clearances must be standardized to obtain reproducible comparisons.

Formability test data for typical stainless steel analyses are compared with low-carbon steel in Table 2. (See Chap. 20, Table 14 and Fig. 22 for additional data.) The superiority of the austenitic stainless steels in stretching operations is indicated by the high work-hardening and bulge test values. The ferritic stainless steels, in comparison, have somewhat limited stretch formability but they are entirely adequate for most forming operations which combine stretching and drawing. All of these stainless steels have excellent drawability as shown by the LDR and strain ratio values.

TABLE 2   Formability Test Data

	Stretchability			Drawability	
		Biaxial bulge height*			
Material	Work-hardening coefficient, n	mm	in.	Strain ratio, $\bar{r}$	Limiting drawing ratio, LDR†
301	0.50–0.70				
304	0.45–0.50	79	3.10	1.0	2.18–2.25
305	0.45				
405	0.20				
409	0.20	62	2.45	1.0–1.5	2.15–2.30
430	0.20	52	2.05		
Low-carbon steel	0.22	63	2.48	1.0–1.8	2.15–2.50

*Biaxial hydraulic bulge test, 178-mm-diameter (7 in.) round die.

$$†LDR = \frac{\text{maximum blank diameter which can be drawn successfully}}{\text{punch diameter}}$$

The excellent inherent properties of these stainless steels make them suitable for practically all forming operations used for carbon steels. However, provisions have to be made for the high strengths, the high work-hardening rates of the austenitic steels and high abrasive action on tools and dies accompanying the higher pressures and loads required for deformation.

EQUIPMENT, TOOLS, AND LUBRICATION

Conventional methods and equipment are used in forming the stainless steels. However, in view of the higher yield strengths and work-hardening rates, 50 to 100% greater load capacities are required than for equivalent operations on low-carbon steel. Presses and dies must have high rigidity and strength to handle the higher forces.

The choice of tool and die materials depends on the operation being performed and the number of parts to be produced. For high production runs, the high-carbon, high-chromium die steels (AISI D series) are usually employed for forming, drawing, blanking, and piercing dies. Forming dies should be highly polished to minimize friction which can lead to galling and tearing. These dies are sometimes nitrided or hard-chromium plated to further reduce friction and wear. Hard aluminum bronze draw rings or inserts also are useful to reduce friction and galling where surface finishes must be preserved, but the die life is usually shorter than when tool steels are used. Alloy cast irons and less abrasion-resistant tool and die steels may be adequate for short runs and developmental purposes.

Lubrication with high viscosity and film strength are necessary to withstand the high pressures and temperatures generated during operations with the stainless steels. Extreme pressure and/or chlorinated oils or emulsions may be required for severe deep-drawing operations to prevent galling. Depending on the severity and type of operation, other less effective types of lubricants (including pigmented paste emulsions and waxes) may be adequate. Some experimentation is usually necessary to determine the most economical and effective practice. Ease of removal is also a factor which must be considered since any surface contamination can have an adverse effect on the appearance and corrosion resistance of the finished part. All lubricants must be removed prior to any annealing treatments.

Shearing   Conventional press equipment is used for shearing the stainless steels. However, press capacity ratings are 20 to 50% less with the stainless steels since presses are usually rated on the maximum thickness of carbon steels which can be sheared.

The shearing action with annealed ferritic and martensitic stainless steels is similar to that of carbon and low-alloy steels. Greater blade penetration is necessary to initiate fracturing with the austenitic steels because of their high ductility and work-hardening rates. Shear knives must be kept sharp and clearances carefully adjusted to prevent dragging the metal over the blade. Hold-down pressures must be proportionally higher to compensate for the high shearing forces required.

Blade relief angles range up to 1½°, depending on the thickness of the material. Blade clearances also depend on the thickness of the material. These should be adjusted where possible to prevent excessive burring. A nominal value is about 5% of the metal thickness.

Shear blades require a combination of impact resistance and wear resistance. For gages up to approximately ¼ in. (6 mm) in thickness, high-carbon–high-chromium tool steels such as AISI D2 are recommended to provide maximum wear resistance with adequate impact strength. For thicknesses up to about ½ in. (12 mm), AISI A2 is recommended for improved toughness. For thicker plates, shock-resistant steels, such as AISI S2 or S5, are usually required.

Bending and Roll-Forming   Bending and roll-forming operations on the stainless steels also require more power than on carbon steels but otherwise the operations are similar. Cold bend limits on annealed materials vary with the composition and thickness. Typical limits are given in Table 3.

TABLE 3   Stainless Steel Bend Limits—Annealed Condition

Stainless type	Thickness, mm (in.)	
	To 6.5 (0.250)	6.5 (0.250) to 12.5 (0.500)
Austenitic	Min. R = ½T, 180° bend	Min. R = ½T, 90° bend
Ferritic (11–17% Cr)	Min. R = T, 180° bend	Min. R = T, 90° bend

R = radius of bend and T = thickness of material.

The high-chromium ferritic steels (up to 27% chromium), such as Types 442 and 446, tend to be brittle at room temperature but can be bent in a press brake by heating to 120 to 200°C (250 to 400°F). These steels are not ordinarily roll-formed.

Temper-rolled austenitic steels may have limited bendability depending on the strength and ductility. Typical bend limits for temper-rolled austenitic steels are shown in Table 4.

Springback in bending the annealed ferritic stainless steels is somewhat greater than with annealed carbon steels but is of the same order of magnitude. However, it is considerably greater with the austenitic steels because of the high rate of work hardening during deformation. In production, springback is usually compensated for by overbending. The amount required is proportional to the yield strength and the radius of the bend, expressed in terms of the thickness of the material being bent. Variations within the composition range of a given grade, Type 301 in particular, can have a pronounced effect on the work-hardening rate and, consequently, on the amount of springback.

The amount of overbending required to make a 90° bend ranges from about 2° with a bend radius equal to the thickness of the material to 12 to 15° with a bend radius equal to 20 times the thickness. The overbend required for ½-hard temper-rolled material is two to three times greater than for annealed material.

TABLE 4   Bend Limits for Temper-rolled Austenitic Stainless Steels

Temper designation	Minimum yield strength		Thickness, mm (in.)	
	MPa	ksi	To 1.25 (0.050)	1.25 to 4.75 (0.050 to 0.187)
¼ hard	860	125	Min. $R = \frac{1}{2}T$, 180° bend	Min. $R = \frac{1}{2}T$, 90° bend
½ hard	1035	150	Min. $R = T$, 180° bend	Min. $R = T$, 90° bend
¾ hard	1205	175	Min. $R = 1\frac{1}{2}T$, 180° bend	
Full hard	1275	185	Min. $R = 2T$, 180° bend	

R = radius of bend and T = thickness of material.

The stainless steels are readily cold-roll-formed into channels, tubing, moldings, and other more complex shapes. In this process the finished shape is formed by a series of contoured rolls which progressively develop the desired shape. Since the strip or sheet can be fed into the machine from a coil, roll-forming lends itself to high production rates in comparison to press-brake bending. Temper-rolled austenitic grades may be specified for bright finish work and/or high strength. The ferritic grades (such as Type 430) may also be skin-passed (No. 2 finish) to provide a bright finish and to prevent stretcher strains during bending.

More roll stations may be required than with carbon steel because of the higher initial strength, work hardening, and springback encountered with the stainless steels. Roll-forming speeds range from 8 to 35 m/min (25 to 100 ft/min). Simple shapes in light gages can be run at the higher speed. Heavy gages, up to ⅛ in. (3 mm), and high-strength materials are run at the lower speed.

Special precautions are necessary to prevent pickup, scoring, and galling on the rolls or strip. These defects detract from appearance, may adversely affect corrosion resistance, and increase finishing costs. Plastic-coated strip is sometimes used to prevent scratching and scoring. Effective lubricants are required in severe operations to maintain surface finishes. Soluble oils may be adequate but, for maximum efficiency, extreme-pressure additives and high-viscosity chlorinated oils may be required.

Choice of roll materials is often based on the production anticipated. However, when roll-forming stainless steels where high pressures and temperatures are generated and surface finishes are important, special attention to the roll designs and roll materials are required to produce the high-quality finishes specified for a stainless application. High-carbon–high-chromium tool steels (D1) hardened to 60 to 65 Rockwell C are recommended for maximum production. Rolls should be polished and may also be chromium-plated to prevent scratching and pickup. In some cases, hard aluminum bronze rolls are used to advantage to preserve surface finishes.

Blanking, Punching, and Piercing   Blanking, punching, and piercing operations are mechanically essentially the same. In blanking, flat sheets are shaped by a punch-and-die setup in a press. Punching and piercing are similar operations except that these usually refer to producing holes in a sheet or blanked form. The processes are essentially shearing operations. The press equipment, punches, and dies must have the strength and rigidity to accommodate the added power requirements. Die materials with high wear resistance are required for extended production runs.

The straight-chromium ferritic stainless steels are comparable to the low-carbon steels except for higher shear strength. Fracturing occurs with about the same depth of cut. The austenitic grades with higher ductility and work-hardening characteristics require a deeper cut to induce fracturing, and die clearances have to be controlled to prevent the metal from being pulled into the die and to control burr formation. Cutting edges must be kept sharp. Tool steels with high abrasion resistance are necessary for extended production runs. Power requirements can be reduced by designing the punches or dies with angular shear cutting edges.

Clearances between the punch and die normally are held to 5% of the metal thickness on a side (10% overall) for sheet and strip gages. Larger clearances cause excessive bending over the die edges and consequently excessive distortion with the tough austenitic steels.

Pierced holes should not be smaller than about 1½ times the metal thickness. In order to maintain flatness and freedom from distortion, the minimum distances between holes or the edges of the blank should not be less than one-half the hole diameter. Increased spacing may be necessary on thin stock, 0.062 in. (1.6 mm) or less.

The selection of die materials depends on the number of parts to be made. For long production runs, the stainless steels require die materials with maximum wear resistance. AISI tool steels A2, D2, and D4 provide increasingly long die life in the order given. Carbides may be used to advantage where high impact resistance is not required. Lubrication is not always required, but for high-speed work soluble oils or chlorinated oils with extreme pressure additives may be required as a coolant and to prevent pickup on tools.

Drawing Drawing is a process by which flat sheet metal is formed into cylindrical or box-shaped components by means of a punch-and-draw ring or die. These operations are usually performed in double-action presses with a blank holder to prevent wrinkling in the flange as the metal is pulled into the die. In a simple drawing operation hold-down pressures on the flange are controlled to permit the flange material to compress and flow into the die with a minimum of stretching. Higher hold-down pressures cause both stretching and drawing. In pure stretching the flange edges are clamped so that practically no metal can flow into the die. A bottom die may be employed in stretch-draw operations to form contoured shapes. Most so-called drawing operations involve both stretching and drawing in varying degrees depending on the complexity of the part being made.

The broad range of properties exhibited by the various stainless steels makes it possible to select a grade to fit the formability requirements assuming that corrosion resistance and other requirements of the application are met.

The austenitic Types 201 and 301, which work harden fastest, are best suited for operations in which stretching predominates. While these grades can be deep-drawn successfully, intermediate annealing treatments are usually necessary where a sequence of drawing operations is required to produce the final shape.

Types 202, 302, and 304, with lower work-hardening rates than Types 201 and 301, are preferred for deep-drawing applications. Several drawing sequences are usually possible without annealing if excessive reductions are not made in any one operation.

Type 305 has the lowest work-hardening rate of the more widely used austenitic steels. Drawability is excellent but the stretchability is somewhat limited. The primary justification for using Type 305 in drawn applications is the possible elimination of annealing treatments between redrawing operations.

High residual stresses induced during fabrication can cause delayed cracking, usually within several hours, in Types 201 and 301. These are most likely to appear at the edges of drawn shapes without a flange. This type of cracking can be prevented by stress-relieving or annealing as soon as possible after fabrication.

All of the austenitic grades are susceptible to stress-corrosion cracking in environments containing chlorides if high residual stresses from fabrication are present. Components which may be exposed in service to environments which can cause stress-corrosion cracking should be annealed after the final drawing operation.

The ferritic stainless steels are similar to the carbon steels in deep drawing. Types 405, 409, and 430 provide a combination of adequate corrosion resistance for many applications, good drawability, and relatively low cost.

Conventional mechanical and hydraulic presses are used for drawing, but up to 100% greater ram force and higher blank-holding pressures are required for the austenitic steels in comparison to carbon steels. Press frames and tooling must have the rigidity and strength to accommodate the higher forces. For critical jobs, hydraulic presses are often preferred because speeds and pressures can be accurately controlled. The austenitic steels are usually drawn at comparatively slow speeds, approximately 6 m/min (20 ft/min), or less. Drawing press equipment and operations with the ferritic steels conform more closely to practices used for carbon steels.

Specific drawing sequences depend on many factors which include the material being drawn, the shape to be made, punch and die radii, the speed of the operation, etc. In general, large initial reductions, which work harden the material excessively, greatly reduce the amount of redrawing possible without annealing. Single draws of 40 to 50% reduction are possible with the austenitic steels but an annealing treatment would be required before any subsequent finishing operation. In the case of Types 201 or 301, delayed cracking could occur unless the part is promptly annealed or stress-relieved. Typical reduction schedules for Types 302 and 304 might be:

1. 45, 30, and 25% with intermediate and final annealing
2. 25, 20, 15, and 10% with no intermediate anneals but possibly a final anneal before sizing or other finishing operations

Drawing sequences for the ferritic steels such as Types 409 and 430 are comparable to those for carbon steels. Single reductions up to about 40%, followed by an anneal, are feasible.

The austenitic steels tend to thicken much more than carbon steels in the sidewalls of deep-drawn cylindrical shapes and in the corners of rectangular shapes. For this reason, clearances between the punch and die of 40 to 45% over the original sheet thickness may be required. Thickening can be controlled to some extent by increasing hold-down pressures to promote stretching. With the ferritic materials, clearances of 10 to 20% over the thickness are usually sufficient. Adequate clearances must be maintained to avoid ironing, particularly with the austenitic steels. The high surface hardnesses developed by cold-working cause scoring and excessive die wear. The high drawing loads required to iron these steels may push out the bottoms of the drawn parts.

Punch and die radii are usually held in the range of 5 to 10 times the material thickness. Small radii limit the amount of reduction possible. Larger radii may cause wrinkling in the sidewalls.

The selection of tool materials for drawing dies depends on a number of factors related to the particular item to be produced. The high pressures and forces necessary to form the stainless steels require tool materials with high abrasion resistance, high strength, and resistance to scoring, galling, and pickup. The choice may also be a compromise between cost and anticipated production. Often, more expensive tool materials with maximum wear resistance and resistance to scoring prove to be the most economical in the long run since maintenance costs on the tools and finishing costs on the fabricated parts are minimized. High-carbon–high-chromium tool steels, such as AISI D2, are commonly used. For long production runs carbide draw rings or inserts in critical high wear areas are advantageous. High-strength aluminum bronze can be used for draw rings and inserts to reduce friction and to prevent scoring and galling where surface finishes have to be preserved.

Because of the high pressures involved in drawing the stainless steels, proper lubrication is essential to reduce friction which can lead to seizing and galling in the dies. Extreme-pressure-type lubricants are often needed for severe deep-drawing operations. These may be oil- or wax-based or water emulsions containing sulfur and chlorine compounds. Pigmented types are also applicable. Depending on the particular job other lubricants may be adequate. Ease of removal after fabrication is also an important consideration since all traces of lubricant must be removed prior to subsequent annealing treatments or before being put into service. Surface contamination can increase finishing costs and adversely affect corrosion resistance.

Spinning Conical, spherical, and bowl-shaped parts, which require several operations with intermediate annealing when drawn, can often be formed in one step by spinning. The shapes are generated over a turning mandrel by applying pressure to a round blank which rotates with the mandrel. The metal is formed over the mandrel either manually or with power-activated tools. In manual operations, the flat blank or a preformed shape is forced over the mandrel with little or no thinning. In compression or shear spinning, sufficient pressure is applied mechanically or hydraulically to actually thin the blank material. Depending on the work material, reductions in thickness of from 50 to 80% are possible without annealing.

Materials with a low work-hardening rate and high ductility are most suitable for manual spinning. Among the stainless steels, Type 305 provides the best combination of properties for manual spinning. The ferritic stainless steels, which also are suitable, have low work-hardening rates but the ductility drops off more rapidly with cold-work than it does for Type 305. As a result, intermediate anneals may be necessary to produce shapes which require severe cold-working. The thicknesses which can be spun manually are limited by the high initial yield strengths of the stainless steels and the limited power available. A thickness of 0.125 in. (3 mm) is usually considered to be the maximum for manual spinning.

In manual spinning, rolls and round-nosed tools of hardened and polished tool steels, or hard bronze to reduce friction, are used. Lubricants which will adhere to the surface, such as soaps and tallow, are usually effective. Spinning speeds depend on the equipment available, the size and shape of the part being produced and, to a large degree, on the operator's skill. In general, the speeds for stainless steels are about one-half those used for carbon steels.

Deformation by compression or shear spinning can be compared to cold-rolling. Most materials which can be cold-rolled successfully are suitable for this process since adequate power is available. The austenitic stainless steels are particularly well suited since they retain relatively high levels of ductility with heavy cold-work. Thicknesses which can be spun and reductions which can be made are only limited by the power available. Where a sequence of operations is required, Type 305 is usually recommended to avoid the necessity for intermediate annealing. Heavy reductions are also possible with other austenitic and ferritic grades but annealing may be required between operations. Water- or oil-based lubricants, which can also act as coolants, are applied to the work area to dissipate the heat which is generated during the reduction in thickness.

Chapter **28**

Forming Parts from Wire

JOHN F. PFEFFER
**Techalloy Company, Inc., Rahns,
Pennsylvania**

Although this chapter will deal principally with forming parts from wire, a brief look at the production of the wire itself will be undertaken to acquaint readers with the material with which they will be working.

PRODUCTION OF STAINLESS STEEL WIRE

This section will cover cold-drawing stainless steel wire in the size range from ½ to 0.002 in. (12.7 to 0.051 mm) in diameter—the bulk of the commercially used sizes required by industry today.

Cleaning and Pickling   Rod stock from which wire is produced is usually $\frac{9}{16}$ to $\frac{7}{32}$ in. (14.29 to 5.56 mm) in diameter. Although it has been hot-rolled and pickled by the primary producing mill, stock is usually put through a final cleaning process to remove any remaining scale, oxide, or foreign matter. Pickling baths are either a mixture of muriatic, sulfuric, and nitric acids or of nitric and hydrofluoric acids. Other cleaning methods (e.g., shot blasting and ultrasonics) are available, but the acid baths have proven to be the most effective and economical.

Coatings   Coatings applied to the wire often act as lubricants in the cold-drawing process. Three important coatings include:

1. *Alkali.* This widely used compound, applied before drawing, is described by various commercial names and trademarks. Relatively new, alkali coatings are highly versatile and their use often permits less intense precleaning of the wire before coating with other types of materials. These coatings also provide an economical and effective lubricant for wiredrawing operations. Alkali-coated wire should be stored in a dry, dehumidified area since certain types are hygroscopic and can become tacky, uneven, and easily scuffed.

2. *Copper.* Some end uses, particularly in cold-heading and spring coiling, require a special coating to act as a lubricating agent when very high pressures, high friction, and severe metal deformation will be encountered. Copper has long been a popular choice to meet these operating conditions.

3. *Lead.* Some wire-forming operations require the use of lead coating as a lubricant. After being coated with lead, the wire coil is normally dipped in a lime solution. The lime picks up powdered soap compound in the die box and draws it into the die for additional lubrication.

Wiredrawing Machines   There are various types of wiredrawing machines, each designed for a specific purpose, size, and capacity. They include the single-block type and the continuous type, with as many as 17 die stations which reduce wire diameter up to a maximum of 80% reduction of area with one pass through the machine. Machines with seven dies generally provide a 25 to 30% reduction of area.

Single-block machines are of both the vertical- and horizontal-spindle types and can draw a size range from ³⁄₃₂ to ½ in. (2.38 to 12.70 mm). Two kinds of continuous drawing machines are in use today: the slip and nonslip types. While the slip type has several inherent limitations, many of these machines are in use for drawing intermediate sizes of wire and for fine sizes, using a wet lubricant. These are known as "wet" drawing machines and the lubricant is a continuously fed solution of water and soluble oil or a soap compound. When drawing very fine wire in the 0.032- to 0.003-in.-diameter (0.81- to 0.076-mm) range and lower, the dies, cones, and capstans are submerged in the lubricant during drawing and the machines operate at speeds of 500 to 3000 ft/min (152.4 to 914.4 m/min). Nonslip drawing machines are highly automated, multiple-station machines with a regulator between each die station to control the speed of the capstan as the wire increases in length and speed after each draw. Uninterrupted production is realized with this highly automated equipment thus allowing the operator ample time to weld coil ends together and remove the drawn wire from the finishing block.

A critical part of the wiredrawing machine is the die itself, consisting of two parts: the carbide nib and the steel die block which supports the nib. Tungsten carbide dies are used to draw stainless steel wire in the size range 0.500- to 0.028-in. (12.7- to 0.71-mm) diameter. Diamond dies are generally used below that range. Six of the critical dimensions of a wiredrawing die are shown in Fig. 1.

Producing Shaped Wire   Stainless steel wire can be cold-rolled into countless variations of cross-sectional shapes (Fig. 2) on Turk's head machines. This special equipment (Fig. 3) operates on the rolling-mill principle, and the die consists of a combina-

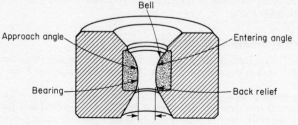

Fig. 1   Six of the critical dimensions in a die are shown here. The die, or nib, is of hard tungsten carbide, inserted in a steel block.

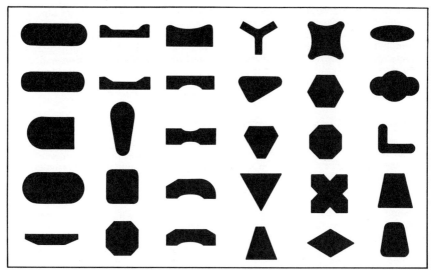

Fig. 2 Typical shapes of drawn wire are shown in these cross sections.

Fig. 3 Specially designed dies roll the required shapes into wire on a Turk's head machine.

tion of three or four rollers with specially designed surface shapes which are adjustable for obtaining specific sizes. These roller dies are mounted on a plate through which standard annealed round wire is drawn. The special shape is rolled into the wire to extremely close tolerances, with fine surface finish and desirable grain structure.

Users of shaped wire obtain substantial savings in their production costs, and metal waste is virtually eliminated. Fabricating steps are reduced since machining is no longer needed to achieve the desired configuration. Starting with preshaped wire increases design capabilities and the cold forming improves strength of the finished parts.

FORMING PARTS FROM STAINLESS STEEL WIRE

The applications for stainless steel wire are growing. Designers are becoming more familiar with its versatility and how to utilize to best advantage its corrosion resistance, high strength at high and low temperatures, and ease of maintenance. Designers are learning how to apply stainless steel to products and equipment where functional performance is the prime requisite. Some characteristics of certain stainless steels, as wire, are described in Table 1.

Stainless steel wire is not a single specific material. Although it is generally referred to in the singular sense, there are actually 60 individual compositions accepted as standard by the American Iron and Steel Institute (AISI), plus many proprietary grades. The designer has a wide range of stainless steels from which the one that will best serve the intended purpose can be selected. There are also a wide range of forming processes by which the wire can be shaped into a finished product.

Cold-Heading   In the forming of parts from stainless steel wire, one of the most widely used production methods is the cold-heading or cold-forming process. The metal is deformed in this process and this condition strain hardens it with a consequent increase in the strength of the steel (See Fig. 4).

Cold-heading, as implied, is a cold-working process. Basically, wire, feeding into a cold-heading machine, is cut to length and inserted in a die so that a bit of this stock protrudes. A punch slams down on the protruding end to form a headlike shape at the end of the wire blank (see Fig. 5). Although cold-heading is usually associated with the production of screws, bolts, rivets, and other fasteners, more elaborate parts such as ball studs, link pins, and even pinion shafts, complete with gears, can be cold-headed. Heading is fast, scrap-free, and produces strong, uniform parts; it is best suited for high-volume production. A cold-heading machine can turn out as many as 27,000 formed pieces per hour.

Guidelines for Deformation Limitations. "Deformation" refers to the amount of metal that must be deformed or moved in the heading operation to produce a finished part. The

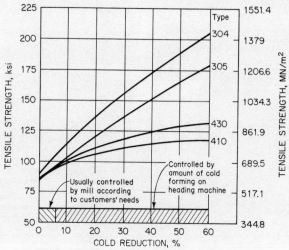

Fig. 4 Effect of cold-working on tensile strength.

TABLE 1   Characteristics and Typical Applications of Certain Grades of Stainless Steel Wire

302 and 302 HQ	Good corrosion resistance, a basic general-purpose type. Can be cold-worked to high tensile strength. Good cold-heading properties. For fasteners with simple head design, springs, food processing equipment.
304	Low carbon variation of 302. Work hardens rapidly. High corrosion resistance, i.e., nitric acid. Good cold-heading properties; for fasteners with simple head design, circuitboard nests, safety lock wire.
305	Lower work-hardening rate than 302, 304; good for severe cold-heading in multiple stage and for thread rolling. Work hardens rapidly. Resists corrosion in severe atmosphere, nitric acid, foodstuffs. For instruments, low magnetic parts.
316	Higher corrosion and pitting resistance than 304. Good strength at high temperatures. Work hardens rapidly. Good cold-heading properties. For fasteners in chemical processing industries, screens for marine use.
321 and 347	Stabilized to permit use in 800–1500°F (425–815°C) range. Work hardens rapidly at room temperature. Has superior resistance to intergranular corrosion. Used for aircraft fasteners, rocket engine parts, furnace parts.
410	A general-purpose, low-cost alloy used where corrosion is moderate. Cold-worked with good results. Heat-treatable. Used for sheet metal screws, bolts, fasteners, springs, pump parts.
430	Good corrosion, heat resistance. Excellent cold-working results. Economical where corrosion is mild. Low work hardening. For all types of fasteners, particularly for recessed heads. Can be upset as much as 3½:1. Resists mild acids and water. For decorative parts.
431	Best corrosion resistance of standard chromium types. Heat treatable for high mechanical properties. For marine and aircraft fasteners.
Tech 10	Work hardens very slowly. Highly suited for most severe cold-heading applications; remains nonmagnetic. Extremely high resistance to atmospheric corrosion and to effects of chemicals and foodstuffs.
Tech 12	Work hardens very slowly. Used for severe cold-heading and upsetting jobs; remains nonmagnetic. Has excellent resistance to corrosion but not equal to Tech 10.
A-286	Has high temperature resistance, good strength and resistance to corrosion up to 1300°F (705°C). For wide range of fasteners in high temperature use, jet engine parts, high-temperature springs.
17-4PH	Good where corrosion resistance is associated with wear, fatigue, erosion, or high stress. Has exceptionally high strength and hardness. Low temperature hardening. For high-temperature fasteners.
15-7PH	Semiaustenitic, precipitation-hardened. Very high strength type, has good formability in annealed condition and corrosion resistance approaching Type 304. May require intermediate annealing. For cold-headed parts, fasteners.
18-9 LW	Low work-hardening, excellent cold-heading properties. Economical for cold-working parts . . . fasteners, ferrules, aircraft and missile parts. Resistance to large variety of corrosives.

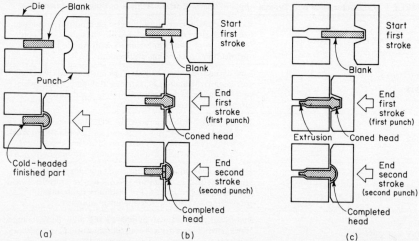

Fig. 5 Basic types of cold-heading operations.[2] (*a*) This is the basic, one-stroke cold-heading process. Although hot-working processes can move greater volumes of metal, only cold-working imparts greater strength to the finished part. Cold-worked metal strain hardens and so is stronger, tougher, and more fatigue resistant than unworked metal. (*b*) Designs calling for severe deformations or intricate shapes may be cold-headed in successive strokes. In this case, the first stroke roughs out the head (the operation is called coning in this example). The second stroke finishes the head and the detailed shape beneath the head. Sometimes cold-heading blanks are preheated (but below the recrystallization temperature of the metal). Cold-heading of preheated metal is sometimes dubbed warm heading, but—technically—is still a cold-working process. (*c*) Cold-heading is often combined with cold extrusion. In this example, the first stroke simultaneously cones the head and extrudes the tail of the part. Ball studs, pinion shafts, and multidiametered fasteners are produced in this way. Sometimes severely deformed parts must be annealed between successive strokes to reduce the strengthening effect of cold-working.

amount of metal to be moved is usually referred to as the "number of diameters in the upset." Successful upsetting is determined by a critical diameter/length ratio. In cold-heading terminology, a "diameter" is a length of wire equal to its diameter. The severity of a cold-heading operation is measured in diameters, or the volume of metal deformed to the length of wire deformed.

For many common steel alloys, severe heading is any cold-forming application where the amount of metal moved is over 2½ diameters, that is, a length of wire 2½ times the diameter of the wire. Average single-stroke heading operations deform from 2¼ to 2½ diameters. Severe deformations usually require additional steps, or strokes, to flow the metal into the final shape.

By heading in two strokes, from 4½ to 5 diameters can be upset as standard practice. Triple stroke headers displace 8 diameters and form specially shaped heads. For stainless steels, recommended heading ratios may differ because these metals may have higher initial hardness and faster work-hardening rates. In some cases preheating and heat treatments between heading operations are required.

Stainless steel fasteners, for example, require two to three strokes, and only 1.5 to 1.7 diameters are moved in the first stroke. In these cases, a so-called coning punch in the first blow allows greater subsequent upsetting ratios. Stainless steel socket screws require three blows, but one blow simultaneously extrudes the shank and upsets the head. In addition, the metal is prewarmed from 600 to 1000°F (316 to 538°C).

Sometimes special methods permit higher deformation ratios. Extruding the shank or stem of a part prior to heading (to reduce the cross section) in effect allows more severe heading than guidelines dictate. The combined effect of extrusion and heading reduces heading severity and is often used to produce fasteners such as socket head cap screws.

Selecting Stainless Steels for Cold-Heading. The selection of stainless steels requires ~~~ selecting carbon or alloy steels for cold-heading. Yet, the cold-
~~~ ~st economical way to produce certain parts from stainless.

The process, being virtually scrap-free, does not waste material. The strengthening that results from cold-heading is an especially valuable asset when working with costly steels because an alloy that is initially less strong than the design requires, and therefore less expensive, can be specified.

Stainless steels are selected mainly because they are heat- and corrosion-resistant, and strong. Some types of stainless steel are more suitable to severe heading designs than others. Types 304, 410, and 430 stainless steel wire are adequately ductile for cold-heading in the annealed condition. But, the 300 series austenitic Cr-Ni stainless steels develop greater strengths than other steels because of their higher rate of work hardening. At the same time, however, they retain good ductility and toughness at these high-strength levels, and so, parts made from these steels permit slight plastic deformation under loading (to distribute stresses during static loading as well as to supply a measure of safety against part failure during occasional overloading).

For parts and fasteners with a simple head design, Type 304 stainless wire is practical. However, from the standpoint of tool and die life, since 304 strongly resists cold-working, recessed head design should be avoided. Table 2 indicates the corrosion resistance and headability rating of certain grades of stainless wire.

Type A-286, a precipitation-hardenable stainless steel, meets specifications that require high strength and oxidation resistance. It withstands temperatures up to 1300°F (704°C) and has low magnetic permeability. Because of this combination of properties, A-286 is used for many critical applications, such as aerospace components and jet engine parts. Other corrosion-resistant steels for cold-heading include Types 305, 316, 410, and 416.

Selecting the best stainless wire is often a matter of compromising a number of trade-offs. For example, the most readily headable steels are not usually the most corrosion resistant. So, to keep heading costs to a minimum and achieve greater tool life, select a grade having the minimum acceptable corrosion resistance for the application. Also, in most cases, the grade that work hardens the least forms the most easily and produces the least amount of die wear and the lowest heading costs. So work hardening (or strength) is compromised by the cost of the part.

The same types of cold-forming equipment used for carbon steel can be used for stainless steel. In general, however, the machine for forming stainless parts should be one size larger than for carbon steels. Also, about twice as much power is needed for stainless parts, especially Cr-Ni work-hardening grades.

Heat Treatments Broaden Design Potentials   In many cases, certain heat treatments in various cold-heading stages can broaden the ratio of deformation of the part and increase design possibilities. Three heat treatments may be specified.

Type 1. The most important one is applied at the wire mill and establishes the metallurgical condition of the raw material. The other treatments are preheating the metal prior to cold-heading, and annealing the blanks between cold-heading steps. These last two process cycles are often established in the shop after experimental runs.

Type 2. The second type of heat treatment often specified for cold-headed parts is preheating the wire stock before it is fed to the heading machine. Although most cold-heading stainless stock can be formed into parts without preheating, the extra step assures better formability and less cracking for minimum rejects. In some cases, preheating allows

TABLE 2   Corrosion Resistance and Headability

Type	Corrosion resistance*	Headability*
302	5	7
302HQ	5	3–4
304	3	5
305	1	2–3
316	2	4
Tech. 10	1	2
Tech. 12	2–3	2
410	7	3
430	6	1
431	5	5
18-9LW	5	3–4

*No. 1 best; no. 7 lowest.

use of a less expensive alloy. The resulting cost reduction may offset the added cost of preheating. Die life, too, increases when cold-heading blanks are preheated. Preheating changes the hardness of the finished part, however, so trial runs must be made to determine how the material reacts.

Type 3. The third type of heat treatment is to anneal parts between successive cold-heading steps to reduce the effects of work hardening. In addition, if subsequent operations such as drilling, turning, or grinding are required, either the metal should be within a soft enough range after forming to permit easy machining, or the formed parts must be annealed. Every effort should be made to select a metal which, when cold-formed, can be used without further heat-treating, especially when the finished part must have a specific hardness. Properly selected stainless grades could eliminate the need for further heat-treating after heading. Such alloys, selected according to their degrees of work hardening, may produce finished parts to the correct hardness.

Design the Part With the Die in Mind   In producing stainless steel parts from wire by cold-heading, the design of the finished part and design of the heading die go hand in hand. Points of maximum deformation in the part, where the grains are heavily elongated and lie close together, are highly stressed locations in the die. It takes considerable experience to identify points of maximum deformation and stress at the tool layout stage. Incorrect die design can overstress the material at these points, too, causing splitting material in the finished part.

Parts should be designed from the outset to give the most favorable conditions for cold-heading, especially avoiding unnecessarily large changes in section and sudden transitions. Also, sharp radii on the outer edges of heads or collars on fasteners should be avoided. Sharp edges rapidly break or wear out dies, and are costly. Sharp radii, when unavoidable, are best produced on high-speed secondary turning or trimming equipment. Secondary operations are not as costly as the special tooling needed to create sharp outside corners in the header.

Some Design Recommendations to Avoid Problems

Corners are Critical. It is difficult to force or flow metal into sharp corners of the die, so generous fillets and corner radii represent the best cold-heading conditions (Fig. 6a).

Square or Rectangular Heads. These require subsequent trimming (while oval or round shapes do not) because the displaced metal usually assumes a cylindrical shape when it is formed in the header (Fig. 6b).

Eccentric or Off-center Formations. Although harder to produce than concentric shapes, certain stainless parts with eccentric cams, serrations or sections can be cold-headed successfully (Fig. 6c).

Hollow Upsets. These require more die maintenance and cracks may form around edges of recess (Fig. 6d).

Concentric Ridges. Added to the underside surface of large, flat sections, concentric ridges make a part easier to eject from the die (Fig. 6e).

Long Sections. Long sections of stainless cold-headed parts are more likely to distort during subsequent heat-treatment operations (Fig. 6f).

Extensions. Lugs, fins, wings, and other extensions can be included in the head design, but the diameter of the blank and configuration of the head determine the size and quantity of such features (Fig. 6g).

Maximum Length. A cold-headed part that can be produced in most machines usually has a maximum length of about 6 in. (152.4 mm). Designs that represent exceptions to this rule may require special machinery (Fig. 6h).

Cold-heading Tolerances. Generally the tolerances are closer than hot-heading tolerances. Parts made on single-stroke cold headers have wider tolerances than parts made from two or more strokes. For example, rivets (which are often formed in single-stroke machines) have tolerances of ±0.015 in. (0.38 mm) except when specified otherwise (Fig. 6i). On the other hand, shanks for rolled threads (which are formed in several strokes) may have only ±0.0015-in. (0.038-mm) tolerance. Generally, small parts can have closer tolerances than large parts.

Four-Slide Wire Forming   Another process for forming wire into parts is performed on the widely used four-slide forming machine. Other types of equipment include punch presses, press brakes, and welding machines. The four-slide machine derives its name from the fact that the principal forming mechanism consists of four slides lying 90° apart in a single plane. The plane of these slides may be aligned horizontally, vertically, or may be made adjustable to any point between the vertical and horizontal axes, depending on the manufacturer of the particular machine.

The name "four-slide" is somewhat of a misnomer since an additional motion, and sometimes two motions, in a direction perpendicular to the plane of the main slides are available. These may be used for additional forming, transferring the workpiece to another forming area or stripping the workpiece from the machine. Typical press-working operations (such as swaging, piercing, coining, drawing, and stamping) can be performed on the

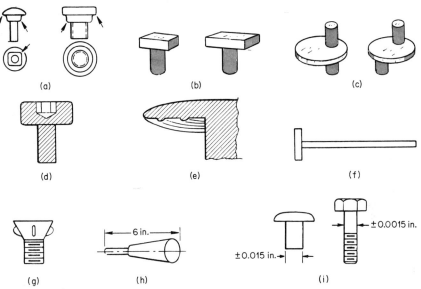

Fig. 6 (*a*) Corners are critical. (*b*) Square or rectangular heads require subsequent trimming. (*c*) Eccentric formations are harder to produce. (*d*) More die maintenance needed for hollow upsets. (*e*) Concentric ridges aid ejection. (*f*) Long sections may distort. (*g*) Extensions can be included in head design. (*h*) Maximum length as cold-headed is 6 in. (15.24 cm). (*i*) Close tolerances possible with cold-heading.

four-slide machine. Other attachments such as drilling, tapping, resistance welding, hopper feeds for assembling, etc., are available.

Four-Slide Forming Sequence. The forming sequence to produce a ring on a four-slide machine is illustrated in Fig. 7. The sequence is as follows: the wire is fed to the proper length. As the wire is cut off, the stock holder on the front slide grips the wire. After the cutoff, the front slide completes its form as shown in Fig. 7*b*. As the front slide completes the form, the left and right tool enter and complete their form as shown in Fig. 7*c*. The rear slide then completes its form. The slides retract, and the part is ejected.

The complexity and accuracy of components produced by the multiple-slide wire-forming method is limited only by the competence and ingenuity of the tool designer.

Swaging and Piercing   In swaging, metal is plastically deformed by means of compressive forces to conform to the shape of the die. The die capacity is difficult to obtain exactly since the total pressure depends on the area to be swaged, the speed of the die, and the amount of restriction to metal flow. An approximate method for computing press capacity is given in the nomograph of Fig. 8. It is based on theoretical yield points and does not account for strain hardening, speed of swage, or restriction to metal flow.

It is recommended that flattening or swaging of wire should be limited to about one-third of the wire diameter. Swaging hardens the stainless steel wire and increases its strength in the swaged area. Some of the wide variety of swaging and piercing operations are shown in Fig. 9. Some design criteria must be observed in piercing holes. They require a wall thickness that is at least equal to the hole diameter. These holes should be spaced a minimum distance of 1 diameter from the end of the wire and similarly minimum spacing between holes should be 1 wire diameter. Most piercing is done in swaged areas

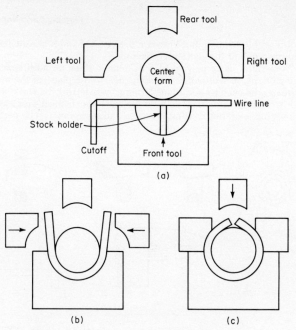

Fig. 7 Ring-forming sequence on four-slide machine.[1]

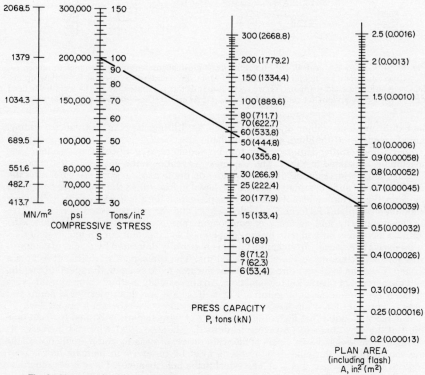

Fig. 8 Nomograph of press capacity required for swaging annealed stainless steel wire.[1]

rather than on round wire. Since piercing reduces the wire's strength to some degree, compensation should be made for this by using slightly larger wire gages or by proper placement on a swaged section.

Bend Radii Formula As a rule of thumb, many wire fabricators say that the minimum bend or radius should be equal to the wire diameter. However, there are instances where, due to temper, type of stainless steel, etc., these rules change. Various formulas

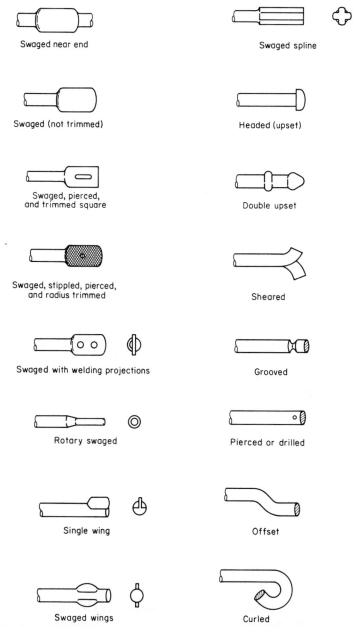

Swaged near end

Swaged spline

Swaged (not trimmed)

Headed (upset)

Swaged, pierced,
and trimmed square

Double upset

Swaged, stippled, pierced,
and radius trimmed

Sheared

Swaged with welding projections

Grooved

Rotary swaged

Pierced or drilled

Single wing

Offset

Swaged wings

Curled

Fig. 9 Typical ends or terminations of wire involving swaging, piercing, and upsetting.[1]

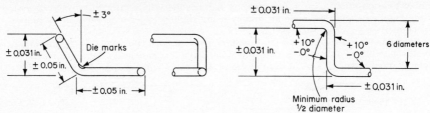

Fig. 10   Multiple-bend tolerances.

have been established, based on experience, and can be found in several reference sources, such as the "Wire Designer's Handbook"[1] published by the American Iron and Steel Institute.

Multiple Bends. Bends formed in press-brake dies need a bend-to-bend dimensional tolerance of ±0.05 in. (1.27 mm). However, the overall plane-to-plane dimension remains ±0.031 in. (0.787 mm). Angles other than right angles need a wider tolerance, ±3°. In the opposite right-angle double bend shown in Fig. 10, perpendicularity tolerance jumps to 10°, all on the plus side, and the minimum spread between parallel legs is 6 wire diameters.

Press-formed Dip Bend. In the press-formed dip bend (Fig. 11), the width of the dip A is limited to at least 2 wire diameters or 0.25 in. (6.35 mm), whichever is larger. With A at a minimum, dip depth B is limited to 4 diameters. Minimum upper-inside radius is 0.1875 in. (4.76 mm). Minimum draft goes from 2 to 3° for the minimum condition of dip width, and die marks will occur inside the dip.

Captive-Hook Bends. Allow 0.094 in. (2.39 mm) for springback and 3 wire diameters of overhang (Fig. 12). Table 3 shows the minimum forming-pin size for a given wire size. With springback, the final hook diameter is somewhat larger. Open hooks need 4 diameters of overhang and a minimum inside radius of ½ diameter or 0.25 in. (6.35 mm), whichever is larger.

Loops. Loops have minimum diameters of twice the wire diameter. Springback opening is at least 0.094 in. (2.39 mm). Severe die marks and deformation occur with minimum bending radii of ½ diameter for the two lower bends (Fig. 13).

Rectangular Wire Frames. These frames have optimal tolerances from an economic standpoint (Fig. 14). Keep the welded seam at least 4 in. (10.2 cm) from the corner to facilitate welding, hold camber to ±0.031 in. (0.787 mm), and set dimensional tolerances at ±0.031 in. (0.787 mm) except that for the welded leg, which should be double, ±0.062 in. (1.57 mm).

The inside radius of the corner should be at least 0.25 in. (6.35 mm) or half the wire diameter, whichever is larger. Corner angles can be held to ±1°. Radius tolerances should be ±0.031 in. (0.787 mm) for 0.25 to 0.375-in. (6.35 to 9.53-mm) wire; ±0.062 in. (1.574 mm) for 0.375 to 1-in. (9.53 to 25.4-mm) wire, and ±0.094 in. (2.39 mm) for wires over 1 in. (25.4 mm). Any time the inside radius is less than wire diameter, die marks and distortion will occur on the inner portion. Flatness of the finished frame can deviate by ±0.031 in. (0.787 mm) on one corner when the other three corners are touching a flat plate. Although some decrease in most of these limits is possible, it will boost cost.

End Trimming. After welding, end trimming should be at angles no greater than 30° to ensure a sound weld as indicated in Fig. 15. Trimmed edges must be free of sharp projections. A flush, or vertical trim still overhangs 0.007 to 0.015 in. (0.18 to 0.38 mm).

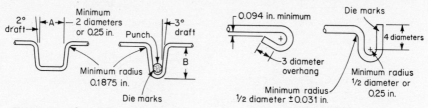

Fig. 11   Press-formed dip bend tolerances.

Fig. 12   Captive hook bend tolerances.

TABLE 3   Bending Limits

Wire size		Bending-pin diameter	
in.	mm	in.	mm
0.331–0.362	8.41–9.19	0.500	12.7
0.243–0.331	6.17–8.41	0.312	7.92
0.192–0.243	4.88–6.17	0.250	6.35
0.105–0.192	2.67–4.88	0.187	4.75
0.105 or smaller	2.67 or smaller	0.125	3.18

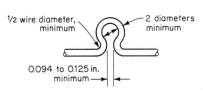

Fig. 13   Loop tolerances.

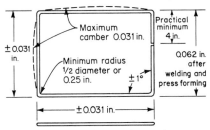

Fig. 14   Rectangular wire frame tolerances.

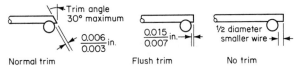

Fig. 15   End trimming tolerances.

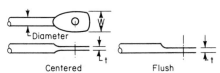

Fig. 16   Flattened or swaged end tolerances.

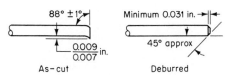

Fig. 17   Wire end condition.

With no trimming, the smaller wire should overhang by half its diameter, or at least 0.062 in. (1.57 mm), ±0.031 in. (0.787 mm). Avoid trimming a large wire welded to a smaller wire.

Flattened or Swaged Ends. Whether flush or centered, swaged or flattened ends have an approximate width of 2¼ diameters less thickness t (Fig. 16). The flattened surface is subject to die marks and a change in physical structure that impairs electroplating finishes. It usually is work hardened and is quite brittle, depending on the ratio of diameter to thickness.

Wire-End Condition. Normal straightening and cutting machines will produce deformation and burr (see Fig. 17) and deburring may be required.

REFERENCES

1. "Wire Designer's Handbook," pp. 36–39, Committee of Rod and Drawn Wire Producers, American Iron & Steel Institute, 1969.
2. Schmid, D. M., and J. F. Pfeffer: Cold Heading High-Performance Alloys, *Mach. Des.*, vol. 64, no. 17, p. 137, Jul. 11, 1974.

Chapter 29

The Powder Metallurgy of Stainless Steels

HARRY D. AMBS*

Manager Technical Service, Glidden–Durkee Division, SCM
Corporation, Johnstown, Pennsylvania

ATHAN STOSUY*

Hoeganaes Corporation, Subsidiary of Interlake, Inc., Riverton, New
Jersey

*Acting as representatives of the Metal Powder Industries Federation.

INTRODUCTION

Stainless steel powder metallurgy (P/M) is a metal fabrication process which combines stainless steel metallurgy with the art and science of powder technology to produce stainless steel shapes and products from particulate materials.

The original efforts to make stainless steel articles by P/M date back to the early 1930s at the Hardy Metallurgical Company. Their approach consisted of mixing elemental powders of iron, nickel, and chromium together in standard 18-8 proportions, pressing the mix into compacts, and sintering in purified dry hydrogen. They obtained a full alloyed austenitic structure and the test pieces exhibited good mechanical properties but only after a sintering cycle of 44 h at 2370°F (1300°C), which was entirely uneconomical.

In 1942, J. Wulff reported on a stainless steel material produced from an alloy powder in which each particle was of true 18-8 composition. This powder was prepared by first heating high-carbon stainless steel scrap to 500 to 750°C to cause precipitation of carbides at the grain boundaries and then boiling the embrittled scrap in a $CuSO_4$-H_2SO_4 solution to cause it to disintegrate. Powder of this type was commercially produced by the Unexcelled Manufacturing Company in New York. The Unexcelled powder was generally difficult to press and had low green strength but, if handled carefully, gave acceptable properties. Some stainless steel parts, mainly filters, were developed through the use of this powder.

In the late 1940s Vanadium Alloys Steel Company started production of a prealloyed stainless steel powder using a modified rotating disintegrator of the F. W. Berk or Comstock design. Because of production problems associated with running it, they soon developed a direct water atomization technique for producing prealloyed stainless steel powders (Batten & Roberts, U.S. Patent 2,956,304). By the 1950s Vasco had a plant producing 40 tons/yr (36,280 kg/yr) of stainless steel powders using 1000-lb (453-kg) induction furnaces and water atomization facilities. This was the start of commercial stainless steel P/M. Today, there are three companies in the United States producing stainless steel powder by water atomization for powder metallurgy with a combined capacity of over 4000 tons/yr (3.63×10^6 kg/yr).

P/M STAINLESS STEEL MARKET

Two of the early successful applications of stainless steel P/M were an airplane wing deicer filter element made by Aircraft Porous Media Company from Type 316 stainless and an automotive manifold heat-control valve bushing made from Type 304 stainless by Amplex Division, Chrysler Corporation. Today, there are hundreds of different parts and filters made annually from stainless steel powders by custom fabricators and in-plant P/M part manufacturers.

In 1973, the total production of powder metallurgy parts in the United States from all materials was at a level of 170,000 tons (154.2×10^6 kg). Stainless steel P/M parts are only approximately 1% of this amount, [1800 tons (1.63×10^6 kg)] as is shown in Fig. 1, but stainless steel P/M still is a young and rapidly growing industry. Figure 2 shows the shipments of stainless steel powders in the United States for the period 1962 to 1973.

Production of P/M stainless steel parts and filters has also been reported in Argentina, Australia, Belgium, Brazil, Canada, France, Germany, Italy, Japan, Mexico, Spain, Sweden, Switzerland, the United Kingdom, and the U.S.S.R.

Powder Prices   The price of atomized stainless steel powder in the United States depends on the grade and quantity purchased. In spite of some downward trends owing to the influence of more efficient powder production and the rising pressures of inflation, this price has remained fairly steady over the years. In 1948, *Iron Age* reported the price of Type 302 stainless steel powder as $0.75 per pound. More recent price ranges for 1-ton lots of some popular grades are shown in Table 1.

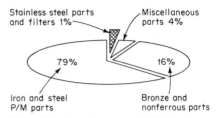

Fig. 1   Distribution by material of P/M parts shipped in 1973.

Use of Stainless Steel P/M   The successful use of the stainless steel P/M technique depends on the proper selection and control of the following:

- Part application, design of part, and quantity required
- Powder alloy selection and preparation of powder for use
- Consolidation technique and tooling
- Sintering cycle and atmosphere
- Secondary and finishing operations

The P/M process is shown in Fig. 3. Most P/M stainless steel parts are made by conventional compacting and sintering. Most stainless steel filters, however, are made by pressureless-mold or gravity sintering.

Almost any stainless steel alloy can be made in powder form by induction melting and water atomization. However, not all are suitable for P/M. The most popular alloys are 316L, 303L, 304L, and 410L. Powders of these alloys have been specifically engineered for use in the P/M process and have closely controlled characteristics of chemistry, particle shape, and particle size. Other alloys such as 347L, 17-4PH, 302B, 434L have also been made but are used to a lesser extent.

Stainless steel P/M parts are used primarily because of their corrosion resistance. The P/M process is chosen over competitive processes mainly because of economics. Stainless

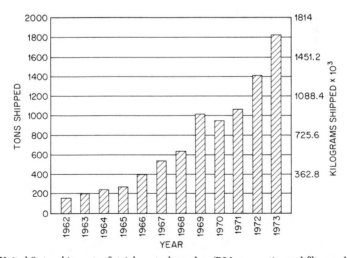

Fig. 2   United States shipments of stainless steel powders (P/M, compacting and filter grades).

steel filters are an exception as the powder process results in controlled permeability which is otherwise unattainable. Stainless steel P/M parts are used in the automotive and marine industries, for hardware, nuts, hinges and fasteners, for machines handling food and drugs, for decorative parts, in aircraft, and in the chemical industry. The chart in Fig. 4 gives an approximation of the relative volume of stainless steel P/M parts used by various

TABLE 1   **United States Prices of Stainless Steel Powder**
2000-lb (907-kg) lots

Grade	Price per pound 1960–1961	Price per pound 1973–1974
303L	$0.81–$0.96	$0.76–$0.97
304L	0.78– 0.96	0.79– 0.96
316L	0.88– 1.08	0.82– 1.00
410L	0.73– 0.90	0.65– 0.81

industries. Stainless steel P/M parts are found in a greater variety of applications than any other P/M material.

STAINLESS STEEL POWDER

While there are several methods by which stainless steel powder can be manufactured, only one, atomization with water, is of commercial importance for the P/M industry. Stainless steel powders can be made by intergranular corrosion, coreduction, and rotating electrode atomization but these powders do not possess the characteristics needed for compacting and sintering. Consequently, there was very little advancement in stainless P/M until the commercial development of the water atomization process for the manufacture of powders.

   Atomization of Powder   Basically, atomization is the disintegration of a molten metal

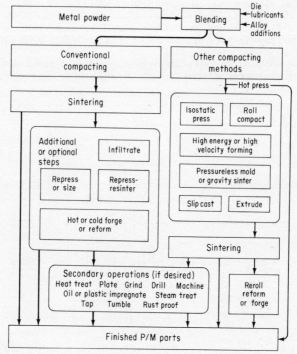

Fig. 3   The power metallurgy processes. *(Metal Powder Industries Federation.)*

stream into droplets which are subsequently collected as powder. Figure 5 is a flowsheet of the water atomization process.

The water atomization of P/M grade stainless steel powder starts with the production of the molten alloy. Melting is usually done in high-frequency induction furnaces of 100 to 3000 lb capacity (45 to 1362 kg).

Raw Materials Used. Because of the stringent chemical requirements of stainless steel powder for P/M, virgin raw materials are used almost exclusively to make up the melt.

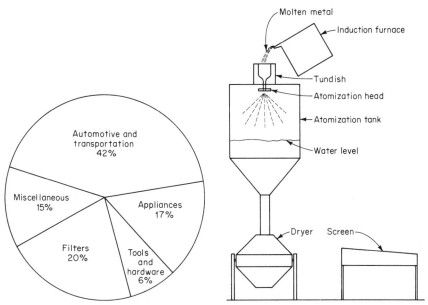

Fig. 4 Approximate market distribution for stainless steel, P/M products (1973).

Fig. 5 Schematic of water atomization process for stainless steel powder.

Pure iron, such as Armco iron or similar material, is used for the basic charge. Low carbon content is of prime importance. Nickel is added as cathode, pellets, or electrolytic nickel, while chromium and molybdenum are added as low-carbon ferroalloys when required. Control of minor elements such as manganese, phosphorus, silicon, and sulfur are important to the viscosity and deoxidation of the melt. Scrap materials are very seldom used. The composition must be rigidly controlled to assure efficient atomization and to give the desired performance properties to the resulting powder.

A protective slag cover is used to minimize the oxidation of the melt, particularly the chromium. When the melt has reached a temperature of about 3000°F (1650°C), the slag is removed and the metal poured into a preheated tundish. In the bottom of the tundish is a ¼- to ½-in. diameter (6.35- to 12.7-mm) orifice which meters the flow of a thin stream of molten metal down into the atomizing chamber.

Atomizing Head. The atomizing unit is located near the top of the atomizing tank and close to the exit port of the tundish. This consists of a series of jet nozzles which are directed downward at an angle so that the jet streams of water converge and intersect at the metal stream to form a V jet. The apex angle between the intersecting water jets is critical and usually established experimentally for each system. Typically it is held at 40 to 45° (0.70 to 0.79 rad) for stainless steel. At a more shallow angle, the molten metal stream will be forced back while an angle too steep will result in inefficient disintegration.

Atomizing Conditions. The impingement of the atomizing medium, water, gas, steam, etc., against the metal stream disintegrates the molten metal into fine droplets. In making stainless steel powder, water is the most commonly used atomizing fluid. Pressures of up to 2000 psi (13.8 MN/m²) are commercially employed depending on particle-size distribution and particle shape required. The higher the pressure, the smaller will be both the

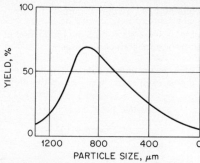

Fig. 6 Low-pressure water atomization.

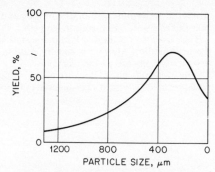

Fig. 7 High-pressure water atomization.

maximum and the average particle size (see Figs. 6 and 7). The stainless steel powders used for compacting are most commonly atomized under conditions which will yield −100 mesh (<150 μm) powder containing 35 to 50% −325 mesh (<44 μm) particles. Table 2 gives the yield and distribution for various atomizing conditions.

The atomized molten droplets of stainless steel then fall freely to the bottom of the atomizing chamber which is filled with water. Most of the droplets have solidified either during atomization or while dropping toward the water. The remaining particles solidify after hitting the water.

Drying and Screening. Periodically, the slurry of metal particles and water is removed and the water is separated from the powder. This is done by centrifuging, filtration, vacuum, or heat. After the powder is completely dry, it is screened to remove the oversize particles or to obtain special screen cuts for filter applications.

Austenitic stainless steel powders do not require any additional treatments. As-atomized, their metallurgical structure is the softest attainable and therefore has maximum compressibility for P/M. However, with martensitic stainless steel such as AISI 410, the as-atomized structure is martensitic and has high hardness and minimum compressibility. Therefore, the powder must be annealed to be useful for P/M. Two annealing treatments are used to improve the compressibility. The first consists of heating the powder to a temperature somewhat below the austenitizing temperature and in essence tempering the martensitic structure. The other method consists of heating to just above the austenitic-phase transformation temperature and then slowly cooling through the critical temperature range. In either case, a protective atmosphere must be used to prevent oxidation. Dry hydrogen is the preferred gas although dissociated ammonia is most commonly used in production. Some sintering takes place during annealing, and a light comminution is required to restore the original particle-size distribution.

Powder Characteristics

Chemistry. Today's stainless steel powders are highly engineered for their intended uses. While most commercial stainless steel alloys can be made in powder form, the

TABLE 2 **Effect of Water Pressure on Yield and Particle Size Distribution of Atomized Stainless Steel**

Atomizing water pressure		Yield of −100 mesh (<150 μm), %	Size distribution of −100 mesh material, %		
psi	MN/m²		−100 +200 (74–150 μm)	−200 +325 (44–74 μm)	−325 (<44 μm)
800	5.5	50	50	30	20
1000	6.9	60	40	35	25
1200	8.3	70	35	35	30
1500	10.3	80	30	30	40
1750	12.1	85	25	30	45
2000	13.8	90	15	25	60

SOURCE: "Powders in Industry," in I. Jenkins (ed.), "The Manufacture and Testing of Metal Powders," p. 255, Society of Chemical Industry, London, 1961.

powder metallurgy industry has standardized on relatively few grades. These are AISI 304L, 303L, 316L, 410L, and 434L. The chemical analyses for these grades (Table 3) generally fall within the limits specified by AISI for the wrought alloys, but in practice are held to tighter tolerances because of the special requirements of powder metallurgy. Slightly higher nickel contents, particularly in 303L and 304L, and low carbon levels are used exclusively.

Some special stainless steel powder alloys and precipitation-hardenable grades have

TABLE 3   Nominal Chemistry of P/M Grades of Stainless Steel Powders

Grade	Ni	Cr	Mo	Si	Mn	S	C	Fe
303L	12.5	17.5		0.7	0.35	0.2	0.02	Bal.
304L	10.5	18.5		0.7	0.25		0.02	Bal.
316L	13.0	17.0	2.1	0.7	0.20		0.02	Bal.
316B	12.5	17.5	2.2	2.4	0.25		0.02	Bal.
410L		13.0		0.7	0.40		0.02	Bal.
434L		17.0	1.0	0.7	0.25		0.02	Bal.

also been developed by powder producers and part fabricators. These compositions usually offer some improved performance for specific applications but are not in general use.

Particle Shape. The shape of stainless steel particles to be used in powder metallurgy is very important since all of the powder properties such as apparent density, flow rate, compressibility, green strength, etc., are in some way influenced by the shape. Control of particle shape is the most critical processing variable. In the manufacture of P/M parts and some filters, for example, an irregularly shaped powder particle is preferred because of the need for green and sintered strength. Although chemistry has some effect on particle shape, the primary control of particle geometry is through the choice of the atomizing media and atomizing conditions. Water will produce the most irregularly shaped powder while inert gas and steam produce a smoother and more rounded particle. Stainless steel filters are sometimes made with more regular or spheroidal powders to achieve better control of permeability. Figures 8 and 9 illustrate the irregular particle shape of water-atomized 316L stainless steel powder.

Powder Microstructure. During atomization, the individual droplets freeze almost instantaneously so that the microstructure of each particle resembles that of a fine-textured miniature casting. A dendritic pattern is formed during solidification with the core

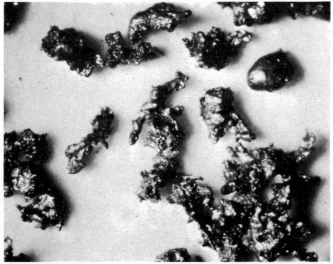

Fig. 8 Irregularly shaped particles of compacting grade 316L stainless steel powder produced by water atomization. Magnification 20×. *(Glidden Metals, Glidden-Durkee Division of SCM Corp.)*

of the dendrites being rich in iron. This delta ferrite causes the particles of an austenitic alloy to be slightly ferromagnetic. The finer particles are more magnetic. After sintering, the structure is homogenized and the part becomes nonmagnetic. Figure 10 shows the cored structure of a particle of 316L powder. Figures 11 and 12 show the microstructure of a 410L particle as-atomized and after annealing.

Powder Properties

Apparent Density. This is the bulk density or the mass per unit volume of the loose powder as determined by Metal Powder Industries Federation Standard MPIF 05 (Amer-

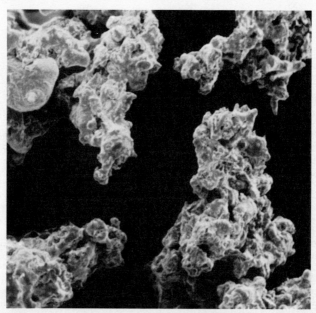

Fig. 9   Scanning electron micrograph of water-atomized 316L stainless steel powder. Original magnification 90×. *(Glidden Metals, Glidden-Durkee Division of SCM Corp.)*

ican Society for Testing and Materials Standard ASTM B 212). It is an important property because it determines the fill requirements of the compacting die. The more irregularly shaped the particles, the lower will be the apparent density and the greater the volume of fill needed to achieve a desired weight. The apparent density of compacting grades of stainless steel powder made by water atomization generally ranges from 2.8 to 3.2 g/cm³. Spherical solid stainless steel powders produced by gas atomization may have an apparent density as high as 5.0 g/cm³.

Flow Rate. This is defined as the time required for a mass of 50 g of powder to flow through an 0.010-in. (0.254-mm) orifice according to MPIF Standard 03 (ASTM B 213). The rate at which parts can be made is often limited by the filling of the die with powder and a faster flow rate can mean higher production rates. Spheroidal stainless steel powders may have flow times of only 15 s, while irregularly shaped powders may require 25 to 30 s. Stainless steel powders have flow characteristics that are more than adequate for most P/M applications.

Sieve Analysis. This is the distribution of particle sizes by weight percent for a representative sample of powder using the sieve series designated by MPIF Standard 05 (ASTM B 215). Stainless steel powders for P/M applications have the typical sieve analysis shown in Table 4.

Stainless steel powders for filter applications are usually supplied as screen cuts or split fractions limiting the particle size to a specific range. A coarse filter may be made from the −20 + 50 fraction which would contain particles between 297 and 841 μm in size.

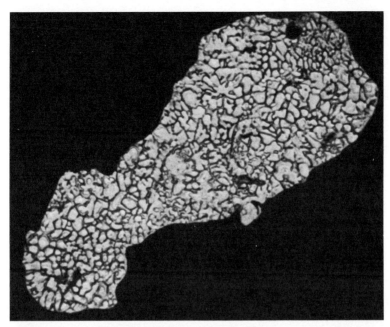

Fig. 10 Microstructure of as-atomized particle of 316L stainless steel powder. Magnification 1000×. *(Hoeganaes Corp.)*

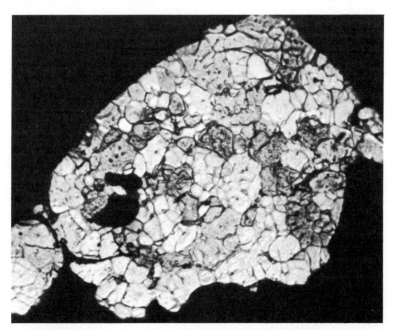

Fig. 11 Microstructure of as-atomized particle of low-carbon 410 stainless steel powder. Magnification 1000×. *(Hoeganaes Corp.)*

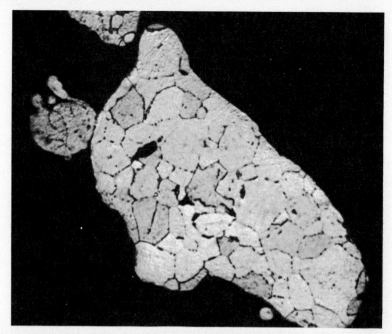

Fig. 12 Structure of 410L powder particle after annealing. Magnification 1000×. *(Hoeganaes Corp.)*

Because of the difficulties of production screening, commercial practice generally allows 5% maximum oversize and 10% maximum undersize on split cuts.

Compressibility. This property, sometimes called compactibility, is a measure of the density achieved when a powder is compacted under a given pressure. The standard test method is described in MPIF 45 (ASTM B 331). Compressibility curves for some stainless steel powders are shown in Fig. 13. The austenitic grades are more compressible than the martensitic grades. Compressibility is a function of the yield strength and rate of work hardening of the alloy, the softness of the particles, the amount of closed internal porosity, the shape of the particles, and the particle-size distribution.

Green Strength. This property, as determined by MPIF Standard 15 (ASTM B 312), is a measure of the transverse rupture strength of the compacted but unsintered powder. It relates to the resistance of the powder to breakage during handling in the manufacture of P/M parts. Water-atomized stainless steel powders have sufficient green strength for most applications but do require more care in handling than iron powders. More regular or spherical stainless steel powders have inadequate green strength for compacting but may be used for pressureless sintering of filters.

Safety Data. Stainless steel powder has no known toxic, radioactive, or pyrophoric hazards other than as a nuisance dust. The 8-h time-weighted average Threshold Limit Value (TLV) for exposure to nuisance dust is 15 mg/m³, as listed in Table G-3 of Part 1910 of the Williams-Steiger Occupational Safety and Health Act of 1970.

TABLE 4 Typical Sieve Analysis of P/M Grade Stainless Steel Powders

U.S. Standard sieve size	Particle size, μm	Weight, %
+100	>149	0– 3
−100 +140	105–149	10–15
−140 +200	74–105	15–25
−200 +325	44–74	20–30
−325	< 44	35–50

Stainless steel powder is classified as a nonexplosive material by the U.S. Bureau of Mines in Report RI-6516, "Explosibility of Metal Powders."

SOURCES OF STAINLESS STEEL POWDER

There are three companies in the United States which produce stainless steel powder for P/M compacting and filter manufacturing. Each employs fluid atomization as the primary method to disintegrate the metal. There are also three foreign companies that atomize stainless steel powders. All of these companies are listed in Table 5.

STAINLESS STEEL P/M PRINCIPLES

The mechanical and physical properties of P/M stainless steel materials are a function of the chemistry of the grade and the manner in which the powder is processed into parts. This section deals with these processing variables and illustrates the effects by reference to laboratory data.

Powder Lubrication   For the manufacture of structural parts, a lubricant must be used with the prealloyed powder to permit high-density compaction and the ejection of the part from the die.

The type and amount of dry lubricant to be mixed with the powder must be selected carefully since the lubricant will affect apparent density, flow rate, green density, green strength, ejection pressure, and the sintered properties. The lubricants most commonly used with stainless steel powders are lithium stearate and synthetic wax, but zinc stearate is also used. Lithium stearate will give the best compressibility but at a slight sacrifice in green strength. The waxes will give higher green strength but they also require higher compacting pressures to reach a given density. Table 6 shows the effect of various lubricants on some processing properties of stainless steel powder.

The amount of lubricant required depends on the die-wall area in contact with the part and the density to which the powder is to be pressed.

Thin parts may only require ½% lubricant while long thin-walled parts may need as

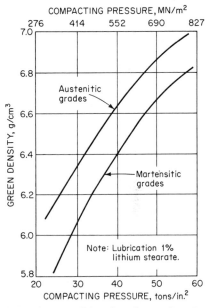

Fig. 13   Compactibility of stainless steel powder.

TABLE 5   Stainless Steel Powder Producers

United States:

Glidden Metals, Glidden-Durkee Div.,
   SCM Corporation, Cleveland, Ohio
Hoeganaes Corporation, Subsidiary
   Interlake, Inc., Riverton, N.J.
Metallurgical International, Inc., New
   Shrewsbury, N.J.

International:

BSA Metal Powders Ltd., Birmingham,
   England
S. A. Floridienne, Brussels, Belgium
Demag-Meer-Pulvermetall GmbH,
   Moenchengladbach, West Germany

TABLE 6   Effect of Various Admixed Lubricants on 316L Stainless Steel Powder

Powder mix	Apparent density, g/cm³	Flow rate, s/50 g	Green density, g/cm³ at 45 tons/in.² (620 MN/m²)	Green strength psi	Green strength MN/m²	Ejection pressure psi	Ejection pressure MN/m²
316L (unlubricated)	2.80	27.0					
w/1/2% lithium stearate	2.92	30.2	6.73	950	6.6	1300	9.0
w/1% lithium stearate	2.98	34.6	6.75	800	5.5	1200	8.3
w/1% powdered synthetic wax	2.80	Int.	6.67	1500	10.3	1450	10.0
w/1% atomized synthetic wax	2.90	Int.	6.72	1100	7.6	1400	9.7
w/1% stearic acid	2.94	24.8	6.54	2100	14.5	1650	11.4
w/1% zinc stearate	2.92	Int.	6.73	1000	6.9	1400	9.7

much as 1½%. In general commercial practice, 1% lubricant is most commonly used. A mixing time of 15 to 30 min is usually sufficient to produce a homogeneous stable mix. Overmixing can result in loss of green strength.

Compacting   Stainless steel powders do not present any unique problems in compacting. They have very good flow and die fill characteristics. Stainless alloys are inherently harder than copper or iron so tool wear can be expected to be somewhat greater than when the latter materials are processed. When processing stainless steels, care must be taken that the press area is completely clean of any other powders such as iron, since even a few particles of iron may cause localized corrosion in the finished parts.

Stainless steel powders are normally pressed at 30 to 60 tons/in.² (414 to 827 MN/m²) to achieve densities of 6.2 to 6.9 g/cm³. Densities higher than 7.0 g/cm³ require multiple processing or densification through high-temperature sintering.

All properties of sintered stainless steel increase with higher densities. Density is a direct result of compacting pressure. Figure 14 shows the relationship between tensile strength, yield strength and hardness as density increases.

Presintering   The green compacts are normally presintered in air or nitrogen at 800 to 1000°F (426 to 538°C) to volatilize and burn off the pressing lubricant. If higher temperatures are used, a protective atmosphere is required. It is important to remove this lubricant because it may cause carburization of the alloy during sintering which would be detrimental to the machinability and corrosion resistance of the austenitic alloys. Those martensitic alloys which contain carbon for hardenability must be presintered in nitrogen.

Sintering Principles   The most important and critical step in the processing of P/M stainless steel is sintering.

In the course of making wrought stainless, severe hot- and cold-working of the ingot and long annealing periods are required to homogenize the structure of the material. This is due primarily to the coarse structure resulting from the slow rate of solidification. Homogenization of stainless powder, on the other hand, is much more easily attained. Figure 15 illustrates the microstructure of a number of pressed particles of atomized 316L powder. The dendritic pattern is easily seen. Figure 16 shows the structure after sintering

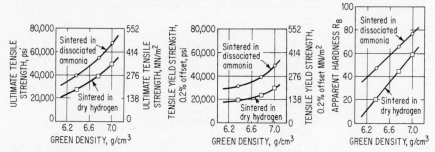

Fig. 14   Effect of density on the tensile and yield strengths, and hardness of sintered 316L stainless steel powder.

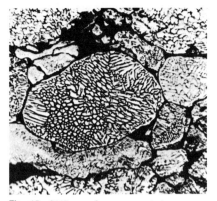

Fig. 15 316L powder as-pressed (green compact). Magnification 500×.

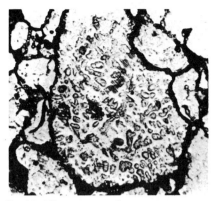

Fig. 16 Microstructures after sintering 5 min at 1950°F (1066°C) in dissociated ammonia. Magnification 500×.

for only 5 min at 1950°F (1066°C). The cored structure is still visible, but the particles already show signs of homogenization. The structure after sintering 30 min at 2050°F (1120°C) is shown in Fig. 17. Here homogenization is almost complete and particle-to-particle bonding is taking place. Figure 18 shows the structure after sintering 120 min at 2400°F (1315°C). Homogenization is complete and considerable grain growth and spheroidization of the pores have taken place. The original particle boundaries have completely disappeared with the formation of a single-phase austenitic structure.

Several phenomena which can take place during sintering are listed in Table 7. The atmosphere, temperature, and time used determine which of these phenomena is predominant during sintering.

Sintering Atmospheres

Hydrogen. This is an active sintering atmosphere. Unless a purified grade of hydrogen is purchased, it is necessary to remove the residual air and moisture. This is accomplished easily by passing the gas through a palladium catalyst to let the oxygen react with the hydrogen. The resulting water is removed by means of activated alumina or molecular sieves. A recent development is a commercial silver-palladium filter which will produce extremely pure hydrogen. The ratio of hydrogen to water vapor determines whether or not surface chromium oxide will be reduced during sintering and during cooling. The dew

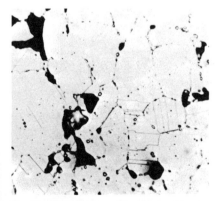

Fig. 17 Microstructure after sintering 30 min at 2050°F (1121°C) in dissociated ammonia. Magnification 500×.

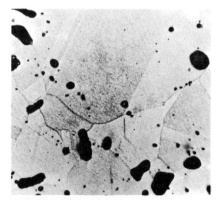

Fig. 18 Microstructure after sintering 2 h at 2400°F (1316°C) in dissociated ammonia. Magnification 500×.

point controlling the reduction-oxidation reaction depends on the temperature. As the sintering temperature is increased, the dew point required for reduction will be less critical, as shown in Fig. 19. Theoretically, at a temperature of 2050°F (1121°C), a dew point of less than −8°F (−22.2°C) at the surface of the powder is required for reduction

TABLE 7   Sintering Phenomena

Oxide reduction
Oxide dissolution
Carburization
Nitriding
Homogenization
Grain growth
Increase in bond area
Change of pore structure

while at 2400°F (1316°C), a dew point of +13°F (−10.6°C) is satisfactory. To maintain reducing conditions in actual practice, it is usually necessary to have a dew point of at least −30 to −40°F (−34.4 to −40°C) in the furnace. Because water vapor is formed during reduction, a sufficient flow of gas is needed to continually remove this water and also the water formed by the reaction between the hydrogen and the air introduced with the parts and through the furnace openings.

During sintering, hydrogen will reduce the surface oxide. The removal of this oxide promotes a greater degree of bonding resulting in better ductility in the sintered product. Yield and tensile strengths increase with density of the parts. The high degree of sintering also results in more dimensional shrinkage than when other atmospheres are used. During cooling, the atmosphere requirement becomes more stringent and this also dictates the need for at least a −30°F (−34.4°C) dew point. Even then some oxidation may take place, but at such a slow rate that it is not noticeable either as a change in mechanical properties or as discoloration. This slight surface oxidation does not appear to be protective against corrosion and cannot be compared to that obtained by chemical passivation.

Dissociated Ammonia. This is the most common commercial atmosphere used for sintering stainless steels and is composed of 75% H_2 and 25% N_2. It contains very little (0.012%) residual ammonia and has a dew point of −50 to −65°F (−45.6 to −54°C) at the generator. A dryer may be used to reduce the dew point to less than −80°F (−62°C) to allow more leeway in the sintering operation. The 25% nitrogen present in dissociated ammonia, although considered neutral for many materials, is far from neutral for stainless steels. Chromium in stainless steel has a high affinity for nitrogen and in dissociated

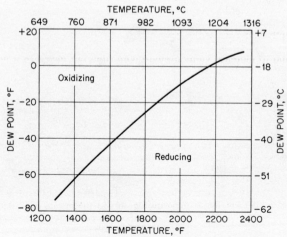

Fig. 19   Oxidation-reduction of Cr_2O_3 with hydrogen.

ammonia nitriding takes place very rapidly. For example, in one test, the nitrogen content of 316L increased from 0.028% in the powder to 0.302% in the part after sintering for 30 min at 2050°F (1120°C)—an increase of more than 10 times. Nitrogen is a strong austenitizer and its effects on mechanical properties are illustrated in Table 8. Even when dilute amounts are present the rate of absorbtion can be substantial. This must be considered if the furnace is not completely purged when switching to a hydrogen atmosphere and traces of nitrogen remain.

Vacuum. Sintering in vacuum will produce properties quite similar to those obtained by sintering in hydrogen: high ductility with relatively low yield and tensile strengths.

TABLE 8   Mechanical Properties of 316L Pressed to 6.85/cm³ and Sintered for 30 min at 2050°F (1120°C) in Various Atmospheres

Property	Sintered in dissociated ammonia	Sintered in hydrogen
Yield strength, (0.2% offset)	39,800 psi (274.4 MN/m²)	26,600 psi (183.4 MN/m²)
Ultimate tensile strength	53,000 psi (365.4 MN/m²)	41,800 psi (288.2 MN/m²)
Elongation in 1 in. (25.4 mm)	7.0%	10.9%
Apparent hardness	67 R_B	47 R_B

Since the vacuum required for the dissociation of the oxides is much greater than that normally attained even in laboratory equipment, the sintering process in vacuum involves the dissolving of the surface oxides. Commercial vacuum sintering of stainless steels is normally done at a partial pressure of approximately 10 μm. Too low a pressure can cause chromium depletion in the alloy.

Backfilling with nitrogen increases the rate of cooling after sintering. When cooling in nitrogen, enough nitriding takes place to make the mechanical properties of stainless steel similar to those obtained by sintering in dissociated ammonia. This phenomenon certainly has to be considered in the evaluation of equipment and processing needs. Backfilling with argon is necessary to achieve maximum ductility.

Sintering Cycles Tensile strength increases with sintering temperature and with sintering time; while the yield strength decreases with increasing temperature and increases with increasing time. These results can be explained as follows: After the surface oxide has been reduced in the initial stage of sintering, the particles bond to each other by solid-state diffusion. This is followed by a gradual increase in the amount of bonding and by an increase in grain size. The two phenomena take place simultaneously, but their rate of growth is influenced differently by the sintering time and temperature. The growth of the bond area depends on both time and temperature while the grain size depends primarily on the temperature. As the bond area increases, there is an increase in both yield and tensile strengths because of the increased actual cross-sectional area of the bonds. On the other hand, it is well known that for a given material the yield strength decreases as the grain size increases. These two effects combine to increase the tensile strength of sintered material with increased sintering time and temperature, and to increase yield strength with time but decrease it with increased temperature.

Figures 20 and 21 show the effect of sintering temperature and atmosphere on the mechanical properties and the dimensional change (calculated from die size) of 316L stainless steel. The decrease in yield strength and increased ductility are readily apparent. Note the high degree of shrinkage when sintering at higher temperatures, especially in hydrogen.

Lengthening the sintering time increases all of the tensile properties and the amount of shrinkage. Figures 22 and 23 illustrate the influence of sintering time on 316L in dissociated ammonia. Sintering in hydrogen or in vacuum will show similar trends, but the curves will be displaced accordingly.

Cooling Rates Regardless of the sintering atmosphere, the rate of cooling from the sintering temperature will have some effect on the properties of sintered austenitic stainless. Fortunately, the rates of cooling normally used give the best combination of strength and ductility. All stainless steels will contain a certain amount of carbon, and when dissociated ammonia is used, nitrogen will also be present. The amount of these

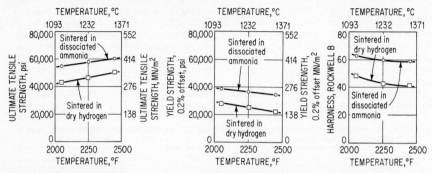

Fig. 20 Effect of sintering temperature on tensile and yield strengths, and apparent hardness of sintered 316L stainless steel pressed to 6.85 g/cm³ and sintered for 30 min in various atmospheres.

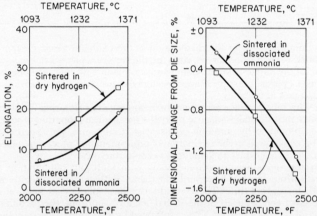

Fig. 21 Effect of sintering temperature on the elongation and dimensional change during sintering of sintered 316L stainless steel pressed to 6.85 g/cm³ and sintered for 30 min in various atmospheres.

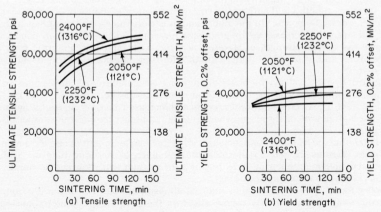

Fig. 22 Effect of sintering time on the tensile and yield strengths of sintered 316L stainless steel pressed to 6.85 g/cm³ and sintered at various temperatures in dissociated ammonia atmosphere.

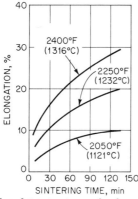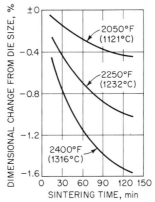

Fig. 23 Effect of sintering time on the elongation and dimensional change during sintering of sintered 316L stainless steel pressed to 6.85 g/cm³ and sintered at various temperatures in dissociated ammonia atmosphere.

elements normally obtained is beyond the limits of room temperature solubility and on cooling, carbides and nitrides both tend to precipitate in the form of fine particles. With extremely slow cooling, such as furnace cooling, the precipitation takes place preferentially at the grain boundaries as is shown in Fig. 24. As a result, there is a noticeable increase in strength and loss of ductility even though the amount of the precipitate is small. But, carbide precipitation is also quite detrimental to machinability. With normal rates of cooling (10 to 30 min) expected from typical P/M production, there is less precipitation at the grain boundaries so the strength is lower but the ductility is higher. This condition is shown in Fig. 25. Very rapid cooling, such as obtained by water quenching, suppresses the precipitation of carbides and nitrides as shown in Fig. 26. This will produce maximum ductility.

The cooling-rate effect in vacuum sintering is largely controlled by the atmosphere in which the parts are cooled. If a nitrogen backfill is used, the properties will be similar to those obtained by sintering in dissociated ammonia. If argon is used, the results will be like those obtained when sintering in hydrogen.

Control of Carbon Content The austenitic grades of stainless steel powders are made with less than 0.03% carbon. In order to retain this low carbon content after sintering

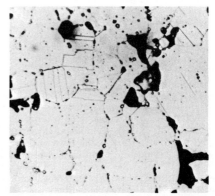

Fig. 24 Microstructure of 316L sintered in dissociated ammonia and cooled extremely slowly to encourage carbide precipitation at the grain boundaries.

Fig. 25 Microstructure of sintered 316L which results from normal rate of cooling in water-jacketed zone of the furnace.

(for maximum corrosion resistance, weldability, or machinability), carbon pickup must be avoided.

First, it is necessary that the solid lubricant used for pressing be completely removed by presintering, since the stearates and waxes are a source of carbon. Sometimes, small loads can be sintered directly by using excessive flow of atmosphere to flush away the volatilized lubricant. In general, two-step sintering is the safest practice.

Other common sources of carbon are soot, residual lubricant in the furnace, or traces of previous furnace atmosphere. It does not take very much carbonaceous material for dissociated ammonia or hydrogen to develop a carburizing potential. Care must be taken to assure that the furnace is clean and the atmosphere being used is pure.

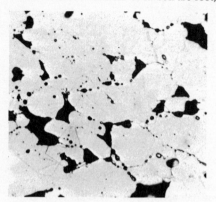

Fig. 26 Microstructure of 316L which results from a rapid water-quench after the sintering cycle.

Processing of Martensitic Grades The martensitic grades, 410 and 420, are used quite extensively in the P/M industry. Pressing and sintering variables have effects similar to those that were shown for the austenitic grades.

The higher carbon grades such as 440A, 440B, and 440C are rather difficult to process because of their tendency to form a continuous carbide network during sintering and are not used for P/M.

Powder is commercially available corresponding to the 410 stainless steel chemistry except that the carbon is usually less than 0.03% in the P/M grade. For many applications, sufficient hardening can be obtained, in spite of this low carbon, by sintering in dissociated ammonia where enough nitrogen is picked up to cause hardening in the normal sintering cycle. However, with the same sintering cycle in hydrogen, the parts will be soft. If furnace hardening is desired but only hydrogen or vacuum is available, graphite must be added to the powder mix prior to pressing. Generally about 0.10% graphite is required when hydrogen is used while 0.20% or more may be necessary when vacuum is used. If the parts are to be machined after sintering in dissociated ammonia, they can be softened by annealing at 1300 to 1400°F (704 to 760°C). Low-carbon martensitic grades sintered in hydrogen or vacuum are generally soft enough for easy machining.

After machining, the parts can be rehardened by heating in dissociated ammonia at about 1850°F (1010°C) and then quenching.

Table 9 shows the effect of sintering atmosphere, graphite additions, and heat-treat conditions on the strength and hardness of 410 stainless steel at a density of 6.7 g/cm³ sintered for 30 min at 2050°F (1120°C).

Stainless Steel Filters Filter materials with controlled permeability are a unique class of P/M stainless steel products. In this specialized area the control of the interconnected passages in the material is of primary concern.

Stainless steel P/M filters are made by forming closely sized powder into a shape with little or no pressure and then sintering to bond the particles together only where they touch so that an open-pore structure is maintained. Generally, lubricants need not be added to the powder as is done when making stainless steel structural parts.

Most of the grades of stainless steel powders are used for filters but the high-silicon grade of 316L (316B) is the most popular. This alloy possesses the particle shape for optimum permeability control. The primary control of permeability is through choice of powder particle size. This principle can be visualized by comparing the size of the openings which would be formed by a volume of grapefruits against a volume of marbles, each having a close-packed structure. The larger particles will produce a coarser filter, even though the total porosity will be the same.

In commercial practice, the properties of sintered filters depend not only on the particle size of the powder used but also on the method by which the loose powder is formed and on the sintering temperature.

For gravity-filled sheet material, the tensile strength will range from about 5000 psi

(34.5 MN/m²) for filters made from a −30 +60 mesh powder (particle sizes from 250 to 590 μm) to about 15,000 psi (103.4 MN/m²) when using −325 mesh (<44 μm) powder. Even though the product may be 40% porous, considerable ductility is obtained by sintering at temperatures above 2300°F (1260°C).

Secondary operations such as light repressing or light rolling of sintered filter sheet not

TABLE 9   Properties of Sintered 410 Stainless Steel

Processing treatment	% graphite added	Sintering atmosphere	Tempering temperature		Ultimate tensile strength		Apparent hardness, R_B
			°F	°C	psi	MN/m²	
As sintered and cooled in	None	NH₃			105,000	724	102
water-jacketed zone of	0.10	NH₃	400	204	99,000	682.6	103
furnace	None	H₂			57,000	393	68
	0.10	H₂	350	177	103,000	710.2	95
Reheated in NH₃ and	None	NH₃	400	204	91,000	627.4	106
oil-quenched from	0.10	NH₃	430	221	102,000	703.3	102
1750°F (950°C)	None	H₂			109,000	751.6	106
	0.10	H₂	430	221	104,000	717.1	105
Reheated in H₂ and	None	NH₃	400	204	106,000	730.9	104
oil-quenched from	0.10	NH₃	400	204	108,000	744.7	104
1750°F (950°C)	None	H₂	400	204	93,000	641.2	95
	0.10	H₂	430	221	116,000	799.8	101

only can control the permeability but also will affect the strength and ductility of the material.

P/M STAINLESS STEEL ENGINEERING

In order to have a successful stainless steel P/M application, there are many factors which must be considered. The application engineer must have the material which will meet the requirements. The designer must consider shape and tolerances. Powder having the desired alloy composition must be available. Dies and tooling must be designed and made. The part fabricator must be able to make the part to meet all specifications. Finally, economics must be evaluated. This section will deal with some principles to help in the decision-making process.

Application of P/M Stainless Steel Powder metallurgy parts and filters made from stainless steel are used in a wide variety of applications and in many different industries. The decision to use stainless P/M must be based on two considerations. First, the configuration of the part must be suitable to the P/M process and second, the selection of stainless steel as the material must offer some advantage over other P/M materials.

Why Use Powder Metallurgy? The choice of powder metallurgy as a manufacturing method may be made for the following reasons:
1. Precise tolerances available
2. Smooth surface finishes
3. Shape suited to P/M manufacturing
4. Controlled porosity for filtration or oil impregnation
5. Controlled mass-to-volume ratio
6. Elimination of subassemblies
7. Elimination of scrap and machining losses
8. Desirable production rates
9. Overall economy

Why Use Stainless Steel? Stainless steel may be selected as the material for a P/M part for the following reasons:
1. Corrosion resistance
2. Nonmagnetic material (300 series)
3. High strength and other mechanical properties
4. Unnecessary to plate for surface finish
5. Heat treatable (400 series)
6. Coefficient of expansion and physical properties

7. Machinability (303)
8. Color and appearance
9. Elevated temperature strength
10. Oxidation resistance

Typical Applications. Shown in Figs. 27 and 28 are a variety of stainless steel P/M parts that are in commercial production. In each example, stainless steel powder metallurgy was chosen over competing metalworking methods because it offered some advantage.

Grade Selection   Even though many stainless alloys are made as powder, certain grades have been designed specifically for P/M use. The grades shown in Table 10 are the most popular, are readily available, and can be used for the bulk of P/M stainless steel applications.

Fig. 27   Some typical P/M stainless steel parts. Starting at left and going clockwise: 1, toothed cam cleat of 304L for a marine application; 2, pump bushing with splined ID of 410L; 3, valve bushing with hex ID of IPM's SS-100; 4, hex nut for kitchen appliance of 303L; 5, acme threaded plug housing of 303L; 6, thrust hub of 316L for a marine application. (*IPM Corp., Div. of Allegheny Ludlum Industries.*)

Figure 29 shows a P/M application in the automotive industry. The mirror mount is bonded to the automobile windshield and the rearview mirror in turn is mounted on the P/M part. The Ford part is made of 316L as the P/M material and has excellent corrosion resistance. The General Motors and Chrysler parts are 434L which has a coefficient of thermal expansion which matches that of the glass, and its corrosion resistance is adequate for the application.

Design of Stainless Steel P/M Parts   The successful application of a stainless steel P/M part starts on the drawing board. The technical principles which pertain to the manufacture of sintered stainless steel parts are different from other metal-forming processes, such as forging, casting or machining. The part designer must be aware of the P/M process to take advantage of its strengths while avoiding its weaknesses.

The production of stainless steel P/M parts follows basic P/M principles but requires slightly more care and knowledge than the more standard bronze or iron P/M technology. Most stainless steel structural parts are made by the press and sinter process; therefore, any part suitable to be manufactured by the P/M process can be made in stainless steel.

Design Rules   When considering the use of a stainless steel P/M part, it is usually best to design originally for P/M rather than to convert to P/M from some other manufacturing process. Powder metallurgy is ideally suited to the production of cylindrical, rectangular, or irregular shapes that do not have large variations in cross section.

Special rules must be followed in the design of parts in order to realize the full advantages of powder metallurgy. These are necessary because of the characteristics and movement of the powder under pressure and operation of a tool set. Adherence to these few fundamental rules will generally result in preferred designs, simplified tooling and production, better economics, and longer part life.

Rule 1—The Shape of the Part Must Permit Ejection from the Die. Although most stainless steel P/M parts can be molded directly into accurate finished shapes, there are some with design requirements that can only be achieved by subsequent machining; for example, undercuts, holes at right angles to the direction of pressing, reverse tapers, reentrant angles, threads, and diamond knurls (as illustrated in Figs. 30 to 35). Corner reliefs can be molded in the direction of pressing as seen in Fig 33. Also, straight serrations (Fig. 35) can be molded. In most instances, parts requiring design features that cannot be molded can be produced economically by first making semifinished shapes by the P/M process, and then machining the desired features.

Rule 2—The Shape of the Part Should Be Such that the Powder Is Not Required to Flow into Thin Walls, Narrow Splines, or Sharp Corners. While parts having thin walls, narrow splines, or sharp corners can be produced by powder metallurgy, adherence to this rule will result in better parts, usually at lower cost. Only minor changes in the design of any part are generally necessary to satisfy these requirements.

Fig. 28 Sintered stainless steel components: 1, 316L knife card; 2, 316L link; 3, quick disconnect handle; 4, 316L ramp; 5, 304L ring tube; 6, 316L clamp; 7, 316L clamp; 8, 410 disc; 9, flow divider from 410; 10, 316L catch; 11, 316L lever; 12, 410 gear; 13, 410 disc; 14, 316L catch; 15, bushing from 410; 16, 316L handle; 17, link latch from 303L. *(Remington Arms Co., Inc. P/M Products Division.)*

TABLE 10   Characteristics of P/M Stainless Steel Grades

316L	Best general-purpose austenitic grade for P/M parts. Combines good corrosion resistance with P/M workability. Has good machinability. Nonmagnetic.
304L	Basic 18-8 grade. Most economical of the austenitic grades. Corrosion resistance and machinability not as good as 316L. Used where ratio of material costs to processing costs is high.
303L	Free-machining austenitic grade. Used for parts requiring extensive secondary machining operations. Corrosion resistance not as good as 304L or 316L.
316B	High silicon version of 316, also designated as 316L-Si. Designed specifically for filter manufacture. Gives superior permeability control and resistance to sulfuric acid. Not generally used for P/M structural parts.
410L	Basic martensitic grade. Heat treatable. Carbon can be added for increased hardness and wear resistance. Fair corrosion resistance.
434L	Basic ferritic grade. Better corrosion resistance than 410L. Color compatible with chrome plate. Has low coefficient of expansion. Economical alloy.

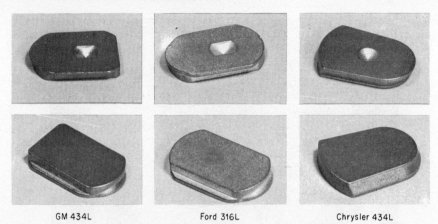

GM 434L   Ford 316L   Chrysler 434L

Fig. 29 Automotive mirror mounts of P/M stainless steel. These are attached to inside of windshield and support rear view mirror. *(Sintered Specialties Division, Panoramic Corp.)*

Original   Preferred

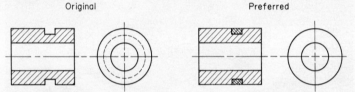

Fig. 30   Undercuts cannot be molded, they must be machined.

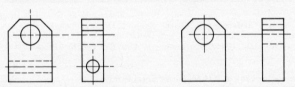

Fig. 31   Holes at right angles to pressing direction must be machined.

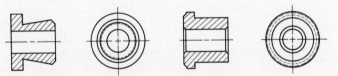

Fig. 32   Reverse taper cannot be molded, must be machined.

Must be machined   Can be molded

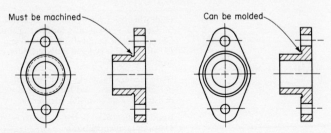

Fig. 33   Corner relief should be specified in molding direction to save secondary machining.

Original   Preferred

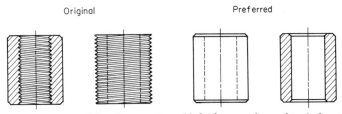

Fig. 34   Internal and external threads cannot be molded. They must be machined after sintering.

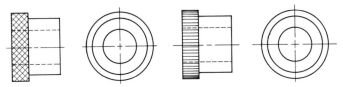

Fig. 35   A diamond knurl cannot be molded but straight serrations can.

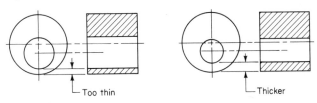

Too thin   Thicker

Fig. 36   Thin sidewalls less than 0.03 in. (0.8 mm) should be avoided.

In general, sidewalls bordering a depression or hole in a P/M part should be thicker than 0.030 in. (0.76 mm) as seen in Fig. 36. Also, abrupt changes in wall thickness should be avoided whenever possible, since nonuniform dimensional changes in thin- and thick-wall sections can result in distortion during sintering. Feather edges (Fig. 37) should be avoided. Rounded corners (Figs. 38 through 40) permit better, more uniform powder flow into the die, and result in higher strength parts than can be obtained with sharp corners.

Rule 3—The Shape of the Part Should Permit the Construction of Strong Tooling. Considerable economy in both tooling and production, as well as improved parts, can often be effected by simplifying shapes. For example, the design should allow a reasonable clearance between the top and bottom punches during the pressing operation. Also, it should be possible to make both the dies and punches without sharp edges. Well-rounded grooves (Fig. 41) are preferable to narrow, deep splines.

Spherical bearings, such as the one seen in Fig. 42, must have flats. Flats (Fig. 43) eliminate the need for sharp edges on the tools and strengthen the dies. Also, 30° (0.51-rad) chamfers (Fig. 44) permit the use of stronger tools, and tapered counterbores (Fig. 45) assist in tool removal. Round instead of odd-shaped holes (Fig. 46) simplify tools and

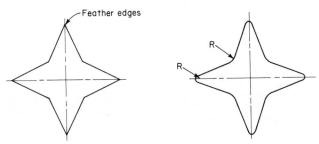

Feather edges

R

R

Fig. 37   Feather edges on parts should be avoided and replaced with radii.

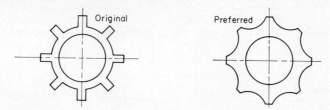

Fig. 38 Rounded internal corners simplify tools and give higher strength parts.

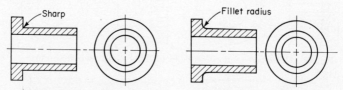

Fig. 39 Fillet radius at base of flange eliminates stress concentration.

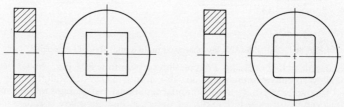

Fig. 40 Rounded corners permit more uniform powder flow in the die.

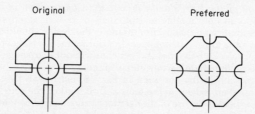

Fig. 41 Narrow, deep splines in the part should be avoided.

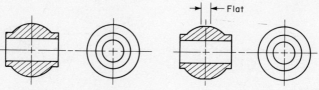

Fig. 42 A completely spherical bearing cannot be molded. A short flat area is necessary.

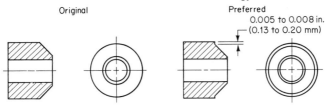

Fig. 43   Flats of 0.005 to 0.008 in. (0.13 to 0.20 mm) eliminate need for sharp feather edges on tools.

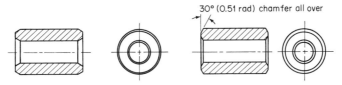

Fig. 44   A 30° chamfer permits the use of stronger tools.

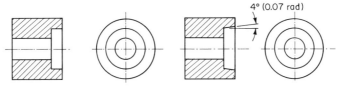

Fig. 45   Slight taper on the counterbore will assist in tool withdrawal.

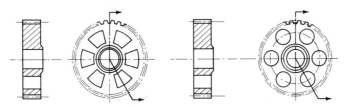

Fig. 46   Round lightening holes will simplify tools and reduce costs.

reduce costs, but very small holes should be avoided if possible to minimize breakage of core pins. A minimum flange overhang of 1/16 in. (1.6 mm) (Fig. 47) is desirable to facilitate production.

Rule 4—The Shape of the Part Should Make Allowance for the Length to which Thin-walled Parts Can Be Compacted. As shown in Fig. 48, the maximum length for thin-wall, hollow cylindrical parts is about 2½ times the diameter of the parts. This ratio can be increased to 4 or more times the diameter for parts having thicker walls.

Rule 5—The Part Should Be Designed with as Few Levels (Diameters) and Axial Variations as Possible. Uniform density and high strength in a multilevel part can best be maintained when the number of levels does not exceed the number of pressing actions

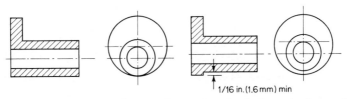

Fig. 47   A 1/16 in (1.6 mm) minimum flange overhang is desired to facilitate manufacture of part.

Original   Preferred

0.032in. min (0.8 mm)

Fig. 48 Length of part should not be greater than two and one-half times the diameter with minimum wall thickness of 0.032 in (0.8 mm).

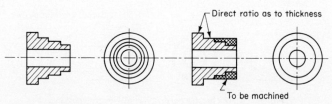

Direct ratio as to thickness

To be machined

Fig. 49 Lower strengths will result if all stepped diameters are molded. Some should be machined.

available in the compacting press. When an excessive number of levels are required (Fig. 49), it may be more practical for the parts manufacturer to compact the part with as many levels as it is practical to obtain, maintaining as uniform a density as possible, and then add the remaining levels by machining. Slots having a depth greater than one-quarter of the axial length of the part (Fig. 50) require multiple punch action and result in higher production costs.

Rule 6—Take Advantage of the Fact that Certain Forms Can Be Produced by Powder Metallurgy which are Impossible, Impractical, or Uneconomical to Obtain by Any Other Method. For example, true involute gear forms (Fig. 51) can readily be made by powder metallurgy, but are difficult to make by other methods because of the undercuts at the bases of the teeth. Also, the tooth form can be modified, when required, to obtain specific shapes, added strength, or other features. Increased fillet radii at the tooth roots facilitate manufacturing and assure maximum strength. Since pressure is applied axially during compacting, radial contours that do not have axial length variations can be produced most readily by powder metallurgy.

Separate keys and keyways for gears, pulleys, bushings, etc., can be eliminated since the key form can be made integral with the part (Fig. 52).

Figure 53 shows two P/M components in a rotary switch. The design was made to take advantage of the ability of powder metallurgy to produce three-dimensional complexity. The stop plate replaced two stainless steel stampings while the P/M stainless steel cover had been a molded wood-flour-filled phenolic.

Press and Sinter Process   The standard manufacturing technique for the manufacture of stainless steel P/M parts involves mixing the prealloyed powder with a lubricant, pressing to the desired configuration, presintering to remove the lubricant, high-temperature sintering, and final finishing.

While these operations are also used for iron or bronze parts, certain points should be noted as pertaining only to stainless steels.

1. Since stainless powders are prealloyed, mixing times need only be long enough to admix the lubricant.

L

Fig. 50 Slots should not exceed one-quarter of the axial length for best economy.

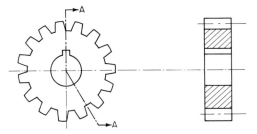

Fig. 51   True involute gears can be made by the P/M process.

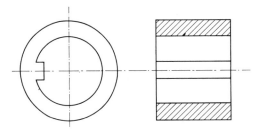

Fig. 52   Keyed bushing can be readily molded, eliminating the need for separate keyways and key.

2. Compacting of stainless steel powders requires slightly higher pressures with 30 to 60 tons/in.² (414 to 827 MN/m²) being common.

3. Pressing rates may be faster, on the order of 500 to 2000 parts per hour.

4. Green strength may be somewhat lower, so extremely fragile parts should be avoided.

5. Cleanliness is extremely important to prevent contamination from iron powders.

6. Tools should be made of carbide to combat wear.

7. The higher apparent density of stainless steel powder permits short, stubby, and stronger tools.

8. Sintering cycles require higher temperatures and longer times, with 45 min to 1 h at 2100 to 2400°F (1149 to 1316°C) being common commercial practice.

9. Dew-point control and purity of sintering atmosphere are most critical.

Fig. 53   The stop plate and cover for this rotary electric switch are fabricated from 316L stainless steel powder. *(Sintered Specialties Division, Panoramic Corp.)*

10. Dimensional change during sintering (shrinkage) is greater than for iron or bronze, so extra tight tolerances are more difficult to achieve.

11. Repressing tools should also be made of carbide, preferable a grade containing TiC or TaC to combat wear and galling.

Shown in Fig. 54 are three parts used in home appliances which are made by stainless steel powder metallurgy. These are excellent examples of the design principles of this technique.

Material Standards To aid the engineer and the designer in the choice of stainless steel material, various industry standards are available. Both the American Society for

Fig. 54 Stainless steel P/M parts used in home appliances. *Left,* 304L insert molded into a rubber impeller for an automatic washer. *Center,* heat-treated 410 knife blades for a food disposal unit. *Right,* 304L sealing ring which is cast-in-place in a die-cast mounting stem for an automatic washing machine. *(Maytag Co.)*

Testing and Materials and The Metal Powder Industries Federation have developed material standards which are commonly used to specify P/M stainless steels. These documents give engineering property information and physical properties that can be used for design purposes.

The MPIF Standards SS-303-P & R, SS-316-P & R and SS-410 N & P describe these stainless steel alloys and the properties expected for two density ranges. These documents are found in MPIF Standard 35 which covers all P/M materials.

The ASTM standard specification B 525-70 covers the austenitic stainless steel grades 304 and 316 for structural parts.

Stainless Steel Filters Sintered filters and porous media are special products produced from stainless steel metal powders. They have the advantages of good mechanical strength, high thermal conductivity, and corrosion resistance as compared to other metallic or nonmetallic products. Stainless steel powder filters are widely used for separating solids from liquids or gas, liquids from gases, liquids from liquids, for acoustical damping, flow control, restrictors, and as breathers.

Most sintered filters are made from AISI 316L or a high-silicon 316L alloy (316B) although 304L and other alloys are also used. Irregularly shaped particles offer the greatest manufacturing flexibility. The following production methods are used for the manufacture of these products.

Loose Powder Sintering. The majority of high-quality filters made by this process use irregularly shaped particles having a relatively narrow split sieve fraction. The particle size is selected to give the desired permeability to the component. Shaped filters or large sheets are produced by filling ceramic molds and then vibrating to pack the powder evenly. The powder and mold together are then placed in atmosphere furnaces for sintering. The sintering temperature is close to the melting point of the alloy in order to obtain strong particle-to-particle bonding. Sheets made in this way may be repressed or rolled after sintering to improve mechanical properties, surface finish and to modify permeability. Sheets can also be cut and formed into tubes or disks and arc welded onto other filter components.

Some filters are made in this manner using closely sized spherical stainless steel powders. These filters have very good filtration characteristics but it is difficult to form the sheets because of lower mechanical properties and limited ductility.

Press and Sinter Process. The procedures here are similar to those used for normal P/M parts except that densities are much lower. Irregularly shaped particles must be used because they have the green strength necessary to hold the filter together. This technique generally produces filters more closely packed and with lower permeability ratings. Sometimes volatile pore-forming agents are added to the powder to obtain higher porosity, but these must be removed prior to sintering and require an additional processing step. Furnace capacity is increased because the mold is not used in the furnace but the low-density green compacts must be handled very carefully due to their friable nature. Secondary pressing operations may be used to change the mechanical and physical characteristics of the sintered filter. One big advantage of press and sinter filters is that the porosity may be changed in certain sections by densifying selected areas. This will result in an edge- or rib-strengthening effect or a variable permeability filter.

A modification of the press and sinter process, continuous powder rolling, is used to make the strip or sheet of filter material at a high production rate.

Slip Casting and Extrusion Processes. Some filters are made by casting a slip of metal powder and a liquid in plaster molds, allowing the cast to dry, breaking away the mold, and sintering the shape. The extrusion process can also be used to make continuous shapes by extruding a paste or slurry of powder, driving off the binder and sintering the extruded billet.

Filtration Principles Filtration is controlled by the size of the pores and the thickness of the filter. The pore structure is three dimensional and not of a constant size. A certain portion of impurities smaller than the pore diameter are removed by the tortuous paths of the porosity. The thicker the filter, the smaller will be the minimum size removed. All larger impurities are blocked. Table 11 and Fig. 55 show some permeability data for gases and liquids for some typical grades of stainless steel filters made from split fractions of stainless steel powders.

Stainless Steel Filter Applications. Stainless steel powder filters are used for a wide variety of applications, including liquid extraction from a gas, particle extraction from a gas or liquid, breathers, fluidized-bed applications, flow control, and pressure control.

They have the desirable properties of being able to be used over a wide temperature range, are corrosion-resistant, have high strength, are formable and weldable, and can be cleaned by reverse flushing.

Stainless steel P/M filters are precision components and are closely checked for permeability and performance. Most filters are sold as complete assemblies containing all the mounting hardware needed for easy installation into the system.

Figure 56 shows typical filters and porous media made from stainless steel powders.

Finishing Operations If the design requires, P/M stainless steel can be drilled, tapped, or otherwise machined to produce a configuration not obtained during pressing. All machining operations should be done with sharp-pointed carbide tools using fine feeds and high speeds. The use of a light spray-mist lubricant is recommended.

TABLE 11   Efficiency of Filtration for Sintered Stainless Steel Filters

| Grade | Mean pore size, μm | Removal ratings, μm | | | |
| | | When filtering liquids | | When filtering gases | |
		Nominal (98%)	Absolute (100%)	Nominal (98%)	Absolute (100%)
C	165	55	160	45	110
D	65	22	55	8	20
E	35	12	35	4	11
F	20	7	25	1.3	3
G	10	3	15	0.7	1.8
H	5	2	12	0.4	1.0

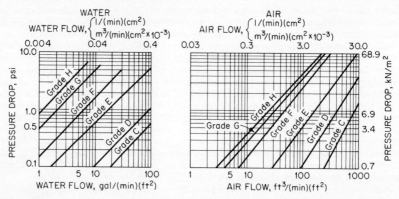

Fig. 55   Flow vs. pressure drop through 1/8 in. (3.2 mm) sintered stainless steel filters. *(Pall-Micro-Trinity Corp.)*

While some parts are used as-sintered, most stainless steel P/M parts are cleaned and finished by a wet tumbling operation in vibratory or barrel finishers to burnish the surface and remove any burrs or sharp corners. A low-temperature bake to remove any entrapped water completes the operation.

Figure 57 shows a number of watertight watch cases that were made from 316L powder. The blind holes for the watchband pins and the through hole for the winding stem were drilled as secondaries. The cavity for the watch works was finish-turned and then threaded to accept the back cover. The sides have been polished to a mirror finish while the face area has been belt sanded. This is a unique example of P/M stainless steel engineering.

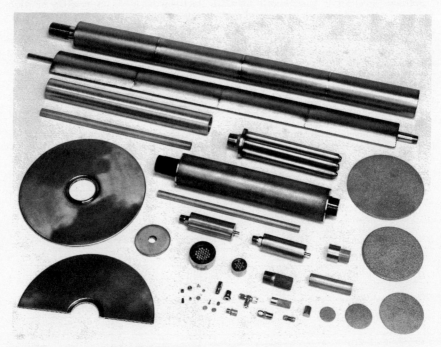

Fig. 56   Assortment of filter cartridge assemblies, porous disks, and seamless tubing of P/M stainless steel filter material. *(Mott Metallurgical Corp.)*

Corrosion Resistance   One of the primary reasons for selecting stainless steel as an engineering material is its corrosion resistance. This is also true for P/M stainless steel. However, the corrosion resistance of P/M grades is not as well documented in the literature as is that for wrought materials. More reliance must therefore be placed on actual environmental testing.

The corrosion resistance of sintered stainless steel depends not only on the environment to which it is exposed but also on the way the material has been processed and on the porosity inherent in the material. It is therefore difficult to assess corrosion resistance except by actual field testing. To a certain degree there is some correlation between the corrosion resistance of wrought material and its P/M counterpart, but the sintered product may be somewhat more prone to corrosion because of the porosity.

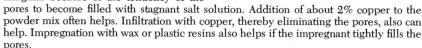
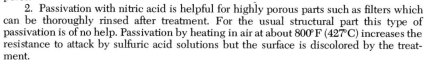

Fig. 57   Stainless steel men's and women's watch cases produced from 316L powder. *(Schild S.A.-Sintec.)*

Several generalities can be stated pertaining to the performance of P/M stainless steel which will be helpful to both the designer and the part producer.

1. Resistance to saline solutions is marginal because of the tendency of the pores to become filled with stagnant salt solution. Addition of about 2% copper to the powder mix often helps. Infiltration with copper, thereby eliminating the pores, also can help. Impregnation with wax or plastic resins also helps if the impregnant tightly fills the pores.

2. Passivation with nitric acid is helpful for highly porous parts such as filters which can be thoroughly rinsed after treatment. For the usual structural part this type of passivation is of no help. Passivation by heating in air at about 800°F (427°C) increases the resistance to attack by sulfuric acid solutions but the surface is discolored by the treatment.

3. High-temperature sintering usually improves the corrosion resistance.

4. For some environments sintering in vacuum gives best results but for others hydrogen or dissociated ammonia is best. There does not seem to be an established pattern.

5. The carbon content must be held as low as possible.

6. The lower the porosity, the better the corrosion resistance.

7. Avoid contamination with iron and other powders. Processing stainless steel with the same equipment used to process other powders usually results in contamination and loss of corrosion resistance.

Test data are constantly being generated and often the parts fabricator can advise on the suitability of P/M stainless to particular corrosive environments.

Stainless Steel P/M Suppliers   For information on fabricators of stainless steel P/M structural parts and filters and powder suppliers, contact the Metal Powder Industries Federation, P.O. Box 2054, Princeton, N.J. 08540.

REFERENCES

1. "Metals Handbook," vol. 4, American Society for Metals, Metals Park, Ohio, 1967.
2. "A.S.T.M. Standards," Part 9, ASTM, Philadelphia, Pa., July 1975.
3. Bhattachary, S., and N. M. Parikh: Optimization of Properties of Powdered Stainless Steel Parts by Statistical Design, *Powder Metall.*, vol. 14, no. 28, 1971.
4. Bishop, E., and G. Collins: Stainless Steel Filters for Nuclear Applications, *Powder Metall.*, vol. 10, no. 20, pp. 192–202, Autumn 1967.
5. Burke, J. J., and V. Weiss: "Powder Metallurgy for High-Performance Applications," Syracuse University Press, Syracuse, N.Y., 1972.
6. Clark, Frances: "Advanced Techniques in Powder Metallurgy," Rowman and Littlefield, New York, 1963.
7. Cliffel, E. M., Jr., W. E. Smith, and A. D. Schwope: Theory and Applications of Controlled Permeability, in H. H. Hausner (ed.), "Modern Developments in Powder Metallurgy," vol. 3, Plenum, New York, 1966.

8. Dixon, R. H. T., and A. Clayton: "Powder Metallurgy for Engineers," Machinery Publishing, London, 1971.
9. Product brochures, Stainless Steel Powder Data Sheets, Glidden Metals, Cleveland, Ohio.
10. Gummeson, P. N.: High Pressure Water Atomization, in John J. Burke and Volker Weiss (eds.), "Powder Metallurgy for High Performance Applications," Syracuse University Press, Syracuse, N.Y., 1972.
11. Hausner, H. H.: "New Types of Metal Powders," Gordon and Breach, New York, 1964.
12. Hirschhorn, Joel S.: "Introduction to Powder Metallurgy," P.M.I.A., Princeton, N.J., 1969.
13. "Stainless Steel Powders Seminar," Product brochures, Hoeganaes Corporation, Riverton, N.J., 1965.
14. Jones, W. D.: "Fundamental Principles of Powder Metallurgy," William Clowes and Sons, London, 1960.
15. Product brochures, Metallurgical International, Inc., New Shrewsbury, N.J.
16. "M.P.I.F. Standards," Metal Powder Industries Federation, Princeton, N.J.
17. "Powder Metallurgy Design Handbook," Metal Powder Industries Federation, Princeton, N.J., 1974.
18. Otto, G.: Vacuum Sintering of Types 410 and 420 Martensitic Stainless Steel, *Proc. Int. Powder Metall. Conf.*, Toronto, 1973.
19. Sands, R. L., G. F. Bidmead, and D. A. Oliver: The Corrosion Resistance of Sintered Austenitic Stainless Steel, in H. H. Hausner (ed.), "Modern Developments in Powder Metallurgy," vol. 2, Plenum, New York, 1966.
20. Sugarman, B., and G. Collins: Porous Stainless Steel Filters; Their Development and Use, in "Symposium on Powder Metallurgy," pp. 188–191, *Special Rep. 58*, The Iron and Steel Institute, London, 1954.
21. Sugarman, B.: Permeability and Mechanical Strength of Porous Stainless Steel Plate, in "Symposium on Powder Metallurgy," pp. 184–188, *Special Rep. 58*, The Iron and Steel Institute, London, 1954.

Chapter 30

Forming Tubular Parts

JAMES L. SCHANCK
Quality Assurance Coordinator, Tubular Products
Division, The Babcock & Wilcox Company, Beaver Falls, Pa.

Many parts and products are made from stainless steel tubing. Some of these are used as straight mill lengths. Others have been bent, flared, flanged, spun, upset, machined, or merely cut to length and used without a contour change. Before making such parts, someone had to ask:

   1. What do we want to do?
   2. How do we want to do it?
   3. What material should be used?
   4. Can the part be made from the chosen steel by the proposed method?

5. Can the chosen steel be bought as tubing and how readily?

These questions bear strongly on each other. But the most important is the last: Is the product available?

Many types of stainless steel are mentioned elsewhere in this handbook. Are they readily available as tubing?

AVAILABILITY OF STAINLESS STEEL TUBING

Tubemaking Method Affects Availability Most of the standard austenitic, martensitic, and ferritic stainless steels can be made into tubing. One can also assume that at least an effort has been made to make tubing of the nonstandard analyses. How successfully that has been done is another question.

Some stainless steels can be made as either seamless or welded tubing; others can be made only as seamless tubing in certain limited size ranges. Some nonstandard grades can be made (practically) by only one process or the other.

The common tubemaking methods include rotary piercing bars, extruding billets, and welding cold-rolled strip.

Rotary Piercing. If a stainless steel has good hot workability, it can probably be made into tubing by rotary piercing. In this method a bar is rotated and squeezed between revolving cones or rolls to generate multiaxial stresses at the bar's center. These stresses weaken the center of the hot bar so that it can be forced (while rotating) over a rigidly held piercer point. Schematics of rotary piercing are seen in Fig. 1. The center of the bar is pushed out by the point and becomes the inner surface of a rough tube hollow. Subsequent operations are performed to size, smooth, and elongate the hollow into a finished tube. Only the final product would be most suitable for forming.

The limitations of the piercing process are (1) the size range of any one mill and (2) the hot workability of the steel being pierced. The first point is obvious. Each mill has its largest and smallest diameter, wall thickness, and length capability. A desired tube size which lies outside a mill's range will not be available. Later cold-finishing steps may expand the effective size range somewhat.

The second factor, hot workability, is not as obvious. The steel, when heated to some optimum forging temperature, must hold together during rotary piercing. Many two-phase alloys will not. Some of the highly alloyed "super" stainless grades, on the other hand, hold together so well that they will stall a mill or just spin and not yield at the center. Sometimes the hot-working range is very narrow and may be hard to hit, given the normal variance in mill furnaces, transfer times, etc. Piercing mill design may also affect the types of steel which can be pierced. Some piercers seem to be gentler than others. These mills might, therefore, have a wider product capability.

Extrusion. Extrusion, which is discussed in Chapter 23, is more (but not wholly) forgiving of steel which would tear up during rotary piercing. The extrusion process can, for instance, accept two-phase alloys more readily than piercing. But there are also alloys that will stall a press which does not have enough power. And there are steels which cannot be extruded at an economical rate (if they can be made into tubing at all).

There also are some stainless grades, both new and old, where the quantity of business projected does not justify even a production trial, regardless of the tubemaking method. In that case, a mill would be reluctant to quote.

Welding Strip. The third method is welding cold-rolled stainless strip. Most of the common austenitic grades, some of the ferritic and martensitic grades, plus a few of the nonstandard grades can be made as welded tubing.

The raw material for stainless steel welded tubing is coils of cut-to-width strip. These coils are rolled to carefully controlled thicknesses. The strip is passed through a series of in-line rolls which curve it into a tubular shape. When the edges are almost touching, the strip travels under or over a head which heats it to above the melting point. Simultaneously, the edges are forced together, fusing them into a good metallurgical bond. A protective atmosphere prevents oxidation at the heated area. The heat may be generated by a tungsten or plasma arc; no filler metal is added.

The availability of welded tubing is governed by size and capability of equipment, quantity of tubing desired, strip availability, and the steel analysis.

To summarize, there are a number of ways in which tubing can be produced. Any one of them may or may not lend itself to making a particular size and grade of stainless tubing.

One producing mill may have different capabilities than another. Economics and quality will vary from mill to mill. Plans or cost estimates must not be based on what might be available. Instead, inquiries to the mills should be made, laying out the tentatively planned grades and probable ways of making the parts. In many cases, the mills can advise right away on availability and economics. A mill may even be able to suggest cheaper and better ways of doing the job.

Steel Type Affects Availability *Austenitic Grades.* Analysis is the strongest determinant of availability. The standard austenitic (300 series) grades are widely available as

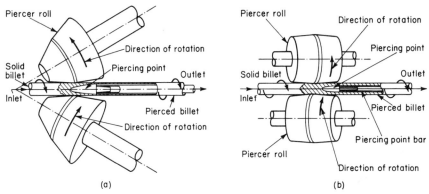

Fig. 1 Schematics of rotary piercing methods: (a) piercing operation in the cone-type mill; (b) Mannesmann piercer with barrel-shaped rolls. *(Babcock & Wilcox.)*

stainless tubing. Naturally, each mill will have its own size limits, methods of manufacture, economic factors, and technical capabilities. Austenitic tubing can be made by rotary piercing, extrusion, or welding. Welded austenitic stainless steel tubing is made by many mills. This ready availability applies to the common Cr-Ni grades, as well as to the stabilized grades, Types 321, 347, and 348.

Some of the free-machining grades are an exception. The ASTM mechanical tube specifications show only those grades which contain selenium. ASTM notes, however, that other grades are available. For instance, some mills can produce Type 303 (with sulfur) in certain sizes, but other mills quote only Type 303Se. Here, hot workability is the main factor. The elements which promote machinability decrease weldability. Therefore, free-machining stainless steel welded tubing is not generally made.

Martensitic Grades. The common martensitic stainless steel grades can be made as seamless tubing over a broad size range. The willingness of a given mill to tackle any one analysis, size, and/or quantity varies widely. What may be technically and economically alluring for one mill might not be for another. Since these grades will air-harden, they are not made as welded tubing. Some limited success has been achieved with Type 410 but, overall, even it is not available as welded tubing.

The higher-carbon–higher-chromium grades of martensitic stainless steel are inherently troublesome. Some are hard to heat-treat and are almost impossible to cold-work. An additional limit to availability is the small number of seamless tube producers. There are many sources of welded tubing, but they do not make the highly hardenable stainless grades.

Ferritic Grades. The nonhardenable, standard ferritic stainless steels, from Type 405 (13% chromium) up to Type 446 (27% chromium), are available as seamless tubing. While these steels are not wholly troublefree, they can be both hot- and cold-worked. This increases the range of sizes available.

Welding of the ferritic stainless steels is limited to only a few producers. The higher the chromium content, the greater the tendency to coarsen the grains in and near the weld. Also, the ferritics are known to be notch-sensitive. They do not act well after welding during operations such as bead swaging and drawing. Some Type 429/430 welded tubing is available from a limited number of producers, but these mills have learned the hard way. They still judge each requirement on its own merits.

As previously mentioned, inquiries to the mills can save a lot of problems if ferritic stainless steel tubing is being considered.

Nonstandard Grades. Nonstandard stainless steel grades must at least be mentioned. Among these are (1) precipitation-hardenable grades, (2) high (8 to 15%) manganese stainless steel, (3) the so-called "super" martensitic stainless steels, and (4) some of the ferritic grades which have been modified for increased corrosion resistance, impact strength, and greater weldability.

It is difficult, even for a person within the tube industry, to comment about the availability of these grades. Many of them have enjoyed little demand, even though they were highly touted outside the tube industry. Some of these steels have questionable hot workability; thus, they may not lend themselves to rotary piercing. Some of them are hard to extrude, also. Welded tubing may be available, but how readily must be determined by inquiring among the suppliers.

Many of the nonstandard grades have not seen enough demand to justify even mill development work. Some are still covered by letters patent; thus, they are not freely available to tube producers. Mills are reluctant to take out a license to produce a grade if there is no foreseeable demand for it.

These comments are vague by necessity. When one of the nonstandard stainless steels, in tubular form, is being considered, the mills should be canvassed for their thoughts. One tube mill or another might have the key to producing such grades.

Mechanical Properties and Availability   The mills often make stainless steel tubing with controlled mechanical properties. This applies to martensitic, austenitic, and some nonstandard grades, but not to the ferritics.

Ferritic Grades—Always Annealed. The ferritic stainlesses, such as Types 405 through 446, are always supplied in the annealed condition. Cold-working to raise their strength and hardness is bad practice; it aggravates their known notch sensitivity. Cold-work does not strengthen the ferritic stainless steels significantly.

Martensitic Grades—Controlled By Heat Treatment. The martensitic grades can be heat-treated (normalized, normalized and tempered, quenched and tempered) to achieve useful strength levels (see Chapter 6). As far as the mills are concerned, heat treatment for properties is applied only to the lower-carbon–lower-chromium grades. The more highly alloyed steels (such as Types 414, 431, 440A, B, and C) are used more in machining operations than for forming; therefore, they must be suitably softened, i.e., annealed. Thus we see Type 410 being heat-treated for properties at the mill (if required), but not other martensitic grades. Furthermore, fabrication (other than machining) by the end user is largely impractical if the desired properties have already been developed. If a user is going to machine and/or form a part, and then heat-treat it, the mill normally supplies annealed tubing.

Nonstandard Grades—Check The Mill. The nonstandard stainless steel grades may or may not be heat-treated or cold-worked at the mill, depending on their end use. If a precipitation-hardenable steel is to be fabricated, it would normally be supplied in the solution-annealed condition. An exception might be a case where only machining is to be done. Otherwise, the fabricator would perform the final heat treatment after machining and/or fabricating. Conversely, there are nonstandard stainless steels which depend on cold work, such as drawing or tube reducing, to achieve final properties. Usually, only a tube mill is equipped to perform such operations. Little fabrication, other than machining, would be practical with such tubes. Where nonstandard analyses are involved, there should be close consultation between the mill, the fabricator and, sometimes, the end user. Such communication will help avoid embarrassing, costly problems.

Austenitic Grades—Cold Work for Strength. Austenitic stainless steel tubing can also be supplied with controlled properties. There are a number of applications which require the corrosion resistance, magnetic properties, and/or impact strength of austenitic stainless steel. But an annealed austenitic stainless steel has relatively low strength. Unlike the martensitic grades, which can be heat-treated, these steels can be hardened only by cold work. They can be supplied in a wide range of cold-worked tempers. Such a product is known as hard-drawn stainless tubing.

Mills cold-work an austenitic stainless steel tube either by cold-drawing or by tube reducing. Drawing can be done in two ways: through a die and over a mandrel (mandrel drawing) or through a die without internal support (sinking). A greater degree of cold-working is achieved by mandrel drawing than by sinking (see Fig. 2).

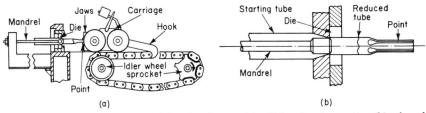

Fig. 2 Schematic diagram of a typical draw bench setup: (a) cold draw bench operation; (b) enlarged section through die and mandrel. *(Babcock & Wilcox.)*

Tube reducing, on the other hand, can impart large amounts of cold work. Tube reducing (sometimes called roto-rocking because of the motion of the dies used) is employed where large reductions of area and wall thickness are needed (see Fig. 3).

The mechanical property levels (tempers) normally associated with hard-drawn austenitic stainless steel are shown in Table 1.

Not all grades and sizes can be hard-drawn equally well. As the alloy content increases, the steel becomes less responsive to cold work. For instance, Types 201, 202, 301, 302, and 304 can be hard-drawn to higher properties than analyses such as Types 305, 316, 317, and 310. Because of their higher nickel contents, the latter grades are more stable and, therefore, do not work harden as much for a given reduction of cross section.

Size affects hard-drawn tube availability even more than analysis, especially if a given size is not suited for the cold-working machinery. Some time ago, one major tube mill studied how size influences the tempers which can be produced. The results of this work are shown in Fig. 4. It is obvious that some sizes are impractical to make; for instance, when the wall thickness approaches one-half the outer diameter. Similarly, when the wall is only a small percent of the diameter, a producer is almost dealing with an eggshell. It is hard to produce such a tube and hold close roundness tolerances. Even worse is the possibility that such a thin-walled tube may pull apart during drawing. Furthermore, machinery limitations and lubricant breakdown must not be overlooked when producing hard-drawn tubing.

The foregoing discussion has been aimed primarily at the standard austenitic grades. There are also some nonstandard, high-manganese austenitic stainless steels that work harden very rapidly. Such steels widen the range of sizes where higher properties can be secured. However, it may be more difficult to secure the lower tempers (⅛ hard) with some of these grades because they work harden so quickly.

Where hard-drawn austenitic stainless steel is being considered, the mills should definitely be consulted. Even experienced users need guidance before buying a new size or grade of hard-drawn stainless tubing.

Ask the Mills About Availability. A knowledge of raw material availability is needed by those who purchase tubes for forming. Since the subject can be complex, it is advisable to discuss a proposed application with the tube producers. They can advise what is and is

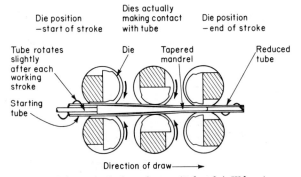

Fig. 3 Schematic of tube reducing. *(Babcock & Wilcox.)*

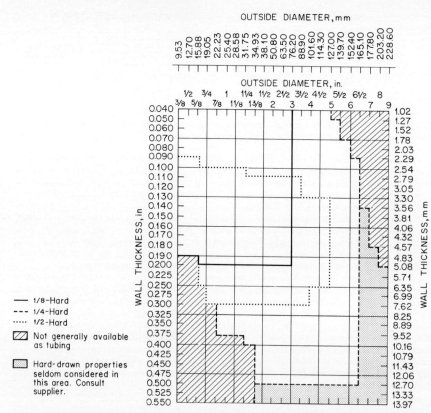

Fig. 4 Effect of tube size on hard-drawn stainless steel tube availability. (*Babcock & Wilcox.*)

not available. They may also be able to suggest how to do a job more simply and less expensively.

FORMABILITY OF STAINLESS STEEL TUBING

All stainless steels can be formed by one means or another; but forming demands practicality. What might be academically possible and interesting may not be economically feasible.

Austenitic Grades Of the stainless steels, the austenitic grades are the easiest to form. They work harden more than the other grades, but can be severely deformed without failure. From tension test data, we find that the annealed austenitics have elongations of 45 to 55% and reductions of area ranging from 55 to 70%. Austenitic tubing can be reduced in cross section as much as 60% if heavy equipment and proper techniques are

TABLE 1 Properties of Hard-Drawn Austenitic Stainless Steel Tubing

Temper	Yield strength, min.		Tensile strength, min.		Elongation, % in 2 in. (50.8 mm), min.
	ksi	MPa	ksi	MPa	
Annealed	30	207	75	517	35
⅛-hard	75–110	517–758	105–140	723–965	20
¼-hard	75	517	120	827	12
½-hard	110	758	150	1034	7
¾-hard	135	930	175	1206	3
Full hard	140	965	185	1275	3

applied. Annealed tubing can also be flared to increase the diameter 25 to 30%. These figures show that austenitic stainless tubing should behave well during bending, spinning, flaring, reducing, etc.

Austenitic steels are usually annealed by holding them at about 1900 to 2050°F (1038 to 1121°C), then quenching in water. This treatment leads to the softest, most formable condition and best corrosion resistance. Good practice calls for an anneal to be applied after forming. An exception would be an application which requires the strength obtained by cold-working.

Most austenitic stainless steels are formed at room temperature, but they can also be hot-worked. Hot-working may be needed to move the metal if (1) large, thick-walled tubes are involved and (2) the amount of deformation is severe. For instance, hot bending and spinning are common operations.

A word of caution is in order. The hot-short range(s) must be avoided. Hot shortness is a condition where a metal's ductility is greatly reduced within certain temperature ranges. Instead of stretching as desired, the metal might pull apart after only a little deformation. The austenitic stainless steels seem to have two hot-short ranges: (1) where the carbides precipitate at grain boundaries and (2) at high temperatures where delta ferrite forms.

Chromium carbides can come out of solution over a fairly wide and uncertainly bounded temperature range, about 900 to 1600°F (482 to 871°C). Any working carried out in that range will also affect carbide precipitation. The major metallurgical changes taking place at the grain boundaries can cause weakness. Results such as those seen in Figs. 5 and 6 might occur. An almost classic case of hot shortness is seen there. The tube shown in Figs. 5 and 6 was bent at too low a temperature. A proper forging range of 2150 to 2250°F (1177 to 1232°C) should have been used. Work should be finished before cooling to 1600°F (871°C), preferably slightly higher. Heating much above of 2250°F (1232°C) could allow delta ferrite to form at the grain boundaries. Again, hot shortness might be found.

Austenitic tubes can also be warm-worked, at less than normal forging temperatures. But heat must be limited to about 800°F (427°C) to avoid carbide precipitation.

Hard-drawn stainless tubing can also be formed. However, the stronger the tubing, the less the ductility (elongation). Thus, forming such tubing severely may be asking too much of it, especially with the higher tempers which have the least ductility (see Table 1). As will be noted later, hard-drawn tubing can be spun if care is taken. Such work is usually done hot. Care must be taken when hot-working hard-drawn tubing since too much heat will destroy the strength derived from the cold work.

Ferritic Grades   Ferritic stainless tubing, such as Types 430 and 446, can also be formed. But since these grades are less ductile, their forming is more difficult than for the austenitic grades. Tensile tests show that the ferritic grades have elongations and reductions of area of about 20 to 30% and 50 to 60%, respectively (compared with 45 to 55% and 55 to 70% for the austenitics). The ferritics are also notch-sensitive. A nick, scratch, or other sharp discontinuity can lead to splitting during cold-working or in the interim after cold-working, but before annealing. This problem worsens with higher chromium contents. Type 446 (27% chromium) would be more notch-sensitive than Type 430 (18% chromium). One way to lessen this effect is to work these grades warm, at 250 to 400°F (121 to 204°C).

While the ferritic grades can be worked at ambient and warm temperatures, it is frequently more practical to form them hot. Here the piece would be heated to 1900 to 2050°F (1038 to 1121°C) before forming starts. The job should be finished before the temperature reaches 1500°F (816°C).

When the ferritics are heated to too high a temperature, they suffer marked grain growth. The larger the grain size, the less ductile and more notch-sensitive they become. Since ferritic stainless steel cannot be heat-treated to refine the grain size, the recommended forging (working) temperature should not be exceeded. Only by working, then annealing, can the grain size be refined.

After the ferritic grades are hot-worked or annealed, they should be cooled rapidly to room temperature. If cooling is too slow through the range of 800 to 1500°F (427 to 816°C), embrittling phases may appear. The hazard is greater at the lower end of the range. There, so-called 885°F (474°C) embrittlement occurs. Ductility and notch toughness suffer here. Water quenching is recommended for fast cooling. Deformation in the range 800 to 1500°F (427 to 816°C) may also promote hot shortness.

Annealing these grades will restore their ductility and enhance corrosion resistance.

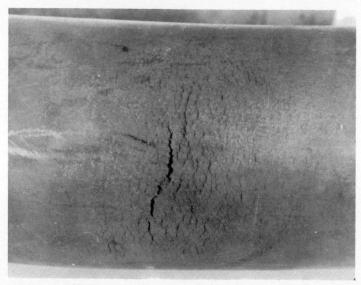

Fig. 5 Failure in an 18-8 type tube which was bent in the hot-short range. Bending was performed at a temperature much lower than the proper range of 2150–2250°F (1177–1232°C). (*Babcock & Wilcox.*)

Type 446 should be annealed at 1600°F (871°C), then rapidly cooled, preferably with water. Type 430 may be annealed at 1500°F (816°C), followed by water quenching or, in the case of thin sections, air cooling. Type 405, also nonhardenable, can be annealed by heating at 1350 to 1500°F (732 to 816°C), followed by air cooling.

Martensitic Grades The martensitic grades will harden if air cooled or quenched from temperatures above 1500°F (816°C). Among the martensitic group are Types 403, 410,

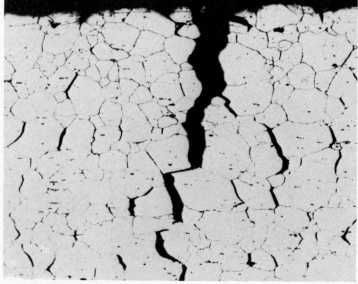

Fig. 6 Intergranular fissuring found at the outer surface of the tube shown in Fig. 5. Etch: electrolytic HNO₃. (*Babcock & Wilcox.*)

420, the 440s and others. These steels cannot be work hardened usefully. Because of their notch sensitivity, they should not be shipped or used in the cold-worked condition. Types 403 and 410 are often used as heat-resisting steels in the annealed condition. When annealed, they can be bent, flared, and worked in other manners, to a certain degree. The higher-carbon-content grades, however, would be machined, then used in the hardened and tempered condition for mechanical parts. Therefore, these grades would almost always be supplied in the annealed condition.

The ductility of the martensitic grades is generally less than that of even the ferritics. Types 403 and 410, with a maximum of 0.15% carbon, have about 30% and 60% elongation and reduction of area, respectively. When the carbon content is higher, as in Types 420 (0.15 to 0.30% C) and Type 440C (about 1% carbon), the ductility drops. Type 420 has a nominal elongation and a reduction of area of 25% and 55%, respectively. Type 440C has nominal values of only 13% and 25%, even in the fully annealed condition. For this reason, a mill cannot supply Type 440C as cold-finished tubing.

As a practical matter, much martensitic stainless steel tubing goes into mechanical uses. Machinability would be more important than ductility. Thus, the higher carbon grades would be shipped from the mills in the fully annealed condition.

Types 403 and 410 may see either heat-resisting or mechanical usage. In the first case, the tubing is supplied in the soft condition. This would allow a moderate amount of forming at room temperature. To soften grades such as these, any of three anneals can be used:

■ Subcritical—heating to and holding at a temperature below the lower critical transformation temperature to effect softening

■ Isothermal—heating to above the critical transformation temperature, then cooling to a temperature at which transformation to a soft ferrite and carbide structure will occur

■ Full—heating to above the critical temperature (austenitizing), then slowly cooling continuously until transformation to soft products is complete

Any of these treatments can be used for Types 403 and 410. Which one to use will depend on the specification being applied, facilities available, the size and number of pieces to be annealed, and the relative cost differences among the methods. The higher-carbon-content grades would require the full anneal to achieve the softest condition.

For mechanical uses, martensitic grades can be heat-treated for strength and hardness. Since this chapter is primarily concerned with forming, hardening and tempering will not be discussed in depth. Also, the quenching and tempering parameters are so numerous that readers should check with the mills, a commercial heat-treater, or perform some heat-treat trials of their own to work out the best thermal cycles. Three precautions will be offered, however.

1. When quenching one of the higher carbon grades, such as Type 440 A, B, or C, oil should be used as the quenching medium. Rapid water cooling could cause cracks during the hardening cycle.

2. After a martensitic stainless has been quenched, it should be tempered without delay. Otherwise, cracking may occur.

3. The temperature range 700 to 1050°F (371 to 566°C) should be avoided for tempering. Using that range leads to erratic impact behavior and lower corrosion resistance. Avoiding this range may restrict the properties obtainable, but perhaps a slight design change could be made to cope with this limitation.

FORMING METHODS

This section will look at the methods commonly used to form stainless steel tubes. Included are bending, spinning, expanding and reducing, upsetting and drawing. Methods of moving metal, rather than removing or joining it, will be discussed. If, as a fabricator, you have problems with machining or joining, you should seek help from Chapters 24 to 26, from the mills, or from experts who deal with such matters routinely.

There is no magic formula that can assure success in forming. Only experience, skill and good equipment can do that. This section points out a number of factors to think about; it does not guarantee success.

Bending   Bending is the most widely employed forming method. Welded fittings are used for many short, tight turns in piping systems. But there are still a great many places where bending is both desirable and necessary. Many plants, such as petrochemical plants, central station boilers, and refineries, have miles of tubing and pipe which wander in complex paths. By using bends, many of the costs and hazards of joints can be avoided.

Stretching and Thinning During Bending. In theory, bending is simple. However, some of the basics cannot be ignored. One must remember that there are inner and outer bend radii. The metal at the outer radius stretches and thins. But the metal at the inner radius is compressed and tends to thicken.

Most bending problems are found at the outer radius. If bending is poorly done, the metal can pull apart in a tensile-type failure or become too thin to meet design criteria. Since many high-pressure units must meet state and local safety codes, thinning must be considered. A tube may actually pull apart if it lacks the required ductility during bending.

While most bending problems are found at the outer radius, the inner radius should not be forgotten. Unexpectedly poor results, such as wrinkling or flattening, may be found there if less than good practice is used.

Calculate the Amount of Stretch and Thinning. Thinning and stretching for large arc bends can be calculated roughly from two formulas. Stretch at the outer radius (and shrink at the inner) can be figured from

$$e = \frac{D}{2R}$$

where e = stretch
$\quad\;\; D$ = tube outer diameter
$\quad\;\; R$ = centerline bend radius.

The elongations of the various steels are generally known or can be determined by tests. Thus, for a given tube size and material, the feasibility of a proposed bend radius can be estimated.

The amount of wall thinning can be approximated from

$$\frac{\Delta T}{T}100 = \left(1 - \frac{1}{\sqrt{1 + e}}\right)100$$

where ΔT = the change in wall thickness
$\quad\;\; T$ = the original wall thickness
$\quad\;\; e$ = stretch, derived from the formula above

It is questionable whether an annealed austenitic tube should be bent if the e value must exceed 35%. The austenitic grades have typical elongations much greater than 35%. But factors other than ductility also govern success. Some of these will be discussed later.

Similar estimates can be made for the annealed martensitic and ferritic grades. In earlier parts of this chapter, it was noted that these steels are not as ductile as the austenitics. Sometimes warming martensitic and ferritic stainless steels to about 250 to 400°F (121 to 204°C) will help. It should be possible, though, to bend them to an e value of at least 20%. This assumes that they have been well annealed.

Hard-drawn austenitic stainless can be bent, but with difficulty and usually not in tempers above ½ hard. Nonstandard stainless grades can also be bent, but to pick a general elongation figure for them would be futile. In this latter case, a metallurgical handbook, the manufacturer's literature, or one of the tube mills should be consulted.

One more word on elongation and bending. Most of the specifications which cover annealed austenitic tubing require an elongation of at least 25 to 35%. Other annealed stainless grades have lower minima. Therefore, if the outer fibers are stretched more than the minimum required amount, the bender enters unguaranteed territory. That is, exceeding the specified minimum elongation will show only that the steel has the required ductility. Past that point, fabricators are on their own. Experience may tell them that a steel will far exceed the required elongation. But sooner or later, they will receive some tubing which has only slightly more ductility than required. Here they might run into trouble if they think every tube lot has typical ductility.

Size and Geometry Are Important. Size is also a factor. Tubes which have large D/T ratios may not require much power to deform them. But they are the most difficult to bend. When the OD/wall ratio is small, relatively more power may be needed. But here the workpiece tends to support itself. That is, it will not buckle, wrinkle or assume an oval shape as readily as a tube with a large ratio. Size is especially important when working with the austenitic grades. They work harden more than the other grades; therefore, even more power may be needed to form them.

The geometry of a bend is important, too. The ratio of the centerline bend radius to the tube's outer diameter (R/D) and the ratio of the diameter to the wall thickness (D/T) should be calculated. The resulting numbers will indicate, in large measure, whether a tube can be bent with (1) no inner or outer support, (2) whether and what type of mandrels should be used, and (3) whether outer support should be employed. Maybe a combination of mandrels and outer support would be needed.

The matter of geometry is treated well in at least two sources. The International Nickel Company has published a fine reference.[1] Although the book is aimed primarily at the austenitic grades, much of the contained information can also be related to other stainless types. The section on bending is especially good. Similarly, the American Society for Metals has issued a handbook[2] on forming all types of metals. The author commends both of these references to the readers.

Figure 7 shows the effects of both size and geometry. While the illustration was derived from carbon steel tubing, tests have shown that it will also apply

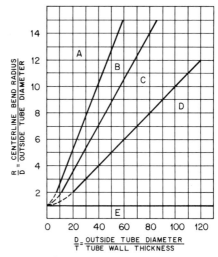

Fig. 7 Effect of tube size and bend radius on equipment setup.[1] Also see Table 2.

to austenitic stainless steels. It can probably be used as a general guide for annealed martensitic and ferritic stainless tubing; but the two formulas for stretch and wall thinning must also be consulted.

From Fig. 7, we see that bending is probably not practical with $R/D \leq 1$. For instance, a 5-in. diameter (127-mm) tube should not be bent to a radius of 5 in. (127 mm) or less, regardless of the wall thickness T. Now assume that we have a tube which is 5 in. (127 mm) OD × 0.125 in. (3.2 mm) thickness. Reference to Table 2 and Fig. 7 shows that different equipment setups would be needed for bends of various radii.

First of all, we find that the tube in question gives us a D/T ratio of 40 [5 in. (127 mm) ÷ 0.125 in. (3.2 mm)]. If we were to bend this to a centerline radius of 60 in. (1524 mm) $(R/D = 12)$, no inner or outer support should be needed. However, to bend the same tube to a 40-in. (1016-mm) radius $(R/D = 8)$, some sort of inner support (plug or other mandrel) and outer support (wiper die) would be advisable. Similarly, bending to a 25-in. (635-mm) radius $(R/D = 5)$ would require a one-ball mandrel but no wiper die, and for a 10-in. (254-mm) radius bend $(R/D = 2)$, a two-ball mandrel and wiper die would be employed.

The foregoing seems to be stated somewhat absolutely. While Fig. 7 seems to define

TABLE 2 Effect of Tube Size and Bend Radius on Equipment Setup [5 in. (127 mm) OD × 0.125 in. (3.2 mm) wall]

D/T	Proposed bend radius, in. (mm)	R/D	Applicable area of Fig. 7
40	60 (1524)	12	A, no inner or outer support needed
40	40 (1016)	8	B, use mandrel and wiper die
40	25 (635)	5	C, use one-ball mandrel and wiper die
40	10 (254)	2	D, use two-ball mandrel and wiper die
40	5 (127)	1	E, bending not practical

the areas sharply, there is actually some overlap. The amount will depend on the tube material and how well it is annealed, the surface smoothness and how well it is lubricated, and the metal temperature, etc. But one thing can be said with certainty: as the bend radius becomes tighter, the degree of care needed becomes greater.

Bending Equipment and Methods. The discussion about Fig. 7 alluded to bending equipment and methods. Here is another area to think about—whether to do the work in-house or to have it done by an outside contractor. If a fabricator needs only a few bends which can be made with simple equipment, maybe the work should be done by the fabricator. But if only a few complex bends are needed, perhaps the work should be farmed out to a well-equipped bending shop. Conversely, if the fabricator's volume of bending is large and repetitive, it might justify the cost of some expensive, but versatile, equipment.

A few paragraphs ago, mandrels and wiper dies were mentioned. Mandrels are tools which are used to control the inner tube contour during bending. Most mandrels are shaped to accommodate round tubing. But, they can also be made to handle square or other tubular shapes. Mandrels may be either solid or flexible. Solid mandrels contact the inner surface at the area of bending only; they do not offer support immediately afterward. Flexible mandrels curve and support a tube both at the area where the bend starts forming and for a little distance afterward. Flexible mandrels, such as the two-ball type, are used for more complicated bends. Mandrels remain stationary during bending; they are fixed on the end of a rod or bar. In other words, the tube moves over the mandrel during bending.

Wiper dies are support pieces which move over (wipe) the outside diameter of a tube while it is being bent. (Or the tube may be moved under the die.) Such dies not only hold a tube in a bending machine, but also help to combat ovality or flattening.

Rotary Bending. Sophisticated bending machines, sometimes called rotary benders, will be discussed only in general terms. For greater detail, the equipment makers should be consulted. The machines can vary widely. They range from large, rugged constructions to smaller, precision mechanisms. Operating speeds can vary according to machine complexity, tube size, analysis and surface condition (smoothness and lubrication). In many respects, the use of such equipment is a mechanical challenge, rather than a metallurgical one.

A rotary bender provides for clamping a tube with the section to be bent at the working area of the machine. A central form then rotates, pulling the tube around its outer surface. Depending on the severity of the bend, a mandrel may or may not be used for internal support. Another similar method wraps the tube around a central stationary form. Here, roundness is maintained by wiper dies which also force the tube around the form. Working is carried out in a horizontal plane in both methods. Therefore, quite a bit of floor space is needed. Because of the strength which can be built into large bending machines (they are usually hydraulic), it is common to handle 8- to 10-in.-diameter (203- to 254-mm) tubes. There are machines which can bend even larger tubes, but the demand for them is slight.

Press Bending. Press bending employs a hydraulic press to push the shaped head of a ram onto a tube which, in turn, is forced into a die or between rollers. The die/rollers back up the tube and allow it only restricted freedom. The method does not usually employ internal support and is widely used for smaller workpieces. Further, little if any lubrication is needed to reduce friction. The production rates depend on the number and complexity of the bends, as well as the operator's dexterity. It is frequently possible to make simultaneous bends in one plane quite rapidly. Sequential bends can be made by advancing a tube through the press by previously set amounts. Press bending is widely applied to less expensive tubing such as that used for furniture, decorative pieces, automobile exhaust systems, etc. For simple configurations, press bending can be automated to increase productivity.

Pulling Around a Template. One of the simpler forms of bending involves pulling a tube around a form or template. This form must be carefully laid out on a large plane surface, usually horizontal. The movement of the tube is confined to one end, while the other leg of the bend is held in place by pegs or other simple hold-down devices. The pulling power may be applied by cables attached to winches or cranes. The method is cumbersome at best. It does not lead to high productivity. In most cases, fairly wide arc bends are made unless some internal support can be imposed. Since the method is used when only a few bends are to be made, the internal support may be provided by filling the tube with (1) a low-melting-point metal, such as "Wood's" metal*, or (2) by filling it with clean, tightly packed dry sand. Heating the tube may lessen the bending force needed and also allow a smaller bend radius to be made. But as noted later, heat should not be applied if a low-melting filler metal is used.

Filling the Tube for Support. A filler is usually considered when only a few tubes must be bent. The method seems simple, but some difficulties are possible. First, there is the question of filling. The filler must be tightly packed or its purpose is defeated. Using a low-melting-point metal for a filler will assure tight packing. But that process is cumbersome and messy: capping the ends, melting the metal, filling the tube with it, removing it after bending is complete, and making sure that the last vestiges are cleaned from the tube surface. The last point is important. Thorough cleaning will help to avoid corrosion and/or contamination. Further compounding the problems of this method is the volume of liquid metal needed for larger tubes. As noted near the end of this chapter, filler metals must be completely removed before heat treatment and/or before the tube is put into service.

Sand filling also has its drawbacks. A method must be found to pack the sand tightly. Tamping alone is usually not effective; therefore, the workpiece must be vibrated to settle the sand. This requires holding the tube upright. As in metal filling, the ends must be shut. Of course, putting on and taking off of end caps or plates is another bother and expense. After the bend is complete, the ends can be opened and the sand removed by tapping the tube. Good practice dictates that the filler be dry and clean, especially if the tube is to be bent hot. During repeated use and careless storage, sand can accumulate grease, oil, and other carbon-bearing substances. These contaminants can promote carburization during heating for bending or subsequent annealing. This will lessen corrosion resistance.

Who Should Do the Bending? Careful thought should be given to the merits of doing a job in-house or having a competent bending shop tackle it. Where experience and equipment are lacking, the decision may be simple. Since requirements, capabilities, and economics vary so widely, each job must be judged on its own merits.

Hot Bending. Without question, most bending is performed at room temperature. But sometimes a tube must be heated for bending. Heating permits tighter-radius bends. The power required will be less since the yield strength decreases with increasing temperatures.

When should a fabricator use hot or warm bending? Not at all if it can be avoided. If cold bending can be performed, no heating equipment will be needed, the metallurgical structure and corrosion resistance will be disturbed less, and cleaning after bending, if needed, will be easier. Hot bending also slows production and increases cost. Furthermore, the surface finish may be degraded by scaling and handling when hot.

There is no widely accepted rule to indicate when bending should be done hot (or warm). The practice is applied to larger sections which would otherwise strain or stall a shop's equipment. Raising the temperature lowers a metal's yield strength and increases the ductility. This means that the metal at the outer bend radius will stretch farther while the metal at the inner radius will compress more readily. Therefore, tighter bends will be possible.

Heat is usually applied uniformly to the tube's cross section. In some cases, however, heat is directed only to the side which will be in compression (inner radius). The major metal deformation will be thrown to the inner radius because of its lower compressive yield strength. This will prevent excessive stretch and wall thinning at the outer radius. When heating is uniform, the tube can either be brought to the forging range or be warmed to a temperature below the hot-short or embrittlement range. (These ranges were discussed earlier in this chapter.)

Heat application to only one side of a tube will generally involve only warming. Trying to heat only one side is not recommended unless one has a wealth of experience. It is difficult to achieve a happy medium between heating uniformly, heating only one side, avoiding the hot-short and embrittlement ranges, etc.

Even tubes which are bent hot may need internal support. While mandrels can be used for hot bending, their use is made more difficult by the presence of heat. As noted below, a

---

*There are several different compositions which melt at or below the temperature of boiling water. A number of these are loosely referred to as Wood's metal or alloy.

lubricant is frequently employed when a mandrel is used. But most common lubricants do not hold up well in the presence of high heat. Also, many lubricants contain carbonaceous materials which can carburize the metal. Carbon can combine with chromium to lessen the effective amount of chromium. In that case, the steel would become less stainless. Therefore, sand filling is sometimes used for internal support when tubes are to be bent hot.

Lubricants. It would not be proper to discuss or recommend a particular lubricant maker's product here. Reference 1 contains a long list of lubricants arranged according to basic type and mentions trade names. It also notes vendors' names and addresses at the time of printing.

Lubrication would almost certainly be required when making a bend with a mandrel and/or wiper die. Both the mandrel and the inner tube surface can be coated with a pigmented lubricant to reduce friction and pickup during bending. Sometimes an oil flow can be introduced through holes in the mandrel while the tube is being bent. Where the wiper dies contact the outer surface, lubrication is not as critical as it is for the mandrel. Here only a snug fit must be maintained, but without the risk of galling and pickup. As noted earlier, special problems are found during hot bending. Lubricant breakdown and carburization must be minimized if at all possible.

Cleaning of the workpiece after bending must also be considered. Therefore, the removal of lubricant is almost as important as its application. For these reasons, a fabricator should consult the lubricant vendors before beginning a project. The subject of cleaning stainless steels has been treated in more detail in Chapter 35.

Spinning This section will deal with spinning as applied to generally available stainless tubing. This excludes thin-wall cylinders which might be made from rolled and welded sheet or plate. Common stainless grades only are considered.

General Considerations. Spinning is often used to change the contours of tubing. The process can either reduce or expand the diameter. Expansion, of course, is almost always limited to areas near the ends. The major use of tube spinning is closing or almost closing the end(s). This technique is used for such products as steam drums made from large-diameter heavy-wall pipe, pressure bottles which must meet ICC regulations, soot-blower elements for central station power plants, and compact, high-pressure gas reservoirs in aircraft-seat ejection systems. Spinning eliminates the need for circumferential welds and end closures.

Wall thickness can also be changed, but that is not usually the aim of the process. However, when spinning is used for wall thinning, the job is certainly not one for the novice.

Tubes for spinning are usually supplied in the annealed condition. A minor amount of hard-drawn (unannealed) austenitic tubing is also used. But experience and care are required to spin hard-drawn tubing. Minor amounts of ferritic stainless steel are also spun; however, such steels are applied only if the use is not critical, i.e., contained pressure is not great and notch toughness is not a service requirement. Best practice would call for annealing after working. The martensitic grades are not spun often; but when they are spun, proper final heat treatments should be applied. These thermal cycles include annealing or hardening (quenching or normalizing) and tempering.

Severe spinning operations can exceed the room-temperature ductility of stainless steels; therefore, heat is often used. The heat is generated by friction, applied externally, or is a combination of both. If the reductions are small, heat generation or application can be minimized.

In most cases, the workpiece is small enough to be handled easily. Therefore, it is possible to rotate the tube rapidly while forcing it against the forming tools. Conversely, the tools may be forced against the piece as it rotates. In these cases, the pressure for deformation is applied both axially to the tube and perpendicularly to the outside diameter. When the pieces to be spun are big (such as large-diameter heavy-wall tubes or hollow forgings), the tools, usually rollers, are rotated about and forced onto the piece being spun. The tube itself remains stationary and heat is applied externally.

Unless spinning is to be done at room temperature, the effect of heat on the tools must be considered. If heat is not a problem, tools can be made of common hardenable grades (AISI 52100, 4150, etc). Chrome plating the tools should minimize pickup and galling, as well as extend their overall life. Where heat is generated or applied, a heat-resisting tool steel would be used. A handbook or manufacturer could give guidance for a proper steel choice here.

Careful Preparation Needed. Tubular blanks for spinning must be prepared with care. The piece should be cut, preferably by machining, so that the ends are reasonably smooth and square. Burrs should be removed. Beveling the edges also helps. These steps will minimize cracking during working. Such details are of utmost importance when the ferritic or martensitic grades are involved. They are notch-sensitive and have less ductility than the austenitics. When spinning is done at normal forging temperatures, these precautions are not as important. They can, however, become critical at room or only warm temperatures. The comments on tube formability should be reviewed, especially as they apply to the ferritic and martensitic grades.

Lubrication. Lubricants may or may not be used for spinning. Their use will depend on the shop involved, equipment being used, and amount of deformation required. Lubricants are normally not needed if roller-type tools are used. However, if tools that rub the workpiece are used, lubricants should be applied. On the other hand, some shops prefer to let friction help heat the piece. Therefore, they use little or no lubricant. The surface would be badly scored if not lubricated. Then later operations (such as machining, tumbling, or blasting) might have to be applied. When lubricants are used, their effect on corrosion resistance must be considered. This subject will be examined next.

Many compounds can be used for lubrication. Of course, some would be eliminated for high-temperature use. For instance, grease and graphite have been used successfully. But if the workpiece becomes very hot, such a lubricant will break down and severely carburize the steel. Carbon will enter the surface and penetrate even deeper at the grain boundaries. Since most common stainless grades are highly susceptible to carburization, corrosion and oxidation resistance may suffer. Similar problems may occur with soapy lubricants which contain nonferrous metal compounds, such as those of zinc. Such metals may penetrate stainless steels at the grain boundaries with disastrous results. Best practice dictates that lubricants be thoroughly removed before any heat treatments are applied. Heat is apt to break down the lubricant and lead to the hazards described above.

There are many makers of lubricant materials. They can best explain the application, use, and removal of their products. A list and general description of many lubricants was cited earlier.[1] In the final analysis, only experience will show which lubricant is best for an operation.

Spinning the Austenitic Grades. Special emphasis will be given here to the austenitic grades. They are the most commonly spun stainless steels. The austenitics are normally supplied annealed. But occasionally they may be used in the hard-drawn (unannealed) condition.

Annealed austenitic tubing is relatively easy to handle. There is ample ductility for most spinning operations. These steels also have high notch toughness. Regardless of the good ductility and toughness, an austenitic tube end must still be prepared carefully to prevent the formation of stress raisers. The points mentioned next may appear to be repetitious; however, they are particularly important when the austenitic grades are involved.

Most stainless steel tube spinning involves heat to aid deformation. Heating lowers the yield strength and increases ductility. Gas flames are commonly used to warm the area to be worked. Rotating the tube under the flame will promote better heat uniformity. Most of the common austenitic stainless steels carburize readily; therefore, the flame should be kept slightly oxidizing or at least neutral. Furthermore, the surface to be heated should be free of dirt, grease, and other contamination. Contamination includes the presence of nonferrous metals, such as copper or brass, which may have been used as shims during cutoff or other operations. The hazards of nonferrous metals on stainless steels were noted earlier. But when such attack is combined with deformation, the steel may almost literally fall apart.

In many, if not most, cases of austenitic tube spinning, gas flames are used only for a preheat. Then the tool/workpiece friction quickly generates the rest of the heat for and during spinning. Sometimes frictional heat can be augmented by electric resistance heating. (Electric resistance can also be used for preheating.) The procedures outlined here heat the area of spinning rapidly. Since heating and deformation are so fast, hot-short reactions do not have time to occur. Here again, coordinated action, plus experience, will determine ultimate success.

Spinning is used primarily to close, or almost close, the ends of stainless steel tubing. As it is moved toward the tube's axis, the steel at the end becomes mushy and is forced together. A pressed or forged weld is made. Some of the oxides from heating, plus any remaining lubricant, tend to be trapped at the center of the closure. This is not very important for noncritical uses. However, for pressure-containing parts, it is common practice to remove this nonhomogeneous area by drilling. Then a plate of sound, similar material is welded in as a replacement. Another frequently used procedure is to drill out the area, then tap it for threaded connectors.

Spinning for closure also causes a thickening of the tube wall as shown in Fig. 8. This photograph shows part of a sectioned Type 304 bottle for compressed gas. The tube had

Fig. 8 Part of a sectioned, partially completed Type 304 pressure bottle. Note the wall thickening near the closure and heat and lubricant discoloration on the surfaces and outer surface scoring. (*Babcock & Wilcox.*)

been hot-spun almost shut, and several things can be noted. The wall starts to thicken at the shoulder of the closure. This thickening becomes even more pronounced nearer the tube axis. There is an accumulation of scale and lubricant on the inner surface where closure neared completion. The dark, heat-affected area is seen clearly on the inner surface. It is not defined as sharply at the outer surface but appears to extend further down the length, well past the shoulder.

After reaching the state shown in Fig. 8, the job is far from finished. Beside having its ends perfected or adapted for fittings, a piece must be cleaned of scale and lubricants (see Chap. 35). If an austenitic stainless tube has been hot-spun, it will contain areas where carbides have precipitated at the grain boundaries. Cleaning with an aggressive acid may then cause intergranular attack in the heat-affected area. Therefore, sand or grit blasting may be the most practical way to clean the inner surface. The outer surface could be cleaned by blasting, grinding, polishing or even machining. The workpiece could then be annealed for maximum corrosion resistance and softness, recleaned (as before and/or by pickling), passivated, then dressed up for cosmetic or commercial reasons. (The martensitic grades, instead of being annealed, may be hardened or tempered.) These procedures should produce a product that is clean, metallurgically homogeneous, and sound.

Spinning Hard-drawn Tubing. There are occasions when it is not possible to use an annealed stainless steel. Annealed material might not be strong enough. But if high notch toughness is required, only the austenitic grades may be suitable. Also, some specification-writing groups will approve only austenitic stainless steels. Even then, products made from them must be rigidly tested. Under these conditions hard-drawn austenitic stainless tubing may be considered.

Before using hard-drawn tubing, the user must ascertain (1) whether unannealed steel can be approved under existing or (officially) modified regulations and (2) whether hard-drawn tubing will be suitable for end uses where the stresses of cold-work can affect corrosion resistance. Stress-corrosion cracking may occur if certain warm media contact stressed stainless steels. If unsure, the fabricator should consult one of the tube mills or a reputable corrosion expert.

Once acceptability is established, material availability has to be considered. Also, what properties are needed? The ductility of hard-drawn tubing decreases as strength increases. Therefore, hot-working may have to be considered. If heat is applied, the cold-work strength may be degraded. Heating in the wrong temperature range will also cause carbides to precipitate. Susceptibility to corrosion will increase. This problem can be minimized or prevented by using low-carbon grades such as Types 304L or 316L or stabilized grades such as Types 321 and 347. Annealing to develop corrosion resistance cannot be done since the strength derived from cold-working would be eliminated.

The strengths and sizes available for hard-drawn stainless steel tubing were explored earlier. If heat is used during spinning, stress relieving may occur. The hardness and strength will decrease accordingly. One must compensate for this effect. In short, the stock for a project must have a strength level higher than that needed in the final product so that even if some strength is lost, it will remain acceptably high. Another method of compensation would be to use a tube with a greater wall thickness and/or smaller outside diameter if the design allows it. But this might affect cost and availability.

To minimize the effects of hot-working, the fabricator must do the job as fast as possible. Preheating should be kept low and localized. The work must be done quickly to minimize heat buildup and consequent heat flow to other parts of the tube. Using hard-drawn stainless for hot spinning may call for some ingenuity. For instance, it might be possible to use selective cooling to limit the flow of heat away from the end and toward the body of the tube. But the most effective remedy will be speed and coordination. At the hottest area of the tube, the properties will approach those of annealed stainless. But as noted before, there is a noticeable wall thickening in this area. The combination of rapid working, residual strength after hot-working, plus wall thickening may be enough to meet the end-use requirements.

The author would strongly advise a novice to avoid spinning hard-drawn stainless tubing, especially if large amounts of deformation are needed. Unless time and money are available for experiments, some or many of which will fail, it is better to let an experienced fabricator do the job.

Precipitation-hardenable Stainless Can Be Spun. Specification criteria can sometimes be met with some of the precipitation-hardenable grades. The steel would have to be chosen carefully. As noted earlier in this chapter, availability of tubing may be limited. But if one of the precipitation-hardenable grades can be made into tubing, it can probably be spun. However, the rules of physical metallurgy which apply to a particular analysis would have to be observed. Some grades require complicated thermal cycles. Sometimes certain furnace atmospheres, such as disassociated ammonia, must be avoided during heat treatment. Ductility varies widely. This will affect workability and method of deformation. Since the precipitation-hardenable grades are so different, their behavior should be discussed thoroughly with the producing mill's metallurgists. This should be done before any purchases are made.

Seek Advice. While the procedures for spinning may seem fairly simple, there are still potential hazards. Thus, more than the usual amount of preparation is advised. The tube mills and other competent sources should be consulted.

Expanding and Reducing Expanding and reducing are frequently applied to stainless tubes. These operations may be done during manufacturing or testing at the mills or during fabrication for use.

Flaring and Flanging. Flaring and flanging are common procedures. If a tube is to be expanded, the ends must be prepared carefully. All rough cuts must be smoothed and notches and burrs removed. Beveling, where permissible, helps. Of course, the annealed austenitics will respond much better than other stainless types. Therefore, we will not consider the martensitic or ferritic grades.

Flares Are Simply Made. Since austenitic stainless steel tubing can be flared without much trouble, it is usually deformed cold and in one step. Most flares are relatively narrow, such as those used for hydraulic or pneumatic connections. But sometimes unusually wide expansions must be made. Here multiple steps and intermediate anneals may be needed. Simple calculations will show whether a proposed expansion will exceed a steel's inherent ductility. If so, multiple steps and anneals would be required.

A flare is commonly made by pressing a cone into the prepared end of a well-supported tube. If surface quality is a concern, scratching and galling must be prevented. Chrome-plated tools may be used for smoothness or a simple lubricant might be applied. The lubricating method will depend on the number of pieces involved. If only a few are to be handled, brush or dip lubrication might be in order. For a large number of pieces, mass lubrication may be more practical. It is also wise to check the tools frequently to see that they are free of grit, dirt, metal pickup, or score marks. Score marks on tools can be mirrored on the workpiece surface. When any of these faults are found, the tools should be cleaned, replaced, or redressed.

Frequently, flared pieces are used in the as-formed state. But if they are to be annealed, they should be thoroughly cleaned before heat treatment. This will help to prevent carburization or other surface contamination.

Flares can also be made by rolling a tool over the inner surface. Rolling leads to a smoother surface. Frictional forces are also avoided. When a flare is formed by rolling, the tube usually remains still as the tool rotates. It is also possible to form a flare by spinning. Here the tube is rotated while a tool is forced into the inner surface. The tool may be a roller type or one which rubs the wall. The latter type of tool is seldom used for flaring.

Flanging More Difficult. Flanging is actually an extension of flaring. In some cases, a flange and the body of the tube may form an angle which is less than 90°. But a flange is normally thought of as being normal to the tube axis.

Making a right-angle flange severely tests a metal's ductility. Such flanges usually are made in at least two steps. The first step makes a flare. The second and/or last step is made with a flat punch and die. The flare is pressed down to make a 90° angle with the rest of the tube. Intermediate anneals are used to restore ductility as needed. The tube must be securely held in a die to prevent collapse of the straight length. This will help to maintain the exact angle and depth desired.

For a flange, end preparation is crucial. The outer edge of the flange is stretched severely. Wall uniformity must be good. If the thickness varies greatly, there may be uneven deformation. Nonuniformity can lead to ripping during forming. Lubrication is usually not used, but sometimes it may be beneficial.

A machine has also been developed for cold rolling 90° flanges. The face of a flange made in this way is smooth enough to permit sealing with gaskets. For the method to work well, the tube must be very concentric. Prior to flanging, backup rings are slipped onto the tubes.

Several Methods of Reducing. Reducing can be performed in several ways. At an end, a tube can be reduced by pushing it through a die or by rotary swaging. Spinning may also be used. Internal support may be needed if there is a danger that the tube will collapse or if control of the ID is important.

Pushing Into a Die. Pushing a tube into a properly contoured die is common. A lubricant may be used to ease the operation. The method does not control ID very precisely, but this is unimportant in most cases. The tube should be well supported to prevent bending and buckling along the length. Usually the tube is gripped just behind the area to be reduced. If very fine inner and outer dimensional control is needed, further finishing operations should be considered, including machining, grinding, or polishing.

Swaging. Swaging is a second method of reduction. It is a common tube mill process which requires some fairly hefty equipment. The most common type of swager contains a rotating sleeve which rolls over a series of balls. The balls act as cams which cause split dies to impact against a tube's outer surface. (The rapid action of the dies against the tube surface is noisy. This noise would have to be considered, especially in an enclosed work area.) As the dies beat against the tube, it rotates in the same direction as the dies. They, in turn, rotate with the sleeve. The tube is advanced at the same time. These movements of the tube help to make working more uniform. Usually this is not a great concern because the reductions commonly made by swaging are small and swaging is not used to make close-dimension work. If the inner dimension must be controlled, it is a simple matter to insert a supporting mandrel. A bar could be used for longer lengths.

Swaging is almost always done cold and without lubrication. Heat could be modestly applied to difficult alloys, such as the ferritic stainless steel grades, but it is usually not needed. Swaging is used primarily on tubes that are about 3 in. (76.2 mm) OD and smaller.

Miscellaneous Methods. There are other, more specialized, ways of expansion and reduction. Many of these methods are suited only to thin-wall tubing. In some cases, such tubing is produced from rolled and welded sheet at the shop where the work is to be done. But some smaller OD, light-wall tubing may be within the tube mills' ranges, too. Inquiries would establish this.

Some of the forming methods which have been used include spinning into split dies, hydraulic expansion into dies (at room or subzero temperatures), and roll-forming against arbors. Combinations of these methods can also be employed.

Cold-forming Cold-forming (also called cold extrusion) will become an increasingly important forming method. This process deforms a prepared slug in a press. Cold-extrusion techniques have been employed for expanding, reducing, and otherwise contouring some relatively complex shapes. The advance of cold-forming will continue as (1) low-work-hardening-rate stainless steel grades are developed, (2) the nature of metal flow is better understood, and (3) lubricant technology moves forward. The main advantages of cold extrusion are high productivity, close dimensional tolerances, and material savings. Many cold-formed parts are close enough to final size so that few or no subsequent finishing operations are required.

Upsetting There are end uses which require heavy stainless steel tubes to have other than straight (plain) ends. Therefore, a fabricator, or more likely a tube mill, may upset the ends to achieve larger or smaller outside and/or inside diameters, lighter or heavier walls, or combinations of modified outside and inside diameters and/or wall thicknesses. Small tubing is rarely, if ever, upset.

Upsetting is a forging operation. It is common to many tube mills and some forging and specialty fabricating houses. Actually, not much stainless tubing is upset. The bulk of upset tubing is made of alloy steel. The equipment needed for the process is quite heavy. Since upsetting is a hot operation, there must also be facilities for heating and reheating the ends.

An upsetting machine contains split dies into which heated tube ends can be placed. The dies, open when a tube is positioned, close to form an encircling chamber around the tube end. A ram then impacts the end of the tube to drive the metal back and also out to the die. The ram carries with it a mandrel to control the inner dimensions.

The upsetting process may involve several stations for making the required forging. There may also be a number of reheating cycles if the job cannot be done quickly enough. The greatest limitation on the size of upsets is the mass and power of the forging equipment.

Lubricants are commonly used to minimize galling and sticking to the tools. However, care must be taken to prevent contamination.

After the forging operation is complete, some grinding or machining will probably be needed to complete the job. Once the proper contour has been made and the piece has been cleaned, annealing can be performed. The usual precautions should be observed to prevent contamination. Since one of the aims of annealing is to promote uniformity, the whole length should be heat-treated, not just the upset ends. The martensitic grades, of course, could be hardened and tempered, if desired.

Cold-drawing and Tube Reducing Cold-drawing and tube reducing are common tube mill processes. A number of companies use these two forming methods as the major operations of their whole business. The redraw mills buy tube hollows from the primary mills, then produce fine, small tubes, using one or both of the methods.

Schematics of cold-drawing and tube reducing have been shown in Figs. 2 and 3. As previously mentioned, these processes are used to make hard-drawn tubing.

Cold-drawing uses tube hollows which have been produced by rotary piercing or extrusion. These hollows must be cleaned, inspected, then conditioned, if necessary, by grinding or machining. Appropriate heat treatments are applied as needed. The tubes must also be pointed (reduced in size) at one end. After pointing, the tubes are lubricated to reduce the frictional forces of drawing.

A prepared tube is then put on the drawbench with its point extending through a die. The die controls the outer shape and size. A mandrel may or may not be used to control the inner dimensions. After the hollow is presented to the drawbench, a carriage (see Fig. 2) comes forward, seizes the point and pulls the hollow through the die. If a mandrel is used, the process is called mandrel drawing. If not, it is called sinking. Sinking applies reducing forces to the outside diameter only. The pulling force for the carriage may be applied by a continuously traveling chain which is picked up by a hook on the carriage or a hydraulic system. Hydraulic benches can be built to draw several tubes at once.

After the tubes are drawn, they are cleaned, cut, heat-treated, cleaned again, inspected, and conditioned if necessary. The drawing cycle can then be repeated or the tubes can be prepared for shipment.

Tube reducing (see Fig. 3) achieves the same end as drawing. The hollows are prepared similarly to tubes for drawing. But they are not pointed. After a prepared hollow is presented to the tube-reducing machine, a tapered mandrel is inserted to control the inner surface during working. Then two semicircular dies are rocked back and forth over the outer surface. The tube being reduced can be advanced or turned at opposite ends of the die travel. After the reducing cycle is complete, the tube can be cleaned, annealed, cut, inspected, conditioned if necessary, and then recycled through tube reducing or shipped from the mill. Or it could also be cold-drawn after the initial tube-reducing cycle.

There are two major advantages of tube reducing (as opposed to drawing). Pointing is not needed; thus, material loss is not as great. Tube reducing can also effect greater reductions of area.

There are three major advantages to cold-finishing stainless steel tubing by drawing or tube reducing. First, various cold-work tempers (strength levels) can be imparted to the austenitic grades. Second, longer lengths and more size combinations can be produced than would otherwise be available. Third, close tolerances can be produced by cold finishing. These points are somewhat academic since, for various reasons, the bulk of stainless steel tubing is normally produced in the cold-finished condition.

For obvious reasons, the heavy equipment needed for drawing or tube reducing is not commonly found among smaller fabricators. These processes are left to the tube mills.

REFERENCES

1. "Forming of Austenitic Chromium-Nickel Stainless Steels," The International Nickel Company, New York, N.Y., 1954.
2. Forming, in "Metals Handbook," 8th ed., vol. 4, American Society for Metals, Metals Park, Ohio, 1969.

Chapter **31**

Foundry Practice

DAVID R. POIRIER
Associate Professor of Manufacturing Engineering, University of Bridgeport, Bridgeport, Connecticut

CASTING FUNDAMENTALS

Role of the Designer   Approximately 1.8 million tons (1633×10^6 kg) of the 21 million tons ($19,047 \times 10^6$ kg) of castings produced in 1973 in this country went into cast steel components. Less than 1% by weight of all metal cast is stainless steel; but those applications test the creativity of the designer because stainless steel castings are used in particularly severe environments. Indeed, by way of emphasizing their applications, stainless steel castings are categorized as either *corrosion-resistant* or *heat-resistant* castings. Common grades suitable for casting are presented and discussed in Chaps. 2, 9, and 10. Heat-resistant castings are used in furnaces for the metallurgical, refinery, and petrochemical industries, and equipment for power plants, cement mills, and steel mills. They are also essential components in turbosuperchargers and gas turbines. The corrosion-resistant castings are used in a wide variety of applications ranging from containing liquids at room temperature and boiling liquids at elevated temperatures to withstanding corrosive gases at temperatures up to $1200°$F ($649°$C).

Engineers and designers should understand the capabilities and limitations of the casting process in order to develop reliable products of high quality and competitive price. When manufacture of a component by casting is considered, the first selection must be the casting alloy and process which can produce the required dimensional tolerance, mechanical properties, and production rate. If a casting is found to be suitable, an estimate should be made of the product cost of alternative processes such as fabrication, forging, or machining. And if it appears that a casting process offers the least cost, the engineer refines the design specifically for the casting process. Obviously, the best castings are produced from designs originating from engineers with a good understanding of the casting processes.

Casting processes offer to the designer several distinct assets: the ability of a liquid to fill a complex shape, production economy, and a wide choice of alloys suitable for use in highly stressed parts where corrosion or heat may be a problem. Casting permits the engineer to place the metal where it is needed and minimize it where there are excesses.

There are inherent problems, too, including internal porosity and inclusions, and surface defects and dimensional variations which require vigilant control of melting, molding, pouring, solidification, cleaning and heat-treating in the foundry.

The design and production of a successful casting requires the simultaneous application of a number of basic sciences: metallurgy, fluid flow, heat transfer, and materials engineering to name a few. Defects such as metal penetration into the mold wall or pinholes have occurred in the past and they still occasionally plague even the most sophisticated casting engineers, despite years of experience and greatly expanded technological know-how. To establish the relationship between the casting processes and good design practice, this chapter attempts to tie together casting fundamentals, casting processes, and design considerations.

Alloy Solidification What happens as the metal solidifies in a casting is crucial, because many of the properties of the finished product arise from the events of solidification. Until fairly recently, when modern techniques of research and inspection were brought to bear on the subject, exactly how a melt solidified was a mystery. Casting was more of an art than a science, and foundry operators tended to be secretive about the techniques they had found successful. Not all features of the solidification process are understood today, but the interaction between solidification theory and foundry practice has been strong in recent years.

Solidification of a casting is a freezing process which begins at the wall of the mold and proceeds inward. In a partially solidified casting there exists a zone of solid metal, a zone of liquid metal and between them a zone where the liquid is transforming into the solid. In the industry this latter zone is termed the *mushy zone*.

All alloys freeze over a range of temperature which depends on alloy content. Low-carbon steel and commercially pure metals freeze in a narrow temperature range (less than 60°C), and certain tin-bronzes have wide freezing ranges (150 to 200°C). The stainless steel alloys fall in between these extremes. Figure 1 depicts the solidification of alloys in molds and typical as-cast grain structures. Figure 1c illustrates a stainless steel casting showing long columnar grains developing at the mold wall and growing into the melt, with a mushy zone forming as solidification progresses toward the thermal center of the casting.

A closer look within the grains during alloy solidification reveals the formation of treelike structures called dendrites (Fig. 2). Dendrites have a layered structure of varying composition—like a candle which has been successively dipped in waxes of different colors. The outer layers are most heavily alloyed. The structure, called coring, is evidence of microsegregation.

As solidification proceeds the dendrites grow until they impinge upon each other, and impurities, low-melting constituents, and microporosity can occur at the interstices between the interlocking dendrites. The properties of cast structures depend on the proper control of these chemical and structural heterogeneities that occur in dendritic solidification.

Solidification Contraction Most metals and alloys, including stainless steel alloys, contract on solidifying; the volume change results from the liquid-solid contraction which is about 3 to 6% for alloys. To counteract this contraction or *shrinkage*, appendages are added to the castings. The appendages are termed *risers*. The behavior of a simple riser-casting system is shown in Fig. 3 where a cube casting and its cylindrical riser are totally enclosed in sand. Solidification occurs simultaneously in both casting and riser, and liquid flows from the riser into the casting; i.e., the riser "feeds" the casting. A riser of optimum size is one which freezes just after the casting has frozen and in which the shrinkage pipe does not extend into the casting. The proper riser size can be calculated by foundry engineers.

Risers also serve as reservoirs of heat which are necessary to establish the thermal gradients in a casting. Risers should be located to promote *directional solidification*, i.e.,

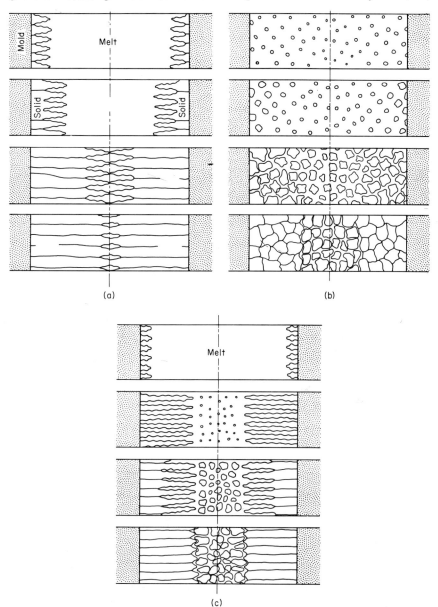

(a)

(b)

(c)

Fig. 1 Modes of solidification of alloys poured in sand molds. (*a*) Stages during solidification of alloys with narrow freezing ranges. (*b*) Stages during solidification of alloys with wide freezing ranges. (*c*) Stages of solidification of alloys which freeze in an intermediate manner. (*Redrawn with permission of the American Foundrymen's Society.*)

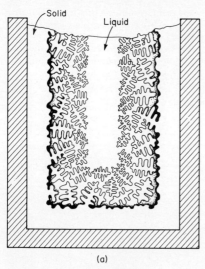 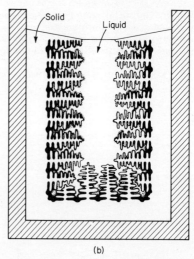

Fig. 2 Formation of dendrites in (a) equiaxial grains and (b) columnar grains. The dendrites depicted here are greatly exaggerated in size.[1]

solidification from a chilled small section by a gradually tapered wall to a larger section which is risered (Fig. 4).

Properly designed risers compensate for solidification shrinkage, but after the casting solidifies, there is additional shrinkage in linear dimensions of about 1 to 2% during cooling to room temperature. Compensation for this solid contraction is furnished by oversizing the pattern with the so-called patternmaker's shrink rule.

Shrinkage problems which occur in making castings can be avoided only by good design and skillful foundry practice. The major problems are hot tears, centerline shrinkage, and dispersed microporosity.

Hot tears and excessive residual stress occur when sections of a casting are restrained from shrinking by either massive cores or molds rammed to high hardness. Such problems are overcome by designing with gradual changes in cross section and by making the molds and cores more collapsible. Generous use of fillets and large radii at joints also help to reduce casting stresses.

Heavy sections can be made to cool faster by adding chills or reducing the mass by coring. Hot tears are particularly troublesome in steel castings if good casting design procedures are ignored. In Fig. 5 some simple classical situations are depicted. Later in this chapter more detail related to casting design is presented.

Centerline shrinkage can occur in alloys such as stainless steel. In long shapes of uniform thickness, there is too little feed metal to fill the entire center of the casting at the end of solidification. Thus a series of voids form at the thermal center of the casting which appear on x-ray negatives of the casting. However, they usually have little or no effect on mechanical properties since they are well removed from casting surface. Fatigue tests of steel castings have demonstrated that centerline shrinkage has no effect on the failure of steel castings subjected to fatigue loading.

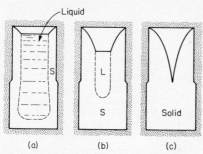

Fig. 3 Solidification of a top risered cube. (a) Near beginning of solidification. (b) During solidification. (c) After solidification.[1]

Stainless steel castings are subject to dispersed microporosity. This defect is microscopic and occurs at the interstices between interlocking dendrite arms and if uncontrolled it does lead to a marked decrease in mechanical properties. The defect can be minimized by promoting directional solidification through steep thermal gradients which decrease the width of the mushy zone. Associated with steep thermal gradients are more rapid cooling rates which tend to decrease as-cast grain size and always decrease the spacing between dendrite branches in the microstructure. Grain size may also be reduced by supplying sufficient grain refiners in some stainless steel alloys. By whatever means grain size and the dendrite branch spacing within the grain are reduced, mechanical

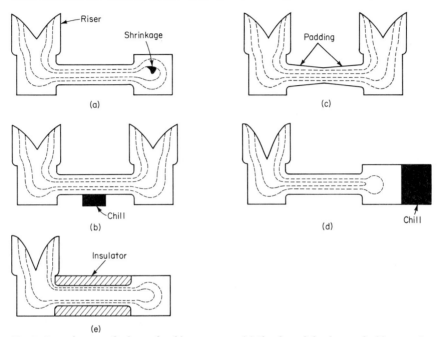

Fig. 4   Several ways to feed an isolated heavy section. (*a*) Shrinkage defect has resulted because the thin section between the riser and heavy section froze first. (*b*) to (*e*) Show ways of providing for *directional solidification* toward the risers.[2]

properties increase. Dendrite arm spacing has been found to be mainly a function of the cooling rate and is independent of grain size itself. At high chilling rates dendrite arm spacing is reduced by an order of magnitude. Since the time to homogenize a cast structure depends on the square of the dendrite arm spacing, homogenizing heat-treatment cycle time can be reduced by two orders of magnitude.

The fluidity of all cast alloys is closely related to superheat, i.e., the difference between the pouring temperature and the liquidus of the alloy. Fluidity is important because it is an index of the filling of detail in thin sections. Where too thin or too extensive a section is designed, a casting is prone to cold shuts during pouring; this defect can be eliminated by increasing the superheat. However, the metal caster is limited to the amount of superheat because metallurgical problems (such as excessive oxidation of alloy elements, gas absorption, and metal-mold reactions) can introduce a whole new set of defects if the metal is poured at too high a temperature. Good foundry practice requires the lowest possible pouring temperature consistent with an acceptable casting.

The product designer should work closely with foundry personnel to ensure that defect-free castings can be made and that faulty castings are not produced because of their inherent design.

Casting Processes   Stainless steel castings can be manufactured in several ways. Today, the major processes are sand casting, shell-mold casting, investment casting, and ceramic-mold casting. In all of these processes, the molds are destroyed after each casting cycle. The molds are designed with a gating system to channel molten alloy into the mold cavity. These channels are called sprues, runners, and gates in sand castings (Fig. 6). Molds may be modified by cores which form holes and undercuts.

After casting liquid metal, the resulting castings require subsequent operations such as trimming, inspection, grinding, and welding repair (if necessary) prior to shipping. A comparison of the major features of different casting processes used for stainless steel

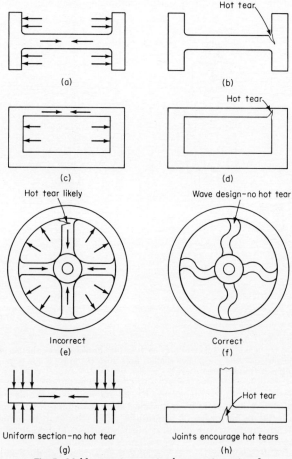

Fig. 5 Mold constraints causing hot tears in castings.[3]

alloy is given in Table 1. The table indicates casting processes which utilize metal molds: permanent-mold casting and die casting. Actually, not until very recently have any steels been cast in significant quantity using these processes because the thermal shock to the metal components of the machinery used, including the die molds, is so severe that the life of the components is short. Because of the inherent high production rate capabilities of die casting, research into the die casting of stainless steels has been so vigorous that, today, that manufacturing option is available.

CASTING PROCESSES

Sand Casting   Silica sand is used more than any other molding material for making stainless steel castings. It is relatively cheap and is refractory enough even for stainless steel casting processes.

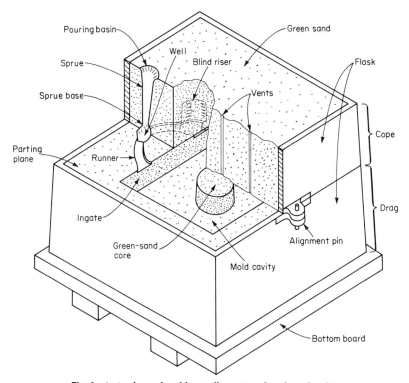

Fig. 6 A simple sand mold partially sectioned to show detail.[2]

Sand molds are made by ramming sand around a pattern in a flask (Fig. 7). The sand is either shoveled by the molder, thrown by a sand slinger, or dropped in from an overhead chute. The molding sand is compacted by jolting several times and squeezing or by jolting alone for larger deep flasks. The pattern is withdrawn, cores are added, and the mold is reassembled and sent on to the pouring station. Patterns are reusable, but the sand molds are broken from the castings after they have cooled sufficiently. The sand is recycled by mulling with some new clay and water to reactivate the old clay. In ferrous casting, the sand is typically bonded with 6 to 8% western bentonite mulled with 2 to 3% water.

In high-pressure molding the compaction pressure exceeds 100 psi (6.9 kN/m²) at the parting plane, which is about 50% more than the pressure used during the 1960s. The greater compaction pressures yield harder, more uniform molds resulting in much less mold wall movement and closer dimensional control of the castings.

Sand molds are made in many sizes and molding can be mechanized in all but the largest sizes. Thus sand molds are produced with hand tools (bench molding) or by jolt-squeeze molding machines, automatic molding, flaskless molding, high-pressure mold-

TABLE 1 Typical Features of Processes for Stainless Steel Castings

Casting process	Maximum size		Minimum thickness		Production rate, parts per hour	Surface finish, μin.	Relative pattern or die cost
	lb	kg	in.	cm			
Sand casting	2×10^5	9×10^4	3/16	0.5	1–15	300–600	1
Shell-mold casting	200	100	3/32	0.2	40–60	100–200	5
Investment casting	100	50	1/32	0.1	40–60	20–125	4
Ceramic-mold casting	1500	700	1/32	0.1	1–15	20–125	3
Permanent-mold casting	300	140	3/16	0.5	40–60	150–500	7
Die casting	100	50	1/16	0.2	100–200	20–125	17

ing, floor molding, and pit molding. Whatever molding method is used, the sand molds must be strong enough to withstand the metallostatic pressure of the molten metal, must resist erosion by the flowing metal during pouring, must be permeable to mold gases, must be refractory, and must strip easily from the casting after cooling.

Sand-clay molding mixtures are used in the green (moistened) or dried conditions. *Green sand molds* are those into which the metal is poured soon after molding, before appreciable drying has occurred. Green sand molds are used more than dry sand molds

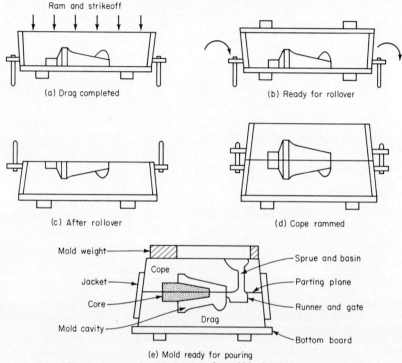

Fig. 7   Steps in the construction of a mold by hand ramming.[2]

because no time is lost or expense incurred in driving off the water, since the mold is used as is. For most work, this practice is satisfactory. Moisture can be controlled enough to prevent excessive steaming at the mold-metal interface, and permeability can be kept high enough to prevent blows caused by release of steam and other gases.

In *dry sand molds*, free moisture is completely removed by heating in an oven. Generally, a harder, stronger mold results from drying, and less mold gases are generated during pouring. Thus dry sand molds produce castings with dimensions more accurate than those achieved with green sand molds, and they are less susceptible to breakage and gas blows than green sand molds. Some of the advantages of dry sand molds are obtained in skin-dried and air-dried molds. In skin-dried molds, only the surface moisture is evaporated by torch or warm air applied briefly to the mold cavity. Air-dried molds are molds that are allowed to stand and surface-dry in air for a considerable time before pouring.

Cores are used to obtain internal configurations in castings. A core inserted in a mold can be seen in Fig. 7. Figure 8 illustrates the steps involved in making a simple core. Cores must burn out and collapse to permit the cast metal to contract freely during solidification and cooling.

Cores are usually made of silica sand bonded with an organic agent such as linseed oil. Cereals are sometimes added to make the mixture stronger. The basic advantage of organic binders for cores (as compared to clays) is that they lose their strength under the heat of the metal (have collapsibility) and can easily be removed from the casting at shakeout.

Cores are made by ramming or blowing the sand into coreboxes. If cores are made in parts, these are pasted together after baking and are rebaked briefly to dry and set the paste. Baking is done in ovens, preferably with circulating air, at about 450°F (230°C). A properly baked core does not produce harmful gases, has adequate strength, and collapses at the right time after metal is poured around it.

Resins are used more and more to replace linseed oil as core binders. Urea formalde-

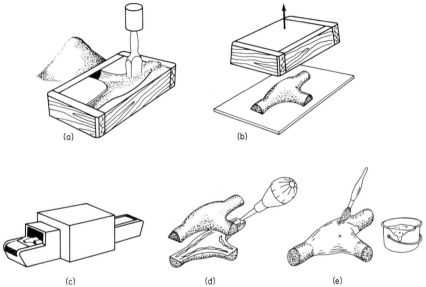

Fig. 8 Making a simple core. (a) Ramming core sand. (b) Drawing the corebox. (c) Baking the core half (in a dielectric oven). (d) Pasting the core halves. (e) "Washing" the core with refractory slurry to improve casting surface finish.[3]

hyde and phenol formaldehyde are the two most widely used. Phenol formaldehyde is more suitable for stainless steel castings than is urea formaldehyde because the latter breaks down at very low temperatures. Urea formaldehyde resin is only suitable in thin-section stainless steel castings. Formaldehydes have the advantage that they can be cured rapidly in dielectric ovens.

Another method of making cores is commonly termed the CO_2 process. In this process, sodium silicate is used as the binder along with organic additions to improve collapsibility. After the core sand is rammed or blown into the corebox, CO_2 gas is passed into the core through a series of vents. The sand immediately becomes strongly bonded as the sodium silicate becomes a stiff gel:

$$Na_2O \cdot xSiO_2 + nH_2O + CO_2 \rightarrow Na_2CO_3 + xSiO_2 \cdot n(H_2O)$$

where $1.6 < x < 4$.

Silicone parting agents are sprayed on the patterns and coreboxes prior to filling them with sand because the cured molds and cores are rather rigid.

Molding with CO_2 sand is more expensive than molding with clay-bonded sand because the binder is more costly. Process costs also tend to rise with CO_2 sand because the shakeout is made more difficult. Even so there are a number of advantages to the process. A few of these are listed below.[2]

1. Conventional equipment for molding and sand mixing is used and the use of baking ovens and core driers can be eliminated.

2. Molds and cores can be used immediately after they are made.

3. Since the cores are not handled in the green condition, there is no need for internal supports in cores.

4. Some improved dimensional accuracy relative to conventional resin-bonded sands is possible because of greater fidelity of pattern or corebox detail in the cured mold.

Sands may also be bonded with air-setting binders or no-bake binders that cure at low temperatures within a reasonable length of time. A number of such binders are available and are known as hot-box or cold-box binders.[2] Organic resins, usually consisting of blends of formaldehyde, urea, and furfural alcohol, cross-link into rigid polymers in the presence of a catalyst such as phosphoric acid. Without the catalyst, the furfural alcohol causes cross-linking slowly over a period of time, whereas in the presence of a catalyst, the cross-linking reaction rate is greatly increased. In such systems, therefore, it is possible to control the cure cycle depending on the composition of the blends selected. In ferrous casting processes the urea component of the mix must be carefully controlled or even eliminated in cores and molds because it promotes pinhole porosity.

A typical core sand mix contains 2% resin and 0.6 to 0.8% catalyst. The setting time is a function of the amount of catalyst, the temperature of the mulled sand, and the mulling time. Since the curing cycle begins as soon as the materials are combined in the muller, the bench life is short.

In the hot-box process the mix must have good flowability. A weak catalyst is used and the mix is blown into the corebox. In the corebox itself, the reaction rate is increased because temperatures of 200 to 260°C are achieved as an exothermic curing action occurs; the core is cured in 30 s. A drawback of the process is that the core must cure before the corebox can be used again.

The cold-box process uses a two-component liquid organic binder. One component is a phenolic resin in solvent form and the second component is a polyisocyanate in solution. In the presence of an airborne catalyst, triethylamine, the phenolic resin combines with the isocyanate group to form a stiff urethane resin. The two binder components are usually used in a 1:1 ratio and, after mixing, about 1 to 2% is added to the sand. The curing time is only 10 to 20 s so it is a simple high-production core-making process. Once the triethylamine has been used, it must be catalytically decomposed and vented to comply with OSHA regulations. In the cured state, the nitrogen content is only 3% of the binder rather than 10% as is found in the hot-box process. Thus, cold-box cores are used in ferrous castings in order to minimize pinhole porosity.

Some large castings are made entirely of cores: individual core sections are fitted together in a pit and rammed in position with backup molding sand or securely clamped. This method is chosen when the design is such that the patterns cannot be drawn from the type of molds usually employed. Core sand is also rammed or blown into flasks and used instead of green molding sand; the mold is then baked like a core. This method is chosen when (1) a casting of extremely accurate dimensions is required, or (2) many cores must be carefully set. Also, core sand molds are sometimes used to improve casting surface finish or to permit the casting of thin sections.

Sand technology in a successful stainless steel foundry is not taken lightly. Accordingly, there are a number of tests available to measure and to control the following properties:[3]

1. Permeability, the capacity of a sand to vent gases away from the mold cavity

2. Hardness, the resistance of the mold surface to deformation by a standard indentor

3. Moisture content

4. Shear and compressive strength, measured on cores or green and dry specimens of molding sand by standard apparatus on standard specimens

5. Hot strength, measured by compression of a standard test piece in a furnace capable of reaching 1650°C

6. Collapsibility, indicated by failure of the specimen at high temperature under load

7. Expansion and contraction characteristics, checked by special attachments to the same furnace

8. Grain size, shape, and distribution, determined by the usual methods for particle classification or petrographic analysis

The relatively low cost and adequate refractoriness (for most purposes) of silica sand has made it the most widely used molding medium in the foundry industry. Other refractories, however, can be mulled with suitable binders and molded in the same manner as silica sand. Some selected refractory materials are listed in Table 2. Many of these materials are used for special purposes, i.e., mold inserts, in the sand-casting process.

In steel foundries, zircon sand ($ZrO_2 \cdot SiO_2$) is used in strategic mold locations to extract heat from a casting somewhat more rapidly than silica sand. Additional advantages of zircon sand as compared to silica are: (1) it possesses a lower coefficient of expansion and undergoes no phase transformation upon heating and so is less liable to produce expansion defects, and (2) its high fusion point prevents metal penetration due to mold-metal reactions at heavy metal sections. *Olivine sand* [$(Mg,Fe)_2SiO_4$] is used for much the same reasons, especially in Europe. *Chamotte* (calcined fire clay) is also occasionally used as a facing material to prevent expansion and penetration defects in ferrous castings. Large castings made in chamotte do not show scabs and sand spots as do ordinary sand castings. Chamotte has a better resistance to erosion by molten steel than silica sand, and it is used for runner blocks and cores as well as molds. Many metal alloys are also cast in plaster molds; however, ferrous alloys cannot be cast into plaster molds because the high pouring temperature destroys the plaster and the sulfur from the gypsum reacts with ferrous metals to give very poor casting surfaces.

TABLE 2   Properties of Selected Refractory Materials

Refractory	Melting point		Linear coefficient of expansion, 30–800°C (80–1470°F), $\times 10^6/°C$
	°F	°C	
Silica (SiO_2)	3115	1710	16.2
Alumina (Al_2O_3)	3670	2020	8.0
Beryllia (BeO)	4660	2570	7.5
Magnesia (MgO)	5070	2800	13.5
Thoria (ThO_2)	5530	3050	9.5
Zirconia (ZrO_2)	4890	2700	6.5
Zircon ($ZrO_2 \cdot SiO_2$)	4800	2650	4.5
Spinel ($Al_2O_3 \cdot MgO$)	3870	2130	8.5
Mullite ($3Al_2O_3 \cdot 2SiO_2$)	3290	1810	5.5
Sillimanite ($Al_2O_3 \cdot SiO_2$)	3290	1810	

Coatings (or washes) are sometimes used on molds and cores to obtain better finish on the castings, including smoother surfaces and less metal penetration. The coatings are refractory, composed of silica flour, zircon flour, or chromite flour. Zircon flour is preferred for most steel foundry applications. The refractory material is a fine powder, and it is mixed with either water or alcohol along with a small amount of bentonite. The coating may be applied by brushing or spraying. The surface is dried with a gas torch or hot air before the mold is closed. Multiple coats of wash are often applied to molds with heavy wall sections to protect the molds from penetration which arises from the diffusion of the metallic vapors through the permeable mold and their subsequent condensation in subsurface mold pores.

Design for Sand Casting. Design factors for corrosion-resistant steel castings and heat-resistant castings do not differ appreciably from those of other castings. For the majority of applications, these alloys are sand-cast using patterns such as those depicted in Fig. 9.

Pattern design is very important to the success of castings. Loose wood or metal patterns should be considered only for large castings or when a few small or experimental parts are being made. Mounted patterns, match-plate patterns, or separate cope and drag patterns are usually used in order to produce dimensionally accurate castings of high quality.

Loose patterns are essentially single copies of the casting to be produced (Fig. 9*b*). A skilled molder is required to gate them properly. Cope and drag patterns are made so that they are split into cope and drag sections of the mold (Fig. 9*a*). These patterns are used for large castings.

Match-plate patterns (Fig. 9*c*) are mounted on plates with the cope patterns on one side and the drag on the opposite side; the risers and the gating system are also attached. Match-plate patterns are used for quantity production in mechanized molding operations. In many production situations, however, it is more economical to produce the cope and drag of the mold with two separate patterns and machines.

In sand casting, minimum section thickness is $3/16$ in. (0.5 cm) or greater, if possible. Somewhat lighter sections are feasible for most of the alloys depending on pattern equipment, casting design, and molding medium selected, but some difficulty is experi-

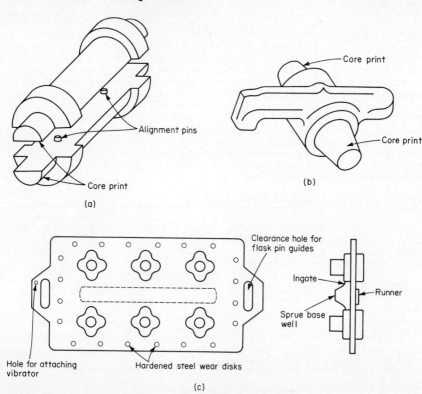

Fig. 9 Pattern equipment for sand molds. (*a*) Cope and drag pattern.[2] (*b*) Single or loose pattern. (*c*) Match-plate pattern.[2]

enced in running thin sections in the straight chromium alloys. Where intricate designs are involved, the greater fluidity of the austenitic Cr-Ni grades is advantageous. On surfaces to be machined, finish allowances of ⅛ in. (0.3 cm) or more are used in the standard casting design, but by using special core inserts and/or washes, it is possible to reduce the allowance.

Dimensional tolerances depend on pattern equipment, design configuration, and casting size. In most situations, overall dimensions and location of cored holes are held to within 1/16 in./ft (0.5 cm/m). Shrinkage is compensated for as noted in Table 3; the figures apply only to unhindered contraction. Because shrinkage varies with the mold resistance to free contraction of the casting, a single shrinkage allowance for a given casting design is necessarily a compromise. When extremely good dimensional accuracy is desired, several different shrinkage allowances are used on a single pattern. Furthermore, an entirely different pattern may be needed to produce the same casting design if different molding methods are employed.

TABLE 3   Patternmakers' Shrinkage for Cast Corrosion-Resistant Alloys*

ACI Type	Shrinkage allowance	
	in./ft	cm/m
CC-50	7/32	1.8
CA-15, CA-40, CB-30	¼	2.1
CE-30, CF-8, CF-8M, CF-12M, CF-16F	5/16	2.6
CH-20, CK-20, CN-7M, CF-8C, CF-20	11/32	2.9

*These values are for unhindered contraction; considerable variation does occur depending on casting shape.

The minimum size of a cast cored hole depends on the accuracy of the hole location and tolerance required. In sand casting, the minimum core diameter is usually not less than one-half the casting thickness or ¼ in. (0.6 cm), whichever is greater. If a cored hole must be located within a tight tolerance with respect to reference surfaces, it is usually better to drill the hole than to core it.

Once a sand mold has been rammed over a pattern, the pattern must be drawn from the mold cavity. The drawing is assisted by rapping or vibrating the pattern, but it is also necessary to taper all surfaces normal to the parting line. This taper is called draft; it usually varies between 1 and 1½°.

Because of high pouring temperatures, stainless steel castings are susceptible to cracking or tearing in the mold. These defects can be caused by the mold resistance to casting, shrinkage, or by influences attributed to design. The obvious correction for mold resistance is to increase the collapsibility of the sand. The metal caster can control the sand by adjusting its composition, but in many situations the defect cannot be eliminated in this way because the design of the casting is faulty. By altering design and avoiding thin sections which freeze prematurely and resist contraction of heavier sections, casting stresses often can be reduced. Uniform sections of castings do not tear, but junctions are constant sources of trouble.

The temperature gradients in solidifying castings must be controlled if sound castings are to be made. Designers should recognize that heavy sections cannot be fed through light sections. For example, consider the T section of Fig. 10. By inscribing circles, we see that the region *d* is a larger mass of metal than regions *a*, *b*, or *c*. Therefore, the metal at the center of the *d* region is a hot spot, i.e., it is the last to solidify. Usually it is not economical to attach a riser to the junction, so it is necessary to rely on feeding through the arms from a riser placed some distance away. But if the arms freeze first, as in this example, shrinkage develops in the junction. Since hot spots freeze last, they are weak, and the metal may also tear where they exist. Therefore, tearing defects are usually associated with shrinkage in junctions.

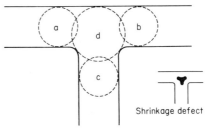

Fig. 10 Method for the determination of hot-spot location by inscribing circles.

It is obvious that the designer should minimize the size of hot spots. Figure 11 illustrates how this can be accomplished by making one joining member as thin as load stresses will allow. X junctions are particularly difficult to cast; improved casting design can be made by the offset method (Fig. 12). In the grid casting of Fig. 13, the designer should replace the X junctions with Y junctions. Good design practice for L junctions is shown in Fig. 14. Notice that in all junctions, sharp internal corners should be avoided. By replacing the sharp corners with fillets, casting quality is improved in several ways:

1. Sharp corners of molding sand, which can be eroded rather easily during pouring, are avoided.

2. Fillets increase the mold surface area exposed to the junctions thereby decreasing junction freezing time.

3. From a purely mechanical design standpoint, fillets reduce stress concentrations significantly (Fig. 15).

If possible, sections should taper toward risers for controlled directional solidification. Since it is the responsibility of the foundry engineer to locate and design the risers, consultation between the designer and the foundry engineer before final design can avoid many headaches for both. For example, it is sometimes stated that uniform sections make the best design. That concept should be questioned when designing castings. Consider the valve body in Fig. 16*a*; this design does not take into account the fact that directional solidification is very beneficial to the final casting. Figure 16*b* is a much better design because the section can easily be fed with proper riser location and sections are joined with generous radii.

Shell-Mold Casting Shell molding is a form of sand casting which is particularly adaptable to mechanization and high production rates. The process also produces stainless steel castings with a better surface finish and closer dimensional tolerances

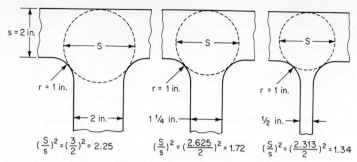

Fig. 11   Increased mass for T-junction designs.[4]

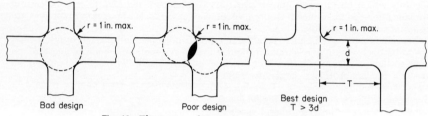

Fig. 12   Elimination of X junction by offset method.[4]

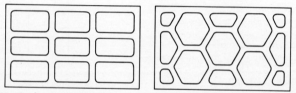

Fig. 13   Replacement of (*a*) X junctions with (*b*) Y junctions in a grid-casting.[4]

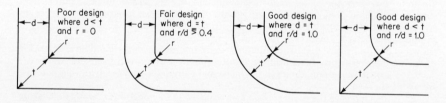

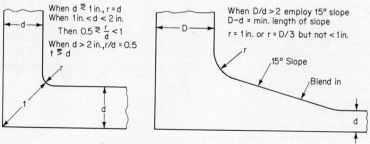

Fig. 14   Design rules for L junctions.[4]

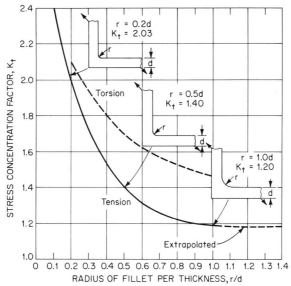

Fig. 15 Stress concentration factors for L junctions.[4]

than can be achieved by the usual sand molds and cores. In the process, which is illustrated in Fig. 17, a phenolic resin is mixed with sand for casting stainless steel. A typical sand is 63% silica sand, 30% zircon, 2% silica flour, and 5% phenolic resin. The pattern is made of metal, preferably cast iron. With a well-made pattern, parts can be made to close tolerances.

The resin and sand mixture is deposited by blowing or dumping onto a pattern heated to 200 to 260°C. The excess sand mixture is shaken off for reuse, and the shell or crust (0.3 to 0.6 cm thick) is removed from the pattern after curing is complete. Halves are matched and located by integral bosses and matching recesses and glued or clamped together to form a mold. Finally, the molds are placed in a metal can and surrounded by backup material to support them during pouring.

Fully automatic shell-molding machines can shell halves of resin-bonded sand every 30 s. This equipment is coupled with a shell-closing machine which joins the two halves of the mold. Close tolerance between the mold halves is maintained, thus minimizing objectional fins in the finished casting.

After the shell-closing operation, the molds are stored until needed. The mold shown in Fig. 17 has a vertical parting line, but many molds have a horizontal parting line if the casting is small.

When the metal is poured, the smooth shell promotes easy flow and the metal is not held back by gas pressure; the porous mold permits gases to escape easily. Since the sand cannot be reused, without pneumatic or thermal reclamation, shell molding is relatively expensive. In view of the cost of pattern and curing equipment, the principal disadvantage of the shell-molding process is that the process is not economical for small quantities.

The shell-molding process has the following advantages over typical green sand molding:[2]

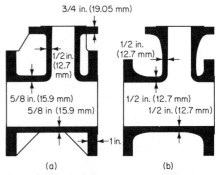

Fig. 16 Valve body designs. (*a*) Design with uniform section thicknesses. (*b*) Preferred casting design for directional solidification. (*Courtesy Steel Founders' Society of America.*)

1. Productivity can exceed that of conventional sand-casting practice.
2. Thin sections (down to 0.025 cm) can be cast.
3. Machining of the castings is reduced, and in some cases, eliminated.
4. Cleaning is considerably reduced; shot blasting is frequently eliminated.
5. Saving of metal through the use of smaller gates, sprues, and risers in the casting process results in a higher yield from the metal.

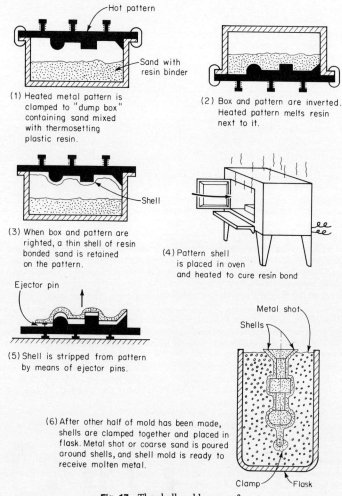

(1) Heated metal pattern is clamped to "dump box" containing sand mixed with thermosetting plastic resin.

(2) Box and pattern are inverted. Heated pattern melts resin next to it.

(3) When box and pattern are righted, a thin shell of resin bonded sand is retained on the pattern.

(4) Pattern shell is placed in oven and heated to cure resin bond

(5) Shell is stripped from pattern by means of ejector pins.

(6) After other half of mold has been made, shells are clamped together and placed in flask. Metal shot or coarse sand is poured around shells, and shell mold is ready to receive molten metal.

Fig. 17 The shell-mold process.[3]

6. Savings in workspace, material handling, and storage are also realized through the use of 90% less molding materials.
7. The cured resins are not hygroscopic, thus permitting prolonged storage of the molds.
8. Closer dimensional tolerances can be obtained (0.2 cm/m) in one-half of a mold and 0.025 cm across the parting line.
9. Better surface finishes are realized (100 μin.).
10. Shell molding is particularly useful for small steel castings (up to 110 lb, or 50 kg).

11. Shell core production is particularly attractive because it reduces core weight and eliminates core ovens.

Castings produced in shell molds often require cores; accordingly, shell cores are often utilized. In fact, shell cores are sometimes used in regular sand molds.

The best dimensional control in sand cores can be obtained with the shell process. Base tolerance for the shell-cored openings in steel castings is ±0.8 cm/m compared to ±2 cm/m for CO_2 cores and ±3 cm/m for baked cores. However, stainless steel castings produced with shell cores will pick up carbon from the resin, resulting in a carburized surface. Shell cores should be avoided in their production unless the cored surface is to be removed by machining or unless precautions, such as coating the cores, are taken in the foundry.

Shell cores do have the advantage of better collapsibility than cores made with other binders. When steel solidifies around a shell core, the core offers little resistance to solidification contraction, and thus prevents the tearing of the solidifying metal. It is for this reason that shell cores are employed in certain thin-wall castings where core restriction is a problem.

The fluidity of liquid steel is enhanced by shell cores. Casting sections as thin as 0.4 cm are easily made against shell cores; against other types of cores, the usual minimum casting section is 0.6 cm.

Investment Casting Investment casting, precision casting, and lost-wax processes are all essentially the same. Investment casting is of particular interest because this process offers greater freedom of design than any other metal-forming operation. Accurate and intricate castings can be made from several alloys, including stainless steels. Parts can be cast to such close tolerance that little or no machining is required. The process is similar to sand casting in that after solidification the mold is broken from the casting. Investment casting is unlike other casting processes in that the pattern, as well as the mold, is expendable.

Dies for the wax patterns can be made of steel, aluminum, soft metals or even rubber, depending on the required tolerances and die-life expectancy.

Investment castings are made by either the *full-mold* process or the *ceramic-shell process*. In the full-mold process (Fig. 18) the expendable pattern unit is coated with a fine colloidal silica wash and dusted with a refractory sand. A slurry is then poured around it and allowed to set. Since there is no parting line, close tolerances can be maintained in all directions. The flask with its contents is vibrated to pack the slurry around the pattern without air bubbles and separate the solid material from the water, which is withdrawn from the top. The flask is then placed upside down in a furnace; the wax pattern melts and runs out, leaving the mold ready for final baking at higher temperatures. After it is baked at the higher temperature, it is ready for pouring while the mold is still hot. Castings are usually poured by gravity with parts arranged in a vertical fashion. Centrifugal, vacuum, or air pressure is also sometimes used to pour metal into the hot mold. After casting, the mold is allowed to cool and then it is broken and the casting removed.

Ceramic-shell casting has proven to be a boon to investment casters because the molds cost considerably less than the molds used in the full-mold process. As in the investment process, patterns are wax-welded to a central sprue (Fig. 19). The assembly is carefully cleaned in a suitable solvent, dipped in a colloidal ethyl silicate gel, and drained for several minutes. When draining stops, it is stuccoed by inserting into a fluidized bed of a fine-grained fused silica. The process of dipping, draining, and stuccoing is repeated. On the third and subsequent stuccoing operations a coarser grade of fused silica is used, usually five coats are sufficient. Over 85% of all precision casting is carried out in ceramic-shell molds.

Wax patterns usually are preferred to plastic patterns because of relative cheapness and because it is easier to construct a tree. Since wax is dimensionally sensitive to temperature, an air-conditioned room is usually provided. Allowances for dimensional control in the investment-casting process must account not only for the changes of the dimensions of the casting itself, but also the wax pattern and the mold. As a liquid, the wax is injected into a die and is subjected to solidification and cooling shrinkage. The ceramic mold changes dimensions because it is heated to high temperatures. The cast metal contracts upon solidification and subsequent cooling. Compensation for all of these dimensional changes must be made in the die from which the wax patterns are made.

The refractories frequently used in investment casting mixes are fine silica sand and silica flour. Other refractories sometimes are used because of higher melting points or improved thermal stability. These include zircon, alumina, and magnesia. Binders include ethyl silicate and magnesium phosphate. Full strength is developed in these binders by firing the molds at relatively high temperatures (980 to 1100°C) after the molds have been dewaxed.

The designer has almost unlimited freedom in design geometry. Investment-casting

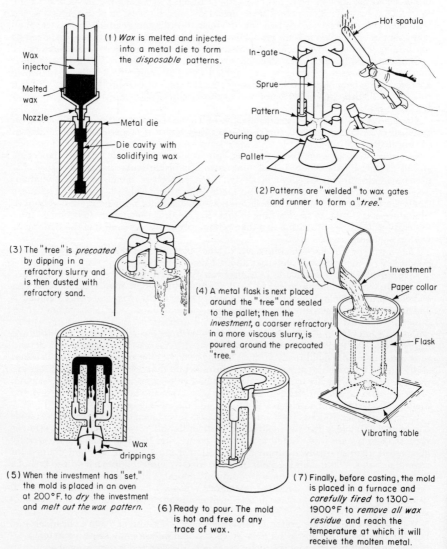

Fig. 18 Preparing a mold for investment casting made by the full-mold process.[2]

plants usually maintain their own toolrooms for in-house manufacture of dies for making the patterns. Complex internal configurations can be produced because the investment-casting engineer can incorporate water-soluble wax cores into the wax pattern. These cores are dissolved from the pattern prior to forming the refractory mold. The castings can be cleaned in a bath of a proprietary salt to remove the refractory mold from cored cavities after casting the stainless steel.

The chief characteristics of investment castings are:

1. Production of castings with good and reproducible dimensional control and excellent surface finish

2. Accommodation of complex geometry avoiding costly joining operations or machining except where machined surfaces are necessary

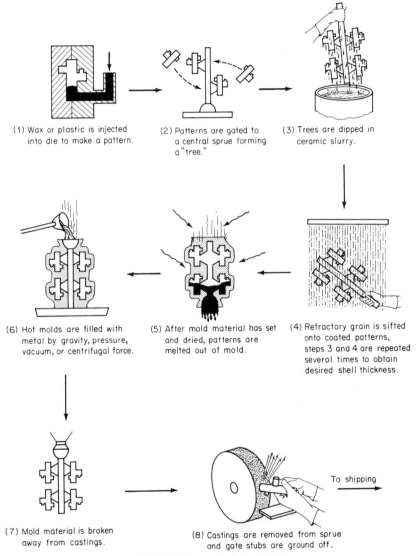

(1) Wax or plastic is injected into die to make a pattern.

(2) Patterns are gated to a central sprue forming a "tree."

(3) Trees are dipped in ceramic slurry.

(6) Hot molds are filled with metal by gravity, pressure, vacuum, or centrifugal force.

(5) After mold material has set and dried, patterns are melted out of mold.

(4) Refractory grain is sifted onto coated patterns, steps 3 and 4 are repeated several times to obtain desired shell thickness.

To shipping

(7) Mold material is broken away from castings.

(8) Castings are removed from sprue and gate stubs are ground off.

Fig. 19   The ceramic-shell process.[2]

3. No parting line as found on castings made by cope and drag methods

4. Higher cost than sand castings

Usually designers of castings think in terms of either the sand-casting process or the ceramic-mold process for castings weighing in excess of 10 lb (4.54 kg). Smaller intricate shapes are identified with investment castings. However, this picture is changing; many 50- to 100-lb (22.7- to 45.4-kg) investment castings have been made. Indeed, some steel castings weighing as much as 500 lb (227 kg) have been made. Thus, even if a component is rather large, the designer should not eliminate the possibility of using the investment-casting process for this reason alone.

Ceramic-Mold Casting   The basic materials used for producing full-mold investment castings are also used to make cope and drag molds. For the cope and drag reusable metal patterns, rather than wax, are used. Cope-and-drag ceramic molds are used in preference to wax-pattern investment casting when castings are too large to be produced by the latter process and when the parting line is not deleterious to the performance or appearance of the casting. The major disadvantage of the parting line is that dimensions across a parting line cannot be controlled as well as dimensions which do not extend across a parting line. Ceramic-mold castings are used, rather than sand castings, when better surface finish or dimensional control is required than can be achieved with sand castings.

The ceramic-mold process, which is also known as cope-and-drag investment casting, has two proprietary variations: Shaw process and Unicast process. Ceramic-mold casting employs mold materials that are refractory, requiring high preheat, and that are suitable for most castable alloys, particularly ferrous alloys. The refractory slurry consists of fine-grained zircon and calcined high-alumina mullites or, in some cases, fused silica. In making a mold, the thick slurry is poured over the metal pattern which is usually mounted on a match-plate (Fig. 20). Before setting completely, the slurry gels. The mold is stripped from the pattern when the gel is firm enough to prevent breakage when drawing from the pattern. The basic difference between the Shaw and the Unicast processes is that in the Shaw process stabilization results from the burn-off of an alcohol binder, whereas in the Unicast process, the mold is stabilized by immersion in a liquid bath or a gaseous atmosphere which cures the gelled slurry. Before pouring, the molds are usually preheated in a furnace to reduce the temperature difference between the mold and the molten metal and to maximize the permeability available through the microcrazed mold structure.

Ceramic molding is suitable for parts weighing as much as 3000 kg (6600 lb) or more. Even on such large castings the process yields castings with excellent accuracy and reproducibility, but as mentioned above, it is impractical to expect the dimensional tolerance across the parting line to be as low as the tolerance within one-half of the mold. The process is more expensive than sand casting because the mold materials are expensive and are not recycled into the process. Ferrous alloys are the ones most commonly cast; they are made into die-casting dies, large-trim dies, components for food machinery, milling cutters, structural components for aircraft, and hardware for aerospace vehicles and atomic reactors.

An as-cast surface finish of 125 μin. or better can readily be achieved. Dimensional tolerances are ± 0.003 cm/cm for the first inch, with incremental tolerances of ± 0.2 cm/m for larger dimensions. Across the parting line an additional tolerance of ± 0.0025 cm should be provided.

Design for Castings Produced in Other Than Sand Molds   The principles of directional solidification and the factors which lead to hot spots, tears, and shrinkage regions in sand castings also apply to castings manufactured in shell molds, investment molds, and ceramic molds.

The dimensional tolerances discussed in the preceding sections on casting design are summarized in Tables 4 through 9. Table 4 applies to sand castings. The other molding processes have been developed primarily to provide improved dimensional accuracy or better surface finishes not usually obtainable with conventional sand molds. Consequently, the dimensional tolerances applicable to these mediums will differ from those for sand castings.

Shell-mold casting is particularly adapted to the production of large quantities of relatively small, high-quality components. Because of reduced draft, greater dimensional accuracy of pattern, and superior stability, this technique permits closer dimensional tolerances than sand-mold castings. Minimum dimensional tolerance for shell-mold steel castings that are not to be machined are shown in Table 5. Recommended minimum section thicknesses as a function of section length are shown in Table 6.

The investment-casting processes are well suited to the production of fine detail and close dimensional tolerances. Close control of dimensions in the wax or plastic pattern, smooth surface and the rigidity of the ceramic investment or shell mold all contribute to

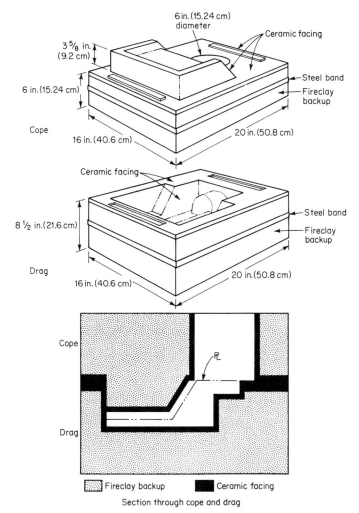

Fig. 20 Cope and drag setup for a ceramic-mold casting. *(Redrawn with permission of American Society for Metals.[5])*

TABLE 4   Suggested Minimum Tolerances for Stainless Steel Castings Produced in Sand Molds

Dimension		Tolerance	
in.	cm	in.	cm
Up to 4	10.2	+0.08, −0.06	+0.20, −0.15
4–8	10.2–20.3	+0.12, −0.06	+0.30, −0.15
8–16	20.3–40.6	+0.19, −0.06	+0.48, −0.15
16–32	40.6–81.3	+0.25, −0.12	+0.64, −0.30
ft	m		
3–8	0.9–2.4	+⅜, −⅜	+0.95, −0.95
8–15	2.4–4.6	+½, −⅜	+1.3, −0.95

TABLE 5   Minimum Dimensional Tolerances for Shell-Mold Steel Castings Not to Be Machined

Dimension	Tolerance	
	in.	cm
Length, in. (cm):		
Less than 4 (10.2)	±0.010	± 0.025
4–8 (10.2–20.3)	±0.015	± 0.038
8–16 (20.3–40.6)	±0.035	± 0.089
16–32 (40.6–91.3)	±0.10	± 0.25
Across the parting line	±0.010	±0.025
Draft	0.002 in./in. min.	
Hole diameter	±0.005 in./in.	
Concentricity	0.002 in./in.	

TABLE 6   Recommended Minimum Section Thickness for Steel Castings Produced in Shell Molds

Length		Minimum section thickness	
in.	cm	in.	cm
Less than 4	10.2	3/16	0.48
4–12	10.2–30.5	1/4	0.64
12–18	30.5–45.7	5/16	0.79
18–48	45.7–122	3/8	0.95
48–80	122–203	1/2	1.27

TABLE 7   Minimum Tolerances for Investment-Mold Steel Castings

Dimension		Minimum tolerance		Dimension		Minimum tolerance	
in.	cm	±in.	±cm	in.	cm	±in.	±cm
Up to 1	2.5	0.005	0.013	6	15.2	0.030	0.076
1½	3.8	0.009	0.023	7	17.8	0.035	0.089
2	5.1	0.010	0.025	8	20.3	0.040	0.10
2½	6.4	0.015	0.038	9	22.9	0.045	0.11
4	10.2	0.020	0.051	10	25.4	0.050	0.13
5	12.7	0.025	0.064				

TABLE 8   Minimum Thickness of Investment Cast Steel Sections

Length		Minimum Thickness	
in.	cm	in.	cm
1/4	0.6	0.03	0.08
1/2	1.2	0.04	0.10
3/4	1.8	0.05	0.13
1–2½	2.5–6.4	0.06	0.15

TABLE 9   Minimum Tolerances of Ceramic-Mold Stainless Steel Castings

Dimension		Tolerance*	
in.	cm	± in.	±cm
Up to 1	2.5	0.003	0.008
1–3	2.5–7.5	0.005	0.013
3–8	7.5–20	0.015	0.038
8–15	20–38	0.030	0.076
Over 15	38	0.045	0.11

*For dimensions across parting line, add ±0.010 to ±0.020 in., (±0.025 to ±0.050 cm).

accuracy. Suggested minimum tolerances for investment castings are shown in Table 7. The minimum thickness that can be produced by the investment-mold process is considerably less than by either sand- or shell-mold castings, primarily because of the higher temperature of the investment mold during pouring. Table 8 shows minimum thickness of sections of investment casting as related to length.

For ceramic-mold castings, the tolerances in dimensional accuracy are given in Table 9. It is usually possible to cast sections in ceramic molds comparable to sections made in investment-casting processes, so Table 8 can be consulted as a guide.

For all processes, and particularly for ceramic-mold casting and investment casting, closer tolerances than presented in Tables 4 through 9 are obtainable by reworking the pattern equipment after test castings have been made. Reproducibility is excellent for investment castings and ceramic-mold castings once the pattern has been established.

The casting designer should carefully consider all specified tolerances. The closer the tolerance, the higher the final cost of the casting. For greater economy, tolerances should only be as close as the application actually requires.

REFERENCES

1. Flemings, M. C.: "Solidification Processing," McGraw-Hill, New York, 1974.
2. Niebel, B. W. and A. B. Draper: "Product Design and Process Engineering," McGraw-Hill, New York, 1974.
3. Taylor, H. F., M. C. Flemings, and J. Wulff: "Foundry Engineering," Wiley, New York, 1959.
4. Steel Casting Design, Engineering Data File No. 1, Steel Founders' Society of America, Rocky River, Ohio.
5. "Metals Handbook," vol. 5, American Society for Metals, Metals Park, Ohio, 1970.

Chapter 32

Die Casting of Stainless Steels

DALLAS T. HURD
President, Ferrodyne Corporation, Cleveland, Ohio

Die casting is the injection of molten metal, usually under pressure, into a closed mold or die in which the metal solidifies into a precise shape. The mold is opened to release the cast part, then closed for another injection of liquid metal to produce another part, and so on. The opening and closing of the molds and the means for the pressure injection of molten metal is commonly provided by a die-casting machine which is designed to be sufficiently large and strong to maintain closure of the die against the pressure exerted by the injection.

Generally automated to a considerable degree, the die-casting process is well established as a major industrial method for producing shaped articles of the light metals, particularly aluminum, zinc, and magnesium. It offers a low-cost, high-volume production route from raw material to finished products. However, the economics of the die-casting process necessarily depend on a relative degree of permanence in the dies themselves, which are expected to resist repeated, severe thermal and mechanical shock for many thousands of casting cycles without deformation or deterioration. With optimum dies and operating conditions, the die-casting process is capable of higher dimensional precision and smoother surfaces than any other hot-forming process for producing metal parts.

For many years, attempts have been made to apply the die-casting process, so highly successful with the low-melting structural metals, to higher-melting metals. Some brass and bronze components are now regularly produced by die casting in spite of die performance limited by the early onset of more or less severe thermal crazing and cracking of the die surfaces. The ability of a die to resist such degradation is, of course, determined in part by the temperature of the metal being cast, and the alloy steels which may operate successfully as dies for many hundreds of thousands of cycles in casting zinc articles may be usable for only a few thousand castings of brass. The economical application of die casting to the ferrous metals, with their considerably higher melting points, was practically impossible until the advent of the refractory metals tungsten and molybdenum in shapes and sizes suitable for fabricating die-casting dies. These metals and their alloys have unusual thermal and mechanical properties which enable them to endure for extended periods the extremely severe conditions of thermal shock imposed by the die casting of iron and steel alloys.

Historically, the refractory metals achieved prominence as the filaments in incandescent electric lamps and electronic tubes. In the 1960s the demands of the aerospace industry for high-temperature materials promoted the development of both tungsten and molybdenum in the form of alloys with improved properties, and as large, massive shapes. At this time, the General Electric Company, long a leader in the technology of the refractory metals, pioneered the application of these metals as dies for the automated casting of irons and steels. By the early 1970s ferrous die casting began to be recognized as a useful production method for shaping stainless and alloy steels, particularly for parts difficult or expensive to fabricate by other methods. Now, for many such applications, ferrous die casting is competitive with forging, investment casting, or machining from mill bar stock.

Advantages of Die Casting Stainless Steels An important economic advantage of ferrous die casting is the ability of the process to utilize low-cost metal scrap as raw material. Scrap generated in the process (such as sprues, runners, etc.) is sufficiently clean to be recycled without further treatment. Further, ferrous die casting may be used to fabricate unusual alloys unobtainable as mill bar stock or forging blank, or to shape alloys difficult or impossible to fabricate by machining. However, die maintenance expense is a much larger factor in the cost of producing steel die castings than it is in the cost of nonferrous die castings. Even at best, the useful performance life of refractory metal dies in the fabrication of steel articles falls short of that experienced in the die casting of aluminum and zinc. On the other side of the economic equation is the substantially greater value of articles fabricated from stainless and high-alloy steels, a value which can support higher die maintenance costs.

It is interesting to note that although the ferrous die-casting process is applicable to a very broad range of alloy compositions ranging from gray iron to tool steels, the stainless steels appear to offer maximum opportunity for exploiting the advantages of the process in the ferrous field. That is, the stainless steel alloys are somewhat easier to shape by die casting than the low-alloy structural steels. Sounder castings with better surfaces are more easily obtained and useful die lives are extended. These effects are believed due to the considerably lower thermal conductivity of the stainless steels compared to the low-alloy structural steels. At the same time, certain benefits in the structure and properties of steel castings are realized as a result of the extremely rapid freezing that occurs in the pressure die casting of ferrous metals in refractory metal dies. The most notable effect with stainless steels is an enhanced resistance to corrosion, since the freezing process in die casting appears to be sufficiently rapid to repress the segregation of interstitial impurities that normally occurs in liquid metal solidification and which has an important bearing on resistance to corrosion. Owing to the unusually fine grain structure which the fast freezing promotes, many ferrous alloys cast as die castings show enhanced response to heat treatment.

Die-Casting Process Stainless steel die castings have been produced from a variety of alloy compositions: AISI 403, 410, 420, 431, and 440 in the martensitic stainless series; AISI 302, 304, 310, and 316 in the austenitic series; and 17-4PH in the precipitation-hardenable series. Casting temperatures generally are in the range of 1500 to 1600°C although at least one stainless steel alloy, IN-856 developed by the International Nickel Company, has been successfully die-cast at temperatures as low as 1250°C, which is not far above the casting temperature of copper-based alloys.

Metal melting is done in coreless electric induction furnaces of up to 200 to 300 kg capacity. Since such melts must be held for extended periods while the die-casting machines are fed with small portions of liquid metal shot-by-shot, it is advisable to provide the furnaces with protective atmospheres of inert gas. Nitrogen can be used for most of the stainless steels in order to protect the melts against the loss of easily oxidizable constituents such as chromium, manganese, silicon, carbon, etc.

Present practice in ferrous die casting is to feed the die-casting machine with molten metal by hand-held ladle from an adjacent melt furnace such as is usual practice in aluminum die casting. The operator ladles the metal from the furnace into the injection system of the machine, then presses the contact button which initiates the pressure injection of the fluid metal into the die. Injection pressures in the range of 300 to 1000 kg/cm² (29.4 to 98.1 MN/m²) are common; that is, from about 5000 to 15,000 psi. The inflow of metal into the die is accomplished in a fraction of a second under the action of the pressure injection system. For most die castings of relatively thin cross section, from a millimeter or so up to a centimeter or two, the actual freezing process occurs within a fraction of a second, and dwell time of castings in the die (the interval of time between the injection of the liquid metal and the opening of the die to discharge the completed casting) generally is in the range of 2 to 4 s.

To avoid "cold shuts" and other defects and to obtain smooth-surfaced castings, the dies are preheated and maintained at an average operating temperature of several hundred degrees, the optimum level depending on the particular metal being cast. A good die-release agent, such as graphite, applied to the die surfaces before liquid metal injection is made, will promote surface smoothness. The more rapid the injection, the better will be the casting smoothness, but usually at the expense of internal soundness and freedom of porosity of the casting. As-cast surfaces can be as smooth as 30 to 50 μin. (0.0008 to 0.0013 mm) with austenitic stainless steel die castings made under optimum conditions.

A skilled operator working at a modern die-casting machine can achieve production rates of a hundred or more casting cycles per hour. Thus, production per operator can be relatively high as compared to many other casting processes, particularly when multiple-cavity dies are being used. For small parts, such dies may comprise up to 10 or more cavities, either all forming the same part or a family of related but different parts at each cycle of the casting process.

Typical casting weights range from a few grams to several kilograms; casting sizes from less than a centimeter in the longest dimension to 20 to 30 cm. Dimensional tolerances of a few hundredths of a millimeter per centimeter may be held; that is, a few thousandths of an inch per inch of casting dimension. Owing to the relatively great difference in coefficient of thermal expansion between the stainless steels and the refractory metals used as casting dies, drafts on external casting surfaces can be zero in most cases, but drafts on internal surfaces must be at least 5 to 10° for free release of the cast parts from core surfaces. Parts with relatively simple geometry can be made in straight-pull two-part

Fig. 1 A diversity of articles produced in stainless steel alloys by the die-casting process: golf club heads, crescent wrench jaws, rifle parts, valve handles, etc. Both austenitic and martensitic stainless steels are represented in this photograph.

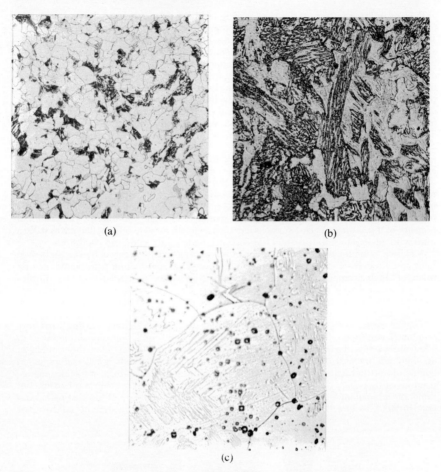

Fig. 2 Photomicrographs showing metallurgical structures of various ferrous metals in parts produced by the die-casting process. (*a*) AISI 1018, (*b*) AISI 4618, (*c*) Type 304.

dies with fixed internal cavity detail. More complex parts can be made in dies having moveable cores or other cavity detail parts that are removed from the castings before or simultaneously with the separation of the main die halves by the die-casting machine. Dies generally are designed with auxiliary pins (ejector pins) to ease the castings from the die cavities as the die-casting machine opens the dies at the end of the casting cycle.

Postcasting Treatment Die-cast stainless steel parts are separated from sprues by cutoff saw or trim press. The austenitic stainless steels (such as AISI 304, 310, etc.) generally need no postcasting heat treatment as they are strong and ductile as-cast. The martensitic stainless steels (like 403, 410, 431, etc.) may be above desired hardness levels as-cast, particularly if carbon levels are near or above specified limits, and may require tempering or annealing to reduce hardness and improve ductility. Parts then can be finished by conventional methods as desirable, such as tumbling, vibratory polishing, buffing, etc. Internal details impossible to cast, such as threaded holes, are added to the parts by the usual machining operations. It generally is found that die-cast stainless steel parts require less finishing than corresponding parts produced by forging or sand-mold casting.

Figures 1 and 2 illustrate the variety of shapes and alloy compositions that are possible to produce as stainless steel die castings.

Chapter 33

Atmospheres for Heat-Treating Stainless Steels

RUSSELL F. NOVY
Chief Metallurgist, Lindberg Division of Sola Basic Industries, Chicago, Illinois

INTRODUCTION

Surfaces of metallic materials are in a constant state of chemical activity due to exposure to ever-changing environments. This continues from the time of manufacture of the primary product at the mills through and beyond the finished manufactured product. Temperature affects the rates of this surface chemical activity. When metallic products are thermally processed at elevated temperatures, the activity increases to a point, depending on the environment, that can cause catastrophic failure. These are the conditions that materials are subjected to during the processes encountered in necessary heat treatment whether it be solution annealing, austenitizing, quenching, aging, tempering, etc.

There are various types of gases and gas mixtures, along with prepared atmospheres, that can be used effectively as protective atmospheres during the heat treatment of stainless steel alloys. The choice depends on "what is good enough to do the job." One is not going to employ an expensive hydrogen gas for annealing a fabricated section of a reworked jet engine when an exothermic type of atmosphere, at 5% of the cost, will suffice. And by the same token, highly stressed fasteners are not going to be heat-treated in a lower-cost atmosphere of dissociated ammonia in preference to hydrogen or argon gas, since the absorption of molecular nitrogen will be detrimental.

SEVEN BASIC ATMOSPHERES

Argon Argon, along with helium, is as close to being a truly inert gas as any of the known gases and, for all practical purposes, can be used in the heat treatment of stainless steels to prevent the possibility of any gas reaction or gas absorption.

Because of its relatively high cost (approximately three times the cost of cylinder nitrogen), its use is usually limited to those high-integrity types of heat-treating equipment where a minimum volume of gas is required to maintain necessary process pressure to give required protection. Therefore, the majority of the processing where argon is utilized is restricted to retorts using high-integrity seals so that minimum usage is experienced.

Argon is in common use as a backfill gas for vacuum furnaces where rapid cooling is necessary at the conclusion of a vacuum environment thermal treatment. Argon is admitted to the vacuum chamber and then is circulated to increase heat transfer and accelerate the required cooling. Because of its inertness, it will not be absorbed by the highly reactive surface of the treated stainless steel as nitrogen gas would be. Where subsequent highly stressed stainless steel materials are being heat-treated, argon will normally be used as a protective atmosphere or as a backfill gas in a vacuum furnace.

Argon is made by compressing, liquefying, and rectifying air. Air contains 0.933% argon by volume. Because of the present high oxygen requirements of the steel industry, argon has become more plentiful in supply as a by-product of the air liquefaction plants. Consequently, it is more economical in cost. Argon gas is usually distributed in cylinders, the most common being the 330 ft³ (9.34 m³) size at 2600 psi (17.93 MN/m²). Where large volumes of argon are used, liquid argon in Dewar containers is available. Because of its method of manufacture, relatively high purity levels can be maintained. A typical analysis is 99.90% argon, 0 to 0.098% nitrogen, 0.001% hydrogen, and 0.001% oxygen.

Helium Helium is also inert and will not combine with any other elements. Helium is used extensively as a protective atmosphere for shielded-inert-arc welding of stainless steel alloys. It is used to some extent in the heat treatment of stainless alloys in much the same type of equipment as argon. However, having a specific gravity of 0.137, second only to hydrogen with 0.069, it is more difficult to contain than argon. Consequently, greater care must be given to the integrity of the heat-treating equipment and associated piping.

Helium is obtained from natural gas fields by liquefaction of natural gas and results in a very pure and dry gas. The greater majority of helium is furnished in 200 ft³ (5.66 m³) cylinders and is comparable in price to argon.

Hydrogen Hydrogen is the most active reducing gas or deoxidizer, highly inflammable and with the lowest specific gravity (0.069) of all known gases. And here lie many of the considerations in using hydrogen as a protective atmosphere at elevated temperatures.

Hydrogen is produced commercially by a variety of methods including the electrolysis of water, separation of dissociated ammonia, and as a by-product in the manufacture of sodium hydroxide. Where large quantities are required on site, purification of steam-reformed natural gas or propane is readily accomplished if capital investment justifies it. Hydrogen from the electrolysis of distilled water is the preferred source for metallurgical purposes.

Hydrogen is usually supplied in cylinders. Small quantities are supplied in steel cylinders containing 193 ft³ (5.49 m³) of hydrogen at 2000 to 2200 psi (13.8 to 15.2 MN/m²) pressure. Larger quantities can be contracted to be supplied in banks of 12 interconnected cylinders on portable dollies containing about 3200 ft³ (90.6 m³). For high volume requirements, trailers are used containing a total of 28,600 ft³ (809.4 m³) of hydrogen in 22-ft-long (6.7-m) steel cylinders at 2500 psi (17.2 MN/m²).

All cylinder hydrogen contains traces of water vapor and oxygen if the source is the electrolysis of water. Other impurities vary depending on the process of manufacture of hydrogen. The impurities can be carbon monoxide, carbon dioxide and methane. This is the reason that the hydrogen best suited for metallurgical purposes is made by the electrolysis of distilled water or the electrolysis of sodium hydroxide.

In most heat-treating processes requiring, as nearly as practical, pure hydrogen, water vapor and oxygen are objectionable. Therefore, this requires purification before using. The removal of these two contaminants is fairly easy to accomplish. To remove oxygen, the hydrogen is passed through a bed of palladium catalyst at room temperature, combining the oxygen with the existing hydrogen to form water vapor. The water vapor is removed by passing the gas through silica gel, activated alumina, or a synthetic zeolite better known by its trade name of molecular sieve. Where activated alumina dryers can remove water vapor to a −60°F (−51°C) dew point, molecular sieve can remove water to less than a −100°F (−73°C) dew point. (Table 1 shows the relationship between dew point and moisture content of gases.)

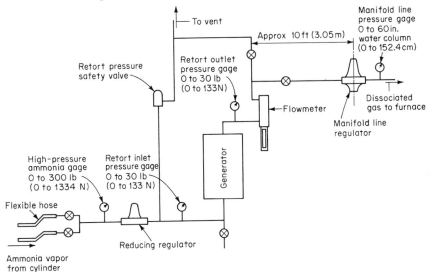

Fig. 1 Schematic flow diagram for ammonia dissociator.

Dissociated Ammonia Where the absorption of molecular nitrogen at elevated temperatures is not detrimental to the product, dissociated ammonia is usually considered a low-cost substitute for a pure hydrogen atmosphere. Dissociated ammonia is 75% hydrogen and 25% nitrogen and, as its name implies, is the result of the dissociation of gaseous ammonia by the reaction:

$$2NH_3 + heat \rightarrow 3H_2 + N_2$$

Ammonia used for dissociation for metallurgical applications must be of high purity and is specified as a refrigeration grade or a metallurgical grade. Refrigeration grade is 99.99% pure while the metallurgical grade is 99.999% pure. Therefore, if these purities hold true, if the dissociator systems (see Fig. 1) are piped tightly, and if they are well conditioned, then the maximum water vapor of the dissociated product will be less than −60°F (−51°C) if the impurity is only water. Since an ammonia dissociator operates through an endothermic reaction, the purity of the dissociated product depends solely on the purity of the ammonia. This is why only the highest grades of ammonia can be considered for use in metallurgical processes. One should never use a lower grade or fertilizer grade of ammonia.

The raw ammonia is supplied from 150- or 300-lb (68- to 136-kg) cylinders, or from bulk storage tanks in sizes ranging from 4000 to 10,000 lb (1814 to 4535 kg) or more. The majority of the dissociator systems depend on the source supply for gaseous ammonia, since this is the easiest and safest way to convey ammonia through a plant facility.

TABLE 1   Relation Between Dew Point and Moisture Content of Gases*

Dew point temperature		Moisture content			Dew point temperature		Moisture content		
°F	°C	lb/1000 ft³	mg/l	Vol %†	°F	°C	lb/1000 ft³	mg/l	Vol %
110	43	3.77	60.5	8.70	16	−8.8	0.160	2.56	0.308
108	42.2	3.57	57.0	8.20	14	−10	0.147	2.35	0.282
106	41.1	3.38	54.0	7.75	12	−11.1	0.135	2.16	0.258
104	40	3.20	51.0	7.30	10	−12.2	0.124	1.99	0.236
102	38.9	3.02	48.5	6.40	8	−13.3	0.114	1.83	0.216
100	37.7	2.86	45.6	6.45	6	−14.4	0.105	1.68	0.198
98	36.6	2.70	43.2	6.10	4	−15.5	0.096	1.54	0.180
96	35.5	2.55	40.8	5.75	2	−16.6	0.088	1.41	0.165
94	34.4	2.41	38.7	5.40	0	−17.7	0.081	1.30	0.150
92	33.3	2.27	36.4	5.05	−2	−18.9	0.074	1.18	0.136
90	32.1	2.14	34.3	4.75	−4	−20	0.0671	1.08	0.124
88	31	2.02	32.4	4.46	−6	−21.1	0.0612	0.982	0.113
86	29.9	1.90	30.5	4.18	−8	−22.2	0.0558	0.896	0.102
84	28.8	1.79	28.7	3.92	−10	−23.3	0.0508	0.815	0.093
82	27.7	1.68	26.9	3.68	−12	−24.4	0.0462	0.742	0.084
80	26.8	1.58	25.3	3.46	−14	−25.6	0.0420	0.674	0.076
78	25.5	1.49	23.9	3.22	−16	−26.7	0.0381	0.610	0.0685
76	24.4	1.40	22.5	3.02	−18	−27.8	0.0346	0.555	0.0619
74	23.3	1.31	21.0	2.84	−20	−28.9	0.0314	0.505	0.0558
72	22.2	1.23	19.7	2.65	−22	−30	0.0284	0.455	0.0503
70	21	1.15	18.4	2.47	−24	−31.1	0.0257	0.410	0.0452
68	19.9	1.08	17.3	2.31	−26	−32.2	0.0232	0.372	0.0407
66	18.8	1.01	16.2	2.16	−28	−33.3	0.0209	0.336	0.0364
64	17.7	0.95	15.2	2.02	−30	−34.4	0.0189	0.303	0.0328
62	16.6	0.89	14.2	1.88	−32	−35.6	0.0170	0.272	0.0294
60	15.6	0.83	13.3	1.75	−34	−36.7	0.0153	0.245	0.0264
58	14.3	0.777	12.5	1.63	−36	−37.8	0.0137	0.220	0.0235
56	13.2	0.725	11.6	1.51	−38	−38.9	0.0123	0.197	0.0210
54	12.1	0.677	10.9	1.40	−40	−40	0.0110	0.177	0.0188
52	11.1	0.632	10.1	1.30	−42	−41.1	0.0098	0.157	0.0167
50	9.9	0.589	9.5	1.21	−44	−42.2	0.0088	0.141	0.0149
48	8.8	0.549	8.81	1.12	−46	−43.3	0.0079	0.127	0.0132
46	7.7	0.511	8.20	1.04	−48	−44.4	0.0070	0.112	0.0117
44	6.6	0.475	7.62	0.966	−50	−45.6	0.0063	0.101	0.0104
42	5.5	0.442	7.08	0.894	−52	−46.7	0.0056	0.090	0.0092
40	4.4	0.410	6.58	0.827	−54	−47.8	0.0050	0.080	0.0082
38	3.3	0.381	6.12	0.765	−56	−48.9	0.0044	0.071	0.0072
36	2.2	0.354	5.68	0.707	−58	−50	0.0039	0.063	0.0063
34	1.1	0.328	5.26	0.653	−60	−51.1	0.0034	0.054	0.0056
32	0	0.304	4.88	0.602	−65	−53.9	0.0025	0.040	0.0041
30	−1.1	0.280	4.50	0.553	−70	−56.7	0.0018	0.029	0.0029
28	−2.2	0.259	4.15	0.511	−75	−59.5	0.0013	0.021	0.0021
26	−3.3	0.240	3.84	0.472	−80	−62.2	0.0009	0.014	0.0015
24	−4.4	0.221	3.55	0.434	−85	−65	0.0007	0.011	0.0010
22	−5.5	0.204	3.28	0.398	−90	−67.8	0.0005	0.008	0.0007
20	−6.6	0.189	3.02	0.367	−95	−70.1	0.0003	0.005	0.0005
18	−7.7	0.174	2.79	0.337	−100	−73.3	0.0002	0.003	0.0003

*At 1 atm (101.3 kN/m²).

†Vapor pressures in atmospheres at various dew point temperatures can be obtained by dividing the values for vol % given in this table, by 100. For parts per million (ppm) of water vapor at various dew point temperatures, multiply values of vol % by 10,000.

SOURCE: Mine Safety Appliances Co.

However, if the dissociator is supplied with liquid ammonia, usually from a multiple-cylinder system, then the dissociator must be equipped with a vaporizer.

Gaseous ammonia is usually supplied from the tanks at relatively high pressures, depending on the fill of the tank and ambient temperature. One can expect supply pressures to range from 50 to 150 psi (0.34 to 1.03 MN/m²). This necessitates pressure-reducing regulators in the supply line to reduce the pressure to approximately 2 to 7 psi (13.8 to 48.3 kN/m²) before introduction into the dissociator retort. It is recommended that supply pressure be reduced in two steps: typically from the tank supply pressure to 15 to 20 psi (103.4 to 137.9 kN/m²) in the first reduction and then to the operating pressure in the second reduction. Many times, if the reduction is taken in one step, one may experience freezing of the reducing or expansion valve at high flow rates, resulting in the throughput of liquid ammonia into the retort. This will adversely affect the dissociation efficiency by reducing the temperature in the dissociator retort and increasing the amount of residual ammonia in the dissociated product. Two-stage pressure reduction will also afford a more stable pressure control of the overall system.

After the reduction of the supply pressure, the gaseous ammonia enters an externally heated retort filled with a suitable catalyst, usually metallic nickel or a nickel-impregnated refractory base material. The heating chamber is controlled at a temperature of 1750 to 1850°F (953 to 1008°C) so that the catalyst bed is maintained at a temperature of 1700 to 1800°F (926 to 981°C). In an efficiently designed system, the residual undissociated ammonia will be in the range of 25 to 75 ppm.

The dissociated product is then cooled through a water-cooled heat exchanger. In some cases the heat of the dissociated product is used as a heat source for the vaporizer in the vaporizing of liquid ammonia. The heat of the dissociated ammonia can also be given up through a gas-to-gas heat exchanger by using the incoming gaseous ammonia as the coolant. After the heat exchanger, the dissociated product is metered through a flowmeter to the distribution manifold and then to the furnace. If the residual ammonia in the dissociated product is deemed excessive, it can be readily lowered to less than 5 ppm by passing the gas through a desiccant dryer filled with either activated alumina or molecular sieve.

The operation of the dissociator is very simple. It can be operated intermittently or continuously at any flow rate from complete turndown up to maximum flow rate. Once the generator is started, the operation is completely automatic. Automatic control safety devices are in effect throughout the generator to prevent dangerous or excessive pressures from being built up in the system. Signal lights and alarm bells immediately warn the operator of any abnormal operation.

One must realize that dissociated ammonia has a relatively low specific gravity, 0.269, compared with air at 1.0, and must therefore always be aware of the integrity of the installation such as tight pipe fittings, gasketed flanges and joints. It is good policy, wherever possible, to use welding in joining or in sealing. Good welding practices are a good guarantee that air infiltration into the hydrogen or dissociated ammonia system will be zero, for all practical purposes.

When using cylinder ammonia at $0.35 per pound, dissociated ammonia atmosphere costs $9.20 per 1000 ft³ (0.28 m³). In areas where bulk ammonia deliveries are available to fill large tank installations, truck deliveries in approximately 4000-lb (1816-kg) lots cost $0.17 per pound ($0.16 per kilogram) and reduce the cost of atmosphere to $4.50 for 1000 ft³ (0.28 m³). When rail tank car deliveries are available in approximately 10,000-lb (4540-kg) quantities, the cost is reduced to $0.085 per pound ($0.039 per kilogram) and the atmosphere cost is about $2.30 per 1000 ft³ (0.28 m³) of dissociated ammonia.

In comparison, cylinder hydrogen costs about $11 to $12 per 1000 ft³ (0.28 m³). In addition, cylinder hydrogen must be purified to remove traces of oxygen and dried by a desiccant before it can be used on stainless steels.

Exothermic Atmosphere   There are many times in the heat treatment of stainless steel products where a bright surface, free of any trace of oxidation, is not absolutely necessary or required. In these cases, the role of the protective atmosphere is to exclude the air, oxygen being the gross oxidizing constituent. Though the heat-treated product is not bright, the surface finish is uniformly discolored with a tight molecular thickness of oxide but free of any flaky loose scale that would otherwise necessitate removal in a subsequent operation.

The exothermic atmosphere fills this role. The exothermic atmosphere, AGA Type 101 to 114, is the least expensive of all prepared protective atmospheres and is extensively used throughout the heat-treating industry as an economical furnace atmosphere.

The exothermic atmosphere is produced by partially burning a preset ratio of air and a hydrocarbon fuel. Under controlled ratios of combustion, a large range of controllable analyses of produced atmosphere can be expected within the following limits: nitrogen, 67 to 87%; carbon monoxide, 0.5 to 11%; carbon dioxide, 4 to 11%; hydrogen, 0.5 to 15%; and under certain conditions, methane may be present in small amounts. The water-vapor content depends on the temperature of the subsequent cooling water and/or subsequent water-removal devices.

The exothermic atmosphere is the most economical of the prepared furnace atmospheres and is produced by the most simple means. Referring to the flow diagram of a typical exothermic generator (Fig. 2), one soon recognizes that it is nothing more than a close-controlled combustion chamber. Again, the atmosphere is produced by partially

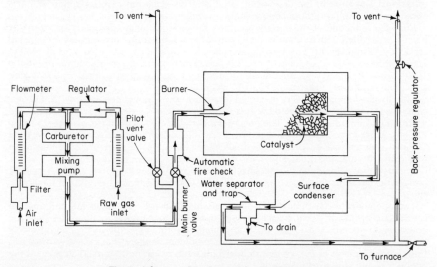

Fig. 2 Schematic flow diagram for exothermic generator.

burning an air-gas ratio where the hydrocarbon gas can be natural, manufactured, propane or butane gas and in some cases, various grades of kerosene.

The air and gas are metered through respective flowmeters, as shown in Fig. 2, with the desired ratio being maintained by a proportional mixer or carburetor. The air-gas mixture is drawn in by a constant-volume–constant-pressure pump, compressed to approximately 16 to 20 oz (4.4 to 5.6 N) and pumped through an automatic firecheck into the combustion chamber via a standard burner block. Here the air-gas mixture partially burns to the completion of the available oxygen. The unburned hydrocarbons pass over the heated catalyst in the rear of the combustion chamber and are further cracked, or dissociated, into constituents of hydrogen and carbon monoxide. The water vapor from the reaction is condensed out of the reacted atmosphere in the water-cooled surface condenser and separated from the atmosphere by means of a separator and a water trap. The water vapor or dew point of the gas generally runs 7 to 10°F (4 to 5.6°C) higher than the temperature of the cooling water. For example, if the cooling water temperature is 60°F (15.6°C), the resulting dew point will be 67 to 70°F (19.3 to 21°C) or 2.25 to 2.47% water vapor.

It must be remembered that the percentage of water vapor, or the dew point, of the resultant atmosphere is dependent on the temperature of the cooling water in the surface condenser. Depending on the locality of the installation, the temperature of this cooling water can change drastically from the summer to winter seasons, experiencing as much as a 45°F (24.8°C) differential. This means a varying analysis. Also, some installations are constantly dependent on recirculated cooling systems in which the water temperature remains fairly high. The efficiency of water removal is lowered in such installations. Where constant water-vapor control is necessary or desired, the atmosphere is passed through a refrigerated cooler designed to cool the gas to some controlled temperature. If the gas is efficiently cooled to 40°F (4.4°C), the dew point will be 40°F (4.4°C) or 0.825% water vapor. This consistency of water-vapor control alleviates many problems in the operation of the atmosphere system and subsequent processes.

There are applications of an exothermic atmosphere that require even lower water-vapor content. In these cases the refrigerated gas is passed through desiccant dryers utilizing materials similar to materials used in dryers for hydrogen, such as activated alumina or molecular sieve. The resultant water vapor will be less than a $-60°F$ ($-51°C$) dew point or 0.0055% water vapor.

The exothermic generator is the principal part of a nitrogen-producing generator where an atmosphere is required to have a high nitrogen content, perhaps with controllable reducing constituents of hydrogen and carbon monoxide. This necessitates the removal of the water vapor and the carbon dioxide. Although the system will not be discussed in detail, the exothermic atmosphere as produced by the exothermic generator is then compressed to pressures, varying on system design, from 20 to 100 psi (138 to 689.5 kN/m²). The compression of the atmosphere will essentially wring out the water vapor to a dew point of 0°F ($-17.7°C$). The atmosphere is then passed through towers of molecular sieve under elevated pressures, adsorbing the carbon dioxide to a resultant content of 0.1% and the water vapor to less than a $-85°F$ ($-65°C$) dew point or 0.0013% water vapor.

As previously mentioned, the exothermically produced atmosphere is the most economical of all produced atmospheres. Depending on cost of fuel and utilities, exothermic atmospheres will have a beginning cost of $0.12 to $0.15 per 1000 ft³ (0.28 m³). Some of this variation in cost will also be due to the ratio of generation, the richer ratios being more expensive than the lean ratios. If the gas is further refrigerated, the cost will be increased $0.02 to $0.03 per 1000 ft³ (0.28 m³). To dry the gas through a desiccant dryer will add an additional $0.05 per 1000 ft³ (0.28 m³) so that the dried exothermic gas costs $0.20 to $0.25 per 1000 ft³ (0.28 m³). Again, the costs vary with the costs of utilities.

Nitrogen   Nitrogen is often considered an inert gas when used as a protective atmosphere for heat-treating ferrous metals at elevated temperatures. However, when utilized under certain conditions for chromium-bearing alloys such as stainless steels, it can become highly detrimental because of the interstitial absorption of nitrogen. This absorption of nitrogen, or nitriding of the alloy, acts as a strengthening mechanism which increases the tensile strength but decreases ductility and elongation. Where highly stressed components are involved, such as aircraft fasteners, this nitriding can be highly detrimental to fatigue life. When intermediate anneals are performed on repeatedly deep-drawn stainless steel shapes, the cumulative absorption decreases the ductility to a point where the effects of the annealing process are negated.

In addition, nitrogen acts much in the same manner as carbon in that it combines with the nitride-forming elements of the alloy, such as chromium, and reduces the corrosion resistance of an austenitic stainless steel. When a nitrided austenitic steel, such as Type 321, is exposed to a hostile environment, an accelerated intergranular attack occurs. This corrosion is a source of stress raisers or concentrators and causes a part to fail readily under repeated stress and/or tension.

Bear in mind, we are referring to heat-treating conditions which promote the phenomenon of the absorption of molecular nitrogen. Again, it is to be emphasized that this is molecular, not nascent, nitrogen. The condition under which this absorption of molecular nitrogen occurs is when the surface of the stainless steel alloy is highly active after being highly reduced and cleaned by the reducing action of a hydrogen or vacuum environment at elevated temperatures. That is why, during a gas-quenching mode in a vacuum furnace after a vacuum thermal treatment, dry pure nitrogen is not used as the quenching medium on parts which are susceptible, such as fasteners and thin-wall corrosion-resistant tubing. After the vacuum thermal treatment, the surface is highly active and will readily absorb nitrogen. That is also why dry dissociated ammonia is not used as a protective atmosphere for certain products (as previously mentioned). It is not because of the very minute percentage of residual ammonia which might be present in the dissociated ammonia but rather, to the fact that the hydrogen component of the atmosphere highly activates the surface of the stainless steel product and consequently promotes and assists the transport of nitrogen.

This does not mean that the use of nitrogen as a protective atmosphere in the heat treatment of stainless steels should be eliminated, because there are many applications where it can be utilized. In the case of vacuum thermal processing, dry nitrogen can readily be used as a backfill quenching gas on those stainless steel products which have a heavy cross section, where the slight amount of absorbed nitrogen is of no consequence. Nor does it apply to those products that will not be subjected to stress or to highly corrosive environments.

Straight dry nitrogen can be used as a protective atmosphere. It takes an exceptionally high-integrity system to maintain a condition that would promote nitrogen absorption since nitrogen is not reducing in nature and the maintenance of an oxide-free surface only depends on the thermal dissociation. Therefore, from a practical standpoint, straight dry nitrogen can be used for many applications. However, the user should not expect the same surface finish obtained after the use of either a hydrogen-bearing or a vacuum atmosphere.

Nitrogen is made or manufactured in various ways, the current and most common being the liquefaction of air. Air contains approximately 78% nitrogen and its is a readily available by-product of the liquid air plants that furnish oxygen to steelmaking facilities. For the small or intermittent user, nitrogen is available in 200 ft³ (5.7 m³) cylinders or in multiple manifolded cylinders on a dolly rack. Where there is high use and/or requirements for high purity, liquid nitrogen is furnished in Dewar containers or cryogenic storage vessels. Nitrogen from a liquid source is inherently very dry and low in other residual gases.

Vacuum   Vacuum is probably one of the environments that has gained the fastest acceptance in the heat treatment of stainless steel. Vacuum is probably best character-ized as a lack of atmosphere. Since the detrimental constituents of a protective atmo-sphere are gaseous in nature, the most valid method to eliminate their effects is to pump

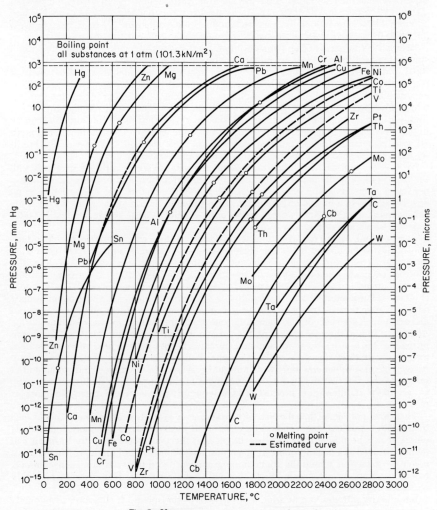

Fig. 3 Vapor pressure-temperature relationship.

them out of the heating chamber. Vacuum levels, at pressures of 1 micron (1 μm) of mercury, are comparable to an atmosphere of 99.995% purity or to a dew point of $-115°F$ ($-82°C$).

Vacuum is achieved in a vacuum-tight high-integrity chamber by exhausting the gaseous contents, by means of an efficient pump, to a level of 5 to 10 μm Hg. This pressure level is usually sufficient for the processing of most stainless steel alloys. The mechanical pump coupled with a Roots-type blower is all that is required as a pumping system for over 90% of the applications involving the thermal processing of stainless steels.

Higher vacuum levels, where required, can be achieved by adding an oil diffusion pump in line with the mechanical pump to achieve levels of less than 1×10^{-6} mm Hg. But for the most part, these vacuum levels are the exception rather than the rule in the normal thermal processing of stainless steels.

The use of vacuum environments is readily applicable to reactive metals susceptible to the formation of hydrides (metals combined with hydrogen), nitrides (metals combined with nitrogen), or oxides (metals combined with oxygen) in gaseous protective atmospheres.

Vacuum levels must be controlled where vaporization of elements may occur at a given thermal processing temperature. The temperature-vapor pressure relationships in Fig. 3 give the vapor points of various elements. To illustrate: if one were brazing a stainless steel assembly under a vacuum environment at 2200°F (1204°C), the vacuum level must be maintained above 1×10^{-3} mm Hg so that the chromium constituent in the alloy will not be vaporized, or "pulled out," and subsequently condense out in a colder portion of the furnace. Also by vaporizing the chromium from the surface, one is also losing a valuable corrosion-resisting constituent of the alloy.

In comparison with other atmospheres, the cost of a vacuum environment is basically that of the electrical utilities, water, and backfill atmosphere used for gas quenching.

Chapter **34**

Surface Hardening of Stainless Steels

WILLIAM G. WOOD
Vice President—Technology/Research and Development
Kolene Corporation, Detroit, Michigan

GENERAL HEAT-TREATMENT REQUIREMENTS

Wide-ranging stainless steel specifications permit the user considerable flexibility in attainable mechanical properties. Tensile strengths in the range of 280 ksi (1930.5 MN/m²) and hardnesses of Rockwell C 60 can be achieved in these corrosion-resistant materials.

Maximum mechanical properties of many of the alloys can frequently be obtained by heat treatment or strain hardening, depending on the grade. One factor that is of prime consideration in any heat-treatment process involving stainless steel is the function of the material in corrosive environments. Particular compositions are generally selected for this fundamental property, and thermal treatments that change corrosion resistance through the formation of new metallurgical phases must be closely examined.

SURFACE-HARDENING REQUIREMENTS

Surface hardening is required in certain applications to improve the gall- and wear-resistant properties of stainless alloys. The general nature of this treatment, in which the maximum attainable wear properties are developed through the formation of hard dispersions, suggests that some chemical change has been made in the metal surface exposed to corrosive environments.

Nitriding   Austenitic and ferritic stainless steels can be surface hardened by gas nitriding. This treatment increases hardness and, by changing friction characteristics, prevents galling and scoring.

The hardness requirements must be limited to surface properties since core properties are unaffected by the heat treatment. Stainless steel parts should be annealed and stress-relieved prior to nitriding, with the exception of the hardenable grades.

The martensitic grades can be hardened and tempered at a temperature above nitriding temperature, 975°F (524°C). The precipitation-hardenable grades, which are also capable of being nitrided, can be treated in the quenched and tempered condition.

Surface preparation prior to nitriding should include the removal of solid particles and oil and grease films. Conditioning is accomplished by removing any oxide which tends to create a passive condition. Mechanical methods or acid pickling are acceptable procedures. Molten salt treatment in a cyanide salt bath which has reducing characteristics is an effective means of preparation where stubborn passive films are encountered.

Nitriding is accomplished at temperatures of 975 to 1020°F (524 to 549°C) in a cycle which may vary from 20 to 48 h. The case depth developed is proportional to time. Knoop hardness values between 800 and 1400 can be obtained from the nitriding treatment depending on the grade of stainless involved. Case depths may range from 0.006 to 0.007 in. (0.015 to 0.018 cm) for the 48-h treatment at 975°F (524°C).

The increase in hardness and improvement of wear resistance is obtained at the expense of the corrosion resistance. The precipitation of the finely dispersed chromium nitrides which are responsible for the wear properties tends to deplete the surrounding matrix of dissolved chromium, effecting a lowering of overall corrosion resistance.

Electroplating   Surface characteristics of stainless steels may be altered by electroplating providing the plated surface has the required resistance to abrasive wear or galling and corrosion. Electroplating has the advantage of having a negligible effect on the microstructure of the base material. Diffusion of atomic hydrogen during the process may create embrittlement problems with some grades.

Chromium plating improves the wear and galling properties of stainless steels. Chromed surfaces have a lower coefficient of friction along with good corrosion resistance. Activation of the surface may be required prior to chromium plating because of the passivating film present on the surface.

Electroless nickel plating has been examined for increasing surface properties of stainless alloys. The plating has good hardness (700 Vickers), wear resistance, and generally an excellent appearance. The deposits are more brittle than equivalent amounts of chromium plating. Since deposition is independent of current density, even complex shapes can be plated uniformly.

As with other surface reactive processes, plating of stainless steels can be retarded by the passive oxygen-rich film present on the surface. After final cleaning, activation is required to remove this film. The treatment may be chemical, such as simple immersion in hydrochloric or sulfuric acids or a combination of the two. Cathodic treatments in electrolytic acids are also effective in surface preparation prior to electroplating.

Boronizing   Stainless steels may also be diffusion-hardened through chemical treatments in boron and boron-containing atmospheres. The reactive boron may be supplied by a molten salt bath media, activated packed powder, or recycled compounded granules.

The process is performed at a temperature in the range of 1650 to 2100°F (899 to 1149°C). The resultant diffusion zone is known for its low coefficient of friction and high surface hardness, which may reach values of 1800 Vickers. Case depths of 0.002 in. (0.005 cm) can be achieved with 1 to 5 h treating time.

Specialized systems are required for salt bath processing including protective atmospheres and fixturing. Pack methods can be performed in standard carburizing-type equipment which is capable of maintaining the required temperature.

The activated packed powder has a short life cycle since the cementation which occurs during the process limits recycling. The granules which contain additives to prevent intergranular oxidation can be partially recycled and a replenishment of 10 to 20% of new compound is required.

The borided 17% Cr steel shown in Fig. 1 was treated for 5 h at 1650°F (899°C). The compound zone consists of two phases of FeB and Fe₂B with some chromium atoms combined with the iron boride. The structure at the interface is characteristic of all borided high-chromium steels.

Carburizing   Stainless steels may be carburized to improve surface hardness and resistance to galling. The availability of substantial amounts of chromium in these

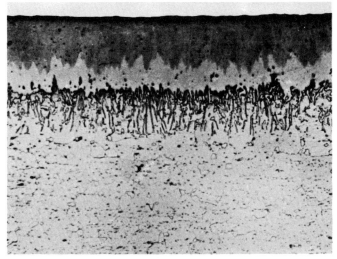

Fig. 1 Boronized surface on stainless steel. (200×.)

alloys promotes the rapid formation of chromium carbides at the surface. The chrome-bearing steels have been carburized to surface hardness values of 700 to 750 Vickers. The precipitation-hardenable stainless steels can be gas carburized to improve resistance to galling. Treatment temperatures up to 1850°F (1010°C) may be required.

In the austenitic grades of stainless steel, much of the chromium carbide formed migrates and is precipitated in the grain boundaries, developing intergranular corrosion susceptibility. Although the carbide distribution tends to be less segregated in the martensitic grades, they too are subject to localized corrosion and especially stress-corrosion cracking.

One of the prime reasons carburizing is not generally recommended for stainless steels is a concern with the overall corrosion resistance of the finished product. Since the stainless properties of the material are directly dependent on the type and quality of alloying elements in solution, a process which tends to precipitate chromium will degrade the corrosion-resistant properties. In addition, since the precipitated chromium has a tendency to exist at the expense of immediate adjacent areas, localized galvanic cells may develop. When carburizing is considered, it must be recognized that surface physical properties are being obtained at the expense of surface chemical properties.

Because of the disadvantages indicated, most of the carburizing performed on stainless steel is not planned and develops because of surface contamination. Carbonaceous compounds such as charcoal, coke, oil, and grease can develop carburizing activity under the proper conditions. Molten salt baths containing percentages of cyanide to prevent decarburization may also become carburizing in contact with stainless steels.

Flame- or Plasma-Sprayed Coatings   These coatings are continuous wear-resistant films fused on the surface. They differ primarily in the method of deposition. Flame-spray coatings are applied from powders which are gas aspirated and carried through a fuel-gas flame. The fuel gas may be an oxygen-acetylene mix or an oxygen-hydrogen mix. In the flame area, the powder is heated to the molten state and immediately deposited on the surface. The wear-resistant surface formed is usually rough and may be applied in coated thicknesses of 0.100 in. (0.254 cm). The coating is readily machinable and final

TABLE 1   Characteristics of Plasma-sprayed Coatings

Metal combination	DPH hardness	Finishing method
Tungsten carbide	700	Diamond wheel grind
Chromium carbide	700	Diamond wheel grind
Nickel chromium	450	Diamond grind
Molybdenum	300	Abrasive wheel grind
Nickel aluminide	170	Machining
Aluminum silicon	95	Machining

dimensions are achieved by machining or grinding. Flame-spray coatings on stainless steels have numerous applications in the aircraft industry, especially in the area of abradable seals.

Plasma coatings are developed from powders ejected through a gun. Plasma coating is formed through the dissociation of argon, hydrogen, or helium by electrical energy which ionizes the gas. The ejected powder is introduced into the area of the ionized gas which, upon recombining to the molecular state, produces extremely high flame temperatures which may reach 10,000 to 30,000°F (5538 to 16,649°C). The molten powder is ejected onto the parts at speeds as high as 700 ft/s (213.4 m/s). Plasma-spray coatings can be applied in a finished condition, finely machined or ground to specified dimensions.

Major applications of plasma coatings are in the area of high wear resistance and part restoration. Table 1 lists the metal combinations normally applied on stainless steels through plasma spray.

Plasma coatings (Fig. 2) find extensive application in the aircraft engine industry where parts are subject to selective and severe wear. The powders provide metallic compositions which are capable of withstanding abrasive wear conditions much more severe than those tolerated by other alloys fully heat-treated. When wear factors are sufficiently severe to produce dimensional changes beyond acceptable tolerances, the part may be removed from service, suitably stripped and again flame or plasma coated.

Age-hardenable austenitic and martensitic stainless steels are commonly surface-hardened by this method. Since the treatment produces a true coating with measurable dimensions, allowances must be made during final finishing. Proper precleaning is of prime importance in obtaining a satisfactory bond between base metal and spray coating.

Liquid Nitriding   Wear and gall resistance of stainless steels can be improved by aerated liquid nitriding. This process is performed in a molten mixture of sodium and

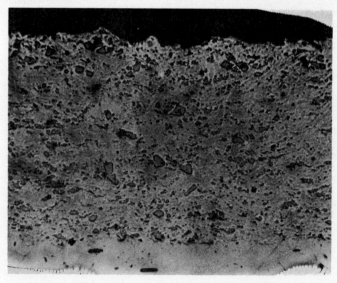

Fig. 2   Tungsten carbide coating on steel. (200×.)

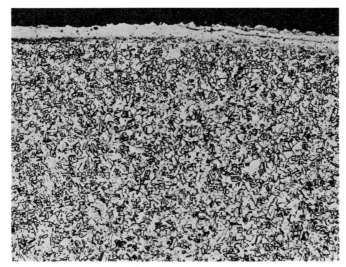

Fig. 3   Liquid nitrided Type 347 stainless steel. (Etchant, 10% HCl.) (200×.)

potassium cyanides and cyanates. Immersion in this molten salt at 1060°F (570°C) develops a physical compound zone in stainless steels that may vary between 0.0002 to 0.001 in. (0.00051 to 0.00254 cm), depending on treatment time. The cases developed in Types 347 and 303 stainless alloys, after hydrochloric acid etching, are shown in Figs. 3 and 4.

Although this wear-resistant surface has a measurable hardness of 70 to 72 Rockwell C, it is tough and ductile. These characteristics are understandable from the x-ray diffraction data which reveals the absence of brittle iron-nitrogen alloys in the molecular range of Fe_2N. The composition of the case is actually epsilon iron nitride (Fe_3N) and iron carbide (Fe_3C) in an iron matrix. A diffusion zone composed of soluble iron and alloy nitride is present immediately below the wear-resistant compound zone. This zone has a hardness gradient between 62 Rockwell C and that of the 1060°F (570°C) tempered core.

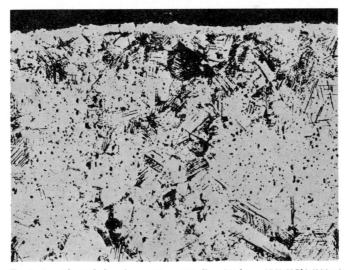

Fig. 4   Liquid nitrided surface on Type 303 alloy. (Etchant, 10% HCl.) (200×.)

The diffused nitrogen-bearing case contributes to improved endurance properties in unnotched structures.

Some loss in corrosion resistance results from the liquid nitriding treatment. Restricting the alloy content of stainless materials through the formation of nitride and carbide depletes adjacent matrix areas. Corrosion data based on weight loss indicates that liquid

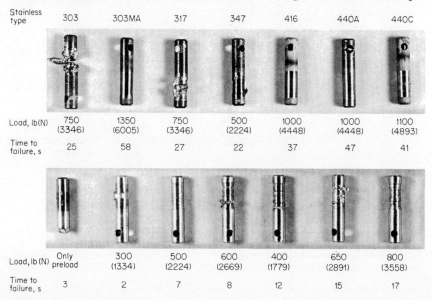

Stainless type	303	303MA	317	347	416	440A	440C
Load, lb(N)	750 (3346)	1350 (6005)	750 (3346)	500 (2224)	1000 (4448)	1000 (4448)	1100 (4893)
Time to failure, s	25	58	27	22	37	47	41
Load, lb (N)	Only preload	300 (1334)	500 (2224)	600 (2669)	400 (1779)	650 (2891)	800 (3558)
Time to failure, s	3	2	7	8	12	15	17

Fig. 5   Faville–LeVally Falex test results. Top row of pins has been liquid nitrided, bottom row was not treated.

nitrided stainless steels lose approximately 50% corrosion resistance but are substantially superior to untreated carbon and low-alloy steels.

Any closely controlled nitriding process should be capable of reproducibility in case depth and diffusion zone and subsequent mechanical properties. The low-temperature liquid nitriding process is controlled in this manner and consequently develops properties that are peculiar to this treatment alone. It is one of the few heat treatments that can produce a wear-resistant hard surface, improve the fatigue properties, and substantially retain the good corrosion resistance of stainless materials in a single operation. In addition, quenching is not required following heat treatment and, therefore, the flexibility in design and final machining is frequently advantageous.

The wear- and gall-resistant properties of liquid nitrided stainless alloys have been extensively documented in production applications and laboratory tests. One of the most visual laboratory tests can be performed on the Faville–LeVally Falex machine. This test involves a standard pin which rotates between two V-shaped jaws which are subjected to constantly increasing loads. A measure of the resistance of the surface to seizing and galling is indicated by the maximum loads sustained in the length of time to seizure. Figure 5 shows two sets of Falex pins. The pins at the top of the illustration have been liquid nitrided while those at the bottom are as-machined. It is apparent that the treatment is effective on most stainless alloys and that substantial improvement in load-carrying capacity can be obtained.

Chapter **35**

The Cleaning
of Stainless Steels

WILLIAM G. WOOD

Vice President—Technology/Research and Development, Kolene
Corporation, Detroit, Michigan

SURFACE CONTAMINANTS

Shop Soils Stainless steel, like any processed metal, is subject to different surface contaminations and each of these requires specialized cleaning. Shop soils, including grease, oil, grit, and metal chips, resulting from machining and fabrication processes, require a combination of dissolution and flotation for their removal. Lubricant residues, including both saponifiable and unsaponifiable oils, graphite, molybdenum disulfide, and silica-type materials, also require some solution of the binding material and dispersion of solid residues.

Conversion Soils A different classification of soils requiring a very specialized approach are the conversion coating types which are actually integral with the surface. This category would include the short-time anneal oxides, which could be formed on continuous product during a few minutes dwell time at 1200 to 1500°F (649 to 816°C), and all the intermediate possibilities up to the long-time box anneal scales formed on Type 430 grades of stainless steels. These variations alone suggest numerous approaches to the problem of obtaining a clean metal surface following heat-treatment operations.

Lubricant-Oxide Mixtures Another group of conversion coatings which can be even more complex than those resulting from in-process annealing are those formed during hot-working, forging, and casting. These scales not only include the multiple oxide combinations which are possible in all heat-treated stainless steels and listed in Table 1, but also may incorporate the elevated temperature lubricants or mold- and core-treating materials which can be combined with oxides to produce some extremely complex scales.

The removal of anneal and hot-work scales requires cleaning processes which either mechanically abrade and attack the surface or chemically react and dissolve the surface or possibly a combination of both.

REMOVAL OF SHOP SOIL

Solvent Degreasing Soils developed during machining or fabricating operations, which are primarily composed of organic binders such as grease, unsaponifiable oils, or

TABLE 1 Predominant Oxide Structures Expected in Stainless Steel Scale Formation

Formula	Name
FeO	Ferrous oxide
Fe_3O_4	Ferrosofferic oxide
Fe_2O_3	Ferric oxide
Cr_2O_3	Chromium sesquioxide
NiO	Nickel monoxide
SiO_2	Silicon dioxide
$FeCr_2O_4$	Chromium spinel
$NiFe_2O_4$	Nickel spinel

waxes, can be removed efficiently by solvent cleaning. Solvent cleaning may be effected by soak tank immersion or spray cleaning if the flash point of the solvent permits this approach.

There are numerous solvents or combinations of solvents available for this type of cleaning and the selection should be based primarily on the composition of the organic binder to be removed. The basic limitation on recirculating solvent solutions depends on the rate at which saturation is achieved in the solution. The final residual film remaining on the cleaned surface will consist of the nonvolatile residue deposited from the evaporation of the solvent "dragged out" on the work. If this residue accumulates too rapidly in the solvent tank, the frequent changing required may destroy the economics of the process.

Vapor Degreasing Vapor degreasing has the decided advantage of introducing fresh solvent onto the contaminated surface on a continuous basis. Therefore, not only is the solvency action at a maximum but any retained solvent will have a minimum residual oil concentration and will leave the lowest possible residue on the surface of the parts being cleaned. Vapor degreasing is more suited to batch work than to continuous processing because of the dwell time required within the degreaser. It also is limited to high organic residue soils and has very little effect on inorganic soils such as grinding residues, lint, soap, and metal chips.

Water-Emulsion Cleaning Shop soils which are composed of equal parts of solid residues and organic binders may be cleaned with water-emulsion solvent cleaners which have the capability of dissolving organic residues along with sufficient flotation properties to remove undissolved solids. These cleaners, which may be composed of 5 to 10% emulsifier with the balance being aromatic or aliphatic solvents or a combination of both, are diluted with water to form a concentration of 2 to 10%. When used as soak tank cleaners, where agitation is limited and the reaction is usually a combination of solvency and flotation, a ratio of 10:1, or 10%, is preferred. These solutions are usually employed at temperatures of 140 to 160°F (60 to 71°C) with relatively long dwell times. The reactions are a combination of solvency with the dispersed solvent particles reacting with the oils or greases on the surface, releasing the inorganic soils which can be wetted by the emulsifier solution and floated to the surface. After thorough rinsing and drying, the parts should be clean.

Emulsion cleaners also are very effective in power washers where they are used at a temperature of 180°F (82°C) in concentrations of 2 to 3%. Here the contact time between the part and the spray may be limited to 1 to 2 min and the reaction must necessarily be of shorter duration than in soak tank cleaners. The cleaning is a combination of solvency, wetting, and scrubbing. Again, the solvency takes place through the action of the dispersed solvent, the wetting results from the solution of the emulsifier, and the scrubbing action is a combination of the impingement of the solvent particles and the water particles on the surface of the metal. Spray-emulsion cleaners are usually followed by a spray rinse which removes any residual trace of cleaner or soil on the surface. It also is very effective for the removal of combinations of organic binders and inorganic solids.

Water-Soluble Alkaline Cleaners Alkaline cleaners are particularly effective in soak tank operations where soils are composed of a combination of saponifiable organic binder and inorganic soil. There are many commercial formulations available on the market for soak tank cleaning comprising caustic soda, soda ash, phosphate, silicate, and wetting agents. They are normally employed at a concentration of 2 to 4 oz/gal (0.22 to 0.43 g/m³) of water at a temperature of 180 to 190°F (82 to 88°C). The parts to be cleaned are immersed for a period of 5 to 20 min, water rinsed, and dried prior to additional operations or shipping. The free alkali in these cleaners will react with the saponifiable material on the surface, forming water-soluble soaps and releasing the solid particles for flotation or settling. These cleaners are very effective in batch operations with the indicated time cycle.

Compounded alkaline cleaners are also used in spray-type washing operations. Here they react with saponifiable material but are capable of removing soils that are composed predominately of mineral oil and solid material since, in power washers, they also effect an impingement action along with their chemical action. Chemically they are capable of producing strong emulsifying and flotation action because of their combined alkaline system. They normally are employed at concentrations of ½ to 1½ oz/gal (0.05 to 0.16 g/m³) at a temperature of 180°F (82°C). The cleaning cycle is preferably followed by a continuous overflow rinse and forced-air drying cycle.

OXIDE AND SCALE REMOVAL

Shot or Abrasive Blasting The oxide coatings developed on the stainless steel during welding, processing, and heat-treating, and those formed during forging and casting mixed with lubricant residues, require the processing indicated in Table 2.

TABLE 2   Scale Removal Methods

Acid pickling
Mechanical abrasion
Salt baths
Salt bath conditioning and acid pickling
Mechanical abrasion, salt bath conditioning, and acid pickling
Other combinations

Sand or shot blasting is satisfactory for removing scales from stainless steel providing the intensity is such that the surface finish of the abradable base metal is not destroyed. This can also be influenced by the size and grade of shot or grit selected and by the length of time the part is exposed to the blasting media.

Another limitation on blast cleaning can be found in the configuration of the part to be finished (Fig. 1). If there are numerous cavities and blind areas that are protected from the impingement pattern of the shot, these, of course, will not be cleaned in a normal production cycle. It is possible to supplement automatic cycles with hand operations to reach the areas where scale is still retained.

There are work-hardening effects from abrasive cleaning and, in a material like stainless steel, which is susceptible to working, this factor cannot be ignored. In most cases, however, it can be controlled and maintained as a shallow surface effect which is not objectionable. Where a problem does exist, it is possible to reduce the amount of abrasive cleaning to an acceptable level and finish the final operation with a chemical cleaner.

Shot or abrasive blasting is, undoubtedly, one of the most rapid methods for removing difficult scale from stainless steel. Batch processing, where a large number of parts are subjected to the abrasive in a closed cabinet and discharged all at one time, is acceptable as long as the part size lends itself to this type of operation. Continuous processing can be effective when the stock can be conveyorized and fixtured or supported on tables, or, in the case of stainless steel strip, passed over rolls. There is little opportunity for part rotation on a continuous basis and usually the shot or grit must be directed at the proper angles to complete the cleaning operation in a single pass. Frequently, shot blasting or grit blasting is combined with chemical cleaning. The shot, in this case, is used to penetrate or loosen the scale allowing the final finishing and cleaning to be accomplished with the chemical solution whether it be molten salt or acid or a combination of both.

Tumbling or Slurry Finishing Small-to-medium-size stainless steel sections can be tumbled or barrel finished to remove light-to-medium scales. With a wide choice of abrasives available, various combinations can be selected to attain the desired finish. Part configuration is not too important since the constant moving action of the part in the media usually allows free access to all blind areas. Abrasive or cutting action should be just sufficient to remove all the scale present but yet not develop rounded corners or edges and dimensional changes unless these are required. After completion of the time cycle required to remove all the scale, the loads are screened to separate work and abrasive, the

Fig. 1 Complex fabrication.

parts are thoroughly rinsed, dried and ready for additional processing. The equipment requirements for tumbling are rather moderate and, because of the nature of the operation, maintenance costs are not excessively high. The media is consumed and must be replaced periodically. This is probably the major cost of the operation. There is an appreciable noise factor associated with this type of finishing even though improvements in design have tended to make this more acceptable in recent years. At the present time, barrel finishing is a batch-type operation, although there are indications that a continuous process will be feasible sometime in the future.

Wire Brushing, Grinding, Flapper-Type Wheel   Several other mechanical methods are available for finishing stainless steel parts. Most of these are necessarily limited to batch operations on individual parts although all of them can be used on continuous strip. Wire brushing uses the scrubbing action of wire bristles to mechanically strip the scale from the surface. Usually the pattern of the brushing action is evident.

Abrasive wheel or belt grinding may be used to remove surface defects from stainless steel mill products at various stages of manufacture. Restrictions on these operations involve the complete removal of grind patterns and grit residues.

Flapper-type wheels are also a type of grinding operation in which a segmented wheel formed from abrasive sheets is employed. The flexibility of this wheel permits wider applications in areas where nonuniformity in a horizontal plane is a problem. The same requirements regarding surface finish and abrasive removal apply.

ACID CLEANING AND PICKLING

Organic Acids   Organic acid chelates and dilute solutions of mineral acids can be used to clean light oxides or scales and free-iron particles from stainless steel surfaces.

The organic compounds are interestingly versatile, combining acid solution activity with sequestrant and buffering properties. Light scale residues can be solubilized with dilute solutions of ammoniated citric acid. Treatments of this type are satisfactory for final cleaning of fabrications for the food and chemical industry. A concentration of 3 to 5% citric acid is preferred and this solution is adjusted with ammonium hydroxide to a pH of between 3 and 4. An operating temperature of 170°F (77°C) will produce good cleaning within acceptable time cycles. Embedded iron particles may contaminate stainless steel surfaces as a result of shot blasting or machining. This free iron produces unacceptable corrosion-resistant properties. Formulated cleaning compositions with dibasic ammonium citrate combined with anionic or nonionic wetting agents are effective in removing these iron particles. An operating temperature of 170°F (77°C) and concentrations of 2 to 5% are preferred.

Citric acid, glycolic acid, and formic acid are used in many equipment cleaning operations including pharmaceutical processing equipment, whiskey storage tanks, steam generators, and nuclear reactors. In addition to their ability to combine with many other chemical compounds, the advantages of using acids of this type for these applications include the low corrosion rate experienced, ability to hold iron in solution, and safe handling properties. A number of manufacturers of these compounds have detailed descriptive literature of specific formulations which may be employed for cleaning stainless steel surfaces.

Dilute Mineral Acids   Dilute mineral acids combined with nonionic detergent systems can be used as single-step cleaning for the removal of oils, soaps, shop soils, light oxides, and free iron. The compounded liquid cleaners of this type are used at concentrations of 15 to 20% by volume and temperatures of 140 to 150°F (60 to 66°C). Soak tank time of 10 to 15 min should produce, after water rinsing, a continuous film without water breaks or the process should be repeated.

Inhibited hydrochloric, phosphoric, sulfuric, and nitric acid solutions, along with various combinations of these, are used for surface activation prior to electroplating, adhesive bonding, nondestructive testing, and welding. They may also be used as a final treatment following buffing, heat-treating, and machining operations. In the latter case, because of the presence of organic soils and lubricating oils, an alkaline soak clean or spray wash is required prior to the acid treatment.

Strong Mineral Acids   Solutions of sulfuric acid (8 to 20%) at temperatures in the range of 160 to 180°F (71 to 82°C) and nitric (15 to 25%)-hydrofluoric (1 to 4%) acid in the range of 120°F (49°C) may be used for treatment of light scales formed during heat-treat operations on the 200-, 300-, and 400-series stainless steels. Immersion times are usually rather long to effect scale removal and the strong concentration of acids employed adds the additional risk of severe etching of surfaces which are exposed selectively to the solution. Nitric-hydrofluoric acid cleaning solutions at various concentrations and temperatures are also used to remove residual scale particles and smut and to produce a uniform white pickle on finished products.

SALT BATH CONDITIONING

Scale Conditioning   Hot-rolled, forged, cast, and many continuous anneal scales require salt bath conditioning prior to acid pickling. Salt baths are almost universally specified when complex mixtures of oxides and lubricants are present. The salt bath treatment reacts with the lubricant present on the surface and converts the complex oxide to a form which is more easily soluble in acid. Depending on the reaction of the salt bath, this may either be a reduced form of the oxide or one oxidized to a more soluble oxygen-rich form.

Types of Molten Salts   There are a number of types of molten salts that are of commercial importance in the processing of stainless steel mill products and fabrications. Table 3 lists several types of conditioning salts available from major suppliers to the industry. All are alkaline base, oxidizing or reducing to the complex chromium, nickel, and iron oxides developed on the surface of the stainless steel.

The operating temperature may vary between 400°F (204°C) and 900°F (482°C). The activity of a particular salt bath depends on the chemical composition of the reacting compounds, with one exception. The exception is when an electrolytic bath is employed and, in this case, the bath is normally neutral as far as oxidation or reduction is concerned, and its activity is determined by the polarity of the workpiece and the current density of the electrical input. Most of the salt baths listed in Table 3 are oxidizing with the exception of item 4, which is reducing in nature.

Oxidizing Salt Baths   The effectiveness of oxidizing salt baths as a conditioning media depends on the conversion of the insoluble complex iron, chromium, and nickel oxides to a more soluble form. The diagram shown in Fig. 2 illustrates that, adjacent to the metal surface, the oxides formed are metal-rich and oxygen-poor and notoriously insoluble in most common pickling acids. The outer surface of the oxidized layer which is immediately adjacent to the gas film is, at the same time, oxygen-rich, and these oxides are relatively soluble in the common pickling acids. It is the ability of the oxidizing salt bath to penetrate this outer oxide and to convert the layers beneath to the completely oxidized form which is responsible for their conditioning action. The chemical reactions which take place in the molten salt bath to effect this are

$$2MO + NaNO_3 = M_2O_3 + NaNO_2 \tag{1}$$
$$C + 2NaNO_3 = CO_2 + 2NaNO_2 \tag{2}$$
$$NaNO_2 + 0.5O_2 = NaNO_3 \tag{3}$$
$$SiO_2 + 2NaOH = Na_2SiO_3 + H_2O \tag{4}$$
$$MoS_2 + 6NaOH + 9NaNO_3 = Na_2MoO_4 + 2Na_2SO_4 + 9NaNO_2 + 3H_2O \tag{5}$$

Equation (1) indicates the oxidation of the metal-rich oxide to the oxygen-rich oxide. Equation (2) is the reaction that takes place with excess carbon or graphite on the surface in which the oxidizing agents in the salt convert the carbon to carbon dioxide. Equation (3) indicates that the oxidizing potential of the bath is maintained [at 900°F (482°C)] through a regenerative reaction with the oxygen in the atmosphere to convert the nitrite

TABLE 3   Cleaning and Conditioning Salt Baths

| | Operating temperature | |
Type	°F	°C
1. High-temperature oxidizing	900	482
2. Reversible electrolytic (oxidizing/reducing)	875	468
3. Intermediate temperature oxidizing	850	454
4. Reducing	750	399
5. Low-temperature oxidizing (chemical)	400	204
6. Low-temperature oxidizing (electrolytic)	400	204

formed to nitrate. Equation (4) is the alkalinity reaction that takes place with any silica present on the surface from extruding or drawing compounds, and Eq. (5) is the same reaction with molybdenum disulfide.

Reducing Salt Baths   The reducing type salt bath (Table 3, item 4), in the reaction with stainless steel oxides, depends on the formation of sodium hydride in the bath which has a reducing reaction according to the following equation:

$$M_2O_3 + 3NaH = 3NaOH + M_2 \tag{6}$$

The process is quite effective on most stainless steel oxides and the reaction time is very similar to that experienced in the oxidizing type salt bath. The problem with the reducing

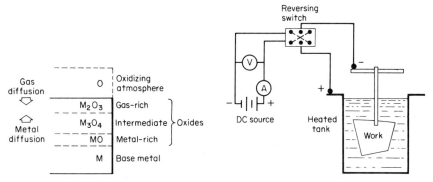

Fig. 2   Simple oxidation diagram.

Fig. 3   Diagram for electrolytic salt bath conditioning.

conditioning bath is that the active chemical depletes and must be replaced on a periodic basis. This requires the introduction of sodium metal into a generator, along with hydrogen gas, to produce the sodium hydride in situ. This produces certain hazards and causes some objectionable conditions as far as operating personnel are concerned.

Electrolytic Salt Baths   The third basic class of molten conditioning salts is the neutral caustic baths which are neither oxidizing nor reducing but are used in conjunction with electrical current. When the workpiece is positive, these baths behave as oxidizing baths and convert the metal-rich oxides to gas-rich oxides. When the workpiece is negative, the baths become reducing in character and are able to convert the metal oxide to the base metal. The simplified electrical diagram for this type of bath is shown in Fig. 3. It can readily be observed from this diagram that, with the one alkaline-base salt bath, both the oxidizing- and reducing-type bath reactions can be developed with a change in polarity. The process is slightly more involved than the other two types of baths because of the necessity of an electrical system which can be complex in reaction because of the resistivity of molten salt baths. The chemical reactions involved with the electrolytic bath at 900°F (482°C) are:

Oxidizing reaction:

$$2MO + 2OH^- = M_2O_3 + H_2O \tag{7}$$

Reducing reaction:

$$MO + 2Na^+ = M^+ + Na_2O \tag{8}$$

Since the reactivity of the bath depends strictly on the electrical current input, there is no chemical depletion and, therefore, if the salt bath is maintained in a sludge-free condition, replacement of drag-out salt is sufficient for maintenance of the bath on a continuous basis.

The 400°F (204°C) electrolytic bath is slightly different from the higher temperature one since the oxidation reaction is the only important one. There is no reduction even though the work may be negative because the bath at 400°F (204°C) does not have sufficient reducing power to produce an oxygen-free metal. The primary reaction of conversion to a more acid-soluble oxide is

$$2MO + NO_3^- = M_2O_3 + NO_2^- \tag{9}$$

Again, this bath maintains its reactivity by producing the opposite reaction at the reduction, or negative, polarity. All of the indicated reactions go to completion but leave a film of oxide on the surface of the metal which is easily removed in the subsequent acid pickling.

ACID PICKLING FOLLOWING SALT BATH CONDITIONING

Mineral Acids The normal pickling procedure following salt bath conditioning involves an initial treatment with sulfuric acid. This pickle has a twofold purpose in that some of the converted oxides are soluble in the sulfuric acid but the pickle solution also neutralizes any residual alkali remaining from the water rinse. Concentrations of sulfuric acid pickling solutions have never been standard and will depend on the preference of the pickling department or the laboratory. Again, their decision is based on whatever works best for the particular oxide condition. A 10 to 15% concentration at 160°F (71°C) is quite common, although variations from 8 to 25% are not unusual. Frequently the sulfuric acid is operating in an electrolytic pickle to increase the effectiveness. A carbon-steel tank with natural rubber lining protected with red shale brick or a polypropylene molded tank can be used to contain the sulfuric acid.

After the sulfuric acid treatment and water rinse, the final pickling is accomplished in a solution of nitric and hydrofluoric acid. This combination also is not standard throughout industry but generally is sufficiently concentrated to remove the last traces of oxide on the surface. In the pickling of stainless steels, the nitric-hydrofluoric solutions are the most effective but also are more likely to cause surface attack. Concentrations are maintained at a ratio of five parts of nitric acid to one part hydrofluoric acid and at a temperature slightly below 120°F (49°C) (above which excess volatilization of hydrofluoric could be experienced). Hydrofluoric acid concentrations of 2 to 3% are most common but 3 to 5% is not unreasonable, although it may be quite expensive to operate a pickle bath at these concentrations. Very low percentages, down to 7 to 8% nitric acid and 0.5% hydrofluoric acid at 120°F (49°C), are frequently specified for straight-chromium-type stainless steels. Certain pickle houses eliminate the hydrofluoric completely, using a straight nitric acid pickle for these grades. A carbon-steel tank lined with polyvinylchloride protected with carbon brick is a recommended pickle tank construction.

Chelated Caustic Pickle Recent years have seen the introduction of alkaline pickle baths based on chelated caustic. These baths are effective and may find wide application in the stainless steel industry providing salt bath conditioning is part of the system. They are completely ineffective on scales in the reduced or metal-rich oxide condition. After treatment in an oxidizing salt bath in which the oxygen-rich layer is formed, the solubility in the chelated caustic solution operating between 220°F (105°C) and 280°F (137°C) is completed within a few minutes. A solution of this composition has the added advantage of not reacting with the base metal, restricting dissolution of metal ions to the scale alone. In this way, the concentration of heavy metals in the pickle solution is minimized.

CONTINUOUS CLEANING OF STAINLESS STEEL STRIP

Hot-Rolled Annealed Strip Cleaning of annealed stainless steel strip on a continuous basis generally follows a standard pattern of salt bath conditioning, water rinsing, sulfuric acid pickle, water rinse, nitric-hydrofluoric pickle, and water rinse. One exception occurs in the cleaning of hot-rolled annealed product. These scales, being the most difficult to remove either because they consist of a double scale or, more likely, because of the effect of long time at temperature, usually require mechanical finishing or a more active chemical cleaning than can be achieved in the normal oxidizing conditioning salt. Mechanical cleaning takes the form of shot or grit blasting, both top and bottom, followed by either salt bath conditioning and acid pickle, or very strong acid pickle alone. A more active chemical cleaning involves the electrolytic salt on a two-furnace system in which the strip is oxidized in the first salt bath furnace and finally reduced to the base metal in the second furnace, followed by a sulfuric acid pickle and a nitric-hydrofluoric pickle to produce a clean strip (Fig. 4).

Process Anneal Scales Process anneal scales, which are more easily cleaned, are usually treated in the salt bath and acid pickle system. It is possible to avoid salt bath conditioning and use excessively strong acid pickles to obtain a clean surface; however, the cost and problems involved with strong acid pickles usually negate this approach. Process anneal scales then are generally removed by one of the following three methods:

1. Oxidizing salt bath conditioning followed by sulfuric acid pickle and nitric-hydrofluoric pickling

2. Electrolytic neutral salt bath conditioning followed by sulfuric acid pickling and nitric-hydrofluoric pickling

3. Low-temperature electrolytic oxidizing salt bath conditioning followed by sulfuric acid pickling

Finish gage material which has a final process anneal is normally cleaned in a straight

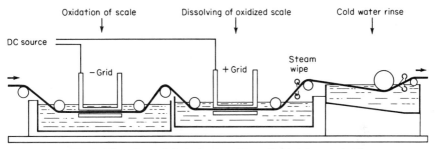

Fig. 4 Electrolytic salt bath cleaning of hot-rolled stainless steel strip.

nitric or hydrofluoric acid pickle or may be cleaned in a low-temperature salt bath followed by a sulfuric acid pickle. If the final annealing is to be in a bright annealing furnace in which oxides are not developed, precleaning is extremely important and may involve either an acid detergent system or an alkaline detergent system or a combination of the two.

Salt Bath Equipment. Salt bath conditioning on a continuous basis requires certain specialized equipment. Effective sludge settling systems are necessary to prevent the reaction products from getting trapped between the strip and the rolls and creating scratch or mar problems on the surface of the strip. A high-temperature steam wipe is necessary to prevent the fast travel of the strip from dragging excessive amounts of salt out of the system and resulting in high operating costs and pollution problems. Synchronized roll drives are also necessary to maintain roll and strip travel in phase to prevent scratching from possible rubbing action.

WIRE PROCESSING

Salt Bath Conditioning Stainless wire processing, because of the very large surface area and the requirement for frequent annealing and subsequent cleaning, presents many specialized problems.

Salt bath conditioning (Fig. 5) is required on wire products as there is no effective way to mechanically abrade tight coils of wire. Also, there is no effective way to introduce current into a coil of wire in a molten salt bath without creating arc burns in areas of high current density. Therefore, conditioning of stainless steel wire is done in either the immersion-type oxidizing or reducing bath. The former generally is preferred because of ease of operation and the latter is sometimes required for certain scales on special grades. Throughput can either be on a continuous strand basis or on a batch-type coil basis with the latter most common because of the longer dwell times required in the molten salt conditioning process.

Batch Processing. Batch-type processing of wire coils requires a salt bath furnace, followed by a water rinse, followed by two to three pickle tanks, depending on the type of material being processed and the recommendations of the pickling department or the metallurgical group. Dwell time in the molten salt may be 10 to 20 min; this is accomplished by having several yokes in the salt bath at the same time and moving them progressively forward. Following the conditioning, the coils are water rinsed and treated in sulfuric acid with approximately a 1- to 2-min cycle. Cycles through the acid are very rapid in order to keep the production cycle going and to keep up with the coils of wire

Fig. 5   Salt bath processing of wire product.

exiting from the salt bath furnace. The sulfuric acid is maintained at 160°F (71°C) and an average concentration would be approximately 10 to 15% sulfuric acid. After sulfuric, the coils again are rinsed followed by a very rapid nitric-hydrofluoric cycle. The nitric-hydrofluoric acid is maintained at a temperature of 120°F (49°C) and at a concentration of approximately 15% nitric and 3% hydrofluoric. Elimination of the hydrofluoric acid or use of a 15% hydrochloric acid is suggested when straight-chromium grades are being processed. Scales on stainless steel wire are resistant to chemical attack and, therefore, are very difficult to remove. Longer salt times and the higher concentrations of acids are required to effect complete cleanliness.

Multiple Strand Systems. Continuous systems for cleaning stainless steel wire, at the present time, are restricted to strand-type operations. Here multiple strands pass over guide rolls simultaneously into a molten salt bath and out through exit rolls into a water quench as shown in Fig. 6. Immersion times are necessarily very short because of the high speeds required for production and limitations on the length of the salt bath. The short dwell times also impose the requirement that this method of cleaning be limited to light soils treated in oxidizing-type salt baths.

The Helicofil System. Another continuous method which has been applied on a limited basis to light pickling systems is the Helicofil method as shown in Fig. 7. Longer dwell times are possible with this system because longer sections can be immersed within a shorter horizontal space. Based on the circumferential formula, πD, for every 3-ft (0.91-m) diameter loop, 9.42 ft (2.87 m) of wire will be immersed. It is even probable that, in the future, an efficient method of introducing electrical current into wire will be possible with the Helicofil system. At the present time, the limitations on a continuous current feed without arcing are quite substantial.

In both the continuous strand method and the Helicofil method the wire passes from

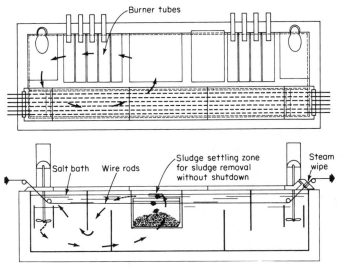

Fig. 6 Multiple-strand wire processing.

the salt bath furnace through some method of wiping, to minimize molten salt drag-out, into a water quench, followed by sulfuric acid pickle, water quench, and nitric-hydrofluoric pickling solution.

PROCESSING OF SHEET AND PLATE

Stainless steel sheet and plate in the hot-rolled annealed condition can be heavily scaled, producing serious problems in cleaning and pickling. Because of configuration, sheet and

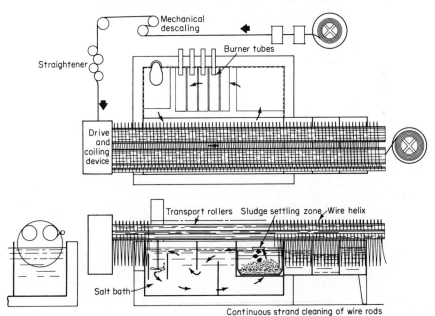

Continuous strand cleaning of wire rods

plate generally are processed in racks (Fig. 8). Continuous systems in which the plates are fixtured individually are also possible.

Hot-rolled annealed scale can be removed from plate or sheet by mechanical finishing or shot-blasting operations. This treatment is more common with plate because the restrictions on surface finish are generally less severe. Shot blasting of plate requires that

Fig. 8   Processing of stainless steel sheets.

it be handled in a system which allows access of the shot to both large surfaces and all four edges of the plate. Following blasting, the plate then passes through a final pickle which can be an immersion-type bath or a spray pickle. The purpose of the pickle in this case is to remove any traces of remaining scale and also to dissolve directly any contaminants present in the blasting media. An initial pickle of sulfuric acid generally is used to dissolve any iron on the surface followed by a final treatment and brightening in nitric-hydrofluoric. Sulfuric concentrations can vary between 10 and 20% from ambient temperature to 160°F (71°C). The final nitric-hydrofluoric pickle can vary in temperature between ambient and 120°F (49°C) with a concentration of 20% nitric and 4% hydrofluoric.

Salt Bath Conditioning. Salt bath conditioning, which can be either the oxidizing or the reducing-type salt bath, must be followed by water rinsing and acid pickling. Salt time of 20 to 30 min is normal. Handling systems should be geared to lower the plate or the fixture which carries several plates into the salt bath. After the conditioning cycle, the system must again return the plates to a horizontal traveling system which can carry them into a spray rinsing, acid pickle, second spray rinse, final acid pickle, and final rinse. Because of the carryover of the alkaline salt, the initial pickle should be 10 to 20% sulfuric at 140 to 160°F (60 to 71°C) which neutralizes the residual alkali as well as solubilizing the scale. Final pickling is accomplished in a 10% nitric plus 2% hydrofluoric acid in either a spray or immersion tank. The plates travel from salt bath conditioning through the pickling system on a continuous conveyor or automated system or are transferred from station to station by a hoist in a manual system.

CAST AND FORGED PRODUCTS

Scale Composition   Cast and forged products present unusual cleaning problems because the scales formed during long-time soaking at high temperature are usually complexed with either mold residues or forging lubricants. The resulting high-temperature glassy slags on the surface can only be removed by mechanical finishing or salt bath

Fig. 9   Miscellaneous turbine blade forgings.

conditioning. Usually, mechanical treatments are limited because of complicated part shape or the critical requirements of small sections.

Oxidizing Salt Bath Conditioning   Cast or forged parts (Fig. 9) can be conditioned successfully in the oxidizing-type salt bath. The initial reactions involved are the oxidation of any organic lubricant residues on the surface and the solubilizing of siliceous materials. The elimination of these residues allows the salt bath to contact the layers of scale, converting metal-rich insoluble oxides to the gas-rich form. This process is aided by the differential thermal expansion that occurs when the metal part and the scale are heated to the operating temperature. The reactions associated with oxidizing salt bath conditioning are as follows:

$$C + 2NaNO_3 = CO_2 + 2NaNO_2 \tag{10}$$
$$CO_2 + 2NaOH = Na_2CO_3 + H_2O \tag{11}$$
$$SiO_2 + 2NaOH = Na_2SiO_3 + H_2O \tag{12}$$
$$2M_3O_4 + NaNO_3 = 3M_2O_3 + NaNO_2 \tag{13}$$
$$NaNO_2 + 0.5O_2 = NaNO_3 \tag{14}$$

Reducing Salt Bath Conditioning   Cast and forged products can also be conditioned in reducing-type salt baths provided the surface scale is not complexed with organic or graphitic residues. If graphite is present on the surface, it is nonreactive in the reducing bath and, therefore, interferes with proper conditioning. Siliceous materials are soluble also in the reducing bath and oxide conversion can proceed according to the following equation after the surface residues have been dissolved:

$$M_2O_3 + 3NaH = 2M + 3NaOH \tag{15}$$

Electrolytic Processing   Another very effective approach to the descaling of cast and forged products involves the electrolytic salt bath. Since the work can be made either anodic or cathodic, it is possible to remove both the organic soils and scales by varying the polarity. With the workpiece positive in the bath, carbonaceous residues are removed according to the following equations:

$$C + 4OH^- = CO_2 + 2H_2O \tag{16}$$
$$CO_2 + 2NaOH = Na_2CO_3 + H_2O \tag{17}$$

With the surface free of organic materials, the polarity of the workpiece is reversed, developing a condition for the removal of the various chromium, nickel, iron, and silicon oxides according to the following general equation:

$$M_2O_3 + 6Na^+ = 2M + 3Na_2O \tag{18}$$

Acid Pickling   After each type of conditioning, thorough water rinsing is required to remove residual alkaline salts which would tend to neutralize the acid pickling solutions. Pickling is accomplished in the usual initial sulfuric acid bath at 180°F (82°C) and a concentration of 20% followed by another water rinse and brightening in a nitric-hydrofluoric concentration of 10 parts nitric acid, 2 parts hydrofluoric acid at 120°F (49°C). Desmutting solutions frequently are used on high-alloy parts which develop smut during the pickling cycle. A typical cycle for processing stainless turbine blades is shown in Table 4.

Processing Methods. Cast and forged products normally are processed in batch-type equipment if their section size prohibits automated systems. The requirements for batch-type processing include a manually operated hoist, overhead rail with positioning of salt bath water rinse and pickle tanks to allow the operator to proceed with a logical sequence during cycling.

When the formed parts are sufficiently small to allow fixture or basket handling, automated continuous conditioning and descaling systems are the most efficient. A diagram of one such system is shown in Fig. 10.

PROCESSING OF BAR, SHAPES AND TUBING

Oxidizing Salt Bath Conditioning   Bars and shapes usually have surface contamination equivalent or quite similar to that experienced with cast and forged products. High-temperature lubricants are required for the severe hot-working operations that are necessary to produce complicated shapes and tubing. These lubricants are generally glass lubricants and are soluble in the conditioning bath. Conditioning in an oxidizing salt bath again requires a solubilizing of these lubricants to expose the surface oxides to

TABLE 4   Cycles for Processing Turbine Blades

Ferrous alloys		Titanium alloys	
Operation	Time, min	Operation	Time, min
Salt bath	10	Salt bath	10
Water quench	2.5	Water quench	2.5
Sulfuric acid	2	Sulfuric acid	2
Cold-water rinse	2	Cold-water rinse	2
Alkaline permanganate	10	Nitric-hydrofluoric acid	1.5
Cold-water rinse	2	Cold-water rinse	1
Sulfuric acid	1	Hot-water rinse	1
Cold-water rinse	1	Air dry	Varies
Nitric acid	1.5		
Cold-water rinse	1		
Hot-water rinse	1		
Air dry	Varies		

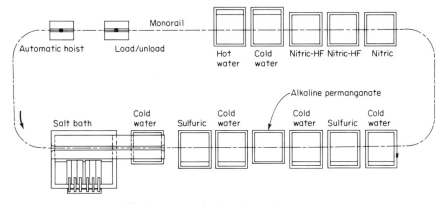

Fig. 10 Automatic batch pickling of forgings.

the reaction of the salt bath. The reactions in the salt bath are identical with Eqs. (12) and (13).

Reducing Salt Bath Conditioning   The reducing salt bath can also be used on bars, shapes, and tubing since organic materials are not present on the surface. The siliceous residues are quite soluble in the caustic-based reducing bath. The chemical reactions in this type of bath are identical with those shown in Eqs. (6) and (12).

One disadvantage associated with the reducing salt bath in operations involving bars and shapes is that long salt baths are required and the large surface area exposed creates problems in maintaining a reducing condition in the bath. Because of the type of work

Fig. 11   Batch pickle house for processing bar, shapes and tubing.

being handled, bars, shapes, and tubing generally are processed in batch-type systems. A complete batch pickle house for these configurations is shown in Fig. 11. After conditioning, the batch loads are water rinsed and pickled in the standard 160°F (71°C), 15% sulfuric acid, followed by water rinse and the 120°F (49°C), 10% nitric and 2% hydrofluoric.

FUTURE TRENDS IN STAINLESS STEEL CLEANING

Future investigations to improve the present methods of cleaning and descaling stainless steel will be directed toward minimizing acid consumption and disposal problems. This can be accomplished through increased application of electrical energy to cleaning systems, whether continuous or batch operations. Electrolytic acid pickling can also reduce the concentration of acids required and the metal attack.

Combinations of mechanical finishing, including abrasive cleaning, flapper-type wheels, and even slurry finishing, will be used with salt bath conditioning. It is quite feasible that the proper combinations will effectively minimize or possibly eliminate acid requirements.

One area of investigation that has been seriously neglected in recent years, but which is expected to grow in the future, is the control of furnace atmospheres to reduce the amount of scale formed in heat-treating operations with a consequent reduction in conditioning and pickling requirements. New scientific equipment which permits exact analyses of molecular surface films will aid in determining the direction of furnace atmosphere control.

Development in the knowledge of chelating systems, along with the introduction of new metal chelates, holds strong promise for the eventual elimination of acid in pickling systems. At the present time, it is quite feasible, with lighter scales that have been oxidized, to completely clean heat-treated parts in a caustic-based chelated solution.

Part **6**

The Applications
of Stainless Steels

Chapter 36

Stainless Steels
in Architecture

A. LEE DOVERSPIKE
Republic Steel Corporation, Cleveland, Ohio

The use of stainless steel as an architectural material has increased steadily through the years. The increased use can be attributed to a number of factors, including a better knowledge of the material, attempts to design something different, and the desire to produce a structure that is not only long lasting, but also nearly maintenance-free.

Early architectural uses of stainless steel were limited to applications where the design architect was looking for a new material to produce a special effect not previously available. In many of these cases stainless was used even though its long-term performance was yet unknown and had to stand the test of time.

The dome and gargoyles of the Chrysler Building in New York City are a prime example of a search for a new material combined with a concern for the durability of the material. The decision to use stainless steel, indeed quite a decision in 1929, was made with the condition that the producing mill would roll and hold additional material in the event that it should ever be needed for replacement. In 1969, after 40 years, it was determined the extra sheets would not be needed, so the mill melted them for reuse.

Periodic cleaning has revealed what stainless producers have long thought—stainless steel will not deteriorate when used for outdoor applications, even in highly corrosive atmospheres (see Fig. 1).

The combination of the two properties of stainless, its durability and its nearly maintenance-free surface, are causing more people to specify stainless than ever before. The cost of most construction materials has been rising at a rapid, yet constant, rate. The cost of many materials has risen more sharply than has that of stainless. However, the cost of maintaining the interior and exterior of the buildings in prime condition has skyrocketed.

Today's architects must think beyond the completion of the building. Their success will be short-lived if the maintenance on a building increases dramatically and unnecessarily over the years.

Architects designing today's schools have awakened to the problem after voters across the country have often said "no" to renewal or new operating levies. A prime example of the switch away from painted carbon steel or aluminum to stainless steel can be seen in the Forest Manor Middle School, Indianapolis, Indiana. Stainless steel, Type 304 with a number 4 polish, was used in the pool area because of the corrosive atmosphere produced by high humidity and high temperatures. It was felt that painted carbon steel would need

Fig. 1 After more than 40 years the dome of the Chrysler Building in New York City shines brightly.

Fig. 2 Stainless steel helps reduce the maintenance costs in high humidity areas. Location: Forest Manor School, Indianapolis, Ind. Architect: James Associates Architects, Indianapolis. Fabricator: Emerson Engineering Company, Indianapolis.

repainting every 2 or 3 years, an expensive job indeed. Aluminum was rejected because of its lack of abrasion resistance. With 3000 youthful students using the facilities per week, the abrasion resistance of stainless steel had to be considered (see Fig. 2).

The use of stainless steel for the walls of a swimming pool has been gaining acceptance in recent years. Painted concrete, long the primary material, had to be patched and

Fig. 3 The 72-ft-high (22-m) mirror-finish stainless steel panels add to the feeling of height and reflect the passage of thousands through the World Trade Center lobby. Architects: Minuro Yamasaki and Emery Roth and Associates, New York. Fabricators and Erectors: Craft Architectural Products Inc., Huntington, L.I., N.Y.

painted every year, particularly in the northern regions of the country. The pools made from painted carbon steel needed extensive scrubbing or painting every year. Both the patching and painting and the scrubbing and painting added considerably to the operating costs of the pools. When stainless steel, Type 304 with a 2B finish, is used, the sides of the pool simply require scrubbing with soap and water and a quick rinse. Concrete bottoms are still often used with the stainless walls, primarily as an "antislip" measure.

The tremendous number of finishes available from the stainless steel producers has been another factor in the increased acceptance of the material. The use of a tampico-brushed finish can add the softness a designer needs to control reflectivity, just as a bright annealed or highly polished surface can introduce a feeling of expansion into the design.

For the lobbies of the World Trade Center in New York City, Minuro Yamasaki chose Type 304 stainless steel with a number 8 architectural mirror finish for the 72-ft (22-m) high lobby walls.

The matched panels were polished and color buffed so that all of the panels had the same hue and reflectivity. To prevent "oil canning," the heavy gage stainless sheets were mounted on thick sandwich panels composed of galvanized steel and compressed flake board. The polished panels were affixed to the galvanized steel with an epoxy bonding agent (Fig. 3).

The availability of "dead soft" stainless has led to the use of stainless steel as a flashing and roofing material. Because of the ease with which it can be formed and its durability and beauty, builders of a number of buildings have used stainless not only as a protective cover but as an integral part of the design.

The Benjamin F. Yak Recreation Center in Wyandotte, Michigan, used a Bermuda-type stainless steel roof with horizontal overlapping seams. Not only is the roof beautiful and functional, but the reflectivity of the surface of the stainless steel has permitted an extended indoor ice skating season without incurring unreasonable operating expenses (see Fig. 4).

Problems unique to certain structures have been solved by using stainless steel. A parking garage in White Plains, New York, wanted to provide protection for the automo-

Fig. 4 The long low roof of the Benjamin F. Yak Recreation Center in Wyandotte, Michigan adds to the beauty of the building and at the same time helps reduce heat penetration into the ice skating area. Architect: Jack W. Yops, Wyandotte. Roofing Contractor: Firegaugh and Reynolds Roofing Contractor.

biles parked in the garage and provide for good ventilation of the exhaust while at the same time allowing a certain degree of natural daylight. The material used was to last indefinitely and was to be maintenance-free. All this was accomplished by using 6 × 10 in. (15 × 25 cm) Type 201 stainless steel blanks fastened to vertical columns, placing one blank on the outside, the next on the inside and repeating the pattern. To add interest to the design, alternating rows of the outside panels have an embossed finish. The other exterior rows have a plain 2B finish. All of the interior panels have a 2D finish. The alternating patterns have created a striking appearance in what might have been just another parking garage.

When a structure is on the roof of a building, consideration must be given to appearance as well as durability. At Kennedy International Airport on Long Island, New York, the exhaust fans from a restaurant in the National Airlines "Sundrome" Terminal were to be covered with stainless steel for esthetic purposes. In selecting the material for the cover, emphasis had to be placed on the nonreflectivity of the material as well as the durability. a satin-polished, low-reflective, number 6 finish on Type 304 stainless steel was used. Care had to be exercised in the selection of the finish to prevent glare from the top of the unit that could hamper a pilot's vision during his final approach to the landing area.

The Cleveland Federal Office Building, Cleveland, Ohio, utilizes stainless steel for both the interior and the exterior of the building. It was the first General Services Administration (GSA) building to specify a stainless steel curtain wall. Stainless steel was also used to cover the colonnade columns at the building's entrance as well as the window washer tracks on the face of the building (see Fig. 5).

The ceiling of the lobby of the Cleveland Federal Office Building is composed of embossed panels of stainless steel. Male and female dies were used to emboss the pattern into the stainless sheets. The 1-in. (2.5-cm) high, 3-in. (7.6-cm) square embossed patterns

Fig. 5 The Cleveland Federal Office Building was the first GSA building to have stainless steel specified as the material for the curtain wall.

Fig. 6 The embossed ceiling of the Cleveland Federal Office Building provides an interesting pattern as well as the illusion of depth.

Fig. 7 The famed "Gateway to the West" arch in St. Louis, Missouri. An observation area inside the apex of the arch permits visitors to view the surrounding countryside.

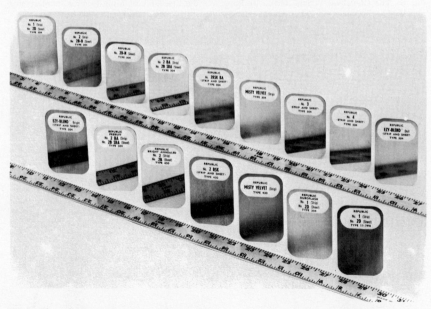

Fig. 8 The reflectivity of standard and proprietary stainless finishes is reflected in a ruler. Republic Steel makes a wide range of finishes for architectural applications. They range from the duller 2D finish, which has a frosty gray appearance and is seldom used, to the 2B mill finish, which is the one most widely used for architectural applications.

are separated by inch-wide flat depressions. The inch-wide recessed area has been painted with a semimatte finish black paint which creates an illusion of greater depth in the embossing (see Fig. 6).

Although known primarily for its durability, stainless steel is quite acceptable as a material for sculpture, which may be used to enhance the lines of a building or as a primary element of a plaza. A downtown renewal project in Kansas City, Kansas, called for a pedestrian mall depicting the terrain of the Kansas countryside. At the east end of the mall, 30 stainless steel pylons, each 20 ft (6.1 m) high and 5 ft (1.5 m) square, stand in a reflecting pool. The pylons represent the tall buildings and grain elevators located in eastern Kansas.

Another example of the use of stainless steel as the prime material for a work of outdoor art is the famed "Gateway to the West" arch on the bank of the Mississippi River in St. Louis, Missouri. The arch, highly reflective in the daytime and beautifully illuminated at night, has become one of the biggest tourist attractions in mid-America (see Fig. 7).

Stainless steel is adaptive. Its high strength-to-weight ratio makes it ideally suited for construction purposes. The wide variety of surface finishes (see Fig. 8) adds immeasurably to the adaptability of stainless steel for virtually any architectural application. Its use mainly depends on the architect's imagination.

Chapter **37**

Stainless Steels in Marine Systems*

B. FLOYD BROWN

Senior Research Scientist, Department of Chemistry, The American
University, Washington, D.C.

The oxide film responsible for the stainlessness of chromium-bearing steels can be broken down mechanically (as at rubbing surfaces within a working wire rope), electrically (as by stray currents) and chemically by certain ions, notably the chloride ion. The effectiveness of the chloride ion in breaking down the oxide film gives rise to the dictum that *stainless steels are not stainless in seawater* unless either (1) cathodically protected or (2) washed by a flow of oxygen-bearing seawater sufficient to keep the oxide film in repair. Despite this dictum stainless steels of various grades are being used in ever-increasing quantities for various purposes in the marine environment, often successfully. *Successful prolonged corrosion-free service of stainless steel in seawater requires sophisticated corrosion engineering, or enormous good fortune.*

*The support of the Office of Naval Research under Contract Number N 00014-68-A-0245-0009 during the preparation of this manuscript is gratefully acknowledged. R. T. Foley, T. J. Lennox, Jr., and M. H. Peterson read the draft and made very helpful suggestions.

Austenitic and martensitic stainless steels have long been used in marine power plants as superheater tubing and turbine blading, respectively. Great pains are taken to keep the chloride level in these power plants low, and as a consequence the technology of this application does not differ in essentials from that of power generation in general. Stainless steels are also being used for bulk chemical containers aboard merchant ships, but certain aspects of this service are sufficiently different from the land-based chemical industry to merit cautionary remarks, which are given in the section on applications.

Success in the design, fabrication, and maintenance of structures for the marine environment requires attention to both mechanical and chemical properties. Purely mechanical brittle fracture is not likely to be a problem with the austenitic types that would be the preferred stainless steels for marine service. Brittle fracture *could* be a problem with ferritic types, depending on temperature, and with martensitic, precipitation-hardenable, and maraging grades. Brittle-fracture properties are not affected by chemical environment, however, so that the fracture considerations treated in Chap. 21 are applicable regardless of service. This chapter concentrates on the special *corrosion* consideration which the marine environment requires for stainless steels and therefore treats only corrosion-related failure modes.

PRINCIPLES

The special failure modes which must be guarded against in the marine environment are due to the presence of appreciable concentrations of chloride ions. Guidance in avoiding these corrosion-related failure modes is preferably sought from research and experience in the sea itself rather than in beaker-size tests using (typically) sodium chloride solution or ferric chloride. The reason for this preference is not so much the many other chemical elements present in seawater (although at times they can make important differences in behavior) as it is the fact that conducting a corrosion experiment in a limited quantity of corrodent may change the corrodent in important ways and produce misleading results. An additional reason to prefer guidance from observations using natural seawater is that marine organisms can affect corrosion behavior to an important degree. Unfortunately there are very few corrosion laboratories sited on full strength seawater which is also relatively uncontaminated, and this limited testing capability hampers the development of marine corrosion data banks. There is an additional factor which limits the amount of quantitative guidance available in the marine corrosion field, and that is that the most preferred candidate materials are those which corrode only very slowly. We have not learned how to characterize their corrosion behavior in a proven manner except by lengthy experiments, typically lasting 1 year or more.

For these reasons the corrosion characterizations given in this chapter are based on limited experimentation and are necessarily largely qualitative and to some extent subjective. The corrosion modes considered are general rusting, crevice corrosion and pitting (taken as a single process), stress-corrosion cracking, and corrosion fatigue.

General Rusting   Most grades of stainless steel perform satisfactorily in the marine atmosphere, except that certain ones discussed below may be susceptible to stress-corrosion cracking. The martensitic steels, typified by Type 410, and ferritic steels, typified by Type 430, may rust in a few months in the marine atmosphere. If this general rusting is objectionable, it may be removed by mechanical polishing. The preferred stainless steels for the marine atmosphere are the austenitics (except, again, as noted in the section on stress-corrosion cracking) because of their greater resistance to staining. Even the austenitics darken with time, and if this darkening is objectionable for esthetic or other reasons, it can be removed by mechanical polishing. General rusting of the stainless steels in seawater is of little or no practical concern.

Crevice Corrosion and Pitting   In seawater, within flanges, at faying surfaces, in other designed crevices such as under bolt heads, and under sessile organisms, silt, fragments of seashells, and a host of other matter, the protective oxide film on stainless steels tends to break down, permitting localized corrosion. Although the cleaning action of initial chemical passivation treatments is desirable, they do not prevent this breakdown, though they may delay it. An example of the consequences of this breakdown and localized corrosion is shown in Fig. 1. Since the corrosion remains localized rather than wandering in turn over the entire surface, it takes the form of pits or of cavities at crevices, with the vast majority of the surface being unaffected. Although pitting and crevice corrosion are considered together here, in practice it is the crevice, rather than a pit in a boldly exposed area, which constitutes the problem in most engineering applications.

Whether pitting or crevice corrosion, the amount of surface affected is so small that the *average* corrosion, as determined for example by dividing the weight of metal corroded by the total metal surface, is *always* exceedingly small for all the stainless steels in seawater. In the older literature, including some handbooks, it is common to see corrosion rates quoted as *average* values, in terms such as "mdd" (milligrams per square decimeter per day) or "ipy" (inches per year). Tabulations so headed read like just the thing the engineer wants, in order to apply a "corrosion allowance." However, the *average* amount of corrosion is of no significance if the real corrosion is concentrated, say under an O-ring, or as a perforating pit in a tank, or as a groove under a crevice which may initiate corrosion fatigue failure. *Average* corrosion rates of stainless steels in seawater are not only fiction, they are always misleading and in the dangerous direction, and such tabulations should be *totally ignored.* A "corrosion allowance" based on average corrosion rate is an invalid concept for stainless steels in seawater.

The local corrosion in crevices and pits in stainless steels in seawater is characterized by highly acidic solution in the corroding area—pH 2 or lower, even though the seawater a fraction of a millimeter away may have a pH of 8. This acidification is due to the hydrolysis of chromic ions according to the equation[1]

$$Cr^{3+} + 3H_2O = Cr(OH)_3 + 3H^+$$
$$pH = 1.60 - \tfrac{1}{3}\log\lfloor Cr^{3+}\rfloor$$

Once this acid condition is established, the oxide film cannot re-form without external intervention, there is no self-stifling mechanism, and corrosion proceeds apace. Methods of external intervention both to prevent this reaction and to stop it once it is proceeding are discussed below.

All the commercial stainless steels made in the United States are susceptible to crevice corrosion and pitting in seawater, but there is a large difference in degree of susceptibility among the various types. These corrosion modes are processes of nucleation and growth, both of which (but predominantly nucleation) are affected by composition and neither of which has been well quantified.

In addition to the other problems of acquiring reliable numerical data on marine corrosion already cited, the problem of reproducibility of crevice-corrosion experiments is an acute one. Crevice corrosion may be observed in one specimen in a matter of weeks, but an apparently replicate specimen at the same site may appear inert for a year or more. For this reason the following categorization of susceptibility of various steels according to their crevice-

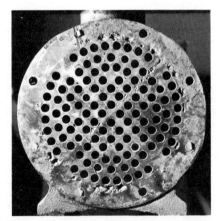

Fig. 1   Crevice corrosion and pitting of Type 316 stainless steel heat exchanger in seawater. Tubes also were perforated. *(Courtesy of M. H. Peterson and T. J. Lennox, Jr., Naval Research Lab.)*

corrosion and pitting behavior must be both qualitative and somewhat subjective:

- Highly susceptible: 200 series, 400 series, and Type 303
- Somewhat susceptible: 300 series (less 303) and the precipitation-hardenable steels, with Type 316 or 316L decidedly superior
- Slightly susceptible: Carpenter 20Cb3

It is thought that the molybdenum in Type 316 is an important factor in its superior performance and probably in the performance of 20Cb3. But this superior performance is largely in low probability of nucleation; once a crevice area or pit becomes active, it may corrode as rapidly as some of the more susceptible steels, perhaps 0.2 in. (5 mm) or more in depth per year.

The experience with new alloys, expecially those containing molybdenum, suggests that other formulations warranting future inclusion in the "slightly susceptible" or even in an "effectively immune" category are distinctly possible, but conservative practice would require prolonged experience in the sea with several heats of the steel for such classification.

Sensitization by welding or by heat treatment (as in stress-relieving a carbon steel weldment clad with stainless steel) degrades the ability of a given type to resist crevice corrosion and pitting. The nature of the crevicing material can make an important difference in kinetics as well, with carbon and vulcanized rubber (containing both sulfur and carbon) being decidedly undesirable materials to have in contact with the steel. Both the probability of nucleation and the rate of crevice attack after nucleation are greater for greater ratios of area outside the crevice to area within the crevice. Increasing temperature also increases the probability of crevice corrosion and pitting. Thus a soot particle from high-sulfur fuel lying on a stainless steel surface warmed by the sun and subject to a moist salt atmosphere has a high probability of initiating a pit.

To give the reader some quantitative feel for the rate of these forms of localized corrosion in seawater, crevice corrosion of the Type 304 specimen extended 0.02 to 0.045 in. (0.5 to 1.1 mm) in depth in 649 days. In the same location and configuration of specimen, the depth for 20Cb3 was 0.004 in. (0.1 mm). Alloys in the "acutely susceptible" category could exhibit as much as either of these in a very few weeks.

The corrosion potentials of most stainless steels in seawater lie in the band between +0.2 to −0.2 V_{SCE}.* Cathodic protection by coupling through a metallic path to enough mild steel to bring the potential of the stainless steel to about −0.6 V_{SCE} has been found effective in mitigating crevice corrosion in 200-, 300-, and 400-series stainless steels, particularly in the preferred 300-series steels, but has been found to be comparatively ineffective in reducing the depth of random pitting [typically about 0.003 in./yr (0.08 mm/yr)] not associated with an obvious crevice.[2]

Cathodic protection to bring the potential to about −1.05 V_{SCE} has been found to be effective in greatly reducing or even eliminating crevice corrosion and also in mitigating random pitting. But cathodic protection of ferritic, martensitic, precipitation-hardenable, and perhaps maraging stainless steels to potentials more negative than about −0.8 V may cause blistering or cracking due to hydrogen. The austenitics appear to be immune to hydrogen cracking from normal cathodic protection, with the possible exception of cold-rolled Type 301. Cathodic protection is not only capable of preventing crevice corrosion, but it can also stop crevice corrosion already in progress by neutralizing the acid solution noted earlier thereby permitting re-formation of the protective oxide film. If zinc anodes are selected for cathodic protection in seawater, they should conform to MIL-A-18001h to be reliable. For reference purpose, the potential of this grade of zinc is about −1.03 V_{SCE}.

Many of the successful applications of stainless steel in the sea can be attributed to cathodic protection provided by a metallic connection to mild steel, low-alloy steel, or cast iron where these more active metals are either uncoated or, at best, have an imperfect paint system, or alternatively where the steel or cast iron and consequently the stainless steel are protected by a cathodic protection system. For example, the stainless steel sonar dome on a ship may receive cathodic protection from the vastly larger area of imperfectly painted hull steel, or alternatively both may be protected by zinc anodes mounted on the bilge keel or by an impressed current system.

The principles by which crevice corrosion and pitting are avoided in the case of the sonar dome are common to several seemingly different situations. Cathodic protection from the steel hull or from the zinc anodes functions adequately to protect the stainless steel under stagnant conditions. Under the turbulent conditions of high-speed runs, the stainless steel dome will not be polarized appreciably (its potential will not be changed nearly as much); but under high-speed conditions enough oxygen is made available to the surface to maintain the oxide film in good repair, and additionally, the flowing seawater counters the tendency for the development of local acidification. It should be noted, however, that in deep crevices, such as in broad flanges, the beneficial external turbulence may not extend into the crevice; the attack within the crevice may be intensified. For this reason some seawater pump shafts are made of 20Cb3.

*SCE = saturated calomel electrode.

The reliability of coatings to prevent localized corrosion of stainless steels in seawater service is not well established, and in fact could contribute to crevice corrosion by supplying the equivalent of a crevice at a defect in the coating.

Mention has been made of pitting or crevice corrosion in the marine atmosphere under soot particles. In general, conservative design practice employing stainless steels for service in the marine atmosphere calls for avoiding crevices or other sites in which salt water can collect and remain, and conservative maintenance practice calls for periodic rinsing away of accumulated salt to avoid pitting or crevice corrosion. Cathodic protection methods are, of course, seldom applicable to the problem of atmospheric pitting from pocketed seawater.

Stress-Corrosion Cracking   This failure mode is virtually unknown in unheated seawater except for the heat-treated high-strength grades. Cracking has been reported in one application of highly cold-drawn Type 316 wire in seawater, and one might be concerned about cracking in cold-rolled Type 301, but the major concern in both these steels when immersed in seawater is crevice corrosion, which may in effect provide sacrificial cathodic protection against cracking.

There have been a limited number of cases of stress-corrosion cracking of heavily cold-worked Types 301, 302, and 303 and also Types 430 and AM 355 stainless steels in the marine *atmosphere* (Fig. 2). These have usually been under circumstances in which brine may have become concentrated by the evaporation of spray, or in which solar heating may have played a role, or both.

If stainless steel tubing is used to heat bulk cargo space, and if the space has been washed down with seawater, care must be taken *not* to activate the heating system until the chloride has been rinsed away with fresh water, for even the premium 300-series grades are acutely susceptible to stress-corrosion cracking in the presence of chloride ions at temperatures above about 50°C (122°F). Forming stresses, assembly stresses, or thermal stresses can be counted on to provide the requisite stress for this failure mode.

Fig. 2 Stress-corrosion cracks in Type 303 stainless steel nuts after service in marine atmosphere. Similar cracking has been observed in cold-rolled Type 301 components in the marine atmosphere. (*Courtesy of W. W. Kirk, The International Nickel Company.*)

The high-strength stainless steels of most current interest for marine applications are the precipitation-hardenable steels. The values of stress-corrosion cracking resistance K_{Iscc} as measured by fracture mechanics methods have been determined for a number of precipitation-hardenable steels in salt water, and the results are plotted in Fig. 3 as a function of yield strength. From the Irwin equation, if one assumes stresses equal to the yield strength and the existence of a long surface crack-like flaw, the flaw would be expected to propagate as a stress-corrosion crack if it is deeper than a critical value given by $a_{cr} = 0.2(K_{Iscc}/\sigma_Y)^2$. Lines representing three values of a_{cr} are drawn in Fig. 3. If, for example, one had to assume the possibility of a flaw as deep as 0.01 in. (0.25 mm), in 17-7PH steel (triangles marked "19" on Fig. 3) stress-corrosion cracks would be expected to grow, because the K_{Iscc} is lower than that line and its critical flaw size would therefore be less than 0.01 in. (0.25 mm). On the other hand, 15-5PH steel (marked "17" on Fig. 3) would not be expected to crack, according to these data.

Another way to interpret the data of Fig. 3 is that for a component containing a standard-sized crack, the load-carrying capability is linearly proportional to its K_{Iscc} value.

Corrosion Fatigue   The corrosion fatigue characteristics of stainless steels in seawater, particularly the 300-series steels, are intermediate between those of unalloyed or low-alloy steels and those of the superalloys. The methodology for containing the corrosion-fatigue problem consists primarily of using the geometric design principles which contain the plain fatigue problem (avoiding sharp fillets, avoiding high local strain ranges at load-transfer sites, etc.) and also avoiding conditions which lead to crevice corrosion or pitting, either of which may cause premature initiation of a corrosion fatigue crack.

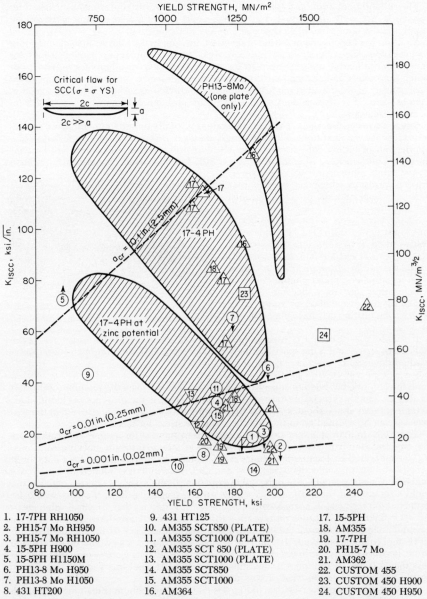

Fig. 3   Resistance to stress-corrosion cracking in salt water by precipitation-hardenable stainless steel alloys. *(After Sprowls, et al.[3] with added information courtesy of C. T. Fujii, Naval Research Lab.)*

1. 17-7PH RH1050	9. 431 HT125	17. 15-5PH
2. PH15-7 Mo RH950	10. AM355 SCT850 (PLATE)	18. AM355
3. PH15-7 Mo RH1050	11. AM355 SCT1000 (PLATE)	19. 17-7PH
4. 15-5PH H900	12. AM355 SCT 850 (PLATE)	20. PH15-7 Mo
5. 15-5PH H1150M	13. AM355 SCT1000 (PLATE)	21. AM362
6. PH13-8 Mo H950	14. AM355 SCT850	22. CUSTOM 455
7. PH13-8 Mo H1050	15. AM355 SCT1000	23. CUSTOM 450 H900
8. 431 HT200	16. AM364	24. CUSTOM 450 H950

FUNCTIONAL APPLICATIONS

Propellers   Propellers for tugs and other work boats may be made of cast stainless steel CF-8, equivalent to Type 304. When the boat is not underway, there is electrical continuity in a metallic path from the propeller shaft through the shaft bearings to the hull, which, as a rule, has a coating sufficiently imperfect to permit the steel hull to cathodically protect the propeller against pitting under stagnant conditions. When the vessel is underway, the lubrication films in the bearings and gears tend to isolate the propeller electrically from the hull, but the relatively high speed of the propeller blades through the water keeps the protective oxide film in repair.

Cast propellers equivalent in composition to Type 410 are also in use, among other purposes, for ice breakers.

Among recent developments in stainless steel technology is the use of duplex austenitic-ferritic stainless steel of 20Cr-8Ni-3.5Mo to cast large propellers (3000 kg) for ocean-going ships.

Vessels working in harbors are particularly likely to experience a high rate of propeller damage from logs and other floating debris, and the capability of field repair of austenitic stainless steel propellers by straightening or welding is an important consideration in their selection.

Pumps Centrifugal pumps employing stainless steel components have demonstrated their reliability for seawater service provided principles discussed earlier are observed. The use of cast CF-8M impellers, corresponding in composition to Type 316, and of 316 shafting would cause no problems with constantly moving water. During downtime, crevice corrosion or pitting could be a serious problem, but this is taken care of by making the pump casing of a more active nonstainless cast iron, with ample wall thickness. The cast iron thus provides cathodic protection during downtime. The cathodic protection afforded by the pump casing might not be capable of polarizing the stainless steel when in operation, but while in operation the flow of water renders cathodic protection unnecessary. Alternatively, during prolonged layup the seawater may be replaced by fresh water.

Bulk Tankages Stainless steel is being used for special bulk cargo containers for materials such as liquefied natural gas (LNG), chemicals, and beverages. The LNG containers are customized to the one cargo, and stainless steel (304L) is used, not for its corrosion resistance, but for its mechanical properties at cryogenic temperatures.

In chemical tankages, stainless steel for sea transport is used for its corrosion resistance, and unlike land-based chemical storage and handling facilities, if the ships are engaged in general tramping, the chemical tankers may transport anything from acetic acid to molasses to xylene. Therefore as a precautionary measure, the preferred steel is Type 316L for valves, cargo pumps, piping, and heating coils as well as for the tanks themselves. The tanks may be of solid stainless or of carbon steel clad with 0.06 to 0.08 in. (1.5 to 2 mm) of stainless steel. Meticulous inspection of cladding for defects and meticulous cleaning and passivation precedes placing these systems in commission.

Usual practice permits washing down chemical tanks with seawater providing they are washed down quickly thereafter with fresh water. Also any stainless steel heaters in the tanks must not be activated until the chloride is thoroughly rinsed away, as noted in the section on stress-corrosion cracking.

Chemical tanks are not designed to be ballasted with seawater because of the hazard of crevice corrosion. If designs should require seawater ballasting, it is possible that a satisfactory cathodic protection system could be developed to control crevice corrosion. In that case the possibility of producing difficult-to-remove calcareous deposits on the stainless steel would have to be taken into consideration.

Heat Exchangers Coolers for captive water systems (Fig. 1) and condensers for steam power plants, the latter where high pollution of intake water makes copper alloys unsuitable, have made use of austenitic stainless steel tubing. The preferred grade is Type 316. Particularly in coastal or estuarine waters, the amount of solid foreign objects and silt entering the condenser tubing constitutes a hazard which must be dealt with systematically. One such system, which is proprietary, employs rubber balls which are circulated through the tubes and exert a squeegee action to clean the tube walls. A minimum flow rate of about 1 m/s is required to prevent attachment of marine organisms and to keep the condenser tubes free from pitting. Unlike some of the nonferrous alloys used for condenser tubing, there is no restriction on the maximum flow rate in stainless steel tubing short of that limited by pumping economics.

O-ring Seals Types 304 and 316 in-line electrical connectors and other fixtures involving O-ring seals have been used widely for various oceanographic and military projects. Where these applications have been successful, the O-ring seal has received cathodic protection from the hull of a ship, an aluminum frame, or other source. Without cathodic protection the O-ring groove invites rapid crevice corrosion, which has caused expensive failures, some as quickly as within a very few weeks.

REFERENCES

1. Peterson, M. H., T. J. Lennox, Jr., and R. E. Groover: *Mater. Prot.*, vol. 9, no. 1, pp. 23–26, January 1970.
2. Lennox, T. J., Jr., R. E. Groover, and M. H. Peterson: *Mater. Prot.*, vol. 8, no. 5, pp. 41–48, May 1969.
3. Sprowls, D. O., M. B. Shumaker, and J. D. Walsh: *Final Rept. on NASA Marshall Space Flight Center Contract No. NAS 9-21487*, 1973.

Additional Literature

Fink, F. W., and W. K. Boyd: "The Corrosion of Metals in Marine Environments," Bayer and Company, Columbus, Ohio, 1970.
Tuthill, A. H., and C. M. Schillmoller, "Guidelines for Selection of Marine Materials," The International Nickel Co., New York, 1966.
LaQue, F. L.: "Guide to Marine Corrosion and Protection," Wiley-Interscience, New York, 1975.

Chapter **38**

Stainless Steels in the Chemical and Process Industries

MARSHALL H. BROWN
Consultant, Wilmington, Delaware

Stainless steels are used widely in the chemical and process industries. All of the various grades are represented to at least some extent, but the major tonnages are in the austenitic grades (particularly AISI Types 304, 304L, 316, and 316L), the ferritic grade Type 430, and, for castings, ACI grades CF-8, CF-8M, and CN-7M. Many applications involve severely corrosive conditions for which no suitable lower cost material is available. However, a major proportion of the stainless steel specified for the chemical and process industries is used in services which are only mildly corrosive but where it is desired to hold product contamination to a minimum for quality control purposes.

The stainless steels are unusually versatile in the range of chemicals and operating conditions for which they are satisfactorily resistant. However, they have a number of limitations which must be recognized and guarded against to avoid failures which might otherwise occur, often under apparently mild conditions. These pitfalls apply particularly to the chemical and process industries and have caused many problems. They will be discussed here only in a practical sense since theory and more detailed background have been presented in Chapter 16.

INTERGRANULAR CORROSION

Susceptibility to intergranular corrosion due to the precipitation of chromium-rich carbides at the grain boundaries (sensitization) can result from welding or improper heat treatment of any of the austenitic stainless steels except the L grades (0.03% carbon maximum) and the stabilized grades containing columbium or titanium. Both the ease and severity of sensitization increase with carbon content. Several evaluation tests are available for the detection of susceptibility to intergranular corrosion as described in ASTM A-262.[1] Material shown to be susceptible may or may not be intergranularly attacked in another environment; this must be established independently by specific tests or service experience. The results of long-term service exposures which provide useful guidelines as to the types of environments which are capable of intergranularly attacking 300-series stainless steels of varying degrees of susceptibility have been presented by Auld[2] and by the High Alloys Committee of the Welding Research Council.[3]

The most damaging environments are hot solutions containing certain inorganic and organic acids, including nitric, sulfuric, phosphoric, formic, acetic, and lactic acids. Severely sensitized material, as determined by evaluation tests, will be intergranularly attacked at a more rapid rate and over a wider range of temperatures and concentrations than mildly sensitized material.

Many instances of failure by intergranular corrosion have been reported, including some which developed very slowly under relatively mild service conditions. For example, an improperly heat-treated cast CF-8 agitator hub casting exposed to a solution containing 28% acetic acid and 0.5% sulfuric acid at a temperature of approximately 50°C failed after 8 years of service.[4] There had been no reduction in section thickness by general corrosion, but intergranular corrosion had proceeded to a depth of approximately $\frac{1}{4}$ in. (6.35 mm) from all exposed surfaces. Failure occurred when three of the four $\frac{3}{4}$-in.-thick (19.05-mm) hub vanes snapped because the remaining $\frac{1}{4}$ in. (6.35 mm) of sound metal was no longer able to withstand the operating load.

The conventional ferritic stainless steels such as Type 430 are also susceptible to intergranular corrosion in the as-welded or improperly heat-treated condition. However, these alloys normally require heat treatment after fabrication for mechanical reasons, thus the corrosion problem is avoided at the same time. In contrast with the austenitic steels, higher temperatures are the most damaging for the ferritics and intermediate temperatures are the most favorable.

STRESS-CORROSION CRACKING

The austenitic stainless steels are subject to cracking without appreciable weight loss when exposed under tensile stress to certain specific media, particularly hot solutions containing chlorides. Cracking is predominantly transgranular, but may be partially intergranular if the alloy is in the sensitized condition. This type of failure is particularly frustrating in operating equipment since it can occur without prior warning and, when discovered, is usually beyond repair.

While chloride stress cracking has been the subject of extensive research for many years, it is still not understood thoroughly. It is not possible to assign safe limits for either chloride concentration or tensile stress. Actually, many failures occur in handling waters or solutions of quite low chloride content where some mechanism exists for concentration of chlorides to a much higher level at the location of attack. And, while high tensile stresses greatly accelerate cracking, it is not possible to reduce them sufficiently by stress-relieving treatments to guarantee against attack under severe conditions. Where practical, lowering of solution temperature can be helpful. While this variable is interrelated with chloride concentration and stress level, most service failures occur with solution temperatures above 70°C, only a small proportion below 60°C, and very few below 50°C.

There is little difference between the various grades of AISI 300-series stainless steels in vulnerability to chloride stress cracking. Material which has been imperfectly heat-treated and pickled in nitric-hydrofluoric acid solution is especially vulnerable since surface intergranular attack has already taken place to provide small crevices which serve as ideal sites for chlorides to concentrate. In such cases cracking is partially or even predominantly intergranular, depending on the severity of sensitization. Stainless steel castings seem to be less vulnerable to chloride stress cracking than wrought material and such failures seldom occur in cast stainless steel valves and pumps.

For operating equipment, proper design to minimize situations which could cause local concentration of chlorides can be very important. Obviously, crevices should be eliminated to the maximum possible extent. In some cases concentration can occur through the hot-wall effect, especially where conditions of uneven heating apply. A particular situation which has caused many failures is inadequate venting of vertical heat exchangers so that the liquid level on the shell side is some distance below the top tube sheet. Under these circumstances chlorides can concentrate on the outer tube surfaces (by evaporation of cooling water of even quite low chloride content) to cause cracking of the upper ends of the stainless steel tubes from the water side. Two special techniques have been developed to combat this problem. In one, known as "safe-ending," 1 ft (30 cm) or so of a more resistant alloy is welded to a stainless steel tube of appropriately adjusted length. In the other, the top portion [1 ft (30 cm)] of the cooling water side of each tube is protected cathodically by spraying with lead.

There are many cases where improved design could have avoided stress-cracking failures. For instance, two flat-bottomed Type 304 tanks used to store a hot process solution were mounted on concrete slabs without adequate provision to prevent seepage of brackish water underneath the tanks. Concentration of chlorides by evaporation was sufficient to cause cracking of the bottoms of both tanks within 60 days. There are a number of known instances where operating equipment was cracked even before startup during a "steaming out" operation following the use of chloride-bearing detergents or solvents for initial cleaning. Cracking has been encountered in the operation of Dowtherm systems when traces of chloride compounds concentrated and condensed together with water in dead spaces where circulation and temperature were at a minimum. Another common cause of failure is the leaching of chlorides from thermal insulation and their concentration on the hot metal surface by evaporation. All commercial insulating materials contain enough chlorides to make this mechanism possible, but some now also contain sodium silicate which acts as an effective inhibitor. Sodium silicate and sodium nitrate are also effective inhibitors in solutions if used in generous amounts, but the expense is usually too great to justify except occasionally in closed systems. Another method of protection which is used occasionally for small parts or areas is to put the surface to be exposed under compression by, for instance, shot peening.

Where operating conditions are too severe to be solved by design or operating changes, it is necessary to use a material which is more resistant to chloride stress cracking and also suitable for the particular process involved. Proprietary alloys often specified for this purpose include Incoloy 800, Carpenter 20 Cb-3, Incoloy 825, Inconel 600, and 18-18-2 (18Cr-18Ni-2Si). Most of these alloys can be cracked by long exposure in the rigorous boiling magnesium chloride test which is often used to screen alloys for vulnerability to chloride stress cracking. However, they are all sufficiently resistant to withstand most service conditions and particularly those concerned with cooling water problems. The ferritic stainless steels, Types 430 and 446, also are used sometimes to avoid chloride stress cracking, but Type 430 has more limited corrosion resistance than the austenitics and Type 446 is not readily weldable. Quite recently new high-chromium ferritic alloys of very low interstitial content have been developed which are claimed to be readily weldable, to have good general corrosion resistance, and to be highly resistant to chloride stress cracking. It is too early to predict just how important a role this new class of alloys will play in future process design, but it appears likely that it will be substantial.

Stress cracking of the austenitic stainless steels also has been reported in a variety of other media, although in many cases chloride impurities probably were actually responsible. However, there is no question that cracking can occur in chloride-free caustic solutions at high temperatures.[5] In the severely sensitized condition, cracks can be developed in high-purity water at high temperatures in the presence of oxygen;[6] in this case the cracks are predominantly intergranular. Severely sensitized austenitic stainless steels are also vulnerable to so-called polythionic acid cracking, which, again, is intergranular.[7] Polythionic acids ($H_2S_xO_8$ where x usually is 3, 4, or 5) are formed by the interaction of a sulfide (often hydrogen sulfide), moisture, and oxygen. It is thus possible to have equipment which has operated satisfactorily within the sensitizing temperature range fail by cracking during a shutdown when moisture and oxygen are introduced into the system.

The hardenable martensitic stainless steels are subject to cracking in acid sulfide solutions if their hardness is above R_c 22 to 25. In this case, the cracking usually is considered to be a form of hydrogen embrittlement. When heat-treated to high strengths (e.g., over 160 ksi [1103 MN/m^2]), these alloys may be cracked in chloride solutions and even in marine or industrial atmospheres.[8]

PITTING

Pitting is localized corrosion which is concentrated in small areas (pits) and may proceed rapidly while most of the exposed surface is essentially unattacked. For stainless steels the most troublesome exposure conditions are those on the borderline of passivity, particularly when chloride ions are present. Oxidizing chlorides (such as cupric chloride or ferric chloride) are especially bad.

Pitting is most likely to occur in stagnant solutions, under deposits, or in crevices, under conditions where concentration cells can form. Care in design can do much to prevent pitting problems. Vessels should be designed so that stagnant areas and sludge buildup are avoided. Relatively little trouble is experienced where velocities are high enough to keep the surfaces clean. Potential crevices should be sought out and eliminated wherever possible; for instance, double fillet welds should be used when practical. If lap joints must be used, they should have continuous welds on both sides. Fabricated vessels should be cleaned thoroughly before being placed in service. Gaskets and washers frequently cause trouble, especially when not properly fitted. For stainless steel tubes, a minimum velocity of 4 to 6 ft/s (1.219 to 1.829 m/s) tends to minimize pitting and helps to maintain the passive film.

In general, the addition of molybdenum to stainless alloys tends to expand the range of passivity and to reduce pitting. In most cases where pitting is a problem, the molybdenum-bearing grades offer considerable advantage over the others.

BORDERLINE PASSIVITY

The stainless steels owe their excellent corrosion resistance to their ability to readily develop passivity. The mechanism of passivity is still a matter of lively debate, but it is usually pictured as a very thin protective oxide film. However, this film must be thought of as being dynamic, rather than static like a coat of paint, i.e., as not being stable in all environments but only in those which are capable of maintaining it by healing breaks as they occur. In general, the presence of oxygen (air) or of other oxidizing agents is favorable for the maintenance of this film, while reducing agents tend to destroy it. In cases of borderline passivity, only a very slight change in conditions may make the difference. For instance, in dilute sulfuric acid at a moderate temperature, corrosion may be negligible so long as a little oxygen is present. But, if the oxygen is displaced by hydrogen (perhaps generated by corrosion of another metal elsewhere in the system), the passive film cannot be maintained and active corrosion will proceed. A slight increase in either acid concentration or temperature could bring about the same result. On the other hand, if a little nitric acid or cupric sulfate were added (both are oxidizing), the surface would remain passive over a considerably broader range of concentration and temperature. Chloride ions seem to be capable of creating local breaks in the film; consequently, if chlorides are present, the environment must strongly favor passivity if the film is to be maintained.

COMPARATIVE GENERAL CORROSION RESISTANCE

In general, the martensitic and ferritic stainless steels show a lower degree of corrosion resistance than the austenitic stainless steels. Types 405 and 410 have considerable usage in the chemical and process industries for mildly corrosive applications where somewhat better resistance than that afforded by carbon steel is required. Types 416 and 420 are employed similarly where better machinability or higher hardness is desired and Type 440 (usually 440C) where wear resistance is the primary objective. The ferritic alloys of higher chromium and low carbon contents are substantially more resistant to corrosion. Type 430 finds numerous applications, including many in services involving nitric acid. Type 446 approaches the austenitics in corrosion resistance but is limited to applications which do not require welding. The newly developed high-chromium ferritic alloys of very low interstitial content are reported to be readily weldable. Since they are not vulnerable to chloride stress cracking, they appear to offer great promise if they can be produced at reasonable cost.

Of the austenitic stainless steels, Type 304 will be used as the basis of comparison. Types 304L, 321, and 347 are equivalent in corrosion resistance but are not susceptible to intergranular corrosion in the as-welded condition. Type 304L is used more commonly since it is lower in cost. Types 316, 316L, 317, and 317L contain molybdenum and are generally more resistant than Type 304 to pitting and to various corrosive media of a nonoxidizing character. Type 303 (free-machining) is considerably less resistant than 304. Types 309 and 310 are most frequently used for high-temperature applications, but the lower carbon (S) grades offer improved corrosion resistance for a few specific applications. The AISI 200-series stainless steels are quite similar to their 300-series counterparts in corrosion resistance. The various precipitation-hardenable grades are slightly to considerably less resistant depending on the alloy and the specific heat treatment employed. Permissible operating ranges, particularly when dealing with nonoxidizing acids, can be extended by the use of proprietary stainless-type alloys of higher nickel content with molybdenum and copper additions such as Carpenter 20 Cb-3 and Incoloy 825. (See Figs. 1 to 3.)

SERVICE PERFORMANCE WITH SPECIFIC CORROSIVES

Nitric Acid   The first large-scale commercial applications for stainless steels in the 1920s were in services involving nitric acid. These first applications were of 15 to 18% Cr steel (now Type 430) and 18Cr-8Ni steel (now Type 304). The necessity for proper heat treatment to prevent intergranular corrosion in nitric acid was demonstrated at once through service failures of improperly heat-treated and as-welded equipment. These difficulties were overcome by postfabrication heat treatments involving slow cooling from about 1450°F (787°C) for Type 430 and rapid cooling from about 2000°F (1093°C) for Type 304. Later the necessity for post fabrication heat treatment of Type 304 was eliminated by the development of the columbium-stabilized grade (Type 347) and later of the extra-low-carbon grade (Type 304L). Both of these show satisfactory resistance to nitric acid in the as-welded condition. The titanium-stabilized grade (Type 321) is not reliable in the as-welded condition for services involving hot nitric acid solutions; even when welded with Type 347 electrodes, it may develop so-called knife-line attack immediately adjacent to the weld.

Type 304L is used widely for all types of equipment handling nitric acid. For a limiting corrosion rate of 5 mils/yr (0.127 mm/yr), it is satisfactory up to the atmospheric boiling point with concentrations up to about 50% and for 10 mils/yr (0.254 mm/yr) up to about 60%. However, if the acid is recirculated so that the corrosion products accumulate, attack in hot solutions at the higher concentrations is accelerated because of the presence of hexavalent chromium ions. The critical level in boiling 65% acid is about 0.004% chromium in the solution and attack increases rapidly with higher Cr^{6+} concentrations. Under such conditions, both increased general corrosion and intergranular corrosion occur, even on stabilized or extra-low-carbon grades. Accelerated corrosion also occurs when dichromates or other strong oxidizing agents (such as vanadates or cerates) are added to hot nitric acid solutions.

When nitric acid is under pressure at temperatures above the atmospheric boiling point, it becomes corrosive to stainless steels at much lower concentrations because of the

Fig. 1 Use of Type 302 stainless steel jacketing on the piping and towers at an ammonia plant has all but eliminated the need for exterior maintenance. *(The International Nickel Company.)*

retention of lower oxides of nitrogen in the system. Even at 5% concentration, a corrosion rate of 5 mils/yr (0.127 mm/yr) is reached at about 250°F (121°C) and 20 mils/yr (0.508 mm/yr) at slightly above 300°F (149°C).

At ambient temperatures, corrosion of Type 304L is almost negligible at strengths up to 94% but increases rapidly with higher concentrations. In storage of very strong acid, the condensate is of higher concentration than the solution so that the upper part of the storage tank begins to corrode when the strength of the solution exceeds about 92%. Aluminum is used commonly for the storage of 95 and 98% nitric acid, but care must be taken that the strong acid is never diluted since the resistance of aluminum decreases rapidly with decreasing concentration.

Type 309Cb is somewhat more resistant under the most severe conditions and occasionally is used where the corrosion resistance of Type 304L is not quite satisfactory. Types 316 and 316L are seldom used for nitric acid service. For Type 316L, exposure to sensitizing temperatures can bring about the formation of so-called submicroscopic sigma which results in intergranular corrosion in hot nitric acid solutions. For cast valves, pumps, etc., ACI grades CF-8 and CN-7M are regularly employed.

Type 430 continues to be used for all types of equipment in the ammonia oxidation process for nitric acid manufacture and many components in nitric acid service. Temperature ranges are somewhat more limited for various concentrations than for Type 304, but it costs less than the austenitic grades and is adequate for many applications. Its principal limitation is that it requires heat treatment after fabrication. For a limiting corrosion rate of 5 mils/yr (0.127 mm/yr), Type 430 can be used up to the atmospheric boiling point at up to about 30% concentration. At 40°C the corrosion rate is less than 1 mil/yr (0.025 mm/yr) up to about 80% concentration. Pure 70% acid is still shipped in Type 430 tank cars, although Type 304L usually is specified for new tank cars to provide

Fig. 2   Sodium cyanide towers are clad in Type 304 stainless. *(E. I. duPont de Nemours & Co.)*

more versatility in the range of chemicals which can be handled and to avoid the necessity of postfabrication heat treatment.

The resistance of chromium steels is related almost directly to chromium content. Type 446, with the highest chromium content of the ferritic stainless steels, is comparable to Type 304L in resistance to nitric acid. However, since it is very difficult to fabricate, it is employed only in the form of seamless tubing and a few special applications. Type 329 (a ferritic alloy of similar chromium content but also containing nickel and molybdenum) shows an appreciably lower corrosion rate in boiling 65% nitric acid but is also difficult to fabricate. Cast chromium stainless steels are seldom used in nitric acid service. For a long time forged Type 430 valves were employed widely but these have largely been replaced with the less expensive cast austenitic grades.

In hot dilute mixtures of nitric and sulfuric acids, the austenitic stainless steels are not attacked appreciably when the ratio of nitric acid to sulfuric acid is 2 to 1 or higher. With very dilute mixtures (about 1 to 1.5% total acid), where the proportion of nitric acid is not sufficient to maintain passivity, Type 443 (20Cr-1Cu) has greater resistance.

Mixtures of nitric and hydrofluoric acids, as used for the pickling of stainless steels, are not only sufficiently aggressive corrodents to clean the surface effectively but are capable of intergranularly corroding even mildly sensitized (imperfectly heat-treated) material. In fact, exposure for 4 h in a 10% HNO_3-3% HF solution at 70°C is a sensitive standard method for the detection of susceptibility to intergranular corrosion. Imperfectly heat-treated material, especially if somewhat overpickled, can have rather severe surface intergranular corrosion. Depending on the service condition, such a surface may encourage trouble from either chloride stress cracking, pitting, or further intergranular corrosion.

Another type of corrosion sometimes encountered in nitric acid service is *end-grain attack*. This occurs usually when the cross-sectional area of bar, rod, or tubular products is directly exposed to the acid. It is believed that the ends of inclusion stringers are attacked initially and thus provide sites for the accumulation of Cr^{6+} ions causing severe localized corrosion in the form of pinholes. This type of corrosion often can be prevented by

Fig. 3   Production unit for organic isocyanates. Type 316 is required for the columns because traces of HCl result in need for resistance to pitting. *(E. I. duPont de Nemours & Co.)*

designing to avoid exposure of cross-sectional areas to the solution. If this cannot be done, the best solution is to cover the exposed "end grain" with weld metal.

Sulfuric Acid   The austenitic stainless steels are resistant to corrosive attack by sulfuric acid within only very limited ranges of concentration and temperature. They are passive in aerated, dilute solutions at low temperatures but become active in solutions that are more concentrated, hotter, or air-free. The addition of oxidizing agents (such as nitric acid, air, or cupric sulfate) will widen the range of usefulness, while the presence of reducing agents (such as hydrogen) will narrow it. Where process requirements permit, additions of small amounts of cupric sulfate to operating solutions containing sulfuric acid sometimes are made specifically to prevent attack on stainless steel equipment. For nonoxidizing (air-free) solutions, Type 304 can be used for only cold, very dilute solutions. While the molybdenum-bearing grades are considerably more resistant than Type 304, the limiting concentration for a corrosion rate of 10 mils/yr (0.254 mm/yr) on Type 316 in air-free sulfuric acid is less than 1% near the boiling point and in the order of 5% at 50°C. Type 316L has equivalent resistance but provides protection against intergranular corrosion in the as-welded condition. Type 317L is slightly more resistant because of its higher molybdenum content and in some borderline services this can make the difference between success and failure. However, for substantial expansion of permissible operating ranges, it is necessary to go to one of the proprietary alloys such as Carpenter 20 Cb-3 or Incoloy 825 which have a higher nickel content and contain both molybdenum and copper. For cast valves and pumps, the corresponding ACI grade CN-7M is the most widely used.

Like carbon steel, the austenitic stainless steels show good resistance to concentrated sulfuric acid at relatively low temperatures. For certain services, especially those involving acid in the 100 to 101% concentration range where carbon steel is less resistant, the higher cost of stainless steel sometimes can be justified. Likewise, in services involving strong mixed acids (sulfuric and nitric acids) the stainless steels can be used at higher temperatures than carbon steel.

The martensitic and ferritic chromium steels are much less resistant to sulfuric acid solutions than the austenitics. In fact, in laboratory tests, these alloys frequently show higher corrosion rates than carbon steel.

Sulfurous Acid The molybdenum-bearing austenitic stainless steels are used frequently in process equipment handling wet sulfur dioxide and sulfurous acid environments. The relative resistance of the various grades is similar to that in sulfuric acid and intergranular corrosion sometimes has occurred adjacent to welds when the extra-low-carbon grades were not specified. Crevice-type pitting has been encountered in some instances when solids accumulated on tank bottoms or on the tops of heating coils. Hot dilute sulfuric acid solutions containing considerable amounts of sulfurous acid are particularly corrosive to the stainless steels.

Phosphoric Acid In pure phosphoric acid Types 316L and 317L are resistant to hot solutions up to about 40% concentration. Intergranular corrosion adjacent to the welds can be avoided by specification of the extra-low-carbon grade. Type 304L is used also within narrower limits. However, in commercial acid containing fluoride and sulfate impurities, severe attack on all stainless steels may occur at much lower concentrations and temperatures depending on the actual analysis.

Hydrochloric Acid All of the stainless steels are attacked rapidly by hydrochloric acid solutions of any appreciable concentration. Of the other halide acids, hydrobromic is almost as corrosive and hydriodic somewhat less. Dilute hydrofluoric acid solutions are very corrosive when hot.

Sulfamic Acid This strong inorganic acid often is used for cleaning stainless steel equipment since it forms readily soluble salts and does not cause pitting or stress-corrosion cracking. The pure acid is quite corrosive to stainless steels. However, the hot 10% solution normally used for cleaning contains ferric ion inhibitor (about 0.20 to 0.25 g/l) which reduces the corrosion rate to less than 1 mil/yr (0.025 mm/yr).

Acetic Acid The austenitic stainless steels are used widely for all types of equipment in acetic acid service. For the pure acid, Type 304 is resistant at glacial strength and all lower concentrations at moderate temperatures and Type 316L is resistant up to the atmospheric boiling point. Specification of the extra-low-carbon grade is desirable for the higher temperature applications in order to avoid intergranular corrosion in fabricated equipment. Anhydrous (100%) acetic acid is considerably more corrosive at the higher temperatures but in mixtures of acetic acid and acetic anhydride, corrosion decreases with increasing anhydride content.

Various impurities encountered in the manufacture or use of acetic acid (particularly chlorides and formic acid) can greatly accelerate corrosion, sufficiently in some cases to necessitate the use of higher alloys. Acetaldehyde, propionic acid, and high boiling by-products of alcohol oxidation also have been reported to activate stainless steels under certain circumstances. For applications involving temperatures above the atmospheric boiling point, a more resistant material may be required even without impurities, especially at higher concentrations.

Cast ACI grades CF-8, CF-8M, and CN-7M are all commonly used for valves and pumps with corrosion resistance under severe conditions increasing in the order listed. Of the ferritic alloys, Types 329 and 446 have had limited use in tubular form where fabrication was not required.

Formic Acid The range of concentrations and temperatures in which the stainless steels remain passive in process equipment is much more limited for formic acid than for acetic acid. Only the molybdenum-bearing grades are used to any appreciable extent, and even these show only moderate resistance to hot solutions at intermediate concentrations. The presence of impurities of a reducing nature or chlorides can encourage activation. Where required, proprietary alloys such as Carpenter 20 Cb-3 and Incoloy 825 have generally given satisfactory performance at all concentrations up to the atmospheric boiling point.

Other Organic Acids   Propionic acid is somewhat less corrosive than acetic and corrosivity decreases further as the length of the carbon chain increases. The austenitic stainless steels often are used for process applications involving these and other organic acids (such as lactic acid, fatty acids, naphthenic acids, phthalic anhydride, etc.) with the molybdenum grades finding application under the most severe conditions. Oxalic acid is an exception which is severely corrosive to the stainless steels.

Organic Compounds   Most organic compounds (such as aldehydes, ketones, alcohols, hydrocarbons, etc.) are noncorrosive to the stainless steels. However, organic chlorides, when wet, can cause serious problems which, depending on specific conditions, can be either (1) general corrosion due to hydrolysis which forms hydrochloric acid, (2) pitting, or (3) stress-corrosion cracking.

Alkalies   The austenitic stainless steels are quite resistant to sodium or potassium hydroxide solutions up to about 100°C and up to about 50% concentration. However, they are seldom used for caustic service since carbon steel is satisfactory at the lower concentrations and temperatures, and nickel or high-nickel alloys are better in concentrated caustic at high temperatures. Furthermore, the stainless steels may be subject to stress-corrosion cracking at temperatures near the atmospheric boiling point at intermediate concentrations and at temperatures well above the boiling point for lower concentrations.

Inorganic Salt Solutions   The stainless steels are highly resistant to solutions of most nonhalide salts which are neutral or alkaline. Salts which hydrolyze to form acidic solutions act like dilute solutions of the corresponding acid; e.g., hot concentrated aluminum sulfate solutions are quite corrosive while solutions of aluminum nitrate are not corrosive. Halide salts which hydrolyze to give acidic solutions generally cause either severe general corrosion or pitting, with iodide salts being the least aggressive. Neutral chloride and bromide solutions usually cause pitting rather than general corrosion and with chlorides there is the added danger of stress-corrosion cracking. Solutions of oxidizing chloride salts such as cupric or ferric chloride are particularly aggressive pitting agents. Hypochlorite solutions also cause severe pitting.

General   As previously mentioned, a major proportion of the stainless steels used in the chemical and process industries are for essentially noncorrosive services where avoidance of product contamination is the major objective. In many cases the nature of cooling water is the variable which determines whether or not the austenitic stainless steels should be used; this, in turn, depends to a considerable degree on the thoroughness of the designer and the fabricator in avoiding possible mechanisms which could concentrate chlorides to cause either stress-corrosion cracking or pitting.

REFERENCES

1. Recommended Practice for Detecting Susceptibility to Intergranular Attack in Stainless Steels, *ASTM Specification A-262.*
2. Auld, J. R.: *Proc. 2nd Int. Cong. Metallic Corrosion,* pp. 445–461, 1963.
3. Subcommittee on Field Corrosion Tests: Intergranular Corrosion of Chromium-Nickel Stainless Steel—Final Report, *Weld. Res. Counc. Bull. no. 138,* February 1969.
4. Brown, M. H., W. B. DeLong, and W. R. Myers: *ASTM Spec. Tech. Publ. no. 93,* pp. 103–120, 1949.
5. Swandby, R. K.: *Chem. Eng.,* vol. 69, p. 186, 1962.
6. Clarke, W. L. and G. M. Gordon: *Corrosion,* vol. 29, no. 1, pp. 1–12, 1973.
7. Samans, C. H.: *Corrosion,* vol. 20, no. 8, pp. 256–262, 1964.
8. Truman, J. E., R. Perry, and G. N. Chapman: *J. Iron Steel Inst. London,* vol. 202, p. 745, 1964.

Chapter **39**

Stainless Steels in Transportation Systems

CHARLES W. VIGOR
JOHN N. JOHNSON
JOSEPH E. HUNTER
Metallurgy Department, Research Laboratories, General Motors
Technical Center, General Motors Corporation, Warren, Michigan

STAINLESS STEEL AUTOMOTIVE TRIM AND DECORATIVE HARDWARE

Present Materials, Applications, and Requirements Five stainless steel alloys are used for virtually all the stainless steel trim and stainless steel decorative hardware on United States automobiles. The use of AISI Type 430 stainless steel is limited largely to interior trim parts. Types 434 and 436, both containing 1% molybdenum and having substantially better resistance to pitting corrosion than Type 430, are used extensively for exterior moldings. Type 434 is used for stampings and rolled sections requiring moderate formability. Type 436, containing 0.5% columbium, is used on parts requiring greater forming strains. Type 201 has still greater resistance to pitting than 434, as well as being more ductile. Type 201 is, therefore, often selected for applications below the automobile belt line where improved corrosion resistance may be desirable and is also selected for parts where Type 436 is inadequate for reasons of ductility or formability. Type 301 is limited largely to use on wheel covers and other parts too difficult to make from AISI Type 201. All five materials (see Appendix I for composition) are used both in the bare and the chrome-flashed condition. For the austenitic grades, the chrome flash serves primarily to provide better color match with adjacent chromium-plated parts or ferritic stainless steel trim. The chrome flash on the ferritic grades serves both to improve corrosion resistance and to provide trim color compatibility. Types 434 and 436 also appear as the exterior surface on trim parts made from stainless steel–aluminum composite materials. Such composites combine the brightness of stainless steel and the galvanic corrosion protection offered by aluminum.

Stainless steel trim material may be offered in any of five general finish categories:

1. A dull gray matte finish produced by cold-rolling, annealing, and pickling.
2. A smoother, more reflective surface than (1), produced by giving that product a skin pass on smooth, highly reflective rolls.
3. A bright, reflective surface produced by final annealing the cold-rolled product under a controlled atmosphere which prevents scaling and oxidation (i.e., bright annealing) prior to the final temper pass.
4. A bright, reflective, prebuffed surface provided by bright annealing, as in (3), followed by continuous buffing. [Alternately, a comparable surface may be obtained by a more rigorous buffing of finish (1).]
5. Patterned finishes.

The austenitic stainless steels are commonly purchased in all five finishes. The first of these is favorable for retaining lubricant in deep drawing and is normally used in severely drawn or formed parts such as wheel covers. Other finishes are used when possible to minimize in-house buffing operations. Typically, the ferritic stainless steels are ordered in the bright-annealed or bright-annealed and prebuffed condition. The former is used to fabricate parts which will subsequently receive a buffing operation. The latter is used for parts where forming conditions and use of protective coatings make it possible to produce a part which requires little or no buffing. This finish is also specified for parts which are to be chrome flashed, as direct chrome flash of a bright-annealed surface leads to the development of a white frosty appearance. Patterned finishes may be used for their aesthetic value on certain parts or for reduced reflectivity on bright trim in the driver's immediate visual path.

Material purchased for automotive trim is usually required to meet certain standards with respect to brightness, buffability and freedom from deleterious surface effects such as orange peel, ribbing, roping, and severe buffing marks. These requirements commonly are established by reference to preestablished visual standards which exhibit a range of quality with respect to variables being controlled.

Brightness refers to the general luster of the material. Qualitative differences in brightness in a material of the same grade and finish generally reflect variations which occur in annealing, pickling, and rolling. The quality of the finish on rolls used in final cold-roll and temper passes is critical to the final finish on the product.

Buffability pertains to the capability of obtaining a satisfactory finished part surface without undue buffing cost. A material's capability for meeting this requirement may be judged by subjecting it to a standardized buffing operation. Laps, seams, carbide segregation, mars and scratches, ribbing and roping, and orange peel all influence buffability.

Orange peel is a surface roughening, visually similar to that seen on the surface of an

TABLE 1 Typical Mechanical Properties for Stainless Trim Materials

Property	Type 201	Type 301	Types 430, 434, 436
Ultimate tensile strength, min., psi (MPa)	100,000 (689.5)	95,000 (655)	72,000 (496.4)
Tensile yield strength, max., psi (MPa)*	60,000 (413.7)	45,000 (310.3)	60,000 (413.7)
Elongation in 2 in. (50.8 mm), min., %*	45	50	22
Hardness, Rockwell 30T, max. †	74	72	72
Cold-bend test*	180° flat on itself without cracking	180° flat on itself without cracking	180° flat on itself without cracking
Cup ductility test	0.025-in. thick—0.400-in. min (0.625-mm) (10.6-mm)	0.020-in. thick—0.430-in. min (0.508-mm) (10.9-mm) 0.025-in. thick—0.450-in. min (0.035-mm) (11.4-mm) 0.030-in. thick—0.460-in. min (0.762-mm) (11.68-mm)	0.015-in. thick—0.280-in. min (0.381-mm) (7.11-mm) 0.022-in. thick—0.300-in. min (0.559-mm) (7.62-mm) 0.020-in. thick—0.320-in. min (0.508-mm) (8.13-mm)

*ASTM A-370
†ASTM E-18.

orange, which occurs when a part is stretched or drawn. This surface effect can be virtually eliminated by specifying grain size 7–8 or less.

Ribbing and roping are terms for the surface ripples or bands of varying height and width which occur in ferritic steels in the direction parallel to rolling. Visually, ribbing manifests itself as bands of differing reflectivity on as-received stock. Roping is the grosser manifestation of these ripples which occurs when the material is strained further in the direction of rolling. Commonly, a material's susceptibility to roping is judged by prestraining the material a specified amount, e.g., 10 to 15%, in the direction of rolling. To date the most effective means of reducing roping and ribbing has been to add 0.20 to 0.75 columbium to the ferritic steel, as in Type 436 alloy.

Chemical composition limits, grain size, mechanical properties, and formability criteria are also commonly specified by the trim manufacturer. These limits serve to define that material within a grade which will successfully make a wide range of parts without resorting to special practice. Mechanical property limits, for one manufacturer, are shown in Table 1.

Since the function of automotive trim is to enhance a vehicle's appearance, the trim material must not only meet high standards for its original appearance but must also maintain that appearance for prolonged periods of service. This requires that it resist pitting, general corrosion, and loss of its original high luster in the wide variety of environments which it may encounter. To this end, stainless steel trim may be required to pass one or more of the accelerated corrosion tests detailed in Table 2.

While the collective or individual correlation of results of these tests with service performance is sometimes questioned, the fact remains that many of these tests were instrumental in evaluating the effects of process and alloy changes instituted at the low point of stainless steel corrosion performance in the late 1950s. These changes have markedly increased the service performance of stainless steel trim.

Despite these improvements, the use of stainless steel trim has declined in the past decade. Table 3 shows the trend in stainless steel use by one manufacturer in the last 4 years. With this trend, the extent of stainless steel trim illustrated in Figs. 1 and 2 is currently found in only a limited number of models. This recent history suggests a continued decrease in solid stainless steel trim as it is replaced by aluminum or stainless steel–aluminum composites. Use of the latter may also decline as they are in turn replaced by aluminum or plastic moldings.

History of Stainless Steel Trim

The Early Years 1928 to 1935.[1] Stainless steel was first used for decorative automotive trim in the United States in 1928. Total stainless steel used in making the 3-in.-diameter (7.6-cm) hub caps in the first application was less than ½ lb (0.23 kg) per car. In 1930, radiator outer shells on some models were made from stainless steel. Roll-formed stainless steel moldings were introduced in 1932. By 1935, stainless steel was being used for radiator grilles and most trim moldings. Competing decorative materials included brass (plated and nonplated), chromium-plated steel and chromium-plated zinc-base die castings. Then, as now, decorative treatment of parts varied from year to year with styling changes or changes in manufacturing techniques. As an example, the radiator outer shell was formed from a welded strip in 1931 rather than from a single sheet. Components previously made in part from the center sheet offal in 1930 reappeared as painted items in 1931.

Two stainless steel alloys were used in these early days. One was a ferritic alloy containing 17% chromium, similar to AISI Type 430, and the other was Type 302 austenitic alloy containing 18Cr-8Ni. Virtually all moldings were made of the former material; difficult-to-form parts such as radiator shells and lamp parts were made from the latter.

Final mill treatments consisted of acid pickling, a light cold-rolling pass, and passivation in a nitric acid dip giving a clear, silver-gray finish. Fine-grain material was generally specified to limit the development of orange peel surface characteristics which would necessitate additional polishing and buffing. Material which had been overpickled or which exhibited fine seams was avoided for the same reason.

Subsequent to forming, the stainless parts were polished and buffed in high-speed production polishing and buffing machines developed specifically for these operations. In the polished condition, sheet was expected to withstand several hundred hours of salt spray without showing rust spots.

TABLE 2 Tests Used to Evaluate the Corrosion Resistance of Stainless Trim

Test	Test solution	Purpose	Reference
Neutral salt spray	5 g NaCl/95 g distilled H_2O	General corrosion resistance	ASTM B117
Copper acetic acid salt spray (CASS)	5 g NaCl/95 g distilled H_2O, 1 g $CuCl_2 \cdot 2H_2O$ and 5.5 ml glacial acetic acid/gal solution	Pitting, general corrosion	ASTM B368
Corrodkote	50 ml distilled H_2O, 0.35 g $Cu(NO_3)_2 \cdot 3H_2O$, 0.165 g $FeCl_3 \cdot 6H_2O$, 1.0 g NH_4Cl, all in 30.0 g of water-washed kaolin	Pitting, general corrosion	ASTM B380
Spot test	10 g $FeCl_3 \cdot 6H_2O$, 5 g NaCl, 2.5 g HCl(conc.), 200 ml distilled H_2O	Detect chromium depletion	Ref. 4
Cyclic immersion test	0.5 g Na_2SO_4, 0.25 g Na_2SO_3, 0.1 g $Na_2S_2O_3$, 52.5 g NaCl, 52.5 g $CaCl_2 \cdot H_2O$, 1050 ml distilled H_2O pH adjusted to 9.3 with dilute NaOH or HCl	Pitting in calcium chloride—slag environment	Ref. 16
Thermographic	As above soaked in dye transfer paper	Pitting in calcium chloride—slag environment	Ref. 16

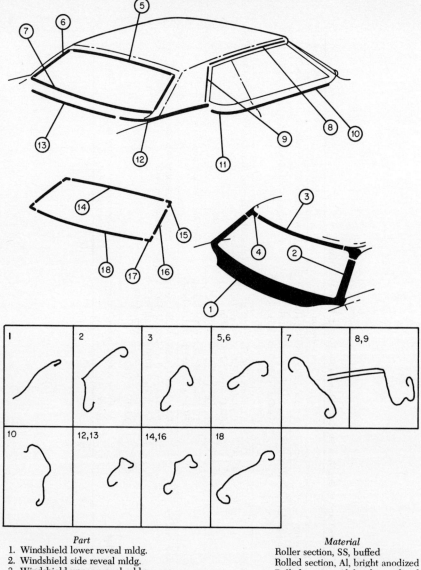

Part	Material
1. Windshield lower reveal mldg.	Roller section, SS, buffed
2. Windshield side reveal mldg.	Rolled section, Al, bright anodized
3. Windshield upper reveal mldg.	Rolled section, Al, bright anodized
4. Windshield upper reveal corner mldg.	Stamping, Al, bright anodized
5. Back window upper reveal mldg.	Rolled section, Al, bright anodized
6. Back window side reveal mldg.	Rolled section, Al, bright anodized
7. Back window lower reveal mldg.	Rolled section, Al, bright anodized
8. Front roof drip mldg.	Rolled section, SS, buffed
9. Rear roof drip mldg.	Rolled section, SS, buffed
10. Front door window reveal mldg.	Rolled section, SS, chrome flash
11. Quarter window mldg. assy.	Zinc die cast, chrome-plated
12. Quarter belt reveal mldg.	Rolled section, SS, buffed
13. Rear belt reveal mldg.	Rolled section, SS, buffed
14. Back window upper reveal mldg.	Rolled section, Al, bright anodized
15. Back window upper corner escutcheon	Stamping, Al, bright anodized
16. Back window side reveal	Rolled section, Al, bright anodized
17. Back window lower corner escutcheon	Stamping, Al, bright anodized
18. Back window lower reveal mldg.	Rolled section, bright anodized

Fig. 1 Upper exterior ornamentation

TABLE 3   Trends in Stainless Steel Use for One Manufacturer 1970–1973 (Exterior and Interior Body Trim)

Year	lb (kg) per car
1970	13.1 (5.94)
1971	8.6 (3.90)
1972	7.8 (3.54)
1973	7.2 (3.27)

The Middle Years 1950 to 1958.[2,3] By the mid-1950s between 18 and 45 lb (8.2 to 20.4 kg) of stainless steel were being used per car for decorative trim. Alloys in use were basically the same as those used in the early 1930s. Type 430 steel was still being used for most stainless steel parts, while Type 301 was used for parts difficult to form or requiring higher yield strength. Parts made from Type 301 included wheel covers and windshield wiper arms while moldings, hub caps, headlamp door and retaining rings, radiator grilles, and similar items were made of Type 430. Type 201 steel had been developed in response to the nickel shortage of the early 1950s but had found only limited uses as decorative trim. Anodized aluminum and plastic were added to the list of decorative trim materials in use, although neither achieved significant use until the early 1960s.

In the mid-1950s, a chromium flash was being applied to many stainless steel parts. This flash generally was applied to the austenitic grades to cover the yellow tint characteristic of these materials and to provide better color match between adjoining chromium-plated or Type 430 steel. This flash was also applied to Type 430, usually on more expensive cars, to achieve greater corrosion resistance and a brighter, richer appearance.

As-received decorative trim stainless steels were still being supplied in the pickled, temper-rolled condition. However, practice differed to the extent that continuous annealing furnaces were in common use, and there was a trend to decreased pickling to provide brighter as-received surfaces which allowed a commensurate reduction in buffing and polishing by the trim manufacturer.

In the mid-1950s, the neutral salt spray test was still used as the standard test for

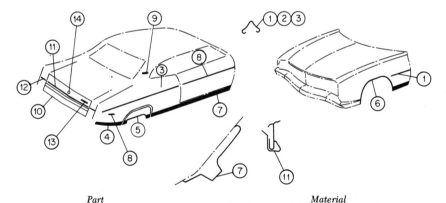

Part	Material
1. Front mldg.	Rolled section, SS, chrome flash
2. Door mldg.	Rolled section, SS, chrome flash
3. Rear fender mldg.	Rolled section, SS, chrome flash
4. Windshield upper	Stamping, SS, chrome flash
5. Wheel cover mldg.	Stamping, SS, chrome flash
6. Front wheel opening mldg.	Rolled section, SS, chrome flash
7. Rocker panel mldg.	Rolled section, SS, chrome flash
8. Rear fender nameplate	Zinc die cast, chrome plate
9. Nameplate sail	Zinc die cast, chrome plate
10. Rear end panel mldg. assy.	Zinc die cast, chrome plate, satin finish and plastic
11. Compartment lid mldg.	Rolled sections, SS, chrome flash
12. Mldg. rear of rear fender	Zinc die cast, chrome plate
13. Compartment lid nameplate	Zinc die cast, chrome plate, paint
14. Compartment lid lock emblem	Zinc die cast, chrome plate, paint

Fig. 2   Lower exterior ornamentation.

stainless steel and was still considered satisfactory. However, by the late 1950s, small etch spots virtually imperceptible to casual observers were being noted by engineers in annual trim inspections of new and recent model cars. Increased pitting was also being observed on Type 430 steel in industrial atmospheres and in areas where calcium chloride was being used for dust control or being used in conjunction with sodium chloride for deicing. Additionally, very severe pitting was starting to be observed in areas such as Pittsburgh, Pennsylvania and Youngstown, Ohio, where crushed steel mill slag was being applied to icy streets and highways for increased traction in winter driving. Other problems of concern were galvanic corrosion of body sheet adjacent to stainless trim material and the increased difficulty of getting the required quantities of low-roping Type 430 required for increasingly complex moldings. These problems led to later technical developments.

Technical Developments Since 1958. In 1959 the white etch occurring on stainless steel trim in service was found to be related to low surface-chromium content, and the etch was duplicated using a ferric chloride spot test. This low surface-chromium content was shown to be due to the depletion of the surface chromium under the time-temperature and atmosphere conditions experienced in continuous annealing in oxidizing atmospheres.[4] That is, at the 1350 to 1650°F (735 to 900°C) and 3 to 5-min processing times in an oxidizing atmosphere, chromium oxidized at the surface more rapidly than it could diffuse to the surface. Subsequent light pickling removed the chromium-rich oxide layer without removing the underlying chromium-depleted layer. Thus, the demand for a brighter as-received product, which eventually led to short-time, low-temperature continuous annealing and reduced pickling, had inadvertently produced a surface with reduced corrosion resistance. Options to correct this problem included:

- Bright annealing to prevent oxidation, and, hence, chromium depletion.
- Removing the chromium-depleted layer by heavier pickling or prebuffing.
- Adjusting annealing conditions to longer times or higher temperatures so that the balance between chromium oxidation and diffusion could be restored.

Most stainless steel suppliers elected the first approach. Installed at the cost of from one to several million dollars each, bright-annealing facilities continuously annealed stainless steel in low-dew-point reducing atmospheres of hydrogen or dissociated ammonia without touching hot metal to the processing rolls.[5] One major supplier elected to follow the second approach, supplying material in the prebuffed condition.[6] Subsequently, in the face of increased demand for prebuffed material, most stainless steel suppliers offered bright-annealed, prebuffed steel.

Elimination of chromium-depleted surface effectively prevented etching of the stainless steel and improved the general corrosion resistance. However, Type 430 stainless steel still had substantially poorer corrosion resistance than the austenitic alloys, particularly with respect to pitting in industrial atmospheres, in calcium chloride, and in the environment imposed by using steel mill slags on icy streets. The efforts of automotive and steel company engineers were, therefore, directed toward obtaining a ferritic alloy with improved pitting resistance. Subsequent evaluation of numerous steels in accelerated tests designed to simulate pitting environments (CASS, Alternate Immersion, Corrodkote, and others) established that an alloy of 1Mo-1Cu added to a 430 base composition had substantially improved resistance to pitting corrosion. Subsequently, the 1% molybdenum addition alone was found to give still better corrosion resistance. This alloy was designated Type 434 and by the mid-1960s had virtually replaced Type 430 as the standard exterior trim alloy. The development and corrosion testing of both 434 and 436 are discussed in references 7 to 19.

Concurrent with the development of Type 434, efforts were made to decrease the ribbing and roping tendency of Type 430. This was prompted by the increasing difficulty in identifying and obtaining sufficient heats of low-roping 430 for the increased number of complex moldings being designed. Subsequent studies to delineate the nature of ribbing and roping showed that peak-to-peak distances of the ripples in ribbed steel were 0.7 to 1.0 mm, with ripple height of 25 to 250 μm.[20] In subjective visual ratings, ribbing was judged to be more severe as the tangent angle of the rib increased. Roping appeared to be simply a grosser manifestation of ribbing encountered when the material was subsequently strained, i.e., peak heights increased and ripples became more discernible. Two theories evolved for both ribbing and roping; one related these phenomena to preferred orientation, the other to carbide banding. The preferred orientation theory, now generally accepted, attributed ribbing and roping to anisotropic flow in adjoining bands of material having different textures.[21] In particular, these phenomena were postulated as being associated with a strong cube face or cube edge texture in a cube-on-corner matrix texture. Development of these textures was attributed to rolling of two-phase structures ($\alpha + \gamma$) produced in annealing. The carbide theory attributed ribbing and roping to the presence of segregated carbides which altered the local deformation characteristics.[22] Research showed that ribbing and roping of some stainless grades could be reduced by hot-working at higher temperatures.[23] However, the most effective means for obtaining material with consistently low roping characteristics in the ferritic trim alloys was to add 0.25 to 0.75% columbium, as in Type 436 steel.[24]

The problem of galvanic corrosion on body panels adjacent to stainless steel trim was also attacked in the mid- and late 1960s.[25] Galvanic corrosion occurred at breaks in the paint surface due to the potential difference between the cathodic stainless steel and the anodic base metal. Solutions to the problem involved using nonconducting clips to interrupt the current path between the molding and carbon-steel panel and providing a material which was anodic to the carbon steel on the underside of the molding or at the faying surface.[26] Metallurgically bonded composite materials of stainless steel and aluminum were developed specifically for this purpose and introduced in the late 1960s.

The latest innovation in stainless steel decorative treatments, still to be exploited in automotive trim, was the development of permanently colored stainless steel.[27]

EXHAUST VALVES

The development of the internal combustion engine as a durable automotive power plant has been paralleled closely by improvements in the stainless steels used in exhaust valves. In early engines where temperatures were low and valve replacement was an accepted practice, ordinary carbon and low-alloy steels were used.[28] Cast-iron and high-speed steel exhaust valves were also used prior to World War I. Beginning in 1919, these materials were gradually replaced by stainless steels of the silicon-chromium type. The "silchrome" alloys gained almost universal acceptance for automotive exhaust valves by 1935. To meet a need for better wear resistance and elevated temperature hardness, sigma-phase alloys of the 24Cr-4Ni-1Mo type were developed. The introduction of leaded fuels in conjunction with increased operating temperatures and the need for improved valve durability created a need for alloys having better high-temperature strength and corrosion resistance, hence, the development of austenitic exhaust valve steels* used in present-day automotive engines.[29]

The properties considered to be important in the selection of materials for exhaust valves are:[30,31]

■ High-temperature creep strength, thermal and mechanical fatigue resistance, and hot hardness.

■ Corrosion and oxidation resistance in the presence of combustion products which can contain such elements as Pb, S, Br, Cl, and V.

■ High-temperature wear resistance in the seat area and low-temperature wear and scuff resistance in the stem and tip area.

Valve steels used in automotive and light-duty truck applications are usually separated into three categories:[32] martensitic, sigma-phase, and austenitic alloys. Compositions of commonly used alloys within each group are shown in Table 4.

Martensitic Alloys The martensitic valve materials usually contain up to 1% carbon and up to 22.0% chromium. Other elements are controlled as dictated by fabrication and operational requirements. In exhaust valve applications, the maximum operating temperature of martensitic alloys is limited to 1200°F (650°C).

Sigma-phase Alloys The sigma-phase valve materials are partially austenitic and are hardenable by precipitation of sigma phase. The alloys are suitable for light-duty exhaust valve applications and have extremely good wear resistance as required in the valve stem area.

Austenitic Alloys Austenitic valve materials contain sufficient amounts of the austenitizing elements Ni, N, and C to be fully austenitic. Usually the composition is adjusted and the carbon and nitrogen levels are sufficiently high so that the alloys can be

---

*Engines used in heavy-duty applications may use nickel-based alloys for exhaust valves. This discussion is limited to iron-based materials.

solution-treated and aged. Austenitic valve materials are useful at operating temperatures up to 1600°F (870°C). Of the three types of exhaust valve steels, the austenitic alloys are by far the most widely used in present-day automotive engines.

While exhaust valve materials can be characterized by the aforementioned properties (such as creep strength, corrosion resistance, etc.), the choice of materials is critically

TABLE 4   Nominal Chemical Compositions of Automotive Exhaust Valve Steels

SAE no.	Commercial designation	Element, wt %							
		C	Mn	Si	Cr	Ni	Mo	Other	Fe
		MARTENSITIC ALLOYS							
HVN 3	SIL 1	0.45	0.40	3.3	8.5				Bal.
HVN 6	XB	0.80	0.40	2.3	20.0	1.3			Bal.
		SIGMA-PHASE ALLOYS							
EV 1	TCR	0.45	0.50	0.50	23.5	4.8	2.8		Bal.
EV 2	TXCR	0.40	4.3	0.80	24.0	3.8	1.4		Bal.
		AUSTENITIC ALLOYS							
EV 3	21-12	0.20	1.3	1.0	21.0	11.5			Bal.
EV 4	21-12N	0.20	1.3	1.0	21.0	11.5		0.20 N	Bal.
EV 5	SIL 10	0.38	1.0	3.0	19.0	8.0			Bal.
EV 6	SIL 10N	0.38	1.0	3.0	19.0	8.0		0.20 N	Bal.
EV 7	2155N	0.20	5.0	0.50	21.0	4.5		0.30 N	Bal.
EV 8	21-4N	0.53	9.0	0.15	21.0	3.75		0.42 N	Bal.
EV 9	TPA	0.45	0.50	0.60	14.0	14.0	0.35	2.40 W	Bal.
EV 10	CAST 14-4	1.0	0.8	3.0	14.5	14.5			Bal.
EV 11	SIL 746	0.70	6.3	0.55	21.0	1.9		0.23 N	Bal.
EV 12	21-2N	0.55	8.3	0.15	21.0	2.2		0.30 N	Bal.
EV 13	GAMAN H	0.53	11.5	2.6	21.0			0.40 N	Bal.

interrelated with such factors as engine and valve train design, engine duty-cycle, and fuel and lubricating oil composition. Final selection of a valve material can only be made after extensive engine evaluation in dynamometer and field tests. Typically, a period of 3 to 5 years is required to fully qualify a valve material for high-volume production.[33]

EXHAUST SYSTEMS

Stainless steels are used in those parts of automotive exhaust systems where corrosion is a major durability problem. A typical exhaust system, shown in Fig. 3, consists of a Y pipe, an intermediate pipe, a muffler, a kickup pipe, a resonator, and a tailpipe. The pipes are formed from seam-welded single- or double-wall tubing. Mufflers are generally of the triflow type and consist of inlet tubes, a turnaround chamber, a return tube, a second turnaround chamber, and outlet pipes. Perforations in the tubes and tuning cans provide high-frequency silencing. Baffles are spot welded to the shell to divide the mufflers into chambers. The shell is usually covered by an asbestos sheet and metal wrap to reduce shell noise. The outer wrap is held in place by a rolled seam at the front and rear head. Resonator construction is similar to that of mufflers except that gas flow is generally straight through and the outer asbestos and metal wraps are not used.

Exhaust systems are subject to both internal and external corrosive environments. Externally, there is an oxidizing environment resulting from exposure of the hot system to ambient air and a corrosive environment resulting from exposure to rain, snow, slush, and accompanying deicing and dust-laying salts. Operating temperatures on the external surfaces range from ambient to 1000°F (538°C). The internal corrosion atmosphere consists of high-temperature exposure to exhaust gases which may range from slightly reducing to slightly oxidizing and low-temperature exposure to exhaust gas condensate. Internal metal temperatures can be as high as 1300°F (705°C). Maximum temperatures usually occur in the pipes ahead of the muffler and in muffler turnaround chambers. Minimum temperatures occur in muffler and resonator dead chambers.

Materials used in producing automotive exhaust systems since World War II have varied.[34] Carbon steel and galvanized steel were used in the late 1940s and early 1950s. Aluminized steel was initially used in the late 1950s and is still the primary material of construction. In single exhaust systems, all parts of the silencing components are made of aluminized steel. In dual systems, the gas stream is split. In these applications, the cold side muffler and both resonators are often constructed with muffler-grade stainless steel

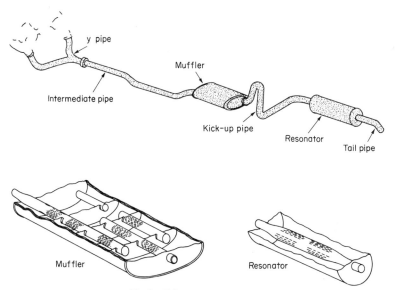

Fig. 3 Exhaust system components.

heads, first and last baffles, and inner shell. Typically, Type 409 stainless steel is used. Performance of this material has been excellent. More extensive use has been limited by high cost and a need for pipe welding and forming technology.

Chromized low-carbon steel has been used since the late 1960s as an alternate to stainless steels in baffles and wraps. One limitation of this material is that seam welding leaves an unprotected anodic joint adjacent to the highly cathodic chromized surface, a condition highly conducive to galvanic corrosion.

Catalytic Converters   In order to comply with the Federal Clean Air Act of 1970, the majority of 1975 automobiles were equipped with catalytic converters. Inasmuch as the converter systems operate at high temperature and must last the lifetime of the vehicle, stainless steels have been specified. The principal type used has been Type 409, the so-called muffler grade of stainless steel. A considerable amount of welding is required for tubing fabrication and for sealing of converter units. To avoid hardening in the heat-affected zones and to otherwise obtain good welding characteristics, most users have adopted low-carbon, titanium-stabilized versions of the 409 grade.

MISCELLANEOUS USES OF STAINLESS STEEL IN AUTOMOBILES

Many small and seemingly insignificant parts of automobiles or automotive subsystems are made of stainless steel. Because of the price premium commanded by stainless steel, all such uses are reviewed continuously for cost/performance benefits. The use of stainless steel for such parts is retained only where justified. Some uses may combine appearance and function requirements, such as the windshield wiper arm, and others completely hidden from view are entirely functional. A few such examples are cited.

Windshield Wipers. Practically all of the externally exposed members of automobile windshield wipers are stainless steel. The principal types used are Type 430 and 434. A special matte finish produced by wire brushing is specified to meet U.S. government regulations regarding antiglare. Another small but vital part in the wiper mechanism is a small ball-stud which connects the wiper motor pitman arm to the linkage connecting the wiper arms. This stud, manufactured from Type 416F stainless, is subjected to wide ranges of environmental conditions and to intermittent motion; freedom from corrosion is a must as this is one of many items which must last the life of the car.

Head Gaskets. For many years head gaskets in automotive engines have been of the metal-asbestos or beaded-metal type as shown in Fig. 4a and *b*. Low-carbon steel is used

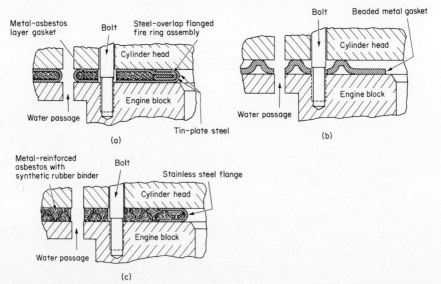

Fig. 4 Three head gasket systems. (*a*) Metal-asbestos layer gasket. (*b*) Beaded metal gasket. (*c*) Metal-cored, flanged composition gasket.

for the metal portions of these gaskets; however, in engines where corrosion is a major problem, as in marine applications, Type 430 stainless steel is commonly used.[35] The trend toward engines with larger displacements and higher horsepowers has led to new developments in head gasket design. A recent innovation is the flanged composition gasket[36] shown in Fig. 4c. The gasket consists of a perforated low-carbon-steel core onto which is bonded a nitrile-rubber-asbestos facing material. Metal flanges are provided around cylinder and/or fluid passage openings. Typically, Type 430 stainless steel is used for the flange material around cylinder openings, the primary requirement being oxidation resistance. In engines where corrosion in the fluid passages is of major concern, Type 321 stainless steel is commonly used for the flange material.

Stainless steel inserts are also used on some asbestos intake manifold gaskets in the vicinity of the exhaust gas crossover passage.[35]

Odometer Shafts.[37] The small shaft which supports the numeral drums of the odometer is Type 416F stainless steel. Freedom from rust is a must if the odometer is to correctly operate for the life of the car.

Seat Belt Mechanism.[37] A tiny shaft not much larger than a matchstick is used in some seat belt mechanisms to prevent belt slippage during sudden deceleration. Both strength and corrosion resistance are important in this application. Cold-drawn Type 303 is used.

Piston Ring Expander. Type 201 stainless steel is used to form the corrugated spring behind piston rings. Type 201 has been found to provide the right amount of work hardening to enhance fatigue strength. In addition, the excellent shearing characteristic of Type 201, i.e., less tendency to form edge burrs, makes the material easier to fabricate.

Radiator Pressure Cap Spring. Hard-drawn Type 304 wire provides both the high modulus and corrosion resistance required.

Hose Clamps. Round wire of either Type 304 or 301 is used for many hose clamps.

USES OF STAINLESS STEEL IN GENERAL
TRANSPORTATION

Trucks Manufacture and marketing of trucks is highly cost competitive. While a pleasing outward appearance is desired, the gleaming stainless steel brightwork used on automobiles has not been adopted by the truck industry. Rather, emphasis is placed on performance, operational economy, durability, and low first cost. Because of the high cost of stainless steels, the trend has been to use either plastic or anodized aluminum where trim or brightwork is involved. Very little stainless steel is used in today's typical truck. Occasionally, however, aluminum is found to be unsatisfactory and the switch back to stainless steel is made. One such typical item is the kickplate just below the door of a truck. One truck manufacturer originally used a 400-series stainless steel, switched to anodized aluminum and back again to stainless steel because of the severity of the corrosion involved.

Trailers In former years many truck trailers were constructed of Type 301 stainless steel. This was the only material which would reliably furnish a 20-year lifetime. Recently, the use of stainless steel in ordinary cargo trailers has declined markedly due to its rising cost. Another factor has been the increasing popularity of trailer leasing which has placed further emphasis on low initial cost. The fast write-off practices allowed for leased equipment further deemphasizes the requirement for long life. There are uses, however, which require stainless steel to meet minimum performance standards, and long life becomes a primary goal to justify the high first cost. The best example of this is the transportation of bulk foodstuffs, especially milk. Bulk transport tanks are subjected to a wash cycle after every use. Included in these wash cycles is the use of strong chemical sanitizers. Stainless steel is the only material which will endure such treatment. A typical milk tank trailer is all-welded construction and is made from 2.8-mm-thick (0.11-in.) Type 304. Much of the welding is autogenous; filler metal, where used, may be 304, 316, or 318. Corrosion due to wash cycles is not a problem for such service and stabilized grades of stainless are not used. One tank may outlast two or three vehicle chassis. Since adoption of bulk milk hauling in the United States, about as many trailers are rebuilt annually as are produced new. Because milk must be transported in a refrigerated condition, most tanks are insulated, making necessary an outer protective cover for the insulation. While aluminum or painted mild steel is satisfactory for the outer sheathing, stainless steel, 0.81-mm-thick (0.032-in.) Type 304, proves to be more economical because painting or reconstruction of the outer sheath are not required during the lifetime of the tank. Another factor affecting the choice of stainless for the sheathing is the high quality "clean" appearance of stainless which enhances the public image of the dairy industry. Ancillary equipment (such as valves, pumps, and connecting lines) are also stainless steel, many of which are castings.

Other Uses The 11% Cr Type 409 stainless steel is being used increasingly to replace mild steel in specialized applications. One such application is for self-contained tanks of firefighting apparatus. Because such equipment must be ready for use at any instant, the storage tanks are always filled with water. Type 409 provides adequate corrosion resistance and is fabricated readily. A feature of these tanks is considerable internal baffling to avoid sloshing during maneuvering of the vehicle.

A new type of shipment practice is that of the cargo box which is both semitrailer body and shipboard container. These are, for the most part, built of carbon steel. The ends of these containers tend to become scuffed during loading and unloading aboard ship. Exposure to the highly humid salt air causes accelerated corrosion wherever a paint film becomes damaged. One manufacturer of containers uses Type 409 corner channels to overcome this problem. A unique feature of this fabrication is that the stainless steel is welded to a cast carbon steel corner piece.

Buses As with trucks, stainless steel is used in buses only where other less costly materials will not perform satisfactorily. The components which are stainless steel appear to be well-established and are not likely to change in future years.

Grab rails in metro transit types of buses consist of an outer jacket of either Type 302 or 430 formed around an inner tube core of carbon steel. Metro transit bus fare box stanchions are also of stainless to resist corrosion due to tracked-in salt; either 400 or 300 series may be used. The largest use of stainless steel on buses, especially for the metro-type bus, is for front and rear bumpers. This approximates 90 kg (198.2 lb) per coach and is 3.4-mm-thick (0.134 in.) Type 304. This is considerably more costly than chromium-nickel plating. However, coach operators favor stainless since their practice of parking coaches "bumper to bumper" in depot areas causes damage to plated bumpers which leads to unsightly rusting. While the stainless steel bumpers ·become severely scarred from this type of abuse, corrosion does not result.

Rapid Transit Rail Equipment   Stainless steel is extensively used in rapid transit rail equipment. The reasons are long life, minimal maintenance, and improved strength-to-weight ratio. This latter reason is most important for equipment which starts and stops frequently since less power is required. By judicious use of stainless grades which can be strengthened by work hardening, principally Types 201 and 301, strength-to-weight ratios up to three times greater than for standard steel construction can be used. Main structural components are often stainless steel which simplifies original construction in that paints or other protective coating systems are not required. Stainless steel greatly minimizes maintenance and upkeep of car interiors, thus making more time available for operational purposes. All-stainless exteriors stand up well to the frequent washings given such equipment. As much as 13 tons (11,791 kg) of stainless steel may be used in a single rapid transit rail car.

Other Rail Equipment

Locomotives. Diesel locomotives contain little stainless steel. This sparing use is controlled mainly by cost considerations. One area where stainless steel is used is the joints in the exhaust system. Temperature and corrosion conditions are modest, allowing Type 410 and 409 to be used.

Rolling Stock. Stainless steel is normally not used in box car or gondola construction. It is used, however, for bulk cargo such as acid or other highly corrosive products. In general, the grades used are the same as would be used for handling stationary equipment.

REFERENCES

1. Thun, E. E. (ed.): "The Book of Stainless Steels," pp. 667–676, American Society for Metals, Metals Park, Ohio, 1935.
2. Durbin, C. O.: Stainless Steel as Automotive Trim, *Proc. Elec. Furn. Conf.*, vol. 16, pp. 103–108, Dec. 5, 1958.
3. Frey, D. N.: Materials for Bright Trim on Passenger Cars, *Proc. Elec. Furn. Conf.*, vol. 16, pp. 110–115, Dec. 5, 1958.
4. Trax, R. V., and J. C. Holzwarth: Effect of Chromium Depleted Surfaces on Corrosion Behavior of Type 403 Stainless Steel, *Corrosion*, vol. 16, pp. 105–108, June 1960.
5. Friedlander, S.: Processing Equipment for Stainless Steel Bright Annealing, *Iron Steel Eng.*, vol. 38, pp. 85–91, May 1961.
6. New Technique Buffs Beauty on Stainless Strip, *Steel*, vol. 148, p. 92, Jun. 19, 1961.
7. McManus, G. J.: Auto Stainless Faces Icy Test, *Iron Age*, vol. 188, pp. 48–49, Nov. 23, 1961.
8. Bush, G. F.: How to Ward Off Corrosion on Stainless Steel Trim, *Iron Age*, vol. 189, Dec. 20, 1962.
9. Zaremski, D. R.: Ice, Snow, Salt and Slag . . . How Stainless Steel Auto Trim Resists Corrosion, *Met. Prog.*, vol. 90, pp. 71–75, September 1966.
10. Bush, G. F.: Progress in the Battle with Corrosion of Automobiles, *Met. Prog.*, vol. 90, pp. 56–67, December 1966.
11. McDougall, J.: Objectives in Corrosion Protection of Bright Decorative Trim and Their Implication, *48th Ann. Tech. Proc. Am. Electroplaters' Soc.*, pp. 120–127, 1961.
12. Nasea, J., Jr., B. E. Tiffany, and G. F. Bush: Research Method of Rating Corrosion of Automotive Trim, *Plating*, vol. 49, pp. 989–997, September 1962.
13. Bush, G. F.: Corrosion of Exterior Automotive Trim, Paper 650A, *SAE Automot. Eng. Cong.*, Jan. 14–18, 1965.
14. Kahler, H. A., and R. E. Harvie: Corrosion Resistance of Trim Materials, paper 650B, *SAE Automot. Eng. Cong.*, Jan. 14–18, 1963.
15. Hill, J. B., W. G. Renshaw, and T. R. Harkens: Three Steps to Arrest Auto Body and Moulding Corrosion, *SAE J.*, vol. 71, July 1963.
16. Fowler, R. M., and C. R. Bishop: New Corrosion Test for Stainless Steel Auto Trim, *Met. Prog.*, vol. 84, pp. 88–90, September 1963.
17. Bush, G. F.: Accelerated Corrosion Tests . . Are They Reliable? *Met. Prog.*, vol. 88, pp. 152–159, October 1965.
18. Redmerski, L. S., and A. Moskowitz: Stainless Steel in Automotive Applications—Corrosion Studies, Paper 680143, *SAE Automot. Eng. Cong.*, Jan. 8–12, 1968.

19. Walker, M. S., and L. C. Rowe: The Application of Electrochemical Techniques to the Study of Corrosion of Automotive Trim Material, *24th Ann. NACE Conf.*, March 1965.
20. Sergott, E. D.: An Analysis of Ribbing in Ferritic Steels, unpublished work.
21. Chao, Hung-Chi: The Mechanism of Ridging in Ferritic Stainless Steels, *Trans. Am. Soc. Met.*, vol. 60, 1967.
22. Chadben, R. M.: Cold-rolled Stainless Steel Finishes and Some Problems Associated with Type 430, *J. Aust. Inst. Met.*, vol. 9, no. 1, pp. 29-37, February 1964.
23. Waxweiler, J. H.: Process of Diminishing Ridging in 17 Chrome Stainless Steels, U.S. Patent No. 2,851,384, September 1958.
24. Evans, C. T., Jr.: Columbium Curbs Wrinkling in Forming Stainless Strip, *Iron Age*, vol. 187, pp. 96-97, Feb. 23, 1961.
25. Bates, J. F.: Preventing Corrosion of Auto-Body Steel Adjacent to Stainless Steel Trim, paper 680144, *SAE Automot. Eng. Cong.*, Jan. 8-12, 1968.
26. Baboian, R.: Clad Metals in Automotive Trim Applications, paper 710276, *SAE Automot. Eng. Cong.*, Jan. 11-15, 1971.
27. Permanently-Coloured Stainless Steel, *Anti Corrosion Methods and Materials*, vol. 19, p. 22, June 1972.
28. Thum, E. E.: "The Book of Stainless Steels," pp. 485-497, American Society for Metals, Metals Park, Ohio, 1935.
29. Cowley, W. E., P. J. Robinson, and J. Flack: Internal Combustion Engine Poppet Valves: A Study of Mechanical and Metallurgical Requirements, *Proc. Inst. Mech. Eng.*, vol. 179, pt. 2A, no. 5, pp. 145-165, 1964-1965.
30. "Metals Handbook," 8th ed., vol. 1, pp. 626-634, American Society for Metals, Metals Park, Ohio.
31. Cherrie, J. M., and E. T. Vitcha: New Automotive Poppet Valve Materials, *Met. Prog.*, vol. 100, no. 3, pp. 54-56, September 1971.
32. "SAE Handbook," Information Report J775, "Engine Poppet Valve Materials," pp. 85-87. Society of Automotive Engineers, Pittsburgh, Pa., 1965.
33. Newton, J. A.: Engineering of the Poppet Valve, *A Symp. Internal Combustion Engine Valves*, Valve Div. TRW Inc., Cleveland, Ohio, 1958.
34. Hunter, J. E.: "Materials for Emission Control Exhaust Systems," talk presented to Porcelain Enamel Institute Forum, Ohio State University, Columbus, Oct. 8, 1971.
35. Watrous, C. A.: Victor Products Div., Dana Corp., private communication.
36. Lillis, S. M.: Getting to the Core of Gasket Sealing, Paper 680027, *SAE Automot. Eng. Cong.*, Jan. 8-12, 1968.
37. Saving with Stainless Components, *Automot. Ind.*, p. 32, Nov. 15, 1974.

Chapter 40

Stainless Steels
in the Food Industry

J. DENNIS SPRAGG

**Product Specialist, Stainless and Special Metals Division, Republic
Steel Corporation, Cleveland, Ohio**

Fertilizer to fondue, "dogs" to donuts, from beginning to end, stainless steels play an
ever-increasing role in the largest industry in the world—"food." To cover the topic, we
will review the growing, processing, storing, serving, and eating of food—and even the
disposal of its wastes and residues.

Since there are many and varied facets to the stainless steel food complex, we may jump
around and even miss a few, but to start somewhere, let's look at the farm. In the soil
preparation, planting, and cultivation of crops, some stainless has been used, primarily in
prevention of erosion or abrasion in plows and planters. Soils can be very abrasive and, at
times, corrosive. Hardenable grades, such as Type 410, play a role by providing long wear
and corrosion resistance in these adverse conditions. After germination, the crops must be
fed, and liquid fertilizers are one of the answers to this need. To store, carry, and apply
this soil food, stainless steel tanks are needed. Types 409 through 316 can be used,
depending on the corrosiveness of the solution—and their use is increasing every year
(see Fig. 1).

When grain or other crops need to be stored, stainless steel is used for construction of
bins, and for chutes and other accessory items. While we are still in the raw food product
area, let us consider milk. Milk is collected by, held in, carried through, and processed in
Type 304 stainless steel equipment. The automatic milkers as well as the walls and stalls
in the milking parlor are Type 304 stainless steel. The tanks, both on the farm and in the
dairy, are usually Type 304 with a polished No. 4 finish, as is the tank truck which
transports the milk. The smooth, pit-free surface of Type 304 provides for the easy and
complete cleanability essential for milk processing and holding equipment (see Fig. 2).

Every dairy uses equipment made of Type 304 in making ice cream, cheese, or other
milk products, and for the pasteurization of the milk. Type 304 is found everywhere there
is milk or where milk products are being processed.

Staying with beverages, let us turn to some of the others. Beer, wine, orange juice,
tomato juice, apple juice—name one and it is processed and stored in stainless steel

Fig. 1 Stainless steel fertilizer tanks similar to this are used to apply liquid fertilizer to many rows of crops at one time. (*John Blue Company, Huntsville, Ala.*)

equipment. Tanks for brewing, fermenting, or cooking; equipment for transferring liquids to settling and holding tanks is most commonly made of Type 304 sheet or plate, with Type 316 being used for certain extremely corrosive areas.

The most common beverage, sometimes overlooked, is potable water. To provide this necessity, purification is a must in most sections of the world. Makers of desalination units have been testing many metals, and stainless steel is one of those being tested. Types 304 and 316 may prove to be the best metals for use as tubing in desalination plants. Systems for purification of water in municipalities, including the filters, holders, pumps, and valves, all use stainless steel. The laboratories connected with the testing of purity in all beverages also use considerable amounts of stainless steel.

Going back to the raw food products, vegetables and fruits, whether they are cooked or frozen for consumer use, are processed through stainless steel equipment. Again, the tanks, vats, and other containers used for processing are made of Type 304 and 316. The cryogenic applications, or "fast freeze," use Type 304, because it has good properties at the low temperatures employed. Federal regulations governing the canning and food processing industries demand a stainless type of material which is rust resistant and can readily be sanitized, thus the predominant and widespread use of Type 304, and some Type 316. Any tour through canneries or processing plants will show that Type 304 is used extensively where equipment is in contact with the food.

Another area of the food processing industry includes meat producers and packers. From hog pens to refrigerator trim, stainless steel is used. All the areas that come in actual contact with the meat must be contaminant-free, thus stainless steel is used for tables, hooks, walls, doors, and heavy cutting equipment. Usually Type 304 is employed, but in some areas Type 430, as well as other ferritic grades, have been used successfully.

Fig. 2 Stainless steel milk trucks have a pit-free interior to facilitate easy cleaning between loads.

Once the meat is cut, it must be packed and refrigerated or frozen. Packaging equipment, as well as freezers, use stainless for cleanliness as well as wearability. Slicers, grinders, and tenderizers—all are made of stainless steel for two main reasons: cleanliness and durability.

For dry process foods (such as cereals, flour, or sugar) stainless steel again is a must. The massive operations needed to provide ample supplies of these foodstuffs can only be maintained efficiently if the processing equipment is made from stainless steel, usually Type 304. The bins, drying equipment, and packaging units all employ various types of stainless steel, depending on the needs of the job. Many large bakeries producing bread for extensive distribution find Type 301 just the material needed for endless belts to carry goods to and through proofing and baking ovens (see Fig. 3).

All these industries are only part of the food industry. We have yet to discuss the home, institutional, and retail preparation (and consumption) of food, as well as the necessity to dispose of the leftovers or wastes.

As we start into the food service industry and look at the quick-serve companies, we suddenly realize they are enormous—over $2½ billion retail sales through thousands of outlets in 1973 for the two largest firms. They employ, as do all of their competitors, stainless steel kitchen equipment from counter tops and spatulas to deep fryers and exhaust hoods. Type 304 stainless steel is evident everywhere. We recognize the equipment in these quick service units because we can see the kitchen as we order. But think of that little family eatery down the street or that wonderful gourmet restaurant you went to last month. They all employ stainless steel for cooking, cutting, cooling, and serving (see Fig. 4).

A look in the Yellow Pages of the telephone directory under "Restaurants" will impress you with how many stainless steel kitchens are around. Every restaurant and tavern has stainless steel sinks and counter tops as well as utensils. At a restaurant or at home, chances are you eat with stainless steel flatware—Type 301 or 430 for forks and spoons and some Type 410 for knife blades as well as high-grade cutlery blades made of Type 420.

Back in the kitchen, we take a closer look at the cookware, the pots and pans. Everywhere we look, stainless steel is evident. One of the types used extensively for pots and pans for home and commercial kitchens is a 3-ply material, stainless-clad carbon steel,

Fig. 3 A stainless steel bread dough mixer is sanitary, easy to clean, and durable enough to withstand years of service. Photograph taken at Schwebel Bakery, Youngstown, Ohio. Unit manufactured by F. H. Langsenkamp Company, Indianapolis, Ind.

Fig. 4 Nearly all of the equipment used in the fast-food market is stainless steel because it is easy to clean, durable, and has an attractive appearance. *(Church's Fried Chicken Inc., San Antonio, Tex.)*

Fig. 5 An automatic disposal, utensil separator, and dishwasher in a school cafeteria employs stainless steel throughout because of the high sanitation requirements. *(Industrial Industries, Houston, Tex.)*

Type 304 on the outside with a carbon core. This provides the good corrosion resistance of stainless steel and the uniform heat transfer of carbon steel. Types 301, 201, and 430 are also utilized in pots and pans and lids or covers.

Not only the equipment for the preparation of the meals, but also the dishwasher and the sinks, as well as parts of the garbage disposal units, are stainless steel. Again, Type 304 is prominent with Types 410 and 430 also being used. All major producers of this equipment use stainless steel to a great extent for its cleanability. Any of the items mentioned for restaurants and homes are even more important for institutional service. Schools, elementary through college; hospitals; penitentiaries; mental institutions—any institutions you can think of that must serve their people food use stainless steel more than any other metal, and Type 304 is usually the alloy (see Fig. 5).

Now that we have all eaten our meal at home or away, we have the leftovers. What we do not salvage for recycling (tomorrow's lunch), we send down a garbage disposal with stainless steel cutters and throat, or we put into a compactor which can use stainless steel parts in the corrosive areas. Still another method of disposal is the incinerator. These units range from small home burners which use a little stainless steel to the large municipal or commercial ones, which are made of Type 309 and Type 442. These alloys provide good high-temperature resistance and long life, thus saving the taxpayers' money. Many of the stacks on these units are also stainless to prevent excessive maintenance.

Anything that comes in contact with food in its many forms should be (and usually is) stainless steel. Although many alloys are available, one is the general, all-purpose stainless steel for the food industry—Type 304.

So, anywhere you enjoy food, stainless steel makes it good.

Bon Appétit!

Chapter 41

Stainless Steels in the Alcoholic Beverage Industry

WILLIAM H. DETWILER
Valley Foundry & Machine Company, Fresno, California

THOMAS I. WILLIAMS
WIT Engineering, Arvin, California

INTRODUCTION

The use of stainless steel in the alcoholic beverage industry does not differ from applications in other areas of the food industry. The 300-series stainless steels are used generally, and on very special occasions a specific stainless steel is required. A special consideration might be a seat material for a valve where high velocities are encountered.

Types 304 or 316 stainless steel are used for various reasons. One is because of high corrosion resistance to alkalines, acids, sterilants and various fermentation by-products. There is also the possibility of product flavor integrity contamination if carbon steels are used. In many instances there are esthetic concerns where the facility is open to public scrutiny. Maintenance costs are drastically reduced because of the lifetime appearance.

Sanitizing with various cleaning compounds is simplified by using stainless steel. A very important consideration to the design engineer is the superior structural properties of stainless steel in pressure vessels. Type 304 stainless steel has a tensile strength of 84,000 psi (579.2 MN/m²) and a yield strength of 42,000 psi (289.6 MN/m²). A value of 80% of either is accepted for design.

Finishes   The application engineer must also determine the finish desired when specifying stainless steel. The finishes available are listed below along with their advantages.

- *Type 1.* Specified on large industrial tanks that will not be polished after fabrication. Normally not used for product, but rather for chemical storage used in process.

- *Type 2B.* Most common finish used in the industry. Bright-annealed and No. 2B finishes are similar. Used in storage and process tanks because of all around strong points. Easy to clean, good appearance. Finish seems to improve with age.

- *Type 2D.* Slightly duller than No. 2B but used for deep drawing. Can easily be polished and buffed after drawing. Used in heat exchangers.

- *Type 3.* Finish is used for esthetic purposes more than functional reasons. Has the obviously polished look without the expense of an exceptionally uniform look.

- *Type 4.* Used where product contact surface is required to be kept clean and very sanitary. Very common in dairy industry.

- *Type 6.* This polish has an "old silver" appearance. Used where severe use is encountered but scratches are not evident, whereas they would be obvious on a brighter finish. Used for drainboards and architectural trim.

- *Type 7.* Nearly a mirror finish and most commonly used for ornamental and architectural applications.

It is very important that the application engineer check with the supplier to determine if a desired finish is available before specifying.

WINE AND BRANDY PRODUCERS

In today's changing alcoholic beverage industry many more uses for stainless steel have developed. Today the wine industry employs stainless steels for a myriad of equipment used in wine production, not to mention the use in the distilling and rectifying fields.

Uses of stainless steel in the wine industry are many; however, most wineries are concerned with parts of machinery, equipment, and pumps that contact the product, although there has been a very strong trend to include the use of stainless steel in supports, frameworks, and exterior reinforcement both for esthetic reasons and to reduce painting and other maintenance costs.

Wineries currently use primarily Type 304 stainless steel, with some use of Type 316 when special cleaning compounds are employed or where the firm produces wine vinegars. Type 304 will not afford sufficient corrosion resistance to the fumes of vinegars or acetic acid mixtures.

Type 304 stainless steel is used as follows:

1. Process piping for transfer of wines and brandy and for pumping of the freshly crushed grapes. Type 304 (ASTM A269) tubing with a 0.065-in. (1.65-mm) wall is the most commonly utilized. The tube is normally pickled and annealed with the weld bead removed. TIG or heliarc welding is the most common joining method.

2. Screw conveyors and screw conveyor troughs, sometimes including the coupling shafts and hanger bearings, are fabricated from Type 304, generally with a Type 2B finish, and fabricated and welded using MIG or a short-arc welding process, employing a high-silicon Type 308 stainless steel wire.

3. Tanks:
    a. Mixing tanks for slurries, filtration precoat tanks and similar process vessels. Type 304 with Type 2B or Type 4 finish is generally used.
    b. Storage tanks for wine. The industry generally uses Type 304 stainless steel storage tanks with a Type 2B finish to supplant or replace preexisting cooperage. Storage tanks of stainless steel are currently used in sizes of a few thousand gallons capacity up to 350,000 gal (1325 m³) capacity. Storage tanks have, in general, replaced previously supplied steel tanks that had specially applied food-grade epoxy linings. In many instances in the larger premium

wineries and in almost all of the common wine producers, stainless steel has replaced the large redwood or oak tank.

   c. Fermenting tanks of Type 304 have become an industry standard, both for the small, medium, and large producers of premium varietal wines, as well as large producers of common wines of generic origin. Many of the smaller fermenting tanks, in the range of 3000 to 30,000 gal (11.4 to 114 m³) capacity, are equipped with outside cooling jackets to properly control temperatures during fermentation of the wines. In some instances, the larger tanks of 40,000 to 100,000 gal (151.4 to 378.5 m³) capacity have stainless steel coils installed in the tank which are used to cool the wines.

4. Filtration equipment in recent years has been produced in stainless steel with the following types in general use:

   a. Pressure leaf filters with stainless steel screens, manifolds and tanks.

   b. Plate and frame filters with the heads and framework or all of the noncontact parts usually in carbon or alloy steel with the plates, frames, manifolds, etc., of stainless steel.

   c. Rotary vacuum filters, usually of the precoat type, with almost all parts of Type 304 stainless steel, Teflon rings, plastic grids, and polypropylene filter cloths.

   d. Micro- or milipore filters of stainless steel are also newly established industry standards.

5. Pumps of stainless steel, mostly Type 316:

   a. Positive rotary

   b. Gear pumps

   c. Centrifugals

   d. Diaphragm

   e. Progressive screw

6. Grape crusher-stemmers are presently constructed of Type 304 stainless steel, with framework or supports of carbon steel. Almost 95% of all crusher-stemmers installed in the past 5 years are stainless steel. Very few domestic or foreign equipment producers are utilizing epoxy-coated carbon steel.

7. Presses:

   a. Presses of the large-diameter continuous-screw variety are fast using all-stainless steel construction, although many utilize nickel-resist screws with other contact parts of stainless steel.

   b. Other presses used in the industry, the majority of which are fabricated of stainless steel, include:

      1. Inflatable bag or pneumatic presses

      2. Horizontal hydraulically or mechanically operated basket presses

      3. Vertical basket presses with press chamber, basket and platen of stainless steel

8. Mechanical screens, commonly called "juice screens," fashioned somewhat the same as any common dewatering screening device, are also fabricated, almost exclusively, of stainless steel, completely replacing those previously fabricated of epoxy-coated carbon steel or wood framework. Dewatering or juice screens employ 16 or 14 gage perforated stainless steel screens or wedge-bar or champfer-bar screens. Some employ the chain and cleat principle with hardwood or nylon brush cleats while others are produced with stainless steel screws with specially wound nylon brushes mounted in a stainless steel holder.

9. Also used almost exclusively are items within the winery such as:

   a. Hose couplings

   b. Valves for tanks and process flow control

   c. Pipe fittings, adapters, hose fittings

10. Bottling equipment produced of stainless steel:

   a. Fillers

   b. Table top chains

   c. Filters

DISTILLERIES

Distilleries are divided into continuous stills and pot stills. All associated equipment in this important segment of the alcoholic beverage industry has been, in the past, primarily constructed of copper, brass, and bronze. Recent trends and innovations have made use of stainless steel more attractive to this industry.

Distillation columns, aldehyde and rectifying columns are made of stainless steel, with weldments stress-relieved to prevent cracking. Because of the heat involved in distillation plus the temperature ranges employed in the common beer or stripping column, stainless steels were not commonly employed. With improved welding technology, these limitations have been eliminated, resulting in a greater use of austenitic stainless steels.

Fig. 1 Dump and screw conveyor of grape crusher with a capacity of 250 tons/h (226,750 kg/h). The dump is constructed of Type 304 stainless steel.

Condensers, dephlegmators and heat exchangers were previously constructed of copper and mild steel shells because of the heat-transfer capabilities. Producers long recognizing the adaptability of stainless steel tubes in these units have, in recent years, specified stainless steel because of its increased corrosion resistance and decreased replacement and maintenance costs.

Product receiving tanks and fermenting vessels are presently constructed of stainless steel, both Type 316 and Type 304.

Process piping, valves, pipe fittings, etc., have for the most part been converted from the traditional bronze or brass construction to Type 316 stainless steel.

Other equipment in the distillery employing widespread use of stainless steel includes:
1. Pumps
2. Filtration equipment
3. Weigh tanks
4. Rectifying and process tanks and vessels
5. Barrel dumping troughs and transfer lines

Rectifying and bottling plants have experienced the most phenomenal growth in use of austenitic grades of stainless steel. Until approximately 1965, the most common grade employed was Type 316; however, since that date the less expensive, more readily available Type 304 has been used.

It is very important to point out that bourbon whiskey cannot tolerate any iron contamination. The presence of even small amounts of iron will burn bourbon black, thereby negating its value as a beverage alcohol. Therefore it is important to properly "passivate" manufactured or fabricated stainless steel equipment in order to guard against this possibility.

The usual passivating method employed by whiskey producers, rectifiers, and bottlers is use of a hot solution of 10% nitric acid, allowing 10 to 15 min contact time. This is

Fig. 2 The Vincent press (right center) and all piping, conveyors, and fermenting tanks are constructed of Type 304 stainless steel.

Fig. 3 These Type 304 stainless steel tanks hold wine for bottling. The building itself is fully insulated and refrigerated to ensure that the wines are kept at the proper temperature for bottling. Tanks have a capacity of 37,000 gal (140 m³).

Fig. 4 Vats of 500- aand 1000-hectoliter (50- to 100-m³) capacity for the fermentation and storage of champagne, constructed from stainless steel Z8 CNDT 17-12.

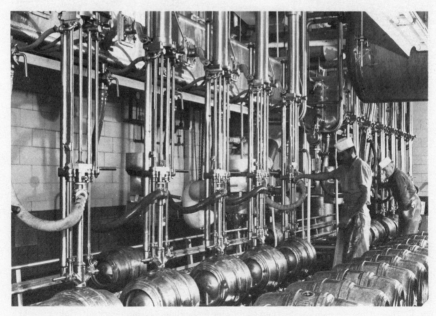

Fig. 5 Type 304 stainless steel beer barrels.

followed by a thorough water rinse and then a wash with an alkaline solution followed by a water rinse. A test for the presence of free iron is then made, usually with a ferroxyl solution. Although there are more extensive methods employed for this passivation procedure, the above has proven effective.

Fig. 6   Brew kettle of Type 304 stainless. *(Nooter Corp.)*

BREWING—BEER INDUSTRY

Brewers have, in past years, always employed steel fermentation tanks with an epoxy food-grade paint coating or the so-called "glass" linings.

In today's economic situation, the brewer is switching to austenitic steels with a preference (until 1967 to 1968) for Type 316. Since that time a very strong trend toward Type 304 has developed.

The brewer's "plumbing" has traditionally been copper or copper- or bronze-based alloys. This trend, too, has changed to an almost exclusive use of austenitic steels.

The brewer of today uses stainless steels for much the same equipment as used in other alcoholic beverage facilities.

Various items of equipment used in the production of alcoholic beverages are shown in Figs. 1 to 6.

Chapter 42

Stainless Steels in Medical Devices

DENES I. BARDOS

Director, Technical Affairs Division,
ZIMMER · USA, Warsaw, Indiana

The requirement for corrosion-resistant materials has historically existed in the broad application spectrum of the health care field. Practically all types of stainless steels have found application ranging from hospital equipment and furnishings to the most delicate of surgical implants to sustain vital human functions.

Application of stainless steels to auxiliary medical areas, such as pharmaceutical processes and hospital furnishings, are not significantly different from industrial applications, such as chemical processing and home furnishings, and will not be discussed here. This discussion will be limited to those stainless steel alloys which have contributed to historical and modern developments in medicine; especially orthopaedics.

THE HISTORY OF STAINLESS STEEL IMPLANTS

Archaeological evidence clearly indicates that surgical procedures were performed in several ancient civilizations. Progress in surgery, however, was slow and mixed liberally with superstition until the latter part of the nineteenth century. Pasteur's and Lister's aseptic surgical techniques, developed around 1883, and shortly thereafter Roentgen's discovery of x-rays in 1895, added a new dimension to orthopaedic surgery. The great step forward in technique outstripped the state of materials art. In the beginning of the twentieth century, surgical techniques were developed for the fixation of bone fractures with a plate and screw combination. Sherman-type bone plates (see Fig. 1) were fabricated from the best available alloy at the time, vanadium steel. By the 1920s, use of vanadium steel Sherman plates became questionable because of poor tissue compatibility. At the time however, no other alloy was available with high strength and good corrosion-resistant properties.

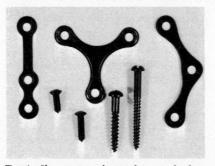

Fig. 1 Sherman-type bone plates made from vanadium steel and some miscellaneous screws of different compositions.

Shortly after the introduction of the 18-8 stainless steels, clinical experiments were conducted to utilize the material for manufacture of surgical implants. This material had far-superior corrosion resistance to anything that had been available up to that time and immediately attracted the interest of orthopaedic surgeons. Bone plates, screws, and other fixation appliances were fabricated and used as surgical implants. Although the material performed better than anything else available, it still showed some susceptibility to attack in the saline environment of the human body. In 1926, when Strauss patented the 18-8 SMO stainless steel, containing 2 to 4% molybdenum and a reduced carbon content of 0.08%, a material was created which promised improved resistance to acid and chloride-containing environments. Results of research in the 1930s were so encouraging that, as a result, the Orthopaedic Committee of the National Research Council assigned a research project to C. R. Murray and C. G. Fink at Columbia University in 1941. The object of the project was to rapidly determine the most desirable metal or alloy for the internal fixation of fractures. The study resulted in recommendation of Type 302 and 316 stainless steel in 1943. Subsequent research at several medical centers across the nation prompted the American College of Surgeons at its 1946 meeting to endorse Types 316 and 317 stainless steels for use in surgical implants.

During the 1960s, the ASTM F-4 Sub-Committee was formed to standardize materials used in surgical implant manufacture. Currently available high-quality stainless steels are now recommended for this application. The desirable properties of low carbon and vacuum or electroslag remelted materials have been recognized and standards covering these materials have been published. Table 1 summarizes the chemical requirements of these ASTM standards. Note that the alloy chemistry is not identical to AISI material standards so that both 316 and 317 grades may fit the specifications.

BIOCOMPATIBILITY

One very important consideration in the selection of surgical implant materials is the compatibility of the material with the human body. Ideally, a metallic implant should be completely inert in the body. However, that is rarely the case. The body environment is

TABLE 1   Chemical Composition of Low-Carbon Stainless Steel Used in Manufacture of Surgical Implants

Carbon	0.03 max.
Manganese	2.00 max.
Phosphorus	0.03 max.
Sulfur	0.03 max.
Silicon	0.75 max.
Chromium	17.00–20.00
Nickel	10.00–14.00
Molybdenum	2.00–4.00
Iron	Balance

extremely hostile to all foreign materials and therefore, the effect of the environment on the implant and the effect of the implant on its host tissue is of primary concern.

Extracellular Body Fluids A surgical implant is constantly bathed in extracellular tissue fluid. Basically water, this fluid contains electrolytes, complex compounds, oxygen, and carbon dioxide. Electrolytes present in the largest amounts are sodium (Na^+) and chloride (Cl^-) ions. A 0.9% salt solution is considered to be isotonic with blood. Other electrolytes present include bicarbonate ions (HCO_3^-) and small amounts of potassium, calcium, magnesium, phosphate, sulfate, and organic acid ions. Included among the complex compounds and present in smaller amounts are phospholipids, cholesterols, natural fats, proteins, glucose, and amino acids. Under normal conditions, the extracellular body fluid is slightly alkaline with a pH of 7.4. Traumatized tissue has been reported to have a significantly lower pH level.

Corrosion Because of the similarities of body fluids and saline solution, corrosion research carried out for marine applications has served as the basis for development of materials for implant use. As a general guideline, materials that exhibit outstanding corrosion resistance in seawater may be considered as candidates for implant applications. On the other hand, if the material's corrosion products contain toxic elements (such as copper, arsenic, mercury and beryllium) which in minute quantities may produce undesirable side effects, it may not be considered further. In addition, the surgical implant may not be protected by plating, painting, coating, or cathodic protection techniques. Body implants must be naturally inert, such as the noble metals, or be protected by a natural passive film, as is the case in accepted biomaterials including stainless steel, Co-Cr-Mo alloy, and the titanium alloys.

The addition of a minimum 2% molybdenum content in Type 316 stainless steel has been shown to reduce the tendency for pitting-type corrosion in chloride environments. Hoar and Mears[1] postulated that chloride ions accelerate the corrosion of stainless steel by penetrating the oxide film. The chloride-contaminated film then loses its passivating quality and a local attack on the metal follows, creating a pit. The exact mechanism by which molybdenum strengthens the oxide film is not clearly understood.

Perhaps the most serious corrosion problem in Type 316 stainless steel is its susceptibility to crevice corrosion. Incidence and extent of this type of corrosion in surgical implants was stressed by Scales, et al. in 1959.[2] Scales' study reported the presence of crevice corrosion in 24% of Type 316L bone plates and screws examined after removal from patients. This record however compares favorably with the presence of crevice corrosion in 51% of 18-8 stainless plates, demonstrating the superiority of the molybdenum-containing grade.

Further significant improvements in corrosion resistance may be obtained by minimizing the nonmetallic inclusion content of Type 316 stainless steel. A routine examination of over 100 Type 316LVM surgical implants,[3] removed for various reasons, did not show evidences of pitting corrosion or general attack but have revealed small areas of crevice corrosion in bone plate/bone screw interfaces. A crevice is usually formed by screw head/bone plate countersink contiguity, initiating the corrosion process. Constant, minute, flexural movement of the highly stressed bone plate aggravates the corrosion damage through fretting of the contacting surfaces.

Tissue Reaction Reaction of the host tissue to metallic implants is affected by many factors including shape and size of the implant, movement between the implant and tissue, extent of corrosion attack, general degradation of the implant, and the biological activity of the resulting by-products of corrosion or degradation.

When an implant is surgically inserted into the human body, the internal environment is greatly disturbed. Hematomas are likely to collect around the implant, resulting in a lowered pH. Laing[4] observed pH values as low as 4.0 in healing wounds. The low pH usually persists until the hematomas are resorbed after several weeks.

The body reacts to the foreign materials in many ways. The immediate reaction is to form layers of fibrous tissue between the implant and healthy tissue. In the presence of corrosion an inflammatory reaction may occur and thickening of the fibrous tissue is observed. Bone resorption has been noted in cases of corroding metallic implants fabricated from vanadium steel. In these cases, actual rust formation resulted, inducing severe clinical complications necessitating the immediate removal of the implants.

The presence of metallic ion concentration around a surgical implant site is almost always measurable. The effect of the metallic ions in the host tissue may vary from a passive tolerance to local reaction or, possibly, broad systemic effects. Ions of cobalt, for example, have been observed in patients with Co-Cr-Mo implants as far removed from the implant as the hair and fingernails. Chromium ions are known to attach themselves to protein molecules and migrate to great distances from the surgical site. Increased nickel concentration in the organs of patients with stainless steel fixation devices in their legs has been reported. In most cases, the body tolerates minute quantities of metallic ions, but it is evident that their concentration should be kept at a minimum.

Biomechanics   Present-day surgical implants must undergo extensive mechanical testing to ascertain their service performance in vivo. In order to perform a valid test, one must understand the load conditions to which an appliance is subjected in the human body. The hip joint provides an interesting example of how a biomechanical analysis may provide information which is not intuitively obvious. Upon first examination, one could logically assume that each hip joint carries half the body weight or full body weight when standing on one leg. Researchers however have shown that muscles acting through complex lever systems may subject the joint to loads in excess of seven times body weight during normal activities such as stair climbing. A 150-lb (68-kg) patient may subject his hip to loads of over 1000 lb (454 kg), demonstrating the need for accurate biomechanical analysis of the loading conditions seen by prosthetic devices in service.

Volumetric considerations, in some applications, limit the maximum allowable cross section of an implant, dictating use of high-strength materials. In addition to high static stresses, the implant is continually subjected to repeated cycles of significantly high loading. Problems involving fatigue fracture have been encountered. Eliminating, or at least minimizing, stress concentrations is often a difficult problem for the designer of implants. Attention to this detail, however, will greatly contribute to the service life of the implant.

INTERNAL FIXATION DEVICES

The most significant contribution of stainless steel to the advancement of modern surgery is in the area of internal skeletal fixation. Since movement of the human body is accomplished through the musculo-skeletal system, any impairment of the skeletal system, due to trauma or disease, results in reduction or complete loss of motion capability. Frequently such conditions also result in severe discomfort and pain to the orthopaedic patient seeking medical treatment.

Basing a decision on a large number of factors, the surgeon may elect to treat the disabling condition conservatively, as in closed reduction of forearm fractures, or surgically, as in cases of femoral (thigh bone) fractures. Surgical reduction of fractures often involves the use of internal, metallic, fixation devices such as bone plates, intramedullary rods, and highly specialized nails. Some of the advantages of internal fixation are:

1. Positive maintenance of fracture surface proximity
2. Early patient mobility and joint movement, in cases of limb fracture
3. Shortened hospitalization and disability times
4. Reduced probability of limb deformity due to malunions

Of the many requirements a surgical implant must meet, strength and corrosion resistance are most important. There is a wide assortment of internal fixation devices. The most common examples are screws, bone plates, nails, bolts, rods, and pins. These may be considered internal splints and fasteners. Figure 2 illustrates typical bone plates fabricated from Type 316LVM stainless steel. Figure 3 illustrates an application of these items.

For the treatment of fracture of the upper femur that in the past has often resulted in severe crippling and serious clinical complication, a combination nail-plate device has been used successfully. The design shown in Fig. 4 is based on the invention of an orthopaedic surgeon in which a three-finned nail for reduction and fixation of the fracture is combined with a strong bone plate securely attached to the shaft of the femur with bone screws as shown in Fig. 5. This device is fabricated from forged Type 316LVM.

Figure 6 illustrates other products for the fixation of long bone fractures for which the high-strength characteristics of stainless steel are most desirable. The products illustrated are inserted into the medullary canal of fractured long bones in order to maintain intimate proximity of the fractured segments, ensuring the alignment of the segments and thus

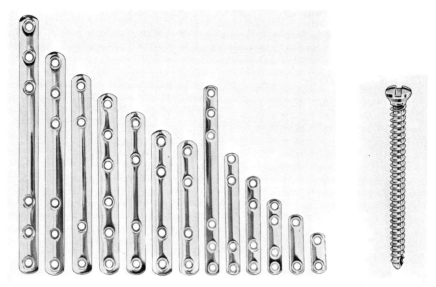

Fig. 2 Type 316LVM bone plates with highly polished and passivated surface. The closeup of the 316LVM bone screw is not to scale.

aiding rapid healing. The most common of these intramedullary rods are the clover leaf design with a hollow interior and cruciform cross-section rod with self-broaching ends to facilitate insertion of the rod into the marrow cavity.

The use of stainless steel surgical implants for the internal fixation of fractures has been growing steadily since World War II. It is estimated that over 50 million fixation devices have been implanted with satisfactory results. Table 2 gives estimated annual use of some of the most popular fixation devices.

Other Orthopaedic Applications Figure 7 illustrates x-rays of a patient with spinal curvature immediately before and after surgical treatment. The dramatic improvement seen in this patient's spinal column is achieved through use of a novel invention by

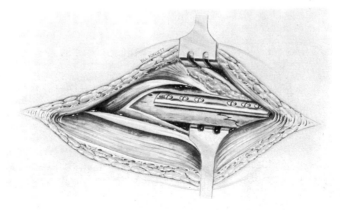

Fig. 3 The segments of a broken bone fastened together with the use of a bone plate and six bone screws. Retractors help to hold soft tissue apart during operation.

orthopaedic surgeon, Dr. P. R. Harrington. The device consists of long, stainless steel rods provided with hooks that apply distraction forces on one side and compressive forces on the other side of the spinal column. In this highly stressed application, the great strength of stainless steel combined with its ductility and biocompatibility are essential requirements for the successful performance of the device.

Figure 8 illustrates an early prosthetic device developed by Dr. P. O. Eicher and used as a substitute for diseased hip joints. Development of this class of implant was pioneered

by Dr. A. T. Moore and other researchers in the 1930s. The early devices consisted of long, narrow stems with highly polished ends or head sections. Surgical implantation of the prosthesis involved radical excision of the diseased femoral head, reaming of the femur's intramedullary canal and forceful insertion of the stem. Thus, a mechanical substitution for one-half of the diseased hip joints was achieved.

Since the early pioneering work, many designs have evolved with steadily improved mechanical qualities culminating in the "total hip joint." With the advent of improved mechanical design and surgical technique, the entire hip joint may now be reconstructed with a metallic femoral component and a polymeric socket component as shown in Fig. 9.

A majority of total hip prostheses are fabricated from a cast Co-Cr-Mo alloy similar to Haynes Stellite 21 alloy. On the other hand, some of the latest styles of hip prostheses are fabricated from premium-quality, cold-worked Type 316L stainless steel. Figure 10 shows one of these styles which offers improvements in mechanical characteristics and joint mobility while decreasing chances of total joint dislocation.

Cast stainless, similar to grade CF-8M, is currently receiving minor attention in the fabrication of total hips. However, this material has considerably lower strength than cold-worked 316L stainless steel.

Fig. 4 The Jewett combination nail-plate device.

SURGICAL IMPLANT MANUFACTURING

Metallurgical Considerations   Optimizing the properties of Type 316 stainless steels requires considerable metallurgical control of the raw materials.

The alloy was designed to have optimal properties when the microstructure reveals the fully austenitic condition, free of second-phase particles or other microconstituents.

In addition to well-balanced chemistry and proper metallurgical condition of the material, one may gain additional improvements by achieving the following requisites:

1. Fine grain size
2. Reduced inclusion content and carbon precipitates
3. Absence of delta ferrite
4. Absence of alloy segregation

Fine grain size ensures better mechanical properties as well as more uniform cold-forming characteristics. Figure 11 shows a typical cold-worked Type 316LVM stainless steel structure with a grain size of 6 as estimated by ASTM Standard E-112. Presence of a fine grain size, as observed in this material, has also been shown to increase fatigue strength. The microstructure shows a very uniform austenitic grain structure with no detrimental carbide, ferrite, or sigma-phase particles present. This microstructure is considered to represent the most desirable metallurgical condition of cold-worked 316LVM for surgical implant applications.

TABLE 2   Estimated Annual Use of Fixation Devices in the United States, 1974

Fixation device	Number of units	Dollar value
Bone plates	67,000	$ 800,000
Intramedullary rods	80,000	900,000
Pins and wires	600,000	2,000,000
Bone screws	1,000,000	2,000,000

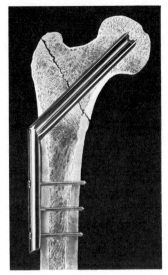

Fig. 5 A combination nail-plate device is shown on a cross section of the femur.

Fig. 6 Type 316LVM intramedullary nails for the fixation of broken long bones.

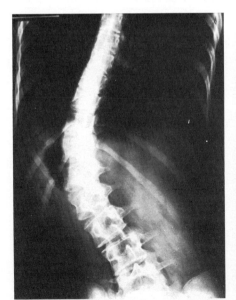

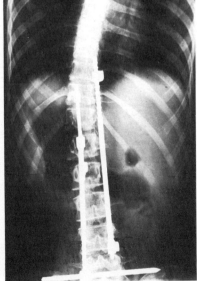

Fig. 7 X-rays of a patient before and after surgical treatment for the correction of curvature of the spine. The remarkable improvement is achieved with the use of cold-worked Type 316LVM rods and hooks.

Fig. 8 The early Eicher prosthesis for hip hemi-arthroplasty.

Fig. 9 The Charnley-type total hip prosthesis.

The role played by nonmetallic inclusions in affecting the properties of Type 316L has been recognized. Reduction of inclusion content is highly desirable. Maximal structural integrity and reduction of fatigue-crack-originating sites in the material are achieved by lowering the permissible level of inclusions. Figure 12 shows a typical as-polished 316LVM cross section for the evaluation of microcleanliness. The procedures described

Fig. 10 Trapezoidal-28 total hip joint, cold-worked Type 316LVM femoral component and ultra-high molecular weight poly-ethylene acetabular component.

Fig. 11 Microstructure of cold-worked Type 316LVM in the proper metallurgical condition. Electrolytic ammonium persulfate etch. [100X (original).]

Fig. 12 Vacuum-remelted Type 316L steel with minimal nonmetallic inclusion content. As-polished. [100X (original).]

in ASTM E-45, Method A, are followed with the exception that Chart III is utilized for low-carbon, vacuum-melted material. The common types of inclusions encountered are sulfides and oxides.

A continuous carbide network along the grain boundaries can significantly reduce the material's resistance to corrosion. Regular grade 316 with a maximum carbon content of 0.08%, when handled properly, is free of this precipitate. The added precaution of reducing the allowed carbon content to 0.03% provides an additional safety factor to assure that the microstructure will be free of continuous carbide network formation. The ability of the alloy vendor to limit the presence of the precipitate is exemplified by routine examination of hundreds of stainless steel shipments revealing no trace of continuous carbide network. Since delta ferrite can pose a problem to implant corrosion resistance, steel producers carefully control the chemistry and utilize elevated temperature homogenization to produce Type 316L essentially free of delta ferrite. Of course, maintaining nickel, an austenite stabilizer, on the high side of specification limits and chromium, a ferrite stabilizer, on the low side of its specification range does much to eliminate the possibility of delta ferrite. The proper balance of chemistry combined with annealing in the proper temperature range practically assures ferrite-free Type 316L.

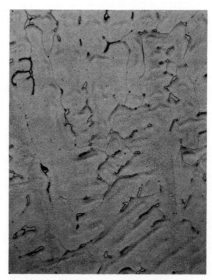

Fig. 13 Microstructure of cast stainless steel used in some surgical implants. Electrolytic ammonium persulfate etch. [100X (original).]

Corrosion resistance of Type 316L can also be appreciably lowered by alloy segregation coupled with second-phase particles in the microstructure. Figure 13 shows alloy segregation in a cast austenitic stainless steel having a chemical composition similar to CF-8M. The structure consists of pools of ferrite in a matrix of cored, coarse-grained austenite. Cast structures with this alloy chemistry invariably show ferrites and some alloy segregation. Homogenization by thermal treatment alone is extremely difficult. Molybdenum, for example, has a low diffusion coefficient in iron-based alloys even at high temperatures and dissolution of the ferrite occurs quite sluggishly.

Manufacturing Considerations Most stainless steel surgical implants are fabricated from cold-worked mill products. The usual metalworking processes are available to the implant manufacturer. Common milling, lathing, drilling and grinding operations are commonly utilized. The feed rates and machine speeds are usually quite low, with most manufacturing difficulties being overcome with proper tooling. Cutting tool geometry must be maintained at a positive face and rake angle to provide free cutting. In the highly cold-worked condition of Type 316 material, the hardness may be in the range of 35 to 40 causing some additional difficulties. Due to the large variety of styles and sizes of implants and the relatively low volume of production, very few operations can economically be fully automated. In fact, most parts require a considerable amount of tooling, and setup time and production rates are further lowered by numerous hand operations. Dimensional specifications are also maintained to very close tolerances.

Very stringent surface requirements are imposed on stainless steel surgical implants. It has been recognized that the mechanical properties and the corrosion resistance of these devices are influenced by their surface condition. Fatigue-crack initiation is significantly lowered when the surface is in the highly polished condition. ASTM F-4 Committee has formulated standards for the surface qualities of stainless steel surgical implants. The following requirements are included in ASTM F-86:

1. The surfaces of metallic implants shall be free of imperfections, such as tool marks, nicks, scratches, cracks, cavities, burrs, and other defects that would impair the serviceability of the device.

2. Surface texture classifications may vary from dull to bright depending on the application and specific area involved on the metallic implant.

3. The surface shall be free from imbedded or deposited finishing materials or other foreign contaminants.

4. The implant surface shall be in the passive condition.

Stainless steels made a significant contribution to the development of modern medicine. Today every doctor has stainless steel tools and instruments ranging from inexpensive disposable hypodermic needles and surgical blades to complicated hand tools designed for specific medical procedures.

Many surgical applications depend on the good mechanical properties and corrosion resistance of Type 316 steel. While research is continuing for improved implantable materials, devices fabricated from this readily available alloy continue to relieve the suffering of millions of orthopaedic patients.

REFERENCES

1. Hoar, T. P., and D. C. Mears: Corrosion Resistant Alloys in Chloride Solutions: Materials for Surgical Implants, *Proc. R. Soc. London,* vol. A294, pp. 486–510, 1966.
2. Scales, J. T., G. D. Winter, and H. T. Shirley: Corrosion of Orthopedic Implants, *J. Bone J. Surg.,* vol. 41B, no. 4, pp. 810–820, November 1959.
3. Unpublished work performed at Zimmer · USA Laboratories.
4. Laing, P. G.: Compatibility of Biomaterials, *Orthop. Clin. of N.A.,* vol. 4, no. 2, pp. 249–273, April 1973.

Chapter 43

Stainless Steels in the Pulp and Paper Industry

KARL-ERIK JONSSON

Technical Service, Gränges Nyby AB,
Nybybruk, Sweden

INTRODUCTION

Corrosion has always been a source of trouble in the pulp and paper industry. It was therefore only natural that this industry was one of the first in which uses were found for stainless steel. This material was used to some extent by the pulp and paper industry as early as the 1920s. Nowadays, its use is very widespread.

It has been estimated that corrosion costs the pulp and paper industry throughout the world, excluding Eastern Europe, over $300 million per year (1971),[1] both in the form of increased investment costs in consequence of more expensive materials, etc., and in the form of higher maintenance costs.

Stainless steels have several properties which are regarded as particularly valuable in the pulp and paper industry, the most important of them being their high corrosion resistance. They also have a high yield strength and a high ultimate tensile strength, which means that lighter and more manageable structures can be obtained compared with many other materials. Furthermore, they have good formability and good weldability, which makes them easy to handle. These properties, particularly the corrosion resistance, may in many cases vary quite considerably between different grades of stainless steels. Many different grades are used in the pulp and paper industry, principally Types 304, 304L*, 316, 316L*, 317, and 317L*. Composition of these steels is shown in Appendix 1, United States.

In Scandinavia, steels corresponding to Types 304, 316, and 317 are used but with a carbon content of 0.05% maximum, whereas the AISI standard permits a maximum content of 0.08%. There is normally no risk of intercrystalline corrosion after welding steels with a carbon content of 0.05%. These steels may therefore often be used instead of steels with a maximum carbon content of 0.03%, i.e., Types 304L, 316L, and 317L. Instead of these steels, equivalent grades such as titanium-stabilized steels are used in some countries. For severe corrosive environments (such as those found in bleach plants), there are also several different special grades with excellent resistance to corrosion. Their composition may vary slightly, depending on the manufacturer. Usually, however, they have higher chromium, nickel, and molybdenum contents than those given in Appendix 1. In addition to austenitic stainless steels, ferritic stainless steels of the AISI Type 400 series and ferritic-austenitic steels, such as Type 329, are also used to some extent, especially in cases where high resistance to stress corrosion is required.

Cast alloys used in the pulp and paper industry are CF-8, CF-3, CF-8M, and CF-3M which have about the same composition as Types 304, 304L, 316, and 316L, respectively. Other cast alloys used are CD-4M Cu and CE-30, which are ferritic-austenitic.

In many pulp and paper mills, one basic stainless grade, and one only, has been adopted as standard, particularly for tubes. Usually this grade is Type 316L. The primary reason for introducing a standard grade is to avoid the risk of using a wrong material by mistake. Thus, if tubes of Type 304L are installed by mistake instead of Type 316L, the risk of corrosion would sometimes increase considerably. In principle, Type 316L can be used instead of Type 304L in most places in a pulp mill. Another major advantage of a single standard grade is that it simplifies stocking.

For an optimum choice between stainless steel grades or other materials, the comparison must cover not only differences in investment costs but also differences in maintenance costs. Any anticipated loss in production must also be taken into consideration. In order to make the right material choice, several different points must be considered. It is important to know, for instance, the concentration and temperature of the medium to be used, as well as the variations which may occur. A very important piece of information is the presence of impurities, both in solid form and in solution. In particular, the chloride content should be investigated. Pressure and pH are also data of interest. In some cases the outside atmosphere plays an important part. Thus Type 316L should be used in bleach plants where the atmosphere is very often aggressive, although Type 304L can well be used for the medium itself. Sometimes information indicating whether the operation is continuous or discontinuous is of interest. It is often useful to know whether the medium is in motion or not. Stainless steels have a higher resistance to pitting in environments containing chlorides if the medium is in motion. Deposits constitute a risk that must constantly be borne in mind and avoided wherever possible. Sometimes, equipment and pipes in pulp and paper mills get encrusted. In such cases, diluted hydrochloric acid, with or without inhibitor, is often used to remove the incrustations or deposits. Unfortunately, hydrochloric acid, with or without an inhibitor, is aggressive to stainless steel and particularly to welds, which are often subject to so-called selective corrosion, the ferrite in the welds being particularly susceptible to attack. The ferrite content should therefore be kept as low as possible. It is generally believed that if the ferrite content is lower than 1%, the risk of corrosive attack in the welds is minimized. If, therefore, hydrochloric acid is to be used for cleaning welded tubes, these should be ordered from the tube manufacturer with a maximum ferrite content in the weld of 1%. Sulfamic acid is sometimes used for cleaning instead of hydrochloric acid with inhibitor, as it does not present any corrosion problems on stainless steels.

The choice of stainless steel grades is often based on previous experience in the same industry. However, it should be borne in mind that there are differences between mills,

---

*Although the low-carbon grades are mentioned, it is possible to use steels with carbon contents up to 0.05%

and these may sometimes be decisive, even if superficially they appear to be rather small. Sometimes, in fact, only very minor changes are needed for a material to start to corrode after previously resisting corrosion. Results obtained from using the same material for similar applications can, therefore, often vary.

PULP AND PAPER PROCESSING

Mechanical Pulping

General. Since no chemicals are used in the production of mechanical pulp, corrosive conditions are not so severe as in the sulfate and sulfite processes. Formerly the use of stainless steel was not so common. However, its use has increased in recent years because stainless steel often provides an excellent economic alternative to other materials which not only have a shorter life but also require more maintenance. The high corrosion resistance of stainless steels means that smooth surfaces are usually retained, so that tubes do not become clogged as easily as in the case of mild steel tubes. Furthermore, the demand for whiteness in the pulp means that stainless steel is used to avoid iron contamination. Since stainless steel need not have any corrosion allowance and has a high yield strength and ultimate tensile strength, structures can often be simpler and less clumsy than with other materials. Consequently, lighter and more manageable stainless pipes can be used instead of heavy cast-iron pipes.

Normally, stainless steel of Type 304L is used in this process. Where there is a so-called closed system (i.e., the process water is reused to reduce water pollution) the water may acquire a certain content of acetic and formic acid, which easily gives a pH value of about 4 to 5. This does not normally constitute a severely corrosive environment for stainless steel, but if in reuse the water acquires a higher chloride content, Type 316L may be a better alternative, particularly at higher temperatures, so as to avoid the risk of pitting or crevice corrosion.

Grinding and Refining. In grinders at least the water showers and sprays should be of stainless steel. Type 304L normally can be used here, but if high temperatures are anticipated, Type 316L should nevertheless be preferred.

When defibering chips in a refiner rather high temperatures are often reached. The chips are also often preheated with steam from the refiner. To ensure high corrosion resistance, parts in contact with water often are made of Type 316L. This also applies to the equipment used for feeding the steam-heated chips.

Screening and Dewatering. Type 304L is used in coarse screens and classifiers usually as screen plates, ends, vats, drums, etc. It is also used in centrifugal cleaners. Sometimes the stock chests are made of Type 304L.

In deckers, it is primarily those parts which are in contact with the pulp that are made of stainless steel. This is done in order to prevent the pulp from being contaminated by corrosion products.

Pipes and associated pumps and fittings used for conveying pulp may appropriately be made of a steel corresponding to Types 304L or 316L especially at high temperatures. The often troublesome risk of clogging will thereby be reduced, since the pipes, with their good corrosion resistance, largely retain the smoothness of their inner surfaces.

High chloride contents of the pulp as well as high temperature will justify the choice of Type 316L instead of 304L for the screening and dewatering equipment. The risk of pitting or crevice corrosion will thereby be minimized. (See Fig. 1.)

Sulfate Pulping

General. Although the sulfate process cannot be regarded as being as corrosive as the sulfite process, certain parts of the equipment can be exposed to fairly corrosive environments. Chemical recovery and the increased reuse of water can also result in slightly increased chloride contents. These may enter the system with seawater-floated timber or through the use of brackish water and, to a certain extent, of chemicals such as glauber salt which contains about 0.3% sodium chloride. Stainless steel is used to advantage at several points in the process where there are severely corrosive conditions, but also at other points where it has been found to be an economically satisfactory alternative.

Cooking. The cooking of chips takes place in alkali solutions with several sodium compounds, the most important of which are sodium hydroxide and sodium sulfide. Batch digesters, usually made of carbon steel, may sometimes be exposed to highly aggressive general corrosion. This may, in some cases, amount to as much as 1 mm/yr. A switch to stainless steel results in a substantial decrease in corrosion. Type 304L is normally used. Where there is a risk of high chloride content in the liquor, Type 316L should be chosen. In some cases, general corrosion has been caused by white liquor splashes on American and Canadian digesters made of Type 316. However, this is probably due to special

Fig. 1 Cylinder press for dewatering mechanical pulp. The drum and vat are made of solid Type 316. *(Sunds AB, Sweden.)*

operating conditions since excellent results have been obtained with stainless steel in Scandinavia. Thanks to the high pH, a relatively high chloride content can be tolerated without risk of stress corrosion or pitting. Continuous digesters do not have working conditions as severe as batch digesters, but despite this both Type 304L and Type 316L are also used—at least in some parts, such as screen plates.

The shell of a digester can be in the form of either a stainless lining in a mild steel vessel or a stainless steel clad plate. New digesters are, today, usually made of solid stainless material. This may be cold-stretched, which increases the strength of the material and thus reduces the necessary wall thickness. The new nitrogen-alloyed variants of Types 304L and 316L with greater strength than the corresponding conventional grades, have also become conceivable alternatives in recent years. Their corrosion resistance compares favorably with corresponding non-nitrogen-alloyed grades. Sometimes the digesters may consist of mild steel with a layer of stainless steel applied by welding. Usually, this coating is performed in at least two different steps. However, certain problems have sometimes been encountered with crack formation in the layers.

The tube system belonging to the digester is often made of Type 304L or Type 316L. The heat-exchanger tubes in the calorisator, other parts of which are often of carbon steel, are also made of stainless steel. These tubes last for about 1 to 3 years for Type 304L, and about 5 years for Type 316L.[2] Tube life varies considerably with the operating conditions. Any risk of stress corrosion due to sodium hydroxide, possibly combined with sodium chloride, is normally fairly small, but there have been cases of stress corrosion. In such cases, replacement tubes of Type 20Cr-4Ni-2Mo and of Type 18Cr-2Mo-0.6Ti with a low carbon content have been used with satisfactory results. Pumps are made of a steel corresponding to Types 304, 316, or 317, depending on the type of environment and the reliability requirements imposed. Mild steel is not sufficient. Type 316L or 317L is normally used for steam and liquor nipples, nozzles, and sleeves although Type 304 is also acceptable in many cases.

Screw conveyors in hot liquor are often made of Type 316L. In some cases Type 304L has lasted only a few months. If these components are made of carbon steel they may develop a corrosion rate exceeding 2 mm/yr.

Blow-off piping can be of mild steel, but is often a steel corresponding to either Type 304L or 316L while blow valves are either of Type 304L or of cast iron with an internal lining of Type 304L. Lye traps and condensers are generally of Type 304L. In the latter, corrosive conditions are so severe that mild steel does not last for any length of time.

TABLE 1   Frequency of Use of Stainless Steel in Evaporators, in Percent[3]

Apparatus component	Material	Evaporation stage number					
		1	2	3	4	5	6
Vapor body	S/S	93	72	1	1	0	0
	S/S clad	6	6	1	1	0	0
	C/S	1	22	98	98	100	100
Heating element shell	S/S	99	79	2	0	0	0
	C/S	1	21	98	100	100	100
Tube sheet	S/S clad	99	79	7	7	6	5
	C/S	1	21	93	93	94	95
Product liquor flash tank	S/S or clad	53					
	S/S internals	2					
	C/S	45					
Tubes	S/S	100	86	61	59	57	61
	C/S	0	14	39	41	43	39

S/S, standard stainless steel trim; S/S clad, carbon steel clad with stainless; C/S, carbon steel.

Washing, Screening, and Dewatering. The blow pits or diffusers are sometimes made of solid stainless steel or of mild steel, lined with Type 304L. When they are made of mild steel only, at least the conical section at the bottom and perforated plates should be made of stainless steel, as these sections are most susceptible to corrosion in combination with wear. In pulp washers the cylinders, vats, etc., are made of Type 304L or preferably, Type 316L. In knotters and screens, pulp-swept parts are normally made of Type 304L or 316L. Centrifugal cleaners are often built with the upper part in Type 304L, while the lower part is sometimes made of a ceramic material in order to withstand the heavy wear which occurs there. The stock chests and tanks are also sometimes made of 304L, usually in the form of linings on mild steel. Vats and strainer plates in deckers are frequently made of Type 304L or 316L. The tubes, pumps, and valves for the pulp may be of a stainless steel corresponding to Type 304L or Type 329 for pumps and valves. The high corrosion resistance will give the tubes smooth surfaces so that there is less risk of clogging or leakage due to corrosion. In cases where high chloride contents in the pulp are envisaged (for instance after the bleaching process), Type 316L should be chosen, particularly at those points where the temperature is relatively high. This grade will probably become generally used in the future as increased water reuse produces higher chloride contents in the system. This applies not only to the tube system but to all parts of the equipment in contact with the pulp.

Liquor Making. During evaporation, corrosive conditions are so severe that stainless steel has proved to be a suitable construction material. In most cases Type 304L is used, but the use of Type 316L is also rather common. Even Type 430 is sometimes an acceptable alternative. An American study[3] covering 94 mills in the United States and Canada gave the frequency of the use of stainless steels in evaporators as tabulated in Table 1. The figures given are in precentages. The corrosive conditions are worst in the first evaporation stages, where it is necessary to use stainless steel. In the last stages, the conditions are such that carbon steels may be used. The stainless tubes in stages 3 through 6 are the result of replacing carbon-steel tubes with stainless tubes. Thus there is a tendency toward increased use of stainless steel in this field of application. New mills have evaporators of stainless material only since these will remain cleaner for a longer time than if they were made of mild steel. Furthermore, there are no deposit problems on the steam side of the tubes and this, too, contributes to increased evaporation capacity.

The weak-black-liquor tank is usually only made of carbon steel, while the heavy-black-liquor tank is often lined with Type 304L.

In the lower sections of the soda recovery boiler there have been problems with severe gas corrosion caused by the sulfurous gases reacting on mild steel tubes. Tubes made of Type 304L or 316L only can be subject to stress corrosion from the inside. One solution to this problem is to use composite tubes consisting of an outer stainless steel layer of Type 304L and an inner layer of mild steel. The risk of stress corrosion on the outside of the tube is very slight.

Causticizing vessels and tanks for green and white liquor are often made of mild steel lined with Type 304L. This also applies to the clarifier and its accessories such as shaft sleeves. In some cases there have been problems with corrosion in combination with erosion of mild steel tubes between the causticizing vessel and the white-liquor tank, which is why Type 304L is a suitable choice in such cases. Pipes for white liquor only can be of mild steel or stainless steel Type 304L.

The scrubber for the combustion gas in lime kilns is made of stainless steel because of the corrosive conditions prevailing in the presence of sulfuric acid condensate. The exposed parts should therefore be made of Type 317L or better, e.g., a copper-alloyed stainless steel such as 20Cr-25Ni-2Mo-2Cu.

Sulfite Pulping

General. The sulfite process is the most corrosive method of making pulp. Calcium bisulfite with an excess of sulfur dioxide was formerly used as cooking liquor. This liquor, which was comparatively acid, could only be used for certain species of wood. By introducing magnesium, sodium, and ammonia as bases for the cooking liquor, different pH values can be obtained, enabling the cooking liquor to be used for most species of wood. As these chemicals are relatively expensive, plants must be constructed for their recovery. Because of pollution restriction regulations, the discharge of calcium bisulfite into water courses is, in most cases, no longer permitted. Consequently, this chemical must be treated in some way, e.g., by evaporation.

Liquor Making. Since the atmosphere in sulfur burners and pyrite furnaces contains sulfur, austenitic Cr-Ni steels should be avoided as these have a limited resistance at elevated temperatures because of the formation of nickel sulfide. This sulfide has a low melting point and therefore reduces the resistance of the material at high temperatures in sulfurous atmospheres. Instead of austenitic steels, ferritic-austenitic steels such as Type 329 can be used. Ferritic chromium steels are also suitable. These grades are, for instance, used in pyrite furnaces as rabbles and in pipes from burners to cooling and washing towers.

Cooling and washing towers are often built with acid-resistant bricks, but the towers are also made of stainless steel. The corrosive conditions are very severe, which is why the upper part is made of Type 316L and the lower part of a steel of Type 18Cr-15Ni-4.5Mo. It is also essential that the spray nozzles work satisfactorily so that the walls are washed continuously.

After going through the cooling and washing towers, some of the sulfurous acid in the condensate may oxidize into sulfuric acid. Both Type 316L and Type 317L have had a limited life in pipes and fans. An acid-resistant steel composed of 20Cr-25Ni-2Mo-2Cu has a higher resistance to sulfuric acid and is therefore more suitable in this case. The piping should also be designed so that drainage can take place.

Acid tanks may be made of mild steel or concrete with an acid-resistant brick lining. Sometimes they may also consist of stainless steel either in the form of lining, clad steel plate, or solid plate. Type 316L is normally used. In some cases sulfuric acid may be formed in the condensate in the hot-acid tank due to oxidation of sulfurous acid. This can easily cause severe corrosion on Type 316L at temperatures above 85°C. One solution to this problem may be to use a stainless steel composed of 18Cr-15Ni-4.5Mo for the upper part of the tank. Another solution is to have a constant excess pressure of sulfur dioxide in the tank so that air cannot be admitted to oxidize the sulfur dioxide. In this case, Type 316L is also usable in the gas phase. The shell can also be protected against corrosion in the gas phase by means of special washing or spraying units. In the tube systems corrosive conditions are not so severe as in the tanks and therefore Type 316L is sufficient.

Cooking. Formerly, digesters were constructed of Type 316L. Nowadays, however, they are usually made of Type 317L or of a steel composed of 18Cr-15Ni-4.5Mo because there have been corrosion problems with Type 316L. Thus in some cases, stress corrosion occurred when chloride content became too high, as can easily happen when chemical recovery is utilized in combination with seawater-floated timber. Stress corrosion has occurred with chloride contents of about 1 g/l (0.001 g/m³). Another type of corrosion which may occur is attack due to condensates consisting of sulfuric acid, i.e., a type of general corrosion at certain points on the surface. The risk of this type of corrosion can be reduced by changing to stainless steels with molybdenum contents higher than 3%.

The digester may consist either of a stainless steel lining in old acid-resistant brick digesters or of stainless steel clad plate. The digester may also be made of solid stainless steel. If a cold-stretched material is used, this will increase the strength of the material and the wall thickness can therefore be made thinner. Recently, the nitrogen-alloyed variants of Types 316L and 317L have also been considered. They have a relatively high yield strength and tensile strength compared with the corresponding conventional grades.

Cast components such as digester necks, emptying bends, pumps, and valves are often made of either CE-30, CF-8M, or CD-4M Cu. Other digester components (such as screen plates) should be made of Type 316L or preferably 317L.

The tubes belonging to the digester and the calorisator are either of Type 316L or 317L. The choice of grade depends on factors such as chloride content, temperature, and cooking liquor. For high-chloride contents and high temperatures, the higher alloyed grade should always be chosen, especially for the heat-exchanger tubes in the calorisator.

Washing, Screening, and Dewatering. Some of the washing is sometimes done in the digester, but the pulp will still contain waste liquor which has to be removed. The blow pits or diffusers may be made of either acid-resistant tile or Type 316L or 317L stainless steel. Type 304L does not have sufficient resistance to the residual liquor in the pulp. Where washing filters are used, the vat and cylinder with wire gauze may be made of Type 316L. The tube system for the weak liquor should also be of Type 316L.

In knotters, screens, and centrifugal cleaners the parts in contact with the pulp are often made of Type 316L since the pulp usually contains small amounts of bisulfite.

Type 304L or preferably 316L is suitable for deckers with tube systems.

The tubes and the equipment that are exposed to bleached pulp should always be made of Type 316L, since bleached pulp usually has a higher chloride content than unbleached pulp.

Chemical Recovery. Before the rather corrosive cooking liquor from the digester is evaporated, it is often stored in waste-liquor tanks. The free sulfur dioxide can readily be oxidized here, forming sulfuric acid condensate. If the temperature of the liquor exceeds about 80°C, a steel composed of 18Cr-15Ni-4.5Mo should be used. This type is quite capable of withstanding such conditions. Water sprays may also be used on the walls, in which case use of Type 316L or 317L is also possible. At temperatures below 80°C, Type 316L or, preferably, 317L may be used without a spraying device as the sulfuric acid condensate in this case is not that aggressive. Tube systems are usually made of Type 316L or 317L. Evaporation takes place in an evaporator at different stages. Investigations [3] have shown that a steel corresponding to Type 316L is a suitable material for all components in the evaporators such as tubes, vapor bodies, liquid flush tanks, vapor pipes, condenser pipes, liquor pipes, valves, pumps, and condensers when calcium bisulfite is evaporated. For evaporation of cooking liquor on magnesium base, Type 316L with 2.75% molybdenum or Type 317L is often prescribed, since the corrosive conditions are considered to be somewhat more severe than for calcium bisulfite. For cooking liquor on sodium base, the conditions are not equally corrosive and therefore Type 316L is used for the first stage and Type 304L or mild steel for the final stages in the evaporators. Mild carbon steels in the final stages have sometimes been replaced by stainless steels, primarily to reduce fouling and secondly to reduce corrosion. The corrosion problems are less severe for cooking liquor on ammonium base.

Semichemical Pulping
General. The semichemical methods of making pulp are divided into two process stages. The first stage involves the use of chemicals for partial dissolving of the lignin in

the wood. In the second stage, the chips are fully defibered in a mechanical way, e.g., in refiners. The method is thus a compromise between the chemical and mechanical methods of manufacturing pulp. The choice of construction materials for different equipment depends to a large degree on the chemical process used in the first stage, e.g., sulfate, sulfite, etc. The most common semichemical method is the NSSC (Neutral Sulfite SemiChemical) process.

Liquor Making and Recovery. Sodium bisulfite is used as NSSC cooking liquor. Type 316L is often used for the liquor-making equipment. Thus the evaporators for evaporating the liquor should be made of Type 316L. Type 304L has also been used, but sometimes corrosion has occurred. The corrosive conditions, however, do vary slightly since there are variations in the NSSC process. Other parts of the recovery system (such as pipes, tanks, etc.) should also be made of stainless steel, usually Type 316L.

Cooking. The corrosive conditions in the digesters can vary somewhat, depending on the composition of the liquor. Since the temperature is relatively high, the corrosion conditions are usually such that they demand Type 316L. In continuous digesters the conditions may permit use of Type 304L. Through liquor recovery the chloride content can easily become quite high, which increases the risk of stress corrosion. The pipe system and auxiliary equipment for the digester should be made of Type 316L. (See Fig. 2.)

Defibering, Washing, and Screening. Corrosive conditions in the stages after the digester depend on whether washing takes place in the digester or not. If the stock contains cooking liquor after the digester, the subsequent stages (i.e., blow tank or stock chest and washing filter) should be of Type 316L. For the screw press, both the screw itself and the other parts in contact with pulp should be made of Type 316L.

In refiners, Type 316L is preferred since the pulp temperature is generally increased by this process. Those parts of the screens and centrifugal cleaners which are in contact with pulp are normally of Type 316L, although Type 304L could also be used. The pipes and pumps are normally made of a steel corresponding to Type 316L.

Wastepaper Pulping   The corrosive conditions involved in making pulp from wastepaper are not normally so severe. The demand for pulp purity and reduced plant maintenance results in the use of Type 304L even where mild steel could well be an alternative. In this process, however, chemicals are sometimes used to remove printing inks in the wastepaper. Low concentrations of sodium hydroxide, sodium silicate, sodium carbonate, etc., normally are used for this purpose. In addition, zinc hydrosulfite and sodium peroxide are also sometimes used. The most suitable steel grade for pulping with addition of the above-mentioned chemicals is Type 316L. This grade will also permit chemicals to be changed and will permit high temperatures to be used for dissolving wet-strength papers in the pulper. In some cases, sodium hypochlorite is also used as a process chemical. As this can be partly converted to sodium chloride, which gives a risk of pitting, Type 316L is a suitable material for protection against corrosive attacks. The addition of chemicals often takes place in pulpers, which may be either of mild steel lined with stainless steel or of solid stainless steel. Other equipment components (such as tube systems, stock chests, screens, washing filters, water extractors, and floation equipment) are also often made of Type 316L. This applies in particular to those parts of the equipment which are in contact with the pulp if a product with a high degree of purity is required.

Bleaching

General. The most common bleaching processes, which involve the use of chemicals such as chlorine, alkali, hypochlorite, and chlorine dioxide, are highly corrosive. This means that stainless steels with a very high corrosion resistance must be used. It may generally be stated that Type 316L is the lowest grade that should be used in bleach plants. When conditions are particularly severe, it is often necessary to use Type 317L or other high-alloyed special grades of stainless steels or titanium.

In addition to the above-mentioned bleaching processes, which are used primarily for sulfite and sulfate pulp, there are also other processes. These involve the use of peroxide or hydrosulfite and are used mainly for mechanical and semichemical pulp.

More stringent demands with regard to the reuse of process water in bleach plants must be expected in the future. This can lead to, among other things, a very sharp increase in chloride content, perhaps up to 10 times the present level.[4] This, in turn, means that corrosive conditions will become much more severe in most bleach plants than they are at present. It is therefore possible that in many cases Type 317L will be needed where 316L is now accepted. Increased use of even higher alloyed stainless steels must also be expected at a number of places where 316L is sufficient today. To a certain extent, new processes such as oxygen bleaching may help to reduce slightly the increase in chloride content, but generally it will be higher than at present.

Chlorination. Mild steel pipes can be used for dry chlorine gas, but stainless steel should be used whenever there is a risk of external corrosion. Moist chlorine gas is extremely

Fig. 2   Continuous digesters at Gruvön, Billeruds AB, Sweden. The NSSC-digester to the right is made of plate clad with Type 316. To the left is a sulfate digester built mainly of mild steel with parts, such as screen plates and piping, made of Type 316L. *(Kamyr AB, Sweden.)*

corrosive, which means that it is usually necessary to have a coated mild steel. The outside coatings have failed in some cases so that external corrosion occurred. Pipes and pumps for conveying pulp to towers may be made of either coated mild steels or a steel corresponding to Type 316L. The mixer is usually made of mild steel covered with rubber, but there are also mixers made of Type 316L despite the fact that this material has a short service life. The reason is that these mixers are easier to repair than mixers with coated surfaces. The bleaching tower is usually lined with acid-resistant tile, since the corrosive conditions are too severe for stainless steel. The tower scraper is usually made of titanium or sometimes of rubber-coated Type 317L. Piping to carry the pulp from the bleaching towers to the filter washing stage is sometimes made of Type 316L or 317L. Pitting problems are sometimes encountered in the welds, particularly when using Type 316L. Rubber-coated tubes, which are relatively common, are not always considered satisfactory. The head boxes are generally of Type 316L or 317L. In some cases, pitting has occurred on the surface above the liquid level. In this case it is possible to clean the surface and coat it with a glass-fiber-reinforced plastic layer to a certain distance below the liquid level. The filter drum and the filter placed around its periphery normally are made of Type 316L or 317L. However, it must be expected that the filter gauze will require replacement after 6 months to 2 years. The vat itself may be made of either acid-resistant tile, plastic, or rubber-coated steel, as the corrosive conditions in this environment are very severe. The white water coming from the filter is very corrosive and the pipes must therefore be of Type 316L or, preferably, 317L. Polyester tubes are also common in this case.

Alkaline Extraction. The alkaline extraction stage is not as corrosive as the chlorination stage. The pH is generally about 10. The temperature can vary from 40°C upwards. Most components in this stage can be made of Type 304L but, since consideration must be paid to the external corrosion which may occur in the aggressive atmosphere at bleach plants, Type 316L is often more suitable.

The piping system for the pulp before and after the tower should be of Type 316L. This also applies to filtrate tubes. This gives better protection against corrosive attacks at high temperatures than Type 304L. The mixer can be of Type 304L or 316L. Pumps are made of cast iron or preferably of a stainless steel corresponding to either Type 304L or 316L. The tower itself usually consists of mild steel with an acid-resistant tile lining, but it can be made of, or lined with, Type 304L or 316L. The feed tube and tower scraper should be of Type 304L or 316L, as should the tower agitator. Type 316L preferably should be used in the washing filter for both cylinder and vat. Type 316L is recommended for the filtrate tank and drain pipe.

Hypochlorite Bleaching. Bleaching in the hypochlorite stage takes place in an alkaline environment with a pH above 8.5 and at temperatures between 30 and 45°C. The corrosive conditions are not quite so severe as in the chlorination stage. The tube system for the pulp is usually made of Type 316L but polyvinyl chloride (PVC) tubes are also used. The mixer is normally made of Type 316L. The bleaching tower usually consists of mild steel lined with acid-resistant tile since the corrosive conditions are too severe for stainless steel. The feed tube is often made of Type 316L or of glass-fiber-reinforced plastic, while the agitator is of Type 316L or, preferably, 317L. Corrosive conditions are very severe at the tower scraper, and this is normally made of Hastelloy C. The filter vat, cylinder, and filter gauze are usually made of Type 316L or 317L. The vat, however, is sometimes made of acid-resistant tile.

Chlorine Dioxide Bleaching. The solution used for chlorine dioxide bleaching is relatively acid, with a pH of 4 to 5, and is highly aggressive, thus placing considerable demands on the corrosion resistance of the materials. Investigations[5] have shown that chlorine dioxide alone cannot attack stainless steels. The attacks do not begin until chloride ions are present. During bleaching, however, chlorine dioxide is reduced, forming chlorides in solution.

The mixer can be of Type 316L or 317L, with a normal life of 2 to 5 years, although longer lives are known. Hastelloy will last 4 to 7 years. The corrosion conditions in the tube system are rather severe and therefore Type 317L should be used. Pumps, however, may consist of a steel corresponding to either Type 316L or 317L. The bleaching tower, where there are very severe corrosive conditions, is usually lined with acid-resistant tile, whereas the agitator is often made of either Type 316L or 317L. The scraper at the top of the tower can be made of Type 317L, which in most cases does not cause any problems. The drum and the gauze in the washing filter can be made of Type 316L. The gauze, however, has a limited life. Vats made of Type 316L have exhibited severe corrosion damage. Type 317L or a higher alloyed grade is therefore a better choice. White-water pipe systems of Type 316L have in some cases suffered corrosive attacks, while Type 317L has given satisfactory service.

Peroxide Bleaching. Peroxide bleaching is a commonly employed method for bleaching mechanical pulp. In some cases, the peroxide bleaching is also used after chlorine dioxide bleaching.

The bleaching liquor usually consists of hydrogen peroxide, sodium hydroxide, and silicates and normally has a pH of 9 to 11. The conditions in this bleaching stage are to some extent similar to those in the alkaline extraction.

In bleach plants which also include stages with chlorine, hypochlorite or chlorine dioxide, all the components which can be made of Type 304L in the peroxide stage should be made of Type 316L in view of the risk of external corrosion in the aggressive bleach plant atmosphere. Somewhat higher chloride contents in the bleaching liquor must also be expected, which means that the liquor will be slightly more corrosive than in, for example, bleaching with peroxide only.

The tube system can be made of Type 304L or 316L, while the pumps should normally be made of a steel corresponding to Type 316. Type 304L or 316L is used for the mixer. The bleaching tower is usually made of mild steel with an acid-resistant tile lining. It could, however, also be made of Type 316L, preferably as a nitrogen-alloyed variant or in a cold-stretched condition. Tower scrapers, agitators, and feed tubes should be made of Type 304L or 316L. The washing filter vat is normally constructed of Type 304L and the drum of Type 316L. The filtrate tank as well as the tubing usually consists of Type 316L.

Hydrosulfite Bleaching. Zinc or sodium hydrosulfite is sometimes used for bleaching mechanical pulp. A two-stage bleaching, with a peroxide stage followed by a hydrosulfite stage, is frequently used. The bleaching liquor consists either of zinc hydrosulfite with a pH of 4.5 to 5.5 or of sodium hydrosulfite with a pH higher than 6.

Those components coming into contact with the hydrosulfite (i.e., the mixer and pulp pipes) should be of either Type 316L or Type 317L. The tower usually consists of mild steel with an acid-resistant tile lining. However, this could conceivably be made of Type 316L or 317L. The tower scraper is usually made of Type 316L. The hydrosulfite solution should be stored in equipment made of either Type 316L or 317L. For equipment coming into contact with the pulp before mixing with hydrosulfite solution, Type 304L or 316L may be used, depending on the chloride content and the temperature.

Papermaking

General. In papermaking, conditions are not as corrosive as in the sulfate and sulfite processes. However, since there are high demands on product purity, coupled with a desire to cut down equipment maintenance, stainless steel has come to be used in many phases of the manufacturing process. The proportion of stainless steel has also increased, since the above factors have become increasingly important.

Recently, the corrosion conditions have also become somewhat more severe as a consequence of the increasing use of closed water systems to reduce effluent. Type 304L is normally used, as is Type 316L, particularly at high temperatures and if there is a risk of high chloride content in the process water. This latter risk is usually incurred when brackish water is used, or with a closed water system. Efforts should therefore be made to ascertain the probable content of chlorides in the water before choosing the grade of stainless steel.

Preparation of Stock. Some stock chests can be made of solid stainless steel or more often of mild steel lined with stainless steel, usually Type 304L. However, it is a question of economy, in terms of investment costs and maintenance, whether stainless steel should be used or not.

Nowadays pulpers are often made of solid stainless steel to prevent corrosion from affecting the raw material for the paper. Pulpers of mild steel are sometimes lined internally with thin stainless sheet. Type 304L is normally used for this purpose, as this has sufficient resistance for the application concerned. If water temperatures are high, Type 316L is preferred. The agitator is also made of stainless steel with Stellite at the tops for good wear resistance.

Beater tubs are often lined with Type 304L to ensure a high degree of purity in the product by preventing corrosion. The same applies to jordan refiners in headboxes, etc. Type 431 is generally used for the knives in beaters and jordan refiners as this grade has high wear resistance. However, Type 431 is sometimes unable to withstand the corrosive conditions, and in such cases a molybdenum-alloyed steel is recommended. In disk refiners, the parts which come in contact with stock are also made of stainless steel, most often Type 316L.

The corrosive conditions in cleaners are not severe, but nevertheless stainless steel is used in screens and centrifugal cleaners for numerous components such as vats and screen plates.

The mixing tanks can be of either solid stainless material or mild steel with a lining of Type 304L or 316L. Tanks for inks should preferably be made of Type 316L to safeguard against corrosion. Further advantages are the clean and smooth surfaces obtained as a result of the high corrosion resistance, and the fact that the tanks can easily be cleaned. Tanks for alum and for starch are often made of Type 304L since this simplifies maintenance.

The tube system is often made of stainless steel. This prevents corrosion and, consequently, contamination of the product, and gives smooth surfaces, which reduces the risk of clogging. For the same reason, pumps and valves are also made of stainless steel. Type

304L or 316L or the equivalent cast alloy, is used, depending on the chloride content and the temperature.

Paper Machine. It is mainly the wet sections in the paper machine (Fig. 3) that are made of stainless steel. The main advantages are reduced maintenance and purer products. Type 304L is normally used, since this is adequate in most cases. However, it must be expected that the chloride content in the stock will increase in the future as an inevitable result of

Fig. 3 Paper machine for newsprint and magazine paper at Kvarnsveden Paper Mill, Sweden. The head box is clad with Type 316 stainless sheet and the piping system is made of Type 316. *(Stora, Sweden.)*

increased water reuse. Where high chloride contents are foreseen, Type 316L should be used. The components made of stainless steel in the paper machine are the headbox, rails, side panels, table rolls, suction boxes and white-water system with savealls and pipe systems. There are normally no corrosion problems with these components when stainless steel is used; however, scrupulous cleanliness is essential in order to avoid clogging in the various machine components. If clogging does occur, the corrosive conditions may deteriorate, sometimes resulting in corrosive attacks such as crevice and pitting corrosion.

There have been some problems with corrosion fatigue on suction couch rolls of Type 304L and 316L. Here, a ferritic-austenitic stainless steel composed of 20Cr-4Ni-2Mo may perhaps solve the problems.

Type 304L or, preferably, Type 316L may be used for the fourdrinier wire. These grades have proved satisfactory in most cases.

REFERENCES

1. Davy, M. F., and W. A. Mueller: Pulp and Paper Industry Worldwide Corrosion Costs, "Pulp and Paper Industry Corrosion Problems," p. 1, National Assoc. Corrosion Engineers, 1974.
2. Macdonald, R. G.: "Pulp and Paper Manufacture, vol. 1, The Pulping of Wood," (2d ed.), McGraw-Hill, New York, 1968.
3. Lankenau, H. G., and A. R. Flores: Survey of Pulp Mill Evaporator Systems Corrosion and the Corrective Measures Taken, *Tappi*, vol. 51, no. 2, p. 53A.
4. Laliberte, L. H.: Corrosion Problems of Stainless Steels in the Bleach Plant, "Pulp and Paper Industry Corrosion Problems," p. 51, National Assoc. Corrosion Engineers, 1974.
5. Passinen, K., and P. E. Ahlers: Corrosion of Acidproof Steel in ClO_2-Solution, *Pap, Puu—Papper och Trä*, vol. 48, p. 549, 1966.

Chapter **44**

Stainless Steels
in the Petroleum Industry

EMIL L. BERECZKY

Metallurgical Engineer, Union Oil Company of California, Los Angeles, California

Corrosion is one of the predominant factors that influence the selection of materials for construction of refinery equipment. Corrosion may be caused by corrosives originating in the crude oil (such as hydrogen sulfide, organic sulfur compounds, chlorides, carbon dioxide, dissolved oxygen, and organic acids), by the chemical compounds used in the refining processes (such as sulfuric acid, sodium hydroxide, etc.), by environmental effects as in outdoor atmospheres, or by the combustion gas in fired heaters.

Hydrogen Sulfide Attack Most important and far reaching in its effect is sulfur, which exists in practically all crude oils and finds its way into almost every refinery operation. It may be generalized that sulfur in refinery streams is corrosive under two conditions:

1. As hydrogen sulfide in the presence of water below the dew point. This condition is usually manifested as straightforward chemical attack except that it may cause stress corrosion in martensitic 400-series stainless steels and precipitation-hardenable stainless steels.

2. As hydrogen sulfide at elevated temperatures with or without the presence of other corrosives. These may be classified as follows:

Elevated Temperature H₂S Attack without Naphthenic Acids and Hydrogen. Although minor amounts of H_2S can be present in crude-oil feed stocks, most H_2S is generated from unstable organic sulfur compounds as a result of heating. For this reason the corrosivity of crude, or process streams, cannot be predicted accurately from the total sulfur content. H_2S generation becomes appreciable at about 500°F (260°C) and is essentially completed at about 900°F (482°C).

The corrosion resistance of steels in sulfur-containing crude oil is strongly dependent on temperature and chromium content, as illustrated by Fig. 1. The corrosivity of other

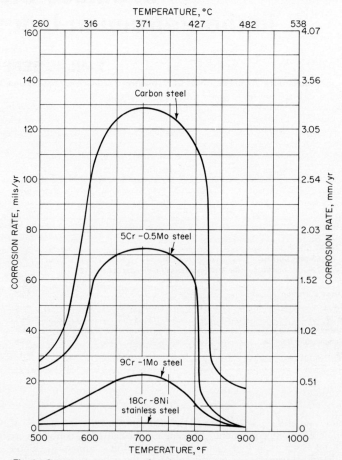

Fig. 1 Comparative corrosion of steels in crude oil containing 1.5% sulfur.[1]

types of crude oils follows similar patterns, except that the actual corrosion rates at various temperatures may differ.

The resistance of 12% Cr and 18Cr-8Ni stainless steels, such as Type 304, to elevated temperature H_2S attack is normally excellent throughout the entire range of temperatures encountered in processing. Possible exceptions may arise wherever very high velocities or flashing of feed may occur such as in localized areas of pumps, heater tubes, or in piping between heaters and fractionating towers. In these cases, molybdenum-containing Type 316 is usually an economic solution.

The 12% Cr stainless steels, specifically Types 410, 410S, and 405, find applications as cladding, exchanger tubing, ballast trays, and pump components. The austenitic 300-series stainless steels are also used for the above items and for heater tubes whenever the ferritic alloys have inadequate corrosion resistance. Experience indicates that the 18Cr-8Ni alloys have better weldability and lower installed cost than many of the straight-chromium alloys. As for disadvantages, it should be noted that the austenitic alloys are susceptible to stress-corrosion cracking, but cracking has been rare in crude and vacuum units.

In recent years Type 430 has found significant usage as welded heat-exchanger tubing, replacing lower chromium alloys because of lower cost and superior corrosion resistance. It should be noted, however, that this alloy should be used with caution in water-containing services because of potential pitting corrosion problems.

Elevated Temperature H_2S Attack with Naphthenic Acid Present. When sour crude oils containing organic acids such as naphthenic (neutralization number 0.5 mg KOH/gr) are heated above 450°F (232°C), corrosion can be much higher than expected from sulfur corrosion alone. In general, higher naphthenic acid contents (as evidenced by higher neutralization numbers) indicate probable increased corrosion rates beyond those predicted from sulfur compounds alone. Precise correlation, however, does not exist as this type of corrosion is governed by many interrelating factors.

Naphthenic acid attack is particularly insidious because it is practically impossible to predict its severity, location or, for that matter, even if it will take place at all. Specific localized conditions, such as velocity, turbulence, impingement, feed vaporization, or condensation can have extreme influence.

Naphthenic acid corrosion reaches maximum at approximately 530°F (277°C) and greatly diminishes above 650°F (343°C). If corrosion rates continue to increase above 530°F, such increase is considered to be caused primarily by sulfur compounds. When naphthenic acids are suspected to be active, a test using coupons of Type 304 and Type 316 alloys can be made; if 304 is attacked and 316 is not, the presence of napthenic acid is considered proven since 304 is almost completely inert to sulfur corrosion but is attacked by naphthenic acids. Naphthenic acid corrosion is observed primarily in oil heater tubes, especially in return bends, heater outlet headers, heater to fractionating tower transfer lines, fractionating tower internals, piping, and pump components. In these instances carbon steel, Cr-Mo alloys, and most 18Cr-8Ni stainless steels are subject to unacceptably high corrosion rates and Type 316 stainless steel is normally the most economic choice. Wherever aggravated corrosive conditions exist, Type 317 stainless steel offers decided improvement over Type 316 to this type of attack.

Elevated Temperature H_2S Attack with H_2 Present. The corrosion products formed in this environment are mostly iron sulfides that provide a poorly adherent nonprotective film on carbon steel and low-chromium steels. It has been observed that as the temperature is raised, corrosion increases without a maximum. The corrosion rate depends on chromium content, as illustrated in Fig. 2, and generally a minimum of 12% Cr content is required in ferrous alloys for protection even in moderately severe environments. The more highly alloyed 18Cr-8Ni stainless steels have excellent resistance to this type of attack and find extensive applications.

Low chromium additions generally do not provide increased corrosion resistance and, surprisingly, can be detrimental, as shown in Fig. 3. Alloying elements other than chromium do not have any significant effect on corrosion resistance in commercial alloys.

It has been observed that corrosion primarily depends on temperature and H_2S content up to 1 mole %. Above this amount, corrosion is almost completely independent of H_2S levels. Total hydrogen pressure, likewise, has insignificant influence. The corrosive attack is strongly influenced, however, by the nature of the hydrocarbon processed and it is lowest in naphtha and considerably higher in heavier stocks (gas oils). Higher concentrations of impurities (such as sulfur, chlorides, organic acids, etc.) in gas oils is thought to be the cause of this phenomenon.

Corrosion rates obtained in short tests of several hundred hours duration are found to be far higher than encountered in commercial units during normal runs and for this reason could be quite misleading.

The H_2-H_2S corrosion at elevated temperatures is controlled by the use of 18-8 austenitic stainless steels such as Types 304, 304L, 321, 347, etc., by cast austenitic-ferritic alloys such as the HF alloy modified to contain ferrite, usually 5 to 15%, and occasionally with 12% Cr alloys. All of these materials except the HF alloy are used for piping, heater and heat-exchanger tubing, pump components, cladding, and reactor internals. The modified

HF alloy is utilized, because of its good elevated temperature strength and excellent resistance to polythionic acid and chloride stress-corrosion cracking, as piping, heater tubes, valve bodies, and reactor internals.

Type 430 is finding increasing application as heat-exchanger tubing because of its excellent resistance to H_2-H_2S, its immunity to stress corrosion, and its economic advantage over the 12% Cr alloys.

Several relatively new proprietary wrought austenitic-ferritic alloys, such as Sandvik 3RE60 and Carpenter 7 Mo, have been developed and are being marketed. These alloys, primarily available in tubular forms, should find increasing acceptance, along with the older cast duplex alloys because of their outstanding resistance to stress corrosion caused by wet sulfidic or chloride environments encountered during operation or shutdown periods.

Polythionic Acid Stress Corrosion These acids, $H_2S_xO_6$, may cause stress-corrosion cracking in fully or partially austenitic stainless steels. Ferritic or martensitic steels are not attacked. Polythionic acids form on metal surfaces when sulfide-bearing corrosion products react with moisture and air (O_2). This condition exists predominantly when equipment is shut down and is opened to the atmosphere. It can be avoided by

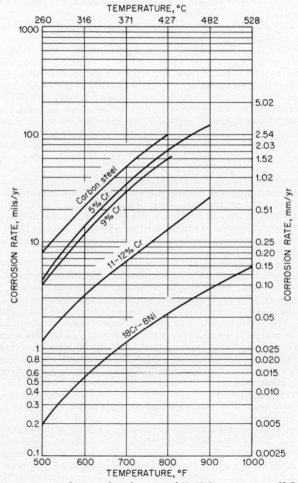

Fig. 2 Corrosion rate curves for several steels in gas-oil-H_2-H_2S environments. $H_2S = 1$ mole %.[2]

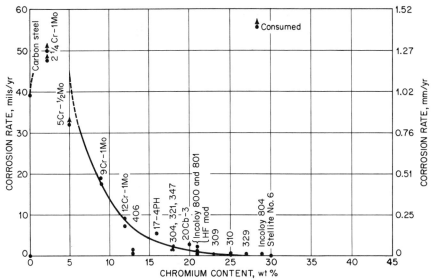

Fig. 3 Effect of chromium content on corrosion rate in high-pressure H_2-H_2S oil environment. H_2S = 1.3 mole %. Tested at 790°F (421°C) for 11,000 h minimum.

maintaining an inert gas purge or by using an alkaline wash to neutralize any acids formed.

As austenitic stainless steels have their greatest use for resisting high-temperature sulfur corrosion, their susceptibility to cracking is of very serious concern, especially so in hydrodesulfurizers and hydrocrackers which utilize very large quantities of austenitic alloys.

Polythionic acid stress-corrosion cracking can be classified as stress-accelerated intergranular corrosion of sensitized alloys. The 18-8 stainless steels, and other austenitic alloys as well, can be sensitized by very long-term exposures at temperatures as low as 600°F (316°C). Sensitization is defined as the presence of grain-boundary chromium depletion to significantly lower levels, to approximately 12% or less, than the bulk chromium content. Grain-boundary attack without stress in most petroleum processing applications is only superficial and insignificant; with stress, applied or residual, cracking can be extremely rapid.

Polythionic acid cracking can be controlled metallurgically by eliminating, or at least minimizing, grain-boundary chromium depletion. These methods are:

1. Solution annealing at temperatures high enough, typically around 2000°F (1093°C), to take into solution the carbides, followed by rapid cooling to ambient temperature. This method is acceptable only if service exposures do not result in sensitization, that is, below approximately 600°F (316°C).

2. Thermal stabilization at an intermediate temperature, typically 1625 ± 25°F (885 ± 14°C) for 4 h minimum to precipitate and agglomerate the portion of carbon that is insoluble at these temperatures. The principal value of this treatment is the reduction of carbon available for causing sensitization in service and the complete stress relief resulting in much reduced susceptibility to stress corrosion.

3. Chemical stabilization by the addition of strong carbide-forming elements such as Ti or Cb, as in Type 321 or 347. This method may reduce susceptibility, depending on past thermal history and in-service conditions, but definitely does not eliminate it. For optimum resistance, these alloys, similar to the unstabilized grades, should be used in the thermally stabilized condition if service-related conditions may result in sensitization.

4. Austenitic-ferritic alloys possess significantly improved resistance to sensitization, and because of this, to polythionic acid cracking. Additional benefit resulting from the presence of ferrite is a superior resistance to chloride stress-corrosion cracking. At first this

type of alloy was available in the cast form only, such as the HF alloy modified to contain 5 to 15% ferrite, but several wrought proprietary alloys have been developed since and should find increasing usage.

It should be noted that the ferrite in these alloys is subject to the 885°F (475°C) embrittlement that results in significant overall reduction in toughness above 675°F (357°C) as shown in Fig. 4.

Embrittlement of Ferritic and Martensitic Stainless Steels Containing at Least 12% Chromium These alloys are susceptible to loss of toughness at normal temperatures due to

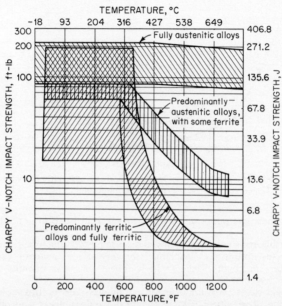

Fig. 4 Schematic representation of embrittlement characteristics of austenitic, ferritic, and austenitic-ferritic alloys upon long-term holding at elevated temperatures.

885°F (475°C) embrittlement when heated above approximately 675°F (357°C), and from the precipitation of sigma phase when heated above 900°F (482°C). The temperature ranges of embrittlement caused by these sources overlap and may be indistinguishable (shown schematically in Fig. 4) for several alloy types.

The degree of embrittlement depends on the composition, especially on the chromium content, temperature of exposure, holding time, and the degree of cold-working. For example, in a 12% Cr alloy embrittlement may not develop until several years of exposure, or depending on specific composition, not at all. In high-chromium alloys, such as Type 446, even short holding times are certain to result in extremely adverse changes in ductility and toughness.

These alloys should not be used for pressure-restraining components such as piping, vessels, etc., above approximately 675°F (357°C) to avoid the real possibility of brittle failure. When this is not possible, the components should be designed and operated with full recognition of their probable service-induced embrittlement, and bending stresses, shock, or impact loading should be minimized to the greatest extent possible.

In spite of this shortcoming, the 12% Cr alloys are extensively utilized in the embrittling range for applications involving non-pressure-restraining components such as cladding, weld overlay, ballast trays, or other internals. Service-induced embrittlement, while present and undesirable, has not presented undue difficulties or hazards in these applications.

The properties of alloys embrittled by 885°F (475°C) embrittlement can be restored by heating above 1000°F (538°C); excessive holding, however, may result in sigma embrittlement, that in turn can be eliminated by heat treatment above 1600°F (870°C).

It should be recognized that the ferrite in ferritic-austenitic duplex alloys (such as in "austenitic" weld deposits, Type 329, HF modified, and various proprietary alloys) is also subject to 885°F (475°C) and to sigma embrittlement. As these alloys vary from the predominately ferritic to the almost fully austenitic with attendant wide variations in their overall embrittlement characteristics, their use above 675°F should take this characteristic into account.

Chloride Stress Corrosion   Austenitic, and to a lesser extent, partially austenitic stainless steels, are susceptible to transgranular stress-corrosion cracking when exposed to tensile stresses at temperatures in excess of approximately 150°F (65°C) in corrosive media containing chlorides.

The major factors having influence on susceptibility for cracking are the composition, especially the nickel content, tensile stress level, ferrite content, and pH. For example, far more severe conditions can be tolerated without adverse affects in alkaline than in acidic environments. This principle is illustrated well by the widespread use of austenitic stainless steels in the chloride-contaminated alkaline solvents used in acid gas removal plants.

Significant improvement in stress-corrosion resistance can be achieved by incorporating at least a small amount of ferrite in the austenitic structure as in weld deposits, in HF modified alloy, and in others. Another practical, though more expensive method, is to increase the nickel content to approximately 45% at which level, for all practical purposes, a virtual immunity is reached.

It should be noted that sensitized 18Cr-8Ni stainless steels can be extremely susceptible to intergranular cracking, even at room temperature, in the presence of tensile stresses in chloride-bearing environments, while higher temperatures are required for transgranular cracking in nonsensitized alloys.

Because at least a trace of chlorides is present in almost all refinery streams involving hydrocarbons, in cooling water, in boiler feedwater, and in the many chemical agents used in the refining processes, the potential for stress-corrosion cracking is widespread and the suitability of austenitic stainless steels must be evaluated carefully for each application with this hazard in mind.

Sulfuric Acid   This chemical has widespread use in several refinery processes such as alkylation, polymerization, and isomerization of light hydrocarbons into gasoline blending stocks. Other important applications include water treatment and pH control.

Sulfuric acid of at least 65% concentration is usually handled at ambient temperatures in carbon-steel equipment except when high velocity or turbulence is present. These conditions, as well as higher temperatures, require the use of austenitic stainless steels, special alloys or other materials. Typical isocorrosion curves for several stainless steels are given in Fig. 5.

The molybdenum-free grades of stainless steels such as Type 304, and to a lesser extent the molybdenum-bearing Type 316, may have erratic resistance and their usability depends on acid concentration, turbulence, velocity, temperature, and aeration. Because of this, a testing program of 18-8 type alloys is frequently advisable before use. Several more highly alloyed stainless steels such as 20Cb-3, Incoloy 825, etc., were developed with improved sulfuric acid resistance and these alloys find extensive applications in the more demanding services such as piping, valves, pumps, and structural components.

Carbonic Acid   Large quantities of hydrogen are utilized in several important refinery operations. The hydrogen is produced for this purpose in specialized plants by reacting steam and methane at elevated temperatures in the presence of a catalyst.

Carbon dioxide, carbon monoxide, and water are also present in the hydrogen produced and must be removed prior to use. As this stream is cooled below its dew point of approximately 350°F (177°C), a carbonic-acid-containing low-pH condensate forms. This condensate, depending on the temperature and pressure, can be extremely corrosive to carbon steel and low-chromium ($\leq$5%) steels, especially at the location of the initial condensation, and corrosion rates on the order of 1.0 in./yr (2.54 cm) have been observed. The addition of as little as 5% chromium to steel results in significant increase in corrosion resistance, as illustrated in Fig. 6. However, at least 12% chromium is required for a tolerable resistance under most conditions. The 12% Cr steels, primarily because of their

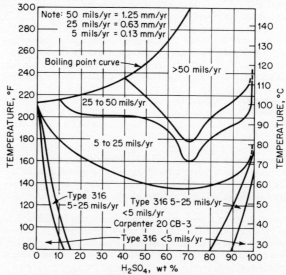

Fig. 5 Iso-corrosion curves for Types 316 and Carpenter 20 Cb-3 stainless steels in sulfuric acid without aeration. These curves are for general guidance only as corrosion may vary with impurities, aeration, velocity, etc. (*Carpenter 20 Cb-3 data from private communication with M. Henthorne.*)

higher cost, are rarely used in this service. The most economic ferrous high alloys are usually Type 304 or 304L stainless steels. These are used as piping, exchanger tubing, cladding, pump wetted compounds, valves, etc., and are immune, for all practical purposes, to the corrosive affects of the acidic condensate.

Alkaline Environments   Highly alkaline materials such as sodium hydroxide are normally handled under conditions that do not require materials other than carbon steel or cast iron. Stainless steels are, however, extensively employed with the moderately alkaline solutions that are used for removal of H_2S and CO_2 acid gases from fuel gases or CO_2 from manufactured hydrogen. Acid gas removal is accomplished with DEA (diethanolamine), MEA (monoethanolamine) and other alkaline solvents, some of them proprietary.

The major portions of the absorption plant and the attendant regeneration section as well, are constructed from carbon steel. Stainless steels are utilized wherever carbon steel is subject to high depreciation rates due to high concentration of contaminants, high velocity, or turbulence, as heat-exchanger tubing, piping, pump components, cladding, and stripper or regenerator column internals.

The usual alloy choice is Type 304 or 316 stainless steel if improved pitting resistance is desired. Column internals are normally 12% Cr or 304 stainless steels.

It should be noted that the alkaline solutions utilized for acid gas removal may contain several hundred parts per million of chlorides originating from the makeup chemicals and, because of this, stress corrosion is a possibility. Reports of cracking problems are rare and the austenitic alloys have demonstrated excellent performance.

In an effort to use materials that are immune to chloride stress-corrosion cracking, some uses of 12% Cr and 17% Cr alloys have been made as heat-exchanger tubing. These materials, however, have generally not shown adequate resistance to pitting in this service.

Elevated Temperature Service   Stainless steels are used for elevated temperature service, defined as above 1000°F (538°C), because of their excellent high-temperature strength, oxidation resistance, and structural stability.

The most common type of corrosion at high temperatures is the same as at ordinary temperatures, namely, oxidation. In commercially important steels, oxidation is reduced by the addition of chromium, the amount needed for passivity depending on the temperature and specific environment.

Gases other than oxygen (such as sulfur dioxide, hydrogen sulfide), halogens, alkali salts, or heavy metal contaminants as well, strongly affect the corrosive conditions. Exposure to mild conditions, for example, below 1200°F (649°C) in oxidizing atmospheres, results in the formation of thin protective oxide film, while exposures to severe conditions may lead to the formation of thick, nonprotective scales.

The chemically stabilized Types 321 and 347 were developed for use in the as-welded condition in corrosive services when an electrolyte is present. They do not improve the corrosion resistance at elevated temperatures. The stabilizing elements, however, do enhance the stress-rupture strength of 18-8 stainless steels to approximately 1325°F (718°C), as shown in Fig. 7.

Occasionally the chemically stabilized stainless steels are selected with the expectation of avoiding sensitization in long-term high-temperature service. Unfortunately, disappointment is the result since stabilized and unstabilized austenitic stainless steels are both sensitized by long-term service-related exposure.

Justification for using other than the lowest cost Type 304 should be evaluated critically for each application, as more often than not this grade represents the best all-round choice among the stainless steels because of high strength, acceptable corrosion resistance, and excellent weldability in the new and aged conditions.

Important high-temperature applications of stainless steels include:
- Heater tubes: Types 304, 316, 321, 347, HF, and HK-40
- Piping: Types 410, 304, 316, 321, and 347
- Heater tube supports: HF, HK, 330

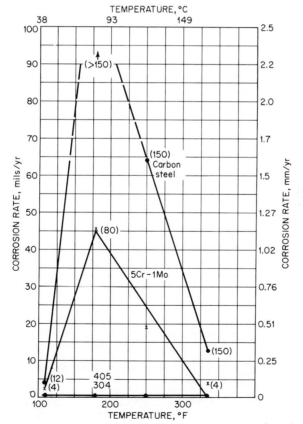

Fig. 6   Hydrogen plant effluent corrosion, 296-day test, CO_2 = 40 psi (276 kN/m^2). *Note:* Number in parentheses is the pit depth. *(Private communication from W. H. Sharp, Shell Development.)*

- Refractory anchors: Types 304, 305, 309, and 310
- Thermowells: Types 446, 304, 316, 321, and 347
- Structural components: Types 304, 316, 321, 347, and alloy 800

Other rather specialized high-temperature uses of stainless steels are associated with the manufacture of hydrogen as in the reformer furnace and in flare tips.

Steam Methane Reformer Furnace. Natural gas or other methane-containing materials are reacted with steam over a catalyst in reformers to produce hydrogen. The reaction is strongly endothermic and therefore requires large heat input. The operating conditions,

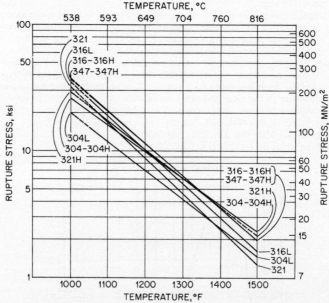

Fig. 7   Average rupture strength curves (100,000 h) for several austenitic stainless steels.[3]

high stresses and temperatures to 1800°F (982°C), thermal shock, and the large relative movement of various components due to heating and cooling cycles, place extremely severe demand on the materials of construction. Various austenitic stainless steels and higher alloys have found extensive use in reformers. These applications are:

1. The catalyst tubes for the reaction are usually fabricated from centrifugally cast alloys with the surfaces in the as-cast condition. There have been applications of tubes with the unsound metal machined off on the inside diameter, but this practice is relatively rare in the United States and generally it is not economical.

The HK alloy has been used in some of the earliest furnaces and it still remains the most widely used alloy for catalyst tubes. The very strong influence of carbon content on stress-rupture strength within the specification range of 0.35 to 0.45% is increasingly being recognized and the minimum carbon content usually is specified at some higher level, such as 0.40%.

The increasingly severe operating conditions, as well as the difficulty encountered with measurement of the tube metal temperatures, have resulted in tube life that is but a fraction of the 100,000-h design. Desire for longer tube life resulted in several applications of tubes with wall thicknesses approaching 1 in. (2.54 cm). The expected increase in tube life, however, has not been attained.

It is believed that thermal gradient stresses in thicker wall tubes are much higher than in thinner wall tubes, thus possibly negating much of the expected gain from the use of additional tube wall.

Other materials with superior rupture strength, such as HP or various proprietary alloys, are increasingly utilized for improved life expectancy. This expectation is based on the reduction of thermal gradient stresses due to thinner walls as well as the improved microstructural stability of these alloys.

2. Outlet "pigtails." These are usually fabricated from wrought Incoloy 800 or occasionally from the similar, nonproprietary alloy 800 piping, in the mill-annealed or solution-annealed condition. Solution-annealed, coarse-grained material is definitely preferred because of higher elevated temperature strength.

3. Outlet header and transfer lines. These have been fabricated from cast HF, HK-40, and HT alloys or wrought Incoloy 800. These cast alloys, while possessing adequate strength, are quite brittle at ambient temperature, especially after aging at operating temperatures. Thus, these cast alloys are quite liable to failure from thermal shock or from mechanical stresses imposed by the movement of the header system. Wrought alloys, in the solution-annealed condition, are increasingly used for headers and definitely are preferred because of their superior ductility.

Blowdown Flare Tips. They are used for combustion of hydrocarbons released into the refinery blowdown system to prevent equipment overpressure during abnormal or upset conditions. Since flare tips are in intermittent service, they are required to resist not only the severe thermal stresses resulting from rapid heating and cooling cycles between ambient and burning gas temperatures, but, in addition, radiant high heat, effects of sulfidizing atmospheres, and severe vibration resulting from combustion resonance.

Failures are usually due to cracking, either because of thermal shock or from the action of polythionic acids on the sensitized alloys when they are relatively cold.

The most commonly used alloys for flare tips are Types 304, 309, 310, and alloy 800. Steam piping that is exposed to high radiant heat is usually made from Type 304. Experiences indicate that Type 310 and alloy 800 have better resistance than Types 304 or 309 in flare-tip service.

REFERENCES

General

1. Nelson, G. A.: "Corrosion Data Survey," National Assoc. Corrosion Engineers, Houston, Tex., 1967.
2. Couper, A. S., and J. W. Gorman: Computer Correlations to Estimate High Temperature H_2S Corrosion in Refinery Streams, *Mater. Prot.*, vol. 10, no. 1, pp. 31–37, January 1971.
3. Smith, G. V.: An Evaluation of the Yield, Tensile, Creep and Rupture Strengths of Wrought 304, 316, 321 and 347 Stainless Steels at Elevated Temperatures, *ASTM Data Ser. 5S2*, 1969.

Specific

1. McConomy, N. F.: High Temperature Sulfidic Corrosion in Hydrogen Free Environment, *Proc. Am Pet. Inst., Sec. 3*, vol. 43, pp. 79–96, 1963.
2. Piehl, R. L.: Correlation of Corrosion in a Crude Distillation Unit with Chemistry of Crudes, *Corrosion*, vol. 16, no. 6, pp. 305t–307t, June 1960.
3. Eroneta, V. G., and A. S. Couper: Crude Unit Corrosion Control Based on Pilot Plant Tests, *Proc. Am. Pet. Inst.*, Div. of Refining, vol. 50, pp. 830–843, 1970.
4. Derungs, W. A.: Naphthenic Acid Corrosion–An Old Enemy of the Petroleum Industry, *Corrosion*, vol. 12, no. 12, pp. 617t–622t, December 1956.
5. Heller, J. J.: Corrosion of Refinery Equipment by Naphthenic Acid, *Mater. Prot.*, vol. 2, no. 9, pp. 90–96, September 1963.
6. Prescott, G. R., and J. J. Heller: A Modified Cast HF Alloy for Hydrocracker Service, *Mater. Prot.*, vol. 7, no. 3, pp. 42–44, March 1968.
7. Carlen, Jan-Christer, and C. Helmer: Development Properties, and Applications of Sandvik 3RE60 Tubes for Refinery Service. *NACE Preprint no. 13*, March 1973.
8. McCoy, J. D.: Corrosion Rates of H_2S at Elevated Temperatures in Refinery Hydrodesulfurization Processes, *Mater. Perform.*, vol. 13, pp. 19–25, May 1974.
9. Samans, C. H.: Stress Corrosion Susceptibility of Stainless Steels and Nickel Base Alloys in Polythionic Acids and Acid Copper Sulfate Solution, *Corrosion*, vol. 20, no. 8, pp. 256t–262t, August 1964.
10. Piehl, R. L.: Stress Corrosion Cracking by Sulfur Acids, *Proc. Am. Pet. Inst. Sec. 3*, vol. 44, pp. 189–197, 1964.
11. Heller, J. J., and G. R. Prescott: Cracking of Stainless Steels in Wet Sulfidic Environments in Refinery Units, *Mater. Prot.*, vol. 4, no. 9, pp. 14–18, September 1965.
12. Flowers, J. W., F. H. Beck, and M. G. Fontana: Corrosion and Age Hardening Studies of Some Cast Stainless Alloys Containing Ferrite, *Corrosion*, vol. 19, no. 5, pp. 186t–198t, May 1963.
13. Kadlecek, P.E.: A Wrought Corrosion Resistant Two-Phase Stainless Steel, *Mater. Prot.*, vol. 10, no. 6, pp. 25–30, June 1971.

14. Scheil, M. A.: Embrittlement of 12 Cr Steels After Exposure to 750° and 900° F, *Am. Soc. Mech. Eng. Pap. no. 51-A-07*, November 1951.
15. Ludwigson, D. C., and H. S. Link: Further Studies on the Formation of Sigma in 12 to 16 Percent Chromium Steels, ASTM *Spec. Tech. Publ. no. 369*, pp. 299–311, 1965.
16. Moller, G. E.: Experiences with 885°F Embrittlement in Ferritic Stainless Steels, *Mater. Prot.*, vol. 5, no. 5, pp. 62–67, May 1966.
17. Malone, M. O.: Sigma and 885°F Embrittlement of Chromium-Nickel Stainless Steel Weld Metals, *Weld. J., Res. Suppl.*, vol. 32, no. 6, pp. 241s–253s, June 1967.
18. Lang, F. S., and J. F. Mason: Corrosion in Amine Gas Treating Solutions, *Corrosion*, vol. 14, no. 2, pp. 105–108, February 1958.
19. Montrone, E. D., and W. P. Long: Choosing Materials for CO_2 Absorption Systems, *Chem. Eng.*, vol. 78, pp. 94–99, Jan. 25, 1971.
20. Ciuffreda, A. R., and B. N. Greene: Survey of Materials and Corrosion Experience in Reformer Hydrogen Plants, *Proc. Am. Pet. Inst.*, Div. of Refining, vol. 52, pp. 549–584, 1972.
21. Nisbet, D. F.: Case History: Failures in a Steam-Methane Reformer Furnace, *Hydrocarbon Process.*, vol. 50, no. 5, pp. 103–105, May 1971.
22. Cantwell, J. E., and R. E. Bryant: How to Avoid Alloy Failures in Flare Tips by Severe Cracking, *Hydrocarbon Process.*, vol. 52, no. 5, pp. 114–117, May 1973.

Chapter 45

Stainless Steels in Nuclear Applications

NATHAN HOFFMAN
and
GORDON KING
Members of the Technical Staff, Liquid Metal Engineering Center,
Atomics International Division, Rockwell International, Canoga Park,
California

Introduction 45-1
Types of Nuclear Reactors of Interest, 1975 to 2000 45-2
    Classification of Nuclear Reactors by Purpose 45-2
    Classification of Electrical Power Reactors by Importance 45-3
    Characteristics of Various Power Reactors 45-3
Use of Stainless Steel in a Nuclear Reactor 45-5
Problems Encountered by a Metallurgist in Using Stainless Steel in the LMFBR 45-6
    Problems Associated with Codes and Standards 45-6
    Problems Associated with Nuclear Radiation 45-8
    Problems Associated with Liquid Sodium 45-10
    Problems Associated with Long Times at High Temperature 45-12
    Problems Associated with World Chromium Availability 45-12
References 45-12

INTRODUCTION

This chapter is divided into three separate parts. The first will be a description of the types of nuclear reactors of interest in the three closing decades of the twentieth century. This topic will emphasize description of hardware. No nuclear applications other than nuclear reactors will be discussed. The second part will concentrate on the use of stainless steel in one such reactor. The third part will cover some of the problems that a metallurgist will encounter in the stainless steel hardware under discussion, with possible solutions.

TYPES OF NUCLEAR REACTORS OF INTEREST, 1975 TO 2000

There are many methods of classifying nuclear reactors. The most obvious ways, perhaps, are by their purpose and their relative importance. Since we are going to be interested in hardware, we will find it most advantageous to classify this hardware by its nuclear, physical, and chemical characteristics. Let us begin, then, by presenting a series of classification tables for nuclear reactors.

Classification of Nuclear Reactors by Purpose At any point in time from 1970 to 2000, there will be reactors of various kinds whose purpose is actually to produce electrical power on a commercial basis. In the United States as of 1974, there are the pressurized water reactors (PWR) and the boiling water reactors (BWR). In the classification of Table 1, these are the "operating plants." At that same point in time, there will be reactors that are being built whose purpose is to demonstrate the commercial feasibility

TABLE 1   Classification of Nuclear Reactors by Purpose

Electrical power:
   Operating plants
   Demonstration plants
Test facilities for evaluating nuclear reactors or material behavior:
   Experimental breeder reactors
   Fast flux test facility
Fissile material production
Research unrelated to generation of power:
   Medical
   Genetic
Advanced reactor concepts—fusion
Propulsion:
   Submarine
   Surface ship
   Airplane
   Nuclear rocket
   Ion engine power supply

of a reactor concept. In the United States circa 1974, this classification would include the liquid metal fast breeder reactor (LMFBR), being built at Clinch River in Tennessee, and the gas-cooled reactor, "Fort St. Vrain" under construction in Colorado. We will classify these as "demonstration plants."

Reactors built to allow engineers and scientists to study nuclear reactor phenomena and the behavior of materials in a radiation field include experimental breeder reactor I (EBR I) and EBR-II in Idaho, and the fast flux test facility (FFTF) in the state of Washington.

Nonbreeder reactors have also been designed and built for the purpose of maximizing the yield of fissile material, e.g., plutonium from uranium 238, rather than electrical power. In the United States, reactors of this type are found at the Hanford Engineering Development Laboratory in Washington.

Reactors whose main purpose is research unrelated to generation of power are found throughout the world, numbering more than 100. The specific applications for these reactors range from neutron diffraction experiments through cancer research to plant mutation studies.

Advance reactor concepts center around nuclear fusion research. As of 1974, laser implosion methods are being explored as the best tool of the fusion process in Ann Arbor, Michigan, Princeton, New Jersey, and Berkeley, California, and at other locations. Although the physics of nuclear fusion appears promising at this time, the associated material problems appear to be too difficult to solve within the next few decades. Of course, such assessments have been made before with respect to technical problems only to have an unexpected solution eliminate the problem.

Nuclear reactors for propulsion purposes have a checkered history. Submarine propulsion by nuclear reactor is one of the glorious stories of modern technology. Propulsion of surface craft by nuclear reactor has proven to be technically feasible but, to date, economically questionable. Aircraft propulsion by nuclear reactor appears to be an abandoned concept although considerable technology was developed in that program. The nuclear reactor concept for heating hydrogen to propel rocket ships through space was perhaps nuclear technology's most brilliant moment . . . while it lasted. The program went through many names, Diablo, Kiwi, Rover, resulting in a complex in western Nevada, where top engineers in rocket engine technology and nuclear science successfully tested a fully developed nuclear rocket engine. Then the project was discontinued, almost all the engineers disbursed, and the complex reverted to inactive status. Nuclear reactors for supplying the electrical power for ion-engine, rocket propulsion went under the name of SNAP-50. This was one of a series of Space Nuclear Auxiliary Power systems. These SNAP programs flourished in the 1960s, but lapsed in the early 1970s. Since the ion engine will eventually be needed by any reasonable extrapolation of our reduced space program into the 1980s and 1990s, a nuclear reactor reminiscent of the SNAP programs may again become a viable engineering project.

Classification of Electrical Power Reactors by Importance   Since our main concern here is with reactors for electrical power, we will now reclassify that topic by means of other tables. Table 2 classifies the electrical power-producing reactor by a chronological estimate of relative importance.

TABLE 2   Classification of Electrical Power Reactors by Importance, 1970 to 2000, in the United States

Operating in 1970 to 1980 period:
   Pressurized water reactor (PWR)
   Boiling water reactor (BWR)
Operating in 1980 to 1990 period:
   Thermal reactors of types prior to 1980
   Liquid metal fast breeder reactors (LMFBR)
   Gas-cooled fast breeder reactors
Operating in 1990 to 2000 period:
   Fast breeder reactors
   Fusion-based reactors (a finite possibility)

Table 2 lists a reasonable estimate of the "relative importance" of various reactors from the electrical power production point of view. Two dark horse reactor candidates for the American scene, Admiral Rickover's light-water, "near" breeder reactor, or the heavy-water moderated reactor could become commercially important before the fast breeder reactor can become the major producer of electricity. Breakthrough on types of reactors now considered commercially uninteresting, such as the three-stage potassium, cesium, water concept or the potassium, organic, water concept could change the estimates listed in Table 2.

Two rather unpredictable considerations affect the accuracy of any estimates of future reactor system usage: environmental activists' effects and mineral availability. Fast breeder reactors have been a favorite target for the environmental activist and they may well succeed in slowing down the introduction of this type of reactor as a major source of electricity. Mineral availability is perhaps even more of a factor in rendering estimates of reactor development activity into dubious quantities than are the questions associated with the environmental activists. Here, the major factor is the amount of uranium ore available to the United States in the decades under consideration. Truly huge quantities of uranium ore would have to be available if the breeder reactor's role as the major reactor system were to be postponed beyond 1990. The mineral availability problem becomes important in unexpected ways. For example, while it is obvious that systems involving cesium depend for their success on the continuous availability of cesium in large tonnages, it comes as a surprise that, by the turn of the century, chromium availability may eliminate nuclear reactors that require stainless steel from consideration as the main source of electricity.

Summarizing Table 2, then, we must note that these estimates may turn out to be far off the mark for reasons other than an unexpected persistency of coal-and-oil-fueled power plants or the sudden advent of some nonnuclear-power-producing technology. Within the nuclear reactor technology itself, enough unknowns exist to preclude firm estimates as to which reactors will dominate in any particular year.

Characteristics of Various Power Reactors   In order to understand the hardware within the types of reactors listed in Table 2, we have to supply more information about the

TABLE 3   Nuclear Characteristics of Various Power Reactors

Energy levels*	Energy of neutrons producing most fission, eV	Possible commercial breeder
Thermal reactor	≤0.5	No
Epithermal reactors	0.5 to 100	No
Fast reactor	>100,000	Yes

Moderators:
  Water (H_2O)
  Heavy water (D_2O)
  Liquid organics (e.g., terphenyl)
  Solids that contain light elements [C (e.g., graphite), BeO, ZrH, etc.]
Fuels:
  Natural uranium (0.7% ^{235}U)
  Slightly enriched uranium (to 5% ^{235}U)
  Highly enriched uranium (to 93% ^{235}U)
  Plutonium-239
  Uranium-233

*From birth in the fission process, the neutrons come off with their highest energy. These fast neutrons have energy levels of several million electron volts. After bouncing off light element nuclei, they are slowed down to more moderate energy levels. In fast reactors, capture of neutrons and consequent fission of nuclei occur when the neutrons are in the >100,000 eV range, so care must be taken not to moderate the neutrons. In epithermal reactors, the energy levels of neutrons being captured are in the 1 to 100 eV range. In thermal reactors, the bulk of the neutrons have moderated down to <1 eV by collisions with light-element nuclei.

reactors themselves. We will do this by classifying reactors according to their nuclear, physical, and thermochemical characteristics in Tables 3, 4, and 5, respectively.

Before we discuss these last three tables, we want to stress again that the main reason for selecting a particular type of reactor for development is the relative availability of natural uranium versus the availability of enriched fuels. If natural uranium is plentiful, a nonbreeder reactor concept is favored. At the opposite end of the spectrum, if natural uranium is in extremely short supply, the fast breeder reactor concept is favored.

Information listed in Table 3 defines for us the term "fast reactor." If most of the neutrons producing fission have energy levels greater than 100 eV, the reactor can change the ^{238}U fraction of natural uranium (99.3% ^{238}U, 0.7% ^{235}U) to a fissionable material while still producing enough heat to generate commercial amounts of electric power. Thus, the fast reactor can be a fast breeder reactor.

Under the subheading "Moderators," we list materials that slow neutrons down so that they can interact more efficiently with fissionable atomic nuclei. Moderators require atoms with atomic weights no more than 12 times the weight of a neutron (H, He, Li, Be, B, or C).

The subheading "Fuels" in Table 3 starts with the term natural uranium, followed by grades of enriched uranium. The term enriched has nothing to do with the grade of uranium ore mined. Whether the uranium is still in the ore in the ground, in concentrate form after mineral beneficiation, or after extraction, the uranium still has its original

TABLE 4   Physical Characteristics of Various Power Reactors

Fuel arrangement
  Heterogeneous
    Metallic fuels
    Dispersion fuels (cermets, e.g., UO_2+ stainless steel)
    Ceramic fuels (uranium carbide, uranium oxide, etc.)
  Homogeneous
    Liquid metal fuels (U + Th in B:)
    Molten salt fuels (UF_4 in LiF-ZrF)
    Aqueous fuels ($UO_2 SO_4$)
Reactor size
  Thermal energy output
  Electrical energy output

TABLE 5   Thermochemical Characteristics of Various Power Reactors

Type of Coolant in Power Reactors of the Future
Liquid sodium
Loop geometry
Pool geometry
Water (H_2O)
Boiling water reactors
Pressurized water reactors
Helium
Light-water near-breeder
Heavy-water (D_2O)
Liquid metals other than pure sodium
Nonoxidizing gases other than helium (A, H_2, N_2)
Carbon dioxide
Air
Liquid organic (terphenyl)
Different Thermodynamic Characteristics
High-temperature reactors
Superheat cycle
Supercritical pressure cycle
Saturated steam cycle
Nominal temperature reactors
Low superheat cycle
Saturated steam cycle
Low-temperature reactors
Low pressure, saturated steam cycle
Process heat, spare heat

isotopic ratio of 99.3% of unfissionable ^{238}U and 0.7% of fissionable ^{235}U. Enrichment here means a method of increasing the fissionable fraction, either by gaseous diffusion of uranium halides through miles of porous barrier, by centrifuge techniques, by electromagnetic techniques, or by breeding with a reactor. Enrichment by the latter method often involves transmutation of uranium to plutonium.

With respect to Table 4, the heterogeneous fuel arrangement is far more important than homogeneous arrangements. The reactor size in terms of power can be defined in terms of the watts of the thermal energy produced or in terms of the smaller number of watts of electrical energy actually generated from that thermal energy.

In Table 5, we have listed first the characteristic that is usually the most important concern of the metallurgist, the type of coolant. The metallurgical problems associated with a sodium-cooled reactor are far different from those of a light-water near-breeder reactor, for example. The list of coolants is in descending order of estimated importance of *future* reactor coolant concepts, as of January 1975. However, the proposed order is certainly open to debate. The items listed under the subheading "Different Thermodynamic Characteristics" are often found in nuclear power plant literature. These terms, however, are not exclusive to nuclear power reactors but also apply to steam-generating plants for producing electrical power in general.

USE OF STAINLESS STEEL IN A NUCLEAR REACTOR

As we have seen in the previous section, there are many types of nuclear reactors. In this section, we will select one type, the sodium-cooled, fast breeder reactor in a loop configuration, and discuss component by component, where stainless steel is used. We will first list the major subsystems of this type of liquid metal fast breeder reactor (LMFBR) in Table 6.

TABLE 6   Major Subsystems of the Loop Configuration LMFBR

Reactor core including in-vessel handling mechanisms
Primary sodium loop
Intermediate heat exchanger
Secondary sodium loop
Steam generator
Inert gas systems

Within the reactor core is, of course, the fuel. The fuel is usually small pellets of uranium oxide or uranium carbide packed into very long, small-diameter tubes. These packed tubes, called fuel rods, are taller than a man but thinner than a man's little finger. These tubes have been made of 20% cold-worked Type 316 stainless steel. Around each tube is wrapped a wire for spacing the tubes a given distance apart. This wire wrap also has been made of stainless steel. A large number of these wire-wrapped, fuel-packed tubes are placed within a hexagonal duct, tube axes parallel to duct axis. These ducts have been made of 300-series stainless steel. A large number of ducts are packed together to form the reactor core. Sodium coolant circulates between individual fuel rods, between fuel rod and hexagonal duct wall, and between adjacent hexagonal ducts. The in-vessel handling mechanism (IVHM) is used for refueling, where an individual hexagonal duct filled with spent fuel rods is lifted out of the core and replaced by a new hexagonal duct filled with new fuel rods. Many parts of the IVHM are made from 300-series stainless steels. The assembly of hexagonal ducts in the core is surrounded by the reactor primary vessel with its cover, guard vessel, and supports. Other components considered part of the core include the reactivity control members.

The primary sodium loop includes piping, valves, fittings, support, heaters, expansion and drain tankage, surveillance systems, pumps, cold traps, plugging meters, bellows, and sodium-purity-measuring hardware. The intermediate heat exchanger is the link between the primary coolant loop and the secondary coolant loop. The somewhat radioactively contaminated coolant in the primary loop gives up some of its heat to the nonradioactive sodium circulating in the secondary loop through a tube-in-shell type of heat exchanger. This sodium-to-sodium heat exchanger is made from 300-series stainless steel. The secondary sodium loop moves hot sodium from the intermediate heat exchanger to the steam generator. The 2.25Cr-1Mo steel is used to eliminate the potential for chloride stress-corrosion cracking in the structure exposed to hot pressurized water. As will be discussed later, the 2.5Cr-1Mo steel, though immune to chloride stress-corrosion cracking, is sensitive to caustic stress-corrosion cracking. Since the bulk of the secondary sodium loop is made from austenitic stainless steel, transition joints between the 2.25Cr-1Mo steam-generator shell and the stainless steel inlet piping must be made.

The inert gas systems include tubing and piping, gas analysis units, on-off valves, relief vent valves, other pressure regulation valves, and vapor traps. This latter hardware is to eliminate sodium vapor from escaping, and is often made of stainless steel.

PROBLEMS ENCOUNTERED BY A METALLURGIST IN USING STAINLESS STEEL IN THE LMFBR

We will now discuss the actual problems that a metallurgist would encounter when using stainless steel in a specific type of nuclear reactor, in this case, the liquid-metal fast breeder reactor. Of course, this section cannot cover all the problems, but certain problems of a recurring nature will be discussed. Some of these are unique to nuclear reactor technology while others are found in many other metallurgical applications. These problems are outlined in Table 7.

Problems Associated with Codes and Standards   One of the major problems facing a metallurgist in the nuclear industry is "knowing the requirements" associated with the codes and standards imposed by the regulatory bodies. The basic requirements for design, materials, fabrication, and examination of a nuclear power plant are provided in the ASME Boiler and Pressure Vessel Code (B&PV code). There are 11 sections in the ASME B&PV code. However, only two are specific to nuclear systems: Section III, "Nuclear Power Plant Components" and Section XI, "In-Service Inspection of Nuclear Reactor Coolant Systems." Three other sections of the code (Section II, Materials; Section V, Examination; and Section IX, Welder Qualification) are general to the overall code as well as being applicable to nuclear systems. The remaining six sections of the code cover the requirements for design, materials, fabrication, and examination of power boilers and pressure vessels for nonnuclear applications.

A nuclear power plant, by its very nature, must be extremely reliable. Recognizing this fact, the formulators of the ASME B&PV code have developed a special section of the code (Section III) in which rules are provided for designing and building metal components which will provide a pressure containment function in a nuclear power system:

Containment systems for which rules are specified by this section of the Code are those components which form structures that may enclose nuclear power systems or that may be connected to other containment components and which are designed to provide a pressure containing barrier for the primary purpose of containing within leakage limits or for the channeling for containment or for controlled disposal, radioactive or hazardous effluents released from nuclear power systems so enclosed.

Section III of the code has been further divided into six subsections in order to assess the importance and criticality of various metal components and structures in the nuclear facility. For example, a metal component can be considered as a class 1, 2, or 3, depending on the application and the level of importance associated with its safe operation. Although Section III does provide rules for the various component classifications, it does not provide guidance in the selection of the class for a specific system. Such guidance is

TABLE 7   Problems Encountered by a Metallurgist in Using Stainless Steel in the LMFBR

Problems associated with codes and standards:
    Nuclear pressure vessel code
    Nuclear standards
Problems associated with nuclear radiation:
    Fuel-rod swelling
    Changes in stainless steel properties
    Adherence of coatings
    Induced radioactivity
    Remote metallography
    Core and out-of-core component maintenance storage tank corrosion
Problems associated with liquid sodium:
    Mass transfer in sodium loops
    Decarburization and carburization
    Friction properties
    Cleaning and design of components
        Caustic stress-corrosion cracking
        Molten caustic grain-boundary attack
Problems associated with long times at high temperature
Problems associated with world chromium availability

derived from systems safety criteria applicable to specific types of nuclear power systems (e.g., pressurized water reactors, boiling water reactors, etc.) as specified in engineering standards or as may be required by regulatory authorities having jurisdiction at the nuclear power plant site:

The owner of a nuclear power plant, directly or through his agent, shall be responsible for determining the appropriate Code Class(es) for each component of the nuclear power plant and shall specify these code classes in the Design Specifications as required.

The metallurgist in the nuclear industry would not normally be faced with the responsibility of establishing the code classification; however, he could be involved in enforcing the requirements as specified in each class.

The broad fields of activity for a metallurgist in the nuclear field would consist of research and development, component testing, new plant construction, or plant operation. Research and development for the metallurgist could consist of such areas as effects of radiation on material properties, wear testing, corrosion studies, etc., and therefore probably would not require a thorough knowledge of the ASME B&PV code. The other three areas (component testing, new construction, and plant operation) would probably involve the code, particularly in the area of new construction, and therefore it is essential that the metallurgist working in these areas understand the code requirements, particularly as they pertain to materials, fabrication, and examination.

Knowing the requirements is no easy chore for a variety of reasons. First, and probably foremost, is the fact that the code is in a constant flux. The base document is reissued every 3 years (1974 is the latest issue), and every 6 months an addendum is released. Two or three years later, it is necessary to review the basic code as well as four or five addenda in order to determine the requirement. This constant change occurs in each of the 11 different sections of the code.

Second, Section III has six different subsections; one general and five specific to particular classes or types of metal components. Each of these five component classifications has its own material, design fabrication and examination requirements. This makes it extremely difficult to commit the individual classification requirements to memory.

In addition to the material subsection of each component classification, where requirements pertinent to materials for that particular Section III classification are given, there is a material section (II) in the ASME B&PV code which contains the various material specifications that are acceptable for code use. There are three parts to Section II, ferrous, nonferrous, and weld rod. The ferrous and nonferrous sections are comprised of material specifications which are similar to ASTM material specifications but consist of only those which are considered appropriate for ASME B&PV code usage. There are approximately 140 material specifications in part A (ferrous) and approximately 70 in part B (nonferrous). The weld rod specifications (part C of Section II) are similar to the American Welding Society (AWS) Specifications. There are approximately 20 of these documents covering both ferrous and nonferrous welding materials which have been adopted by the ASME B&PV code.

In summary, the ASME B&PV code recognizes approximately 320 material standards. These are materials that, when used in accordance with the design rules of the ASME code, are considered acceptable for code applications. Materials which are not included in this group of 230 specifications cannot be used in metal components and structures fabricated to ASME code.

A new generation of nuclear power plants, the LMFBR, is in the development stages. This new generation of reactors brings with it a new series of standards. This new standard program, reactor development technology (RDT), is designed to use the ASME code as the base document, adding requirements as deemed necessary. Thus, the requirements for this latest nuclear program are provided in RDT standards which, whenever possible, modify ASME B&PV code base requirements. Therefore, when "determining the requirements" in the RDT program, a metallurgist must not only review the requirements of the ASME code and applicable addenda but also the RDT standards and the amendments. (The RDT standard program is in a constant state of change, similar to the ASME code, with the periodic issuance of amendments.)

Needless to say, knowing the requirements in this system of codes and standards can be very demanding. The complexities of the system are demonstrated, for example, in reviewing the weld filler-wire requirements just prior to the issuance of the 1974 ASME code. In order to summarize these requirements, 18 different sections of four different documents had to be reviewed.

Another typical example of the difficulty of knowing the requirements would be the procurement of a welded stainless steel pipe fitting (manufactured by forming out of plate and welding). A supplier furnishing such a fitting would have to invoke 14 first-tier referenced documents and at least 15 second-tier documents. Each of these documents, in most cases, has anywhere from one to five amendments or addenda. Indeed, one of the major problems facing the metallurgist in the nuclear industry is determining exactly what requirements are applicable and then storing this information in some easily retrievable manner.

Problems Associated with Nuclear Radiation   Radiation damage of 300-series stainless steel is so severe in fast reactor core applications that a strong effort is being made to eliminate the use of austenitic stainless steel as the duct and cladding material. This damage is of three types: radiation hardening, swelling, and He embrittlement. Radiation hardening is due to dislocation formation formed by displacements of atoms from their lattice sites during neutron bombardment and the subsequent rearrangement of these atoms. Under certain conditions, the atomic rearrangement will result in the formation of cavities, usually called voids. This results in an increase in the volume of the stainless, and the phenomenon is called swelling. When reactions between fast neutrons and iron, nickel, and chromium atoms cause transmutation reactions to occur that produce helium nuclei, the helium tends to accumulate as bubbles in the grain boundaries, leading to premature intergranular failure during service. Some consideration is being given to slowing down the accumulation of helium in the grain boundary by designing an alloy that retains the helium as small bubbles within the matrix. One approach to such alloy design is to provide many nucleation sites for the helium bubbles within the grains. In thermal reactors, helium generation is due to transmutations of tramp boron atoms within the stainless steel. In fast reactors, the major alloy constituents of stainless produce the helium.

Properties of stainless steel can change in a high enough neutron flux field. Ductility of annealed stainless steel can be reduced while the ductility of cold-worked stainless steel can be improved (Table 8). Stainless steel parts in the core in addition to fuel rods may be affected. Radiation can cause an increase in the rates of reactions that are normally so slow

TABLE 8   Effect of 3.5×10^{22} n/cm^3 (E > 0.1 MeV) Fluence on Stainless Steel

Alloy	Treatment	Condition	Test temperature, C	Yield strength, MPa	Tensile strength, MPa	Elongation, % Uniform	Total
316	A	Control	500	146	479	36.4	37.0
316	A	Irradiated	500	482	545	6.5	6.0
316	A	Control	600	136	423	34.6	36.9
316	A	Irradiated	600	251	376	13.7	14.9
316	B	Control	500	616	694	3.0	3.5
316	B	Irradiated	500	557	625	3.9	4.1
316	B	Control	600	525	596	4.5	6.7
316	B	Irradiated	600	391	463	4.0	4.3
316	C	Control	500	825	863	2.9	3.1
316	C	Irradiated	500	595	667	3.2	3.6
316	C	Control	600	698	756	2.6	2.9
316	C	Irradiated	600	438	519	4.5	5.0
321	D	Control	500	220	442	15.0	16.3
321	D	Irradiated	500	604	653	3.7	4.2
12R72	E	Control	500	112	390	25.5	26.5
12R72	E	Irradiated	500	565	603	4.1	4.8

PRE-IRRADIATION TREATMENTS

Designation	Treatment	Condition
A	980°C/1 h + 760°C/8 h	Solution-annealed and aged
B	980°C/1 h + 760°C/8 h + 22% cold-rolled	Solution-annealed, aged, and cold-rolled
C	1120°C/30 min + 25% cold-rolled	Solution-annealed and cold-rolled
D	Mill-annealed	Mill-annealed
E	1100°C/1 h + 825°C/8 h	Solution-annealed and aged

Strain rate = 0.02 min^{-1}; 15-min hold at test temperature prior to testing.

as to allow metastable states to exist as apparent equilibrium states. At temperatures not too far from room temperature, for example, the equilibrium state of many 300-series stainless steels is not the face-centered-cubic (fcc) structure that is usually predominant. The equilibrium state is usually metal carbides precipitated out in a body-centered cubic (bcc) solid solution. Transition states between the fcc and bcc include various supersaturated solid solutions, and these may be formed. Even dissolution rates of phases in the molten sodium environment may be increased. The adherence of coatings on stainless steel can be severely affected by a radiation field. Thus, not only new coatings need to be checked out in the appropriate radiation field, but even changes in coating application technique must be thoroughly checked out in a radiation field. Since uncoated stainless steel usually has unacceptable galling and seizing characteristics, the usual coatings on stainless are low-friction hardfacing, applied either by diffusion coating methods, welding techniques, detonation gun spray, plasma arc techniques, spray and fuse methods, or electroplating. The latter three methods, in particular, are suspect in a strong radiation field.

Induced radioactivity is one of the most obvious problems that concerns a metallurgist associated with nuclear energy. Failure analysis methods for core components must include remote metallography capability, but this is only a small part of the metallurgist's concern. Material selection of both in-core and primary loop out-of-core components must take into consideration component maintenance which now becomes a major effort. Highly radioactive wear-debris or mass-transferred precipitate can deposit on surfaces well away from the core in the primary loop, making certain surfaces of a component radioactive. Failure of a screw or other minor part of the component is not the quickly fixed situation that it would be in a nonradioactive application. Cracks in stainless steel piping in particular become a far more difficult problem in a radioactive environment.

A most important metallurgical problem associated with nuclear reactors is the long-term storage of radioactive wastes. Corrosion of storage vessels by aqueous solutions of radioactive salts can be minimized by storing only dried wastes, but corrosion by soil moisture can still occur. Double wall tankage (double containment) appears to be a desirable approach. Even using dried radioactive waste, liquids may still have to be pumped around and corrosion of the transfer system is a metallurgical concern. Methods of ascertaining whether corrosion has initiated may be required along with the instrumentation that assures no leakage is occurring.

Problems Associated with Liquid Sodium   One of the major concerns of the metallurgist dealing with a sodium-cooled reactor is mass transfer of chemical elements from one part of the sodium loop to another. The driving force of this mass transfer can be the difference in activity of an element in one alloy as compared with its activity in another alloy under isothermal conditions. More commonly, the activity gradient that causes the mass transfer is due to a temperature gradient along Type 304 stainless steel piping in the loop. An example of a chemical element transferring from one alloy to another is decarburization of 300-series stainless steel and carburization of a cooler 300-series stainless steel component. At sodium velocities of main interest in an LMFBR, the rate at which mass transfer of an element occurs is a function of the diffusion constant in liquid sodium, the degree of saturation of the sodium, the ratio of sodium volume to stainless steel area, and the stagnant, subboundary-layer thickness. Both dissolution and redeposition are a function of these parameters except that redeposition depends on the degree of supersaturation rather than the degree of saturation. The time t to reach a concentration of solute c in liquid sodium solvent can be expressed as

$$t = \frac{-\Delta}{D} \frac{V_{melt}}{A_{stainless}} \ln\left(1 - \frac{c}{c_{sat}}\right)$$

where Δ = stagnant subboundary layer, cm
  D = diffusion coefficient of solute in liquid sodium at loop temperature, cm^2/s
  V_{melt} = sodium volume, cm^3
  $A_{stainless}$ = area of sodium–stainless steel interface
  c = concentration of solute in sodium after time t in any units
  c_{sat} = concentration of solute in sodium at saturation at temperature of dissolving metal measured in same units as c

This equation assumes that diffusion through a stagnant subboundary layer is the slowest process and, hence, the rate-determining process. Certain effects become apparent upon studying this equation. Dissolution rates slow down as sodium builds up in solute concentration as it flows along a pipe. Since the stagnant subboundary layer varies in thickness roughly as the laminar boundary layer does, dissolution rate is quite sensitive to the flow patterns of the sodium. Since precipitation acts in a similar manner, the metallurgist must be alert to the chemical hydrodynamics of the sodium–stainless steel system. Usually precipitation is of much more practical concern than dissolution. Areas of very thin boundary layer (such as in valves where the flow of sodium is changed suddenly in direction or rapidly accelerated) can cause such an increase in precipitation kinetics that growths occur on those valve surfaces. Such growths can also be observed where the system is coldest, i.e., where the degree of supersaturation is the highest. The metallurgist must be sure that component design is such that these growths will occur in areas that do not interfere with component operation.

Decarburization is a special case of mass transfer. Here, the metallurgist concerned with austenitic stainless steel is concerned with the migration of carbon out of the stainless into the sodium. Individual carbon atoms dissolved in austenite will leave the stainless, diffuse through the stagnant subboundary layer, and eventually convectively mix into the flowing sodium. Interestingly, carbides seem to be metastable for kinetic reasons in flowing sodium, though, as the carbon level of the stainless steel matrix drops, the carbide begins to dissolve into the solid solution. Austenite matrix then serves as a conduit for putting carbide carbon into sodium solution. If the carbon level in the sodium builds up towards saturation, the kinetics of decarburization become very slow. If the system provides a sink for removing carbon (such as a zirconium hot trap or a cooler 300-series stainless steel component), then the stainless can begin to decarburize at a significant rate when system temperatures exceed 500°C. Carburization can occasionally also be deleterious to 300-series stainless steel. Ferrite parts can cause carburization of austenite in sodium systems.

The friction and self-welding properties of 300-series stainless steel in sodium are such that the metallurgist should never let a designer make rubbing surfaces out of stainless steel unless galling, seizing, and self-welding somehow do not interfere with the performance of a part. Coating one side of a rubbing couple with a hardfacing while allowing the other surface to remain stainless is not the answer, since the hardfaced surface soon becomes coated with stainless, bringing all the resultant problems. Stainless bolts threaded finger-tight will have to be drilled out. Parts undergoing slight rubbing due to thermal expansion and contraction will weld together to form joints that may be strong enough to cause failure through some other section of the structure. Such seizing problems are a function of sodium-purity level, with increased purity giving the worst seizing. Actual reactor sodium, however, is usually purer than that available in many test vessels, so any uncoated stainless steel surface in potential rubbing contact in sodium should be hunted down and eliminated by the metallurgist.

The cleaning of stainless steel components exposed to sodium must always be of paramount consideration to the LMFBR metallurgist. This consideration must begin in the design stage. Obviously, drainability of sodium must be considered but other, less obvious, considerations are vital to cleaning, such as designing for disassembly and cleaning facility handling. The metallurgist must be familiar with sodium cleaning procedures in order to evaluate a component design, and then should participate in preparation of specific cleaning procedures for the component being designed, including the extent of disassembly and handling points for required hoists.

There are two main reasons for concern about cleaning: caustic stress-corrosion cracking and molten caustic grain-boundary attack. Caustic stress-corrosion cracking in stainless steels is a sudden failure in a brittle mode, often transgranular in habit, associated with the simultaneous presence of three environmental effects: (1) aqueous caustic solution, (2) temperatures between 150 and 400°C, and (3) the presence of residual or applied stress. Since caustic raises the boiling point of water to a point near 400°C at atmospheric pressure, maintaining temperatures above 100°C is not effective as in the case of chloride stress-corrosion cracking. Apparently, areas near unannealed welds always have sufficient residual stress to allow this brittle type of failure to occur. If steam or water is used to clean welded parts of stainless steel that have been exposed to sodium, the parameter that must be controlled is temperature. There have been indications that sensitized stainless steel may undergo intergranular stress-corrosion cracking in aqueous caustic solution at lower temperatures than that associated with transgranular stress-corrosion cracking. Alcohol cleaning has been proposed as a way of avoiding the careful control required for successful cleaning of sodium-exposed stainless steel parts by steam or water mist. In the case of cleaning loops or entire systems, the required process control for steam or mist cleaning is probably excessive and either loop disassembly or an alcohol process should be considered.

The problem of molten caustic grain-boundary attack is associated with failure to clean the sodium off sufficiently before exposure to some oxygen or moisture source and subsequent reheating, generally in inert gas or vacuum, to temperatures above 500°C. If a cap of sodium carbonate has not formed on any retained caustic, exposure to molten sodium will dissolve the caustic away before the grain boundaries are attacked. Thus, only caustic somehow isolated from the sodium pool can cause the molten caustic grain-boundary attack.

Liquid sodium is such an excellent heat conductor and quenching medium that thermal transients are of concern. The plunging of hot metal into relatively cool liquid sodium results in no vapor film that limits heat transfer. Metallurgists must consider, therefore, the effects of expected thermal transient conditions on adherence of coatings and thermal fatigue aspects. In general, the temperature range of the thermal fluctuations do not span an austenite-to-martensite range or a ferrite-to-austenite range. Thermal stresses induced can, however, affect the kinetics of carbide precipitation in the 300-series stainless steels.

Problems Associated with Long Times at High Temperature   A major source of worry for the metallurgist in the LMFBR program is the 20 years in the 500 to 600°C range that some structural alloys must survive under load. In alloys with low stacking-fault energies, precipitates come out along crystallographic directions within individual grains (slip-plane decoration) and cause an apparent brittle failure in a normally ductile alloy. Such slip-plane decoration can even channel fatigue cracks along these directions of nil ductility and result in jagged cracks with crystallographic orientation that bear little resemblance to the usual fatigue-crack morphology. The precipitating phase may even be one unknown. Although present theories on sensitization postulate that chromium depletion near the grain boundary should be alleviated after very long times at sensitization temperatures as chromium within the grains diffuses into the depleted region, 20-year data have not been accumulated under LMFBR conditions. Perhaps the grain-boundary carbides change stoichiometry and lattice parameter over the 20 years and new interface stresses are created. More predictable than the microstructure extrapolations are creep effects, though these effects strongly depend on interstitial atom content and grain size. Activation energies for creep of stainless steel need to be worked out experimentally as a function of chemical content and stress level. Creep of pure metals is just beginning to be understood and many of our concepts about that phenomenon are based on generalizations that are valid only under certain highly restrictive conditions. Considerable applied research effort is required in the area of 304H stainless steel creep behavior theory in addition to the also required massive cumulation of creep-rate data on this alloy.

Problems Associated with World Chromium Availability   A surprising problem for the metallurgist intent on using stainless steel in the LMFBR is associated with the world supply of chromium. Our power requirements for the year 2000 will require such vast amounts of structural alloy that there may not be enough chromium in the world to allow the power plant structural alloy to contain 18% chromium. Perhaps other families of stainless steel with far less chromium will be candidate alloys, or perhaps stainless steels will be employed only on a very limited basis and alloys such as the 2.25Cr-1Mo steels will begin to be the workhorse alloys for nuclear plants.

REFERENCES

1. Types of Nuclear Reactors, "Steel for Nuclear Nuclear Applications," United States Steel Corp., Pittsburgh, 1967.
2. "The Nuclear Industry: Issues in the 1970's," Atomic Industrial Forum, New York, 1972.
3. Coghill, D. F., "The Nuclear Industry 1971–1972 Index," Esco Corporation, Portland, Ore., 1972.
4. Garr, K. R., A. G. Pard, and D. Kramer: The Effect of Neutron Irradiation on Types 316, 321, and Sandvik 12R72 Stainless Steels, *AI-AEC-13130*, Atomics International, Canoga Park, Calif., 1974.

Chapter 46

Stainless Steels in High-Pressure Hydrogen

ANTHONY W. THOMPSON
Science Center, Rockwell International, Thousand Oaks, California

There are a variety of stainless steel applications which involve high-pressure hydrogen gas. ("High pressure" usually means greater than 15 MPa, or about 2200 psi.) Because of the risk of a catastrophic failure if brittle, delayed fracture occurs, it is important that material selection for such applications be made carefully. The same is true for environments other than gaseous ones, such as chloride-containing aqueous solutions, in which hydrogen may be available to the steel at high fugacity; those environments are discussed in Chaps. 16, 17, and 37. This chapter will be concerned with hydrogen and hydrogen-containing gases.

Before high-pressure hydrogen applications can be discussed, it is necessary to summarize the behavior of stainless steels in the gaseous environment. Much of the information on such behavior is in the form of government reports or is scattered through the literature, and consequently it will be drawn together here in usable form. Once the patterns in material behavior are presented, alloy selection for applications can be discussed in close relation to that behavior.

MATERIAL BEHAVIOR IN HYDROGEN

There are two aspects of material behavior with which to be concerned when selecting an alloy for high-pressure hydrogen service. One is the short-time or "instantaneous" behavior, where little or no entry of hydrogen into the metal occurs by diffusion. Such behavior

TABLE 1   Effect of High-Pressure Hydrogen on Martensitic and Precipitation-hardenable Steels

Alloy	Yield strength, MPa	Loss* in ultimate tensile strength, %		Loss* in reduction of area (RA), %		Ref.
		Unnotched	Notched	Unnotched	Notched	
Type 410	1325	21	78	80	73	1
Type 440C	1625	60	50	~100	~100	1
17-7PH	1035	8	77	94	60	1
AFC 77	~1400	~75				3

*Defined in Eq. (1); all tests at 69-MPa pressure.

is modeled by a tensile or fracture mechanics test in high-pressure gas. The second is the behavior of the material when hydrogen has been introduced into the lattice, as would occur by accumulation during prolonged exposure to hydrogen in service. This behavior can be simulated by tests on specimens which have been supersaturated by gas-phase or electrolytic charging. Different applications may dictate different emphases on these two behavior types when selecting a material, as will be discussed, but both will be important in most cases, particularly since the two behaviors are often different from each other. In general, then, a material can only be chosen with confidence when data from both types of tests are available. Many of the existing data, however, relate only to the first behavior type and thus should be used with care.

Hydrogen can cause several mechanical properties to be degraded, including tensile strength and ductility. The magnitude of the degradation ranges from materials like Type 410, a martensitic steel, which loses considerable ductility as well as 80% of its notched strength in hydrogen gas,[1] to austenitic materials, like Type 316, which show no detectable changes in either ductility or strength when tested in hydrogen.[1,2] Strength losses are especially dangerous because they can lead to failure at unexpectedly low operating stresses. Ductility losses are of less concern, although such losses can mean a reduction in fracture toughness, and lowered resistance to either sustained-load crack growth or fatigue in hydrogen.

As will be seen below, the available evidence indicates that martensitic and precipitation-hardenable (PH) steels perform poorly in high-pressure hydrogen, ferritic and unstable austenitic steels are intermediate, and stable austenitic steels perform well. Austenitic-ferritic or duplex steels have been little studied, but appear to lie in the intermediate to good range. Data for each of these structural categories are presented separately below.

Martensitic and Precipitation-hardenable Steels   As Chaps. 6 and 7 demonstrate, these steels have high strength, due in part to the martensitic structures which they share. Their behavior in hydrogen is poor, as is the behavior of microstructurally similar conventional high-strength steels. Table 1 summarizes data on a few stainless steels of this type. Where possible, high-pressure hydrogen data are compared to data from tests in helium at the same pressure, since the high-pressure medium can affect the ductility. Also of importance is a comparison of notched and unnotched performance, particularly at high strength levels. Losses in properties observed in high-pressure hydrogen (usually 69 MPa, or 10,000 psi) are defined in Eq. (1)

$$\text{Loss} = \frac{\text{property in He} - \text{property in H}_2}{\text{property in He}} \tag{1}$$

where He and H_2 refer, respectively, to high-pressure helium and hydrogen.

The steels in Table 1 all show very large ductility losses. They also show substantial losses in notched strength. None could be considered for use in high-pressure hydrogen unless a barrier or liner technique (discussed below) were used to prevent access of the gas to the steel. Although more information would be welcome, it is expected that other steels in these two categories would perform equally badly in hydrogen.

Ferritic Steels   The only data available on this type is for Type 430; it is the most widely used alloy of the type. Type 430 loses 32% of its notched strength in 69-MPa hydrogen;[1] it also loses 42% of its smooth-bar reduction of area (RA) and 69% of its notched reduction of area.[1] The strength loss is not quite as severe as for the steels in Table 1 but is large enough, in combination with the ductility losses, to make Type 430 unacceptable for hydrogen service. Emphasis is given to that conclusion by the observation of surface cracking and brittle-fracture topography in this alloy.[1] It has been

TABLE 2   Effect of High-Pressure Hydrogen on Austenitic Steels

Alloy (AISI)	Yield strength, MPa	Loss* in ultimate tensile strength, %		Loss* in reduction of area (RA), %		Ref.
		Unnotched	Notched	Unnotched	Notched	
304L	200	11	13	59	52	1,2
305	350†	3	11	4	11	1
309S	220	0	2	0	0	5
316	215	0	0	0	0	1,2
321	220	0	12	10	64	6
347	460†	0	9	0	9	7

*Defined in text; Type 321 and 347 data are for tests in 34.5-MPa gases, others for 69 MPa.
†Cold-worked (see text).

pointed out[4] that the ferritic and martensitic steels, in fact, behave similarly on an equal-strength basis. This conclusion adds weight to the recommendation not to use ferritic stainless steels in high-pressure hydrogen.

Austenitic Steels   Behavior of austenitic stainless steels in high-pressure hydrogen ranges from marked ductility loss to no apparent damage. A single categorization therefore cannot be made for these steels, and the statements which are sometimes seen that austenitic steels are "immune" to hydrogen effects are not accurate.

As mentioned above, there is a *general* correlation of hydrogen resistance with austenite stability. Comparison of quite different steels, e.g., Types 304L and 310, illustrates this (see below). For steels which are less different, however, the correlation works less well. It is fair to say that there are too many exceptions to the correlation for it to serve as a reliable rule.

Table 2 shows data for austenitic steels in the format of Table 1, with both notched and unnotched properties. It will be noted immediately that the hydrogen-induced property losses are far less severe, particularly the strength losses, than for the martensitic and precipitation-hardenable steels. Of the list, Types 309S and 316 are clearly the least-affected alloys. The data for Types 305 and 347 are for cold-worked material;[1,7] results for annealed material (see below) show greater damage. Results from one of the investigations[1] on Type 316 also refer to cold-worked material, but show no difference from annealed data[2] in either strength or ductility loss.

In general, the austenitic steels are of lower strength and higher toughness than the ferritic, martensitic, and precipitation-hardenable alloys, and consequently the degree of notch sensitivity is much less. Experimenters have recognized this by omitting notched bar tests in many cases. The available smooth-bar data are shown in Fig. 1 with results from Table 2 on smooth-bar reduction of area of annealed materials for comparison. Very generally, the materials at the left of the figure are less stable than those at the right, although there are some prominent exceptions. The proprietary steel 18Cr-15Mn (Tenelon, United States Steel Corp.) forms no martensite when deformed; neither do 21Cr-6Ni-9Mn (21-6-9, Armco Steel Corp.), 22Cr-13Ni-5Mn (22-13-5, Armco Steel Corp.), or 15Cr-25Ni (solution-treated A-286, Ref. 9). Yet these four steels differ considerably in their extent of hydrogen-induced RA loss.

It should be pointed out in connection with both Fig. 1 and Table 2 that the usual scatter in RA data is about 2 or 3%, and RA loss results of that magnitude should be considered as essentially equal to zero. Note also that although the RA loss shown for

Type 321 is not great, surface cracking was observed after testing,[6] a phenomenon usually associated with steels which perform poorly, such as Type 304L.[1,2,10]

An important point to be noted in Fig. 1 is the high RA loss in annealed Type 347, compared to the data on cold-worked Type 347 in Table 2. The composition of this alloy is similar to that of Type 304L, since its higher carbon is removed from solution by Nb + Ta stabilizing additions; data of Fig. 1 in fact show a similarity of Types 304L and 347 performance in hydrogen. But moderate cold-work improves hydrogen resistance of Type 347, just as it does for Type 304L in hydrogen-producing environments.[10] Presumably the same effect would be noted in Type 305, so that data for annealed Type 305 would reflect

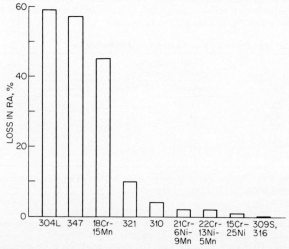

Fig. 1 Loss in RA for several austenitic stainless steels in the annealed condition. Nonstandard steels designated by composition (see text). Source of data: 304L, 347, 18Cr-15Mn, 310, 316[2]; 309S[5]; 321[6]; 22Cr-13Mn-5Ni[8]; 21Cr-6Ni-9Mn, 15Cr-25Ni[9].

greater susceptibility to hydrogen than does Table 2. On the other hand, *severe* cold-work of Type 304 increased hydrogen damage.[3]

Temperature reduction generally worsens hydrogen effects somewhat; for example, in Type 321, the RA loss increases from 10 to 16% in going from 300 to 144 K.[6] Similarly, the ductility loss in Type 310 increases from ~ 0 at 355 K, to over 30% at 225 K.[2] At least in the case of Type 310, there is no martensite formed during deformation even at temperatures as low as 77 K, so this effect is not a manifestation of a change in austenite stability.

There are relatively few data on austenitic stainless steels for other types of mechanical behavior. Investigation of low-cycle fatigue, high-cycle fatigue, and fracture toughness of cold-worked Type 347 showed no degradation by 34.5 MPa hydrogen gas,[7] although as noted above, some effect might have been observed in the annealed material. Creep-rupture properties of Type 347 at 951 K were likewise unaffected by hydrogen.[7] Sustained-load crack growth experiments on Type 321 showed [6] little or no effect of 34.5-MPa hydrogen, even when the 25-mm-thick (1-in.) specimens were loaded at the unstable fracture stress intensity, 35 MPa $\sqrt{m}$ (32 ksi $\sqrt{in.}$); all crack extension observed was in the form of blunting. In the same vein, cracks in Type 304L have been found to extend only by blunting, when gross yielding commenced.[11]

Austenitic-Ferritic or Duplex Steels The only steel of this category to have been investigated, a 26Cr-6.5Ni composition,[3] showed little loss in strength in high-pressure hydrogen. No ductility measurements were made. Other relevant data have been obtained on Type 309S heat-treated to contain varying amounts of delta ferrite, up to 10%, and then tested in 69-MPa hydrogen.[9] No changes in strength or ductility relative to tests in air were detected, which is also the result noted in Table 2 for single-phase Type 309S. This suggests that, at least for small volume fractions of ferrite, it is the austenite which determines hydrogen performance. On that somewhat tentative basis, it would appear that these steels have a potential for acceptable performance in hydrogen, but clearly more work is needed before recommendations for use could be made.

Other Considerations in Austenitic Steels   The results just described clearly indicate that the austenitic stainless steels perform best in high-pressure hydrogen tests. It is therefore appropriate to consider other aspects of the behavior of these steels.

Warm-Work Effects. There have been several studies of the effect of warm-work on hydrogen performance of austenitic steels, and the effects are significant. Usually the warm-work has been performed by high-energy-rate forging (HERF), at temperatures in the range 1090 to 1200 K (1500 to 1700°F). The combination of deformation rate and

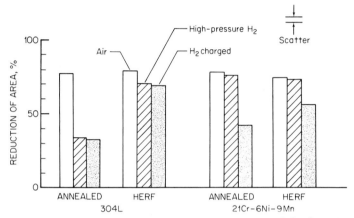

Fig. 2   Ductility of AISI Type 304L and 21Cr-6Ni-9Mn steels in the annealed and HERF conditions (discussed in text). Tests conducted in air, in 69-MPa hydrogen, or after hydrogen charging.[9]

temperature permits strengthening through retention of a deformed substructure. For example, the yield strength of Type 304L has been increased from 200 to 520 MPa (29 to 75 ksi) by HERF deformation.[9]

The strength increase is of value, but the interesting point is the concomitant increase in resistance to hydrogen damage. Figure 2 shows a comparison of annealed and HERF microstructures for two austenitic steels.[2,9] The improvement due to the HERF process is evident. It would thus appear that even the less successful steels in Fig. 1 can be used in high-pressure hydrogen, provided that appropriate warm fabrication procedures are devised for the product form to be used. Cold-work is also useful to a limited extent, as has been described.

Hydrogen Charging Compared to High-Pressure Gas. The data presented above are for "instantaneous" tests in 34.5- or 69-MPa hydrogen, except for part of Fig. 2. Included in Fig. 2 are ductility data for tests on material thermally charged to a supersaturated condition. Typical charging conditions might consist of exposure to 24-MPa hydrogen at 475 K for 14 days. As was mentioned, these "internal" hydrogen results are of importance because they represent the performance to be expected of a material exposed to hydrogen in service for a prolonged period. For example, the charging conditions quoted above would be equivalent to a 10-year exposure at ambient temperature under 69-MPa pressure.

Figure 2 shows that for Type 304L, the high-pressure and charged hydrogen have similar effects, for both annealed and HERF conditions. But for 21-6-9, the charged hydrogen is distinctly more damaging, even for the HERF condition. If the data for charged hydrogen in annealed 21-6-9 had been used instead of high-pressure data in Fig. 1, 21-6-9 would lie between Type 347 and 18Cr-15Mn, and would be classed as an undesirable steel for hydrogen service.

A similar change occurs with 18Cr-15Mn steel when hydrogen-charged;[11] the RA loss increases from 31% in 69-MPa gas, to 47% for charged smooth bars. A less dramatic instance is that of Type 309S, which, when hydrogen-charged, showed[5] an unnotched RA loss of 16% and a notched RA loss of 38%, instead of the zero losses for 69-MPa hydrogen recorded in Table 2.

It must therefore be reemphasized that high-pressure *and* charged hydrogen data can be important in selecting an alloy for hydrogen service. As has been emphasized before,[12] results of these two types of tests are not necessarily alike. And for long-term service in high-pressure hydrogen, even at ambient temperature, the performance of charged material can be at least equally as important as performance in a high-pressure gas test.

APPLICATIONS

Stainless steel is used in a variety of high-pressure hydrogen applications. Most of these involve hydrogen transmission and storage, ranging from small laboratory gas-handling systems, to industrial installations in the thousands of cubic feet range, and to fuel storage and handling systems for rocket engines. In all these applications, there is considerable concern for failure prevention, since the most common mode of hydrogen failure (brittle, reduced-strength fracture after an unpredictable delay period) is potentially catastrophic. Both the stored energy of the pressurized gas (sometimes called, from the gas law, PV energy) and the chemical energy of possible ignition or explosion can be released very rapidly in a failure, with destructive consequences for both the failed part and also for surrounding equipment and personnel.

Materials selection for high-pressure hydrogen service therefore goes beyond the usual kinds of questions an engineer might ask about a prospective choice, such as "Is it strong enough?" or "Is its corrosion resistance high enough to ensure an economical lifetime?" The engineer must also ask, "Is there a risk, even a small risk, of delayed failure?" The question is not easy to answer, for there is no standardized test, like a fracture toughness test, to use as a standard. As with stress-corrosion cracking, it is necessary to do extensive simulation and prototype testing to give even a partial answer. In what follows, therefore, a very conservative approach to materials selection will be outlined, with the understanding that extensive and detailed engineering tests could justify less conservative choices in particular applications. There is too little known about failure in hydrogen, either scientifically or in the engineering sense, to justify any other course.

Stainless Steel Structures   The relatively high cost of stainless steels means that they are used as structural materials only when the system is small or when safety and reliability requirements are paramount. Nonstructural uses will be discussed in the next section.

The most common structural applications are in hydrogen-bearing corrosive gas systems or in relatively small gas-handling systems, where they include piping and tubing; compressor parts; small storage vessels; gages, valves, and fittings; and various other hardware. Such parts have been known to fail in hydrogen service, such as Bourdon tubes in pressure gages which had been made of a martensitic stainless steel. The strength losses shown in Table 1 mean that it is unsafe to use martensitic or precipitation-hardenable steels in high-pressure hydrogen, and probably ferritic steels as well. It appears, therefore, that only for austenitic steels does adequate information exist to permit structural applications in hydrogen.

In practice, such applications are in fact generally met with an austenitic steel, frequently Type 304 or 304L. As Fig. 1 shows, however, such a choice is not risk-free, and Type 316 would appear preferable. It should be mentioned in this connection that steel cleanliness is important. Inclusions or stringers can not only be as large as a tubing wall thickness or a machined valve body wall, and thus cause leaks, but also can act as sites at which hydrogen can accumulate during service, creating an internal pressure equivalent to that on the high-pressure side. Such sites are potential failure nuclei. In cases where reliability is essential, a vacuum-melted steel or even a vacuum-arc remelted steel should be specified, and critical parts radiographed before installation.

Requirements for higher yield strength than the 200 to 250 MPa (29 to 36 ksi) of the 300-series austenitic steels can be met by use of one of the nitrogen-strengthened steels, such as 21-6-9 (Fig. 1), or by use of warm-forming, which raises strengths to 500 to 700 MPa (73 to 100 ksi).[9] The need for strength above that level would necessitate a nonaustenitic structural alloy with stainless steel protection (see below).

Welding of stainless steels usually has little effect on hydrogen performance, although good weld quality to minimize inclusion content is essential. The presence of delta ferrite has been shown not to be deleterious in Type 309S,[9] and it may be concluded that the small amounts of ferrite usually formed will not adversely affect other austenitic grades. There is also evidence[3,5] that sensitization has little or no effect on high-pressure hydrogen performance.

Very little has been published about stainless steels at elevated temperatures in high-pressure hydrogen. The creep-rupture performance of Type 347 was unaffected by hydrogen at 951 K,[7] but ductility losses in an 18Cr-8Ni steel, which were roughly comparable to those shown in Fig. 1, were observed after a 14,000-h exposure at 810 K under 24MPa hydrogen.[13] The latter case emphasizes the point raised earlier about long-term hydrogen exposure in service, and is distinct from cases of "hydrogen attack,"[14] a phenomenon to which austenitic stainless steels are largely immune.

Nonstructural Uses In cases where either the low strength or high cost of an austenitic stainless steel would prohibit its use as a structural material, such as in a hydrogen pipeline or a large hydrogenation reactor vessel in a refinery, such steels may still be used as liners. These restrict access of the high-pressure gas to the (susceptible) structural material because their hydrogen permeability is low. In such designs it is essential to ensure reliability of the liner; even though the liner is not load-bearing, leakage or failure is very likely in turn to cause catastrophic failure of the structure. In fact, applications at even moderately elevated temperature require attention even to the hydrogen which *diffuses* through the liner, and accumulates between the liner and the vessel wall. This is avoided by loosely bonding the liner, or even inserting thin spacers, to create a leak path and avoid any pressure buildup. The hydrogen can be vented through weep holes in the vessel, or through a single vent which is monitored so that sudden increases in flow, due to leaks, are detected.

The statement is sometimes encountered that the need for liners cannot be great since refineries pipe hydrogen at up to 7 MPa in conventional steel pipes and the gas is routinely distributed in alloy steel cylinders at 14 to 15 MPa. But those pressures, which are not high by the definition in this chapter, do cause surface cracking in the interior of gas cylinders. And an attempt to reduce the weight of commercial cylinders through use of high-strength steel resulted in hydrogen-induced delayed failures.[3] It is only the low strength level and low operating stress which make gas cylinders and low-pressure piping reliable. Higher pressures, use of higher strength materials, or a requirement of rigorous safety and reliability, all dictate use of liners.

Liner materials can be chosen from a longer list of stainless steels than can structural materials, since fracture behavior should be of lesser concern. Steels of body-centered cubic (bcc) structure, however, as in martensitic and ferritic steels, would in general be avoided because their permeability to hydrogen is high. An austenitic structure, with its much lower diffusivity, is ordinarily preferred. Any stainless steel liner, however, can serve the function of isolating the structural material from high-pressure hydrogen if the liner is vented. Fabrication and installation requirements for liners will generally dictate choice of an alloy with good formability and weldability.

Another use of stainless steels which is nonstructural is that of bolts used to fasten flanged fittings in moderate-pressure systems. The bolts, with sharp stress raisers in the threads, will be less tolerant of hydrogen than the piping material, and may need to be of a more compatible alloy.

SUMMARY

The behavior of stainless steels in high-pressure hydrogen has not been studied sufficiently to provide thorough knowledge for materials selection. It appears, however, that the substantial losses in both strength and ductility exhibited by martensitic and precipitation-hardenable steels constitute too poor a performance to be considered for high-pressure use unless protected by a liner. The ferritic and austenitic-ferritic or duplex steels have not been extensively studied, but appear to occupy an intermediate position such that their use could be considered for liners but not, in general, for structural uses.

The austenitic steels as a class perform fairly well and may be suitable for structural uses; some of them offer greater reliability than others. Specific applications will dictate the balancing required among available properties in the various steels, including not only the high-pressure gas and charged-hydrogen performance but also strength, weldability, etc. The risk of delayed failure always has to be guarded against, and careful consideration of hydrogen performance is essential for safe and reliable use of stainless steels in high-pressure hydrogen.

REFERENCES

1. Walter, R. J., and W. T. Chandler: Effects of High-Pressure Hydrogen on Metals at Ambient Temperatures, *Rept. R-7780-1 (Access no. N70-18637)*, Rocketdyne Div., Rockwell International, Canoga Park, Calif., February 1969.
2. Louthan, M. R., G. R. Caskey, J. A. Donovan, and D. E. Rawl: Hydrogen Embrittlement of Metals, *Mater. Sci. Eng.*, vol. 10, pp. 357–368, 1972.
3. Fidelle, J.-P., R. Bernardi, R. Broudeur, C. Roux, and M. Rapin: Disk Pressure Testing of Hydrogen Environment Embrittlement, pp. 221–253, "Hydrogen Embrittlement Testing," *ASTM Spec. Tech. Publ.* 543, 1974.
4. McGuire, M. F., R. F. Hehemann, and A. R. Troiano: Stress Corrosion Cracking and Hydrogen Embrittlement in 410 Stainless Steel, "L'Hydrogene dans les Metaux," vol. 2, pp. 325–329, Éditions Science et Industrie, Paris, 1972.
5. Thompson, A. W.: The Behavior of Sensitized 309S Stainless Steel in Hydrogen, *Mater. Sci. Eng.*, vol. 14, pp. 253–264, 1974.
6. Walter, R. J., and W. T. Chandler: Influence of Gaseous Hydrogen on Metals, *Rept. NASA CR-124410*, Rocketdyne Div., Rockwell International, Canoga Park, Calif., October 1973.
7. Harris, J. A., and M. C. van Wanderham: Properties of Materials in High Pressure Hydrogen at Cryogenic, Room, and Elevated Temperatures, *Rept. PWA FR-4566 (Access no. N71-33728)*, Pratt and Whitney Aircraft, W. Palm Beach, Fla., June 1971.
8. Odegard, B. C., and A. J. West: Thermomechanical Behavior and Hydrogen Compatibility of 22-13-5 Stainless Steel, *Mater. Sci. Eng.*, vol. 19, pp. 261–268, 1975.
9. Thompson, A. W.: Ductility Losses in Austenitic Stainless Steels Caused by Hydrogen, pp. 91–102, "Hydrogen in Metals," American Society for Metals, Metals Park, Ohio, 1974.
10. Thompson, A. W.: Hydrogen Embrittlement of Stainless Steels by Lithium Hydride, *Metall. Trans.*, vol. 4, pp. 2819–2825, 1973.
11. Louthan, M. R.: Effects of Hydrogen on the Mechanical Properties of Low Carbon and Austenitic Steels, "Hydrogen in Metals," pp. 53–75, American Society for Metals, Metals Park, Ohio, 1974.
12. Walter, R. J., R. P. Jewett, and W. T. Chandler: On the Mechanism of Hydrogen-Environment Embrittlement of Iron- and Nickel-base Alloys, *Mater. Sci. Eng.*, vol. 5, pp. 99–110, 1969–70.
13. "Metals Handbook," vol. 1, p. 601, American Society for Metals, Metals Park, Ohio, 1961.
14. Nelson, G. A.: Metals for High-pressure Hydrogenation Plants, *Trans. ASME*, vol. 73, pp. 205–213, 1951.

Chapter 47

Stainless Steels in Aircraft and Aerospace*

LAWRENCE J. KORB

Supervisor, Metals, Space Shuttle Orbiter, Space Division, Rockwell International, Downey, California

INTRODUCTION

The increased performance demanded of aircraft and aerospace vehicles over the past 20 years has emphasized the need to select the most desirable materials for each application. There are many important design requirements which must be accommodated, but most

*The author wishes to acknowledge the valuable contributions made by W. A. Reinsch, H. Taketani, R. W. Chester, and A. Hurlich.

important are those of weight and cost. Studies are usually made of several material and design concepts to arrive at the optimum weight-cost trade-off for each major component or structure. It is generally conceded during the preliminary design period that the reduction of each pound of weight on an aircraft is worth $200 to $300 ($440 to 660 per kg) during the life of the vehicle, whereas each pound reduction in a space vehicle is often worth $30,000 ($66,000 per kg) or more. Reduction in weight is reflected directly in the reduction of fuel costs, the reduction in the size of the power plant or launch system, or in increased performance—such as increased speed or payload.

Stainless steels have played an important role in aircraft and aerospace designs. The apparent design advantages of stainless steels are their combined properties of high strength, high stiffness, excellent corrosion resistance, high resistance to wear, ability to operate over a wide range of temperatures, and their relative low cost and ease of fabrication. Stainless steels occupy a middle ground between aluminum and titanium both with respect to raw material costs and ease of fabrication. They operate efficiently in environments too corrosive for aluminum or low-alloy steels or in temperature ranges too severe for either aluminum or titanium. There are five major areas where stainless steels have been widely used in aircraft and aerospace: high-temperature structures, pressure vessels, fluid lines and fittings, fasteners, and mechanical systems. Some of the design applications for stainless steels typical of these areas are discussed below.

HIGH-TEMPERATURE STRUCTURES

Two excellent examples of the use of stainless steel for high-temperature structures are the skins of the XB-70 aircraft and the heat shield substructure of the Apollo spacecraft. Both designs employed brazed honeycomb sandwich construction made from precipitation-hardenable stainless steels. The XB-70 skins were designed and fabricated in the 1955 to 1965 period. The Apollo heat shield substructure was an extension of this technology and was designed and fabricated in the 1961 to 1970 period.

XB-70 Valkyrie The XB-70 skin used PH15-7Mo sandwich face sheets brazed to a resistance welded core of either PH15-7Mo or 17-7PH and heat-treated to an RH 1050 condition (200 ksi [1379 MN/m²] ultimate strength). It was designed for service in the −65 to +900°F (−53.9 to 482°C) range.[1] Initial designs used skins as thin as 0.008 in. (0.20 mm) and cores as thin as 0.00075 in. (0.019 mm). Experience indicated that practical minimum gages of 0.012 in. (0.30 mm) for skins and 0.001 in. (0.03 mm) for cores were necessary to avoid intercell dimpling of face sheets, excessive handling damage and difficult repairs, and excessive "puckering" of cell walls in deep sandwich cores. Sandwich panels were generally in the 0.25 to 4-in. (6.35 to 101.6 mm) thickness range. Panel dimensions were limited by brazing facilities and handling considerations to sizes of approximately 10 by 20 ft (3.05 by 6.1 m). Both single- and double-curvature panels as well as flat panels were made. Edge close-out members were made from 17-4PH heat-treated to the H950 temper. Weld lands were provided on the panel edges to accommodate strength reductions in the heat-affected zones. Initially panels were made using chemically milled skins; later it was found that chemical milling of face sheets after panel brazing resulted in higher quality brazes and less damage. Masking was provided in the weld bead areas where face sheets were spliced and panel edges required sealing from chemical milling solutions. To accommodate highly localized stresses, different densities of core were often spliced together within a single panel prior to brazing.

The brazing cycle was selected in a range to accomplish the austenite conditioning of the face sheet and core. The brazing alloy used, LCT 80/20, is basically a silver-based alloy, containing copper, indium, and palladium (69Ag-18.5Ni-6.2Cu-4.5In-1.8Pd-0.16Li) to which a small quantity of lithium was added to deoxidize the surface and permit proper alloy flow. The braze alloy was impregnated into a nickel matrix foil carrier. All brazing was performed in sealed retorts evacuated and backfilled with argon. Brazing could either be accomplished by furnaces or blankets employing nickel-chromium strip heaters. Initial hardening cycles were selected to accommodate the flow requirements of the brazing alloy. Flow of the brazing alloy along sandwich core nodes increased sandwich efficiencies under compressive load. Braze-alloy flow had to be balanced in such a manner that fillet starvation of the core-to-face sheet bonds did not occur. A minimum core-to-face fillet of 0.006 to 0.010 in. (0.15 to 0.25 mm) was required, the size depending on core thickness, depth and cell size.

Cooling rates were controlled and the final aging temperatures were selected to ensure that both transformation and design properties were achieved. The cooling rates recognize the slow cooling imposed by large masses of tooling and had to be carried out without jeopardizing transformation or causing premature precipitation. The cooling cycle further assures completion of the austenitic-martensitic transformation prior to the precipitation hardening. The aging cycle was then adjusted to provide the desirable combination of strength and toughness.

Apollo Command Module   The stainless steel heat shield for the Apollo command module formed the substructure to which the ablative reentry-protective material was attached.[2] It was designed for service from −150 to +600°F (−101 to 316°C). To provide the toughness needed at the lower temperatures, vacuum-melted PH14-8Mo was required for the face sheets. Edge members used 17-4PH heat-treated to a H1150M condition (135 ksi [931 MN/m²] ultimate tensile strength) to ensure maximum cryogenic toughness as verified through Charpy V-notch impact tests.

The heat shield consisted of three major sections, each free to expand and contract independently of the others. The forward heat shield was a dome shape, the crew compartment heat shield was a conical shape, and the aft heat shield was a dish shape approximately 13 ft (3.96 m) in diameter (Fig. 1). Stainless steel face sheets varied from 0.050 to as low as 0.008 in. (1.27 to 0.20 mm), depending on the loads involved. Sandwich depths varied from 0.50 in. (12.7 mm) on the crew compartment section to 2 in. (50.8 mm) in the aft heat shield. As with the B-70, core splicing was widely used. The aft heat shield, for example, contained three different core cell sizes and gages (³⁄₁₆ in. by 0.0015 in. (4.76 by 0.04 mm), ⅛ in. by 0.004 in. (3.18 by 0.10 mm), and ³⁄₁₆ by 0.003 in. (4.76 by 0.08 mm)).

Brazing and thermal processing were similar to that used for the B-70 except that full martensitic transformation required cooling to −140°F (−96°C) using a nitrogen quench and that slight modifications were made in the cooling rates and aging times resulting in a BCHT 1050 heat treatment (190 ksi [1310 MN/m²] minimum tensile ultimate strength). A comparison between the two cycles is shown in Table 1.

After brazing, panels did not often achieve the mold line tolerances of ±0.030 in. (±0.76

Fig. 1   Fabrication of Apollo AFT heat shields.

TABLE 1   Braze Cycle Heat Treatments

Cycle	PH15-7Mo (RH1050)	PH14-8Mo (BCHT 1050)
Braze, °F (°C)	1740 ± 25 (949 ± 14)	1740 ± 25 (949 ± 14)
Cool, min	61–90	1–90
Transformation, °F (°C); h	25 (−4); 3	−140 (−96); 3
Age, °F (°C); min	1065 ± 10 (574 ± 5.6); 60–75	1050 ± 10 (565 ± 5.6); 60–75

mm) required by design. Shot peening became an effective method of bringing panels into contour. Panels were clamped into place to avoid mismatch between face sheets and edge members during welding after having both the core and all braze alloy removed for a 0.120-in. (3.05-mm) distance to prevent overheating (and debonding) of the brazed core. Minimum distortion was achieved during welding by simultaneously welding both sandwich face sheets to the edge members. This balanced the shrinkage in the weld zone and avoided weld peaking.

PRESSURE VESSELS

Stainless steels have been widely used in three different types of pressure vessels in the aerospace industry: large liquid launch vehicles, high-strength cryoformed pressure vessels, and low-pressure fluid containers.

Large Liquid Launch Vehicles   Extensive use of stainless steel has been employed in the Atlas, the Centaur, and the Delta launch vehicles in the 1955 to 1975 period. A brief description of the technology involved is presented below.

Atlas and Centaur. The Atlas vehicle was the first American intercontinental ballistic missile. It was also used to launch the Mercury spacecraft, and, when used with the Centaur second stage, it launched the Pioneer, Surveyor, and Mariner series space probes. Both the Atlas (Fig. 2) and Centaur were fabricated from extra cold-rolled Type 301 stainless steel. The Atlas is approximately 120 in. (3.05 m) in diameter and 80 ft (24.38 m) long and contains tanks for liquid oxygen and jet propulsion fuel (kerosene). The Centaur, approximately 120 in. (3.05 m) in diameter and 35 ft (10.67 m) long, was the first booster system to employ both liquid hydrogen and liquid oxygen.

The 300-series austenitic stainless steels, because of their excellent corrosion resistance, ease of fabrication, good cryogenic properties, and their ability to be cold-rolled to very high strength levels are quite attractive for use in large cryogenic launch missiles. Type 301 can be cold-rolled to produce the highest strength efficiency, while Types 304L and 310 result in more ductile joint designs (see Table 2 and compare mechanical properties noted in Table 5, Fig. 12, and Fig. 13, Chap. 20). Both the Atlas and Centaur used Type 301 in pressure-stabilized monocoque structures with no internal stiffening or supporting members.[3,4] Skin thicknesses ranged from 0.010 to 0.030 in. (0.25 to 0.76 mm). Tanks are built up from overlapping ring segments and capped by bulkheads made from gore sections stretch-formed from half or three-quarter hard Type 301 stainless steel. Internal bulkheads separated the fuel from

Fig. 2   Atlas vehicle.

TABLE 2 Mechanical Properties of Resistance Spot Welds in Stainless Steel Sheet Alloys*

Alloy	Test temperature		Shear strength		Cross-tension strength		Tension/shear ratio
	°F	°C	lb/spot	N/spot	lb/spot	N/spot	
60% cold-rolled Type 301, 0.011 in. (0.28 mm) thick	+75	24	390	1735	213	947	0.55
	−320	−196	470	2091	70	311	0.15
	−423	−253	379	1686	65	289	0.17
50% cold-rolled Type 304L, 0.012 in. (0.30 mm) thick	+75	24	409	1819	256	1139	0.63
	−320	−196	634	2820	265	1179	0.42
	−423	−253	666	2962	306	1361	0.46
75% cold-rolled Type 310, 0.010 in. (0.25 mm) thick	+75	24	293	1303	168	747	0.57
	−320	−196	422	1877	202	898	0.48
	−423	−253	464	2064	232	1032	0.50

*All data represent averages of 20 to 100 replicate tests.

the oxidizer. The Centaur required a vacuum-insulated sandwich bulkhead made from stainless steel face sheets and a glass fiber reinforced core. All joining used fusion welding or overlap seam welding for sealing and was reinforced by resistance spot-welded doublers where required to maintain joints at 100% efficiency.

The increased joint efficiency of Types 304L and 310 have been attributed to their higher nickel contents. Tests have shown that Type 310 remains completely austenitic even when cold-rolled to a 75% reduction and strained at −423°F (−253°C). Although nickel enhances the cryogenic ductility, it does so at the expense of cryogenic strength. In order to increase the structural efficiency on the Centaur vehicle, Type 301 steel was used and a 0.003-in. (0.08-mm) interleaf of nickel foil was placed between spot-welded joints. This resulted not only in higher strength than without the foil, but in greater fatigue resistance (Table 3). The nickel also enhanced the ability of x-rays to determine the quality of spot welds.

Delta. The Delta launch vehicle has launched nearly 100 satellites through the period from the early sixties to 1975 (Fig. 3).[5] The second stage of the Delta is fueled by aerozine 50, a mixture of hydrazines, and uses nitrogen tetroxide as the oxidizer. These propellants do not require the use of insulation, a necessity with liquid hydrogen or liquid oxygen, but are highly toxic as well as hypergolic. Aerozene 50 is readily decomposed in the presence of rust; therefore stainless steel is desirable. Type 410 is used for both tanks which are designed integral with the second-stage structure (Fig. 3). Both manual and machine welding are employed using the gas-tungsten-arc welding (GTAW) process, a modified Type 410 stainless welding wire (AMS 5821), and argon gas for shielding. Subsequent to welding, the structure is heat-treated to 170 ksi (1172 MN/m²) minimum ultimate tensile strength as shown in Table 4.

High-Strength Cryoformed Pressure Vessels   Stainless steel pressure vessels fabricated by the cryoforming process are among the most efficient small pressure vessels on a strength-to-weight basis. In this process, a pressure vessel is fabricated by rolling or forming a low-silicon, Type 301 stainless steel sheet, welding with either Types 310 or 301 welding wire, then expanding the vessel approximately 15% into a female die cavity with liquid nitrogen. During the process the stainless steel attains extremely high cold-worked properties. Additional hardening can be accomplished by subsequent aging (Table 5). Where increased thickness is required, such as for structural or fluid system attachments, a machined boss can be welded onto the vessel prior to its expansion.

Since titanium is undesirable for liquid-oxygen storage because of impact sensitivity,

TABLE 3   Effect of Nickel Foil on Mechanical Properties of Complex Weld Joints in the Type 301 Full-Hard Stainless Steel*

Thickness	Test temperature		Nickel foil in joint	Tensile strength of complex weld joint		Stress range from 0 to		Fatigue properties	
	°F	°C		ksi	MN/m²	ksi	MN/m²	Number of cycles to first leak	Number of cycles to fracture
0.011 in. (0.28 mm)	+75	24	No	207	1427	145	1000	462	945
	+75	24	No	207	1427	180	1241	196	319
	+75	24	Yes	210	1448	140	965	459	1531
	+75	24	Yes	210	1448	186	1282	362	496
	−320	−196	No	269	1855	140	965	>2000	>2000
	−320	−196	No	269	1855	214	1476	350	389
	−320	−196	Yes	288	1986	140	965	>2000	>2000
	−320	−196	Yes	288	1986	214	1476	>2000	>2000
	−423	−253	No	236	1627	140	965	275	736
	−423	−253	No	236	1627	170	1172	100	200
	−423	−253	Yes	307	2117	140	965	>4000	>4000
	−423	−253	Yes	307	2117	170	1172	>900	1225

*All data represent averages of two or three replicate tests.

Fig. 3 Delta second-stage booster tank structure.

cryoformed stainless steel is one of the most efficient designs presently available. Its efficiency, when described by parameters of the ratio of its burst pressure and volume to its weight P_bB/W, is approximately 800,000 in. (20,320 m). The largest vessel fabricated to date is approximately 38 in. (96.5 cm) in diameter. More than 900 pressure vessels had been fabricated by this process during the period from 1966 to 1974 by Ardé, Inc.[6]

Under development in 1975 were pressure vessels with cryoformed stainless steel liners and high-strength filamentary overwrap materials, such as "Kevlar" 49 (an aromatic amide produced by Du Pont). These composite tanks are projected to be up to 33% more efficient than those produced from titanium alloy Ti-6Al-4V. Stainless steel liners are highly desirable because of their high strength, corrosion resistance, low cost, fabricability, and high toughness to resist cyclic fatigue.

Low-Pressure Fluid Containers Low-pressure fluid containers are made from austenitic stainless steels because of their corrosion resistance, ease of fabrication, and ability to resist damage in minimum gages, typically as low as 0.010 in. (0.25 mm). These tanks are normally fabricated from Types 321 or 347 stainless steel in the annealed condition.

TABLE 4   Thermal Treatment of Delta Second-Stage Booster Tank Structure (Type 410)

Thermal treatment	Temperature °F	°C	Time, min.	Remarks
Stress relief	1225 ± 25	663 ± 14	60–75	Air cool
Austenitizing	1450 ± 25	788 ± 14	30–40	Rapidly heat to 1710°F (932°C)
	1710 ± 10	932 ± 6	90–95	Cool uniformly to below 1200°F (649°C) (in 3.25 min); air cool
Tempering	600 ± 10	315 ± 6	105–120	Air cool

TABLE 5   Properties of Cryoformed Stainless Steel Pressure Vessels (Type 301)

Properties	Unaged Spheres	Cylinders	Aged Spheres	Cylinders
F_{tu}, ksi (MN/m²)	210 (1448)	240 (1655)	260 (1793)	290 (2000)
F_{ty}, ksi (MN/m²)	190 (1310)	215 (1482)	235 (1620)	260 (1793)
Elongation, %	12	12	10	10
K_{IC} welds, ksi $\sqrt{\text{in.}}$ (MN/m³/²)	80 (87.9)	80	80	80
K_{IC} parent metal, ksi $\sqrt{\text{in.}}$ (MN/m³/²)	100 (110)	100	100	100

The Orbital Workshop used 10 such tanks each containing 600 lb (272.1 kg) of potable water.[7] The tanks measure 30 in. (76.2 cm) in diameter by 50 in. (127 cm) in length and were made from fusion-welded Type 321. Water was expelled by pneumatically actuated stainless steel bellows. Stainless steel is preferred to aluminum in high-purity spacecraft water systems because of its superior behavior in the presence of biocides and its freedom from corrosion and joining problems where stainless lines are used.

FLUID LINES AND FITTINGS

Stainless steel is an ideal material for aircraft and aerospace fluid service because of its corrosion resistance, ease of forming, and its wide choice of joining techniques. Nearly all commercial aircraft use stainless steel for hydraulic lines while the latest military aircraft use titanium for maximum weight reduction. Titanium, although more efficient on a weight basis, is more costly and does not lend itself to brazing or welding on vehicle assembly.

Material Selection   A designer may be faced with several questions in the use of stainless steel for fluid lines: whether to select a seamless or a welded and drawn tube, whether to use annealed or cold-reduced tubing, which alloy to choose, and what type of joining method to employ. In recent years the quality of welded and drawn tubing has become equal to that of seamless tubing and most aerospace companies no longer distinguish between the two in fluid system designs. The choice of cold-reduced tubing over annealed must depend on the need for weight reduction, the type of joining technique used (which could anneal the joint), and the severity of forming requirements.

Stainless steel has been used principally as Type 304L, AM-350, or the 21-6-9 alloy tubing, the latter now becoming the most commonly used. Table 6 summarizes alloy usage in recent aircraft.

While Type 304 had been the traditional choice for early commercial jets, Type 304L was used in early spacecraft (Gemini, Apollo, LM). Both are limited in strength as compared to AM-350 or 21-6-9 (Table 7). Type 304L was selected in preference to Type 304 to avoid carbide precipitation during welding or brazing and in preference to Types 321 or 347 because of its superior wetting characteristic during brazing. AM-350 was used on the XB-70 experimental bomber and the C-5A aircraft. Recent aircraft and spacecraft use the 21-6-9 alloy because of its higher strength when compared to Types 304 or 304L and its better corrosion resistance, lower cost, and ease of fabrication when compared to AM-350. The 21-6-9 alloy does require larger bend radii (3D versus 1D) than Type 304L and requires better fitup on assembly since lines are much more difficult to flex into position. The minimum practical gage of the 21-6-9 alloy tubing is generally considered to be 0.016-in. (0.41-mm) wall in sizes up to and including 0.750-in. (19.05-mm) diameter.

TABLE 6   Stainless Steel Tubing Usage in Typical Aircraft and Spacecraft

Alloy	Vehicle	Alloy	Vehicle
AM-350	XB-70	304L	Apollo
	C-5A		Gemini
	CH-53E		Lunar Module
	Concorde		Space Shuttle Orbiter
21-6-9	747		
15% cold-reduced	DC-10	316	Saturn SIVB/1B
	A-300		
	S-3A	321	Saturn SIVB/1B
	L1011		
	Space Shuttle Orbiter	347	Saturn SIVB/1B
304	C-130A		
	F-5E		
	A-9		
	707		
	727		
	Spartan missile		
	Delta space vehicle		
	Saturn S1VB/1B		

TABLE 7   Properties of Stainless Steel Tubing

Alloy	Ultimate tensile strength		Tensile yield strength		Elongation, %
	ksi	MN/m²	ksi	MN/m²	
AM-350 CRT	185	1275.6	140	965.3	15–25*
21-6-9 15% cold-reduced	142	979.1	100	689.5	16
21-6-9 annealed	100	689.5	60	413.7	40
304 ⅛ hard	105	724	75	517.1	20
304L ⅛ hard	95	655	60	413.7	25
304 annealed	75	517.1	30	206.9	40
304L annealed	65	448.2	30	206.9	30

*Dependent on wall thickness.

Stainless steel has been joined by swaging, brazing, or welding in systems up to 4000 psi (27.6 MN/m²).[8] Both permanent and separable connectors are employed. Separable joints for many years involved the use of flared tubing with B-nut fittings of AN, MS, or MC configurations. Limited leakage or seepage in hydraulic systems was tolerated in aircraft. B-nut fittings were not satisfactory for spacecraft service where joints often were required to be helium leak-tight to prevent the escape of pressurant gases or toxic propellants. B-nuts have been largely replaced by machined separable fittings which are permanently joined to the tube ends by either brazing, welding, or swaging. These fittings are made from either 17-4PH, 15-5PH or 300-series stainless, depending on the design.

Joining Methods   Several different brazing or welding concepts have been employed, all involving automatic equipment. Brazing is accomplished with Au-Ni or Au-Cu-Ni alloys, the most widely used being 82Au-18Ni and 81.5Au-16.5Cu-2Ni. Because of the recent high prices of gold, some development is proceeding with silver braze alloys. Brazing requires inert gas shielding on both the interior and exterior of the tubing to ensure an oxide-free surface for wetting during the braze cycle. Joints are brazed at temperatures from approximately 1800 to 2000°F (982 to 1093°C). Good braze-alloy flow requires that a capillary gap of 0.001 to 0.006 in. (0.025 to 0.152 mm) be maintained. To facilitate brazing, diametric tolerances of tubing are held to +0.004 (0.102 mm), −0.000 in. and unions to +0.001 (0.025 mm), −0.000 in. Brazing is limited to approximately 1 in. (25.4 mm) diameter maximum because of the difficulty of maintaining the proper capillary gap and of transferring heat to the tube ends through the union with portable induction brazing equipment. While brazed joints are easily fabricated and have a high initial acceptance rate, usually greater than 97%, they are more expensive than swaged joints (due to the cost of x-rays, argon, braze alloy, etc.) and more difficult to repair.

Swaged joints are low in cost, quickly fabricated, and as with brazed or welded joints, will develop the full burst strength of the tube. They are not, however, as strong in axial or torsional loads. Permanent joints now in use are swaged from the exterior and require a silicone rubber seal, thus limiting their service to temperatures from −65 to +275°F (−54 to +135°C). Separable connectors are swaged by internal swaging tools and are not temperature-limited in this regard.

Welded joints may or may not employ a sleeve. The advantage of the sleeve is that it assures better axial fitup of the welded joint, provides filler metal for the joint, and permits the full strength of cold-reduced tubing to be developed. Stainless welds produced by the GTAW process are smooth with little drop through on the back side, therefore making the process suitable for sizes down to 0.25 in. (6.35 mm). The maximum diameter for joining does not appear to be limited, as is the case with brazing or swaging. Where sleeves are used, they are normally sized to within 0.002 in. (0.05 mm) of the tube diameter. An axial gap between tube ends should be less than one-half the thickness of the tubes and sleeve combination. To replace a welded component often requires the use of two welds and an additional length of tube to compensate for the loss in length due to the removal of the weld bead. Where possible weld sleeve designs which eliminate crevices on the fluid side are preferred to prevent crevice corrosion. Typical swaged, brazed, and welded joints are shown in Fig. 4.

Fittings, such as tees and elbows, for aircraft or aerospace systems are generally not available unless purchased from a source which sells their proprietary brazing methods.

Therefore many aerospace companies machine their own fittings from bar stock of the same alloy as the tubing. Austenitic stainless bar does contain inclusions. Fittings made in this manner may contain a small percentage of rejects. To preclude this, either a vacuum-melted alloy such as 304L can be procured, or bar stock can be reforged to break up and reorient inclusions and tighten grain boundaries to avoid leakage paths.

FASTENERS

Stainless steel fasteners are not widely used in aircraft applications because of either cost or weight considerations, but are widely used in spacecraft. Most modern aircraft use aluminum rivets, titanium pin and collar fasteners, and cadmium-plated low-alloy steel

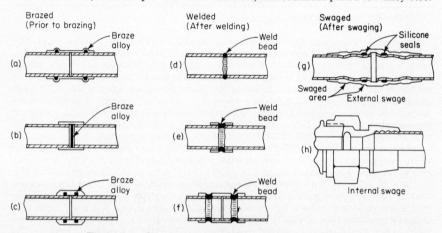

Fig. 4   Typical permanent tubing joints in stainless steels (cross sections).

bolts and nuts. The space environment imposes two requirements on fasteners which eliminate the cadmium-plated low-alloy steels:

1. Service temperatures from −250 to +1000°F (−157 to +538°C)
2. Lubricating coatings which do not sublime in space

Because of this, A-286 bolts and screws mated to silver-plated A-286 nuts were used for the Apollo command and service modules. For tension applications, both 200 and 140-ksi (1379- and 965-MN/m²) (NAS 1000 series) bolts are used, while for shear applications 84-ksi (579 MN/m²) bolts (NAS 1100 series) are widely used on the Apollo and Space Shuttle orbiter. Pin and collar fasteners of A-286 are being used in tension on the Space Shuttle Orbiter where studies have indicated they are more reliable than titanium.

MECHANICAL SYSTEMS

Stainless steel is widely used as machined parts in various mechanical systems such as latches, gears, hinges, rods, fittings, etc. Steel is selected over aluminum or titanium where a rigid part is required. Here, the high modulus of elasticity governs. This is particularly evident in mechanisms and structural parts where space is limited. Steel also has a higher tolerance for elevated temperatures, and often replaces aluminum at temperatures above 250°F (121°C) and titanium at temperatures in 700-1000°F (371 to 538°C) range. Where steel is required, stainless steel alloys are often selected to avoid the necessity of providing corrosion protection, or where corrosion protection would interfere with the function of the part. Further, parts requiring impact-resisting surfaces, or sliding surfaces, are often designed in stainless steel. The stainless grades are available in a wide selection of product forms, sizes, and strength levels up to about 220,000 psi (1517 MN/m²) minimum ultimate tensile strength. Above this strength level, the alloy steels are used, and the disadvantages of coatings in all but "inert" environments must be dealt with.

In the high-strength ranges, the most commonly used stainless steels are PH13-8Mo,

TABLE 8   Comparison of High-Strength Stainless Steel Alloys Used in Mechanical Systems

Properties	PH13-8Mo	15-5PH	17-4PH	CUST 455
Strength	High	Medium	Medium	High
Machinability	Good (55)	Good (55)	Good (55)	Good (55)
Weldability	Good	Good	Good	Good
Corrosion resistance	Good	Good	Good	Good
Heat treatment	One-step	One-step	One-step	One-step
Transverse ductility	Good	Good	Limited	Good
Magnetic	Yes	Yes	Yes	Yes

Note: Machinability index of 55 is based on a scale with free-machining carbon steel at 100.

15-5PH, 17-4PH, and Custom 455. A summary of design characteristics provides some comparison (Table 8).

The applications of the 300-series stainless steels are common and provide the maximum corrosion resistance of all the stainless steels. They are also nonmagnetic. Most commonly used are Types 303Se or 303S compounded with selenium (Se) or sulfur (S) to improve the machinability of the basic 300-series compositions. By these chemical additions, the machinability index is increased from a rather poor 40 to a very respectable 65. Often such designs are limited to applications not involving tension due to their poorer transverse properties. The 300-series alloys without additions include Types 302, 304, and 316.

Type 316 has the best corrosion resistance of all the 300 series, with similar properties in other respects. To assure good corrosion resistance in welds, a low-carbon modification, Type 316L is recommended. For other welded applications, Types 347 or 321 are recommended, again to assure good corrosion resistance in welded areas.

Several 400-series alloys are used for specialized applications. They are limited in their corrosion resistance, and are heat-treatable by quenching and tempering similarly to alloy steels. Type 416 enjoys some use, where corrosion is not limiting, for automatic screw machine stock because of its high machining index (85). Another in this series, Type 431, has been used for fittings, particularly in mechanisms such as bomb racks. The 400-series alloys are widely used in solenoid valves where their magnetic properties aid in valve actuation. Type 440C, as well as 17-4PH, enjoy wide application in bearings and races because of their hardness and corrosion resistance.

REFERENCES

1. Reinsch, W. A.: Personal correspondence, December 1974.
2. Gatzek, L. E., R. P. Olsen, L. J. Korb, and H. M. Clancy: Materials and Fabricating Methods for the Apollo Spacecraft, *Met. Prog.*, vol. 89, no. 2, February 1966.
3. Hurlich, A., and W. G. Schenck: Evaluation and Application of Stainless Steels in Cryogenic Environments, *ASTM Spec. Tech. Publ. no. 369.*, 1965.
4. Hurlich, A.: Metals and Fabrication Methods Used for the Atlas, *Met. Prog.*, vol. 76, no. 5, November 1959.
5. Taketani, H.; Personal correspondence, December 1974.
6. Cozewith, A.; Personal correspondence, December 1974.
7. Chester, R. W.; Personal correspondence, December 1974.
8. Korb, L. J., L. W. Myers, and J. Soja: Spacecraft Plumbing Systems, *Met. Prog.*, vol. 91, no. 2, February 1967.

Chapter **48**

Stainless Steels in Fasteners

JOHN MENGEL
Vice President—Marketing, ITT Harper, Morton Grove, Illinois

INTRODUCTION

An analysis of standard fasteners, such as bolts and screws, reveals that all have certain characteristics in common. Further, their differences can be classified as shown in Fig. 1. Thus, the fasteners may have some or all of these parts: head, driving recess, shoulder, unthreaded shank, threaded shank, and point. Certain combinations of these components, because of usage, are considered standard. Others are nonstandard, but nearly any combination can readily be produced.

   Basic Considerations In modern fastening technology, the object is to reduce the friction between the nut and the bolt, or the mating parts. The ideal fastening condition is obtained when the nut is driven on the bolt, or the bolt into the mating part, without friction and up to the bolt's elastic limit. It is not necessary that the bolt shank fit deadtight into the clearance hole if the proper tension is placed on the fastener, since the fastener should rely on tension, rather than its fit, for holding power.

Some general rules of good fastening technique are:

1. Use a larger number of fasteners of small diameter, rather than fewer large diameter fasteners.

2. Use fasteners with as near frictionless threads as possible. Fastener threads must be clean of dirt. Machine screws, bolts, and nuts should be lubricated.

3. Use a definite torque in driving the fastener to a certain percentage of the fastener's elastic limit. Examples of suggested maximum torquing values for 18-8 and Type 316 stainless steels are shown in Table 1. Note that the table refers to "18-8." This term encompasses Types 302, 303, 304, and 305, depending on whether the fastener is hot-formed, cold-headed, or machined.

Thread Forms   The modern Unified and American Standard screw thread has evolved from threaded parts used by clockmakers and gunsmiths of the seventeenth and eighteenth centuries. Three principal systems of screw threads gradually developed around the world: the Unified and American Standard Form, the British Whitworth Form, and the European Metric Form. These are discussed in detail below. It is interesting to note, however, that certain thread forms exist which are peculiar to certain industries. Many water meters have their own thread standards, just as they did

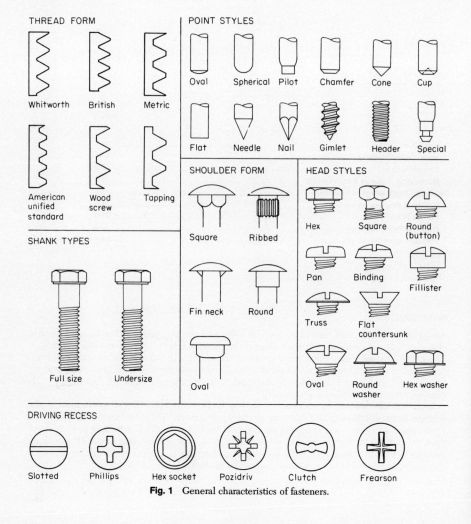

Fig. 1   General characteristics of fasteners.

TABLE 1   Suggested Maximum Torquing Values for Stainless Steel Bolts*

Bolt size	18-8	Type 316
	VALUES ARE STATED IN IN.-LB (J)	
2-56	2.5 (0.28)	2.6 (0.29)
2-64	3.0 (0.34)	3.2 (0.36)
3-48	3.9 (0.44)	4.0 (0.45)
3-56	4.4 (0.50)	4.6 (0.52)
4-40	5.2 (0.59)	5.5 (0.62)
4-48	6.6 (0.75)	6.9 (0.78)
5-40	7.7 (0.87)	8.1 (0.92)
5-44	9.4 (1.06)	9.8 (1.11)
6-32	9.6 (1.08)	10.1 (1.14)
6-40	12.1 (1.37)	12.7 (1.44)
8-32	19.8 (2.24)	20.7 (2.34)
8-36	22.0 (2.49)	23.0 (2.60)
10-24	22.8 (2.58)	23.8 (2.69)
10-32	31.7 (3.58)	33.1 (3.74)
¼″-20	75.2 (8.50)	78.8 (8.90)
¼″-28	94.0 (10.62)	99.0 (11.19)
⁵⁄₁₆″-18	132 (14.92)	138 (15.59)
⁵⁄₁₆″-24	142 (16.05)	147 (16.61)
³⁄₈″-16	236 (26.67)	247 (27.91)
³⁄₈″-24	259 (29.27)	271 (30.62)
⁷⁄₁₆″-14	376 (42.49)	393 (44.41)
⁷⁄₁₆″-20	400 (45.20)	418 (47.23)
½″-13	517 (58.42)	542 (61.25)
½″-20	541 (61.13)	565 (63.85)
⁹⁄₁₆″-12	682 (77.07)	713 (80.57)
⁹⁄₁₆″-18	752 (84.98)	787 (88.93)
⅝″-11	1110 (125.43)	1160 (131.08)
⅝″-18	1244 (140.57)	1301 (147.01)
¾″-10	1530 (172.89)	1582 (178.77)
¾″-16	1490 (168.37)	1558 (176.05)
⅞″-9	2328 (263.06)	2430 (274.59)
⅞″-14	2318 (261.93)	2420 (273.46)
1″-8	3440 (388.72)	3595 (406.24)
1″-14	3110 (351.43)	3250 (367.25)
	VALUES ARE STATED IN FT-LB (J)	
1⅛″-7	413 (560.03)	432 (585.79)
1⅛″-12	390 (528.84)	408 (553.25)
1¼″-7	523 (709.19)	546 (740.38)
1¼″-12	480 (650.88)	504 (683.42)
1½″-6	888 (1204.13)	930 (1261.08)
1½″-12	703 (2157.4)	732 (992.59)

*Based on dry product wiped clean.

80 years ago. And, many gas fixtures have their specialized thread forms, including left-handed leads, to prevent the uninitiated from installing unsafe fittings in gas lines.

The fine thread series of the Unified and American Standard, as distinct from the coarse thread series, came into existence years ago through the efforts of the Society of Automotive Engineers. It was felt that more threads per inch permitted better wrenching because of the smaller helix angle. Although some of the advantages claimed for fine threads have been disproved, they still have great popularity in certain industries.

Unified Thread Form. This form encompasses both the Unified Coarse Thread UNC (Fig. 2*a*) and the Unified Fine Thread UNF (Fig. 2*b*). It is used for most of the bolts, nuts, screws, and other threaded products made in the United States and Canada. The fine thread series is distinguished from the coarse by the greater number of threads per inch

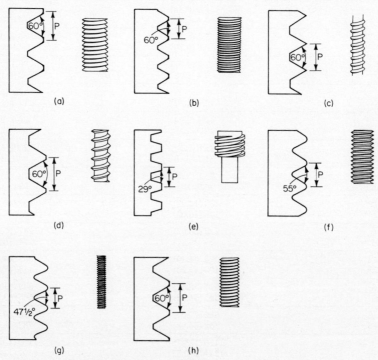

Fig. 2 Thread forms. (*a*) Unified coarse thread, UNC. (*b*) Unified fins thread, UNF. (*c*) American Standard Wood Screw. (*d*) American Standard Tapping Screw. (*e*) American Standard Acme. (*f*) British Standard Whitworth. (*g*) British Association Standard. (*h*) European Metric.

applied to a specific diameter. It is recommended for general use in automotive and aircraft work where wall thickness requires a fine thread.

American Standard Thread Form. Three forms are contained within this group:

1. *American Standard Wood Screw Thread.* Interchangeability of parts is not a prerequisite for wood screw thread forms since the threads cut into the workpiece and do not mate with tapped holes. The form illustrated in Fig. 2*c* is in accordance with American Standard B18.6.1-1961.

2. *American Standard Tapping Screw Thread.* Interchangeability is not a requirement for tapping screw thread forms. The form shown in Fig. 2*d* meets American Standard B18.6.4-1966.

3. *American Standard Acme Thread.* This thread form is used chiefly for producing traversing motions. American Standard B1.5-1952 standardized acme threads into two classes: (1) general purpose with clearance on all diameters for free movement and (2) centralizing threads, with more limited clearance at the major diameter between external and internal threads (Fig. 2*e*).

British Thread Form. Two forms are described:

1. *British Standard Whitworth Thread.* The crest and root of this thread form are rounded. The form is in general use in the United Kingdom. This thread form is also used in the British Standard Fine Screw Threads (BSF), British Standard Pipe Threads (BSP), and British Standard Conduit Threads (BSC) (see Fig. 2*f*).

2. *British Association Standard Thread.* This screw thread system (Fig. 2*g*) is recommended by the British Standards Institution for use in preference to the BSW and BSF systems for all screws smaller than ¼ in. (6.35 mm).

European Metric Thread Form. This thread form is similar to the Unified American Standard except the depth of the thread is greater. This system has been adopted by most European countries using the metric system, by Japan, and by the Soviet Union, either in whole or in part (Fig. 2*h*).

Mechanical Property Requirements   Minimum mechanical property requirements for a range of stainless steel fasteners are described in Table 2, based on Industrial Fasteners Institute Standard 104. The data, intended for use in industrial engineering applications, are based on tests of full-sized fasteners. Testing the fastener, rather than the material from which it is formed, gives the designer an advantage because higher strengths generally can be used in design considerations. Lack of this product information in the past often led to over-design.

INDUSTRIAL APPLICATIONS OF FASTENERS

Fasteners are ubiquitous. Because of their very broad use, only four major industries will be examined.

Chemical Process Industries   Since corrosion resistance is an important aspect of product reliability, the careful selection of fasteners is inherent in any attempt to achieve corrosion-resistant assemblies. An excellent and conservative practice in this industry is to use fasteners made of alloys that are actually more corrosion-resistant than the materials they hold together. This practice is often desirable because corrosion-weakened fasteners may lead to a more immediate failure, with more serious consequences, than the same amount of corrosive attack elsewhere in the assembly.

Fluid Flow. Pumps used in the chemical process industries embrace a large variety of types and sizes. Fastening requirements vary with the pump type. Bolts, nuts, studs, screws, and washers are used, for example, to connect the pump to its bearing frame, to attach piping to the pump, and to assemble the stuffing box. Here, the corrosive nature of the liquid being pumped, the atmosphere in which the pump is located, and the possibility of galvanic attack require care in the selection of a fastener material. Choices often made include 18-8, Type 410, and Carpenter 20. Pipe and fittings present similar problems of attachment and are fastened in much the same manner as pumps and valves. The fastener must resist the corrosive environment in which the equipment is located. Fasteners for valves should be fabricated from the same material as the valve or from a more noble metal. Examples of applications include assembling the yoke to the body, attaching valve bodies to bonnets, attaching handwheels, etc.

Size Reduction and Enlargement. While most crushing and grinding equipment is made of steel, special requirements, such as the size reduction of corrosive material may lead to the use of other metals. Generally, the fasteners used will be similar in composition to the parts being joined. But, at times, stainless steel bolting is used even with a carbon steel assembly, especially where the assembly must be taken apart periodically. Cutters, shredders, chippers, and dicers perform variations of crushing and grinding and are subject to the same problems and requirements.

Mixing and Blending. Typical examples of fastener use in this area include hex head bolts with nuts and lock washers for the paddle blades. Stainless steel is often specified because of its strength, hardness, and corrosion resistance.

Stainless steel fasteners are also used in areas such as fractionation, distillation, heat transfer, separation, and filtration. Equipment is subjected to a corrosive environment, requiring a careful selection of fasteners.

Maintenance. Maintenance is the key to efficient, uninterrupted production. The use of corrosion-resistant fasteners can delay maintenance needs and can speed up disassembly for inspection.

Marine Industry   Very often, the fastenings on ships and boats are used where the joints have to be taken apart and reassembled from time to time. This is when the corrosion resistance of the fastener assumes its greatest economic advantage. One factor that must always be kept in mind in dealing with various metal combinations in seawater is galvanic corrosion. As a general rule, the fastener alloy, if it is not the same as the material being joined, should be lower in the galvanic series (more noble) than the material being joined.

TABLE 2 Mechanical Requirements for Stainless Steel Fasteners

Grade*	General description of material	Full-size bolts, screws, studs		Machined test specimens of bolts, screws, studs				Nuts	
		Yield‡ strength, min., psi (MN/m²)	Tensile strength, min., psi (MN/m²)	Yield‡ strength, min., psi (MN/m²)	Tensile strength, min., psi (MN/m²)	Elongation, %, min.‡	Hardness Rockwell, min.	Proof load stress, psi (MN/m²)	Hardness Rockwell, min.
303-A	Austenitic stainless steel, solution annealed	30,000 (206.85)	75,000 (517.13)	30,000 (206.85)	75,000 (517.13)	20	B75	75,000 (517.13)	B75
304-A	Austenitic stainless steel, solution annealed	30,000 (206.85)	75,000 (517.13)	30,000 (206.85)	75,000 (517.13)	20	B75	75,000 (517.13)	B75
304	Austenitic stainless steel, cold-worked	50,000 (344.75)	90,000 (620.55)	45,000 (310.28)	85,000 (586.08)	20	B85	90,000 (620.55)	B85
304-SH	Austenitic stainless steel, strain hardened	See Note§	See Note§	See Note§	See Note§	15	C25	See Note§	C20
305-A	Austenitic stainless steel, solution annealed	30,000 (206.85)	75,000 (517.13)	30,000 (206.85)	75,000 (517.13)	20	B70	75,000 (517.13)	B70
305	Austenitic stainless steel, cold-worked	50,000 (344.75)	90,000 (620.55)	45,000 (310.28)	85,000 (586.08)	20	B85	90,000 (620.55)	B85
305-SH	Austenitic stainless steel, strain hardened	See Note§	See Note§	See Note§	See Note§	15	C25	See Note§	C20
316-A	Austenitic stainless steel, solution annealed	30,000 (206.85)	75,000 (517.13)	30,000 (206.85)	75,000 (517.13)	20	B70	75,000 (517.13)	B70

Designation	Description								
316	Austenitic stainless steel, cold-worked	50,000 (344.75)	90,000 (620.55)	45,000 (310.28)	85,000 (586.08)	20	B85	90,000 (620.55)	B85
316-SH	Austenitic stainless steel, strain hardened	See Note§	See Note§	See Note§	See Note§	15	C25	See Note§	C20
XM7-A	Austenitic stainless steel, solution annealed	30,000 (206.85)	75,000 (517.13)	30,000 (206.85)	75,000 (517.13)	20	B70	75,000 (517.13)	B70
XM7	Austenitic stainless steel, cold-worked	50,000 (344.75)	90,000 (620.55)	45,000 (310.28)	85,000 (586.08)	20	B85	90,000 (620.55)	B85
384-A	Austenitic stainless steel, solution annealed	30,000 (206.85)	75,000 (517.13)	30,000 (206.85)	75,000 (517.13)	20	B70	75,000 (517.13)	B70
384	Austenitic stainless steel, cold-worked	50,000 (344.75)	90,000 (620.55)	45,000 (310.28)	85,000 (586.08)	20	B85	90,000 (620.55)	B85
410-H	Martensitic stainless steel, hardened and tempered	95,000 (655.03)	125,000 (861.88)	95,000 (655.03)	125,000 (861.88)	20	C22	125,000 (861.88)	C22
410-HT	Martensitic stainless steel, hardened and tempered	135,000 (930.83)	180,000 (1241.10)	135,000 (930.83)	180,000 (1241.10)	12	C36	180,000 (1241.10)	C36
416-H	Martensitic stainless steel, hardened and tempered	95,000 (655.03)	125,000 (861.88)	95,000 (655.03)	125,000 (861.88)	20	C22	125,000 (861.88)	C22
416-HT	Martensitic stainless steel, hardened and tempered	135,000 (930.83)	180,000 (1241.10)	135,000 (930.83)	180,000 (1241.10)	12	C36	180,000 (1241.10)	C36

TABLE 2 Mechanical Requirements for Stainless Steel Fasteners (Continued)

| 430 | Ferritic stainless steel | 40,000 (275.80) | 70,000 (482.65) | 40,000 (275.80) | 70,000 (482.65) | 20 | 70,000 (482.65) | B75 | 70,000 (482.65) | B75 |

*Grade designations: A, solution annealed; SH, strain hardened; H, hardened and tempered at 1100°F (593°C) min.; HT, hardened and tempered at 525°F ± 50°F (274°C ± 28°C); HF, hot-forged.
†At 0.2% offset.
‡In 2 in. (50.8 mm) or 4 diameters.
§Strain-hardened austenitic stainless steel bolts, screws, studs, and nuts shall have the following mechanical properties:

| | Bolts, screws, studs | | | | Nuts |
| | Tested full size | | Machined test specimens | | |
Product size, in. (mm)	Yield strength, min., psi (MN/m²)	Tensile strength, min, psi (MN/m²)	Yield strength, min., psi (MN/m²)	Tensile strength, min, psi (MN/m²)	Proof load stress, psi (MN/m²)
To ⅝ (15.88)	100,000 (689.5)	125,000 (861.85)	90,000 (620.55)	115,000 (792.93)	125,000 (861.88)
Over ⅝ to 1 (15.88–25.4)	70,000 (482.65)	105,000 (723.98)	65,000 (448.18)	100,000 (689.5)	105,000 (723.98)
Over 1 to 1½ (25.4–38.1)	50,000 (344.75)	90,000 (620.55)	45,000 (310.28)	85,000 (586.08)	90,000 (620.55)

Pulp and Paper Industry This industry experiences severe corrosion problems because of the nature of its operations.

Barking. Hydraulic barking focuses high-pressure jet streams of water on the logs, encouraging steady corrosion of all components. Mechanical barking places high stress on critical areas and involves continuous maintenance and replacement. 18-8 or Type 316 fasteners are recommended.

Pulping. There are several approaches to pulping:

1. *Mechanical.* Logs are ground against a revolving abrasive stone. 18-8 fasteners are recommended.

2. *Sulfite.* All of the sulfite processes are highly corrosive. Recommended stainless fastenings are Types 316, 309, and Hastelloy C. These alloys are especially valuable for target plates in the blow pit and for all digester fittings.

For magnesia-based pulping, Type 316 and Hastelloy C are recommended.

3. *Semichemical.* The neutral sulfite, semichemical pulping employs a dilute acid solution in which Type 309 fasteners offer superior performance. Type 316 is also recommended.

4. *Alkaline.* Soda pulping and kraft or sulfate pulping are both alkaline processes. Fasteners associated with the digester dump valve and digester body should be of Type 316 or 18-8.

Digesters, Diffusers, Vacuum Washers, Bleach Liquor Evaporators, and Pulp Screens. The same type of stainless steel fastener recommended for the digester, 18-8 or Type 316, should also be used for the blow tanks, diffusers, brown stock washers, knotter screens, and fire screens. Nearby fasteners, such as motor mountings, are also subject to corrosion if not made of stainless steel.

Pulp Bleaching. When sodium chlorite or sodium peroxide are used in the bleaching process, Type 316 fasteners should be specified. That alloy is also recommended when hydrogen peroxide, zinc hydrosulfite, and calcium hypochlorite are used in the bleaching process.

Stock Preparation. Types 316 and 18-8 have proved to be superior fastener alloys. Stock chest fittings, agitators, beater bars, and pipe connections should also be fastened with these alloys.

Fourdrinier and Cylinder Paper Machines. Austenitic stainless steels and Monel are now used extensively for shower pipes, midfeathers, slices, aprons, headbox linings, save-all trays, and doctor blades. Fasteners of similar metal should be used for all these applications.

Pollution Control Industry Both water and air pollution control are receiving greater attention. Each area encounters problems that require the use of stainless steel fasteners.

Water Pollution. Components of water pollution control systems include:

1. *Filters.* Normally constructed of carbon steel, but stainless steel is being specified more frequently to reduce maintenance problems. Type 316 is the suggested fastener alloy. When carbon steel components require frequent disassembly, 18-8 is suggested.

2. *Adsorption Columns.* Type 18-8 fasteners are a good choice if the columns are specified in stainless steel, or to attach parts that require maintenance.

3. *Activated Sludge and Aerators.* Stainless steel fasteners, generally 18-8 or Type 316, are used to connect the aeration blades to the main driving hood. Bolts, nuts, and washers are used. Stainless steel locknuts are sometimes specified to prevent loosening due to vibration.

4. *Thermal Cooling Units.* Cooling towers are usually constructed either of pre-stressed concrete slabs or redwood sections. In the former, 18-8 or silicon bronze U bolts and nuts are used to support the pipes. In the redwood towers, each section is bolted together, most commonly with either Type 304 or naval bronze fasteners.

Air Pollution. In equipment such as dust collectors, fabric filters, and electrostatic precipitators, 18-8 is a preferred fastening material. More severe corrosion or oxidation conditions are encountered in wet scrubbers, afterburners, and adsorbers. The wet scrubbers can use Type 18-8 fasteners, but Type 316 or Carpenter 20 should be specified under extreme conditions of corrosion. Afterburners, operating at temperatures from 800 to 1600°F (426 to 871°C), require Types 309, 310, or 321 fasteners.

Appendixes

Appendixes

Specifications of the Stainless Steel Producing Countries

DONALD PECKNER
Consultant, Santa Monica, California

I. M. BERNSTEIN
Professor of Metallurgy and Materials Science, Carnegie-Mellon University, Pittsburgh, Pennsylvania

The material which follows this short introduction represents composition data obtained from the specifications of the various countries that produce stainless steel. Most of the data refer to wrought steels. When cast steels are described, that is indicated in the title of the table. In addition to the chemical compositions described in this Appendix, the reader is referred to Table 1, Chapter 1, which compares AISI grades with their approximate equivalents produced by other nations; and to two tables in Chapter 2: Table 7, which compares the equivalent specifications for corrosion-resistant cast steels; and Table 8, which makes the comparison for heat-resistant cast steels.

The tables which follow only note chemical composition. Details on mechanical properties, permissible length, width, and thickness variations, etc., the usual structure of a specification, can be obtained by consulting the actual specifications noted on each of the tables. Sources of the specifications are as follows:

CZECHOSLOVAKIA: FERROMET Foreign Trade Corp., P. O. Box 779, Prague 1

EUROPEAN ECONOMIC COMMUNITY: Commission des Communautes Europeennes, Rue de la Loi 200, B-1040 Brussels, Belgium

FRANCE: Chambre Syndicale des Producteurs D'Aciers Fins et Spéciaux, 12, rue de Madrid, Paris (VIIIe)

GERMANY, EAST: Council for Standardization, Berlin, DDR

GERMANY, WEST: Verein Deutscher Eisenhüttenleute, Breite Strasse 27, 4000 Düsseldorf 1

GREAT BRITAIN: British Standards Institution, British Standards House, 2 Park Street, London W1Y 4AA

HUNGARY: METALIMPEX, P. O. Box 330, Budapest 62

INDIA: Indian Standards Institution, 9 Bahadur Shah Zafar Marg, New Delhi 110001

ITALY: Centro Inox, piazza Velasca, 10, 20122 Milan
JAPAN: Japanese Standards Association, 1-24, Akasaka 4, Minate-ku, Tokyo 107
POLAND: Polski Komitet Normalizacji i Miar, ul. Elektoralna 2, 00-139 Warsaw
ROMANIA: METALIMPORTEXPORT, 8 Edgar Quinet Street, Bucharest
SOVIET UNION: GOSSTANDART USSR, Department for Foreign Relations, Leninskiy Prospekt 96, Moscow M-49
SPAIN: CENIM, Ciudad Universitaria, Madrid 3
SWEDEN: Sveriges Standardiseringskommission, Box 3295, 103 66 Stockholm 3
UNITED STATES: American Iron and Steel Institute, 1000 16th Street N.W., Washington, D.C. 20036

EDITOR'S NOTE: The newly revised Austrian specification, "Steel Plates for Boilers and Pressure Vessels," issued 1 August 1976, was received too late to be included in the tables which follow. The specification, ÖNORM M3121, includes nineteen stainless steels within its ambit. Copies can be obtained from Österreichisches Normungsinstitut, Leopoldsgasse 4, A-1021 Vienna 2, Austria.

CZECHOSLOVAKIA Stainless and Heat-resisting Steels
Specification: Ceskoslovenska Statni Norma (CSN4)

Standard number	Composition, %								
	C, max.	Mn, max.	P, max.	S, max.	Si, max.	Cr	Ni	Mo	Other elements
17020	0.08	0.90	0.040	0.035	0.70	12.0–14.0			
17021	0.15	0.90	0.040	0.035	0.70	12.0–14.0			
17022	0.16–0.25	0.90	0.040	0.035	0.70	12.0–14.0			
17023	0.26–0.35	0.90	0.040	0.035	0.70	12.0–14.0			
17024	0.36–0.45	0.90	0.040	0.035	0.70	12.0–14.0			
17027	0.15–0.25	0.90	0.040	0.035	0.70	14.0–16.0			
17029	0.40–0.50	0.90	0.040	0.035	0.70	14.0–16.0			
17040	0.10	0.90	0.040	0.035	0.70	16.0–18.5	0.60 max.		Ti ≤ 0.30
17041	0.15	0.90	0.040	0.035	0.70	16.0–18.5	0.60 max.		Ti ≤ 0.30
17042	0.90–1.05	0.90	0.040	0.035	0.70	16.0–18.0			
17047	0.15	0.80	0.045	0.035	0.80	20.0–23.0	0.60 max.		Ti ≤ 0.70
17061	0.18	0.80	0.045	0.035	0.80	23.0–26.0	0.60 max.		Ti ≤ 0.70
17062	0.16	0.60	0.040	0.035	0.50	23.0–26.0	0.60 max.		
17113	0.15	0.60	0.040	0.035	0.80–1.30	6.0–7.5			Al 0.40–1.00
17115	0.40–0.50	0.60	0.040	0.035	2.80–3.50	7.50–9.50			
17125	0.15	0.80	0.040	0.035	1.00–2.00	12.0–14.5			Al 0.60–1.20
17132	0.18–0.26	0.50–1.20	0.040	0.030	0.50	10.5–12.5	0.40 max.		V 0.20–0.60
17134	0.17–0.23	0.50–1.00	0.035	0.030	0.25–0.60	10.6–12.5	0.30–0.80	0.8–1.2	W 0.30–0.60 V 0.20–0.35
17153	0.20	1.00	0.045	0.040	1.30	23.0–27.0	2.0 max.		
17225	0.12	2.00	0.040	0.035	1.00	13.0–15.0	10.0–12.0		
17240*	0.08					18.5	10.0		

CZECHOSLOVAKIA Stainless and Heat-resisting Steels *(Continued)*
Specification: Ceskoslovenska Statni Norma (CSN4)

Standard number	Composition, %								
	C, max.	Mn, max.	P, max.	S, max.	Si, max.	Cr	Ni	Mo	Other elements
17241	0.12	2.00	0.045	0.030	1.00	17.0–20.0	8.0–11.0		
17242	0.25	2.00	0.045	0.030	1.00	17.0–20.0	8.0–11.0		
17246	0.12	2.00	0.045	0.030	1.00	17.0–20.0	8.0–11.0		Ti $\geqslant 5 \times$ (C − 0.03)
17248*	0.10					18.0	10.5		
17249*	0.03					18.5	11.0		Ti $\geqslant 5 \times$ C
17251	0.20	1.50	0.035	0.035	2.00	18.0–21.0	8.0–11.0		
17252	0.12	1.50	0.045	0.035	1.50	19.0–22.0	36.0–40.0	4.50–6.50	$4 \times$ C $\leqslant$ Ti $\leqslant 1.00$
17253	0.25	1.50	0.035	0.035	1.50	19.0–22.0	36.0–40.0		
17254	0.12	0.40–1.20	0.050	0.035	0.80	19.5–22.0	4.50–5.80		Ti 0.30–0.60
17255	0.25	1.50	0.045	0.030	2.00	23.0–27.0	18.0–22.0		
17331	0.07–0.15	0.40–1.00	0.045	0.030	0.20–0.80	12.0–15.0	11.0–14.0	0.70–1.50	W 1.00–2.00 V 0.30–0.80 Ti $\leqslant 1.00$

17335	0.12	1.00–2.00	0.045	0.030	0.80	13.5–16.5	34.0–38.0	1.50–2.50	W 2.70–3.70 Ti 1.20–1.90
17345	0.15	2.00	0.045	0.030	1.50	16.00–19.0	9.00–12.0	1.50–2.50	
17346*	0.08					17.5	12.5	2.25	
17347	0.12	2.00	0.045	0.030	1.50	16.0–19.0	9.00–12.0	1.50–2.50	Ti $\geq$ 5 × (C − 0.03)
17348*	0.10					17.5	12.5	2.25	Ti $\geq$ 5 × (C − 0.03)
17349*	0.03					17.5	12.5	2.25	
17350*	0.03					17.5	13.5	2.75	
17351	0.08	0.30–0.80	0.045	0.035	0.90	15.5–17.0	5.50–7.00		Al $\leq$ 1.00 Ti 0.50–1.00
17352*	0.08					17.5	12.5	2.75	
17353*	0.10					17.5	13.5	2.75	Ti $\geq$ 5 × (C − 0.03)
17356*	0.08					17	14.5	3.5	Ti $\geq$ 5 × (C − 0.03)
17460	0.12	7.00–10.0	0.060	0.035	0.90	17.0–20.0	4.00–6.00		N 0.10–0.25
17471	0.05–0.12	14.0–17.0	0.045	0.035	0.60–1.50	16.0–19.0	1.20–2.00		N 0.32–0.42

*Denotes average composition.

EASTERN EUROPEAN ECONOMIC COMMUNITY Stainless and Heat-resisting Steels
Specification: COMECON PC4-70

Type	C, max.	Mn, max.	P, max.	S, max.	Si, max.	Composition, % Cr	Ni	Mo	Other elements
1	0.08	0.80	0.035	0.025	0.80	12.00–14.00			
2	0.08	1.00	0.035	0.025	1.00	11.50–14.00			Se 0.10–0.30
3	0.09–0.15	1.00	0.035	0.025	1.00	12.00–14.00			
4	0.15–0.25	0.80	0.035	0.025	0.80	12.00–14.00			
5	0.26–0.35	0.80	0.035	0.025	0.80	12.00–14.00			
6	0.36–0.45	0.80	0.035	0.025	0.80	12.00–14.00			
7	0.12	0.80	0.035	0.025	0.80	16.00–18.00			
8	0.10	0.80	0.035	0.025	0.80	16.00–18.00			$5 \times C \leqslant Ti \leqslant 0.80$
9	0.11–0.17	0.80	0.035	0.025	0.80	16.00–18.00	1.50–2.50		
10	0.17–0.25	0.80	0.035	0.025	0.80	16.00–18.00	1.50–2.50		
11	0.90–1.05	0.80	0.035	0.025	0.80	17.00–19.00			
12	0.15–0.30	8.00–10.00	0.050	0.025	0.80	12.00–14.00	3.70–4.70		
13	0.12	8.00–10.50	0.050	0.025	0.80	16.00–18.00	3.50–4.50		N 0.15–0.25
14	0.12	2.00	0.035	0.025	0.80	17.00–19.00	8.00–10.00		
15	0.08	2.00	0.035	0.025	0.80	17.00–19.00	9.00–11.00		
16	0.03	2.00	0.035	0.025	0.80	17.00–19.00	10.00–12.50		
17	0.12	2.00	0.035	0.025	0.80	17.00–19.00	8.00–10.00		$5 \times C \leqslant Ti \leqslant 0.80$

18	0.08	2.00	0.035	0.025	0.80	17.00–19.00	9.00–11.00		$5 \times C \leq Ti \leq 0.70$
19	0.12	2.00	0.035	0.025	0.80	17.00–19.00	11.00–13.00		$5 \times C \leq Ti \leq 0.80$
20	0.08	2.00	0.035	0.025	0.80	17.00–19.00	10.00–13.00		$10 \times C \leq Nb \leq 1.1$
21	0.08	2.00	0.035	0.025	0.80	16.00–18.00	11.00–14.00	2.00–2.50	$5 \times C \leq Ti \leq 0.17$
22	0.03	2.00	0.035	0.020	0.80	16.00–18.00	12.00–15.00	2.00–2.50	
23	0.08	2.00	0.035	0.025	0.80	16.00–18.00	14.00–16.00	3.00–4.00	Ti 0.30–0.60
24	0.07	2.00	0.035	0.020	1.00	16.50–18.50	19.00–21.00	2.00–2.50	Cu 1.80–2.20 $7 \times C \leq Ti \leq 0.70$
25	0.06	2.00	0.035	0.020	0.80	22.00–25.00	26.00–29.00	2.50–3.00	Cu 2.50–3.50 Ti 0.50–0.90
26	0.35–0.45	2.00–3.00	0.035	0.025	0.80	8.00–10.00			
27	0.35–0.45	1.90–2.60	0.035	0.025	0.80	9.00–10.50		0.70–0.90	
28	0.12	1.00–1.80	0.035	0.025	0.80	12.00–14.00			Se 0.80–1.80
29	0.15	0.80–1.50	0.035	0.025	0.80	17.00–20.00			Se 0.70–1.20
30	0.15	1.00	0.035	0.025	0.80	24.00–27.00			$5 \times C \leq Ti \leq 0.90$
31	0.10–0.20	2.00	0.035	0.025	0.80–2.00	17.00–20.00	8.00–11.00		
32	0.20	1.50	0.035	0.025	2.00–3.00	19.00–22.00	12.00–15.00		
33	0.20	1.50	0.035	0.025	1.00	22.00–25.00	17.00–20.00		
34	0.20	1.50	0.035	0.025	2.00–3.00	24.00–27.00	18.00–21.00		

EUROPEAN ECONOMIC COMMUNITY **Stainless Steels**
Specification: Euronorm 88-71

Short designation	C, max.	Mn, max.	P, max.	S, max.	Si, max.	Cr	Ni	Mo	Other elements
						Composition, %*			
FERRITIC STEELS									
X6Cr13	0.08	1.0			1.0	11.5–14.0	≤ 0.50		
X6CrAl13	0.08	1.0			1.0	11.5–14.0	≤ 0.50		Al 0.10–0.30
X8Cr17	0.10	1.0			1.0	16.0–18.0	≤ 0.50		
X8CrTi17	0.10	1.0			1.0	16.0–18.0	≤ 0.50		Ti ≥ 7 × C ≤ 1.0
X10CrS17	0.12	1.5			1.0	16.0–18.0	≤ 0.50	≤ 0.60†	P ≤ 0.060 S 0.15–0.35
X8CrMo17	0.10	1.0			1.0	16.0–18.0	≤0.50	0.90–1.30	
MARTENSITIC STEELS‡ (INCLUDING CUTLERY STEELS)									
X12Cr13	0.09–0.15	1.0			1.0	11.5–14.0	≤ 1.00		
X12CrS13	0.08–0.15	1.5			1.0	12.0–14.0	≤ 1.0	≤ 0.60†	P ≤ 0.060 S 0.15–0.35
X20Cr13	0.16–0.25	1.0			1.0	12.0–14.0	≤ 1.0		
X30Cr13	0.26–0.35	1.0			1.0	12.0–14.0	≤ 1.0		
X40Cr13	0.36–0.45	1.0			1.0	12.5–14.5	≤ 1.0		
X45Cr13	0.42–0.50	1.0			1.0	12.5–14.5	≤ 1.0		
X14CrS17	0.10–0.17	1.5			1.0	16.0–18.0	≤ 0.50	≤ 0.60†	P ≤ 0.060 S 0.15–0.35
X21CrNi17	0.17–0.25	1.0			1.0	16.0–18.0	1.5–2.5		
X105CrMo17	0.95–1.20	1.0			1.0	16.0–18.0	≤ 0.75	0.35–0.75	

Austenitic Steels	C			Cr	Ni	Mo	Others
X3CrNi1810	0.030	2.0	1.0	17.0–19.0	9.0–12.0§		
X6CrNi1810	0.07	2.0	1.0	17.0–19.0	8.0–11.0§		
X10CrNi18 9	0.12	2.0	1.0	17.0–19.0	8.0–10.0		
X10CrNiS18 9	0.12	2.0	1.0	17.0–19.0	8.0–11.0	≤ 0.60†	$P \leq 0.20$ $S\ 0.15{-}0.35$
X8CrNi1812	0.10	2.0	1.0	17.0–19.0	11.0–13.0		
X12CrNi17 7	0.15	2.0	1.0	16.0–18.0	6.0–8.0		
X6CrNiTi1810	0.08	2.0	1.0	17.0–19.0	9.0–12.0		$Ti \geq 5 \times C \leq 0.80$
X6CrNiNb1810	0.08	2.0	1.0	17.0–19.0	9.0–12.0		$Nb + Ta \geq 10 \times C \leq 1.0$¶
X3CrNiMo17 12 2	0.030	2.0	1.0	16.0–18.5	11.0–14.0	2.0–2.5	
X6CrNiMo17 12 2	0.08	2.0	1.0	16.0–18.5	10.5–13.5	2.0–2.5	
X6CrNiMoTi17 12 2	0.08	2.0	1.0	16.0–18.5	10.5–13.5	2.0–2.5	$Ti > 5 \times C \leq 0.80$
X6CrNiMoNb17 12 2	0.08	2.0	1.0	16.0–18.5	10.5–13.5	2.0–2.5	$Nb + Ta \geq 10 \times C \leq 1.0$
X3CrNiMo17 13 3	0.030	2.0	1.0	16.0–18.5	11.5–14.5	2.5–3.0	
X6CrNiMo17 13 3	0.08	2.0	1.0	16.0–18.5	11.5–14.0	2.5–3.0	
X6CrNiMoTi17 13 3	0.08	2.0	1.0	16.0–18.5	11.5–14.5	2.5–3.0	$Ti \geq 5 \times C \leq 0.80$
X6CrNiMoNb17 13 3	0.08	2.0	1.0	16.0–18.5	11.5–14.5	2.5–3.0	$Nb + T \geq 10 \times C \leq 1.0$¶
X3CrNiMo18 16 4	0.030	2.0	1.0	17.5–19.5	14.0–17.0	3.0–4.0	

*Unless otherwise indicated, P ≤ 0.040 for the ferritic and martensitic steels. P ≤ 0.045 for the austenitic steels. S ≤ 0.030.
†At the choice of the producer.
‡The structure is preponderantly martensitic.
§In seamless tubes, the maximum nickel content may be increased by 1%.
¶Tantalum and niobium are reported together as niobium content.

FRANCE Stainless and Heat-resisting Steels
Specifications: AFNOR NFA 35-572, 35-578, 35-580, 36-209, 35-576

AFNOR	Composition, %								
	C, max.	Si, max.	Mn, max.	P, max.	S, max.	Cr	Ni	Mo	Other elements
Z2CN18-10	0.03	1.00	2.00	0.040	0.030	17.00–19.00	9.00–11.00		
Z2CND17-12	0.03	1.00	2.00	0.040	0.030	16.00–18.00	11.00–13.00	2.00–2.50	
Z2CND17-13	0.03	1.00	2.00	0.040	0.030	16.00–18.00	12.00–14.00	2.50–3.00	
Z2CND19-15	0.03	1.00	2.00	0.040	0.030	18.00–20.00	14.00–16.00	3.00–4.00	
Z5CMDU21-08	0.06	1.00	1.00	0.040	0.030	20.00–22.00	7.00–9.00	2.20–2.80	Cu 1.00–2.00
Z6C13	0.08	1.00	1.00	0.040	0.030	11.50–13.50	$\leqslant 0.50$		
Z6CA13	0.08	1.00	1.00	0.040	0.030	11.50–13.50	$\leqslant 0.50$		Al 0.10–0.30
Z6CN18-09	0.07	1.00	2.00	0.040	0.030	17.00–19.00	8.00–10.00		
Z6CND17-11	0.07	1.00	2.00	0.040	0.030	16.00–18.00	10.00–12.00	2.00–2.50	
Z6CND17-12	0.07	1.00	2.00	0.040	0.030	16.00–18.00	11.00–13.00	2.50–3.00	
Z6CND17-12B*	0.08	1.00	2.00	0.040	0.030	16.00–18.00	11.00–13.00	2.00–2.50	
Z6CNDNb17-12	0.08	1.00	2.00	0.040	0.030	16.00–18.00	11.00–13.00	2.00–2.50	$Nb + Ta \geqslant 10 \times C \leqslant 1.00$
Z6CNDNb17-13	0.08	1.00	2.00	0.040	0.030	16.00–18.00	12.00–14.00	2.50–3.00	$Nb + Ta \geqslant 10 \times C \leqslant 1.00$
Z6CNDNb17-13B*	0.04–0.08	1.00	2.00	0.040	0.030	16.00–18.00	12.00–14.00	2.00–2.50	$Nb + Ta \geqslant 8 \times C \leqslant 1.00$
Z6CNNb18-11	0.08	1.00	2.00	0.040	0.030	17.00–19.00	10.00–12.00		$(Nb + Ta) \geqslant 10 \times C \leqslant 1.00$
Z6CNNb18-12B*	0.08	1.00	2.00	0.040	0.030	17.00–19.00	11.00–13.00		$Nb\ 8 \times C \leqslant 1.00$
Z6CNT18-11	0.08	1.00	2.00	0.040	0.030	17.00–19.00	10.00–12.00		$Ti \geqslant 5 \times C \leqslant 0.60$
Z6CNT18-12B*	0.08	1.00	2.00	0.040	0.030	17.00–19.00	11.00–13.00		$Ti\ 4 \times C \leqslant 0.60$
Z6CNU17-04	0.07	1.00	1.00	0.040	0.030	15.50–17.50	3.00–5.00	1.00–1.60	Cu 2.50–4.50
Z6CNUD15-04	0.07	1.00	1.00	0.040	0.030	13.50–15.50	3.00–5.00	1.00–1.60	Cu 2.50–4.50
Z6NCTDV25-15B*	0.03–0.08	1.00	2.00	0.030	0.030	13.50–16.00	24.00–27.00	1.00–1.50	V 0.1–0.5 $Al \leqslant 0.4$ Ti 1.7–2.3

Grade	C	Si	Mn	P	S	Cr	Ni	Mo	Other
Z8C17	0.10	1.00	1.00	0.040	0.030	16.00–18.00	≤ 0.50		
Z8CA7	0.10	0.50–1.00	1.00	0.040	0.030	6.00–8.00			Al 0.50–1.00
Z8CD17-01	0.10	1.00	1.00	0.040	0.030	16.00–18.00	≤ 0.50	0.90–1.30	
Z8CN13-13	0.10	1.00	2.00	0.040	0.030	12.00–14.00	12.00–14.00		Cu ≤ 2.00
Z8CN18-12	0.10	1.00	2.00	0.040	0.030	17.00–19.00	11.00–13.00		
Z8CN20-11	0.10	1.00	2.00	0.040	0.030	19.00–21.00	10.00–12.00		
Z8CNDT17-12	0.10	1.00	2.00	0.040	0.030	16.00–18.00	11.00–13.00	2.00–2.50	Ti ⩾ 5 × C ⩽ 0.60
Z8CNDT17-13	0.10	1.00	2.00	0.040	0.030	16.00–18.00	12.00–14.00	2.50–3.00	Ti ⩾ 5 × C ⩽ 0.60
Z8CNDT17-13B*	0.05–0.10	1.00	2.00	0.040	0.030	16.00–18.00	12.00–14.00	2.00–2.50	Ti ⩾ 4 × C ⩽ 0.70
Z8NC32-21	0.10	1.00	1.50	0.040	0.030	19.00–23.00	31.00–34.00		Al 0.15–0.60 / Ti 0.15–0.60
Z10C13	0.12	1.00	1.00	0.040	0.030	12.00–14.00			
Z10C24	0.12	1.50	1.00	0.040	0.030	23.00–26.00			
Z10CAS18	0.12	0.50–1.50	1.00	0.040	0.030	17.00–19.00			Al 0.70–1.20
Z10CAS24	0.12	0.50–1.50	1.00	0.040	0.030	23.00–26.00			Al 1.20–1.70
Z10CF17	0.12	1.00	1.50	0.060	0.150	16.00–18.00	≤ 0.50	(⩽ 0.60)	
Z10CN18-09	0.12	1.00	2.00	0.040	0.030	17.00–19.00	8.00–10.00		
Z10CN25-13	0.08	0.60	2.00	0.040	0.030	22.00–24.00	12.00–14.00		
Z10CNF18-09	0.12	1.00	2.00	0.060	0.150	17.00–19.00	8.00–10.00	(0.60)	
Z10CNT18-11	0.12	1.00	2.00	0.040	0.030	17.00–19.00	10.00–12.00		Ti ⩾ 5 × C ⩽ 0.80
Z10CNWT17-13B*	0.07–0.12	1.00	1.00	0.040	0.030	16.00–18.00	12.00–14.00		W 2.50–4.00 / Ti 4 × C ⩽ 0.80
Z12C13	0.08–0.15	1.00	1.00	0.040	0.030	11.50–13.50	≤ 0.50		
Z12CF13	0.15	1.00	1.50	0.060	0.150	12.00–14.00	≤ 0.50	(⩽ 0.60)	

FRANCE Stainless and Heat-resisting Steels (Continued)
Specifications: AFNOR NFA 35-572, 35-578, 35-580, 36-209, 35-576

AFNOR	C, max.	Si, max.	Mn, max.	P, max.	S, max.	Cr	Ni	Mo	Other elements
Z12CN17-08	0.08–0.15	1.00	2.00	0.040	0.030	16.00–18.00	6.50–8.50		
Z12CN25-20	0.15	1.00	2.00	0.040	0.030	23.00–26.00	18.00–21.00		
Z12CNS25-20	0.15	1.50–2.50	2.00	0.040	0.030	23.00–26.00	18.00–21.00		
Z12NC37-18	0.15	1.00	2.00	0.040	0.030	16.00–19.00	36.00–39.00		
Z12NCS35-16	0.15	1.00–2.00	2.00	0.040	0.030	14.00–17.00	33.00–36.00		
Z12NCS37-18	0.15	1.50–2.50	2.00	0.040	0.030	16.00–19.00	36.00–39.00		
Z15CN20-12	0.20	1.20	2.00	0.040	0.030	19.00–21.00	11.00–13.00		
Z15CN24-13	0.20	1.00	2.00	0.040	0.030	22.50–25.00	11.00–14.00		
Z15CNS20-12	0.20	1.50–2.50	2.00	0.040	0.030	19.00–21.00	11.00–13.00		
Z20C13	0.15–0.24	1.00	1.00	0.040	0.030	12.00–14.00	⩽ 1.00		
Z20CNS25-04	0.15–0.25	0.80–1.50	2.00	0.040	0.030	24.00–27.00	3.00–3.50		
Z30C13	0.25–0.34	1.00	1.00	0.040	0.030	12.00–14.00	⩽ 1.00		
Z40C14	0.35–0.45	1.00	1.00	0.040	0.030	12.50–14.50	⩽ 1.00		
Z100CD17	0.90–1.20	1.00	1.00	0.040	0.030	16.00–18.00	⩽ 0.50	0.35–0.75	

*B 0.0010–0.0060%.

GERMANY, EAST Stainless and Heat-resisting Steels
Specifications: TGL 7143-63, 7061-63

Type	Number	C, max.	Si, max.	Mn, max.	P, max.	S, max.	Cr	Ni	Mo	Ti	Other elements
							Composition, %				
X3CrNi 18.10	6970	0.04	0.80	1.00–2.00	0.040	0.030	17.0–19.0	9.00–11.0			Cu ≤ 0.30
X5CrNi 18.10	6950	0.07	0.80	1.00–2.00	0.040	0.030	17.0–19.0	9.00–11.0			Cu ≤ 0.30
X5CrNiMo 18.11	8870	0.07	0.80	2.00	0.040	0.030	16.5–18.5	10.5–12.5	2.00–2.50		Cu ≤ 0.30
X7Cr14	4680	0.08	0.60	0.60	0.040	0.030	13.0–15.0				Cu ≤ 0.30
X8Cr17	4620	0.10	0.80	1.00	0.040	0.030	16.0–18.0				Cu ≤ 0.30
X8CrMoTi 17	8860	0.10	0.80	1.00	0.040	0.030	16.0–18.0		1.50–2.50	7 × C – 0.9	Cu ≤ 0.30
X8CrNi 12.12	6960	0.10	0.80	1.00–2.00	0.040	0.030	11.5–13.5	12.0–14.0			Cu ≤ 0.30
X8CrNiMoTi 18.11	9800	0.10	0.80	1.00–2.00	0.040	0.030	16.5–18.5	10.5–12.5	2.00–2.50	5 × C – 0.7	Cu ≤ 0.30
X8CrNiTi 18.10	8940	0.10	0.80	1.00–2.00	0.040	0.030	17.0–19.0	9.00–11.0		5 × C – 0.7	Cu ≤ 0.30
X8CrTi 17	7790	0.10	0.80	1.00	0.040	0.030	16.0–18.0			7 × C – 0.9	Cu ≤ 0.30
X10Cr13	4640	0.09–0.15	0.60	0.60	0.040	0.030	12.0–14.0	≤ 0.60			Cu ≤ 0.30
X10CrMnNiN 17.9.4	9840	0.12	0.80	8.00–10.5	0.050	0.030	16.0–18.0	3.50–4.50			N ≤ 0.25 Cu ≤ 0.30
X10CrNi 18.9	6940	0.12	0.80	1.00–2.00	0.040	0.030	17.0–19.0	8.00–10.0			Cu ≤ 0.30
X12CrMoS 17	7090	0.10–0.17	1.00	1.00	0.040	0.250	15.5–18.0		0.20–0.30		Cu ≤ 0.30
X12CrNi 17.7	6980	0.15	0.80	1.00–2.00	0.040	0.030	16.0–18.0	7.00–8.00			Cu ≤ 0.30
X12MnCr 18.12	6340	0.15	0.80	17.0–19.0	0.080	0.030	11.0–13.0	1.50–2.50	0.30–0.80		Cu ≤ 0.30
X20Cr 13	4650	0.16–0.24	0.60	0.60	0.040	0.030	12.0–14.0	≤ 0.50			Cu ≤ 0.30
X20CrMo 13	7070	0.16–0.24	0.60	0.60	0.040	0.030	12.0–14.0	≤ 1.00	1.00–1.30		Cu ≤ 0.30
X22CrNi 17	6950	0.15–0.25	0.80	0.80	0.040	0.030	16.0–18.0	1.00–2.50			Cu ≤ 0.30
X35CrMo 17	7080	0.30–0.40	0.80	0.80	0.040	0.030	15.5–18.0	≤ 1.00	1.00–1.30		Cu ≤ 0.30
X40Cr 13	4670	0.35–0.44	0.60	0.60	0.040	0.030	12.0–14.0	≤ 0.50			Cu ≤ 0.30

GERMANY, EAST Stainless and Heat-resisting Steels (Continued)
Specifications: TGL 7143-63, 7061-63

Type	Number	C, max.	Si, max.	Mn, max.	P, max.	S, max.	Composition, % Cr	Ni	Mo	Ti	Other elements
X90CrMoV 18	9260	0.85–0.95	0.80	0.80	0.040	0.030	17.0–19.0	≤ 0.50	1.00–1.30		V 0.07–0.12
X8CrNiTi 18.10	8940	0.10	0.80	1.00–2.00	0.040	0.030	17.0–19.0	9.00–11.0		5 × C − 0.7	Cu ≤ 0.30
X10CrAl 7	6450	0.12	1.20–1.80	0.50	0.040	0.030	5.50–7.00				Al 0.70–1.10
X10CrAl 13	6460	0.12	1.20–1.80	0.50	0.040	0.030	12.0–14.0				Al 1.00–1.80
X10CrAl 18	6470	0.12	1.20–1.80	0.50	0.040	0.030	17.0–20.0				Al 0.70–1.20
X10CrAl 24	6480	0.12	1.20–1.80	0.50	0.040	0.030	23.0–25.00				Al 1.20–1.70
X12NiCrSi 36.16	8150	0.15	1.50–2.00	2.00	0.040	0.030	15.0–17.0	34.0–37.0			
X15CrNiSi 20.13	8120	0.20	2.00–2.50	1.50	0.040	0.030	19.0–22.0	12.0–14.0			
X15CrNiSi 25.20	8130	0.20	2.00–2.50	1.30	0.040	0.030	24.0–26.0	19.0–21.0			
X20CrNiSi 25.4	8140	0.15–0.25	0.80–1.30	2.00	0.040	0.030	24.0–26.0	3.50–4.50			

GERMANY, WEST   Stainless and Heat-resisting Steels
Specifications: DIN 17440(1967), VDEH Werkstoffblatt 470-60 and 490-52; DIN 17224, DIN 17225, Stahleisenliste

Werkstoff number	Type	Composition, %								
		C, max.	Mn, max.	P, max.	S, max.	Si, max.	Cr	Ni	Mo	Other elements
1.4000	X7Cr13	0.08	1.00	0.045	0.030	1.00	12.00–14.00			
1.4001	X7Cr14	0.08	1.00	0.045	0.030	1.00	13.00–15.00			
1.4002	X7CrAl13	0.08	1.00	0.045	0.030	1.00	12.00–14.00			Al 0.10–0.30
1.4006	X10Cr13	0.08–0.12	1.00	0.045	0.030	1.00	12.00–14.00			
1.4016	X8Cr17	0.10	1.00	0.045	0.030	1.00	15.50–17.50			
1.4021	X20Cr13	0.17–0.22	1.00	0.045	0.030	1.00	12.00–14.00			
1.4024	X15Cr13	0.12–0.17	1.00	0.045	0.030	1.00	12.00–14.00			
1.4028	X30Cr13	0.25–0.35	1.00	0.045	0.030	1.00	12.00–14.00	≤ 1.00		
1.4034	X40Cr13	0.40–0.50	1.00	0.045	0.030	1.00	12.00–14.00			
1.4057	X22CrNi17	0.15–0.23	1.00	0.045	0.030	1.00	16.00–18.00	1.50–2.50		
1.4104	X12CrMoS17	0.10–0.17	1.00	0.045	0.250	1.00	15.50–17.50		0.20–0.30	
1.4112	X90CrMoV18	0.85–0.95	1.00	0.045	0.030	1.00	17.00–19.00		1.00–1.30	V 0.07–0.12
1.4113	X8CrMo17	0.07	1.00	0.045	0.030	1.00	16.00–18.00		0.90–1.20	
1.4120	X20CrMo13	0.17–0.22	1.00	0.045	0.030	1.00	12.00–14.00		1.00–1.30	
1.4122	X35CrMo17	0.33–0.43	1.00	0.045	0.030	1.00	15.50–17.50	≤ 1.00	1.00–1.30	
1.4125	X105CrMo17	0.95–1.20	1.00	0.045	0.030	1.00	16.00–18.00		0.40–0.80	
1.4300	X12CrNi18 8	0.12	2.00	0.045	0.030	1.00	17.00–19.00	8.00–10.00		
1.4301	X5CrNi18 9	0.07	2.00	0.045	0.030	1.00	17.00–20.00	8.50–10.00		
1.4305	X12CrNiS18 8	0.15	2.00	0.045	0.20	1.00	17.00–19.00	8.50–10.00		
1.4306	X2CrNi18 9	0.03	2.00	0.045	0.030	1.00	17.00–20.00	10.00–12.50		
1.4310	X12CrNi17 7	0.12	2.00	0.045	0.030	1.00	16.00–18.00	7.00–9.00		
1.4311	X2CrNiN18 10	0.03	2.00	0.045	0.030	1.00	17.00–19.00	9.00–11.50		N ≤ 0.20

GERMANY, WEST   Stainless and Heat-resisting Steels (Continued)
Specifications: DIN 17440(1967), VDEH Werkstoffblatt 470-60 and 490-52; DIN 17224, DIN 17225, Stahleisenliste

Werkstoff number	Type	Composition, %								
		C, max.	Mn, max.	P, max.	S, max.	Si, max.	Cr	Ni	Mo	Other elements
1.4319	X5CrNi18 7	0.07	2.00	0.045	0.030	1.00	16.00–18.00	7.00–8.00		
1.4401	X5CrNiMo18 10	0.07	2.00	0.045	0.030	1.00	16.50–18.50	10.50–13.50	2.00–2.50	
1.4404	X2CrNiMo18 10	0.03	2.00	0.045	0.030	1.00	16.50–18.50	11.00–14.00	2.00–2.50	
1.4406	X2CrNiMoN18 12	0.03	2.00	0.045	0.030	1.00	16.50–18.50	10.50–13.50	2.00–2.50	N ≤ 0.20
1.4420	X5CrNiMo18 11	0.07	2.00	0.045	0.030	1.00	16.50–18.50	9.00–12.00	1.20–1.70	
1.4427	X12CrNiMoSi18 11	0.12	2.00	0.06	0.15–0.35	1.00	16.50–18.50	10.50–13.50	2.00–2.50	
1.4429	X2CrNiMoN18 13	0.03	2.00	0.045	0.030	1.00	16.50–18.50	12.00–14.50	2.50–3.00	N ≤ 0.20
1.4435	X2CrNiMo18 12	0.03	2.00	0.045	0.030	1.00	16.50–18.50	12.50–15.50	2.50–3.00	
1.4436	X5CrNiMo18 12	0.07	2.00	0.045	0.030	1.00	16.50–18.50	11.50–14.00	2.50–3.00	
1.4439	X3CrNiMoN17 13 5	0.04	2.00	0.045	0.030	1.00	16.50–18.50	12.50–14.50	4.00–5.00	N 0.10–0.20
1.4449	X5CrNiMo17 13	0.07	2.00	0.045	0.030	1.00	16.00–18.00	12.50–14.50	4.00–5.00	
1.4460	X8CrNiMo27 5	0.10	2.00	0.045	0.030	1.00	26.00–28.00	4.00–5.00	1.30–2.00	
1.4465	X2CrNiMoN25 25	0.03	2.00	0.045	0.030	1.00	24.00–26.00	22.00–25.00	2.00–2.50	N 0.08–0.16
1.4505	X5NiCrMoCuNb20 18	0.07	2.00	0.045	0.030	1.00	16.50–18.50	19.00–21.00	2.00–2.50	Cu 1.8–2.2 Nb ≥ 8 × C
1.4506	X5NiCrMoCuTi20 18	0.07	2.00	0.045	0.030	1.00	16.50–18.50	19.00–21.00	2.00–2.50	Cu 1.8–2.2 Ti ≥ 7 × C
1.4510	X8CrTi17	0.10	1.00	0.045	0.030	1.00	16.00–18.00			Ti ≥ 7 × C
1.4511	X8CrNb17	0.10	1.00	0.045	0.030	1.00	16.00–18.00			Nb ≥ 12 × C

Werkstoff-Nr.	Kurzname	C	Mn	P	S	Si	Cr	Ni	Mo	Sonstige
1.4512	X5CrTi12	0.08	1.00	0.045	0.030	1.00	10.50–12.50	≤ 0.50		Ti ≥ 6 × C
1.4523	X8CrMoTi17	0.10	1.00	0.045	0.030	1.00	16.50–18.50		1.50–2.00	Ti ≥ 7 × C
1.4532	X7CrNiMoAl15 7	0.09	1.00	0.030	0.030	1.00	14.00–16.00	6.50–7.50	2.00–2.50	Al 0.75–1.50
1.4541	X10CrNiTi18 9	0.10	2.00	0.045	0.030	1.00	17.00–19.00	9.00–11.50		Ti ≥ 5 × C
1.4550	X10CrNiNb18 9	0.10	2.00	0.045	0.030	1.00	17.00–19.00	9.00–11.50		Nb ≥ 8 × C
1.4568	X7CrNiAl17 7	0.09	1.00	0.045	0.030	1.00	16.00–18.00	6.50–7.50		Al 0.75–1.50
1.4571	X10CrNiMoTi18 10	0.10	2.00	0.045	0.030	1.00	16.50–18.50	10.50–13.50	2.00–2.50	Ti ≥ 5 × C
1.4573	X10CrNiMoTi18 12	0.10	2.00	0.045	0.030	1.00	16.50–18.50	12.00–14.50	2.50–3.00	Ti ≥ 5 × C
1.4577	X5CrNiMoTi25 25	0.07	2.00	0.045	0.030	1.00	24.00–26.00	24.00–26.00	2.00–2.50	Ti ≥ 10 × C
1.4580	X10CrNiMoNb18 10	0.10	2.00	0.045	0.030	1.00	16.50–18.50	10.50–13.50	2.00–2.50	Nb ≥ 8 × C
1.4582	X4CrNiMoNb25 7	0.06	1.50	0.045	0.030	1.00	24.00–26.00	6.50–7.50	1.30–2.00	Nb ≥ 10 × C
1.4583	X10CrNiMoNb18 12	0.10	2.00	0.045	0.030	1.00	16.50–18.50	12.00–14.50	2.50–3.00	Nb ≥ 8 × C
1.4724	X10CrAl13	0.12	0.60	0.040	0.030	1.50–2.00	11.00–13.00			Al 1.00–1.30
1.4742	X10CrAl18	0.12	1.00	0.045	0.030	0.70–1.20	17.00–19.00			Al 0.70–1.20
1.4747	X80CrNiSi20	0.75–0.85	0.80	0.035	0.030	1.75–2.50	19.00–21.00	1.00–1.70		
1.4762	X10CrAl24	0.12	1.00	0.040	0.030	1.20–1.50	23.00–25.00			Al 1.20–1.70
1.4828	X15CrNiSi20 12	0.20	2.00	0.045	0.030	1.80–2.30	19.00–21.00	11.00–13.00		
1.4841	X15CrNiSi25 20	0.25	2.00	0.045	0.030	1.50–3.00	23.00–26.00	19.00–22.00		
1.4845	X12CrNi25 21	0.15	2.00	0.045	0.030	0.75	24.00–26.00	19.00–22.00		
1.4873	X45CrNiW18 9	0.40–0.50	0.80–1.50	0.035	0.030	2.00–3.00	17.00–20.00	8.00–10.00		W 0.80–1.20
1.4922	X20CrMoV12 1	0.16–0.22	0.40–0.70	0.040	0.030	0.15–0.40	11.50–12.50	0.30–0.60	0.90–1.10	V 0.25–0.35

GREAT BRITAIN Stainless and Heat-resisting Steels
Specifications: B.S. 970, Part 4; B.S. 1449, Part 4

British Standard	Replaces En-	C, max.	Mn, max.	P, max.	S, max.	Si, max.	Cr	Ni	Mo	Other elements
284S16		0.07	7.00–10.00	0.060	0.030	≤ 1.00	16.50–18.50	4.00–8.50		N 0.15–0.25
301S21		0.15	0.50–2.00	0.045	0.030	0.20–1.00	16.00–18.00	6.00–8.00		
302S17		0.08	0.50–2.00	0.045	0.030	0.20–1.00	17.00–19.00	9.00–11.00		
302S25	58A	0.12	0.50–2.00	0.045	0.030	0.20–1.00	17.00–19.00	8.00–11.00		
303S21	58M	0.12	1.00–2.00	0.045	0.15–0.30	0.20–1.00	17.00–19.00	8.00–11.00		
303S41	58M	0.12	1.00–2.00	0.045	0.030	0.20–1.00	17.00–19.00	8.00–11.00		Se 0.15–0.30
304S12		0.03	0.50–2.00	0.045	0.030	0.20–1.00	17.50–19.00	9.00–12.00		
304S15	58E	0.06	0.50–2.00	0.045	0.030	0.20–1.00	17.50–19.00	8.00–11.00		
304S18	58E	0.06	0.50–2.00	0.045	0.030	0.20–1.00	17.50–19.00	9.00–11.00		
305S19		0.10	0.50–2.00	0.045	0.030	0.20–1.00	17.00–19.00	11.00–13.00		
309S24		0.15	0.50–2.00	0.045	0.030	0.20–1.00	22.00–25.00	13.00–16.00		
310S24		0.15	0.50–2.00	0.045	0.030	0.20–1.00	23.00–26.00	19.00–22.00		
312S24		0.15	0.50–2.00	0.045	0.030	0.20–1.00	23.00–26.00	16.00–19.00		
315S16	58H	0.07	0.50–2.00	0.045	0.030	0.20–1.00	16.50–18.50	9.00–11.00	1.25–1.75	
316S12		0.03	0.50–2.00	0.045	0.030	0.20–1.00	16.50–18.50	11.00–14.00	2.25–3.00	
316S16	58J	0.07	0.50–2.00	0.045	0.030	0.20–1.00	16.50–18.50	10.00–13.00	2.25–3.00	
317S12		0.03	0.50–2.00	0.045	0.030	0.20–1.00	17.50–19.50	14.00–17.00	3.00–4.00	
317S16		0.06	0.50–2.00	0.045	0.030	0.20–1.00	17.50–19.50	12.00–15.00	3.00–4.00	
320S17	58J	0.08	0.50–2.00	0.045	0.030	0.20–1.00	16.50–18.50	11.00–14.00	2.25–3.00	Ti 4 × C – 0.50

		C	Mn	S			Cr	Ni		
321S12	58B + 58C	0.08	0.50–2.00	0.045	0.030	0.20–1.00	17.00–19.00	9.00–12.00		Ti 5 × C – 0.70
321S20	58B + 58C	0.12	0.50–2.00	0.045	0.030	0.20–1.00	17.00–19.00	8.00–11.00		Ti 5 × C – 0.90
325S21	58M	0.12	1.00–2.00	0.045	0.15–0.30	0.20–1.00	17.00–19.00	8.00–11.00		Ti 5 × C – 0.90
326S36		0.12	1.00–2.00	0.045	0.030	0.20–1.00	18.50–20.50	10.00–13.00	2.25–3.00	Se 0.15–0.30
347S17	58F + 58G	0.08	0.50–2.00	0.045	0.030	0.20–1.00	17.00–19.00	9.00–12.00		Nb 10 × C – 1.00
403S17		0.08	1.00	0.040	0.030	0.80	12.00–14.00	≤ 0.50		
405S17		0.08	1.00	0.040	0.030	0.80	12.00–14.00	≤ 0.50		Al 0.10–0.3
409S17		0.09	1.00	0.040	0.030	0.80	11.00–13.00	≤ 0.70		Ti 5 × C – 0.60
410S21	58A	0.09–0.15	1.00	0.040	0.030	0.80	11.50–13.50	≤ 1.00		
416S21	56AM	0.09–0.15	1.50	0.040	0.15–0.30	1.00	11.50–13.50	≤ 1.00	≤ 0.60	
416S29	58BM	0.14–0.20	1.50	0.040	0.15–0.30	1.00	11.50–13.50	≤ 1.00	≤ 0.60	
416S37	58CM	0.20–0.28	1.50	0.040	0.15–0.30	1.00	12.00–14.00	≤ 1.00	≤ 0.60	
416S41	56AM	0.09–0.15	1.50	0.040	0.030	1.00	11.50–13.50	≤ 1.00		
420S29	56B	0.14–0.20	1.00	0.040	0.030	0.80	11.50–13.50	≤ 1.00	≤ 0.60	
420S37	56C	0.20–0.28	1.00	0.040	0.030	0.80	12.00–14.00	≤ 1.00		
420S45	56D	0.28–0.36	1.00	0.040	0.030	0.80	12.00–14.00	≤ 1.00		
430S15	60	0.10	1.00	0.040	0.030	0.80	16.00–18.00	≤ 0.50		
431S29	57	0.12–0.20	1.00	0.040	0.030	0.80	15.00–18.00	2.00–3.00		
434S19		0.10	1.00	0.040	0.030	0.80	16.00–18.00	≤ 0.50	0.90–1.30	
441S29		0.12–0.20	1.50	0.040	0.15–0.030	1.00	15.00–18.00	2.00–3.00	≤ 0.60	
441S49		0.12–0.20	1.50	0.040	0.030	1.00	15.00–18.00	2.00–3.00	≤ 0.60	Se 0.15–0.30
442S19	61	0.10	1.00	0.040	0.030	0.80	18.00–22.00	≤ 0.50		

HUNGARY Stainless and Heat-resisting Steels
Specifications: MSZ 4359-72; MSZ 4360-72

Type	C, max.	Si, max.	Mn, max.	P, max.	S, max.	Composition, %		Mo	Ti	Other elements
						Cr	Ni			
H8	0.20	0.80–2.00	2.00	0.040	0.030	17.00–20.00	8.00–11.00	⩽ 0.50		Cu ⩽ 0.30
H9	0.20	1.00	1.50	0.040	0.030	22.00–25.00	17.00–20.00	⩽ 0.50		Cu ⩽ 0.30
H10	0.20	2.00–3.00	1.50	0.040	0.030	24.00–27.00	18.00–21.00	⩽ 0.50		Cu ⩽ 0.30
H12	0.12	1.00–1.50	1.00	0.040	0.030	12.00–14.00	⩽ 0.60	⩽ 0.50		Al 0.70–1.20 Cu ⩽ 0.30
H13	0.12	0.80–1.50	1.00	0.040	0.030	17.00–20.00	⩽ 0.60	⩽ 0.50		Al 0.70–1.20 Cu ⩽ 0.30
H14	0.12	0.80–1.50	1.00	0.040	0.030	23.00–26.00	⩽ 0.60	⩽ 0.50		Al 1.20–1.70 Cu ⩽ 0.30
H15	0.15–0.25	0.80–1.30	2.00	0.040	0.030	24.00–27.00	3.50–4.50	⩽ 0.50		Cu ⩽ 0.30
H16	0.12	1.00	1.00	0.040	0.030	16.00–18.00	⩽ 0.60	⩽ 0.50		Cu ⩽ 0.30
H17	0.20	1.00	1.50	0.040	0.030	23.00–27.00	⩽ 0.60	⩽ 0.50		N ⩽ 0.25 Cu ⩽ 0.30
KO1	0.08	1.00	1.00	0.040	0.030	12.00–14.00	⩽ 0.60		⩽ 0.20	
KO2	0.09–0.15	1.00	1.00	0.040	0.030	12.00–14.00	⩽ 0.60		⩽ 0.20	
KO4	0.10	1.00	1.00	0.040	0.030	16.00–18.00	⩽ 0.60		5 × C − 0.80	
KO6	0.10	1.00	1.00	0.040	0.030	16.00–18.00	⩽ 0.60	0.90–1.30	⩽ 0.20	
KO11	0.16–0.25	1.00	1.00	0.040	0.030	12.00–14.00	⩽ 0.60		⩽ 0.20	

KO12	0.26–0.35	1.00	1.00	0.040	0.030	12.00–14.00	≤ 0.60		≤ 0.20	
KO13	0.36–0.45	1.00	1.00	0.040	0.030	12.00–14.00	≤ 0.60		≤ 0.20	
KO14	0.95–1.20	1.00	1.00	0.040	0.030	16.00–18.00	≤ 0.60	0.30–0.75	≤ 0.20	
KO16	0.11–0.17	1.00	1.00	0.040	0.030	16.00–18.00	1.50–2.50	≤ 0.50	≤ 0.20	
KO17	0.18–0.25	1.00	1.00	0.040	0.030	16.00–18.00	1.50–2.50	≤ 0.50	≤ 0.20	
KO21	0.15–0.30	1.00	8.00–10.00	0.040	0.030	12.00–14.00	3.70–4.70	≤ 0.50	≤ 0.20	
KO31	0.12	1.00	8.00–10.50	0.040	0.030	16.00–18.00	3.50–4.50	≤ 0.50	≤ 0.20	N 0.15–0.25
KO32	0.12	1.00	2.00	0.040	0.030	17.00–19.00	8.00–11.00	≤ 0.50	≤ 0.20	
KO33	0.08	1.00	2.00	0.040	0.030	17.00–19.00	9.00–11.00	≤ 0.50	≤ 0.20	
KO34	0.08	1.00	2.00	0.040	0.030	17.00–19.00	10.00–13.00	≤ 0.50	≤ 0.20	$10 \times C$ $5Nb \leq 1.10$
KO35	0.08	1.00	2.00	0.040	0.030	16.00–18.00	11.00–14.00	≤ 0.50	$5 \times C - 0.70$	
KO36	0.12	1.00	2.00	0.040	0.030	17.00–19.00	8.00–11.00	≤ 0.50	$5 \times C - 0.80$	
KO37	0.08	1.00	2.00	0.040	0.030	17.00–19.00	9.00–11.00	≤ 0.50	$5 \times C - 0.70$	
KO38	0.03	1.00	2.00	0.040	0.030	16.00–18.00	12.00–15.00	2.00–2.50	≤ 0.20	
KO40	0.06	1.00	2.00	0.040	0.030	22.00–25.00	26.00–29.00	2.50–3.00	0.50–0.90	Cu 2.50–3.50
KO41	0.03	1.00	2.00	0.040	0.030	17.00–19.00	10.00–12.50	≤ 0.50	≤ 0.20	
KO42	0.12	1.00	2.00	0.040	0.030	17.00–19.00	11.00–13.00	≤ 0.50	$5 \times C - 0.80$	
KO43	0.08	1.00	2.00	0.040	0.030	16.00–18.00	14.00–16.00	3.00–4.00	0.30–0.60	
KO44	0.07	1.00	2.00	0.040	0.030	16.50–18.50	19.00–21.00	2.00–2.50	$7 \times C - 0.70$	Cu 1.80–2.20

HUNGARY Stainless and Heat-resisting Steel Castings
Specification: MSZ 21053-72

Type	Composition, %										
	C, max.	Si, max.	Mn, max.	P, max.	S, max.	Cr	Ni	Mo	Ti		Other elements
A6X8CrNiMo 18 10	0.08	1.50	2.00	0.040	0.040	17.00–19.00	9.00–11.00	2.00–3.00			
A6X8CrNiTi 19 10	0.08	1.50	2.00	0.040	0.040	17.00–20.00	8.00–11.00		⩾ 5 × C		
A6X15Cr13	0.15	1.50	1.00	0.040	0.040	12.00–14.00	⩽ 1.00				
A6X15CrNi 18 10	0.15	1.50	2.00	0.040	0.040	17.00–19.00	8.00–11.00				
A6X15CrNiMo 18 10	0.15	1.50	2.00	0.040	0.040	17.00–19.00	9.00–11.00	2.00–3.00			
A6X15CrNiMo 18 12	0.15	1.50	2.00	0.040	0.040	17.00–19.00	11.00–13.00	3.00–4.00			
A6X15CrNiMoCu 21 30	0.15	1.50	2.00	0.040	0.040	19.00–22.00	28.00–31.00	2.00–3.00			Cu 3.00–4.00
A6X15CrNiMoTi 18 10	0.15	1.50	2.00	0.040	0.040	17.00–19.00	9.00–11.00	2.00–3.00	⩾ 5 × C		
A6X15CrNiTi 18 10	0.15	1.50	2.00	0.040	0.040	17.00–19.00	8.00–11.00		⩾ 5 × C		
A6X15MnCrNiN 9 19	0.15	1.50	8.00–10.00	0.040	0.040	17.00–20.00	4.00–5.00				N 0.15–0.25
A6X20Cr13	0.15–0.25	1.50	1.00	0.040	0.040	12.00–14.00	⩽ 1.00				
A6X20Cr18	0.15–0.25	1.50	1.00	0.040	0.040	17.00–19.00	⩽ 1.00				
A6X20CrNi 17 2	0.15–0.25	1.50	1.00	0.040	0.040	16.00–18.00	1.50–2.50				
A6X30Cr14	0.25–0.35	1.50	1.00	0.040	0.040	13.00–15.00	⩽ 1.00				
HAöCr7	0.25	1.00–2.00	0.50–0.90	0.040	0.040	6.00–7.00		⩽ 0.50			
HAöCr17	0.15–0.50	0.90–2.50	1.00	0.040	0.040	16.00–18.00	⩽ 0.60				
HAöCr27	0.50–0.80	2.00	1.00	0.040	0.040	25.00–30.00					
HAöCr30	1.20–2.00	2.00	1.00	0.040	0.040	28.00–32.00					
HAöCrNi	0.40	1.00–2.50	1.00	0.040	0.040	24.00–26.00	19.00–21.00				

INDIA   Stainless and Heat-resisting Steels
Specification: Indian Standard No. 1570 (Part V)—1972

Serial no.	Steel designation	C, max.	Si, max.	Mn, max.	Cr	Ni	Mo	Ti	Nb	Other elements
						Composition, %				
1	04Cr13*	0.08	1.0	1.0	11.5–14.5					Al 0.10–0.30
2	12Cr13*	0.09–0.15	1.0	1.0	11.5–14.0	≤ 1.0				
3	20Cr13*	0.16–0.25	1.0	1.0	12.0–14.0	≤ 1.0				
4	30Cr13*	0.26–0.35	1.0	1.0	12.0–14.0	≤ 1.0				
5	40Cr13*	0.36–0.45	1.0	1.0	12.5–14.5	≤ 1.0				
6	05Cr17	0.10	1.0	1.0	16.0–18.0	≤ 0.50				
7	15Cr16Ni2	0.10–0.20	1.0	1.0	15.0–18.0	1.5–3.0				
8	105Cr18Mo50	0.90–1.20	1.0	1.0	16.0–19.0	< 0.50	≤ 0.75			
9	02Cr18Ni11	0.030	1.0	2.0	17.0–20.0	9.0–13.0				
10	04Cr18Ni11	0.08	1.0	2.0	17.0–20.0	9.0–13.0				
11	07Cr18Ni9	0.12	1.0	2.0	17.0–19.0	8.0–10.0				
12	10Cr17Ni7	0.15	1.0	2.0	16.0–18.0	6.0–8.0				
13	04Cr18Ni10Ti20	0.08	1.0	2.0	17.0–19.0	9.0–12.0		5 × C – 0.80		
14	04Cr18Ni10Nb40	0.08	1.0	2.0	17.0–19.0	9.0–12.0			10 × C – 1.0	
15	04Cr17Ni12Mo2	0.08	1.0	2.0	16.0–18.5	10.5–14.0	2.0–3.0			
16	02Cr17Ni12Mo2	0.030	1.0	2.0	16.0–18.5	10.5–14.0	2.0–3.0			
17	04Cr17Ni12Mo2Ti20	0.080	1.0	2.0	16.0–18.5	10.5–14.0	2.0–3.0	5 × C – 0.8+		
18	10Cr17Mn6Ni4N20	0.15	1.0	5.5–7.5	16.0–18.0	3.5–5.5				N 0.25 max.
19	15Cr25Ni20	0.20	1.0	1.50	23.0–27.0					N 0.25 max.
20	15Cr24Ni13	0.20	1.5	2.0	22.0–25.0	11.0–15.0				
21	20Cr25Ni20	0.25	2.5	2.0	24.0–26.0	18.0–21.0				
22	45Cr9Si4	0.40–0.50	3.25–3.75	0.30–0.60	7.50–9.50	≤ 0.50				
23	80Cr20Si2Ni1	0.75–0.85	1.75–2.25	0.20–0.60	19.0–21.0	1.20–1.70				

*For free-cutting varieties at serial numbers 1 to 5, sulfur and selenium content shall be as agreed to between purchaser and manufacturer.
+For electrode steel Nb–10C to 1.0 in place of Ti.

ITALY Stainless and Heat-resisting Steels
Specification: UNI 6900-71

Type	Composition, %								
	C, max.	Mn, max.	P, max.	S, max.	Si, max.	Cr	Ni	Mo	Other elements
X6Cr13	0.08	1.00	0.040	0.030	1.00	11.50–14.00	≤ 0.50		
X12Cr13	0.09–0.15	1.00	0.040	0.030	1.00	11.50–14.00	≤ 1.00		
X20Cr13	0.16–0.25	1.00	0.040	0.030	1.00	12.00–14.00	≤ 1.00		
X30Cr13	0.26–0.35	1.00	0.040	0.030	1.00	12.00–14.00	≤ 1.00		
X40Cr14	0.36–0.45	1.00	0.040	0.030	1.00	12.50–14.50	≤ 1.00		
X8Cr17	0.10	1.00	0.040	0.030	1.00	16.00–18.00	≤ 0.50		
X16Cr26	0.20	1.50	0.040	0.030	1.00	24.00–27.00			N ≤ 0.25
X6CrAl13	0.08	1.00	0.040	0.030	1.00	11.50–14.00	≤ 0.50		Al 0.10–0.30
X10CrAl12	0.12	0.60	0.040	0.030	1.50–2.00	11.00–13.00			Al 1.00–1.30
X8CrMo17	0.10	1.00	0.040	0.030	1.00	16.00–18.00	≤ 0.50		
X16CrNi16	0.10–0.20	1.00	0.040	0.030	1.00	15.00–17.00	1.50–2.50		
X14CrNi19	0.16	1.00	0.040	0.030	1.00	18.00–20.00	1.50–2.50		
X12CrNi17 07	0.15	2.00	0.045	0.030	1.00	16.00–18.00	6.00–8.00		
X10CrNi18 09	0.12	2.00	0.045	0.030	1.00	17.00–19.00	8.00–10.00		
X5CrNi18 10	0.06	2.00	0.045	0.030	1.00	17.00–19.00	8.00–11.00		
X8CrNi19 10	0.04–0.10	2.00	0.040`	0.030	0.75	18.00–20.00	8.00–12.00		
X2CrNi18 11	0.03	2.00	0.045	0.030	1.00	17.00–19.00	9.00–12.00		
X8CrNi18 12	0.10	2.00	0.045	0.030	1.00	17.00–19.00	11.00–13.00		
X6CrNi23 14	0.08	2.00	0.045	0.030	1.00	22.00–24.00	12.00–15.00		

Designation									
X16CrNi23 14	0.20	2.00	0.045	0.030	1.00	22.00–24.00	12.00–15.00		
X6CrNi25 20	0.08	2.00	0.045	0.030	1.50	24.00–26.00	19.00–22.00		
X22CrNi25 20	0.25	2.00	0.045	0.030	1.50	24.00–26.00	19.00–22.00		
X2CrNiMo17 12	0.03	2.00	0.045	0.030	1.00	16.00–18.50	11.00–14.00	2.00–2.50	
X5CrNiMo17 12	0.06	2.00	0.045	0.030	1.00	16.00–18.50	10.50–13.50	2.00–2.50	
X8CrNiMo17 12	0.04–0.10	2.00	0.030	0.030	0.75	16.00–18.00	11.00–13.50	2.00–2.50	
X2CrNiMo17 13	0.03	2.00	0.045	0.030	1.00	16.00–18.50	11.50–14.50	2.50–3.00	
X5CrNiMo17 13	0.06	2.00	0.045	0.030	1.00	16.00–18.50	11.00–14.00	2.50–3.00	
X8CrNiMo17 13	0.04–0.10	2.00	0.030	0.030	0.75	16.00–18.00	11.00–14.00	2.50–3.00	
X2CrNiMo18 16	0.03	2.00	0.045	0.030	1.00	17.50–19.50	14.00–17.00	3.00–4.00	
X6CrNiMoNb17 12	0.08	2.00	0.045	0.030	1.00	16.00–18.50	10.50–13.50	2.00–2.50	Nb + Ta ≤ 1.00
X6CrNiMoNb17 13	0.08	2.00	0.045	0.030	1.00	16.00–18.50	11.50–14.50	2.50–3.00	Nb + Ta ≤ 1.00
X6CrNiMoTi17 12	0.08	2.00	0.045	0.030	1.00	16.00–18.50	10.50–13.50	2.00–2.50	Ti ≤ 0.80
X6CrNiMoTi17 13	0.08	2.00	0.045	0.030	1.00	16.00–18.50	11.50–14.50	2.50–3.00	Ti ≤ 0.80
X6CrNiNb18 11	0.08	2.00	0.045	0.030	1.00	17.00–19.00	9.00–12.00		Nb + Ta ≤ 1.00
X8CrNiNb18 11	0.04–0.10	2.00	0.030	0.030	0.75	17.00–19.00	9.00–13.00		Nb + Ta ≤ 1.00
X10CrNiS18 09	0.12	2.00	0.200	0.350	1.00	17.00–19.00	8.00–11.00	≤ 0.60	
X16CrNiSi25 20	0.20	2.00	0.045	0.030	1.50–2.50	24.00–26.00	19.00–22.00		
X6CrNiTi18 11	0.08	2.00	0.045	0.030	1.00	17.00–19.00	9.00–12.00		
X8CrNiTi18 11	0.04–0.10	2.00	0.030	0.030	0.75	17.00–19.00	9.00–13.00		
X12CrS13	0.08–0.15	1.50	0.060	0.350	1.00	12.00–14.00	≤ 1.00	≤ 0.60	
X10CrS17	0.12	1.50	0.060	0.350	1.00	16.00–18.00	≤ 0.50	≤ 0.60	

JAPAN Chemical Composition of Stainless and Heat-resisting Steels[a]

STAINLESS STEELS

Notation	Composition, %									
	C, max.	Si, max.	Mn, max.	P, max.	S, max.	Ni	Cr	Mo	Cu	Other elements
Austenitic:										
SUS 201	0.15	1.00	5.50–7.50	0.060	0.030	3.50–5.50	16.00–18.00			N 0.25 max.
SUS 202	0.15	1.00	7.50–10.00	0.060	0.030	4.00–6.00	17.00–19.00			N 0.25 max.
SUS 301	0.15	1.00	2.00	0.040	0.030	6.00–8.00	16.00–18.00			
SUS 302	0.15	1.00	2.00	0.040	0.030	8.00–10.00	17.00–19.00			
SUS 303	0.15	1.00	2.00	0.20	0.15	8.00–10.00	17.00–19.00	c		
SUS 303Se	0.15	1.00	2.00	0.20	0.060	8.00–10.00	17.00–19.00			Se 0.15 min.
SUS 304	0.08	1.00	2.00	0.040	0.030	8.00–10.50	18.00–20.00			
SUS 304L	0.030	1.00	2.00	0.040	0.030	9.00–13.00	18.00–20.00			
SUS 305	0.12	1.00	2.00	0.040	0.030	10.50–13.00	17.00–19.00			
SUS 305J1	0.08	1.00	2.00	0.040	0.030	11.00–13.50	16.50–19.00			
SUS 308	0.08	1.00	2.00	0.040	0.030	10.00–12.00	19.00–21.00			
SUS 309S	0.08	1.00	2.00	0.040	0.030	12.00–15.00	22.00–24.00			
SUS 310S	0.08	1.50	2.00	0.040	0.030	19.00–22.00	24.00–26.00			
SUS 316	0.08	1.00	2.00	0.040	0.030	10.00–14.00	16.00–18.00	2.00–3.00		
SUS 316L	0.030	1.00	2.00	0.040	0.030	12.00–15.00	16.00–18.00	2.00–3.00		
SUS 316J1	0.08	1.00	2.00	0.040	0.030	10.00–14.00	17.00–19.00	1.20–2.75	1.00–2.50	
SUS 316J1L	0.030	1.00	2.00	0.040	0.030	12.00–16.00	17.00–19.00	1.20–2.75	1.00–2.50	
SUS 317	0.08	1.00	2.00	0.040	0.030	11.00–15.00	18.00–20.00	3.00–4.00		
SUS 317L	0.030	1.00	2.00	0.040	0.030	11.00–15.00	18.00–20.00	3.00–4.00		
SUS 321	0.08	1.00	2.00	0.040	0.030	9.00–13.00	17.00–19.00			Ti ≥ 5 × C
SUS 347	0.08	1.00	2.00	0.040	0.030	9.00–13.00	17.00–19.00			Nb + Ta ≥ 10 × C

Grade									
SUS 384	0.08	1.00	2.00	0.040	0.030	17.00–19.00	15.00–17.00		
SUS 385	0.08	1.00	2.00	0.040	0.030	14.00–16.00	11.50–13.50		
Austenitic-Ferritic:									
SUS 329J1	0.08	1.00	1.50	0.040	0.030	3.00–6.00	23.00–28.00	1.00–3.00	
Ferritic:									
SUS 405	0.08	1.00	1.00	0.040	0.030	b	11.50–14.50		Al 0.10–0.30
SUS 429	0.12	1.00	1.00	0.040	0.030	b	14.00–16.00		
SUS 430	0.12	0.75	1.00	0.040	0.030	b	16.00–18.00		
SUS 430F	0.12	1.00	1.25	0.060	0.15	b	16.00–18.00	c	
SUS 434	0.12	1.00	1.00	0.040	0.030	b	16.00–18.00	0.75–1.25	
Martensitic:									
SUS 403	0.15	0.50	1.00	0.040	0.030	b	11.50–13.00		
SUS 410	0.15	1.00	1.00	0.040	0.030	b	11.50–13.50		
SUS 410J1	0.08–0.18	0.60	1.00	0.040	0.030	b	11.50–14.00	0.30–0.60	
SUS 416	0.15	1.00	1.25	0.060	0.15	b	12.00–14.00	c	
SUS 420J1	0.16–0.25	1.00	1.00	0.040	0.030	b	12.00–14.00		
SUS 420J2	0.26–0.40	1.00	1.00	0.040	0.030	b	12.00–14.00		
SUS 420F	0.26–0.40	1.00	1.25	0.060	0.15	b	12.00–14.00	c	
SUS 431	0.20	1.00	1.00	0.040	0.030	1.25–2.50	15.00–17.00		
SUS 440A	0.60–0.75	1.00	1.00	0.040	0.030	b	16.00–18.00	d	
SUS 440B	0.75–0.95	1.00	1.00	0.040	0.030	b	16.00–18.00	d	
SUS 440C	0.95–1.20	1.00	1.00	0.040	0.030	b	16.00–18.00	d	
SUS 440F	0.95–1.20	1.00	1.25	0.060	0.15	b	16.00–18.00	d	
Precipitation Hardening:									
SUS 630	0.07	1.00	1.00	0.040	0.030	3.00–5.00	15.50–17.50	3.00–5.00	Nb + Ta 0.15–0.45
SUS 631	0.09	1.00	1.00	0.040	0.030	6.50–7.75[e]	16.00–18.00		Al 0.75–1.50

Remark: SUS 329J1 may be added with the alloy element not specified in the table if necessary.

A1-27

JAPAN   Chemical Composition of Stainless and Heat-resisting Steels[a] (Continued)

HEAT-RESISTING STEELS

Notation	C, max.	Si, max.	Mn, max.	P, max.	S, max.	Ni	Cr	Mo	W	Co	Other elements
Austenitic:											
SUH 31	0.35–0.45	1.50–2.50	0.60	0.040	0.030	13.00–15.00	14.00–16.00		2.00–3.00		
SUH 309	0.20	1.00	2.00	0.040	0.030	12.00–15.00	22.00–24.00				
SUH 310	0.25	1.50	2.00	0.040	0.030	19.00–22.00	24.00–26.00				
SUH 330	0.15	1.50	2.00	0.040	0.030	33.00–37.00	14.00–17.00				
SUH 661	0.08–0.16	1.00	1.00–2.00	0.040	0.030	19.00–21.00	20.00–22.50	2.50–3.50	2.00–3.00	18.50–21.00	N 0.10–0.20 Nb + Ta 0.75–1.25
Ferritic:											
SUH 446	0.20	1.00	1.50	0.040	0.030	[f]	23.00–27.00				N 0.25 max.
Martensitic:											
SUH 1	0.40–0.50	3.00–3.50	0.60	0.030	0.030	[f]	7.50–9.50				
SUH 3	0.35–0.45	1.80–2.50	0.60	0.030	0.030	[f]	10.00–12.00	0.70–1.30			
SUH 4	0.75–0.85	1.75–2.25	0.20–0.60	0.030	0.030	1.15–1.65	19.00–20.50				
SUH 600	0.15–0.20	0.50	0.50–1.00	0.040	0.030	[f]	10.00–13.00	0.30–0.90			V 0.10–0.40 N 0.05–0.10 Nb + Ta 0.20–0.60
SUH 616	0.20–0.25	0.50	0.50–1.00	0.040	0.030	0.50–1.00	11.00–13.00	0.75–1.25	0.75–1.25		V 0.20–0.30

Remark: Ferritic and martensitic bars may contain up to 0.30% Cu.

[a] Applicable to all standards for wrought products which follow.
[b] Not more than 0.60% may be contained.
[c] Not more than 0.60% may be added.
[d] Not more than 0.75% may be added.
[e] For SUS 631 for wire rod and wire, the nickel content shall be 7.00 to 8.50% and the notation shall be SUS 631J1.
[f] Contains not more than 0.60% nickel.

JAPAN   Stainless Steel Bars
Specification: JIS G 4303 (1972)

Present notation	Old notation	Structural classification
SUS 201		
SUS 202		
SUS 301	SUS 39B	
SUS 302	SUS 40B	
SUS 303	SUS 60B	
SUS 303Se		
SUS 304	SUS 27B	
SUS 304L	SUS 28B	
SUS 305		
SUS 305J1		
SUS 308		
SUS 309S	SUS 41B	Austenite
SUS 310S	SUS 42B	
SUS 316	SUS 32B	
SUS 316L	SUS 33B	
SUS 316J1	SUS 35B	
SUS 316J1L	SUS 36B	
SUS 317		
SUS 317L		
SUS 321	SUS 29B	
SUS 347	SUS 43B	
SUS 384		
SUS 385		
SUS 329J1		Austenite-ferrite
SUS 405	SUS 38B	
SUS 429		
SUS 430	SUS 24B	Ferrite
SUS 430F		
SUS 434		
SUS 403	SUS 50B	
SUS 410	SUS 51B	
SUS 410J1	SUS 37B	
SUS 416	SUS 54B	
SUS 420J1	SUS 52B	
SUS 420J2	SUS 53B	Martensite
SUS 420F		
SUS 431	SUS 44B	
SUS 440A		
SUS 440B		
SUS 440C	SUS 57B	
SUS 440F		
SUS 630	SUS 80B	Precipitation-hardenable
SUS 631		

JAPAN   Hot-rolled Stainless Steel Sheet and Plate
Specification: JIS G 4304 (1972)

Present notation	Old notation	Structural classification
SUS 202		
SUS 302	SUS 40HP	
SUS 304	SUS 27HP	
SUS 304L	SUS 28HP	
SUS 305	SUS 62HP	
SUS 309S	SUS 41HP	
SUS 310S	SUS 42HP	Austenite
SUS 316	SUS 32HP	
SUS 316L	SUS 33HP	
SUS 316J1	SUS 35HP	
SUS 316J1L	SUS 36HP	
SUS 317	SUS 64HP	
SUS 317L	SUS 65HP	
SUS 321	SUS 29HP	
SUS 347	SUS 43HP	
SUS 329J1		Austenite-ferrite
SUS 405	SUS 38HP	
SUS 429		Ferrite
SUS 430	SUS 24HP	
SUS 434		
SUS 403	SUS 50HP	
SUS 410	SUS 51HP	Martensite
SUS 631		Precipitation-hardenable

JAPAN   Cold-rolled Stainless Steel Sheet and Plate
Specification: JIS G 4305 (1972)

Present notation	Old notation	Structural classification
SUS 201		
SUS 202		
SUS 301	SUS 39CP	
SUS 302	SUS 40CP	
SUS 304	SUS 27CP	
SUS 304L	SUS 28CP	
SUS 305	SUS 62CP	
SUS 309S	SUS 41CP	
SUS 310S	SUS 42CP	Austenite
SUS 316	SUS 32CP	
SUS 316L	SUS 33CP	
SUS 316J1	SUS 35CP	
SUS 316J1L	SUS 36CP	
SUS 317	SUS 64CP	
SUS 317L	SUS 65CP	
SUS 321	SUS 29CP	
SUS 347	SUS 43CP	
SUS 329J1		Austenite-ferrite
SUS 405	SUS 38CP	
SUS 429		
SUS 430	SUS 24CP	Ferrite
SUS 434		
SUS 403	SUS 50CP	
SUS 410	SUS 51CP	
SUS 420J2		
SUS 440A		Martensite
SUS 631		Precipitation-hardenable

JAPAN   Hot-rolled Stainless Steel Strip
Specification: JIS G 4306 (1972)

Present notation	Old notation	Structural classification
SUS 201 SUS 202 SUS 301 SUS 302 SUS 304 SUS 304L SUS 309S SUS 310S SUS 316 SUS 316L SUS 321 SUS 347	 SUS 39 HS SUS 40 HS SUS 27 HS SUS 28 HS SUS 32 HS SUS 33 HS SUS 29 HS SUS 43 HS	Austenite
SUS 329J1		Austenite-ferrite
SUS 405 SUS 430 SUS 434	SUS 38 HS SUS 24 HS	Ferrite
SUS 410 SUS 420J2 SUS 440A	SUS 51 HS	Martensite
SUS 631		Precipitation-hardenable

JAPAN   Cold-rolled Stainless Steel Strip
Specification: JIS G 4307 (1972)

Present notation	Old notation	Structural classification
SUS 201 SUS 202 SUS 301 SUS 302 SUS 304 SUS 304L SUS 309S SUS 310S SUS 316 SUS 316L SUS 321 SUS 347	 SUS 39 CS SUS 40 CS SUS 27 CS SUS 28 CS SUS 32CS SUS 33CS SUS 29CS SUS 43CS	Austenite
SUS 329J1		Austenite-ferrite
SUS 405 SUS 430 SUS 434	SUS 38CS SUS 24CS	Ferrite
SUS 410 SUS 420J2 SUS 440A	SUS 51CS	Martensite
SUS 631		Precipitation-hardenable

JAPAN   Stainless Steel Wire Rod
Specification: JIS G 4308 (1972)

Present notation	Old notation	Structural classification
SUS 302 SUS 303 SUS 303Se SUS 304 SUS 304L SUS 305 SUS 305J1 SUS 309S SUS 310S SUS 316 SUS 316L SUS 321 SUS 347 SUS 384 SUS 385	SUS 40 WR SUS 60 WR SUS 27 WR SUS 62 WR SUS 63 WR SUS 32 WR	Austenite
SUS 430 SUS 430F	SUS 24 WR	Ferrite
SUS 410 SUS 416 SUS 420J1 SUS 420J2 SUS 440C	SUS 51 WR	Martensite
SUS 631J1		Precipitation-hardenable

JAPAN   Stainless Steel Wire
Specification: JIS G 4309 (1972)

Class	Notation	Structural classification
Soft No. 1	SUS 303-W1 SUS 303Se-W1 SUS 304-W1 SUS 304L-W1 SUS 305-W1 SUS 305J1-W1 SUS 309S-W1 SUS 310S-W1 SUS 316-W1 SUS 316L-W1 SUS 321-W1 SUS 347-W1	Austenite
Soft No. 2	SUS 303-W2 SUS 303Se-W2 SUS 304-W2 SUS 316-W2 SUS 430-W2 SUS 430F-W2 SUS 410-W2 SUS 416-W2 SUS 420J1-W2 SUS 420J2-W2 SUS 440C-W2	Austenite Ferrite Martensite
Half-hard	SUS 304-W1/2H SUS 316-W1/2H	Austenite

JAPAN   Heat-resisting Steel Bars
Specification: JIS G 4311 (1972)

Present notation	Old notation	Structural classification	Remarks
SUH 31 SUH 309 SUH 310 SUH 330	SUH 31B SUH 32B SUH 33B SUH 34B	Austenite	Mainly for valves Mainly for heat- and oxidation-resisting applications
SUH 661			For high heat-resisting applications
SUH 446		Ferrite	For oxidation-resisting application
SUH 1 SUH 3 SUH 4	SUH 1B SUH 3B SUH 4B		Mainly for valves
SUH 600		Martensite	Mainly for heat-resisting applications
SUH 616			Mainly for heat- and oxidation-resisting applications
SUH 304 SUS 316 SUS 317 SUS 321 SUS 347 SUS 405	SUS 27B SUS 32B SUS 29B SUS 43B SUS 38B	Austenite	
SUS 430	SUS 24B	Ferrite	Conforms to JIS G 4303 Stainless Steel Bars
SUS 403 SUS 410 SUS 410J1 SUS 420J1 SUS 420J2 SUS 431 SUS 440A SUS 440B SUS 440C	SUS 50B SUS 51B SUS 37B SUS 52B SUS 53B SUS 44B SUS 57B	Martensite	
SUS 630 SUS 631	SUS 80B	Precipitation-hardenable	

JAPAN   Heat-resisting Steel Sheet and Plate
Specification: JIS G 4312 (1972)

Notation	Old notation	Structure	Remarks
SUH 309 SUH 310 SUH 330 SUH 661	SUH 32P SUH 33P SUH 34P	Austentite	Mainly used for heat- and oxidation-resisting applications For heat-resisting applications at higher temperature
SUH 446	SUH 6P	Ferrite	For oxidation-resisting applications
SUS 304	SUS 27HP or SUS 27CP	Austenite	Conforms to JIS G 4304 Hot-rolled Stainless Steel Sheet and Plate or JIS G 4305 Cold-rolled Stainless Steel Sheet and Plate
SUS 316	SUS 32HP or SUS 32CP		
SUS 317	SUS 64HP or SUS 64CP		
SUS 321	SUS 29HP or SUS 29CP		
SUS 347	SUS 43HP or SUS 43CP		
SUS 405	SUS 38HP or SUS 38CP	Ferrite	
SUS 430	SUS 24HP or SUS 24CP		
SUS 403	SUS 50HP or SUS 50CP	Martensite	
SUS 410	SUS 51HP or SUS 51CP		
SUS 631		Precipitation-hardenable	

JAPAN Stainless Steel Castings
Specification: JIS G 5121–1975

Class	Symbol*	C, max.	Mn, max.	P, max.	S, max.	Si, max.	Composition, % Cr	Ni	Mo	Other elements
1	SCS1	0.15	1.00	0.040	0.040	1.50	11.50–14.00	1.00 max.	0.05 max.	
2	SCS2	0.16–0.24	1.00	0.040	0.040	1.50	11.50–14.00	1.00 max.	0.05 max.	
11	SCS11	0.10	1.00	0.040	0.040	1.50	23.00–27.00	5.00–7.00	1.50–2.50	
12	SCS12	0.20	2.00	0.040	0.040	1.50	18.00–21.00	8.00–11.00		
13	SCS13	0.08	2.00	0.040	0.040	2.00	18.00–21.00	8.00–11.00		
14	SCS14	0.08	2.00	0.040	0.040	1.50	17.00–20.00	10.00–14.00	2.00–3.00	
15	SCS15	0.08	2.00	0.040	0.040	1.50	17.00–20.00	10.00–14.00	1.75–2.75	Cu 1.00–2.50
16	SCS16	0.03	2.00	0.040	0.040	1.50	17.00–20.00	12.00–16.00	2.00–3.00	
17	SCS17	0.20	2.00	0.040	0.040	2.00	22.00–26.00	12.00–15.00		
18	SCS18	0.20	2.00	0.040	0.040	2.00	23.00–27.00	19.00–22.00		
19	SCS19	0.03	2.00	0.040	0.040	2.00	17.00–21.00	8.00–12.00		
20	SCS20	0.03	2.00	0.040	0.040	2.00	17.00–20.00	12.00–16.00	1.75–2.75	Cu 1.00–2.50
21	SCS21	0.08	2.00	0.040	0.040	2.00	18.00–21.00	9.00–12.00		10 × C ≤ Nb + Ta ≤ 1.35
22	SCS22	0.08	2.00	0.040	0.040	2.00	17.00–20.00	10.00–14.00	2.00–3.00	10 × C ≤ Nb + Ta ≤ 1.35
23	SCS23	0.07	2.00	0.040	0.040	2.00	19.00–22.00	27.50–30.50	2.00–3.00	Cu 3.00–4.00
24	SCS24	0.07	1.00	0.040	0.040	1.00	15.50–17.50	3.00–5.00		Cu 2.50–4.00 Nb + Ta ≤ 0.45 N 0.05 min.

*Centrifugally cast steel pipe shall be noted by adding -CF to the symbol, e.g., SCS 2-CF.

JAPAN Heat-resistant Steel Castings
Specification: JIS G 5122-1975

Class	Symbol	C, max.	Mn, max.	P, max.	S, max.	Si, max.	Cr	Ni	Mo
							Composition, %		
1	SCH 1	0.20–0.40	1.00	0.040	0.040	1.50–3.00	12.00–15.00	1.00 max.	12.00
2	SCH 2	0.40	1.00	0.040	0.040	2.00	25.00–28.00	1.00 max.	
3	SCH 3	0.40	1.00	0.040	0.040	2.00	12.00–15.00	1.00 max.	
11	SCH11	0.40	1.00	0.040	0.040	2.00	24.00–28.00	4.00–6.00	
12	SCH12	0.20–0.40	2.00	0.040	0.040	2.00	18.00–23.00	8.00–12.00	
13	SCH13	0.20–0.50	2.00	0.040	0.040	2.00	24.00–28.00	11.00–14.00	
15	SCH15	0.35–0.70	2.00	0.040	0.040	2.50	13.00–17.00	33.00–37.00	
16	SCH16	0.20–0.35	2.00	0.040	0.040	2.50	13.00–17.00	33.00–37.00	
17	SCH17	0.20–0.50	2.00	0.040	0.040	2.00	26.00–30.00	8.00–11.00	
18	SCH18	0.20–0.50	2.00	0.040	0.040	2.00	26.00–30.00	14.00–18.00	
19	SCH19	0.20–0.50	2.00	0.040	0.040	2.00	19.00–23.00	23.00–27.00	
20	SCH20	0.35–0.75	2.00	0.040	0.040	2.50	17.00–21.00	37.00–41.00	
21	SCH21	0.25–0.35	1.50	0.040	0.040	1.75	23.00–27.00	19.00–22.00	
22	SCH22	0.35–0.45	1.50	0.040	0.040	1.75	23.00–27.00	19.00–22.00	

Notes:
1. Types 2, 3, and 11 to 22 may contain up to 0.50% molybdenum.
2. Type 2 may contain up to 4.00% nickel depending on agreement between the purchaser and manufacturer.
3. Types 13, 21, and 22 may contain up to 0.20% nitrogen. However, in such cases the minimum elongation stated in the specification shall not apply.
4. If Type 22 is supplied as centrifugally cast pipe for high-pressure applications, nickel, chromium, and phosphorus content shall be 20.00 to 23.00, 23.00 to 26.00 and 0.30% max., respectively.

POLAND Stainless and Heat-resisting Steels
Specifications: PN-71-H-86020, H-86022

Type	Composition, %								
	C, max.	Si, max.	Mn, max.	P, max.	S, max.	Cr	Ni	Mo	Other elements
H5M	0.15	0.50	0.050	0.035	0.030	4.50–6.00	≤0.50	0.45–0.60	
H6S2	0.15	1.50–2.00	0.70	0.040	0.030	5.00–6.50	≤0.60		
H9S2	0.35–0.45	2.00–3.00	0.70	0.035	0.030	8.00–10.00	≤0.60		
H10S2M	0.35–0.45	1.90–2.60	0.70	0.035	0.030	9.00–10.50	≤0.50	0.70–0.90	
H13JS	0.12	1.00–1.30	0.80	0.040	0.030	12.00–14.00	≤0.50		Al 0.80–1.10
H13N4G9	0.15–0.30	0.80	8.00–10.00	0.050	0.030	12.00–14.00	3.70–4.70		
H16N36S2	0.15	1.50–2.00	2.00	0.045	0.030	15.00–17.00	34.00–37.00		
H17	0.10	0.80	0.80	0.040	0.030	16.00–18.00	≤0.60		
H17N2	0.11–0.17	0.80	0.80	0.040	0.030	16.00–18.00	1.50–2.50		
H17N13M2T	0.08	0.80	2.00	0.045	0.030	16.00–18.00	11.00–14.00	2.00–2.50	Ti 5 × C–0.70
H18	0.90–1.05	0.80	0.80	0.040	0.030	17.00–19.00	≤0.60		
H18JS	0.12	0.80–1.10	0.80	0.040	0.030	17.00–19.00	≤0.50		Al 0.70–1.20
H18N9S	0.10–0.20	0.80–2.00	2.00	0.045	0.030	17.00–20.00	8.00–11.00		
H18N10MT	0.10	0.80	2.00	0.045	0.030	17.00–20.00	9.00–11.00	1.50–2.20	Ti 5 × C–0.80
H18N25S2	0.30–0.40	2.00–3.00	1.50	0.035	0.025	17.00–19.00	23.00–26.00		
H20N12S2	0.20	1.80–2.50	1.50	0.045	0.030	19.00–22.00	11.00–13.00		
H23N13	0.20	1.00	2.00	0.045	0.030	22.00–25.00	12.00–15.00		
H23N18	0.20	1.00	1.50	0.045	0.030	22.00–25.00	17.00–20.00		
H24JS	0.12	1.30–1.60	1.00	0.045	0.030	23.00–25.00	≤0.50		Al 1.30–1.60
H25N20S2	0.20	2.00–3.00	1.50	0.045	0.030	24.00–27.00	18.00–21.00		
H25T	0.15	1.00	0.80	0.045	0.030	24.00–27.00	≤0.60		Ti 4 × C–0.80

POLAND Stainless and Heat-resisting Steels (*Continued*)
Specifications: PN-71-H-86020, H-86022

Type	Composition, %								
	C, max.	Si, max.	Mn, max.	P, max.	S, max.	Cr	Ni	Mo	Other elements
H26N4	0.20	2.50	0.80	0.045	0.030	24.00–28.00	4.00–5.00		
OH13	0.08	0.80	0.80	0.040	0.030	12.00–14.00	≤0.60		
OH13J	0.08	1.00	1.00	0.040	0.030	11.50–14.00	≤0.60		Al 0.10–0.30
OH17N4G8	0.07	0.80	7.00–9.00	0.050	0.030	16.00–18.00	4.00–5.00		N 0.12–0.25
OH17N12M2T	0.050	1.00	2.00	0.045	0.030	16.00–18.00	11.00–14.00	2.00–3.00	Ti 5 × C – 0.60
OH17N16M3T	0.08	0.80	2.00	0.045	0.030	16.00–18.00	14.00–16.00	3.00–4.00	Ti 0.30–0.60
OH17T	0.08	0.80	0.80	0.040	0.030	16.00–18.00	≤0.60		Ti 5 × C – 0.80
OH18N9	0.07	0.80	2.00	0.045	0.030	17.00–18.00	9.00–11.00		
OH18N10T	0.08	0.80	2.00	0.045	0.030	17.00–19.00	9.00–11.00		Ti 5 × C – 0.70
OH18N12Nb	0.08	0.80	2.00	0.045	0.030	17.00–19.00	10.00–13.00		Nb 10 × C – 1.10
OH22N24M4TCu	0.06	0.17–1.00	1.20–2.00	0.045	0.030	20.00–22.00	24.00–26.00	4.00–5.00	Ti 5 × C – 0.70 Cu 1.30–1.80
OH23N28M3TCu	0.06	0.080	2.00	0.045	0.030	22.00–25.00	26.00–29.00	2.50–3.00	Ti 0.50–0.90 Cu 2.50–3.50
OOH17N14M2	0.03	0.080	2.00	0.045	0.030	16.00–18.00	12.00–15.00	2.00–2.50	
OOH18N10	0.03	0.80	2.00	0.045	0.030	17.00–19.00	10.00–12.50		

Grade	C	Si	Mn	P	S	Cr	Ni	Mo	Other
1H13	0.09–0.15	0.80	0.80	0.040	0.030	12.00–14.00	≤0.60		
1H17N4G9	0.12	0.80	8.00–10.50	0.050	0.030	16.00–18.00	3.50–4.50		N 0.15–0.25
1H18N9	0.12	0.80	2.00	0.045	0.030	17.00–19.00	8.00–10.00		
1H18N9T	0.10	0.80	2.00	0.045	0.030	17.00–19.00	8.00–10.00		Ti 5 × C – 0.80
1H18N9T selekt	0.10	0.80	2.00	0.035	0.030	17.00–18.50	10.00–11.00		Ti 5 × C – 0.80
1H18N12T	0.10	0.80	2.00	0.045	0.030	17.00–19.00	11.00–13.00		Ti 5 × C – 0.80
2H13	0.16–0.25	0.80	0.80	0.040	0.030	12.00–14.00	≤0.60		
2H14	0.16–0.25	0.80	0.80	0.040	0.030	≥13.00	≤0.60		
2H17	0.15	1.20	0.70	0.040	0.030	16.00–18.00	≤0.60		
2H17N2	0.17–0.25	0.80	0.80	0.040	0.030	16.00–18.00	1.50–2.50		
2H18N9	0.13–0.21	0.80	1.00–2.00	0.045	0.030	17.00–19.00	8.00–10.00		
3H13	0.26–0.35	0.80	0.80	0.040	0.030	12.00–14.00	≤0.60		
3H14	0.26–0.35	0.80	0.80	0.040	0.030	≥13.00	≤0.60		
3H17M	0.33–0.43	1.00	1.00	0.045	0.030	15.50–17.50	≤1.00	1.00–1.30	
4H13	0.36–0.45	0.80	0.80	0.040	0.030	12.00–14.00	≤0.60		
4H14	0.36–0.45	0.80	0.80	0.040	0.030	≥13.00	≤0.60		
4H14N14W2M	0.40–0.50	0.80	0.70	0.030	0.030	13.00–15.00	13.00–15.00	0.25–0.40	W 2.00–2.75
50H21G9N4	0.47–0.57	0.50	8.00–11.00	0.030	0.030	20.00–22.00	3.25–4.50		N 0.38–0.50

POLAND Stainless and Heat-resisting Cast Steels
Specifications: PN-73-H-83159, PN-71-H-83158

Type	Composition, %							
	C, max.	Mn, max.	P, max.	S, max.	Si, max.	Cr	Ni	Mo
LH7S2	1.25–1.35	1.0	0.040	0.035	2.20–2.80	6.0–7.0		
LH18S2	1.35–1.50	0.40	0.040	0.035	1.90–2.50	17.0–19.0		
LH26	0.40–0.60	0.80	0.040	0.035	≤1.00	25.0–27.0		
LH29S2	1.45–1.60	1.00	0.040	0.035	1.50–2.10	28.0–30.0		
LH17N8	≤0.25	1.50	0.040	0.035	≤1.50	16.5–18.5	7.5–8.5	
LH19N14	≤0.25	1.00	0.040	0.035	≤1.50	18.0–20.0	13.0–15.0	
LH23N18	≤0.25	1.50	0.040	0.035	≤1.80	22.0–24.0	16.5–18.5	
LH25N19S2	≤0.25	0.60	0.040	0.035	2.00–3.00	24.0–26.0	17.5–19.5	
LH14	0.15–0.25	0.40–0.60	0.035	0.035	0.30–0.70	13.0–15.0	≤1.0	
LH17N	0.15–0.25	0.50–0.90	0.035	0.035	0.20–0.60	16.0–18.0	1.5–2.5	
LH18N9	≤0.15	2.0	0.035	0.035	1.50	17.0–19.0	8.0–11.0	
LH18N11M	≤0.15	2.0	0.035	0.035	1.50	17.0–19.0	9.0–11.0	2.0–2.5
LOH18N11M	≤0.07	2.0	0.035	0.035	1.50	17.0–19.0	9.0–11.0	2.0–2.5

ROMANIA Stainless and Heat-resisting Steels
Specification: STAS 3583-64

Type	C, max.	Si, max.	Mn, max.	P, max.	S, max.	Cr	Ni	Mo	Ti	Other elements
7C120	0.08	0.60	0.60	0.035	0.030	11.00–13.00	≤0.60			Cu ≤ 0.30
7NbNC180	0.08	0.80	1.00–2.00	0.035	0.030	17.00–19.00	11.00–13.00			Nb ≤ 1.20 / Cu ≤ 0.30
7NC180	0.08	0.80	1.00–2.00	0.035	0.030	17.00–19.00	9.00–11.00			Cu ≤ 0.30
7TC170	0.08	0.80	0.70	0.035	0.030	16.00–18.00	≤0.60		$5 \times C - 0.80$	Cu ≤ 0.30
7TNC180	0.08	0.80	1.00–2.00	0.035	0.030	17.00–19.00	9.00–11.00		$5 \times C - 0.60$	Cu ≤ 0.30
8TMoNC170	0.10	0.80	1.00–2.00	0.035	0.030	16.00–18.00	12.00–14.00	1.80–2.50	0.30–0.60	Cu ≤ 0.30
10AzMNC170	0.12	0.80	8.00–10.50	0.035	0.030	16.00–18.00	3.50–4.50			N < 0.25 / Cu ≤ 0.30
10C170	0.12	0.80	0.70	0.035	0.030	16.00–18.00	≤0.60			Cu ≤ 0.30
10NC180	0.12	0.80	2.00	0.035	0.030	17.00–19.00	8.00–10.00	≤0.20		Cu ≤ 0.30
10TNC180	0.12	0.80	2.00	0.035	0.030	17.00–19.00	8.00–9.50	≤0.20	$5 \times C -0.70$	Cu ≤ 0.30
12C130	0.09–0.15	0.60	0.60	0.035	0.030	12.00–14.00	≤0.60			Cu ≤ 0.03
12TC250	0.15	1.00	0.80	0.035	0.030	24.00–27.00	≤0.60		$5 \times C - 0.80$	Cu ≤ 0.30
14NC170	0.11–0.17	0.80	0.80	0.035	0.030	16.00–18.00	1.50–2.00			Cu ≤ 0.30
15NC230	0.20	1.00	2.00	0.035	0.030	22.00–25.00	17.00–20.00			Cu ≤ 0.30
15SNC200	0.20	2.00–3.00	1.50	0.035	0.030	19.00–22.00	12.00–15.00			Cu ≤ 0.30
20C130	0.16–0.24	0.60	0.60	0.035	0.030	12.00–14.00	≤0.60			Cu ≤ 0.30
22MNC130	0.15–0.30	0.80	8.00–10.00	0.035	0.030	12.00–14.00	3.70–4.70			Cu ≤ 0.30
30C130	0.25–0.34	0.60	0.60	0.035	0.030	12.00–14.00	≤0.60			Cu ≤ 0.30
40C130	0.35–0.44	0.60	0.60	0.035	0.030	12.00–14.00	≤0.60			Cu ≤ 0.30
40MoSC100	0.35–0.45	1.90–2.60	0.70	0.035	0.030	9.00–10.50	≤0.60	0.70–0.90		Cu ≤ 0.30
40SC90	0.35–0.45	2.00–3.00	0.70	0.035	0.030	8.00–10.00	≤0.60			Cu ≤ 0.30
90C180	0.90–1.00	0.80	0.70	0.035	0.030	17.00–19.00	≤0.60			Cu ≤ 0.30

ROMANIA Stainless and Heat-resisting Steel Castings
Specification: STAS 6855-64

Type	Composition, %								
	C, max.	Si, max.	Mn, max.	P, max.	S, max.	Cr	Ni	Mo	Ti
T10MTMoNC170	0.12	1.00	1.50	0.035	0.030	16.50–18.50	10.50–12.50	2.00–2.50	5 × C
T10MTMoNC175	0.12	1.00	1.00–2.00	0.035	0.030	16.00–19.00	11.00–13.00	3.00–4.00	5 × C
T12C130	0.15	0.70	0.60	0.035	0.030	12.00–14.00	≤0.60		
T12MSMoNC180	0.15	0.50–2.00	2.00	0.035	0.030	17.00–19.00	9.00–11.00	2.00–2.50	
T12MSNC180	0.15	0.50–2.00	2.00	0.035	0.030	17.00–19.00	8.00–10.00		
T15MoC90	0.20	1.00	0.35–0.65	0.050	0.040	8.00–10.00		0.90–1.20	
T20SNC250	0.25	1.50–2.50	1.50	0.040	0.030	23.00–27.00	18.00–21.00		
T22C130	0.16–0.24	0.70	0.60	0.035	0.030	12.00–14.00	≤0.60		
T35MSNC260	0.30–0.40	1.50–2.50	1.50	0.035	0.030	23.00–27.00	13.00–15.00		
T40SC130	0.30–0.50	2.00–3.00	1.00	0.035	0.030	12.00–14.00			
T75SC260	0.50–1.00	0.50–1.30	0.50–0.80	0.100	0.080	26.00–30.00			

SOVIET UNION Stainless and Heat-resisting Steels
Specification: GOST 5632-72

| Number | Designation | Composition, % | | | | | | | | |
		C	Mn, max.	P, max.	S, max.	Si, max.	Cr	Ni	Mo	Other elements
							1. MARTENSITIC STEELS			
1-1	15Kh5	≤0.15	0.5	0.030	0.025	0.5	4.5–6.0			
1-2	15Kh5M	≤0.15	0.5	0.030	0.025	0.5	4.5–6.0		0.45–0.60	
1-3	15Kh5VF	≤0.15	0.5	0.030	0.025	0.3–0.6	4.5–6.0			W 0.4–0.7 V 0.4–0.6
1-4	12Kh8VF	0.08–0.15	0.5	0.030	0.025	0.6	7.0–8.5			W 0.6–1.0 V 0.3–0.5
1-5	40Kh9S2	0.35–0.45	0.8	0.030	0.025	2.0–3.0	8.0–10.0			
1-6	40Kh10S2M	0.35–0.45	0.8	0.030	0.025	1.9–2.6	9.0–10.5		0.7–0.9	
1-7	15Kh11MF	0.12–0.19	0.7	0.030	0.025	0.5	10.0–11.5		0.6–0.8	V 0.25–0.40
1-8	18Kh11MNFB	0.15–0.21	0.6–1.0	0.030	0.025	0.6	10.0–11.5	0.5–1.0	0.8–1.1	Nb 0.20–0.45
1-9	20Kh12VNMF	0.17–0.23	0.5–0.9	0.030	0.025	0.6	10.5–12.5	0.5–0.9	0.5–0.7	W 0.7–1.1 V 0.15–0.30
1-10	11Kh11N2V2MF	0.09–0.13	0.6	0.030	0.025	0.6	10.5–12.0	1.5–1.8	0.35–0.50	W 1.6–2.0 V 0.18–0.30
1-11	16Kh11N2V2MF	0.14–0.18	0.6	0.030	0.025	0.6	10.5–12.0	1.4–1.8	0.35–0.50	W 1.6–2.0 V 0.18–0.30
1-12	20Kh13	0.16–0.25	0.8	0.030	0.025	0.8	12.0–14.0			
1-13	30Kh13	0.26–0.35	0.8	0.030	0.025	0.8	12.0–14.0			
1-14	40Kh13	0.36–0.45	0.8	0.030	0.025	0.8	12.0–14.0			
1-15	30Kh13N7S2	0.25–0.34	0.8	0.030	0.025	2.0–3.0	12.0–14.0	6.0–7.5		
1-16	13Kh14N3V2FR	0.10–0.16	0.6	0.030	0.025	0.6	13.0–15.0	2.8–3.4		Ti ≤ 0.05 V 0.18–0.28 W 1.6–2.2 B ≤ 0.004

SOVIET UNION Stainless and Heat-resisting Steels (Continued)
Specification: GOST 5632-72

Number	Designation	Composition, %								
		C	Mn, max.	P, max.	S, max.	Si, max.	Cr	Ni	Mo	Other elements
1-17	25Kh13N2	0.2–0.3	0.8–1.2	0.08–0.15	0.15–0.25	0.5	12.0–14.0	1.5–2.0		
1-18	20Kh17N2	0.17–0.25	0.8	0.035	0.025	0.8	16.0–18.0	1.5–2.5		
1-19	95Kh18	0.9–1.0	0.8	0.030	0.025	0.8	17.0–19.0			
1-20	09Kh16N4B	0.05–0.13	0.5	0.030	0.025	0.6	15.0–17.0	3.5–4.5		Nb 0.05–0.20
					2. MARTENSITIC-FERRITIC STEELS					
2-1	15Kh6SJu	≤0.15	0.5	0.030	0.025	1.2–1.8	5.5–7.0			Al 0.7–1.1
2-2	15Kh12VNMF	0.12–0.18	0.5–0.9	0.030	0.025	0.4	11.0–13.0	0.4–0.8	0.5–0.7	W 0.7–1.1 V 0.15–0.30
2-3	18Kh12VMBFR	0.15–0.22	0.5	0.030	0.025	0.5	11.0–13.0		0.4–0.6	W 0.4–0.7 V 0.15–0.30 Nb 0.2–0.4 B ≤ 0.003
2-4	12Kh13	0.09–0.15	0.8	0.030	0.025	0.8	12.0–14.0			
2-5	14Kh17N2	0.11–0.17	0.8	0.030	0.025	0.8	16.0–18.0	1.5–2.5		
					3. FERRITIC STEELS					
3-1	10Kh13SJu	0.07–0.12	0.8	0.030	0.025	1.2–2.0	12.0–14.0			Al 1.0–1.8
3-2	08Kh13	≤0.08	0.8	0.030	0.025	0.8	12.0–14.0			
3-3	12Kh17	≤0.12	0.8	0.035	0.025	0.8	16.0–18.0			
3-4	08Kh17T	≤0.08	0.8	0.035	0.025	0.8	16.0–18.0			Ti 5 × C − 0.80
3-5	15Kh18SJu	≤0.15	0.8	0.035	0.025	1.0–1.5	17.0–20.0			Al 0.7–1.2
3-6	15Kh25T	≤0.15	0.8	0.035	0.025	1.0	24.0–27.0			Ti 5 × C − 0.90
3-7	15Kh28	≤0.15	0.8	0.035	0.025	1.0	27.0–30.0			

4-1	20Kh13N4G9	0.15–0.30	8.0–10.0	0.050		0.8	12.0–14.0	3.7–4.7	
4-2	09Kh15N8Ju	≤0.09	0.8	0.035	0.025	0.8	14.0–16.0	7.0–9.4	Al 0.7–1.3
4-3	07Kh16N6	0.05–0.09	0.8	0.035	0.025	0.8	15.5–17.5	5.0–8.0	
4-4	09Kh17N7Ju	≤0.09	0.8	0.030	0.020	0.8	16.0–17.5	7.0–8.0	Al 0.5–0.8
4-5	09Kh17N7Ju1	≤0.09	0.8	0.035	0.025	0.8	16.5–18.0	6.5–7.5	Al 0.7–1.1
4-6	08Kh17N5M3	0.06–0.10	0.8	0.035	0.020	0.8	16.0–17.5	4.5–5.5	3.0–3.5
	5. Austenitic-Ferritic Steels								
5-1	08Kh20N14S2	≤0.08	1.5	0.035	0.025	2.0–3.0	19.0–22.0	12.0–15.0	
5-2	20Kh20N14S2	≤0.20	1.5	0.035	0.025	2.0–3.0	19.0–22.0	12.0–15.0	
5-3	08Kh22N6T	≤0.08	0.8	0.035	0.025	0.80	21.0–23.0	5.3–6.3	Ti 5 × C − 0.8
5-4	12Kh21N5T	0.09–0.14	0.8	0.035	0.025	0.80	20.0–22.0	4.8–5.8	Ti 0.25–0.50 / Al ≤0.08
5-5	08Kh21N6M2T	≤0.08	0.8	0.035	0.025	0.80	20.0–22.0	5.5–6.5	1.8–2.5 / Ti 0.20–0.40
5-6	20Kh23N13	≤0.20	2.0	0.035	0.025	1.0	22.0–25.0	12.0–15.0	
5-7	08Kh18G8N2T	≤0.08	7.0–9.0	0.035	0.025	0.8	17.0–19.0	1.8–2.8	Ti 0.20–0.50
5-8	15Kh18N12S4TJu	0.12–0.17	0.5–1.0	0.035	0.030	3.8–4.5	17.0–19.0	11.0–13.0	Ti 0.4–0.7 / Al 0.13–0.35
	6. Austenitic Steels								
6-1	08Kh10N20T2	≤0.08	2.0	0.035	0.030	0.8	10.0–12.0	18.0–20.0	Ti 1.5–2.5 / Al ≤ 1.0
6-2	10Kh11N20T3R	≤0.10	1.0	0.035	0.020	1.0	10.0–12.5	18.0–21.0	Ti 2.6–3.2 / B 0.008–0.020 / Al ≤ 0.8
6-3	10Kh11N23T3MR	≤0.10	0.6	0.025	0.010	0.6	10.0–12.5	21.0–25.0	1.0–1.6 / Ti 2.6–3.2 / B ≤ 0.02 / Al ≤ 0.8
6-4	37Kh12N8G8MFB	0.34–0.40	7.5–9.5	0.035	0.030	0.3–0.8	11.5–13.5	7.0–9.0	1.1–1.4 / Nb 0.25–0.40 / V 1.25–1.55

SOVIET UNION Stainless and Heat-resisting Steels (Continued)
Specification: GOST 5632-72

Number	Designation	Composition, %									
		C	Mn, max.	P, max.	S, max.	Si, max.	Cr	Ni	Mo	Other elements
6-5	10Kh14G14N3	0.09–0.14	13.0–15.0	0.035	0.020	0.7	12.5–14.0	2.8–3.5		
6-6	10Kh14G14N4T	≤0.10	13.0–15.0	0.035	0.020	0.8	13.0–15.0	2.8–4.5		Ti 5 × (C − 0.02) −0.6
6-7	10Kh14AG15	≤0.10	14.5–16.5	0.045	0.030	0.8	13.0–15.0			N 0.15–0.25
6-8	45Kh14N14V2M	0.40–0.50	0.7	0.035	0.020	0.8	13.0–15.0	13.0–15.0	0.25–0.40	W 2.0–2.8
6-9	09Kh14N16B	0.07–0.12	1.0–2.0	0.035	0.020	0.6	13.0–15.0	14.0–17.0		Nb 0.9–1.3
6-10	09Kh14N19V2BR	0.07–0.12	2.0	0.035	0.020	0.6	13.0–15.0	18.0–20.0		W 2.0–2.8 B ≤ 0.005 Nb 0.9–1.3 Ce ≤ 0.02
6-11	09Kh14N19V2BR1	0.07–0.12	2.0	0.035	0.020	0.6	13.0–15.0	18.0–20.0		W 2.0–2.8 B ≤ 0.025 Nb 0.9–1.3 Ce ≤ 0.02
6-12	40Kh15N7G7F2MS	0.38–0.47	6.0–8.0	0.035	0.020	0.9–1.4	14.0–16.0	6.0–8.0	0.65–0.95	V 1.5–1.9
6-13	08Kh16N13M2B	0.06–0.12	1.0	0.035	0.020	0.8	15.0–17.0	12.5–14.5	2.0–2.5	Nb 0.9–1.3
6-14	08Kh15N24V4TR	≤0.08	0.5–1.0	0.035	0.020	0.6	14.0–16.0	22.0–25.0		Ti 1.4–1.8 B ≤ 0.005 W 4.0–5.0 Ce ≤ 0.025
6-15	03Kh16N15M3	≤0.03	0.8	0.020	0.015	0.6	15.0–17.0	14.0–16.0	2.5–3.0	
6-16	03Kh16N15M3B	≤0.03	0.8	0.020	0.015	0.6	15.0–17.0	14.0–16.0	2.5–3.0	Nb 0.25–0.50
6-17	09Kh16N15M3B	≤0.09	0.8	0.035	0.020	0.8	15.0–17.0	14.0–16.0	2.5–3.0	Nb 0.6–0.9
6-18	15Kh17AG14	≤0.15	13.5–15.5	0.035	0.020	0.8	16.0–18.0	≤0.6		N 0.25–0.37
6-19	12Kh17G9AN4	≤0.12	8.0–10.5	0.035	0.020	0.8	16.0–18.0	3.5–4.5		N 0.15–0.25
6-20	03Kh17N14M2	≤0.03	1.0–2.0	0.035	0.020	0.8	16.0–18.0	13.0–15.0	2.0–2.8	
6-21	08Kh17N13M2T	≤0.08	2.0	0.035	0.020	0.8	16.0–18.0	12.0–14.0	2.0–3.0	Ti 5 × C − 0.7

No.	Grade	C	Mn	S	P	Si	Cr	Ni	Mo	Other
6-22	10Kh17N13M2T	≤0.10	2.0	0.035	0.020	0.8	16.0–18.0	12.0–14.0	2.0–3.0	Ti 5 × C − 0.7
6-23	10Kh17N13M3T	≤0.10	2.0	0.035	0.020	0.8	16.0–18.0	12.0–14.0	3.0–4.0	Ti 5 × C − 0.7
6-24	08Kh17N15M3T	≤0.08	2.0	0.035	0.020	0.8	16.0–18.0	14.0–16.0	3.0–4.0	Ti 0.3–0.6
6-25	12Kh18N9	≤0.12	2.0	0.035	0.020	0.8	17.0–19.0	8.0–10.0		
6-26	17Kh18N9	0.13–0.21	2.0	0.035	0.020	0.8	17.0–19.0	8.0–10.0		
6-27	12Kh18N9T	≤0.12	2.0	0.035	0.020	0.8	17.0–19.0	8.0–9.5		Ti 5 × C − 0.8
6-28	04Kh18N10	≤0.04	2.0	0.035	0.020	0.8	17.0–19.0	9.0–11.0		
6-29	08Kh18N10	≤0.03	2.0	0.035	0.020	0.8	17.0–19.0	9.0–11.0		
6-30	08Kh18N10T	≤0.03	2.0	0.035	0.020	0.8	17.0–19.0	9.0–11.0		Ti 5 × C − 0.7
6-31	12Kh18N10T	≤0.12	2.0	0.035	0.020	0.8	17.0–19.0	9.0–11.0		Ti 5 × C − 0.8
6-32	12Kh18N10E	≤0.12	2.0	0.035	0.020	0.8	17.0–19.0	9.0–11.0		Se 0.18–0.35
6-33	03Kh18N11	≤0.03	2.0	0.035	0.020	0.8	17.0–19.0	10.5–12.5		
6-34	06Kh18N11	≤0.06	2.0	0.035	0.020	0.8	17.0–19.0	10.0–12.0		
6-35	03Kh18N12	≤0.03	0.4	0.030	0.020	0.4	17.0–19.0	11.5–13.0		Ti ≤ 0.005
6-36	03Kh18N12T	≤0.03	2.0	0.035	0.020	0.8	17.0–19.0	11.0–13.0		Ti 5 × C − 0.6
6-37	12Kh18N12T	≤0.12	2.0	0.035	0.020	0.8	17.0–19.0	11.0–13.0		Ti 5 × C − 0.7
6-38	08Kh18N12B	≤0.03	2.0	0.035	0.020	0.8	17.0–19.0	11.0–13.0	1.0–1.5	Nb 10 × C − 1.1
6-39	31Kh19N9MVBT	0.28–0.35	0.8–1.5	0.035	0.020	0.8	18.0–20.0	8.0–10.0		Ti 0.2–0.5 Nb 0.2–0.5 V 1.0–1.5
6-40	36Kh18N25S2	0.32–0.40	1.5	0.035	0.020	2.0–3.0	17.0–19.0	23.0–26.0		
6-41	55Kh20G9AN4	0.50–0.60	8.0–10.0	0.040	0.030	0.45	20.0–22.0	3.5–4.5		N 0.30–0.60
6-42	07Kh21G7AN5	≤0.07	6.0–7.5	0.030	0.030	0.7	19.5–21.0	5.0–6.0		N 0.15–0.25
6-43	03Kh21N21M4GB	≤0.03	1.8–2.5	0.030	0.020	0.6	20.0–22.0	20.0–22.0	3.4–3.7	Nb 15 × C − 0.8
6-44	45Kh22N4M3	0.40–0.50	0.85–1.25	0.035	0.030	0.7–1.0	21.0–23.0	4.0–5.0	2.5–3.0	
6-45	10Kh23N18	≤0.10	2.0	0.035	0.020	1.0	22.0–25.0	17.0–20.0		

SOVIET UNION Stainless and Heat-resisting Steels (Continued)
Specification: GOST 5632-72

Number	Designation	Composition, %								
		C	Mn, max.	P, max.	S, max.	Si, max.	Cr	Ni	Mo	Other elements
6-46	20Kh23N18	≤0.20	2.0	0.035	0.020	1.0	22.0–25.0	17.0–20.0		
6-47	20Kh25N20S2	≤0.20	1.5	0.035	0.020	2.0–3.0	24.0–27.0	18.0–21.0		
6-48	12Kh25N16G7AR	≤0.12	5.0–7.0	0.035	0.020	1.0	23.0–26.0	15.0–18.0		N 0.30–0.45 B ≤ 0.010

Notes:
1. The following symbols are added after a dash at the end of the designation to indicate the method of melting:
(Ш) Electroslag remelting; (ВД) vacuum arc remelting; (ВИ) vacuum induction melting.
2. When electroslag melted, steels 10KhN23T3MR, 03Kh16N15M3, and 03Kh16N15M3B have a maximum sulfur content of 0.015%.
3. Compositional deviations of elements are not to exceed the following:

Element	Range, %	Allowance, %
C	Up to 0.10	±0.01
	0.10–0.25	±0.02
	Over 0.25	±0.05
Ti	Up to 1.0	±0.05
	Over 1.0	±0.10
S	As shown in table	±0.005
P	All	±0.005
N	All	±0.02
V	All	±0.02
Nb	Up to 5.0	±0.02
	Over 5.0	±0.10
Mo	Up to 5.0	±0.02
	Over 5.0	±0.10
Al	Up to 5.0	±0.02
	Over 5.0	±0.02
W	Up to 5.0	±0.05
	Over 5.0	±0.10

4. Titanium content is not to exceed 0.02% for steels 12Kh18N9, 08Kh18N10, and 17Kh18N9. If there is no prior agreement, titanium content is not to exceed 0.05%. For steels 03Kh18N11, 03Kh16N15M3, 03Kh17N14M2, 09Kh15N8Ju, 07Kh16N6 and 08Kh17N5M3, titanium content is not to exceed 0.05%.

5. A maximum copper content of 0.3% is permitted for all steels shown in the table.

6. Nickel-free steels may contain up to 0.6% nickel.

7. If not shown in the standard, or agreed upon, Cr-Ni steels may contain up to 0.3% Mo, 0.2% W, and 0.2% V.

8. Steels containing tungsten can have a molybdenum content not exceeding 0.3%. If the tungsten content decreases, molybdenum can increase in the ratio 2:1.

9. When used for glass melting, 15Kh28 should have a silicon content of 0.4%.

10. Elements not shown in the table are not permitted in the analysis.

11. The steel designation consists of the elements, with numbers identifying contents. Small amounts are not identified. The numbers preceding the designation represent either maximum or median carbon content. The letter "A" (designating nitrogen) is not permitted at the end of the designation.

12. Only the designation shown may be used to identify the steels.

13. If there is any disagreement, then the parties must use precise chemical analysis to establish the composition of the steel.

SPAIN Stainless Steels
Specification: UNE 36 016-74

Class	Symbol	Composition, %								
		C, max.	Mn, max.	P, max.	S, max.	Si, max.	Cr	Ni	Mo	Other elements
F3110	X6Cr13	0.08	1.00	0.040	0.030	1.00	11.50–14.00	0.50 max.		
F3111	X6CrAl13	0.08	1.00	0.040	0.030	1.00	11.50–14.00	0.50 max.		Al 0.10–0.30
F3113	X8Cr17	0.10	1.00	0.040	0.030	1.00	16.00–18.00	0.50 max.		
F3117	X10CrS17	0.12	1.50	0.060	0.15–0.35	1.00	16.00–18.00	0.50 max.	0.60 max.	
F3114	X8CrTi17	0.10	1.00	0.040	0.030	1.00	16.00–18.00	0.50 max.		$5 \times C \leqslant Ti \leqslant 0.80$
F3401	X12Cr13	0.09–0.15	1.00	0.040	0.030	1.00	11.50–14.00	1.00 max.		
F3411	X12CrS13	0.08–0.15	1.50	0.060	0.15–0.35	1.00	12.00–14.00	1.00 max.	0.60 max.	
F3402	X20Cr13	0.16–0.25	1.00	0.040	0.030	1.00	12.00–14.00	1.00 max.		
F3403	X30Cr13	0.26–0.35	1.00	0.040	0.030	1.00	12.00–14.00	1.00 max.		
F3404	X40Cr13	0.36–0.45	1.00	0.040	0.030	1.00	12.50–14.50	1.00 max.		
F3405	X46Cr13	0.42–0.50	1.00	0.040	0.030	1.00	12.50–14.50	1.00 max.		
F3423	X46CrMo16	0.42–0.50	1.00	0.040	0.030	1.00	15.50–17.50	1.00 max.	1.00–1.50	V 0.20 max.
F3427	X15CrNi16	0.10–0.20	1.00	0.040	0.030	1.00	15.00–18.00	1.50–3.00		
F3503	X2CrNi19-10	0.03	2.00	0.045	0.030	1.00	18.00–20.00	8.00–12.00		
F3504	X6CrNi19-10	0.08	2.00	0.045	0.030	1.00	18.00–20.00	8.00–10.50		
F3507	X10CrNi18-09	0.12	2.00	0.045	0.030	1.00	17.00–19.00	8.00–10.00		
F3508	X10CrNiS18-09	0.12	2.00	0.20	0.030	1.00	17.00–19.00	8.00–10.00	0.60 max.	
F3513	X8CrNi18-12	0.10	2.00	0.045	0.030	1.00	17.00–19.00	11.00–13.00		
F3517	X12CrNi17-07	0.15	2.00	0.045	0.030	1.00	16.00–18.00	6.00–8.00		
F3523	X6CrNiTi18-11	0.08	2.00	0.045	0.030	1.00	17.00–19.00	9.00–12.00		$5 \times C \leqslant Ti \leqslant 0.80$
F3524	X6CrNiNb18-11	0.08	2.00	0.045	0.030	1.00	17.00–19.00	9.00–12.00		$10 \times C \leqslant Nb \leqslant 1.00$
F3533	X2CrNiMo17-12-03	0.03	2.00	0.045	0.030	1.00	16.00–18.00	10.00–14.00	2.00–3.00	
F3534	X6CrNiMo17-12-03	0.08	2.00	0.045	0.030	1.00	16.00–18.00	10.00–14.00	2.00–3.00	
F3535	X6CrNiMoTi17-12-03	0.08	2.00	0.045	0.030	1.00	16.00–18.00	10.00–14.00	2.00–3.00	$5 \times C \leqslant Ti \leqslant 0.80$

SPAIN   Cast Stainless Steels
Specification: UNE 36257

Class	Symbol	Composition, %								
		C, max.	Mn, max.	P, max.	S, max.	Si, max.	Cr	Ni	Mo	Other elements
F-8401	AM-X12Cr13	0.015	1.0	0.04	0.04	1.5	12.0–14.0	1.0 max.	0.50 max.	
F-8402	AM-X30Cr13	0.20–0.40	1.0	0.04	0.04	1.5	12.0–14.0	1.0 max.	0.50 max.	
F-8403	AM-X15CrNi17	0.25	1.0	0.04	0.04	1.5	16.0–18.0	1.5–2.5		
F-8404	AM-X40Cr28	0.50	1.0	0.04	0.04	1.5	25.0–30.0	4.0 max.		
F-8411	AM-X7CrNi20-10	0.08	1.5	0.04	0.04	2.0	18.0–21.0	8.0–11.0		
F-8412	AM-X2CrNi19-10	0.03	1.5	0.04	0.04	2.0	17.0–21.0	8.0–12.0		
F-8413	AM-X7CrNiNb20-10	0.08	1.5	0.04	0.04	2.0	18.0–21.0	9.0–12.0		$8 \times C \leqslant Nb \leqslant 1.0$
F-8414	AM-X7CrNiMo20-10	0.8	1.5	0.04	0.04	2.0	18.0–21.0	9.0–12.0	2.0–3.10	
F-8415	AM-X2CrNiMo19-11	0.03	1.5	0.04	0.04	2.0	17.0–21.0	9.0–13.0	2.0–3.0	
F-8416	AM-X7CrNiMo20-11	0.08	1.5	0.04	0.04	1.5	18.0–21.0	9.0–13.0	3.0–4.0	
F-8417	AM-X6NiCrMoCu29-20	0.07	1.5	0.04	0.04	1.5	19.0–22.0	27.0–31.0	2.0–3.0	Cu 3.0–4.0

SWEDEN   Stainless and Heat-resisting Steels
Specification: SIS-14-

| Standard | Composition, % | | | | | | | | |
	C, max.	Si, max.	Mn, max.	P, max.	S, max.	Cr	Ni	Mo	Other elements
2301	0.08	1.00	1.00	0.040	0.030	12.00–14.00	≤0.50		
2302	0.09–0.15	1.00	1.00	0.040	0.030	12.00–14.00	≤1.00		
2303	0.18–0.25	1.00	1.00	0.040	0.030	12.00–14.00	≤1.00		
2304	0.28–0.35	1.00	1.00	0.040	0.030	12.00–14.50	≤1.00		
2317	0.20–0.26	0.10–0.50	0.30–0.80	0.035	0.035	11.00–12.50	0.30–0.80	1.00–1.40	V 0.25–0.35 N 0.030–0.060
2320	0.10	1.00	1.00	0.040	0.030	16.00–18.00	≤0.50		
2321	0.17–0.25	1.00	1.00	0.040	0.030	16.00–18.00	1.25–2.50		
2322	0.25	1.00	1.00	0.040	0.030	24.00–28.00			
2324	0.10	1.00	2.00	0.045	0.030	24.00–27.00	4.50–6.00	1.30–1.80	
2325	0.08	1.00	1.00	0.040	0.030	16.00–19.00	≤0.50	1.30–2.00	
2331	0.12	1.00	2.00	0.045	0.030	17.00–19.00	7.00–9.50		
2332	0.07	1.00	2.00	0.045	0.030	17.00–19.00	8.00–11.00		
2333	0.05	1.00	2.00	0.045	0.030	17.00–19.00	8.00–11.00		
2337	0.08	1.00	2.00	0.045	0.030	17.00–19.00	9.00–13.00		Ti 5 × C ≤ 0.80
2338	0.08	1.00	2.00	0.045	0.030	17.00–19.00	9.00–13.00		Nb + ½ Ta 10 × C ≤ 1.00
2340	0.10	1.00	2.00	0.045	0.030	16.50–18.00	8.00–10.00	1.30–1.80	

No.	C	Si	Mn	P	S	Cr	Ni	Mo	Other
2343	0.05	1.00	2.00	0.045	0.030	16.00–18.50	10.50–14.00	2.50–3.00	
2346	0.12	1.00	2.00	0.060	0.15–0.35	17.00–19.00	8.00–11.00	≤0.60	
2347	0.05	1.00	2.00	0.045	0.030	16.00–18.50	10.50–14.00	2.00–2.50	
2348	0.03	1.00	2.00	0.045	0.030	16.00–18.50	11.00–14.00	2.00–2.50	
2350	0.08	1.00	2.00	0.045	0.030	16.00–18.50	10.50–14.00	2.00–2.50	Ti 5 × C ≤ 0.80
2352	0.03	1.00	2.00	0.045	0.030	17.00–19.00	9.00–12.00		
2353	0.03	1.00	2.00	0.045	0.030	16.00–18.50	11.50–14.50	2.50–3.00	
2361	0.08	1.50	2.00	0.045	0.030	24.00–26.00	19.00–22.00		
2366	0.05	1.00	2.00	0.045	0.030	17.50–19.50	13.00–16.00	3.00–4.00	
2367	0.03	1.00	2.00	0.045	0.030	17.50–19.50	14.00–17.00	3.00–4.00	
2370	0.05	1.00	2.00	0.045	0.030	17.00–19.00	8.00–11.00		N 0.15–0.22
2371	0.03	1.00	2.00	0.045	0.030	17.00–19.00	9.00–12.00		N 0.15–0.22
2374	0.05	1.00	2.00	0.045	0.030	16.00–18.50	10.50–14.00	2.50–3.00	N 0.15–0.22
2375	0.03	1.00	2.00	0.045	0.030	16.00–18.50	11.00–14.00	2.50–3.00	N 0.15–0.22
2380	0.08–0.15	1.00	1.00	0.060	0.15–0.35	12.00–14.00	≤1.00	≤0.60	
2383	0.10–0.17	1.00	1.50	0.060	0.15–0.35	16.00–18.00	≤0.50	≤0.60	
2570	0.08	1.00	2.00	0.025	0.025	13.50–16.00	24.00–27.00	1.00–1.50	V 0.10–0.50 Al ≤ 0.35 Ti 1.90–2.30 B 0.003–0.010

UNITED STATES Stainless and Heat-resistant Steels

From: Stainless and Heat-resisting Steels Products Manual, AISI, 1974

Type	UNS Number	C, max.	Mn, max.	P, max.	S, max.	Si, max.	Cr	Ni	Mo	Other elements
							Composition, %			
201	S20100	0.15	5.50–7.50	0.060	0.030	1.00	16.00–18.00	3.50–5.50		N 0.25
202	S20200	0.15	7.50–10.00	0.060	0.030	1.00	17.00–19.00	4.00–6.00		N 0.25
205	S20500	0.12–0.25	14.00–15.00	0.060	0.030	1.00	16.50–18.00	1.00–1.75		N 0.32–0.40
301	S30100	0.15	2.00	0.045	0.030	1.00	16.00–18.00	6.00–8.00		
302	S30200	0.15	2.00	0.045	0.030	1.00	17.00–19.00	8.00–10.00		
302B	S30215	0.15	2.00	0.045	0.030	2.00–3.00	17.00–19.00	8.00–10.00		
303	S30300	0.15	2.00	0.20	0.15	1.00	17.00–19.00	8.00–10.00	0.60*	
303Se	S30323	0.15	2.00	0.20	0.060	1.00	17.00–19.00	8.00–10.00		Se 0.15 min.
304	S30400	0.08	2.00	0.045	0.030	1.00	18.00–20.00	8.00–10.50		
304L	S30403	0.030	2.00	0.045	0.030	1.00	18.00–20.00	8.00–12.00		
	S30430	0.08	2.00	0.045	0.030	1.00	17.00–19.00	8.00–10.00		Cu 3.00–4.00
304N	S30451	0.08	2.00	0.045	0.030	1.00	18.00–20.00	8.00–10.50		N 0.10–0.16
305	S30500	0.12	2.00	0.045	0.030	1.00	17.00–19.00	10.50–13.00		
308	S30800	0.08	2.00	0.045	0.030	1.00	19.00–21.00	10.00–12.00		
309	S30900	0.20	2.00	0.045	0.030	1.00	22.00–24.00	12.00–15.00		
309S	S30908	0.08	2.00	0.045	0.030	1.00	22.00–24.00	12.00–15.00		
310	S31000	0.25	2.00	0.045	0.030	1.50	24.00–26.00	19.00–22.00		
310S	S31008	0.08	2.00	0.045	0.030	1.50	24.00–26.00	19.00–22.00		
314	S31400	0.25	2.00	0.045	0.030	1.50–3.00	23.00–26.00	19.00–22.00		
316	S31600	0.08	2.00	0.045	0.030	1.00	16.00–18.00	10.00–14.00	2.00–3.00	
316F	S31620	0.08	2.00	0.20	0.10 min.	1.00	16.00–18.00	10.00–14.00	1.75–2.50	
316L	S31603	0.030	2.00	0.045	0.030	1.00	16.00–18.00	10.00–14.00	2.00–3.00	

Type	UNS	C	Mn	P	S	Si	Cr	Ni	Mo	Other
316N	S31651	0.08	2.00	0.045	0.030	1.00	16.00–18.00	10.00–14.00	2.00–3.00	N 0.10–0.16
317	S31700	0.08	2.00	0.045	0.030	1.00	18.00–20.00	11.00–15.00	3.00–4.00	
317L	S31703	0.030	2.00	0.045	0.030	1.00	18.00–20.00	11.00–15.00	3.00–4.00	
321	S32100	0.08	2.00	0.045	0.030	1.00	17.00–19.00	9.00–12.00		Ti 5 × C min.
329	S32900	0.10	2.00	0.040	0.030	1.00	25.00–30.00	3.00–6.00	1.00–2.00	
330	N08330	0.08	2.00	0.040	0.030	0.75–1.50	17.00–20.00	34.00–37.00		
347	S34700	0.08	2.00	0.045	0.030	1.00	17.00–19.00	9.00–13.00		Cb + Ta 10 × C min.
348	S34800	0.08	2.00	0.045	0.030	1.00	17.00–19.00	9.00–13.00		Cb + Ta 10 × C min. Ta 0.10 Co 0.20
384	S38400	0.08	2.00	0.045	0.030	1.00	15.00–17.00	17.00–19.00		
385	S38500	0.08	2.00	0.045	0.030	1.00	11.50–13.50	14.00–16.00		
403	S40300	0.15	1.00	0.040	0.030	0.50	11.50–13.00			
405	S40500	0.08	1.00	0.040	0.030	1.00	11.50–14.50			Al 0.10–0.30
409	S40900	0.08	1.00	0.045	0.045	1.00	10.50–11.75			Ti 6 × C min. or 0.75 max.
410	S41000	0.15	1.00	0.040	0.030	1.00	11.50–13.50			
414	S41400	0.15	1.00	0.040	0.030	1.00	11.50–13.50	1.25–2.50		
416	S41600	0.15	1.25	0.060	0.15 min.	1.00	12.00–14.00		0.60*	
416Se	S41623	0.15	1.25	0.060	0.060	1.00	12.00–14.00			Se 0.15 min.
420	S42000	Over 0.15	1.00	0.040	0.030	1.00	12.00–14.00			
420F	S42020	Over 0.15	1.25	0.060	0.15 min.	1.00	12.00–14.00		0.60*	
422	S42200	0.20–0.25	1.00	0.025	0.025	0.75	11.00–13.00	0.50–1.00	0.75–1.25	V 0.15–0.30 W 0.75–1.25
429	S42900	0.12	1.00	0.040	0.030	1.00	14.00–16.00			
430	S43000	0.12	1.00	0.040	0.030	1.00	16.00–18.00			
430F	S43020	0.12	1.25	0.060	0.15 min.	1.00	16.00–18.00		0.60*	
430FSe	S43023	0.12	1.25	0.060	0.060	1.00	16.00–18.00			Se 0.15 min.

UNITED STATES Stainless and Heat-resistant Steels (Continued)
From: Stainless and Heat-resisting Steels Products Manual, AISI, 1974

Type	UNS Number	Composition, %								
		C, max.	Mn, max.	P, max.	S, max.	Si, max.	Cr	Ni	Mo	Other elements
431	S43100	0.20	1.00	0.040	0.030	1.00	15.00–17.00	1.25–2.50		
434	S43400	0.12	1.00	0.040	0.030	1.00	16.00–18.00		0.75–1.25	
436	S43600	0.12	1.00	0.040	0.030	1.00	16.00–18.00		0.75–1.25	Cb + Ta 5 × C min. 0.70 max.
440A	S44002	0.60–0.75	1.00	0.040	0.030	1.00	16.00–18.00		0.75	
440B	S44003	0.75–0.95	1.00	0.040	0.030	1.00	16.00–18.00		0.75	
440C	S44004	0.95–1.20	1.00	0.040	0.030	1.00	16.00–18.00		0.75	
442	S44200	0.20	1.00	0.040	0.030	1.00	18.00–23.00			
446	S44600	0.20	1.50	0.040	0.030	1.00	23.00–27.00			N 0.25 max.
501	S50100	Over 0.10	1.00	0.040	0.030	1.00	4.00–6.00		0.40–0.65	
502	S50200	0.10	1.00	0.040	0.030	1.00	4.00–6.00		0.40–0.65	
	S13800	0.05	0.10	0.01	0.008	0.10	12.25–13.25	7.50–8.50	2.00–2.50	Al 0.90–1.35 N 0.010 max.
	S15500	0.07	1.00	0.040	0.030	1.00	14.00–15.50	3.50–5.50		Cu 2.50–4.50 Cb + Ta 0.15–0.45
	S17400	0.07	1.00	0.040	0.030	1.00	15.50–17.50	3.00–5.00		Cu 3.00–5.00 Cb + Ta 0.15–0.45
	S17700	0.09	1.00	0.040	0.040	1.00	16.00–18.00	6.50–7.75		Al 0.75–1.50

*Optional.
Note: For some tube-making processes it is necessary that the nickel content of several of the austenitic grades be slightly higher than shown in the above tables. The producer should be consulted for the appropriate nickel ranges for such grades.

Comparison of U.S. Government Specifications for Stainless Steel

Specification	Form	SAE	Nearest corresponding number — AISI	AMS
MIL-S 853A (Ships) Supersedes Mil-S-853 (Ships)				
Class 1, Types A, B, C		30304	304	5639
Class 2, Types A, B, C	Bars and forgings, except for reforging (For reforging bars and billets, see MIL-S-862A)	30302	302	5636A, 5637A
Class 3, Types A, C, E, F		51410	410	5613C
Class 4		51430	430	5627
Class 5, Types A, F		51420	420	5620B, 5621
Class 6, Types A, C, E		51416	416	5610E
Class 7, Types A, B, C		30303F	303	5640E, 5641A, 5742
Class 8, Type A		30321 or, 30347	321 or, 347	5645F, 5646D
Class 9, Types A, C		30317	317	
Class 10, Types A, E, F		51431	431	5628B
Class 11, Type A		30310	310	
Class 12		30325	325	5651C
Class 14, Types A, E, F				
MIL-S 854 (Ships) Amend 4 Supersedes 47S20 (INT)				
Class 1, Cond. A	Plate, sheet, strip, and shapes	30304	304	5513
Class 2, Cond. A, B, C, D, E		30302	302	5515C, 5516E, 5517D, 5518C, 5519E
Class 3, Cond. A		51410	410	5504C
Class 4, Cond. A		51430	430	
Class 8, Cond. A		30321 or 30347	321 or 347	5510E, 5512B
Class 9, Cond. A		30316	316	5524B
Class 11, Cond. A		30310	310	5521B
MIL-S-861A (Ships) Supersedes MIL-S-861 (Ships)				
Class 403	Bars		403	
Class 410		51410	410	5613C
Class 405			406	
Class 422				
MIL-S-862A Supersedes MIL-S-862 (Ships)				
Classes similar to MIL-S-853 A (Ships)	Bars and billets (for reforging only)	See MIL-S-853A (Ships)		

Comparison of U.S. Government Specifications for Stainless Steel (Continued)

Specification	Form	Nearest corresponding number		
		SAE	AISI	AMS
MIL-P-1144A (Ships) Used in lieu of JAN-P-1144	Seamless and welded pipe	30304 30316 30321 or 30347	304 316 321 or 347	
MIL-S-4043 (USAF) Amend. 1	Plate, sheet and strip		304L	5511A
MIL-S-5059A (ASG) Amend. 1 Supersedes MIL-S-5059	Plate, sheet and strip	30301 30302 30316	301 302 316	5515C, 5517D, 5518C, 5519E 5513, 5516E 5524B
MIL-T-5695B (ASG) Supersedes MIL-T-5695A	Seamless and welded tubing	30304	304	5560C, 5565C, 5566C
MIL-W-6713 Supersedes AN-W-24	Wire	30302	302	5688C
MIL-S-6721A Supersedes MIL-S-6721	Plate, sheet and strip	30321 30347 30347	321 347 347	5510E 5512B 5512B
MIL-T-6737A (ASG) Amend. 2 Supersedes MIL-T-6737	Welded tubing	30347 30321	347 321	5575E 5576A

Comp. 304, Comp. 316, Comp. 321 or 347 (MIL-P-1144A); Comp. 301, Comp. 302, Comp. 316 (MIL-S-5059A); Grades C, Cond. A, B (MIL-W-6713); Comp. Ti, Comp. Cb, Comp. Cb-Ta (MIL-S-6721A); Comp. 347, Comp. 321 (MIL-T-6737A)

MIL-T-6845, Amend. 5 Supersedes AN-T-86		Seamless and welded tubing– hydraulic	30304	304	5566C
MIL-T-6846, Amend. 1 Supersedes AN-T-43		Seamless and welded tubing– hydraulic	30304	304	5566C
MIL-S-7720, Amend. 1 Supersedes AN-S-771	Comp. 302 Comp. 303S Comp. 303Se Comp. 316	Bars and forging stock	30302 30303F 30303F 30316	302 303 303Se 316	5636A, 5637A, 5639 5640E, 5641A, 5742 5640E, 5641A, 5742 5648B, 5649
MIL-T-8504 (ASG) Amend. 2 Supersedes MIL-T-6846		Seamless and welded tubing– hydraulic	30304	304	5566C
MIL-T-8506 Amend. 1		Seamless and welded tubing	30304	304	5560C, 5565C, 5566C
MIL-T-8606 (ASG)	Comp. G347 Comp. G321	Seamless and welded tubing	30347 30321	347 321	5571A 5570F
MIL-T-8808	Comp. G347 Comp. G321	Seamless and welded tubing– hydraulic	30347 30321	347 321	5571A 5570F
MIL-S-17759 (Ships)	Cond. A, B, C, H	Bars, billets, forgings and wire		17-10P	
MIL-S-17996 (Ships)	Class 1 Class 2	Sheet and other wrought forms		201	

Comparison of U.S. Government Specifications for Stainless Steel (Continued)

Specification	Form	SAE	AISI	AMS
			Nearest corresponding number	
MIL-T-18063 (Ships) Amend. 1 (for radioactive systems service)	Comp. 304 Comp. 304L Comp. 347	Seamless and welded pipe and tubing	30304	304 304L	5560C, 5565C, 5566C 5647 5570F, 5575E
MIL-S-18170 (Ships) Amend. 3 (for radioactive systems service)	Comp. 304 Comp. 304L Comp. 347	30304 30347		304 304L 347	5639 5647 5646D
MIL-S-18171 (Ships) (for radioactive systems service)	Comps. identical to MIL-S-18170(Ships) Amend. 3	Plate, sheet, and strip		See MIL-S-18170 (Ships) Amend. 3	
MIL-S-18732 (ASG) Supersedes AN-QQ-S-770a		Bars	51431	431	5628B
MIL-S-25043A (ASG)		Plate, sheet, and strip		17-7PH	5528, 5529
AIR FORCE—NAVY AERONAUTICAL SPECIFICATIONS					
AN-W-24	Grade G	Wire	30302	302	5688C

Specification	Composition	Form			
AN-S-757	Comp. Ti	Plate, sheet, and strip	30321	321	5510E
	Comp. Cb		30347	347	5512B
AN-QQ-S-770a Amend. 1		Bars	51431	431	5628B
AN-S-771 Amend. 1	Comp. G	Bars	30302	302	5636A, 5637A
	Comp. MCR		30316	316	5648B, 5649
	Comp. FMS		30303F	303	5640E, 5641A, 5742
	Comp. FMP		30303F	303	5640E, 5641A, 5742
	Comp. FM Se		30303F	303	5640E, 5641A, 5742
AN-QQ-S-772a Amend. 1	Comp. G	Plate, sheet, and strip	30302	302	5515C, 5516E, 5517D, 5518C, 5519E
	Comp. MCR		30316	316	5524B
AN-WW-T-855, Amend. 2		Seamless tubing	30304	304	5560C
AN-WW-T-858		Seamless tubing	30321 or 30347	321 or 347	5570F, 5571A
FEDERAL SPECIFICATIONS					
QQ-W-423	Comp. FS 302	Wire	30302	302	5688C
	Comp. FS 304		30304	304	5697
	Comp. FS 310		30310	310	
	Comp. FS 316		30316	316	5690E
	Comp. FS 410		51410	410	
	Comp. FS 420		51420	420	
	Comp. FS 430		51430	430	
QQ-S-763b Supersedes QQ-S-00763a Rev. 1 and MIL-S-854 (in part)	Class 202	Bars, shapes and forgings		202	
	Class 302		30302	302	5636A, 5637A
	Class 303		30303F	303	5640E, 5641A, 5742
	Class 303Se		30303F	303 Se	5640E, 5641A, 5742
	Class 304		30304	304	5639
	Class 304L			304L	5647
	Class 305		30305	305	
	Class 309		30309	309	5650

Comparison of U.S. Government Specifications for Stainless Steel (Continued)

Specification	Form	SAE	AISI	AMS
			Nearest corresponding number	
Class 310	Bars, shapes and forgings	30310	310	3651C
Class 316		30316	316	5648B, 5649
Class 316L			316L	
Class 317		30317	317	
Class 321		30321	321	5645F
Class 322			17-7PH	5644
Class 324			17-4PH	5643C
Class 347		30347	347	5646D
Class 350				
Class 355				
Class 403			403	
Class 405			405	
Class 410		51410	410	5613C
Class 414		51414	414	5615B
Class 416		51416	416	5610E
Class 416 Se			416Se	5610E
Class 420		51420	420	5620B, 5621
Class 430		51430	430	5627
Class 430F		51430F	430F	
Class 430F Se			430FSe	
Class 431		51431	431	5628B
Class 440A		51440A	440A	5631
Class 440B			440B	
Class 440C		51440C	440C	5630C

Plate, sheet, and strip

QQ-S-00766b Amend. 1 Supersedes MIL-S-854 (in part)			
Class 440F	51440F	440C	5632A
Class 440FSe	51440F	440C	5632A
Class 446	51446	446	
Class 201		201	
Class 202		202	
Class 301	30301	301	
Class 302	30302	302	5515C, 5516E, 5517D, 5518C, 5519E
Class 304	30304	304	5513
Class 304L		304L	5511A
Class 305	30305	305	5514A
Class 309	30309	309	5523
Class 310	30310	310	
Class 316	30316	316	5521B
Class 316L		316L	5524B
Class 321	30321	321	
Class 323			
Class 347	30347	347	5510E
Class 348		348	
Class 410	51410	410	5512B
Class 430	51430	430	5504C
Class 446	51446	446	

Appendix **2**

Proprietary Alloys

This Handbook has, for the most part, avoided the use of commercial trade names. For valid reasons, some references to proprietary alloys have invariably appeared in the text. To assist the reader in identifying the basic composition of these alloys, a listing of them has been assembled in alphanumeric order. Unlike Appendix 1, which states the composition ranges found in the various national specifications, this appendix generally lists the average composition of each steel noted.

Proprietary Alloys

Alloy	Average composition, %								
	C	Mn	Si	P	S	Cr	Ni	Mo	Other
A-286	0.05	1.4	0.4			15	26	1.25	Ti 2.15 Al 0.2 V 0.3 B 0.003
AF-183	0.30	18				12.5	16	3	N 0.2 V 0.08
AL-386	0.05								
Alloy 15	0.15–0.25					10–13	1–2	0.50	
Almar 362	0.03					14.5	6.5		Ti 0.8
AM 350	0.10	1.0	0.4			16.5	4.25	2.75	N 0.1
AM 355	0.15	1	0.4			15.5	4.25	2.75	N 0.1
Allegheny HWT	0.07			0.30	0.30	17.75–18.75	0.50		$12 \times C \leqq Ti \leqq 1.0$ Al 0.15
Allegheny MF-1	0.04					11			Ti 0.5
Allegheny OR-1	0.04					12.5	0.25		Al 3.2 Ti 0.4
Allegheny 216	0.05	8.3				19.8	6		N 0.35
Allegheny 216L	0.03	8.3				19.5	6		N 0.35
AM 363	0.04					11	4		Ti 0.25
Armco 15-16WR	0.5		4.85			15	17		W3 Cb 0.25
Armco 18SR	0.04					18	0.30		Al 2.0 Ti 0.40
Armco 18-2Mn	0.10	12				18	1.6		N 0.34
Armco 21-6-9	0.4	9				20.5	6.5		N 0.27

Alloy	C	Mn	Cr	Ni	Mo	Other
Armco 22-4-9	0.55	8.5	20.5	3.5		N 0.4
Armco 22-13-5	0.06	4–6	20.5–23.5	11.5–13.5	1.5–3	N 0.2–0.4, Cb 0.1–0.3, V 0.1–0.3
Armco 300	0.08		17	7		
Armco 400	0.025		12.5			Al 0.20
Boron Stainless	0.08		18–20	8–14		B 1-2
Carpenter 7 Mo	Equivalent to Type 329					
Carpenter Stainless No. 5-F	0.10		13–14.5		0.4–0.6	
Carpenter Stainless No 20 Cb-3	0.07		19–21	32–38	2–3	Cu 3–4, $8 \times C \leq Cb + Ta \leq 1$
Carpenter Stainless No. 404	0.05		11–12.5	1.25–2		
Croloy 15-15N	≤0.15		14.75–18	13.5–16.5	1.25–1.85	W 1.0–1.85, Cb + Ta 0.8–1.3, N ≤ 0.15
Croloy 16-1	0.035		14–16	1–1.5		Al 2–2.5
Croloy 16-6PH	0.03–0.06		14.75–15.75	6.25–7.25		Ti 0.70–0.90, Al 0.35–0.45
Croloy 20 Mod.	≥0.08		20.5	≥0.3		Al 2.25
Croloy 299	0.18	14.7	17.2	1.45		N 0.36

Proprietary Alloys (Continued)

Alloy	Average composition, %								
	C	Mn	Si	P	S	Cr	Ni	Mo	Other
Croloy 302 B Mod.	0.08	2–3				17–19	11–14		
Croloy 20-2Al	0.08					20–21.5	0.3		Al 2–2.5
Croloy 299	0.12–0.25	14–15.5				16.5–18	1.2–1.7		N 0.32–0.40
Croloy 303S	0.15				0.15	17–19	8–11		
Crucible 16-16-1	≥0.10	16				16	1		N 0.18
Crucible 18-16	0.05					18	16		
Crucible 223	0.08	12				15.5	0.50	0.50	Cu 1, N ≥ 0.25
Crucible AFC-77	0.15					14.5		5	Co 13, V 0.4
Crucible Bright E2	0.08					10.5–11.75	0.5		5 × C ≤ Ti ≤ 0.75
Crucible Bright E3	0.08					12	0.5		Ti 5 × C
Crucible E-3NT	0.08					13	0.5		Al 0.10–0.30
Crucible T303 Plus X	0.15	2.5–4.5				17–19	7–10	0.6	
Custom 450	≥0.05					14.5–16.5	5.5–7.0	0.5–1.0	Cu 1.25–1.75, Cb ≥ 8 × C
Custom 455	0.03					11.75	8.5		Ti 1.2, Cb 0.30, Cu 2.25
Cryogenic Tenelon	0.10	15				17.5	5.5		N 0.38
Discaloy	0.04					13.5	26	2.75	Ti 1.75, Al 0.10, B 0.005

	C	Mn	Si	N	Cr	Ni	Mo	Other elements
E-Brite 26-1	0.005				25–27		0.75–1.5	Cu ≤ 0.20 N 0.015 Cu + Ni ≤ 0.50
Eastern Alloy No. 20, Escalloy 20	0.07				19–21	24–30	2–3	Cu 3–4 8 × C ≤ Cb + Ta ≤ 1
EME	0.10				19	12		W 3.2 Cb 1.2 N 0.15
Glidden 303L, Cold Stream 303L	0.013				17.6	12	0.04	
Glidden 316LSi	0.018		2.33		17.4	12.3	2.18	
Glidden 410 L, Ancor 410L, Coldstream 410L	0.017				12.5			
Greek Ascoloy	0.12				13	2		W 3
Hastelloy Alloy C	≤0.02				14.5–16.5	Bal.	15–17	Co 2.5 W 3–4.5 Fe 4–7 Zr ≤ 0.35
HNM	0.30	3.5	0.5	0.23	18.5	9.5		
IN-856	0.07	17	3		18.5	9		
Inconel Alloy 600	0.08				15.5	76		Fe 8 Cu 0.25
Incoloy Alloy 800	0.05				21	32.5		Ti 0.38 Al 0.38 Cu 0.38 Fe 46
Incoloy 825	0.03				21.5	42	3	Ti 0.9 Al 0.10 Cu 2.25 Fe 30

Proprietary Alloys (Continued)

Alloy	Average composition, %								
	C	Mn	Si	P	S	Cr	Ni	Mo	Other
Incoloy Alloy 825	0.03					21.5	42	3	Ti 0.9 Al 0.10 Cu 2.25 Fe 30
JS700	0.03	1.7				21	25	4.5	Cb 0.3
Jal Head 12-15	0.08					11–13	14–16		
Jethete M152	0.14					11.25	2.9	1.6	V 0.3 N 0.35
JS-700	0.03					21	25	4.5	Cb ≥ 8 × C
Kromarc 55	0.04	9.5				16	20	2.25	
Kromarc 58	0.02	10				15	22	2.25	B 0.008 Zr 0.01 N 0.23 V 0.25
Lapelloy C	0.22					11.5	0.30	2.75	Cu 2 N 0.08
Nitronic 32	0.1	12				18	1.6		N 0.35
Nitronic 33	0.05	13				18	3.25		N 0.30
Nitronic 40	0.04	9				20.5	6.5		N 0.30
Nitronic 50	0.06	5				22	13	2	Cb 0.20 V 0.20 N 0.3
Nitronic 60	0.08	8	4			17	8.5		N 0.14
OR-1	≥0.08					12.5	≥0.5		Al 3 Ti 0.6
PH 12-9Mo	0.035					11.85	8.65	1.5	Al 1.65 N 0.005
PH 13-8Mo	0.035					12.75	8.2	2.15	Al 1.1 N 0.005

Alloy	C		Cr	Ni	Mo	Other
PH 14-8Mo	0.03		14.4	8.2	2.25	Al 1.17
PH 15-7Mo	0.07		15.1	7.1	2.25	Al 1.17
Pyromet 538	≥0.03	9	20	6.5		N 0.27
RA 311	0.15	2.5	20	25		
Republic 14-6Ti	≥0.05		14.5	6.5		Ti 0.75
Sandvik 2RE10	0.02	1.75	24	20		
Sandvik 2RK65	0.02		19.5	25	4.5	Cu 1.5
Sandvik 2RN65	0.02		17.5	24	4.7	
Sandvik 3R19	0.03		18.5	10.3		N 0.18
Sandvik 3R69	0.03		17.4	12.8	2.8	N 0.18
Sandvik 12R72HV	0.10		15	15	1.2	Ti 0.40 B 0.0065
Sandvik 5RA90	0.05		17.4	13.4	2.7	Cu 2 Ti 1
Sandvik 3RE60	≤0.03		18.5	4.7	2.7	
Sandvik 3RE60	0.03	1.65	18.5	4.7	2.7	
Tech 10	0.08		16	18		
Tech 12	0.08		12	15		
UHB 44L	≥0.03		26	5	1.5	
UHB 904L	≥0.02	1.75	20	25	4.5	Cu 1.5
Uniloy 302 HQ	0.08		17–19	9–10.5		Cu 3–4
Uniloy 303 MA	0.15	0.11–0.16	17–19	8–10	0.40–0.60	Al 0.60–1.0
Uniloy 332, AL 332	≥0.05		20.5	32.5		Al 0.40 Ti 0.40
Uniloy 888	≥0.5	9	7.5	7.5		V 1.5
USA met	0.07–0.13		16.5–17.5	7.4–8.3	0.18–0.8	

Proprietary Alloys (Continued)

Alloy	Average composition, %								
	C	Mn	Si	P	S	Cr	Ni	Mo	Other
USS 18-18-2	0.07		2			18	18		
USS Tenelon	0.10	15				18			N 0.40
Z8 CNDT 17-12	≥0.10					15–19	10–14	2–3	Ti ≥ 4 × C
12R72	0.10	1.8				15	15	1.2	Ti 0.40 B 0.006
15-5PH	0.04					15.1	4.6		Cb + Ta 0.27 Cu 3.3
16-15-6	0.07	7.5				16	15	6	N 0.35
16-25-6	≥0.08					16	25	6	N 0.15
17-4PH	0.04					16	4.25		Cb + Ta 0.27 Cu 3.3
17-7PH	0.07					17	7		Al 1.17
17-10P	0.12			0.30		16.7	10.2		
17-14Cu Mo	0.12					16.0	14.3	2.5	Cb 0.45 Ti 0.25 Cu 3.0
18-3Mn	0.05	13				18	3.3		N 0.30
18-5Mn	0.10	15				17.5	5.5		N 0.38
18-9LW	0.1					17–19	8–10		Cu 3–4
18Cr-2Mo-0.6Ti	≥0.03					18		2	Ti 0.6
18Cr-8Ni-2Si	0.07		2			18	8		
18Cr-15Ni-4.5Mo	≥0.03					18	15	4.5	
18Mn	0.10	15				18	0.2		N 0.40
20Cr-4Ni-2Mo	≥0.03					20	4	2	
20Cr-25Ni-2Mo	≥0.03					20	25	2	2 Cu

Alloy	C	Mn	Si	P	S	Cr	Ni	Mo	Other
19-9DL	0.3	1.1	0.6			19	9	1.25	W 1.2, Cb 0.4, Ti 0.3
19-9DX	0.3	1.0	0.55			19.2	9	1.5	W 1.2, Ti 0.55
19-9WX	0.11					20.5	8.5	0.5	W 1.55, Cb 1.3, Ti 0.2
26-2	0.005					25	0.4	2.2	V 0.04
203EZ	≤0.08	5-6.5		0.18-0.35		16-18	5-6.5	≤0.50	Cu 1.75-2.25
204	0.06	8.0				18	5		N 0.20
211	0.05	6.0				17	5.5		Cu 1.5
216	0.06	8.3				20	6	2.5	N 0.37
248SV	≤0.04					16	5	1	
249SV	≤0.06					18			
254SLX	≤0.02					20	25	4.5	Cu 1.5
302Cu	≥0.10					18	9		Cu 3.5
303Cu	≤0.15			≤0.15	>0.10	17-19	8-10		Cu 2.5-4, Se ≤0.10
303Pb	≤0.15			0.12-0.25		17-19	8-10	≤0.60	Pb 0.12-0.30
304LN	0.03					18-20	8-10.5		N 0.10-0.15
308L	0.021					20	10		
309Cb	≤0.08					22-24	12-15		8 × C > Cb ≤ 1
309Cb + Ta	0.08					22-24	12-15		Cb + Ta 8 × C ≤ 1.0
309SCb	0.08					22-24	12-15		Cb 8 × C ≤ 1.0
310Cb	0.08					25	20		Cb 10 × C
312	0.15					30	9		

Proprietary Alloys (Continued)

Alloy	Average composition, %								
	C	Mn	Si	P	S	Cr	Ni	Mo	Other
316B	0.02	0.25	2.4			17.5	12.5	2.2	
316Cb	0.08					16.25–17.25	11–14		Cb 9 × C ≤ 1.0
318	0.08					17–19	10–14	2–3	Cb + Ta 10 × C
322	0.08					17	7	0.70	
326	0.05					25–27	6–7		Ti 0.25 max.
330HC	0.40					19	35		
332	0.04					21.5	32		
347FSe	0.08				0.15–0.30	17–19	9–13		10 × C ≤ Cb + Ta ≤ 1.0
347Se	0.04			0.14		18	11		Se ≥ 0.15 10 × C ≤ Cb + Ta
393M	≤0.06					13.5			
410Cb	0.13					12			Cb 0.15
410S	0.08					11.5–13.5	≤0.6		
414L	0.06					12.5–13	2.5–3	0.50	Al 0.03
420FSe	≥0.15					12–14		≤0.60	P or Se ≥ 0.07
425	0.58					14			

Grade	C				Cr	Ni	Mo	Other
430M	0.06				16		1.8	
430Ti	0.10				16–19.5	0.75		5 × C ≤ Ti ≤ 0.75
430Ti-Al	≤0.07				17.75–18.75	0.50		Al 0.15 12 × C ≥ Ti ≤ 1.1
434F	0.03			0.3	17.5		1	
440FM	0.95–1.20			0.15–0.30	16–18		≤0.75	
440FSe	0.95–1.20				16–18		≤0.75	Se 0.15–0.30
443	0.20				18–23			Cu 0.90–1.25
434L	0.02	0.25	0.7		17		1	
453S	≤0.10				26	5	1.5	
664MV	≤0.05	8			18	5.5		N 0.2
739S	≤0.17				13.5		1	
832MV	≤0.05				18	9.5		
832SK	≤0.05				17	11.5	2.7	
832SL	≤0.05				17	15	4.5	
832SN	≤0.05				18.5	14.5	3.5	
832SV	≤0.05				17	10	1.5	

Index

DUANE S. REVES,
BOX 293,
BRUNO, SASK.